P9-CBI-857

akistan

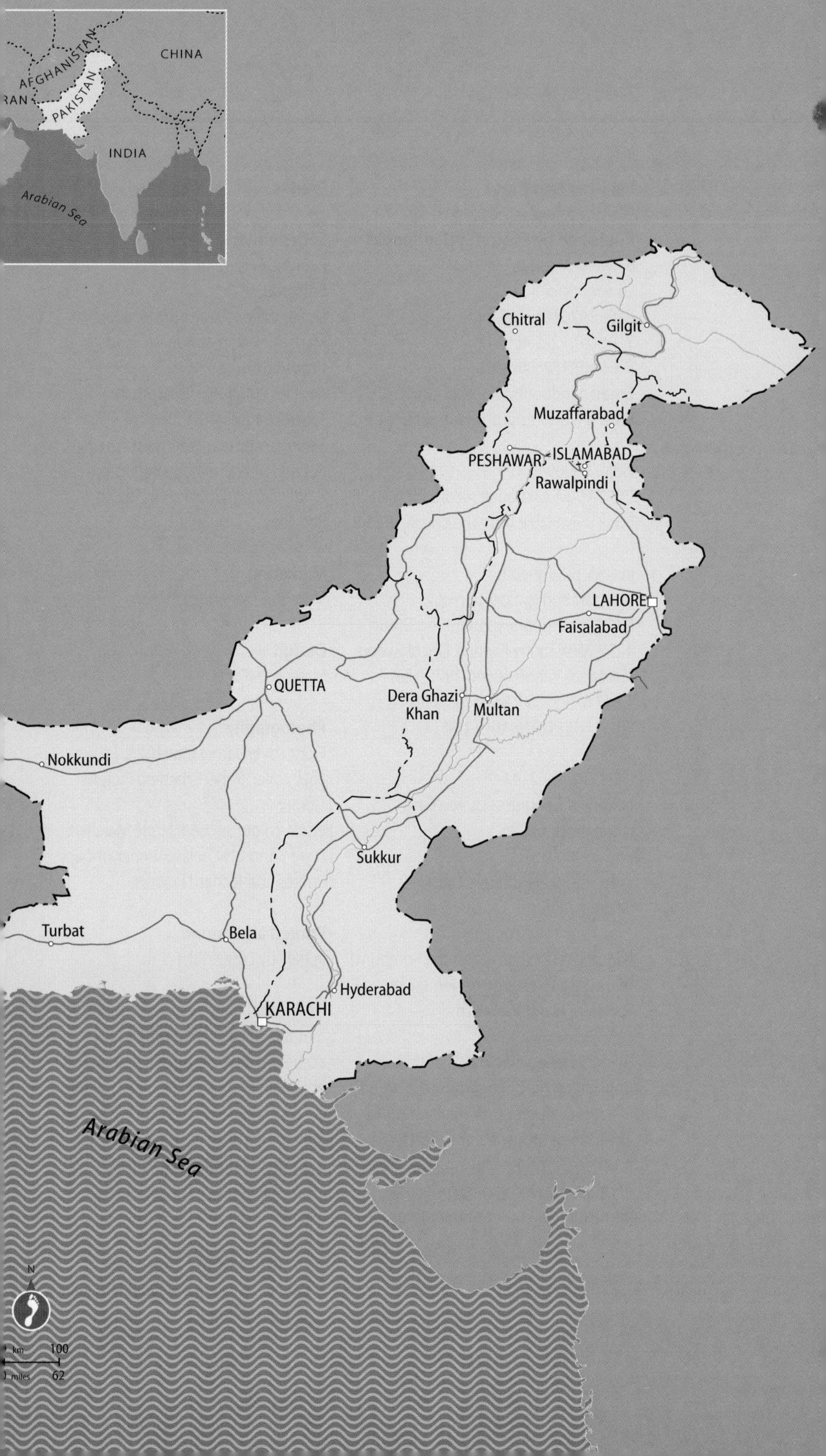

CHINA
AFGHANISTAN
RAN
PAKISTAN
INDIA
Arabian Sea

Chitral
Gilgit
Muzaffarabad
PESHAWAR
ISLAMABAD
Rawalpindi
LAHORE
Faisalabad
QUETTA
Dera Ghazi Khan
Multan
Nokkundi
Sukkur
Turbat
Bela
Hyderabad
KARACHI
Arabian Sea

N
km 100
miles 62

Pakistan Handbook

Published by Footprint Handbooks
6 Riverside Court
Lower Bristol Road
Bath BA2 3DZ. England
T +44 (0)1225 469141
F +44 (0)1225 469461
Email handbooks@footprint.cix.co.uk
Web www.footprint-handbooks.co.uk

ISBN 1 900949 37 7
CIP DATA: A catalogue record for this book is available from the British Library

In USA, published by
Passport Books, a division of
NTC/Contemporary Publishing Group
4255 West Touhy Avenue, Lincolnwood
(Chicago), Illinois 60646-1975, USA
T 847 679 5500 F 847 679 24941
Email NTCPUB2@AOL.COM

ISBN 0-8442-2144-9
Library of Congress Catalog Card Number: 98-68296

Second edition

Credits

Series editor
Patrick Dawson
Editorial
Senior editor: Sarah Thorowgood
Maps: Alex Nott and Jo Williams
Production
Pre-Press Manager: Jo Morgan
Typesetting: Ann Griffiths
Maps: Kevin Feeney, Richard Ponsford, Robert Lunn and Claire Benison
Proof reading: Howard David and Rod Gray

Marketing
MBargo, Singapore

Design
Mytton Williams

Photography
Front cover: Jamie Marshall
Back cover: Robert Harding Picture Library
Inside colour section: Jamie Marshall, Dave Winter, Nicholas Sumner, Impact Photos and Richard Powers

Printed and bound
in Italy by LEGOPRINT

Footprint Pakistan Handbook

Ivan Mannheim and Dave Winter

"All things considered there are only two kinds of men in the world – those that stay at home and those that do not."

Rudyard Kipling

Foreword

Imran Khan

A combination of misinformation and lack of knowledge about Pakistan has contributed to the fact that the country has never attracted tourists in large numbers. Many people see Pakistan as an inaccessible and even hostile place, when the truth is that there are few people more welcoming to foreigners than Pakistanis if an effort is made by the visitor to respect their precious culture and traditions.

Pakistan is a land of huge diversity and each of its four provinces - Punjab, Sind, North West Frontier Province and Baluchistan - have their own dialects, foods, landscapes and customs. Sind is best appreciated for its wonderful handicrafts and its Sufi traditions; Punjab for its Mughal monuments, and above all for its cuisine; Baluchistan accounts for 43 percent of the land mass of Pakistan, and its largely unexplored, uninhabited and rugged terrain combining mountains, deserts and a beautiful coastline; whilst NWFP has its own unique charm, and is the cradle of the Gandharan (Buddhist) civilization.

Since childhood, however, my greatest passion has been for the Northern Areas of Pakistan. The magic of being surrounded by some of the highest mountains in the world is unequal to anything else I have ever experienced. Since the construction of the Karakoram Highway in the early 1970s, this area has been opened up to travellers wishing to experience this incredible and unspoilt beauty from the highest road in the world, which reaches 4,733 metres at the Khunjerab Pass on the Silk Road to China.

Another special place for me is Pakistan's Salt Range, which lies between the Jhelum and Indus rivers in the Punjab. It is a low mountain range, rich in salt and other minerals and teeming with wildlife. It is also a geologist's dream – on several occasions I have found fossils of trees. It is also where the Hindu vedas were written, and there are many only recently discovered ancient sites such as the ruins of a city called Tuleja, which I discovered by chance one day.

Sadly the wilderness, wildlife and ancient monuments are threatened by a fast-growing population and a lack of interest in conservation. We in Pakistan have to work fast to preserve the beauty for our future generations.

I know of no book that I would recommend more highly to the visitor than the Footprint Pakistan Handbook. Dave Winter and Ivan Mannheim have written a comprehensive, authoritative and positive guide to a fascinating and endlessly surprising country. Here you can uncover the wild beauty and history that Pakistan has to offer, and more importantly, find your way around the country with ease whilst on the road.

Come and visit us - you will find that you are more than welcome.

Contents

9

10

A foot in the door

Highlights

Asia's best kept secret is about to be revealed. Now that India and Nepal are so firmly established as major tourist destinations, more and more travellers are looking to Pakistan as the unspoilt travel destination of South Asia. Yet Pakistan deserves this title in its own right, and not merely by default.

People Visitors to Pakistan are all agreed upon one thing: the warmth of the welcome afforded to them by the people. The international media often paints a negative picture of fanaticism, violence and danger, yet visitors to Pakistan should prepare themselves instead for a lesson in human warmth, generosity and hospitality. You are far more likely to find yourself accepting endless invitations to stay or eat in people's homes than reporting a theft or mugging. The sheer diversity of peoples, cultures and traditions makes travelling in Pakistan a continually fascinating experience. Indeed, Pakistan may be considered to be several countries rolled into one. Travelling from one part of Pakistan to the next you encounter not just different landscapes, but also different ethnic groups, cultures, clothing, cuisine and languages.

Mountains As the meeting point of the Karakoram, Himalaya and Hindu Kush ranges, the north of Pakistan encompasses soaring mountains of rock, ice and snow, huge sweeping glaciers, and lofty plateaux. Here is the highest concentration of peaks over 7,000 metres anywhere on earth, including K2, the second highest mountain in the world. Such an environment may seem inhospitable, yet there are also high pastures carpeted in summer with grass and flowers, rich forests and dazzling islands of fertile irrigated green amidst the bare rock. Whatever the immediate surroundings, this region is undeniably one of breathtaking and unforgettable beauty.

Karakoram Highway Much of Pakistan's mountain splendour has been opened up to the outside world by the construction of the Karakoram Highway, or KKH. This 1,300 kilometre-long engineering miracle links the Pakistani capital Islamabad with Kashgar, one of China's legendary Central Asian cities. Literally blasted out of rock in places, this road never fails to impress. Yet a journey along the KKH is not just about scenery, as spectacular as the views are. Former independent kingdoms, the very inspiration of popular myths such as James Hilton's Shangri La, are now beginning to come to terms with the 20th century, welcoming visitors to their once isolated mountain fastnesses, whilst still retaining their ancient charm. The spectacular Sunday Market at Kashgar meanwhile provides an unforgettable feast for the senses, and for many people is in itself reason enough to undertake a journey along the KKH.

History and culture A visit to Lahore reveals something of the richness of Pakistan's historical and cultural heritage. It was here that the great Mughal emperors of the 16th and 17th centuries, Akbar, Jahangir, Shah Jahan and Aurangzeb, built lavish monuments of outstanding beauty. Many of these, the Badshahi Mosque, Lahore Fort and Jahangir's Tomb (to name just a few), still survive in all their glory. Such monuments give you tantalizing glimpses of a bygone era, yet it is their connection with the present which is perhaps the most fascinating aspect of this city, for Lahore is still a thriving, dynamic centre of culture and learning, just as it was under the Mughals.

Peshawar boasts an equally illustrious history, and indeed also flourished under the Mughals. Today, however, the contrast with Lahore couldn't be greater, the romance and atmosphere of this city reflecting its 'frontier' setting close to the historic Khyber Pass. In the colourful bazaars of the Old City, Pathan tribesmen from the surrounding tribal areas mingle with traders from all over Central Asia, playing out scenes which appear to have changed little over the centuries.

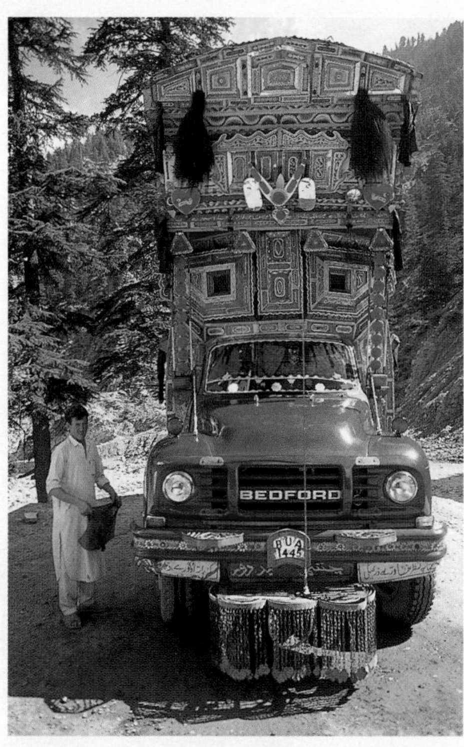

Page 7: The "Great Leader" and father of Pakistan, Mohammed Ali Jinnah, was born in Karachi in 1976. Following his death in 1948, the Quaid-e-Azam was buried in this splendid mausoleum in the city of his birth. It is noted for its neat fusion of traditional and modern styles.
Left: brightly coloured Bedford truck.
Below: drammatic granite 'Cathedral Spires' (Tupopdan) stand guard over the Karakoram Highway at Passu.

Above: the Badshahi Mosque in Lahore was built for the Emperor Aurangzeb in 1673-74. Its enormous courtyard is said to hold 100,000 worshippers, making it one of the largest mosques in the world.
Left: stall in the Rajah bazaar, commercial heart of Rawalpindi , Punjab.
Next page: one of Pakistan's most striking monuments is the semi-ruined 13th century tomb of Bibi Jalwindi at former capital town of Uch Sharif, Punjab.

A rich history

Indus Valley Civilization

Although the modern state of Pakistan has only recently celebrated its 50th anniversary, it has a history that stretches back to the very beginnings of human civilization, spanning numerous empires and dynasties. Each has left its own legacy. The great Indus Valley Civilization, comparable in importance to the ancient civilizations of Egypt and Mesopotamia, has left behind the cities of Moenjo Daro and Harappa. Both are visually stunning, as well as representing amongst the most significant archaeological remains in South Asia.

Gandharan civilization

Few would think of Pakistan as having played a central role in the development of Buddhism, yet it was here that the Gandharan civilization flourished. A visit to the museums at Peshawar and Taxila reveals the subtle beauty of the Gandharan artistic style, a unique fusion of Graeco-Roman and Oriental influences.

Islamic legacy

The early Muslim period provides us with a series of spectacular shrines and monuments, such as the semi-ruined tombs at Uch Sharif and the delicately restored shrines of Multan. Yet this isn't just archaeology. The shrines of the Sufi saints who spread Islam throughout the region, notably in Sind, are more than just bricks and mortar; they are living centres of worship, where daily acts of pilgrimage and devotion keep alive the message of these early wandering mystics.

Mughals and the British

Perhaps the most impressive era in terms of architecture was that of the Mughals, who were responsible for much of the magnificence of Lahore. Many Mughal monuments were later embellished and adapted by the Sikhs to produce distinctive new forms such as the funerary memorials of Guru Arjun Dev and Maharaja Ranjit Singh. The British also left a lasting and prominent influence. Many of the public buildings they built are striking pieces of architecture, blending Gothic and Mughal styles in a splendidly ostentatious manner; posting a letter at Lahore's stunning General Post Office could hardly be described as a mundane experience.

Diverse cultures

Pakistan's position on the subcontinent is often likened to a zone of contact, with centuries of migration and invasion, as well as the intermingling of new arrivals with indigenous populations, explaining this diversity of peoples. Compare, for example, the fair-skinned and green/blue-eyed Pathans of NWFP and Baluchistan with the dark-haired and dark-eyed Punjabis. Both are of Aryan descent, yet somewhere along the line the bloodstock of other groups has filtered its way in. Likewise, the Sindhis and Baluch may be defined as distinct ethnic groups, though both extend far beyond the boundaries of modern Pakistan, into India and Iran respectively.

Amongst the mountains and valleys of northern Pakistan live myriad groups that reflect both centuries of contact via the various strands of the Silk Road, and long periods of isolation. The people of Hunza (who claim to be descended from the armies of Alexander the Great), are followers of the Ismaili branch of Islam, whilst the darker skinned people of Nagar are Shia Muslims. Yet these two groups are neighbours, living just a short distance apart on the opposite banks of a river. Or consider the Gojalis, linked by geography and religion to the people of Hunza, yet by language and ethnicity to the nomads of Central Asia. Similarly, the Baltis of Baltistan are followers of the Shia branch of Islam, yet ethnically and linguistically their closest ties are to Buddhist Tibet. Dotted amongst these groups are small pockets of peoples who do not appear to fit in anywhere, such as the Kalash of Chitral, incorrectly labelled as 'kafirs', or 'non-believers', despite their complex religion. The joy of travelling in Pakistan is to encounter these different groups, learn about their varying ways of life, and to see how they fit into this entity called 'Pakistan'.

A land of adventure

Exploring the mountains Not surprisingly, Pakistan's stunning mountains have been attracting professional and amateur climbers for decades. They also offer some of the most spectacular trekking imaginable. In terms of sheer scope and variety, northern Pakistan arguably surpasses any other region in the world, offering a range of opportunities to cover all tastes and inclinations, with everything from easy day-walks to demanding treks of up to three weeks or more. Even if trekking completely turns you off, the mountains are still within easy reach. As well as travelling along the KKH, which takes you right through the heart of this awesome landscape, you could hire a jeep for the demanding but equally exhilerating journey on rough tracks between Gilgit and Chitral, or up onto the high Deosai Plateau. You can even view K2 and the host of other high peaks which surround it from the comfort of a PIA Boeing 737 as it undertakes a round-trip 'air safari' from Islamabad.

The wild frontier Pakistan's North West Frontier Province (NWFP) takes its name from the days of the Raj, when this was indeed a frontier region over which the British struggled to exert their control. Then, as now, the war-like Pathan tribes of the area refused to be completely subdued, maintaining their autonomy in an uneasy truce with the authorities. Even today, when you travel through the tribal areas of NWFP, you are advised to stick to the main road; as soon as you stray from the road, Pakistani state law is replaced by tribal law and you are beyond the reach of the authorities.

The Khyber Pass Just 50 km to the west of Peshawar is the legendary Khyber Pass. Its fame derives from the fact that it was of enormous strategic importance to the British, representing the 'gateway of India'. To visit the pass, which lies in the territory of the Afridi tribe, you must take an armed escort. Recently, the British-built steam railway which climbs to the top of the pass has been reopened. A ride on this remarkable railway line, with its 34 tunnels and 92 bridges, is an experience not to be missed.

Darra Adam Khel Whenever the local political situation permits, the authorities in Peshawar allow tourists to visit what is perhaps the most unusual town in Pakistan. Darra Adam Khel, just over 40 km to the south of Peshawar, is a small, dusty one-street town with a strong 'wild west' feel to it. But rather than the usual mixture of shops selling food, household goods et cetera, practically the only thing you will find on sale here is guns; everything from tiny pen-guns which slip neatly into your top pocket, to Kalashnikovs and full-size rocket launchers. Even more amazingly, all these weapons are made in the town itself, using the most primitive of machine tools.

The unexplored south The southern half of Pakistan is rarely visited in any great detail by tourists, though it also conceals many fascinating attractions. Explore the mysterious Cholistan desert by jeep, or better still, by camel. Discover isolated desert fortresses with a 'lost-in-time' feel about them, abandoned cities and tombs that the outside world appears to have passed by, or the tented settlements of nomadic tribes scratching a living out of this harsh environment. Enjoy a cup of tea on the banks of the mighty Indus as it flows down through the heartlands of Pakistan, or cycle along the shady, tree-lined canals that branch from this river, its life-giving waters transforming the vast surrounding plains into fertile farmland. Marvel at the rugged beauty of Baluchistan's inhospitable landscape, or venture into the bizarre moonscape of the Makran coastal region.

Left: one of the most popular day walks in northern Pakistan involves crossing a couple of spectacular suspension bridges over the Hunza river, near Passu.

Below: a man having his head shaved in the Sunday market in Kashgar, the town that stands at the end of the Karakoram Highway in China.

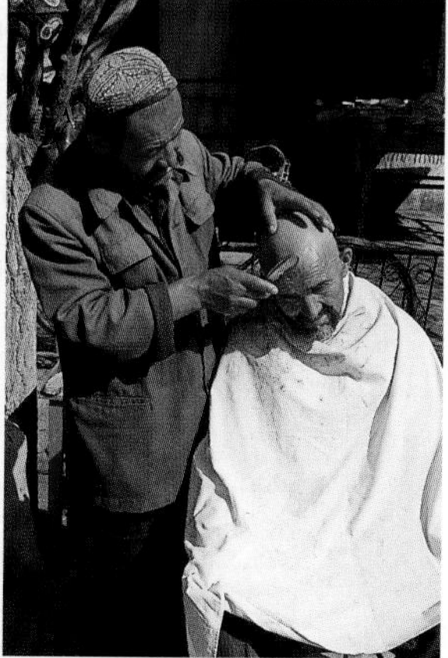

Above: the beautifully sited Passu village in Gojal, Upper Hunza, is the base for some of Pakistan's best day-walks and short hikes.

Left: a young girl plays outside her house in Melishkar, on the path up to one of Hunza's greatest viewpoints at Duikar.

Sights, sounds and smells of Pakistan

Wherever you go in Pakistan, you're never quite sure what's around the next corner. This is nowhere more so the case than in the country's towns and cities, which have a sense of vibrancy and exuberance that is a hallmark of all the great metropolises of the subcontinent. A wander around a Pakistani town is an assault on all five senses.

The bazaars Jostling for space in the crowded bazaars, you will find almost everything under the sun which might appeal, fascinate or appal; pungent, brightly coloured spices piled high into neat conical mounds; a bewildering variety of fresh fruits and vegetables; great chunks of meat hanging rudely amidst hovering clouds of flies; glittering displays of gold and silver bridal jewellery, all intricately and painstakingly fashioned by hand; medical quacks peddling highly dubious-looking arrays of elixirs for every possible ailment you can imagine; beautiful hand-woven rugs, hand-knotted carpets, printed and embroidered fabrics, intricately carved woodwork and other handicrafts. The list is truly endless, and whether you simply want to wander through, taking it all in, or hunt for bargains to take home, the only limit to what you might discover is your own stamina!

Food Aficianados of that great British institution, the Indian restaurant, may be surprised to learn that many of these are in fact run by Pakistanis. Indeed, a firm favourite such as the 'Balti' (absolutely nothing to do with Baltistan) is derived from the Pakistani *karahi*. Watching this spicy dish of braised meat and vegetables being cooked in its distinctive heavy iron wok amidst leaping flames is almost as enjoyable as eating it! The array of dishes awaiting you is truly mouth-watering; there are *tandoori* and *tikka* dishes from Punjab, the *chapli kebab* (a round flat burger made from mince, chopped onions, egg and tomato) from NWFP, *sajji* (a whole leg of lamb roasted on an open fire) from Baluchistan, and a whole host of others.

Contrasts Perhaps most striking of all are the ever-present contrasts to be found at every turn. Stand and watch the scribes congregated outside the post office writing letters on behalf of the illiterate, then wander next door to the recently opened internet café. Listen to the muezzin call the faithful to prayer from the mosque's minaret, then check out the latest Hindi-pop tunes from Bollywood in the bootleg cassette shop. Watch a middle-class 'VVIP' ('Very Very Important Person') in his latest Japanese four-wheel drive vehicle stuck in a traffic jam alongside a camel-drawn cart, a carbon monoxide-pumping auto-rickshaw, an elaborately decorated truck and a spectacularly overcrowded bus. See Wasim Akram smack a cricket ball to all parts of the stadium, then watch a small boy repeat those same shots using a home-made bat in a game of street cricket; there's no tea interval here, just a quick break whilst passing cars drive through the centre of the 'pitch'. Or see the polo players in Lahore who would not look out of place in the company of Prince Charles at Windsor, and then watch the version played in the Northern Areas, which is best described as rugby-cum-wrestling on horseback.

Surprises Most of all, Pakistan is a land of surprises; travelling through the remotest backwaters of Baluchistan, you might suddenly find yourself the honoured guest in the palatial residence of a local tribal chief (educated at Oxford or Harvard no doubt); just as you are at the end of your tether at the overwhelmingly male-dominated social set up, you might meet an outspoken Pakistani woman campaigning to promote female education. There is always something or someone around the next corner ready to shatter any simple generalizations or stereotypes you may be tempted to construct for yourself.

Clockwise from top left: *market day at Sialkot, an important industrial centre in Punjab famed for the sports goods it produces (including the footballs used in the 1998 World Cup); Pakistan excels at a number of sports, notably cricket, hockey and squash, so bats, sticks and raquets are produced locally; cinema advertising billboards at Mansehra, on the Karakoram Highway; available nationwise (of course) a Coca Cola delivery van; kite fighting is a popular pastime, here ground glass is added to the threads enabling combatants to cut their rivals' kite strings.*

2

Essentials

Essentials

Planning your trip

Where to go

Pakistan is a land of contrasts; not just in terms of landscapes, but also in terms of peoples and cultures. In many ways it is several countries rolled into one, and so the best way to visit it, time and money permitting, is to travel slowly and extensively. Each of the regions described in detail in this *Handbook* has something different to offer, and noted below are just some of the highlights.

Karakoram Highway/ Northern Areas

Karakoram Highway There's an old saying about 'getting there being half the fun'. This is certainly true of the journey along the KKH, where you can marvel not just at the natural landscape, but also at the ingenuity of man.

Fairy Meadows and Nanga Parbat Be captivated by the world's ninth highest mountain, and Pakistan's most accessible 8,000 metres plus peak, from your camping spot in a flower-strewn alpine meadow.

Gilgit to Chitral This is one of Pakistan's most beautiful but challenging journeys, and still relatively few visitors attempt it. Yet transport connections are improving, and for those prepared to rough it a bit, or use their feet, the attractions are almost limitless. The wonderfully rural Ishkoman and Yasin valleys provide engaging diversions off the main jeep track, whilst Khalti Lake must be one of Pakistan's most beautiful spots. Or why not head up to the Shandur Pass, perhaps in time to catch the world's most spectacular polo tournament.

Concordia The trek along the Baltoro glacier to Concordia brings you into the presence of a host of peaks over 8,000 metres, including K2, the second highest mountain in the world. It's a long and demanding trek, but also perhaps the most spectacular in the world.

Hushe valley This beautiful valley is dominated by the towering majesty of Masherbrum peak to the north. It is accessible by jeep as far as the tiny village of Hushe, from where you can undertake numerous walks and treks. For the serious trekker, this valley also provides an alternative route into or out of Concordia, over the demanding Gondogoro La.

Deosai plateau This vast expanse of land above 4,000 metres represents an extension of the Tibetan plateau in geographical terms. Snowbound for most of the year, in early summer it is carpeted in bright flowers of every description. It is also home to the rare Himalayan Brown Bear.

Chalt and the Chaprot Valley The word 'rustic' can almost have been invented for the Chaprot Valley, with its charming walks through the fruit orchards and wheat fields.

Rakaposhi This beautiful 7,788 metres snowy peak becomes a familiar sight to those travelling up and down the KKH. It is at its most striking in the early morning light or sunset glow. For an even better appreciation, you can hike up to its base camp from Minapin in a relatively straightforward two-day return trip.

Karimabad, Altit and Duikar Karimabad, its scaled down neighbour Altit, and the viewpoint at Duikar high above, are the most popular spots in the famous Hunza Valley. Beautiful mountain views in all directions, charming people, village atmosphere, and a good choice of accommodation, continues to draw visitors. And despite what some might say, these villages are far from being "too touristy".

The road to China The KKH does not end at the Pakistani border, so there's no need to finish your trip there. With a Chinese visa and a double-entry Pakistani visa, it's possible to head up to the Chinese Central Asian town of Kashgar for its fabulous Sunday Market, spend a few days at the beautiful Kara Kuli (lake), and then return to Pakistan.

Essentials

NWFP

Peshawar The bazaars of Peshawar's Old City are a truly fascinating and absorbing experience, as well as being an excellent place to shop for everything from carpets to spices. Peshawar museum, though not as large or famous as Lahore's, is also highly impressive.

Khyber Pass A trip by steam train on the narrow-gauge railway line from Peshawar to the historic Khyber pass takes you through the wild Tribal Areas of the Afridi Pathans. From the top of the pass you can see (but sadly not go) across the border into Afghanistan.

Takht-e-Bhai Sites such as Taxila may be more famous, but the beautifully preserved and strikingly situated ruins of the Gandharan Buddhist monastery of Takht-e-Bhai are full of atmosphere and sure to inspire a sense of wonder at this ancient civilization.

Chitral In the extreme north of NWFP, the Chitral region is the setting for some truly stunning mountain scenery. It's not as well known as Hunza or Baltistan (or as frequently visited), but every bit as impressive.

Kalash valleys Three small valleys in Chitral are home to the unique non-Muslim Kalash people, whose beliefs and way of life provide a fascinating and colourful contrast to Pakistan's otherwise male-dominated society.

Azad Jammu and Kashmir

Thickly forested valleys Sadly scarred by a bitter dispute that has lasted half a century and has put the most attractive spots 'out of bounds' to visitors, it is still possible to visit some of AJ&K's famous alpine valleys.

Mirpur Find out more about the life of the average Pakistani in Britain by visiting this small town in southern AJ&K. Urdu or Kashmiri language skills are not required; just an understanding of Brummie and Yorkshire accents.

Baluchistan

Quetta Although there is little in the way of historic monuments here (Quetta was largely destroyed by an earthquake in 1935), Baluchistan's provincial capital has a friendly, relaxing atmosphere about it. You can also find a dazzling array of colourful Baluchi rugs, carpets, embroidered fabrics, jewellery, antiques and other items in the bazaars.

Ziarat Within easy reach of Quetta, the hill resort of Ziarat has a refreshingly cool climate, making it a great place to escape from the summer heat. The surrounding hills and valleys, with their extensive juniper forests and cool streams, offer numerous opportunities for walking and hiking.

Bolan Pass Baluchistan's only rail link with the rest of Pakistan runs through the historic Bolan Pass, providing one of the most dramatic and memorable train rides in the country.

Sind

Karachi This may not be the most beautiful city, and it suffers more than its fair share of inter-communal tension and violence, but it does have a number of attractions associated with the life and times of the founder of the nation, Mohammad Ali Jinnah. His mausoleum is one of the finest monuments built in Pakistan since independence.

Makli Hill and Thatta Covering a substantial area, and featuring over one million tombs, Makli Hill is considered to be the world's largest necropolis. The adjacent town of Thatta features the simple but splendid lines of the Mughal era Shah Jahan Mosque.

Sehwan Sharif Sufi saints did much to spread the message of the Prophet Mohammad throughout Sind, and at Sehwan, the last resting place of a noted 13th century Sufi mystic, you can experience living, breathing Islam in an intense atmosphere charged with piety, devotion and hope.

Moenjo Daro Perhaps the most important archaeological site in South Asia, Moenjo Daro represents the Indus Valley Civilization at its peak, some 3,500-4,500 years ago. The state of preservation of this ancient city is a marvel even to those with only a passing interest in archaeology.

Punjab

The Salt Range This little visited region features panoramic views, all-but-forgotten Hindu temples and pilgrimage sites, plus a huge salt mine that provides the mineral from which the region draws its name.
Lahore Lahore probably has more 'unmissable' sights than any other Pakistani city. Its Mughal heritage is beautifully encapsulated by the magnificent Badshahi Mosque, Lahore Fort, Shalimar Gardens and Jahangir's Tomb, whilst priceless items from all periods of Pakistan's history are on display in the magnificent Lahore Museum. Do not miss the Shrine of Data Ganj Baksh, or a stroll through Lahore's Old City.
Multan Although the heat and dust can be extremely trying at the 'wrong' time of year, Multan has a cluster of magnificent shrines, tombs and monuments that reflect the city's strategic importance at the crossroads of the sub-continent.
Uch Sharif Few visitors make it down to Uch, which is a great shame since the tombs here are one of Pakistan's greatest sights. Approaching them from the town, you are confronted by a series of superb brick built tombs, fabulously embellished with stunning glazed tile mosaic. But as you get closer, you realize that half of each tomb is missing, a victim of the changing course of the Chenab river. Far from reducing the impact of these magnificent buildings, this seems to enhance their appeal.
Fort Derawar and the Cholistan Desert Hire a jeep (or a camel) and head off into Pakistan's largest desert, where you will find a series of spectacular fortresses looming out of the dunes and scrub.

When to go

Pakistan can be visited at any time of year, the best season varying according to the region to be visited. Very broadly, the southern half of the country (Sind, Punjab, Baluchistan and southern NWFP) is best visited from late autumn to early spring (November to March) when temperatures are pleasantly cooler. During the summer, most parts of the plains are extremely hot and travelling around is hard work. The northern half of the country (northern NWFP, Northern Areas and parts of Punjab) are best visited from late spring to early autumn (April to October). During the winter, most of the mountainous north is snowbound, and not easily accessible. The main trekking season in the Northern Areas and NWFP extends from June to September. For details of holidays and festivals in Pakistan, see page 53, and for information on travelling in Pakistan during Ramadan, see page 55.

What will it cost?

The cost of living in Pakistan remains well below that of industrialized countries. Food, accommodation and transport are exceptionally cheap by western standards. Budget travellers can expect to get by on as little as US$10 a day by staying in the cheapest hotels (sometimes in dormitories), eating at cheap 'local' restaurants, and by travelling by the cheapest means. By increasing your budget to around US$20 a day you will be able to experience a significant improvement in the standard of accommodation, as well as allowing you to travel on a more luxurious form of transport (buses with reserved seats, a sleeper on a train etc). Sleeping, eating and transport options are available in Pakistan for all budgets, whether travelling with a backpack or a suit bag.

What to take

Most travellers take far too much. Remember that practically everything is available in Pakistan, at least in the major cities. We have not included a comprehensive list of what to take (if you cannot pack your own bag, perhaps you should stay at home), but here are a few points worth bearing in mind.

A rucksack is the most practical if you intend to do a lot of moving around (and essential if you intend to trek), but does instantly classify you as a 'backpacker'. Some people prefer a hybrid backpack/suitcase on which the straps can be zipped out of sight, turning you into a 'respectable' tourist where need be.

Appropriate clothing depends on the season and area in which you will be travelling. In summer, light, loose-fitting cottons are a must. A *shalwar kameez* (baggy pants and long, loose-fitting over-shirt) can be bought very cheaply in Pakistan, off the peg or tailor-made, and is ideal in hot, humid weather. It also helps you to blend in a little and draws a warm response from Pakistanis to see you wearing their national dress. Footwear should likewise be as airy as possible for hot weather; comfortable sandals or light canvas trainers are a good bet. In the mountains warm clothing is essential. Note that in winter it gets very chilly even on the plains. It is important for both men and women to dress modestly; shorts, singlets etc are likely to cause offence. For women a scarf to cover their heads where necessary is very useful. See also the advice for women travellers.

If you are on **medication**, bring sufficient supplies. It is probably readily available, but brand names may differ and stocks may be out of date. Some medicines deteriorate rapidly in hot conditions. Contact lens cleaning equipment is available only in the main cities. Likewise for tampons and contraceptives. **Insect repellents** are generally less effective than the stronger western varieties, although good mosquito coils are readily available. Strong sunscreen can be difficult to find away from larger cities.

Spare **passport photos** are very useful for any bureaucratic dealings. Take **photocopies** of all important documents in case of loss or theft (also leave a set with friends at home or, ideally, in Pakistan). Photos of family and home are an excellent way of bridging the cultural gap and are always generate great interest. Postcards of home make good gifts.

Budget travellers should bring their own **padlock** to use in cheaper hotels where doors are often secured by a padlockable bolt. A **cotton sheet** sleeping bag is also very useful for when the available sheets are dirty. A secure **money belt** is the best way to carry money and documents.

Although **photographic** products are available in the larger cities, it is highly recommended that you bring all your film and batteries from home. If you do run out, Fuji in Rawalpindi has the freshest film stock (see Rawalpindi Essentials).

Tours and tour operators

In Pakistan

Adventure Tours Pakistan, PO Box 1780, House 55, Street 53,G-9-1, Islamabad, T252759, F252145. Trekking, climbing, jeep safaris. Run by Ashraf Aman the first Pakistani to climb K2. ***Adventure Travel***, PO Box 2062, 15 Wali Centre, 86 South Blue Area, Islamabad, T822728, F821407. Indus boating, camel safaris, climbing, trekking, jeep safaris, special interest tours (including to Kashgar and Kyrgistan). ***Baltistan Tours***, PO Box 604, Link Road, Satellite Town, T2626, F2180. Branch office PO Box 1285, House 14, Street 44, F-6/1, Islamabad, T270338, F278620. Local handlers for *KE Adventure Travel* (see below). ***Indus Guides***, 108A, C-II, Gulberg III, Lahore, T872975, F5712529. Special interest tours, jeep safaris, Indus boating, camel safaris, trekking. ***Hindukush Trails***, House 37, Street 28, F-6/1, Islamabad, T277067, F275031. Trekking, climbing, jeep safaris. Specializing in Chitral. Run by Chitral's former ruling family. ***Karakoram Treks and Tours***, 1 Baltoro House, Street 19, F-7/2, Islamabad, T829120, F271996. Trekking, climbing, jeep safaris and special interest tours (Northern Areas). ***Nazir Sabir Expeditions***, PO Box 1442, Islamabad, T853672, F250293. Specializing in climbing expeditions (Nazir Sabir was the second Pakistani to climb K2), also treks and jeep safaris. ***North Pakistan Treks, Tours and Expeditions***, PO Box 463, Islamabad, Pakistan, T281655, F260835. Trekking, mountaineering, jeep safaris. ***Omar Travels***, No 8, Shahid

Essentials

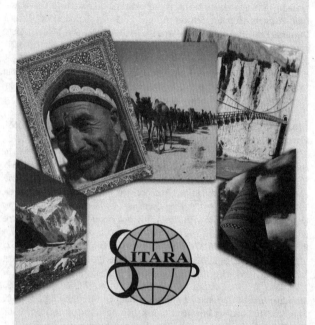

Plaza, Blue Area, Islambad, T815409, F275006. *Pakistan Guides*, PO Box 1692, 3rd Floor, 62/2 Bank Road, Rawalpindi, T524808, F539497. Run by Kaiser Khan, 20 years experience, offers a wide range of specialized expeditions and tours. ***Pakistan Tours Ltd***, 24 Flashman's Hotel, The Mall, Rawalpindi T563038, F565449. Affiliated to PTDC but operating as a commercial concern, full range of services, able to offer tailor-made packages. ***Sitara Travel Consultants***, Waheed Plaza, 3rd floor, 52 West, Jinnah Avenue, Blue Area, PO Box 1662, Islamabad, T813372, F279651. Also has offices located in Tashkent and Canada. Full range of services, including tours of Central Asia. ***Trans-Pakistan Adventure Services***, PO Box 2103, Apt 8, 2nd Floor, Muzaffar Chambers, Fazl-e-Haq Road, Jinnah Avenue, T274796, F274838. Special interest tours, jeep safaris (including Makran coast), trekking, climbing. ***Travel Walji's***, Walji's Building, 10 Khabayan-e-Suhrawardy, PO Box No 1088, Islamabad, T270757-58, F270753. Pakistan's largest travel agents, full range of services. Also with offices in Karachi and Lahore (see respective city Directories). Smaller regional companies are listed in the Directories of the relevant towns/cities.

Abroad ***Allibert***, 14 Rue de l'Asile Popincourt, 75011 Paris, France, T01-48061661, F01-48064722. Or. Route de Grenoble, 38530 Chapareillan, France, T76452226, F76452728. ***Club Adventure***, 122 Rue d'Assas, 75006 Paris, France, T4806116. ***Encounter Overland***, 267 Old Brompton Road, London SW5 9JA, UK, T0171-3706845, F0171-2449737. ***Exodus***, 9 Weir Road, London SW12 0LT, UK, T0181-6730859, F0181-6730779. ***Explore Worldwide***, 1 Frederick Street, Aldershot, Hants GU11 1LQ, UK, T01252-319448, F01252-343170. ***Hann Overland***, 2 Ivy Mill Lane, Godstone, Surrey RH9 8NH, UK, T01883-743861, F01883-743912. ***High Places***, Globe Works, Penistone Road, Sheffield, S6 3AE, UK, T0114-2757500. ***Himalayan Kingdoms***, 20 The Mall, Clifton, Bristol BS8 4DR, UK, T0117-9237163. ***Himalaya Trekking***, Constant Erzeijstraat 49, 3523 Vt Utrecht, Netherlands, T030-871420. ***Inner Asia Expeditions***, 2627 Lombard Street, San Fransisco, CA94123, USA, T415-9220448, F415-3465535. ***KE Adventure Travel***, 32 Lake Road, Keswick, Cumbria CA12 5DQ, UK, T017687-73966, F017687-74693. ***Mountain Travel***, 6420 Fairmount Avenue, El Cerrito, CA 94530, USA, T415-5278100, F415-5257710. ***Travelbag Adventures***, 15 Turk Street, Alton, Hampshire, GU34 1AG, UK, T01420-541007. ***Wilderness Travel***, 801 Allston Way, Berkeley, CA 94710, USA, T415-5480420, F415-5480347.

Special interest travel

The ***Adventure Foundation***, which has offices at the *Adventure Inn* in Islamabad (see page 197) can organize **horse riding**, **ballooning** and **paragliding.** One of Pakistan's greatest attractions is the opportunities it offers for **trekking** and **climbing**. A selection of the main treks (and shorter walks) are covered in the travelling text of the *Pakistan Handbook* (described at the point of departure), and there is also a section providing detailed practical information for anyone planning a trek (see page 67). Many of the tour operators listed above specialize in trekking and climbing expeditions. They can also organize other adventure activities such as **jeep safaris** through the mountains of northern Pakistan or **camel safaris** in the Cholistan desert. Long stretches of the Indus are navigable and a couple of the tour operators offer **boating** trips on this formidable river. We are not aware of any tour operators within Pakistan with **white-water** rafting/canoeing equipment or expertise, though many of the rivers in NWFP and the Northern Areas have great potential for this sport. There is a book on the subject; *Paddling the Frontier; a Guide to Pakistan's Whitewater*, by Wickliffe Walker.

Although Pakistan has enormous potential for **skiing**, facilities are poorly developed and you will have to bring all your own equipment. The Austrian-built chairlift at Malam Jabba (see page 383), where there are several good slopes, was at the time of writing still not operational, though the hotel there is now open. Check with PTDC in Islamabad for the latest situation. The *Adventure Foundation* can also provide information and help you with organizing a skiing expedition in Pakistan.

Sports

Some visitors plan their trip around the itinerary of a visiting **cricket** side. Pakistan is an excellent place to see international cricket; not only is there a unique atmosphere inside the stadiums, but tickets are readily available and extremely cheap (under £1 to see international cricket is not bad!). In the winter of 2000-2001 the England team will be touring Pakistan for the first time since 1987(fixtures from the England and Wales Cricket Board will be available in early 2000, T0171-4321200).

Wildlife

In Sind there is excellent birdwatching in **Haleji Lake Bird Sanctuary**, and a wide range of wildlife (including the Sind Ibex) in **Kirthar National Park**. Visits to both of these can be organized through the Sind Tourist Development Corporation (STDC) and Sind Wildlife Management Board (see page 100). Visits to the **Hazerganji Chiltan National Park** in Baluchistan (home to the Chiltan Markhor) can be arranged through the Quetta Forestry Department (see page 150). Visits to the **Deosai National Park** in Baltistan (home to the Himalayan Brown Bear) can be arranged through the Himalayan Wildlife Project (see page 516). The **Chitral Gol National Park** (see page 404) provides a refuge for Snow Leopards and Black Bears.

Finding out more

The tour operators and other organizations mentioned above are best placed to give further information on organized tours and specialist interest travel in Pakistan. On a more general level, the government-run **Pakistan Tourism Development Corporation (PTDC)** has a number of information centres abroad, though on the whole they are of little help. Their web site is www.tourism.gov.pk. The various branches of PTDC within the country, and their provincial offshoots are likely to be of more help, though their usefulness varies.

Before you travel

Visas

Regulations regarding visas are subject to change, so it is essential to check the current situation with the issuing embassy. All foreign nationals require a valid visa for visiting Pakistan, with a few exceptions. Tourist visas are valid for a period of 90 days (though some embassies, eg Beijing, sometimes only issue 30 day visas). Single, double and multiple entry visas are available. Single and double entry visas must be used within six months of the date of issue. Multiple entry visas are valid for a period of one year. In the case of double or multiple entry visas, each visit is restricted to a period of 90 days. If you are travelling up to Kashgar (China), and then returning to Pakistan, it makes things easier if you obtain a double-entry visa in advance.

Certain countries have visa abolition agreements with Pakistan, allowing nationals of those countries to visit Pakistan without a visa for periods of between 30-90 days. These agreements in particular are subject to frequent change, so check with your nearest Pakistan embassy.

For details of visa extensions see page 201.

Cost

Visa fees vary according to your nationality, and are subject to frequent changes. Given opposite are the fees (£ sterling) charged by the Pakistani embassy in London for single entry tourist visas in January 1999. Note that foreign nationals must provide proof of residency in the UK if applying there, and in some instances may be required to apply in their home country in any case.

***Australia** £40; **Denmark** £43; **France** £20; **Germany** £15; **UK** £40; **USA** £33*

Travel tip

Be prepared for conflicting advice from Pakistani embassies abroad and from immigration officials inside Pakistan. For example, the Pakistan High Commission in London may tell you that British passport holders visiting Pakistan for less than 30 days do not require visas. However, when your plane lands at Karachi, immigration officials may issue you with a 72 hour transit visa (meaning that you will have to go to Islamabad to extend it), or even simply tell you that you can't come in without a visa! The moral of the story: always get a visa in advance if possible.

Transit visas These are issued *only at the discretion of immigration officials*. Visitors are strongly advised to obtain a full visa beforehand if at all possible; converting a transit visa into a full tourist visa is time consuming, and can only be done in Islamabad. Transit visas are usually only valid for 72 hours, though you may get seven days if arriving overland in Pakistan from China (see page 573). Coming from Iran, travellers were being issued with 72 hour transit visas at the Taftan border without any problems in late 1998, and the Home Department in Quetta (See Useful addresses in the Quetta Directory) was extending these to seven days. Transit visas are rarely given at the Pakistan-India border (see page 281).

Foreigners' registration Note that all foreign tourists, except nationals of UK, UAE and Australia, are required to register if staying more than 30 days in the country (see page 31 in the 'Touching down' section below). See also section on 'Permits for restricted areas' in the 'Touching down' section.

Pakistani embassies around the world

For foreign embassy listings in Pakistan, see under individual city in the 'Directory' section.

Australia, PO Box 648, 4 Timbarra Crescent, O'Malley Act-2606, Mawson, 2607 Canberra, T2901676. **Consulates:** Sydney T2677250, Melbourne T6087153. ***Austria***, Hofzeile 13, A 1190, Vienna, T367381. ***Bangladesh***, NE (C) 2, Road 71, Gulshan, Dhaka, T885387. ***Belgium***, Avenue Delleur 57, Brussels 1170, T6738007. ***Canada***, Burnside Building, 151 Slater Avenue, Suite 608, Ottowa, Ontario K1P 5H3, T2387881, F2387296. **Consulates:** Toronto T2501255, Montreal, T8452297. ***China***, 1 Dong Zhi Men, Wai Da Jie, San Li Tun, Beijing 100600, T5321217. **Consulate:** Hong Kong T28270681. ***Denmark***, Valeursvej 17,2900 Hellerup, Copenhagen, T31621693. ***France***, 18 Rue Lord Byron, Paris 75008, T45622332. **Consulate:** 10 Boulevard Jules Favre, 96006 Lyon, T78529680. ***Germany***, Rheinallee 24, 53173 Bonn, T95530. ***India***, 2/50-G Shantipath, Chanakyapuri, New Delhi110021, T600603. ***Indonesia***, 50 Jalan Teuku Umar, Jakarta, Pusat, T3144008. ***Iran***, Koocha-e-Ahmed, Eatmadzadeh, Block 1, Jamshedabad Shomali, Tehran, T394330. **Consulates:** Mashad T29845, Zahedan T23666. ***Italy***, Via Della, Camillucia 682, 00135 Rome, T36301775. **Consulates:** Genoa T3628554, Naples T7532865. ***Japan***, 2-14-9 Moto Azabu, 2 Chome, Miato-Ku, Tokyo, T34544861. **Consulate:** Osaka T2262483. ***Kazakhstan***, 25 Tulebayeua, Alma Ata, T331502. ***Malaysia***. 132 Jalan Ampang, 50450 Kuala Lumpur, T2418877. ***Myanmar (Burma)***, PO Box 581, A-4, Diplomatic Quarters, Payay Road, Rangoon, T22881. ***Nepal***, PO Box 202, Panipokhari, Kathmandu, T418446. ***Netherlands***, Amaliastraat-8, 2514 JC, The Hague, T3648948. ***New Zealand*** (Consulate) 251 Kapa Road, Kohimarama, Auckland 5 N-2, Auckland, T3072238. ***Norway***, Eckersbergsgata 20, 02244 Oslo, T555197. ***Philippines***, Alexander House, 132 Amorsolo Street, Legaspi Village, Makati Metro, Manila, T2776. ***Portugal***, Avenida da Republic20-1, 1000 Lisbon, T3538547. ***Russia***, 17 Ul Sadova Kudrinskaya, Moscow, T2503991. ***Singapore***, 20-A Nazim Road, Singapore 1025, T7376988. ***Spain***, Avda, Pio XII, 11, 28016 Madrid, T3459138. **Consulates:** Barcelona T2574230, Bilbao T4320845, Seville T228921. ***Sri Lanka***, 211 De Saram Place, Colombo 10, T696301. ***Sweden***, Sergels Tong 12, 14 TR11-57, Stockholm, T203300. **Consulate:** Gothenburg T812124. ***Switzerland***, Bernastrasse 47, Ch-3005, Berne, T3525063.

Tajikistan, Tajikistan Hotel, Dushanbe, T275153. ***Thailand***, 31 Soi Nana Nua Sukhumvit (3) Road, Bangkok 10110, T2532557. ***Turkey***, Iran Caddesi No. 37, Gazi Osman Pasa, Ankara, T4271410. ***UK***, Visa section, 34 Lowndes Square, London SW1X 9JN, T0171-6649200 (recorded visa info T0891-880880). **Consulates:** Bradford T661114, Birmingham T2334123, Glasgow T4295335, ManchesterT2881349. ***USA***, 2315 Massachusetts Avenue NW, Washington DC 20008, T9396200, F3870484. **Consulates:** New York, T8795800, Los Angeles T4410167, Boston T2675555, Chigago T8537630, San Francisco T7780677. ***Uzbekistan***, Tchilanzar Street 25,Tashkent, T771003.

Vaccinations

There are a number of health-related matters which must be tackled up to a month before arriving in Pakistan (notably vaccinations and malaria-prevention measures). See the 'Health' section on page 56 for full details.

Money

Currency

Pakistani currency is the **Pakistani Rupee** (usually just referred to as the 'rupee' and written as 'Rs'). Notes come in denominations of Rs 1,000, 500, 100, 50, 10, 2 and 1. The Rupee is divided into 100 paise, although the coins of 50, 25, 20, 10 and 5 paise are gradually disappearing. The lower denomination notes are slowly being replaced with coins. Unlike in India, currency notes are usually accepted whatever their condition, unless they have been seriously damaged or defaced. Obtaining change for larger currency notes can be difficult in remoter areas; it is well worth accumulating a good supply of smaller notes. For details of the 'cost of living' in Pakistan, see 'What will it cost?' in the 'Planning your trip' section (page 21).

How to take your money

It is worth giving some advance thought to the way in which you will carry your travelling funds. **US$** is the most widely accepted currency, followed by **£ Sterling**. Other European currencies can generally only be changed in the five main cities. US$ has shown the greatest stability recently, while £ Sterling has been subject to significant fluctuations. A secure money-belt worn beneath your clothing is the best way to carry your documents and travelling funds, although it is worth having a few other 'stashes' in case of emergencies (eg some money hidden in your day-pack, some in your luggage etc).

Cash It is unwise to carry all your travelling funds in the form of cash. However, it is advisable to have some hard currency cash for use in emergencies (or when banks are shut). A good mix of high and low denomination (recently issued) US$ bills is the best bet.

Travellers' cheques This is the best way to carry the bulk of your travelling funds since they can be replaced if lost/stolen. Note, however, that even the well-known brands of travellers' cheques rarely live up to their advertising when it comes to replacing lost cheques in Pakistan. **US$** and **£ Sterling** are the two most widely accepted currencies, with other currencies only really being convertible in the state capital cities. Like cash, you tend to get marginally better rates on larger denominations. ***American Express*** travellers' cheques are probably the best bet, largely because with offices in Islamabad, Karachi, Lahore and Islamabad, replacing lost travellers' cheques should (in theory) be more straightforward. Make sure that you keep your travellers' cheques purchase receipts separate from the cheques themselves. When buying your travellers' cheques, whenever possible go to the offices of the company issuing the cheques (eg for American Express cheques go to an Amex office) rather than an agency (eg a travel agents or building society that also sells Amex travellers' cheques); this will speed things up if you need them replaced.

Bank exchange rates: January 1999

US$1	*49.29*
UK £1	*81.24*
Aus $1	*31.26*
Can $1	*32.48*
NZ$1	*26.83*
Yen 100	*43.82*
DM1	*29.14*
Dutch Gilda 1	*25.93*
French Franc 1	*8.62*
Spanish Peseta 100	*34.83*
Italian Lira 1,000	*29.79*

***NB** These are bank exchange rates; on the open market you can get significantly higher rates (see below).*

Credit cards Currently you can only really use a credit card at most of the **L** and **A** category hotels, and at the tourist and handicraft shops in the five main cities. It can still be difficult to buy a plane ticket with a credit card. American Express card holders can use their cards to buy travellers' cheques at Amex offices, or to cash personal cheques there, whilst Visa and Mastercard holders can obtain (Rupee) cash advances on their cards at the international banks in the main five cities (though this is a time consuming process, and can involve a hefty commission fee).

Changing money

Banks ***National Bank of Pakistan***, ***Habib Bank*** and ***United Bank Limited*** are authorized to change foreign currency and travellers' cheques, as are foreign banks such as ***ANZ Grindlays***, ***American Express*** and ***Citibank***. Commission rates vary from bank to bank, so it is worth shopping around. American Express do not charge a commission for changing their own travellers' cheques. Note that outside of the main towns, Pakistani banks must obtain current exchange rates from their head offices; these usually don't arrive until late morning, leaving little time to conduct any transactions. It should also be noted that the further you move away from a large city, the poorer the rate you are likely to get. For example, if you are travelling up the KKH, the rate in Rawalpindi will be better than the rate in Gilgit, which will be better than the rate in Karimabad, which in turn will be better than the rate in Sust. Changing money (and especially travellers' cheques) can be a tediously time-consuming process.

Licensed money changers These are to be found in most towns and cities. They are perfectly legal and provide a much quicker service for changing cash and travellers' cheques. **NB** At the time of research, there was a significant difference between the official bank exchange rates and the open market (or so-called 'kerbside') rates being offered by licensed money changers. Thus, in late 1998, UK£1was fetching around Rs 95 for cash and Rs 90 for travellers' cheques, while US$1 was fetching around Rs 60 for cash and Rs 55 for travellers' cheques. This was a reflection of the dire state of the Pakistani economy and the lack of confidence in the Rupee; if and when the situation improves, the gap between the official bank rate and the 'kerbside' rate is likely to narrow.

Hotels Many of the larger hotels will also change foreign currency, and in some cases travellers' cheques, but generally at slightly lower rates than the banks.

Black market Unlicensed money changers generally offer identical rates to their licensed counterparts, but will not issue you with currency-exchange receipts. Those who approach you in the bazaars are likely to be working on a commission basis; they are often not the most trustworthy of characters and are best avoided.

Currency-exchange receipts You will receive a currency-exchange receipt when changing money through a bank or authorized dealer. You may be required to produce such receipts if you wish to reconvert rupees upon departure, or when buying international air tickets inside Pakistan.

Transferring money to Pakistan American Express and ANZ Grindlays can make instant money transfers to their banks in Pakistan, but charge a high fee. National Bank of Pakistan and Habib Bank branches abroad charge less, but can take two to three days. The cheapest option is to have a bank draft posted out to you personally by priority mail.

Reconverting rupees on departure Banks at the airports and land crossing points will be able to reconvert Rupees upon your departure, although they generally only have US$ cash. You will have to show currency-exchange receipts to the value of the amount you wish to reconvert.

Getting there

Air

Pakistan is easily accessible by air from just about any part of the world. The direct flying time is around nine hours from London, around 17 from New York, and about six hours from Bangkok. Pakistan is extensively served by its own national airline, **Pakistan International Airlines** (PIA), in addition to all the major (and many minor) airline companies. Thus it is possible to find rock-bottom discounted fares, in addition to the luxury associated with the more upmarket airlines.

Previously, most airlines served Karachi, with only a limited number of companies flying into Islamabad. However, for a number of reasons (including relatively high landing fees and a 'security' surcharge that airlines feel should be the responsibility of the government), many are switching operations from Karachi to Islamabad. Flying into Islamabad makes a lot of sense if you intend spending all your time in the north. For details of Quaid-e-Azam Airport in Karachi see page 97. For details of Islamabad International Airport see page 211. There are also a limited number of international flights into Lahore.

A flight bought from a discount ('bucket') shop in London will cost around £300 return (London-Karachi-London), whilst a return to Islamabad costs from £500 (London-Islamabad-London), though it pays to shop around. If money (and not time) is your key consideration, you can fly to Karachi and then travel overland to Islamabad. Alternatively, internal flights are very cheap when bought in Pakistan (see 'Getting around – Air' below).

Overland

Pakistan is very much part of the overland route between Europe and Southeast Asia, and beyond. Iranian visas are becoming increasingly easy to obtain, and the options for continuing on from Pakistan are wide ranging. The Karakoram Highway (KKH) provides onward access to China and Central Asia, whilst travelling on to India has never been easier. Addresses of foreign embassies in Pakistan are to be found in the 'Directory' information in Islamabad (and to a more limited extent in Karachi, Lahore and Quetta). **NB** For those arriving with their own vehicle, it is important to have the correct *Carnet de Passage*. See 'Getting around – private vehicles' for further details (page 45).

To/from India

Despite their long frontier, there is only one recognized border crossing between Pakistan and India, located between Lahore and Amritsar. The border towns are **Wagah** (23 kilometres from Lahore) on the Pakistani side, and **Attari** (39 kilometres from Amritsar) on the Indian side. The border should be open on every day of the year, although it is worth enquiring locally about holiday arrangements. See page 281 for further details.

Because of the sensitive nature of relations between the two states, it is worth getting your visas in advance (they are nigh on impossible to get on the border). Indian visas are only available in Islamabad (most nationalities are required to present a 'letter of recommendation' from their embassy), whilst Pakistani visas are only available in New Delhi (same 'letter' required). For further details about India, we quite naturally recommend the excellent Footprint *India Handbook*.

To/from China and Central Asia For those travelling on to China, it is essential to obtain a visa in advance since **they are not available on the border**. The Chinese embassy in Islamabad issues visas in one to three days (usually requiring a 'letter of recommendation' from your embassy). It is not permitted to take private vehicles into China unless prior arrangements have been made (this can take months, and also works out to be very expensive). In theory this restriction also applies to bicycles (the visa application form at the Chinese embassy in London states that a special permit for bicycles is required); in practice this rule is rarely enforced, and those cycling from Pakistan up to Kashgar (China) are unlikely to be challenged or 'encouraged' to load their bike onto a bus.

Pakistani border formalities are completed at **Afiyatabad/'New' Sust** on the KKH, whilst Chinese formalities are completed at **Tashkurgan**. For those arriving in Pakistan from China it is generally possible to get a seven-day transit visa on the border (extendable in Islamabad), though this involves unwanted hassle, and so you should get your visa in advance if possible. The only Pakistani embassy/consulate in China is in Beijing, some 4,000 kilometres from the Pak-China border (and they have a tendency to only issue one month, as opposed to three month, visas)! This border crossing is weather dependent, though it is generally open from 1 May until mid/end of November. For further details on crossing the border between Pakistan and China, see pages 573 and 578.

From the Chinese city of Kashgar it is possible to travel on to **Kyrghizstan** via the Tourgat Pass, although you will need a Kyrghiz visa in advance (available in Islamabad) and a permit to cross the pass (which can be arranged in Kashgar). It is also possible to travel on from Kashgar to Urumqi, and then from there to **Kazakhstan** (visas in Islamabad). A seldom undertaken, but much talked about, option from Kashgar is to travel to Lhasa in **Tibet** via Mount Kailash. Since permits for this gruelling trip are not available in Kashgar, this journey is technically illegal, though a number of travellers continue to attempt it. For full details of travelling on from Kashgar, see page 594.

To/from Iran The only official border crossing point between Pakistan and Iran is at **Taftan**, 84 kilometres from the Iranian city of Zahedan and over 600 kilometres from Quetta in Pakistan. Trains run between Zahedan and Quetta, although they are very slow (minimum 32 hours), or you can make the journey by bus which is much quicker (around 15 hours) but less comfortable. For further details of this border crossing, see page 169.

There is an Iranian embassy in Islamabad, and consulates in Peshawar, Lahore, Karachi and Quetta. At the time of researching, the Iranian consulate in Quetta claimed that it was issuing transit visas (usually valid for seven days and extendable by a further week once inside Iran) to tourists within 10 days. This represents a massive improvement on the situation a few years ago when the process took a minimum of one month. What's more they were not demanding that dreaded 'letter of recommendation'. Some readers have also written to say that the Iranian consulate in Lahore is issuing visas without too much hassle. Bear in mind, however, that the situation is liable to change without warning.

The Pakistani embassy is located in Tehran, with consulates in Mashad and Zahedan, but you are strongly advised to obtain your Pakistani visa before leaving home (especially given the limited time available on an Iranian transit visa).

To/from Afghanistan

At the time of going to press, visas for Afghanistan were only being issued to accredited journalists and aid workers. Tragically, Afghanistan continues to be deeply embroiled in civil war, and although the situation changes from week to week, there appears to be little hope of an end to the fighting in the foreseeable future. It is **not safe** for foreigners to visit; apart from the very real risk of getting caught up in fighting, there is the added danger from several million landmines remaining in the country. The Mine Clearing and Planning Agency report 20-25 'mine incidents' in Afghanistan every day.

Should the situation improve sufficiently, this beautiful country would once again form part of the overland route between Europe and Asia. It would also link Pakistan with the Central Asian republics. The two main border crossings are at Torkham, on the Khyber Pass between Peshawar and Jalalabad, and at Chaman, between Quetta and Kandahar. Most of Pakistan's border with Afghanistan is however extremely porous. If you are keen to find out about the current situation in Afghanistan, Peshawar is the best place to get up-to-date information. There are over a hundred NGOs still based there, working with Afghan refugees in Pakistan and across the border in Afghanistan itself. **ACBAR** (Agency Co-ordinating Body for Afghan Refugees) and **ARIC** (ACBAR Resource and Information Centre) share premises in Peshawar's University Town (see Useful addresses in the Peshawar Directory). They issue monthly news summaries of the situation in Afghanistan and have an excellent library.

Sea

Although Karachi is a major sea-port, it is not really served by passenger liners. There is a weekly passenger ferry service linking Karachi and Dubai (48 hours, US$150-325 return depending upon class of cabin), as well as pilgrim ships to Saudi Arabia during the *hajj* season.

Touching down

Getting in

Visas and passports

Having a visa before you arrive will save you considerable hassle. See the 'Before you travel' section above for details of visa requirements (page 25). You are strongly advised to carry your passport with you at all times; you may be required to produce your documents at check posts, particularly when crossing between provinces, entering tribal or restricted areas, and travelling around AJ&K or along the KKH.

Visa extensions It is currently only possible to extend your visa, or convert a transit visa into a full tourist visa, in Islamabad. For full details see page 201.

Foreigners' registration

This formality is the source of much confusion in Pakistan, seemingly amongst officials as well as tourists; hopefully it will be done away with entirely in the not too distant future. The following describes the situation in 1998, as confirmed by the relevant officials in Islamabad, Peshawar, Quetta and Karachi. Nationals of Britain, Australia and the UAE are not required to register. All other foreigners visiting Pakistan for more than 30 days are required to formally register their presence as a 'resident' in the country before the 30 days are up. This can be done in most towns and cities through the Foreigners' Registration Office or Senior Superintendent of Police (SSP). Bring two passport photos and you will be issued with a **Certificate of Registration** and **Residential Permit**. Before leaving Pakistan you must then apply for an **Exit Permit** from the last town you stay in; take your Certificate of Registration and Residential Permit to the Foreigners' Registration/SSP office and you will be issued with the Exit

Essentials

Business hours *There is considerable regional variation in business hours. Timings often differ for winter and summer. Note that during Ramadan most offices and businesses are only open from 0800/0900-1200/1300. The weekly public holiday has now been shifted from Friday to Sunday. What this means in effect is that Friday has virtually become a half-day (with most offices/businesses closing at 1200 for Friday prayers, and many not re-opening during the afternoon), while Saturday has also in many cases become a de-facto half-day (with many government offices closing mid-afternoon). Generally, the following hours apply:*
Banks: *Monday-Thursday 0900-1200, 1400-1600, Friday 0900-1130, Saturday 0900-1200, Sunday closed.* ***Government offices****: Monday-Thursday 0900-1200, 1400-1600, Friday 0900-1130, Saturday 0900-1200, Sunday closed.* ***Museums:*** *usually open 0900-1700 in summer (1600 winter), closed Wednesday.* ***Post Offices:*** *Monday-Thursday 0900-1500 (some later), Friday 0900-1130, Saturday 0900-1200, Sunday closed.* ***Shops:*** *Monday-Saturday 0900-1900, closed Sunday (and closed for prayers1200-1400 on Friday).* ***Telephone offices:*** *usually open 24 hours/7 days in larger towns.*
Electricity *220/240 volts, 50/60 cycle AC. Most plug sockets are of the round two-pin variety. Some round 3-pin sockets are found in larger hotels. Power cuts or "load shedding" is common, particularly in remoter areas. Power surges can be a problem; delicate electrical equipment such as laptops should be protected by a surge adaptor.*
Time *Pakistan is 5 hours ahead of Greenwich Mean Time (GMT+5).*
Weights and measures *The official system of weights and measures is metric. However, miles are sometimes still quoted on older distance markers and by the older generation. Cloth merchants and tailors still generally work in yards. Locally used weights include the tola (around 12 grammes) and the seer (just under 1 kilo).*

Permit. **NB** There have been instances where travellers have been told that they must obtain their Exit Permit from the same office as they originally registered at. This is not the case. If this happens to you, enlist the help of the nearest PTDC office.

Permits for 'Restricted Areas' Sensitive or unstable areas in Pakistan are often designated 'Restricted Areas' and can only be visited with a permit (usually called a 'No Objection Certificate', or NOC) issued by the relevant authority. Such 'Restricted Areas' include the Federally Administered Tribal Areas, parts of Baluchistan, parts of NWFP, parts of the Northern Areas and most of AJ&K. Permits are usually obtained in the regional capital, and full details of procedures for applying are given in the relevant pages of the travelling text.

Many areas that are potentially dangerous, for example parts of Karachi and Sind, are not designated 'Restricted Areas' and you remain free to visit. Warnings about specifically dangerous places are given in the relevant pages of the travelling text. See also the general warning on safety on page 35.

Vaccination requirements Officially you must have a Yellow Fever vaccination certificate if arriving from a country where the disease is endemic. In practice this is rarely enforced. All foreigners coming to Pakistan for more than one year are required to produce a certificate confirming they do not have HIV/AIDS (though again this is rarely enforced). See page 56 for information on staying healthy.

Duty free allowance The official list of items which can be imported free of duty by foreign tourists makes for amusing reading ("one electric smoothing iron, one portable electric hot plate, one hair dryer for lady tourists only"). Basically all items which may be reasonably required can be brought in. Alcohol is forbidden; if found it is usually 'confiscated' by customs officials against a receipt which in theory allows you to reclaim it on leaving; don't count on it. With a little gentle persuasion they sometimes relax the rules; try saying that it is a gift for Christian friends. The official limit on tobacco is 200 cigarettes or 50 cigars or 1lb of tobacco. Officially, gifts should not exceed Rs 1,000 in value. Cameras and camcorders can be imported free of duty. However, these and other valuable items or professional equipment, including jewellery, laptop computers etc, should be declared to customs and recorded in your passport, and must be brought out again personally.

Duty free shopping

Karachi airport has the reputation of being one of the cheapest places for duty free shopping in the world, though alcohol is not available. If you fly via Dubai, Bahrain or Abu Dhabi, you will also have access to a bewildering range of electrical and other goods. There are duty free shops in the main cities of Pakistan, but they have a very limited selection of goods.

Currency regulations

There are no restrictions on the amount of foreign currency (cash or travellers' cheques) tourists can bring in to Pakistan, or take out with them when they leave. However a limit of just Rs 100 of local currency can be brought in or taken out.

Export restrictions

The export of antiquities is prohibited. Jewellery up to the value of Rs 25,000 bought in Pakistan, provided it is not made wholly or mainly of gold, can be exported free of duty, but you must be able to produce foreign exchange encashment receipts up to the value of the jewellery. Other items, including carpets, can be exported up to the value of Rs 75,000 provided you obtain an Export Permit. This is a time consuming process; ask for help from the dealer you bought the goods from, or from PTDC officials. You will need the sales receipt, encashment receipts up to the value of the value of the goods, and photocopies of these and the relevant pages of your passport.

Departure tax

Note that an airport departure tax is charged on all international departures. In early 1999 this was Rs 600 for first class passengers and Rs 400 for economy. A Foreign Travel Tax of Rs 500 is charged on all international tickets purchased in Pakistan. An airport tax of Rs 100 is also charged on domestic flights (usually included in the price of the ticket). There are no departure taxes for land crossings, although a sizeable 'tax' is incorporated into your bus ticket fare for the trip from Sust across the Khunjerab Pass into China.

Arrival points

Airports If you are 'touching down' at Quaid-e-Azam airport in Karachi, see page 97, or at Islamabad International Airport see page 211.
Land borders If arriving by land, see the following pages for the relevant information: India page 281; China pages 573 and 578; and Iran page 169.

Tourist information

Tourist offices

Pakistan Tourism Development Corporation (PTDC) This is the government-run tourist information department, with offices (of variable levels of usefulness) in all the main towns and cities (see the relevant Directories for addresses and comments), plus a series of motels in the **A-B** price categories (though rumours persist that eventually they will all be privatized). Their head office is at College Road, F-7/2, Islamabad, T9202766, F294540 (open 0900-1600, Friday 0800-1230, Sunday closed).

PTDC is also complemented by various provincial tourist information offices; **Sind Tourism Development Corporation (STDC)**, see Karachi Directory; **Culture and Tourism Cell (CTC)**, see Quetta Directory; **Tourism Development Corporation of**

Punjab (TDCP), see Lahore Directory; **Azad Jammu and Kashmir (AJ&K Tourism Department)**, see Muzaffarabad Directory; and **Sarhad Tourism Corporation**, see Peshawar Directory.

Student travellers Anyone in full-time education is entitled to an International Student Identity Card (ISIC). These are issued by student travel offices and travel agencies around the world. In Pakistan they entitle you to a 50 percent discount on rail tickets. The ISIC head office is: ISIC Association, Box 9048, 1000 Copenhagen, Denmark, T45-33939303.

Disabled travellers Pakistan makes no specific considerations for disabled travellers, and travel here (particularly on public transport) would be extremely demanding. Further information on options for disabled travellers is available from the following organizations, though they currently have nothing specific on Pakistan: Mobility International, PO Box 10767, Eugene, OR 97440, USA, E info@miusa.org; or RADAR (based in London), T0171-2503222, F0171-2500212.

Gay and lesbian travellers Homosexuality is illegal in Pakistan, although few cases ever seem to be brought to court and the harsh punishments are rarely enforced. Many visitors are surprised by the common sight of young Pakistani men holding hands, or being physically intimate in public (seeing two policemen or soldiers walking down the street hand in hand remains an extraordinary sight). Generally, this is just a sign of friendship, and does not mean that they are gay. However, a number of commentators are now beginning to bring up the previously taboo subject of pre-marriage homosexuality. Foreign visitors, whether homosexual or heterosexual, are advised to avoid all displays of physical affection in public.

Rules, customs and etiquette

Pakistan is an extremely hospitable country where visitors are generally treated with great respect. It is important to reciprocate that respect and to show sensitivity towards cultural norms in order to avoid giving offence.

Conduct You will be judged to a large extent by the way you dress; a neat and clean appearance will command more respect and get a better response in any situation. Scanty or tight-fitting clothes cause great offence to Muslims. For their own safety and wellbeing, women need to take particular care over this, although it applies just as much to men. Open displays of affection between couples also cause offence and are not acceptable in public. It is common however to see young Pakistani men walking around hand in hand.

Courtesy It never pays to be rude or discourteous in Pakistan; doing so will invariably make things more difficult than they might otherwise be. Likewise, direct confrontation is never a good idea and is the surest way of eliminating any hope of achieving your aims in a particular situation. Unfortunately bureaucracy can be a major headache in Pakistan, with reams of red tape surrounding even the simplest of tasks. Bureaucrats are a law unto themselves and can be rude, obstructive and unhelpful. The only way to deal with this is to be patient, polite and firm. Open displays of anger or frustration only serve to delight them.

Visiting mosques and shrines Non-Muslims are welcome in most mosques and shrines, though there are exceptions. Always remove your shoes before entering. A thick pair of socks are useful for walking across baking hot floors. It is particularly important to dress modestly, not exposing anything more than head, hands and feet. Women should also cover their heads. Never walk directly in front of someone who is praying.

Hands

The left hand is considered unclean in Pakistan and should never be used for eating. More accurately, the rule is that the left hand should not be raised to the mouth, or dipped into a communal dish during a meal. It is perfectly acceptable to hold your *roti* in the left hand and tear bits off with the right. Avoid offering or accepting things with the left hand.

Women

Social etiquette regarding Pakistani women varies enormously. In remote, rural and tribal areas women are rarely seen at all and only go out in public with a full *burqa*. In the major cities, upper and middle class women at least are free to move around as they please. They are often well educated and highly westernized. In most circumstances, women do not shake hands with men, and offering your hand is likely to cause confusion and embarrassment. Men should never take photographs of women without their consent, or more importantly that of their male escort. Female tourists are more likely to be given permission to take photos of women but should never take it for granted.

Begging

Beggars are less common in Pakistan than in India, although they are found in large numbers around bus and train stations. The standard advice is that it is better to give to a recognized charity working with the poor than to make largely ineffectual handouts (though this is really a matter of personal judgement). Two particularly deserving charities working in Pakistan include the Edhi Foundation (Rangila Street, Boulton Market, Sarafa Bazaar, Karachi, 74000) and the Shaukat Khanum Memorial Cancer Hospital and Research Centre (see page 270). In larger cities, beggars are often being exploited by syndicates which cream off most of their daily takings.

Tipping

Tipping is generally expected in more expensive restaurants, although many also have a service charge. 10 percent is considered generous; five percent or rounding off with loose change is perfectly acceptable. Use your discretion. Beware of nodding at waiters as they bring you your change; they are liable to interpret this as an indication that they can pocket the money as a tip.

Photography

Photography of military installations, airports, railway stations, bridges and dams is prohibited. Do not take photos of women without permission.

Safety

Many travellers, particularly those arriving from India, are primed with horror stories about the dangers of travelling in Pakistan. Almost always they are very pleasantly surprised. With some notable exceptions, Pakistan is probably one of the safest countries in South Asia for foreign tourists. Basic common sense is the key to ensuring your safety and security in the majority of situations.

Specific information on travelling in Pakistan can be obtained from the following government advisory bodies, although their advice tends to be on the 'pessimistic/safe' side (for example, whilst we were researching this second edition of the *Pakistan Handbook*, the British Foreign & Commonwealth Office was advising travellers not to got to Pakistan; needless to say we had no problems): ***US State Department's Bureau of Consular Affairs***, Overseas Citizens Services, Room 4800, Department of State, Washington, DC 20520-4818, USA, T202-6474225, F202-6473000, internet http://travel.state.gov/travel_warnings.html. ***British Foreign & Commonwealth Office***, Travel Advice Unit, Consular Division, 1 Palace Street, London, SW1E 5HE, UK, T0171-2384503 (Pakistan desk T0171-2702385), F0171-2384545, internet www.fco.gov.uk/. ***Australian Department of Foreign Affairs***, Canberra, Australia, T06-62613305, internet www.dfat.gov.au/consular/ advice/pakistan.html.

Personal safety

Certain areas of Pakistan are dangerous for foreigners to travel in or visit. The most notable of these are the Tribal Areas of NWFP and Baluchistan, which are in any case restricted and require permits to visit. Rural Sind was for many years a no-go area due to banditry, although the situation has recently improved. Likewise, remoter parts of Baluchistan, NWFP and even Punjab can be dangerous for foreigners. Note that, up till now at least, Karachi has been more or less safe for foreigners; despite the tragic situation there, violence is restricted to remote suburbs far from the city centre. Detailed information and advice is given in the relevant sections. However, situations can change rapidly so it is always essential to check with tourism officials and/or the police regarding the current situation. Take heed of advice given by locals. If you are heading into a dangerous area or volatile situation, someone will almost invariably materialize to warn you, beg you not to go, or offer you a safe refuge.

When travelling in remoter areas, it is always a good idea to register your presence with the local police and/or the Deputy/Assistant Commissioner. The latter are generally well informed, helpful and speak good English. Women should not travel alone in remoter areas.

Theft "Trust in God, but tie your camel!" Never leave valuables and important documents in your hotel room. This applies even to more expensive hotels. If the room is secured by a padlockable bolt, use your own padlock, not the one supplied by the hotel; anyone can stay in the room and get a key cut. Take particular care in cheaper hotels, and in crowded bus or railway stations where it is easy for someone to slip away with your bags. Organized gangs and pickpockets do operate in larger cities. When on the move it is a good idea to secure any zips on your bags with a padlock.

Confidence tricksters These are far rarer than in other countries of South and Southeast Asia. In general people are surprisingly honest and straightforward. If someone offers to help you out or show you round, they are unlikely to be after something in return. However, you must still be on your guard, particularly in larger cities. Lahore has a bad reputation for confidence tricksters.

Police The police are something of an unknown quantity in Pakistan. In larger centres they are generally helpful, but in remoter areas they sometimes do not speak any English. Wherever you are, they can be corrupt. If you do have anything stolen, report it immediately to the police and be sure to get a copy of the police report if you intend to claim against your insurance. It is a good idea to enlist the help of someone who speaks good English. If you run into problems with corrupt police in remoter areas, insist on being taken to the nearest Deputy Commissioner or Assistant Commissioner.

Drugs Hashish, or *charas*, is readily available throughout Pakistan, with the exception of the Northern Areas. In many places, including Islamabad, there are profuse quantities of low grade cannabis growing wild. The authorities periodically get embarrassed by this and have it cut down and destroyed ... by burning it in huge bonfires around the city! In many communities it forms an integral part of the social fabric, particularly amongst the Pathans of NWFP and Baluchistan. However, it is also illegal and foreigners should be extremely careful. There is no guarantee that someone offering to sell you hashish will not then go and inform the police. Penalties are stiff and, for larger quantities, generally involve a lengthy prison sentence. If you are intent on smoking, avoid actually buying it; most Pakistanis who indulge in the habit will be happy to share a smoke with you. Some travellers report instances of hashish being planted on them by corrupt police. If your bags are searched, try to ensure that this is done publicly and keep a close eye on what is going on. Such occurrences are thankfully rare. Don't even consider trying to smuggle drugs out of the country; Pakistan is recognized as a major drug producing country on the international scene and customs officials are generally on the alert.

Advice for women travelling alone

Travelling in Muslim countries is undoubtedly harder for women than for men, and more so for women travelling alone. Even when travelling with a male companion or in a group, women need to be particularly aware of the cultural context. Most Pakistani women never travel alone, and outside of the main cities they are rarely seen in public. This in itself can make travelling around hard work. Certain remoter and tribal areas are not safe for women on their own; specific warnings are given in the relevant sections. The widely held perception of western women is based on the images in western magazines, films and satellite TV, which portray them as having 'loose' sexual morals. This, along with the fact that in their rigidly segregated society many young Pakistani males openly admit to feeling sexually frustrated, can lead to problems of sexual harassment. Cases of violent sexual assault are however extremely rare and a firm, unambiguous response will deal with most situations. In public, the best approach is to make a scene. Any form of impropriety towards women is a gross violation of the tenets of Islam and someone is bound to come to your aid; the perpetrator meanwhile will quickly vanish in a cloud of shame. It is worth remembering that a good Muslim would consider it improper to be alone with a female in private, so any attempt to contrive such a situation should set alarm bells ringing.

Many female travellers in Pakistan strongly advise adopting the local dress of *shalwar kameez* (baggy trousers and long over shirt which comes down to the knees) and *dupatta* (scarf) to cover the head in more conservative areas. This is a matter of choice. The important thing is to wear baggy, loose-fitting clothes that do not highlight the lines of your body, and not to expose anything more than head, hands and feet. A scarf is always useful for covering up further if you begin to feel exposed or uncomfortable in a given situation; it is also very good protection against the sun. Some women argue that it makes absolutely no difference to a determined male what you are wearing. However, given that actual harassment is relatively rare, the main object of dressing modestly is to show respect for Islamic values and not cause offence.

If you are put off the idea of visiting Pakistan by the above, don't be. Plenty of women travel around Pakistan and the majority are very enthusiastic about the country. While it can be very demanding, there are also distinct advantages. In the vast majority of situations women are treated with great respect. Seasoned female travellers in Pakistan argue that they get the best of both worlds. As a foreigner they are generally accorded the status of 'honorary males' in public, while in private they have access to female society, from which men are excluded. Pakistani women, although largely invisible in public life, are a dominant force in family life at home. When invited to a Pakistani household, male guests are usually confined to the guest room while women are whisked away behind the scenes into the 'real' household, where they can meet wives, mothers, sisters and other members of the extended family. Other advantages include getting to sit in the best seats at the front of buses and in special women's compartments on trains, and going straight to the front of lengthy queues.

Where to stay

Hotels

Throughout this book hotels are indicated on maps with a ■ symbol.

There is a vast range of accommodation options across Pakistan, both in terms of price and facilities. On the one hand there are international standard hotels, with facilities (and prices) to match the best in the world, whilst at the other end of the scale it is possible to find cheap and safe dormitory accommodation for as little as US$2 a night.

The international class hotels tend to be found only in the state capitals. Outside the main cities, hotels that fall into our **C** price category may be the highest grade

Hotel price categories

For a quick-reference guide to our price coding, see inside the front covers of the book.

Exact prices for hotel rooms are not quoted; price categories are used instead. Note that categories are based upon the cost of a double room, and are not star ratings. These categories are designed to include any taxes, and are peak season rates (before bargaining).

***L** Rs 5,000 + The '**L**' stands for 'luxury', with full facilities for the business and leisure traveller to the highest international standard. Most are part of a multi-national chain and are found only in Islamabad, Rawalpindi, Karachi, Lahore, Quetta and Peshawar.*

***A** Rs 2,000-5,000 There are often some good deals in this category ('**L**' hotels bargained down to '**A**' prices). Full international class facilities, such as central air-conditioning, dish TV, pool and leisure activities, choice of restaurants, business centre, etc.*

***B** Rs 1,000-2,000 These rooms generally feature many of the facilities of an '**A**' category hotel, but without the feeling of luxury. You should expect a/c, TV/dish and hot water, although there may not be a pool, business centre, or choice of restaurants. Some of the older (faded glory) government-run places fall into this category, though really they belong in the price category below.*

***C** Rs 700-1,000 Often the highest category of hotel in medium and small towns, though not always the best value. Sometimes the entrance and reception area is more grand than '**D**' category hotels, but the quality of the rooms are no better despite the higher price. For this price you should expect a/c, hot water, and possibly a TV.*

***D** Rs 400-700 Rooms in this category are amongst the most variable. They tend to be better furnished than those in the category below, often with a/c, TV, and perhaps a hot shower. Alternatively, they are just overpriced '**E**' category rooms. There is often a good deal of scope for bargaining in this category.*

***E** Rs 200-400 Hotel rooms are likely to have a carpet, and the bathroom is more likely to have a shower than a bucket and scoop. Some hotels in this category will have a few rooms with the added luxury of a/c, priced in the category above.*

***F** Rs 100-200 The cheapest double rooms available usually fall into this category. Most will have an attached bathroom, often a basic affair with squat toilet and a tap/bucket/scoop style shower. In hotels aimed at foreign backpackers there are some excellent rooms in this category; elsewhere things are a bit more variable.*

***G** under Rs 100 Extremely variable. In popular tourist areas (eg Gilgit, Hunza, Chitral, Baltistan etc) this may be a dormitory bed in a well-run backpacker place. Elsewhere, it may be a squalid private room, usually with a shared bathroom. There are some real bargains in this category, but also some real 'nightmares'.*

available. Budget hotels (**E**, **F** and **G**) are usually found in even the smallest of places. Always ask to see a room before accepting it.

Hotel facilities A major difference between hotel accommodation in Pakistan and India is that, almost without exception, even the cheapest hotels in Pakistan have **attached bath and toilet facilities**. There are exceptions to this rule, and some hotels offer cheaper rooms where such facilities are shared. If contemplating such a deal, check both the room and the bathroom before committing yourself. It should also be noted that an attached toilet can sometimes be something of a mixed blessing! In most hotels, toilets tend to be of the Asian 'squat' variety, rather than the Western WC. They are easy to adapt to and usually more hygienic. Many toilets in Pakistan are unable to cope with toilet paper, so a separate waste-paper basket is provided. With the exception of hotels in the **L** and **A** categories, the word 'bath' is used to denote 'bathroom' as opposed to a 'bathtub'. Most bathrooms are equipped with either a shower, or some sort of tap/bucket/scoop combination. In many hotels, hot water is only available during certain times of the day. Towels, soap and toilet paper are rarely provided in budget hotels.

Many parts of Pakistan experience **power cuts**, or 'load-shedding' as it is euphemistically termed. It is worthwhile having a good torch handy. Many mid-price hotels have their own generators, although they tend to be unpleasantly noisy. Erratic or rationed **water supply** is another problem that you may encounter. If your bathroom has a bucket, it is recommended that you keep it full at all times so that it is still possible to flush the toilet during water cuts. Few hotel sinks have plugs. **NB** It should be assumed that tap water, even in expensive hotels in big cities, is **not** safe for drinking or cleaning teeth.

Only the more expensive hotels have central **air-conditioning** (a/c); elsewhere a/c rooms are cooled by individual units and occasionally 'air-coolers'. Many hotels in the **D** and **E** category will have a number of identical rooms, but with a/c, and priced in the **C** category. If you are paying extra for a/c, make sure that the unit is working properly. Almost all rooms, even in the cheapest hotels and dormitories, have a **fan**. Most hotels can arrange **laundry** services very cheaply. Charges are per item, typically around Rs 15-30 depending on the size, though at luxury hotels prices can be much higher.

In cheaper hotels you may well be sharing your room and bathroom with a whole host of **animal life**, notably cockroaches, ants and geckos (harmless house lizards). Poisonous or dangerous animals are extremely rare, though bed bugs are far more common (and should be dealt with by changing room/hotel). Very few hotels have mosquito nets or effective mosquito screens. See 'Health' for information on how to deter mosquitoes.

Resthouses and inspection bungalows

In many remote areas, notably in the Northern Areas, NWFP and AJ&K, the only accommodation available is in the form of government run 'resthouses' and 'inspection bungalows'. These tend to be two to three bedroom bungalows that are used by travelling officials. In theory, a booking chit should be obtained from the department's regional headquarters, although at some it is possible to just turn up and request a room. Note, however, that visiting officials always have priority over tourists, even those who have a booking chit. Such resthouses are generally well furnished, clean, and remarkably good value (usually **E-F** category), though the best located ones tend to be permanently full. They are usually cared for by a *chowkidar* (watchman/caretaker) who may be ab+le to provide basic meals on request.

Railway retiring rooms

Railway stations in some of the larger towns have 'retiring rooms' that can be used by passengers holding a/c and first-class sleeper tickets. They are cheap (**F**), but are frequently full. Bedding is generally not provided and they are extremely variable in cleanliness.

Hostels

There are a number of Youth Hostels in Pakistan run by the Pakistan Youth Hostel Association (National Office, G-6/4, Garden Road, Aabpara, Islamabad, T826899; branch office, House 110-B, Gulberg III, Lahore, T878201). IYHA members pay Rs 55 per night (Rs 30 student) for a single-sex dorm bed, or non-members can buy a daily 'welcome ticket' (Rs 60 in addition to daily bed fee). One year IYHA membership can be bought for Rs 360. The maximum stay is limited to three days and there is an early evening curfew. The hostels are extremely variable, often inconveniently located, whilst the best ones seem permanently full. There are also YMCA, YWCA and Salvation Army hostels in some cities, and although cheap they tend to be either permanently full or very poor value.

Camping

Officially designated campsites are few and far between, although those trekking in the north will find almost unlimited camping options. Many hotels will allow you to pitch a tent in their grounds for a modest fee.

Travel tip: off-season rates and bargaining

In parts of the country popular with domestic tourists (eg Murree and the Galis, Swat Valley, Kaghan Valley etc), accommodation prices soar by two or three times during the peak season. ***NB*** *'Peak season' does not necessarily just refer to a time of year; accommodation prices also inflate at weekends (Friday-Sunday) and during public holidays. Visiting such places outside of peak periods can reduce costs, though you will have to ask for discounts rather than have them 'given' to you.*

In recent years, more and more hotels have been built, whilst the number of tourists visiting Pakistan has remained constant (or even declined). Thus, it is worthwhile haggling about room prices wherever you are, whatever time of year, or whichever type of hotel you are at. It is not just the budget 'backpacker' places that are open to bargaining; the 5-star international class hotels are also desperate for business and some are currently offering Rs 8,000 a night rooms for a mere Rs 4,000. When negotiating a price for a room, make sure you establish whether this rate includes all taxes (these can add 20 percent to the price).

Essentials

Getting around

Air

Pakistan has an extensive air network, linking all the key cities and major district centres. It is worth noting that internal flights are considerably cheaper when bought in Pakistan, rather than when booked and paid for abroad. For example a Karachi-Islamabad flight on PIA will cost around US$180 when bought in London, but just US$75 when booked and paid for in Pakistan. There are also savings to be made by flying on 'night-coaches' (services that leave/arrive at inconvenient times during the night or very early mornings).

The state-run carrier **PIA** operates a comprehensive network of flights across the country (see map), with a fleet that ranges from the latest 747s and Airbuses, through to propeller-driven Fokker F27s. Note that the flight schedules listed in this *Handbook* are based on PIA's 1998 timetable. It is worth picking up a copy of the latest timetable (which also includes fares) from the larger booking offices if you intend doing a lot of flying. Since the early 1990s, PIA has been joined on the major routes by a number of private commercial airlines; **Aero Asia, Bhoja Air** and **Shaheen Air**. Fare structures are similar, though it is worth flying Aero Asia just to hear the "travellers' prayer" from the Qur'an that is played just before take-off. Read over the tannoy in a Vincent Price 'Hammer House of Horror' style, it closes with the line (just as the pilot guns the engines) "remember, we must all return to our Creator". Not on this flight, we hope.

PIA's Domestic Air Network

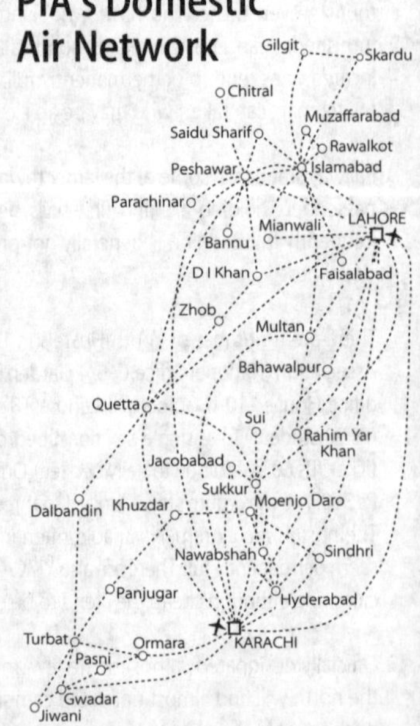

Rail information in the Pakistan Handbook

Major train services are identified by a name, eg Khyber Mail, and smaller ones by their number. The trains listed in this Handbook tend to be those offering the quickest, most direct daily services between destinations, in addition to all classes of ticket. Where possible, a choice has been offered between morning and afternoon services, although on many routes there are more services than those listed.

The train information follows this format: ***Destination, Name of train, Departure time, journey length****. eg* ***Lahore****, Shalimar Exp, 0630, 17 hours; Tezgan, 1630, 19 hours. The major cities also have a 'box' listing four categories of train fares to all key destinations. Train times and fares in this Handbook are based on the October 1998-April 1999 Pakistan Railways Time and Fare Table. Exact timings of trains tend to chang slightly each season. For those intending to travel extensively by train, it is worth purchasing a copy of this booklet, available from most train stations for Rs 5. The labyrinthine rules and regulations governing rail travel contained within it also make for some highly entertaining reading.*

There are a couple of spectacular flights over the mountains from Islamabad into the Northern Areas, as well as PIA's magnificent 'Karakoram Air Safari' (see page 477 and 'Islamabad/Rawalpindi – transport' for further details).

Security on internal flights is tight, with even hand luggage often having to pass through two or three x-ray machines. You may even be requested to remove batteries from cameras and place them in the aircraft hold.

Train

Like India, Pakistan has an extensive network of railways that can provide a relatively comfortable and reasonably fast way of covering large distances, in addition to offering the opportunity to see the countryside and experience a slice of Pakistani society on the move. The main backbone of the system runs in a broad arc north-south between Peshawar and Karachi, via Rawalpindi and Lahore, with an important branch line to Quetta, and various other branches throughout Punjab, Sind and parts of Baluchistan and NWFP.

Fare structure

There are three categories of trains in Pakistan (Express, Mail, Passenger), and six classes of ticket.

A/c Sleeper fares are generally on a par with air travel, although they become very competitive if you obtain a discount (see below). They tend to be quite luxurious, in private compartments sleeping either two or four, and sometimes have private toilets. The a/c can get cold at night, although on occasion it doesn't work at all. **A/c Sitter** and **A/c Lower** are seats in the air conditioned carriage. Tickets for air conditioned berths and seats can be bought up to **one month** in advance, although they tend to sell out quickly on most journeys.

First Class Sleeper berths are also quite comfortable, and can be reserved up to **15 days** in advance. **Economy** class is basically a reserved first class seat which can also be booked 15 days in advance. If you are joining a popular service (eg Karachi to Lahore) halfway through its journey, this may well be the highest class of ticket that you can buy at short notice. You would probably not want to take this class for any journey beyond eight hours.

Rail travel tips

Although it is possible to travel exceptionally cheaply by using the lower classes of rail travel, conditions can become very crowded and quite unpleasant. If your budget can stretch to it (bear in mind the discounts available), it may be worth moving up a class or two for the sake of your sanity. Having said that, travelling unreserved can be an exhilarating experience; a total immersion in the sights, sounds and smells of Pakistan.

Security, particularly at night, can be a concern. Luggage should ideally be padlocked to the racks, and valuables never left unattended, even for a second. Money belts should be worn out of sight, underneath clothing.

Women travelling alone, or in groups, can ask for tickets in women-only compartments. If men come into these compartments, demand that they leave. It is worth asking for upper berths, which offer some protection against theft, and can be used in the daytime when the lower seats may all be occupied by sitting passengers.

Always carry plenty of liquid. Bottled water and/or juice and soft drinks in cartons are the safest options. Tea is also widely available, as are snacks and sweets. On many trains, cheap, good quality meals can be ordered from railway catering staff. The drugging and robbing of unwary foreigners by seemingly friendly families offering food and drink is nowhere near as prevalent as in India, although it may be something worth bearing in mind.

If you wish to upgrade your ticket it is worth making a friend of the all important ticket inspector, although generally you will face great competition from other passengers.

Below Economy is **Second** class, available with reserved or unreserved seats, and sometimes referred to by travellers as 'Livestock Class'. If you are travelling unreserved on long or popular journeys, conditions can be quite miserable. Then again, it is very cheap ... The best option in this class is to reserve a sleeper berth for long journeys; only the top berth can be used as a sleeper during the day. Tickets can be bought from **15 days** in advance up until time of departure. If you are very lucky, the ticket inspector may be able to upgrade you.

Discounts Foreign tourists and foreign students who have the patience to deal with a degree of bureaucracy are able to take advantage of some excellent discounts offered by Pakistan Railways. Foreign tourists (except Indians) are eligible for a **25 percent discount** on most fares, whilst holders of an ISIC International Student Card are entitled to a remarkably generous **50 percent discount**. This means that you can travel, for example, the 1,260 kilometres between Karachi and Lahore for a little over US$3, or for US$12 in the luxury of an a/c berth.

The procedure for obtaining these discounts can be quite time-consuming however, sometimes taking the best part of a day. You must first obtain a letter from the local **PTDC** office confirming that you are a foreign tourist or a foreign student (most easily done in the latter case if you can produce an ISIC card). You will need to state which train you intend taking, which class of ticket, and on which date, so a prior visit to the railway ticket office may be necessary to check availability. You should then take the letter along to the **Commercial Department** of Pakistan Railways. These offices are not always located at the train station or at the main ticket office, although directions are given in the text for finding them in cities where they are located elsewhere. (**NB** It is sometimes possible to go directly to the Commercial Dept with your student or tourist ID without first obtaining a letter from the PTDC). The Commercial Dept will then eventually issue you with a certificate stating the date, class, and specific train on which you wish to undertake your journey. This certificate should then be taken to the booking office where the discounted ticket can be purchased. If in the meantime that service has sold out, you have to start all over again. The process must also be repeated every time you want to buy a ticket, in each town you visit.

Road

Bus

The bus network in Pakistan is extensive, providing a cheap and convenient means of getting around, and reaching all those places that the train cannot reach. There is a distinctive nomenclature associated with road transport in Pakistan, and some grasp of the terminology used is extremely useful. Inter-city buses are often referred to as **big buses** or **coaches**, denoting vehicles of varying degrees of comfort designed to seat 50 or so. The degree of comfort is nominally indicated by a prefix such as 'deluxe' or 'super deluxe'. Any bus without this prefix, or referred to as a **local bus**, is likely to have unreserved seating, will carry more people inside (and possibly on the roof also) than you would think possible, will crawl along at 20 kilometres per hour, have little legroom, and will be an extremely uncomfortable (but cheap) way to travel.

A far better bet is to travel with one of the many private bus companies, on their so called **'Flying Coaches'.** These are generally slightly more expensive, but are quicker, more comfortable (sometimes with air-conditioning), and usually have the assurance of a reserved seat. Booking in advance means that you are more likely to get a 'good' seat, although it is difficult to reach that happy compromise between comfort (seats near the front) and safety (seats away from the front).

The most comfortable form of bus transport in Pakistan is the **Coaster**, somewhere in size between a coach and a minibus. Seating is usually reserved, and the vehicle is usually air-conditioned. Below the coasters in size are the **minibuses**, used for shorter inter-city trips, some long distance runs and for around-town transport. In the West, such a vehicle would probably seat 12, but in Pakistan they generally hold up to 18 passengers, plus driver and driver's assistant. Legroom can be a problem, or a nightmare on a long trip. Minibuses are often referred to by their manufacturer's name, eg **Hiace** (Toyota) or **Transit** (Ford), though sometimes they are simply called **wagons**.

Smaller vehicles used for transport around town, and for short runs between towns, are usually Suzuki mini-wagons, referred to as **Suzukis** or **wagons**. In some rural areas, converted pick-ups are used for public transport. They are frequently referred to as **Datsuns**, whoever their manufacturer is.

Car/jeep hire

Self-drive car hire is only available in the major cities, particularly Islamabad/Rawalpindi. If you opt for this be sure to carefully check the hire terms in case of an accident, and also the roadworthiness of the vehicle before you drive off. More commonly, car hire in Pakistan refers to a car and driver. Larger hotels generally have a car and driver hire desk, as have most travel agents, with typical fees being around Rs 500-800 per day plus a per kilometre charge. In more remote regions, notably the Northern Areas, it is possible to hire jeeps for half, one or multi-day trips. This is a great way to get around, and is extremely competitive when shared amongst a group. See the relevant Transport sections for an indication of prices.

Cycling

More and more foreign cyclists are to be spotted on Pakistan's roads, particularly on the popular Karakoram Highway route. The majority are travelling on high-tech imported mountain or touring bikes. Another option is to buy a Pakistani or Chinese cycle in Pakistan. These are fairly cheap (around Rs 2,500 new with an almost identical re-sale value), very solid and can be easily and cheaply repaired almost anywhere without any worries about finding spare parts. However, they are also very slow and heavy, with cast-iron frames and just one gear (difficult to get going but plenty of

The hazards of road travel in Pakistan

In theory, vehicles in Pakistan drive on the left! If you drive yourself, or are cycling, it is essential to take great care. Pedestrians, cattle and a wide range of other animals roam at will. It can be particularly dangerous when driving after dark because few vehicles are ever lit. The general rule of night-driving in Pakistan seems to be to kill your lights as you approach an on-coming vehicle, and then hit them with the full beam just before you pass! Similarly, use of the indicator lights does not necessarily mean 'I am turning right/left'; it can also be read as 'Please overtake me to the left/right'!

There is next to no training for would be drivers, and the test is a farce. Licences are invariably obtained through bribery, and as a result there are very real dangers from poor judgement and suicidal overtaking manoeuvres. The general rule on Pakistan's roads is 'might is right'. These dangers apply to both visitors with their own vehicles, and those travelling on buses and other forms of public transport. Pakistani newspapers are full of stories of buses "turning turtle", followed invariably by the lines "driver is absconding".

Accidents often produce large and angry crowds,so if you have an accident it is best to leave the scene and report it to the police as quickly as possible thereafter. It is probably also worth informing your own embassy.

momentum once you do!). They are only really viable on the flatter terrain of the plains, although you do meet the occasional determined individual struggling up the KKH on one.

Although geared bikes are now being imported and manufactured in Pakistan (you can find Taiwanese mountain bikes on sale in Islamabad's Blue Area for around Rs 5,000), foreigners on imported cycles still attract a lot of attention, particularly in more remote areas. Keep an eye on your bike during meal and drink stops; adults and children alike are prone to fiddle with gear levers, brakes, and the occasional small hand may find its way into your paniers. Respect for the Islamic sense of decorum should be maintained, and lycra cycling shorts should **not** really be worn, and certainly **not** by women.

Almost all buses in Pakistan, including those that make the journey across the border into China, are happy to take cycles on the roof. Make sure that your cycle is properly secured; it will probably sustain more damage being rattled around on the roof than through using it. Expect to pay 50-100 percent extra on the fare.

Many who cycle the Karakoram Highway report unpleasant experiences on the long stretch through Kohistan, from Thakot Bridge to Chilas. Women cyclists should not tackle this stretch of the road alone. It may be worth conserving your energy, taking a bus, and using the time that you have saved to explore the more hospitable valleys further north. In many of the more popular backpacker hotels it is likely that you will meet other cyclists with whom you can exchange information. Look out also for the 'rumour books' at many of these hotels. They often have detailed information written by other cyclists. This *Handbook* has detailed information for cyclists on the Karakoram Highway. The 'routes' information describes in great detail distances, gradients, accommodation and refreshment stops at and between all the main towns and sites.

There is also endless potential for exploring the southern half of the country on a cycle. Most of the canals that irrigate the plains have good tracks running alongside them which are ideal for cycling and blissfully free of traffic.

Some degree of maintenance competence is required, particularly if you have problems in more remote areas. A tool kit and spares should be carried, especially by those with imported cycles, although local cycle repair shops are extremely resourceful and able to carry out the most unlikely of improvisations.

Hitch-hiking

Because public transport is so cheap in Pakistan, the concept of hitch-hiking is virtually unknown. One exception is along the Karakoram Highway, particularly in the more northerly parts. Trucks do sometimes give lifts, but they are impossibly slow, rarely averaging more than 40 kilometres per hour. The Western 'thumbs-up' sign is unknown; just flag the vehicle down. Some drivers will expect at least the equivalent bus fare for giving you a lift. It is not advisable for women to hitch-hike alone.

Private vehicles

With Iranian visas becoming increasingly easy to obtain, more and more people are bringing their vehicles through Pakistan as part of their overland trip. If bringing your own motor vehicle, a *Carnet de Passage* (carnet) is essential. These are usually obtained from a motoring organization in your own country. Pakistan will accept both AIT and FIA carnets, although if you are continuing on to India (and Nepal) you will need an AIT carnet. Most carnets now feature both logos. If in doubt, contact the AA in Lahore. It is currently not possible to take a vehicle into China without prior arrangement, an expensive and time-consuming business.

Fuel Both petrol and diesel are widely available in Pakistan, though the latter is much cheaper. Petrol is rarely above 92 octane and tends to be particularly 'dirty'.

Local transport

Auto-rickshaws Cheaper than taxis, auto-rickshaws are the most convenient way of getting round many towns, although visitors should note that the variety found in Pakistan are even smaller than those found in India, and it is quite a squeeze to fit in two adults with backpacks. Very few have working meters, so it is essential to agree the fare in advance. Note that in heavy city traffic, you are much more vulnerable in a rickshaw than in a taxi.

Local buses If you are staying in larger towns and cities for only a short time it is unlikely that you will get to grips with the local bus system. Routes are difficult to understand, the buses are often impossibly crowded, and it can be very brutal getting on and off the still moving bus. However, if you are determined, you will generally find someone who will ensure that you are on the right bus.

Minibuses Many towns have minibus or Suzuki services which operate on a fixed route, but pick up and drop passengers on request. They are quicker than local buses, but equally crowded.

Taxis Pakistan's taxi drivers are generally less money-grasping than those in India, and over charging is less frequent. Nevertheless, it is always advisable to fix the price in advance. Do not be afraid to bargain, although you should be realistic; it is unlikely that you will pay the same as a local person. An exception to this general pattern of honesty is to be found at the airports, most notably Karachi, where you may be asked for 10 times the correct fare. In many of the larger towns, there are numerous brand new, comfortable, yellow taxis, many of which have working meters that the drivers are prepared to use.

Tongas Horse drawn carts, or tongas, are still found in many cities, operating on fixed routes, and pulled by mangy beasts usually revealing their entire rib cage.

Keeping in touch

Language Urdu is the national language of Pakistan and is spoken by most people, at least to some degree (it is the 'first' language of just eight percent of the population). There are four major regional languages, Sindhi, Punjabi, Baluch and Pashto, plus numerous minor languages and dialects. English is the main language of commerce and business, and is widely spoken. Even in remote areas you are likely to find someone (often the local teacher) who speaks at least a little English. See under 'Culture' for further details of the variety of languages found in Pakistan, page 633. For a glossary of useful Urdu words and phrases, see the 'Footnotes' section at the end of the Handbook.

Postal services Postal services in Pakistan are on the whole reliable. Note that **PO Box** numbers are frequently used within Pakistan as a way of eliminating 'lost at point of delivery' problems. It is a good idea to take letters to a Post Office where you can hand mail over for franking on the spot (to prevent your stamps being stolen!). Mail between Europe and the major cities of Pakistan generally takes four to seven days, and seven to 10 days from North America to Pakistan. Outgoing mail is often slightly slower.

Parcels sent from Pakistan have to be sown up in cloth, though they must first be inspected at the post office (and have a customs declaration form completed, with one attached to the parcel itself); some GPOs have packers who will do the sowing for you. Sending parcels is a tedious and time-consuming process. GPOs in the larger cities also have an **International Speed Post (ISP)** service for parcels; parcels to Europe, USA or Australia cost Rs 500 for 500 grammes and then Rs 250 for each additional 500 grammes. Central Exise Duty of 12.5 percent is applicable. Parcels to Canada, France, Germany, Sweden and the Netherlands are charged 30 percent extra due to surcharges in these countries.

Poste Restante facilities are available at most GPOs, and mail is held for up to three months. American Express offices also have "clients' mail" services for those with Amex cards or travellers' cheques.

Telephone services

See inside front covers for a list of telephone area codes in Pakistan

The telephone system in Pakistan continues to undergo change, with the installation of fibre optic lines and the conversion to digital exchanges. The only drawback with such improvements is that telephone numbers in Pakistan change with monotonous regularity, though the situation is improving and in the long-term should stabilize. The number for **telephone enquiries** in major towns is T17. Standard emergency numbers include: **Police** T15; **Fire** T16; **Ambulance** T115, with additional local numbers for each city. Some major companies (eg airlines etc) now have 'universal access numbers' (UAN), allowing the same number to be dialled from any city (they start with T111 followed by six digits). See the inside cover flap for a list of the dialling codes for major Pakistani towns and cities.

Most of the country (with the exception of points along the KKH north of Gilgit) now has **international direct dialling (IDD)**, and having to book calls in advance is slowly becoming a thing of the past. Telephone offices (sometimes called Telegraph Offices), most of them run by ***Pak Telecom***, are the cheapest places to make international calls from, though they tend to be busier. You may also find that instead of making your call from a booth, you may just have a phone pushed across a counter to you; not the most intimate setting for speaking to a loved one, or for finding out third division football results. Rates from *Pak Telecom* telephone offices in 1998 were as follows; UK Rs 68 per minute (though to other European countries they can be much more expensive); USA Rs 74 per minute; Australia Rs 85 per minute. Note that there is a three minute minimum for international calls.

Best short wave frequencies

*The BBC's World Service transmissions to South Asia have been greatly enhanced in recent years by the leasing of a relay transmitter in Tashkent. Ironically, the same transmitter had previously been used by the Soviet regime to block out the BBC's services. The frequencies marked in **bold** are the best. Signal strength varies throughout the day, with lower frequencies generally better at night. At times the East Asia Service, and indeed the African Service, are clearer than the South Asia Service. The BBC's nightly "South Asia Report" offers a good, up to the minute insight into events in the sub-continent. For programme listings contact BBC, PO Box 76, Bush House, London, WC2B 4PH (www.bbc.co.uk/worldservice/); VoA, Washington, DC20547 (www.voa.gov/). **BBC World Service (London)** 5975, 6195, 7105, **9740**, **11750**, **12095**, 15070, **15310**, 15400, 18080.*

Privately run **public call offices (PCOs)** are usually slightly more efficient. Calls are more expensive, but there is no three minute minimum. Making international calls from **hotels** will incur an extortionate 'surcharge'. **NB** It is not possible to call 'collect' ('reverse-charges') from Pakistan; the nearest you can get is to phone through the number of your hotel from a telephone office or PCO and get the person to call you back there.

Fax

Fax (Facsimile) services are rapidly becoming widespread in Pakistan, with fax machines installed in many hotels. You can also send faxes from most Telegraph Offices and PCOs.

Internet services

At the time of writing, internet and email facilities are only really available in the regional capitals and main cities (notably Karachi, Quetta, Lahore, Rawalpindi, Islamabad and Peshawar), though this is bound to change during the life-span of this *Handbook*. Away from the main cities, international NGOs, larger hotels and major travel agents may allow you to send/receive email on their systems.

The **British Council** runs cyber-stations in its libraries, though hours are restricted (usually closing at around 1800). Other cyber-stations can be found in the larger cities, though few are open seven days a week or around the clock. Most charge between Rs 50-100 per hour for on-line access. The 'business centres' in the luxury hotels offer extended hours, although they haven't yet fully got to grips with a key principal behind internet/email (ie that you only pay for the cost of a local telephone call). Some ask for Rs 200-300 per hour for on-line access, or charge a flat Rs 200 fee just to send an email (leading to the ridiculous situation where it is often cheaper to send a fax, which more or less defeats the point of email).

Media

Newspapers There are currently at least six English language daily newspapers available – *The News* (probably the best), *Dawn*, *Frontier Post*, *The Muslim*, *The Nation*, *The Pakistan Times* – although not all are available nationally, and all can be difficult to find outside of the main cities. Unfortunately, Pakistan's newspapers are a major disappointment, being filled with "reports of chief ministers condoling deaths, announcements of new schemes to benefit the poor, and statements put out by opposition leaders ... they are, by and large, boring compilations of press releases" (Emma Duncan). The letters and editorial pages are full of poorly constructed rants about how "the West is ignorant of Islam" and "only sees Muslims in the form of inaccurate stereotypes", but then goes on to present a view of Western society that is completely ignorant and full of inaccurate stereotypes ("totally immoral and sex-obsessed ... no family values ... only concerned with making money"). The sports pages are reasonable, though in a country with little interest in tennis, there are a surprising number of photos of Martina Hingis and Venus Williams!

Several of the papers can be read on-line: *Dawn* (www.dawn.com/); *The Nation* (www.brain.net.pk/nation/); *The News* (www.jang-group.com/thenews/index.html). English and American papers can be read at the British Council and American Centre respectively, or can be bought in some Islamabad and Karachi bookshops and in the top hotels.

Magazines What Pakistan lacks in the quality of its newspapers, it makes up for in its magazine output. For a good summary of the contemporary political, economic, sporting and fashion scene in Pakistan, there are several informative periodicals available. *The Herald* and *Newsline* both appear monthly, covering the political and social scene in Pakistan in some depth. The reporting is of a high standard, and the contributors are not afraid to criticize the government, opposition, or the religious parties. Other interesting magazines include *Pakistan Illustrated* and *Politics and Business*. *Newsweek* and *Time* are available from most book stands.

Television and radio Pakistan's two state-run television stations (Ptv 1 and Ptv 2) have little to offer the foreign visitor. The nightly news in English (at 1800) is very much in the "what the Prime Minister did today" mould, with very poor coverage of international events (unless the Prime Minister is making yet another trip abroad). STN, meanwhile, shows short slots of CNN, BBC, TNT Movies etc that it has bought, though it is sometimes off air (when, allegedly, it hasn't paid its bills).

In recent years there has been a truly phenomenal growth in the number of people with access to satellite television stations. Almost all upper and middle class households, all top-end hotels, and more and more restaurants, tea houses and hotels are sprouting satellite dishes. Murdoch's Star TV Network is now beamed direct from Hong Kong into the remotest villages and households. What the long term impacts of this will be is hard to say, but it is now possible to sit in a chai shop in strictly Shia Muslim towns such as Skardu, where it is rare to even see a woman on the streets, and watch uncensored episodes of 'Baywatch'! Foreign tourists, particularly women, may feel very uncomfortable watching 'MTV' etc in such situations.

Although satellite TV carries both CNN and BBC World Service Television, those who want to keep up to date with news, world affairs and English football results, should consider carrying a short-wave radio (see box below).

Food and drink

Food

At its very best, Pakistani food can be superb; at its worst, bland and uninspiring. Meat-eaters are particularly well served, with delicious chicken, mutton and beef served in most restaurants. The style of cooking is often referred to as *Mughlai*, hinting at the Mughal and Afghan influences introduced into the South Asian diet over a period of six centuries. Cream and *ghee* (clarified butter) are favourite cooking mediums, with meat as the main focus of the meal. Dishes are generally less spicy than in India, although they are often oilier. Spicy kebabs, meat balls and minced meat are common, as are *Tandoori* dishes – marinated meat cooked in a special clay oven. *Karahi* (*'balti'*) meals, consisting of chicken or meat cooked and served in a thick metal wok with spicy tomatoes and chillies, are very popular in Pakistan, and are being rapidly adopted in the 'curry-houses' of Bradford and London. Although rice is available, wheat is the staple. Most meals are eaten with either *chapatis* or *nan* (see Food Glossary, page 659). There are regional specialities across Pakistan (eg seafood in Karachi), although these are discussed as they occur.

Travellers arriving from India may find the variety of dishes on offer in Pakistan less inspiring. Vegetarians and vegans are not well served. Although dishes of spinach, potatoes, okra, peas and the ubiquitous *dhal* (lentils) can be excellent when well prepared, all too often they are simply overcooked mush. In many areas, particularly transport stops, all that is on offer is dhal and chapati, okra and chapati, or poor quality mutton and chapati (see Health Information for tips on eating healthily). Snacks such as samosas, bhajis and good quality biscuits can be found all across Pakistan.

Chinese and Western

All the main cities have restaurants offering reasonable imitations of Chinese food. Western 'fast food' is becoming increasingly common across the country. In fact, amongst the middle-classes the words 'fast food' are seen more as a style of cuisine than as a derogatory term describing nutritionally poor food. *KFC*, *Pizza Hut* and now *McDonalds* have, or are in the process of opening, branches in all the major cities.

Western-style breakfasts are generally available, with the emphasis on fried eggs, boiled eggs or omelette. Porridge and inferior cornflakes can also be found, but those seeking an egg, bacon and sausage fry-up are likely to be disappointed (although some of the large department stores in Karachi and Islamabad that specialize in expensive imported foodstuffs for the expatriate community sell bacon, and non-pork sausages). Reasonable quality Western chocolate is becoming more commonplace, but fans of cheese are recommended to bring their own.

Eating out

Restaurants are indicated by a ● symbol on the maps throughout this book.

Almost all hotels, whatever their status or category, have either a restaurant or dining hall, and they can often be very good value. Eating out in Pakistan is far cheaper than in the West, even at the top-end restaurants (although restaurants in five-star hotels are often priced on a par with the West).

Most restaurants in Pakistan have 'family rooms'; sometimes a separate room, or simply an area partitioned off by a curtain or screen. Pakistani families almost always use this facility, so any travelling couples or females who want to avoid unwarranted attention are recommended to follow suit. Note that children are extremely welcome in even the most expensive restaurants and staff invariably go to great lengths to accommodate them.

In some smaller towns the choice of restaurant and cuisine may be limited to 'meat and chapati' places, where various parts of recently dead animals are hung up outside to tempt you in. In such circumstances it is generally best to follow the example of the local people and select the busiest one. There are also numerous roadside snack-sellers, offering tempting samosas, pakora, burgers etc. Obviously, health risks may well be increased, so it is wise to only eat things that you have seen freshly cooked.

Drink

Drinking water

Public water supplies, even in large cities, are nearly always polluted and unsafe to drink. This applies to both tap water in your hotel room, and water served in a jug at the dining table. Bottled mineral water is widely available, although not all bottled water is mineral water; some is simply purified water from an urban supply. Check the seal of the bottle when buying, and reject any that appears to have been resealed or tampered with. Many people begrudge spending one or two dollars a day on bottled water, but if it reduces the likelihood of illness it must surely be worth it. (See Health Information for further information on purifying water.) **NB** It is important to use pure water for cleaning teeth.

Beverages and soft drinks

Tea, or *chai*, is the universal drink of Pakistan. It is generally made by throwing equal handfuls of tea and sugar into a pot, adding equal parts of UHT (long-life) milk and water, and bringing the whole thing to the boil. It is very sweet, but remarkably refreshing. Ask for chai, or 'Pakistani tea'. If you do not want sugar (*chini*) or milk (*dudh*), you should say so when ordering. Many places offer 'separate tea' or 'English tea', with a pot of tea, milk and sugar served separately. Chinese-style green tea is available in many areas. Coffee is rarely found outside the bigger hotels, and even then it is generally of the 'instant' variety.

Bottled, carbonated drinks such as 'Pepsi', 'Coca-Cola', '7-Up' and 'Fanta' are found almost everywhere, although prices rise as you move away from the main cities (eg Rs 7 in Islamabad, Rs 10 in Gilgit, or Rs 20 in a five-star hotel). Cartons of fruit juice, most notably mango, are also widely available. In season, fresh mango, orange and banana shakes are common. **NB** Ice cubes should be considered unsafe because the water source is likely to be contaminated.

Alcohol

Pakistan is officially a dry country. Non-Muslim foreigners are, however, permitted to purchase locally produced beers and spirits on production of a special permit. Obtaining the permit does require a certain degree of persistence. The permits are available from the Excise and Tax Department in major cities, although they are only valid for the city or district within which they are issued. You will require your passport, photocopies of the relevant pages and some passport size photographs. Although the fee for the permit is small (Rs 50), it can often only be paid at a certain bank on the other side of town from the permit office. The current allowance is nine litres per month, which can usually be bought from the more expensive hotels. Some top-end hotels have special bars where guests (and sometimes non-guests) can buy and consume alcohol. Murree Beer (advertised as being glycerine free!) can be remarkably good, although you do come across the odd rogue bottle. Varieties of whisky, gin, rum and vodka are also available. It is not permitted to bring alcohol into the country, although customs officers generally turn a blind eye to reasonable quantities, or 'confiscate' it against a receipt.

Entertainment

Nightclubs and bars

Pakistan is the wrong country if you are seeking nightclubs and bars. In cities with large expatriate communities, such as Islamabad, Karachi and Peshawar, there are thriving social scenes, although they are difficult to penetrate for the casual, short-term visitor. Legendary nights out in Islamabad include the Saturday night swill at the Australian embassy, followed by a trip to *Muddy's Café* at the Marriot Hotel, where you may see women in sleeveless shalwar kameezes! (see Islamabad 'Essentials').

There's normally a big Tuesday night drink up at the *Rose and Crown*, the bar at the British Deputy High Commission in Karachi, although it is **strictly invitation only**. For those desperate for a drink and Western company, contact the *Karachi Hash House Harriers* on a Monday night (see Karachi 'Essentials').

Cinemas

Far more accessible is the key local entertainment centre, the cinema. Pakistan's film industry is based around Lahore ('Lollywood', as opposed to Bombay's 'Bollywood'), and like their Indian counterparts, Pakistani films tend to be a combination of high-octane, non-stop violence, with sloppy love songs and coy love scenes intermittently interspersed. Pakistan does, however, produce some quality dramas, although they are not really accessible to non-Urdu speakers. Many cinemas in the larger cities show Western films, although these too are invariably of the 'action' variety. Fans of Arnie, Stallone, Bruce Lee and James Bond are well served.

The atmosphere in a Pakistani cinema is something akin to a boy's night out, which is what it is. You rarely see a woman in a cinema in Pakistan, and consequently Western women (including those accompanied) often feel extremely uncomfortable and intimidated.

Sport

Pakistan is one of the world's most fanatical sporting nations. Many play sport, even more watch it, but everybody has got an opinion on it. Pakistan is a young state, little more than 50 years old, and is still trying to come to terms with its own sense of identity. One of the key collective experiences in Pakistan's nation-building process came in the field of sport. In a country that was founded on a religious concept rather than an ethnic or nationalist sense of belonging, that has fought and realistically lost three wars with its neighbouring rival, has spent just under half of its independent life under martial law, and where no civilian elected government has ever served its full term, there have been few events that have brought the people of Pakistan as closely together as the victory of their **cricket** team in the World Cup Final in Melbourne on 25 March, 1992. The fact that their opponents were their old colonial masters, the English, made the victory even sweeter.

Yet it is not just in the sport of cricket that Pakistan excels. They have won many **hockey** World Championships and Olympic medals, and in Jahangir Khan and Jansheer Khan, Pakistan dominated world **squash** for a decade. In the recent past the World Amateur Snooker Champion has come from Lahore, and though Pakistan is yet to make its mark at international level, all the major cities have a thriving football ('soccer' to you philistines) scene. Some claim that the original form of **polo** was first played in the north of Pakistan, as it still is today. The more refined version is played in Lahore. **Golf** is becoming increasingly popular amongst the middle classes, with plenty of opportunities to play in the larger cities. **Horse and camel racing** still take place, though betting is illegal, and **sailing** and **diving** are available off the Karachi coast.

Shopping

There is an enormous variety of souvenirs, handicrafts, tribal jewellery, clothing, precious and semi-precious stones and other goods available in Pakistan, reflecting the country's rich resources and diversity of cultural traditions. The most exciting places to hunt for goods are the traditional bazaars of the old quarters of towns and cities. This is where you can often find the best bargains. In the more frequently visited places there are usually plenty of tourist shops in the main shopping areas of the modern parts of town. These often have an excellent range of goods on offer, all brought together under one roof, though prices tend to be higher. Most of the luxury hotels also have tourist shops. They tend to be the most expensive, though sometimes the quality of the goods is considerably higher than in the markets. In major cities you will often find government-run emporiums for regional handicrafts.

Bargaining is very much a part of everyday life in Pakistan, particularly in the bazaars and in tourist shops. There are exceptions to the rule (some government-run places for example are fixed-price, and sometimes traders will not budge an inch), but on the whole the initial price you are quoted will be much more than the seller is actually prepared to accept. Some people find this off-putting, or fear that they are constantly being 'ripped-off', but the whole bargaining process can be enormously enjoyable if entered into in the right spirit. It's important to keep thing in perspective; most things in Pakistan are after all very cheap by Western standards. If you have set your heart on something, ask yourself what it is worth to you and use that as a benchmark.

Carpets

These are a major industry in Pakistan, making a significant contribution to export earnings. They are generally hand-woven and hand-knotted and made of wool, silk or a mixture of the two. The main centres of carpet making are around Karachi, Multan, Quetta, Lahore, Faisalabad, Muzaffarabad and Peshawar. There is a huge variety of indigenous tribal designs, many of them very striking, particularly in NWFP,

Baluchistan and lower Sind. The majority of the other designs are borrowed and adapted from other major carpet producing countries such as Iran, Afghanistan and Turkey. Peshawar and Quetta are perhaps the best places to shop for carpets, particularly ones brought over from Afghanistan, though you will find them on sale in most towns and cities. *Kilims* (flat-woven carpets) are significantly cheaper (and lighter) than knotted carpets, making them a practical and good value option.

Ceramics Clay and terracotta pottery and utensils continue to be of great practical importance throughout Pakistan. Multan and Hala (near Hyderabad) are famous for their glazed pottery employing bright blues and whites. Bahawalpur is famous for its paper-thin *Kaghazi* pottery. Many of the designs of urns, pitchers, bowls and pots seen today are almost identical to those uncovered at Indus Valley sites around the country. Persian and Greek influences meanwhile resulted in distinctive long-necked, narrow-based vessels. A related craft which also came from Persia is that of glazed tile making, still known in Pakistan as *Kaashi*, after the town of Kashan in Iran. Sind (Thatta and Hala) and Punjab (Lahore, Multan and Uch Sharif) are most famous for this craft. As with the glazed pottery, blue and white are the most popular colours, with the geometric designs in Sind giving way to a more floral emphasis in Punjab. Distinctive glazed blue tile work is used to decorate many of the great mosques in Pakistan.

Embroidery This has developed to a fine art, with distinctive regional designs and patterns. The Sindhi *Gajh* is a lavishly embroidered wedding shirt incorporating traditional mirror work, worn by brides. The *Pushk* is found mostly in Baluchistan, with the most intricate examples coming from the Makran coastal region. It is characterized by matching embroidered cuffs and a pouch called a *pudo* in the centre of the lower half of the front of the shirt. *Phulkari*, literally meaning 'flowering', is found all over Punjab, and in the Swat valley and Hazara districts of NWFP. Traditionally, silk thread is used on plain Khaddar cloth. The floral patterns suggested in the name are usually abstracted into geometric motifs, although in Punjab the floral emphasis is retained to a greater extent. The *bagh* (garden) design involves the entire surface of the cloth being covered in intricate stitching. The gold or silver wire embroidery work on wedding suit and ceremonial clothes is known as *Zari* and probably originated in Mughal times. In the north, the *chunghas* (loose cloaks) of Patti cloth found in Swat, Gilgit and Chitral are often beautifully embroidered around the collars, lapels and cuffs.

Jewellery Gold and silversmiths and jewellers constitute one of the largest communities of craftsmen in Pakistan. Most distinctive is the chunky silver tribal jewellery of Sind, Baluchistan and NWFP. Much of the gold and silver jewellery made and sold in the cities however is intricately fashioned and very delicate. Peshawar's Andarshah bazaar is perhaps the most dazzling place to look for jewellery, although even the smallest towns will have a jeweller where one can see work in progress. Sind, Punjab and Baluchistan are famous for their enamelled silver, and for gold and silver inlaid with semi-precious stones. In Baluchistan, NWFP and the Northern Areas it is possible to find beautiful items of lapis lazuli jewellery, much of it originating from Afghanistan.

Leatherwork Leatherwork is an important craft in Pakistan. Traditionally perhaps the most important product was the leather *mashk* or water bag. Today the main products include items such as jackets, handbags, belts, shoes and sandals. Shoes and sandals are widely available with each province having its own distinctive designs. Handbags and leather jackets are made to very high standard for export and can be bought very cheaply within Pakistan. There is also an important tradition of leather bookbinding, often intricately decorated and embossed, in centres such as Lahore, Peshawar and Hyderabad.

Metalwork

Peshawar is famous for its hammered brass and copper metalwork, with a huge range of items including plates, trays, boxes, vessels etc. These can also be found in Lahore and across most of northern Punjab, but the bazaars of Peshawar's Old City are the best place to look.

Textiles

Textiles are found throughout the country and display a huge variety of designs and techniques. *Khaddar* is the simplest cotton weave, used mostly in the traditional shalwar kameez. The *Lungi* is a draped cloth used in NWFP as a turban, and in Sind also as a bridegroom's sash and scarf. The standard pattern is the *charkhana*, made up of small squares. Some of the best examples can be found in Multan. *Sussi* is another popular cotton weave with bright multi-coloured striped patterns. It is found primarily in Sind. *Khes* is a patterned and bound double weave cloth used all over Pakistan for bedcovers and sometimes as shawls. *Bandhni* or *Chunri* is the distinctive tie-dye decoration of cloth, traditionally used by the women of Sind and Cholistan on *dupattas* (long scarves). The most popular form is a pattern of small dots arranged in geometrical designs. In addition to the woven designs, block printing is a popular form, with the *Ajrak* designs of Sind generally considered amongst the best. Designs are invariably brightly coloured, with a traditional emphasis on blues (derived from the indigo plant) and also reds. The traditional designs include the *kakkar* (cloud), *charkha* (spinning wheel) and *badaam* (almond). *Patti* is a thick woollen cloth usually in a trill or herring-bone weave, typically found in the Swat, Chitral and Gilgit areas. Azad Kashmir is famous for its fine *Pashmina* woollen shawls. *Rilli* combines various decorative techniques such as printing, painting, applique and embroidery to produce colourful patchwork quilts.

Woodwork

The Swat valley is perhaps the most famous for its intricately carved architectural woodwork and furniture, although woodcarving is common throughout the mountainous north. In Swat, where the craft was undoubtedly most developed, it no longer seems to be practised, with most items offered for sale having been removed from old houses in the valley. In Sind and the Dera Ghazi Khan and Multan areas of Punjab, brightly lacquered woodwork is popular. These areas, and centres such as Dera Ismail Khan, are famous for their brass and bone-inlaid woodwork.

Holidays and festivals

The following is a list of national public holidays and Islamic holy days (usually public holidays). Note that the precise timing of Islamic holy days is linked to the sighting of the new crescent moon (at Mecca), although there is sometimes a discrepancy in the formal sighting between different sects of Islam. Islamic holy days are unfortunately often a time of sectarian tension (and even violence) between Sunnis and Shias.

National public holidays

Pakistan Day (23 March), marks the 1956 resolution proclaiming the Republic of Pakistan. **International Labour Day** (1 May). **July Bank Holiday** (1 July), although most businesses and government offices remain open. **Independence Day** (14 **August**), celebrates the founding of Pakistan in 1947, and is marked by a grand military parade in Islamabad and the opportunity to buy Pakistani flags and patriotic badges (including missile-shaped ones bearing the motto 'crush India'). **Defence of Pakistan Day** (6 September), commemorates the Pak-India war of 1965, and features a military parade in Islamabad and numerous column inches in the newspapers dedicated to this great 'victory'. **Urs of Mohammad Ali Jinnah** (11 September), death anniversary of the founder of the nation. **Mohammad (Allama) Iqbal Day** (9 **November**), the birth anniversary of the great Urdu poet, who in 1930 proposed a separate state for the Muslims of South Asia. **Birthday of Mohammad Ali Jinnah** (25

Public and religious holidays, 1999 and 2000

April 1999
28th Ashoura
May 1999
1st International Labour Day
June 1999
7th Chhelum (40 days after Ashoura)
28th Moulid an-Nabi
July 1999
1st July Bank Holiday
August 1999
14th Independence Day
September 1999
6th Defence of Pakistan Day
11th Urs of Mohammad Ali Jinnah
November 1999
9th Mohammad Iqbal Day
December 1999
9th Ramadan (until 8 January 2000)
25th Birthday of Mohammad Ali Jinnah
31st Bank Holiday
January 2000
8th Eid el-Fitr (end of Ramadan 1999)

March 2000
19th Eid el-Adha
23rd Pakistan Day
April 2000
17th Ashoura
May 2000
1st International Labour Day
27th Chhelum (40 days after Ashoura)
June 2000
17th Moulid an-Nabi
July 2000
1st July Bank Holiday
August 2000
14th Independence Day
September 2000
6th Defence of Pakistan Day
11th Urs of Mohammad Ali Jinnah
November 2000
9th Mohammad Iqbal Day
December 2000
25th Birthday of Mohammad Ali Jinnah
31st Bank Holiday

December). **Bank Holiday** (31 December), although many businesses and government offices remain open.

Islamic holy days

The Islamic Calendar begins on 16 July 622 AD, the date of the *Hijra* (`flight' or `migration') of the Prophet Mohammad from Mecca to Medina in modern Saudi Arabia, which is denoted as 1 AH (Anno Hegirae or year of the Hegira). The Islamic or *Hijri* calendar is lunar rather than solar, each year having 354 or 355 days, meaning that annual festivals do not occur on the same day each year according to the Gregorian calendar. As a very general rule, Islamic holy days move 10 or 11 days earlier each year according to our Gregorian (solar) calendar.

The 12 lunar months of the Islamic calendar, alternating between 29 and 30 days, are: *Muharram, Safar, Rabi-ul-Awwal, Rabi-ul-Sani, Jumada-ul-Awwal, Jumada-ul-Sani, Rajab, Shaban, Ramadan, Shawwal, Ziquad and Zilhaj.*

Ras as-Sana (Islamic New Year) 1st Muharram. The first 10 days of the year are regarded as holy, especially the 10th. **Ashoura** 9th and 10th Muharram. Anniversary of the killing of Hussain, grandson of the Prophet Mohammad, commemorated by Shia Muslims. The Ashoura procession, with men beating and flagellating themselves, is a moving sight, although the possibility of Sunni-Shia tension at this time means that foreign tourists are usually kept well away. If you are in, say, Gilgit or Baltistan, you may be confined to your hotel. In Rawalpindi, however, you may be encouraged to observe the proceedings close up. Ashoura also celebrates the meeting of Adam and Eve after leaving Paradise, and the end of the Flood. **Moulid an-Nabi** Birth of the Prophet Mohammad. 12th Rabi-ul-Awwal. **Leilat al-Meiraj** Ascension of Mohammad from the Haram al-Sharif in Jerusalem. 27th Rajab. **Ramadan** The holiest Islamic month, when Muslims observe a complete fast during daylight hours (sometimes referred to as 'Ramazan' in Pakistan). Businesses and Muslim sites operate on reduced hours during Ramadan. 21st Ramadan is the *Shab-e-Qadr* or `Night of Prayer'. **Eid el-Fitr** Literally `the small feast'. Three days of celebrations, beginning first Shawwal, to

Travelling during Ramadan

The holy month of Ramadan is perhaps the most important in the Islamic calendar, and certainly the one period of the year when every day life is most dramatically affected. All Muslims are required to observe a total fast (which includes liquids and also smoking) between the hours of sunset and sunrise. Exceptions are made for the sick (or very elderly), pregnant women, travellers and young children.

From the point of view of the tourist travelling in Pakistan, it is important to bear in mind the implications of this. Some people advise against visiting Pakistan during Ramadan. Such advice is really overstating the case (although if you are coming specifically for business it may be worth avoiding, since offices generally close by midday and significantly less gets done). To begin with, for the next 10 years or so Ramadan falls during the winter months when days are shorter and cooler, making it much less of an ordeal. In the main cities it is always possible to obtain food at any time of day from the larger hotels and restaurants (Chinese restaurants are usually a good bet). Even in smaller towns, many restaurants are happy to serve non-Muslims, who are after all exempt, usually discreetly at the back of the dining hall. Bear in mind, however, that in remote areas smaller hotels sometimes close during Ramadan. Many bus and railway stations provide special facilities in deference to the exemption of travellers. It is always possible to buy fruit from the markets, and biscuits, cakes etc from bakeries to take back to your hotel room.

Although it can certainly be more demanding travelling in Pakistan during Ramadan, there are also advantages. For non-smokers, bus and train journeys suddenly become far more pleasant. While tempers can sometimes begin to fray towards the end of the day, the actual breaking of the fast after sunset, which is marked by a snack called Iftar (several large meals follow on) is always a warm and friendly moment, with people invariably inviting you to share in their food. Likewise, the end of Ramadan, marked by Eidel-Fitr, is an occasion for huge celebrations and feasting characterized by outpourings of generosity and goodwill. Such moments are what a visit to Pakistan is all about.

Both authors of this Pakistan Handbook have spent a number of Ramadans in Pakistan, and we feel that it can be one of the most rewarding times to visit the country. We certainly do not agree with the contention in one guidebook that Pakistan "is no fun at all during Ramadan".

mark the end of Ramadan. **Eid el-Adha** Literally `the great feast' or `feast of the sacrifice'. Four days beginning on 10th Zilhaj. The principal Islamic festival, commemorating Abraham's sacrifice of his son Ismail, and coinciding with the pilgrimage to Mecca. Marked by the sacrifice of a sheep, by feasting and by donations to the poor.

Other regional holidays and festivals

The following are just a selection of some of the regional holidays and festivals. Check locally for exact dates. For the date of Urs (death anniversaries) at specific shrines and tombs around Pakistan, see the relevant section of the travelling text.

Kitdit (late February) is a 'coming of spring' festival celebrated in Gojal. **Bo Pho/Taghun** (late February/early March) is celebrated in Hunza, Nagar and Gojal, and celebrates the first ploughing/sowing of the year (wheat). **Basant** (spring, usually late March) is a grand kite-flying festival held in Lahore, heralding the arrival of spring. **Nauroz** (21 March) is celebrated in parts of the Northern Areas and NWFP, and marks the pre-Islamic vernal equinox (arrival of spring). **Baisakhi** (mid April) is a Sikh holy day centred on the Panja Sahib Gurudwara in Hasan Abdal. **Shandur Pass Polo** (late

July/early August) is a spectacularly situated polo tournament (see page 501), although it suffers from the fact that the date is often set according to a whim. **Ginani/Chinir** (late June/early July) is celebrated in Hunza, Nagar and Gojal to mark the first wheat harvest of the year. **Taqt Nashina** (11th July) is fervently celebrated in all Ismaili areas to mark the ascension of the present Aga Khan to the position of leader of the Ismaili community. **Aga Khan's first visit** to Hunza (1960) is commemorated each year on 23 October. **Jashan-e-Gilgit** (1 November), also known as the 'Gilgit Uprising', is commemorated in the town by a week-long polo tournament. **Aga Khan's first visit** to Gojal (1987) is commemorated each year on 18 November. **Aga Khan's birthday** (13th December) is celebrated each year in Ismaili areas. **Tumishiling** (21 December) is a festival held in Hunza and Nagar to celebrate the death of Shri Badat of Gilgit.

Health

The following information has been compiled by Dr David Snashall, Senior Lecturer in Occupational Health, United Medical Schools of Guy's and St Thomas' Hospitals and Chief Medical Adviser, Foreign and Commonwealth Office, London, with added comments and recommendations specific to Pakistan from Dr Martin Taylor, Kensington Street Health Centre, Bradford, West Yorkshire.

Travellers to Pakistan are exposed to health risks not encountered in Western Europe or North America. Because much of the area is economically underdeveloped, serious infectious diseases are common, as they were in the West some decades ago. Obviously, business travellers staying in international hotels and tourists on organized tours face different health risks to travellers backpacking through rural areas. There are no absolute rules to follow; you will often have to make your own judgement on the healthiness of your surroundings. With suitable precautions you should stay healthy.

There are many well qualified doctors in Pakistan, most of whom speak English, but the quality and range of medical care diminishes rapidly as you leave the major cities. If you are in a major city, your embassy may be able to recommend a list of doctors. If you are a long way from medical help, some self-treatment may be needed. You are more than likely to find many drugs with familiar names on sale. Always buy from a reputable source, and check date stamping. Vaccines in particular have a much reduced shelf-life if not stored properly. Locally produced drugs may be unreliable because of poor quality control and the substitution of inert ingredients for active drugs.

Before travelling

Take out good medical insurance. Check exactly what the level of cover is for specific eventualities, in particular whether a flight home is covered in case of an emergency, whether the insurance company will pay any medical expenses directly or whether you have to pay and then claim them back, and whether specific activities such as trekking or climbing are covered. Have a dental check up, and take spare glasses (or at least a glasses prescription) if you wear them. If you have a long-standing medical problem such as diabetes, heart trouble, chest trouble or high blood pressure, get advice from your doctor, and carry sufficient medication to last the full duration of your trip. You may want to ask your doctor for a letter explaining your condition.

Vaccination and immunization

If you require travel vaccinations see your doctor well in advance of your travel. Most courses must be completed in a minimum of four weeks. Travel clinics may provide rapid courses of vaccination, but are likely to be more expensive.

The following vaccinations are recommended:

Typhoid This disease is spread by the insanitary preparation of food. A single dose injection is now available (*Typhim Vi*) that provides protection for up to three years. A vaccine taken by mouth in three doses is also available, but the timing of doses can be a problem and protection only lasts for one year.
Polio Protection is by a live vaccine generally given orally, and a full course consists of three doses with a booster every five years.
Tetanus If you have not been vaccinated before, one dose of vaccine should be given with a booster at six weeks and another at six months. 10 yearly boosters are strongly recommended. Children should, in addition, be properly protected against diphtheria, mumps and measles.
Infectious Hepatitis If you are not immune to hepatitis A already, the best protection is vaccination with *Havrix*. A single dose gives protection for at least a year, while a booster taken six months after the initial injection extends immunity to at least 10 years. If you are not immune to hepatitis B, the vaccine *Energix* is highly effective. It consists of three injections over six months before travelling. A combined hepatitis A & B vaccine is now licensed and available.
Malaria For details of malaria prevention, see below.

The following vaccinations may also be considered:

Tuberculosis The disease is still common in the region. Consult your doctor for advice on BCG inoculation.
Meningococcal Meningitis and Diphtheria If you are staying in the country for a long time, vaccination should be considered.
Japanese B Encephalitis (JBE) Immunization (effective in 10 days) gives protection for around three years. There is an extremely small risk in Pakistan, though it varies seasonally and from region to region. Consult a travel clinic or your family doctor.
Rabies Vaccination before travel gives anyone bitten more time to get treatment (so particularly helpful for those visiting remote areas), and also prepares the body to produce antibodies quickly. The cost of the vaccine can be shared by three persons receiving vaccination together.
Smallpox, **Cholera** and **Yellow Fever** Vaccinations are not required, although you may be asked to show a vaccination certificate if you have been in a country affected by yellow fever immediately prior to travelling to Pakistan.

Common problems

Intestinal upsets

Intestinal upsets are due, most of the time, to the in sanitary preparation of food. Do not eat uncooked fish, vegetables or meat (especially pork, though this is highly unlikely in Pakistan), fruit with the skin on (always peel fruit yourself), or food that is exposed to flies (particularly salads).

Tap water should be assumed to be unsafe, especially in the monsoon; the same goes for stream or well water. Bottled mineral water is now widely available, although not all bottled water is mineral water; some is simply purified water from an urban supply. If your hotel has a central hot water supply, this is generally safe to drink after cooling. Ice for drinks should be made from boiled water but rarely is, so stand your drink on the ice cubes rather than putting them in your drink. For details on water purification, see box.

Heat treated milk is widely available, as is ice cream and milk produced by the same methods. Unpasteurized milk products, including cheese, are sources of tuberculosis, brucellosis, listeria and food poisoning germs. You can render fresh milk safe by heating it to 62°C for 30 minutes, followed by rapid cooling or by boiling. Matured or processed cheeses are safer than fresh varieties.

Diarrhoea is usually the result of food poisoning, occasionally from contaminated water. There are various causes: viruses, bacteria, protozoa (like amoeba and giardia), salmonella and cholera organisms. It may take one of several forms, coming on suddenly, or rather slowly. It may be accompanied by vomiting or by severe abdominal pain and the passage of blood or mucus (when it is called dysentery).

How do you know which type you have and how do you treat them? All kinds of diarrhoea, whether or not accompanied by vomiting, respond favourably to the replacement of water and salts taken as frequent small sips of some kind of rehydration solution. Proprietary preparations, consisting of sachets of powder which you dissolve in water (ORS, or Oral Rehydration Solution) are widely available in Pakistan, although it is recommended that you bring some of your own. They can also be made by adding half a teaspoonful of salt (three and a half grams) and four tablespoonfuls of sugar (40 grams) to a litre of safe drinking water.

If you can time the onset of diarrhoea to the minute, then it is probably viral or bacterial, and/or the onset of dysentery. The treatment, in addition to rehydration, is Ciprofloxacin (500 milligrammes every 12 hours). The drug is now widely available.

If the diarrhoea has come on slowly or intermittently, then it is more likely to be protozoal (ie caused by amoeba or giardia). These cases are best treated by a doctor, as should any diarrhoea continuing for more than three days. If medical facilities are remote a short course of Metronidazole (*Flagyl*) may provide relief. This drug is widely available in Pakistan, although it is best to bring a course with you. If there are severe stomach cramps, the following drugs may help: Loperamide (*Imodium, Arret*) and Diphenoxylate with Atropine (*Lomotil*).

Thus, the lynch pins of treatment for diarrhoea are rest, fluid and salt replacement, antibiotics such as Ciprofloxacin for the bacterial types and special diagnostic tests and medical treatment for amoeba and giardia infections.

Salmonella infections and cholera can be devastating diseases and it would be wise to get to a hospital as soon as possible if these were suspected. Fasting, peculiar diets and the consumption of large quantities of yoghurt have not been found useful in calming travellers' diarrhoea or in rehabilitating inflamed bowels. As there is some evidence that alcohol and milk might prolong diarrhoea, they should probably be avoided during and immediately after an attack. Antibiotics to prevent diarrhoea are probably ineffective and some, such as Entero-vioform, can have serious side effects if taken for long periods.

Heat and cold

Full acclimatization to high temperatures takes about two weeks, and during this period it is normal to feel relatively apathetic, especially if the relative humidity is high. Drink plenty of water, use salt on your food and avoid extreme exertion. When you are acclimatized you will feel more comfortable, but your need for plenty of water will continue.

Tepid showers are more cooling than hot or cold ones. Remember that, especially in the mountains and deserts, there can be a large and sudden drop between temperatures in the sun and shade, and between night and day. Dress accordingly.

The burning power of the tropical sun is phenomenal, especially at altitude. Always wear a wide brimmed hat and use some form of sun cream or lotion. Normal temperate sun tan lotions (up to factor seven) are not much good. You will need to use the types designed specifically for the tropics or for mountaineers/skiers, with a protection factor between seven and 25 (dependent on skin type). Glare from the sun can cause conjunctivitis, so wear good quality UV protection sunglasses on beaches and snowy areas. There are several variations of 'heat stroke'. The most common cause is severe dehydration, so drink plenty of non-alcoholic fluid. Sun-block and cream is not widely available in Pakistan, so you should bring adequate supplies with you.

Insects

These can be a great nuisance. Some of course are carriers of serious disease. The best way to keep mosquitoes away at night is to sleep off the ground with a mosquito net, and to burn mosquito coils containing Pyrethrum (available in Pakistan). Aerosol sprays or a 'flit' gun may be effective, as are insecticidal tablets which are heated on a mat which is plugged into a wall socket. These devices, and the refills, are not widely available in Pakistan, so if you are taking your own make sure it is of suitable voltage with the right adapter plug. Bear in mind also that there are regular power cuts in many parts of Pakistan.

A better option is to use a personal insect repellent of which the best contain a high concentration of Diethyltoluamide (DEET). Liquid is best for arms, ankles and face (take care around eyes and make sure you do not dissolve the plastic of your spectacles). These are available in Pakistan (eg *Mospel, Repel*), although it is recommended that you bring your own supply. Aerosol spray on clothes and ankles deter mites and ticks. Liquid DEET suspended in water can be used to impregnate cotton clothes and mosquito nets.

If you are bitten, itching may be relieved by cool baths and anti-histamine tablets (care with alcohol or driving), corticosteroid creams (great care and never use if hint of infection) or by judicious scratching. Calamine lotion and cream are of no real use, and anti-histamine creams have a tendency to cause skin allergies and are, therefore, not recommended.

Bites which do become infected (common in Pakistan) should be treated with a local antiseptic or antibiotic cream such as Cetrimide, as should infected scratches. Skin infestations with body lice, crabs and scabies are unfortunately easy to pick up, particularly by those travelling cheaply or trekking to mountain grazing pastures. Use Gamma benzene hexachloride for lice and Benzylbenzoate for scabies. Crotamiton cream alleviates itching and also kills a number of skin parasites. Malathion five percent is good for lice, but avoid the highly toxic full strength Malathion used as an agricultural insecticide.

Malaria

Malaria is a risk in Pakistan. It remains a serious disease and you are strongly advised to protect yourself against mosquito bites and to take prophylactic (preventive) drugs. Recommendations on prevention change, so consult your family doctor or see the further information at the end of this section. However, the current combination of anti-malarial drugs for use in Pakistan requires a daily dosage of *Proguanil* (brands such as Paulidrine) and a weekly dosage of *Chloroquine* (various brands). For those unable to use these particular drugs, your doctor may suggest the use of *Mefloquine*, although this tends to be more expensive, less well tried, and more likely to encourage side effects. Start taking the tablets one week before exposure and continue to take them for four weeks after leaving the malarial zone.

The subject of malaria prevention is becoming more complex as the malaria parasite becomes immune to some of the older drugs. In particular, there has been an increase in the proportion of cases of falciparum malaria which is particularly dangerous. Some of the preventive drugs can cause side effects, especially if taken for long periods of time, so before you travel you must check with a reputable agency the likelihood and type of malaria in the areas you intend to visit. Take their advice on prophylaxis, but be prepared to receive conflicting advice. **Do not use the possibility of side effects as an excuse not to take drugs**. In one General Practice in Britain dealing with a lot of travellers to Pakistan, no complications of anti-malarial drugs have been seen in the last five years. On the other hand, there have been several cases of malaria, some serious, in travellers who had not taken prevention seriously.

You can catch malaria even when taking prophylactic drugs, although it is unlikely. If you do develop symptoms (high fever, shivering, severe headache, sometimes

Water purification

There are various ways of purifying water in order to make it safe to drink. Dirty water should first be strained through a filter bag, and then boiled or treated. Bringing water to a rolling ***boil*** *at sea level is sufficient to make water safe for drinking, but at higher altitudes you have to boil the water for longer to ensure that all the microbes are killed.*

Various sterilizing methods can be used and there are propriety preparations containing ***chlorine*** *(eg 'Puritabs') or* ***iodine*** *(eg 'Pota Aqua') compounds. Chlorine compounds generally do not kill protozoa (eg giardia). Prolonged usage of iodine compounds may lead to thyroid problems, although this is rare if used for less than a year.*

There are a number of ***water filters*** *now on the market, available both in personal and expedition size. There are two types of water filter,* ***mechanical*** *and* ***chemical****. Mechanical filters are usually a combination of carbon, ceramic and paper, although they can be difficult to use. Ceramic filters tend to last longer in terms of volume of water purified. The best brand is possibly the Swiss made Katadyn. Although cheaper, the disadvantage of mechanical filters is that they do not always kill viruses or protozoa. Thus, if you are in an area where the presence of these is suspected, the water will have to be treated with iodine before being passed through the filter. When new, the filter will remove the taste, although this may not continue for long. However, ceramic filters will remove bacteria, and their manufacturers claim that since most viruses live on bacteria, the chances are that the viruses will be removed as well. This claim should be treated with scepticism.*

Chemical filters usually use a combination of an iodine resin filter and a mechanical filter. The advantage of this system is that according to the manufacturers' claims, everything in the water will be killed. Their disadvantage is that the filters need replacing, adding a third to the price. Probably the best chemical filter is manufactured by Pur.

diarrhoea) seek medical advice immediately. The risk of disease is obviously greater the further you move from the cities into rural areas with primitive facilities and standing water.

Infectious hepatitis (jaundice)

Medically speaking there are two types. The less serious but more common is **hepatitis A**, a disease frequently caught by travellers, and common in Pakistan. The main symptoms are yellowness of eyes and skin, lack of appetite, nausea, tiredness and stomach pains. The best protection is careful preparation of food, the avoidance of contaminated drinking water, and scrupulous attention to toilet hygiene.

The other, more serious, version is **hepatitis B**, which is acquired as a sexually transmitted disease, from blood transfusions or injection with an unclean needle, or possibly by insect bites. The symptoms are the same as hepatitis A, but the incubation period is much longer.

You may have had jaundice before or you may have had hepatitis of either type without becoming jaundiced, in which case it is possible that you could be immune to either form. This immunity can be tested for before you travel.

There are various other kinds of viral hepatitis (C, E etc) which are fairly similar to A and B, but currently vaccines do not exist for these.

Essentials

Altitude sickness

Acute mountain sickness (AMS) can strike from about 3,000 metres upwards. It is more likely to affect those who ascend rapidly (eg by plane, or by not allowing sufficient acclimatization time whilst trekking), and those who over-exert themselves. Teenagers seem to be particularly prone. It can affect you even if you have not had problems at altitude before.

On reaching heights above 3,000 metres, heart pounding and shortness of breath, especially on exertion, are almost universal responses to the lack of oxygen in the air. Acute mountain sickness takes a few hours or days to come on and presents with headache, fatigue, dizziness, loss of appetite, nausea and vomiting. Insomnia is common and often associated with a suffocating feeling when lying down in bed. Keen observers may note that their breathing tends to wax and wane at night and their faces tend to be puffy in the morning – this is all part of the syndrome. If the symptoms are mild, the treatment is rest, painkillers for the headache (preferably not Aspirin based), and anti-sickness pills for vomiting. Oxygen may help at very high altitudes but is unlikely to be available.

The best way of preventing acute mountain sickness is a relatively slow ascent and, when trekking to high altitudes, some time spent in the foothills getting fit and adapting to moderate altitude is beneficial. On arrival at places over 3,000 metres, a few hours rest and avoidance of cigarettes, alcohol and heavy food will help prevent the problem. **Should the symptoms be severe or prolonged, it is best to descend to a lower altitude and to re-ascend slowly or in stages.** Symptoms disappear very quickly even with a few hundred metres of descent. If a staged ascent is impossible because of shortage of time, the drug Acetazolamide is proven to prevent minor symptoms, but some people experience funny side effects, and it may mask more serious symptoms. The usual dose is 500 milligrammes of the slow release preparation each night, starting the night before ascending above 3,000 metres. The drug will not prevent severe altitude sickness.

There is a further, albeit rare, hazard due to rapid ascent to high altitude; a kind of complicated mountain sickness presenting as acute pulmonary oedema or acute cerebral oedema. Both conditions are more common the higher you go. Pulmonary oedema comes on quite rapidly, with breathlessness, noisy breathing, cough, blueness of the lips and possibly frothing at the mouth. Cerebral oedema usually presents with confusion, going on to unconsciousness. Anyone developing these symptoms should be evacuated from the mountain as a medical emergency.

Other problems experienced at high altitude are sunburn, excessively dry air causing skin cracking, sore eyes (it may be wise to leave your contact lenses out) and stuffy noses. It is unwise to ascend to high altitude if you are pregnant (especially in the first three months), or if you have a history of heart, lung or blood disease, including sickle cell. Do not ascend to high altitude in the 24 hours following scuba-diving (though the opportunity is unlikely). Rapid descent from high altitude may aggravate sinus and middle ear infections and make bad teeth ache. The same problems are sometimes experienced during descent at the end of a plane flight.

Remember that the mountain ranges of Northern Pakistan are very high, very cold, very remote and potentially very dangerous. Do not travel in them alone, if you are ill, or if you are poorly equipped. Telephone communication can be extremely difficult, mountain rescue all but non existent, and medical services extremely basic. Despite these various hazards (mostly preventable) of high altitude travel, many people find the environment healthier and more invigorating than at sea level.

AIDS

In Pakistan, AIDS is increasing in prevalence with a pattern typical of developing societies. Thus, it is not wholly confined to the well known high risk sections of the population, ie homosexual men, intravenous drug abusers, prostitutes and the children of infected mothers. Heterosexual transmission is now the dominant mode and so the main risk to travellers is from casual sex. For most visitors to Pakistan, the chances of casual sex are minimal. The same precautions should be taken as when encountering any sexually transmitted disease.

The AIDS virus (HIV) can be passed via unsterile needles which have previously been used to inject a HIV positive patient, but the risk of this is very small indeed. It would, however, be sensible to check that needles have been properly sterilized, or better still, disposable needles used. The chance of picking up hepatitis B in this way is much more of a danger. If disposable needles are carried as part of a proper medical kit, customs officials in Pakistan are not generally suspicious.

The risk of receiving a blood transfusion with blood infected with the HIV virus is greater than from dirty needles because of the amount of fluid exchanged. Supplies of blood for transfusion are now usually screened for HIV in reputable hospitals, so the risk may be small. Catching the AIDS virus does not necessarily produce an illness in itself; the only way to be sure if you feel you have been at risk, is to have a blood test for HIV antibodies on your return to a place where there are reliable laboratory facilities. The test does not become positive for many weeks.

Bites and stings

If you are unlucky enough to be bitten by a venomous snake, spider, scorpion, centipede or sea creature, try (within limits) to catch the animal for identification. Failing this, an accurate description will aid treatment. See the information on rabies (below) for other animal bites.

The reactions to be expected are fright, swelling, pain and bruising around the bite, soreness of the regional lymph glands (eg armpits for bites to hands and arms), nausea, vomiting and fever. If, in addition, any of the following symptoms supervene get the victim to a doctor without delay: numbness, tingling of face, muscular spasm, convulsions, shortness of breath or haemorrhage. Commercial snake bile or scorpion sting kits may be available but are only useful for the specific type of snake or scorpion for which they are designed. The serum has to be by injection into a vein, so it is not much good unless you have some practice in making such injections. If the bite is on a limb, immobilize the limb and apply a tight bandage (not a tourniquet) between the bite and the body. Be sure to release it for 90 seconds every 15 minutes. Do not try to slash the bite and suck out the poison because this will do more harm than good. Reassurance of the bitten person is important. Death from snake-bite is extremely rare. Hospitals usually hold stocks of snake-bite serum, though it is important to have a good description of the snake, or where possible, the creature itself. The best precaution is not to walk in snake territory with bare feet, sandals or shorts, and not to touch snakes even if assured they are harmless.

If swimming in an area where there are poisonous fish such as stone or scorpion fish (also called by a variety of local names) or sea urchins on rocky coasts, tread carefully or wear plimsolls. The sting of such fish is intensely painful but can be helped by immersing the stung part in water as hot as you can bear for as long as it remains painful. This is not always very practical and you must take care not to scald yourself. At certain times of the year, coincidental with the best surfing season, stinging jelly-fish can be a problem off the coast of Karachi.

Avoid spiders and scorpions by keeping your bed away from the wall, look under lavatory seats (if you come across any), and inside your shoes in the morning. Dark dusty rooms are popular with scorpions, particularly in Chitral. In the event of being bitten, consult a doctor.

Other afflictions

Rabies is endemic in Pakistan. If you are bitten by a domestic or wild animal, do not leave things to chance. Scrub the wound immediately with soap and water/disinfectant. Try to capture the animal (within limits). Treatment depends on whether you have already been vaccinated against rabies. If you have (and this is worthwhile if you are spending lengths of time in developing countries) then some further doses of vaccine are all that is needed. Human diploid cell vaccine is best, but expensive; other, older types of vaccine such as that made of duck embyos may be the only type available. These are effective, much cheaper and interchangeable generally with the human derived types. If not already vaccinated then anti-rabies serum (immunoglobulin) may be required in addition. It is wise to finish the course of treatment whether the animal survives or not.

Dengue fever is present in Pakistan. It is a viral disease, transmitted by mosquito bites, presenting severe headache and body pains. Complicated types of dengue known as haemorrhagic fevers occur throughout Asia, but usually in persons who have caught the disease a second time. Thus, although it is a very serious type, it is rarely caught by visitors. There is no treatment; you must just avoid mosquito bites.

Athlete's foot and other fungal infections are best treated by sunshine and a proprietary preparation such as Canesten or Ecostatin.

Influenza and respiratory diseases are common, perhaps made worse by polluted cities and rapid temperature and climatic changes.

Intestinal worms are common, and the more serious ones such as hook worm can be contracted by walking barefoot on infested earth.

Leishmaniasis can be a serious disease taking several forms. It is generally transmitted by sand flies, which should be avoided in the same way as mosquitoes.

Prickly heat is a very common itchy rash, and can be avoided by frequent washing and wearing loose clothing. It is helped by the use of talcum powder to allow the skin to dry thoroughly after washing.

Returning home

It is important to take your anti-malaria tablets for four weeks after your return. Malaria can develop up to one year after leaving a malaria area. If you do become ill, with fever, make sure your doctor knows about your travel. If you have had attacks of diarrhoea, it may be worth having a stool specimen tested in case you have picked up amoebic dysentery, giardiaisis or other protozoal infections. If you have been living rough, a blood test may be worthwhile to detect worms and other parasites.

Further information

The following organizations give information regarding well trained English speaking physicians throughout the world: *International Association for Medical Assistance to Travellers, 745, 5th Avenue, New York, 10022; Intermedic, 777, Third Avenue, New York, 10017.*

Information regarding country by country malaria risk can be obtained from: *Malaria Reference Laboratory*, UK, T0891-600350 (recorded message, premium rate); *Liverpool School of Tropical Medicine*, UK, T0891-172111 (recorded message, premium rate); *Centre for Disease Control, Atlanta, USA*, T404-3324555.

The *London School of Hygiene and Tropical Medicine*, Keppel Street, London, WC1E 7HT, UK, publishes a strongly recommended book titled "The Preservation of Personal Health in Warm Climates". The organization *MASTA (Medical Advice Service for Travellers Abroad)*, T (UK) 0171-6314408 will provide up to date country by country information on health risks.

Further information on medical problems abroad can be obtained from: *"Travellers' Health: How To Stay Healthy Abroad", edited by Richard Dawood (Oxford University Press)*, recently updated, with good information on travel to more out-of-the-way places. A new edition of the HMSO publication *"Health Information for Overseas Travel"* is now available.

Further reading

Pakistan (notably Islamabad, Rawalpindi, Lahore and Karachi) is an excellent place to buy books. Not only are they cheap compared with the 'West' (there are many locally printed reprints), it is also possible to find recently published versions of books that have been out of print for years. The books listed below comprise a highly selective and subjective list, although reading just a small selection will help give an insight into all things Pakistani. Those marked with an * are our particular favourites.

Books

History Allchin, B and R, 1982, *"The Rise of Civilisation in India and Pakistan"*; the most authoritative survey of the origins of Pakistani and Indian civilization. Barth, F, 1985, *"The Last Wali of Swat"*; Miangul Jahanzeb's own account of the history of Swat and his period of rule. Caroe, O, reprints, *"The Pathans"*; first published in1958 and widely regarded as the definitive study. Collins, L and Lapierre, D, reprints, *"Freedom at Midnight"*; easily digestible history, though distinctly pro-Gandhi and sadly under-estimating Jinnah's role in partition. Dani, AH, 1995, *"Peshawar: Historic city of the Frontier"*; detailed history of Peshawar and environs. Dani, AH, 1991, *"The History of the Northern Areas"*; the definitive study. Easwaran, E, 1984, *"A Man to Match his Mountains"*; highly readable, if at times a little misty-eyed, account of the life of Abdul Gaffar Khan, the 'Frontier Gandhi'. Fa Hsien, reprints, *"A Record of Buddhist Kingdoms"*; account of this monk's fifth century journey through the region. Hassan, MU, 1992, *"Mehergargh: the Oldest Civilization in South Asia"*; concise readable analysis. Robertson, GS, reprints, *"The Kafirs of the Hindu Kush"*; written at the turn of the century and now dated in many respects, but still considered amongst the most authoratitive works on the Kalasha people. Robinson, F (ed), 1989, *"Cambridge Encyclopedia of India, Pakistan"*; excellent and readable introduction to many aspects of South Asian society. Reprints are available of the *"Imperial Gazetteer of India"*, which covers most of Pakistan at the provincial and district level. Often rich in cultural and historical information, they also provide an interesting (and often humourous) insight into British colonial perceptions of the region.

'Great Game' and colonial exploits Biddulph, J, reprints, *"Tribes of the Hindoo Koosh"*. Durand, A, 1899, *"The Making of a Frontier"*. French, P, 1995, *"Younghusband"*; excellent new biography of this fascinating character. Hopkirk, P, 1990, *"Great Game: On Secret Service in High Asia"**; highly readable account of the Great Game and the history of Central Asia. Keay, J, 1977, *"When Men and Mountains Meet"**; excellent historical companion whilst travelling in this area.

Keay, J, 1979, *"The Gilgit Game"**; ditto above. Knight, EF,1894, *"Where Three Empires Meet"**; classic colonial writing, unintentionally hilarious. Schomberg, RCF,1935, *"Between the Oxus and the Indus"*; entertaining, but bigoted, colonial writing.

Politics

Burki, Shahid Javed, *"Pakistan: A Nation in the Making:*; and *"Pakistan: The Continuing Search for Nationhood"*. Duncan, E, 1989, *"Breaking the Curfew: A Political Journey Through Pakistan"**; one of the best books on Pakistan available, compulsory reading for anyone interested in modern Pakistan. Harrison, SS, 1981, *"In Afghanistan's Shadow: Baluch Nationalism and Soviet Temptations"*; in depth analysis of Baluch nationalism in its geo-political context. Lamb, C, 1991, *"Waiting for Allah: Pakistan's Struggle for Democracy"**; similar to Emma Duncan's book, though not quite so well written. Mir Ahmed Yar Khan Baluch, 1975, *"Inside Baluchistan: a political autobiography of the Khan of Kalat"*; an interesting insight into the politics of Kalat state, relations with the British, and merger with Pakistan. Wolpert, S, 1984, *"Jinnah of Pakistan"**; the definitive biography of Jinnah, though for a long time versions sold in Pakistan excluded details of Jinnah's penchant for pork sausages. Wolpert, S, reprints, *"Zulfi Bhutto of Pakistan"*; authorised biography that papers over some of the cracks, though nevertheless fascinating. Yousaf, M and Adkin, M, 1992, *"The Bear Trap: Afghanistan's Untold Story"**; fascinating insight into Pakistan's involvement in the Afghan war from the former head of the Afghan Bureau of the Inter Services Intelligence (ISI). Includes an interesting summary of the various theories surrounding Zia's death.

Religion

Ahmed, Akbar, 1996, *"Living Islam"*; based on the BBC series of the same name, this is an excellent introduction. Baldick, J, 1989, *"Mystical Islam: An Introduction to Sufism"*. Chaudhry, Mhd Sharif, 1991, *"Women's Rights in Islam"*. Holt, Lambton, Lewis (eds), 1970, *"The Cambridge History of Islam"* (two volumes).

Art and architecture

Ahmad Nabi Khan, reprints, *"Islamic Architecture of Pakistan"*. Mumtaz, KK, reprints, *"Architecture in Pakistan"*.

Fiction

Kipling, R, 1901, *"Kim"*; the classic novel that gave prominence to the expression 'Great Game'. Kipling, R, reprints, *"The Man Who Would Be King"*; classic adventure story of two deserters from the British Indian army who find themselves revered as royalty in a remote valley of the Northwest Frontier. Rushdie, S, 1983, *"Shame"*; bitterly sharp critique of South Asian life. Singh, K, 1956 (reprints), *"Train to Pakistan"*; Khushwant Singh's first novel gives a moving insight into the trauma that accompanied partition.

Travel writing

Danzinger, N, 1987, *"Danzinger's Travels: Beyond Forbidden Frontiers"*; highly readable account of travel through Turkey, Iran, Afghanistan, Pakistan, China and Tibet, though rather self-important. Denker, D, *"Sisters on the Bridge of Fire"*; familiar theme (woman travels through Northern Pakistan), but reasonably well executed. Fairley, J, 1975, *"Lion River: The Indus"*. Hopkirk, P, *"Quest for Kim"*; poorly reviewed search for the story behind Kipling's classic, research wasn't helped when the author lost most of his notes! Jamie, K,1990, *"The Golden Peak: Travels in Northern Pakistan"*; Uneventful, but beautifully written account of a young woman's travels through Northern Pakistan. Marqusee, M, 1996, *"War Minus The Shooting"*; subtitled "a journey through South Asia during cricket's World Cup", this book will appeal even to those who do not follow the game. Moorhouse, G, *"To The Frontier"*; well written account of a journey through the region. Murphy, D,1965, *"Full Tilt: Ireland to India on a bicycle"*; great fun and inspirational. Murphy, D, 1977, *"Where The Indus Is Young: a winter in Baltistan"*; account of a winter spent in Baltistan by the author and her young daughter, though rather self-important (sort of 'it's alright for me to come here, but it will be terrible when all those tourists arrive'). Newby, E, 1958, *"A Short Walk in the Hindu Kush"*; one of the best travel books ever written, details a hilarious expedition to Nuristan (in Afghanistan).

Guidebooks Lonely Planet, 1998, *"Karakoram Highway"*; much improved background information though written in that LP style that you either love or hate, hotel descriptions are minimalist. Lonely Planet, 1998, *"Pakistan"*; hard to see why anyone would buy this, continues to perpetuate the myth that you can't visit Sind or Baluchistan, lots of Punjab towns are missing altogether, whilst information on the north is sparse (it keeps referring you to its more detailed KKH and trekking books), comparatively few maps, improved background information. Lonely Planet, 1996, *"Trekking in the Karakoram & Hindukush"*; written by two authors who have probably trekked more in Pakistan than any other foreigners, very detailed information (including the unreliability of available maps), though if you are trekking with a guide you probably won't require the detailed daily route description (though this is invaluable if trekking without a guide). Shaw, I & Shaw, B, 1993, *"Pakistan Trekking Guide"*; carefully researched over five years, but as a result parts were already out of date at publication. Swift, H, 1990, *"Trekking in Pakistan and India"*; well written, lots of interesting and useful information, but now well out of date. For those continuing on to India, we thoroughly recommend **Footprint's** *India Handbook*, updated and published every year.

Specialist texts Ali, S & Dillon Ripley, S, *"Handbook of the Birds of India and Pakistan"*; available in compact edition, or five volumes. Dani, AH, *"Chilas: City of Nanga Parbat"*; excellent guide to petroglphs found in North Pakistan. Jettmar, K, *"Rock Carvings and Inscriptions in the Northern Areas of Pakistan"*; ditto Dani. Khan, Fazle Karim, 1991, *"A Geography of Pakistan".* Messerli, B & Ives, J, 1989, *"Himalayan Crisis: Reconciling Development and Conservation"*; excellent review of the controversial debate over environmental change in the Himalaya.

Web sites

Finding good web sites still remains something of a matter of hit and miss, though the following have all proved useful.

www.tourism.gov.pak PTDC's web site.
www.city.net/countries/pakistan
Www.samilan.com

Maps

Good maps are very difficult to come by in Pakistan, so you are advised to bring your own. The most detailed country map available is the **Nelles Verlag** 1:500,000 'Pakistan' map (Nelles Verlag also do a 'Himalaya' map covering northern Pakistan, parts of Afghanistan and north India, Nepal, Bhutan, Bangladesh and Tibet). More up to date is the **Geo Centre** 1:2 million 'Afghanistan/Pakistan' map in the World Map series. If coming overland, the **Kummerly + Frey** 1:4 million 'Proche-Orient' map is useful, covering Turkey and the Middle East, Iran, Afghanistan, Central Asia, Pakistan and parts of China and India. Major routes are accurately marked.

Survey of Pakistan produce a wide selection of country, regional and town maps, although most are of limited value. The 1:2 million 'Road Map of Pakistan' is one of the better country maps but is difficult to read. Some of the provincial and district maps are good (and quite pretty). Town maps are generally out of date and none too accurate (eg the 'Northern Areas' map doesn't even show the Karakoram Highway!). Survey of Pakistan maps are available from their head office; Murree Road, Faisabad, Rawalpindi, T450808, open 0900-1700, closed Friday, Saturday. You must select the maps you want from a catalogue at reception and they will be brought down to you. Be sure to keep the receipt and 'authorization' form to show to customs if necessary. Note that some of these maps are huge (two metres by two metres) and are hardly practical for navigation (though they make excellent wall posters).

PTDC have town plans and maps of most major cities and tourist destinations, although these generally only give an overview and are not sufficient for finding your way around.

For details of **trekking** maps and where they can be obtained see page 71.

Trekking

Northern Pakistan offers some of the best trekking in the world. The Karakoram, Himalaya and Hindu Kush ranges which dominate the Northern Areas and NWFP are truly spectacular, and offer a range of hiking and trekking opportunities to cover all tastes and inclinations, with everything from easy day-walks to demanding treks of up to three weeks or more.

Yet the potential of this region remains for the most part undiscovered. With the exception of one or two areas (the trek to the base camp of K2 in particular is far and away the most popular in Pakistan, and experiences many of the problems found in the Everest region of Nepal), trekking in Pakistan is generally completely free of crowds and pollution. The days when European explorers set out to fill in the 'blanks on the map' may be past, but this region remains one of the least comprehensively mapped in the world and is still full of adventure and excitement.

Aside from the natural beauty of the mountains and the peaceful, unspoilt solitude they offer, perhaps the most rewarding aspect of trekking in Pakistan is the contact it brings with the peoples who inhabit this beautiful and yet harsh environment. With one or two notable exceptions (see below), the peoples of northern Pakistan are friendly, hospitable and open in a way which seems to be characteristic of mountain people throughout the world. In Pakistan this is complemented by a fascinating variety of cultures; moving from one valley to the next it is often possible to witness a complete change in the traditions, lifestyle, language and ethnic origins of the people.

General points

Trekking in Pakistan is more demanding than in countries such as Nepal and even India, where facilities are so far developed that luxuries such as 'tea-shop trekking' are an option. In Pakistan this is not the case. Any trek involves having all the supplies and equipment, as well as the physical stamina, to be completely self-sufficient if need be. Most treks, if crossing a pass, rise to a minimum of 4,000 metres and can reach anywhere up to 5,500 metres. The terrain can be very demanding, crossing glaciers, glacial moraine, scree slopes and fast-flowing rivers, and involving numerous steep ascents and descents in the course of even a gradual overall climb. In this context, physical fitness, proper acclimatization and careful planning are crucial to your enjoyment and safety on a trek.

This section aims to provide detailed practical information on how to plan and organize a trek. The notes on specific treks which appear in the main travelling text aim only to give a general insight into what to expect (those treks which have been covered first-hand by the editors are indicated and treated in more detail, the remainder have been compiled from other sources).

We believe that any step-by-step descriptions of trekking in Pakistan should be treated with a healthy degree of scepticism. Mountain topography changes rapidly; avalanches, landslides, glacial action, flooding and erosion all conspire to make a mockery of the concept of a fixed route. Bridges may be destroyed; paths washed away and re-routed along the opposite sides of valleys, or rendered completely impassable; glaciers inevitably shift, and with them the best routes across them. Other variables such as the season, specific weather conditions and even the time of the day, can make the difference between the route across a pass being easily followed or waist-deep in snow, and rivers being easily fordable or impassable raging torrents.

There is simply no substitute for up-to-the-minute, first hand information about a particular area or route. Local tour operators are often a good source of information and can be very helpful. Talk to other trekkers and climbers; in Chitral, Gilgit and Skardu they are easily found, often congregating in specific hotels. Talk to local people; this is invariably the best source of information, although it can be misleading and must be carefully sought. The concept of 'local' also needs to be treated carefully; specific information, unless given by an experienced guide, is only likely to be accurate if the person giving it is actually from the particular valley.

Ecology and conservation

The mountains of northern Pakistan, as well as being very beautiful, also represent an extremely fragile environment. The growth of mountaineering and trekking undoubtedly poses a serious threat to the ecology of the region. Unfortunately, climbers and trekkers often appear to be the least aware, or least concerned, about the dangers.

Firewood For many, part of the romance of trekking is associated with 'wilderness' images of sitting around campfires under a starlit sky. While certainly appealing, the cutting and burning of firewood is perhaps the most immediate and dramatic cause of environmental degradation. Forests are all too scarce in most of northern Pakistan and are under serious threat. There is no justification for trekkers and climbers to light fires; they have (or should have) their own stoves and fuel. More importantly, they should ensure that their porters are likewise equipped. Existing forest and scrub is already under heavy pressure from local people and all of it is allocated on a collective basis to local communities. A contingent of porters arriving in another valley and collecting firewood to cook their evening meal are eating into the stock of firewood which will be collected and used during the harsh winter that follows the tourist season. It is ultimately up to you to ensure that your porters have kerosene stoves, and use them.

Pollution Litter is perhaps the most needless legacy of trekking and climbing groups. For some inexplicable reason, having spent small fortunes employing porters to carry their precious supplies for them, most people appear to think it perfectly acceptable to leave the associated waste in the mountains. Why not pay that little bit extra to have it carried out? (Or carry it out yourself?) With a just a bit of forethought it is possible to significantly reduce the amount of waste that your supplies will generate in the first place; discard any surplus packaging beforehand; decant as much as possible into re-usable containers (generally lighter and more practical anyway). Paper can be burnt, but not plastics. Remember that even biodegradable items take a long time to degrade in cold, dry, high altitude conditions. Dig a pit for shitting in (at least 30 metres from water supplies and above the high water mark of rivers). Avoid contaminating rivers, streams and water channels with detergents; they are likely to be someone's drinking water supply lower down. Burn toilet paper or better still, get used to using water instead. Anyone who has trekked the Annapurna "Andrex Trail" in Nepal will appreciate the outcome of 'my little bit ...' attitudes.

Types of trekking

Organized treks There are a large number of foreign and local 'adventure travel' tour operators offering specialized trekking services in Pakistan. Foreign tour operators are the most expensive. Their main advantage is that everything is done for you; pay your money and you will be looked after from the airport until you return, with everything in between, short of actually walking, taken care of. If you can afford it and have limited time, this is undoubtedly the best way of avoiding the inevitably time consuming process of planning and organizing a trek. Reputable foreign companies generally offer an excellent service, with carefully planned treks and experienced overseas staff and local guides combining to minimize the possibility of a hitch.

Many local tour operators are extremely competent and easily able to match the services of foreign companies, for less money. They are also generally very flexible, allowing you to plan your own itinerary and change it if necessary. However, liaising with local companies from abroad can (though not necessarily) be more difficult. If going through a smaller company it is essential to ensure that all the details regarding jeeps, guides, and porters etc are clear beforehand. It is worth shopping around between the various companies to find the best deal.

For a list of major overseas and Pakistani tour operators offering trekking services, see page 22. Smaller local trekking agencies are included in the Directory sections of Chitral, Gilgit and Skardu.

Self-organized treks

By choosing to join an organized trek, all the responsibility for hiring porters and guides, buying supplies, arranging transport etc, is passed to the tour operator. The second option is to undertake all these aspects of the planning and preparation yourself. The main advantage of this is that it generally works out cheaper. The main disadvantage is that the planning and preparation is a time consuming process and ultimately you will have to deal with any problems which may arise yourself. Be prepared to invest a few days at least organizing your trek. Read the information below on organizing a trek.

Independent trekking

The third option is the simplest and by far the cheapest. Hiring porters and guides is an expensive business. For two people for anything more than a few days, you soon encounter the logistical realities of having to hire porters to carry food for the porters, and enter a steep spiral of costs. If you are travelling on a budget, trekking independently is likely to be the only option. It is essential however that you have at least some experience of trekking, as it involves carrying all your own equipment and supplies, and finding your own way along the route. Trekking alone is not advisable. Many trekking areas in Pakistan are extremely remote and isolated, sparsely populated and without any reliable system of rescue; if you sustain an injury or get lost, you are on your own. The main disadvantage of this form of trekking is that, since you must be completely self-sufficient, your range is greatly limited. Assuming a maximum load of around 20 kilograms (which is a hefty weight to lug around at high altitude), you are likely to be able to trek for no more than five days at a time. The great advantage is that you do not have a retinue of porters following you around everywhere, and are free to camp where you choose, as oppose to being tied to the porters' recognized overnight stops.

One approach is to aim for a compromise which may either involve hiring a freelance guide to accompany you, carrying an equal load, or to hire one or two porters en-route. If you hire porters in the area in which you are trekking, they will have a good knowledge of routes and their condition, and extend your range considerably. Hiring on an informal basis is easily done; it is often possible to set out without any porters or guides and then simply hire a local farmer or shepherd for a section of the trek, to get you across a difficult pass for example.

Classification of treks

A 'trek' is officially defined as any route which does not exceed 6,000 metres in altitude. Treks are classified into 'open', 'restricted' or 'closed' zones.

Open zone The majority of treks fall into the open zone category, meaning that you are free to undertake the trek without a guide and without first gaining any official permission.

Restricted zone Treks in restricted zones require that you obtain an official trekking permit for the particular trek you wish to undertake (see below) and that you employ a government-registered guide. Restricted areas include a 48 kilometre zone approaching any of Pakistan's international borders (16 kilometres in Azad Kashmir), parts of Chitral and the most popular treks in Baltistan (for example the Baltoro Glacier trek to Concordia and the base camp of K2). A full list of government-approved treks in restricted zones is given in the booklet *Trekking Rules and Regulations* (1996 edition), available from the PTDC head office in Islamabad (see Tourist offices in the Islamabad Directory). Restricted zone treks included in the *Pakistan Handbook* are identified as such in the trek notes. However, the list of restricted zone treks is liable to change, so you should check for yourself before setting off on a trek.

Closed zone These areas are generally the most sensitive in political and military terms, for example the Siachen area close to the disputed Line of Control with India. They are off-limits to trekkers unless they are able to obtain special permission, which is very rarely granted. If you wish to trek in a closed zone you really need to have contacts in high places. Alternatively, try applying through one of the major local trekking agencies, which is more likely to have the relevant contacts and so give your application at least some chance of success.

Mountaineering Venturing above 6,000 metres is classified as 'mountaineering', for which a separate permit is needed. Mountaineering expeditions must pay a 'royalty' according to the altitude of the peak they are attempting and must be accompanied by a government-appointed liaison officer. Expeditions are governed by a series of rules and regulations as laid down by the Tourism Division of the Ministry of Culture, Sports and Tourism. They are outlined in a booklet entitled "Mountaineering Rules and Regulations" (1996 edition), available from the PTDC head office in Islamabad.

Choosing a trek

There is a huge variety of treks in Pakistan, with enormous variations in the level of difficulty. Choosing the right trek is extremely important. Most obviously, the trek you undertake should match your level of fitness; unless you are fairly fit, setting off on a long, hard trek is likely to be an exhausting experience, and so not particularly enjoyable. Likewise, if you have flown directly to Chitral, Gilgit or Skardu, it is essential that you acclimatize properly before undertaking any strenuous treks. If you have the time, the best approach is to do one or two shorter, easier treks first, before attempting anything more strenuous. It is well worth undertaking a programme of physical fitness training before you go. Bear in mind also that some treks do involve a certain level of technical difficulty, be it traversing glaciers, walking on snow, or fording rivers, which can be dangerous unless you (or your guide) have the experience and equipment to deal with the conditions. Note that if you wish to trek independently, you must trek in an open zone, where a permit and registered guide are not required.

'Dangerous' areas

A number of areas in northern Pakistan, despite being in open zones, are inherently dangerous. These are invariably 'tribal' areas where banditry has been the norm for centuries, and remains so even today. The main areas where this is the case are **Indus Kohistan** (which includes all the side valleys leading off from the KKH in the area; the Jalkot, Tangir, Kandia, Darel and Thor valleys, as well as the route between Chilas and

Babusar Pass), **Daimar District** (the approaches to the north side of Nanga Parbat from the KKH, also inhabited by Kohistanis), **Swat Kohistan** (the valleys north of Kalam leading over into the Gilgit river valley) and **Dir Kohistan** (the routes leading east from around Dir into Swat).

This does not mean that trekking is not possible in these areas, but that you need to take extra care. It is strongly advised (and in some cases officially required) that you trek with a reliable local guide and first inform the local authorities of your intended itinerary. The Deputy or Assistant Commissioners of each of these areas are the best people to turn to; they will be able to vet your guide, or help find one, and also advise you as to whether a particular area is safe at a given time.

Female trekkers

Women are advised not to trek alone in Pakistan. Even in the areas which are otherwise safe for women travellers, the spectacle of a woman walking through the mountains on her own is likely to cause serious offence and result in misunderstandings and problems. News of your presence would certainly spread like wildfire and be likely to attract more than just idle curiosity from local people.

The only real option for solo women travellers is either to link up with other groups, or to hire a reliable guide to accompany you. In the latter case, going through a recognized company with a reputation to uphold is the best way to ensure your safety. Alternatively, make sure that a competent authority is informed as to the trek you are undertaking, and the identity of your guide (make sure the guide is aware of this also).

Health

Read the Health section (page 56) for detailed information on staying healthy. Pay particular attention to the sections on acclimatization, altitude sickness and hypothermia. The golden rule is to allow plenty of time for acclimatization and to descend carefully to a lower altitude if the symptoms of altitude sickness manifest themselves. Avoiding hypothermia is largely a question of being properly equipped and observing basic common sense.

Getting sick is unpleasant at the best of times; while trekking it can also be dangerous in that you might be several days walk from the nearest medical facilities, which are likely to be fairly basic anyway. The most common problems are diarrhoea and stomach upsets due to contaminated food and water. The best insurance against any form of diarrhoea is to take meticulous care over personal hygiene and the preparation of food, and to purify any water which has not been collected directly at source from a spring. If you have hired a cook, it is essential that he understands the importance of hygiene and proper food preparation; most locals have a far higher tolerance than foreigners, so it is usually necessary to directly supervise their cooking, initially at least. See the Health section regarding the medical treatment of diarrhoea and the purification of water.

The other main risk while trekking is of injury. Trekkers are strongly advised to learn about the basics of first aid; there are various courses available in Europe and North America. All trekking groups in restricted areas are officially required to have at least one member with some knowledge of first aid.

Maps

Maps of northern Pakistan are fairly limited and vary greatly in their accuracy and reliability. Even the best available trekking maps are really only reliable on the main trekking routes. Within Pakistan there is little or nothing which is of any use to trekkers, so it is essential to obtain all your maps before leaving home.

The **US Army Map Service (AMS) U502 series** covers most of northern Pakistan at a scale of 1:250,000 in a series of eight sheets (two further sheets covering the border with Afghanistan are restricted). Published in the 1950s and '60s, most existing roads and jeep tracks are not shown, while village names are woefully inaccurate. However, they do on the whole give accurate information as to the topography and are useful in planning a trek (**NB** each map has a 'reliability' diagram dividing the map into poor/fair/good areas). Published in colour, they are also the most detailed in terms of contour information. International boundaries are not marked.

A book entitled **Mountaineering Maps of the World; Karakoram, Hindu Kush, Pamir and Tien Shan** published in Japan in 1978 at a scale of 1:200,000 also covers most of northern Pakistan. Although the text is in Japanese, the maps themselves are labelled in Roman script. They are on the whole reasonably accurate. The main disadvantage is that this hefty volume is very expensive and quite difficult to find.

For the Karakoram range, the **Swiss Foundation for Alpine Research** 'orographical sketch map' in two sheets at a scale of 1:250,000, or the 'trekking map' in three sheets at a scale of 1:200,000 are the best available. Published in 1990, they are generally the most accurate, at least in terms of village names, trails and mountain topography (newer jeep tracks are often not marked). International boundaries with India and China are not marked. **Leomann** also publishes a good set of four trekking maps of Gilgit, Hunza and Baltistan at a scale of 1:200,000.

There are also several more detailed maps. The excellent **Deutsche Himalaya Expedition** 1:50,000 maps in two sheets, one covering Nanga Parbat and the other Minapin Glacier were published in 1934 but updated in 1980. The Chinese **Institute of Glaciology, Cryopedology and Desert Research, Acedemia Sinica** published an excellent map of the Batura Glacier at a scale of 1:60,000 in 1978. There is also a Japanese map of the Baltoro Glacier at a scale of 1:100,000, published on the basis of the 1977 Japan-Pakistan K2 Expedition.

Buying maps

Most of the maps mentioned above can be obtained from the following places: ***Cordee Books***, 3A De Montford Street, Leicester LE1 7HD, UK, T0116-2543579, F0116-2471176. ***Edward Stanford Ltd***, 12-14 Long Acre, London WC2E 9LP, UK, T0171-8361321, F0171-8360189. ***Geo Buch Verlag***, Rosental 6, D-800, Munchen 2, Germany. ***ILH Geo Center***, Schockenriestrasse 40A, Postfach 800830, D-700 Stuttgarte 80, Germany. ***Libreria Alpina***, Via C Coronedi-Berti, 4, 40137 Bologna, Zona 3705, Italy. ***Maplink***, 25 East Mason Street, Santa Barbara, CA 93101, USA. ***Michael Chessler Books***, PO Box 2436, Evergreen, CO 80439, USA, T800-6548502. ***Travel Bookshop***, Rindermarkt 20, 8001 Zurich, Switzerland. ***US Library of Congress; Geography and Map Division***, 101 Independence Avenue, Washington, DC 20540, USA.

Organizing a trek

Permits

Permits for treks in restricted zones have to be applied for through a government-registered tour operator. Applications must be made in Islamabad, at the Tourism Division, 13-T/U, College Road, F-7/2 (next door to the PTDC office, in the same building), T9202766, F294540. Applications (in duplicate) must identify the relevant trek, give exact dates and a list of all people going on the trek, including passport details and two photos per person. A fee of US$20 per head is charged. Insurance must also be provided for all porters and guides. If the trek is one of those listed in the *Trekking Rules and Regulations* booklet, permits are generally issued within 24 hours (if not, the procedure takes a minimum of 15 days, and you are required to take a Liaison Officer with you, as well as a registered guide). Though the tour operator will deal with all the paperwork, the guide and group leader must present themselves at the offices of the Tourism Division for a briefing beforehand. **NB** The above information was correct at the time of research. However, there are concerted efforts to reduce the bureaucratic red tape associated with trekking in Pakistan; hopefully there will be constructive changes to the rules in the near future.

Guides

The guide is undoubtedly the most important component of any organized trek, and can make the difference between a trek being a highly enjoyable and rewarding success, or a complete disaster. The best guides will have experience of organizing and leading treks, and an understanding of the peculiarities of foreigners; particularly with respect to health, hygiene and fitness, but also in terms of their interest and motivation towards trekking (for example wanting time to enjoy and camp in the most picturesque spots). They will also have detailed knowledge of the particular trek you are setting off on.

It is crucial that you are able to communicate satisfactorily with your guide; in most circumstances this is determined by their grasp of English. Hiring a guide who is from the specific area in which you are going to trek is an enormous advantage. As well as being very familiar with the trek itself, he will be in a position to introduce you to local people (particularly family, friends or relations) along the way. This can make a trek infinitely more rewarding and open up a whole new world which would otherwise be far more difficult to connect with. The best guides will also take responsibility for hiring porters, ideally dealing with people with whom they are already familiar. This can be a great help when it comes to dealing with any disputes which may arise concerning porters.

Given the profitability of the profession it is not surprising that there is no shortage of people offering their services as guides. The main distinction is between government-registered guides, who are officially permitted to lead trekking groups, and unofficial guides. Government-registered guides are generally either working for one or more of the foreign/local trekking companies, or on a freelance basis, or as is commonly the case, a combination of the two. They are generally reliable, although there is a great deal of variation in their level of competence. All will have a certificate confirming their status as registered guides (if someone is unable to produce one they are probably not registered). With unofficial guides, there is a much greater element of chance.

Both registered and unofficial guides, if they are any good, will have built up a collection of letters of recommendation from previous clients. This is invariably the most revealing indicator of their competence. Ultimately however, and particularly in remoter areas, choosing a guide is largely a matter of intuition; at the least, you should get a sense of whether you feel comfortable putting yourself in that person's hands, and whether you are prepared to spend the duration of your trek with them. Local trekking companies will have their own register of guides; if you explain that you wish to organize your own trek they are usually willing to recommend an available guide.

It is usual practice to pay guides on a daily basis, as oppose to by stages (see below). Rates vary a great deal between different areas and according to the experience/competence of the guide, whether they are registered and the difficulty of the trek to be undertaken. In 1998, the daily wage for guides generally ranged from around Rs350 up to Rs700. As a rule it is worth paying more for a guide with a proven reputation and experience; often it can end up saving a great deal more in the long run.

Porters

The terms and conditions on which porters are hired are the most frequent source of disputes and misunderstandings. If you have a good guide they will hopefully be able to foresee and avoid such difficulties. But however good your guide, it is crucially important that you involve yourself with the hiring of porters and are able to satisfy yourself that all the terms and conditions of their employment have been discussed, understood and agreed.

Porters are traditionally paid by the stage. Stages are more or less established, again according to tradition, along each particular route. Most disputes arise out of the fact that an average day's trek will usually cover at least two porter's stages, meaning that the rate of payment you agree with your porters is not per day, but per stage. At lower altitudes this can end up being very expensive; over flat terrain, a porter's stage may be no more than a couple of hours walk. Make sure that it is crystal clear as to whether you are paying your porters by the day or by the stage, and establish beforehand the number of stages on a particular trek. The official line on porters is that they should cover between 10-13 kilometres per day, although in practice this has little or no relevance. One option is to negotiate a fixed payment for the porters for the whole trek. Other related points to clarify before setting off include payment on rest days or in case of forced halts due to bad weather (officially full pay), payment for the return trip (officially half pay) and transport arrangements if the porters will be returning home by road. A good idea is to write out an informal 'contract' for your porters, covering all details of payment, transport, food and clothing. It is also well worth making a list of your porters so that you can get them to sign against their names (or tick them off) after paying them.

Food and Clothing There are a number of government regulations regarding food and clothing for porters (outlined in the *Trekking Rules and Regulations* booklet). Again it is essential to establish exact arrangements beforehand. In practice porters often prefer to be paid a daily rate in lieu of their food ration and to make their own arrangements for food, particularly if trekking through their own areas where they can eat with relations and friends. Make sure though that porters take adequate food if you are heading beyond any settlements. Government rules stipulate that each porter must be equipped with rubber shoes, gloves, sunglasses and two pairs of socks, as well as a stove/fuel and tarpaulin sheet per eight porters. At higher altitudes they require in addition a jacket, and if walking on snow, proper boots. Again in practice little of this is adhered to, although the rubber boots are often expected. However, each year a number of porters die in accidents, usually related to inadequate equipment. If you are going to be trekking across ice or snow, it is your responsibility to ensure that porters have the right equipment; rubber shoes are not adequate. Indeed, rubber shoes must be the most grotesquely inappropriate kit for porters wherever they are walking; canvas shoes are not that much more expensive and are far more comfortable.

Clothing and equipment

Proper clothing and equipment is essential for trekking in northern Pakistan. It is possible in summer on lower altitude treks to get away with surprisingly little, but if the weather turns bad you could find yourself in serious trouble. At higher altitudes weather conditions can get extremely nasty very suddenly at any time of year. The following is not a comprehensive list, but covers the main essentials.

Clothing In terms of warmth, a good combination is to have a high quality 'fleece' type jacket and a waterproof/windproof jacket to go over it in extreme conditions. Full thermal underwear is also very warm and relatively light. It is through the extremities of the body that most heat is lost, so good gloves, socks and a woollen hat are vital. In most circumstances it can get quite hot during the daytime so light, loose-fitting, cotton clothing is the most practical. Many people swear by the traditional Pakistani *shalwar kamiz* as the ideal loose-fitting, light-weight, quick-drying attire. A broad-brimmed sun hat is invaluable for protection against the sun

Footwear is largely a question of personal preference. The most important thing is to have adequate ankle support, for which boots are essential. Good quality leather boots with a metal *shank* in the sole are the most robust and supportive, but some people prefer to go for lighter-weight canvas or synthetic boots. Trainers can be very comfortable and perfectly adequate on many treks, but they do not give any ankle support and therefore increase the likelihood of a sprained ankle or worse. On the other hand they are very pleasant to change into after a days walking, and invaluable for fording streams.

Equipment A good sleeping bag (minimum four-season, preferably five; a cotton sleeping bag liner will increase the warmth of a sleeping bag considerably), a sleeping mat and a tent able to withstand strong winds (domed or tunnel tents are generally the best) are essential. If you are carrying your own load, a good framed rucksack is vital and worth spending money on. Women should choose a rucksack specially designed for wider hips. If you are taking porters, a day pack is still necessary (your porters will rarely be in the same place as you en route). Other essentials include a first-aid kit, a water bottle to carry with you while walking, torch, sun cream (minimum factor 15) and sun block, lip cream (sunburnt lips are no fun), sunglasses (note that cheaper sunglasses can seriously damage your eyes by encouraging your pupils to dilate without actually filtering out harmful rays) and snow glasses if you are likely to spend much time above the snow-line. In an emergency, a 'survival blanket' (insulating silver sheet) and 'bivvy bag' (reinforced plastic sack large enough to crawl into) are potential life-savers; be sure to carry them with you if trekking with porters. A telescopic ski pole is useful for balance when fording rivers, traversing scree slopes and if walking on snow or ice. Other more specialized equipment such as ice-axes, crampons, ropes etc are only of value if you have experience in using them in the relevant conditions.

Cooking equipment is an important consideration. Kerosene or petrol stoves are most practical in that fuel is readily available, even in fairly remote areas (a fine-gauze strainer is very useful for filtering out impurities). High tech stoves such as the MSR are the lightest and most efficient. Older designs or locally made kerosene stoves have the advantage of being more readily serviceable, particularly the latter, for which spares are available in any bazaar. Make sure that you have spares of all the main components before setting out; most failures are related to the pump (make sure it is properly oiled) and to blockages in the vapourising jets (take lots of needle 'pokers'). Aluminium one litre fuel containers are best, but large groups will need a larger plastic jerry can (the latter are readily available in most bazaars in five, 10 and 25 litre sizes). Butane/propane gas (Gaz) stoves are lighter, but finding refills is difficult (though not impossible) and you face the problem of getting them onto flights. They also generally have less heating power than kerosene/petrol. The best are those that re-seal themselves automatically when dismantled. A pressure cooker is a good idea, particularly at higher altitudes where it can save significant amounts of fuel and is the only way to force water up to 100°C. A large foldable plastic water container saves numerous trips to collect water at camp.

Hiring/buying equipment

It is best to bring your own equipment, though it is becoming increasingly possible to hire equipment in Pakistan. Many of the local trekking agencies have built up a comprehensive range of equipment from previous expeditions, including sleeping bags, tents, ice axes, crampons, ropes etc. Some agencies are in a position to fully equip a large group for even the most demanding treks. Apart from Islamabad, where the larger trekking agencies have their head offices, Skardu and Gilgit have the widest range; Chitral has relatively little. Details of what is available and from whom is given in the regional sections.

Rawalpindi and Gilgit are the best places to buy equipment, although there is a certain amount available in Skardu and Chitral. Most readily available are army surplus items such as sleeping bags, ground sheets, jackets etc, although all tend to be heavy. Left-over expedition equipment is sometimes available and trekking agencies are sometimes willing to sell equipment.

Whether hiring or buying second-hand equipment, be sure to check that it is in good condition. Hiring ropes is not a good idea unless you are sure of their condition. Boots are much better brought from home. Buy new boots well in advance and take time to break them in properly.

Food The most important thing is to ensure a balanced diet (proteins, fats, vitamins, minerals, carbohydrates and fibre) and an adequate intake of calories (anywhere between 3,000 and 4,500 depending on your weight, metabolism and level of activity). Vitamin and mineral deficiencies are the most likely when trekking. Vitamin supplements are a good idea (many vitamins quickly deteriorate in even relatively fresh fruit and vegetables). Salts are rapidly lost from the body through perspiration and must be replaced. Carbohydrates (eg wheat, rice, sugar) are your main source of instant energy and need to be consumed in increased quantities; pasta is the most easily and efficiently converted carbohydrate energy source.

The main consideration in planning what food to take on a trek is whether you intend to rely on what is available in Pakistan or to bring your own supplies from home. A combination of the two gives the most flexibility and variety. The standard porters' fare of chappatis, rice, dhal, vegetables and tea (with lots of milk and sugar) is actually very nutritious and is available in any bazaar. The fastest cooking varieties of lentils are *mung* and *masoor*. It is often possible to obtain fresh dairy products from shepherds when trekking through summer pastures, but don't rely on it (remember also that milk and cheese will not have been pasturized). Other items readily available all over Pakistan include pasta, biscuits, porridge, dried fruit, nuts and fresh seasonal fruits and vegetables, dried milk, tea, sugar, salt and spices. Items such as tinned and freeze-dried foods, stock cubes, coffee, honey and jam, yeast extract, tomato ketchup and other condiments are available in major cities such as Islamabad/Rawalpindi, but can sometimes be found in Chitral, Gilgit and Skardu.

The most useful items to bring from home include freeze-dried/dehydrated foods (packet soups, though available in Pakistan, are generally pretty foul), instant noodles, high-energy foods such as chocolate bars, glucose tablets etc. Note that many of these items can often be found in Chitral, Gilgit and Skardu, having been left behind by previous expeditions; it is a matter of luck though as to what is actually available.

Sind

Sind

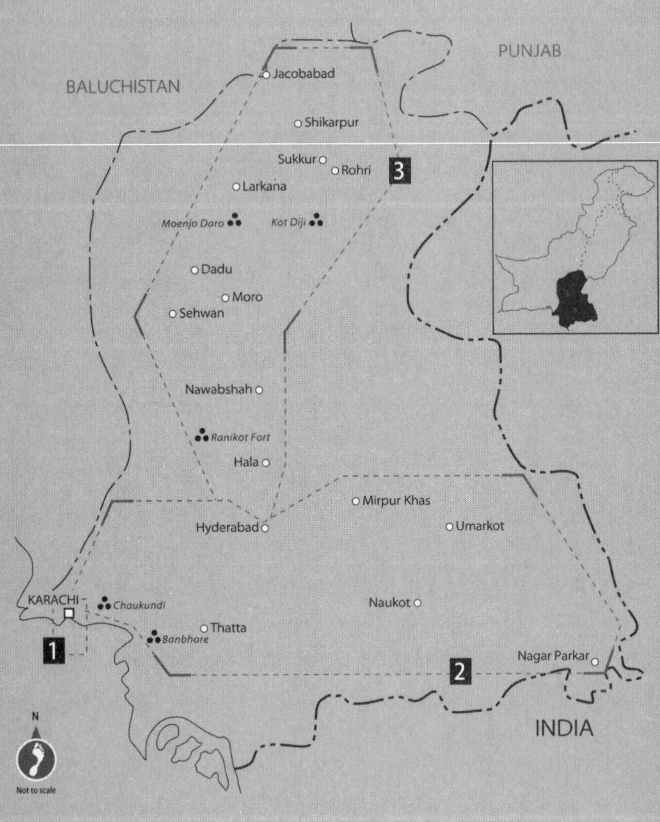
PUNJAB
BALUCHISTAN
Jacobabad
Shikarpur
Sukkur
Rohri
3
Larkana
Moenjo Daro
Kot Diji
Dadu
Moro
Sehwan
Nawabshah
Ranikot Fort
Hala
Mirpur Khas
Hyderabad
Umarkot
KARACHI
Chaukundi
Naukot
Thatta
Banbhore
1
Nagar Parkar
2
INDIA
N
Not to scale

Text Divisions

In recent years, few visitors to Sind have ventured beyond the city limits of the major international air gateway of Karachi. However, Sind has much to offer visitors, including some of the most important archaeological sites in South Asia (perhaps the world), in addition to desert adventures, beaches, and the living cultural museums of the state's many Sufi shrines. Whilst travel in the interior has been difficult in recent years, the situation has now changed drastically and no problems were encountered during extensive travels in late 1998. The situation may change, so check with your embassy and PTDC, and take advice from other travellers before setting out.

Best time to visit *Winter and spring (November-March) are very pleasant in Sind, although nights can be chilly, particularly in desert regions. Sind can become very hot in summer, with some of the world's highest temperatures recorded in the state. Sea breezes can have a cooling influence in the south, although humidity tends to be higher.*

Ins and outs

The Sind capital of Karachi remains the main international arrival point, and for many visitors this is their first taste of Pakistan. Karachi has good transport connections with the rest of the country, so if you feel that you don't want to explore Sind, it is easy to find plane and train connections on to Punjab and NWFP.

Those wishing to get the most out of Sind may like to consider travelling from Karachi to Hyderabad via the National Highway, then continuing to Sukkur via the East Bank of the Indus. Those returning to Karachi may like to do so via the West Bank of the Indus and the Super Highway, thus completing the grand loop. Those with less time, upon reaching Sukkur, can use it as a base from which to visit Moenjo Daro, before continuing north into the Punjab or northwest into Baluchistan.

Background to the area

Covering around 18 percent of Pakistan's surface area (about the size of England), the geography of Sind is dominated by the Indus River. Indeed, the very name Sind, one of South Asia's oldest regional names, is derived from the local name for the Indus River, and ultimately gave its name to India. Because of its strategic location, Sind has had a long experience of influence from outside. Sind is home to more Baluchis than Baluchistan, received more Muslim migrants at Partition than any other state, and due to the urban 'pull' of Karachi, has continued to experience mass internal migration from NWFP, the Northern Areas and the Punjab. In addition, refugees from civil wars and political change in Afghanistan, Iran, Bangladesh, Sri Lanka and India have continued to be drawn to Sind, and Karachi in particular. Despite problems of sectarianism, hyper urbanization, regional inequalities and an uncertain political future, Sind contributes significantly to the economy of Pakistan. Sind accounts for approximately 30 percent of GDP, 21 percent of agricultural GDP, 47 percent of manufacturing GDP and 42 percent of construction.

Modern Sind

Politics in Sind has been dominated in recent times by two main parties. Sind has been the traditional power base of the **Pakistan's Peoples' Party** (PPP); a party formed on socialist lines in the late 1960s by Zulfikar Ali Bhutto. However, the party is dominated by the ruling feudal families of Sind, in whose interest the traditional socialist values are in stark contrast. To perpetuate their grip over the peasantry, it is not unusual for the landed families to offer candidates to rival political parties in order to maintain their vested interests.

The second major political party of Sind, the **Mohajir Qaumi Movement** (MQM), represents the overwhelmingly urban mohajir community (Muslims from India who came to Pakistan at Partition). The rise of this movement dates to the early eighties, when disillusionment with access to reserved government job and education quotas prompted the mohajir community to press for greater rights within the framework of Pakistan. More radical members of the community call for the recognition of a mohajir state within Pakistan. The MQM has recently changed its name to the **Muttahida Qaumi Movement**.

Warning about travel in Sind

Though guidebooks have a responsibility to readers to warn of possible dangers that they may encounter on their travels, they also have a responsibility to be rational and not alarmist in the advice that they offer. Certain guidebooks published during the 1990s have basically told readers that the interior of Sind should be considered completely off limits. Whilst recognizing that there are some risks attached to travelling in Sind, the editors of the Pakistan Handbook feel that these dangers have been overstated.

True, dacoity (banditry) and kidnapping are large scale industries in the interior of the state, but these crimes are usually committed in remote, rural areas. It is also possible to reduce these threats significantly by taking a number of precautionary measures. The main roads through interior Sind are generally safe, with most places that are of interest to tourists being located on these roads. You should, however, avoid travelling by road at night. Before commencing a trip into Sind it is worth seeking advice on the current situation from PTDC, STDC, travel agents, embassies and other travellers, though you should be prepared for conflicting advice. PTDC and STDC are likely to be optimistic in their prognosis, whilst embassies are likely to be pessimistic (an official at the British Deputy High Commission in Karachi told me privately that their warning is vague and general since nobody from the consulate ever goes there).

Unlike some other guidebooks, all the information here on 'interior Sind' has been researched first-hand. I have personally travelled extensively around Sind in 1993, 1995 and 1998 without armed guards and without incident. It is really a matter of personal choice when it comes to assessing the potential risks. Dave Winter.

During much of the 1980s and 1990s, Sind saw the complete collapse of the rule of law in many parts, notably in Karachi. Much of the antagonism is between the PPP and the MQM, and has manifested itself in the form of murder and kidnapping, with each new outrage generating a revenge attack. The situation has also been complicated in urban areas by a major split within the MQM, with the 'Altaf' faction frequently blaming the ruling government (through the police and army) of covertly supporting the rival 'Haqqiqi' faction. And whilst the feuds festered in the cities, gangs in the rural areas took advantage of the breakdown in law and order and fell back upon those ancient professions of 'dacoity' (banditry) and kidnapping.

The army's 30-month 'Operation Clean-up' that began in May 1992 has been largely successful in rural Sind, making travel here a far less risky option than before. However, the seemingly arbitrary nature of the operation has alienated many Karachites, particularly the mohajir community, and the situation has in many ways worsened.

Neither the PPP nor the Pakistan Muslim League have been successful in resolving the crisis in Karachi whilst heading the federal government, and it seems unlikely that there will ever be a cessation to the violence without the participation of all interested and aggrieved groups. In the meantime, a series of stop-gap measures are being introduced, such as the recently initiated military courts (cases are tried before three military judges, and 'justice' is dispensed within 30 days, with no right of appeal to the civilian courts). However, like the oft rumoured threat of imposition of direct rule from Islamabad, these measures seem sure to inflame the situation.

Karachi

Population: 10 million
Phone code: 021
Colour map 2, grid

From modest beginnings as the old fishing village of Kalachi-jo-Goth at the mouth of the Indus, Karachi has grown into a mega-city, ranking amongst the greatest metropolis in the world. As capital of Sind Province, and former capital of Pakistan, Karachi represents the country's major commercial, industrial, financial and educational centre, as well as having the premier port and international airport.

As the main international gateway, Karachi provides most visitors with their first contact with Pakistan. Don't be put off by first impressions, and in particular don't judge the city (or indeed the whole country) by the rapacious taxi-drivers who will greet you at the airport. Karachi does not have to be the type of place to get into, then get out of, as quickly as possible. True, it cannot compete with Lahore for historical attractions, or with Peshawar for atmosphere, but it is certainly worth a few days of anybody's time.

Ins and outs

Getting there Karachi still provides the main air link to the outside world, as well as having a number of domestic connections. The airport is located 12 kilometres east of the city, and is connected by taxi service. For full details of the airport, including getting there and away, see the 'box' on page 97. Karachi has excellent train connections to the rest of the country, although on some trains, particularly fast services to Lahore, sleepers, AC and 1st Class are often fully booked for 2 weeks ahead. There are 2 major stations in Karachi: ***Karachi City*** and ***Karachi Cantt***. There are several bus stations and private bus offices scattered across the city, so where you arrive rather depends upon where you came from and who you travelled with. For full details see 'Transport' below.

Getting around Like many other South Asian cities, Karachi's public buses are impossibly crowded, routes are confusing, and getting on and off the still moving buses can be dangerous. Taxis and rickshaws are a far more practical way of getting around. Most of Karachi's modern fleet of yellow taxis have working meters that the drivers are prepared to use. Otherwise, the fare should be agreed upon before commencing the journey. Outside the central areas, particularly in residential districts, drivers will expect to be directed to the destination. It is worth having the destination clearly written on paper that can be used to ask directions from passers-by. Rickshaws are cheaper than taxis, but more vulnerable in Karachi's chaotic traffic.

History

Early history Karachi originated from a collection of small islands – Baba, Shamspir, Keamari and Manora – around a bay that acted as a natural harbour. A harbour at this site is mentioned by Pliny and Ptolemy, writing in the 2nd century. Indeed, Karachi may be the place at which Alexander the Great's admiral Nearchus assembled his fleet in 326 BC to sail to the Euphrates.

However, it was the arrival of the **British** in the mid-19th century that really changed the settlement's fortunes. Having occupied the Talpur fort on Manora island in 1839, the British annexation of Sind four years later saw the provincial capital shifted here, and within 30 years the population had expanded three-fold to some 57,000.The latter half of the 19th century saw the rapid growth of Karachi's infrastructure, including the opening of the Sind Railway in 1861 and the construction of the Mereweather Pier at the port in 1882. Many early buildings from this period (Masonic Hall, Frere Hall, Mereweather Tower, Empress Market), can still be seen today. A water supply and underground drainage system was completed in 1894, and electricity was provided in 1914. An aeroplane landed in Karachi for the first time in 1918. The pace of Karachi's expansion and development was enhanced by the city's strategic location during the Second World War, and by 1941 the population of Karachi was over 350,000.

Partition of the sub-continent and the emergence of Pakistan dramatically transformed the city once more. Despite the exodus to India of most of the Hindu population, the massive influx of refugees more than doubled Karachi's population from 420,000 in 1948 to over one million by 1951. Over 60 percent of Karachi's population were immigrants, bringing with them a culture and society quite distinct from both that of earlier Karachi and rural Sind. Known as **mohajirs**, a term associated with the Prophet's flight from Mecca, these refugees continue to dominate political life in Karachi today.

Refugees and migrants continued to flood into Karachi at the rate of 300 per day. In 1960, with Karachi's primacy threatening to distort the whole economy of Pakistan (the population doubled to over two million in the decade 1951-61 alone), Gen Ayub Khan decided to move the capital away, to the new city of Islamabad.

Recent history

Despite losing its capital city status, Karachi continues to attract significant numbers of refugees and internal migrants. The 1981 census conservatively estimated Karachi's population to be eight million, though it may well be 10 million plus by the end of the millennium (the 1998 census remains controversial). Nearly seven percent of Pakistan's population (some argue 10 percent), and 22 percent of Pakistan's urban population live in a city that fails miserably to match population growth with the provision of infrastructure and services. Statistics are contentious, but it's estimated that only one third of homes have piped water, a quarter sewerage, and there are only facilities to collect and dispose of 25 percent of the city's one million kilos of daily rubbish. As Karachi's population increases annually by six percent, availability of services increase by a miserly one and a half percent. Just one of Karachi's many slum settlements, Orangi, has itself over one million residents. Yet despite this, Karachi contributes 15 percent of GDP, 25 percent of federal revenue, 72 percent of the nation's issued capital, with 50 percent of national bank deposits held here. Karachi is both a very rich and a very poor city.

It is also a city that faces acute ethnic, sectarian and criminal violence that is threatening to destroy Karachi. The 1990s have seen a situation in which thousands of people have been killed each year in a seemingly endless spiral of violence that fills hundreds of column-inches in the local and international press. The killings are linked to tensions

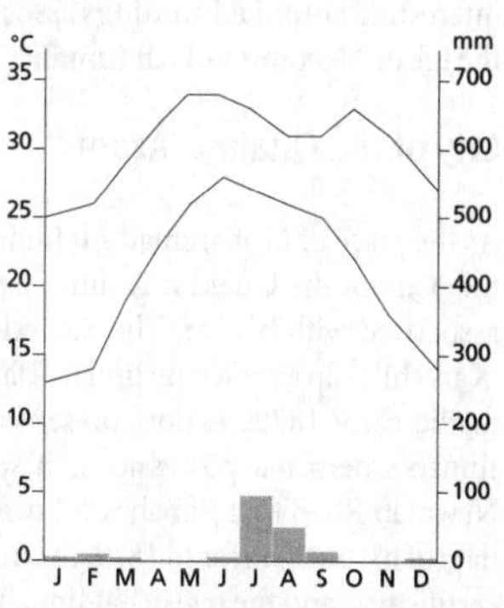

The best time to visit is undoubtedly during the cooler winter months.

Safety in Karachi

Certain parts of Karachi are considered 'high risk', where the possibility of being caught in indiscriminate firing must be considered. These areas include Orangi, Korangi, North Karachi, Nazimabad, Liaquatabad, Malir, Pak Colony, Pathan Colony and Faisal Colony. Although this list seems extensive, it should be considered that there is no reason for a tourist to need to go to any of these districts. Those arriving at Quaid-e-Azam Airport in the middle of the night are advised to remain there until day break before heading in to town.

With car-snatching becoming increasingly common, it is recommended that all vehicles should carry conspicuous as well as hidden security markings (ie sand-blasting engine and chassis numbers on front and rear windscreens). Four-wheel drive vehicles appear to be most commonly targeted. Travelling accompanied appears to reduce the risk of attack. If you are involved in a snatch situation do not attempt to offer any form of resistance.

between native Sindhis, mohajirs, Pathans, Biharis, Punjabis, as well as those wishing to exploit the Sunni-Shia split, reflecting the huge ethnic mix of the city. Allegedly fanning the flames of sectarian tension are the Indian intelligence agency RAW, the CIA, mysterious "Western powers", and whichever organization fits in with the particular conspiracy theory that you believe. More realistically, the situation is the culmination of a number of tragic events. Rival political factions have divided the city into small fiefdoms, and although operating under these covers, they are effectively criminal gangs who rule through terror and extortion. The police, demoralized and poorly paid, are both unable to take effective action, and party to the criminality. The problem is compounded by the ready availability of cheap, high-tech guns (a legacy of the Afghan war), and the drug trafficking mafia who take advantage of the deteriorating security situation to enhance huge profits. At the time of going to press, there appears to be no let-up in the cycle of violence.

Sights

Highlights

'People-watchers' will find **Clifton Beach** and the open air laundry at **Dhobi Ghat** to be two of Karachi's most interesting sights. Karachi's many **bazaars and markets** make for good shopping and wandering. The city has some interesting **colonial buildings** associated with the period of British rule and the life of **Mohammad Ali Jinnah**.

City of the Quaid-e-Azam

Wazir Mansion As the place of Mohammad Ali Jinnah's birth, Karachi is often referred to as the 'City of the Quaid-e-Azam' ('Great Leader'), and has several buildings associated with his life. The second floor apartment, **Wazir Mansion** (see 'Karachi' map), rented by Jinnah's father when he moved to the booming city in the early 1870s is now preserved as a museum, housing a number of Jinnah's personal possessions. It was in this elegant balconied house on Newman Road that Jinnah was born, though there is some dispute as to the date of his birth. Prior to 1879, the municipality of Karachi did not issue birth certificates, and the register at Jinnah's first school records his date of birth as

20 October 1875. Jinnah always claimed that he was born on Christmas Day 1876, and this date is still celebrated as a holiday in Pakistan. The irony of the significance of the date that Jinnah claimed is not lost on his principal biographer Wolpert. Jinnah attended the first Muslim educational complex to be built in Sind, Karachi's **Sind Madrassa-tul-Islam**, although records show that he was withdrawn after several years due to "long absences".

Quaid-e-Azam House Museum

Located on Shahrah-e-Faisal Rd, opposite *Avari Towers Hotel* (see 'Karachi Centre' map), is the superbly refurbished former home of Jinnah. It was known as Flag Staff House when occupied by General Gracy, commanding officer of the British Army in Sind until 1946. Following Partition it became the official residence of Jinnah as first Governor General of Pakistan, although he rarely stayed here. The main building is built of limestone block, with a wooden trussed roof finished with red ceramic Mangalore tiles. Standing in its own grounds, this beautiful Anglo-Indian mansion was opened as a museum in late 1993. The private apartments, bedrooms, study and drawing room of Jinnah and his sister Fatima have been meticulously recreated with original furniture and personal artefacts including the Quaid-e-Azam's Paris-made spat shoes.

Quaid-e-Azam's Mausoleum

Situated on a low rise to the east of M A Jinnah Rd (see 'Karachi' map), the tomb of the Quaid-e-Azam shows a neat fusion of traditional and modern Islamic architectural styles. Standing on a 54 square metres platform, the white marble mausoleum has high, pointed arches filled with copper grills, in the North African style. The cool and airy interior has a Japanese tiled ceiling, a four tiered Chinese crystal chandelier, and an Iranian silver railing around the cenotaph. There is a regular changing of the guards. Also within the terraced gardens are the tombs of Pakistan's first Prime Minister, Liaquat Ali Khan, and Jinnah's devoted sister, Fatima. A photograph of the Mausoleum opens the 'Foot in the door' section of this Handbook.

Beaches and harbours

Beaches west of Karachi

An almost uninterrupted line of beaches stretch for several hundred kilometres west of Karachi, along Baluchistan's Makran coast into Iran. However, few foreign tourists would choose Karachi, or indeed Pakistan, as the destination for a beach holiday. Beaches tend to become busy at weekends, and the attention of camel owners, cold drink vendors and souvenir salesmen can make the experience far from relaxing. Foreigners are something of a rarity, and soon become the centre of attention. Women in particular may feel very uncomfortable. Even the most non-revealing one-piece bathing suit will attract crowds of staring men, and a two-piece is just asking for hassle. Unless you're on a private or hotel-owned beach, women (and to a certain extent men) may feel more comfortable swimming in a hotel pool. It is worth remembering the cultural context: most women in South Asia bathe in the sea fully clothed. That said, the beaches around Karachi are ideal for people-watching and observing Pakistanis at play.

Warning During the monsoon season from June to August, currents are strong and the sea is dangerously rough. In May and June jellyfish make sea bathing unpleasant.

Several beaches, **Sandspit**, **Hawkes Bay** and **Paradise Point**, can be reached by car from the town (45 minutes) or by bus from **Lea Market** (one and a half hours). **French Beach**, at the centre of Hawkes Bay, and some 40 kilometres from Karachi, is for the exclusive use of foreigners and privileged

Karachi

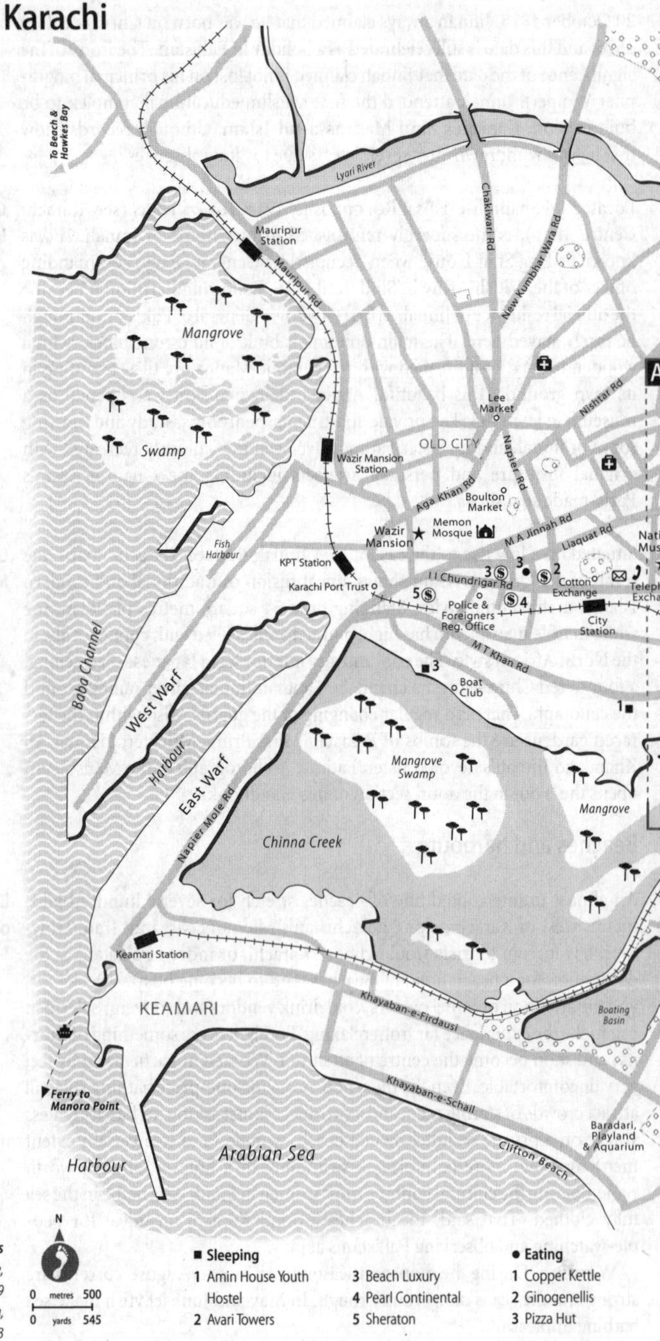
To Beach & Hawkes Bay
Lyari River
Chakiwari Rd
New Kumbhar Wara Rd
Mauripur Station
Mauripur Rd
Mangrove
Swamp
A
Lee Market
Nishtar Rd
OLD CITY
Napier Rd
Wazir Mansion Station
Aga Khan Rd
Boulton Market
Fish Harbour
Wazir Mansion
Memon Mosque
M A Jinnah Rd
Liaquat Rd
National Museum
KPT Station
Karachi Port Trust
I I Chundrigar Rd
Cotton Exchange
Telephone Exchange
Police & Foreigners Reg. Office
City Station
M T Khan Rd
Boat Club
Baba Channel
West Warf
Harbour
East Warf
Napier Mole Rd
Mangrove Swamp
Mangrove
Chinna Creek
Keamari Station
KEAMARI
Khayaban-e-Firdausi
Boating Basin
Ferry to Manora Point
Khayaban-e-Schall
Baradari, Playland & Aquarium
Clifton Beach
Harbour
Arabian Sea
N
0 metres 500
0 yards 545
Related maps
A Karachi centre, page 89
B Saddar area, page 93
■ Sleeping
1 Amin House Youth Hostel
2 Avari Towers
3 Beach Luxury
4 Pearl Continental
5 Sheraton
● Eating
1 Copper Kettle
2 Ginogenellis
3 Pizza Hut

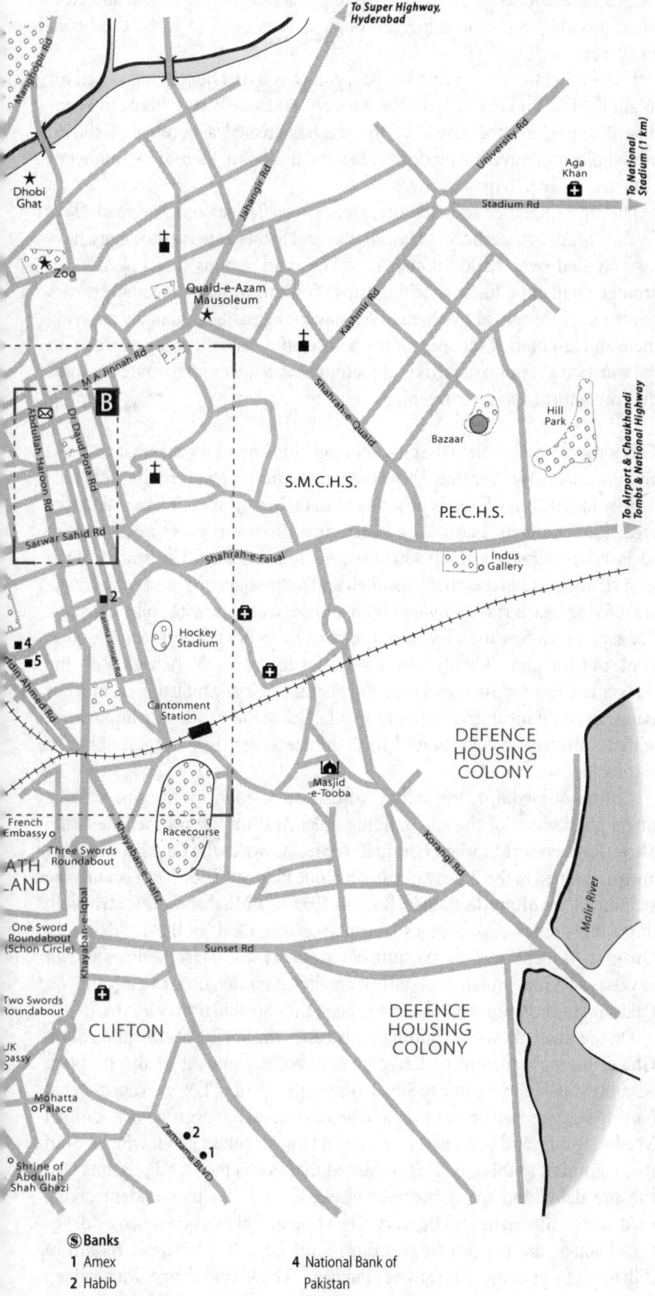

Banks

1 Amex
2 Habib
3 Karachi Stock Exchange (KSE)
4 National Bank of Pakistan
5 Standard Chartered

Pakistanis, and offers a greater degree of privacy. The rocky beach and clear water are ideal for snorkelling, although visitors need to bring their own equipment.

Continuing west along Hawkes Bay, you pass **Baleji Beach**, renowned for its snorkelling and diving, past the **Karachi Nuclear Power Plant** to **Paradise Point**. Here, the action of the sea has created a number of stacks, blow-holes and wave-cut platforms. Beyond this point, there are a number of attractive isolated bays and coves.

During September and October, giant *Green Turtles* and *Pacific* or *Olive Ridley Turtles* come ashore at Hawkes Bay and Sandspit to lay their eggs, having travelled over 1,500 kilometres. PTDC and various travel agents can arrange night-time turtle watching trips. You can witness the female turtles select a suitable spot above high tide to lay the eggs, before quickly covering them and re-entering the sea, but not before, some say, shedding a tear. With the constant attention of birds and roaming dogs, the mortality rate amongst the young turtles is extremely high.

Clifton Beach

This is the closest beach to the city, although this very factor makes it polluted and unsuitable for swimming. Developed as a health resort in the 19th century by the British, Clifton is now one of Karachi's most exclusive residential areas (see 'Karachi' map). The beach area, however, is where the entire socio-economic strata of Karachi life comes to enjoy itself. The beach is lined with stalls selling snacks, trinkets, shell and onyx souvenirs, and camel owners offering beach rides. *Funland* is an amusement park with roller coasters, dodgems and a bowling alley, and is perhaps Karachi's greatest social leveller. Look out for poor, scruffy young boys terrifying spoilt, rich girls on the dodgems. *Playland*, on the Marine Drive, was originally built as a casino, but is now a restaurant and amusement arcade. Below the arcade is an **aquarium**, with an interesting collection of fresh and seawater fish, and a number of turtles.

Clifton Viewpoint, the yellow sandstone pavilion on the promenade, offers good views of the surrounding area. Also on the promenade is the **Shree Ratneswar Mahdevi Hindu Temple**, known as the Caves of Mahdevi and mentioned in the Ramayana. Inland, one kilometre northeast, stands the red sandstone **Mohatta Palace**. Built in 1933 in a Mughal-Gothic style with imposing domes and cupolas, the palace was used as the residence of Quaid-e-Azam's sister Fatima, until her death in 1967. It is sometimes known as Qasr-e-Fatima Jinnah. Now all but derelict, it is often used as a location on Pakistani fashion shoots. For a few rupees, the chowkidar may let you in.

On the small hill above Clifton Beach stands the **Shrine of Abdullah Shah Ghazi**, the patron saint of Karachi. A direct descendant of the Prophet, Abdullah Shah Ghazi came to Sind in the ninth century. Legend suggests that his ship was wrecked off the coast and he was one of the few survivors. A noted Muslim mystic and preacher, he gained a large devotional following in Sind that continues to this day. It is suggested that over a thousand pilgrims visit the site daily, and many more at weekends, to join the resident fakirs, medicants, musicians and beggars. On Thursday nights *qawwalis*, or devotional songs, are performed and during his *Urs* (20-22 Islamic month of Zilhaj) pilgrims come from all over Pakistan. The square shrine, with a green and white striped dome, is typical of Sufi shrines all across Sind. Beneath the tomb, the sweet water spring that flows from the rock is attributed to the saint's mystic powers.

Keamari Harbour

Strategically placed on the Arabian Sea, Karachi has taken advantage of its fine natural harbour to become one of the key ports in the region. Not only is the port critical to the Pakistani economy, it is also the key point of entry for goods in transit to Afghanistan. For the tourist, it is possible to hire boats for **crabbing** expeditions. The best time for crabbing is late afternoon, after the

Karachi Centre

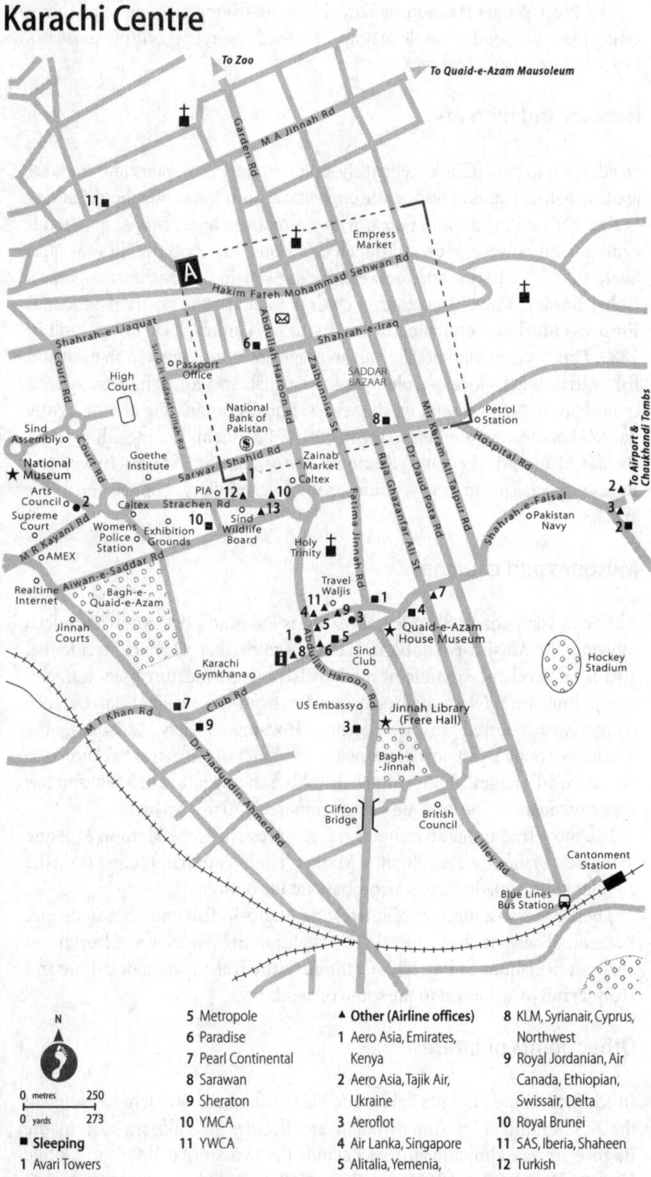

■ **Sleeping**
1 Avari Towers
2 Holiday Inn Crowne Plaza
3 Marriot
4 Mehran
5 Metropole
6 Paradise
7 Pearl Continental
8 Sarawan
9 Sheraton
10 YMCA
11 YWCA

● **Eating**
1 Cafe Grand
2 Coconut Grove
3 Village Garden

▲ **Other (Airline offices)**
1 Aero Asia, Emirates, Kenya
2 Aero Asia, Tajik Air, Ukraine
3 Aeroflot
4 Air Lanka, Singapore
5 Alitalia, Yemenia, Finnair, Korean
6 Cathay Pacific, Thai, Olympic
7 Gulfair, Zimbabwe
8 KLM, Syrianair, Cyprus, Northwest
9 Royal Jordanian, Air Canada, Ethiopian, Swissair, Delta
10 Royal Brunei
11 SAS, Iberia, Shaheen
12 Turkish
13 Qantas, South African, China, Shaheen

Related maps
A Saddar area*, page 93*
Karachi*, page 86*

monsoon. Rs 800 should cover an evening's boat hire, including cooking your catch, although you will need to bargain hard. Trips can also be arranged through Karachi travel agents. You can then go to Zainab Market in Saddar and buy a "I caught crabs in Karachi" t-shirt! From the harbour it is possible to take a ferry launch to **Manora Point**, site of a quiet beach, an old Talpur fort, a couple of British churches and a ruined Hindu temple.

The **West Wharf Harbour** is Karachi's main fishing pier, and is an interesting place to spend a couple of hours. Seafood represents one of Pakistan's key foreign exchange earners.

Bazaars and markets

In addition to providing excellent shopping, Karachi's bazaars and markets are fascinating places to wander through and absorb the atmosphere. **Saddar** is Karachi's main shopping area, with numerous carpet shops, handicraft centres and jewellers on Abdullah Haroon Rd, Zaibun Nisa St and Shahrah-e-Iraq. In the lanes between Saddar's main thoroughfares operates **Bohri Bazaar**, Karachi's colourful cloth market. To the north of Saddar is **Empress Market**, dominated by the 50 metres Gothic clock-tower, built in 1889. This covered market sells fruit and vegetables, groceries, fresh meat and fish, and is used by local people. The noise, smells and colourful activity are a typical South Asian assault on the senses. Equally fascinating are the tightly packed bazaars and markets to the north of M A Jinnah Rd, including **Jodia Bazaar**, **Juna Market** and **Khajoor (date) Bazaar**. **Sarafa (jewellers) Bazaar** specializes in heavy, traditional silver jewellery, copper and brass articles.

Mosques and churches

Although Islamabad's Shah Faisal Masjid is Pakistan's best known modern mosque, the **Masjid-e-Tooba** in Karachi's upmarket 'Defence' residential area is an excellent example of modern Islamic architecture (see 'Karachi' map). Built in 1969 through subscription from the residents of Defence (sometimes referred to as Defence Housing Society Mosque), the Masjid-e-Tooba's vast, low dome, with a diameter of 72 metres, is claimed to be the world's largest. The central hall holds a congregation of 5,000 and has superb acoustics. The mosque's single minaret is 70 metres high.

In a more traditional style, but equally impressive, is the **Memon Mosque** in the west of the city, near Boulton Market. The lofty minarets taper from the cupolas at the top, down to narrow bases at the bottom.

There are also a number of interesting Anglo-Indian churches in central Karachi. These include the 1882 Anglican **St Andrew's Church** on Shahrah-e-Liaquat, **St Patrick's Catholic Cathedral** on Shahrah-e-Iraq, and **Holy Trinity Cathedral** to the south of Saddar.

Other points of interest

In addition to the Mohatta Palace and Flag Staff House, Karachi has some of the best examples of Anglo-Indian architecture in Pakistan. Set in the **Bagh-e-Jinnah** (Jinnah Gardens), stands the two-storied Venetian-Gothic **Liaquat Hall**. Built in 1865 as the **Frere Hall**, the building has been substantially redecorated in Islamic style by the renowned Pakistani artist **Sadequan**. It houses a library and a permanent exhibition of the artist's work.

Further examples of Karachi's Victorian heritage include the red sandstone **Sind High Court** on Court Rd, complete with cupolas, balconies and pillars. Opposite stands the 19th century **Sind Assembly Building**. Other examples of Karachi's earliest buildings include the **Masonic Hall** (1845), now offices of Sind Wildlife Management Board, and the **Mereweather Tower** (1892), in the heart of the business district.

National Museum of Pakistan

Formerly housed in Frere Hall, the National Museum of Pakistan was moved to this purpose built building in Burns Garden, Dr Ziauddin Ahmed Rd, in 1970 (1000-1700, Rs 4, closed Friday, see 'Karachi Centre' map). Despite having some remarkable exhibits, there is little sense of the dynamism of archaeological research and the significance of recent developments in work on such important themes as the early Indus Valley Civilization.

Pre and proto-historic gallery 5000-1500 BC. Despite some gaps, this period is very well represented with some remarkable exhibits from Amri (c 3500-2200 BC), Kot Diji (c 3500-2500 BC), Harappa (c 2600-1900) and Moenjo Daro (c 2500-1500).

Gandharan gallery Exhibits from Gandhara sites in Taxila, Peshawar, Swat, Dir, Punjab and parts of Sind, dating from third century BC to sixth-seventh century AD. This gallery is attached to a small room displaying some **Hindu** sculptures dating from the sixth to 11th century.

Islamic gallery Includes ceramics, glass, textiles, metalware and scientific instruments such as globes and astronomical instruments dating from ninth to 14th century. Also some impressive pottery, coins and textiles excavated from Banbhore, dating from the eighth to 10th century. Exhibits from the late Mughal period include arms and armoury as well as carpets.

Freedom Movement gallery Photos from events in the life of Mhd Ali Jinnah, details of the formation and work of the All India Muslim League, the table at which Jinnah presided over the first Govt of Pakistan cabinet meeting, plus some of Jinnah's personal artefacts.

Ethnology gallery Three dimensional models representing cultural life in different regions of the country, including Kafiristan. Handicrafts, jewellery, fabrics, utensils and furniture.

The second floor **Manuscripts Hall** is currently closed to visitors.

Karachi zoo and Dhobi Ghat

Karachi **zoo** on Nishtar Road (see 'Karachi' map) is a depressing experience for animal lovers, but a great place for people watching. The 'interesting optical play' of 'half-man half-fox' is worth the Rs 2 entrance fee alone. Wednesday is ladies-only day and very colourful. About one kilometre north of the zoo, on the Lyari River, is the **Dhobi Ghat**, a fascinating giant outdoor laundry stretching for several kilometres along the river bank, and one of Karachi's great (and free) sights (see 'Karachi' map).

Essentials

Sleeping

■ on maps
Price codes: see inside front cover

Karachi has a wide choice of hotels, although prices here are generally more expensive than in the rest of Pakistan. The top hotels are of international standard (generally Rs 7,000-8,000 per night) and advance booking is often required, though don't be afraid to ask for discounts (between 30-50 percent is often available). The moderately priced and cheapest hotels are mainly in the Saddar area. Those around Lea Market, City Station and Cantt Station are best avoided.

More expensive hotels

L ***Avari Towers***, Fatimah Jinnah Rd, T5660100, F5680310, E avari@atsales.khi.sdnpk.undp.org. Full facilities including suites and 'club rooms', pool, gym, tennis, choice of restaurants, though not quite the feel of luxury as found at the *Sheraton* or *PC*. **L** ***Holiday Inn Crowne Plaza*** (formerly *Taj Mahal*), Shahrah-e-Faisal, T5660611, F5683146. Full facilities, deluxe and executive rooms, suites, business centre, pool, squash, choice of restaurants. **L** ***Karachi Marriott*** (formerly *Holiday Inn*), 9 Abdullah Haroon Rd, T5680111, F5681610. Popular *Nadia* coffee shop, *Suzie Wong* Chinese restaurant, fitness centre with pool, squash, tennis, business centre plus shopping arcade. **L** ***Karachi Sheraton***, Club Rd, T5681021, F5682875, E kshbcl@cyber.net.pk. Superb facilities, also features 'smart rooms' fully equipped for business travellers, plus split-level *Shalimar Court* rooms overlooking pool for long stay guests, choice of restaurants. Recommended. **L** ***Pearl Continental***, Club Rd, T111505505, F5681835, E pchki@ppsl.khi.erum.com.pk. The *'PC'* is probably the most luxurious in town, suites and deluxe suites available (Rs 15,000-20,000), full facilities including pool (Rs 400 day charge to non-residents), gym and health club, a/c squash courts, tennis, business centre, choice of 5 restaurants. Recommended.

A ***Beach Luxury*** (*Avari* chain), off MT Khan Rd, T5611031, F5611625, E beachlux@khi.comsats.net.pk. Harbour views (popular for video shoots), little run down for a luxury class hotel, though reasonably priced, a/c, pool, restaurants (seafood speciality). **A** ***Mehran***, Shahrah-e-Faisal, T5660851, F5677019. Central a/c, furnished rooms, fridge, dish TV, modern tiled bath, reasonable value though avoid damp and musty rooms. **A** ***Paradise***, Shahrah-e-Iraq, T5680011. 296 rooms, central a/c, dish TV, phone, bath, breakfast included, very friendly staff, only good value at half the quoted price.

B ***Al-Mustafa***, Raja Ghazanfar Ali Rd, T5661047, F5660500. New hotel, 40 a/c rooms, though still overpriced. **B** ***Metropole***, Club Rd, T5660145, F5684301. Karachi's oldest colonial period hotel, despite refurbishment it doesn't match the price tag, staff unhelpful, don't waste your time. **B** ***Midway***, out near the airport, rather overpriced rooms and usually no water in the pool. **B** ***Sarawan***, Raja Ghazanfar Ali Rd, T516001, F5680278. Central a/c, dish TV, fridge, standard rooms not very big (deluxe slightly larger with a couple of chairs), attached bath small and old fashioned, some rooms smell rather damp, coffee shop, good value buffet in restaurant, airport pick-up, facilities don't match the price. **B** ***Sky Towers***, Raja Ghazanfar Ali Rd, T5675211, F512331. Fairly new hotel, a/c, dish TV, phone, breakfast included.

Mid-price hotels

C ***Airport***, Stargate Rd, near airport, T4570141. A/c rooms, pool, a little run down but reasonable value. **C** ***Jabees***, Abdullah Haroon Rd, T512011. Central a/c, dish TV, grubby carpets, average bathroom, overpriced (popular with Russian 'business women'). **C** ***Sarah***, 30 Parr St, T5677560, F5677540. Central a/c but rooms very run down.

D ***Gulf***, Dr Daud Pota Rd, T5661235, F5682388. Non a/c rooms are reasonable value, those with a/c rather overpriced. **D** ***Holiday***, Dr Daud Pota Rd, T5661232, F566123. At the cheaper end of the **D** category (with some rooms in the **E** category), recently redecorated and refitted, very clean rooms, some with balcony, modern tiled bathrooms, friendly, a good place for backpackers to begin/end their stay in Pakistan. Recommended. **D** ***Royal City***, Sarmad Rd, T5680247. A/c rooms (some windowless), some dish TV, extraordinary toilets (squat loos converted into western ones), overpriced (though it does have a/c). **D** ***United***, Dr Daud Pota Rd, T515010, F514483. Fan, attached bath, some balconies, reasonable rooms popular with local businessmen. **D-E** ***Reliance***, Dr Daud Pota Rd, T516212. Run down rooms, filthy curtains, some rooms a/c.

Budget hotels

E ***Al-Dubai***, Sohrab Katrak Rd, T5685670. Some rooms windowless though reasonable, attached bath bare but clean, not bad value. **E** ***Al-Salatin***, Dr Daud Pota Rd, T5671093. Fan, attached bath, very similar to neighbouring *Gulf* and *United*. **E** ***Holiday***, see under

D above. **E-F** There are numerous hotels in this price category, often with very little to distinguish between them. They include: **E-F** *Al-Bilal*, Sohrab Katrak Rd, T5681176. **E-F** *Al-Haram*, Sohrab Katrak Rd. **E-F** *Al-Kabir*, Shahrah-e-Iraq, T5683690. **E-F** *Al-Mashriq*, Marian Manzil Rd, T5681004. **E-F** *Al-Sadaat*, Sarmad Rd, T5688586. Not bad value. **E-F** *Ambassador*, Dr Daud Pota Rd, T514200. **E-F** *Falcon*, Zaibun Nisa Rd (recently busted by the Khidmat Committee and charged with being a brothel). **E-F** *Golden City*, Sarmad Rd, T5685753. Fairly new, reasonable. **E-F** *Ocean*, Sohrab Katrak Rd, T5681922. **E-F** *Pak-International*, Marian Manzil Rd.

F *Amin House Boy Scout Assoc Youth Hostel*, off Mt Khan Rd, Sultanabad, T5684657. Very basic dorm (**G**), and sometimes basic rooms available, though very remote and rather run down. **F** *Chandni*, Dr Daud Pota Rd, T511487. Currently closed. **F** *Data Darbar*, Dr Daud Pota Rd. Basic. **F** *Karachi*, Sohrab Katrak Rd. Fan, attached bath rather grubby, sheets not very clean. **F** *Khyber*, Hakim Fateh Mohammad Sehwan Rd. Very basic and noisy. **F** *Paris*, MK Talpur Rd, T524411. Basic and run down. **F** *Salvation Army Hostel*, 78 NI Lines, Frere St, near Empress Market, T7214260. Dorms and some doubles. **F** *Shalimar*, Blenkin St, off Dr Daud Pota, T529491. Basic and run

Sind

Saddar Area

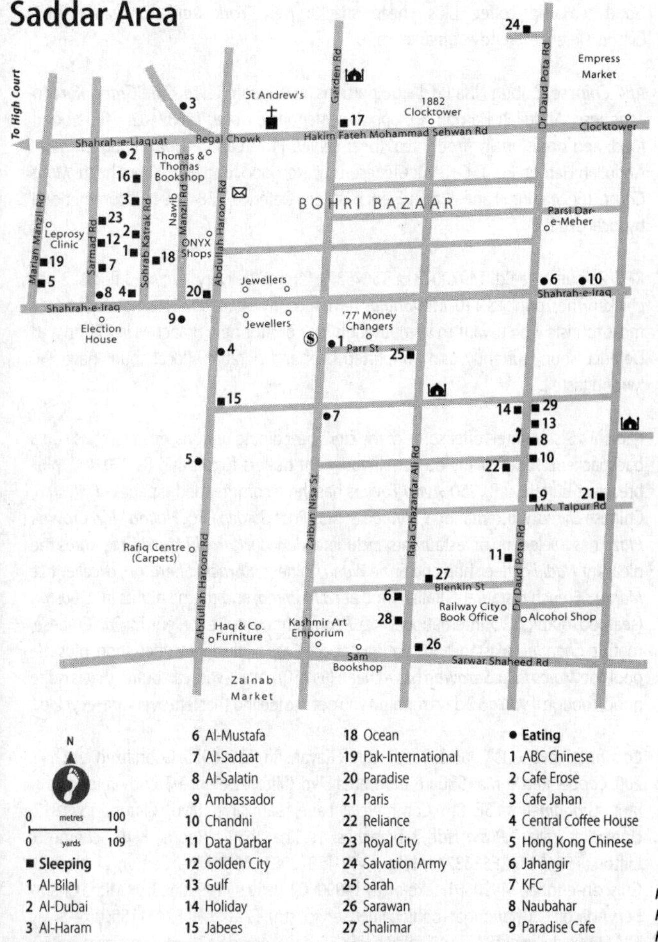

■ **Sleeping**
1 Al-Bilal
2 Al-Dubai
3 Al-Haram
4 Al-Kabir
5 Al-Mashriq
6 Al-Mustafa
7 Al-Sadaat
8 Al-Salatin
9 Ambassador
10 Chandni
11 Data Darbar
12 Golden City
13 Gulf
14 Holiday
15 Jabees
16 Karachi
17 Khyber
18 Ocean
19 Pak-International
20 Paradise
21 Paris
22 Reliance
23 Royal City
24 Salvation Army
25 Sarah
26 Sarawan
27 Shalimar
28 Sky Towers
29 United

● **Eating**
1 ABC Chinese
2 Cafe Erose
3 Cafe Jahan
4 Central Coffee House
5 Hong Kong Chinese
6 Jahangir
7 KFC
8 Naubahar
9 Paradise Cafe
10 Persian Bakery

Related maps
***Karachi**, page 86*
***Karachi centre**, page 89*

down. **F** ***YMCA Hostel***, Strachen Rd, opposite PIA. T5686927. Need to pay a 30 day temporary membership fee plus returnable Rs 100 deposit, dorms often crowded, run down, not good value. **F** ***YWCA Hostel***, MA Jinnah Rd. T7732738. Safe, women only hostel in own grounds, dorms, meals available, 2200 curfew.

● *on maps*

Eating

Budget eating *Jahangir*, Shahrah-e-Iraq. Good value Pak food, chicken Rs 50, mutton Rs 40, dhal Rs 15, excellent egg curry Rs 20, breakfast available. ***Naubahar***, Shahrah-e-Iraq. Huge, cheap dining hall, including 'student biryani'. There are also numerous cheap eating places around Saddar, Empress Market, Lee Market and Boulton Market. See also under 'hotel restaurants'.

Cafés ***Avari Bake & Take*** at the *Avari Hotel*. Offers cheap meals in a coffee-shop atmosphere, including a good value 'eat-all-you-can' buffet for Rs 125 (1600-1900). ***British Council*** has a garden café (see 'Cultural Centres' below). ***Café Erose***, Sharah-e-Liaquat. Tea, coffee and snacks. ***Central Coffee House***, next to *Jabees Hotel*, Abdullah Haroon Rd. Good tea and coffee plus cheap snacks; ***New York Café***, Zamzama Blvd, Clifton/Defence. Trendy upmarket café.

Chinese & Southeast Asian ***ABC Chinese***, Zaibun Nisa Rd. Large portions, reasonable value. ***Café Grand Korean Japanese***, Abdullah Haroon Rd, opposite *Metropole Hotel*, T5682402. Offers good food, and occasionally 'frothy tea' (beer served in a teapot). ***Hong Kong Chinese***, Abdullah Haroon Rd, T5681971. Chinese-run, a/c, good food, Rs 200 per head. ***Ming Court***, 16c Stadium Lane-1, near French Bakery, Defence, T5841694. Recommended by local expats.

Fastfood ***KFC***, Zaibun Nisa Rd, T4970018 or T5675371 for free delivery. A/c on 3 floors, 2 pcs chicken/fries/drink Rs 110. ***McDonalds*** have recently opened in Nazimabad (an area most tourists won't want to visit), though look out for new branches in Clifton and Defence soon, currently using imported beef and potatoes (local spuds have the 'wrong taste').

Hotel restaurants Karachi's 5-star hotels offer some of the city's best dining options, even for those on a backpacker budget. Many do eat-all-you-want buffets for around Rs 300-400, plus breakfast buffets at Rs 250. ***Avari Towers*** has the recommended Japanese *Fujiyama*, Chinese *Dynasty*, international *Shangrila*, plus *Roof Garden BBQ*. ***Holiday Inn Crowne Plaza*** has a selection of restaurants, including *Mexican*. ***Karachi Marriott*** features the pleasant *Nadia* coffee shop and *Suzie Wong* Chinese. ***Karachi Sheraton***, excellent *Le Marquis* French restaurant, Italian food at *La Mamma*, and theme nights in *Al Bustan* (seafood, Arabic BBQ, international etc). ***Pearl Continental***, excellent *Tai Pan* Chinese, rooftop *Chandni* Pakistani and continental, the *Grapevine* lobby coffee shop, plus the poolside *Marco Polo*. ***Sarawan*** has a cheap (Rs 150) eat-all-you-can buffet that is quite good, though if you go 2 days running you get the feeling that left-overs are recycled.

International & mixed menu ***Coconut Grove***, Arts Council Building, MR Kayani Rd, T2626975. Good fixed lunch Rs 200. ***Copper Kettle***, Mall Square, Zamzama Blvd, Clifton/Defence. Trendy café/restaurant. ***Ginoginelles***, 5E 8th Commercial Lane, Zamzama Blvd, Clifton, T571812. Upmarket Italian. ***Pizza Hut***, 3 branches: 10 Khayaban-e-Roomi, KDA Scheme 5, Clifton, T5865347, F5868243, take-away T5872081; 36-B Hina Center, Block 13-A Gulshan-e-Iqbal, T4990601, take-away T4990602, delivery T4990603; 93 Mitha Chambers Adj., off I.I. Chundrigar (behind Shell service stn), T2411147, F2411150, take-away T2411148, delivery T2411149: salad bar Rs 75, garlic bread Rs 30, regular pizzas Rs 350, large pizzas Rs 500, look out for special offers.

Bars

The ***Rose & Crown*** at the British Deputy High Commission is fun, but by invitation only. Those desperate for a beer may like to contact the *Karachi Hash House Harriers* (see under 'Sports – running' below). Liquor permits are available from the Excise Dept, Block 11, Sind Secretariat, opposite Tughlaq House (arrive early with photocopies of your passport, visa, entry stamp). The ***Pearl W Store*** alcohol shop at the south end of Dr Daud Pota Rd does not seem too bothered if foreigners don't have a permit (though none of the beer is refrigerated).

Entertainment

Clubs

Karachi Boat Club, Boat Club Rd, off MT Khan Rd, T552057. Founded in 1881, an exclusive members only club specializing in rowing, with close links with the ***Sind Club***, Abdullah Haroon Rd, T5661417, also members only. Both are proud of their reputation of allowing membership only to those of reputable background, as opposed to money. Other clubs include the ***Karachi Gymkhana***, Club Rd, T5689186 and the ***Yacht Club***, Grindlays Building, Chundrigar Rd, T2412127.

Sports

Most of the 5-star hotels allow long-term Karachi residents to join clubs that allow unlimited access to their sports and leisure facilities. **Cricket:** Karachi's ***National Stadium*** is one of Pakistan's key venues for Test and 1-day Internationals (located to the northeast, past the Aga Khan Hospital, just off Pir Sibghat Ullah Shah/Stadium Rds). Check press for fixtures. Informal matches are played in Bagh-e-Jinnah and on any piece of flat (and not so flat) ground. **Diving**: the diving season is from mid-October to mid-March. **Buleji**, 30 kilometres west of Karachi has some reef diving and snorkelling. Contact *Karachi Diving and Salvage Agency*, T224201. **Fishing**: see under 'Beaches' in 'Sights' above. **Hockey**: the *Hockey Club of Pakistan* is based at the Hockey Stadium (see 'Karachi Centre' map). **Horse riding**: you may get to ride a camel on Clifton Beach. Horse racing takes place at the **Old Race Course Ground**, just south of Cantt Station. **Rowing:** try the *Karachi Boat Club* (see under 'Clubs' above). **Running**: for those who want to jog around a Karachi suburb, the very hospitable ***Karachi Hash House Harriers*** meet every Monday evening. For details of the 'on-on' and 'down-down' contact the *Pearl Continental* reception on Monday afternoon. **Squash**: try the 5-star hotels. **Swimming:** the *Pearl Continental* allows non-residents to use their pool (Rs 400 per day). For details of sea swimming, see under 'Beaches' in 'Sights' above. **Tennis**: try the 5-star hotels. **Yachting**: try the ***Karachi Boat Club*** or ***Yacht Club*** (see under 'Clubs' above).

Theatres

See under 'Cultural Centres' in the directory.

Shopping

Bookshops

Thomas & Thomas, Shahrah-e-Liaquat, opposite Regal Chowk, Saddar. Has a good selection of imported books, plus books on Pakistan. ***Ferozsons***, Main Clifton Rd, T570527. Also has a good range. ***Sam Bookshop***, Sarwar Shaheed Rd, Saddar. Has a limited selection though some interesting books on Pakistan. Most of the 5-star hotels also hold a limited selection of novels.

Carpets

Pakistan is a top producer of hand-knotted wool and silk carpets. They are woven in the traditional style but are less expensive than the Persian originals. There are numerous carpet shops in Karachi, with the greatest concentration around the southern end of Abdullah Haroon Rd, Zaibun Nisa Rd and around the *Hotel Metropole*. The largest in Karachi is ***Afghan Carpet Warehouse***, D/16, Block 8, Chowdary Khaliquzzaman Rd, Clifton, T532690, with branches at the major hotels.

Clothing Reasonable quality, cheap 'western' clothing (jeans, t-shirts, shorts etc) are available at **Zainab Market** at the south end of Saddar (including tasteful "I caught crabs in Karachi" t-shirts). There are a number of 'boutiques' selling better quality Pakistani and 'western' clothes in Saddar, Defence, and notably on the upmarket Zamzama Boulevard in Clifton/Defence.

Duty free Imported goods (including electrical, excluding alcohol) are available at ***Karachi Duty Free***, Shahrah-e-Faisal.

Gemstones and jewellery All the major hotels have jewellers in their arcades although prices are higher than in other parts of town. There are numerous jewellers in Saddar, on Abdullah Haroon Rd, Shahrah-e-Iraq and Zaibun Nisa Rd. A modern jewellers bazaar is located at Liaquatabad Shopping Centre, opposite Super Market.

Handicrafts The ***Afghan Carpet Warehouse*** has a particularly good selection (see under 'Carpets' above). There are also numerous government and privately run handicraft emporiums at the south end of Abdullah Haroon Rd and Zaibun Nisa St in Saddar, and around the *Metropole Hotel*. A noted upmarket handicrafts/antiques shop is ***Design Shop***, 4-C, Sunset Lane 3, Phase II Extension, Defence, T5892228.

Leather goods Hand-made bags, jackets, coats, shoes and boots are good buys. ***Asian Leather Kraft***, ***Dice Gifts***, ***Mr Leather***, *Sheraton Hotel*, T522240. **English Boot House**, Zaibun Nisa St, T441649 and numerous others on Abdullah Haroon Rd.

Photography Most of the shops selling cameras and film are concentrated along Hakim Fateh Mohammad Sehwan Rd at the north end of Saddar (though if you can wait until you get to Lahore or Rawalpindi you'll get fresher film stocks).

Supermarkets Western food, cosmetics, toiletries, consumer goods etc are available from ***Agha Supermarket***, Supermarket Roundabout, Clifton.

Transport

Local Transport **Car hire** Most of the major hotels offer car and driver hire. ***Avis*** at *Travel Walji's* charge US$10 plus per kilometre a day minimum with discounts for weekly rates.

Long Distance Transport **Air** The domestic terminal is located adjacent to the international terminal at Quaid-e-Azam Airport. For details of getting to/from the airport, and facilities there, see 'box'. For airline booking offices see 'Directory – airline offices' below. On domestic flights look out for discounts on 'night coaches'.

Domestic PIA: **Bahawalpur**, Thursday, Saturday; **Bannu**, Monday, Wednesday, Thursday; **DG Khan**, Tuesday, Thursday, Sunday; **DI Khan**, Monday, Tuesday, Friday, Saturday; **Faisalabad**, 2 flights per day; **Gwadar**, daily, 2 flights on Thursday, Friday, Saturday; **Hyderabad**, Wednesday, Thursday, Saturday, Sunday; **Islamabad**, 5-9 flights daily, Rs 3400; **Jacobabad**, Monday, Wednesday, Thursday, Saturday, Sunday; **Jiwani**, Friday; **Kadanwari**, Monday, Thursday; **Khuzdar**, Monday, Tuesday, Thursday, Saturday; **Lahore**, 8 flights per day, Rs 2820; **Mianwali**, Friday, Sunday; **Moenjo Daro**, Monday 0630, Tuesday 0645, 1400, 1415, Wednesday 0645, 1500, Thursday 0630, 1300, 1400, Friday 0645, Saturday 0700, 1530, Sunday 0645, 1600, Rs 2200 return; **Multan**, 1-3 flights daily; **Pasni**, Monday, Tuesday, Wednesday, Thursday, Saturday; **Peshawar**, 2-3 flights daily, Rs 3,400; **Quetta**, 3 flights per day; **Rahim Yar Khan**, 1 flight daily; **Sehwan Sharif**, Monday, Thursday, Friday; **Sui**, Tuesday, Saturday; **Sukkur**, 2-3 flights daily; **Turbat**, 2-3 flights per day; **Zhob**, Monday, Tuesday,

Quaid-e-Azam International Airport, Karachi

Location *Karachi's airport is located 12km east of the city centre. The domestic terminal is adjacent to the international one. The airport (sometimes known as Mohammad Ali Jinnah Airport) has been recently refurbished and is quite modern.*

Getting there and away *Some of the upmarket hotels have a free airport transfer. A metered taxi between the city centre and the airport should not cost more than Rs 100, though it is rare that you ever pay less than Rs 150 (with Rs 200 being more likely). Don't forget to bargain, and set the fare before you get in the taxi. Emerging from Karachi airport can be one of the most unpleasant experiences during your visit to Pakistan; be alert since porters and taxi drivers will hassle you mercilessly, and will generally ask for ten times the correct taxi fare. Don't give in to the bastards. A desperately crowded bus (D-3) runs from the road outside the airport to Saddar.*

Arrival/departure formalities *Upon **arrival** you will be required to fill out a disembarkation card, and occasionally a health card also. The mysterious 'Form C' is rarely offered. The disembarkation card is collected at passport control. Having collected your baggage, pass through customs (foreigners are rarely stopped, though airport security may check to see that your luggage tags match). Banks, domestic flight ticket offices and taxis are now available. Upon **departure**, note that you are theoretically only allowed inside the terminal building 3 hours before your flight leaves (this rule may be waived for foreigners). You then pass through security (including bag x-ray) before you can check in. Check-in clerks will collect the departure tax (Rs 400 economy, Rs 600 club/first class). Fill in the embarkation card which is collected by passport control, and then proceed to the departure lounge. There is a further security check (x-ray and body search) before embarkation.*

Domestic flights *PIA, **Aero Asia**, **Bhoja Air** and **Shaheen Air** all have offices just outside the arrivals terminal where you can buy tickets for onward domestic flights. Note that these are considerably cheaper when bought in Pakistan rather than abroad.*

Services ***Banks** at the airport are open 24 hours (cash and travellers' cheques), though rates are marginally inferior to those available in town. Upon departure, change back Rupees before passing through immigration. **Left luggage** facilities are not available at the airport. **Duty Free** is available to passengers arriving and departing. Alcohol is not available, though cigarettes are incredibly cheap (US$8 for 200). **Porters** are available, though they are extremely keen to rip you off; agree a fee in advance. **Cafeteria** is located on the 7th floor and is open 24 hours.*

Saturday. **Aero Asia**: **Lahore**, 3 flights per day; **Islamabad**, 3 flights per day; **Multan**, 1 flight per day; **Peshawar**, 1 flight per day. **Bhoja Air**: **Lahore**, 2 flights per day, Rs 2,670; **Islamabad**, Monday, Wednesday, Friday, Rs 3,260; **Multan**, Monday, Wednesday, Friday, Rs 1,835. **Shaheen Air**: **Lahore**, 1 flight per day, Rs 2740; **Islamabad**, 1 flight per day, Rs 3,280.

International Karachi remains the main international gateway, despite the withdrawal of several airlines recently. See 'Getting there – Air' in the 'Essentials' section (page 29).

Train Reservations should be made in advance at the City booking office, including trains departing from Cantt. For student and foreign tourist discounts go to the Commercial Dept above the Upper Class booking office (go to the PTDC and get a

Selected train fares from Karachi

	A/C sleeper	*A/C sitter*	*1st class sleeper*	*Economy*
Bahawalpur	*Rs 902*	*Rs 522*	*Rs 600*	*Rs 290*
Hyderabad	*Rs 300*	*Rs 174*	*Rs 100*	*Rs 175*
Lahore	*Rs 1,395*	*Rs 733*	*Rs 550*	*Rs 255*
Larkana	*Rs 564*	*Rs 360*	*Rs 230*	*Rs 95*
Multan	*Rs 1,086*	*Rs 630*	*Rs 413*	*Rs 195*
Peshawar	*Rs 1,839*	*Rs 1,063*	*Rs 715*	*Rs 350*
Quetta	*Rs 938*	*Rs 591*	*Rs 391*	*Rs 110*
Rawalpindi	*Rs 1,671*	*Rs 962*	*Rs 649*	*Rs 195*
Sukkur/Rohri	*Rs 658*	*Rs 383*	*Rs 242*	*Rs 100*

certificate there first). The trains to the following destinations are those that offer the most direct daily services, plus all classes of ticket. **Hyderabad** 16 trains per day (City and Cantt). **Lahore** *Shalimar Exp* (Cantt), 0600, 17 hours; *Tezgam* (Cantt), 1545, 19 hours. **Multan** *Shalimar Exp* (Cantt), 0600, 12 hours; *Tezgam* (Cantt), 1545, 14 hours. **Peshawar** *Awam Exp* (Cantt), 0745, 32½ hours; *Khyber Mail* (Cantt), 2200, 32½ hours. **Quetta** *Bolan Mail* (City), 1030, 26 hours; *Sind Exp/45* (City), 0700, 25 hours; *Baluch Exp* (Cantt), 1845, 15 hours. **Rawalpindi** *Awam Exp* (Cantt), 0745, 28 hours; *Tezgam* (Cantt), 1545, 25 hours. **Rohri/Sukkur** *Shalimar Exp* (Cantt), 0600, 6 hours; *Sukkur Exp* (Cantt), 2230, 9 hours. Railway information: T117, T2415016.

Long distance buses If travelling long distance, trains are a far more comfortable option. It is inadvisable to travel by bus at night around Sind. ***Blue Lines***, outside Cantt railway station, T5660821, run hourly buses to **Hyderabad** (2½ hours via the Super Highway) for Rs 40, some of which continue via the Indus east bank to **Sukkur** (further 8 hours, Rs 170). They also have services to **Lahore**, though the train journey is much better. ***New Khan Road Runners***, also at Cantt station, offer similar services (**Lahore** Rs 450, 24 hours). ***Qalandri Coach***, T4923721, and ***Qadri Coach***, T4938294, operating from Sabzi Mandi on University Rd (opposite *Shahzhob Hotel*) have daily services to **Quetta** (Rs 250, 12 hours), though again the train is preferable.

Local buses For **Chaukundi Tombs/Kinjhar/Makli Hill/Thatta/Hyderabad** depart from **Lea Market** (ask a taxi/rickshaw to drop you at 'Thatta bus stand'). These services depart when full. Local buses to **Mirpur Khas** leave from **Boulton Market.** Local buses for **Khuzdar** and **Las Bela** leave from **Shedi City Rd** and **Mollah Maddar** respectively, both to the north of **Lea Market**.

Directory

Airline offices Many of the airline offices are located at, or close to, the major hotels. At *Avari Towers*: ***American Airlines*** and ***Canadian***, T526466. ***Biman***, T510069. ***Egypt Air***, T5661125. ***Interflug***, T512235. ***Japan***, T510161. ***Uzbek***, T5675943. At *Karachi Marriott*: ***Air France***, T5681071. ***British Airways***, T5686071. At *Karachi Sheraton*: ***Kuwait Airways***, T5685754. ***Malaysian Airlines***, T5682434. At *Pearl Continental*: ***Lufthansa***, T5685811, F5680872. ***Malev Hungarian***, T5681290. At *Holiday Inn Crowne Plaza*: ***Aeroflot***, T5685640. Opposite *Holiday Inn Crowne Plaza*, Shahrah-e-Faisal. ***Tajik***. ***Taron***, T7789261. ***Turkmen***, T7783473. ***Ukraine***. At *Hotel Metropole*: ***Alitalia***, T511097. ***Austrian Airlines***, T510241. ***Cathay Pacific***, T5660391. ***KLM***, *T5689071, F5683345*. ***Royal Jordanian***, T5660458. ***SAS***, T515893. ***Swiss Air***, T5684643. ***Thai***, T5660160. ***United***, T5684731. ***Yemenia***, T5678182. At Services Club Building, Mereweather Rd: ***Air Lanka***, T5662679. ***Iberia***, T510360. ***Royal Nepal***, T514431. ***SAS***, T510346. ***Singapore Airlines***, T5660330. ***Gulf Air***, Kashif Centre, Shahrah-e-Faisal, T5675231 (24 hrs T45791434). At PIA Building, Strachen Rd: ***Air Portugal***, T510600. ***Qantas***, T513636. ***KLM***, Club Rd, T6637620. At *Mehran Hotel*: ***Iran***,

T515001. ***Syrian Arab Airlines***, 6 Club Rd, T5680889. At Lakson Square (behind PIA), ***Emirates***, T5683377. ***Kenya***, T5685730. ***Turkish***, T5685766. At other locations: ***Air China***, 25c 24th St, Block 6, PECHS, T435570. ***Indian Airlines***, G-3/B, Court View Apartment, Court Rd, T5681577. ***Balkan Bulgarian***, Bridge Apartments Shopping Arcade No 4, Clifton Rd, T5677696. ***Saudi***, 5th floor, Al Sehat Centre, Sarfraz Rafiqui Shaheed Rd, T5682525. ***PIA*** has an efficient booking office (domestic and international) on Strachen Rd, T5689631. ***Aero Asia*** have offices in Lakson Square (behind PIA), T5681078, F5682004, and opposite the *Holiday Inn*, T7782851. ***Bhoja Air***, T5682337. ***Shaheen Air***, 157-B Clifton Rd, Clifton, T5872191. Domestic flights can be booked and paid for at Quaid-e-Azam airport. When reconfirming international flights, you may be asked for photocopies of your passport, visa and entry stamp.

Banks Most of the banks have their head offices on I.I. Chundrigar Rd, and offer foreign exchange. ***American Express***, T2630260 *and* ***Hongkong Bank***, T2630386 are both at the Shaheen Commercial Complex, Dr Ziauddin Ahmed Rd. The former offers foreign exchange, inefficient client's mail, whilst the latter has an ATM machine (visa/plus/global access). There are licensed moneychangers on I.I. Chundrigar, and in the block south of Zainab Market, though few exchange TCs. The banks at the airport are open 24 hrs, though the rates are inferior to those available in town. Hotels offer foreign exchange at poor rates.

Communications **GPO:** I.I. Chundrigar Rd. There are branch post offices at the north end of Abdullah Haroon Rd in Saddar, and in the *Hotel Metropole* block. **Post Restante:** available at the GPO. ***American Express*** (see 'Banks') offers an inefficient client's mail service. **Internet/email:** the business centres in the 5-star hotels offer internet/email services, but at a price (between Rs 200-300 per hour). ***Real Time***, Saifee House, opposite Amex, T2634705 (open 0900-1700) has internet access at Rs 145 per hour. Your best bet is the ***British Council*** or ***Goethe Institute***, both at Rs 50 per hour (see 'Cultural Centres'). **Telephones:** Central Telegraph Office is on I.I. Chundrigar, just east of GPO. Top hotels offer international calls – at a price. There are very few PCOs in Saddar (there's one just south of *Hotel Holiday*, Dr Daud Pota Rd); there's an international phone box outside the post office on Abdullah Haroon Rd, Saddar (a man stands there selling phonecards during the day).

Cultural centres *Arts Council of Pakistan*, Strachen Rd. The small AR Afridi Art Gallery has an interesting collection of works by contemporary Pakistani artists. There is also a small reference library and reading room, as well as an exhibition hall, shop selling English and Urdu books, paintings and greeting cards and an open air theatre. Check with the Programme Officer for details of events. This place has no money, so the new outdoor theatre remains half built. ***Alliance Francaise***, Plot St, 1 Block 8, Sch No5, Clifton, T5874302. ***American Centre***, 8, Abdullah Haroon Rd, T5685170. ***British Council***, 20 Bleak Hse Rd, T512036, Mon-Fri 1000-1800, Sat 1000-1300, recent British papers, plus cyber station (Rs 50 per hour). ***Goethe Institute***, 256 Sarawar Shaheed Rd, T5683124, F5683413, Mon-Fri 0900-1700, Sat 0900-1300, also has a cyber station (Rs 50 per hour). ***Islamic Chamber of Commerce***, St 2/A, Block 9, Clifton, T5874910. ***Japan Cultural Centre***, 233 El Lines, Somerset St, T516439. ***Pakistan American Cultural Centre***, 11 Fatima Jinnah Rd, T513836. ***Pakistan National Centre***, 191 A, SMHS, T43133.

Embassies & consulates ***Afghanistan***, 30/2, 9th St, Phase V, Khayaban-e-Shamsi, Defence, T5842263. ***Bangladesh***, 19, Chowdhury Khaliquzzaman Rd, Clifton, T514907. ***Canada***, 136, Beach Luxury Hotel, T5687275. ***China***, Plot No ST20, Block 4, Clifton, T572471. ***Denmark***, F50, Feroz Nana Rd, Kehkashan Block 7, T535048. ***France***, 12/A, Mhd Ali Bogra Rd, Bath Island, T5873797. ***Germany***, F-95 Khayaban-e-Roomi, Block VII, Clifton, T5870234. ***India***, 3, Fatima Jinnah Rd, T512542 (temporarily closed by Govt of Pak, 1995). ***Iran***, 81, Shahrah-e-Iran, Clifton, T5874370. ***Ireland***, 1-A/1, Saba Ave, Phase V Extension, Defence, T5876955. ***Italy***, 85, Clifton, T531007. ***Japan***, 233, Raja Ghazanfar Ali Rd, T5681331. ***Nepal***, 418-419A, Qamar Hse, 4th Floor, MA Jinnah Rd, T2416776. ***Netherlands***, 4A, Ch Khaliquzzaman Rd, T5680670. ***New Zealand***, c/o Commercial Union Ass Co, CU Building, 74/1-A, Lalazar, MT Khan Rd, T5611071. ***Russian Fed***, 8/26, Flench St, Bleak Hse Rd, T512852. ***Spain***, 1, 1st Floor, Services Club Extn Building, Mereweather Rd, T510306. ***Sri Lanka***, House No B-49, 12th St, Gulshan-e-Faisal, Bath Island, Clifton, T537782. ***Sweden***, 5/6, Chartered Bank Chamber, II Chundrigar Rd, T2415697. ***Switzerland***, 98, Clifton, T5873987. ***Turkey***, D264, Block 5, Kehkashan, Clifton, T5874194. ***UK***, York Place, Runnymede Lane, Clifton, T5872431, F5874014. ***USA***, 8, Abdullah Haroon Rd, T5685170 (24 hrs T5681606). ***Uzbekistan***, D-I/66, Block IV, Clifton.

Hospitals & medical services The best hospital in Pakistan, recommended by most overseas missions, is Karachi's ***Aga Khan University Hospital***, Stadium Rd, T4930051. Other well equipped hospitals include: ***Civil***, Baba-e-Urdu Rd, T7729719. ***Holy Family***, Soldier Bazaar, T7218991. ***Jinnah Post Graduate Medical Centre***, Rafiqui Shaheed Rd, T520039. ***Liaquat National***, Stadium Rd, T419612. ***Marie Adelaide Leprosy Clinic***, Mariam Manzil, off Shahrah-e-Liaquat, T5683106. Other useful nos: ***Edhi Blood Bank*** T413151. ***Edhi Ambulance Service*** T683432.

Libraries See under 'Cultural Centres'.

Places of worship *Muslim*: Defence Society Tooba Mosque; Memon Mosque near Boulton Mkt; Pearl Continental Hotel Mosque, and countless others. ***Christian***: Holy Trinity, Zaibun Nisa St; St Andrews near Empress Mkt; St Patrick's Roman Catholic Cathedral, Shahrah-e-Iraq. ***Hindu***: Shree Ratneswar Mahdevi Temple, Clifton Beach. ***Parsi*** Parsi Dar-e-Meher, Daud Pota Rd, Saddar.

Tour companies & travel agents All the large hotels have their own (and private) travel agents, plus there are numerous tour companies around the *Hotel Metropole*. Particularly recommended are: ***Travel Walji's***, 13 Services Mess, Mereweather Rd, T5661865, F5662563, E travelw@paknet3.ptc.pk. Acts as agents for *Avis* car rental (US$10 per day plus kilometres charge for car and driver), one day tour of Karachi US$8 per person, one day excursion to Chaukundi/Makli Hill/Thatta US$8 per person, day trips to Gaddani (enquire), guided tours to Moenjo Daro (return flight is Rs 2,200, plus US$15 per person). ***Raza Khan Tours***, 109 Sheraton Shopping Arcade, Club Rd, T5682111 offers city tours, crabbing tours, turtle watching trips, plus guided group tours to Thatta/Makli/Chaukundi and to Moenjo Daro. ***Sitara Travel Consultants***, No 105, 1st floor, Trade Tower, Abdullah Haroon Rd, T5683887, F7771950.

Tourist offices *PTDC Information Centre*, Shafi Chambers, Club Rd, T5681293. Mon-Fri 0800-1800 (closed Sat-Sun and 1300-1500 Fri). OK for free maps, but not much else (unless you're desperate to sign a visitor's book). Don't run any tours (they refer you to private companies) and have no real information on the security situation in interior Sind. ***Sind Tourism Development Corporation (STDC)***, 114-115, Block C, Sea Breeze Plaza, Shahrah-e-Faisal, T778 2706/2695. Offer daily tours to Chaukundi, Makli and Thatta for Rs 3,000 including guide, for Kinjhar Lake Resort, Haleji Lake bookings and some information on travelling in Sind (when the office is open!). ***Sind Wildlife Management Board***, Strachen Rd, T5683176 can help with information on Kirthar National Park and Haleji Lake.

Useful addresses Karachi's main **Police Station** and the **Foreigner's Registration Office**, T2333737/2416930, are both on I.I. Chundrigar Rd. For advice on visa extensions contact **Directorate of Immigration and Passports**, T5681135. There is a **Women's Police Station** just off Strachen Rd (see 'Karachi – Centre' map).

Useful phone numbers Police: T15. Fire: T16.

Excursions from Karachi

Manghopir

Some 30 kilometres north of central Karachi is the shrine to the Muslim saint, **Pir Mangho**. Arriving in Sind from Arabia in the 13th century, he is said to have meditated in a nearby cave until his death at the age of 150. Next to his shrine are two hot sulphur springs, reputed to help sufferers of rheumatism and skin diseases. The Marie Adelaide Leprosy Clinic has a rehabilitation centre nearby, often staffed by GAP year students from Edinburgh University. The shrine is guarded by a number of snub-nosed crocodiles, said to have been inadvertently brought to the place in the form of head lice by Pir Mangho. Manghopir is best reached by taxi since public transport means passing through some of Karachi's more volatile suburbs.

Gaddani Beach

Although strictly speaking in Baluchistan, Gaddani Beach is best reached as an excursion from Karachi (48 kilometres). Gaddani is famous as one of the world's largest ship-breakers, where, at high tide, giant supertankers are beached and then reduced to scrap by hand. Although still an impressive sight today, increased taxation on the scrap has made the industry less profitable than in the past, and thus the beach no longer resembles the ship's graveyard that it did previously. The main town is set slightly inland, with a small fishing village (and picnic spot) to the west. There are reports of a government-run guesthouse being opened here. The main ship-breaking activity is strung along the beach to the east. In theory, a government permit is required from the town of **Uthal** to visit Gaddani, although this is extremely inconvenient. Many foreigners report having reached Gaddani both by private car and public bus without the necessary documentation, though there is the risk of being turned back at the police check-post on the Hub River, or at Gaddani itself. A little bit of baksheesh it said to go a long way.

Buses from Karachi's **Lea Market** run as far as **Hub** (two and a half hours), although there's no regular transport for the 22 kilometres from here to the beach. The simplest way to get to Gaddani is through one of the Karachi travel agents such as *Travel Walji's*, or you could enquire at the PTDC. Whichever way, it's worth the effort.

Lower Sind

Travelling through Lower Sind between Karachi and Hyderabad gives some idea of the impact that perennial irrigated agriculture has had upon the region. **The National Highway** (NH) to the east runs through the rich plains of canal irrigated land. The NH provides the more interesting route between Karachi and Hyderabad. The 197 kilometres journey can be completed in three and a half hours, though there are several interesting stops along this route, most notably **Chaukundi Tombs, Makli Hill** and **Thatta**. Note that overnight accommodation is rather poor and basic.

The western route between the two cities, the **Super Highway** (SH), runs through uncultivated desert, illustrating the bareness of a hot land without water. This quicker alternative route is 175 kilometres long, and can be covered in two and a half hours. The SH skirts the lower reaches of the limestone Kirthar Range, crossing some of the southernmost ridges of Sindh Kohistan, although its only real sight, **Kirthar National Park**, is currently off-limits to visitors.

The large industrial city of **Hyderabad** has a number of points of interest, as well as acting as the gateway to the **Thar Desert**.

Kirthar National Park

Colour map 2, grid B3

The Super Highway (SH) leaves Karachi to the northeast. At the marker stone 80 kilometres from Karachi (near to the cement works and industrial estate), a four-wheel drive track leads north to **Kirthar National Park**. Covering some 3,000 square kilometres of rolling hills and valleys, Kirthar is one of four UNESCO registered parks in Pakistan. It provides a protected refuge for a number of endangered species including Urial sheep, Sind ibex (wild goat), chinkara and the migratory visitor, the Houbara Bustard. There are also reported to be leopards and desert wolves in the park. The best time to visit is in winter between November-January. Forest hideouts are provided, and there are two Visitors' Centres at **Khar** and **Kharchat**. Also within the National Park is **Ranikot Fort**, though this is perhaps more accessible from the route along the West Bank of the Indus (see page 119). **NB** Due to the uncertain security situation in interior Sind, Kirthar National Park is currently considered off-limits to visitors.

Sleeping **E** *Resthouse*, Khar Centre (park HQ). Basic facilities bookable through *Sind Wildlife Management Board* (see 'Karachi – Tourist Offices').

Transport There is no public transport to or from the park, and the journey should only really be attempted in a four-wheel drive vehicle. To reach the park, turn off the Super Highway at the marker stone 80 kilometres from Karachi (near to the cement works and industrial estate). The park is located 72 kilometres north of the Super Highway, via Zero Point and Karchat. Note that there is an alternative route into Kirthar via Hub Dam and Khar.

Chaukundi Tombs

Colour map 2, grid C2

The site is thought to date from the 13th-16th century and is generally attributed to the *Jokhio* and *Baluch* tribes. The superbly carved sandstone tombs are built out of rectangular slabs placed one on top of the other in pyramidal fashion, some reaching four metres high. They stretch for several kilometres along a low ridge with the centre-piece being two large domed mausoleums, although more outlying tombs are simply piles of stones. Women's graves carry carved reproductions of jewellery (bracelets, anklets, earrings) while the men's show spears, swords, shields and even horsemen. These style tombs are found only in Sind and Baluchistan (particularly along the Makran coast). The intricate carved designs are still found in textiles, pottery, jewellery and wood carvings in Sind and Baluchistan today.

Transport

The tombs can be reached by taking the Thatta or Gharo **bus** along the NH from Karachi's Lea Market (Rs 15), and can easily be visited as a half-day trip. There is a small sign in English, just beyond the 26 kilometres road marker. To return to Karachi or continue towards Thatta, simply flag down a passing bus. Various Karachi travel agents also incorporate Chaukundi Tombs as part of a day trip from Karachi.

Banbhore

Colour map 2, grid C3

Ruins from the Scythian-Parthian, Hindu-Buddhist and Arab periods of influence are spread over an extensive area here. The remains of a fort with walls and bastions are distinctly traceable, and further excavations have revealed the plan of a well fortified harbour town. It has been suggested that Banbhore could be the site of the ancient Hindu port city of **Debal**, although this remains speculation. The town is thought to have declined rapidly in the 13th century, possibly due to further invasions, although the shifting course of the Indus was certainly a major constraint upon Debal's ability to function as a port.

Debal was the port where the 17-year-old Arab commander **Mohammad Bin Qasim** is believed to have landed in 711/712 AD at the head of the forces of the Baghdad Caliphate. The Arab army, having secured the towns of the delta, proceeded north along the Indus, bringing Islam to the sub-continent, and occupying Multan within a few months. Kufic inscriptions on the Grand Mosque, indicating construction in the eighth century, suggest that it is the earliest known mosque in South Asia, and some of the oldest Muslim coins have been found here. A semi-circular stone mansion and a large mud brick house also date to this period. The most important Hindu remains include a Siva temple. Excavations, begun in 1958, have also revealed first century BC pottery, similar in style to that found at Taxila (see page 218) suggesting a link with Alexander. Superb glass and ceramics from Banbhore are displayed in the National Museum in Karachi, and other artefacts are exhibited at the small on-site museum. ■ *April-September 0800-1200, 1400-1830; October-March 0900-1600, closed first Monday of month.*

Transport

The site is just off the NH at Gharo, 38 kilometres beyond Chaukundi Tombs. Take a Gharo or Thatta bus from Karachi's Lea Market. Various Karachi travel agents also incorporate Banbhore as part of a day trip from Karachi.

Haleji Lake Bird Sanctuary

As one of Asia's most important waterfowl sanctuaries, Haleji Lake is populated by some 70 varieties of migratory aquatic birds, including flamingoes, pelicans, herons, egrets and pheasant-tailed jacanas as well as marsh crocodiles. Special hides and a Visitors' Centre are provided for bird-watchers. *Dak Bungalows* can be booked through the Chief Engineer, Karachi Water and Sewerage Board which supplies water to Karachi from this reservoir.

Transport The sanctuary is 18 kilometres along the NH from Gharo (Thatta-bound buses from Karachi's Lea Market).

Sind

Makli Hill

Colour map 2, grid C3

This is one of the most visually stunning archaeological sites in Pakistan. Covering 15½ square kilometres and said to contain over one million tombs, it is considered to be the world's largest necropolis. The tombs and mausoleums are seen as the most substantial remains of Sind's greatness between the 14th and 18th centuries, with many belonging to kings, queens, saints, governors, military commanders, philosophers and poets. They are divided into three distinct historical groupings.

Ins and outs Makli Hill is a low ridge disecting the NH just before Thatta. It is best reached by a Thatta-bound bus from Karachi's Lea Market. Various Karachi travel agents also incorporate Makli Hill as part of a day trip from Karachi. The nearby Rest House appears disused so see under Thatta or Kinjhar. There is a restaurant, *Makli Inn*, near site entrance.

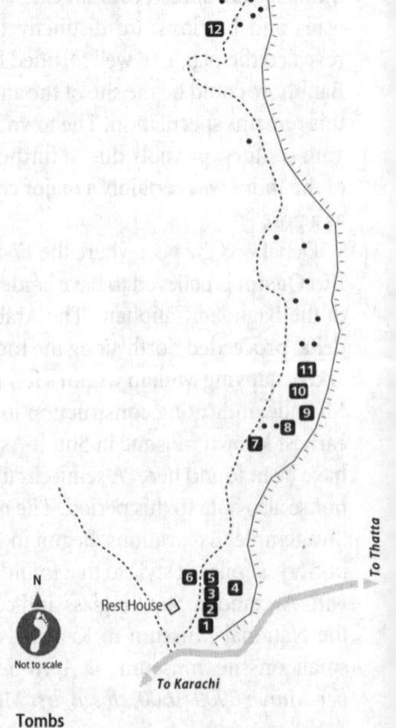

Sights

The best preserved tombs are on the north side of the National Highway. From the gate the initial group of monuments date from the most recent Mughal period (16th to 18th century). The first major tomb on the right, standing on a high plinth in a courtyard, is that of **Mirza Jani Beg** (d 1599), the last Tarkhan ruler. Octagonal with a domed roof, the tomb shows the use of glazed blue and unglazed brown tiles which are still produced in Thatta today. The next major tomb on the right is that of **Mirza Tughal Beg** (d 1679) and has twelve carved sandstone pillars supporting a domed roof.

Perhaps the most imposing tomb on the hill is that of the former Mughal Governor of Sind, **Isa Khan**

Tarkhan the younger (d 1644), which stands in a large square courtyard surrounded by a high wall. The chowkidar has the key to the gate. Similar in style to buildings at Fatehpur Sikri near Agra, the mausoleum comprises a buff coloured square tomb chamber, exquisitely carved inside and out right up to its domed roof. It is surrounded by a double-storey pillared verandah, the upper section roofed by a series of smaller domes. The verandah offers fine views of the whole Makli necropolis.

To the east is a smaller building in the same style housing the tombs of Isa Khan's *zenana* (harem), and carved in a similar fashion to those at Chaukundi. The tomb of **Dewan Shurfa Khan** (d 1638), a little to the northwest, is exceptionally well preserved. In its own courtyard, this solid square tomb's exterior is decorated with blue and turquoise glazed tiles whilst the interior is elaborately fashioned in red, white and blue.

The second group of tombs belong to the Arghun and Tarkhan rulers of the 16th century. Sadly many of these carved sandstone tombs are in a poor state of repair, although the squat, octagonal tomb of **Prince Sultan Ibrahim** (d 1559) is an exception.

Between the second and final collection of tombs stands the shrine of the Sufi saint **Abdullah Shah Ash'abi**. Painted in garish colours, the centrepiece of the shrine is a marble mausoleum, decorated with mirrored tiles, tinsel streamers and heavy with the smell of incense. The shrine is busy with activity as devotees from all over Sind come here seeking blessings, so demonstrating the power of piestic Islam in the region.

The third group of tombs, several kilometres further north, belong to the 14th to 16th century Samma Dynasty, frequently referred to as the Golden Age of Sind. The oldest tomb on the hill with any great historical interest belongs to **Jam Nizamuddin** (d 1508), and has a façade that is very much in the Hindu style. It has been suggested that it was either built with materials from ruined Hindu temples, with idolatrous emblems removed, or that the style is a result of employing Hindu craftsmen in its construction.

Thatta

Colour map 2, grid C3

The new town of Thatta has been identified with the site of both **Debal** and Alexander's **Patala**. It is suggested that Alexander rested his army here following their long march south, whilst his admiral, **Nearchus**, assembled his fleet at the port before sailing down the Indus to the sea. Before that, it is believed to feature in the Hindu epic *Mahabharata*.

Thatta was sacked by Shah Beg Arkhan in 1521, the Portuguese in 1555, and by its own ruler Mirza Jani Beg in 1591 whilst resisting Akbar's forces. Despite its turbulent history, Thatta was described by a visitor in 1699 as a rich and thriving city, and a great artistic centre. At this time it is said to have had 400 schools and seminaries, "being famous for learning, theology, philosophy and politics". Within 150 years, however, war, plague, drought, malaria in the surrounding lowlands and the shifting course of the Indus, had led to its decline.

Be careful how you pronounce the name of this town because it is remarkably similar to the Urdu word for 'bollocks'.

Ins and outs

Thatta is located 98 kilometres east of Karachi, and is best reached by taking a bus along the NH from Karachi's Lea Market (the nearest train station is inconveniently located). Various Karachi travel agents also incorporate Thatta as part of a day trip from Karachi. To continue north or south, flag down a bus from the main street.

Sights The **Shah Jahan Mosque**, built between 1644 and 1647, was a gift from **Shah Jahan** in recognition of the hospitality he received in Thatta whilst seeking refuge from his father, Jahangir. A contemporary of one of Shah Jahan's other great buildings, the Taj Mahal, the mosque is built in the form of a great caravanserai, a large court enclosed by a double arcaded corridor of 93 domed compartments. This serves the purpose of carrying the words of the Imam to all parts of the mosque. The decorative turquoise and white tile work is reminiscent of the great Persian mosques of Isfahan and Shiraz in Iran. The gateway at the east entrance was added when the mosque was refurbished in 1959.

Shah Jahan Mosque

The **Dagbir Mosque** on the outskirts of town, one of the earliest examples of this style in Sind, was previously known for its superb tile work but it is now in a poor state of repair. Built by **Mir Khushro Khan** in 1588, it has a superbly sculptured mihrab.

Much of the old mud and brick centre of the town has been bulldozed, although several multistoreyed houses with carved wooden balconies remain. Many of the old houses use *Munghs*, or 'windcatchers' on their roof to 'catch' and circulate cool breezes into the rooms below. On Friday mornings, on the mud-flats on the edge of town, greyhound races take place, complete with mechanical hare.

Sleeping & eating Describing nearby Makli at the turn of the century, Capt Wood suggested "Here neither labour nor expense has been spared for giving the dead better accommodation than the living". The same could be said of Thatta's hotels today. **F** *Jehan Zeb*, **G** *Agha Mohammad*, **G** *Al-Haufez* and **G** *Al-Kadar Muzaffarkhana* are all pretty basic with filthy rooms and filthy bathrooms. There are a number of basic restaurants on the main highway. The *STDC restaurant* opposite Shah Jehan Mosque is occasionally open.

Kinjhar Lake

Colour map 2, grid C3

From Thatta the National Highway turns northeast to run up the west bank of the Indus. After 22 kilometres a road to the left runs to **Kinjhar Lake**. This lake was constructed for irrigation purposes by linking two smaller lakes, the Sunheri and Kinjhari. Over 32 kilometres long and six kilometres wide, this attractive lake previously supplied water to Karachi, but is now being marketed as a tourist resort. Fishing and boating are available.

Sleeping & eating The old **E** *Old Resort* has been abandoned, and the **C-D** *Tourist Resort* remains a major disappointment. When originally built, the 8 deluxe and 16 standard split level cabanas were very appealing. Now, after years of neglect and maltreatment at the hands of day-trippers, they are in a very poor state of repair, with non-working a/c, broken windows and no hot water. Don't pay more than Rs 300. The pleasantly situated restaurant is overpriced with little choice. Bookings can be made at the *STDC* in Karachi.

Transport

Local bus from Karachi's Lea Market pass the turn-off, or as part of tour (see Karachi).

Hyderabad

The strategic location of Hyderabad, formerly at the apex of the Indus delta, has been recognized by all invading armies from those of Mohammad bin Qasim in 711, to the British forces of Charles Napier in 1843. Today, Hyderabad is Pakistan's fourth largest city, and a centre of industrial production. Almost 12 percent of Sind's urban population live in Hyderabad. It also acts as a gateway to the Thar Desert, along Pakistan's international border with India.

***Population:** about 2 million*
***Phone code:** 0221*
Colour map 2, grid B3

Ins and outs

Getting there

The city airport is located to the southwest (Rs 100 taxi ride), with connections to a number of other cities. Hyderabad is also well served by trains, being on the main Karachi-Multan-Lahore-Rawalpindi-Peshawar route. It is also a significant road junction, linked to the Indus Highway (to Sukkur via the west bank of the Indus), the National Highway (to Sukkur via the east bank of the Indus), the Super Highway (the faster west route to Karachi) and the National Highway (the more interesting east route to Karachi). Hyderabad has no one central bus station, and thus arrival and departure points are spread across the city (see map and 'Transport' below).

Getting around

The local bus service is incomprehensible to the short term visitor; you're better off walking or taking one of the many rickshaws that choke Hyderabad's streets. Expect to pay around Rs 20 between any 2 points.

History

The site upon which the city of Hyderabad stands has a history of settlement dating back to pre-historic times, when the nearby hills of Ganjo Taka were used as a place of worship. Hyderabad traces its origins back to the Hindu ruler Nerun, who built a fort, or *kot* , at the site. The fort at Nerun Kot was occupied by Buddhists when Mhd bin Qasim conquered Sind in 711/712, and the young Arab General built a mosque on the site of an earlier Buddhist temple. During the 16th and 17th centuries, Nerun Kot was the district headquarters of the Arghun Empire ruled from the nearby city of Thatta, and came to be known as Hyderabad after its founder, **Hyder Quli Arghuni**.

In 1758-59, the changing course of the Indus gave an unexpected boost to Hyderabad's strategic location. Leaving its old bed at a point north of Hyderabad, and turning west, the Indus abandoned almost 150 kilometres of its old course. Not only did this action wash away Narsapur, one of the intended capitals of Mian Muradyab Khan, it also flooded **Khudabad**, the old capital of the Kalhora Mirs in Dadu district. In 1786 **Ghulam Shah Kalhora,** ruler of all Sind, selected Hyderabad as the most eligible site for a large

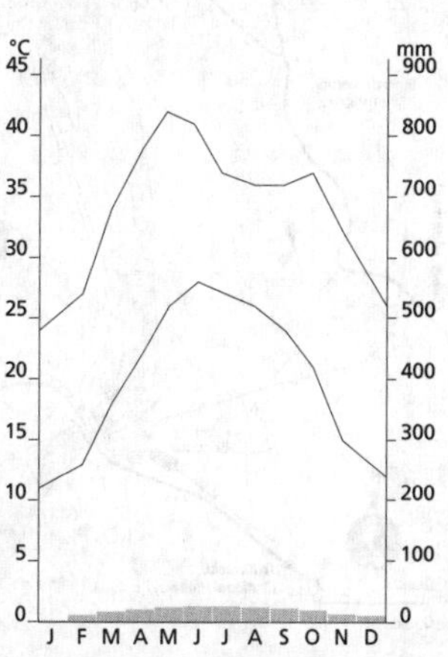

The best time to visit is during the cooler winter months (November to March).

defensible capital. Hyderabad remained the Kalhora's capital until their defeat by the Baluchi **Talpur Mirs** in 1782. The Talpur Mirs occupied Hyderabad until the arrival of the British.

Looking to establish an effective presence in Sind, the **British** had already forced the rulers of Khairpur and Hyderabad to open the Indus for unrestricted navigation in 1831. In 1843, the British annexed Sind, defeating the Talpur forces at a forest near Hyderabad. In September of that year, the British shifted the capital of Sind to Karachi.

Post Partition, Hyderabad experienced a rapid influx of Muslim refugees from India. Like Karachi, Hyderabad has suffered from tensions between the native Sindhi population, and the mohajir community. In September 1988, on a day that came to be known as Black Friday, 186 men, women and children were killed and a further 250 wounded as gunmen went on the rampage through the city. A similar incident occurred in May 1990 when, emerging from Hyderabad Fort, crowds of mohajirs fronted by women and children were fired upon by the police. Thirty one people were killed. However, the thirty month military 'Clean-up' operation in Sind appears to have brought a greater degree of stability to Hyderabad than is being experienced in Karachi.

Sights

Highlights Wandering around the narrow streets inside the **Fort** is a pleasant way to spend some time. The **Kalhora Tombs** and the **Tombs of the Talpur Mirs** are also worth visiting.

The Fort (Qila) Built in 1768 on the order of **Ghulam Shah Kalhora**, Hyderabad Fort stands on the southern extremity of a rocky limestone outcrop that dominates the surrounding plain. This unique strategic location has been enhanced by the perpendicular extension of the plateau supporting the outer fortification wall.

The fort was occupied as a court by the Kalhora ruler during a period in Sindhi history that is recalled with great pride. Successful improvements in irrigation techniques brought economic prosperity, and Sindhi poetry reached its

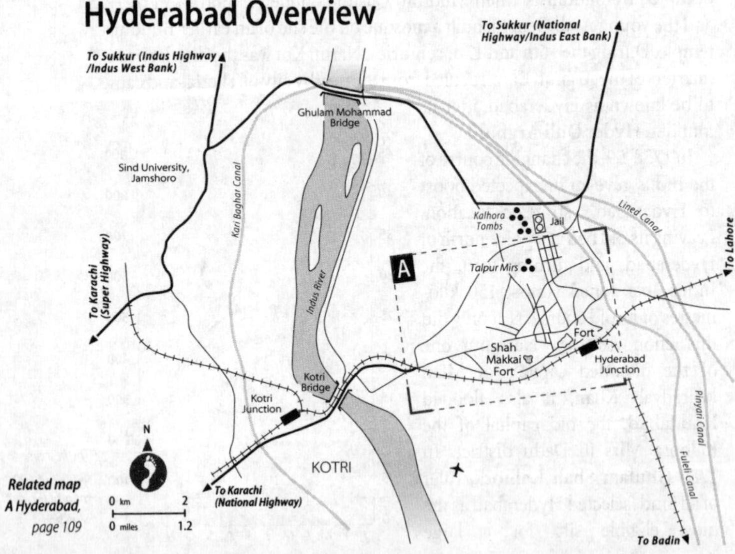

Related map A Hyderabad, page 109

zenith in the compositions of **Mian Shah Inayat** and **Shah Abdul Latif**. The request on the fort's foundation stone, dating from 1768, "Oh God, Bring peace to this city", appeared fulfilled until Ghulam Shah Kalhora's death in 1772.

The period that followed, however, is recalled as a tyrannical era until the **Talpur Mirs** finally defeated the last Kalhora ruler in 1782 and brought peace to the city. The Talpurs occupied the fort and used it as a palace until their defeat by the British in 1843 at the nearby forest of Miani.

Only parts of the 15 metres high outer wall, a circular tower and the main gate remain intact. Much of the interior section was destroyed during the siege, and many sections fell into disrepair through subsequent neglect. Finally, an explosion in the arsenal in 1906 destroyed much of the *Pukka* (brick built) fort. The small **Museum** has a number of interesting exhibits, including weapons, clothes and portraits from the Talpur period. Summer 0700-1400, Winter 0900-1600. Closed Friday and Saturday. It is fascinating to wander through the narrow streets and alleys of the residential area within the fort's walls.

Shah Makkai Fort

Nearby is the **Shah Makkai Fort** or *Kachcha* (mud built) *Qila*, built in 1771 by Ghulam Shah Kalhora to protect the mausoleum of **Sheikh Mohammad Makkai**. This Muslim saint (born in Mecca, hence the title Makkai), settled in the area some 500 years earlier with his wife, daughter of a Hindu ruler. Although most of the fort is in ruins, the shrine itself attracts devotees from all over Sind, particularly on the saint's *Urs* or death anniversary.

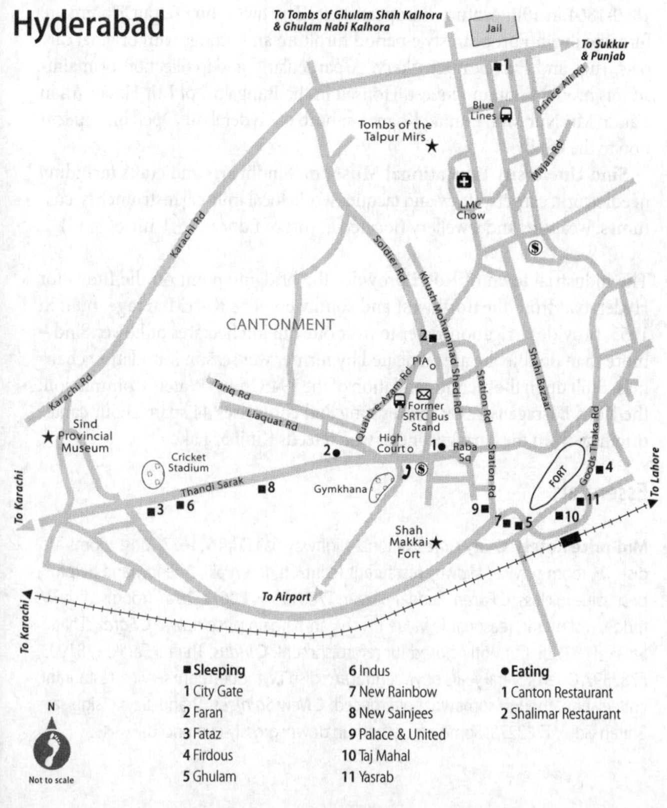

Kalhora Tombs To the north of the city, behind the Central Jail, are the 21 **Kalhora Tombs**. The ornate tombs of the Kalhora rulers are decorated with geometric and floral designs, the most impressive of which belongs to **Ghulam Shah Kalhora**. Despite the loss of the dome, now replaced by a flat roof, the square tomb with an octagonal chamber retains some fine blue and white tile work and carved marble detail.

Tombs of the Talpur Mirs The **Tombs of the Talpur Mirs**, south of the *Hotel City Gate*, although of better general construction than the Kalhora tombs, are less impressive from an architectural point of view. Located in two compounds, the buildings are covered with glazed tiles which are considered to be poor when compared to older work at Thatta. Built between 1812-1857, much research on the tombs has been undertaken by the Institute of Sindhology at Jamshoro, near Hyderabad.

Qadam Gah of Hazrat Ali In the centre of the city is the slab of stone with the hand and footprints of Hazrat Ali, the Prophet Mohammad's son-in-law and 4th Caliph of Islam.

Museums

Sind Provincial Museum This well designed, beautifully laid out and clearly labelled museum is located in Wahdat Colony near Niaz Stadium and Polytechnic. **Section 1**: archaeological display covering whole span from pre-history to the British period; **2**: Sindhi crafts; **3**: children's section.

Talpur House Museum A private museum in a house built between 1860-1864 in 19th century European style. The two room Talpur Harem are furnished with European style period furniture and fittings with original carpets, rugs and European crockery. A particularly good collection of manuscripts brought out on request. Housed in the Bungalow of Mir Hasan Ali in Tando Mir Nur Mohammad Khan, a suburb of Hyderabad. Open on application to the family.

Sind University Educational Museum Sindhi arts and crafts including needlework, carpets, straw and lacquer work, local musical instruments, costumes, weapons and jewellery (located at Inst of Education, Univ of Sind).

Kotri Barrage The industrial town of **Kotri** provides the bridging point on the Indus for Hyderabad from the northwest and southwest. The **Kotri Barrage**, built in 1955, provides irrigation water to over one million hectares of Lower Sind – more than double the area irrigated by former wet season inundation channels. Built upon the recommendation of the 1945 Indus Waters Commission, the Kotri Barrage is 1,000 metres long and comprises 44 spans. Four canals originate from the barrage, one of which feeds Kinjhar Lake.

Essentials

Sleeping

■ *on map*

Price codes: see inside front cover

Mid-price hotels **C** *City Gate*, National Highway, Jail Rd, T611677. Most rooms a/c. dish TV, room service, *Midway* restaurant (cont/Chinese/Pak), "friendly and helpful", best value in class. **C** ***Faran***, Saddar Bazaar, T780194, F780671. 26 a/c rooms, dish TV, fridge, restaurant, reasonable value if you can bargain price down. **C** ***Fataz***, Thandi Sarak, T782125. Currently closed for refurbishment. **C** ***Indus***, Thandi Sarak, T781903, F782397. Open several years now, central a/c, dish TV, fridge, room service, restaurant, coffee shop, though somewhat overpriced. **C** ***New Sainjees***, Thandi Sarak (sign says Bhitah Gdn), T782275. Some a/c, rather run down, grossly overpriced.

Selected train fares from Hyderabad Junction

	A/C sleeper	A/C sitter	1st class sleeper	Economy
Karachi	Rs 300	Rs 174	Rs 100	Rs 41
Lahore	Rs 1,232	Rs 714	Rs 473	Rs 220
Mirpur Khas	Rs 141	Rs 84	Rs 44	Rs 17
Multan	Rs 923	Rs 534	Rs 347	Rs 155
Peshawar	Rs 1,671	Rs 962	Rs 649	Rs 315
Rawalpindi	Rs 1,513	Rs 838	Rs 567	Rs 265

Budget hotels Most of the budget hotels are in the area between the railway station and the fort. Note that many of them are reluctant to accept foreigners. **F** ***New Rainbow***, Station Rd. Quite basic though reasonable value, attached bath. **F** ***Taj Mahal***, Goods Naka, T780592. Reasonable value if you can persuade the manager to let you stay, some a/c, attached bath. **F** ***Yasrab***, Goods Naka, T28006. Friendly, fan, attached bath, clean enough, best bet for backpackers. **G** ***Firdous***, Goods Naka, **G** ***Ghulam***, Station Rd, **G** ***Palace***, Ghazi Abdul Karim Rd and **G** ***United***, Ghazi Abdul Karim Rd are all very basic.

Eating

• on map

The ***Midway*** restaurant at the *City Gate Hotel* serves good à la carte continental, Chinese and Pakistani food. ***Canton***, Ghari Khatta, serves generous Chinese and Pakistani dishes. ***Shalimar***, Thandi Sarak (opposite Gymkhana Club), has good Chinese food. There are numerous basic restaurants in the station area.

Entertainment

Sports Cricket: The Cricket Stadium is on Thandi Sarak, though it's a long time since Test or 1-day Internationals have been played here.

Shopping

Handicrafts The main shopping area is near the fort, south of town. Shahi Bazaar, at 2 kilometres one of the longest in Pakistan, is a maze of narrow crowded lanes with small shops selling a wide variety of goods including jewellery, shoes, lacquerware, handloom textiles, Sindhi embroidery and appliqued *Rillis*.

Local transport

Car hire The *City Gate Hotel* has a car and driver rental service (approximately Rs 500 per day + kilometres charge).

Long Distance Transport

Air PIA fly to **Islamabad**, Thursday, Sunday; **Karachi**, Tuesday, Thursday, Saturday, Sunday; **Lahore**, Tuesday, twice Thursday, Saturday, twice Sunday; **Moenjo Daro**, Wednesday; **Sui**, Saturday; **Sukkur**, Saturday.

Train Karachi hourly, 2-3 hours. **Lahore** *Shalimar Exp*, 0830, 15 hours; *Tezgam*, 1815, 16 hours. **Mirpur Khas** every 2 hours, 1 hour. **Multan** *Shalimar Exp*, 0830, 10 hours; *Tezgam*, 1815, 11 hours. **Peshawar** *Awam Exp*, 1020, 30 hours; *Chenab Express*, 2205, 33 hours. **Rawalpindi** *Awam Exp*, 1020, 25½ hours; *Tezgam*, 1815, 22 hours. **Rohri/Sukkur** *Shalimar Exp*, 0830, 4 hours; *Sukkur Exp*, 0128, 6 hours.

Long distance buses *Blue Lines*, Capri Cinema, 1 block south of *City Gate Hotel*, T615558, run hourly a/c coaches via the Super Highway to **Karachi** (2½ hours, Rs 45); 8 buses per day to **Sukkur** via the Indus East Bank (8 hours, Rs 140); 4 buses per day to **Lahore** (21 hours, Rs 400); and some services to **Larkana** (7 hours, Rs 120). Crowded local buses run via the National Highway (**Kinhjar Lake, Thatta, Makli Hill**) to **Karachi** from the bus stand near Tayyab Complex, off Quaid-e-Azam Rd (this was the old ***SRTC*** bus stand prior to privatization). Local buses and minibuses north bound via the Indus East Bank to **Sukkur** run from Pathan Colony, 1 block west of the *City Gate Hotel*. Local buses to **Mirpur Khas** run from the New Bridge bus stand, though trains are more convenient.

Directory **Airline offices** *PIA*, Saddar Bazaar, 1 block south of *Faran Hotel*, T784228. **Banks** *National Bank of Pakistan*, Ghari Khatta (opposite High Court). Offers foreign exchange (cash only). **Communications** GPO: Saddar Bazaar, 2 blocks south of *Faran Hotel*. **Telephones:** *Pak Telecom*, Ghari Thatta. **Hospitals & medical services** *Liaqat Medical College Hospital*, LMC Market, Hirabad. **Tour companies & travel agents** If looking to book a tour into the Thar Desert, you're better off trying travel agents in Karachi.

Thar Desert

Colour map 2

To the east of Hyderabad, the **Thar Desert** defines the eastern boundary of Sind. Running from the Rann of Kutch in the south, the Thar extends north into the Cholistan Desert, and east into India's Rajasthan Desert. The international boundary runs for over 500 kilometres through the Thar, yet prior to Partition, the desert was more of a route than a barrier to trade and movement. Relatively cool winters and the short distances between trading towns on the Indian side make the desert more accessible than the seemingly hostile appearance suggests. In fact, one and a half million people live in the south-easterly Tharparkar division of the desert, at a population density of 53 per square kilometres.

Visiting the Thar Desert

Though Hyderabad is the main access point to the Thar Desert, the small village of Naukot is in fact the gateway to the area. In recent years, concerns over the security situation in interior Sind has meant that the embryonic 'desert tours' tourist industry that was evolving in Naukot has all but collapsed. Until the market picks up in response to demand, one cannot be certain of being able to hire suitable vehicles in Naukot. It is possible, however, to arrange desert guides in Naukot. Although a network of local buses connect the various settlements in the Thar, foreigners wishing to explore this area are generally encouraged to do so as part of an organized tour. The best place to organize a vehicle and guide is at one of the reputable travel agents in Karachi.

It is essential to ensure that your vehicle is mechanically sound, and that you take adequate spares and supplies. Shovels, gloves, water, fuel, cutting tool or axe and a compass are essential. There are no accurate maps of the region. Prior to commencing a journey into the Thar, it is advisable to contact PTDC in Karachi and your own embassy to check on the latest security situation in the region. Dave Winter spent three days travelling in this region in 1998 without incident. Where possible, you should avoid travelling by road at night, and you should avoid approaching the sensitive border area. Basic accommodation is available in **E-F** *Resthouses* at Mithi, Islamakot and Nagar Parkar, although you should check with the Deputy Commissioner in Mirpur Khas whether it is possible to book them.

Mirpur Khas

Phone code: 023
Colour map 2, grid B4

The road east to the district headquarters of **Mirpur Khas** (65 kilometres), passes through fringes of the Thar Desert that have been transformed by irrigation. The **Rohri Canal** is the chief feeder from the Sukkur Barrage supplying perennial water to the minor canals that irrigate the banana, mango, sugar cane, rice and wheat crops. There is little of interest to tourists in Mirpur Khas, and the nearby Kahujo Daro stupa is in a very poor state of repair.

Sleeping & eating Outside the train station are a collection of miserable, filthy **G** category hotels such as the *Pakistan Guest House*. You're better off pushing on to Umarkot.

Transport

Trains run every 2 hours to **Hyderabad** (1 hour, Rs 17). 2 trains per week travel the 193 kilometres east of Mirpur Khas to the settlement of **Khokhropar** on the Indian border (though the line across the border is long closed). Every Wednesday (0800) a train runs along the metre-gauge line via **Digri** (2¾ hours) to **Naukot** (4¾ hours), from where it loops back up to **Pithoro** (8½ hours). Mirpur Khas can also be reached by bus from Hyderabad's New Bridge bus stand, though trains are more convenient. Buses to **Umarkot** leave from outside the train station.

Umarkot

Colour map 2, grid B5

The road to the desert town of **Umarkot** (74 kilometres) is rough and dusty, yet the countryside gives little impression of aridity. The region is irrigated by the **Nara Canal**, the easternmost of the Sukkur Canals. Cotton and sugar cane cultivation are particularly prominent, and six kilometres east of Mirpur Khas is a major sugar refining plant. **Umarkot** stands between the Marwar and Indus Valley, and the foundation of the town is usually attributed to Umar, first king of the Summa Dynasty (1050-1350 AD). In the 13th century it was occupied by the Rajput, Parmar Soda, one of who's successors, Rana Pashad, played host to Humayun during his flight from the Afghan ruler of North India, Sher Shah Suri. It was in Umarkot that Humayun's young Sindhi wife Hamida gave birth to the future Mughal Emperor **Akbar** (b.1542). One kilometre north of the town, a stone marking the birthplace is said to have the wrong date by six years.

The town of Umarkot is dominated by the earthen brick **fort** built by the Kalhora ruler **Nur Mohammad** in the 18th century. The tapering fortification walls are constructed of unbaked bricks, with baked brick semi-circular bastions at its four corners and either side of the arched doorway. The central tower offers fine views of the surrounding area. A small one room museum next door has a well labelled collection of Mughal armoury, miniature paintings, coins and various treatise and documents. Winter 0900-1600, Summer 0800-1200, 1400-1700, closed first Monday of the month. Umarkot is also renowned locally for its fine embroidery and handloom cloth.

Sleeping

You may be able to book the **E** *Circuit House* through the Deputy Commissioner in Mirpur Khas (the chowkidar is reluctant to admit you otherwise). The 3 **E-F** hotels, *Al Hyder*, *City Heart* and *Kharoonjhar* are all fairly basic, but clean enough and superior to anything Mirpur Khas has to offer.

Transport

Buses to Umarkot leave from outside Mirpur Khas train station. With an early start, it is perfectly feasible to visit Umarkot as a day trip from Hyderabad.

Naukot

Colour map 2, grid C4

The real gateway for trips deep into the Thar is **Naukot**, 80 kilometres south-east of Mirpur Khas. This small town can be reached by road from either Umarkot or Mirpur Khas, although the road from the latter is in a better state of repair. A daily train also runs on a loop line from Mirpur Khas (Wednesday, 0800, 4¾ hours, return Monday, 1156). A desert bus service runs from Naukot via **Mithi** and **Islamakot** to **Nagar Parkar**. Those who are on a tour with a Karachi based travel agent will generally be camping. Otherwise, check with the Deputy Commissioner in Mirpur Khas to see whether it is possible to book the **E** *Resthouses* in Mithi, Islamakot and Nagar Parkar.

South and East of Naukot

Located several kilometres from Naukot, on the road to Mithi, stands the impressive **Naukot Fort**. Built by the Talpurs in 1814, the fort was reoccupied by the Pakistani army during the 1971 war with India. The desert road continues to **Mithi**, a centre for Thar handicrafts, particularly woollen blankets and embroidery work. The Rajput influence is very much in evidence in this southeasterly corner of Pakistan. In fact, 37 percent of the population of the Tharparkar administrative district are Hindus, and Mithi has a number of important Hindu temples including **Temple of Nag Devta** (Snake Temple). There is also a shrine to the 11th century Muslim saint, **Sayed Ali Shah**.

The topography of the land beyond Mithi comprises rough outcrops of wind carved rocks, interspersed with sand blown from the Rann of Kutch. In places, dunes have formed. Xerophytic shrubs and coarse grasses provide the only vegetation. **Islamakot** (40 kilometres) is an ancient Rajput town, and has a predominantly Hindu population. Save The Children Fund have a number of development programmes in the area. To the north of Islamakot is **Chachro**, a famous peacock centre. It was occupied by Indian troops during the 1971 war, and is now said to be the centre of the cross-border smuggling trade.

The desert road passes the old **Jain Temple of Gori** (45 kilometres), built in the late 14th century, before reaching the last truly desert town of **Virawah** (22 kilometres). Incredibly, the nearby ruined town of **Parinagar** was a flourishing port in the sixth century, at a time when the channels of the Rann of Kutch were still navigable.

Beyond Virawah, the desert gives way to the low, volcanic Karunjhar Hills where Pakistan's most southeasterly town, **Nagar Parkar** stands. Nearby at **Bhodesar**, are the remains of three ancient Jain structures built in 1375 and 1449, and a mosque dating from the same period. The sensitivity of the border with India makes it impossible to travel any further east or southeast.

Figurines found at Moenjo Daro (see page 123)

Central and Upper Sind

Central and Upper Sind have a number of fascinating, though rarely visited attractions. On the East bank of the Indus River lies the shrine to the great Sufi scholar **Shah Abdul Latif**, as well as the impressive **Kot Diji Fort**. Meanwhile, on the West bank of the Indus River, is the shrine to another great Sufi mystic at **Sehwan**, as well as the impressive and historically important remains of the Indus Valley Civilization city of **Moenjo Daro**. At the gateway to Upper Sind, providing access into neighbouring Baluchistan and Punjab, and with a number of interesting attractions of their own, are the 'twin' cities of **Sukkur** and **Rohri**.

The Indus East Bank

The east bank route between Hyderabad and Sukkur is far more densely populated than the west bank. It crosses an endless succession of former inundation canals taking off from the right bank of the Indus. Slightly lower than the left bank, the rising waters of the Indus were trained through cuts and led away by canals, making this the granary of Sind.

NB The National Highway (NH), the main road route to the north of Pakistan, is comparatively fast and dangerous. Might is right on this road, so be prepared to get out of the way as drivers attempt risky overtaking manoeuvres in unlikely places. The tangled wreckage of vehicles beside the road is testament to those overtaking manoeuvres that did not come off. A road widening scheme is underway as far as Ranipur, which may make this journey less nerve-wracking. There is no real suitable accommodation along this route, though it is possible to visit all the key sites in a one-day journey between Hyderabad and Sukkur. Alternatively, these sites can be visited as excursions from Hyderabad and Sukkur.

Miani

Colour map 2, grid B4

The forest here (10 kilometres north of Hyderabad along the NH) is the site of the 1843 battle where Napier's forces defeated the Talpur Mirs, ending the 60 year reign of the Baluchis. Napier, who had 2,800 men and 12 artillery pieces, defeated the 22,000 man Talpur army, inflicting over 5,000 fatal casualties. A small memorial remembers the 256 British casualties. There is a *Forest Rest House* and children's park at the site.

Bhit Shah

Colour map 2, grid B3

Holy to all Sindhis, this village houses the shrine of the great poet and Sufi saint **Shah Abdul Latif**. Born in nearby **Hala** in 1689 to a wealthy Hyderabad family, Shah Abdul Latif renounced material comforts for a life of contemplation. He selected a sand dune, *bhit*, as the site of his spiritual environment and spent his life studying both Hindu and Muslim ideas, although the latter became dominant. He is regarded as Sind's (and Sindhi's) foremost poet, and the *Risalo* his greatest work.

Following his death in 1752, Nur Mohammad Kalhora constructed the shrine over his grave. Built in typical Sindhi architectural style, the mausoleum has carved limestone domes and minarets, and is decorated with patterned floors, frescoes and beautiful blue and white tile work. Next to the shrine is a mosque with a superb mirror-tiled ceiling. Each year at the *Urs* anniversary (14th-16th of Islamic month of Safar, end of May 1999, mid-May 2000), thousand of devotees come to the shrine of Shah Abdul Latif to listen to his songs and poetry, and to take part in the ecstatic dances of the dervishes, entering a trance-like state to the beating of drums.

A small museum near the shrine contains a collection of local handicrafts, paintings and musical instruments. There are also a number of waxworks re-enacting favourite Sindhi stories.

Transport Buses from Pathan Colony, Hyderabad, about 50 kilometres south along the NH. To continue north or return to Hyderabad simply flag down a passing bus.

Hala

Colour map 2, grid B3

The town of **Hala** (26 kilometres north of Bhit Shah along the NH) is a famous handicraft centre, particularly renowned for its blue and white ceramics and woven *susi* cloth. The old town was severely damaged during Indus flooding, so a new town, marked by the white and blue tiled archway, was relocated on the National Highway. Hala was the birth place of **Makhdoom Nooh** (b 1505), reputed to have realigned Shah Jahan's mosque at Thatta towards Mecca through the power of a night spent in prayer.

Brahmanabad/Mansura

Colour map 2, grid B4

Almost 35 kilometres east of the NH from Hala, via **Shahdadpur**, is a large mass of ruins, the question of who's identity is a source of controversy. When Mhd Bin Qasim conquered Sind, a fierce battle took place for the Hindu town of **Brahmanabad**. Under Arab rule this town came to be known as **Mansura**, although its exact location is in dispute due to its changing orientation to the shifting course of the Indus. Major Raventry claimed that Brahmanabad stood not on the Indus but on the 'lost river' – **Hakra**. The location of Brahmanabad has also variously been attributed to Kalan Kot, Banbhore and indeed Hyderabad, although in 1854 Bellasis seemed to fix Brahmanabad at this spot. Cunningham has also identified the site with the **Harmateila** of Greek history where Ptolemy was wounded. Excavations have suggested that both a Hindu town (Brahmanabad) and a Muslim town (Mansura) existed at this site. Reasons for the town's decline are uncertain, although earthquake and the shifting course of the Indus have been offered as two possible explanations.

Kot Diji

Colour map 3, grid C3

On a small mound at the side of the NH, 226 kilometres north of Hala, are the remains of the ancient settlement of **Kot Diji**. First excavated in 1955, the site stands on one of the rare outcrops of limestone that are part of the Rohri Hills to the north. Dating between 3500-2500 BC, there are two distinct parts to the site. One comprises a citadel and ruling class residency whilst the other is plebeian residency. Excavation of the upper levels revealed characteristic Harappan pottery whilst the lower levels brought evidence of an unknown pre-Harappan culture, designated as Kot Diji. Distinct forms of pottery were found at this level depicting a new type of ceramic industry. Another interesting feature is evidence of the production and use of sun and oven dried bricks.

On a raised limestone outcrop to the east of the NH stands the magnificent **Kot Diji Fort**. Built between 1803 and 1830 by **Mir Sohrab Khan** to serve as a military stronghold and administrative headquarters, the largely brick built fort dominates the surrounding area. The outer wall runs for over 2,700 metres and is reinforced by rounded bastions and strategically placed towers. The entrance is in the southeast corner on the opposite side to the NH. A steep winding climb passes through three imposing defensive gateways fortified with metal spiked gates to repulse attacks on elephant. At the top stands the Mir's residential quarters, including the plaster floral motif decorated harem. There is a stone pavilion to the north, and a number of cells dating to the period when the fort was utilized by the British as a central state prison.

Sind

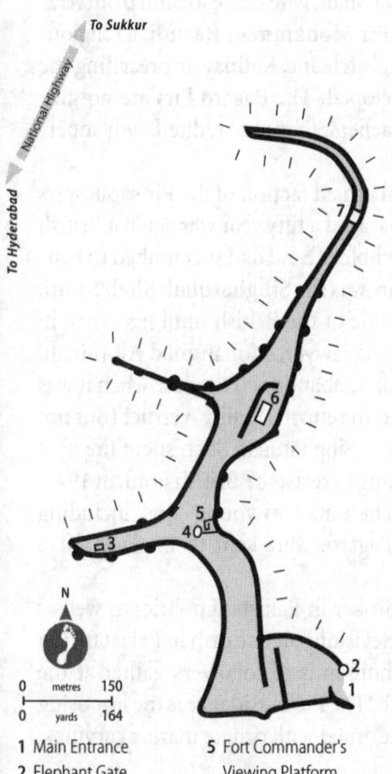

Transport

You can hop on or off any bus running along the NH as it passes Kot Diji. Perhaps the easiest way to visit is as a day trip from Sukkur.

Khairpur

Colour map 2, grid A4

An important regional centre within Sukkur Division (24 kilometres north of Kot Diji), the town was founded around 1787 by **Mir Sohrab Khan Talpur**, and remained an independent state until 1947. There are a number of impressive tombs of the ruling Talpur princes, the most striking of which is the tomb of **Mir Karam Ali Khan Talpur**, built in 1812. The town was described by a visitor in the 1840s as "the dirtiest, unhealthiest town in Sind".

Khairpur borders the *pat* desert to the east, where impervious clay soils hold up the groundwater. Much of the surface configuration has been changed by the provision of irrigation from the Sukkur Barrage. This has allowed the area under cultivation during the *rabi* (winter) season to be increased by 500 percent, with

Kot Diji Fort

the main crop being wheat. A variety of other crops are grown locally, including rice, sugar cane, oil seeds, dates and mangoes.

However, despite benefiting greatly from the construction of the Sukkur Barrage, the region has experienced severe environmental damage as a result of the raising of the watertable. Despite the efforts of the Salinity and Reclamation Projects, some of the worst examples of waterlogging and salinization can be seen in the region. This phenomenon is particularly striking from the air. The waterlogging has also led to a sharp increase in the incidence of malaria.

Pirjo Goth

Colour map 2, grid A4

Several kilometres off the National Highway, west of Khairpur, **Pirjo Goth** is the home town of the **Pagaro Pirs**. The ancestry of this family of hereditary religious leaders dates back to Pir Bakadar Shah, who came to Sind from Arabia. However, it was during the time of **Pir Mohammad Rashdi**, a religious leader who travelled as far as Jaisalmer, Kutch and Kathiawar preaching the message, that the movement really developed. The Pagaro Pirs are not just revered as great religious leaders and teachers, they are credited with supernatural powers.

During the late 19th century, a radical armed faction of the Pir's followers evolved. Known as the **Hurs**, this group waged a fifty year war against British occupation at a time when virtually the whole of Sind had succumbed to British rule. The most revered of the rebel Pirs was **Pir Sibghatullah Shah Saani**, who remained a constant thorn in the side of the British until his arrest in 1930. At his trial an up and coming young lawyer, Mohammad Ali Jinnah, defended the Pir, although it appears that he abandoned the case when it was obvious that the British were determined to return a 'guilty' verdict (but not before he had charged Rs 100,000 in fees). Sibghatullah Shah spent the next 10 years in and out of prison for continuing to resist the British until, in 1943, he was sentenced to death and hung. The Pir's two young sons, including **Shah Mardan Shah**, the current Pir Pagaro, were sent to England for a 'proper' education.

Today, Pir Pagaro is a major powerbroker in Pakistani politics as well as being credited as the owner of the first television satellite dish in Pakistan! On 27th of the Islamic month of Rajab, thousands of followers gather at the *dargah*, or shrine, to the Pirs in Pirjo Goth. The Pir's residence is the imposing four-storeyed red sandstone building, adorned with ornate marble carvings.

Transport Minibuses to Pirjo Goth (Rs 10) run from the small yard on Workshop Rd in Sukkur, near the *Forum Inn*.

The Indus West Bank

The Indus Highway, running along the west bank of the Indus, passes through some of South Asia's most important proto and pre-historic sites. Despite appearing barren and inhospitable, the hills to the west witnessed the earliest development of settled agriculture in South Asia, some 10,000 years ago. Goats and sheep are known to have been domesticated in the region at least 16,000 years ago, and along with the Potwar Plateau in Punjab, the Brahmaputra valley, and the central Indian peninsula around the Krishna and Tungabhadra Rivers, these west borderlands were one of the key South Asian regions at the beginning of the Neolithic period.

Further, the route passes through the heart of one of the world's great pre-modern cultures, the Indus Valley Civilization. From 2500 BC to around 1800 BC, Moenjo Daro was the centre of a civilization that embraced the entire plains area of the Indus, and beyond.

Long after the Indus Valley Civilization had collapsed, the region remained the centre of power under a number of dynasties, most notably the Kushan Empire. Under their great leader, Kanishka, who converted to Buddhism in the first century AD, the Kushans spread their power south from the north-west passes, building stupas such as that on the citadel at Moenjo Daro.

The great Chinese traveller Hiuen Tsang followed this route between 643-44 AD, as did the Arab armies of Mohammad bin Qasim 70 years later.

The road, far quieter than the National Highway on the east bank of the Indus, runs along the flat river plain, skirting the Kirthar Mountains to the west. This limestone range runs for 240 kilometres north to south in an eastward curving direction. Although the apparent dearth of vegetation makes the hills look barren, the scrub and grass support the sheep and goats of nomadic tribes, as well as wild ibex and urials. Along streams, and where the soil is rich and irrigated, rice, wheat and oilseeds are grown.

Ranikot Fort

Colour map 2, grid B3

The fort was first mentioned in 1812 when an older fort, possibly eighth century or even dating back to the Scythians, was refurbished by the Talpur Mirs. Splendid in its isolation, it is assumed that the fort was intended to defend a long since abandoned trade route between Thatta and Central Asia through the Kirthar Hills. The massive defensive walls are visible from several kilometres away, and from the south resemble the Great Wall of China. The battlements near the entrance are sandstone, elsewhere they are shale and limestone, and a sheer limestone rock face protects the northern flank. With a circumference of 25 kilometres, it is one of the world's largest forts.

Ins and outs

Leaving Hyderabad across the Ghulam Mohammad Barrage to the west, you join the Indus Highway. At 75 kilometres from Hyderabad, you reach the **Sann** crossroads. Leaving the Indus Highway here, the rough jeep track to the fort (32 kilometres) passes through barren hills, dotted with scrub and stunted trees. There is no public transport to the fort, although it may be possible to hire camels in Sann for the trip. **NB** The fort has previously been used as a hide-out by bandits, so it is recommended that you take advice on safety before planning a trip.

You enter through the easterly **Sann Gate**, where the River Rani used to flow out. There are several pools with fish, small waterfalls and a fresh water spring where the river enters the fort through the **Mohan Gate** (west). The others are **Amri Gate** (north) and **Shahper Gate** (south). One of two forts within the master fort, **Miri Fort** formerly housed the Talpur Mirs and their harem, and stands on a small hillock in the centre. To the north is the fortified citadel, **Shergarh Fort**. The fort offers excellent views.

Amri

Colour map 2, grid B3

Seemingly little more than a mound made of generations of mud houses built on top of one another, **Amri** is in fact an important prehistoric site (20 kilometres north of the Sann crossroads). In 1929, excavations by the archaeologist NG Majumdar revealed artefacts contemporary with Moenjo Daro. Lower levels, however, revealed a previously unknown ceramic style that extended the period of Amri's occupation from 3500 BC to 2200 BC. Full excavations at the site's three main mounds were not completed until 1962, but revealed three occupations superimposed above one another. Glazed and moulded pottery from the Mughal period were found at the upper level, below which were pieces from the late and mature level of Harappan occupation. At the lowest level was found pottery that showed no affinity with Harappa or Moenjo Daro and has been named **Amri-ware**. The most important pieces are exhibited at the National Museum in Karachi.

The original inhabitants of Amri pre-date the Harappan people, and represent a quite distinct culture. As opposed to the predominantly black-on-red style of Indus Valley pottery, Amri-ware typically uses fine buff and pale pink paste in bands around the mouth of the vessels, with geometric patterns infilled with checkered work, chevrons and diamonds. **Potsherds** dating from 3000 BC and also **Indus bricks** of a millennium later have been found.

The absence of a large settlement has led to the belief that the Amri people lived in scattered villages, possibly using a somewhat better placed, larger and more important village as a centre for trading. The pastoral tribes appear to have preferred the hills, with sheltered valleys and springs. They were slowly forced to move from the west through pressure of population on the land and the changes in climate, and were not attracted by the plains of the Indus. Their

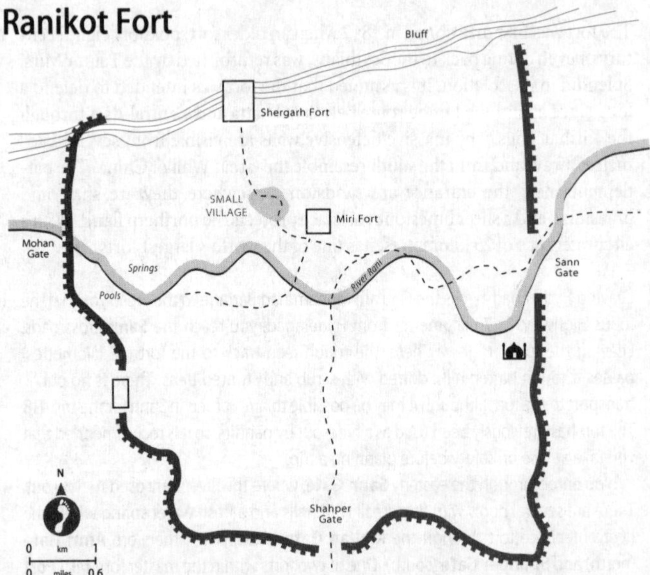

settlements appear in the valleys along the Sind-Baluchistan border, forming a pattern similar to that of the Baluchis thousands of years later.

Sehwan

Colour map 2, grid B3

Formerly known as Siwistan, **Sehwan** may be the oldest continuously occupied town in Sind. The site has been associated with Sindimana, where Sambos king of the hillmen surrendered to Alexander the Great. The **fort**, whose remains lie across the deep and narrow valley to the north of town, was used by Alexander, and is known locally as the 'Kafir Qila'. The town was later used in the 4th century as the Buddhist capital of Chandagupta II's ascetic brother, and then conquered in the 8th century by Mhd bin Qasim when the Buddhist population refused to fight. Commanding the Lakhi Pass, Sehwan has been a key strategic location for all invaders in the region.

Sehwan is famous for the shrine of the 13th century Sufi saint **Hazrat Lal Shahbaz Qalander** (Divine Spirit of the Red Falcon). Born in Afghanistan as Sheikh Usman Merwandi, he came from the 11th century **Qalander** order of wandering sufis who gave up everything worldly to devote themselves to propagating a religion free from orthodox rituals. The saint was renowned for his scholarship in Persian and Arabic, and for his miracles. He claimed to be the last direct descendant of the Prophet, helping the local people in times of disaster, and amazing them with his miracles.

The original 14th century **tomb**, decorated with tiles and calligraphy, had a 17th century surround, partly constructed of wood, with beaten silver ornamentation on the railings and spires. However, this was partially destroyed when the original dome roof collapsed, and the shrine has been substantially rebuilt. Almost all pious rulers of Sind or Sewistan have contributed something to the shrine over the years, with the most recent gift being the magnificent gold covered doors at the south gateway, presented by the Shah of Iran. The rebuilding programme here is well under way, and will eventually double the size of the present enclosure.

A visit to the shrine is one of the highlights of a journey around Sind, as there is an intense atmosphere charged with piety, devotion and hope. The narrow bazaars leading to the shrine, with their food and souvenir stalls, service the stream of pilgrims, fakirs, miracle-seekers as well as Sehwan's numerous beggars. Indeed, the 1919 Gazetteer of Sind claims "the population is largely composed of beggars". The number of visitors swells on Thursday, and peaks during the annual Urs (18th-19th of Shaban, end of November 1999, mid-November 2000). Each evening at 1800, the congregation join in the devotional dance of the dervishes. To the accompaniment of gongs and the rhythmic beating of giant drums, the disciples express their devotion through dancing, music and poetry. The men and women dance separately, reaching a trance-like state, although watching the women can be disturbing. Kneeling on the floor, they swing their heads around and around with remarkable intensity, their long hair sweeping the ground like 'headbangers' at a Heavy Rock concert, before collapsing in a state of exhaustion. The hour of dancing used to be timed using a **waterclock**, in the form of a pot with a hole which fills and sinks after 15 minutes, though it has disappeared during recent rebuilding work.

Sleeping

D-E *STDC Motel* (bookable in Karachi) is the best bet. A/c, attached bath. **E-F** *Indus Rest House*, Station Rd, opposite GPO, T230. Has large bare rooms, some with a/c, attached bath, basic but OK for 1 night. **G** *Lajpal*, Lajpal Rd, near mosque, T444. Extremely basic, noisy, reasonable restaurant.

The world's tallest man

*For many years the Shrine of **Hazrat Lal Shahbaz Qalander** was not Sehwan's only attraction. Until his death from kidney failure in mid-1998, a common sight at the shrine was **Alam Channa** – the world's tallest man. Born in the small village of Bachal Channa in 1953, he became a khadim (attendant) at the shrine in the early 1970s, using his great height to "keep an eye open for pickpockets and eve-teasers". Recorded in the Guinness Book of Records as being 231.7 centimetres, he was perfectly suited for such a role. Twice married (once to a 181 centimetres Pathan, and once to a woman of a 'mere' 140 centimetres), Channa's height had obvious drawbacks – 16 metres of cloth was required just to make one made-to-measure shalwar kameez! Having represented Pakistan abroad at a number of international parades, Channa also founded a charitable trust to help the poor and needy. He is buried in Shahbaz Colony in Sehwan, at the Amir Hamza mosque whose construction he helped to fund.*

Transport **Air** **Karachi**: Monday 0820; Thursday 0820 1725; Friday 1810. **Moenjo Daro**: Thursday 1420; Friday 0805. **Sukkur**: Thursday 1420; Friday 0805.

Bus Buses running between Hyderabad and Larkana/Sukkur via the west bank of the Indus will drop/pick up passengers here (though heading north it's often only possible to go as far as Larkana).

Around Sehwan

Across the road, to the west of Sehwan, is the large marshy area covered by **Manchar Lake**, caused by the overflowing of the right bank of the Indus and the drainage of a large area of the Kirthar Hills. Like most major rivers that flow north-south in the north hemisphere, the action of the Earth's rotation causes the Indus to cut into its west bank. The dry season area of the lake, 36 square kilometres, expands rapidly to 510 square kilometres when the excess high season flow of the Indus drains off into the lake. As the Indus returns to its low stage during the winter, water starts flowing back to the river from the lake. Effectively, Manchar Lake acts as a great safety valve for the Indus in a similar way that the Tonle Sap acts for the Mekong in Cambodia. However, the effect of upstream dams in reducing the flow of the Indus has lead to the steady deterioration of the lake.

The community of **Mohana** fishermen that live on the lake use traditional methods of catching fish, such as submerged baited lines and driving the fish into nets. They also have an ingenious method of catching herons and water fowl that involves placing a stuffed egret on their heads as a decoy, and then wading neck deep to net their unwary prey. The Mohanas' large, flat bottomed boats characteristically have high prows and usually accommodate a family in two rooms. You reach the lake by driving from **Bubak** to the embankment of the **Dunister canal** where you can hire a boat or walk the three kilometres along the bank.

The road between Amri and Sehwan Sharif passes close to the foothills of the Kirthar Range at the only point in Sind where Cretaceous rocks are exposed at the surface. A basaltic fissure flow forms the crest of the range, and numerous thermal springs break the surface in the foothills. The four sulphurous springs at **Lakhi Shah Saddar** draw people in search of cures for rheumatism and skin ailments. The nearby cave where the Muslim saint Shah Saddar came to meditate is now a shrine.

Khudabad

Built during the rule of **Yar Mohammad Kalhora** (1701-1718), this town became the capital of Sind under the Kalhoras until 1768, when the subsequent changing course of the Indus led to its decline. In 1781 the Talpurs raised the city. In fact, the town is so diminished in size that its two main monuments appear out of place. The huge **Jami Masjid** (Friday Mosque) beside the road is big enough to hold almost 2,000 people. The **Tomb of Yar Mohammad Kalhora** is two kilometres off the NH, although it is now in a poor state of repair.

Dadu/Moro

Colour map 2, grid B3

The Indus Highway bypasses the district headquarters of **Dadu.** This is probably just as well since the forests around Dadu are considered to be Pakistan's "heartland of banditry for 800 years", and prior to the army's anti-bandit drive the police travelled in armoured cars. From Dadu it is possible to cross the bridge at **Moro** to the Indus east bank.

Sind

Moenjo Daro

Not only one of the most important archaeological sites of South Asia, for its age, Moenjo Daro is one of the most stunningly restored and preserved prehistoric sites in the whole world.

Phone code: 0741
Colour map 2, grid A3

Ins and outs

There are several options for visiting Moenjo Daro. Many visitors fly in from Karachi, spend some time at the site, then depart again by air the same day. Trains also serve the site, though arrival and departure times tend to be inconvenient. Most budget travellers reach Moenjo Daro as an excursion from Larkana, 26 kilometres away (see below). For 'getting there' information, see 'Transport' below.

Inside the entrance is the ***National Bank of Pakistan***, offering foreign exchange, a fixed price Sindhi handicraft shop and the helpful **PTDC** office (T0741 60906). To the right lie the Water and Soil Investigation Laboratory, the ***Archaeological Dak Bungalow*** (see below), a canteen and the museum. Even by March, temperatures get uncomfortably hot, and as there is virtually no shade on the site, it is essential to take sun-block and water.

History

Moenjo Daro represents the culmination of a long period of development within the Indus region. In some places early Indus Valley settlements can be traced back to the Neolithic, and the pottery of the whole Indus system may go back to 4000 BC or even earlier. With the development of the Kot Diji style of pottery came also greater uniformity

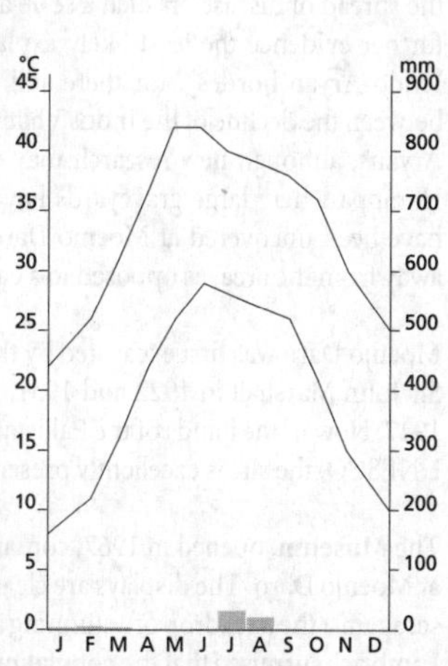

The best time to visit is between November and March

throughout the region, heralding the extraordinary political and cultural unity of the Harappa-Moenjo Daro city culture.

An interesting feature of the civilization is the complete absence of any evidence of warfare; no weapons have ever been found, nor evidence of a warrior class. Some scholars feel that the existence of a specifically non-violent religion was the unifying force which led the civilization to evolve and prosper so successfully. Trade was also extensive, both internally and abroad – with South India, Afghanistan, Egypt and Mesopotamia.

Although the majority of the Indus Valley towns were in what is now Pakistan, there are several important sites in India – the port of **Lothal**, **Rangpur** and **Rojidi** in modern Gujarat, **Kalibangan** in Rajasthan, **Banavli** in Punjab and **Alamgirpur** to the north of Delhi. Yet of all the sites known today Moenjo Daro and Harappa stand out by virtue of their scale and their complexity. The significance of the Indus Valley Civilization is comparable with the two other great ancient civilizations, Egypt and Mesopotamia. The fact that no written records have been discovered and the remnants of the script itself remains undeciphered still leaves the field open to contrasting interpretations of the rise, function and decline of the cities.

Dating the city Both the dating of the city and the causes of its decline remain unclear. Early dating relied on the comparison of objects found in Harappan cities with similar objects found in Mesopotamia, and dated the Indus Valley settlements at between 2500 and 1500 BC. Subsequent analysis, aided in places by radiocarbon dating has suggested an even earlier rise in some parts of the valley, and a decline by 1750 BC at the latest. But what caused the decline is even more speculative than the dating.

The city's decline As you walk back from the lower city past the citadel towards the museum, the fragile nature of the environmental balance is obvious. Any one change might well be enough to tip the balance between success and failure. Probably it was a combination of events. In Lambrick's view, the natural flooding of the Indus may have caused it to move its course massively, resulting in the abandonment of vital agricultural land. Such a change could have been brought about by earthquakes in what is still a highly active earthquake zone.

Flooding itself may have wiped out large parts of the city, or encouraged the spread of disease on such a scale as to decimate the population. Short of further evidence the least likely explanation seems to be the arrival of the "Indo-Aryan hordes", for there still seems a gap of at least two centuries between the decline of the Indus Valley Civilization and the first arrival of the Aryans, although new research may change this view. Significantly, unlike Harappa where large graveyards have been discovered, very few skeletons have been uncovered at Moenjo Daro, perhaps suggesting a gradual move away from the area, as opposed to a cataclysmic ending.

Early excavation Moenjo Daro was first excavated by the Indian Archaeological Survey under Sir John Marshall in 1922 and 1931, and then by Sir Mortimer Wheeler in 1947. Now in the hands of the Pakistan Archaeological Survey, supported by UNESCO, the site is excellently presented.

Tour of the site The **Museum**, opened in 1967, contains the most important artefacts found at Moenjo Daro. The displays are clearly labelled and well presented, and are set against the backdrop of a stunning artist's impression of the city at its peak. Lambrick surmised that the population of Moenjo Daro may have been about

35,000, but more recent research (taking account of a whole new area of settlement) suggests doubling or even trebling that figure.

The city left behind it abundant evidence of its high quality of life. Many **copper and bronze tools** and decorative objects have been found, the ore probably having come from mines in Rajasthan. Copper and bronze vessels in the late stages of the city show highly developed form, the work of craft specialists.

Gold objects are quite common – beads, pendants and ornaments. Allchin and Allchin argue that the light quality of the gold point to a source as far afield as Karnataka in South India, to the Neolithic settlements that were clustered around the bands of quartz reef gold at Hatti. Silver and other metals were also common for works of sculpture, such as the famous figure of the dancing girl.

The museum also contains seals and sealings, with as yet undecipherable characters, as well as images of tigers, rhinos, elephants, crocodiles, unicorns and bulls. Terracotta images of animals, some with moving parts, are thought to be toys, and there are also games involving dice and what appear to be chessboards. There are also exhibits from the pre-Moenjo Daro sites of Kot Diji (3370-2655 BC), and Amri (3660-3360 BC). Timings April-September 0830-1230, 1430-1730; October-March 0900-1600.

The main gate is due north of the citadel. It is best to walk up the path and steps to the top of the citadel, now capped by the ruins of a second century Buddhist stupa. From here you get an excellent idea of the layout of the whole city, and can follow a broadly circular path, well marked out with paved footpaths where necessary, to take you round the main built up areas of the city.

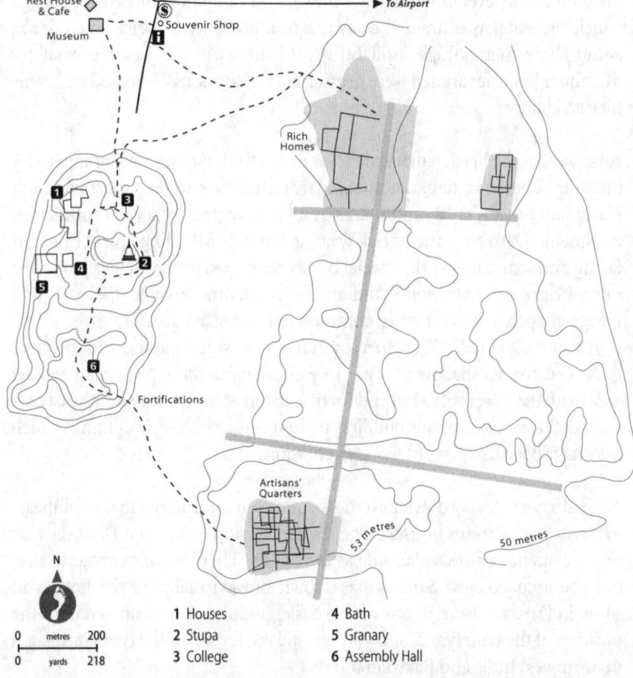

The citadel From the top of the mound you get a commanding view of the citadel below and around the central height. The evidence of town planning, an important feature of the major cities, is all around. Moenjo Daro, in common with Harappa and Kalibangan, has its citadel at the westernmost point of the complex, built up on a mound of bricks. This would have raised the most important area of the city above the floods of the Indus that regularly inundated the town.

The surface level now is more than 10 metres higher than it was when Moenjo Daro's first houses were being built, and have been submerged under the ever increasing deposits of silt. The 13 metres high brick embankment here was probably also a defence against flooding. The long axis in all three cities runs north-south. To the east was a lower city – mainly residential houses. The large mural in the museum suggests that the citadel (probably also residential areas) was surrounded by massive brick fortifications. Although the layout of the streets is not absolutely precise, the main pattern is of the wider streets running from north-south and a series of narrower east-west streets. The width seems to be deliberately graded, the widest being twice the second and four times the width of the lanes.

The civic buildings As you walk down from the top through the citadel area immediately to the west of the stupa, you see other features common to the cities: the presence of civic and administrative buildings, **the great bath** (referred to as the "royal bath", though there is little evidence of the political structure of the society other than that of its buildings and domestic artefacts) and possibly a **granary**.

Whatever the uncertainties of interpretation, the buildings are extraordinarily impressive. The bath, 12 metres by seven metres and three metres deep, with flights of steps into it at each end, has "changing" cubicles along the side. It may have been used for ritual bathing. If you walk down from the edge of the bath to the level immediately below it you can follow the sluice through which the water was drained away – a beautifully made brick-lined drain, about three metres high. Still further to the west you can see what Sir Mortimer Wheeler argued were **granaries**, 27 blocks criss-crossed with ventilation channels.

Harappan brick work All around is the **brick work** which was one of the hallmarks of Harappan city building. There is a remarkable standardization of size. The most common Harappan brick was 28 centimetres by 14 centimetres by seven centimetres. At Moenjo Daro sun-dried brick was used mainly for filling, burnt brick for facing and structural work. Special bricks were used for particular purposes: sawn bricks for bathrooms and in the residential area to the east, and wedge-shaped bricks for wells, common in the eastern quarter.

If you walk about 200 metres south from the stupa mound and the great bath, you cross a shallow valley before climbing to the second main citadel area, with the **Assembly Hall** and **fortifications** at the extreme southeast corner. All that remains of this building are four rows of five-brick plinths, which may have been the bases of wooden columns.

The artisans' quarter The path goes steeply down past the fortifications and across to the southeast to a group of 'artisans houses'. The residential sites in Moenjo Daro show as much evidence of town planning as the citadel. There is a wide range in size, but the archaeologist Sarcina has shown how virtually all the houses in Moenjo Daro conform to one of five basic modules. The main variant is the position of the **courtyard**, and you can still see several of the types in villages in northwest India and Pakistan today.

Saving Moenjo Daro

At present, approximately one-third of Moenjo Daro has been excavated. The last major excavation was undertaken in 1965 by the American George F Dales, although problems of waterlogging meant that the dig could not be completed. It was soon realized that unless immediate action was taken to reduce the impact of water-table rise and the effects of salinity, the site would suffer permanent and irreversible damage.

It is estimated that the water-table needs to be lowered by some 10 metres, and for that purpose 27 tubewells and many cemented disposal channels have been dug to lower the water-table and drain away saline water. Stone pitching has also been introduced to counter seepage from the Indus, just 1½ kilometres away. Cultivation of the traditionally thirsty rice crop has also been banned in the immediate vicinity.

The Water and Soil Investigation Laboratory monitors the water-table level daily, and claims that it has been lowered to the necessary depth. However, during the frequent power cuts, the tubewells are unable to operate, and the level rises once more. Thus, there is a slight improvement, but not a permanent solution.

Other conservation measures include isolation of structures from saline water by installing damp proof courses, underpinning and mudcapping parts that have already decayed, and providing mud poultice treatment in order to desalinize standing structures.

Almost every house had a bathroom (shown by a sawn brick pavement with a surrounding curb). Walking down the narrow streets, drain pipes and vertical chutes for toilet waste disposal, are clearly visible. In the lower city are brick drains, covered over with other bricks or sometimes slabs of stone, and in the south zone there are small, barrack-like houses. One of the most remarkable features are the excavated wells which now stand proud of the ground by as much as four metres. The repeated silt deposition was matched by the raising of the brick lining.

The high class residential quarter

Walk north again from the southernmost group of houses in the lower city along the broad main street that links the artisans' area with the main higher-class residential area. The remarkable scale of the road suggests it may have been used for triumphal processions. At the top of a slight slope look across the low valley between the south and north settlements to the magnificent view of the upper class residential area in front of you. Houses are superbly preserved, and high walls separate both broad streets and narrow lanes. The main street was probably lined with stalls and shops and inside the buildings to the west of this main street is a series of variously labelled rooms. Wheeler suggested that a building where the stone sculpture of a seated figure was found, was a temple.

Essentials

Sleeping & eating

E ***Archaeological Resthouse***, just inside main gate (reservations through Dept of Archaeology and Museums, 27-A Al-Asif Building, Shaheed-e-Millat Rd, Karachi, T4521821). The **D** ***PTDC Motel*** has still not been completed. Alternatively, stay in Larkana (see below). The *Resthouse* has a small café, though you usually need to arrange meals in advance.

Transport

Air The airport is a short distance from the site entrance (T0741 46583/60344). The PIA shuttle bus will usually drop you there. **From Hyderabad**: Wednesday 1605. **To**

Hyderabad: Tuesday 0905; Saturday 1745. **From Islamabad**: Monday 2345; Tuesday 1005 2345; Wednesday 1005 2345; Thursday 1005 2345; Friday 2345; Saturday 1200 2345; Sunday 1005 2345. **To Islamabad**: Monday 1030; Tuesday 0905 1555; Wednesday 1730; Thursday 1030; Saturday 1745; Sunday 1820. **From Karachi**: Monday 0630; Tuesday 0645 1400 1415; Wednesday 0645 1500; Thursday 0630 1300 1400; Friday 0645; Saturday 0700 1530; Sunday 0645 1600 (Rs 1,100 one-way, Rs 2,200 return). **To Karachi**: Monday 1030; Tuesday 0905 1555; Wednesday 1730; Thursday 1030; Saturday 1745; Sunday 1820. **To Sukkur**: Tuesday 1530; Wednesday 0825; Thursday 1515 1530; Friday 0900.

Train From Karachi: *Bolan Mail*, departs 1030, arrives 2000; *Khushal Khan Khattak Express*, departs 1930, arrives 0400 (a/c sleeper Rs 596, a/c sitter Rs 343, 1st class sleeper Rs 220, economy Rs 95), these services continue on to **Quetta**. **To Karachi** (via **Kotri Junction** for **Hyderabad**): rather inconvenient, *Bolan Mail* departs 0423, *Khushal Khan Khattak Express* departs 2306, these services originate in **Quetta**. You will need to take a tonga between the station and the site (Rs 30).

Bus Dokri-bound buses from the Bakrani bus stand in **Larkana** run to the junction 5 kilometres from Moenjo Daro (1 hour), from where you can take a tonga to the site (Rs 30).

Larkana

Phone code: 0741
Colour map 2, grid A3

This busy market town is situated at the place where the Kalhoras first established themselves, and begun to dig canals for irrigated agriculture. The town's location is commercially significant, lying on the route from Karachi to Shikarpur and the Bolan Pass, and under the British it became Sind's greatest grain mart. The town is noted today as the home town of the late Zulfikar Ali Bhutto.

The only antiquity in Larkana is the dilapidated remains of a fort that has been used in turn as an arsenal, a jail, a hospital, a store room for the Camel Corps and a lunatic asylum. Larkana is a good base from which to visit Moenjo Daro.

Sleeping & eating

■ *on map*
Price codes: see inside front cover

C ***Sambara Inn***, Raza Shah Kabor Rd, T44391. Central a/c, dish TV, pool, garden, good restaurant, keen and friendly staff, best in town. **D** ***United***, 2nd floor, Royal Rd, T61863. Some rooms a/c though fairly simple, TV, restaurant. **E** ***Asia***, off Station Rd, behind PIA, T60007. Not bad value, particularly for a/c rooms, TV, restaurant. **E** ***Gulf***, Bunder Rd, T22282. Some rooms a/c, fairly basic, restaurant. **F-G** ***Mehran***, Station Rd, T61077. Very basic rooms, not particularly clean attached bath, restaurant.

Transport

Air The airstrip is at Moenjo Daro (see above).

Train From **Karachi**: *Bolan Mail*, departs 1030, arrives 2040; *Khushal Khan Khattak Express*, departs 1930, arrives 0540 (see 'Moenjo Daro' for approximate fares), these services continue on to **Quetta**. To **Karachi** (via **Kotri Junction** for **Hyderabad**): rather inconvenient, *Bolan Mail* departs 0350, *Khushal Khan Khattak Express* departs 2230, these services originate in **Quetta**.

Bus The General Bus Stand is to the north of town, next to the stadium. Buses depart when full for **Sukkur**. For south bound travellers, your best bet is ***Blue Lines***, near *Hotel Asia*, T61943, who run a/c coaches to **Karachi** (9½ hours, Rs 160) via **Hyderabad** (7 hours, Rs 120). Local buses for **Moenjo Daro** run from Bakrani bus stand, near the Attaturk Memorial. Take a Dokri-bound bus and ask to be let down at the Moenjo

Daro junction (28 kilometres). From here a tonga will take you the 5 kilometres to the site (Rs 30).

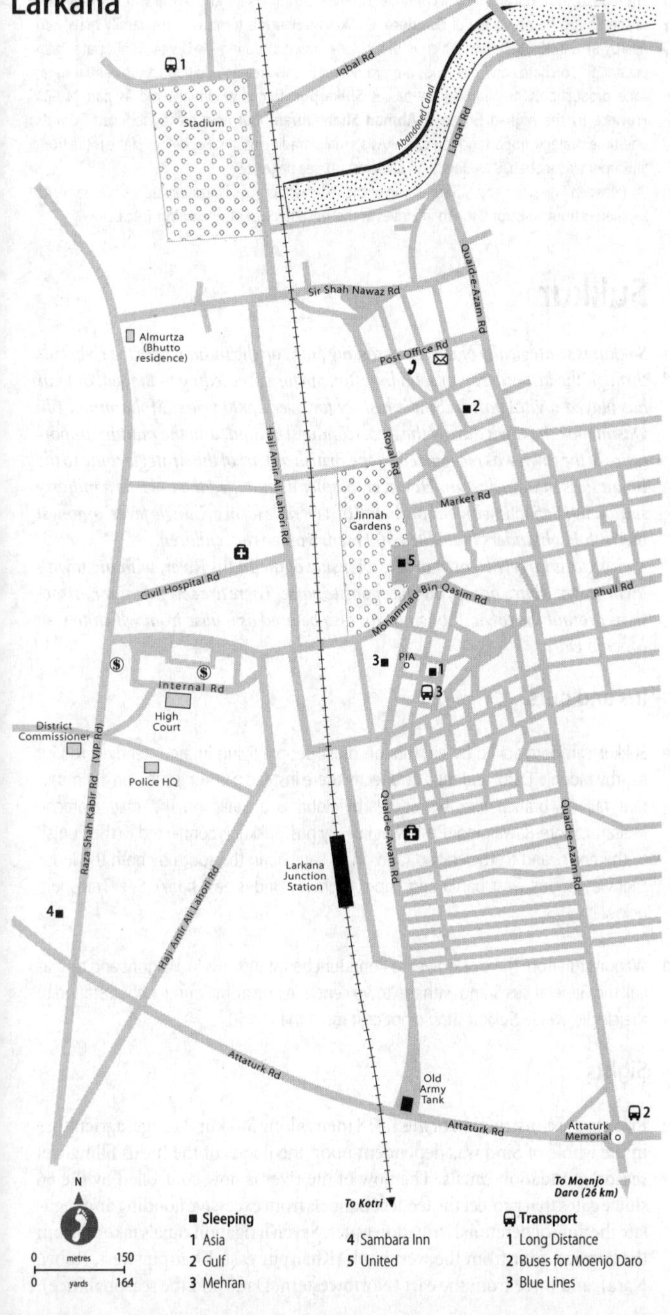

Directory **Airline offices** *PIA*, Station Rd, T60338/60344. **Banks** Use the *National Bank of Pakistan* at Moenjo Daro. **Communications** **GPO:** Burghry Bazaar, Post Office Rd. **Telephone:** Pak Telecom, Post Office Rd. **Hospitals & medical services** *Almas Medical Centre*, Station Rd, T60303. *Civil Hospital*, Civil Hospital Rd. **Tourist offices** *PTDC* is at Moenjo Daro.

Road to Shikarpur and Sukkur The road to Shikarpur and Sukkur continues northeast from Larkana and passes within 1 kilometre of the Bhutto home village of **Naudero**. Zulfikar Ali Bhutto's tomb is in the family graveyard nearby at Gari Khudabaksh, which is particularly crowded during his Urs (4 April). Date palm plantations, orchards and rice fields are prominent in this area, in addition to substantial sugar cane production. The Highway by-passes **Shikarpur**, formerly administered as part of Sibi Province by the Afghan Governor **Ahmed Shah Durani**, but now greatly reduced from its one-time strategic importance on one of Asia's major trading routes. For details of the route from Shikarpur via Jacobabad to Quetta (in Baluchistan), see page 165.

Between Shikarpur and Sukkur, some of the worst effects of salinization are visible. Some 42 kilometres from Shikarpur, the road arrives at the western outskirts of **Sukkur** (see below).

Sukkur

***Phone code**: 071*
Colour map 2, grid A4

Sukkur is strategically placed at a crossing point on the Indus where the river cuts through the last outcrop of solid limestone before proceeding to the sea. Sukkur has played a vital part in Sind's history for over 2,000 years. Mohammad Bin Qasim took the town during the Arab conquest of Sind, and the military importance of the town was recognized by the British as part of the strategic route to the Bolan Pass in Baluchistan. However, Napier abandoned the town as a military station in 1845 following the outbreak of a terrible form of 'jungle fever' amongst the 78th Highlanders that killed 500 men, women and children.

Sukkur is largely located on the west side of the Indus River, with the town's 'twin' town, Rohri, occupying the opposite bank. There are several minor attractions around the town, though it can also be used as a base from which to visit Moenjo Daro.

Ins and outs

Getting there Sukkur can be reached by air, though most people flying in are intending to visit nearby Moenjo Daro, and thus fly directly there instead. Sukkur itself is on an important railway branch line, whilst nearby Rohri is actually on the main Karachi-Multan-Lahore-Rawalpindi-Peshawar line. By bus, Sukkur is connected to the Punjab to the north, and to Hyderabad (and on to Karachi) in the south by both the Indus Highway (Indus west bank) and Super Highway (Indus east bank). See 'Transport' below.

Getting around Wagons run from the clocktower to Rohri Junction station (Rs 5). Wagons and tongas link the General Bus Stand with the town centre. A ride from Rohri Junction station to the clocktower in Sukkur should not cost more than Rs 50.

Sights

Sukkur Barrage Prior to the construction of the 1,418 metres long Sukkur Barrage, agriculture in the whole of Sind was dependent upon the floods of the Indus filling wet season inundation canals. The flow of the river is now controlled by the 66 sluice gates that protect the feeder channels from excessive flooding and regulate the flow of perennial irrigation water. Seven irrigation canals take off from the barrage: four from the west bank (Khairpur east, Khairpur west, Rohri, Nara), and three from the east (Northwestern, Dadu and the seasonal Rice).

The total irrigated area dependent upon the Sukkur Barrage is in the region of 2.98 million hectares, provided through over 75,000 kilometres of canals. Planned as far back as 1847, the project was inaugurated by the then Governor of Bombay, Sir George Lloyd in 1923 and completed as the Lloyd Barrage in 1932 at a cost of Rs 40.4 million. After the barrage was completed however, Sind has been directly affected by use made in winter of water upstream. Further, the unlined (kachcha) canals of previous irrigation systems have brought problems of increased salinity and waterlogging. There are usual Pakistani photography restrictions at the Barrage.

The Minaret of Masum Shah

During the reign of the Mughal Emperor Akbar, **Masum Shah** (1594-1618) was appointed as his Nawab, or Governor, of Sukkur. In 1614 he built the pencil shaped minaret. The tower is 84 foot high, circumference at the base is 84 foot and there are 84 steps leading to the lantern at the top. The spiral staircase is very narrow in places but there are fine views from the top. Sadly, photography is forbidden. At the base of the minaret is the **Faiz Mahal**, an octagonal building with a glazed brick dome, that was built by Masum Shah as a pavilion.Masum Shah is buried in the adjacent tomb.

Sukkur

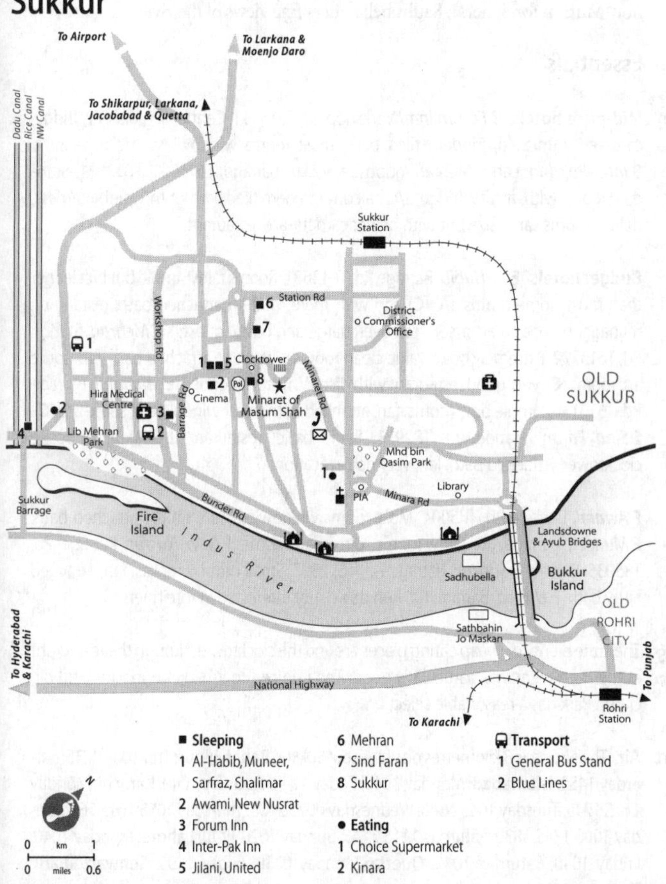

Mausoleum of Shah Khairuddin Jilani To the east of the town, this is the tomb of a religious scholar and wandering founder of a spiritual dynasty who settled in a nearby cave until his death in 1609 at the reputed age of 116. The shrine was built in 1760, although the blue enamelled dome and tiled façade were restored by Sindhi craftsmen only 40 years ago.

Sadhubella One of the most intriguing places of interest in Sukkur is the active Hindu complex on the island of **Sadhubella**. The symbolism of an outpost of Hinduism in predominantly Muslim Pakistan is not lost on the devotees attending the temples on this rocky island in the Indus. Sadhubella is thought to have emerged as a separate island from Bukkur around 1550 AD. Founded some 150 years ago by **Baba Bankhandi Maharaji**, the complex includes a monastery, an ashram, temples to Hanuman, Siva and Ganesh as well as a library containing Dharmic books in Hindi, Sindhi and English. The first entry in the visitor's book is, surprisingly, by General Zia ul-Haq, former martial law ruler of Pakistan, who visited in 1985.

The main temple contains a shrine to the founder, and is decorated with statues of Hindu deities and scenes from Hindu mythology. It is generally possible to visit the island from the Sukkur riverbank although Muslim visitors may require prior permission from the DC's office (this rule is usually waivered for non-Muslim foreigners). Sadhubella offers fine views of the river.

Essentials

Sleeping
■ *on map*
Price codes: see inside front cover

Mid-price hotels **B** *Forum Inn*, Workshop Rd, T613011. Central a/c, dish TV, fridge, carpeted, furnished, modern tiled bath, most rooms windowless, a/c restaurant. **B** *Inter-Pak Inn*, Lab-e-Mehran, opposite Sukkur Barrage, T613051, F613621. Standard rooms with dish TV, fridge, a/c, balcony, modern tiled bathroom, grubby carpets, deluxe rooms same size but with newer carpets, a/c restaurant.

Budget hotels **E** *Al-Habib*, Barrage Rd, T613681. Rooms fairly simple but bit cleaner than most, some rooms a/c (**C**) and with more modern attached bath, restaurant, manager bit of a smart-arse, "staff overcharge and hassle guests". **E** *Mehran*, Station Rd, T613792. Extremely good value clean rooms with clean attached bath, fan, some a/c rooms (**C**), very good restaurant with dish TV. Recommended. **E** *Shalimar*, Barrage Rd, T612156. Simple bare rooms, fan, attached bath, most windowless, some a/c (**C**). **E** *Sind Faran*, Station Rd, T82921. Fairly basic, restaurant. **E** *Sukkur*, opposite clocktower. Attached bath, fan, very noisy location.

F *Awami*, Barrage Rd, T85004. Most rooms windowless, fan, simple attached bath. **F** *Muneer*, Barrage Rd. Dirty rooms, dirty bathrooms. **F** *New Nusrat*, Barrage Rd, T85035. Closed. **F** *Sarfraz*, Barrage Rd, T612397. Small grubby rooms, fan, attached filthy bath. **F** *United*, Barrage Rd. Run down, not interested in foreigners.

Eating
● *on map*

There are plenty of cheap eating places around the clocktower, though the restaurant at the *Hotel Mehran* is particularly good. The ***Choice*** supermarket opposite Mhd bin Qasim Park has a reasonable selection.

Transport **Air** The airport is 8 kilometres northwest of Sukkur. **Bahawalpur**: Thursday 0735; Saturday 1450. **Islamabad**: Monday 1040; Friday 1040; Saturday 1040. **Karachi**: Monday 1115 1745; Tuesday 1045 1640; Wednesday 0925 2105; Thursday 1055 1615 1640; Friday 1000 1745 1830; Saturday 1115 1745; Sunday 1020 1740. **Lahore**: Monday 1040; Friday 1040; Saturday 1040. **Quetta**: Monday 0750; Friday 1505. **Sehwan Sharif**: Thursday 1615.

Bus The chaotic General Bus Stand is to the west of town (see map). Buses depart when full to **Hyderabad** and **Karachi** via the Indus East Bank, though north bound few go beyond **Rahim Yar Khan** (Rs 40, change here for points further north). Heading south, most buses use the National Highway (east bank of the Indus). For points along the west bank (eg **Moenjo Daro, Sehwan Sharif**) you usually have to change at **Larkana**. *Blue Lines*, Workshop Rd, run a/c coaches along the National Highway to **Karachi** (10½ hours, Rs 170) via **Hyderabad** (8 hours, Rs 140) at 0730, 0930, 1030, 1200, 1400, 1800, 2130, 2230. Minibuses to **Pirjo Goth** run from a small yard on Workshop Rd, near *Forum Inn* (Rs 10).

Train Although trains run from Sukkur to Sibi and Quetta, the main railhead for trains north (**Punjab**), west (**Quetta**) and south (**Hyderabad/Karachi**) is at **Rohri Junction** (see below).

Directory

Airline offices *PIA*, opposite Mhd bin Qasim Park, T24547. **Communications** GPO: Minaret Rd. **Telephones:** next to GPO, Minaret Rd.

Sukkur to Rohri

Rohri is reached from Sukkur by crossing the twin bridges via **Bukkur Island** in the centre of the Indus. On the north of this 300 metres wide limestone island is a simple shrine to **Sadra-u-din Badshah**, a contemporary of **Lal Shahbaz Qalander** whose shrine is at **Sehwan**. The ancient ruined mud fort to the south, occupied by Mhd Bin Qasim, is now a military base so access is denied. It is perfectly feasible to walk from central Sukkur to the bus/train stations in Rohri, though three-wheelers and horse-carts link the two.

Rohri

Phone code: 071
Colour map 2, grid A4

In 1875, Lt Twemlour of the Asiatic Society of Bengal found evidence to suggest that Rohri was a flourishing place in neolithic times, making it one of the oldest sites of human habitation in South Asia. Rohri has been a sacred site to Muslims due to the association of Saiyads who settled here, and in 1545 Mir Mohammad Kalhora built a shrine – Mu-e-Mubarak – to receive a hair of the beard of the Prophet. On 2 March each year the sacred relic is displayed to the public.

Sights

In the old part of town, a little difficult to find, stands the **Akbari Mosque**, built in 1583 by an officer of the Emperor Akbar. At the south side is a tall, green domed gateway with a blue, green and brown tiled façade. The mosque, a low white building, has a highly decorated mirrored mihrab. A madrassa, or Koranic school, is attached.

Just below the Ayub Khan arch railway bridge, on a raised mound, stands the **Sathbahin Jo Maskan**, a shrine to the legend of seven virgin sisters who locked themselves away and swore never to look upon the face of any man. This attractive site is entered through a small domed gateway. The shrine is 200 metres long and 50 metres wide and has a rectangular central raised plinth of red baked bricks. At each corner stands a five metres high blue tiled minaret. A number of sandstone tombs, carved with text from the Koran and similar in style to those at Chaukundi, stand on the plinth. There are fine views across the river to Sukkur, and of the **Ayub Khan** and **Landsdowne Bridges**. Below the bridges, along the west bank of the Indus, reside

Selected train fares from Rohri Junction

	A/c sleeper	*A/c sitter*	*1st class sleeper*	*Economy*
Bahawalpur	*Rs 506*	*Rs 293*	*Rs 176*	*Rs 80*
Hyderabad	*Rs 445*	*Rs 260*	*Rs 160*	*Rs 70*
Karachi	*Rs 658*	*Rs 383*	*Rs 242*	*Rs 100*
Multan	*Rs 630*	*Rs 360*	*Rs 231*	*Rs 100*
Peshawar	*Rs 1,390*	*Rs 799*	*Rs 534*	*Rs 255*
Quetta	*Rs 546*	*Rs 321*	*Rs 198*	*Rs 85*
Rawalpindi	*Rs 1,193*	*Rs 681*	*Rs 457*	*Rs 210*

communities of the **Mohana boat people**, an indigenous ethnic group found in several parts of Sind.

Sleeping & eating See under Sukkur.

Transport **Train** Rohri Junction is an important railhead for Sind, Punjab and Baluchistan. **Karachi** 14 trains daily, 6-9 hours. **Lahore** *Shalimar*, 1240, 10½ hours; *Tezgam*, 2245, 11½ hours. **Multan** *Shalimar*, 1240, 5½ hours; *Tezgam*, 2245, 6 hours. **Peshawar** *Awam Exp*, 1530, 24 hours; *Khyber Mail*, 0450, 25 hours. **Quetta** via **Sukkur, Jacobabad** and **Sibi** *Quetta Exp*, 0605, 11 hours; *Abbaseen Exp*, 2215, 18 hours. **Rawalpindi** *Awam Exp*, 1530, 20 hours; *Tezgam*, 2245, 18 hours.

Bus Buses north and south bound can be flagged down on the National Highway.

Sukkur to Baluchistan

From Sukkur it is possible to travel northwest to **Quetta**, Baluchistan, via **Shikarpur**, **Jacobabad**, **Sibi** and the **Bolan Pass**. For a detailed description of this route, see Baluchistan chapter (page 165).

Sukkur to Punjab

There are two routes north from Sukkur into **Punjab**. The west route travels via **Shikarpur** (42 kilometres), **Kandkhot** (64 kilometres), former outpost of the Sind Horse Regiment, **Kashmor** (47 kilometres), famous for its lacquer work and Baluch rugs, and onto **Dera Ghazi Khan** (346 kilometres).

The east route passes through the town of **Ghotki** (67 kilometres). The main mosque, built in 1747 by Pir Musan Shah, is one of the largest of its era in Sind. Constructed of burnt bricks, 35 metres long and 20 metres wide, it has an extensive courtyard and is surmounted by a cupola covered with glazed tiles. The NH continues north via **Ubauro** (41 kilometres), site of a mosque built in 1552, onto **Reti**, the last railway stop in Sind. 12 kilometres south of here, on a dry former bed of the Indus, lie the ancient ruins of **Vijnot**. A contemporary of Brahmanabad, this extensive city is believed to have been destroyed by an earthquake. It is also thought to be the 'Pinchen-po-pu-lu' mentioned by the Chinese traveller Hiuen Tsang. The NH continues north to **Sadiqabad** (29 kilometres), in **Punjab**. For detailed description of routes north to Lahore (but described in reverse, ie north-south), see Punjab chapter (page 290).

Baluchistan

Baluchistan

Text Divisions

An old saying, variously ascribed to the Pathans or Persians, describes this huge tract of land as "the dump where Allah shot the rubbish of creation". While the saying is a reference to the often barren and inhospitable landscape, strewn with the forbidding mountainous rubble of geological processes, it also neatly encapsulates many people's attitude towards Baluchistan. Despite, or perhaps because of, its strategic significance, it remains the least developed province of Pakistan, and the least accessible. Distances are enormous, roads (often little more than dirt tracks) are relatively few in number, and there is just one rail link with the rest of the country. Yet Baluchistan is also a land of stunning beauty and bewildering contrasts. The hospitality and warm, open friendliness of its people meanwhile make the physical difficulties of exploring this fascinating region all the more rewarding.

Best time to visit *Generally speaking, spring (March to May) and autumn (September to November) are the ideal times. This is when the days are pleasantly cool and the air crisp and haze-free, though at night it gets distinctly chilly. In spring the valleys are carpeted in wild flowers, and in autumn the orchards heavy with ripe fruits. The summer months are very hot, even in Quetta, though the nearby hill resort of Ziarat averages a pleasant 27°C. Down on the plains, for example at Sibi, summer temperatures reach as high as 52°C. During winter it gets bitterly cold throughout the province, with temperatures dropping to as low as minus 19°C at Ziarat, and minus 2°C in Sibi.*

Ins and outs

Travel in Baluchistan

Aside from the huge distances involved, and the often poorly developed infrastructure, the greatest obstacles facing tourists are the tight restrictions placed on travel in the province by the Provincial Government. This is due to the perceived threat of kidnapping and banditry in the region. There are areas where banditry or feuding amongst different tribal groups presents a danger, and there have indeed been a number of isolated, but highly publicized, incidents involving foreigners over the years. However, most officials, particularly those who actually live and work in Baluchistan, admit that the dangers have been vastly exaggerated. The Baluch, Brahui and Pathan tribes of Baluchistan are in fact amongst the most warm-hearted, sociable and hospitable people one could hope to meet, and this is overwhelmingly reflected in most peoples' experiences.

At the time of going to press, the following routes were classified as **open**; Quetta to Sukkur via the Bolan Pass; Quetta to Karachi via Khuzdar and Kalat on the RCD Highway; Quetta to Taftan, on the Iranian Border; Quetta to Dera Ghazi Khan via Ziarat or via Qila Saifullah. **NB** Foreigners are allowed to travel freely along these routes, but not to divert off the main highways. The following routes and areas were classified as **restricted**; Quetta to Chaman, on the Afghanistan border; Quetta to Dera Ismail Khan via Zhob (Fort Sandeman); the Makran Coast.

Applying for Permits

Applications for permits (known as 'No Objection Certificates', or 'NOCs') to travel through restricted areas should be made directly to the Home Department of the Provincial Government in Quetta (see under Useful Addresses in the Quetta Directory). You will need to provide a precise itinerary, with dates, and a photocopy of the relevant pages of your passport, including the visa page. Under recommendations passed by the Provincial Government in 1997, permits (where granted) are supposed to be issued within one day. In practice however you should be prepared for quite a bit of waiting around. **NB** Obtaining permits for restricted areas is significantly easier if you are travelling as a part of a package tour. Jeep 'safaris' along the Makran coast for example are perfectly possible if organized through a recognized tour operator.

Background

People

There are three main tribal groups in Baluchistan; the **Baluch**, **Brahui** and **Pathans**. The term Baluch, literally meaning 'wanderer' or 'nomad', is often used very loosely to describe the various tribes inhabiting Baluchistan. In some contexts it indicates a class rather than an ethnic group, as in Makran where the Baluch were traditionally a land owning middle class.

The origins of the Baluch and Brahui are unclear. Their own popular belief, based on ballads and legends, traces their ancestry back to two tribes, the Baluch and Kurds, who inhabited the Aleppo valley in Syria before migrating slowly eastwards through Persia and finally settling in what became known as Baluchistan. The Kurds arrived first, settling around Kalat, where they still dominate. They were known as the *Brahimi*, after Mir Ibrahim who led them through Persia, which evolved into the *Brahui* of today. The Baluch, who had stayed longer in Aleppo, were finally driven out by the Umayyads and spread out along the sea coast, arriving in Baluchistan later. Others suggest that the Baluch were Aryans who migrated from northern Iran in the 11th century, or that they are of Arab extraction and arrived shortly before the Arab invasions of the seventh century. The Brahui are considered by some to be of Dravidian origin, their language bearing many similarities to south Indian languages such as Telegu.

The Pathans are now the largest tribal group in Baluchistan, their numbers having been swelled by the arrival of Afghan refugees in huge numbers. The Pathans are found mostly in the northeast of Baluchistan, their traditional home being around Takht-e-Suleiman, although sizeable minorities exist elsewhere in the province, particularly in the east, around Sibi.

The Tribal System

There are in effect two tribal systems in Baluchistan. Amongst Pathans it is based on a close kinship amongst groups descended from a common ancestor. The Baluch and Brahui tribes on the other hand represent a confederacy which is more a political entity, with groups of separate origin clustering round a head group or *Sardar Khel*. In Makran, the various groups live independently of each other, with no tribal system uniting them.

Bride Price

Amongst many of the Pathan and Baluch tribes of Baluchistan and NWFP, and also in some parts of Sind, the system of bride price is practised. In contrast to the dowry system practised in the Punjab, payment is made by the bridegroom and his family to the bride's parents. The money is then used towards the wedding expenses and to equip the bride appropriately when she moves to her husband's household. Amongst more affluent families, land and other fixed property is often given. Critics of the system point out that the bride price often either comes straight back to the bridegroom's family on their marriage, or is kept by the bride's family and used for other purposes. In a system of arranged marriages, a bride may be 'sold off' to the highest bidder, with no consideration of her interests.

Literature

The Baluch and Brahui tribes have a long oral tradition of poetry, folk songs and ballads. These formed the only means by which tribal histories could be handed down from generation to generation. The *Daptar Shah* is a Chronicle of Genealogies in verse form, and much of the early history of Baluchistan is pieced together from such oral traditions. Many ballads date from the Rind era (1400-1600) and relate in colourful detail the epic battles fought between the different tribes, the origins of their feuding and the heroic deeds of their warriors. When not dealing with war, the ballads tell of tragic and passionate romances. During the Ahmadzai period (1600-1850), the poetic literature becomes more complex and introspective, reflecting perhaps the greater stability and safety of the times. It was only towards the end of this period that some of these ballads and poetry began to be committed to writing, partly through the work of various European scholars. Today the literary tradition in Baluchistan remains strong, and there is many a young poet willing to perform his verses in front of appreciative audiences.

Vegetation and wildlife

Despite the image of Baluchistan as a barren wasteland, the province contains the largest reserves of **Juniper forests** in South Asia, and the second largest in the world, with two large tracts around Ziarat and Loralai covering approximately 85,000 hectares. Other smaller tracts are found around Kalat to the south and in the Suleiman mountains to the north. The species found in Baluchistan is *Juniperus excelsa*, known as *Apurs* in Brahui and *Obusht* in Pashto. It is extremely slow-growing, increasing by just one metre in 60 years. The largest trees are estimated to be in the order of 2,000 years old. Due to its slow rate of growth, the Juniper is under severe threat in Baluchistan (as elsewhere in south Asia) where it is cut for firewood and building materials. It is protected under law, although restrictions on the felling of this tree are difficult to implement and the existing tracts continue to decrease in size. As well as their inherent value in providing protection against soil erosion, these forests also harbour a wide range of associated flora and fauna, including many important medicinal plants. Other important trees found in Baluchistan include **pistachio**, **wild olive**, **tamarisk**, **pine** and *Pesh Mazri*, a kind of small palm.

Baluchistan is home to the **Chiltan Markhor**, a distinct sub-species of wild goat that in now endemic to the province and found only in the Hazerganji Chiltan National Park, just outside of Quetta. The **Baluchistan Black Bear**, related to the Himalayan Brown Bear, is also unique to Baluchistan. Wolves and jackals are found in the hills, as well as foxes, wild ass, wild boar and occasionally leopards. Important birds include the **Chakor**, a distinctive game bird, and several migratory species, including the **Houbara Bustard**, sand grouse, cranes and various duck, which pass through Baluchistan on their way from Central Asia to warmer winter habitats in India and Pakistan. All of these have come under threat from excessive hunting, which despite legislation to control it, remains widespread amongst the élites of Pakistan. The Houbara Bustard in particular is threatened by visitors from the Gulf States, who hunt the bird with falcons.

Quetta

Phone code: 081
Colour map 3, grid B1

Quetta, the provincial capital of Baluchistan, was regarded at the turn of the century as one of the most desirable stations in the north of British India, and was popularly known as 'Little London'. The wide, tree-lined main boulevards and spacious cantonment still survive, but today Quetta has been overtaken by heavy traffic and pollution and the image of a city "refreshed by jasmine scented breezes" is one that is sadly long gone. All the same, at an altitude of 1,676 metres above sea level, its climate is refreshingly cooler than on the plains. Surrounded by high mountains of bare rock – the steep slopes of Murdar rising immediately to the east, Takatu and Zarghun further off to the north, and Chiltan to the west – its setting is a dramatic one. Nearly half the population of Baluchistan live within an 80 kilometre radius of Quetta, with the town itself having a fairly even mix of Pathans, Baluch and Brahui.

Ins and outs

Getting there Quetta is very remote from the rest of Pakistan; unless you are coming from or heading to Iran, a visit here involves a lengthy detour. Given the distances involved, by far the easiest way to reach Quetta is by air. PIA offers regular connections with Karachi, Lahore, Islamabad, Peshawar and a number of smaller towns. Flights should be booked well in advance as they are often full. Rail services to and from Karachi have been greatly improved by the introduction of the *Baluchistan Express*, which makes the journey in just 15 hours (as opposed to 22 or 25 hours on the other express services). The rail journeys to Lahore, Rawalpindi and Peshawar are extremely long (25, 31 and 38 hours respectively), since the train must first head southeast, over the Bolan Pass and down to Rohri (near Sukkur) before joining the main railway artery between Karachi and Peshawar. Unless you have a sleeper, you really need to break the journey. Quetta is also connected by rail with Zahedan (Iran) via the Taftan border crossing, though this journey is much quicker by bus. A combination of a/c coaches, buses, Coasters and minibuses operate along all the routes radiating from Quetta.

Getting around

Auto-rickshaws are the main form of local transport in Quetta. Taxis are readily available, and will also undertake longer journeys from Quetta. The local bus service is useful for getting to and from the long-distance bus station, but it is generally crowded, and not that easy to get to grips with. The centre of Quetta is reasonably compact and can be covered fairly easily on foot.

History

Known originally as Shal or Shalkot, Quetta is thought to have existed as a permanent settlement since prehistoric times. The old fort in the north of the city (the name Quetta is derived from 'kwatta', meaning 'fort' in Pashto), is situated on a low mound formed of the debris of continuous occupation, perhaps for 11,000 years. In 1883, the British started excavations to build an arsenal in the fort and unearthed various items, including a prehistoric ring-stone and corn crusher made of jasper, and a Greek bronze statue of Heracles, suggesting links with the Graeco-Bactrian Empire. It is also likely that Alexander's general Crateros marched via Quetta on his return to Persia earlier in 326 BC. Just a quarter of the total depth of the mound was excavated and today the fort remains in use by the military. In 1985, during excavation work for the building of the Serena Hotel just 500 metres away, more items were discovered, including two gold bullocks, alabaster and terracotta vases and two semi-precious stones set in gold.

Until the rise of Brahui power in the 18th century, Quetta's fortunes were closely linked to those of Afghanistan and Persia. It formed part of the kingdoms of Amir Sabuktagin and Mahmud of Ghazni during the 11th century, before passing into the hands of their successors, the Ghorids. Later, Kandahar and with it Quetta was ruled by the Mongols under Ghengis Khan. The Mughal emperor Hamayun stopped in Quetta on his retreat from India in 1543 and his son Akbar controlled it until 1556, when it was lost to the Persians before being retaken 40 years later.

The British first occupied Quetta between 1839-1842, at the time of the First Afghan War when it formed part of Kalat state, but then abandoned it until 1877 when it was permanently occupied under a treaty between the British and the Khan of Kalat. Despite its strategic importance between the Bolan and Khojak passes, it was not until after this time that Quetta grew into a regional centre of any significance, at the hub of rail and road links with the rest of the empire and its frontiers. In 1935 the town was almost completely destroyed by a devastating earthquake. Only the cantonment area to the north of the Habib Nullah survived; nearly all of the areas to the south date from after this time.

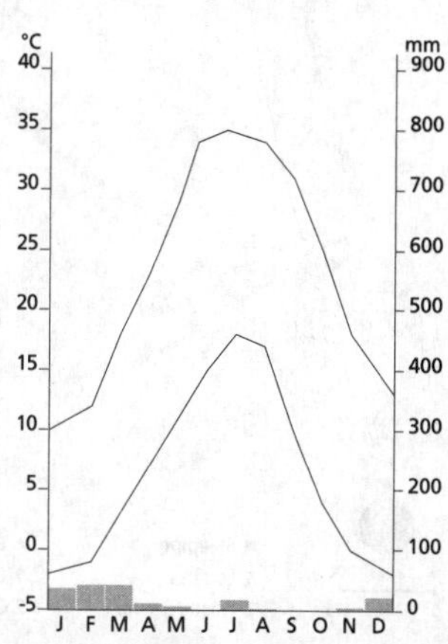

The best time to visit is between March-May or September-November

Sights

With most of the city dating from after 1935, Quetta has little in the way of historic attractions. The two museums, though very small, are both worth a visit. The bazaars meanwhile are colourful and lively, and have a wide range of excellent handicrafts on offer, both Baluchi and Afghan (see below under

Shopping). There are also several interesting excursions which can be undertaken from Quetta (see below under Around Quetta).

Baluchistan Archaeological Museum Originally established in 1906 as the McMahon Museum, it was devastated in the 1935 earthquake. Many of the exhibits were also destroyed, while others were transferred to Calcutta. The museum was re-established in 1972 and since then has been shifted to different premises several times. It is currently hidden away in a small rented building on Fifal Road, to the east of the centre

Quetta: Overview

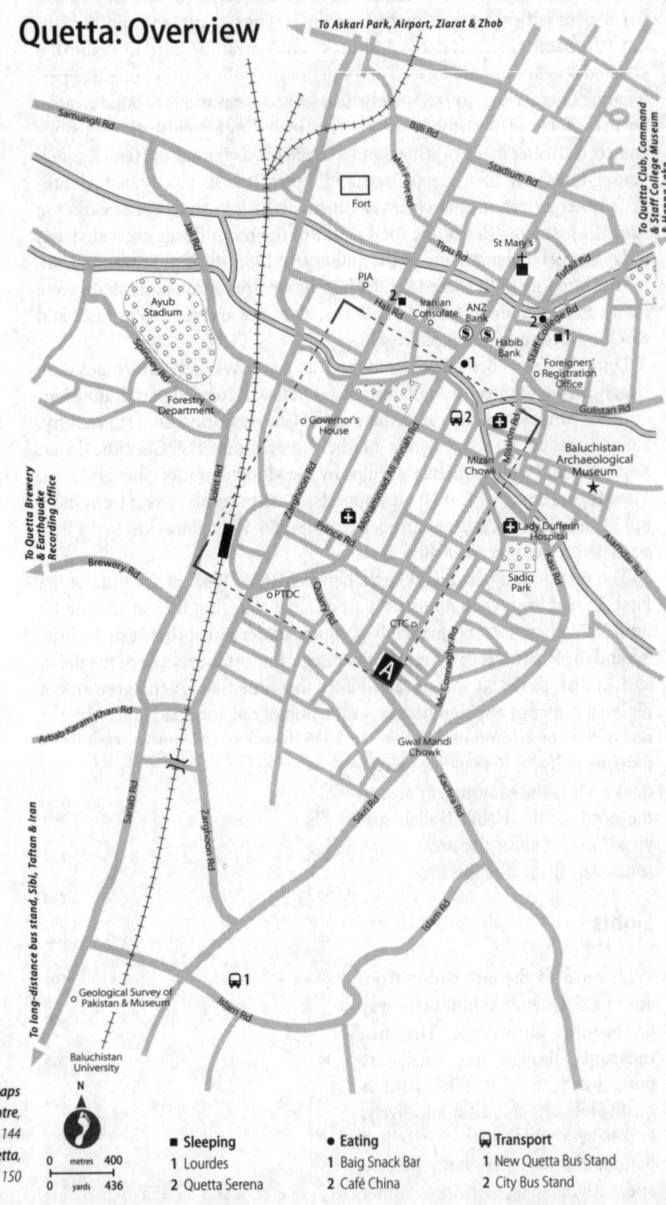

Related maps
A Quetta Centre, page 144
Around Quetta, page 150

Sleeping
1 Lourdes
2 Quetta Serena

Eating
1 Baig Snack Bar
2 Café China

Transport
1 New Quetta Bus Stand
2 City Bus Stand

of town. The search continues for a larger, more central and permanent home for the collection.

Most interesting are the intricately modelled figurines, beautifully decorated pottery pieces, ceramic tiles and terracotta seals from various sites around Baluchistan, dating back as far as 3500 BC, including some recent additions from Mehrgarh and Naushero. Other stone and shell implements date from around 7000 BC. There is also an armoury, with various antique guns and swords, including one sword which was supposedly used to kill a British commander, and a collection of Persian and Arabic manuscripts and Qur'ans, including one written by Aurangzeb.

■ *0800-1400, Friday 0800-1200, closed Sunday. Rs 2. The location of the museum seems an unlikely one, being tucked away down a residential street. Follow Alamdar Road east from Mizan Chowk, turn left and then first right and follow this street until you arrive at the museum on your left, opposite a mosque.*

Command and Staff College Museum

Built in 1905, this was the residence of Colonel (later Field Marshal) Montgomery, before being inaugurated as a museum in 1979 by President Zia. There is an interesting collection of military regalia, as well as oil paintings, photos, albums and Montgomery's original office furniture. The Command and Staff College still has a high reputation internationally and there are usually officers based here on exchange visits from around the world.

■ *Off Staff College Road, Cantonment (follow Staff College Road northeast for approximately three kilometres and turn left at a roundabout to enter the compound in which it is situated; you will be asked for ID, so bring your passport). 1500-1730 in winter and 1700-1930 in summer. Free. It is best to arrange your visit in advance with the army administration, T920917-6611, though getting hold of the right person can be difficult; employ the help of the PTDC or CTC.*

Earthquake Recording Office

Brewery Road leads east out of town, past Quetta Brewery, and then climbs steeply up towards the Earthquake Recording Office, situated on Chiltan Hill. On the way up, there are commanding views out over Quetta and the surrounding mountains.

Essentials

Sleeping

■ *on maps*
Price codes: *see inside front cover*

L ***Quetta Serena***, Shahrah-e-Zarghoon, PO Box 109, T820071, F820070. The only international-standard luxury hotel in Quetta, this establishment also has lots of character. Tastefully built and furnished to reflect traditional Baluchi architecture, right down to the smallest details of the room décor. Centrally located with pleasant gardens and orchards within the grounds. All business and recreational facilities including conference/function rooms, swimming, tennis and squash, as well as access to the nearby Quetta Golf Club. Excellent restaurants (see under Eating, below). Selection of shops in lobby and Bazaar Court. Foreign exchange. All usual guest services, as well as baby sitting. Recommended.

A ***Lourdes***, Staff College Rd, PO Box 68, T829656, F841352. This is the oldest hotel in Quetta. Comfortable rooms with all mod cons. Pleasant gardens. **Camping** allowed, very good value at Rs 80 per person, with use of toilet/shower facilities. Also parking for camper vans et cetera (bus/truck Rs 350, van/car Rs 250, motorcycles Rs 150). Restaurant. Used by many of the overland companies, this can be a good place to find out the latest information on travel in Iran. Recommended

C ***Qasr-e-Gul***, Suraj Ganj Bazaar, T825192. Comfortable rooms with a/c, TV/dish and attached bath. Restaurant. Centrally located.

D *Gul's Inn*, Ali Bhoy Rd, T821926, F63145. Rather tatty (and very '70s) rooms with fan, TV/dish, phone and attached bath. Restaurant. Centrally located but overpriced. **D** *Islamabad*, MA Jinnah Rd, T824006. Clean rooms with a/c, fan, TV/dish, phone and attached bath. Also slightly cheaper non-a/c rooms. Restaurant. Modern, rather characterless hotel. **D** *Qasr-e-Naz*, MA Jinnah Rd, T822821. Spotlessly clean rooms with fan, TV/dish, phone and attached bath. Modern, rather characterless hotel. **D** *Quetta International*, Prince Rd, T836574, F836573. Modern hotel with a glass extravaganza of a lobby. Clean rooms with fan, TV/dish, phone and attached bath. Restaurant.

Quetta Centre

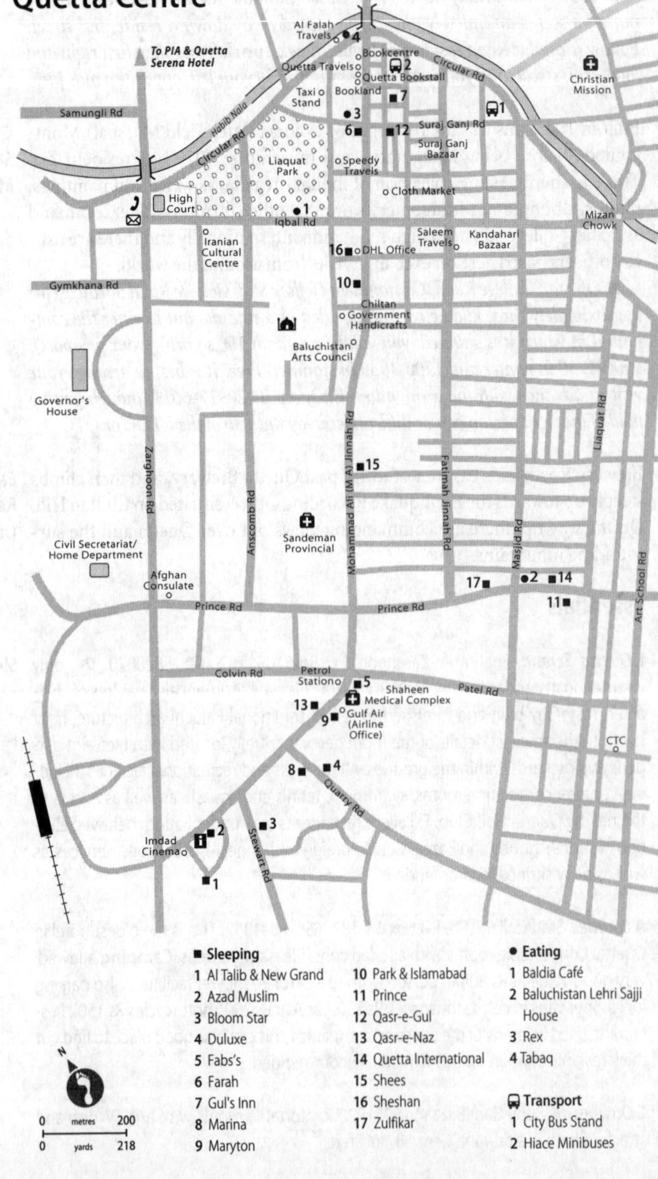

Baluchistan

E *Shees*, MA Jinnah Rd, T823015. Reasonable rooms with fan, TV/dish, phone and attached bath. Restaurant. **E *Bloom Star***, Stewart Rd, T833350, F833353. Clean, comfortable rooms with fan and attached bath. Lovely, quiet garden. Off-road parking. Restaurant. Well run, very pleasant hotel. Good value. Recommended. **E *Deluxe***, Quarry Rd, T831537. Spotlessly clean rooms with fan, phone and attached bath. Restaurant. Nice, but a bit noisy. **E *Fabs's***, MA Jinnah Rd, T825762. Spotlessly clean rooms with fan, TV/dish and attached bath. Recently opened hotel with a very 'Islamic' feel to it. **E *Farah***, MA Jinnah Rd, T844064. Rather run-down rooms with fan, phone and attached bath. Restaurant. **E *Marina***, Quarry Rd, T840765. Clean room with fan and attached bath arranged around central concrete courtyard. Also more expensive rooms with a/c, phone and TV/dish. **E *Maryton***, MA Jinnah Rd, T/F825764. Clean rooms with fan, TV, phone and attached bath. Modern, rather nondescript building. **E *Sheshan***, off MA Jinnah Rd, T844461. Simple but clean rooms in modern building with fan, phone and attached bath, some rooms with balcony. Restaurant. **E *Zulfiqar***, Prince Rd, T822720, F822634. Reasonable rooms with fan, phone and attached bath (and TV/dish for Rs 50 extra). Pleasant, peaceful small courtyard/garden. Restaurant. Recommended.

E/F *New Grand*, MA Jinnah Rd, behind Imdad Cinema, T843906. Simple but large, pleasant rooms with fan and attached bath.

F *Al Talib*, off MA Jinnah Rd, behind Imdad Cinema, T843906 (shares phone with *New Grand* hotel). Lovely old building. Simple but large, pleasant rooms with fan and attached bath. Quiet, secluded garden. Recommended. **F *Azad Muslim***, MA Jinnah Rd, T824269. Rather tatty rooms with fan and attached bath arranged around courtyard/garden. Off-road parking. Popular with budget travellers and another good place for picking up current information on overland travel through Iran. PTDC information centre. Restaurant. **F *Park***, MA Jinnah Rd, T843649. Small, mediocre rooms with fan, phone and attached bath. **F *Prince***, Prince Rd, T842662. Reasonably clean rooms with fan and attached bath.

Eating

● *on maps*

Chinese At the top of the range, the *Quetta Serena* hotel's ***Xuelian*** restaurant offers excellent à la carte Chinese cuisine for around Rs 500 per head upwards. The popular ***Café China***, Staff College Rd (opposite Lourdes Hotel), T841367, is more modest, but serves good Chinese meals for around Rs 200-250 per head. It can get very busy and may be worth booking in advance.

Pakistani/continental The *Quetta Serena* hotel's ***Ziarat Coffee Shop*** offers breakfasts and excellent lunch (1200-1500) and evening (1900-2300) barbecue buffets of Pakistani and continental cuisine (Rs 310 and Rs 315 respectively). If you want to treat yourself without completely ruining your budget, this is the place to do it. Many of the other hotels in Quetta also have restaurants serving a variety of Pakistani and continental cuisine; the restaurants at the ***Qasr-e-Gul*** and ***Farah*** hotels are both reasonable. You can eat well at either for around Rs 200 per head.

The ***Rex*** restaurant, off MA Jinnah Rd, serves reasonable continental and Pakistani cuisine for around Rs 100-150 per head, as does the ***Tabaq***, on Circular Rd (and also some Chinese dishes). There are several cheap restaurants on Circular Road, just to the west of *Tabaq*, serving good curries, *karahis* et cetera.

Sajji houses Quetta is famous for its *sajji*, which consists of whole legs of lamb roasted on an open fire. Traditionally this is served with extra-thin *roti* and goats' milk yoghurt. There are several places which specialize in *sajji* and serve nothing else. Two good ones are the ***Lehri Sajji House***, to the east of MA Jinnah Rd (near *Qasr-e-Gul* restaurant), and ***Baluchistan Lehri Sajji House***, on Prince Rd (near its junction with Masjid Rd). A serving of *sajji* (enough for 2 people) costs around Rs 200.

Snack bars and juice stalls There are several snack bars and juice stalls at the north end of MA Jinnah Road and in the streets around *Gul's Inn* and *Qasr-e-Gul* hotel. The snack bars serve a mixture of Western-style fast foods (burgers, chips et cetera) and Pakistani snacks (roast chicken, samosas et cetera). The juice stalls serve excellent freshly squeezed fruit juices and milkshakes.

Cafés The ***Baldia Café*** has outdoor seating in a pleasant patio garden. It has a nice, relaxed atmosphere about it, being a popular place amongst locals to meet, exchange gossip and read the papers. You can enjoy a pot of tea or cold drink here, and they also serve snacks and light meals from 1200-1500 (not Friday).

Bakeries There are a couple of good bakeries on Circular Road, opposite the *Tabaq* restaurant, which sell hot snacks as well as groceries, cakes, sweets and other goodies.

Entertainment To the northwest of Quetta centre, on the road to the airport, is the large, recently-established **Askari Park**. During the summer, regular cultural events are held here; contact the CTC (see under tourist offices) for more information. ***Baluchistan Arts Council*** (*Idra Saqafat*), MA Jinnah Rd, T824016, has occasional cultural events including music, theatre and poetry, and is a good source of information on other cultural events in Quetta. Attached to it is an Art Gallery, which exhibits works by contemporary local artists, while upstairs there is the Sandeman Library. The *Serena* hotel also occasionally hosts cultural events.

Sports The ***Ayub Stadium***, off Jail Rd, has a variety of facilities. Check with CTC or PTDC for details of events here. The ***Golf Club***, Club Rd, off Staff College Rd is part of the ***Quetta Club***, where there are also squash courts. Foreigners can make use of facilities as the guest of a member. The *Serena* hotel has squash and tennis courts, and a swimming pool, which are available to non-guests for a fee. There are facilities for boating on Hanna Lake.

Shopping These days there are far more tourist shops in Quetta than there are tourists, and you will inevitably find yourself having to fend off shop owners and their touts trying to lure you into their shops. Once inside a particular shop you will come under considerable pressure to buy, but it's a good idea to look around to get an idea of what's on offer, and compare quality and prices. There are dozens of tourist shops towards the north end of MA Jinnah Road, selling Baluchi and Afghan carpets, Baluchi embroidery work (often brightly decorated with mirrors), antiques, jewellery, carved onyx, semi-precious stones et cetera. More such places are to be found in the shopping arcades and alleyways around the *Gul's Inn* hotel, in Suraj Ganj Bazaar (to the south of Suraj Ganj Road), and along the northern end of Liaquat Road. Kandahari Bazaar, along the section of Iqbal Road between Fatimah Jinnah Road and Masjid Road (and in the narrow streets just to the south), specializes in Afghan carpets. ***Balochi Art***, on Circular Rd (next door to *Al Falah Travels*), specializes in Baluchi embroidery work, including excellent embroidered caps. The ***Chiltan Government Handicrafts Centre***, off MA Jinnah Rd, has a good selection of handicrafts. Prices are fixed (on the high side, though the quality is good) and you should be able to look around in peace (in theory at least). There are also several tourist shops in the *Quetta Serena* hotel with a wide range of merchandise, though prices here are considerably higher than in the bazaars.

Books There are 3 bookshops close to each other along MA Jinnah Rd (***Bookland***, ***New Quetta Bookstall*** and ***Book Centre***), all with a good selection of books in English, as well as foreign newspapers and magazines. The bookshop at the *Quetta Serena* hotel is also worth trying.

Selected fares and flying times from Quetta

To	*Fare (Rs)*	*Flying time (approximately)*
Karachi	2,440	1 hour 15 minutes
Islamabad	2,920	1 hour 25 minutes
Peshawar	2,620	1 hour 30 minuets
Lahore	2,920	1 hour 25 minutes
Zhob	1,180	1 hour
Dera Ismail Khan	1,480	1 hour 40 minutes (plus stop en route)
Turbat	2,360	2 hours 5 minutes

NB *Flying times are for direct flights by jet (where applicable); on flights to Karachi, Islamabad, Peshawar and Turbat there are also slower Fokker F27 flights which stop en route, and in some cases (notably Quetta-Peshawar) are cheaper.*

Local transport

To/from the airport The easiest way of getting to and from the airport is by taxi. The fare seems to be pretty much fixed at Rs 150 (one way). You may be able to negotiate an auto-rickshaw for slightly less.

Taxi/car hire The main taxi stand is in an open square between Liaquat Park and Circular Rd. There are 2 companies, the ***Pakistan Yellow Taxi Federation***, T844031 and the ***Quetta Taxi Stand***, T844032. Journeys within Quetta should not cost more than Rs 100. The former quotes considerably cheaper prices for long-distance journeys. Note that for long-distance journeys, fares vary according to road conditions as well as distance. The following return fares were being quoted in 1998 (but be sure to establish clearly how long you wish to spend at a place, as this will obviously also effect the price); Hanna Lake Rs 600; Hazerganji Chiltan National Park Rs 800; Ziarat Rs 1,700; Bolan Pass Rs 1,500; Sibi Rs 2,000 (one way); Chaman Rs 2,000. Ask at PTDC for hire of four-wheel drive vehicles.

Auto-rickshaws These are ubiquitous in Quetta and the main form of local transport. Perhaps because their engines are not adjusted for the higher altitude, their exhaust fumes are particularly noxious, billowing out in a thick blue cloud. Fares are more or less fixed (Rs 20-50 depending on the distance/time). Some drivers try to charge tourists higher rates, but less so than elsewhere in Pakistan.

Bus Local buses operate between the City Bus Stand on Circular Road and the Long-Distance Bus Station on Sariab Road, to the south of Quetta. There are also local bus services between the City Bus Stand to the New Quetta Bus Stand.

Long-distance transport

Air Airport T880166. Quetta is served only by PIA, which operates flights to **Karachi** 1-4 daily; **Islamabad** 1-2 daily; **Peshawar** 1 daily except Friday; **Lahore** Monday, Tuesday, Friday, Sunday; **Sukkur** Monday, Friday; **Dera Ismail Khan** Wednesday, Thursday, Sunday; **Dera Ghazi Khan** Sunday; **Zhob** Wednesday, Thursday, Sunday; **Turbat** Monday, Tuesday, Friday, Sunday; **Panjgur** Wednesday, Sunday; **Dalbandin** Tuesday, Sunday.

Train Booking office T9201066. Enquiries T117. The booking office is located in a separate building directly opposite the main entrance to the station. Sleepers and a/c must be booked well in advance; they often sell out as soon as they go on sale (15 days before the departure date)

Selected rail fares from Quetta (in Rupees)

To	A/c Sleeper	A/c Sitter	1st Sleeper	Economy
Karachi	*1,019*	*591*	*400*	*180*
Peshawar	*1,755*	*1,013*	*704*	*330*
Rawalpindi	*1,586*	*912*	*630*	*295*
Lahore	*1,317*	*760*	*518*	*240*
Multan	*1,002*	*580*	*389*	*175*
Chaman	—	*152*	—	*35*

Peshawar: *Abbaseen Exp* (via Jacobabad, Sukkur, Multan, Faisalabad and 'Pindi), 1800, 38 hours.

Rawalpindi: *Quetta Exp* (via Jacobabad, Sukkur, Multan and Lahore), 1130, 31 hours; the *Abbasseen Exp* is slightly slower, taking 33½ hours, and if on time arrives in 'Pindi at an ungodly hour.

Lahore: *Chiltan Exp* (via Jacobabad, Dera Ghazi Khan and Multan), 1300, 29½ hours; the *Quetta Exp* is faster, taking 25 hours.

Karachi: *Baluchistan Exp* (via Hyderabad), Monday, Thursday, Saturday, 1730, 15 hours; *Bolan Mail* (via Jacobabad, Larkana and Moenjo Daro), 1515, 22 hours; *Sind Exp* (via Jacobabad and Hyderabad), 2000, 25 hours.

Sibi: all of the services listed above stop in Sibi, taking around 5 hours.

Chaman: *Q-847*, Wednesday, Friday, Sunday, 0900, 4¼ hours, departs from Chaman for the return journey at 1445.

Zahedan (Iran): *Taftan Exp* (via Taftan border crossing), Saturday, 0815, 32 hours (**NB** actual journey time to Zahedan depends on border formalities, to Taftan is 24 hours), leaves Zahedan each Monday at 1725 for the return journey.

Bus The **Long-Distance Bus Station** has been moved to a ridiculously inconvenient location around 8 kilometres to the south of Quetta. Bus and coach services operate from here to most major towns and cities in Pakistan.

The **New Quetta Bus Stand** (also inconveniently located to the south of the main city, close to Satellite Town), which was originally the starting point for long-distance services, now officially only has services to 'local' destinations within Baluchistan, although some long-distance buses still operate from here.

A number of **private coach companies** have booking offices along the southern end of MA Jinnah Road, with overnight services to **Karachi** and **Taftan**.

Hiace minibuses operate from the streets just to the east of the north end of MA Jinnah Road, near the *Gul's Inn* hotel. There are fairly regular services from here to **Ziarat**, **Loralai**, **Zhob**, **Dera Ghazi Khan** and **Chaman**. The frequency of services depends very much on the season and passenger demand.

The **City Bus Stand** also has some Hiace minibus services for **Ziarat**, though this bus stand is mostly for local services within Quetta.

Directory **Airline offices** ***PIA Booking Office***, 17 Hali Rd, T820861. Open 7 days, 0800-1800. Efficient service for both domestic and international bookings. ***Gulf Air***, MA Jinnah Rd, T839849. You can reconfirm international flights with other airlines at any of the travel agents listed below. **Banks** ***Habib Bank***, Habib Bank Complex, at the junction of MA Jinnah Rd and Gulistan Rd (see Quetta Overview map) exchanges cash and TCs quickly and efficiently. ***ANZ Grindlays***, opposite Habib Bank, gives cash advances against Visa cards. They charge a flat rate of Rs 500 for cashing TCs. Most of the tourist shop owners in Quetta are also in the unofficial money changing business, and will change cash (and sometimes TCs) at the higher 'kerbside' rate. **Communications** **Post:** The GPO is on Zarghoon Rd, opposite the junction with Iqbal Rd. Open 0800-1400, 1500-1900, closed Sun. The poste restante counter is only open in the morning. **Telephone:** The telegraph office is next door to the GPO. Open 7 days, 24 hrs. You can make international calls from here, and send faxes (though they will insist on keeping the original!) and telexes. **Internet:** The *Serena* hotel offers Internet access at its ***Global Business Centre***, though its rates are exorbitant (Rs 500 per hour for Internet access, or Rs 100 per email message sent). Much better value is ***Geonet***, Serena Bazaar (within the hotel grounds, but an independent outfit run by the friendly Sher Bahadur), T835380. Rs 150 per hour for Internet access (minimum 30 minutes). **Courier:** ***DHL*** have an office on MA Jinnah Rd, T844421. **Embassies & consulates** *Iranian Consulate*, Hali Rd, T843098. Open 0800-1500, closed Fri. In 1998 the situation regarding applying for Iranian transit visas in Quetta appeared to have dramatically improved, with the consulate here claiming to issue transit visas routinely within around 10 days. You need to bring along a couple of passport photos, fill out a form and pay the relevant fee (they were quoting fees of Rs 3,100 for UK nationals, Rs 1,900 for Australians and free for US citizens!). Note however that the situation regarding Iranian transit visas can (and often does) change very suddenly. Check first before making the journey to Quetta in the expectation of a transit visa; it's a long way back to Islamabad. ***Afghan Consulate***, Prince Rd, T9202681, F9202549. This consulate represents the Taliban regime in Afghanistan. At the time of writing it was only issuing press visas for Afghanistan with authorization from the embassy in Islamabad. There is no British Consulate, but there is a **British Representative** in Quetta (currently Mr Malcom Bennett); c/o Sir William Halcrow and Partners Ltd, BCIP, House 231/233, Block 4, Taktu Rd, Sattelite Town, Quetta, T440790, F443263. **Hospitals & medical services Hospitals:** ***Sandeman Provincial Hospital***, MA Jinnah Rd, T9203334 (casualty). ***Saleem Medical Complex***, MA Jinnah Rd, T827104. ***Lady Dufferin Hospital***, McConnaghy Rd, T821488. ***Christian Hospital***, Mission Rd (also known as Mission Hospital), T824906. **Chemists:** There are a number of chemists along MA Jinnah Rd, most opposite the hospital complex. There are more at the entrance to the ***Saleem Medical Complex*** hospital, and a 24 hr dispensary inside, opposite the enquiry desk. **Tour companies & travel agents** The following travel agents are able to book and reconfirm domestic and international flights; ***Al-Falah Travels***, Circular Rd, T824681. ***Quetta Travels***, MA Jinnah Rd, T842903, F844029. ***Speedy Travels***, Adalat Rd, T836592, F836595. **Tourist offices** *PTDC Tourist Information Centre*, Azad Muslim Hotel, MA Jinnah Rd, T825826. Open 0900-1500, Fri 0900-1200, closed Sunday. Helpful and friendly staff, able to offer good advice on current travel conditions in Baluchistan. The PTDC Motels at Ziarat and Khuzdar can also be booked here. ***Culture and Tourism Cell*** (CTC), Najmuddin Rd, T828417. The CTC was established by the provincial government to promote culture and tourism in Baluchistan. Although still limited in terms of resources, they are very helpful. They operate a number of their own motels and resthouses in Baluchistan, including at Ziarat and Loralai, and plan to open their own Tourist Information Centre. **Useful addresses Police:** (emergency), T15 or T9202555. **Ambulance:** T9203334. **Foreigners' registration:** Office of Deputy Inspector General (DIG) of Police, Special Branch, Staff College Rd, T9201742. Open 0900-1500, Fri 0900-1200, closed Sunday. **Permits and visa extensions:** Political Section II, Home Department, Room 50, Block 1 (1st Flr), T9201878. In theory at least, this office should issue permits to visit restricted areas within 1 day. They can also provide a 7 day extension on 72 hour transit visas obtained at Taftan. **Commissioner:** T9201406. **Deputy Commissioner:** T9202244.

Around Quetta

Hanna Lake and Urak Valley

A popular outing is to Hanna Lake, 10 kilometres east of Quetta. The lake is surrounded by bare mountains and has been developed into a picnic spot with two cafés, *Lake View* and *Oasis*, offering snacks and drinks. Small picnic huts of dubious aesthetic quality are dotted around the lake. There is a children's playground and boats for hire giving access to a tiny artificial island in the centre of the lake. During the summer it gets very busy, particularly on holidays.

The Urak Valley is particularly beautiful in spring and autumn, when its plentiful orchards are in blossom or laden with fruit. The village of Urak is at the top of the valley and close by is Urak Tangi, another popular picnic spot with a small restaurant, open from April to September.

Ins and outs

Leave Quetta on Staff College Road and continue straight on at the roundabout and turning for the Command and Staff College Museum, taking the next major turning right onto Urak road. There are several simple restaurants along the way serving tea, cold drinks and food. Just after a check post, fork left and soon after fork left again (right to Urak valley). The route is well signposted. During summer there are regular buses from the City Bus Stand. A taxi will cost around Rs 600 return.

Hazerganji Chiltan National Park

Situated 20 kilometres southwest of Quetta, to the west of the Mustang road, Hazerganji (literally "of a thousand treasures") Chiltan was established as a National Park in 1978. It covers 32,500 acres of hills and valleys in the Chiltan range, including Chiltan Peak (3,264 metres). Its most important inhabitant is the Chiltan Markhor, a wild goat once fairly common in Baluchistan, before being hunted almost to extinction. Now found only in the park, it is registered as an endangered species and carefully protected. The park is also home to the Straight Horned Markhor, 'Gad' wild sheep, leopards, wolves, Striped Hyena, wild cats, hare, porcupine and the Afghan Tortoise, as well as cobras, pythons and vipers. Birds are also plentiful; the Chukor Partridge, whose distinctive call can be heard throughout the park, is the most common. Others include the Seesee Partridge, warblers, shrikes, Rock Nuthatches and Blue Rock Pigeons, as well as Golden Eagles, Bearded Vultures, Sparrow Hawks and Peregrine Falcons. Over 200 species of plants have so far been identified. The main trees are Pistachio, Juniper, Olive, Fig, Ash and Almond. In spring the ground is carpeted in flowering tulips and poppies. There is a small **Natural History Museum** in the park with various pressed dried flowers and grasses and stuffed birds and mammals. From the main road the lower slopes of the park are not readily distinguishable from surrounding areas. Viewed from higher up however, the denser vegetation cover of the fenced off area is clearly visible. Further into the park, much of the area is thickly wooded.

Around Quetta

Ins and outs

Follow Sariab Road south past the University and after 8 kilometres take the right fork (left to Sibi). Around 9 kilometres further on a signposted right turn leads up to the park along a gravel track. The track climbs gently for 3 kilometres to the museum. Further on there is an observation post and nearby a small ***Rest House*** (3 rooms), both of which offer excellent views back down onto the plateau.

You must obtain a **permit** to visit the park, obtainable from the Forestry Department, Spinney Road, Quetta, T9202240. You can also arrange with them to stay in the rest house; well worth it for the splendid views. Rangers are on hand to show you round and point out the wildlife. Allow a minimum of a full day for a worthwhile visit. A taxi will cost around Rs 800 for the return trip. Buses bound for Mustang (which can be caught from the New Quetta Bus Stand) pass the turning for the park. It may also be possible to arrange transport through the Forestry Department.

Zhob narrow-gauge railway

The old narrow-gauge railway line which once connected Quetta with Zhob was closed down in 1985 and has fallen into disrepair. There are, however, plans to reopen a section of the line between Quetta and Muslimbagh. En route, the line passes through Khanozai, billed during the British period as the highest railway station in Asia. If the plan ever gets off the ground, the *Quetta Serena* hotel intends to hire a private carriage (in the past they offered special excursions by train to the Bolan pass, though for the time being at least, these have been discontinued). Check with the *Quetta Serena*, or CTC/PTDC, for details.

Quetta to Ziarat

Follow the route as for Dera Ghazi Khan (see below) as far as **Ziarat Mor** (52 kilometres), continuing straight at this junction. The road climbs up through barren hills of mud and rock. 50 years ago the area was well wooded, but acute deforestation has exposed the land to heavy erosion, creating what appears in places almost to be a moonscape. At **Kach** (72 kilometres) there is a check post and a few tea shops, overlooked by an old fort up on a ridge.

An alternative route to Kach, on a rough jeep track, leaves Quetta on Staff College Road. Continue straight on past the turning right to Hanna Lake. The track winds its way past Kach dam, over a saddle between Takatu and Zarghun mountains, down past the village of Gundak and through denuded hills to Kach, 52 kilometres by this route.

The main road to Ziarat, in poor condition beyond Kach, continues east, following the river past orchards and the small settlements of Kahan, Verchoum, Kawas, Zindra, Chena and Pechi, to arrive at Ziarat. The cover of Juniper trees on the hills gradually increases towards Ziarat. Narrow gorges ('*Tangi*') lead off at various points on either side. The most accessible of these are **Kawas Tangi**, north of Kawas, the **Manna Valley**, north of Zindra, **Fern Tangi**, on a track leading south, just past Pechi, and **Sandeman Tangi**, north of the road just before it passes through the archway marking the start of Ziarat. The latter is the most popular, being easily accessible from Ziarat. All these gorges offer excellent walking and picnic spots.

Ziarat

Phone code: 0833
Colour map 3, grid A2

Ziarat was first developed as a summer retreat by the British. It is the only major hill station in southern Pakistan, and still extremely popular in summer when its climate is pleasantly cool. The season generally runs from April to October. Outside of these months the resort largely closes down; during winter it is usually completely snowbound.

Ins and outs Situated 133 kilometres from Quetta, Ziarat is easily accessible by road. Regular minibuses make the journey in around 3 hours (Rs 50); the frequency of services varies according to the season and demand. A taxi will cost around Rs 1,700-2,000 for the return trip, though visiting Ziarat as a day-trip involves a lot of travelling; an overnight stop here is recommended. Some minibuses operate between Quetta and Loralai via Ziarat (see below), provided the route is passable. The resort's hotels, bus station and various public buildings (post office, telegraph office, hospital etc) are all strung out along the main road as it passes through the town.

Sights The resort itself has a slightly dilapidated atmosphere, though the surrounding hills are a hiker's paradise. The Juniper forests surrounding Ziarat are amongst the oldest in the world, with some of the trees said to be as much as 5,000 years old. Deforestation has however taken its toll, and in places the hillsides have only a thin cover. Under a recent government initiative, gas stoves and subsidized bottles have been distributed amongst the villagers in an attempt to limit the cutting of trees for firewood.

Ziarat was a favourite retreat of Mohammad Ali Jinnah, and the **Quaid-e-Azam's Residency**, in which he spent his last days, has been preserved as a museum, with all the furniture arranged as it was when he died in 1948. Built by the British in 1882, this two-storey building with wooden verandas and balconies is situated up on the hillside looking out over the valley. A jeepable track continues up past the Residency to **Prospect Point** (six kilometres), a massive shoulder of rock which at 2,713 metres gives spectacular views across the whole valley. From higher up on the ridge behind there are views south toward **Mount Khalifat**, the highest peak in Baluchistan at 3,485 metres. Three kilometres further on, the road leads down to the **Shrine of Baba Kharwari**, known popularly as Baba Mian Abdul Hakim. It is from this shrine, or *ziarat*, that the resort gets its name.

Sleeping & eating **NB** Hotels are often heavily booked in summer so it is worth making advance reservations. Prices in the cheaper hotels can become inflated when it is busy. Unless otherwise indicated, hotels close for the winter. **B** ***PTDC Complex***, T356. Comfortable though somewhat overpriced rooms and villa accommodation. Restaurant. Book through PTDC in Quetta. **D** ***Shalimar***, T353. Clean, comfortable rooms. Well run. *Juniper Restaurant*. Recommended. Open all year round. **E** ***Tourist Rest House***, situated at east end of town, no phone. Book through CTC in Quetta. 3 comfortable rooms. Good value. Recommended. Slightly cheaper hotels are around the bus stand, including the **F** ***Grand***, open all year round, and behind it, the **E** ***Sanobar***, T308. Others include the **E** ***Rising Star***, T238, and **E** ***Ziarat***, T226.

Meals at the restaurant of the *PTDC Complex*, or at the *Shalimar* hotel's ***Juniper***, should be booked in advance. There are also a couple of simple Pakistani-style restaurants and snack places around the bus stand.

Quetta to Loralai via Ziarat

The Ziarat road offers a scenic alternative route between Quetta and Loralai. Although more direct, it is much slower than the main route via Muslimbagh and Qila Saifullah, the road being in poor condition for much of the way. To the east of Ziarat the road deteriorates considerably, disappearing altogether for stretches as it follows the stony bed of the river. It is 23 kilometres to **Chautair**, a small village with some basic accommodation. During summer it makes a quieter alternative to Ziarat, and is in some ways more beautiful, the surrounding hills being much more densely wooded. Just before the village, a track leads north to **Chautair Tangi**, giving access to a valley beyond it. The road continues through **Wani**, **Raigora** and **Sanjawi** (62 kilometres). Just before the latter a track leads southwest to Harnai (see below). It is a further 28 kilometres to Loralai, on the route to Dera Ghazi Khan.

An alternative route to Sibi

Around two kilometres to the east of Kach, on the road to Ziarat, a rough track leads off to the right, passing through **Mangi**, **Khost**, **Harnai** and **Spin Tangi** to eventually arrive at Sibi. Before the British secured the Bolan Pass, this was the route used between Sibi and Quetta. The railway line also originally passed this way, but the terrain proved too unstable and it was re-routed through the Bolan Pass. A branch railway line still operates between Sibi and Khost. From Mangi there is access to **Chappar Rift**, a spectacular limestone gorge which cuts through the line of the mountains. This was one of the major obstacles for the railway line and presented a great challenge to the engineers building it. Tunnels were dug through the mountains either side of the rift, which was spanned by an iron girder bridge. The District Gazetteer describes how the work was carried out "... by letting down workmen with ropes from the top of the cliff several hundred feet above the point of operation. The first man down had to gain a footing by driving a crowbar into the perpendicular wall; after the first crowbar others were driven in, and then a platform was erected from which blasting operations could begin. So singular and difficult a piece of engineering has probably seldom or never been accomplished before. Six openings were made on one side of the cliff for one tunnel and six on the other, and galleries driven into them till points were reached from where the main tunnel could be constructed right and left, so that the work could be carried on by 14 separate gangs; and in this way the whole tunnel was blasted out in a few months." From Harnai another track branches north through the **Harnai Gorge** to rejoin the main Ziarat-Loralai road at Sanjawi. The route is a breathtaking one, blasted into the side of a precipitous cliff-face. To explore this fascinating area you need your own four-wheel drive transport, and a guide who is familiar with the terrain.

Quetta to Dera Ghazi Khan via Loralai

If you are heading for Multan or Lahore, the road from Quetta to Dera Ghazi Khan provides a much more direct alternative to the main highway out of Baluchistan (which runs southeast through the Bolan pass via Sibi and Jacobabad, to Sukkur in Sind). The scenery along the way is very beautiful in places.

Ins and outs

There are two roads east from Quetta to Loralai. One via Ziarat and the other via Muslimbagh and Qila Saifullah. They join at Loralai for the remainder of the way to Dera Ghazi Khan. The route via Muslimbagh and Qila Saifullah, described here, is longer but the road is better and considerably faster. See above, under Ziarat, for details of the route via Ziarat. There are regular buses between Quetta and Loralai (an obvious place to break the journey), and between Loralai and Dera Ghazi Khan. There is also a weekly flight from Quetta to Dera Ghazi Khan. At the time of writing, there were no restrictions on travel along this route, nor was it considered particularly dangerous.

Quetta to Loralai

Head northwest out of Quetta on the Chaman road, past the turning for the airport. The road crosses the Chaman railway line and passes through **Baleli Check post.** It is 25 kilometres to **Kuch Lak,** a small town whose population has been swelled significantly by Afghan refugees. Turn right in the main bazaar (straight on for Chaman) and continue on a good two-lane road to the junction known as **Ziarat Mor** (52 kilometres). Turn left here for Muslimbagh (straight on for Ziarat). The road, now single lane, passes rich orchards of apples, plums, almonds and pomegranates to arrive at **Dil Sora** (79 kilometres), a small settlement with simple restaurants and teashops. Further on, the road crosses and re-crosses the old narrow-gauge track, now abandoned, which once connected Quetta with Zhob. **Khanozai** (or Khan Mehtarzai, 96 kilometres) once had the distinction of being the highest railway station in Asia at 2,222 metres. To the north are the mountains of the Toba Kakar range, and beyond the Afghan Border. It is a further 22 kilometres on to **Muslimbagh**, formerly known as Hindubagh. This is the largest village before Loralai, with a reasonably sized bazaar. There is an ***Irrigation Dept Rest House***, although arranging to stay here may be difficult.

Baluchistan

Beyond Muslimbagh, the number of orchards decrease and the landscape gives way to a wide plateau supporting only meagre vegetation. To the south, across the plateau, is a large Afghan refugee camp, known locally as the 'Muslimbagh Mohajir Camp'. The road passes through the small village of Nisai and then once again through scattered orchards, to arrive at the small settlement of **Qila Saifullah** (180 kilometres). This is a popular stopping place with bus and truck drivers, and there are several simple restaurants lining the main road. There is also a basic hotel here, the **E** *Taj*.

Turn right one kilometre beyond Qila Saifullah to head south towards Loralai (straight on for Zhob). The road winds its way up through barren hills, emerging onto a plateau and traversing it. The surrounding scenery is in places quite spectacular, with a distinctive table-topped mountain to the west of the road. It is then a steady, gradual descent, past patches of cultivation, to Loralai, 252 kilometres from Quetta.

Loralai

Phone code: 0821
Colour map, grid B3

Loralai, formerly known as Pathan Kot, is the headquarters of Loralai District. It is a small bazaar town with a separate cantonment area several kilometres to the north which was established by the British between 1890-1897. There is little of interest in the town, which has a vaguely threatening atmosphere to it, perhaps a reflection of the fierce independence of the Pathan tribes which predominate in the area. The complete absence of women is matched only by the abundance of guns and drugs being openly paraded through the bazaar. You are expected to register with the police if staying overnight.

Sleeping & eating

The best accommodation is at the **E** ***CTC Tourist Rest House***, situated in the cantonment area. It has no phone; bookings should be made through the CTC in Quetta (see under Tourist Offices, in the Quetta Directory). Also worth trying is the **E** ***Government Rest House***, which must be booked through the Deputy Commissioner, T2442, or the Assistant Commissioner, T2905. There are a number of fairly basic hotels along the main bazaar in the centre of town. The 2 better ones are the **F** ***Pakiza***, T2417 and **F** ***Spinza***, T3403, both with restaurants. More basic is the **G** ***Gul***, T2437 (hotel sign in Urdu only). As well as the hotel restaurants, there are various basic restaurants in the main bazaar.

Transport

There are fairly regular bus and minibus services to **Dera Ghazi Khan** (8-10 hours) and **Quetta** (5 hours), with several departures through the morning. There is no bus station as such, with buses and minibuses departing from various points along the main bazaar.

Loralai to Fort Munro

East of Loralai the old single-lane road is in poor condition for much of the way, with sections of it having been eroded or washed away. There are several rivers which have to be forded. Repairs are ongoing, with the elements taking their toll each winter. Known in the past as 'Robbers Road', the British never really managed to subdue the tribes of the surrounding countryside. Up until very recently, they continued to raid traffic along this route.

The road passes through green and fertile countryside with fruit orchards intercropped with wheat, and climbs gently through low hills to **Mekhtar** (79 kilometres), a small village with tea shops and basic food. The road then climbs steeply, passing the tiny village of **Kingri** (139 kilometres), before descending steadily to **Rakhni** (184 kilometres), a small bazaar town. Turn left at the T-junction in the bazaar. The road again climbs steeply, this time into the mountains of the Suleiman range, crossing the border into Punjab, to arrive at the village of **Khar** (200 kilometres), where a track leads south to the nearby hill station of Fort Munro.

Fort Munro

Colour map 3, grid B4

Founded by Sir Robert Sandeman and named after Colonel Munro, a former Commissioner of the district, this hill station (1800 metres) was established by the British as a retreat from the summer heat and remains the only one in southern Punjab. It is situated on what appears from below as a steeply-sided, perfectly conical hill. From the main road a track zigzags its way up the side. During summer, it is busy with visiting officials and tribal chiefs, many of whom have their own summer residences here, while in the winter it is all but deserted. Fort Munro has a peaceful air about it and makes a relaxing place to stop. There are plenty of opportunities for walks in the surrounding area.

Sleeping & eating

The only accommodation here is the ideally situated **C** ***TDCP Rest House***, reasonable rooms with attached bath. Good restaurant. Excellent views. Open all year round. Bookings can be made through TDCP in Lahore.

Transport

During the summer there are generally direct bus services between Fort Munro and Dera Ghazi Khan. Irregular buses run to and from Khar on the main road, but out of season you really need your own transport.

Fort Munro to Dera Ghazi Khan

The main road continues east from the turning for Fort Munro, descending steadily through spectacular mountain scenery onto the Indus plain, to arrive at Dera Ghazi Khan, 282 kilometres from Loralai and 534 kilometres from Quetta. There are a total of 3 river fordings along this last stretch. These can be tricky to negotiate after rains, particularly at **Sakhi Sarwar**, site of a famous shrine to a Sufi saint. Bear in mind that even when the weather appears fine, these seasonal streams can be swollen by rainfall occurring a long way off in the mountains.

Dera Ghazi Khan

Phone code: 0641
Colour map 3, grid B5

Known generally by its abbreviated form, DG Khan, this dusty bazaar town is the headquarters of the district of the same name. Originally, the town in fact formed part of Baluchistan and today the people are still predominantly Baluchi or Pathan. However, under the British, in what was generally perceived to be a politically motivated move to weaken the Baluch tribes, the town and surrounding areas were allocated to Punjab. This is the home town of the former Pakistani president, Mr Leghari, although it shows no sign of having benefited from his position of power in terms of its civic amenities. Many of the streets are unpaved, and after rains are churned up into deep mud by the heavy traffic in the town. The main thoroughfare, Faridi Bazaar, is where most of the hotels, restaurants, shops et cetera are located.

Sleeping & eating

The best hotel in town is the **D** *Shalimar*, Faridi Bazaar, T62105. Rooms with a/c, TV/dish and attached bath. Restaurant. More modest is the **D/E** *Pakeeza*, Faridi Bazaar, T63305. Reasonable rooms with attached bath and fan. Also more expensive a/c rooms. Parking. Restaurant. Good value and friendly. Recommended. There are several more basic hotels along Faridi Bazaar, including **F** *New Al-Madina*, T65665, **F** *Al Marhaba*, T63522 and **F** *Fourways*, T62807, all with restaurants. The *Shalimar* hotel's restaurant serves good Pakistani and Chinese cuisine, while the *Pakeeza* hotel's restaurant serves reasonable Pakistani cuisine and is a/c. As well as the other hotel restaurants (all fairly basic), there are a number of simple restaurants along Faridi bazaar.

Transport

Air The agent for PIA in DG Khan is *Travel Point*, T63160, F62408. There are 3 flights weekly to **Islamabad**, **Karachi** and **Lahore** (Tuesday, Thursday, Sunday), and 1 flight weekly to **Quetta** (Thursday).

Train The railway station is inconveniently situated several kilometres outside town. The *Chiltan Express* passes through here en route between Quetta and Lahore. Heading for **Lahore** (via Multan) it passes through at 0515, while heading for **Quetta** (via the Bolan Pass) it passes through at 2255. The *Khushal Khan Khattak Express* passes through en route between Peshawar and Karachi. Heading for **Peshawar** (via Mianwali and Attock) it passes through at 1750, while heading for **Karachi** (via Larkana and Moenjo Daro) it passes through at 1000. Note that long delays are common on both these routes.

Bus There is a new bus station around 2 kilometres outside of town, but much more convenient are the various 'luxury' coach companies with ticket offices and bus stands in Faridi Bazaar. These include: *New Khan Road Runners*, T62580, with services to **Lahore**, Rs 150, 8-9 hours, and **Islamabad/Rawalpindi**, Rs 220, 12 hours; *City Linkers*, T65692, with services to **Lahore** and **Karachi**, Rs 350, 15 hours. There are a number of depots for local buses and minibuses along Faridi Bazaar and a larger one behind Faridi Bazaar, though these may be forced to relocate to the new bus station in the future. Local buses and minibuses operate services to **Muzaffargarh** and **Multan**, as well as to **Loralai** (and **Fort Munro** in summer). The only direct service to **Dera Ismail Khan** is by way of the **Bannu** bus. Alternatively, local buses run to **Taunsa**, from where there are services on to DI Khan, though it's quicker to go up the east bank of the Indus, via Muzaffargarh.

Routes

From DG Khan a good road continues east, across the Indus River and past Ghazi Ghat, to Muzaffargarh (60 kilometres) and Multan (94 kilometres, see page 297).

The Throne of Solomon

Takht-e-Suleiman (literally the 'throne of Solomon') is the highest peak in the Suleiman range at 3,375 metres. Suleiman is frequently mentioned in the Qur'an. In addition to the wisdom for which he is famous in the Old Testament, he is recognised in Islamic tradition as one of the great Prophets, a figure of enormous power who could commune with birds and insects, and who claimed the whole earth as his domain. According to local myths, he used to journey to the top of Takht-e-Suleiman on a magic carpet and offer prayers there to the one true God. There is an open-air mosque enclosure on the summit of the mountain, said to mark the spot where Suleiman would land. Just below, protruding from the sheer cliffs, is a slab of rock (the 'Takht'), where he is said to have prayed. The summit is a popular place of pilgrimage (or ziarat), with local beliefs holding that childless women who make the pilgrimage will be blessed with fertility.

The Suleiman range in general has also become a focus for pilgrimages dedicated rather more to Mammon than God. The higher reaches of these mountains (above 2,900 metres) are clad in rich forests of Chilghoza pine (Pinus gerardiana), as well as Blue pine (Pinus walichiana), Wild ash and other trees lower down. These forests provide a unique natural habitat for a great deal of wildlife, including the indigenous Suleiman Markhor (Capra falcon erigerardiana). Unfortunately, the forests are increasingly being exploited as a lucrative source of timber to be sold to outside contractors. Deforestation is becoming a major problem, particularly on the western slopes of the range, where relatively easy access allows camels to be used to transport the timber down to the nearest roads. On the eastern side, where the approaches are much steeper, the timber has to be carried manually, an extremely slow and laborious, and often dangerous, process. Quite apart from the environmental impact, the indiscriminate cutting of the Chilghoza pine for timber is particularly tragic, given that the edible Chilghoza nut is extremely valuable, selling for around Rs 1,000 per kilo in the markets of larger towns.

DG Khan lies on the west bank route along the Indus. In either direction this road is a narrow single lane, subject to flooding in places. By no means a fast road, it makes a peaceful alternative to the busy National Highway on the opposite bank.

The road south from DG Khan runs through irrigated agricultural land, giving way increasingly to desert as you move further southwards. The main settlements along the way are Jampur (48 kilometres), Rajanpur (114 kilometres), Mithankot (130 kilometres; linked by a bridge of boats with the east bank town of Chacharan), Rohjan (188 kilometres), Kashmor (236 kilometres, just inside Sind, with access to the east bank via the Guddu Barrage), Kandkhot (283 kilometres), and Shikarpur (347 kilometres), on the route between Sukkur and Quetta (see page 157).

Heading north from DG Khan, the road passes through the small villages of Shah Sadruddin and Shadan Lund (51 kilometres). Just north of Shadan Lund the road forks. Straight ahead takes you across the Indus via the Taunsa Barrage on a dual rail/road bridge, to join a quiet road running close to the banks of the Indus, parallel to the National Highway, 4 kilometres north of Kot Addu. The fork left crosses the canal and continues up the west bank to arrive at Taunsa Sharif (70 kilometres).

Taunsa Sharif

Colour map 3, grid A5

Taunsa Sharif (literally 'holy Taunsa'), is a small town famous for its shrine and mosque to **Pir Mohammad Suleiman Shah**. Built in 1855 by the Nawab of Bahawalpur, this impressive mosque, complete with clock tower, is housed in a large courtyard with a pond. The outside of the dome is decorated with blue tiles and marble from Jaipur, while inside it is lavishly ornate. A passage-way leads through to a second building, housing the tomb itself. The annual Urs is held in the first week of the Muslim month of *Safar*. There is no accommodation in Taunsa, other than the extremely basic and best avoided *Café Mahabou Sulaiman*, by the bus stand. Buses and minibuses run services to DG Khan, DI Khan and, via the Taunsa Barrage, to various destinations on the east bank, largely on the basis of demand. The road north of Taunsa is subject to flooding, with a potentially difficult river fording just short of DI Khan.

Quetta to Dera Ismail Khan via Zhob

This route is a spectacular one. The Zhob valley, with an elevation of not less than 1,300 metres, is relatively fertile with frequent oases supporting vineyards and rich orchards of apples, apricots, peaches, pomegranates, plums, almonds, walnuts and melons. The valley is perhaps at its most beautiful during spring, when it blossoms with wild lavender, tulips, hyacinths, poppies and irises, or in autumn when the weather is pleasant and the orchards heavy with fruit. There is frequently heavy snowfall in winter, while in summer temperatures can reach 40°C. To the north, the peaks of the Toba Kakar range rise to over 3,000 metres, while to the south a range of lower hills expose fantastic patterns of folded rock strata. In places you can see ridges rising out of the plain which look for all the world like the backbones of dinosaurs. East of Zhob the road cuts through the northern parts of the Suleiman Range, skirting round the mighty Takht-e-Suleiman.

Ins and outs The route northeast from Quetta via Zhob to Dera Ismail Khan in southern NWFP is unfortunately still restricted, and appears likely to remain so. This is primarily because the section between Qila Saifullah and Zhob is considered particularly dangerous due to feuding and banditry amongst the local tribes. Locals however point out that there have been no incidents involving foreigners along this route in recent years. Travellers can check the latest situation with the PTDC/CTC or the Home Department in Quetta. Naturally, we would not advise contravening official restrictions on travel, but if you are intending to attempt this route by public transport, it is worth noting that Hiace minibuses are generally not checked as thoroughly as larger buses. Frequent buses and minibuses make the journey between Quetta and Zhob in around 8 hours. Another alternative is to fly from Quetta to Zhob, and then continue by road from there. From Zhob to Dera Ismail Khan takes anything from 7 to 10 hours depending on road conditions and the type of vehicle. If you are travelling with your own vehicle, note that this is an extremely arduous route, particularly once inside NWFP, where the road disappears altogether for long stretches and one must follow the course of stony river beds or rough tracks cross-country. After rains, such sections often become impassable.

Quetta to Zhob Follow the route for Dera Ghazi Khan as far as **Qila Saifullah** (180 kilometres). Continue straight on at the junction just east of the town (right for Loralai). The road follows the Zhob River and the old narrow-gauge railway, closed since 1985, passing the settlements of **Tanga** (68 kilometres), **Mina Bazaar** (102 kilometres) and **Badinzai** (120 kilometres), before arriving at Zhob (140 kilometres). There are tea shops and simple restaurants at the settlements along this section of the road, but little else.

Zhob

Phone code: 0822
Colour map 3, grid A4

Zhob (pronounced 'Jhob') is the headquarters of Zhob district, a combination of tribal and 'settled' areas. The population is predominantly Pathan and has grown significantly in recent years with the influx of Afghan refugees. Situated close to the Afghan border and linked by road with the tribal areas of South Waziristan, it has also developed as an important market for smuggled goods.

History

The town is an ancient one, known originally as Apozai, and has been a centre for settlement at least as far back as 3000 BC. Excavations were first carried out by Sir Auriel Stein in 1924 and later by Fairservis in 1950, with finds including leaf-shaped arrowheads and female figurines which have been dubbed 'Zhob Goddesses'. The Zhob valley appears to have acted as an ancient caravan route, the Gomal Pass connecting early settlements such as Mundigak in Afghanistan with Indus Valley settlements to the east. Today the valley is still used by groups of *Powindahs* (literally 'wanderers' or 'nomads'), who migrate between the uplands and plains each spring and autumn. In 1889 the British captured the town and renamed it Fort Sandeman after Sir Robert Sandeman, the first Agent to the Governor General of Baluchistan. For the British it was an important garrison town, central to their Forward Policy, and they were quick to develop road and rail links with the rest of British India.

Sights

There are two forts, situated on rocky ridges overlooking the town's large cantonment area. One is still home to the Zhob Militia, founded in 1890 and now part of the Frontier Corps, while the other was Sandeman's Fort, a grand Victorian structure which now houses the Political Agent. The two are supposedly linked by an underground tunnel. Unless you have official connections, you are unlikely to be allowed to visit. The town's main bazaar area is lively and colourful, but if you are travelling through without a permit you are advised to keep a low profile.

Sleeping & eating

G ***Adil***, located at Purana Adha. Basic but reasonably clean rooms upstairs with shared toilet/shower facilities. Restaurant below. **G** ***Amarat***, located near the main mosque, in Amarat bazaar. Basic but reasonable rooms arranged around a small concrete courtyard/shopping arcade. There are also a couple of ***Government Rest Houses***; if you have a permit, you may be able to stay in one of these. There are a number of simple restaurants in the main bazaar.

Transport

Air **PIA Booking Office**, 10A Market Road ('PIA Chowk'), T412875. Airport, T412954. PIA operates daily flights (except Friday) to **Islamabad** (stopping en route in **Dera Ismail Khan** and **Peshawar**), and 3 flights weekly to **Quetta** (Wednesday, Thursday, Saturday) and **Multan** (Monday, Tuesday, Saturday).

Road The small bus stand known as **'Purana Adha'** has regular Hiace minibus services to **Quetta** (Rs 100, 8 hours). Nearby there is a larger bus stand (known locally as **'big bus Adha'**) with less regular Coaster, bus and four-wheel drive pick-up services to **Daraban** and **Dera Ismail Khan** (Rs 100-150, 7-10 hours). Some services also operate from the main bazaar, waiting around the roundabout known as 'PIA Chowk'.

Zhob to Dera Ismail Khan

NB The route north from Zhob into NWFP, passing through **Tanai** (120 kilometres) and **Ramzak** (200 kilometres), before eventually arriving at **Bannu** (326 kilometres), is through the sensitive tribal/border areas of North and South Waziristan, and is strictly off limits to foreigners. You are strongly advised against travelling on this route.

The main route east from Zhob passes through **Kapip**, surrounded by vineyards, and then starts to climb gradually. Eventually the wide valley begins to narrow and the peaks of the Suleiman range loom up ahead. The road enters a narrow gorge with walls of sheer rock rising up thousands of metres on either side. **Dhanasar**, on the opposite bank of the river, has a check post and small fort. A small steel girder arch by the side of the road marks the border with NWFP. A little further on is **Mughal Khot** (85 kilometres), a small settlement at the top of the gorge with a check post. Here the road abruptly turns to a rough gravel track which descends slowly down the eastern flanks of the Suleiman range, giving spectacular views. A long, difficult stretch follows, often impassable after rains, along the course of a stony riverbed to **Domanda**, an oasis with a couple of tea shops and basic restaurants.

From Domanda the main route follows a wide loop via Sheikh Mela and Darazinda to Daraban. A more direct route leads directly northeast to Daraban. The direct route is very rough (only really passable in a four-wheel drive), following a riverbed for most of the way and involving some deep and difficult fordings. This was the route of the old British road, traces of which are still visible in places. Going by the longer but easier route via Darazinda, **Takht-e-Suleiman**, previously hidden by a series of ridges, comes slowly into view to the southwest. There are a few teashops and basic restaurants in **Darazinda**, and around 5 kilometres further on a Frontier Constabulary fort and check post of the same name. The road then cuts through a ridge of low hills and crosses a wide stony plain, part of the *Daman* plains which stretch for around 120 kilometres north-south between DI Khan and DG Khan, sandwiched between the Suleiman mountains to the west and the Indus River to the east. A little further on is **Daraban** (167 kilometres, full name Daraban Kalan, to distinguish it from Daraban Khurd, south of DI Khan), the largest settlement between DI Khan and Zhob. There is a Frontier Constabulary post, complete with a ***Rest House***, here, as well as some shops and simple restaurants in the main bazaar. From here it is a further 58 kilometres along a single lane road to Dera Ismail Khan, a total of 225 kilometres from Zhob and 545 kilometres from Quetta. For details of DI Khan and routes from there, see page 362.

Quetta to Sukkur via the Bolan Pass

The route southeast from Quetta, through the historic Bolan Pass and down onto the Kachhi plains, has for centuries acted as a thoroughfare for conquerors, traders and nomads alike, providing the easiest access south of the Khyber Pass between the Iranian Plateau and the plains of the Indus. During spring and autumn, nomadic groups with their caravans of camels, horses, donkeys, sheep and goats can still be seen making their seasonal journey between the highlands and the plains.

Ins and outs This remains the most important land route to and from Baluchistan. The road down to Sukkur (on the National Highway) is a good quality metalled one, and much of the public transport running between Quetta and Karachi favours this route over the more direct but slower RCD Highway. This is also the route taken by the only railway line linking Quetta with the rest of Pakistan.

The railway The railway through the Bolan Pass is a remarkable feat of engineering (and a spectacular train journey), with a total of 17 tunnels and numerous bridges and culverts carrying it down onto the plains. On the journey up from Sibi, a second engine is attached to the train to help push it up gradients which reach one in 25 in places. Plans to build a Frontier Railway connecting Quetta with the rest of British India were first drawn up in 1876, when Lord Lytton's

Forward Policy was initiated. It was not until 1879 that work began on the first phase, with a line as far as Sibi being completed in 1880.Work on the next phase, known as the 'Harnai Military Road', began in earnest in 1884 and the line as far as Quetta was opened in 1887. This section of the line ran via Harnai, Khost, Chappar Rift and Bostan. Although a branch line still operates from Sibi as far as Khost, further on the terrain proved too unstable after rains, and the route was abandoned in favour of the present route through the Bolan Pass. This second line however proved to be equally problematic. In 1889, just after it was completed, more flooding resulted in substantial subsidence and much of the line had to be rebuilt on a new alignment.

South to Sibi

Head south on Suriab Road, past the University, and after seven kilometres bear left at the fork (right for the Iranian border and RCD Highway to Karachi). An alternative route from New Quetta Bus Stand joins the Sibi road south of this fork. The main road crosses the wide Quetta plain, running parallel to the railway line, before crossing it and climbing gently to the town of **Kolpur** (25 kilometres), which marks the start of the Bolan Pass. The pass, stretching for 96 kilometres, is in fact more accurately a gorge which cuts through the Central Brahui Range giving access to the plains below.

From Kolpur it is a steady descent all the way down to the plains. The road crosses back and forth over the Bolan River, also passing under the railway line several times. Inscribed above the entrance to one of the tunnels, the name "Mary Jane" is visible from the road, commemorating the wife of the chief engineer who died of an illness while her husband worked on the railway. The occasional tunnels below the railway are remnants of the line which subsided when it first opened.

The road passes the turning left to **Mach**, situated on the other side of the river, clustered around the train station. Mach was at the epicentre of the 1935 earthquake and was completely destroyed. Shortly before the turning there is a stretch of green with date palms on the opposite bank, which was the site of the old town of Mach (in Baluchi, *mach* means 'date'). Today it makes a pleasant picnic spot. Beyond Mach, the road descends steeply and then passes numerous simple coal mines cut into the hills on either side. The gorge meanwhile opens out to a wide braided river bed. Around 25 kilometres from Mach there is a rough track to the right which leads 16 kilometres up to Pir Ghaib.

Pir Ghaib

Permits are no longer required for this short excursion to the hot sulphur springs at Pir Ghaib. The rough track, which has been repaired and is now passable in a four-wheel drive, climbs for 15 kilometres to a series of rock pools dotted around the area, each surrounded by shady palm trees. There is a shrine here, dedicated to the Sufi saint from whom the spot gets its name. Traces of an ancient water channel can still be seen, ascribed by locals to the early Arab invaders and constructed of lime and cement, running from Pir Ghaib to Khajuri, about four kilometres away. Pir Ghaib makes an excellent picnic place. If you have your own transport, it is accessible as a long day trip from Quetta. There are plans to further improve access and provide facilities for tourists.

Routes

Around four kilometres on from the turning to Pir Ghaib is **Bibi Nani Bridge**. In 1986 this bridge was completely washed away by flash floods, and each year it comes under similar threat, though when damaged it is promptly repaired. The road follows the east bank of the river, descending steadily, before crossing again to the west bank. The river, for much of the year a dry stony bed, is up to 15 kilometres wide around here. Further on, around 40 kilometres from Sibi, the **Pinjera Bridge** carries the road back over to the east bank. From here the valley narrows once again to a gorge, passing through a couple of tunnels. At **Bolan Weir** there is a check post and traditional mud fort with a mosque inside. The archaeological site of Mehrgarh is 10 kilometres from here, on the banks of the Bolan River, reached by a rough track leading to the villages of Sanni and Shoran.

Mehrgarh

Colour map 3, grid B2

This archaeological site, first excavated in 1974 by a French team, is one of the most important in Pakistan. The site has provided evidence for the emergence of settled agriculture in South Asia around 8,500 BC, far earlier than previously imagined by archaeologists. It has also provided strong evidence to suggest that the great Indus Valley Civilization which later flourished in Pakistan emerged from these first indigenous settlements, rather than being imported by groups migrating from Egypt, Persia or Central Asia, as originally believed.

Ins and outs You really need your own transport (preferably four-wheel drive), and a guide. PTDC/CTC in Quetta can arrange transport, and perhaps a guide from the museum (they will also be able to advise you about the security situation in the area, which is subject to periodic feuding between the local Bugti and Raisani tribes). The nearest accommodation is at Sibi.

History The earliest part of the settlement, on the high bank of the Bolan River at the north end of the site, was probably a camp of nomadic pastoralists. By 8,000 BC there were well developed villages with agriculture and the beginnings of animal domestication, indicating that settled agriculture occurred in Baluchistan at least as early as it did further west in the traditional 'cradle of civilization', the Fertile Crescent of the Zagros mountains. Hunting continued to complement agriculture, with elephants, wild water buffalo and Nilgai deer amongst those killed. Cereals were also introduced remarkably early, with local varieties of barley and wheat being grown by 8,000 BC, and cotton by 5,000 BC. Primitive items of pottery began to appear from around 6,000 BC, complemented by more sophisticated wheel-thrown pottery, some of it elaborately decorated with geometric designs, from around 5,500 BC. By around 4,500 BC there is evidence that copper was being smelted, though bronze artefacts only start to appear in significant quantities during the second half of the third millennium BC. As well as Mehrgarh's pottery and ceramics, perhaps the most fascinating finds are the terracotta figurines, both animal and human, which become steadily more sophisticated during each period of occupation.

Visiting Mehrgarh Despite its enormous archaeological significance, a visit to Mehrgarh is only for the specialist or the dedicated. Today there is little to see apart from the outlines and foundations of buildings, with all the pottery and other artefacts having been removed to various museums. The displays at the small museums in Sibi and Quetta, and at the National Museum in Karachi, give the best insight into the culture and way of life of these ancient settlements. Excavations shifted some time ago from Mehrgarh to Naushero, 15 kilometres away, where the evidence of a transition from the last period of Mehrgarh to the Indus Valley period has been found.

Routes From Bolan Weir, the road continues past patches of cultivation, emerging onto the flat, wide **Kachhi plain** before reaching **Dadhar**, surrounded by woods and irrigated farmland. There is a stretch of bazaar along the main road, but the town itself is off to the right. Beyond Dadhar the land gives way once more to a barren alluvial plain with a sparse cover of scrub and grass. The road crosses the Nari River and the railway line before arriving in Sibi, 163 kilometres from Quetta.

Sibi

Phone code: 0831
Colour map 3, grid B2

Headquarters of Sibi Division, Sibi is the largest town in Baluchistan after Quetta, with a population of over 100,000. Today it is famous for its **Horse and Cattle Fair**, which is held each year during the first two weeks of April. The fair attracts politicians and other important figures from all over Pakistan, as well as tribesmen from the surrounding areas, and is an excellent place to shop for local Baluchi handicrafts. Sibi is also famous (along with Dadhar and Jacobabad), for being amongst the hottest places in South Asia, with summer temperatures sometimes exceeding 50°C. There is a Persian proverb which loosely translates as; "Oh Allah, having created hot places like Sibi and Dadhar, why bother to conceive of hell?"

History

Although certainly an ancient town, its origins are unclear. There is mention of a tribe known as the Sibi or Sibia in the chronicles of Alexander's expedition to South Asia in 325 BC, perhaps the original inhabitants of the area. Local tradition meanwhile holds that it gained its name from Sewi, a Hindu princess of the Sewa Dynasty. The Brahman king Rai Chach ruled over the area for a period, before it came under the control of the Arab Muslim invaders in the eighth century. Later it was ruled over by Mahmud of Ghazni after he captured Multan in 1004. In 1487 it became the capital of the short-lived kingdom of Mir Chakkar Rind. It was first attacked by the British in 1841 before being captured by them in 1878 during the Second Afghan War and named Sandemanabad after Sir Robert Sandeman. The annual Horse and Cattle Fair developed from the *Shahi Jirga*, a traditional meeting of tribal elders, which was revived by Robert Sandeman in 1882 as a means of encouraging the tribal chiefs of the area to take responsibility for ensuring peace and stability in a region which had been subject to continual and bloody feuds. The Jirga still takes place today as part of the fair.

Sights

Sibi Museum This small museum is housed in the former Queen Victoria Hall, built in 1903 and later known as the Jirga Hall (it was here that the Jirgas of tribal chiefs organized by Sandeman were held). It has an interesting, well displayed collection of pieces from Mehrgarh, Naushero and Pirak (south-west of Sibi). The pottery found at Pirak, which dates from 1800-800 BC, is of a different technique and style to that found at Mehrgarh and Naushero, being adorned with distinctive geometric designs. It has been suggested that the presence of terracotta toy camels indicates that the inhabitants of this site migrated from Central Asia, the home of the camel during this period. Pirak is also significant in that it has provided the earliest evidence of double cropping, with the winter crop of wheat and barley being supplemented by a spring crop of rice, sorghum and millet. There is also a small collection of traditional Baluchi jewellery and embroidered

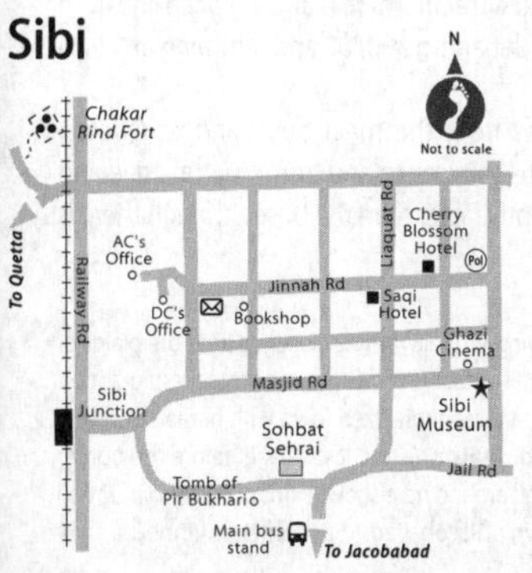

clothes, photos of archaeological and historical sites and artefacts from around Baluchistan, and photographs and text relating to Baluchistan's relations with Pakistan and Jinnah following Independence. ■ *Open 0900-1600, Friday 0900-1200, closed Wednesday.*

Sohbat Serai One of several built by the powerful Sardar Sohbat Khan, this impressive *caravanserai* consists of a large central courtyard with rooms around the outside. It is shaded by large, old trees and in one corner there is a mosque. The walls, inside and out, are decorated with glazed blue tiles. During the annual Jirga, the tribal chiefs would stay here, each bringing with them their own entourage of cooks and servants. Today part of the building is given over to a school. Government officials are accommodated here during the Horse and Cattle Fair. It is managed by the Itthad ('unity') Trust, T3063. Just to the west of the Sohbat Serai, on the opposite side of the road, is the tomb of **Pir Bukhari**, a famous saint from Bukhara in present day Uzbekistan.

Chakkar Rind Fort Northwest of the centre of town, overlooking the railway and river, is the impressive mud fort of Mir Chakkar Rind, dating from the 15th century. Inside the crumbling walls there are two large conical structures which served as grain stores. The fort is within walking distance of the centre of town if the weather not too hot, or else tongas are readily available. **NB** To the east of the fort is a restricted military area; be careful where you point your camera.

Sleeping & eating

Accommodation in Sibi is very limited and very basic. Incredibly for such a hot place, there are no hotels with air conditioning. During the annual Fair you are unlikely to get a room unless you have contacts or have booked well ahead. **NB** Foreigners are required to register with the police if staying overnight. **F** ***Saqi***, Jinnah Rd, T2428. This is the only hotel with reasonable rooms and clean bedding. The **G** ***Cherry Blossom***, nearby, is more basic. There are a number of ***Government Rest Houses***, bookable through the Deputy Commissioner, T2610. Tourists are unfortunately no longer generally allowed to stay in the Sohbat Serai. There are a number of basic but reasonable restaurants along Liaquat and Jinnah Road.

Transport

Train All the trains running to and from Quetta along this route stop at Sibi. Services to **Quetta** (around 5 hours) stop here at 0120, 0250, 0355, 0450, 0915 and 1055. Note however that they are often way behind schedule by the time they pass through. Heading in the opposite direction they are more likely to be on time, passing through around 5 hours after their departure from Quetta (see under Quetta Transport) en route to **Peshawar, Rawalpindi, Lahore** and **Karachi**. There is also a branch line from Sibi to **Khost** (6 hours), with a daily service departing at 0700 and returning at 1345.

Bus There are regular buses and coaches from the main bus stand to **Quetta, Jacobabad, Shikarpur** and **Sukkur**. Minibus services to and from Quetta arrive and depart from Masjid Road. They are significantly faster than the buses, though there is usually a hectic scramble for seats.

Routes

From Sibi, the main road heads southeast, following the railway line closely, across the plains of the Kachhi Desert to **Bellpat** (66 kilometres), a small bazaar town with some simple restaurants. It is a further 48 kilometres to **Dera Murad Jamali**, a reasonably sized town with bazaars and very basic accommodation, set in fertile irrigated land. **Jhatpat** is the last village before the border with Sind, marked by the course of a canal. The land around here shows signs of heavy salinization in places. Just across the border in Sind is the town of Jacobabad, 158 kilometres from Sibi.

Jacobabad

Colour map 3, grid C3

The town of Jacobabad is named after General John Jacob, the remarkable Political Superintendent of the Upper Sind Frontier Region between 1847-1858. Jacob was responsible for laying out the town, and indeed for transforming the surrounding countryside from virtual desert to fertile agricultural land and bringing an end to the anarchic feuding and banditry which characterized the area. Although his rule was strict and uncompromising, he is still revered as the man who brought peace and relative prosperity to the region. He is also one of only two Englishmen whose names remain attached to a town in Pakistan by popular consent, the other being Abbott of Abbottabad.

Jacob's grave, with an arched gate decorated with blue tiles above it, can still be seen today in a graveyard to the right of the main road as you enter the town from the north. His former **Residency** is now occupied by the Deputy Commissioner. An ingenious clock, built by Jacob and incorporating lunar and solar calendars, is housed in the building, where it continues to work. The **Victoria Tower**, a whitewashed stone clock tower, stands nearby in the bazaar. The town itself is today a dusty, somewhat chaotic place with little to indicate the carefully ordered planning which went into its construction.

Sleeping & eating

The **D/E** *Palace*, Quaid-e-Azam Rd, T3395, has basic a/c rooms with attached bath, as well as cheaper rooms with just a fan and attached bath. The **D/E** *Mehran* offers a similar deal. There are various basic restaurants in the main bazaar.

Transport

Train Railway enquiries, T2711. Rail services are the same as for Sibi, passing through 2¼ hours earlier/later. In addition, the *Khushal Khan Khattak Exp* also passes through here en route between Karachi and Peshawar. Heading for **Karachi**, it passes through at 1800, while heading for **Peshawar** it passes through at 0935, though going in either direction it is often subject to long delays. There is also a local service, the *S-304 Passenger* to **Larkana**, departing daily at 1500 (7 hours).

Road There are regular bus and minibus services to **Sibi, Quetta, Shikarpur** and **Sukkur**.

Routes

From Jacobabad it is a further 43 kilometres on to **Shikarpur**, a historically important trading town with an interesting covered bazaar. Founded as a municipal town in 1617, its trading links with Afghanistan and Central Asia go back much further. Traders from Shikarpur travelled very extensively and, before being driven out following the revolution in 1949, were influential in Sinkiang, the westernmost province of China. The road continues through Lakhi to **Sukkur** (42 kilometres), see page 130.

Quetta to Chaman

The route from Quetta to the Afghanistan border post at Chaman is a restricted one requiring permits, and is likely to remain so for the foreseeable future. The main worry from the point of view of Pakistani officials is the large numbers of Afghan refugees along the border, over whom they have little or no control. Widespread trafficking of weapons and drugs coupled with periodic feuding between the various tribal groups does make for a potentially dangerous situation, although the area is on the whole relatively peaceful. If you are intent on going, you are advised to take a local guide who is known in the area. An overnight stay is not recommended.

Ins and outs

There are regular buses and minibuses which make the journey between Quetta and Chaman in around 3 hours. There is also a train, the *Q-487 Passenger*, departing from Quetta at 0900 every Wednesday, Friday and Sunday. It takes 4½ hours and leaves Chaman for the return journey at 1445.

The railway The narrow-gauge railway line initially follows the old line between Quetta and Zhob, before branching northwest at Bostan. It then climbs steadily, skirting the northern slopes of **Mount Takatu** and at one point doing a complete loop to pass over itself. Shortly before Chaman, it passes through a four kilometre tunnel, the longest in Asia, under the **Khojak Pass**. The British engineer in charge of the tunnel dug from both ends and is reputed to have attempted suicide when it failed to meet in the middle. It was eventually completed in 1892.

The road Follow the route for Dera Ghazi Khan as far as **Kuch Lak** (25 kilometres), continuing straight past the right turn in the bazaar for Ziarat and Muslimbagh. The road winds its way through a spectacular landscape of low mud hills of red and ochre, eroded into outlandish shapes, and past orchards and water channels emerging from underground *karez*.

At **Yaro** a road forks off to the right, towards **Pishin**. The Pishin valley is one of the major areas of karez irrigation and is surrounded by over 5,000 hectares of vineyards and orchards. It is also famous for its duck shooting. During the British period, Pishin was a vitally important cantonment area and the road to the town crosses an old runway, now abandoned, dating from the Second World War. The town itself has little of interest and is off-limits to foreigners.

The main road passes two large Afghan refugee camps at **Saranan** and **Jungle Piralizai** and crosses the **Lora River**, which flows into the Hamun-e-Lora near Dalbandin (on the Taftan road). **Qila Abdullah** (78 kilometres) is the last settlement before the pass. The railway enters the tunnel under the **Khojak Pass** shortly after **Shelabagh** station. There is a check post here. The road climbs up through bare rocky hills to the top of the pass, which at 2,273 metres gives excellent views on a clear day across the plains of southwest Afghanistan towards **Kandahar**. The hills were once wooded with pistachio trees, but these were cut down and used in the building of the railway. There is a *Rest House* at the top of the pass, but you are unlikely to get permission to stay here. The road winds its way down to Chaman (113 kilometres), situated at the foot of the pass.

Chaman is a small, chaotic bazaar town, with all the atmosphere of the 'Wild West', Pathan style. The town was established by the British in 1889, replacing Old Chaman, 11 kilometres to the south, which lost its importance with the building of the railway line.

From Chaman it is a further 105 kilometres to Kandahar. Although much of Afghanistan is now firmly under the control of the Taliban, only journalists and aid workers are currently being allowed entry.

Quetta to Iran

The route to Taftan on the Iranian border runs through a forbidding, inhospitable and often spectacular landscape, combining wide expanses of desert and semi-desert with barren mountains exposing twisted, folded strata of igneous rock. In summer it is uncomfortably hot, with temperatures reaching well into the forties, and all year round there are frequent dust storms. The route passes through the Chagai district of northwest Baluchistan, close to the border with Afghanistan.

Ins and outs

Regular buses, Coasters and Hiace minibuses make the journey between Quetta and Taftan in 13-14 hours, travelling overnight to arrive at the border in the morning. It is possible to make the journey in daylight by taking local transport between the towns en route, but this is likely to involve an overnight stop along the way. Dalbandin, though the most logical place to stop being roughly half way, has very poor accommodation and is best avoided if possible. Toyota pick-ups operate fairly regular passenger services between the main towns, leaving when full. They are more expensive than the buses, but significantly faster, particularly where the road is in poor condition. The train is more comfortable than the long distance buses but much slower; the quoted time is 24 hours to Taftan and a further 8 hours through the border and on to Zahedan, although long delays on the border are common. The road between Quetta and Taftan has been much improved in recent years. However, there are still stretches which are unsurfaced (particularly between Dalbandin and Nok Kundi), and in places it is subject to periodic flash floods which are liable to wash away whole sections. Inside Iran, road conditions are excellent.

Routes

Follow the route south out of Quetta, as for the RCD highway to Karachi. At the bottom of the Lak Pass, bear right at the fork (31 kilometres). The road winds its way through low hills and stony plains with isolated patches of cultivation and small settlements, passing check posts of the Chagai Force at **Sheikh Wasil** and **Gulandur Post**, the latter with a traditional mud fort on the hillside overlooking the road. Soon after emerging onto a wide desert plain you arrive at Nushki (114 kilometres). Fork right off the main road to reach the town.

Nushki
Colour map 1, grid A5

Nushki, the headquarters of Chagai District, is a small bazaar town, its population considerably swelled by Afghan refugees. The present town was built by the British in 1899, after they had taken over the administration of the area from the Khan of Kalat. There is a simple *Rest House* offering basic facilities, Pakistani-style restaurants in the bazaar and a small bus station with local buses to Quetta and Dalbandin.

Kharan

Around 20 kilometres beyond Nushki a rough track bears off southwest, leading eventually to Kharan, site of the impressive **Karez Fort**. The fort, just outside the main town, was one of 11 built by Sardar Azad Khan in the 18th century. It is the largest and best preserved, covering over 300 square metres with thick mud brick walls, a three-storey building and the remains of four wells.

Ins and outs Kharan is extremely remote, even by Baluchistan's standards and there are no facilities. To visit it is necessary to organize your own transport, either in Quetta or Nushki. A four-wheel drive and local guide is recommended. With an early start, it is feasible as a day trip from Nushki. **NB** A permit may be necessary. You should register your travel plans with the Commissioner in Nushki or Kharan and check that the road is passable.

History Originally part of Persia, Kharan emerged as a separate Princely State, home to the Nousherwani tribe, in the 18th century. It came under the loose control of Kalat State for a time before turning its allegiance to Afghanistan. Yacoob Shah, the Sardar during the period of British expansion in Baluchistan, resisted British control but was killed by his uncle Nadir Shah who then accepted a quasi-independent status as a protectorate in 1911. After Independence it maintained its internal autonomy within Pakistan until 1952, when its militia was disbanded and ruler stripped of his power. In 1953 it was made into a separate District. Covering over 36,000 square kilometres, it is for the most part desert, although there are considerable areas of cultivated land along the Baddo and Mashkel Rivers.

Routes The main road to Taftan continues west from the turning for Kharan, across wide open plains and rocky mountains to **Padag** (213 kilometres). Although no more than a cluster of buildings, there is a small, well-kept *Rest House* here and good water supply. Further west, roughly half way between Padag and Dalbandin, the shallow seasonal lake of **Hamun-e-Lora** is visible to the north, covering over 600 square kilometres. For much of the year, it is a dry saline expanse, acquiring a thin sheet of water during the winter months. Green onyx is mined in the vicinity.

Dalbandin
Colour map 1, grid A4

Dalbandin, 297 kilometres from Quetta, is the largest town on the route, and since early times was an important staging post on the Seistan Trading Route, though today there is nothing of interest. The bazaar is strung out along the main road, consisting mostly of mechanics' workshops. It has a small airport, but despite this, and its position roughly halfway between Quetta and the border, only the most basic of accommodation is available. There is the **G** *Pakistan* and a couple of others, but they are all very dirty and an overnight stop here is worth avoiding if possible. Around 30 kilometres north of the town there is a large Afghan refugee camp known as Gardi Jungle.

Transport **Air** PIA booking office, London Road, T210519. 2 flights weekly to **Karachi** via **Turbat** (Tuesday, Sunday). 2 flights weekly to **Quetta** (Tuesday, Sunday).

Road Toyota pick-ups and Hiace minibuses run to Taftan and Quetta, leaving from the main bazaar when full. Long distance buses in both directions pass through at night; they are best caught at the police check post at the edge of town where they are guaranteed to stop, though there is no guarantee of a seat.

Routes Continuing west, the road passes through stony desert stretching for miles on either side, with the volcanic Chagai Hills to the north, barely visible in the distance. **Yakmach** (353 kilometres) is a small oasis town with greenery and palm trees relieving the surrounding drab grey and a small *Rest House* offering basic but reasonable accommodation. **Nok Kundi** (464 kilometres) is the next town. There is a large cantonment area and a simple *Rest House* here. From Nok Kundi it is a further 113 kilometres to the Iranian border at Taftan, a total of 606 kilometres from Quetta. Shortly before Taftan, a track leads north to Saindak, now the site of a major mining project which aims to exploit the deposits of copper and lead that are found here.

Taftan

Phone code: 0886
Colour map 1, grid A1

Taftan is everything one would expect of a remote border post. It is a dusty, ramshackle town with a forlorn, half-built atmosphere. There are a few shops offering a curious range of smuggled goods ranging from plastic kitchenware to tinned food, a couple of very basic restaurants and the customs and immigration buildings. Money changers wander around armed with plastic carrier bags full of Rials and small pocket calculators.

The **border** opens daily from 1000-1300 and 1600-1800. Leave plenty of time for Customs and Immigration formalities which can be very lengthy, especially for private vehicles which are often thoroughly searched, particularly when coming from Pakistan.

Sleeping

E/F *PTDC Motel*, T302. Simple but clean rooms. Dorm rooms also available. Accommodation can be arranged in the Customs House and private vehicles can also park in the compound there.

Transport

Train Heading for **Quetta**, the *Zahedan Express* leaves Taftan each Monday at 1505 (in theory at least; when it actually sets off depends on how long it takes to get through the Iranian and Pakistani border formalities). Heading for **Zahedan**, it leaves at 0840 every Saturday, though it is much quicker to cross the border individually on foot and pick up transport on the Iranian side.

Road Buses, Coasters and Hiace minibuses to **Quetta** wait around on the Pakistani side of the border, usually departing in the late afternoon or early evening (or when full). On the Iranian side of the border (known as Mirjavé, or Mirjawa) there are usually minibuses or Toyota pick-ups waiting to ferry passengers to Zahedan, the first major town inside Iran, 84 kilometres away. The journey takes around 1½ hours, on a road that puts most of Pakistan's main highways to shame.

Quetta to Karachi

The RCD Highway (standing for Regional Co-operation for Development) was built as part of a programme initiated in the 1960s to link Turkey, Iran and Pakistan by road. The section between Quetta and Karachi was the only part within Pakistan to be completed.

Ins and outs

Originally, the RCD Highway consisted of a rather basic single-lane road, heavily pot-holed sections of which are still in use. However, in recent years much of it has been upgraded to a better quality 2-lane highway. The journey between Quetta and Karachi can be completed in 1 long day; buses usually take 13-14 hours. Alternatively, there is reasonable accommodation at Khuzdar, roughly half way between Quetta and Karachi. There is also an airport at Khuzdar, with flights connecting it with Karachi, Turbat, Gwadar and Moenjo Daro.

Routes

Head south out of Quetta on Suriab Road, and bear right after 9 kilometres (left to Sibi). The road climbs gradually, past the turning on the right to Hazerganji National Park (13 kilometres) and up to the **Lak Pass**, overlooked by a small mud fort and behind it a modern communications post. From here it descends steeply with good views over the wide plain below. At the bottom of the pass, the road to Taftan and the Iranian border forks off to the right. The RCD Highway continues straight, crossing the railway line for Taftan and passing through orchards and fields to arrive at Mastung (50 kilometres).

Mastung The small town of Mastung, set in fertile orchards and fields of wheat, is the headquarters of Mastung district. Despite the fertile environment, these are tribal areas, and though generally peaceful, the Deputy Commissioner's house, enclosed by large walls and fortress-like bastions, gives an indication of the potential for trouble. Most of the houses are of mud and straw; there is no hotel and little of interest. The Deputy Commissioner (T0823-2675) can arrange for accommodation in the *Government Rest House* if necessary, although foreigners are not encouraged to stay.

Routes From Mastung, the main road continues south over a wide open plain, through the Kad Khucha section of Mastung division. The scattered settlement of **Manguchar** (105 kilometres), in Kalat division, is surrounded by orchards of apples, apricots, pomegranates and almonds. There is a petrol pump, basic restaurants/tea stalls and a few small shops here. It is a further 40 kilometres on to Kalat.

Kalat

Phone code: 084
Colour map 1, grid A6

Kalat was the seat of power of the influential Khans of Kalat, whose state grew to become the largest and most powerful in Baluchistan. The old town of Kalat was almost completely destroyed in the earthquake of 1935 and today there is little to indicate its historic importance. The ruins of the **fort** and its walls, which enclosed the old town, can still be seen spread out over a low ridge of the Shah-e-Mardan hill. Dominating the town was the **citadel** or *Miri* of the Khan of Kalat, an impressive five-storey structure. A **Hindu temple** to Kali, perhaps a remnant of Sewa rule stood within the walls, which boasted 10 bastions and three gates. The present town is situated just north of the ridge, on level ground. It is to the east of the main road, across a seasonal stream. Most of the buildings are of traditional mud and straw construction. The new palace of the present Khan of Kalat is situated behind the bus stand. Just south of the town, perched on a small hill to the west of the main road, there is the mosque and shrine of an 11th century Shia saint, **Sheikh Abdul Qadir Gilani**. To the east of Kalat is the **Harboi range**, which boasts peaks of around 3,000 metres in altitude, deep gorges and rich Juniper forests. There are plans to develop the more easily accessible parts of this range into a summer resort.

History Little is known about the early history of Kalat, which is thought to have been inhabited from a very early stage. It is known also as Kalat-e-Sewa, perhaps after the Hindu **Sewa Dynasty** which is said to have ruled here for a time. During the 15th century, the Brahui tribe of **Mirwaris** succeeded in ousting the Mughals and established Kalat as a more or less independent state. Kalat town remained the capital of their successors, the **Ahmadzai Khans** until Independence. **Nasir Khan I** ruled as the Khan of Kalat for 44 years from 1750 to 1794. He is viewed as one of the great historical rulers by the Brahui, and referred to as Nasir the Great. Under his rule, Kalat State grew to encompass some 71,593 square miles, including the divisions of Sarawan, Kachhi, Jhalawan, Kharan and Makran. Kalat town became an important trading centre on the route between Afghanistan and India. With the arrival of the British and the building of the railway line to Quetta, its importance as a trading centre declined.

Sleeping & eating There is one very basic hotel in the main bazaar, the **G** *Mughal*, and a *Government Rest House*, bookable through the Commissioner (T087-2654). There are several basic restaurants in the bazaar.

Routes

From Kalat the road climbs to a low pass and then descends through hills to a wide plateau. At **Surab**, 70 kilometres from Kalat, a road branches off to the west, leading to Panjgur (320 kilometres) and on to Turbat (598 kilometres), a long, arduous journey on rough tracks. The main town of Surab is a short distance down this road. There is a check post at the junction, tea shops and a petrol station. The main route south continues across wide plains with mountains rising up on either side. The rugged and barren landscape is interspersed by small settlements and patches of cultivated land. The road crosses a low pass before arriving at the town of Khuzdar, 163 kilometres from Kalat.

Khuzdar

Colour map 1, grid B6

The town of Khuzdar, set in a wide plain, is the largest settlement on the RCD Highway. A turning east off the highway takes you into the main town. Although there is little of interest, it makes a convenient stopping point, being roughly half way between Quetta and Karachi, and has reasonable accommodation. The large cantonment area spreads out to the south, on the other side of the river.

Baluchistan

Sleeping & eating

■ *on maps*
Price codes: see inside front cover

E *PTDC Motel*, RCD Highway. Clean rooms with fan and attached bath. Restaurant. **F** *Rizwan*, Azadi Chowk. Clean rooms with fan and attached bath. Good value. Restaurant. **G** *Prince*, Masjid Rd. Cheaper and more basic. Restaurant. Opposite is the similar **G** *Holiday*, also with restaurant.

Transport

Air PIA booking office, Khoral Road, T412225. 4 flights weekly to **Karachi** (Monday, Tuesday, Thursday, Saturday). 2 flights weekly to **Turbat** (Tuesday, Saturday). One flight weekly to **Gwadar** (Monday). 2 flights weekly to **Moenjo Daro** (Monday, Thursday).

Road The main bus stand is at Azadi Chowk. There are long-distance **buses** to **Karachi, Quetta, Panjgur** and **Turbat**. Also regular **minibuses** to **Kalat, Quetta** and **Bela**.

Routes

The RCD Highway south from Khuzdar passes through terrain which alternates between wide expanses of plateau surrounded by mountains, and the rough, barren hills of the **Pab Range**. The road passes through the scattered settlement of **Wad**, followed soon after by **Urnach**, where there are a few basic restaurants, tea shops and a petrol pump. At **Sunaro**, set in an open plain, there are extensive chrome mines. The next settlement is **Kohan**, consisting only of a few houses and a check post. From here the road follows the course of the Porali River, with scattered villages and isolated clumps of date palms along its banks, before eventually emerging onto open plains. Shortly before Las Bela, a road, metalled for a short distance, branches off west towards Bedi Dat and Turbat in Makran. The main road bypasses Las Bela (228 kilometres from Khuzdar), which is reached by a left turn soon after the Turbat turning.

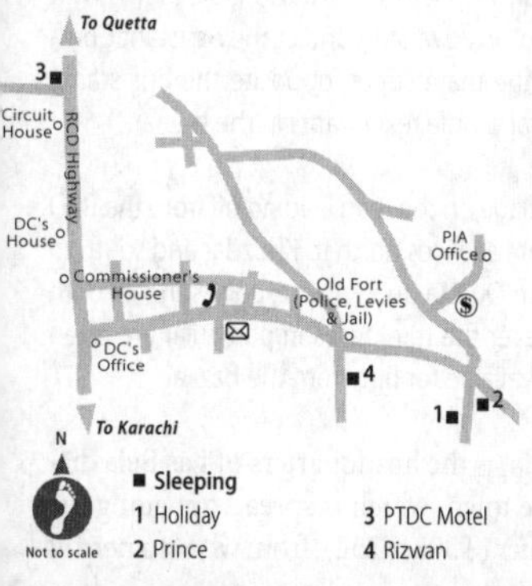

Las Bela

Colour map 1, grid C5

The large village of Las Bela is set in fertile surroundings, with plentiful date palms and trees giving the area a tropical feel. The village itself retains its traditional Baluchi character, most of the houses still being of mud and straw construction, with wooden beams and simple lattice work.

Distinctive open-sided chimneys also serve to catch the daytime breezes, ventilating the houses during summer.

This was the capital of the old state of Las Bela which was Buddhist during the seventh century, before the arrival of Rai Chach in 631 AD, and later the Arab general Mohammad Bin Qasim. It then existed as a semi-independent division of Kalat, rebelling against it in the 19th century. After independence, Kalat State was divided up and Las Bela became a separate District. The Lassi, with their own language of the same name, form the main tribal group around Las Bela. They are thought to have originated from Sind and been converted from Hinduism. As amongst the Makranis, Lassi women are allowed a share in inheritance.

Sights The small **main bazaar**, consisting of a covered street with small wooden shops, is colourful and interesting; good quality embroidered blouses and coarse woven rugs and pannier bags can be found here.

Sandeman's Grave Halfway between the bus station and the bazaar, a track leads off to the east, across a tributary of the nearby Porali River, to the garden and grave of Colonel Sir Robert Sandeman, who died of an illness here in 1892, while on tour as the Chief Commissioner of Baluchistan. The dome over the tomb was built by the *Jam* or ruler, Jamali Khan, who became a close friend of Robert Sandeman, and the shady gardens which he laid out are still well maintained and popular as a picnic spot.

Mausoleum of General Mohammad Haroon Just to the north of the village is a domed mausoleum, thought to be that of an Arab General, Mohammad Haroon. The mausoleum is set in a small enclosure and tended by a chowkidar. Inside are five graves, two of them placed together.

Gondrani Caves Approximately 15 kilometres north of Bela, in a narrow side ravine off the main Porali River, there are numerous caves carved into the sheer rock face, thought to date from the Buddhist period. A local legend relates how during the time of Solomon, a king reigned here, whose daughter, Buddul Jumaul, was so beautiful that she attracted the attentions of demons who killed seven of her suitors, all brothers, and tried to carry her off. Saif-ul-Muluk, son of the king of Egypt, arrived there about this time, fell in love with the princess, killed the demons and took her hand in marriage as a reward. The couple then brought peace and security to the area during their reign, and won the loyalty and respect of the people. The story provides an interesting comparison with the legend of Saiful Muluk lake in the Kaghan valley.

Sleeping & eating The ***Government Rest House*** is a classic piece of Colonial architecture set in a pleasant garden and manages to retain much of its atmosphere. It has reasonable rooms with attached bath and fan. It is necessary to book in advance; contact the Assistant Commissioner, T002-3366. A turning west off the main street, opposite the bus stand, leads up to the Rest House. There are several simple restaurants in the bazaar.

Transport The bus stand is to the south of the main village on the road leading off from the RCD Highway. Local buses and minibuses operate services north to Khuzdar and south to Uthal. There is also the through-traffic from Quetta and Karachi, consisting of both minibuses and large buses/coaches. However the minibuses in particular are often already full. A few jeeps and pick-ups are available for hire from the bazaar.

Uthal
Colour map 1, grid C6

Uthal, 60 kilometres to the south of Bela, is the headquarters of Las Bela district. There is nothing of interest in the town, which is spread out along the road, although the Deputy Commissioner (T308, F252), from whom a permit is officially required to visit Gaddani Beach, is based here. The only accommodation is in the *Government Rest House*.

Routes

From Uthal it is a further 115 kilometres to Karachi. The road passes within a couple of kilometres of Siranda Lake. Further on, there is a crossroads; the turning west here leads to a dam on the lake. At the small village of **Winder** there is a bazaar with tea shops and simple restaurants. Around 7 kilometres before arriving in Hub Chowki, there is a turning west to Gaddani Beach (see page 101), signposted "Gaddani Customs House".

Hub Chowki

Colour map 1, grid C6

Hub Chowki is a bustling industrial town which has risen to prominence with the building of the Pakistan's largest oil-fired power station here. There are no hotels, although the *Government Rest House* has comfortable a/c rooms, bookable through the Deputy Commissioner, T251. There are several basic but reasonable restaurants in the bazaar.

Routes

Just south of the town the road crosses the Hub River, which marks the border between Sind and Baluchistan. There is a check post here. The last section of the route passes through an increasingly industrialized landscape, before entering Karachi's sprawling suburbs.

The Makran

Sir Thomas Holditch, Surveyor General of India at the turn of the century, vividly described Makran's "brazen coast washed by a molten sea" and, inland, the "gigantic cap-crowned pillars and pedestals balanced in a fantastic array about the mountain slopes... with successive strata so well defined that they possess all the appearance of massive masonry construction...standing stiff, jagged, naked and uncompromising". The landscape of Makran is certainly amongst the most outlandish and spectacular in Baluchistan, prompting comparisons with a moonscape, though one might doubt that the moon could possess such bizarre scenery. Some of the most striking scenery can be found in the vicinity of the coastal town of Gwadar, which is also where the nicest hotel in the region is located.

Ins and outs

Permits

In 1998 it was still necessary to obtain a No Objection Certificate to visit the Makran. The region's strategic significance, close to the Straits of Hormouz, as well as the considerable amount of cross-border smuggling which goes on with Iran, make the area somewhat sensitive. Applications for permits must be made to the Home Department of the Provincial Government in Quetta (see under Useful Addresses in the Quetta Directory). In theory at least, you should be given an answer within one day. It is worth contacting the CTC in Quetta before applying; they will be able to help you with booking accommodation, which may improve your chances of being issued with a permit.

Getting there

Air By far the easiest and most practical means of reaching the Makran is by air. There are airports at Turbat, Jiwani, Gwadar, Pasni and Ormara, with regular flights linking these centres to Karachi and Quetta.

Bus Long-distance buses operate from Quetta to Turbat (minimum 30 hours), going via Panjgur, and from Khuzdar to Panjgur and Turbat. There are also long-distance buses from Karachi to Turbat (minimum 26 hours), going via Bedi Dat, and along the coast between Karachi, Pasni and Gwadar. Services on the coastal route are erratic.

Road Distances in the Makran are enormous and the road system all but non-existent. The network of rough jeep tracks are often made impassable by the sudden bursts of heavy rainfall characteristic of this region. A four-wheel drive is strongly recommended, as is a guide who is familiar with the area. Some specialist tour operators now run jeep safaris in the Makran and are usually able to offer tailor-made packages; see under Travel Agents in Karachi, Lahore or Islamabad.

Travelling from Quetta, a rough track branches southwest from the RCD Highway at Surab (213 kilometres south of Quetta). From Surab it is a further 320 kilometres to Panjgur, in the Rakhshan River valley. From here, a track leads south to cut through the Central Makran Range and then follows the Kech River west to reach Turbat, 280 kilometres from Panjgur.

From Karachi, the main route is north to Bela on the RCD Highway and then west via Bedi Dat and Hoshab. The coastal route branches west earlier, skirting Siranda Lake and Miani Hor, and then bears north along the Hingol River for a while before swinging southwest to Ormara and continuing west, touching the coast again at Pasni and Gwadar. This latter route is however little used, being extremely difficult and often impassable, particularly between Ormara and the RCD Highway.

The region

The Makran region is predominantly mountainous, with three parallel ranges running east-west. The southernmost is the **Makran Coastal range**, a line of low hills rising no higher than 65 metres. Next is the **Central Makran range** which reaches heights of over 1,300 metres, and to the north of this is the **Siahan range** separating Makran from Kharan.

The coast itself is deeply indented and marked by frequent table-topped promontories and peninsulas of white clay cliffs capped with coarse limestone, notably at Gwadar, Pasni and Ormara. The coastal belt is a mixture of sand and stony desert with occasional oases supporting the small fishing villages. It is within this coastal belt that the most spectacular scenery of eroded pillars and pedestals occurs. Between the Coastal and Central ranges is the narrow, fertile **Kech valley**, famous as the main growing area of Makran's 300

Makran Coast

Alexander's march through the Makran

In 326 BC, the Greek Macedonian King, Alexander the Great, led his army into the subcontinent through the high mountains of the Hindu Kush, advancing east as far as the River Beas before retreating and turning south to pass through Sind on his way to the Arabian Sea. He then elected to march with his army back to Greece across the wastes of Makran. He sent one of his generals, Crateros, by a more northerly route via the Mula Pass, Quetta and Helmand, while another general, Nearchus, sailed the fleet along the coast. Alexander, meanwhile, set off across the Makran, hoping by taking this route to be able to keep his fleet supplied with provisions. Some also suggest that Alexander, by no means ignorant of the difficulty of the route, was inspired by the challenge of successfully leading his army across a country which had reduced the armies of Semiramis and after her Cyrus to a mere handful of people. His ambition was nearly his undoing, The Makran, as for those before him, proved to be a merciless adversary. Alexander's march is described in detail by the historian Arrian:

"The blazing heat and want of water destroyed a great part of the army, and especially the beasts of burden, which perished from the great depth of the sand, and the heat which scorched like fire, while a great many died of thirst. The great distances also between the stages were most distressing to the army. When they traversed by night all the stage they had to complete and came to water in the morning, their distress was all but entirely relieved. But, if, as the day advanced, they were caught still marching owing to the great length of the stage, then suffer they did, tortured alike by raging heat and thirst unquenchable. Thus some were left behind on the road from sickness, others from intolerable thirst … some of the men were overcome by sleep on the way, but on awaking afterwards, those who still had some strength left, followed close on the track of the army and a few out of many saved their lives by overtaking it. The majority perished in the sand like shipwrecked men at sea.

Many of them besides came by their death through drinking, for, if, when jaded by the broiling heat and thirst, they fell in with abundance of water, they quaffed it with insatiable avidity till they killed themselves. When their provisions ran short, they came together and killed most of the horses and mules. They ate the flesh of these animals, which they professed had died of thirst and perished from the heat. When the army on one occasion lay encamped for the night near a small winter torrent for the sake of its water, the torrent became swollen by rains and came rushing down in so great a deluge that it destroyed most of the women and children of the camp followers, and swept away all the royal baggage and whatever beasts of burden were still left. The soldiers themselves, after a hard struggle, barely escaped with their lives, and a portion only of their weapons".

The portion of the army sailing with the fleet likewise suffered heavily, with many dying through disease, malnutrition and lack of water. Crateros meanwhile encountered no major obstacles on his return march. Alexander eventually arrived home to Babylon with a much reduced army. He died shortly after, in 323 BC.

varieties of dates. North of this, between the Central and Siahan ranges, is the wider but less fertile **Rakhshan valley**, with Panjgur as the main centre.

All the rivers in Makran are seasonal, being reduced to dry beds with occasional pools during dry weather, and filling rapidly to form fast flowing torrents after rain. The **Dasht River**, formed by the union of the Nihing and Kech Rivers, is the largest in the region, draining into Gwatar Bay, just west of Jiwani, close to the Iranian border. The **Kech River**, with its tributaries the Gish and Kil, steadily widens as it flows west through the Kech valley, reaching over two kilometres in width at Turbat. The **Shadi River** rises close to

Jamgwang, south of Turbat, and flows south, east and then south again, fed by various hill torrents and tributaries along the way, to drain into the sea just north of Pasni. Further east, the **Basol** winds a tortuous course through the high clay ridges of the Coastal Range before draining into the sea west of Ormara. The **Hingol River** is the largest in Baluchistan, although it is not strictly speaking in Makran, flowing for the most part through Jhalawan District and for a short stretch through Las Bela. Its major tributaries are the Mashkai, Nal, Arra and Mar.

The coastal waters of the Arabian Sea are rich in fish, including tuna, snapper, groakers, grunters, sardines, skate and shark, as well as lobster and shrimp.

The people

Although frequently referred to as Makranis, the people of Makran are essentially Baluch. While they are divided into distinct groups and differentiated according to social status, the absence of a tribal system based on organized political or ethnic units is unique in Baluchistan. The dominant classes, traditionally wealthy landowners, include the Gichkis, Nausherwanis, Mirwaris and Bisanjaus. The middle classes, of smaller landowners, consist of a large number of family groups, the more important of which are the Rinds, Rais, Hots, Kalmatis, Kauhdais, Shehzada and Jadgals or Jats (meaning cultivators). The lower classes consist of occupational groups and are considered to be the aboriginals of Makran. The Meds are fishermen and appear to have much in common with the Ichthyophagoi (fish eaters) described by Arrian. Interestingly, their patron saint is Sakhi Tangav, whose tomb is at Dadhar, on the Kachhi plains near Sibi, suggesting that they originated from that area. The Meds remain amongst the poorest groups in Makran. For three months of the year from May to July, the seas are very rough and the fishing poor, forcing many to take loans from businessmen. Loans are then repayed in fish, prices being dictated by the moneylender, with the result that the fishermen are caught in a cycle of debt which renders them in effect bonded labourers. The Koras, who are sailors, are a branch of the Med. The Darzadas are agricultural labourers and although found scattered all over the Makran, they are concentrated around the Kech valley and Panjgur where they are known as Nakibs. The Loris are traditionally artizans (blacksmiths, carpenters, goldsmiths et cetera) or else musicians and story tellers. Many of them are nomadic.

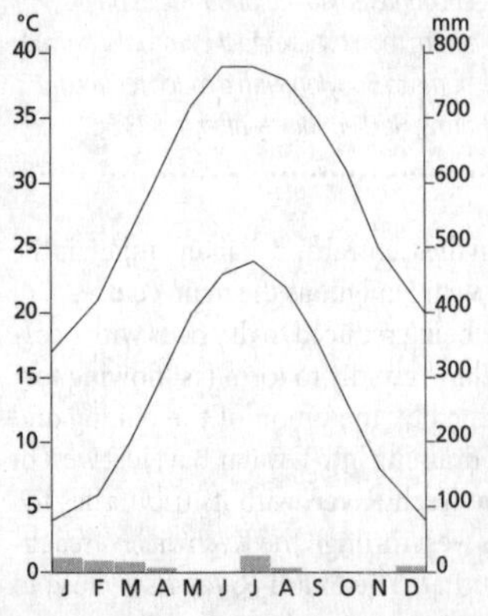

The best time to visit is between October and March

Women occupy a unique position in Makrani society as compared with the rest of Baluchistan. On marriage, as elsewhere, a bride-price is paid by the bridegroom and his family. However, instead of a cash payment to the bride's father, this traditionally consists of land, ornaments and servile dependants, all of which become the personal property of the bride. Women are also entitled to inherit a portion of their parents' property. Thus women are often the wealthy partner in a marriage, with the man being in effect dependent on his wife's wealth. The relatively strong status of women is reflected also in the tradition of attributing the qualities of a child to the mother.

Religion

A sect, known as the **Zikri**, are still to be found in the Makran, particularly around Turbat, where they have established a position of strength in the business community. The Zikri sect is associated to the Mahdevi movement which was started in the 15th century by Sayid Mohammad Joneri, who proclaimed himself a *Mahdi* ("rightly guided one"). One of his followers, Mullah Mohammad is thought to have brought the faith to Makran, perhaps arriving with the Buledais tribe from Helmand. Although they consider themselves to be Muslims, the Zikri are frowned upon by orthodox Islam and there have been attempts by various parties in Baluchistan to have them declared non-Muslims and classified as a religious minority. The all important *Hajj* to Mecca is replaced by an annual pilgrimage to Koh-e-Murad ('hill of fulfilment'), near Turbat, where some believe the Mahdi is buried. The term Zikri is derived from the Arabic Dhikr or Zikr, literally meaning 'remembrance' and more loosely translated as 'litany', in reference to the importance attached to the reciting of the name of God amongst the Zikris. This practice of Zikr replaces the prayers of orthodox Islam.

Local animistic and elemental beliefs, which existed before the advent of Islam, still exert a strong influence, particularly amongst the Meds. Most diseases are considered to be the result of a person being possessed by a spirit or *Gwat*. Patients are first taken to the local *Mat*, somewhat akin to a Shaman, who induces a trance in the patient and speaks through them to the Gwat. Conditions are then agreed for the Gwat to leave the afflicted person, usually involving the holding of a *Leb*, or meeting, at which there is further chanting and induced trances until the Gwat is appeased.

Elsewhere, orthodox Islam has been intermingled with various local beliefs. The most striking example of this can be found in the practice of *shepar-ja*, a type of worship or religious rite. It is confined to people of slave extraction, the patron saint, Sheikh Farid Shakar himself having been a slave. The ceremonies, involving frenzied chanting and dancing to the rhythm of drums, have been associated with the fetish worship of Africa, although the songs and chanting are in Urdu and Sindhi.

The Rifai are another unusual sect found in the Makran, particularly amongst the Meds and Koras of Gwadar. The Rifai are named after their leader Saiad Ahmad Kabir of Iran. At religious meetings they chant verses to the accompaniment of drums and, working themselves into a frenzy, pierce their skin with sharp spikes.

Turbat

Colour map 1, grid C2

Turbat is the Divisional Headquarters for the Makran and has grown considerably in recent years to become an important data processing centre. However, the development of industry and enterprise is restricted by the absence of surfaced roads linking it with the rest of the country. The town, of little interest in itself, consists of a dusty bazaar and main street, with most of the new development spread out over a wide area to the south.

Miri Kalat, situated around 10 kilometres west of Turbat, on the north bank of the Kech River, is an important historical site with the ruins of a large fort perched on top of a high mound. Excavations have revealed evidence of continuous occupation from at least the Harappan period (2700 BC) until around 100 years ago. Little remains of the fort's walls and towers, although it is likely that the high mound on which the fort is situated conceals older walls, perhaps up to 10 metres high, buildings and artefacts chronicling over 4,500 years of habitation. An Italian team has been involved in excavating the site in recent years, although until there is a comprehensive plan for the conservation and management of the site, it is unlikely to be fully excavated.

Sleeping **D** *Gul Rang*, Main Rd, T413002, F413004. Comfortable rooms with a/c, TV and attached bath. Best hotel in town. Good restaurant. **E** ***Mulla Jan***, Main Rd, T412763. Reasonable rooms with fan and attached bath. Pleasant garden. Restaurant. **F** ***Muree***, Main Bazaar, T412213. Basic but relatively clean rooms with fan and attached bath. Restaurant.

Eating The restaurant in the *Gul Rang* hotel serves good food. *Mulla Jan's* restaurant is also reasonable. The *Muree* hotel has a basic restaurant and there are several other similar restaurants in Main Bazaar and Main Road.

Directory **Useful telephone numbers** *Deputy Commissioner's Office*, T413202. ***Commissioner's Office***, T413244. ***Police***, T412222.

Transport **Air** PIA Booking Office, Commissionery Road, T412322 (turn right out of *Gul Rang* hotel, follow the road round to the left, past a left turn – the road to the airport – and the building is clearly visible on the left-hand side). Regular flights to **Karachi** (up to 4 daily). 4 flights weekly to **Quetta** (Monday, Tuesday, Friday, Sunday). 3 flights weekly to **Pasni** (Tuesday, Wednesday, Thursday), **Khuzdar** (Monday, Tuesday, Saturday) and **Panjgur** (Wednesday, Friday, Saturday). 2 flights weekly to **Gwadar** (Thursday, Sunday) and **Dalbandin** (Tuesday, Sunday). 1 flight weekly to **Ormara** (Wednesday).

Road There are long-distance **buses** to **Karachi** (via Bela) and **Quetta** (via Panjgur) departing from Main Road. Toyota **pick-ups** operate passenger services to **Pasni**, **Gwadar** and **Jiwani**, departing from Main Bazaar.

Turbat to Gwadar

It takes approximately six hours to cover the 190 kilometres from Turbat to Gwadar. The road is an un-metalled jeep track and a four-wheel drive is recommended. The track heads south from Turbat through an area of barren rocky hills formed of shales and clay, with distinct strata of rock breaking through in vertical ridges. After approximately 20 kilometres it forks; left to Piderak, a picturesque oasis with the remains of an old fort, and on to Pasni (115 kilometres), and right to Suntsar (150 kilometres), headquarters for the Dasht area, on the route between Mand and Jiwani. Taking the right fork, the track crosses a wide plain and passes through some low hills before bearing east to skirt round the edge of a higher range of hills. After 55 kilometres, just before Piri Chat (previously known as Kikki), bear left at a second fork (right to Suntsar). From here it is another 55 kilometres to the coast road. The track bears south to cut through a low point in the hills, and runs parallel to the seasonal Belar River. At the small oasis of Talar there are a few buildings and basic restaurants and tea stalls. The track continues over a wide expanse of open, sparsely vegetated plains with occasional oases and low barren hills before reaching the coast road. From here it is 60 kilometres to Gwadar. The track passes the scattered settlement of Nalent and the coastal village of Kappar to the south, before crossing the seasonal Karwent River. Here you pass through a spectacular landscape of low mud hills, heavily eroded into deeply fluted fingers and outlandish shapes. The track then passes a large flat-topped hill to the south, known as Koh-e-Mehdi. Soon after is Gwadar airport. For the remaining 12 kilometres into the centre of the town, the road is metalled.

Gwadar

Phone code: 0204
Colour map 1, grid C2

The town of Gwadar is the largest of the fishing villages along the coast. It is spread out along a narrow spit of land extending out to sea, with East and West bays on either side. At the southern tip of the spit, steep cliffs rise up to a wide peninsular platform, known as Koh-e-Bahtil, which fans out into a hammerhead some 10 kilometres in length and two kilometres wide. The greatest attraction here is undoubtedly the miles of deserted beaches which stretch in both directions from Gwadar. Although generally more exposed, the beaches on the West Bay side are more pleasant, as well as being more easily accessible (this is also where the attractive *Gwadar Tourist Motel* is located, see below).Fishing forms the main source of income in Gwadar, with the waters of the Arabian Sea yielding excellent catches of tuna, *Ghor* and shellfish. Today many of the traditional wooden boats of the Meds are motorized, and a jetty able to handle larger vessels has been built in East Bay.

History

Gwadar is probably amongst the oldest settlements along the Makran Coast, although nothing is known about its ancient history. As a maritime port, it was certainly heavily influenced by sea-trade, which from an early period extended throughout the Gulf, Arabian Sea and Indian Ocean region. During the 16th century, Portuguese ships arrived at Gwadar and established a fortified post on top of Koh-e-Bahtil overlooking the town, the remains of which can still be seen today. When they left in 1581, they destroyed the town.

During the 18th century, Makran came under the loose control of Kalat. Nasir Khan, the Khan of Kalat, granted Kalat's portion of Gwadar's revenue (and by implication suzerainty over the port) to Sayid Sultan, an estranged brother of the Sultan of Muscat who had taken refuge in Makran. Sayid Sultan subsequently overthrew his brother to gain the Sultanate of Muscat. The exact terms of the agreement between Sayid and Nasir are unclear; some maintain that Gwadar was in effect given as a gift in perpetuity while others argue that Sayid was supposed to relinquish control if ever he regained Muscat. In the event, Gwadar and a considerable area of the surrounding land remained a part of Muscat, and later Oman, until it was bought back by the Pakistani Government in 1957. Many of the people retain joint citizenship of Oman and Pakistan, and there are large numbers of Pakistanis from Gwadar working in Oman.

Sights

The old bazaar and fish markets are situated on the East Bay side. From the main square and bus stand, a series of narrow alleys lined with old wooden houses and shops lead through to the fish markets, where the day's catch is displayed for sale. Further along is the new jetty. The Governor's House and many of the administrative buildings are on the West Bay side, as well as the rest house and hotel. The police station, built in the style of a fort, is a good example of the distinctive Omani architecture typical of this area.

Mausoleum of Baba Sheikh Abdullah This mausoleum, situated in a graveyard at the foot of the cliffs represents a piece of architecture unique in the Makran. As well as being constructed of stone in a region where sun-dried bricks are the prevalent building material, it is topped by an onion-shaped dome of a type not found elsewhere in the region. An inscription inside gives the date 1468. However, it is possible that it is much older. One theory suggests that the mausoleum underwent a major transformation at some stage, having originally been identical in design to the tombs found at Chaukundi in Sind.

Koh-e-Bahtil A link road zigzags its way up the side of Koh-e-Bahtil. In a depression on top are two small lakes formed by a *band* (dam) which catches all the rain water run-off from the surrounding area. The origins of the dam are unclear. While local tradition dates it to the period of Portuguese occupation, it has also been suggested that the workmanship is indicative of a much earlier period and bears striking similarities to buildings in Yemen dating from around the time of Christ. A local tradition tells of a powerful Arabic tribe settled on the Arabian Peninsular, who were forced by political upheavals and ecological changes to abandon their home, and came to settle on Koh-e-Bahtil which they transformed into a fertile orchard. Today the area, shaded by trees and dotted with pools, is a popular picnic spot. To the north, up on the cliffs overlooking the town, are the remains of a stone wall, said to be the ruins of the settlement established by the Portuguese. The best views out over Gwadar can be obtained from here.

Mud volcanos Near to the village of Dhur, to the east of the airport, below the tall cliffs of Koh-i-Mehdi, there is a small mud volcano, known locally by the Persian name *Dharya Chamag*, literally 'eye of the sea' or *Chandra Kups*, 'moon volcano'. It consists of a small pool in the centre of a low mound from which muddy sea water bubbles up at certain times, apparently under the influence of the tides. A number of these mud volcanoes are to be found elsewhere along the Makran coast, the largest reportedly being over 100 metres tall. Nearby, villagers collect sea water in large shallow beds where it evaporates leaving behind deposits of salt which are collected into large mounds. The salt is used in the drying of fish, particularly *Ghor*, which can then be stored for up to three years.

Essentials

Sleeping & eating Hotel facilities are limited, with just 2 options, both in West Bay, near the Governor's house. The government's **D** ***Fish Harbour Rest House*** has a/c rooms with attached bath, but little in the way of character. Book through the Deputy Commissioner, T2355. Much more picturesque is the **E** ***Gwadar Tourist Motel***, T2688. Owned by the CTC, it is currently being leased out to the enormously friendly and hospitable Bakshi Baluch. 4 rooms with fan and attached bath. Pleasant garden and veranda looking out to sea. The restaurant serves excellent fish. Recommended. There are a number of basic restaurants around the main square in East Bay.

Transport **Air** PIA Booking Office, T2222 (situated on Airport Road, just south of the main square and bazaar. New premises under construction at the main fork on Airport Road, north of the town). The airport is 12 kilometres north of Gwadar. Regular flights to **Karachi** (1-2 daily). 2 flights weekly to **Turbat** (Monday, Saturday). 1 flight weekly to **Jiwani** (Friday) and **Panjgur** (Thursday).

Road There are long-distance **buses** to **Karachi** (via Turbat and Bela), as well as irregular local buses along the coast, east to **Pasni** and west to **Jiwani**. Toyota **pick-ups** operate regular passenger services to **Turbat**.

Car Hire Toyota pick-ups can be hired, with driver, from the main square and provide the most practical means of visiting surrounding areas. The return trip to Jiwani costs around Rs 2,000, and to Pasni around Rs 2,500.

Gwadar to Jiwani

A four-wheel drive and guide is necessary for this route west along the coast to Jiwani. The road is largely non-existent, with long stretches across open desert and mud flats, marked only by the tyre tracks of previous vehicles.

The road branches west just before the airport. The first few kilometres pass through an area of sand dunes which are liable to drift across the road, making progress difficult. Further on, a track branches off to the right, leading up to the recently completed Akra Kaur Dam which, it is hoped, will provide Gwadar with adequate supplies of fresh drinking water. The main track crosses a bridge over the course of the Akra River before emerging onto the wide desert expanses of the coastal belt. The track is at times very rough, passing over deeply corrugated mud flats. Visible to the north are the Garok mountains, and to the south the jagged outline of the Shabi hills. A water pumping station marks the turning south to the fishing village of **Pishukan**, also once part of Oman. The levies post here was originally built by the Omanis and closely resembles the police station in Gwadar.

From Pishukan there is an alternative route west, following the coastline closely. This route, running along the south flank of the coastal hills, gives the best views of their heavily eroded features, which have in places left improbable looking pillars and spires rising out of the desert and huge boulders hollowed by the wind into fragile shells with jagged, pitted surfaces. At the tiny village of **Gunz**, further west along the coast near Jiwani, a definite European/Greek influence is discernible in the features of the people, who also speak a slightly different dialect. The origins of the village's name are also unclear; Gunz is not a Baluchi or Makrani word, and some suggest that it is a corruption of 'guns'. The main route continues west from the turning to Pishukan, across open desert, before bearing gradually southwest to reach the village of Jiwani.

Jiwani

Colour map 1, grid C1

Jiwani was an important base for the British during the Second World War, and the remains of RAF barracks and other buildings can be seen up on the hill behind the village. The nearby officer's mess is now occupied by the Pakistan Navy. The creek or *Hor* behind Jiwani was also used by the navy as a repair yard for ships, which could be sailed in during the spring tides and re-floated the following year.

A large graveyard near the village is thought to date from the period of the Arabic invasions during the seventh century. One of the gravestones, ornately decorated and surrounded by a border, is inscribed in Arabic, with the names Ibrahim and Mohammad just discernible. If indeed dating from the seventh century, the presence of a graveyard here is interesting as tradition at that time dictated that the dead from an expedition had to be transported home for burial. One theory suggests that the ship returning home with those killed in fighting ran into problems and was forced to land at Jiwani, where the corpses were buried for want of a means to preserve them.

Other graveyards in the villages surrounding Jiwani are thought to have even older origins, with gravestones bearing floral designs, similar to those found near Bela, and thought to date from the time of Rais Jamu, ancestor of the Med population in the region. Elsewhere there are shallow vertical graves topped by small cairns in which, according to a local legend, people in ancient times used to entomb themselves, committing suicide in the face of famine.

Sleeping & eating The only accommodation here is at the *Government Rest House*, pleasantly located on low cliffs overlooking the bay. Comfortable, though somewhat run down. It must be booked in advance through the Deputy Commissioner in Gwadar. There are basic restaurants in the bazaar.

Transport **Air** PIA Booking Office, T289. There is one flight weekly to **Karachi** via **Turbat**, departing Friday morning.

Road Local **buses**/Toyota **pick-ups** operate irregular services to **Gwadar**.

Gwadar to Pasni

The first section of the route from Gwadar to Pasni is the same as for Turbat. Continuing east past the turning north for Turbat, the rough track runs through wide expanses of sand dunes. The route passes north of the village of **Kandasole** and then on to **Chakole**. Soon after, a track bears off north into the **Kalag** hills. The main track passes close to the airport before arriving in Pasni, approximately 170 kilometres from Gwadar.

Pasni

Colour map 1, grid C3

The town of Pasni is today the second largest fishing port along the Makran coast after Gwadar. When it was burnt by the Portuguese in 1581, it was described as a "rich and beautiful city". In the early 1900s it rose in prominence above Gwadar, being closer to the regional centre of Turbat. The mini-port here was completed in 1989 with the help of a German company, and now handles much of the fish catch, some of which is partly dried for export to Sri Lanka, while the rest is taken directly to Karachi for sale or export.

Sleeping & eating There is only one hotel in Pasni, the **E** *Marwi*, T210303. Simple rooms with fan and attached bath. Restaurant. There are some basic restaurants in the bazaar. Foreigners should register with the Assistant Commissioner's Office, T210529.

Transport **Air** PIA Booking Office, Aslam Shah Market, T210501. Daily flights (except Friday and Sunday) to **Karachi**. 3 flights weekly to**Turbat** (Tuesday, Wednesday, Thursday). 1 flight weekly to **Panjgur**.

Road Long-distance buses operate to **Karachi** (via Turbat). Local buses and Toyota pick-ups operate to **Gwadar** and **Turbat**.

Punjab

Punjab

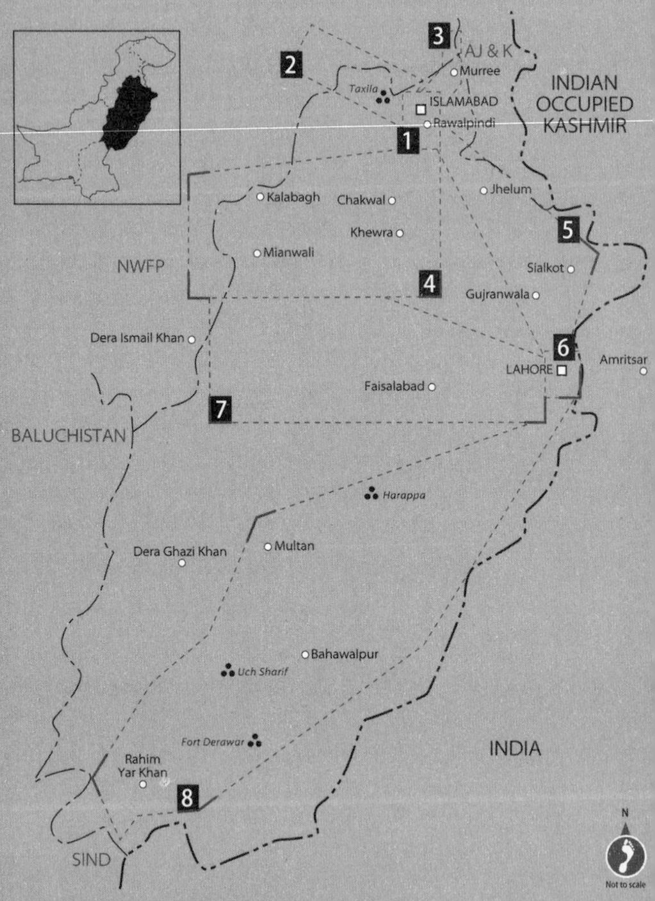
1
2
3
4
5
6
7
8
AJ & K
Murree
Taxila
ISLAMABAD
Rawalpindi
INDIAN
OCCUPIED
KASHMIR
Kalabagh
Chakwal
Jhelum
Khewra
Mianwali
NWFP
Sialkot
Gujranwala
Dera Ismail Khan
LAHORE
Amritsar
Faisalabad
BALUCHISTAN
Harappa
Multan
Dera Ghazi Khan
Bahawalpur
Uch Sharif
Fort Derawar
INDIA
Rahim
Yar Khan
SIND
N
Not to scale

Text Divisions

The most populous state in Pakistan, Punjab derives its name from the "five waters" ('punj' meaning five, 'ab' meaning water) that are tributaries of the Indus. Lying at the crossroads of Asia, the Punjab has seen an endless succession of invaders, all of whom have left their mark on the history, language, religion, culture, literature and architecture of the region. Despite this history of cultural invasion, however, Punjab displays greater cultural homogeneity than say, Sind, and most Punjabis are descended from the Indo-Aryans who migrated into South Asia during the second millennium BC.

Punjab's heritage can be best seen by the tourist in the great Mughal and Anglo-Indian buildings of Lahore, the stunningly restored shrines of Multan, the beautiful tombs at Uch Sharif, and in a string of spectacular desert forts strung across the Cholistan Desert to the southeast.

Best time to visit Visiting the Punjab at a suitable time of year will greatly enhance your enjoyment of the state and its attractions. It's not much fun traipsing around the great sights of Lahore and Multan with the temperature in the 40°s, and humidity over 90 percent! Winter (November-February) is the best time to visit, although Punjab is still pleasant in spring and autumn. Winter nights can be cold, however, and woollens required. Rainfall can be heavy in the monsoonal belt in July, August and September.

Ins and outs

Lying at the heart of Pakistan, most visitors pass through the Punjab at some point, and thus it can be approached from a number of directions. Although Karachi (in Sind) remains the main international air gateway, increasing numbers of visitors are flying directly into Islamabad (this makes a lot of sense if you are heading directly to the north). Pakistan's capital, Islamabad, actually stands in the Punjab, although administratively it occupies a separate status. It, along with its 'twin' city of Rawalpindi, acts as the gateway to the Karakoram Highway, and whether you travel this route north-south or south-north, it is likely that you will travel through Islamabad/Rawalpindi at some point. Thus, this chapter of the *Pakistan Handbook* begins with a description of "Islamabad/Rawalpindi" (including excursions in the immediate area), then follows with details of points of interest along the route to Peshawar in NWFP ("Islamabad/Rawalpindi to Peshawar"). The following two sections then describe areas within easy access of Islamabad/Rawalpindi, ie "Murree and the Galis" and "The Salt Range".

The chapter then describes in detail the key points along the GT Road between Islamabad/Rawalpindi and Lahore that other guides ignore, in the "Islamabad/Rawalpindi to Lahore" section. Visitors arriving from India enter the Punjab from the east, via the provincial capital of Lahore, and this fabulous 'unmissable' city justifies its own section in the chapter, "Lahore". There are a number of minor points of interest described in the "West of Lahore" section, before the chapter concludes with the many highlights of Pakistan to be found in "Southern Punjab". Such sites usually form stop-over points for people travelling between Lahore and Karachi (or vice-versa).

Punjab: the dominant state?

Although there is an even distribution of seats between the four provinces of Pakistan in the Senate (Upper House) of the legislative assembly, the National Assembly (Lower House) is dominated by the Punjab. Over half of the seats (115 out of 217) in the country's sovereign legislative body are in the Punjab, and although this reflects the fact that half of Pakistan's population live in this state, the other states see it as an attempt by Punjab to dominate the nation. The almost total Punjabi domination of the army, and to a lesser extent Pakistan's powerful civil service, is deeply resented by the other states of the federation, and is seen as a Punjabi plot to exert hegemony over the country.

Nowhere is this controversy greater than in the matter of **Kalabagh**. A small town in the Salt Range area of the Punjab (see page 242), Kalabagh is the proposed site for a controversial new hydro-electric power generating and irrigation scheme on the Indus. The idea of building a dam here dates back to 1954. Desperate to meet its energy shortfall, the government of Punjab revived the scheme in the early 1990s. However, the project was blocked by the Sind and NWFP governments. The reduced flow of the Indus downstream from the dam would have an adverse affect on agricultural production in many areas of their provinces, they argued. Furthermore, it would displace huge numbers of people. According to WAPDA's own estimates, a total of 83,000 people would be displaced by the dam, but other estimates put the figure as high as 400,000. Bitter memories remain of the broken compensation promises following the construction of the Tarbela Dam. The fate of important historical sites such as Attock Fort are not even considered in impact assessment reports, and there are many other sites of enormous archaeological significance which would be submerged. Experts also suggested that the

Travel in the Punjab

Punjab is probably the most stable state in Pakistan, and has been relatively untouched by the ethnic and criminal tension currently gripping Sind, the tribal quarrels affecting Baluchistan and NWFP, and the instability created by the problem of Kashmir.

*However, in recent years there has been a significant upsurge in sectarian violence between the majority Sunni sect of Islam and the minority Shia sect. Early in 1994, a new quasi-religious/political party formed to "protect the rights of their community". The Shia **Sipah-e-Mohammad Pakistan** (SMP) is considered by many commentators to be the most militant religious organization in the country, responsible for upping the stakes in Punjab's sectarian divide. The SMP, however, argues that it is merely protecting its community from the militant Sunni organization that has "become a byword for violent anti-Shia fanaticism", the **Sipah-i-Sahaba Pakistan** (SSP). It is a confrontation that the country cannot afford. Both organizations have their power bases in remote areas that tourists are unlikely to visit, although it is worth keeping your ear to the ground as the situation develops.*

unique geology of the Salt Range means that wells in the area would turn brackish.

For a while the project was shelved, but in the summer of 1998 Nawaz Sharif revived it. Current estimates put the cost of the project at a staggering US$9bn, a seemingly impossible sum for a country said by many to be on the verge of bankruptcy. Leaving aside the cost, Nawaz Sharif's determination to have the project completed is seen by many as evidence of his bias towards his home province. It is Punjab which will benefit most, they argue, both in terms of increased electricity generation and irrigation potential, while NWFP and Sind bear the brunt of the social, economic and environmental impacts. Given that Punjab is already by far the wealthiest province in Pakistan, and the most influential politically, this is seen as just another example of Punjab exerting its hegemony over the rest of the country.

Islamabad and Rawalpindi

The contrast couldn't be greater between the twin cities of Islamabad and Rawalpindi. Islamabad is Pakistan's modern, neatly planned capital, built in the 1960s and laid out according to a grid pattern, with sectors for government, commerce, residential, recreational and industrial use. Rawalpindi meanwhile is a sprawling, congested, chaotic and typically South Asian city, with its old bazaars, Cantonment and Saddar areas. Both are growing rapidly and the master plan envisages that the two cities will one day form a single urban mass, with Islamabad encircling the central core of Rawalpindi. Most people pass through these cities at some stage, without paying them much attention beyond sorting out whatever business they have here or organizing their onward journey, but if you do have the time, they are worth exploring in a little more detail.

Ins and outs

Getting there An increasing number of international flights go directly to Islamabad/Rawalpindi, making this the first point of arrival in Pakistan for many visitors, and a far more convenient starting point if you are heading for the mountains. There are also frequent internal flights connecting Islamabad/Rawalpindi with most major towns and cities. Pakistan's main railway artery passes through Rawalpindi, providing links to Lahore and ultimately Karachi (with a branch to Quetta) in one direction, and on to Peshawar in the other. The main bus station, Pir Wadhai, is a chaotic place, inconveniently located for both Islamabad and Pindi, but for major routes you can find services which arrive at and depart from Murree Road and the Saddar area of 'Pindi; a much more practical arrangement.

Getting around Rawalpindi sits astride the old Grand Trunk Road (GT Road) on its route between Peshawar and Lahore, while Islamabad is situated to the north, nestling right up against the foothills of the Margalla range. The two are connected by the Murree road, which runs north from 'Pindi's Cantonment and Saddar Bazaar areas, passing close to the heart of the Old City, to arrive eventually at a large intersection known as Faisabad, from where a broad highway leads northwest to Islamabad's Zero Point.

A steady stream of intercity buses and minibuses connect Islamabad and Rawalpindi. The buses (large, brightly decorated Bedfords) are impossibly slow, stopping at every opportunity to pick up passengers, and best avoided. The minibuses (Toyota Hiace or Ford vans) are extremely cramped but much faster. Taxis are the most comfortable option, though the 15 kilometres trip between Pindi's Saddar area and Islamabad will cost Rs 200 or more, as compared with less than Rs 10 on the buses. Taxis are by far the most convenient way of getting to and from the airport. Within Rawalpindi you have the choice of auto-rickshaws or taxis, as well as horse-drawn tongas around Rajah Bazaar and Committee Chowk. The intercity buses are also useful for getting from Saddar to points along Murree Road. Within specific areas of 'Pindi, walking is also an option. Islamabad is too spread out to walk around.

The intercity buses are useful for getting between the main centres (Zero Point, Aabpara Market, Supermarket and Jinnah Supermarket). There are also local bus/minibus services to other districts of the capital, but on the whole taxis are the most convenient; if they do not have a working meter, always agree a price before getting in.

Islamabad - Rawalpindi Overview

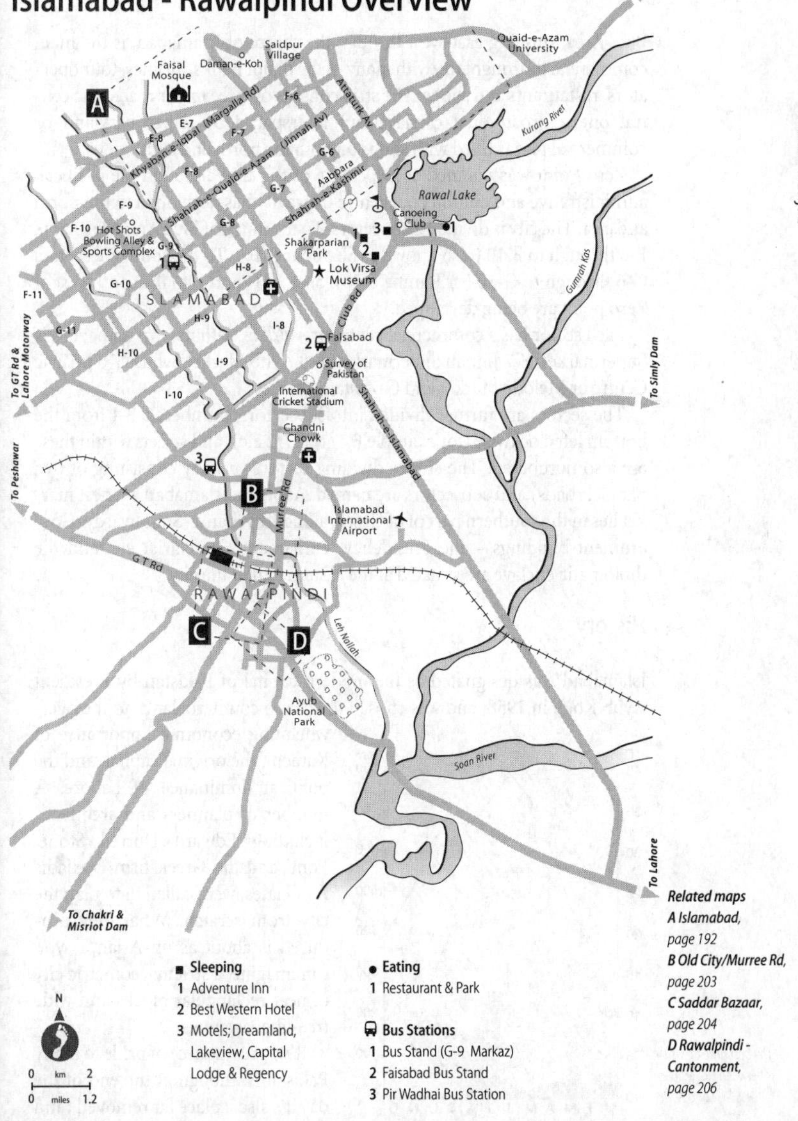

Related maps
A Islamabad, page 192
B Old City/Murree Rd, page 203
C Saddar Bazaar, page 204
D Rawalpindi - Cantonment, page 206

Islamabad

Phone code: 051
Colour map 4, grid A4

Islamabad is often dismissed as a modern, bland and characterless city. Certainly, if you are wrestling with its bureaucrats or plodding round the airline offices or embassies or wherever, it's not exactly the most inspiring of places. But it does have its attractions. Its saving grace is the abundance of open woodland and greenery in amongst all the development, and the natural beauty of the nearby Margalla hills. This is the only urban experience you'll come across in Pakistan which isn't accompanied by choking atmospheric pollution.

Layout

Blue Area, running east-west through the centre of Islamabad, is the main commercial thoroughfare, with many of the major banks, airlines, tour operators, restaurants and shops. The strip consists of three major roads (the central one a broad dual carriageway) interspaced by either parkland or commercial plazas lined with shops on both the north and south sides.

Zero Point was planned as the centre of the city, although the political, administrative and commercial centre of gravity has developed to the north and east. The city is divided into sectors. To the north of Blue Area are sectors F-6 through to F-10 (also known as Shalimar 6-10). To the south are sectors G-6 through to G-10 (or Ramna 6-10). Sectors H and I, to the southwest of Zero point are being developed.

Each sector has a commercial centre or *Markaz*, with its own name; F-6 is Supermarket, F-7 Jinnah Supermarket, F-8 Ayub Market, while G-6 is Civic Centre or Melody Market and G-7 Sitara Market.

The sectors are further divided into subsectors, numbered 1-4 from the bottom left clockwise (for example F-7/1, F-7/2 etc), and streets within these are also numbered. The streets dividing sectors (usually consisting of two parallel roads) and subsectors are named. Aabpara, Islamabad's oldest market lies in the southern part of of G-6/1, along Khyaban-e-Suhrawardy. Government buildings – the Presidency, Parliament, Secretariat etc, and the diplomatic enclave are situated at the eastern end of the city.

History

Islamabad was designated as the modern capital of Pakistan by President Ayub Khan in 1958, and was chosen to act as a counterbalance to the overwhelming economic importance of Karachi, the original capital, and the political dominance of Lahore. A number of planners and architects, including Edward Durrell Stone, Ponti and the Greek firm Doxiadis Associates, were called in to plan the city from scratch. What they produced is about as un-Asian as you can imagine; a strictly geometric city of neat rectangular blocks and wide tree-lined avenues.

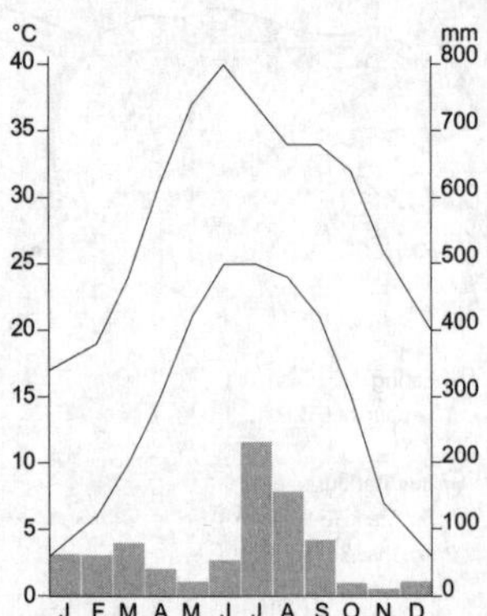

The best time to visit is between November and April

It's a great source of pride to many Pakistanis, though at the end of the day it's also a place far removed (and in many ways very isolated) from the rest of Pakistan. True to its modern image, it's home to some of Pakistan's more daring modern architecture, particularly some of the foreign missions in the diplomatic enclave, as well as the government buildings which reflect the grandeur and scale of the city plan. Elsewhere there are some interesting fusions of 20th century post-modernism and traditional Islamic architecture.

Sights

Margalla Hills

The Margalla hills spread over an area of 12,000 hectares, rising to a maximum height of 1,580 metres. The area has been designated as a National Park in an attempt to curb the encroachment of quarrying and developers, and to protect the rich flora and fauna. The hills offer numerous opportunities for walks and longer hikes, just minutes from the city centre (see under Excursions from Islamabad, page 216, for more details).

Daman-e-Koh

The viewpoint at Daman-e-Koh occupies a spur of the Margalla hills overlooking Islamabad. A road winds its way up to the viewpoint from the north end of 7th Avenue, passing first through beautiful woods with various walking trails before climbing into the hills. There are a couple of snack bars at the turning for the viewpoint, and at the viewpoint itself there is the *Kashmirwala's* restaurant (see Eating, below), with its terrace offering great views of Islamabad. There are a number of short walks around the spur.

Saidpur Village

Saidpur is situated to the east of Daman-e-Koh and reached by a road leading north from the top end of F-6 (the turning is signposted). This small traditional village, surrounded by mango trees, was predominantly Hindu before Partition, and the springs in the area were considered holy. You come first to the school, which is housed in a former Hindu temple. If you follow the stream to the right of the school as you face it, you come to a couple of potters' workshops where you can see the beautifully decorated traditional items of pottery which are still produced here.

Faisal Masjid

Built with funds gifted by King Faisal Bin Abdul Aziz of Saudi Arabia and designed by a Turkish architect, this mosque is one of the largest in the world, with 88 metres high minarets resembling rockets. It is said to hold 100,000 worshippers. The main prayer hall is an unique tent-like structure with eight faces, rising to 40 metres at its summit. The raised courtyard boasts huge expanses of polished marble. There is a bookshop, library and lecture hall belonging to the Islamic Research Centre, and a restaurant to the rear. Signs state that photography is strictly forbidden, but this is applied only in the main prayer hall.

Islamabad Museum

This small museum has an excellent selection of artefacts with rooms covering the prehistoric, Indus Valley, Gandharan, Arabic and Islamic periods. Although no match for the major museums at Peshawar, Lahore and Karachi, the presentation is very good. Well worth a visit, particularly if you lose interest quickly in larger museums.

■ *House 41, Street 3, E-7, T9223826. 0900-1630, Friday 0930-1230, 1430-1630, Wednesday closed. Free. Heading west from the east end of Gomal Road, take the first right (Street 2) and then the first left (Street 3); the museum is two-thirds of the way down on the right.*

Nurpur Shahan This small village is situated three kilometres to the northeast of the Diplomatic Enclave and is famous for the shrine of the 17th century saint, Hazrat Syed Shah Abdul Latif or Barri Imam (holy man of the woods), who lived for 12 years in a nearby cave. Pilgrims arrive in large numbers for the annual *Urs* (death anniversary) in May and there is music and prayers every Thursday evening. There is a path leading up to the site of his cave, on a hillside to the northeast, around two hours walk.

Shakarparian The low hill overlooking Islamabad, to the south of the main road between Zero Point and Aabpara, has been kept as the Shakarparian Park. There are east and west viewpoints at the top, giving good views of the Margalla Hills to the north, Rawal Lake to to the east, Kahuta to the southeast (the centre of Pakistan's nuclear technology research programme) and Rawalpindi to the south. It's a very popular area for a stroll, particularly in the evening, when the lights of the city make for an attractive sight. There are various snack bars and a restaurant at the east viewpoint. The hill is forested and there are various walking trails.

Lok Virsa The Lok Virsa complex is on Garden Avenue, to the south of Shakarparian hill. Lok Virsa is Pakistan's National Institute of Folk Heritage. They are active in promoting the tremendous wealth and variety of traditional arts and

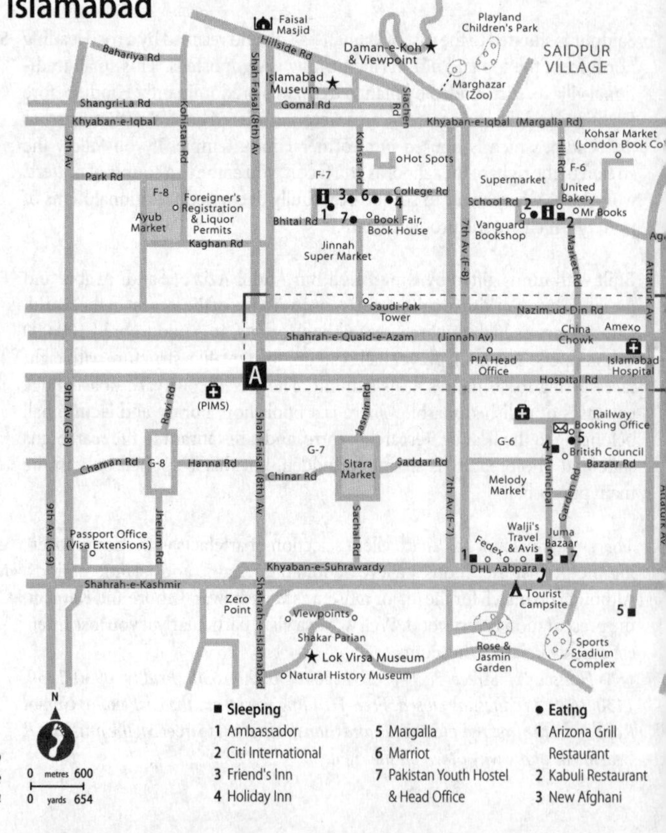

Related map A Islamabad - Blue Area, page 194

crafts in Pakistan and have published a valuable range of social research material and reprints of old folk tale collections. Their sound archive is the largest existing collection of Pakistani songs, balards, interviews etc, while the video archive has films on folk performances, customs and traditions. The **museum** here houses an interesting selection of handicrafts, including some beautiful costumes, textiles, jewellery, musical instruments, pottery and carved pieces, displayed according to area, use and motif. There is also a good research **library** (incorporating the sound and video archives), an open air **theatre** and a **bookshop**.

■ *PO Box 1184, Garden Avenue, Shakarparian, T9203983, F9202042. Summer 0900-1900, winter 0900-1700, closed Friday and public holidays. Rs 10 (students Rs 5). Either walk there from Zero Point, over Shakaparian hill, or take a taxi.*

Pakistan Museum of Natural History

The museum is housed in the basement of a newly built block for the natural sciences research department of Islamabad University. ■ *Garden Avenue, Shakarparian, T9219983, F221864. 0800-1800, closed Sunday. Free. Either walk there from Zero Point, over Shakaparian hill, or take a taxi.*

Punjab

Rose and Jasmine Garden

Within walking distance of Aabpara, the best time to visit is during spring, when the gardens are in flower and there are shows of over 250 varieties of roses and a dozen jasmines. Out of season it is somewhat disappointing.

Rawal Lake

This large lake, formed by a dam across the Kurang River, is the main water supply for Islamabad. There are extensive reed-beds around the northern side of the lake, home to a wide variety of birds and wildlife. There is a restaurant and various snack bars around a terraced garden by the dam, on the south side of the lake, as well as rowing boats and small motor boats for hire nearby. The Canoe Club, on the track up to the dam, has open membership giving the opportunity to enjoy canoeing on the lake (see Sports below).

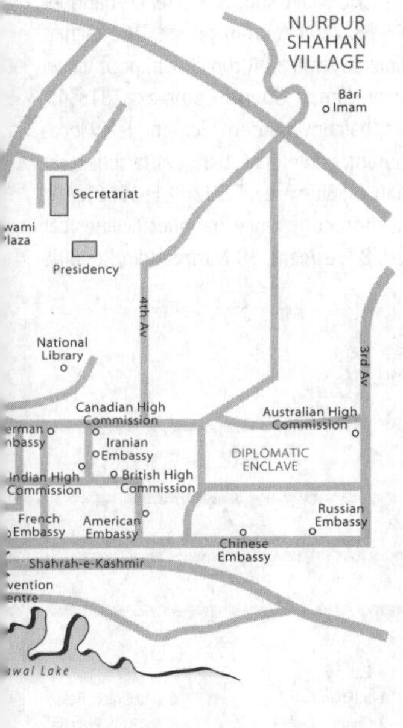

4 Pappasalli's Italian
5 Zenose Restaurant
6 Shifang Chinese
7 Taj Mahal

Essentials

Sleeping

■ *on maps*
Price codes: see inside front cover

More expensive hotels **L** *Best Western*, Club Rd, near Rawal Dam, PO Box 2319, T277460, F277469. A/c, TV/dish, phone, minibar, attached bath. Alcohol served in rooms. Restaurant, coffee shop, business centre, conference/banquet facilities, car hire, shop. Situated away from the city centre, comfortable and nicely furnished but rather overpriced. **L** ***Holiday Inn***, G-6, Civic Centre, Municipal Rd, PO Box 1373, T827311, F273273. 5-star international hotel, though not as luxurious as the *Marriott*. Restaurant, coffee shop, business centre, conference/banquet facilities, shopping mall, travel agents (*Thai, Royal Jordanian, Swissair* and *Singapore Airlines* GSAs), car hire. Plans to completely refurbish the ground floor with an indoor swimming pool, sauna and health club have yet to be undertaken. **L** ***Marriott***, Aga Khan Rd, Shalimar 5, PO Box 1251, T826121, F820648. Islamabad's most luxurious 5-star international standard hotel, Chinese and Pakistani restaurants, swimming pool, health centre, business centre, full conference/banquet facilities, shopping mall, car hire, foreign exchange (guests only). Alcohol served in rooms. The 24 hour Coffee Shop often acts as an ad hoc press club. The *Muddy's Café* is a disco/nightclub – Islamabad's first – in all but name. It is worth asking about special off-season packages and special offers.

A ***Hotel de Papáe***, 16D West, Blue Area, T273427, F273182. A/c, TV/dish, IDD, attached bath, restaurant, coffee shop, *Ewest* nightclub (members/couples only), conference and banquet facilities, business centre, car hire, recently opened, exceedingly glitzy. **A** ***Regency***, Club Rd, near Rawal Dam, T279275, F279276. A/c, TV/dish, IDD, attached bath, restaurant, coffee shop, conference/banquet facilities, business centre. Recently opened, very comfortable, well-run and friendly. Recommended.

B ***Adventure Inn***, Garden Av, PO Box 1807, T272537, F274625. A/c, TV/dish, phone, attached bath, restaurant, garden. Offices of the *Adventure Foundation* located here (see under Sports). Pleasant, leafy location away from city centre, well-run and comfortable but a little overpriced. **B** ***Ambassasor***, Khayaban-e-Suharwardhy, T824011, F821320. A/c, TV/dish, phone, attached bath, small but pleasant garden at rear, restaurant, well-run, good value. Recommended. **B** ***Capital Lodge***, Club Rd, PO Box 2322, T823463. A/c, fan, phone, TV, attached bath, restaurant, conference hall. A bit run-down/overpriced. **B** ***Civic International***, 13 West, Blue Area, Jinnah Avenue, T273740, F274450. A/c, TV/dish, phone, car hire, *Usmania* restaurant (Chinese) next door. **B** ***Dreamland Motel***, Club Rd, T829072, F829077. A/c, fan, phone, TV, attached bath, rooms a bit dank and overpriced. Restaurant, coffee shop, conference/banquet facilities. **B** ***Lakeview Motel***, Club Rd, T821386, F822394. A/c, fan, phone, TV, attached bath. Restaurant, banquet/conference facilities. Overall a bit run-down, poor value. **B** ***Margala Motel***, 1 Kashmir Highway, near Jinnah Sports Complex, T813345, F274054. A/c, TV/dish, phone, attached bath, balcony, garden. Pleasant, leafy location, comfortable rooms, good value. Restaurant, conference/banquet facilities, car hire. **B** ***Marina International***, 109 West, Jinnah Av, Blue Area, T271309, F819661. A/c, fan, TV/dish, attached bath, restaurant, coffee shop, conference/banquet facilities, car hire. OK, but a bit run-down and overpriced. **B** ***President***, 1B Nazimuddin Rd, Blue

Islamabad - Blue Area

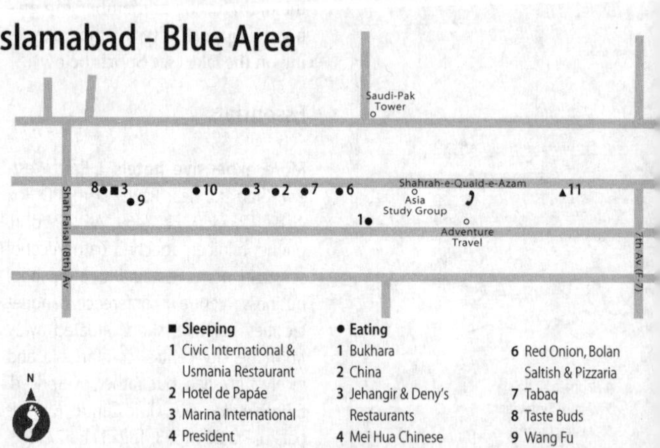

■ **Sleeping**
1 Civic International & Usmania Restaurant
2 Hotel de Papáe
3 Marina International
4 President

● **Eating**
1 Bukhara
2 China
3 Jehangir & Deny's Restaurants
4 Mei Hua Chinese
5 Omar Khayam Iranian
6 Red Onion, Bolan Saltish & Pizzaria
7 Tabaq
8 Taste Buds
9 Wang Fu
10 Yummies 36 & Le Café

Area, F-6, T277142, F270595. A/c, TV/dish, phone, attached bath, restaurant, coffee shop, conference/banquet facilities, comfortable, friendly staff.

Mid-price hotels Guest Houses (B-C) An alternative to upper range hotels in Islamabad are the privately run Guest Houses in residential areas. They are very good value with the quality of accommodation matching that of **A-B** category hotels (although without the shopping and leisure facilities), often at half the price. Popular with aid-workers and other expats who do not have permanent residences and wish to avoid the more impersonal large hotels. Many are part of the Islamabad Guest House Association and have details of other affiliated guest houses. A selection is listed here, but there are many more: ***Continental House***, 94 Nazim ud-Din Rd, F-8/4, T256670, F262144. ***International House***, House 12, 7th Avenue, F-6/1, T827098, F827562. ***Lords Inn***, House 13, Street 28, F-6/1, T824380, F812132. ***Marco Polo Inn***, House 12D, Street 13, F-7/2, T824979, F9204014. ***Pearl House***, 22A College Rd, F-7/2, T822108, F278165. ***Shelton House***, House 11, Kaghan Rd, F-8/3, T856956, F282247. **D** ***Citi International***, Block 7, Markaz F-6, Supermarket, T822295. Fan, attached bath, bit shabby but OK.

Punjab

Budget hotels G *Islamabad Youth Hostel*, Garden Rd, G-6/4 (near Aabpara), T826899. Generally clean, good value, separate male/female dorms, self-catering facilities. Non-members must buy a "welcome ticket" (Rs 60), or you can buy full membership to the IYHA for 1 year (Rs 360), students pay Rs 30 for a bed, adults Rs 55. Maximum stay 3 days in the summer, popular with Pakistani students and often full. **G** *Tourist Camp Site*, opposite Rose and Jasmine Garden, near Aabpara. Strictly foreigners only. Maximum stay 2 weeks (officially). For the princely sum of Rs 8 you can set up tent here, or you can stay in one of their basic dormitory 'bungalows' for Rs 15 per person (fan, no bed/bedding, doss down on the floor). If you are really strapped for cash, they will even let you sleep out under the stars here for Rs 3! Vehicles can be brought inside (big buses Rs 20, vans/cars Rs 10, motorcycles Rs 2). There are shared toilet and shower facilities, reasonable shade and usually an interesting collection of Nigerian refugees, overlanders, skinflints and oddballs. Very basic but equally friendly and good value.

Eating

● *on maps*

Most restaurants in Islamabad are to be found in the commercial markets at the centre of each sector (Supermarket, Jinnah Supermarket, etc), and spread out along the western half of Blue Area between 7th and 8th avenues.

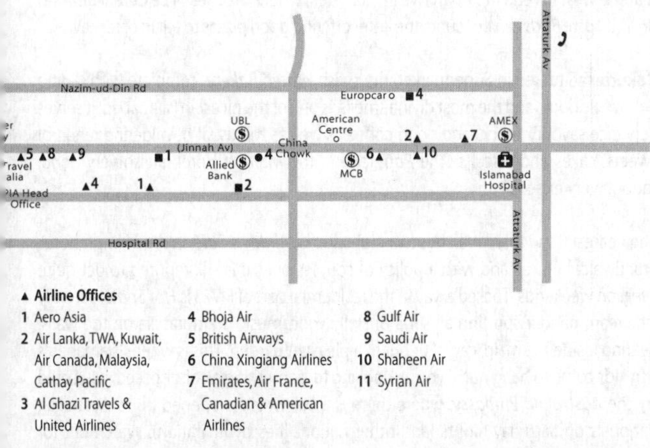

▲ **Airline Offices**

1 Aero Asia
2 Air Lanka, TWA, Kuwait, Air Canada, Malaysia, Cathay Pacific
3 Al Ghazi Travels & United Airlines
4 Bhoja Air
5 British Airways
6 China Xingiang Airlines
7 Emirates, Air France, Canadian & American Airlines
8 Gulf Air
9 Saudi Air
10 Shaheen Air
11 Syrian Air

Pakistani The luxury and more expensive hotels all have restaurants serving good Pakistani dishes in elegant surroundings (the *Marriott* hotel's ***Nadia*** is probably the fanciest). Most of the mid-range and cheaper hotels also have their own Pakistani restaurant, though often you end up paying more for the surroundings than the food. ***New Afghani***, Jinnah Supermarket, F-7 Markaz, T829444. An unassuming restaurant serving excellent Pakistani/Afghan food at very reasonable prices. Eat well for Rs 100-200 per head. Recommended. ***Zenose***, Melody Market. An open-air restaurant serving excellent *karahis, tikkas* and other meat dishes, all fried, grilled, griddled etc in front of you in a dramatic display of flaring hot fat and flames. Dishes from around Rs 100 upwards. Recommended. ***Kabuli***, Supermarket, F-6 Markaz. Reasonable Pakistani/Afghan food for around Rs 100-200 per head. ***Kashmirwala's***, Daman-e-koh, T/F815496. Occupies a prime position at Daman-e-Koh (see Sights above), with wonderful views out over Islamabad. Somewhat cavernous dining hall geared up to catering for special occasions and big groups. Lovely terrace. Buffet lunch/dinner laid on in season.

Chinese The *Marriott* hotel's ***Dynasty*** is undoubtedly the best (and most expensive). ***Wang Fu***, 106 West Jinnah Avenue, Blue Area, T271306. Looks very swish and comfortable. Around Rs 250 per head upwards. There are plenty more Chinese restaurants dotted around Islamabad, for example ***Shifang*** in Jinnah Supermarket, though many of them are somewhat bland.

Italian ***Pappasallis***, Block 13E, Jinnah Supermarket, F-7 Markaz, T273960. Excellent Italian restaurant, continues to maintain its high reputation. Gets busy on weekends. Eat well for around Rs 300-400 per head, or takeaway a pizza/pasta for Rs 175-325 (also home delivery). Recommended.

Iranian ***Omar Khayyam***, Jinnah Avenue (West), Blue Area. Islamabad's only Iranian restaurant. Has an excellent reputation amongst the expat community. Around Rs 300-400 per head. Recommended.

Continental/other ***Arizona Grill***, F-7 Markaz, T824576. Recently opened, American-style restaurant, pleasant décor, well-run, serves steaks, chicken dishes, seafood, also Italian and Mexican cuisine, around Rs 300 per head, good value all-you-can-eat buffet from 1200-1600 for Rs 200. Recommended.

Fast food Western-style fast food places serving burgers, chips, pizza etc can be found in the commercial areas at the centre of each sector. The biggest concentration is at the western end of Jinnah Ave in Blue Area, where the likes of ***Le Café***, ***Yummies 36*** and ***Taste Buds*** can be found, the latter offering good pizzas to eat in or takeaway.

Bakeries Situated in Supermarket, the swish ***United Bakery***, complete with sliding automatic doors and the most divine smells, is one of the nicest in Islamabad. It serves very nice savoury snacks and good coffee as well as the usual bewildering range of sweets, cakes and biscuits. The ***Patisserie*** in the *Marriott* Hotel is also very good, though very expensive.

Entertainment The nearest thing Islamabad has to a nightclub is ***Muddy's Café***, in the *Marriott* hotel. Strictly alcohol-free and with a policy of couples only, it is still reputed to get quite lively on weekends. Tucked away in the residential part of F-7/3 is ***Hot Spots***, a trendy ice cream parlour sporting all sorts of Hollywood/music memorabilia on the walls. Seating inside the main 'cabin' or out in a pleasant garden. This is where Islamabad's rich kids come to hang out. If you are looking for something alcohol-based, you could try the ***Australian Embassy***, where there is a bar which is opened up to Australian nationals on Saturday nights (and other nationalities by invitation). Watch out for

Obtaining a Liquor Permit

To obtain a liquor permit you must go to the Central Excise and Taxation Office, Ayub Market, F-8 Markaz. You need to obtain and fill out an application form, buy court fee stamps (Rs 1 per unit per month, available from the lawyers practicing in the square) and submit your application along with photocopies of the relevant pages of your passport. Your passport will be stamped and signed and you will receive a liquor permit. Be prepared for lots of hanging around. One unit is equal to one litre of spirits or around 12 bottles of beer. The permits are valid only for Islamabad, where they can be used at the Marriott Hotel. An additional "fee" may also be charged, though this is essentially a baksheesh.

shady characters hanging around outside in the hope of fleecing drunken backpackers. Non-Muslim foreigners can also apply for a **liquor permit** (see box) which allows them to obtain alcohol from the Marriott Hotel.

Sports The *Adventure Foundation*, based in the *Adventure Inn* hotel (see above), organizes **horse riding** around Islamabad, **trekking** tours in the Northern Areas, **skiing** near Abbottabad, **ballooning** near Thal and Multan, and also **paragliding**. With the exception of horse riding, which can be arranged at relatively short notice, contact them well in advance if you are interested in any of these activities. ***Hot Shots***, Fatima Jinnah Park, F-9, T111008008, F251915. Open 1000-2200. This fancy new complex features a state-of-the-art **bowling alley** (Rs 200 per person per game for non-members), a **snooker hall** (Rs 75 per person per game for non-members), a small outdoor **swimming pool** (Rs 175 per person per day, separate timings for men/women), and a **health club** complete with gym, aerobics, jacuzzi and steam bath (by membership only, minimum 1 month, or try negotiating a special arrangement with the management). There is also a café/snack bar and a shop. ***Islamabad Canoe Club***, Rawal Lake (correspondence; Mike Semple, Club Secretary, Agricultural Farm No 25B, near Model Village, Chak Shahzad, Islamabad, T241855; or c/o Channel 7 Communications, T217307). Situated close to the dam, this small friendly club will allow non-members to hire out canoes for Rs 50 per person per hour. Membership costs Rs 100, plus a monthly charge of Rs 300, allowing unlimited use. ***Islamabad Golf Club***, Club Rd, T829321. Situated next door to the highly exclusive members-only *Islamabad Club*, the golf club allows non-members to use the course for Rs 700/500 on weekends/weekdays respectively. The *Marriott* Hotel has a good **health club** and **swimming pool**, both of which are open to non-guests for a fee.

Shopping

While most foreign tourists get excited about the prospect of battling their way through the crowded chaos of Rawalpindi's Rajah Bazaar, most Pakistanis are far more interested in the orderly, relaxed and 'modern' shopping experience which Islamabad offers. The commercial centres of each sector (Supermarket, Jinnah Supermarket, Melody Market etc) have more in common with the shopping malls of Europe or North America than the bazaars of Asia. You can find everything here you would expect to find at home, as well as an excellent selection of Pakistani handicrafts, antiques, souvenirs etc.

Aabpara is Islamabad's oldest market, selling household items, fabrics and spices. Nearby is the **Covered Market** for meat, fruit and veg, and the **Juma (Friday) Bazaar**, which can be a good place to hunt for handicrafts. **Kohsar Market**, F-6/3, has a couple of good grocery stores catering for the expat community, and an excellent bookshop (see below). There are also usually various stalls selling handicrafts. **Supermarket** and **Jinnah Supermarket**, at the centre of F-6 and F-7 respectively, are both major shopping complexes, with a selection of chemists, clothing shops, convenience stores, photographic shops, handicrafts/antiques/souvenir shops, bookshops, restaurants, etc. **Blue Area** is the main commercial thoroughfare; many of the banks, travel agents, airlines etc have their offices here. The western section of Blue Area also has a number of restaurants, while around the junction of Jinnah Avenue with 7th Avenue there are several carpet and handicraft shops. **Itwar (Sunday) Market** is held on Sundays near Peshawar Mor; primarily an agricultural market, it's worth visiting for the spectacle if nothing else.

Books Islamabad is well supplied with bookshops offering a wide range of books on Pakistan's history, culture, political and economic development etc, many of them not readily available abroad. Most of the guidebooks to Pakistan are available as well as some maps. There are also a number of second-hand bookshops in Supermarket and Jinnah Supermarket where books can be exchanged. For new books, the following are recommended. ***The London Book Co***, 3 Kohsar Market, F-6/3, T823852. ***Vanguard Books***, Lok Virsa Blding, Supermarket, F-6/1 (right on the southwest corner of Supermarket), T270328. ***Mr Books***, Supermarket, F-6 Markaz (more or less directly opposite where Market Road joins from the south). Also worth a try, though more for specialist books, is the ***Pak Book Corporation***, Modern Way Block, Aabpara, G-6/1 (upstairs, next door to *DHL* office).

Local transport

To & from the airport If you want to go directly between Islamabad and the airport you will need to take a taxi. To go by public transport, take a Suzuki heading for Rajah Bazaar, get off at Liaquat Chowk and then pick up an Islamabad-bound bus/minibus from there. See box 'Islamabad International Airport', page 211, for more detailed information.

To & from Rawalpindi See also Ins and outs, page 188, and Rawalpindi Local transport, page 210. Arriving from Rawalpindi, the large brightly coloured Bedford buses link Faisabad, Zero Point, Aabpara, Supermarket, Jinnah Supermarket, Faisal Mosque and Ayub Market, and then double back along the same route. Minibuses – numbers 1 and 6, with a red stripe on the side – follow the same route, bearing east at Supermarket towards the Secretariat; number 1 goes via the GPO and number 6 via PIA's main office.

To & from Pir Wadhai bus station First take a Rawalpindi-bound bus or minibus as far as Faisabad, then pick up a bus/minibus to Pir Wadhai from there.

Around Islamabad The intercity buses and minibuses are useful for getting between the various markets. In addition, minibus number 120 runs north from Aabpara to Melody Market, then west to Sitara Market, Peshawar Mor (the junction of Shahrah-e-Kashmir with 9th Ave, useful for the Passport and Immigration office) and G-9 Markaz (known as Karachi Co). Heading in the opposite direction from Aabpara, the same minibus runs east along Khayaban-e-Suhrawardy, and then northeast towards Nurpur Shahan village and Bari Imam, passing close to the French, German and Canadian embassies, and within walking distance of the Iranian, Indian and British embassies. Minibus number 105 follows the same route. Suzukis also run due east from Aabpara along Khayaban-e-Suhrawardy (known as Embassy Road further east), passing the French, American, Chinese, Russian and Australian embassies en route to the Qaid-e-Azam University.

Taxis are readily available, and many even have working meters (but check first). An average journey (say between Aabpara and Supermarket) should not cost more than Rs 20-30, though you may have to bargain.

Car hire **Europcar**, 10-11 Shahid Plaza, Nazimuddin Road, Blue Area, F-6 (next door to *President* hotel), T822920, F275912. Chauffeur-driven only. Cheapest car (Toyota Corrola) Rs 1,800 per 24 hours, plus Rs 10 per kilometre. **Avis**, PO Box 1088, Waljis Building, 10 Khayaban-e-Suhrawardy (next door to *Travel Walji's)*, T270751, F270753. Choice of self-drive and chauffeur-driven. Cars from Rs 1150 per day, plus Rs 200 per day for CDW (Crash Damage Waiver) and Rs 4 per kilometre. Amex, Visa and Mastercard accepted.

Long distance transport

Air/Train/Road Are all covered under Rawalpindi Long distance transport, see page 211. There is a **railway booking office** in Islamabad, on the east side of Melody Market, T9207474. Open 7 days, 0830-1630. Tickets can be booked a maximum of 15 days in advance. The main **PIA Office** is in Blue Area (see below). There is a bus station at G-9 Markaz (Karachi Co), with regular coasters and minivans (some a/c) to Lahore, Peshawar, Murree and Abbottabad.

Directory

Airline offices **Domestic:** *PIA*, 49 Blue Area, T816051. Open 0830-1800, 7 days. Airport counter, T591071, open 24 hours, 7 days. ***Bhoja Air***, 8A Potohar Plaza, Blue Area, T828123, F824179 (airport T591300, F590716). ***Shaheen Air International***, 33 Buland Markaz, Jinnah Ave, Blue Area, T813916, F813964. ***Aero Asia***, Block 12-D, SNC Centre, Blue Area, T271341. **International:** ***Air Canada***, 12 Shahid Plaza, Nazimuddin Road, Blue Area, T823040, F824030. ***Air France***, 3001 Jinnah Ave, Blue Area, T824096, F820181. ***Air Lanka***, 2 Shahid Plaza, Nazimuddin Rd, Blue Area, T279795, F278207. ***Alitalia***, Jinnah Ave, Blue Area, T823442, F829550. ***American***, 1D Rehmat Plaza, Blue Area, T273173, F828844. ***British***, No 10, Block 51, Blue Area, T274070, F274078. ***Cathay Pacific***, 14 Shahid Plaza, Nazimuddin Rd, Blue Area, T821936, F271010. ***China Xinjiang***, Shop 3, Sohrab Plaza, Block 32, Jinnah Ave, Blue Area, T273446, F273448. ***Emirates***, 1D Rehmat Plaza, Blue Area, T811677, F215998; ***Gulf***, No 2, 52 West, Waheed Plaza, Blue Area, T271650, F271655. ***Iberia***, 1D Rehmat Plaza, Blue Area, T824718, F829550. ***KLM***, 1A Shahid Plaza, Nazimuddin Rd, Blue Area, T829685, F823795. ***Kuwait***, 3 Shahid Plaza, Nazimuddin Rd, Blue Area, T822727, F272195. ***Malaysia***, 4 Shahid Plaza, Nazimuddin Rd, Blue Area, T273382, F820122. ***Royal Jordanian***, Holiday Inn hotel, T274222, F270673. ***Singapore Airlines***, Holiday Inn hotel, T821555, F824413. ***Swissair***, Holiday Inn hotel, T822677, F822798. ***Thai***, Holiday Inn hotel, T272140, F823735. ***TWA***, 12 Shahid Plaza, Nazimuddin Rd, Blue Area, T823040, F824030.

Banks *American Express*, 1E, Ali Plaza, Blue Area, PO Box 1291, T272425, F828783. Open Mon-Thur 0900-1330, 1430-1700, Friday 0900-1230, 1430-1700, Saturday 0900-1300, closed Sunday. Efficient exchange service for cash and TCs, also cash advances for Amex card holders, and Clients' Mail service. Just a few doors down, the ***Bank of America*** will give cash advances against most major credit cards for a 2 percent commission. There are dozens more banks spread across Blue Area, many of which also do foreign exchange. In Melody Market, behind the *Holiday Inn* hotel, the ***National Bank of Pakistan*** changes cash and TCs. ***Thomas Cook*** is represented through *Travel Walji's* (see below, under Tour companies & travel agents). They issue TCs (through National Bank of Pakistan or United Bank Ltd) and replace lost/stolen ones, but do not cash them or deal in foreign exchange.

Communications **Post:** *GPO*, Civic Centre, Municipal Rd. Open Mon-Thur and Sat 0900-2000, Fri 0900-1130, 1530-2000, closed Sunday. Poste Restante and Express Post service available. There are also post offices in the major markets, including one on the southwest corner of Jinnah Supermarket, near to the PTDC tourist information office. **Courier:** *DHL*, Zarin Chambers, IT Centre, Khayaban-e-Suharwardy, G-6/1, T823545, F275246. ***FedEx***, 1 Ghosia Plaza, Khayaban-e-Suharwardy, G-6/1, T2744020, F274041. **Telephone:** Central Telegraph Office, Attaturk Av, Shalimar 5. Open 7 days, 24 hours. Fax and telex services also available. There is also a telephone office at Aabpara, opposite the *Tourist Camp Site*, a Pak Telecom Customer Services Centre in Blue Area, just west of 7th Ave, and PCOs in the major markets. **Internet:** One of the better internet cafés in Islamabad is ***Cyber City***, 13 Mezzanine, Beverly Centre, 56-G Blue Area, Jinnah Ave, T822940, F822364. Internet access Rs 80 per hour. Another is ***Super Composing Centre***, 3-D Supermarket, F-6 Markaz, T279349, F277450. Internet access Rs 75 per hour.

Cultural centres *Alliançe Francaise*, House 10, Street 16, F-6/3, T210744. Films and other events for the French expat community. *American Center*, 60 Blue Area, Jinnah Ave, T824001. Periodicals, audio-visual and US Information Service materials. *Asian Study Group*, Malik Complex, 80 West, Jinnah Ave, Blue Area, T815891. Formed in the 1970s by members of the expat community, it now has a wider membership and holds regular lectures and cultural evenings, as well as sightseeing trips and walks in the Margalla hills. The ASG have published a number of papers and booklets. Members can make use of the small library which includes some videos. Annual membership Rs 200. *British Council*, 14 Civic Centre, G-6 Markaz, T829041. Geared up primarily to promote education opportunities in the UK, but tourists can browse through the British papers in the library and watch BBC World TV. *Lok Virsa*, PO Box 1184, Garden Ave, Shakarparian Hills, T9203983, F9202042. Open 0930-1330, 1430-1700 (1900 in summer), closed Fri and public holidays. Primarily a museum and library (see under Sights, above), but also hosts occasional cultural events.

Embassies & consulates *Afghanistan*, House 8, Street 90, G-6/3, T824506, F824504. *Australia*, Diplomatic Enclave, T824345, F821112. *Austria*, House 13, Street 1, F-6/3, T279238, F828366. *Belgium*, House 14, Street 17, F-7/2, T827091, F822358. *Canada*, PO Box 1042, Diplomatic Enclave, T279100, F279110. *China*, Diplomatic Enclave, Ramna 4, T817279, F821116. *Denmark*, PO Box 1118, House 9, Street 90, G-6/3, T824724, F823483. *France*, Diplomatic Enclave, T278730, F825389. *Germany*, Diplomatic Enclave, T279430, F279436. *India*, Diplomatic Enclave, T272680, F823386. *Iran*, Diplomatic Enclave, T276271, F279588. *Italy*, 54 Margalla Rd, F-6/3, T829106, F829026. *Japan*, Diplomatic Enclave, T279320, F279340. *Jordan*, PO Box 1189, House 131, Street 14, E-7, T823460, F823207. *Kazakstan*, House 2, Street 4, F-8/3, T262924, F262806. *Lebanon*, House 6, Street 27, F-6/2, T278338, F826410. *Nepal*, House 11, Street 84, G-6/4, T278051, F217875. *Netherlands*, PIA Bldg, 2nd Flr, Blue Area, T279512, F279513. *Russian Federation*, Diplomatic Enclave, T278671, F826552. *South Africa*, House 48, Margalla Rd, F-8/2, T262356, F250114. *Spain*, Diplomatic Enclave, T279480, F279489. *Sri Lanka*, 135C Margalla Rd, F-7/2, T828723, F828751. *Switzerland*, PO Box 1073, Diplomatic Enclave, T279292, F279286. *Syria*, 30 Hill Rd, F-6/3, T279471, F279472. *Thailand*, House 10, Street 33, F-8/1, T280586, F256730. *Turkey*, PO Box 2183, House 58, Attaturk Ave, G-6/3, T278749, F278752. *Turkmenistan*, House 22A, Nizamuddin Rd, F-7/1, T274913, F278799. *UK*, PO Box 1122, Diplomatic Enclave, T822131, F823439. *USA*, Diplomatic Enclave, T826161, F214222. *Uzbekistan*, House 6, Street 29, F-7/1, T820779, F278128.

Hospitals & medical services Private Hospitals: *Al-Shifa International*, H-8, T446801. *Islamabad Hospital*, opposite American Express, Blue Area, T272350, F275846. **Public Hospitals:** *Capital Hospital*, Street 31, G-6/2, T9221334. *Pakistan Institute of Medical Sciences (PIMS)* Hospital Complex, Faisal Avenue, G-8/3, T859511. *Federal Government Services Hospital (Poly Clinic)*, Hospital Rd, G-6/3, T9218300. **Chemists:** There are chemists in the commercial areas at the centre of each sector, in Blue Area (concentrated around China Chowk), and at each of the hospitals listed above.

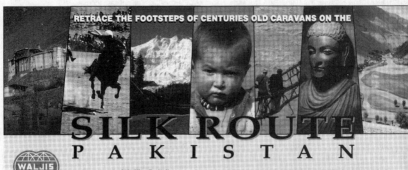

Libraries ***National Library of Pakistan***, Constitution Ave Building, near Parliament House, T812787. Open 0900-1700, closed Sat and Sun. European and Oriental languages, Pakistan collection, manuscripts and rare materials, periodicals and newspapers. ***PTDC Head Office***, House 2, Street 61, F-7/4, T811011. Good collection of books on Pakistani regional history and culture. In addition, the ***American Center***, ***Asian Study Group***, ***British Council***, ***French Cultural Centre*** and ***Lok Virsa*** (see above, under Cultural centres) each have their own libraries.

Tour companies & travel agents ***American Express Travel Services***, 1-E, Ali Plaza, Blue Area, T272425, F828783. Full range of services. ***Sitara Travel Consultants***, Waheed Plaza, 3rd floor, 52 West, Jinnah Avenue, Blue Area, PO Box 1662, T813372, F279651. Offer a wide range of services, including tours of Central Asia. ***Travel Walji's***, Walji's Building, 10 Khayaban-e-Suharwardy, PO Box 1088, T270757-58, F270753. One of Pakistan's largest and longest running travel agents. Generally reliable and efficient. Also representatives for *Thomas Cook*. ***Omar Travels***, No 8, Shahid Plaza, Blue Area, Islambad, T815409, F275006. ***Bukhari Travel and Tourism***, 2 Mohammad Plaza, near American Center, Blue Area, T276076, F272480. National and international ticketing. ***Adventure Travel***, 15 Wali Centre, 86 South, Blue Area, T212490, F214580. Specializing in organized treks etc. **NB** For a more extensive list of companies specializing in trekking, see page 22.

Tourist offices ***PTDC Tourist Information Centre***, College Rd, F-7/2, T9202766, F294540. Open 0900-1600, Fri 0800-1230, Sun closed. This is the main headquarters for PTDC. The information centre is reasonably helpful, and will also arrange tours. However they are poorly informed regarding travel in much of NWFP, Baluchistan and Sind (wait till you get to Peshawar, Quetta or Karachi to get sensible advice from the PTDC offices there). Trekking and mountaineering permits are issued from the office next door, though these days only when applied for through a recognized tour operator. There is another ***PTDC Tourist Information*** at Supermarket, F-6/1, T9204027. Open 0900-1500, Fri 0900-1200, closed Sun. Useful primarily for information on Islamabad/Rawalpindi and the immediate vicinity.

Punjab

Useful addresses Police: ***Emergency:*** T15 or T823333. ***Aabpara police station***, Post Office Rd (next to GPO), T828265. ***Margalla police station***, Ayub Market, F-8 Markaz, T850340. ***Kohsar police station***, Jinnah Supermarket, F-7 Markaz, T812393. ***Foreigners' Registration Office***, near SSP Office, Ayub Market, F-8 Markaz (if coming by bus ask for Zafar Chowk), T246116 (central exchange). **Visa Extensions:** ***Passport and Immigration Office***, Peshawar Mor, G-8/1, T260773. Open 0800-1500, Fri 0800-1200, Sun closed. Tourist visas can be extended by three months, and transit visas converted into tourist visas. Bring photocopies of the relevant pages of your passport, fill out the form and you should be issued with an extension on the spot. To get there, catch minibus No 120 from Aabpara (or take a taxi) and ask for 'Peshawar Mor'. This is the junction of Shahrah-e-Kashmir with 9th Avenue. At this junction, double back along the service road which runs parallel to the north of Shahrah-e-Kashmir and take the first turning heading north. The passport office is a short way up on the right. Holders of non-tourist visas (for example working/student visas etc) must first obtain approval from the Ministry of the Interior, Block R, Secretariat. This may also be the case if yu wish to convert a single entry tourist visa to a double entry. **No Objection Certificates:** Section Officer, FATA, Ministry of State and Frontier Regions, Room 232, Block S, Secretariat. The staff here deserve prizes for raising Pakistani bureaucracy to previously uncharted heights of obstructiveness. **Travel Permits:** *Tarbela Dam*, Section Officer, 4th Flr, Block R, Secretariat, T920729, or contact the Protocol Officer, WAPDA, Tarbela Dam Project, Tarbela, T568941 (sometimes WAPDA will issue permits directly, at other times they require clearance from the Secretariat).

Rawalpindi

Phone code: 051
Colour map 4, grid A4

Rawalpindi is a sprawling city, and one of the fastest growing in Pakistan, with three-quarters of the capital area's combined population. Though it lacks any major monuments or sites of historical significance, its lively and colourful bazaars have plenty of atmosphere.

Layout

The British Cantonment area, focused on The Mall (a part of the old Grand Trunk Road), was once a separate settlement. It had barracks and spacious residential area for the military and civilians, its own offices, clubs and churches. The Saddar area which developed to the northeast is today the main commercial area, with numerous hotels, restaurants, banks, shops, travel agents etc. To the north of Saddar, beyond the railway line and across the Leh River, is the crowded Old City, centred around Fowara Chowk and Rajah Bazaar. In addition to The Mall, the most important transport artery is Murree Road, which runs north towards Islamabad.

History

Although there's nothing much to see in terms of historic monuments, Rawalpindi is an ancient city. There is evidence that a Buddhist settlement existed here, contemporary with Taxila. The first Muslim invader, Mahmud of Ghazni, gave the ruined city as a gift to a Ghakkar Chief, but it remained deserted until restored by Jhanda Khan in 1493.

Rawalpindi served as a strategic base for the Mughal Emperor Jahangir and later, during the 19th century, was developed as a Sikh trading centre. After the Second Sikh War the British gained control in 1849 and made Rawalpindi the Army's General HQ for the northern region. Its importance was further increased by extending the railways to it and building a large complex of military cantonment buildings. Today it is still the headquarters of the country's Armed Forces.

Sights

Rajah Bazaar

The area around Rajah Bazaar is the commercial heart of the old market town of Rawalpindi. Five roads radiate from Fowara Chowk, and tiny alleys with crowded bazaars and craftsmen practising their skills wind their way between these roads. It's a fascinating area to explore and shop around in, for anything from jewellery, handicrafts and fabrics to smuggled electrical goods (see Shopping, below). Walking east from Fowara Chowk along Trunk Bazaar/Iqbal Road, off to the left roughly half way along you can see an old Hindu temple (one of several which once graced this area), now somewhat derelict and partially occupied as a private home.

Ayub National Park

This sprawling park, covering over 900 hectares, is situated on the GT Road to the southeast of the Cantonment area. There is a lake for boating, bridle paths, an aquarium, open-air garden restaurant and theatre, as well as a Japanese garden.

Liaquat Memorial Hall and Gardens

Originally known as Company Bagh but renamed after Liaquat Ali Khan, the first prime minister of Pakistan, who was assassinated here in 1951. There is a library and a large auditorium where occasional art exhibitions, cultural shows and plays are staged.

Old City/ Murree Rd

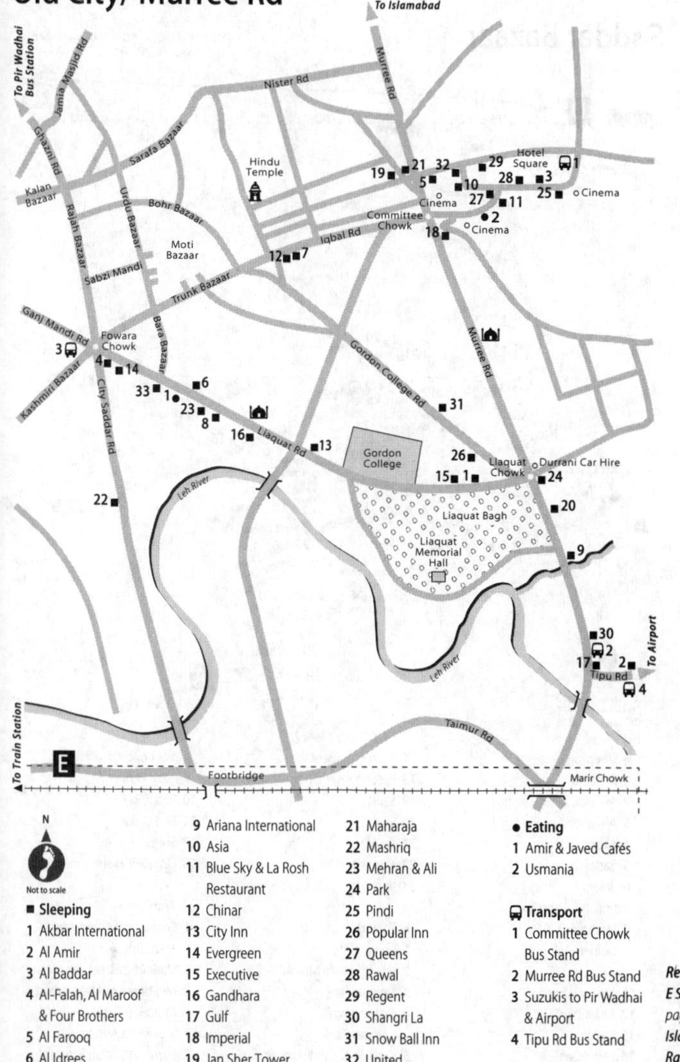

Related maps
E Saddar Bazaar, page 204
Islamabad - Rawalpindi Overview, page 189

Army Museum and Library Various items of military regalia, including paintings, weapons and uniforms, and a collection of books on Pakistan's military history are on display here. ■ *Iftkhar Road. 0800-1400, closed Friday. Free.*

Essentials

Sleeping

■ *on maps*
Price codes: see inside front cover

There are over 250 hotels spread over Rawalpindi, a small selection of which are given below. Most of the hotels are concentrated in the **Saddar/Cantonment** area, which is Rawalpindi's real commercial centre. The more expensive ones are in the Cantonment area, along the Mall, while the mid-range and cheaper ones are in the Saddar area.

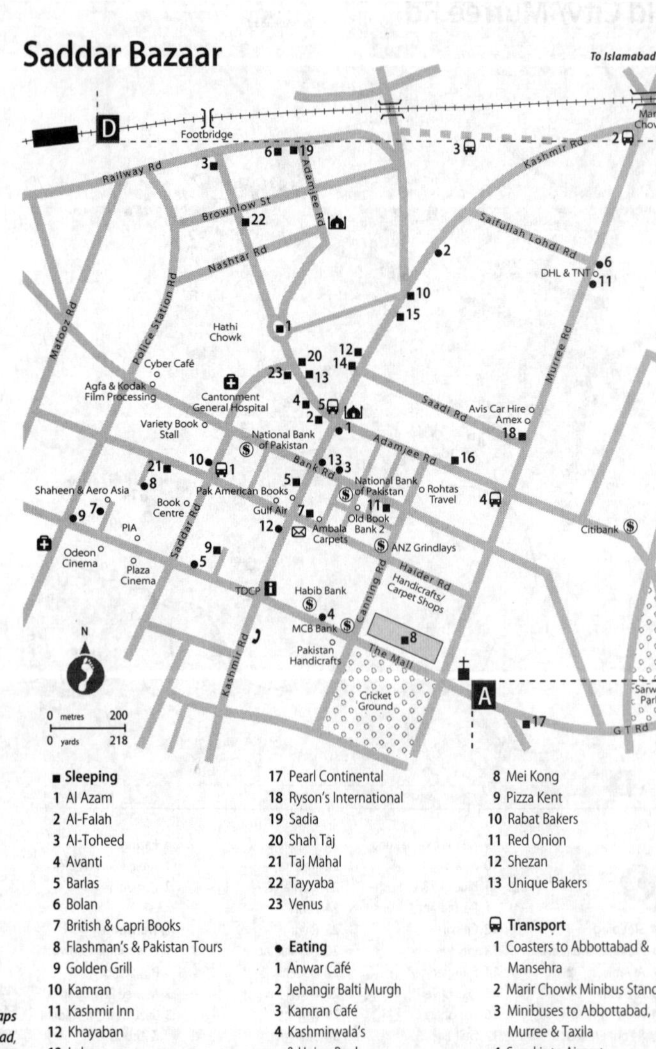

■ **Sleeping**
1 Al Azam
2 Al-Falah
3 Al-Toheed
4 Avanti
5 Barlas
6 Bolan
7 British & Capri Books
8 Flashman's & Pakistan Tours
9 Golden Grill
10 Kamran
11 Kashmir Inn
12 Khayaban
13 Lalazar
14 Marhaba
15 New Kamran
16 Paradise Inn
17 Pearl Continental
18 Ryson's International
19 Sadia
20 Shah Taj
21 Taj Mahal
22 Tayyaba
23 Venus

● **Eating**
1 Anwar Café
2 Jehangir Balti Murgh
3 Kamran Café
4 Kashmirwala's & Union Bank
5 Kim Fah & Saudi Airlines
6 Lasania
7 Mainland Chinese
8 Mei Kong
9 Pizza Kent
10 Rabat Bakers
11 Red Onion
12 Shezan
13 Unique Bakers

Transport
1 Coasters to Abbottabad & Mansehra
2 Marir Chowk Minibus Stand
3 Minibuses to Abbottabad, Murree & Taxila
4 Suzukis to Airport
5 Suzukis to Rajah Bazaar

Related maps
A Islamabad, page 192
D Old City/Murree Rd, page 203

A second focus for hotels (mid-price and budget) is around **Committee Chowk** on Murree Road, the square here having been dubbed 'Hotel Square'. The location is a convenient compromise for both Islamabad and 'Pindi, and there is a bus stand for Peshawar. It is also within walking distance of Rajah Bazaar and Rawalpindi's Old City. However, 'Hotel Square' does have the distinct atmosphere of a building site about it; coupled with the noise of the bus stand, this does not make it the most attractive of locations.

More hotels can be found around **Liaquat Chowk** on Murree Road; those on Murree Road itself are not particularly appealing, but there are good ones in the **B** and **E-F** categories just off, it on Liaquat Road and Gordon College Road.

There are also plenty of budget hotels around **Fowara Chowk** (the heart of the Old City). These tend to be very basic, though if you want to be right in the thick of things, this is the place to be.

More expensive hotels At the time of researching, most luxury hotels were offering substantial discounts (as much as 60 percent in some cases) in an attempt to attract guests. However, you should still watch out for the additional taxes which are added to the advertised room rates in the more expensive hotels. These amount to a whopping 20.5 percent in many cases. **L** ***Pearl Continental***, PO Box 211, The Mall, T566011, F563972. Rawalpindi's most luxurious hotel, full facilities to international standards, including swimming pool, health club, tennis courts, golf and squash by arrangement, business centre, foreign exchange, shopping mall, travel agents, Continental, Pakistani and Chinese restaurants, alcohol served in rooms only. **A** ***Shalimar***, off the Mall, PO Box 93, T562901, F566061. Comfortable international-standard hotel, choice of restaurants, poolside BBQ, banquet hall, conference facilities. **A** ***Rysons International***, 111/10-D Murree Rd, T514884, F514914. A/c, fan, TV/dish, IDD, attached bath, restaurant, business centre, modern comfortable hotel, though a little expensive. **A-B** ***Flashman's*** 17-22 The Mall, T581480. Rather old government-run establishment, has seen better days, overpriced, rooms in new block are better (and more expensive), restaurant, swimming pool, tennis courts, banquet hall, conference facilities, office of Pakistan Tours Ltd (a semi-private tour operator with close links to PTDC) on hotel grounds. **A-B** ***Kashmirwala's Tourist Inn***, 2 The Mall, T583186, F581554. Situated above Union Bank, central a/c, TV/dish, phone, attached bath, undergoing refurbishment at time of writing, should be a comfortable, high standard hotel when it reopens. **B** ***Akbar International***, Liaquat Rd, opposite Liaquat Bagh, T532001, F557642. Central a/c, TV/dish, phone, attached bath, banquet hall, restaurant, clean comfortable rooms, good value. **B** ***Executive***, Liaquat Rd, opposite Liaquat Bagh, T541190, F541299. Central a/c, fan, TV/dish, phone, attached bath, banquet hall, restaurant, clean comfortable rooms, good value.

Mid-price hotels There is a wide selection of hotels in the mid-price range, and an equally wide variation in the quality of the accommodation offered. Don't be afraid to ask to see other rooms in a particular hotel, or bargain over the price.

Saddar/Cantonment **C** ***British***, GPO Chowk, Haider Rd, T527187. Central a/c, fan, phone, attached bath, also cheaper **D** category rooms without a/c, rather shabby and run-down, friendly owner, restaurant. **C** ***Holiday Crown Palace***, 232-B Iftikhar Khan Rd, T568068, F583960. Central a/c, phone, TV/dish, restaurant, helpful staff, good value. **C** ***Paradise Inn***, PO Box 1018, 109 Adamjee Rd, T568594, F567048. Choice of rooms with a/c and TV/dish or fan only, all rooms with phone, attached bath and pleasant balcony, clean but a little expensive, restaurant, rooftop BBQ, almost every taxi driver at the airport appears to have a deal going with this hotel whereby they will try to bring you here for a commission. **D** ***Avanti***, Adamjee Rd, T566905. A/c, fan, phone, attached bath, best rooms at front. **D** ***Golden Grill***, 7B The Mall, T512842,

F562230. Central a/c, TV/dish, phone, attached bath, reasonably clean, restaurant. **D** *Marhaba*, 118 Kashmir Rd, T566021. Central a/c, TV/dish, phone, attached bath, restaurant, rather decrepit and overpriced hotel.

Liaquat Chowk/Murree Rd **C** *Amir International*, Tipu Rd, T500902, F500894. A/c, fan, phone, TV, attached bath, convenient for Tipu Rd/Murree Rd bus stands but *very* noisy (and rather musty) rooms. **C** *Park*, Murree Rd, Liaquat Chowk, T73284, F74161. A/c, TV, phone, attached bath, some cheaper rooms with fan only, nice old building set back from road, though some rooms a bit dank and with no external window. **D** *Ariana International*, Murree Rd, opposite Liaquat Bagh, T599260, F501741. Fan, phone, attached bath, pleasant clean rooms, good value, but smelly stream-going-on-open-sewer flowing past outside. **D** *Kashmir International*, Murree Rd, Liaquat Chowk, T502962, F502964. Fan, room cooler, phone, TV, attached bath, rather mediocre for price. **D** *National City*, Murree Rd, Liaquat Chowk, T555236, F558084. A/c, fan, TV/dish, phone, attached bath, rooms OK but nothing special.

Committee Chowk **C** *Al-Baddar*, Hotel Square, Committee Chowk, T502380, F502330. Central a/c, fan, TV/dish, phone, foreign exchange, restaurant, rooftop BBQ, banquet hall, rather expensive, rooms a bit damp and tacky. **C** *Blue Sky*, Hotel Square, Committee Chowk, T557629, F501517. Central a/c, fan, phone, TV/dish, attached bath, reasonably clean and pleasant rooms, *Larosh* restaurant downstairs. **C** *Imperial*, Murree Rd, Committee Chowk, T559677. A/c, TV/dish, phone, cheaper **D** category rooms without a/c, restaurant. **C** *Jan Sher Tower*, Muree Rd, Committee Chowk, T532144, F532163. A/c, TV, phone, attached bath, restaurant, modern building, clean comfortable rooms, good value. **C** *Rawal*, Hotel Square, Committee Chowk, T556241, F552134. Central a/c, phone, TV/dish, attached bath, foreign exchange, banquet hall, restaurant, posh furnishings but a little run-down and overpriced. **C** *Regent*, Hotel Square, Committee Chowk, T540099, F500480. Central a/c, fan, TV/dish, phone, attached bath, restaurant, newly refurbished, spotlessly clean, comfortable. **D** *Al-Farooq*, Hotel Square, Committee Chowk, T556200. A/c, TV/dish, phone, attached bath, also cheaper **E** category rooms without a/c and TV/dish, restaurant, generally rather shabby hotel. **D** *United*, Hotel Square, Committee Chowk, T556205. Central a/c, fan, phone, TV/dish (cheaper **E** category rooms without TV/dish), clean, fairly good value.

Rawalpindi - Cantonment

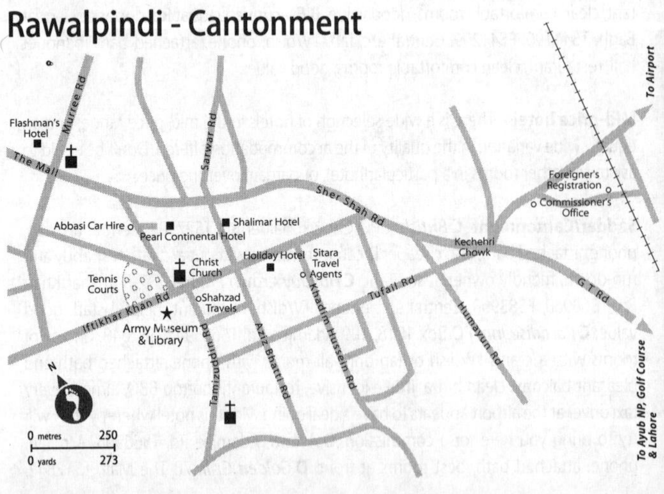

Budget hotels Most of the budget accommodation is found in the Saddar area. Budget hotels can also be found at Committee Chowk and Liaquat Chowk. There are plenty of other places scattered all over Rawalpindi, but often the rooms are really grotty, and in some cases foreigners are not really welcome. Women travelling alone should exercise caution; the *Popular Inn* near Liaquat Chowk is probably the best option in this respect, if only because you are likely to meet other foreigners there.

Saddar/Cantonment **E** *Barlas*, 51-52 Kashmir Rd, T522152. Fan, attached bath, rather basic and not very appealing, restaurant. **E** ***Kashmir Inn***, Bank Rd, T563742. Cooler, fan, attached bath, fairly basic. **E** ***Khayaban***, Kashmir Rd, T568823. Fan, phone, attached bath (no shower), a little pricy. **E** ***New Kamran***, Kashmir Rd, T582040. Fan, phone, attached bath, simple but clean rooms, parking in small but pleasant courtyard area. **E** ***Taj Mahal***, 32 Haider Rd, T586802. Fan, phone, attached bath, fairly clean, good value, restaurant. **E** ***Tayyaba***, Mohammadi St, T514591. Fan, attached bath, reasonably clean, best rooms at front. **F** ***Al-Azam***, Hathi Chowk, Adamjee Rd, T565901. Fan, attached bath, the double rooms with balconies are best, avoid the singles which are windowless boxes, pretty shabby throughout but friendly staff, restaurant for breakfast, snacks etc, good budget option. **F** ***Al-Falah***, Adamjee Rd, T580799. Fan, attached bath, choice of rooms with or without carpet, reasonably clean, restaurant, friendly staff, good budget option. **F** ***Al-Toheed***, Mohammadi St, T510430, fan, attached bath, restaurant, basic. **F** ***Bolan***, Railway Rd, T563416. Fan, attached bath, restaurant, basic. **F** *Lalazar*, Hathi Chowk, Adamjee Rd. Fan, attached bath, basic/grotty but cheap. **F** ***Saadia***, Railway Rd, T568625. Fan, attached bath, basic, clean restaurant downstairs. **F** ***Shah Taj***, Hathi Chowk, Adamjee Rd. Fan, attached bath, basic/grotty but cheap. **F** ***Venus***, Hathi Chowk, Adamjee Rd, T566501. Fan, attached bath, basic/grotty but cheap.

Committee Chowk **E** *Asia*, Committee Chowk, T70898. Fan, phone, attached bath, hotel looks pretty grotty from outside but rooms are in fact reasonably clean. **E** *Maharaja*, Committee Chowk, T70391. Fan, phone, attached bath, rather noisy/grotty, restaurant. **E** ***Pindi***, Committee Chowk, T558809. Fan, phone, attached bath, simple but reasonably clean, upper floors incomplete though building work appears to be on permanent hold. **E** ***Queens***, Committee Chowk, T553201. Fan, phone, TV, attached bath, restaurant, oldest establishment in Hotel Square, reasonably OK, due for renovation soon.

Liaquat Chowk/Murree Rd **E** *Shangri La* (not part of chain), Liaquat Chowk, Murree Rd, T408108. Fan, phone, attached bath, some rooms with a/c, hotel overall a bit dank and run-down. **E-F** ***Popular Inn***, G-261 Gordon College Road, near Liaquat Bagh, T831885. Fan, attached bath, choice of singles/doubles (Rs 150/250) or dorm beds (Rs 100), simple but spotlessly clean, nick-named 'Japanese House' for its popularity amongst Japanese travellers, currently the most popular choice amongst backpackers generally, friendly/helpful staff (but watch out for the afternoon break when they close the restaurant and reception in order to clean). **F** ***Snow Ball Inn***, H-40 Gordon College Rd, T553327. Fan, attached bath, rather tatty rooms, restaurant downstairs.

Around Fowara Chowk Heading southeast from Fowara Chowk along Liaquat Rd there are dozens of **E-F** category hotels. They include the ***Al-Falah***, ***Al-Maroof***, ***Four Brothers***, ***Evergreen***, ***7 Brothers***, ***Al-Idrees***, ***Mehran***, ***Ali***, ***Antepara***, ***Ghandara*** and ***City Inn***. There is often a large variation in the quality of rooms within each hotel, though overall none are particularly appealing.

Heading east from Fowara Chowk along Trunk Bazaar/Iqbal Rd, next door to each other are the **E** ***Al-Siraj***, 63-E Iqbal Rd, T550400 and **E** ***Chinar***, 62-E Iqbal Rd, T74366.

Both provide fairly basic rooms with fan, phone and attached bath. They are noisy but the location is great for the bazaars of the Old City.

Heading south from Fowara Chowk along City Saddar Rd is the **F** ***Mashriq***, City Saddar Rd, T542970. Fan, attached bath, basic, rather dirty and noisy, restaurant, bookings/departures for *Hameed Travels* coasters to Gilgit. Next door is the **F** ***Taimur International***, City Saddar Rd, T550894. Fan, attached bath, good clean rooms.

Eating

● *on maps*

Pakistani The luxury and more expensive hotels all have restaurants serving good Pakistani dishes in elegant surroundings (the *Pearl Continental* hotel's ***Marco Polo*** is the best). The restaurants in the *Shalimar* and *Rysons International* hotels are also of a high standard. Those in the **A-B** and **B** category hotels tend to be more into their furnishings than their cuisine. The restaurant in *Kashmirwala's* hotel on The Mall was closed at the time of writing for refurbishment, though if it maintains its former standard it will be worthy of a recommendation when it reopens.

At **Committee Chowk** there are 2 good restaurants next door to each other, the ***Usmania*** and ***Larosh***, both serving a wide range of Pakistani dishes in comfortable surroundings for around Rs 150-250 per head.

In **Saddar**, the ***Anwar Café***, on the corner of Adamjee Rd and Kashmir Rd, is the epitome of a traditional cheap Pakistani restaurant; simple and crowded, with a constant stream of *karahis*, *tikkas*, curries etc, being fried and grilled out front, in full view of passers-by and diners alike. Eat well for around Rs 100-150. Recommended. To the north of the main centre of Saddar, the popular ***Jehangir Balti Murgh***, 132 Kashmir Rd, T563352, also serves excellent *karahis*, *tikkas*, *kebabs* etc and has a pleasant garden. Gets busy in the evenings. Eat well for around Rs 100-150. Recommended. The clean and unassuming ***Kamran Café***, on Bank Rd, near the junction with Kashmir Rd, serves Pakistani/continental food and is a good place to come for light meals, snacks and refreshments.

On **Murree Road**, a little to the north of Saddar proper, the ***Lasania*** and ***Red Onion*** restaurants serve Pakistani and Continental/fast-food, though they are both geared up more to dealing with large groups and special occasions.

Around **Fowara Chowk** there are numerous cheap eateries, particularly heading southeast along Liaquat Road; the ***Amir*** and ***Javed***, next door to each other usually both do brisk business, offering a standard selection of *karahis*, *tikkas*, meat/veg curries etc.

Chinese The *Pearl Continental* hotel's ***Tai Pan*** restaurant is the best Chinese in Rawalpindi. There are numerous others (all in the **Saddar** area), but despite the choice the food is generally pretty mediocre. A full meal will come to around Rs 200-250 per head, though you can eat reasonably well for half that if you are selective. ***Shezan***, Kashmir Rd, T565743. Fairly popular, reasonable food. ***Chung Pa***, Majeed Plaza, 163 Bank Rd, T564577. Overpriced, usually empty. ***Mei Kong***, off Haider Rd. Looks a bit run-down and also usually empty. ***Kim Fah***, The Mall. OK food. Beer served in teapots; Rs 150 for 500 millilitres bottle. ***Mainland Chinese***, off The Mall. Nothing special.

Fast food There are numerous cheap fast-food places, snack bars and Pakistani-style restaurants dotted around Saddar. ***Burger Express***, Kashmir Rd (next door to the *Anwar Café*). Burgers, fries, milkshakes etc. ***Pizza Kent***, The Mall. Serves overpriced pizzas to a middle-class clientele. There is a good ***fresh juice bar*** next door to the *British* hotel on Haider Rd.

Bakeries The *Pearl Continental* hotel's ***Baker's Boutique*** offers delicious pastries, cakes, ice creams etc, and real coffee. After that, the best bakery in Rawalpindi is probably ***Rahat Bakers***, off Bank Rd, T564373, F521059. Excellent selection of sweets,

Punjab

cakes, biscuits etc, as well as tasty savoury snacks. A good place to search out some breakfast variety. ***Unique Bakers***, corner of Kashmir Rd and Bank Rd, have a good reputation, though there is less choice. Numerous other smaller bakeries can be found around Saddar.

Entertainment

There is not a huge amount going on in Rawalpindi in terms of entertainment, with most cultural events and the like taking place in Islamabad. The *Pearl Continental* hotel sometimes hosts events. Otherwise, the various **cinemas** dotted around Saddar and Committee Chowk are the main source of entertainment for ordinary Pakistanis. These include the ***Ciroz***, Haider Rd; the ***Gullistan*** and ***Shabistan***, Committee Chowk; and the ***Riaz***, further north on Murree Rd.

Sports There is an 18 hole **golf** course adjoining Ayub Park and **boating** on the lake in the park itself. There is a **cricket** ground off the Mall, though the international Test Match is on Stadium Road, just off Murree Road (near Faisabad). The *Pearl Continental* hotel has a **swimming pool** and **health centre**, both of which are open to non-guests for a fee.

Shopping

The main shopping areas are Saddar, Rawalpindi's modern commercial centre, and Rajah Bazaar, the still-thriving heart of the Old City. The streets and tiny alleys around **Rajah Bazaar** each contain their own smaller bazaars, with the various trades grouped together in traditional Asian style. Many of the buildings here still retain their original intricately carved wooden balconies and whenever the bazaars escape the press of modern traffic, it is easy to feel yourself slipping back a century or so. **Kalan Bazaar** is the main cloth market. **Sarafa Bazaar** sells intricate hand-worked gold and silver jewellery as well as brass, copper and tin utensils. **Moti Bazaar** is the women's market with beads, hair braids, shawls, make-up etc. **Trunk Bazaar** combines metal trunks with other items of ironmongery and practical goods; there is a good fishing tackle shop around 200 metres down on the right (coming from Fowara Chowk). **Bara Bazaar**, named after a smuggling town in NWFP near the border with Afghanistan, is full of smuggled electrical goods and other items. **Bohr Bazaar** contains medical shops, both western and traditional, while **Rajah Bazaar** itself centres around stalls of vegetables, spices and dried fruits and nuts, piled high in colourful arrays.

Saddar has a good selection of antique, jewellery and handicraft shops. On The Mall, near the junction with Canning Road, there is ***Pakistan Handicrafts***. Towards the eastern end of Haider Road there are 3 shops grouped together – ***Craft House***, ***Kashmir Handicrafts*** and ***Ganemede*** – which between them offer a good selection of handicrafts and carpets. ***Ambala Carpets***, on Haider Road by the *British* hotel, also has a good selection of carpets and rugs. On Sundays there is a market with handicrafts, second-hand books and numerous other items, which spreads out along Kashmir Road, centred on the junctions with Haider, Bank and Adamjee Roads.

Bookshops There are several bookshops around Saddar, including ***Capri*** on Haider Rd, by the *British* hotel, ***Pak-American Commercial***, upstairs on Kashmir Rd, by the *Barlas* hotel, ***Book Centre***, on Saddar Rd, and ***Variety Book Stall***, on Bank Rd, near the junction with Saddar Rd. Between them they offer a reasonable selection of books, magazines and newspapers, though on the whole the bookshops in Islamabad are better. There are also a couple of reasonable second-hand bookshops; try ***Old Book Bank***, just off Kashmir Rd, or ***Old Book Bank 2***, just off Bank Rd.

Photography The best bet for fresh film stocks (including slide films) in Rawalpindi (and Pakistan) is the ***Fuji*** headquarters next door to *American Express*, 112-D Rahim Plaza, Murree Rd, T581146, F581148 (*Sensia 100* Rs 210, *Velvia* Rs 300).

Vehicle repairs/mechanical Near the railway in Saddar, on Adamjee Road and the road running parallel to it to the west, there are numerous vehicle breakers, car and motorcycle mechanics, tyre repair shops etc. Heading south from Fowara Chowk along City Saddar Road there are plenty of general mehanical/engineering workshops for welding and machine tool jobs. There are also several workshops here specializing in restored (and unused) classic British motorcyles; an immaculate pre-unit Matchless or Triumph will set you back around £1,000 …

Local Transport

To & from the airport See box 'Islamabad International Airport'. If you are intent on catching a Suzuki to the airport, those running from Rajah Bazaar can be picked up at Liaquat Chowk or the corner of Murree Road and Tipu Road. Those running from Saddar Bazaar start at the eastern end of Adamjee Road and run via the Cantonment area.

To & from Islamabad See also under Islamabad. Arriving back from Islamabad along Murree Road, intercity buses and microbuses turn into Haider Road and drive along the length of it picking up passengers. They then turn right to loop up past the railway station, coming back down to Kashmir Road and following it up to join Murree Road at Marir Chowk. This means that there is no northbound public transport along Murree Road for the first stretch between The Mall and Marir Chowk.

To & from Pir Wadhai bus station Getting to and from Pir Wadhai by public transport with luggage is a pain. A taxi or auto-rickshaw between Pir Wadhai and Saddar should cost around Rs 40-50, but if you are catching one at Pir Wadhai you will have to bargain hard to get the price down to double this. Try teaming up with other Pakistanis heading into town. Suzukis operate between Pir Wadhai and Fowara Chowk, but they are always very cramped and you have to change there for Saddar. Alternatively, there are minibuses which run between Pir Wadhai and Faisabad (the major junction at the north end of Murree Road), from where you can pick up local intercity buses and microbuses heading into 'Pindi or Islamabad.

Taxis are readily available throughout Rawalpindi. If they do not have a working meter always agree a price before getting in.

Auto-rickshaws are also readily available throughout Rawalpindi. They are not much cheaper than taxis, though if you can put up with their exhaust fumes they can be more convenient in some situations.

Suzuki A useful Suzuki route is between Saddar (starting/finishing by the mosque at the junction of Adamjee Road and Kashmir Road) and Rajah Bazaar (starting/finishing at Fowara Chowk).

Horse-drawn tongas are available at both Fowara Chowk and Committee Chowk. They have somewhat more romantic appeal than taxis and auto-rickshaws, though they are hopelessly impractical amidst Rawalpindi's relentless motorized congestion.

Car hire Avis, 7 Rahim Plaza, Murree Road (next door to Amex), T520210. Choice of self-drive and chauffeur-driven. Cars from Rs 1,150 per day, plus Rs 200 per day for CDW (Crash Damage Waiver) and Rs 4 per kilometre. Amex, Visa and Mastercard accepted. ***Pearl Continental***, T566011 ext 4573. Chauffeur-driven cars only, from Rs 2,500 per day. ***Abbasi Tours***, Masood Akhtar Rd, opposite Pearl Continental, T516733. Cheapest self-drive car Rs 1,500 per day, unlimited mileage, no insurance. There are dozens of small car hire firms at Committee Chowk; heading north along Murree Rd, turn right at the junction with Iqbal Rd and then immediately right again, and they are along this first stretch of road.

Islamabad International Airport

Location *The airport is situated around 12 kilometres from Islamabad's Zero Point and 7 kilometres from the Saddar/Cantt area of Rawalpindi. The International and domestic terminals are contained within the same complex.*

Getting there and away *Many of the more expensive hotels offer an* ***airport shuttle*** *service for guests. If you have an advanced booking, arranging to be picked up should be no problem (and very useful if you find yourself arriving at some ungodly hour of the night). A metered* ***taxi*** *between the airport and Islamabad should cost around Rs 100, and Rs 50-60 for Rawalpindi. However securing a fare for less than double this at the airport takes some persistence. Taxi drivers are at their pushiest and prices at their highest immediately around the entrance to the airport building. If you walk out to the taxi ranks in the car park you should be able to get a better deal, while on the main road outside the airport gates you stand a chance of getting a ride for the standard fare. There are also tiny* ***Suzukis*** *which run between the airport and Rawalpindi (either to Adamjee Road in Saddar, or to Rajah Bazaar). These cost just a few Rupees but are very cramped indeed and not really suitable if you have lots of luggage, though they do have small roof racks. They do not go into the airport itself, but terminate at a stand a few hundred metres along the main road from the airport entrance (leaving the airport, turn right out of the gates).*

Arrival/departure formalities *Upon* ***arrival*** *you will be required to fill out a disembarkation card, and occasionally a health card also. The disembarkation card is collected at passport control. Having collected your baggage, pass through customs (foreigners are rarely stopped, though airport security may check to see that your luggage tags match). Upon* ***departure****, note that you are theoretically only allowed inside the terminal building 3 hours before your flight leaves (this rule may be waived for foreigners). You must pass through security (including baggage x-ray) before you can check in. Check-in clerks will collect the departure tax (Rs 400 economy, Rs 600 club/first class). Fill in the embarkation card which is collected by passport control, and then proceed to the departure lounge. There is a further security check (x-ray and body search) before embarkation.*

Domestic flights *PIA,* ***Aero Asia, Bhoja Air*** *and* ***Shaheen Air*** *all have offices just outside the arrivals terminal where you can buy tickets for onward domestic flights. Note that these are considerably cheaper when bought in Pakistan rather than abroad.*

Services ***Banks*** *at the airport are open 24 hours (cash and travellers' cheques), though rates are marginally inferior to those available in town. There are branches of the National Bank of Pakistan and Habib bank in the baggage collection hall. Outside the building there are more foreign exchange counters, as well as touts for money changers (**see page 214**). Also outside is the* ***Tourist Information*** *counter (24 hours), as well as offices for some of the luxury* ***hotels*** *(the Marriott, Holiday Inn, Pearl Continental and Shalimar).* ***Left luggage*** *facilities are not available at the airport.* ***Duty Free*** *is available to passengers arriving and departing. Alcohol is not available, though cigarettes are incredibly cheap (US$8 for 200).* ***Porters*** *are available and should have the correct fee displayed on a badge. There is a* ***Café/Snack bar*** *outside and another in the terminal, but both are basic.*

Long distance transport

Air See box for information on Islamabad International Airport.

Domestic The information given below was correct at the time of writing, but all the airlines make minor modifications to their schedules on a regular basis. Contact the airline, or a travel agent, for exact timings. Flights to Lahore, Karachi and Quetta should be booked well in advance. **PIA Bahawalpur** 1 flight daily; **Bannu** (via

Flights to Gilgit and Skardu

Flights to Gilgit and Skardu are handled separately from other domestic flights. They are subject to weather conditions, needing clear visibility in order to operate; a few days of bad weather soon results in a large backlog of passengers. PTDC have a quota of 2 seats specifically for tourists on each flight; if there is a long waiting list it is worth trying for these. The decision as to whether or not to cancel a flight is only made at the last minute (note that it can be cloudy in Islamabad, but if it is clear in the mountains the flight will still go). If a flight is cancelled, you must reconfirm your ticket if you want to try again the next day, or you can get a full refund. To do either, return to the PIA Northern Areas office (around the side of the main building in 'Pindi, and a separate counter in Islamabad) at around 1100 the same morning. Flights to Skardu are by Boeing 737 jet and less frequently subject to cancellation, while those to Gilgit are by smaller, older Fokker F27 propeller planes. In both cases the flight is a spectacular one. Sit on the right for views of Nanga Parbat, or try asking if there is any possibility of a peek in the flight deck for some really awesome panoramic views. *See also page 477.*

Peshawar) Monday, Tuesday, Friday; **Chitral** (via Peshawar) Monday, Tuesday, Wednesday, Friday, Saturday (weather permitting); **Dera Ghazi Khan** Tuesday, Thursday, Sunday; **Dera Ismail Khan** 1 flight daily; **Faisalabad** 1 flight daily, 2 flights Tuesday; **Gilgit** 2-3 flights daily (weather permitting); **Hyderabad** Thursday, Sunday; **Karachi** 5-8 flights daily; **Lahore** 7-10 flights daily; **Mianwali** Friday, Sunday; **Moenjodaro** (via Karachi) 1-2 flights daily; **Multan** 2-3 flights daily; **Muzaffarabad** Monday, Tuesday, Wednesday, Thursday, Saturday; **Parachinar** Monday, Wednesday, Friday; **Peshawar** 2-4 flights daily; **Quetta** 1-2 flights daily; **Rawalakot** Tuesday, Thursday, Saturday; **Saidu Sharif** 1 flight daily, except Saturday; **Skardu** 1 flight daily; **Sukkur** Monday, Friday, Saturday; **Zhob** 1 flight daily, except Friday; **Air Safaris** should be booked through PIA's office in Islamabad; **Aero Asia Karachi** 4 flights daily; **Lahore** 1 flight daily; **Peshawar** 2 flights daily; **Shaheen Air Karachi** 1 flight daily, except Sunday; **Lahore** Monday; **Bhoja Air Karachi** Monday, Wednesday, Saturday.

International: most international flights to and from Islamabad are with PIA and British Airways, though these are now complemented also by Saudi and Xinjiang. In addition, Shaheen Air operates a once-weekly flight (Sunday), and Aero Asia a twice weekly flight (Sunday, Friday) from Islamabad to Dubai.

Train The railway station is situated on the northern edges of Rawalpindi's Saddar area. There is a Pakistan Railways info centre and booking office in Islamabad, at Melody Market, T9207474, as well as at the station. Student and foreign tourist concessions can be obtained from the Commercial Dept at the station. Sleepers and a/c must be booked well in advance; they often sell out as soon as they go on sale, which is 15 days before the departure date. The following is a selection of the most convenient services from 'Pindi.

Karachi; *Tezgam*, 0800, 25½ hours; *Awam Exp*, 1225, 28 hours; *Zulfiqar Exp*, 1435, 29 hours; *Chenab Exp* (via Faisalabad), 0045, 34½ hours; *Khyber Mail*, 0235, 28½ hours; **Lahore**; All the trains for Karachi listed above stop in Lahore, except for the *Chenab Exp*. They take around 5½-6 hours from 'Pindi. In addition, there are 3 services to Lahore only; *Subuk Kharam*, 0700, 5 hours; *Subuk Raftar*, 1630, 5 hours; *Night Coach*, 2345, 4¾ hours; **Quetta**; *Quetta Exp* (via Lahore), 0715, 31½ hours; *Abbaseen Exp* (via Faisalabad), 2230, 35½ hours; **Multan**; All the trains for Karachi listed above stop in Multan. In addition, there is the *Multan Exp* (via Faisalabad), 2015, 13½ hours; **Peshawar**; *Awam Exp*, 1215, 4 hours; *Zulfiqar Exp*, 1530, 4 hours; *Khyber Mail*, 0200, 4 hours; *Chenab Exp*, 0310, 4 hours; *Abbaseen Exp*, 0355, 4 hours. These often arrive

Selected domestic fares and flying times from Islamabad

To	*Fare (Rs)*	*Flying time (approximately)*
Gilgit	*955/2,500**	*1 hour*
Karachi	*3,400***	*1 hour 55 minutes*
Lahore	*1,300*	*1 hour 15 minutes*
Peshawar	*700*	*1 hour*
Quetta	*2,920*	*1 hour 25 minutes*
Skardu	*1,085/2,500**	*1 hour*

** Flights to Gilgit and Skardu are subsidized for Pakistanis. Foreigners pay the higher rate. At the time of writing, the fare for foreigners was being raised by Rs 30 each month, though to judge from other comparable fares it must be pretty near its ceiling.*
*** Cheaper 'Night Coach' fares are available to Karachi for around Rs 2,600.*

extremely late in 'Pindi, having come all the way from Karachi and Quetta; the *211 Passenger*, 0720, 6 hours, originating in Lahore is slower, but at least stands a better chance of passing through 'Pindi on time; **Kohat**; *188 Passenger*, 0600, 5¼ hours; **Havelian (via Taxila)**; *R-455 Passenger*, 0630, 3¼ hours; *Hazara Exp*, 1630, 3½ hours.

Punjab

Bus Pir Wadhai, the main bus station, is inconveniently situated on the northwest outskirts of Rawalpindi and southwest outskirts of Islamabad. See under Local Transport for details of getting to and from it. There are services to all major cities and towns from here, but it is a large and chaotic place and locating the correct bus can be confusing. Conductors and touts compete to hustle you aboard their bus. While it can be difficult to avoid ending up here when you arrive by bus, it is possible to catch a bus to practically anywhere from more convenient locations around Rawalpindi without trekking all the way out to Pir Wadhai. ***Masherbrum Tours*** and ***NATCO*** (Northern Areas Transport Company), both of which operate services to **Gilgit**, originate here. Between them the 2 companies offer regular departures throughout the day (and also a couple during the night), with a choice of simple, 'deluxe' and 'a/c deluxe' buses (Rs 280-380). The trip takes a minimum of 14 hours, though 17-19 hours is the norm.

Committee Chowk The bus stand here has regular a/c coaches and coasters to **Peshawar**, Rs 40, 3½-4 hours. These depart when full, though you rarely have to wait more than half an hour or so before one is ready to go.

Murree Road/Tipu Road On Murree Road itself, next door to the *Shangri La* hotel, there is the ***New Flying Coach*** ticket office, T504840, with a/c coach services to **Lahore (via motorway)** departing every half hour from 0830-2400, Rs 130, 4½ hours. There are also slower a/c Coasters to **Lahore (via GT Road)** departing every hour from 0700-0100, Rs 101, 6 hours. Around the corner in Tipu Road, either side and opposite the *Amir International* hotel, there are bus stands which between them offer a combination of buses, Coasters and Hiaces to **Sarghoda** and **Lahore (via GT Road)**.

Marir Chowk Where Kashmir Road joins Murree Road there is a bus stand with regular Hiaces to **Sialkot**, **Mianwali**, **Gujranwala**, **Chakwal**, **Jhelum** and various other towns in this area. A little more than half way along the street leading west from Marir Chowk parallel to the railway there is a bus stand with regular Hiaces to **Murree**, **Abbottabad** and **Taxila**. All these Hiace services simply depart when full.

City Saddar Road The *Mashriq* hotel on City Saddar Road (due south from Fowara Chowk) also acts as the office for ***Hameed Travel Services***, T542970 which operates a daily Coaster service to **Gilgit**, Rs 330, 14 hours (minimum), departing at 1500.

PIA's Air Safari

PIA operates a weekly 'Air Safari' taking passengers by 737 for a quick spin to K2 and back. This flight leaves each Saturday at 0900 (weather and demand permitting) and lasts one hour 45 minutes. Check with PIA's Islamabad office to see if it is running (T816051). If you have only a limited amount of time in Pakistan, or are unable to visit the Northern Areas, this is the ideal way to get a ring-side view of some of the world's most awesome and spectacular mountains.

Saddar There are various locations around Saddar from where you can catch buses. On the corner of Haidar Road and Saddar Road there are Coasters departing every half hour between 0600-2100 to **Abbottabad**, Rs 40, and **Mansehra**, Rs 45. ***TDCP*** (*Tourism Development Corporation of Punjab*), T564824, operate Hiaces to **Murree**, Rs 30, departing every half hour, and a/c buses to **Lahore (via motorway)**, Rs 150 (including lunchbox), half a dozen departures daily, phone for exact times. Also a/c buses to **Faisalabad**, Rs 130, half a dozen departures daily, phone for exact times. Tickets and departures from their office on the corner of Kashmir Road and The Mall.

Directory

Airline offices *PIA Booking Office*, 5 The Mall, Rawalpindi, T568071, F583793. Open 7 days 0700-2100 (closed Fri 1230-1430); outside office hours call airport reservations, T591071. The Northern Areas office, T567011 (for flights to Gilgit and Skardu) is around the side of the building and is open 7 days 0700-1700 (closed Fri 1230-1430). All the other major airlines have their head offices in Karachi. The following have General Service Agents (GSAs) in 'Pindi. ***British Airways***, Pearl Continental Hotel, The Mall, T564702, F567710. ***Gulf Air***, King Associates, 53-6 Haider Rd, Saddar, T522934, F522935. ***Iraqi***, United Travels, 8 Mobee Plaza, Haider Rd, T581969. ***Royal Jordanian***, World Travel Consultants, T563242. ***Saudi Arabian***, Southern Travels, T814992.

Banks *American Express*, PO Box 96, Rahim Plaza, Murree Rd, T566001, F582863. Open Mon-Thur 0900-1330, 1430-1700, Fri 0900-1230, 1430-1700, Sat 0900-1300, closed Sun. Efficient exchange service for cash and TCs (Thomas Cook as well as Amex), also cash advances for Amex card holders, and Clients' Mail service. There are dozens of banks dotted around Rawalpindi's Saddar area, most of which do foreign exchange. ***National Bank of Pakistan*** does not charge any fee for cashing TCs. ***ANZ Grindlays*** charges an exorbitant Rs 500 fee for cashing TCs, but they do give cash advances against Visa cards. There are several licensed **money changers** to be found in the shopping plaza on the corner of Kashmir Rd and The Mall (in the same complex as the office of the Tourism Development Corporation of Punjab – TDCP). They can generally change TCs as well as cash, and depending on the economic situation may be able to offer substantially better rates than the banks. Several licensed money changers are also to be found at the Suzuki depot near the airport.

Communications **Post:** the GPO is on Kashmir Rd, just south of junction with Haider Rd. Open Mon-Thur and Sat 0900-2000, Fri 0900-1130, 1530-2000, closed Sun. Poste Restante (at rear of building) and Express Post service available. **Telephone:** the PakTelecom office is on Kashmir Rd, just south of junction with The Mall. Open 7 days 24 hours. Fax and telex services also available. There are various PCOs (including 'World Call') dotted around Saddar offering local/national/international phone (and in some cases fax) services. **Internet:** the most convenient internet café in Rawalpindi is the ***Cyber Café***, College of Information Technology, top floor, Majeed Plaza, Bank Rd, T511686. Open 0900-2300. Internet access Rs 35 per hour, or if you join up as a member you can pay in advance for 25, 50 or 100 hours at Rs 30, 25 or 20 per hour. Less conveniently located (half way to Faisabad on the Murree Rd) is ***Web Links***, office 12, 2nd flr, Resham Plaza, Chandni Chowk Murree Rd. Internet access Rs 30 per hour. The internet cafés in Islamabad generally offer faster connections, though they are also more expensive. **Courier:** ***DHL***, T823545, and ***TNT***, T565314. Both have offices next door to each other in Gul-e-Akra Plaza, Murree Rd, south of Marir Chowk.

Cultural centres See under Islamabad.

Selected Rail Fares from Rawalpindi (in Rupees)

	A/c sleeper	*A/c sitter*	*1st sleeper*	*Economy*
Karachi City	*1,495*	*860*	*595*	*315*
Lahore	*380*	*220*	*140*	*70*
Multan	*710*	*415*	*270*	*135*
Bahawalpur	*800*	*460*	*310*	*150*
Jacobabad	*1,170*	*675*	*455*	*240*
Quetta	*1410*	*810*	*560*	*295*
Peshawar	*260*	*155*	*90*	*40*
Kohat	*265*	*155*	*90*	*41*
Taxila Cantt	—	*40*	—	*9*

Embassies & consulates See under Islamabad

Hospitals & medical services The 2 main hospitals are the ***Rawalpindi General***, Murree Rd, T847761, and the ***Cantonment General***, Saddar Rd, T562254. Both have dispensaries, and there are various pharmacies dotted around Saddar area. Medical facilities are better in Islamabad.

Libraries See under Islamabad

Tour companies & travel agents ***Pakistan Tours Ltd*** (PTL), a branch of PTDC, are situated in the grounds of Flashman's Hotel. They offer a number of package tours and also tailor-made arrangements for groups and individuals. Willing to cater for all budgets. ***Pakistan Guides***, PO Box 1692, 3rd Floor, 62/2 Bank Road, T524808, F539497. Run by Kaiser Khan, 20 years experience, offers a wide range of specialized expeditions and tours.

Tourist offices At the time of writing, the *PTDC* office in *Flashman's* hotel was closed; nearest office in Islamabad. *TDCP* (Tourism Development Corporation of Punjab), 44 Mall Plaza (inside shopping plaza on the corner of Kashmir Rd and The Mall), T564824, F568421. Information and package tours to Murree and the Galis, Kaghan valley, Swat valley, Chitral, Gilgit and Hunza. Also tickets and departures for minibus service to Murree and a/c bus services to Faisalabad and Lahore (see under Transport).

Useful addresses **Police:** Police Station Rd, Saddar Bazaar, T564760. **Foreigners registration:** Senior Superintendent of Police, Civil Courts, off Willian Rd. **Visa Extensions:** See under Islamabad.

Excursions from Islamabad and Rawalpindi

There are several interesting excursions which can be made from the capital. The Margalla hills offer endless walking opportunities. The famous archaeological remains at Taxila, dating back to the sixth century BC, are just 40 kilometres away. The Tarbela Dam, also easily accessible from Islamabad, is a spectacular sight, particularly when full. If you are limited for time, it is also possible to visit the hill stations such as Murree and Thandiani as longer excursions from Islamabad, as well as places further afield to the north and northwest.

Margalla Treks

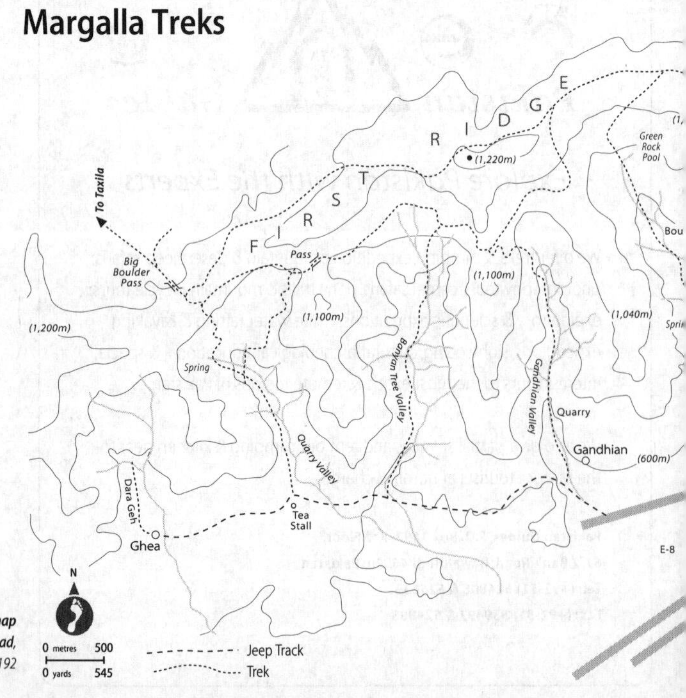

Related map
A Islamabad, page 192

Margalla hills

The **Margalla hills** are also known as the **Islamabad National Park**. Formed of limestone, they cover an area of about 12,000 hectares. Numerous nature trails wind around the hills and valleys, offering a choice for walkers and hikers of distances covering one and a half kilometres to 15 kilometres (a total length of 110 kilometres), and ranging from heights of 640-1,580 metres. As well as a wide selection of short walks and half to full-day hikes, there are also longer treks which can take up to two to three days; go prepared for these with the best maps and a compass. The easy trails can be undertaken in 'trainers' but several are stony and require strong shoes or walking boots. You can start several treks from Islamabad on foot. The best season is October-April but even in these relatively cooler months, mid-day can be very hot. Be prepared for heavy rain in January and February and chilly nights.

Follow the trails, avoid short cuts, as it is easy to get lost (and the thorn bushes can be painful), and carry drinking water with you. In the dry season there is the added risk of fire. The Asia Study Group's *Hiking Around Islamabad* (1992 Revised edition) has very good detailed maps and lists the different possibilities in the Margalla hills and a few further north. The Capital Development Authorities *Trekking in the Margalla Hills* is not accurate enough for the longer trails. **NB** We have received reports of a number of 'incidents'. Women should not hike here alone.

The row of hills facing Islamabad is called the '**First Ridge**' with a number of valleys and ravines with pools, springs and waterfalls, cutting into them from the plains. Some valleys have descriptive names; *Dara Baliman* (Quarry Valley), *Santari* (Banyan Tree Valley), *Nurpur Sara* (Rock Pools Valley), *Rata Hotter* (Leopard Valley) among others. The next row, parallel to the first and separated from it by the deep *Nilan Nullah*, is known as the '**Second Ridge**'. The only motorable road through the hills is the Pir Sahawa Road, which starts from the Khayaban-e-Iqbal (or Margalla Road), near the Zoo, and runs up to the 'First Ridge' eastward. A jeepable track continues east from Pir Sahawa where there is a *Forest Rest House*. Tracks come down to the Nilan Nullah from the Pir Sahawa Road.

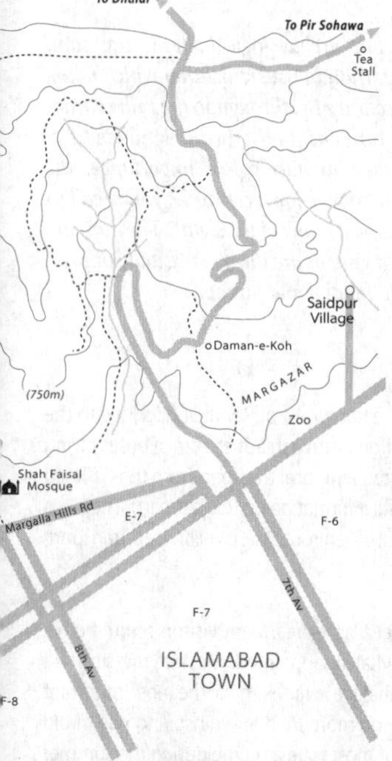

The short walks start near the Zoo (Marghazar), or from Daman-e-Koh or Pir Sahawa. Picnic spots have 'Shades' which can be crowded on Fridays. You can reach the highest point in the hills (1,640 metres) from Pir Sahawa. If you are with children keen on bathing, try the Rock Pools Valley which you can get to by driving up north of Nurpur Shahan village, parking near the Mandiala water works. The longer hikes taking from four to eight hours or two to three days are described in the Asia Study Group's booklet.

Vegetation The hills have been planted with subtropical local as well as non-indigenous ornamental plants with evidence of the primary forest only at the higher levels. The slopes below 1,000 metres have dry, semi-evergreen vegetation, with acacia and olive predominating. Shrubs protect against soil erosion. On the higher slopes, taller pines are common, particularly *Pinus roxburghii* and also the white oak, *Quercus incana*, which can be a fire hazard. There are numerous other species including *sheesham* and the wild date palm, *Phoenix sylvestris*, the silk cotton tree, *Bombax ceiba*, and the Peepul, *Ficus religiosa*.

Ornamental species include jacaranda, bottlebrush, eucalyptus, amalthus, lilies and chir. In the spring, the plants, strikingly similar to European flora, flower in March until mid-April when they die down. Then around the beginning of July, the barren ground comes to life again with flora of Southeast Asia. A good guide available in Islamabad is *Wild flowers of Rawalpindi-Islamabad Districts* by Nasir and others (1987).

Wildlife Hunting has been banned and afforestation carried out. Animals and birds now include rhesus monkeys, barking deer, jackal, wild boar, porcupines, mongoose, pangolin (scaly anteater), the rare leopard in the winter as well as black partridges and birds of prey and a large number of butterfly species. Cheer pheasants which had become virtually extinct have been successfully re-introduced. Poisonous snakes include cobra, krait, and Russell's viper. They hibernate in the winter, but take care when walking off the paths in the warmer months. The ASG has published a list of birds by Corfield which supplements the handy ***Guide to the birds of the sub-continent*** published by Collins. If you are keen to identify butterflies, try ***Butterflies of India*** by Chas and Antram or ***Butterflies of the Himalaya*** by Mani.

Taxila

Phone code: 0596
Colour map 4, grid A4

Taxila represents one of the most important archaeological sites in Pakistan. This was the capital of the rich Gandharan Buddhist civilization which flourished in Pakistan from at least the sixth century BC through to the fifth century AD, evolving and changing over the centuries as it absorbed the influences of various conquering empires. Despite their archaeological importance, the remains themselves elicit mixed responses from visitors; certainly, you need lots of imagination to conjur up the former glory of many of the sights. The museum however is excellent and definitely worth a visit, as are the most visually impressive sites, namely Jaulian, Dharmarajika, Jandial and Sirkap.

Ins and outs

Getting there Taxila is situated around 35 kilometres to the northwest of Rawalpindi, a little to the north of the GT Road. It is easy to get to and from, with a steady stream of buses plying along the GT Road in both directions, and frequent local transport from the GT Road to the site itself (see Local transport for useful information on this last part). There are also trains from Rawalpindi which stop at Taxila en route to Havelian (see Transport, below).

Visiting the sites The various sites at Taxila are spread out over a large area. Many visitors return from a tour of the archaeological remains somewhat disappointed. Most of the sites are poorly labelled and for the non-specialist, what are in fact some of the most important excavations in the world can appear to be no more than an uninspiring pile of old stones. Perhaps the greatest problem is that most tourists come during the summer months, when daytime temperatures often reach well above 40°C. Combined with the lack of shade and the considerable amounts of walking involved, this can make for exhausting work. Visiting in winter is infinitely preferable. In any case, it is well worth starting as early as possible, perhaps using the hottest part of the day to visit the excellent museum and to rest, and then making use of the relatively cooler evening hours for more sight-seeing. For the non-specialist, it is also worth being fairly selective as there is a great deal to see. Those with a special interest will certainly want to spend more than a day here. A possible tour, if you have limited time and are willing to hire a tonga/taxi, is to start early at Jaulian, then visit Jandial and Sirkap, send your transport round to Dharmarajika and walk there from Sirkap. Finish with a tour of the museum.

History

The site at Taxila has been occupied from at least the **Neolithic** period. Excavations at **Sarai Khola**, three kilometres southwest of Taxila City, have shown a succession of occupations, the earliest having several pit dwellings with ground stone axes and burnished pottery. However, until recently it was widely believed that the town first came to prominence when the whole area was incorporated into the **Achaemenid Empire** of **Cyrus the Great** (558-530 BC).

In an inscription of 519 BC the third Achaemenid Emperor, **Darius I**, claimed possession of Gandhara, and soon after of "Hindush", a region which may well have covered most of the Punjab. By then Taxila was already the centre of a major university, attracting students from as far afield as modern Patna. It occupied a strategically important site on one of the ancient world's most important trade routes. If you stand at the monastery of **Jaulian** today you can still gain a sense of the advantage that its site offered, with the hills behind and the broadening lowlands spreading out below.

Recent excavations by the Cambridge-Pakistan team have produced evidence which supports the finds of Sir Mortimer Wheeler at **Charsada** to suggest that Taxila was founded possibly as early as 1000 BC. It probably retained a degree of independence throughout the period of Persian rule.

Punjab

Taxila

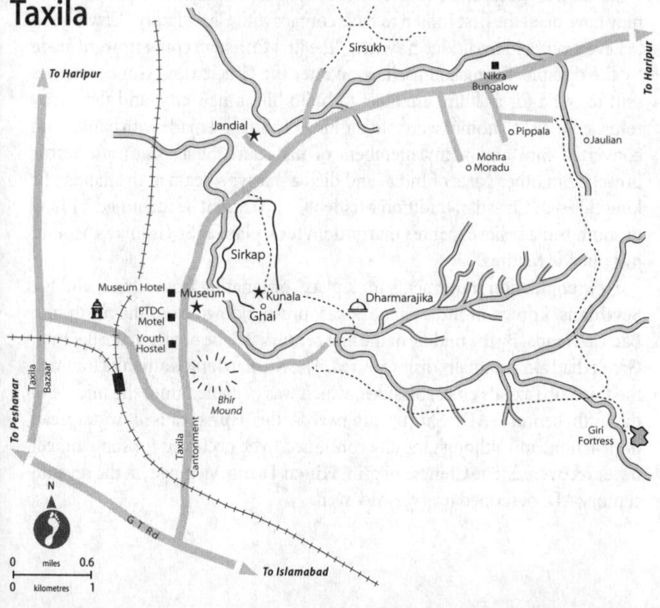

When **Alexander the Great** arrived it was certainly still a centre of learning and culture, for Alexander himself is recorded as having philosophical discussions with naked ascetics. However, the Greek occupation of Taxila was extraordinarily brief, and their influence at this period slight.

They were succeeded around 310 BC by **Chandragupta Maurya**. The contacts with the Greeks were maintained through the reign of his son **Bindusara**, who is recorded as having sent a request to the Greek King Antiochus for "a present of figs, wine and a sophist". According to Basham, Antiochus responded by sending figs and wine, but sent a message to the effect that "Greek philosophers were not for export". During this period Bindusara's son **Asoka**, who was to become one of India's greatest kings, became the Mauryan Viceroy in Taxila, and the Mauryan influence remained strong throughout his rule.

In the fourth century BC Taxila enjoyed a reputation for learning at least equal to that of Varanasi, with which it was contemporary. However, Taxila was particularly noted for its secular studies. **Caraka**, a master of medicine, **Kautilya**, the Brahman adviser in statecraft to the Emperor Chandragupta and **Panini**, author of the most famous Sanskrit grammar, all worked in Taxila. Throughout this period, the city of Taxila was focused on the area that now is known as the **Bhir Mound**.

From the middle of the third century BC Taxila became the scene of a series of invasions from the northwest. Bactrian Greeks under **Euthydemus** gained sufficient independence to break away completely from the Mauryan Empire, establishing a bridgehead for the introduction of western ideas into India. Their widespread coinage gives some impression of the extent and length of their rule, and it seems that Western theories of astrology and medicine, as well as Sanskrit drama, entered at this time. However, by the second half of the second century BC, Bactria was occupied by Parthians and the Greeks in Taxila and its region became isolated. At the beginning of the second century BC the Bactrian Greeks built a new and quite different city at Taxila, known as **Sirkap**

Basham suggests that one of the last of the Bactrian kings, **Gondophernes**, may have been the first Indian to have contact with Christianity. "If we are to believe a very old tradition" he writes "the first Christian converts were made by the disciple Thomas himself, soon after the Crucifixion. Gondophernes sent to Syria for a skilful architect to build him a new city, and the envoy returned with St Thomas who told the king of a city not made with hands, and converted him and many members of his court. St Thomas afterwards preached in other parts of India, and died a martyr's death at the hands of a king called in Christian tradition **Misdeos**, who cannot be identified". Many in south India believe that his martyrdom took place at St Thomas's Mount, just outside Madras.

New population movements took place, originating from China, and the **Scythians**, known in India as the Sakas, pressed down from the north into Bactrian lands. By the middle of the first century BC the power of the Bactrian Greeks had almost totally disintegrated. The Kushan king **Kanishka** founded the third of Taxila's cities, **Sirsukh**, which was occupied until the middle of the fifth century AD. Shortly afterwards the **Huns** caused widespread destruction, and although the city continued to be occupied for some time it never recovered. The Chinese pilgrim **Hiuen Tsang**, visiting it in the seventh century AD, described it as very decayed.

Sights

Taxila Museum

Built during Sir Mortimer Wheeler's time to house the fruits of his exhaustive excavations, this excellent museum is notable for its first class examples of Gandharan sculpture and art, giving some idea of the full splendour of Taxila in its heyday. There is also an impressive collection of coins and silver ornaments in a small room off the main hall (ask to be shown if the room is locked).

■ *Open 0830-1230, 1430-1730 in summer (1 April-30 September). 0800-1600 in winter (1 October-31 March). Closed first Monday of each month for cleaning. Admission Rs 4.*

Bir Mound

Covering the area of land to the south of the museum, and visible from the road, this is the oldest of the sites, dating from the sixth to second centuries BC, and was partially excavated by Sir John Marshall. There is little to see here; the excavations suggest that the settlement was a jumble of unplanned alleys and streets packed tightly together.

Dharmarajika

From the car park at the end of the road, follow the clearly marked path down into a small ravine, across two streams and then up a steep hill that conceals the stupa and surrounding buildings until you are nearly there. The stupa and monastery at the centre of this site possibly date from Asoka's time in the mid-third century BC. The main stupa, 15 metres high, was enlarged after its initial construction and some of the decoration on its east side was added in the fourth century AD.

Originally there was a series of small *votive stupas* (built by wealthy devotees) around the main building, and a series of chapels. If you walk round the stupa to the east side along one of the two processional paths that are a feature of Buddhist stupas you will see the great cut where treasure hunters looked for the relics of the Buddha. When Asoka converted to Buddhism after the great Kalingan War in modern Orissa in India, it is said that he disinterred the Buddha's remains from their casket at Vaisali and distributed them to eight major stupas across his empire, of which Dharmarajika is one. The best preserved work on this main stupa, the band of ornamental stone carving on the east side of the base, dates from the 4th and 5th centuries.

Immediately to the south of the main stupa is another comparatively well preserved though much smaller stupa, notable for the carvings of a series of Buddhas shown wearing local Kushan style dress. Walking north past the east side of the main stupa you pass a chapel in the northeast corner of the compound. There are representations of two of the Buddha's feet, large enough to have supported a statue 11 metres high. To the north again and on slightly higher ground is the large enclosed space of a former monastery, occupied for as much as 600 years from the first century BC. Immediately to the north of the main stupa is a bathing tank, some votive stupas and a building that may have housed an image of the reclining Buddha. Just to the southwest of the main stupa, near the entrance to the complex, is an apsidal ended "chapel".

Sirkap

It is possible to take the path from the northwest corner of Dharmarajika, and to walk through a narrow valley up to the stupa and monastery of Kunala on a hill, before going down into Taxila's second city, Sirkap. Alternatively, follow the road north past the PTDC Motel; the turning is signposted to the right.

Hiuen Tsang related how the **Kunala stupa** was built on the spot where Kunala, Asoka's son, had his eyes put out at the instructions of his stepmother. As is true of many stupas, the outer shell contains an earlier and much smaller stupa, in this case barely three metres high. The smaller one may date from the first century BC, while the larger structure around it dates from the third century AD. You get an excellent view of the city from the stupa.

The remains of Sirkap that have been excavated (just a small part) show a north-south main street, fortified at the north end, and regularly spaced lanes. Most of the buildings come from the beginning of the second century BC through to 85 BC. One feature of the houses is their underground rooms, approached through trap doors.

You need imagination to recapture what Sirkap must have been like when it was occupied. As at Moenjo Daro, the main street at Sirkap was probably lined with shops with two-storey houses behind them, arranged round courtyards. Halfway down the main street on the east side is the shrine of the **Double-Headed Eagle**, a first century AD stupa. Immediately to its south is a small **Jain stupa**. At the extreme south end of the street, again on the east side, is the royal palace, now largely invisible.

Jandial The turning left for Jandial (also signposted) is a little further along the main road from Sirkap. This temple shows obvious signs of its Greek ancestry. It comprised a square inner sanctuary, a meeting hall and a courtyard. Its entrances were flanked by Ionian columns. The existence of a solid tower between the sanctuary and back porch, which would have allowed the rising and setting sun to be observed, have been taken to suggest that this was probably used for **Zoroastrian** worship. It dates from the beginning of the Christian era.

Sirsukh The signposted turning left for Sirsukh is about one kilometre further along the main road from Jandial. There is very little to see on the site, which was only partially excavated.

Jaulian It is a short steep climb from the car park to the monastery, but you are rewarded with a magnificent view over the plains below. These are perhaps the most impressive and evocative remains visible today. The site is fully enclosed and there is always a caretaker in attendance.

The entrance is to the lower court leading to the main stupa. This is nothing like the scale of Dharmarajika, but it is far more fully decorated. Some of the surrounding votive stupas have inscriptions in **Kharoshthi** script. Some of the most important sculptures and relics are in the museum. While several of these stupas date from as late as the fifth century, the main monastery to the west comes from the second century. However, the plaster statues of the Buddha are copies of the originals which are in the museum. Surrounding the monastery courtyard are monks, cells, originally with plastered and painted walls, rather than the bare stone which now survives.

Essentials

Sleeping & eating **C** *PTDC Motel*, T0596-2344. 3 a/c rooms, 2 non a/c (**D** category), comfortable and clean, restaurant, PTDC Tourist Information Centre (phone number as for hotel), gift shop. **E** *Museum*, no phone. Basic though reasonable rooms with fan, restaurant. **G** *Youth Hostel*, 2 double rooms with attached bath, 12-bed dorm (2 toilets, valuables lockers), common room, kitchen, garden (camping), clean, pleasant, well kept youth hostel, excellent value.

There are two comfortable Archaeological Dept *Rest Houses*, one on the museum grounds, and another, *Nikra Bungalow*, opposite the turning to Jaulian. Unfortunately, they are for Archaeological Dept guests only, officially at least. You could try making a reservation with the Curator of the museum (T2495), or with the Director General of Archaeology, Govt of Pakistan, Karachi at least 10 days in advance.

The a/c restaurant at the *PTDC Motel* is the best. The one at the *Museum* hotel is much more basic, but perfectly adequate. There are plenty of cheap eateries in Taxila bazaar, and along the GT Road by the turning for the bazaar.

Shopping

The ***Asian Arts*** gift shop in the *PTDC Motel* has a wide selection of jewellery, antiques, clothing, souvenirs etc, and a good (though overpriced) collection of books and postcards (note that some books and postcards are on sale at the museum ticket office, where they are likely to be cheaper). There are a number of craft shops selling replicas of Gandharan pieces, as well as traditonal stone pestle and mortars, along from the PTDC. The museum kiosk sell booklets and pamphlets about Taxila. If available, *Gandhara, an Instant Guide to Taxila*, is recommended.

Local transport

Coming from Rawalpindi by public transport, get off at the Taxila Bypass junction (soon after the Margalla Pass; the junction is marked by a roundabout with a tank in the middle). From here you can catch a Haripur-bound bus or minibus for a couple of rupees, which will take you right past the Taxila Museum. This is a much quicker, easier and cheaper way of getting to the site than continuing along the GT Road to the turning for Taxila Bazaar (this turning is marked by shops, restaurants and bus stops on the GT Road, as well as a pedestrian footbridge over the road). From the Taxila Bazaar turning there are regular Datsuns and Suzukis, or you can hire a taxi or horse-drawn tonga. But whichever mode of transport you choose, you will have to bargain hard since the drivers here have cottoned on to the possibility of charging tourists hugely inflated prices. A tonga or taxi should not cost more than around Rs 30; the Datsuns and Suzukis should really charge a couple of rupees per passenger, but will probably insist that they only do private bookings for foreigners.

To get around the various sites, which are spread over a large area, you can hire a tonga or a taxi from outside the PTDC Motel. A tonga to visit all the main sights (allow at least 6 hours) should cost around Rs 250, but make sure it is clear exactly where you want to go and for roughly how long. A taxi (for around 3 hours) should cost about Rs 300, but you may have to bargain hard. Organizing transport through PTDC is likely to be a little more expensive, but also more reliable. During winter, a bicycle is an ideal way of getting around, although they are not available for rent in Taxila.

Bus Any Peshawar-bound bus from Rawalpindi will take you past Taxila, though the a/c coaches which run from Committee Chowk will charge you the full fare for Peshawar. A cheaper and more convenient option is to catch a Hiace minibus from the bus stop by the railway near Marir Chowk (see under Rawalpindi Transport). The trip takes around 30 minutes, depending on the traffic leaving Rawalpindi. To return (or continue on to Peshawar), go back to the GT Road and pick up a bus there. If you are heading back to Rawalpindi, try to get a bus which is going to Saddar, rather than Pir Wadhai. If the bus is going to Pir Wadhai, get off when it leaves the GT Road and catch another bus on to Saddar from there.

Train The train station at Taxila is within easy walking distance of the museum and hotels. The *R-455 Passenger* from Rawalpindi to Havelian leaves Rawalpindi at 0630, passing through Taxila at 0720. The *211 Passenger* to Peshawar is scheduled to leave Rawalpindi at 0720 and pass through Taxila at 0815, but since it starts in Lahore it is often late. Returning, the *212 Passenger* from Peshawar passes through Taxila at 2000. The *Awam Express* from Peshawar passes through at 1112. The *Hazara Express* and *R-456 Passenger*, both coming from Havelian, pass through at 1224 and 2254 respectively. Note that these timings are subject to minor changes; consult the latest *Pakistan Railways Time and Fare Table* booklet and check at the station.

Tarbela Dam

Colour map 4, grid A4

Tarbela is the world's largest earth-filled dam. Construction work on the dam began in 1968 as part of Pakistan's response to the Indus Waters Treaty of 1960. It was funded in part by contributions from a number of foreign countries (including India), administered by the World Bank and built by a European consortium led by the Italian firm Impreglio. Designed to store nearly 14 million cubic metres of water and generate 2.1 million KW of electricity, the dam is still not complete due to unforseen technical difficulties and design defects. Some experts have criticized it as a dangerous venture in what is an unpredictable earthquake zone. The build-up of silt in the lake, reducing its storage capacity, has proved to be a far greater problem than expected.

The best views of the dam are from its eastern side. From Ghazi the road passes through a check post and climbs through woods to viewpoints overlooking the two enormous sluice gates. The extensive 'town' of Tarbela which grew up to house the army of technicians and engineers involved in constructing and maintaining the dam is spread across the hillside amongst the woods. Late August/early September are usually peak flow times, when at least one of the gates is open, unleashing a massive cascade of white water that thunders down before hitting concrete breakers at the bottom and exploding hundreds of feet into the air in a spectacular fountain. The sight is a truly awesome one. The road then passes through a second check post and crosses the sluice gates before following the banks of the huge lake created by the dam and descending past more viewpoints to follow the base of the dam across to the other side. The road which runs along the top of the dam is closed to the general public; it may be possible to use it if visiting as part of an official tour.

Ins and outs Officially you must obtain permission from the Secretariat in Islamabad (see under Useful addresses in the Directory) in order to visit Tarbela, and make arrangements with WAPDA if you want a guided tour. In practice however, trying to organize anything through the Secretariat or WAPDA is a waste of time unless you have someone influential behind you. If not, your best bet is simply to turn up at WAPDA's office in Tarbela and hope that there is someone sympathetic on duty. Alternatively, you can travel across the dam by public transport from Ghazi to Topi without a special permit, though this does not give you the chance to stop at the viewpoints. A private car is likely to attract more attention and get you tangled up with the bureaucrats. The viewpoints, and access to the route across the dam, are open only during daylight hours. There are regular buses from Hasan Abdal to Ghazi, and from there to Topi, from where you can either return to the GT Road at Jehangira or continue west towards Mardan (see page 371). There is also a direct road from Haripur to Ghazi. **NB** No photography in the vicinity.

Islamabad and Rawalpindi to Peshawar

The route from Islamabad to Peshawar along the GT Road is described below. It is a fast but very busy route, lined for much of the way with industrial developments. From Zero Point go southwest on Shahrah-e-Kashmir for 14 kilometres before turning right onto the GT road for Peshawar (going straight here takes you onto the new Islamabad-Lahore Motorway, see page 236). Coming from Rawalpindi, get onto The Mall and keep following it northwest, past a right turn for Pir Wadhai and Faisabad, and then straight across the Islamabad-Lahore Motorway/Shahrah-e-Kashmir junction. A short distance on from the junction is the turning left towards Fatehjang, Kushalgarh and Kohat. The main road continues on to the Margalla Pass (28 kilometres).

Margalla Pass

The climb up to the Margalla Pass is very gentle and the pass itself unimposing, despite its historical importance. Sir Olaf Caroe described it as the real division between Central and South Asia. The pass is marked by a distinctive **granite obelisk** to the left of the road, erected in 1868 "by friends, British and Native, to the memory of Brigadier-General John Nicholson CB, who after taking a hero's part in four great wars, fell mortally wounded, in leading to victory the main Column of assault at the great siege of Delhi, and died on 22 September 1857, aged 34. The wars referred to were the two Sikh wars, the First Afghan War and the War of Independence (or Mutiny, depending on your perspective).

The route taken by the GT Road through the pass is identical to that of the **Shahi road** built by **Sher Shah Suri**, and a walk up to Nicholson's obelisk takes you onto a section of the old cobbled road. This route can be traced back over 2,000 years to the campaigns of Chandragupta Maurya in 324 BC which took the Mauryan Empire onto the soils of modern Afghanistan.

Routes

The GT Road descends gently from the pass. After about one kilometre there is a roundabout with a tank in the centre. The fork off to the right here is signposted 'Taxila Cantonment' and leads through the cantonment to Taxila's museum and archaeological sites. For details on **Taxila** see above: Around Islamabad. This road also leads on to Haripur and the KKH (see page 429). A second turning right for Taxila, which leads through the bazaar town, is about two kilometres further on, marked by a footbridge across the GT Road. Immediately after the second Taxila turning, there is a turning right to **Wah Cantonment**, another of the routes taken by traffic heading onto the KKH. **NB** The centre of Wah Cantonment, with its large army ordinance factory is officially off-limits to foreigners. A little further on is a signposted turning left to **Wah Moghul Gardens**.

Wah Moghul Gardens

Wah is supposed to have received its name from the exclamation of the Emperor Jahangir – "wah" ('beautiful') – when he saw the beauty of the valley! The gardens were used as one of numerous resting places by the Mughal emperors en route to Kashmir. Today they are somewhat dilapidated, though with a little imagination you can get some idea of their former glory. They make for a nice shady picnic spot, but unless you have your own transport and some spare time, they are not really worth stopping for.

Hasan Abdal

Colour map 5, grid C2

Hasan Abdal, famous as an important Sikh pilgrimage centre, is a just a little further on from Wah Gardens, and 48 kilometres from Islamabad. The focus of pilgrimage is an early 19th century Sikh temple, **Panja Sahib Gurudwara**, situated in the centre of the village, a 10 minute walk to the north of the GT Road (from where it is visible). Gaining entry can sometimes be difficult, with some of the custodians operating a Muslims and Sikhs only policy. Try smiling sweetly and looking pilgrim-like?

Inside the *Gurudwara* (Sikh temple) there is a stone with a hand imprint reputed to be that of **Guru Nanak**, the founder of Sikhism. A clear, icy spring emerges forcefully from beneath the stone bearing the handprint, feeding an artificial pond which surrounds the central shrine of the temple. According to one legend it was through the intervention of the Sikh founder that the spring was created. Asking a Muslim saint, Baba Wali, for a drink of water, the mystic threw down a huge boulder at his feet. Guru Nanak placed his hand on it where it fell, leaving his hand impress on the stone and causing a spring to well up from underneath it. The **Baisakhi Festival** is held here each April and still attracts Sikh pilgrims from India. **Baba Wali's Shrine** is on the flat-topped hill overlooking the town, with views in all directions. It takes about one hour to walk up to the shrine.

Opposite the entrance to the Gurudwara is a large stone pool, also fed by the spring, and used for swimming and washing. Beside it, a street leads to the Mughal period **Maqbara Hakiman** (tomb of the *hakims*, or doctors). The tomb is built of small bricks covered in lime plaster and originally decorated

The GT Road: Islamabad/ Rawalpindi to Peshawar

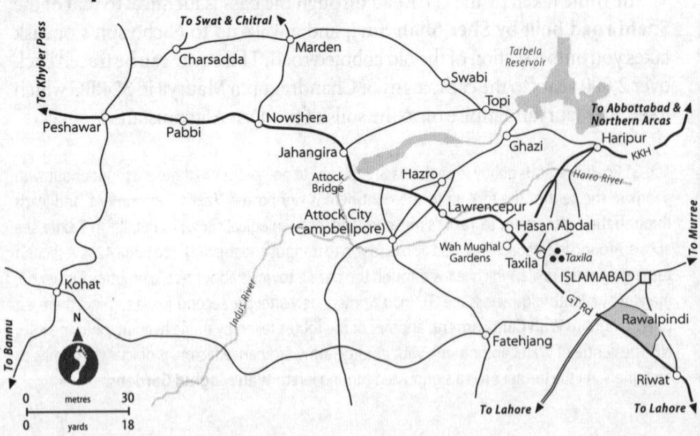

with frescoes. Much of the plaster has come away, but otherwise it is largely complete, and a good example of Mughal funerary architecture. In front of it is another stone pool, this one containing *Mahseer,* a large species of carp, which have been bred here for generations. Both the tomb and the pool are contained within a rectangle of massive cut stones forming something like a raised platform. Further on, a gate leads through into a beautiful walled garden with a simple tomb in the centre. This tomb was built for the Mughal governor Khwaja Shamsuddin Khawafi. He however died and was buried in Lahore in around 1599, and subsequently Akbar ordered that it be used for the *hakims* Abdul and Himan Gilani. According to the sign which points the way there, the tomb is of Lala Rukh.

Sleeping & eating

On the north side of the GT Road, a little to the east of the turning for Hasan Abdal, are 2 hotels, the **E** ***Mesum Tourist Inn***, behind the Caltex petrol station, and the **E** *Frontier*, just east of it. Both offer basic but reasonably clean rooms with fan and attached bath.

There are several restaurants along the GT Road, opposite the turning for the centre of Hasan Abdal, which serve local freshwater fish, deep fried in batter and sold by the kilo or half kilo (Rs 140/70).

Transport

Picking up public transport heading in either direction from Hasan Abdal is fairly easy, with most local buses plying along the GT Road stopping here to drop off and pick up passengers. The faster long distance buses and minibuses plying directly between Islamabad/Rawalpindi and Peshawar are less likely to stop, though if they have any spare seats they will do so.

Hasan Abdal to Attock

Just beyond Hasan Abdal there is a turning right which joins the main road from Wah to Haripur. The GT Road continues west, crossing the Harro River and passing the town of **Lawrencepur**, named after the 19th century British Resident of Lahore, Sir Henry Lawrence. Immediately after the town there is a turning right, the first of three leading up to **Tarbela Dam** (see above: Around Islamabad). Further on there is a turning left to Attock City (marked on some maps by its old name of Campbellpore), then the second turning right to Tarbela, then another turning left to Attock City and the Pak Aeronautical Base of Kamra, followed by the last turning right to Tarbela, signposted for the towns of Shadikhan and Hazro along the way. Finally there is a third turning left for Attock City, before the GT Road crosses the Indus at Attock itself.

Attock

Phone code: 0597
Colour map 5, grid C2

Historically, this was an important crossing point, along with Hund to the north. **Akbar's Fort** on the east bank, built in the 1580s, dominates the gorge, its rambling walls and large crenellations clearly visible to the south of the road. Today the fort is occupied by the Pakistani military and is closed to the public. **Sher Shah Suri's Caravanserai** is below the fort, right by the road. Attock was also the crossing point for the Shahi Road from Delhi to Kabul, and the large caravanserai served as a resting place for travellers. The walls, with living quarters built into them, enclose a large square courtyard with a mosque inside. Steps lead up onto the walls which are remarkably well preserved, though with some cement repairs to the crenellations, giving good views across the Indus and up to the Fort behind. A signposted track leads up to the caravanserai, just west of the turning up to the Fort, or there are steps leading directly up from the road. The turning south on the west bank of the river leads through the village of Khairabad past the old two-storey road/rail bridge built by the British from 1880-81 (now closed to vehicle traffic), and continues on to Nizampur and Khwala Khel before joining the Islamabad-Kohat road near Kushalgarh. The roads south from Attock City on the east bank are in better condition. **Attock City**, with its railway station and some interesting colonial and pre-colonial architecture, is southwest of the bridge crossing, 18 kilometres by road.

Sleeping, eating & transport There is the **D *Indus View*** on the GT Road, east of the bridge, reasonable rooms, restaurant, friendly staff. There are several cheap eateries along the GT Road. As with Hasan Abdal, picking up public transport in either direction is fairly easy.

Routes The bridge across the Indus at Attock marks the boundry between Punjab and NWFP. A little further on is **Jehangira**, where a bridge crosses the Kabul River, the start of the road up to Swabi (26 kilometres), see page 371. The GT Road continues west, passing through **Akor Khattack** to arrive at Nowshera.

Nowshera

Colour map 5, grid C1

The town has a large British built cantonment area and is today still an important military base for the Pakistan army. Just before the main town there is a turning north which crosses the Kabul River on a toll bridge and leads up to Mardan (22 kilometres, see page 366) on a good, fast dual carriageway. Civilian traffic is diverted around the cantonment area which is closed to the public. There is little of interest for the general tourist.

Sleeping & eating There are 2 hotels near the bus stand, both with restaurants. E ***Shobra***, Shobra Chowk, GT Rd, T3177. Some a/c rooms. F ***Spark***, Cavalry Rd, T2101. The ***Friends Corner*** restaurant is nearby, on the GT Rd.

Routes From Nowshera it is a further 44 kilometres on to Peshawar. The road first passes through the town of **Pabbi** and then runs through an increasingly industrial landscape, before entering the suburbs of Peshawar and finally the city itself (see page 338).

Murree and the Galis

To the northeast of Islamabad, on a series of outlying Himalayan spurs, lie a series of settlements that were developed by the British as hill resorts. Known as 'hill stations', they were used by the British administration and their families to escape the summer heat of the Punjab plains. With their cool summers and brisk winters, they remain popular today with Punjabi tourists and expatriate staff in Islamabad.

The most developed of the hill stations, **Murree**, is 64 kilometres from Islamabad and can be reached by car in under two hours along a good quality, winding alpine road. However, on weekends and holidays the road can be packed with traffic, and drivers should be prepared to encounter suicidal overtaking manoeuvres on the bends.

Road to Murree

The toll road from Islamabad/Rawalpindi passes **Chattar Bagh** (20 kilometres), a tacky picnic spot being developed by TDCP, with mini-zoo, water park, nature trail, children's playground and restaurant. From here, the road gently climbs to the small village of **Tret** (40 kilometres) at an elevation of nearly 1,000 metres, where pines first appear. Most public buses and minivans stop at **Charra Pani** (18 kilometres) for tea and photos, before continuing to **Ghora Gali** (at 1,600 metres). Prior to the provision in 1907 of motor transport on this route, this was the point between Rawalpindi and Murree where the carriage horses were changed. Ghora Gali is also the site of the old Murree Brewery. Several kilometres beyond here, at **Bansra Gali**, is the prestigious Lawrence College. Initially established as an asylum for army orphans, it became one of British India's, and now Pakistan's, most reputable education establishments. The road climbs through a sharp south bend at **Sunny Bank** to **Murree**.

Murree

Despite losing its position as summer capital of the British Indian Empire to Simla in 1876, Murree remains the most popular of Pakistan's hill stations. This was the birthplace in 1863 of one of Britain's most celebrated explorers, Francis Younghusband (see Patrick French's excellent biography, Younghusband).

Phone code: 0593
Colour map 5, grid C3

The best season to visit is April to June, although weekends and holidays remain busy all year round. In Summer, Murree can become ridiculously crowded with Punjabi day-trippers taking advantage of the refreshing climate. Yet winter weekends, particularly January to March, attract equally large numbers of

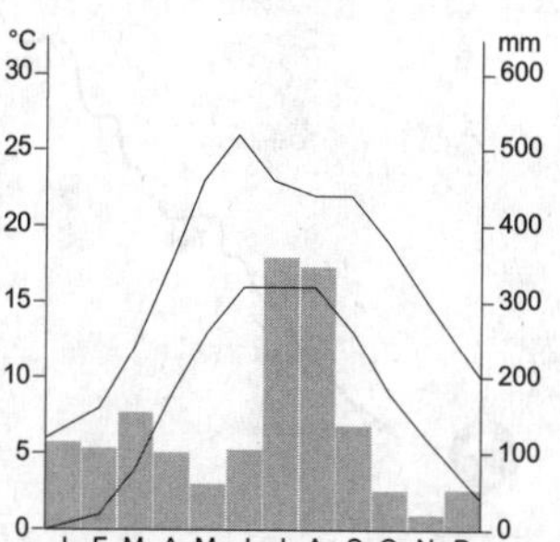

The best time to visit is between April and Junel

Punjab

visitors keen to experience their first encounter with snow. You will need light woollens and cottons in summer and heavy woollens in winter.

Ins and outs

Getting there Buses from Rawalpindi (Rs 15) drop passengers at the bus yard at the bottom of Cart Road.

Getting around A 1972 ordinance bans motor vehicles from the Mall during summer (with the exception of those carrying the President, Prime Minister or certain VIPs), but Murree often suffers from traffic jams of the human variety. The vehicle ban does not apply, however, to buggy-loads of spoilt, fat, rich children, pushed up the hill by scowling Kohistani youths. It is also possible to take pony and donkey rides.

Murree & the Galis

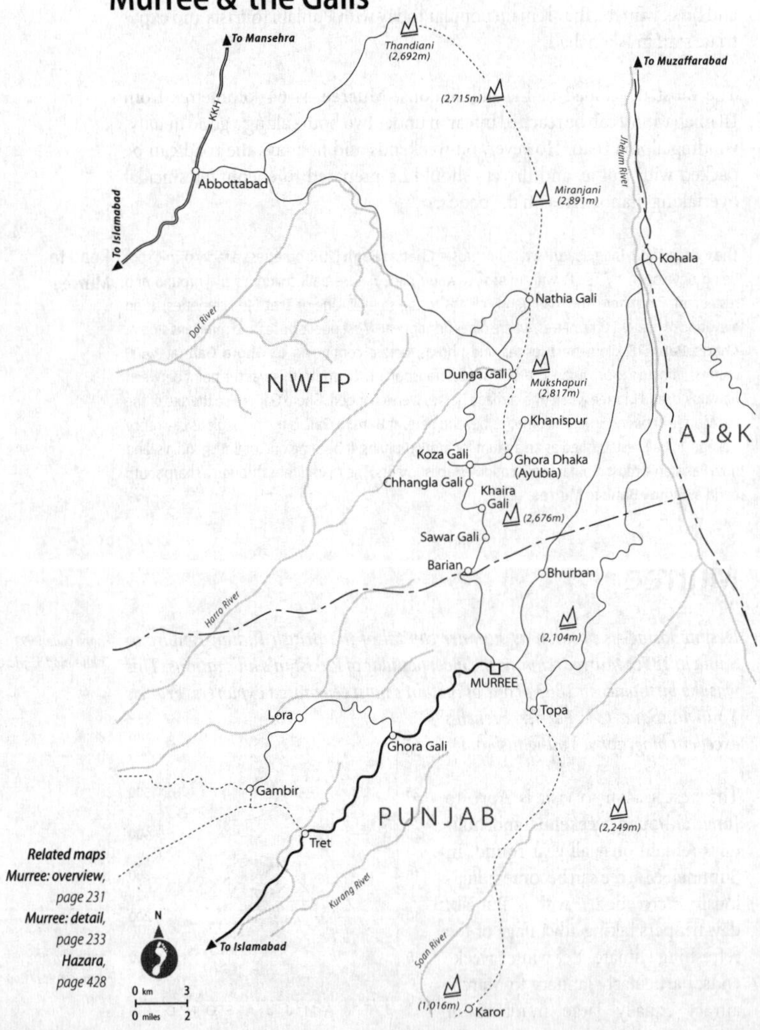

Related maps
Murree: overview, *page 231*
Murree: detail, *page 233*
Hazara, *page 428*

Sights

Despite its ability to draw large numbers of tourists all year round, there are not that many places of interest within the town itself. Beside the views, the main attraction in Murree is a stroll along **The Mall**. Lined with cafés, restaurants and souvenir shops, the Mall is a popular meeting point, as well as being the place to 'be seen'.

At the northeast point of the ridge upon which Murree stands, **Kashmir Point** offers fine views across the Jhelum River and Pir Panjal range into Kashmir. Several kilometres along the ridge to the southwest, **Pindi Point** overlooks the twin cities of Islamabad and Rawalpindi below. The scene is particularly attractive on a clear night. From Pindi Point, the Wonderland **chair-lift** makes the return trip (Rs 40) to the road several kilometres below (and continues to run in all weathers, including snow storms).

Murree does retain a certain colonial air, with its neat bungalows, summer cottages, gardens and churches, but the recent rapid pace of unplanned development is threatening to engulf the town.

Murree: overview

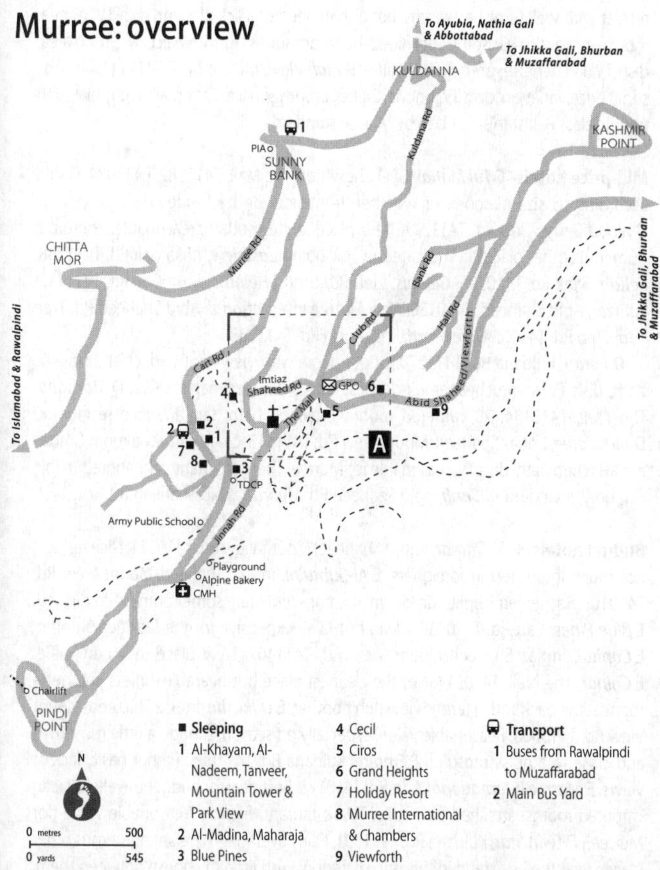

Sleeping
1 Al-Khayam, Al-Nadeem, Tanveer, Mountain Tower & Park View
2 Al-Madina, Maharaja
3 Blue Pines
4 Cecil
5 Ciros
6 Grand Heights
7 Holiday Resort
8 Murree International & Chambers
9 Viewforth

Transport
1 Buses from Rawalpindi to Muzaffarabad
2 Main Bus Yard

Related map
A Murree: detail, page 233

Essentials

Sleeping

■ *on maps*
Price codes: see inside front cover

Murree's hotels are expensive by Pakistani standards, and most are priced 1 or 2 categories above the price category that their facilities merit. During the high season (April-September), on holidays, at weekends, and when the manager feels like it, prices double or treble. Do not be afraid to bargain at any time of the year. Unless otherwise stated, all bathrooms have hot water. Blankets are usually provided. Those listed below are categorized according to their high season tariff, and are just a selection of the hotels found in Murree.

More expensive hotels A-B ***Cecil***, Imtiaz Shaheed/Mount View Rd, T411131, F411133. Best in town. Has more expensive suites, ultra expensive deluxe suites, plus cheaper rooms in the annexe. Prices halve in off season. Dish TV, phone, tennis, children's park, lawns, conference hall, car rental, restaurant, superb views. Given that lesser quality hotels charge similar rates, hotel is good value.

B ***Brightlands***, Imtiaz Shaheed/Mount View Rd, T410270. Colonial building that looks undecorated since the British left, large furnished rooms with sitting area, bath, dish TV, phone, but rather tatty (**C**), plus larger and slightly nicer suites (**B**), but not as luxurious as the price suggests, bargain very hard. **B** ***Ciros***, Abid Shaheed Rd, T411891. All large family rooms, has potential but very grubby for the price, dish TV/video. **B** ***Lockwood***, Imtiaz Shaheed/Mount View Rd, T410112, F411543. Another colonial retreat with well furnished rooms, but also in need of a lick of paint, dish TV, phone, room service, also has some very nice 2-bedroom suites (**A**) with balcony, sitting area, dish TV, kitchenette, pretty good value. **B** ***Mall View***, off The Mall, T411111. No seasonal price variation, dish TV, phone, 24 hour room service, sitting area, popular with middle class Pakistanis, not bad by Murree standards.

Mid-price hotels C ***Taj Mahal***, GPO Chowk, off The Mall, T411082, F411084. Priced according to size of room, or whether 'front-side' or 'back-side', dish TV, phone. **C** ***Wood Berry***, Club Rd, T411212. New place, quite modern, reasonable. There are numerous other places in this category, including ***Eastview***, Jihka Gali Rd, T411238. ***Felton***, Bank Rd, T410795. ***Gillanis***, Club Rd. ***Grand Heights***, Jihka Gali Rd, T411711. ***Lalazar***, Abid Shaheed, T410150. ***New Murree International***, Abid Shaheed Rd. ***Tree Top***, Club Rd, T410029. ***Viewforth***, Viewforth Rd, T411268.

D ***Faran***, Kuldana Rd, T411270. Upper floors with views not bad, clean, modern bath, dish TV, some cheaper windowless boxes (**E**), reasonable value. **D** ***Marhaba***, The Mall, T410184. 20 carpeted rooms, attached bath, fan, TV, nice restaurant. **D** ***Mussiaree***, Imtiaz Shaheed/Mount View Rd, T411513. Clean carpeted rooms, modern attached bath, dish TV, reasonable for Murree. There are many other hotels in this category, including ***Al-Sana***, Abid Shaheen Rd. ***Mehran***, Abid Shaheen Rd.

Budget hotels E ***Al-Qamar***, Imtiaz Shaheed/Mount View Rd, T410311. Nice terrace, not much interested in foreigners. **E** ***Al-Subtaini***, Imtiaz Shaheed/Mount View Rd, T410106. Rather jerry-built, run-down, incompetent staff, some rooms with dish TV. **E** ***Blue Pines***, Cart Rd, T410230. Clean but fairly expensive for the facilities on offer. **E** ***Capital***, Imtiaz Shaheed/Mount View Rd, T411407. New place, not bad value. **E** ***Chinar***, The Mall, T410244. Not the cleanest place but bearable, unless you get a room at the back with a terrific view don't bother. **E** ***Dilkusha***, Imtiaz Shaheed/Mount View Rd, T410006. Reasonable value, especially off season, though a little run-down and close to a noisy mosque. **E** ***Empire***, Kuldana Rd, T411085. Rather basic, lack of views. **E** ***Murree International***, Cart Rd, T410173. Best deal for budget travellers, clean carpeted rooms, attached bath, dish TV, restaurant, friendly, reasonable value (for Murree). **E** ***Twin Star***, Kuldana Rd, T411301. Fairly average. There are numerous other places near the bus stand in this price category with little to choose between them, including ***Al-Khayam***, T410870; ***Al-Madina***; ***Al Nadeem***; ***Holiday Resort***; ***Maharaja***; ***Mountain Tower***, T411331; ***Park View***, T410741, "overpriced and very drab"; ***Tanveer***, T410197.

F ***Al Saud***, The Mall. Very basic and noisy.

Eating

● *on maps*

Most hotels have a restaurant/dining hall, though there are a number of popular places to eat along The Mall. 'Fast food' places are popular (and in Pakistan, particularly Murree, this is not a derogatory description, but a fashionable type of cuisine). Those serving fast food, Chinese, Pakistani and continental dishes include: ***Aladdin's Fun House***; ***Red Onion***, offers pizza, burgers, fast food etc; ***Sam's***; ***Usmania***; ***Lahore Broast Inn***, good roast chicken. ***Lintott's*** on The Mall have reasonable meals for Rs 80-100, good club sandwiches Rs 50, and fine ice-cream sundaes Rs 50, served by ancient waiters keen on tips.

Entertainment

Sports Golf: 9-hole course at **Bhurban**, open May-October (members only in high season). **Horse riding:** Tired nags are available to carry children up to Kashmir Point.

Shopping

Bookshops *Book Galerie*, The Mall, has some English titles plus *Time*, *Newsweek* etc; *Hammed Books*, next door, has a smaller choice.

Punjab

Murree: detail

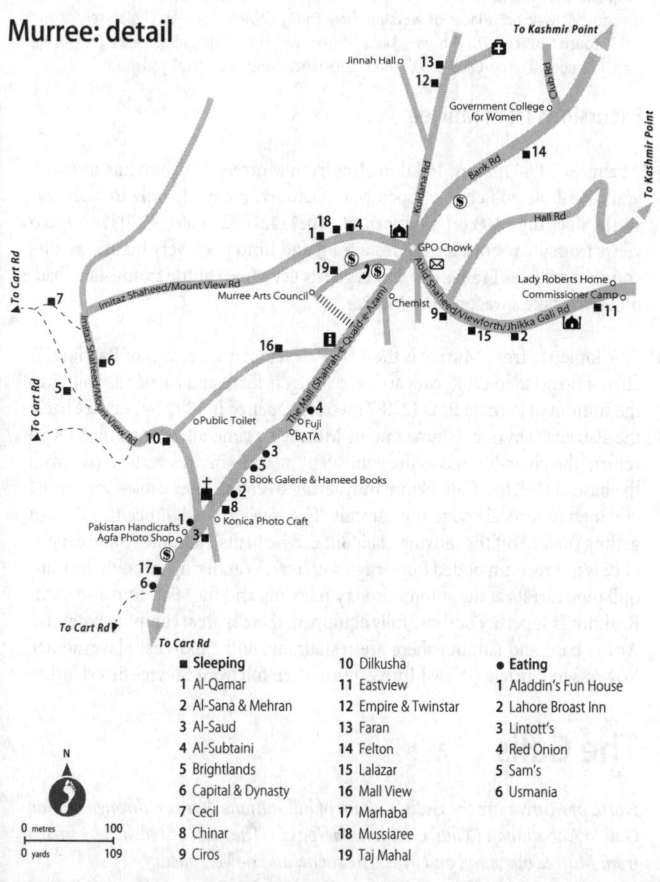

Handicrafts *Pakistan Handicrafts*, The Mall. Run by the 'Punjab Small Industries Corporation', this 'fixed price' shop is a real Aladdin's Cave of stuff (accepts credit cards). It's a good starting point for getting some idea of prices. There's plenty of rubbish available in the 'handicraft' shops in Murree.

Photography *Konica Photo Craft*, The Mall. D&P, sells film (including slide, Rs 200).

Long distance transport

Long distance buses 'Luxury' coasters to **Rawalpindi** run when full from the bus yard on Cart Road (Rs 25, 1 hour), or you can take a regular minibus for Rs 15. Minibuses run when full to **Ayubia, Bhurban** and **Patriata/'New Murree'** (Rs 20) from here, and there are occasional buses or coasters all the way to **Lahore** (Rs 150, 7 hours). A 'deluxe' bus also runs to **Lahore** at midday from Chambers Hotel, and during peak season **TDCP** also runs a service. There are a couple of slow buses each day from the Cart Road bus stand to **Abbottabad** via **Nathia Gali**. Buses on their way from Rawalpindi to **Muzaffarabad** pass through Sunny Bank (Rs 30).

Directory

Airline offices *PIA* agent is down in Sunny Bank. **Banks** *National Bank of Pakistan*, Bank Rd, behind GPO, but doesn't do foreign exchange. **Communications** GPO: *GPO Chowk*, The Mall, local landmark. **Telephones:** *Public Call Office*, above Habib Bank, GPO Chowk, The Mall (open summer Mon-Sat 0600-2400, Sun 0700-1100 1500-2000; winter Mon-Sat 0800-2000, Sun 0700-0900 1500-2000). **Hospitals & medical services** Chemists: *M/S A Rauf Chemist*, The Mall. **Hospitals:** *CMH Hospital*, junction The Mall/Cart Rd, mainly for military personnel, otherwise go to Islamabad/Rawalpindi. **Places of worship** *Holy Trinity Church*, The Mall, English service Sun 1015. **Tourist offices** *TDCP* have a kiosk on The Mall (T410730) and an office on Cart Rd (T410729, open summer 0800-2000; winter 0830-1600), but they can't tell you much.

Excursions from Murree

Bhurban

At almost 2,000 metres, 16 kilometres from Murree, **Bhurban** has an excellent nine-hole golf course (open May-October, members only in high season). **Sleeping A** *Pearl Continental*, T051-427082, F051-427081. Superb views from a/c rooms, terrace restaurant and from pool, very luxurious, discounts available. **Transport** Hotel guests get a free shuttle from Islamabad, otherwise take a wagon from Murree.

Patriata

19 kilometres from Murree is the TDCP developed attraction of **Patriata**. A chair-lift and then cable-car carries passengers three and a half kilometres to the summit of Patriata Peak (2,187 metres). Opened in 1990 by Nawaz Sharif, the Patriata 'Skyride' is now one of Murree's prime attractions. For Rs 80 return, the chair-lift makes the equivalent of a 250 metres vertical rise from the base at Gulehra Gali, before transfering to eight seater cable-cars for the 209 metres vertical rise to the summit. The views are magnificent, although getting on and off the moving chair-lift can be brutal, and the whole experience is not recommended for vertigo sufferers. Wandering through the tranquil pine forests at the summit is very relaxing, and the vista across towards Kashmir is superb. For those fully equipped, there is great camping potential. At the base and summit there are restaurants and childrens' playgrounds. Wagons to Patriata ('New Murree') run when full from Murree bus stand.

The Galis

North of Murree are the Galis, a chain of hill stations that run through Nathia Gali to Abbottabad ('Gali' is Hindko for 'pass'). They can be reached by suzuki from Murree bus stand and by less frequent, and slower, buses.

Routes

The first village on the road to Abbottabad is **Barian**, on the border between Punjab and NWFP. (Although most of these Galis are within the NWFP administrative sphere of influence, their proximity to Murree makes it logical to include them within the Punjab section.) From Murree, the road climbs steadily to **Chhangla Gali** at 2,762 metres (**E** *Summer Inn*). Several kilometres from here, at **Koza Gali**, the road divides, the left fork continuing via Dunga Gali and Nathia Gali to Abbottabad.

The right fork runs 3 kilometres to **Ayubia** (2,416 metres). Formerly known as Ghora Dhaka, the settlement was renamed after the former President of Pakistan, General Ayub Khan. Ayubia is used as the collective name for the cluster of resorts of Chhangla Gali, Khanispur and Ghora Dhaka, as well as the national park to the east of the road. At Ayubia, a chair-lift (Rs 40) runs to a minor peak, offering good views across the national park. **Sleeping E** *Ayubia Palace*, *Summer Inn*, **F** *Al Madina*.

A 3 kilometre road through the pine forests along the spur offers a pleasant walk to **Khanispur**. Locals speak of tigers and leopards in the hills, although there are certainly packs of rhesus monkeys and grey languors. There are excellent views across to Kashmir from here. **Sleeping F** *Kashmir View* (follow sign for 'Armour Hut'), **F** *Youth Hostel*.

To reach Nathia Gali, return to Koza Gali and take the other road fork. Transport to Nathia Gali is more regular from here than Ayubia. There is also a cross-country short cut (6 kilometres) along the 'pipe-line' from Ayubia to Nathia Gali, although this should not be attempted in poor weather or after rain. It is possible to walk the 13 kilometres road to Nathia Gali in about 4 hours, passing through the hamlets of Toheedabad (2,370 metres) and Kundla (2,340 metres). The road is subject to land-slip blockages after prolonged rain, and may be inaccessible from December-February due to snow. 3 kilometres before Nathia Gali is the small resort of **Dunga Gali** (2,439 metres). **Sleeping C** *Mukshpuri*, **F** *Green Valley*, behind which is 2,817 metres Mukshpuri Peak.

Nathia Gali

Nathia Gali (2,500 metres) is the summer headquarters of the NWFP government, and despite recent unplanned development, is still very picturesque. It retains something of a colonial air, with the wooden St Matthews Church, Governor's House and attractive bungalows. Dominating the view to the northeast is the 2,981 metres **Miran Jani**, which can be climbed in three hours. A path lies to the right and below the Governor's House. Just before you reach the house you will see track below you and some easy paths running down to it from the road. Follow the track with the electric poles along it. After approximately one kilometre the track forks, with electric poles leading left. Take neither of these: take the rough track directly ahead that winds up through forest and meadow to Miran Jani. The only stiff climb is just before the hill itself. On clear days you can see Nanga Parbat to the north, and across the Jhelum River to the Pir Panjal range. It is also possible to make the two to three day hike north to the attractive Gali of **Thandiana** (see page 433), although it is only reachable by road from Abbottabad. There are Resthouses en route at Palakot and Biran Gali.

Sleeping

The better hotels are on Nathia Gali's upper road. **B** *Greens*, T868261, F868244. Dish TV, phone, conference hall, skiing (January-February), restaurant. The **C** hotels, including *Park Plaza*, *Pines Shangrila*, *Valley View* are all in need of some repair. The budget hotels are down on the lower road, including **E/F** *Allys*, *International*, *Karachi*, *Madina*, *Marhaba*, *Peshawar*, *Swiss*, although the 2 best are **E** *Kamran* and **E** *Skyways*. A link road runs from opposite Skyways to the upper part of town.

Routes

Abbottabad is a further 2 hour drive along the fairly rough road, via the Pak Air Force base at Kalabagh.

The Salt Range

Easily accessible from both Islamabad and Lahore, the Salt Range is a little visited area of great natural beauty. It's predominantly rural, and as such is a world away from the frenetic crush of the big cities. As well as being visually stunning in places, the Salt Range has a number of specific attractions, including the largest salt mine in the world (excellent guided tours available) and a number of decaying but fascinating Hindu temples and pilgrimage sites.

Ins and outs

The recently opened Islamabad-Lahore Motorway cuts right through the Salt Range, giving excellent views of its landscape and geology. There are exits off the motorway at Balkasar (for Chakwal), at Kallar Kahar and at Lilla (for Pind Dadan Khan). Most of the places of interest are concentrated in the eastern part of the Salt Range, with the town of **Chakwal** acting as a convenient 'gateway' to the area. There are 2 roads leading to Chakwal. The first (and best) road leaves the Islamabad-Lahore GT road just south of Mandra, running parallel to the railway. The second turning is just northwest of Sohawa. There are direct buses from Rawalpindi (Marir Chowk bus station) to Chakwal, or you can pick up transport bound for Chakwal from Mandra, Jhelum, Gujar Khan and Dina. The rail branch from Mandra to Chakwal is now closed. Bus and minibus services between all the places of interest covered below are reasonably frequent (Malot is one exception), though they are much scarcer after nightfall and on Fridays. For a guided tour of the region, ask at PTDC in Islamabad. Alternatively, hiring a car for 2 or 3 days would allow you to explore the area in detail at your leisure.

Salt Range

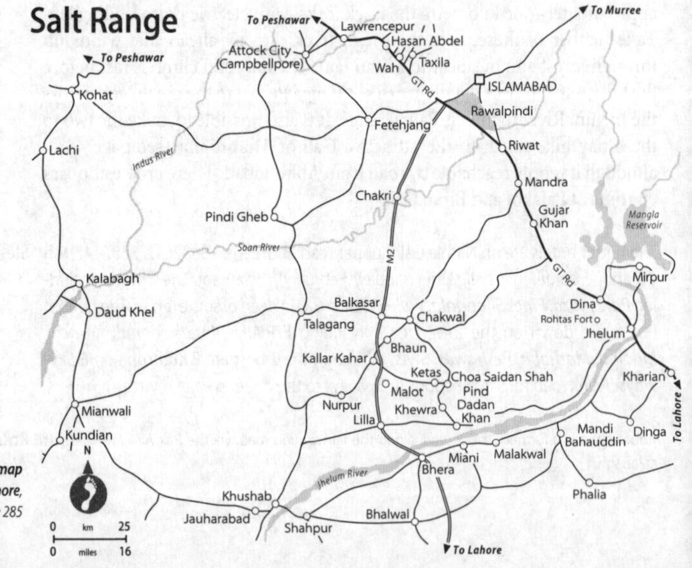

Related map
West of Lahore, page 285

The area

The Salt Range is formed of two parallel lines of hills running east-west roughly between Jhelum and Mianwali, to the north of the Jehlum River. Varying in height between 750 and 1,500 metres, the climate is noticeably cooler during summer. Much of the area is extremely fertile, supporting a variety of crops and a range of wildlife, including wolves, urial, deer and wild boar. Geologically the area is fascinating, with the folding of the earth's crust along this thrust zone producing sharp jutting outcrops of rock strata, some dating from 600 million years ago. Archaeologically the area is highly significant, having revealed evidence of a 'Pebble Culture' contemporary to the nearby Soan Culture of the Potwar Plateau dating from the Palaeolithic period. It is also of historical significance, with many Buddhist and Hindu sites dating from the Singhapura Buddhist and Kashmiri Hindu period. Until Partition, much of the area remained predominantly Hindu.

Chakwal

Phone code: 0573
Colour map 5, grid C2

Chakwal is the largest town in the area, with a bustling main bazaar and lively agricultural markets. Otherwise, it is of little interest in itself, being useful primarily as a transport hub, with frequent services in all directions. There are two hotels here, the **F** *Azeem International*, T0573-51725, friendly and reasonable, and the basic **G** *Gulbarak*, T3071 (hotel sign in Urdu only), both with restaurants.

Choa Saidan Shah

Colour map 5, grid C2

Taking the road from Chakwal to Choa Saidan Shah, the northern slopes of the Salt Range, with their distinctive folded rock strata exposed in sharp jutting outcrops, slowly come into view. Choa Saidan Shah is named after the saint **Saidan Shah Shirazi** who is reputed to have transformed the area from a desert by causing a spring to emerge (*Choa* meaning spring). The small village is nestled at the foot of a valley and surrounded by orchards of loquat, pomegranate, peach and guava. Roses are also grown and used in the production of perfume and local medicines. The saint's shrine is set back from the main bazaar in a courtyard. The annual *Urs* is held in the first week of April.

Sleeping

There is a ***Civil Resthouse*** situated in one of the orchards up on the hillside on the road towards Ketas and Kallar Kahar. It is reserved for officials but if not in use, it may be possible to book it through the Deputy Commissioner in Chakwal, T2615. In the same compound there is a ***District Council Resthouse***. The only other accommodation is the very basic **G** ***Hajji***, in the main bazaar. Daybreak in the village is heralded by a raucous chorus of geese.

Choa Saidan Shah to Khewra

The road climbs from Choa Saidan Shah, passing the ICI pumping station at Watli Spring (which supplies water to the large ICI Soda Ash factory at Khewra), then follows a level stretch of fertile plateau, sown in spring with striking yellow rapeseed, before passing a right turn to the ICI limestone quarry at Dandot (four kilometres). The road then cuts through the main ridge/escarpment of the Salt Range, emerging on the other side to give spectacular panoramic views down onto the wide plain of the Jhelum River. The town of Khewra and the ICI Soda Ash plant are clearly visible. The road winds steeply down off the Salt Range, passing a turning to another limestone quarry at Tober, before reaching Khewra.

Khewra Salt Mine

Colour map 5, grid C2

Situated at the base of the Salt Range, this is the largest salt mine in the world in terms of area. The salt deposits found here stretch in seams up to 90 metres thick along the whole length of the Salt Range, covering over 250 square kilometres. Only a tiny portion has so far been mined. The salt found here is a remnant of the Tethys Ocean which evaporated slowly during the Eocene period, some 60 million years ago.

Legend has it that Alexander the Great first extracted salt from the range in 327 BC. Written records suggest that salt began to be mined from around 600 AD with the arrival of the Muslim emperor Sultan-e-Usmania. The local Janjua tribe are also thought to have mined the salt from the 13th century. The Mughals began larger scale commercial mining in the 15th century and by the 19th century it had been taken over by the British, who called it Yayo Mine. In 1932 electric trains were introduced; before that steam engines were used, and the salt deposits in many of the tunnels are blackened from the soot. Today, 2,300 salt cutters are employed in the mine, which produces around 600 tonnes of salt per day, making it the second largest in the world in terms of output.

Ins and outs It is no longer necessary to obtain a permit in advance to visit the salt mine. Guided tours, conducted by the Pakistan Mineral Development Corporation (PMDC), cost US$4 per person. In theory the mine is open to visitors Monday-Saturday 0900-1600, but in practice they receive few visitors and the official guide is very unlikely to be around on Fridays or Saturdays. PTDC in Islamabad insist that you can just turn up, but it might be a good idea to contact the manager of the mine in Islamabad in advance, particularly if you are planning to stay at their resthouse (Manager Salt, PMDC, Plot 13, H-9, Islamabad, T855290).

Visiting the mine Visitors are shown round a small section at ground level where mining has been discontinued. In all, the mine has 17 levels; five levels reaching 122 metres above ground level, and 11 levels reaching 610 metres below ground level. Each level has a series of four parallel tunnels interconnected at regular intervals. The mine is ventilated by a network of 12 air shafts which also act as a drainage system during the rainy season. Mining is carried out in a series of chambers to the sides of the tunnels in what is known as the "room and pillar method". In many of the old chambers, which were dug down to a depth of around 25m, ground-water has seeped in, creating large ponds of salt saturated water, or brine. This brine forms a second important product of the mine, being pumped out to supply the ICI factory with one of the raw materials for the production of Soda Ash (the others are fresh water from Watli Spring, and limestone from the various quarries in the Salt Range).

The ceiling of the largest chamber, which was mined from the top down, is 72 metres high, with stairs cut into the walls. The whole chamber was mined by hand and the walls are criss-crossed with the lines of the chiselling work. Today the salt is blasted with dynamite.

A small mosque consisting of a low walled enclosure of hewn salt bricks has been constructed in the mine. Lights concealed inside the walls cause the translucent bricks to glow with various hues and shades. Elsewhere, the seepage of water through the ceiling has resulted in the formation of beautiful salt stalactites and stalagmites

Sleeping

The *PMDC Resthouse* in Khewra is at the disposal of visitors to the mine, providing it is not being used by visiting officials. It is simple but clean and well maintained, with a pleasant garden.

Around Khewra

Seven kilometres south of Khewra is **Pind Dadan Khan.** Named after the Rajput chieftain Dadan Khan who ruled here during the 17th century, this town was once an important centre of trade and was raised to a municipality by the British in 1876. Today its importance has waned, although its old narrow bazaars are still colourful and lively. There are some interesting examples of colonial architecture, including the *tahsildar's* (tax collector's) office and civil administration buildings, built in 1890.

Just before the town there is a road east which passes through Haranpur and Dhariala. From Dhariala there is a road north to Rawal and the cement factory at Gharibwal. To the northeast are the remains of a **Mughal gate** at Baghanwala. Beyond that are the ruins of **Nandana Fort** on a huge rock blocking the narrow gorge which formed the ancient gateway to the Salt Range. The main road continues past Jalalpur before crossing the Jhelum River at Rasul Barrage to Rasul. The road then passes through Chillianwalla and Dinga to join the Islamabad-Lahore GT Road at Kharian.

Choa Saidan Shah to Kallar Kahar

This route follows a stretch of wide plateau running along the middle of the Salt Range and is particularly beautiful in late winter and early spring when the fields are bright yellow with the flowering mustard crop. The road climbs from Choa Saidan Shah first to Ketas (five kilometres).

Ketas

Colour map 5, grid C2

In the village of Ketas are the extensive **Satghara Hindu Temples,** centred around a large pool and spring. According to legend, the pool was formed of tears from Siva's eye as he wept over the death of his wife Parvati. Tears from his other eye fell near Amjer in Rajasthan, forming a second pool.

The oldest temple, up on the hill overlooking the complex, has a narrow staircase inside which leads up onto the roof, giving good views over the site and surrounding hills. It is thought to date back as far as the eighth to 10th century, although the top layer of plasterwork is of a much later date. Lower down the hill there is a fort and next to it a large building which was a Sanskrit language university where the famous Muslim scholar Al Burani came to study (also with good views from the roof), as well as a bathing and resthouse complex, and various small shrines down by the road.

The complex is now in a state of dereliction, but before Partition used to attract thousands of Hindu pilgrims every February. Hindus continued to visit in large numbers until recently, when the Babri Mosque incident at Ayodhya in India soured relations between Hindus and Muslims. One particularly beautiful temple on the other side of the road was destroyed as a result, and has been replaced by a modern white concrete structure. Auriel Stein suggests that the main temple complex may mark the site of the Buddhist university and shrines at the centre the capital of the Singhapura Kingdom that existed in the Salt Range from the sixth to seventh centuries AD.

Sleeping

To the north of the road through Ketas there is a **D** *TDCP Motel*. Reasonable rooms with fan and attached bath. Next to the temple complex on the hillside there is a

G ***Youth Hostel***. Recently renovated. Friendly caretaker. If you are on a budget, this makes an ideal base from which to explore the Salt Range.

Ketas to Kallar Kahar From Ketas the tree-lined road continues along the plateau, passing various small coal mining works before descending and then crossing the Islamabad-Lahore motorway to arrive in Kallar Kahar (28 kilometres).

Kallar Kahar

Phone code: 0573
Colour map 5, grid C2

The salt lake (from which the village gets its name) and surrounding marshes at Kallar Kahar are particularly beautiful at sunrise. The lake is also good for birdwatching, attracting large numbers of migrating birds. At the southwest corner there are orchards dating from the 16th century when the Mughal emperor Babur, en route from Kabul to Delhi, was reputedly so taken by the beauty of the lake that he ordered extensive gardens to be laid out. There is also a throne cut out of solid rock, the *Takht-e-Babri*, from where Babur is supposed to have enjoyed the view of the lake and addressed his army. Up on the hillside by the road to Khushab is the shrine of **Sheikh Abdul Qadir Jilani**, which offers good views over the lake. Kallar Kahar is also famous for its six springs, which are attributed to the Sufi saint **Baba Freid Ganj Shakar**. Local legend relates how Baba Freid was teased by a woman who refused to give him water from an existing spring, saying that it was contaminated. The saint subsequently cursed the spring, making the water undrinkable. Continually harassed by petitions of remorseful villagers, he eventually relented and caused the six springs to emerge.

Punjab

Sleeping There is a **D** ***TDCP Resort***, T0573-51725 on the south side of the lake, offering comfortable though somewhat overpriced rooms with attached bath, fan and heater, and a reasonable restaurant, as well as a small playground/fair and boats for hire. There is a forlorn collection of caged birds and monkeys at the entrance.

Malot

Colour map 5, grid C2

The village of Malot is situated to the south of the main road between Kallar Kahar and Choa Saidan Shah. Above the village on a large rocky outcrop at the very edge of the Salt Range's southern cliffs, stand the remains of two Hindu temples. Malot is worth a visit as much for the temples as for the spectacular views from the edge of the sheer cliffs down onto the Jhelum plains. Clearly visible from here is the new Islamabad-Lahore motorway, snaking out of the Salt Range onto the plains and crossing the Jhelum River.

The two temples at Malot were built in the Hindu Kashmiri style of the eighth to 10th centuries. Standing in such an exposed position and built of sandstone, they have been heavily weathered, but the detailed carved reliefs on the sides are still discernible. The larger and better preserved of the two temples has a later Sikh watchtower built on top of it, which replaced the original stepped pyramidal roof. Originally there was a fort here, encompassing the village and temples and covering five square kilometres. It was here that the last of the Hindu Shahi rulers, Raja Mal, was forced to embrace Islam by Mahmud of Ghazni in the early 11th century. Later, in the 16th century, Daulat Khan Lodhi, the last of the Delhi Sultans, was defeated here by the Mughal emperor Babur.

Malot village owes its comparative wealth (the stone houses in the village are well built and most have running water, electricity and telephone) to its strong representation in the Pakistan army, with a large number of the villagers occupying high ranks. There are plans to build a tourist resthouse here.

Ins and outs

The village can be reached by intermittent public transport from Kallar Kahar in the form of Toyota pick-ups, or you could try hitching from the turn-off. To hire a pick-up to take you there on a private basis should not cost more than Rs 300 for the round trip. Leaving Kallar Kahar on the Choa Saidan Shah road, the turning for Malot is the first one you come to on the right after crossing the motorway (there is a tea/snack stall on the corner). From the turning it is approximately 10 kilometres to Malot.

Routes

From Kallar Kahar a road leads northeast back to Chakwal (22 kilometres) via Bhaun. Another road leads southwest towards Khushab. After 38 kilometres there is a turning to the right which leads back north to Talagang (see below), with the possibility also of branching east towards Mount Sukesar (1522 metres), the highest peak in the Salt Range. The Khushab road climbs up through the Salt Range to give spectacular views from its precipitous southern cliffs down over the Jhelum plains, before descending steeply onto the plains and arriving at the town of Khushab.

West to Mianwali

From Chakwal you can continue west to Mianwali (144 kilometres) via Talagang (43 kilometres). After around eight kilometres the road crosses the Islamabad-Lahore motorway. The road runs through flat countryside, for the most part cultivated, occasionally giving way to grass and scrub and in places heavily eroded. From **Talagang** there is a road south towards Khushab and north towards Islamabad via Fatehjang. Continuing west the road to Mianwali gradually approaches the western extremities of the Salt Range, lower here than to the east, but still impressive. The road passes close to the large picturesque **Nambal Lake**, situated right at the foot of the Range, and as it starts to climb you get good views down onto the lake, which attracts large numbers of migrating birds. Emerging on the southern edge of the Salt Range, there are views down onto the plains before the road descends, passing through flat irrigated land planted with rice to arrive at Mianwali.

Mianwali

Phone code: 0459
Colour map 4, grid B3

The town is headquarters of Mianwali District, an area of great agricultural importance, irrigated by a network of canals fed by the water gathered from the Chashma Barrage to the south and the Jinnah Barrage to the north. There is little of interest in the town itself, although it has a claim to fame as the birthplace of Imran Khan. The main reason for coming here is to visit the Chashma Barrage to the south.

Sleeping

The 3 hotels near the bus stand on Shahrah-e-Fiazaya are reasonable. All have restaurants and gardens. **E/F** *Faisal*, T30367. Choice of a/c and non a/c rooms with fan and attached bath. **E/F** *Sharzad*, T32706. Choice of a/c and non a/c rooms with fan and attached bath. **G** *Al-Abbas*, T31923. Basic rooms with fan and attached bath. Near the railway station there is the very basic **G** *Ghazi Lasani*, T2978.

Transport

Train Sargodha; *RC-140*, 0710, 4 hours. **Multan**; *Mehran Exp*, 2256, 9 hours. **Lahore**; *Passenger 220*, 1845, 11¾ hours. **Karachi**; *Khushal Khan Khattak Exp*, 0142, 31 hours. **Mari Indus (Kalabagh)**; *Passenger 219*, 0632, 2 hours. **Rawalpindi**; *RC-145*, 0705, 6 hours; *Mehran Exp*, 0100, 6 hours. **Peshawar**; *Khushal Khan Khattak Exp*, 0147, 8 hours.

Bus There are regular services – a mixture of buses and minibuses – from the main bus stand to Lahore, Peshawar, Bannu, Dera Ismail Khan and Multan. They depart when full.

Chashma Barrage

Colour map 4, grid B2/3

Spanning the Indus 35 kilometres to the south of Mianwali is the Chashma Barrage, one of six built across the river. Completed in 1971 at a cost of Rs 399 million, it created a lake 360 square kilometres in area. The main headworks with the sluice gates and openings are situated at the western end of the barrage, and have a maximum discharge capacity of 950,000 cusecs.

Ins and outs There is no regular public transport to the barrage. To get there, follow the Sarghoda road south out of Mianwali and bear right after 8 kilometres at a fork. The road crosses the main canal headworks, with 3 canals branching off it, and follows the left bank of the southwesterly branch. After 8 kilometres turn right at a crossroads. The road crosses the canal before arriving at Kundian. Turn left and follow the road for around 5 kilometres to the barrage. Alternatively you can follow a track beside the main canal south from Mianwali, taking the right hand branch at the headworks. Soon after the narrow gauge railway crosses the canal, there is a bridge over the canal. Turn right onto this road and follow it to Kundian.

Sleeping There is a ***WAPDA Resthouse*** in the main WAPDA complex on the east side of the barrage, but due to its location next to the Atomic Energy Council complex, they are not keen on accommodating tourists. Contact the Project Director at Chashma, T045202-41289. Generally permission must be gained from the head office in Islamabad. There is another resthouse on the west side, up on the hillside with spectacular views looking out over the Indus and the barrage. This belongs to the Canals Dept, and must be booked through their office in Dera Ismail Khan. Again, tourists are not encouraged. It is probably better to visit the barrage as a day-trip from Mianwali. Alternatively there is the basic **G** ***Al-Massoum***, T41006 at Kundian.

Northern Kafir Khot From the western end of the barrage you can reach the **Northern Kafir Khot**, five kilometres to the north on a rough track. Situated in the Marwat Hills with fine views in all directions, these sprawling ruins of a Hindu Shahi fortress cover a large area, with well preserved walls along the northern ridge and the remains of some Hindu temples inside.

Routes The road south from Mianwali leads down through the Thal desert, parts of which have now been turned into fertile land by the canals feeding from the Jinnah and Chashma Barrages. The road passes a turning west at Dullewala (121 kilometres) across the Indus to Dera Ismail Khan, before eventually arriving at Muzaffargarh (282 kilometres). Alternatively, a road crosses the Chashma Barrage and follows the west bank of the Indus to Dera Ismail Khan (see page 362).

The road north from Mianwali leads to Kalabagh (54 kilometres). Be sure to fork left across the Jinnah Barrage, as the old rail/road bridge across the Indus further on only carries light vehicles. The Jinnah Barrage was completed in 1942 but did not provide irrigation to the Thal desert until after Independence in 1947.

Kalabagh

Colour map 5, grid C1

The setting for the town of Kalabagh is a spectacular one. Surrounded by imposing mountains to the north, east and west, the Indus emerges from its narrow gorge here, spreading lazily across the plains to the south. The town itself, nestled on the steep west bank of the Indus, is a tightly packed jumble of old wooden houses, often intricately carved, and narrow bazaars. The hills here are the western extension of the Salt Range and thick deposits of rock salt can be seen along the banks of the river. Old wooden boats ply up and down the river, powered by engines lashed precariously to the side with long propeller shafts reaching down into the water. The old rail/road bridge gives excellent views onto the town.

Sleeping & eating

There are a couple of basic hotels in the town, and the usual selection of cheap eateries.

Transport

On the opposite bank from Kalabagh is Mari Indus, now the terminus for the branch line from Daud Khel, which once continued on to Bannu and Tank. The *Passenger 219* leaves Mari Indus each afternoon at 1700 to make the journey to Lahore via Faisalabad. It stops at every station en route, taking a painfully long 13½ hours to reach Lahore; definitely for enthusiasts only. Buses and minibuses for Kohat pass through Kalabagh on their way from Mianwali, and vise-versa. Buses for Bannu can be caught at the junction with the Jinnah Barrage road, a few kilometres to the southwest of the town.

Routes

From Kalabagh a road leads northwest through rugged mountains to join the Bannu-Kohat road just south of Lachi. The route is usually passable in an ordinary car, although there are several fordings where bridges are being constructed or repaired, which can render it impassable after rains. Another road leads southwest from Kalabagh to Lakki and then on to join the DI Khan-Bannu road.

Islamabad and Rawalpindi to Lahore

The route from Islamabad and Rawalpindi to Lahore described here follows the historical route of the **Grand Trunk Road**. First built in the fourth century BC by the Mauryan Emperor Chandragupta, the route was developed by the Mughals in the 16th and 17th centuries to link their major cities of Kabul, Peshawar, Rawalpindi, Lahore and Delhi to Bengal in the east. For over two millennia, this route has seen the constant passage of invaders, traders and

Islamabad/Rawalpindi to Lahore

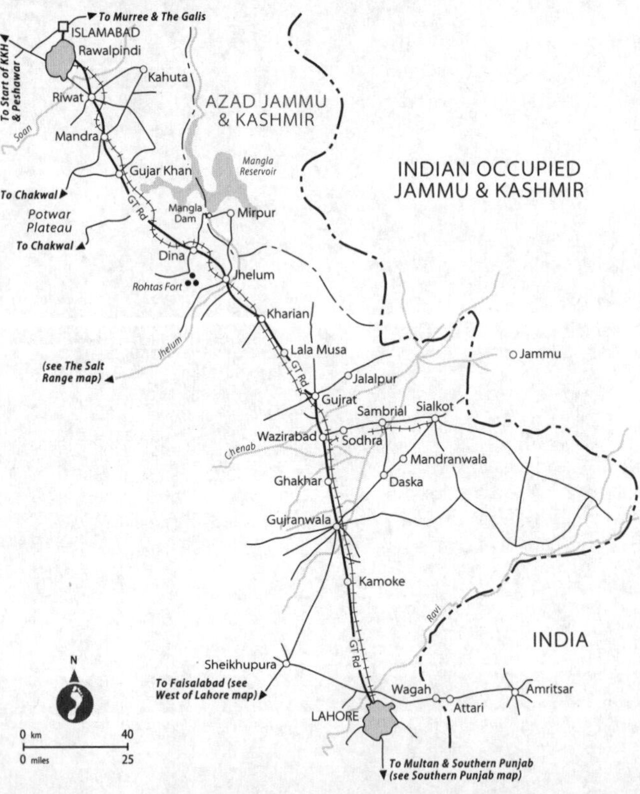

pilgrims, as well as facilitating the spread of new ideas, technologies and religions. For almost its entire length, including those sections that lie within the borders of India, the route is referred to as the GT Road.

NB A quicker route between Islamabad/Rawalpindi and Lahore is provided by the new toll road, the **M2 Motorway** (three and a half hours as opposed to six, see 'Salt Range' map). Although it's fascinating to see a modern six-lane highway with no traffic on it (locals resent the tolls, and are afraid of car-jacking due to lack of traffic), the Grand Trunk Road is a far more interesting route (though very dangerous due to the narrowness of the road and the speed of the traffic).

Riwat

Colour map 5, grid C2

This small village lies some 25 kilometres south of Rawalpindi, at the heart of the **Potwar Plateau** (see page 624 for background details). The overall impression around here is of a 'moon' landscape, with eroded cliffs and bluffs sculptured out of the weathered alluvium. Several kilometres to the west of the road lie the reasonably well preserved remains of a 16th century **Gakhkhar Fort**, built by the former rulers of the Potwar Plateau, the Gakhkhars. Remains of the fort include some of the outside walls, the main gate, a mausoleum and a mosque.

On the banks of the Soan, immediately north of Riwat, is the site of an extraordinary collection of **Middle and Upper Palaeolithic** stone tools, and widespread evidence of settlement by man's earliest ancestors over 100,000 years ago.

Ins and outs

Jhelum-bound minibuses from Rawalpindi's Marir Chowk bus stand will drop you here.

Manikyala Buddhist stupa

About eight kilometres south of Riwat is a small blue and white sign indicating the location of the **Manikyala Buddhist stupa**, the largest of several stupas in the area, and visible in one of the many clumps of banyan trees some two kilometres off the GT Road. Coins found in the stupa suggest that it dates from the time of Kanishka's successor in the first century AD, but it may have been rebuilt as late as the eighth century by Yasovarma of Kanauj, who replaced the relics and included his own gold coins. The dome of the **stupa** is over 30 metres high and 40 metres in diameter. About three kilometres north is another stupa identified by General Cunningham as that referred to by the Chinese traveller Hiuen Tsang as the "**stupa of the body-offering**". 300 metres to its south is the "stupa of the blood offering". Evidently Hiuen Tsang recounted the legend that in a previous life the Buddha had offered his body to ease the hunger of seven tiger cubs. The stupa of the body offering was opened by General Court (a French officer employed by Ranjit Singh) who found three cylindrical caskets made of gold, silver and copper. Four gold coins of the Emperor Kanishka were found in the gold box, seven silver Roman denarii in the silver box dated no later than 43 BC, and eight copper coins, again from Kanishka, were in the copper box.

Ins and outs

Jhelum-bound minibuses from Rawalpindi's Marir Chowk bus stand will drop you here.

Excursions from the GT Road

Lying some 54 kilometres south of Rawalpindi, via the settlement of **Mandra** (where a road branches southwest off the GT Road to Chakwal in the **Salt Range**, see page 236) and the market town of **Gujar Khan**, is the small roadside town of **Dina.** This makes a good base from which to make a couple of excursions off the GT Road. To the west lies **Rohtas Fort** (seven kilometres) and **Tilla Jogian Hill** (22 kilometres), whilst to the east is **Mangla Dam** (16 kilometres). Dina has a couple of hotels: **F** *Al Kousar*, GT Rd, T892. Some a/c, restaurant recommended, good value; **F** *Iqbal*, GT Rd, T630624. Jhelum-bound minibuses from Rawalpindi's Marir Chowk bus stand will drop you at Dina.

Rohtas Fort

Colour map 5, grid C3

Located seven kilometres off the GT Road at Dina, the imposing Rohtas Fort is one of the finest castles on the sub-continent. Commanding the gorge of the Kahan River, the fort was ordered built by Sher Shah Suri in 1543 to prevent the return from exile of his defeated enemy Humayun, and to subdue the local Gakhkhar tribes. The fort also commands a section of the old Grand Trunk Road. The outer fortification wall runs for over four kilometres, following the natural contour of the hill upon which the fort stands, and is reinforced at intervals by 68 bastions and 12 gates.

Punjab

Ins and outs

Local charabanc buses (Rs 10) run from Dina to Rohtas village inside the fort, entering through the Khwas Khani Gate. Ascertain in advance as to whether you are hiring the whole vehicle ('special', Rs 100). There are no toilet facilities within the fort, but it is possible to get cold drinks in Rohtas village. Walking around the fort requires some strenuous work, with lots of backtracking as many of the high walkways along the outer walls end in precipitous drops.

History

Legend has it that Sher Shah Suri commanded his architect Shahu Sultani to build a massive and impregnable fort in three years. Unaware of the grandness of Sher Shah's designs, the fort that Shahu Sultani constructed was considerably smaller than the Emperor had envisaged, and on seeing the completed structure, Sher Shah ordered the architect to be beheaded. As an act of clemency, however, he allowed the architect a further two years to build a fort more in keeping with his wishes. In the event, Sher Shah died in battle

Rohtas Fort

shortly after, and the fort took a further decade to build. The fort is named after the fort at Rohtas in Bengal, scene of one of Sher Shah's great victories.

In fact, within 10 years Sher Shah's successors had abandoned the fort without it ever seriously being attacked. It is even suggested that far from being impregnable, the fact that some of the gates are remarkably easy of access, the construction techniques in places are poor, and that it would require a large army to hold it meant that the fort was something of a military liability. Despite this, Rohtas Fort remains a spectacular sight.

Tour of the fort

The **Sohail Gate** is the most impressive, its image often used to grace Pakistani tourism brochures. Built in the typical Pathan style of the era, it stands 20 metres high and is flanked by two massive rounded bastions. The central gate is topped with seven defensive merlons. Its name is said to derive from the famous saint Sohail Bukhari, although it is argued that the name is taken from the Sohail star that rises above the gate.

Continuing clockwise around the fort's perimeter, you pass through the **Shah Chand Wali Gate** in the wall that divides the inner fort, or citadel, from the outer, main fort. Near to this gate is the shrine of Shah Chand Wali, a holy man who worked on the fort's construction without taking wages right up to his death. The incongruous looking pavilion standing on the small hillock just inside the inner fort is the **Haveli Man Singh**. Built by Man Singh (d 1614), one of Akbar's most famous Rajput generals, the building is made of brick and plaster, rather than the stone used elsewhere in the fort. Its domed roof is topped by a Hindu style lotus emblem. Beyond the haveli is the **Rani Mahal**, the remains of an engraved sandstone minaret.

Immediately to the west of the haveli stands the **execution tower** (*burj*). Built primarily for dealing with rebellious princes and traitors, the execution

Rohtas Fort

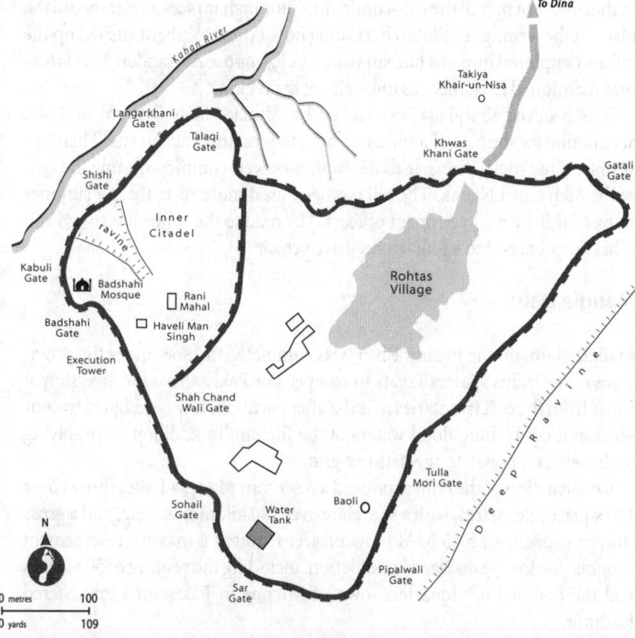

tower has a raised platform with a hole at its centre through which the unfortunate victims were thrown.

West and southwest from the high outer walls lie deep, highly eroded ravines that look set to claim parts of the fort walls. In places the soft sandstone foundations have become worn away, leaving the walls supported only by the durable mortar with which they were constructed.

Continuing along this outer wall you pass the **Badshahi Gate** and the **Shahi** ('royal') **mosque**, a small prayer chamber standing in a courtyard. Facing Kabul, to the northwest, is the striking **Kabuli Gate**. Over three metres wide and flanked by two bastions, a flight of 60 steps leads down to one of the fort's *baolis*, or freshwater wells.

Facing the Kahan River is the **Shishi Gate**, taking its name from the glazed tiles used in the spandrels of the outer arch. Erosion, partly from the river, has greatly cut into the fort at this point. Other gates on the inner fortress include the 15 metres high **Langarkhani Gate** and the **Talaqi Gate**. Talaqi means 'divorce', although it is sometimes translated as 'condemned', and it is considered unlucky to enter through this gate, following the experience of Sabir Suri who contracted fever shortly after entering through here. On the north wall stands **Mori** or **Kashmiri Gate** (facing Kashmir), and the splendid **Khwas Khani Gate**. The latter was named after Sher Shah's commander and is the main entrance to the fort as you arrive from Dina. Outside the Khwas Khani Gate, on the road to Dina, is the **Takiya Khair-un-Nisa**, shrine of the daughter of one of Sher Shah's ministers. Khair-un-Nisa was said to have been a warrior of some repute, and she fought alongside her Emperor at a number of battles.

The gates along the east wall, **Gatali**, **Tulla Mori** and **Pipalwala** are smaller and less interesting than those on the south, west and north side.

Tilla Jogian Hill

A further 15 kilometres west of Rohtas Fort is one of the higher peaks in the **Salt Range** (see page 236), the 990 metres **Tilla Jogian**. On the summit lie the remains of a monastery that may well be one of the oldest religious institutes in the northern part of the sub-continent. Cunningham sees a reference to the place in the writings of Plutarch, relating how Porus' elephant rushed up the hill and implored him in a human voice not to oppose Alexander. Tilla is further mentioned in numerous folk-tales of the region.

It is believed that Tilla was sacked by Ahmad Shah Durrani in 1748, accounting for the lack of antiquated buildings on this ancient site. There is a shrine on the rocky pinnacle to the west, however, commemorating the visit of the Sikh Guru Nanak. The hill has been used more recently as a summer retreat for British Government officers. The road to the summit is rough and is best approached in a four-wheel drive vehicle.

Mangla Dam

Colour map 5, grid C3

Mangla Dam, on the Jhelum River, was completed in 1968 under the provisions of the Indus Waters Treaty to compensate Pakistan for the diversion of water from the east tributaries to India after partition. It was designed to conserve and control the flood waters of the Jhelum, in addition to supplying hydro-electric power to the national grid.

Construction of the dam produced a reservoir, **Mangla Lake**, spread over 160 square kilometres, with a shoreline over 400 kilometres long, and a gross storage capacity of 5.55 MAF. The project required a massive resettlement programme for the displaced population, including the resiting of 50 villages and the regional headquarters town of **Mirpur** in Pakistani administered Kashmir.

In terms of height, Mangla Dam does not figure amongst the world's highest dams. However, volume-wise, Mangla is the world's 10th largest (Aswan High Dam, in Egypt, is 20th). There are several parts to the dam. To the east is the power house, fed by five 480 metre tunnels and capable at peak production of 1170 mw of HEP. Inside the power house is a stunning 20 metres by 100 metres mural painted in 1967 by the famous Pakistani artist **Sadequain**, and depicting workers from prehistoric times to the 'Sputnik' age. The main dam runs for 3,353 metres at the crest, and at the centre is a hill surmounted by an old Gakhkhar fort. The viewing area offers panoramic views of the surrounding area and photography is permitted. There is a small café and children's play area. The fort houses an aquarium with specimens of fish (including a stuffed 30 kilogram monster), that are commercially farmed in the lake. At the west end of the dam lie the main and emergency spillways, designed to cope with over one million cusecs of excess water.

Ins and outs

For a full tour of the dam, contact WAPDA Chief Engineer at Mangla. The dam is located 16 kilometres east of the main GT Road at Dina, and can be reached by public transport from the main highway. Mirpur-bound minibuses from Rawalpindi can also drop you here. Beyond Mangla Dam it is possible to continue to the Azad Kashmir town of **Mirpur** (see page 284).

Returning to the GT Road: Jhelum

Phone code: 0541
Colour map 5, grid C3

Though built on an ancient mound that has provided coins from the Greek period and a lingam from the seventh or eighth century, Jhelum is a relatively modern town. The 19th century Gothic church (to the west of the town) was used as a refuge by British families during the 1857 Mutiny, though there is little of interest to tourists in this military town.

Sleeping

Jhelum's 4 basic hotels are grouped together in the Cantt area (left out of the train station, then first right), with little to choose between them. **E-F** *Faran*, T3161. ***Mehwish***, T2877. ***Paradise***, T4267. ***Zeelaf***, T3698.

Ins and outs

Jhelum is located just off the main GT Rd. To travel north to Islamabad/Rawalpindi, east to Mangla and Mirpur, or to all destinations south, bus services are more regular from Dina (see above). Minibuses from Jhelum to Dina run from just north of Chandni Chowk. Minibuses from Rawalpindi's Marir Chowk bus stand, or Lahore's Australia Chowk bus stand, will drop you in Jhelum.

Gujrat

Phone code: 0541
Colour map 5, grid C3

Gujrat is a typical middle-sized Punjabi market town, though it does have ancient origins. It is associated with the fifth century BC capital of the Rajput ruler Bachan Pal, and also with the fourth century BC battle in which **Alexander the Great** defeated the Indian king Puru (Greek: Poros). Alexander is said to have been so impressed by the dignity in defeat of the captive king that he restored his kingdom as a vassal, and on the withdrawal of the Greek forces, left Puru as ruler of Punjab.

More recently, Gujrat was the scene of the final battle of the **Second Sikh War** (21 February 1849) that led directly to the British annexation of Punjab. General Thackwell, present at the battle, describes the fighting courage of the Sikhs: "Sikhs caught hold of the bayonets of their assailants with their left hands and closing with their adversaries, dealt furious blows

The 'rat children' of Gujrat

During his lifetime, many childless women would come to pray with Shah Daula in the hope of producing offspring. Following his death, a mythology developed that suggested that women praying at the shrine would be blessed with children, but the price to pay would be high. The first born would be a deformed baby with a shrunken head, known as a chuha or 'rat child', and would have to be given up to serve the shrine. Should the parents fail to hand over the child, all their subsequent offspring would also be chuha.

However, questions have been raised in recent years about the exploitation of the chuhas (of which there are an estimated 10,000 in Pakistan). It has been suggested that these unfortunates are actually being controlled by a "mafia" who supposedly buy the children to look after them, but then use them to make money through begging. An article in a British newspaper (The Guardian, 29/6/98) even suggested that these 'rat children' could make around $10 a day from begging, "a very lucrative business considering that's twice the amount a civil servant makes".

Perhaps even more alarming are the allegations that many of these 'rat children' were not actually born with any disability, but were subsequently deformed using some barbaric medieval-like head brace. When I interviewed one of Shah Daula's descendants in 1995, he maintained that the children were born with a congenital disease called microcephaly, and that great efforts were being made to dispel the myths connecting the 'rat children' to the shrine. And further investigations by Pakistan's leading genetic scientist, Dr Qasim Mehdi, have proved inconclusive (other than dispelling the notion of genetic inheritance).

In many regards, the government seems reluctant to intervene, fearing that it may upset religious sensibilites, although it has been suggested that the minister of religious affairs, Raja Zafar-ul-Haq, believes that the children "must have been deliberately deformed" (The Guardian, 29/6/98). The ministry has now taken over the running of the shrine, though greater efforts need to be made to dispel the myths surrounding it, and to protect the chuhas.

with their right ... This circumstance alone will suffice to demonstrate the rare species of courage possessed by these men".

Sights Gujrat's only real attraction is the modest shrine to the 17th century local saint, **Pir Shah Daula of Baghdad**, who is best known for his association with the *chuhas*, or 'rat children' (see 'box'). He arrived in Gujrat during the reign of the Mughal Emperor Shah Jahan, and soon became known for his good deeds (notably providing food, shelter and clothing to the poor). His mausoleum stands in a courtyard just off an alley lined with stalls selling devotional paraphernalia (you may have to ask directions to find it). It is a low white building with a pillared verandah, a green domed roof, and eight small minarets. Above the tombs of the saint and his wife, the interior of the tomb is decorated with mirrored tiles inset with intricate geometric designs in red, green, blue and black. The shrine attracts many devotees during the saint's Urs in late June. For further details see Sheikh Parvaiz Amin Naqshbondy's *"Hazrat Syed Kabeer-ud-Din Shah Daulah"* (Umar Publication, available in Lahore bookshops).

Sleeping & eating **D-E** *Faisal*, GT Rd, T28731. Overpriced. **E** *Soufis*, GT Rd. Basic rooms but good restaurant. **E-F** *Neshaman*, Railway Rd. Basic. **E-F** *New Melody Inn*, Railway Rd, T26037. Clean, good value, some a/c, restaurant recommended. **E-F** *Noor*, opposite City Police Station. Very basic for the price.

Transport Minibuses from Rawalpindi's Marir Chowk bus stand, or Lahore's Australia Chowk bus stand, will drop you in Gujrat. Wagons run north and south from GT Road.

Sialkot

Phone code: 0432
Colour map 4, grid B6

Sialkot is one of Pakistan's most important industrial centres, particularly noted for its production of sports goods, surgical instruments, and, rather bizarrely, bag-pipes! It has a typically Pakistani chaotic old town centre, with a fascinating labyrinth of narrow streets, crowded bazaars, and constant donkey cart jams. And if you can get someone to point you in the right direction, it has several sights that are worth seeking out (although, incredibly, some guidebooks omit this town altogether!). NB The map here is grossly simplified.

Ins and outs

Getting there Sialkot is located some 42 kilometres east of the GT Road. If coming from the north, the turn off is at Wazirabad, and from the south, the route is via Gujranwala. Sialkot is best reached by bus from Rawalpindi's Marir Chowk bus stand, or Lahore's Australia Chowk bus stand. You are likely to be dropped at the General Bus Stand just off the main Wazirabad Road (see map).

Getting around A rickshaw from the General Bus Stand to the town centre will cost about Rs 25, although tongas run along this route (Rs 3). The centre is compact enough to walk around.

Punjab

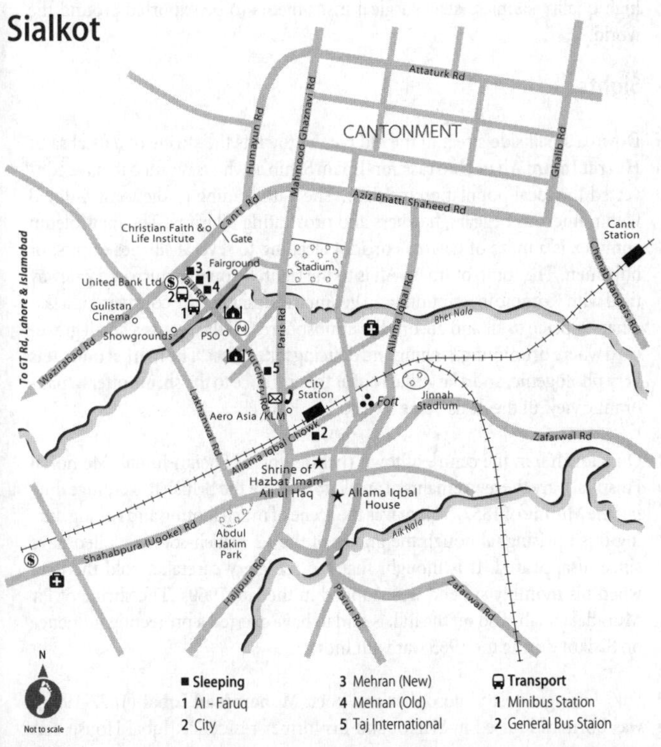

Sialkot at the World Cup

Sialkot is also noted for the sporting goods that it produces, though in recent years this appears to be more a source of infamy than fame. Though many of the world's major sports goods manufactures are represented in Sialkot, the question of child labour keeps rearing its ugly head. It was with delight that Pakistan announced that it was supplying the footballs for the Euro '96 championship in England, and the Adidas balls for the 1998 World Cup in France, but this announcement was accompanied by film footage that seemed to suggest that the replica balls were being hand-stitched by young children. Whether these were 'official' balls or 'bootlegs' is open to debate, though there is little doubt that the use of child labour is a major problem yet to be fully addressed in Sialkot. Many of the sports goods factories around town have signs declaring "child labour not used", and though this is true of the more reputable firms, there are plenty of others where this is not the case.

History

Sialkot has ancient roots, and is associated with King Manender's second century BC capital Sagala. During Mughal times, Sialkot's *koftars* were renowned for their fine craftsmanship with swords and daggers, and though the demand for these items declined with the introduction of the rifle in 1857, an unexpected opportunity to modify their craft arose in 1905 when the local American Mission Hospital needed some equipment replaced. There are now some 500 factories in Sialkot (employing around 100,000 persons) that produce high quality stainless steel surgical instruments to be exported around the world.

Sights

Shrine of Hazrat Imam Ali ul Haq Down a small side street in the old part of town is the shrine of a local saint **Hazrat Imam Ali ul Haq** (ask for 'Imam Sahib'), who is reputed to have converted the local population to Islam. The path leading to the tomb is lined with numerous beggars, hawkers and prostrating pilgrims. The mausoleum complex is a maze of narrow corridors leading to several shrines of pirs, or holy men. The tomb of Imam Ali is to the right, through a mirrored gateway tiled with Koranic inscriptions and geometric designs. The courtyard is a fascinating place to sit and absorb the atmosphere. To the rear is a small graveyard where drumming, singing and dancing takes place. The market outside is very photogenic, and a large flat roof at the entrance to the shrine offers a panoramic view of the deals being struck.

Fort On a low hill in the centre of town (behind the Al Sheikh Jinnah Memorial Hospital), are the few remains of an old fort where the British took refuge during the Mutiny of 1857. Sialkot was the scene of much looting and rioting during this uprising, although the graves of the 12 British soldiers killed have since disappeared. It is thought that the cemetery caretaker sold the land when his monthly stipend was stopped in the late 1960s. The shrine of Pir Muradala Shah, also on the hill, is said to have exerted a protecting influence on Sialkot during the 1965 war with India.

Allama Iqbal House Pakistan's greatest philosopher and poet, **Mohammad Iqbal** (1877-1938), was born and raised in Sialkot and his former residence, Iqbal House, has been turned into a small museum containing some of his personal belongings and work. Another place of interest is the 17th century tomb of the great Muslim scholar, Mian Abdul Hakim (on Khadam Ali Road near Saddar Hospital).

Essentials

Sleeping & eating

■ *on map*
Price codes:
see inside front cover

A ***Taj International***, Kutchery Rd, T265305, F265048, E tajhtl@skt.brain.net.pk. Brand new hotel (1997), standard rooms large, well furnished, central a/c, dish TV, fridge, minibar, modern attached bath, plus very nice deluxe rooms (larger with dining area), plus suites, 2 restaurants, business centre, small pool, plans for a gym, easily the best in town, friendly. Recommended. **D** ***Mehran (New)***, Wazirabad Rd, T264889. Clean but windowless rooms, modern attached bath, some rooms with a/c and dish TV (**C**), restaurant, not bad. **F** ***City***, Allama Iqbal Chowk, opposite railway station, T288559. Basic doubles. **F** ***Mehran (Old)***, Jail Rd, T554889. Basic and noisy. **G** ***Al-Faruq***, Jail Rd. Small cell-like rooms, shared bath, very basic. Most of the hotels have their own restaurants. There are lots of very cheap places to eat opposite the General Bus Stand.

Shopping

Sports goods Naturally, this is the place to get all your football, hockey and cricket accessories. One of the most reputable firms is *Sublime Sports (Pvt) Ltd*, who provided the footballs for the 1998 World Cup (that England were cheated out of).

Long distance transport

Train Sialkot is on an inconvenient branch line (change at Wazirabad to go anywhere).

Long distance buses The **General Bus Station** is chaotic, with lumbering bus running to most destinations. Immediately to the south is the more manageable **minibus station**. Most services depart when full. **Faisalabad** (Rs 80, 4 hours, 8 per day); **Islamabad** (Rs 90, 4 hours, 4 per day); **Lahore** (Rs 45, 2½ hours, hourly); **Peshawar** (Rs 130, 7 hours, 6 per day); **Rawalpindi** (Rs 90, 4 hours, hourly).

Directory

Banks *UBL*, Wazirabad Rd, and ***Bank of Punjab*** Allama Iqbal Chowk, opposite railway station, offer foreign exchange. **Communications** GPO: south end of Paris Rd. **Telephones:** ***Pak Telecom*** at the south end of Paris Rd.

Gujranwala

Phone code: *0431*
Colour map 4, grid B5

Another typical Punjabi market-town, albeit with a large industrial base, the modern town produces fans, air conditioners and fridges as well as being a centre of steel production. Gujranwala's greatest attraction for visitors is a stroll through the old town area: one reader has written to say "the main bazaar is huge (about one mile square) and is fascinating, with thousands of tiny alleys; everyone raves about Peshawar Old City bazaar, but after living in Gujranwala, Peshawar was nothing special". The town also has a cricket stadium that frequently hosts one-day international matches.

Ins and outs

Getting there

The town is located 34 kilometres south of Wazirabad, although it is actually bypassed by the GT Road. If arriving by 'local' bus (from Gujrat or Sialkot), you will be dropped off in the town centre. If coming on a 'flying coach' between Rawalpindi and Lahore, you may well be dropped off on the bypass, 3 kilometres either north or south of town. The main road through the centre of Gujranwala is still referred to as GT Road.

Gujranwala

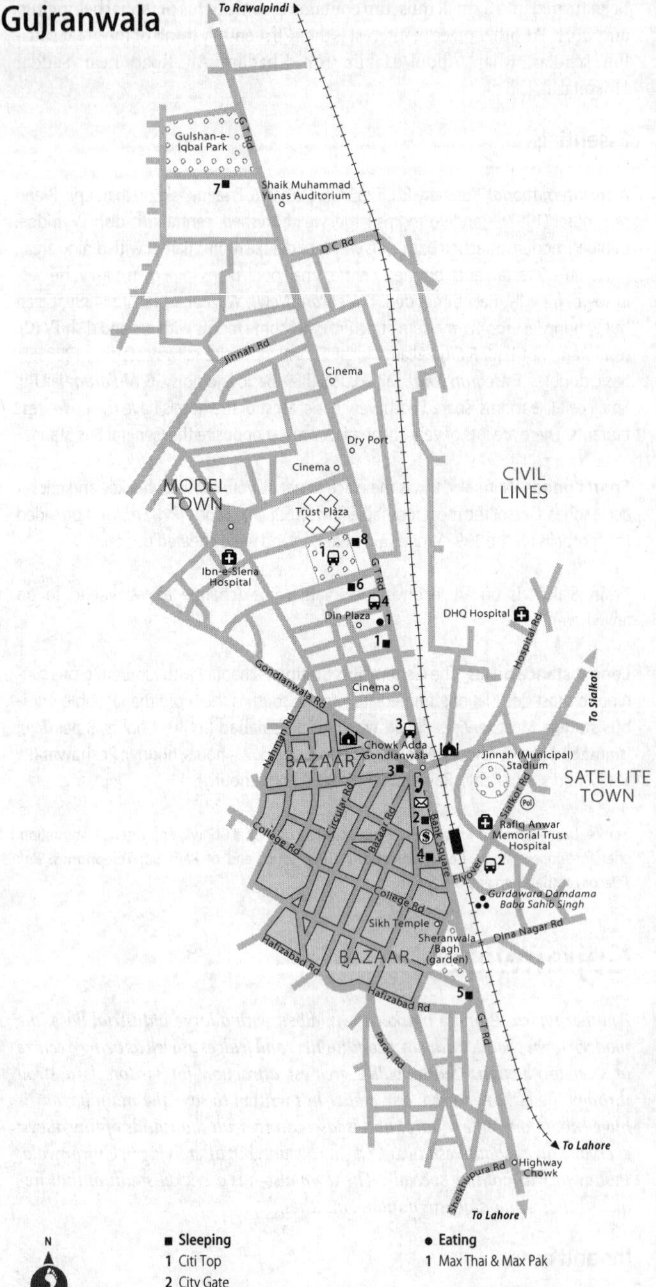

To Rawalpindi
G T Rd
Gulshan-e-Iqbal Park
7
Shaik Muhammad Yunas Auditorium
D C Rd
Jinnah Rd
Cinema
Dry Port
Cinema
MODEL TOWN
CIVIL LINES
Trust Plaza
8
1
Ibn-e-Siena Hospital
6
4
Din Plaza
1
1
DHQ Hospital
Hospital Rd
To Sialkot
Gondlanwala Rd
Cinema
Nahman Rd
3
Chowk Adda Gondlanwala
BAZAAR
3
Jinnah (Municipal) Stadium
SATELLITE TOWN
Circular Rd
Bazaar Rd
Sialkot Rd
College Rd
2
Bank Square
Rafiq Anwar Memorial Trust Hospital
4
Flyover
2
Gurdawara Damdama Baba Sahib Singh
College Rd
Sikh Temple
Dina Nagar Rd
Sheranwala /Bagh (garden)
Hafizabad Rd
BAZAAR
5
Hafizabad Rd
Paraq Rd
G T Rd
To Lahore
Sheikhupura Rd
Highway Chowk
To Lahore

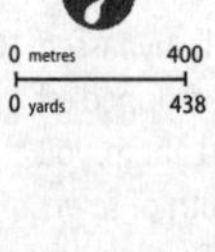

N
0 metres 400
0 yards 438

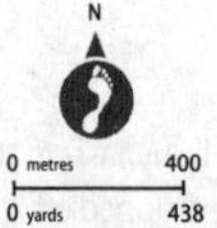

Sleeping
1 Citi Top
2 City Gate
3 Gujranwala
4 Imran
5 Lepari
6 Marhaba
7 Shelton
8 VIP

Eating
1 Max Thai & Max Pak

Buses
1 General Bus Station
2 Minibuses to Sialkot & Lahore
3 Minibuses to Gujrat & Lahore
4 Minibuses to Sargodha

Punjab

Getting around

The town centre is compact enough to walk around. If you are dropped off on the GT Road/bypass, you can take a suzuki into town (Rs 4).

History

Due to its strategic location on the central Punjab plain, **Gujranwala** has had a turbulent history at the hands of advancing and retreating armies on their way to and from India. Although no longer a major garrison town like Jhelum, Gujranwala has a long history of providing army recruits; during the First World War, one in 12 of the male population was recruited into service.

Gujranwala was the first district in which Sikh domination of the Punjab was established, following the capture of the town in 1765 by **Charat Singh**. The capital he established here was used by his son **Mahan Singh**, and his grandson **Ranjit Singh**, until the capture of Lahore by the latter in 1799. To the southeast of the town is the *Samadh*, or octagonal tower, that Ranjit Singh built in memory of his father. The tall pavilion contains a number of Hindu works of art, including scenes from the *Mahabharata* . In 1891, the Deputy Commissioner, Ibbetsen, commissioned a marble monument at the site of Ranjit Singh's birth. Another Sikh building, **Qila** (Fort) **Didar Singh**, c 1850, lies 16 kilometres west of the town on the Hafizabad road.

Essentials

Sleeping
■ *on map*
Price codes:
see inside front cover

B ***Shelton***, opposite Gulshan-e-Iqbal Park, off GT Rd, T259501, F259500. Best in town but little real competition, well furnished a/c rooms, central a/c, dish TV, fridge, minibar, modern bathroom, a/c restaurant, but no real sense of luxury. **C** ***Lepari***, Khawaja Plaza, near Sheranwala Bagh, GT Road, T219853, F250714. Quite large old-fashioned rooms, a/c, dish TV, modern attached bath, plus much bigger deluxe rooms, restaurant. **D** ***Citi Top***, near Din Plaza, GT Rd, T266997. Simple rooms with fan, attached bath, basic but clean, some a/c rooms (Rs 200 extra), dish TV, fridge, discounts negotiable, friendly staff, good Chinese/Pakistani restaurant, good value. Recommended. **D** ***Gujranwala***, Chowk Adda Gondlanwala, off GT Rd, T299308, F236622. Manager friendly but a bit of a smart-arse, large rooms moderately clean, fan, Madonna posters, grubby attached bath, TV in sitting area, 3 a/c rooms, a bargain at half the price. **E** ***VIP***, near Trust Plaza, opposite General Bus Station, T299383. Fairly simple rooms, attached tiled bath, some rooms with a/c and dish TV (**D**), reasonable restaurant, noisy location. **F** ***City Gate***, near Bank Square, GT Rd, T216372. Rather sleazy, very basic filthy cells, dark, no fan, horrible attached bath. **G** ***Imran***, GT Rd, opposite railway station, T219339. Dark, very basic, shared bath; **G** ***Marhaba***, opposite General Bus Station. Basic and noisy.

Eating
● *on map*

Gujranwala is famous in Pakistan for its barbecued quail (Lahorites have been known to drive here to buy it). ***Grand Hotel***, near GPO, GT Road, "serves excellent chicken tikka and quail". ***Max Thai*** and ***Max Pak***, Din Plaza, GT Road, serve Thai and Pakistani food respectively. There are numerous cheap and basic restaurants around the bus and train stations.

Entertainment

Sports Cricket: *Jinnah (Municipal) Stadium*, just behind the train station, is a low concrete bowl (little shade) used mainly for one-day internationals. In 1987 this was the scene of the 7th worst World Cup bowling performance of all time, and the worst by an Englishman (Derek Pringle's 10-0-83-0).

Long distance transport

Train Gujranwala is on the Rawalpindi-Lahore line, though buses tend to be more convenient.

Long distance buses The **General Bus Stand** is just off GT Rd, to the north of town. In addition to the dinosaur buses, there are a/c coasters to **Faisalabad** (Rs 65), **Lahore** (Rs 30), **Mirpur** (Rs 50) and **Rawalpindi** (Rs 80). There are also minibuses to **Gujrat** (Rs 20) and **Jhelum** (Rs 30). There is a small yard on Sialkot Road (near junction with GT Road) with minibuses to **Lahore** (Rs 18) and **Sialkot** (Rs 16). There is a minibus stand on GT Road just north of Chowk Adda Gondlanwala, with services to **Gujrat** and **Lahore** (depart when full). Just north of Din Plaza are minibuses to **Sargodha**.

Directory **Banks** There are numerous banks and moneychangers on 'Bank Square', opposite fly-over, that offer foreign exchange. **Communications** **GPO:** GT Rd, opposite the fly-over. **Telephones:** ***Pak Telecom***, next to GPO. **Couriers:** ***DHL***, Trust Plaza, near General Bus Station, T284486. **Hospitals & medical services** ***DHQ Hospital***, Civil Lines. ***Ibn-e-Siena Hospital***, Model Town. ***Rafiq Anwar Memorial Trust Hospital***, Sialkot Rd.

Routes The GT Road continues south from Gujranwala, after 60 kilometres crossing the **River Ravi**, and entering **Lahore** (7 kilometres).

Lahore

The city of Lahore is considered by many Pakistanis, and certainly most Punjabis, to be the cultural capital of the country. Tourist brochures are keen to quote Punjabi proverbs to emphasize Lahore's uniqueness – "Lahore is Lahore" – and its importance – "East or West, Lahore is best", and there is no doubt that Lahore ranks with Agra, Fatehpur Sikri and Delhi as one of the great centres of Mughal architecture. With its magnificent Islamic monuments, spectacular reminders from the era of British rule, chaotic old city bazaars, plus modern status as the film and fashion centre of Pakistan, Lahore remains high on the list of Pakistan's "unmissable" sights.

Phone code: 042
Colour map 4, grid B5

Ins and outs

Getting there

Lahore's airport is located 5 kilometres east of the city, with taxis charging Rs 100 for the trip. Minibus 32 runs between the airport and the railway station, and minibuses 1 and 24 between the airport and The Mall. The main railway station is Lahore Junction, which is on the main Peshawar-Rawalpindi-Karachi route. Minibuses from the border with India also arrive here. Most visitors arriving by bus use the private bus companies that arrive and depart at the chaotic area around Australia Chowk.

Getting around

Minibuses run on numbered fixed routes around the city, though you can get on and off where you please. The main minibus termini are outside Lahore Junction train station and just to the north of the fort. Note that these minibuses are usually impossibly crowded. Below are a selection of the main routes: 24 Pearl Continental to Lahore Museum via Shahrah-e-Quaid-e-Azam; 1 Salvation Army via Lahore Museum to Fort; 12 Railway station via Shalimar Gardens to Indian border; 33/33a Wahdat Colony (Naqsha stop) via Shahrah-e-Quaid-e-Azam to railway station; 34 Qaddafi Stadium via Salvation Army, Charing Cross to railway station; 43 Main Gulberg to railway station via Salvation Army and Charing Cross. Ubiquitous rickshaws will take you anywhere (maximum fare should be Rs 50 between any 2 points), although the choking fumes make this an unpleasant way to travel. Taxis cost about double the rickshaw fares.

History

Early history

The first recorded history of Lahore probably dates to 630 AD, when **Hiuen Tsang** referred to a large Brahmanical city that he visited on his way to Jullundhur. To Muslims, however, the foundation of Lahore dates to 1021, when **Mahmud of Ghazni** brought Islam to the city. Lahore subsequently became capital of the Ghaznavid Empire, entering a golden age in which great scholars such as **Data Ganj Baksh** settled here, and great Persian poets such as **Masud Saad Salman** first composed those mournful songs about the city that are still sung today.

In the centuries that followed Lahore was captured and ruled by the **Ghauris**, **Khaljis**, **Tughlaqs**, **Sayyids**, the **Lodis** of the Delhi Sultanate, in addition to being attacked and occupied by the **Mongols** of **Genghis Khan** and by **Timur** (Tamerlane).

Mughal period The zenith of Lahore's history, however, dates to the period of **Mughal** rule that effectively began when **Babur** defeated the Sultan of Delhi, **Ibrahim Lodi**, at the first battle of Panipat in 1526. This era marked the construction of some of the finest monuments in the Mughal Empire.

Babur died shortly after this victory (1530) and within 10 years his son **Humayun** had been driven out of the area by the Afghan king **Sher Shah Suri**. Humayun remained in exile for 14 years, but following the death of Sher Shah, he retook Lahore without opposition on 23 February 1555.

Like his father before him, Humayun died shortly after his victory (1556), but under his successor **Akbar**, Lahore's fortunes were revived in 1584 Lahore was made capital of the Mughal Empire. For 14 years Akbar made Lahore his headquarters, directing his campaigns and military operations from there, as well as holding court. Although there are records of an earlier fort at Lahore dating back to 1180, the foundation of the great **Lahore Fort** is attributed to the twelfth year of Akbar's reign. He also rebuilt the walls surrounding the old city and the 12 entrance gates, one of which bears his name. Lahore enjoyed a period of economic prosperity under Akbar, as well as great literary achievement in the works of the Persian poets **Urfi** and **Faizi**.

Following Akbar's death in 1605, Lahore continued to flourish under his son **Jahangir**. He was particularly fond of Lahore, adding several buildings to the fort as well as building **Anarkali's Tomb**. Jahangir is buried in the imposing tomb that was built by his son and successor **Shah Jahan** seven kilometres northwest of Lahore. The tomb of Jahangir's wife, **Nur Jahan**, is nearby.

Born in Lahore, Shah Jahan left his mark upon the city in the form of some of the finest buildings and gardens. The most beautiful buildings in the fort, including the **Shish Mahal**, **Naulakha Bunga**, **Moti Masjid** as well as much of the **Diwan-e-Aam** were built by Shah Jahan. The **Wazir Khan Mosque** was also built during his reign, and many of the great Mughal gardens, including the **Shalimar Gardens**, were initiated by Shah Jahan. He was succeeded in 1658 by his son **Aurangzeb**. A great Islamic reformer, in addition to enlarging the fort, Aurangzeb constructed the magnificent **Badshahi Mosque**.

However, in the power vacuum that followed Aurangzeb's death in 1707, Lahore had a turbulent experience, being attacked, lost and retaken by three different Mughal kings, and by the Sikhs four times, before finally falling after two attempts to the Afghan **Ahmad Shah Durrani** in 1759. In 1799 Lahore was eventually captured by **Ranjit Singh**.

The Sikhs During the forty year rule (1799-1839) of Ranjit Singh, Sikh power in the Punjab was consolidated. However, although Ranjit Singh added some fine architectural features to the city, including the **Gurdwara of Arjan Singh**, he is best remembered by Muslims as a vandal of some repute. Most of the gardens were neglected, and a great deal of marble and many of the precious inlaid stones were removed to embellish the Golden Temple at Amritsar. Indeed, it is claimed that Ranjit Singh removed enough marble from the Muslim mausoleums in Lahore to build two Golden Temples.

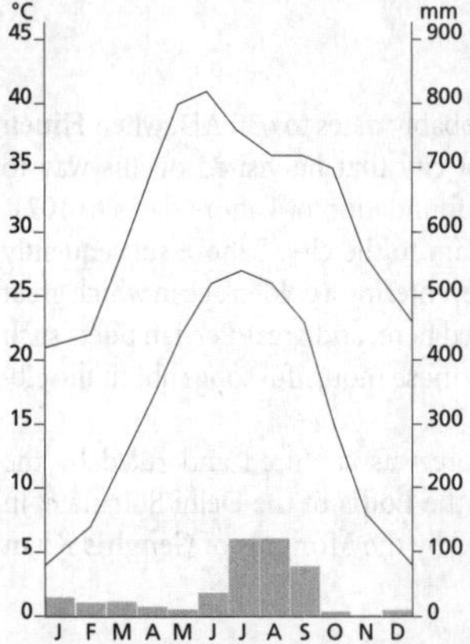

The best time to visit is between November and March

British rule

Following the death of Ranjit Singh, the real victors in the succession struggle that followed were the British. At the conclusion of the Second Sikh War in 1849, Maharaja Dalip Singh was pensioned off to Norfolk and the city was officially handed over to the British.

The British occupied Lahore for almost a century, during which time they built some fine colonial buildings which combined the Gothic and Victorian with the Mughal style. These include the **High Court**, **Lahore Museum**, **Aitchison College**, the old **University campus**, **General Post Office**, **Tollinton Market** and a number of churches. Restoration work was carried out by the Archaeological Department on many of the Mughal buildings, and those which had been turned into offices, storerooms and living quarters were returned to their original functions.

Independence

Lahore played a key role in the partition of India and the subsequent creation of Pakistan, but also witnessed some of the worst excesses of this less than amicable divorce. On 23 March 1940, the All India Muslim League met in session at Lahore under the stewardship of Mohammad Ali Jinnah. The conference culminated in the passing of the historic **Lahore Resolution of 1940** that paved the way for the partition of India and the creation of the new state of Pakistan.

The decision to divide the Punjab between India and Pakistan was looked upon with a deep sense of foreboding by many observers, and right up until the boundary awards were announced, many Sikhs and Hindus in Lahore believed that the city would be 'awarded' to India. When the awards of the Radcliffe Boundary Commission were announced on 17 August 1947, Lahore descended into anarchy. The city resembled one vast refugee camp, with Hindus and Sikhs abandoning all their valuables in order to dash east in fear of their lives, whilst caravans of plundered and mutilated refugees arrived in Lahore from India. Reports speak of railway carriage doors being opened at both Lahore and Amritsar stations, and pouring out onto the platforms the blood of the slaughtered occupants.

Modern Lahore

Though maintaining the tradition of a rich cultural heritage through modern applications, such as innovation in film, fashion and design, the city is changing rapidly, and today represents one of Pakistan's major industrial bases. Nevertheless, the evidence of Lahore's glorious past (notwithstanding events at partition) remain for everyone to see.

Best time to visit

Sightseeing in Lahore is definetely more fun during the cooler months of the year (October-March). In these months it is feasible to cover fairly long distances (for example The Mall to the Fort/Old City area) on foot, though at other times you will almost certainly need to flag down rickshaws.

Sights

Highlights So many to choose from, though the following should not be missed: Badshahi Mosque; Lahore Fort; Old City; Lahore Museum; Jahangir's Tomb; Shalimar Gardens. If you can only spare a day in Lahore, TDCP offer good value 'morning' and 'afternoon' tours of the city (see under 'tourist offices' below).

Badshahi Mosque

Built for the Emperor Aurangzeb in 1673-74, the Badshahi Mosque is Lahore's most striking building. Modelled on the great Jami Masjid in Delhi, it has an impressive 20 metres high gateway and a central prayer chamber

Lahore City

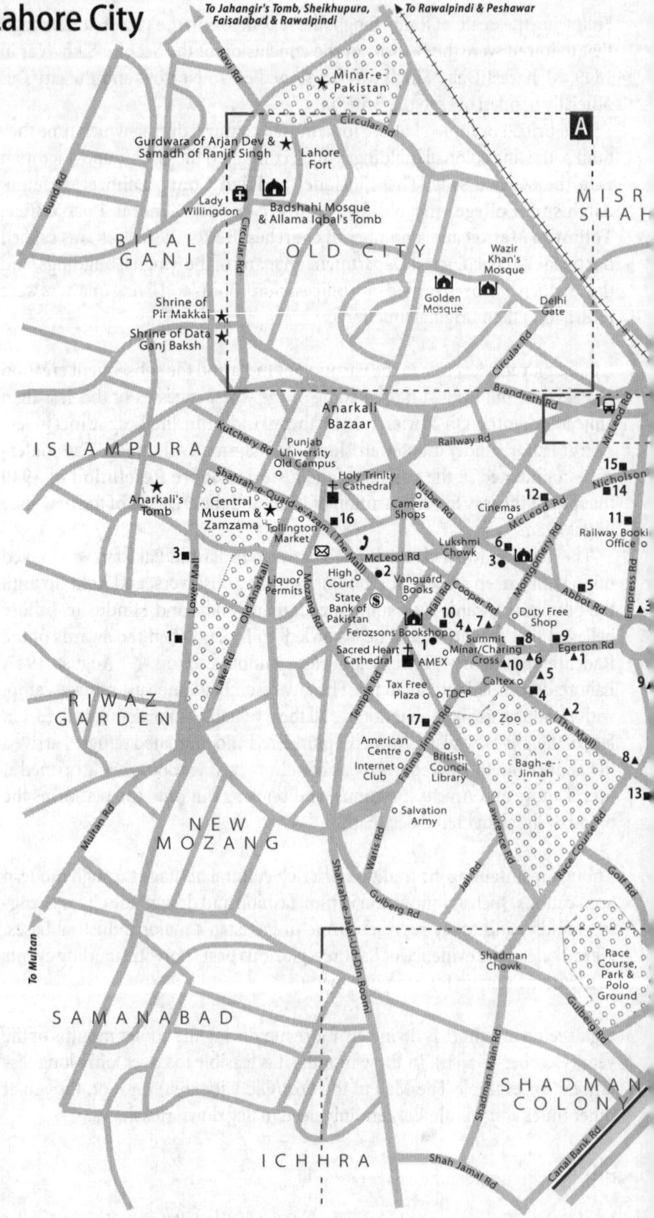

■ **Sleeping**

1 Al-Noor
2 Ambassador
3 Amer
4 Avari
5 Bahktawar
6 Bombay, National, Sanai, United
7 CC Motel
8 Faletti's & Tourist Information
9 Holiday Inn
10 Indus
11 Kashmir Palace
12 Orient
13 Pearl Continental
14 Shah Taj
15 Shobra
16 YMCA
17 YWCA

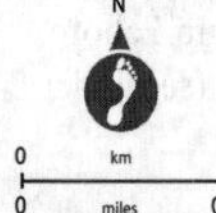

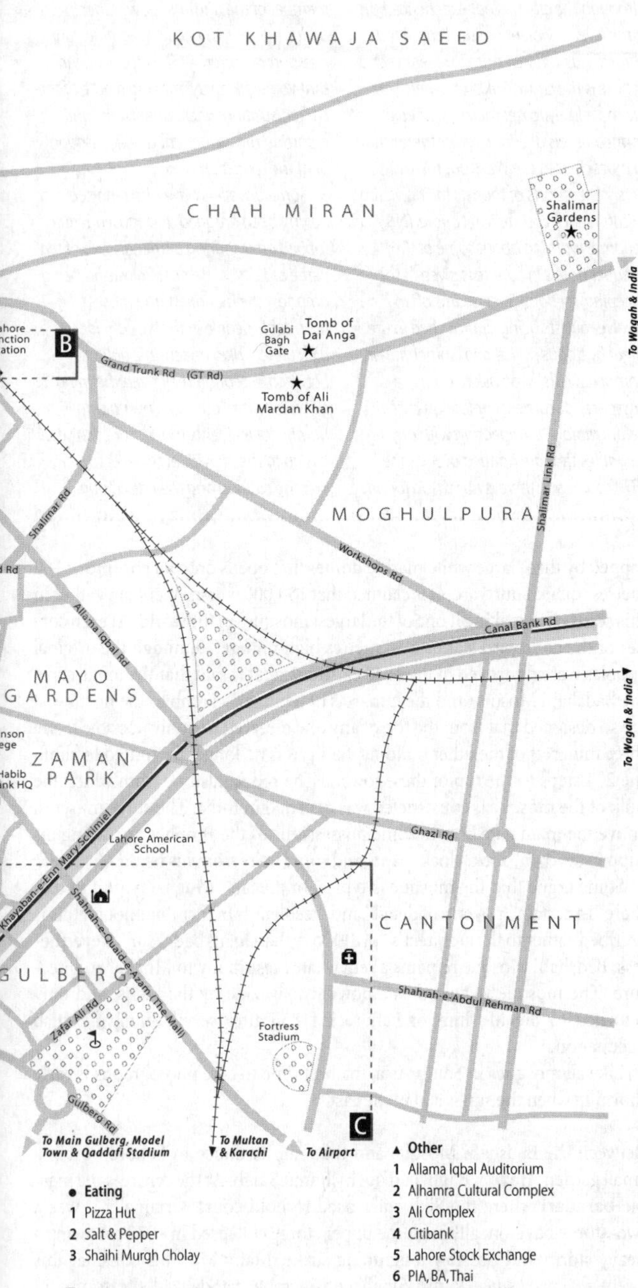

● **Eating**
1 Pizza Hut
2 Salt & Pepper
3 Shaihi Murgh Cholay

Transport
1 Australia Chowk/ McLeod Rd Flying Coaches

▲ **Other**
1 Allama Iqbal Auditorium
2 Alhamra Cultural Complex
3 Ali Complex
4 Citibank
5 Lahore Stock Exchange
6 PIA, BA, Thai
7 Provincial Assembly
8 Punjab Governor's Residence
9 US Consulate
10 WAPDA House

Related maps
A Lahore Old City, *page 266*
B Australia Chowk/ McLeod Rd, *page 274*
C Gulberg, Wahdat Colony & New Garden Town, *page 276*
Lahore Fort, *page 264*

Warning

Although the city has not experienced the same level of violent political crime that Karachi has suffered from in recent years, Lahore is the city in Pakistan where you are most likely to get tricked, robbed or conned. Levels of crime are far ***lower*** *than in most cities in the West, but there are persistent reports of tourists falling victim to confidence tricksters in Lahore. (****NB*** *A separate warning about some of the cheaper hotels in Lahore is given in the 'Sleeping' section.) Such scams often involve tourists being approached in the street by bogus policemen (sometimes in unmarked cars) who ask to examine passports, documents or foreign currency, before rapidly disappearing with any valuables that are handed over. As the PTDC point out, there is no reason for any member of the authorities, whether in uniform or not, to need to examine your passport or currency. They recommend that you walk away, making a note of the car registration where applicable, and reporting the incident at a police station or at the tourist office.*

Some travellers have also reported having been drugged and subsequently robbed after sharing a "friendly cup of tea" in the old city. With most Pakistanis being amongst the friendliest and most hospitable people in the world, it is difficult to strike the sensible balance between accepting their overwhelming generosity, and paranoia over a small number of incidents that occur each year. It is up to the individual traveller to exercise caution and their discretion.

topped by three large white marble domes that opens onto an enormous 160 metres square courtyard. It is claimed that 100,000 worshippers can gather in this courtyard, making it one of the largest mosques in the world. At each corner of the courtyard stands a 50 metres high minaret, although the original cupolas were destroyed in the 1840 earthquake. It is said that the minarets of the Badshahi Mosque and the minarets of Jahangir's Tomb to the northwest are so designed that from the top of any one minaret, it is only possible to see three minarets of the other building. Sadly, it is no longer permitted to climb the 204 steps to the top of these towers. The red sandstone from which the bulk of the mosque is constructed was quarried in India. The small museum above the main gate houses some possessions of the Prophet, including his slippers, turban, stick, cloak, pants and some hairs from his beard.

Some argue that the mosque is typical of the later Mughal period in that there is a certain "poverty of detail" and "feebleness of form", although this is ascribed rather to the architect's "orthodoxy than to his bad taste". Nevertheless, Badshahi Mosque remains a remarkable testimony to Mughal architecture. The mosque was used as a powder magazine by the Sikhs, and only returned to the Muslims of Lahore in 1856 after seven years of British occupation.

Like all mosques in South Asia, the best time to take photographs is early morning when the sun is still in the east.

Hazuri Bagh

Between the Badshahi Mosque and the main entrance to Lahore Fort is a small garden, **Hazuri Bagh**, laid out by Ranjit Singh. At the centre is the marble **baradari** where the Sikh ruler used to hold court. Originally it was a two-storey pavilion, although the upper storey collapsed in 1932 following a heavy storm and possibly a lightning strike. Many Muslims consider this sweet revenge, since Ranjit Singh considerably vandalized the tombs of Jahangir and Asaf Khan to procure the marble for this baradari.

In the southwest corner of the garden stands the **Mausoleum of Allama Iqbal** (1873-1938), Pakistan's greatest poet and expounder of the 'two-nation theory' that led to the creation of the Muslim homeland in South Asia. The red sandstone and marble tomb is built in a mixture of Afghan and Moorish styles, and was paid for by monies raised through public subscription. Following Partition, poor relations between India and Pakistan made it difficult to import the Jaipur sandstone to complete construction, and the tomb lay unfinished for several years. The *ta'weez* of the tomb is of lapis, a gift from Afghanistan, and is engraved with verses from the Qu'ran. The walls of the mausoleum are decorated with couplets from some of Iqbal's *ghazals*.

Gurdwara of Arjan Dev

Just to the north of the Hazuri Bagh is the **Gurdwara of Arjan Dev**, the fifth Guru who completed the *Adi Granth* (the Holy Book of the Sikhs), and initiated work on the Golden Temple at Amritsar. Built by Ranjit Singh, the gurdwara is made conspicuous by its heavily gilded fluted dome, and is a centre of Sikh pilgrimage. The interior ceiling is said to be richly decorated with tracery and inlay, although the complex is only open to Sikhs. Legend suggests that the Guru was swallowed by the waves whilst bathing in the Ravi in 1606, although others suggest that he was executed for supporting Jahangir's rival Khusro.

Also within a walled enclosure is the *Samadh* that holds the ashes of Ranjit Singh. Built in a mixture of Hindu and Muslim styles, the building is also said to have a fine interior. The two buildings are best seen from the vantage point of Lahore Fort.

Lahore Fort

With its counterparts in Delhi and Agra, **Lahore Fort** represents one of the three great forts built by the Mughals. Covering a vast area, some 375 metres by 300 metres, the fort contains some of the most impressive secular Mughal buildings in South Asia. Embellished with carved red sandstone, marble, *pietra dura* work, glazed coloured and *kashi* tile work, plus frescoes depicting royal pleasures, it is more a palace than a fort.

It is thought that there have been a succession of earlier forts on this site dating back at least to 1180, although the basis of what we see today was begun during the reign of Akbar. Later additions were made by Jahangir, Shah Jahan and Aurangzeb. The fort was later occupied by the Sikhs and then the British.

Tour of the fort

The following route takes in all the key buildings. Open daily Summer 0700-1930, Winter 0830-1730 (Rs 4).

Enter the fort through the **Alamgiri Gate (4)**. Built by Aurangzeb in 1674, it is a massive gateway flanked by semi-octagonal bastions overlooking the Hazuri Bagh. There is a small souvenir shop **(5)** just inside the gate.

If you walk uphill and then turn left down the ramp, you come to the **Shah Burj Gate (6)**. This entrance is credited to Shah Jahan, and was built for the exclusive use of royalty. The Persian inscription dates the gate to 1631-32, and was built under the supervision of Shah Jahan's architect, Mamur Khan. The elaborate *kashi* tile work shows a marked Persian influence, although the painted frescoes are a reminder of the Hindu craftsmanship incorporated into Mughal architecture.

Inside the Shah Burj Gate, to the left, is the **Hathi Paer (7)**, or Elephant Path. The 58 steps provide access for the royal entourage, mounted on elephants, to the private royal apartments.

At the top of the Hathi Paer is the **Shish Mahal (8)**, or Palace of Mirrors. Enclosed in a courtyard with a tank and fountains at its centre, the Shish Mahal was used as the royal residence of Shah Jahan, and is one of the most beautiful buildings in the fort. It is decorated with convex mirror mosaic, known as *aiena kari*, set in arabesque patterns of white cement on the ceiling, walls and spandrels of the arches. The ceiling is supported by six pairs of slender fluted pillars. The fretted marble *jalies*, or screens, are of exceptional craftsmanship.

On the west side of the courtyard is the marble pavilion known as **Naulakha Bunga (9)**, so named because it reputedly cost Shah Jahan nine lakh rupees (Rs 900,000) to build. It is decorated in a style known as *pietra dura*, inlaid with semi-precious stones such as agate, jade and lapiz.

Continuing along the north wall of the fort, you reach the **Khilwat Khana (10)**, or private sleeping chamber of Shah Jahan. Outside is the **Paien Bagh** (Ladies' Garden), used exclusively by the women of the harem. The paths were said to be lined with fragrance giving flowers, cypresses and dwarf fruit bearing trees.

Opposite the garden is the **Hamman-e-Sheik (12)**, the royal bath house. The building has a dressing room, (**Jama Khana**), a warm room (**Nim Garm**), and a hot room, **Garm**. It is based on the design of a Turkish bath, with an underground heating system.

Shah Jahan's Quadrangle (13) is at the centre of the north wall, and comprises a white marble colonnaded pavilion, **Diwan-e-Khas (14)** (Hall of Private Audience) and the **Khawabagh-e-Shah Jahan (16)**, or private quarters of Shah Jahan. The Diwan-e-Khas was built in 1645, and was used by the king to receive state dignitaries and distinguished guests. Next to the Khawabagh-e-Shah Jahan is the Fort Curator's office, and the new Lahore

Lahore Fort

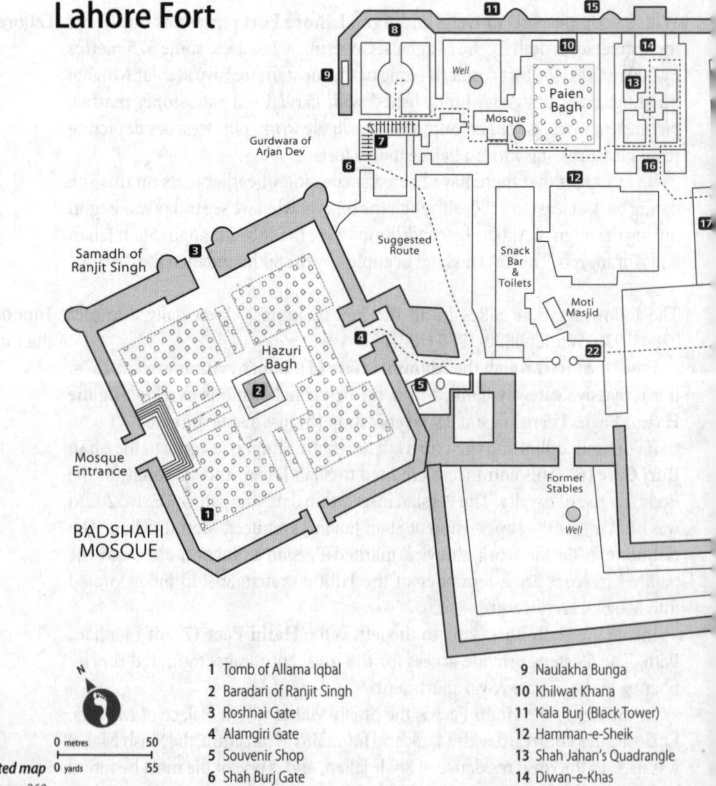

1 Tomb of Allama Iqbal
2 Baradari of Ranjit Singh
3 Roshnai Gate
4 Alamgiri Gate
5 Souvenir Shop
6 Shah Burj Gate
7 Hathi Paer
8 Shish Mahal
9 Naulakha Bunga
10 Khilwat Khana
11 Kala Burj (Black Tower)
12 Hamman-e-Sheik
13 Shah Jahan's Quadrangle
14 Diwan-e-Khas
15 Lal Burj (Red Tower)
16 Khawabagh-e-Shah Jahan

Related map
Lahore City, page 260

Fort Museum **(17)** (Summer 0830-1230 1430-1730, Winter 0900-1600).

In the northeast corner of the fort is **Jahangir's Quadrangle (18)**. Started by Akbar but completed in 1618 by Jahangir, it is flanked to the east and west by carved red sandstone columns. The quadrangle measures 112 metres by 74 metres, and has a central tank and fountains. The British built tennis court has long since gone. The main building to the north of the quadrangle is the **Bari Khawabagh-e Jahangir (19)** that was used by Jahangir as a sleeping chamber, but now houses relics of the Mughal period.

The south side of the quadrangle is completed by the **Diwan-e Aam (20)**, or Hall of Public Audience. The rear court, or **Daulat Khana-e-Khas-o-Aam (21)**, was built during the reign of Akbar, and has at its centre the **Jaha Roka** (State Balcony). Here, the Emperor held court and granted audience to the nobility. The rest of the Diwan-e-Aam was built by Shah Jahan, and comprises 40 pillars standing on a raised rectangular platform.

Proceeding back towards the main gate, the first major building encountered is the **Makatib Khana (22)**, or Secretariat. Built by Jahangir, it is here that the *muharirs* (clerks) kept the palace records.

The final building of significance is the **Moti Masjid**, so named because of its pearl-shaped dome. This white marble mosque, built by Shah Jahan but recently renovated, is in keeping with those at Delhi and Agra.

Next to the mosque are the snack bar and toilets.

Punjab

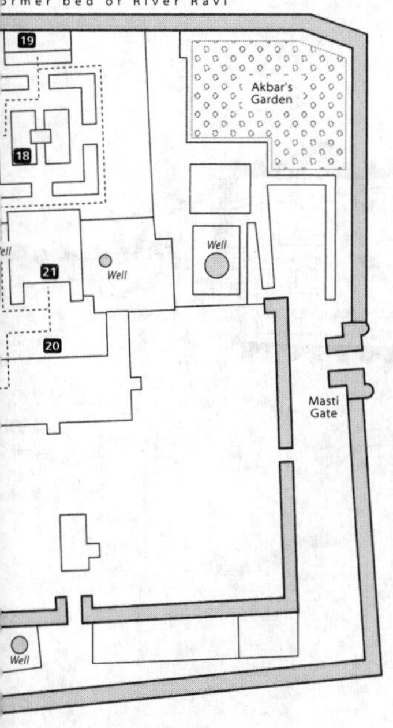

17 Fort Curator's Office & New Museum
18 Jahangir's Quadrangle
19 Bari Khawabagh-e-Jahangir
20 Diwan-e-Aam
21 Daulat Khana-e-Khas-e-Aam
22 Makatib Khana

------ Suggested Route

The Old City

Most of Lahore's key Mughal monuments are located in and around the old walled city. The original nine metres high defensive walls were built during the reign of Akbar, and allowed daytime access to the city through 12 large gates. The Sikh ruler Ranjit Singh later strengthened the crumbling walls, and added a defensive moat to the north.

Although only some of the 12 original gates remain, the old city is still very much alive and it is fascinating to wander through the narrow bazaars. A good route to follow enters through the **Delhi Gate** to the east, although it is almost inevitable that you will get lost at some stage. Immediately inside the Delhi Gate is a useful tourist information centre (housed in a former baths complex). Continuing along the narrow bazaar, you come to the **Wazir Khan Mosque** on the left. The mosque was built in 1643 by the physician **Alamud Din Ansari**, a native of Chiniot. History records that he was rewarded for curing Jahangir's wife Nur Jahan of a foot malady, and later rose to the position of *Wazir* during the reign of Shah Jahan, taking the title of **Wazir Khan**. The mosque is renowned for its use and execution of inlaid pottery decoration in the wall panelling. Close inspection reveals that each section of detail is a separate piece of pot or tile, and the work is strictly inlay and not painted decoration. There are also superb arabesque frescoes in the interior. The mosque is divided into five compartments, each surmounted by a dome, and opening onto the courtyard. A tall minaret stands at each corner of the courtyard. For some small baksheesh, one of the small boys will take you on to the roof of the gate for a fine panoramic view of the old city. The shrine below the mosque's courtyard bears the tomb of the Sufi saint Hazrat Mira Basha (Sayed Ishak Shah).

Continuing through the bazaar, you come to a fork. The right fork leads to Lahore Fort and Badshahi Mosque, the left leads to the **Golden Mosque**. Built in 1753 by Bikhari Khan, the Golden or **Sunehri Mosque** stands on a raised plinth, and gets its name from its three large gilded domes and gold capped 10 metre minarets. Legend suggests that Bikhari Khan was a favourite at the court of the former ruler of Lahore, Mir Mannu. However, following the demise of the Mir, his widow had her maid servants beat Bikhari Khan to death with their shoes!

Continuing west, the route passes through the fascinating **Brass Bazaar**, before turning south (left) into the colourful **Shah Alami Market**. It includes the Kashmiri Bazaar, Suha Bazaar, Dabbi Bazaar and Chatta Bazaar where craftsmen still work with copper, brass and silver. You can exit the old city south through the old site of the **Shah Alami Gate**.

Lahore Old City

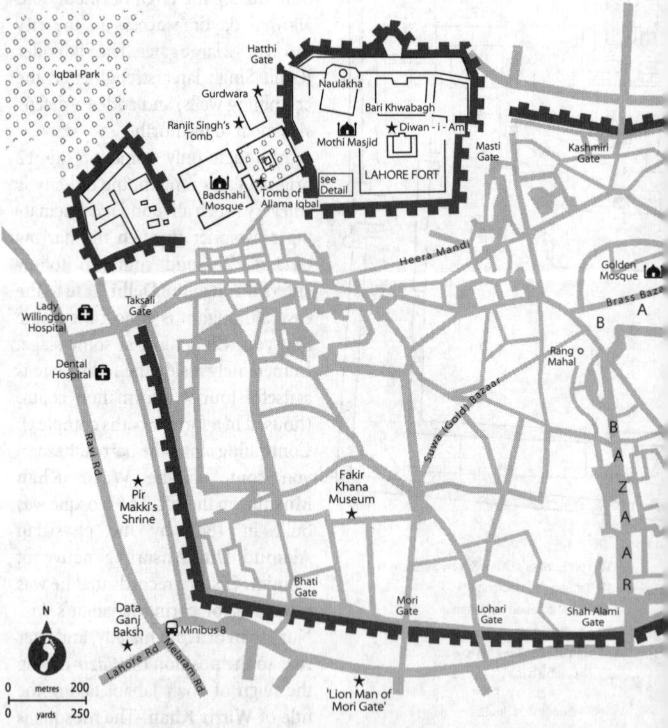

Also within the old city walls is the **Faqir Khana Museum**, approached through the **Bhati Gate**. This private museum belongs to the family of Faqir Azizuddin who was Ranjit Singh's Foreign Minister. It is a treasure house of artistic masterpieces including paintings, sculptures, porcelain, carpets and ancient manuscripts.

Just outside the Mori Gate is the self-styled **'Lion Man of Mori Gate'**, a medical "quack" who, incredibly, has two fully grown Asiatic lions in a small cage in his shop. He sells 'medicine' for "sexual vigour" (one tablet to be taken at night with milk)! Another interesting part of the Old City is **Heera Mandi**, Lahore's traditional red-light district. If demand is sufficient, TDCP will arrange tours to see the 'classical musicians' and 'traditional dancing girls' perform here.

Shrine of Data Ganj Baksh

Located a little to the west of Bhati Gate is the **Shrine of Data Ganj Baksh**, often referred to as the the patron saint of Lahore. A renowned Islamic scholar and author of the classic book on Sufism 'Kashful Mahjoob', he came to Lahore in the early 11th century and remained there until his death in 1072 (although some recent biographies place his death in 1092). Although born Abul Hasan Ali, he was given the title Data Ganj Baksh – 'Bestower of treasures' – in recognition of his help amongst the poor and needy. An inscription above the main gate translates: "He who calls at your shrine, Never returns disappointed". Today there are several buildings attached to the shrine which serve the public, such as a dispensary, hospital, an organisation to help destitute women, and a public kitchen where food is distributed to the poor.

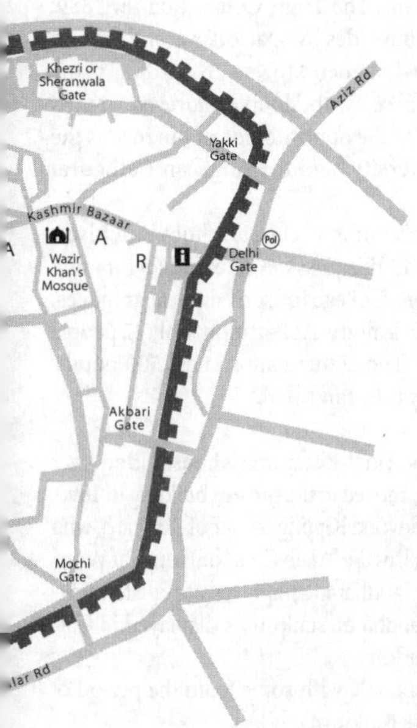

The shrine is a small octagonal marble building, with white marble supporting pillars and intricately carved screens through which to view the sarcophagus. The original mausoleum was built by the Ghaznavid Sultan Ibrahim, although later embellishments have been added by Akbar, Aurangzeb and several dignitaries in the employ of the Sikh rulers.

Adjoining the tomb is a large marble courtyard, with arched domed cloisters on the north and south sides. To the west is a splendid modern mosque. The entrance is in black mirrored glass, cut into the shape of three domes, reflecting the image of the shrine opposite. Two tall rocket-shaped minarets stand on either side. The carpet inside is in the style of Mughal frescoes, and the mihrab wall has extensive wooden panelling. The basement area is a popular place to read and discuss the Qu'ran.

The shrine is always busy, although visitor numbers peak on Thursday evenings, and during the saint's Urs (20th Safar, early June

1999, late May 2000). Suitably dressed visitors are made very welcome. Don't miss this place.

Shrine of Pir Makki On Ravi Road, just to the north of Data Ganj Baksh's shrine, is the tomb of Aziz-uz-Din, a Muslim holy man who came to Lahore in the closing period of Ghaznavid rule. Because he came from Mecca he became known as **Pir Makki**.

Anarkali's Tomb In the grounds of the Punjab Secretariat on the Lower Mall stands **Anarkali's Tomb**. Legend has it that Anarkali (literally Pomegranate Blossom) was either a wife of the Emperor Akbar, or a favourite in his harem. Catching a glimpse of a smile pass between Anarkali and his son Prince Salim (later Emperor Jahangir), Akbar suspected them of having an affair and in a fit of fury had Anarkali buried alive. When Jahangir later became Emperor he raised a mausoleum to Anarkali, engraving a mournful Persian couplet on the cenotaph: "Ah, could I behold the face of my beloved once again, I would offer thanks unto God until the day of Resurrection".

Unfortunately this romantic tale has been dismissed as a piece of fiction, originating from Finch, an English traveller who visited Lahore in 1611 on an indigo selling trip. The tomb is thought to contain the body of Sahiba Jamal, a wife of Jahangir.

The tomb is on a hexagonal base, with a domed octagonal tower at each corner and a huge central dome supported on eight arches. It is now in a poor state of repair, having been previously used as a residence of Ranjit Singh's son Kharak, and later by the Italian General Ventura whilst in the employ of Ranjit Singh. The British converted it into an office, and then into the 'Mother Church' of the diocese until the cathedral was completed.

The Mall Lahore has some of the finest examples of the Gothic-Victorian-Mughal style of architecture on the sub-continent. Many are positioned along **The Mall**, since renamed Shahrah-e-Quaid-e-Azam. The **High Court**, built in 1889, features a central hall surrounded on four sides by spacious verandahs and topped by two 30 metre towers and two 20 metre towers. Next door is the splendid red brick **General Post Office**, with double storeyed arched verandahs and domed corner towers. On the opposite side of the road is the red brick old campus of **Punjab University**, and the Anglican **Cathedral Church of the Resurrection**.

Further east along The Mall is Pakistan's most exclusive school, **Aitchison College**. Set in its own extensive grounds, this classic Anglo-Indian building was established by the British as a Chief's College for sons of local grandees, most of whom were remnants of the Sikh Empire. At Partition, only 42 people were left in the school, including staff. Today there are some 2,500 pupils. Aitchison's most famous recent old boy is Imran Khan.

Lahore Central Museum The museum is the oldest and one of the best in Pakistan and is housed in another fine colonial building. Founded in 1864, it moved to the present building in 1890. The museum's first curator was John Lockwood Kipling, father of Rudyard, who referred to the museum in his classic "Kim" as the 'Ajaib Ghar' or House of Wonders. Some of the collections, notably the Gandharan sculptures, are outstanding.

The pride of the collection are the **Gandharan** sculptures displayed in Gallery 2, including the famous 'Fasting Buddha'.

The **Coin Collection** is extremely valuable with some from the period of Alexander the Great, the Guptas and the Buddhists.

■ *Open daily except Saturday, the first Wednesday of the month and the following: Eid-ul-Fitr, Eid-ul-Zoha, Eid e Milad-un-Nabi, 9th and 10th*

Muharram, 1 May, 11 September. Winter (1 October-15 April): 0900-1600. Summer (16 April-30 September): 0800-1700. Times may change without notice. Entry Rs 5, camera Rs 10, video Rs 50. Free conducted tours and a good printed guide available at the entrance.

Zam zama

Standing on a traffic island in the road outside the museum is the famous **Zam zama** gun. "He sat, in defiance of municipal orders, astride the gun Zam-Zammah on her brick platform opposite the old Ajaib-Gher – the Wonder House, as natives call the Lahore Museum. Who holds Zam-Zammah, that 'fire-breathing dragon', holds the Punjab; for the great green-bronze piece is always first of the conqueror's loot." (Rudyard Kipling, "Kim", 1901).

Immortalized by Kipling in the opening lines of "Kim", this mighty cannon is so named because on firing, it resembles a lion's roar. Cast in copper and bronze collected as public levy in 1757 under the orders of Ahmad Shah Durrani, the gun saw action in the Battle of Panipat in 1761. It was later acquired by Ranjit Singh and became something of a symbol of the Sikh Empire, although it was badly damaged in the Multan campaign of 1818. It was subsequently retired to Lahore Fort, and then moved to its present site in 1870.

At the east end of The Mall, at its junction with Fatima Jinnah Road, is the **Summit Minar**. Standing in a small park known informally as **Charing Cross**, this 50 metre minar was opened in 1977 by Zulfikar Ali Bhutto to commemorate the Islamic Summit held in Lahore in February 1974. At the base of the engraved marble obelisk is a small arcade displaying gifts from the participating countries. The small pavilion houses a Qu'ran inscribed with gold leaf.

Parks

In contrast to the densely packed streets of the old city, Lahore has a large number of open spaces and some notable parks. To the north of the Badshahi Mosque is **Iqbal Park**, a popular recreational spot on weekends and holidays. At the centre is the **Minar-e-Pakistan**, a 60 metre tower built to mark the spot where the Lahore Resolution of 1940 was passed. There are fine views of the fort, Badshahi Mosque and the whole city from the top. Using the stairs negates the need to join the long queues for the lift, and also gives access to the less crowded viewing platforms at different levels. In typical Pakistani style, the lift at this national monument is operated by a man sitting on top of the cage, hot-wiring the lift motor.

The **Bagh-e-Jinnah**, formerly the Lawrence Gardens, were laid out off The Mall in 1860. They are a popular leisure spot for Lahore residents. At the centre is the former Montgomery Hall, now the **Jinnah Library**.

Next to the Bagh-e-Jinnah is **Lahore Zoo**. The zoological gardens were laid out on this eight hectare site in 1872, and contain the usual collection of depressed animals that would be better off dead. The Punjab Wildlife Dept who run the zoo are particularly proud of the bear hill and elephant/rhino house that are based on those at London Zoo. Sadly, these style of structures are now considered by progressive zoos as being unsuitable for keeping animals.

The **Race Course Park** to the southeast of the Bagh-e-Jinnah is popular with families at weekends, as well as being a venue for **polo** matches (check local press for fixtures). The polo played here is much more akin to the sort that Prince Charles plays in Windsor than to the variety played in the north of Pakistan.

Shaukat Khanum Memorial Cancer Hospital and Research Centre

Most people will know Imran Khan through their newspaper's sports section. He was, after all, one of the greatest all-rounders that cricket has ever seen. When he retired in 1992, he was one of only four men to have scored 3,000 runs and taken 300 wickets in Test cricket (3,807 runs at an average of 37.69 and 362 wickets at 22.81 each). His finest sporting moment came in Melbourne in March 1992, when, as captain of Pakistan, he lifted the World Cup.

Others know Imran through their newspaper's society and gossip pages. As one English newspaper once put it, "hapless English, Australian and West Indian opponents were by no means his only conquests. Newspaper cuttings files bulge with débutantes, film starlets and aristocats who have been caught by the wickedly handsome Imran". Even his marriage to Jemima, the "beautiful blond daughter of tycoon Sir James Goldsmith", made headlines in countries with no interest in cricket. The couple now live in Lahore's upmarket Zaman Park with their son (plus another child due as we go to press).

However, Imran Khan's greatest achievment comes far away from the cricket field, and is rarely mentioned when the (British) tabloid press are looking to do a hatchet job on him. In 1985, Imran's mother died of cancer. Had the illness been diagnosed earlier, it is possible that she could have been successfully treated. Realizing the lack of diagnostic facilities in Pakistan, particularly for the poor and those unable to afford treatment abroad, Imran set about raising funds to build a modern yet affordable cancer hospital in Pakistan. On 24 December 1994, having raised almost $40mn, the Shaukat Khanum Memorial Cancer Hospital and Research Centre (named in memory of Imran's mother) opened its doors. The remarkable fact is that much of the money raised through public subscription came not from Pakistan's upper and middle classes, but from the country's poor, with the average donation being around Rs 200. Such is Imran's popularity and trustworthiness amongst his countrymen.

The objectives of the hospital are to provide the highest quality diagnostic and therapeutic care to patients with cancer, irrespective of their ability to pay. The hospital also aims to be at the cutting edge of innovation and involved in every aspect of cancer research. In the first 2½ years, the hospital has registered and examined 15,914 patients and received 81,783 outpatient visits (with 7,743 patients found to have cancer). 20 percent of the patients have been children, with over 300 million Rupees having been spent on free treatment (around 65 percent of patients).

The annual running costs of the hospital exceed US$7.5mn, much of which is raised through public donation. Donations can be sent to: Shaukat Khanum Memorial Cancer Hospital and Research Centre, 7-A, Block R-3, MA Johar Town, Lahore, T042-5180725, E skmt@lhr.comsats.net.pk; Imran Khan Cancer Appeal, (reg. charity no. 1000580), 171a, High Street Kensington, London, W8 6SH, UK, T0171-9374141, F0171-9374142; Imran Khan Cancer Appeal, (IRS No 13-3626299), 440 Ashland Avenue, Lexington, Kentucky, USA 40502, T1606-2665330, F160-62695763, E nkburko@pop.uky.edu.

Short excursions from Lahore

Jahangir's Tomb Across the River Ravi, seven kilometres northwest of Lahore, is the **Tomb of Jahangir**, the Mughal emperor who ruled from 1605 to 1627. He died at Rajauri in Kashmir, but expressed a wish to be buried in Lahore and is now the only Mughal emperor buried in Pakistan. 10 years after the emperor's death his son, Shah Jahan, constructed the mausoleum under the supervision of Jahangir's widow, **Nur Jahan**.

Sited in the attractive walled garden **Dil Kusha**, the mausoleum is a single-storey square structure of decorated marble on red sandstone, with four corner minarets and a projecting entrance at the centre of each side. The corner minarets rise to 30 metres in five stages, are inlaid with zigzag bands of variegated marbles and blocks of yellow stone, and topped with white marble cupolas. Similar in style to the Itimad ad Daulah (built in Agra by Nur Jahan for her father), the disproportion between the height of the base and the minarets gives the tomb an odd appearance – almost as if another storey or a large central dome is missing.

The building is divided into a series of vaulted compartments, with rosettes and arabesques over the arches. The interior is embellished with frescoes, *pietra dura* inlay and coloured marble. In the inner chamber is the white

Punjab

marble sarcophagus, decorated with the black marble inlay, listing the 99 names of God. The Persian inscription reads: "The illuminated resting place of His Majesty, Nur-ud-Din Mohammad Jahangir Badshah AH 1037". About 10 years ago the River Ravi broke its banks, flooding the tomb; the 'high tide' mark can still be seen on the walls about half a metre from the floor.

The original edifice of the tomb was far grander, but Ranjit Singh removed the choicest ornaments to adorn the Golden Temple at Amritsar. At one stage it was even used as the residence of Amise, a French general in the Sikh army.

Outside the Dil Kusha garden is the **Akbari Serai**, a Traveller's Rest House of the same period. The open courtyard is flanked by a raised terrace and 180 cells, each fronted by a verandah. The serai has two grand gateways to the north and south, and a red sandstone three domed mosque to the west. In the enclosure beyond the mosque is the **Tomb of Asaf Khan**. Brother of Nur Jahan, and father of Mumtaz Mahal (the lady of the Taj Mahal), Asaf Khan was Shah Jahan's Prime Minister. Following his death in 1641, Shah Jahan built this tomb to house Asaf Khan's remains. Octagonal in shape, with a high bulbous dome, the tomb was one of the main victims of Ranjit Singh's recycling methods.

Further west, across the railway tracks, are the remain's of **Nur Jahan's Tomb**. She died in 1645 and was buried in the mausoleum that she had erected for herself. Once richly decorated with floral fresco paintings on lime plaster, most of the embellishments were removed by the Sikhs. The minarets have gone, the marble platform and the sandstone facing are new, and the tomb is little more than a shell.

■ *Rs 4 entrance. Buses 6 and 23 from the railway station take about 20 minutes to reach the tombs, although it is easier to go by rickshaw or taxi (Rs 50).*

Kamran Baradari On a small island in the Ravi, just below the new Ravi Bridge, is the Kamran Baradari, a small pleasure pavilion built by Mirza Kamran, son of Babar. It is a popular picnic spot and can be reached by hired pleasure-boat.

Shalimar Gardens

The 'Shalimar' ('abode of love') Gardens were laid out in 1637 on the instructions of Emperor Shah Jahan. Designed by Ali Mardan Khan, it was a royal pleasure garden. Over 450 metres long and enclosed within high walls for privacy, with its marble pavilions with carvings, *pietra dura* inlay work and fresco paintings, a marble waterfall, ornamental ponds and over 400 fountains, the gardens provided an alternative residence for the royal family. Sadly they have nothing of their former beauty.

Jahangir's Tomb

Char baghs The gardens were laid out on the principle of two "char baghs" (quartered gardens) separated by a terrace in the centre. Water tanks drawing from the canal supplied water up to the height of the highest level, which then cascaded down. The highest 'Farah Baksh', reserved for the royal family, is where you enter the gardens, although when it was laid out the entrance was at the other end, enabling privacy to be maintained at each higher level. This top terrace is divided into quarters, but the original decorations on the once grand buildings have virtually disappeared.

The Emperor's sleeping chamber where you enter, the pavilion to house the *harem* and the ladies in waiting to the west and the *Diwan-e-Khas* (Hall of Private Audience) to the east, were the finest buildings of the garden. Steps lead down to the next terrace, about four metres lower, and water was channelled down to the water tank and numerous fountains in the centre. The royal entertainers performed for the Emperor who sat on the marble platform here. To the east are the Turkish Baths. The lowest terrace contained the *Diwan-e-Am* (Hall of Public Audience). The garden was stocked with flowering plants and decorative shrubs from all corners of the Mughal Empire.

The Mughals chose to be 'formal' in their design rather than 'natural', "the aim being to discipline nature and not to imitate it" as Percy Brown puts it. "A regular arrangement of squares, often subdivided into smaller squares to form the favourite figure *char bagh* or fourfold plot".

Punjab

■ *The Shalimar Gardens are located eight kilometres east of Lahore. Open daily: Summer 0800-1800, Winter 0800-1630. Entrance Rs 4. For some small baksheesh (Rs 15) the chowkidar may turn the fountains on for you! Chilled drinks are on sale in the Sikh guest house which was added in the 19th century. The toilets are near the Turkish Baths. You can reach the gardens by driving east down GT Road or from Jahangir's Tomb on the Bund Road. Approximately 20 minutes from the Railway Station on Bus 3, 12 or 17. It is best visited when the flowers are in bloom in February and March. The shallow niches in the marble wall (a feature of Mughal architecture) were used for hundreds of lamps. The gardens are illuminated on Wednesday and Saturday nights.*

Other monuments on the GT Road

On the GT Road on the way to the Shalimar Gardens are a number of other Mughal buildings. To the left, just past the Museum of Science and Technology, is the **Gulabi Bagh Gate**. Constructed in 1655 by the Persian noble and Admiral of the Fleet **Mirza Sultan Beg**, the gate stands at the entrance to the long since disappeared **Gulabi Bagh**, or Rose Garden.

Inside the remains of the Rose Garden, to the north, is the **Tomb of Dai Anga**. Known as Zebun Nisa Begum, she was the wet-nurse of Shah Jahan. The tomb is dated to 1671, is rectangular in shape with a central dome and four corner towers. The decorative mosaic work that adorned the tomb was another victim of Ranjit Singh.

Across the GT Road is the **Tomb of Ali Mardan Khan**. Formerly Governor of Qandahar under the Safvids, he migrated to India and presented himself at the court of Shah Jahan in 1631. A skilled administrator and engineer, he built a number of canals during his tenure as Governor of Punjab, including the one that feeds the Shalimar Gardens. The mausoleum was built following his death in 1657.

Essentials

Sleeping

Warning Be very careful of the cheap hotels around the station area, particularly in Brandreth (Nishtar), Railway and McLeod Roads. Persistent reports speak of theft from rooms, sometimes involving drugged food and drinks. Other travellers tell of having to pay large bribes to police after having drugs planted in their rooms. As a very general rule, hotels that send touts to the bus and railway station are **not** recommended. Further, when checking into a hotel, it is useful to memorize all your passport and visa details, so that you don't have to refer to, and reveal the location of, your money belt. Be suspicious of hotel managers that demand to inspect your passport themselves. If once you're in your room there are repeated knocks at your door with requests to 're-check your passport', 'check the bathroom's plumbing', 'make sure you have a towel/soap' etc, then it may be time to pack your bag, and leave quickly. It may be worth paying slightly more, and staying at a more reputable hotel for the duration of your stay in Lahore.

More expensive hotels

■ *on maps*
Price codes:
see inside front cover

L *Avari*, 87 Shahrah-e-Quaid-e-Azam, T6310646, F6365367, E avarigst@lht.comsats.net.pk. All the facilities associated with a top flight hotel including pool, business centre and choice of restaurants (see below). **L** *Holiday Inn*, 25-26 Egerton Road, T6310077, F6314515, E holiday@inn.brain.net.pk. 120 rooms, some suites, full facilities including rooftop pool, separate sex gyms, choice of restaurants. **L** *Pearl*

Australia Chowk/ McLeod Rd

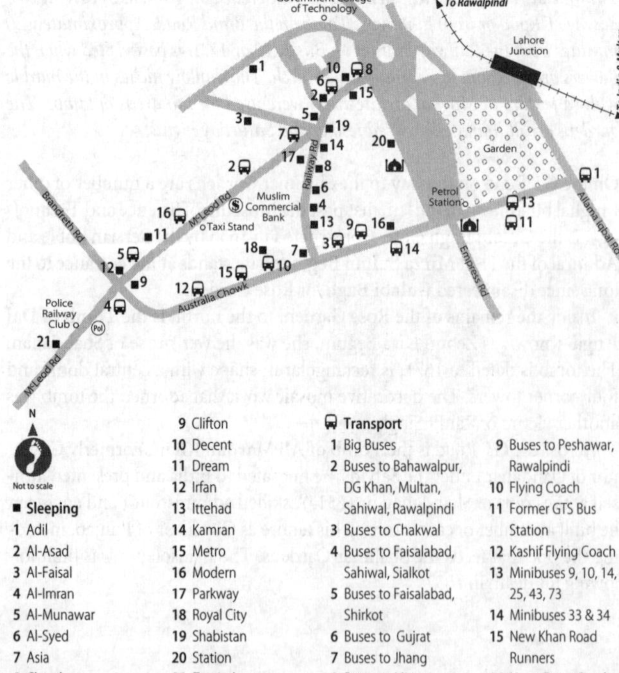

Related map
***Lahore City**, page 260*

Lahore street names

Post Partition, many of Lahore's colonial street names have been changed, though many Lahorites still use the former British names. Key changes include: The Mall/ Shahrah-e-Quaid-e-Azam; Queens Road/Fatimah Jinnah Road; Brandreth Road/Nishtar Road; Empress Road/Shahrah-e-Bin-Baddis; Ferozpur Road/Shahrah-e-Jalal-ud-Din Roomi. Main Boulevard Gulberg is often referred to as Main Gulberg.

Continental, Shahrah-e-Quaid-e-Azam, T6360210, F6362760, E pclhr@hotel.lhr.erum.com.pk. Lahore's most luxurious hotel, particularly the spectacular new wing (the plain exterior of the building belies the opulence inside), full range of facilities including pool, separate sex gyms, tennis, squash, choice of 6 restaurants (see below), cyber café, business centre, highly recommended if you can afford it.

A *Ambassador*, 7 Davis Rd, T6316820, F6301868. Large hotel, central a/c, dish TV, restaurant; **A *Best Western***, 36 Liberty Market, Gulberg III, T5758811, F5712800, E bwsl@brain.net.pk. Away from city centre, central a/c, dish TV, minibar, 24 hour room service and coffee shop, business centre, but without real feeling of luxury. **A *Faletti's***, Egerton Rd, T6363946, F6364819. Fine old colonial hotel that has very much gone to seed, rooms quite large, well furnished, dish TV, fridge, a/c, but rather musty and smelly, now looking hugely overpriced, even the *Ava Gardner Suite* as used by "the renowned showbiz of Hollywood" during the filming of 'Bhawany Junction' in 1955 (the last time the hotel was decorated?) is poor value.

B *Amer*, Lower Mall, T7115015, F7115013. Central a/c, dish TV, fridge, room service, restaurant, car rental, airport pick-up. **B *Sanai***, 1 Abbot Rd, T6316501, F6317047. Large, well furnished central a/c rooms, modern bathrooms, though hotel permeated by a musty smell, officious security guard.

Mid-price hotels

C *Bakhtawar*, 11 Abbot Rd, T6316761, F6316762. Large a/c rooms, some with dish TV, fridge, reasonable value. **C *Indus***, 56 The Mall, T6302856. Recently refurbished, a/c, dish TV, fridge, attached bath, reasonable rooms, rates are negotiable and this could be good value if you get a 25 percent discount. **C *Bombay***, 1 Abbot Rd. Under construction. **C *National***, 1 Abbot Rd, T6367184, F6363152. Large rooms, modern tiled bath, a/c, dish TV, fridge, 24 hour room service, 2 restaurants, reasonable value though street-facing rooms are noisy (even on upper floors). **C *Rise***, 22 Commercial Zone, Liberty Market, T5750695. A/c, dish TV, phone, restaurant. **C *Shah Taj***, 13 Nicholson Rd, T6313821, F6279174. A/c rooms are clean with dish TV, modern tiled bath, but many windowless, non a/c rooms are smaller and rather dirty. **C *United***, 1 Abbot Rd, T6366046. A/c, dish TV, fridge, but bathrooms rather basic given the price.

D *CC Motel*, 105a Shahrah-e-Quaid-e-Azam, T6360346. Rather run-down motel, a/c, better value if you can negotiate a big discount, rather remote. **D *Kashmir Palace***, 14 Empress Rd, T6316700, F6316709. "Hot water, friendly and helpful staff, TV and phone in all rooms, clean and safe". **D *Orient***, 74 McLeod Rd, T7223906. Carpeted rooms clean enough, bathrooms basic but OK, some a/c rooms in **C** category, no restaurant but room service available, not bad value. **D *Shobra***, 55 Nicholson Rd, T6364959, F6374797. Reasonable a/c rooms, though noisy location above bus company.

Budget hotels

E *Al Noor*, Rewaz Gdns, Lower Mall, T7115281. Some a/c, restaurant, rather run-down. **E *Asia***, Railway Rd, T6366449. Average rooms, attached bath, staff a bit pushy but OK. **E *Clifton***, Australia Chowk/McLeod Rd, T6366740. Reasonable rooms, clean attached bath, some a/c rooms (**C**), one of the better hotels in the area. **E *Metro***, Railway Rd. Cheap rooms, attached bath, reasonable value. **E *Parkway***, 1 McLeod Rd, T6365908, F6366029. Another one of the area's hotels that is usually considered 'safe', simple rooms with attached bath, clean enough. There are plenty of other **E-F-G** hotels in the Australia Chowk/McLeod Rd/Railway Rd area, though all are pretty noisy and some discretion is required (see 'warning').

F *Afzaal Tourism Family Guest House*, 17a Wahdat Park, Wahdat Colony, T7561165, mobile 0342 255910. Some way from the city centre but definitely worth the effort of getting here, 3 rooms in the family home (pay per bed), very clean and friendly, meals available, use of fully equipped kitchen, Mr Afzaal is very approachable and full of information on Lahore, also has a camping ground with pool used by overland companies, a quiet and safe budget choice, highly recommended (getting there: your best bet is to phone in advance and see if Mr Afzaal can pick you up, otherwise take wagon 33, 33a, 77 to Naqsha Stop on Wahdat Rd – look out for the *'Broadway Bakery'* – and ask directions from there. A rickshaw from the city centre is about Rs 50).

G *PYHA Youth Hostel*, 110-B/3 Firdous Market, Gulberg, T878201. Reasonable dorm accommodation, but often full and inconveniently located (minibus 43). **G** *Salvation Army Hostel*, Fatima Jinnah Rd. Closed in 1995. **G** *YMCA*, 16 The Mall, T7581758. Usually full of long term Pakistani residents, very run-down, mainly dorms, restaurant open during Ramadan. **G** *YWCA*, Fatima Jinnah Rd, T6304707. Taking advantage of travellers who turn up in the locality only to find the *Salvation Army* closed, the *YWCA* is now very busy. However, the dorm and family rooms are usually occupied by long term Pakistani residents, and all travellers are herded into one large room where 10 or so bed bug ridden mattresses have to serve as many as 40 people dossing down on the floor – roll over, and you end up in the arms of your neighbour, some women justifiably complain that 75 percent of the guests at this women's hostel are now men, there is also a problem with the water supply, poor value.

Gulberg, Wahdat Colony & New Garden Town

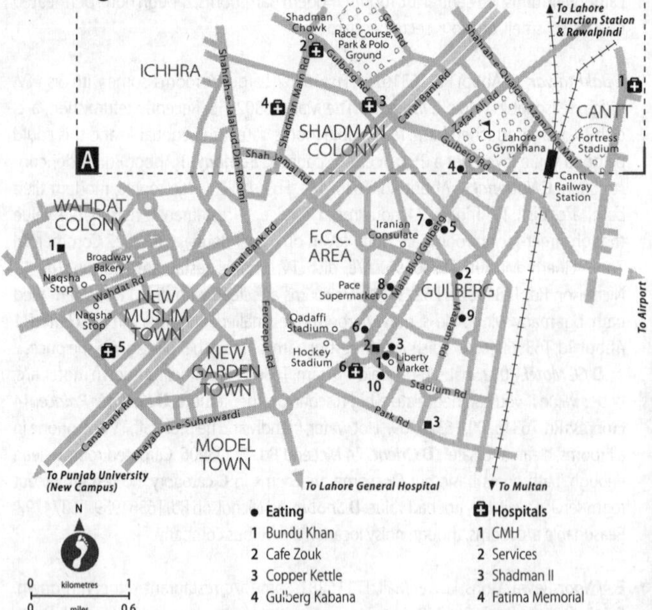

Sleeping
1 Afzaal Tourist Family Guesthouse
2 Best Western
3 PYHA Youth Hostel

Eating
1 Bundu Khan
2 Cafe Zouk
3 Copper Kettle
4 Gulberg Kabana
5 Gulberg Tabaq
6 Kababeesh
7 McDonalds
8 Tai Wah & Yeefah
9 Village
10 Yummy 36

Hospitals
1 CMH
2 Services
3 Shadman II
4 Fatima Memorial
5 Sheikh Zaid
6 United Christian

Related map
A Lahore City, page 260

Punjab

Eating

Lahore offers arguably the best dining options in Pakistan.

● *on maps*

Budget eating

Shaihi Murgh Cholay (sign in Urdu), opposite *National Hotel*, Abbot Rd. Offers meat eaters the opportunity to try a selection of very cheap Pakistani dishes. Recommended. The restaurant at the ***National Hotel*** itself has been recommended by a reader. There are numerous other cheap eating places around the railway station, on and around The Mall, and in the Old City (though hygiene is questionable).

Cafés

Café Zouk, Maalam Rd, Gulberg. "Smart place ... good atmosphere (Rs 200)". ***Yummy 36***, opposite Liberty Market. "Best ice cream in Lahore".

Chinese & Southeast Asian

Lungfung, Kashmir Rd. "Good Chinese food, not loaded with MSG, not cheap". ***Sim Was***, Main Blvd, Gulberg. "Very, very good (Rs 300-350 per head) ... possibly nicest in Lahore". ***Tai Wah***, Main Blvd, Gulberg III, north of *Pace Supermarket*. Received some good reviews. ***Yee Fah***, Main Blvd, Gulberg III, north of *Pace Supermarket*. Recommended as one of Lahore's best Chinese, "excellent food ... a/c ... spotless ... about Rs 150 per head". There are also numerous other a/c Chinese restaurants on Main Blvd Gulberg.

Fast food

KFC, Barket Market, Garden Town, T5882604. Huge, 2 pcs chicken/fries/drink Rs 110. ***McDonalds***, Main Blvd, Gulberg II. Opened October 1998 (making national news!), minibus 43 stops outside. ***Salt & Pepper***, The Mall, opposite High Court. Unpretentious 'fast food'.

Hotel restaurants

Avari has the *Fort Grill* (daily lunch and dinner buffet, Rs 250), *Kim's* (featuring 'Tex-Mex' on Monday, plus Arabian, Southeast Asian etc on other nights), *Tollington* outdoor BBQ, *Dynasty* Chinese, and a Japanese restaurant opening soon. ***Holiday Inn*** features a rooftop poolside BBQ, *Orchids* restaurant, plus coffee shop. ***Pearl Continental*** has the 24 hour *Marco Polo Café* (fabulous breakfasts Rs 200-280, eat-all-you-want breakfast buffet Rs 140, or pancakes and syrup Rs 115, tea/coffee Rs 60), the outdoor BBQ *Bukhara*, the Chinese *Taipan* and a soon to be opened *Mexican Steakhouse*.

International & mixed menus

Copper Kettle, Liberty Market. "Great, with good atmosphere ... leave room for dessert (Rs 150)". ***Gulberg Kabana***, Main Blvd, Gulberg I, T5750573. Very fashionable place, receives rave reviews, around Rs 200 per head. ***Gulberg Tabaq***, Main Blvd, Gulberg II, T5757037. One of Lahore's most renowned restaurants, expect to pay around Rs 200 per head. ***Kings and Queens Pizza***, Fortress Stadium. "Pretty good". ***Pizza Hut***, 73 The Mall, T6370123, takeaway T6370126, delivery T6370161, F6375260 (formerly site of *Caspian Restaurant*). Very keen service, a/c, salad bar Rs 75, garlic bread Rs 30, regular pizzas Rs 350, large pizzas Rs 500, look out for special offers, also at 89/B-1, Gulberg III, MM Alam Rd, Aligarh Chowrangi, T5758440, takeaway T5751456, delivery T5757603, F5753223; ***Saloos***, WAPDA Building, The Mall, T6367137, rather mixed reviews but good choice.

Pakistani & 'Moghul'

Bundu Khan, Fortress Stadium and Liberty Market branches. "Very lively ... very good", Rs 100-120 per head; ***Kababeesh***, south end of Main Blvd, Gulberg III, offers "tastee place for tasteful people", pleasant outdoor setting for meat lovers; See also under 'budget eating'.

Bars & nightclubs

There are no bars as such, although 'permit rooms' can be found at the *Avari*, *Faletti's* and *Pearl Continental* hotels. Liquor permits are available from the difficult to find Excise and Taxation Dept, Room 47, 2nd flr, Mozang Rd (just off The Mall, see map). Open Monday-Thursday 0900-1230, Friday 0900-1100, Rs 25 per month (to be paid at State Bank of Pakistan, Regal Chowk branch, The Mall). Take photocopies of passport, visa, entry stamps etc.

Nightclubs 'Nocturnal' entertainment is available in the Heera Mandi area of the 'Old City'. TDCP (see 'tourist offices') can arrange tours to see the 'classical musicians and dancing girls'. Unaccompanied foreigners visiting places in this red-light area should be wary of being saddled with a hefty 'cover-charge'.

Entertainment

Cinemas Abbott Rd and McLeod Rd (notably at their junction at Lukshmi Chowk) have numerous cinemas showing Urdu-language films. ***Gulistan***, Abbott Rd, ***Plaza***, Fatima Jinnah Rd, and ***Regal***, The Mall, are the best bet for fairly recent English-language films.

Sports **Cricket** **Qadaffi Stadium**, Ferozepur Road, T871031, is the headquarters of Pakistani cricket, and venue for international test and 1-day (including day-night) matches (including the 1996 World Cup Final). It is Pakistan's best cricket stadium, although less important matches are played at **Iqbal Park**, **Lahore Gymkhana** and in the **Bagh-e-Jinnah**. **Flying** *Lahore Flying Club*, Walton Airport. **Football** **Qadaffi Stadium** and **Fortress Stadium** (see map). **Golf** *Lahore Gymkhana*, Upper Mall, T870390; *Railway Golf Club*, off The Mall. **Hockey** **National Hockey Stadium**, near Qadaffi Stadium (also has a **cycling** track). **Polo** Race Course Park, off The Mall (rub shoulders with Charles and Camilla types, this is very different to the version found in the north), check local press for fixtures. **Swimming** Most of the top hotels allow non-guests to use their pools, though the ***Pearl Continental*** is probably the best (Rs 350). **Tennis** Enquire at the top hotels.

Theatres See under 'cultural centres' below.

Festivals

Basant Kite-flying festival to herald the arrival of spring (usually late March), at its most spectacular in the Old City, rather informal (though in the past religious leaders have tried to ban it, suggesting it's "unislamic!")

Drama festival Every other year (next 1999), in March, organized by the Rafi Peer Theater Workshop (check local press).

Mela Chirgan 'Festival of Lights' is held over the last weekend in March, in honour of the mystic and folk poet Shah Hussain (d. 1599), and his friend Madho Lal Hussain who is buried with him, the latter having converted to Islam from Hinduism. People from all over the Punjab, including peasants and fakirs, gather near the Shalimar Gardens on the esplanade, where the mausoleum is illuminated on Shah Hussain's urs. This, and the arrival of spring, is greeted with music, dancing, sports and magic shows.

National Horse and Cattle Show Held at the Fortress Stadium each year in late October/early November. The festival features livestock from all over Pakistan, as well as folk dancing, a military tattoo, displays of tent-pegging and camel dancing!

Puppet festival Every other year in October (next 2000), Lahore hosts an international puppet festival.

Urs of Data Ganj Baksh Death anniversary of Lahore's 'patron saint' (see above), held the 18-20th Safar (Islamic calendar, approximately early June 1999, late May 2000), highly recommended.

Shopping

Bookshops Most are found on The Mall, including: ***Classic Bookshop***, ***Ferozsons*** (best selection, including maps), ***Multiline Books***, ***Vanguard Books***. Most of the top hotels have bookshops, notably ***Arts & Oriental Books*** at *Faletti's Hotel*.

Carpets Lahore is a centre of carpet weaving, although potential buyers should note that it is a post-Partition phenomenon, and thus carpets offered are unlikely to be antiques. Most retail outlets are along The Mall, in the main hotel arcades, and in the upmarket Gulberg area. One reader has recommended ***Ahsan Carpets***, 13 Nicholson Road, near *Shah Taj Hotel*, T6310619.

Clothing Latest Pakistani fashions are to be found in the boutiques in Liberty Market and on Main Gulberg.

Duty free Can be found on Cooper Road and Lawrence Road (opposite TDCP), though neither sell alcohol. Most electronic and imported goods are to be found on Main Gulberg.

Gemstones and jewellery Can be found in shops along The Mall, at Liberty Market, and in the hotel arcades (notably ***Kim's Crafts*** at the *Avari*). Other treasures, as well as modern items and some real junk can be unearthed in ***Anarkali Bazaar*** running north from opposite Lahore Museum, and in the various bazaars of the Old City (notably *Suwa Bazaar*).

Handicrafts See 'gemstones and jewellery' above.

Leather goods ***Panorama Shopping Arcade*** on The Mall (opposite *Pizza Hut*), has been recommended by one reader, particularly ***Guys N Girls***, T6371139, "has a factory on site and will make requested modifications, $50-70 for excellent and well-made leather coats".

Maps See under 'bookshops' above.

Photography Freshest film stock (especially slides, Rs 260 for Kodak Elite 100) is at ***Kodak Express***, The Mall (near *Ferozsons*). The northwest end of Nisbet Road is where all the photographic shops are congregated.

Supermarkets ***Pace Supermarket***, 124 Main Gulberg (open daily 0900-2300) has all manner of imported items, including food, toileteries, clothes, videos etc, takes Visa/Mastercard. There is also an internet club on the 3rd floor (Rs 60 per hour).

Transport

Local Transport

Car hire Available through most major hotels and tour companies.

Long distance transport

Air International: *Aero Asia*: **Dubai**, Monday, Wednesday, Thursday; *Bhoja Air*: **Dubai**, Tuesday, Thursday, Saturday, Sunday; ***PIA***, **Abu Dhabi**, **Amsterdam**, **Bangkok**, **Copenhagen**, **Dharan**, **Dubai**, **Frankfurt**, **Jeddah**, **Kuwait**, **London**, **Manchester**, **New Delhi**, **New York**, and **Riyadh**; ***Shaheen Air***: **Abu Dhabi**, Wednesday, Saturday;

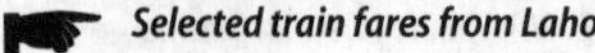

Selected train fares from Lahore

	A/c sleeper	A/c sitter	1st class sleeper	Economy
Bahawalpur	Rs 553	Rs 354	Rs 226	Rs 95
Hyderabad	Rs 1,232	Rs 714	Rs 473	Rs 220
Larkana	Rs 1,046	Rs 602	Rs 402	Rs 185
Karachi	Rs 1,395	Rs 733	Rs 550	Rs 255
Multan	Rs 489	Rs 287	Rs 176	Rs75
Peshawar	Rs 641	Rs 366	Rs 231	Rs 100
Quetta	Rs 1,316	Rs 760	Rs 501	Rs 235
Rawalpindi	Rs 428	Rs 248	Rs 154	Rs 70
Sukkur/Rohri	Rs 957	Rs 551	Rs 358	Rs 165

Dubai, Monday, Thursday.

Domestic: Look for discounts on 'night coaches'. Most domestic flights are subject to a 2 percent increase every month! The daily newspapers carry a full daily flight schedule. ***Aero Asia***: **Islamabad**, daily; **Karachi**, daily. ***Bhoja Air***: **Karachi**, 2 flights daily, Rs 2,670; **Multan**, Monday, Wednesday, Friday. ***PIA***: **Bahawalpur**, 2 flights daily; **Bannu**, Monday, Wednesday, Friday; **DG Khan**, Tuesday, Thursday, Sunday, Rs 1,960; **Hyderabad**, Wednesday, 2 flights Thursday, Saturday, 2 flights Sunday; **Islamabad**, 7-8 flights daily; **Karachi**, 3-6 flights daily; **Mianwali**, Friday, Sunday, Rs 1,240; **Multan**, 2 flights daily, Rs 1,480; **Muzaffarabad**, Monday, Tuesday, Wednesday, Thursday, Saturday; **Peshawar**, 2 flights daily, Rs 1,720; **Quetta**, Monday, Tuesday, Friday, Sunday; **Rahim Yar Khan**, Monday, Wednesday, Thursday, Friday, Saturday, Sunday, Rs 1,900; **Sukkur**, Monday, Friday, Saturday. **Shaheen Air**: **Islamabad**, Sunday, Rs 960; **Karachi**, daily, Rs 2,750.

Train Lahore's magnificent main station (known as Lahore Junction) was built by the British in 1860 in Gothic-Mughal style. Complete with towers, turrets and battlements it was obviously built to be defended. The **Railway Reservation Office** for all classes of advanced bookings is 1 kilometre south of the station, behind the Pakistan Railways HQ (large, red sandstone building) on Empress Road. The concession permit for tourist and student discounts, however, must first be obtained from the rather difficult to find Commercial Office within this complex (though you may need a letter from PTDC first). Railway reservations T9201772; Railway enquiry T117.

Lahore is on the main Peshawar-Rawalpindi-Lahore-Karachi route and the following are just a selection of the quickest trains, offering all classes of tickets and arriving at convenient times. **Karachi** *Shalimar Exp*, 0600, 17 hours; *Tezgam*, 1355, 19 hours. **Rawalpindi** *Awam Exp*, 0535, 5½ hours; *Tezgam*, 1115, 5½ hours. **Peshawar** *Zulfikar Exp*, 0845, 11 hours; *Khyber Mail*, 1920, 10 hours. **Quetta** *Chiltan Exp*, 1100, 28 hours; *Quetta Exp*, 1330, 27 hours. **Multan** *Shalimar Exp*, 0600, 5 hours; *Tezgam*, 1355, 5 hours.

Long distance buses Lahore's main bus transport hub is the chaotic area around Australia Chowk, McLeod Road and Nicholson Road, close to the main railway station. In theory there are timetables, though in practice buses only depart when full. Destination boards are mainly in Urdu; shout out where you want to go and somebody will show you to the right bus. These privately run 'flying coaches' will take you just about anywhere you will want to go, with numerous rival companies operating on the same routes. Fares are standard, so pick the bus that looks the most comfortable (or is nearest to leaving). On main routes (Rawalpindi, Multan etc) there are often services around the clock; on other routes, from early morning until early evening. Tickets can be bought in advance on longer routes (to reserve a 'better' seat), though most

Crossing the border between Pakistan and India

The only recognized land border crossing between Pakistan and India is 23 kilometres east of Lahore, at ***Wagah*** *on the Pakistani side and* ***Attari*** *on the Indian side (35 kilometres from Amritsar). The border is open from 0900-1500 all year round (though check locally about national holidays). Private vehicles with an AIT carnet de passage can be driven across the border (a slow process), or you can cross by train (not recommended since it can take 5-6 hours for the whole train to clear customs), or by a combination of bus/on foot (the quickest method).* ***NB*** *In February 1999 a trial run was given to a direct Delhi-Lahore bus service (with the Indian PM on board). It is not clear whether this will become a permanent fixture, although currently we are unable to recommend its use since various Hindu Nationalist groups have threatened to "stop it at all costs".*

Facilities/formalities *There are* ***money-change*** *facilities on either side of the border (note that it is illegal to take Indian Rupees into India).* ***Customs*** *staff seem keen to examine foreigners' luggage; women in particular may find the customs/immigration staff on either side to be rather sleazy. Note that Indian Standard Time is 30 minutes ahead of Pakistani time.*

The changing of the guards and flag-lowering ceremonies on either side of the border are becoming something of a tourist attraction (TDCP in Lahore arranges trips), as both countries try to outdo each other in the precision of their troops' drill. The tallest people that you are likely to see in either Pakistan or India are the soldiers participating in this rivalry.

Train *The Amritsar Express leaves Lahore at 0900 every Monday and Thursday, arriving at Wagah at 0930. Officially, it is supposed to then leave Wagah for Amritsar 2 hours later, arriving in the city at 1230, though delays of 6 hours are common. The Amritsar Express also leaves Amritsar at 1125 every Monday and Thursday, arriving at Wagah at 1225 and supposedly then arriving in Lahore at 1400 (though don't count on it).* ***NB*** *At the end of November the train is usually restricted to Sikh pilgrims only.*

Bus/foot *Aim to cross the border as early in the day as possible and allow at least 1 hour for formalities. From Lahore, take minibus 12 from outside the main railway station (Rs15), although sometimes it is necessary to change vehicles half way at Jallo (also minibus 12). Having walked across the border (porters are available for those with lots of luggage, though you have to change between Indian and Pakistani porters half way), and completed formalities on both sides, there are buses (Rs 50), rickshaws (Rs 250) and taxis (Rs 500) to take you the 35 kilometres to Amritsar.*

Those arriving in Pakistan from India should find minibuses (No 12, Rs 15) available to take them as far as Lahore Junction railway station. Otherwise, there are taxis (though you will have to bargain hard to get a fair price of around Rs 200).

passengers just turn up and go. One of the most reputable firms is ***New Khan Road Runners*** and its sister company, ***New Khan Road Panthers***, T6363855.

Australia Chowk area **Bahawalpur** (Rs 175, 9 hours); **Chakwal** (Rs 85, 5 hours); **D G Khan** (Rs 155, 10 hours); **Faisalabad** (Rs 55, 3 hours); **Gujranwala** (Rs 30, 1 hour); **Gujrat** (Rs 50, 1½ hours); **Karachi** (Rs 450, 24 hours); **Multan** (Rs 150, 7 hours); **Peshawar** (Rs 125, 10 hours); **Rawalpindi** (Rs 105, 6 hours, or Rs 180, 3½ hours via service along new motorway); **Sahiwal** (Rs 50, 3 hours); **Sialkot** (Rs 45, 2½ hours).

Other *Daewoo Express*, Ferozpur Road, near Qadaffi Stadium, T5863743, have fast buses to **Rawalpindi** via the motorway (Rs 250, 3½ hours, every 30 minutes). ***New Blue Lines***, *Shobra Hotel*, Nicholson Road, T6364959, has a daily bus to **Karachi** (Rs 450, 24 hours); ***New Khan Road Runners***, *Shobra Hotel*, run hourly buses to **Multan** (Rs

132, 7 hours). *TDCP*, 4-A Lawrence Road, T6369687, F636986, have comfortable a/c coaches to **Multan** (0930 1100 1600 2200 2300, Rs 150, 7 hours), **Murree** (2355, Rs 200, 7 hours), and **Rawalpindi** (0900 1400 1700 2355, Rs 170, 3½ hours via motorway).

Directory

Airline offices At Ali Complex, 23 Empress Rd: ***Air Canada***, T6305229. ***Cathay Pacific***, T6369558. ***Shaheen Air***, T6316855. ***Singapore***, T6303269; ***Uzbekistan***, T6312138, plus ***Aeroflot***, ***Air Lanka***, ***Austrian***, ***Continental***, ***Cyprus***, ***Japan***, ***Kenyan***, ***Oman***, ***SAS*** and ***Swissair***. **At Avari Hotel:** ***American Airlines*** and ***Canadian***, T6279045. ***Lufthansa***, T6365168. **At WAPDA House, The Mall:** ***Air France***, T6314420, F6361930. ***Alitalia***, T6360825. ***KLM***, T6363746. ***British Airways***, Transport House, Egerton Rd, T6300701. ***Emirates***, 85 The Mall, T6372990. ***Gulf***, 25 Davis Rd, T6369731. ***Indian Airlines***, Ambassador Hotel, Davis Rd, T6360014. ***Kuwait***, 15a Davis Rd, T6368206. ***Malaysia***, PIA Tower, Egerton Rd. ***PIA***, PIA Tower, Egerton Rd, T62705234/62705267. Huge queues. ***Syrian Arab***, Ambassador Hotel, Davis Rd, T6305484. ***Thai***, Transport House, Egerton Rd, T6316235. ***Turkish***, 85 The Mall, T6303503.

Banks *American Express*, 112 Rafi Mansion, The Mall, T6376472 (Mon-Thur 0900-1330 1430-1700, Fri 0900-1230 1430-1700, Sat 0900-1330, Sun closed). Upstairs for foreign exchange, downstairs for clients' mail; ***Citibank***, Charing Cross, The Mall, T111222222 (Mon-Thur 0900-1330, Fri-Sat 0900-1230). 24-hour ATM machine, cash advance on Visa cards. ***Hongkong Bank***, in the grounds of the *Avari Hotel*, has an ATM (visa/plus/global access). ***Société General***, 6th Flr, PIA Tower, Egerton Rd. There are numerous other banks and money changers on The Mall offering foreign exchange.

Punjab

Communications **GPO:** this magnificent Anglo-Indian building is on The Mall, T7243580. **Poste Restante:** at the GPO. **Internet:** ***British Council***, see 'cultural centres' below, best value cyber station, Rs 50 per hour. ***CyberCafé Pakistan***, 106-G, Phase 1, Defence Society, Lahore-13, T5729901. ***Internet Club***, 28 Fatima Jinnah Rd, open 24 hrs, Rs 70 per hour. ***Lahore Internet Club***, 222 G. Raja Cenyre, Gulberg III, T5761822, Rs 50 per hour. ***Noori International Space Net***, 77-78/G Sadiq Plaza, 69 The Mall (near junction of The Mall and Lawrence Rd), T6370389, E spacenet@thegym.net (open Mon-Sat 0900-2000, Rs 70 per hour). ***Pace Supermarket***, 124 Main Gulberg (open daily 0900-2300), has an internet café on the 3rd Flr, Rs 60 per hour. The 5-star hotels all offer email facilities, though at ridiculous prices (Rs 200 per email!). **Telephones:** The *Central Telephone Office* is on the corner of The Mall and McLeod Rd, opposite GPO (open 24 hrs). **Couriers:** *DHL*, Mini Market, Gulberg, T5757010.

Cultural centres *Alhamra Cultural Complex*, 68 The Mall, T6360040. Open-air theatre, drama hall, 2 theatres, art gallery, main venue for the performing arts. ***Alliance Française***, 20-E/2 Gulberg III, T876043. ***British Council***, 32 Mozang Rd, T6362497 (Mon-Sat 0930-1830). Library, recent British papers, videos, good value cyber station. ***Pak-German Cultural Centre*** (formerly Goethe Institute), 92-E/1 Gulberg III, near 7-Up factory, T877113.

Embassies & consulates You will usually be referred to your embassy in Islamabad. Notable exceptions are ***USA***, 50 Empress Rd, New Shimla Hills, T6365530; and ***Iran***, 55 Shadman-II, near Canal Bank Rd, T7590926 (bus 8, minibus 1, 27, 43), which is reputedly issuing visas again ("easier and cheaper than Islamabad, no need for a letter of introduction").

Hospitals & medical services **Chemists:** most of the all-night pharmacies are located outside the hospitals (a daily list is supplied in the newspapers). **Hospitals:** ***Dental Hospital***, T310261. ***Edhi ambulance***, T444460. ***General Hospital***, T5810891. ***Mayo***, Gowal Mandi, T9211101. ***Medical Centre***, Gulberg III, T881906. ***Shaukut Khanum Memorial Cancer Hospital***, 7-A, Block R3, Johor Town, T5180725, F5180720, E skmt@paknet1.ptc.pk. ***Sheikh Zaid***, Canal Bank Rd, T5865731. ***United Christian Hospital***, Gulberg, T870373. ***United Lady Willingdon***, near Lahore Fort, T7659001. For medical emergencies T310130.

Libraries *British Council*, see under 'cultural centres' above. ***Jinnah Library***, Bagh-e-Jinnah, The Mall (open daily 0800-2000). ***Punjab Public Library***, Old Anarkali Rd, T7325487.

Places of worship *International Christian Fellowship*, FC College, near Qadaffi Stadium, Sun 0900-1100 1830-2030. ***Catholic***: Sacred Heart Cathedral, Lawrence Rd. ***Protestant***: Cathedral Church of the Resurrection, Shahrah-e-Quaid-e-Azam; Eng service Sun 0730 1800.

Tour companies & travel agents *Travel Walji's*, Ali Complex, 23 Empress Rd, T6366246, F6366146. There are numerous other at WAPDA House, along The Mall, and at the top hotels.

Tourist offices *PTDC*, Room 3, *Faletti's Hotel*, Egerton Rd, T6306528. Some keen young (female) staff, brochures and maps, city tours (see below); ***TDCP***, 4-A Lawrence Rd, T6369687, F636986. Offers a number of 'deluxe' coach services (see above), as well as 2 good value guided city tours in a/c minibus, tour runs even if there's only 1 passenger (with pick-up points here, *Faletti's*, *Holiday Inn*, *Ambassador*, *Pearl Continental* and *Avari* hotels): ***Morning Tour*** 0830, 3½ hrs, Badshahi Mosque, Lahore Fort, Jehangir's Tomb, Noor Jehan's Tomb, Lahore Museum, Rs 300. ***Afternoon Tour*** 1430 (1530 in winter), 3½ hrs, Shalimar Gardens, Old City, Shahi Hamman, Wazir Khan's Mosque, Golden Mosque, Haqqis Handicrafts shop. They also offer winter tours of Southern Punjab.

Useful addresses & phone numbers *Foreigners' Registration Office*, 63 Kutchery Rd. ***Pakistan Automobile Association (AA)***, 155 Chenab Block, Iqbal Town, T445320. If continuing to India, you will need an AIT (and not a FIA) *Carnet de Passage*. The AA here can complete the necessary paperwork – for a price! ***Police***, T15 or T6361239. ***Fire***, T16. ***Ambulance***, T115 or T414737.

Longer excursions from Lahore

Jallo Park

(27 kilometres east) Re-vamped and re-opened in 1995, Jallo Park is the pride and joy of the Tourism Development Corporation of Punjab. Covering a 200 hectares site, the park is now being billed as the 'Pakistani Disneyland'. In addition to the fairground rides and water park, there are extensive gardens, a children's zoo, a forest research centre, a Japanese garden, a small museum and a boating lake. Despite the heavy crowds at weekends and holidays, Jallo Park is a pleasant picnic spot. The park is on the GT Road to the Indian border and can be reached by half-hourly trains from Lahore, minibus 12 from outside the station or by taxi (Rs 20).

Sheikhupura

(34 kilometres west) Formerly known as Jahangirabad, Sheikhupura has a Mughal fort that was built by the Emperor in 1619 for use as a hunting lodge. The fort is built of brick rather than the stone more common of Mughal forts, and there are said to be tunnels from the basement to the Hiran Minar (six kilometres) and to Lahore (34 kilometres)! The fort was later used by the Sikh princess Rani Nakayan, and her private quarters are decorated with superbly preserved frescoes depicting dancing girls, hunts, court scenes and images of the Guru Nanak. The chowkidar claims that the fort was used for 25 years by the Pakistani police as a "torture cell". A letter of authorization from the Department of Archaeology at Lahore Fort is officially required for entry.

A further four kilometres along the Sargodha Road is the turn off for Jahangir's **deer park** (two kilometres). The centre-piece to the park is a square artificial lake, with a causeway and arched pavilion in its centre that makes an ideal picnic spot. The tall carved octagonal memorial tower, **Hiran Minar**, was built by the Emperor in memory of his pet antelope 'Maharaj'. The minaret has 99 steps. Sheikhupura now has a cricket stadium that is used for one-day internationals.

Chhanga Manga

(68 kilometres southwest) Initially established as a timber plantation in the last century by the British, the 5,000 hectares Chhanga Manga National Park is said to be the oldest planted forest in South Asia. The park is now a wildlife reserve and holiday resort, with boating lake and model train ride. TDCP have a **D** *Motel* and restaurant in the grounds, bookable in Lahore. The park is located just off the GT Road, on the way to Multan.

West of Lahore

There are a number of places of minor interest to tourists located to the west of Lahore. There are really two logical routes for exploring this region, with numerous side excursions.

One route is via **Sheikhupura** (34 kilometres, see page 283), **Faisalabad** (96 kilometres) and **Jhang** (76 kilometres), before the road divides, offering options of travelling a) on to **Khushab** (132 kilometres) and **Mianwali** (89 kilometres, see page 241); b) via Nageriwala (96 kilometres) and Darya Khan (40 kilometres), then across the Indus into NWFP and **Dera Ismail Khan** (22 kilometres, see page 362); or c) via Ahmadpur Sial to **Muzaffargarh** (183 kilometres), then across the Indus to **Dera Ghazi Khan** (60 kilometres, see page 156).

The second route heads west and then northwest from Lahore, passing through **Chiniot** (34 kilometres) and **Sargodha** (54 kilometres) on the way to **Mianwali** (see page 241). The route then crosses the Indus close to **Kalabagh** (48 kilometres, see page 242), leaves Punjab and enters NWFP, and continues to **Bannu** (see page 360). Some of the towns towards the end of this route are described in fuller detail in the 'The Salt Range' section (see page 236).

To orientate yourself consult the 'West of Lahore' map (below).

Faisalabad

In the words of one local tourism official, "there is nothing of interest to a tourist in Faisalabad"! Locals are fond of referring to the city as "the Manchester of Pakistan", though this does a disservice to the dynamic northern English city. The city today is a focus for agricultural and industrial production, with little to

Phone code: 041
Colour map 4, grid B4

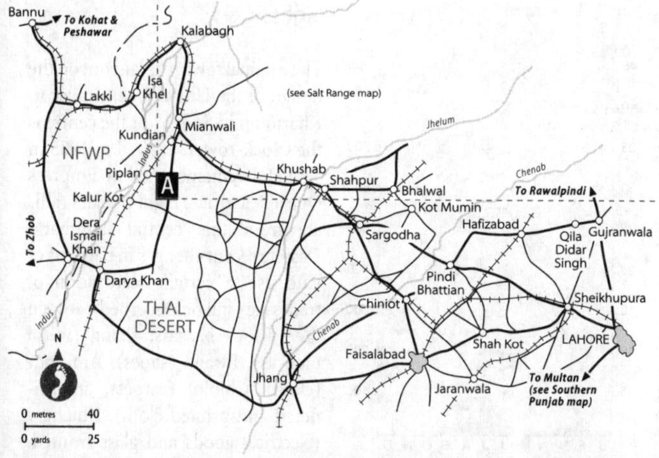

Related map
A The Salt Range, page 236

see unless there's a cricket match on. Faisalabad was, however, the birthplace of the late (and great) Nusrat Fateh Ali Khan (1948-97).

Ins and outs

Getting there Faisalabad is located about 96 kilometres west of Lahore (3 hours), along a terribly surfaced road. The airport is 9 kilometres southwest of town, on the Jhang Road. The railway station is on a fairly obscure branch line, so most visitors arrive by bus. You should try to get down as the bus passes through the town centre, otherwise it's a long walk back (or Rs 30 rickshaw ride) from the main bus station to the north-east of town (see map). To catch a bus, however, it's best to get on at the main bus stand.

Getting around The town centre is compact enough for walking (but floods when it rains), though the bus stand is a long walk away.

History

Founded in 1890 as Lyallpur, after the then Lieutenant Governor of the Punjab Sir James Lyall, the town was renamed Faisalabad in 1977 in honour of the Saudi Arabian king. The status of Faisalabad as Pakistan's third largest city belies the town's recent and modest beginnings. Until the construction of the **Lower Chenab Canal** in the 19th century, most of the district was a vast tract of scrub-land known as Sandal Bar. Local tribes battled for possession of the limited pastures, with a grazing tax, *tarni*, being paid by the lesser tribes to the dominant ones. This system continued until the arrival of the British. The provision of irrigation that led to the development of the canal colonies established Faisalabad as a centre of cotton production, and provided the catalyst in the town's industrialization process. As a large agricultural market, the city is known as the granary of the region, and is the site of Pakistan's oldest and foremost **Agricultural University**. Faisalabad is also the centre of the Pakistani textile industry.

Faisalabad has experienced phenomenal population growth since Pakistani independence, rising from a population of a mere 72,000 in 1947, to over 420,000 within four years of Partition. Today the population is around two million.

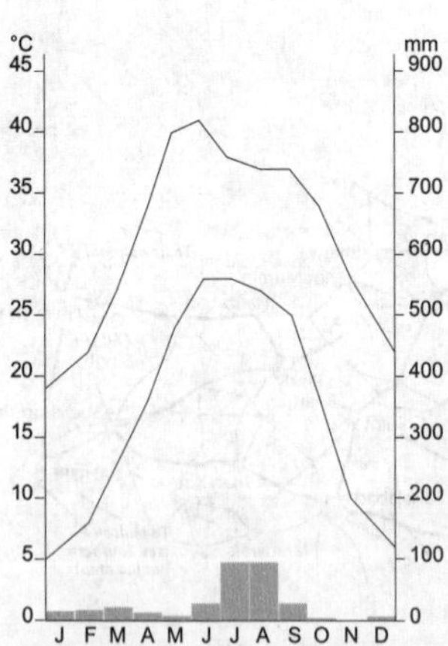

The best time to visit is between November and March

Sights

The original town was laid out on the design of the Union Jack, similar to Khartoum in Sudan. At the centre is the **Clock-tower**, erected in 1905 in "grateful remembrance of Empress Queen Victoria". Eight bazaars radiate from this central landmark. Despite recent changes in patterns of land use, a certain segregation of trades can still be discerned between the various bazaars; Jhang (metal utensils), Bwana (shoes), Aminpur (cloth), Chiniot (carpets, embroidered and printed cloth), Kutchery (electrical goods and glass fronted, upmarket shops), Rail (cloth and jewellery), Karkhana (agricultural implements and products) and Montgomery (brokers, money lenders and financial services).

Essentials

Sleeping

■ *on map*
Price codes: see inside front cover

The cheapo hotels are concentrated in the various bazaars around the clock-tower. Few have English signs, and some are hard to find.

L *Serena*, Club Rd, T600428, F629235. Opened by the Aga Khan in 1987, has all modern facilities in traditional style building, including pool, tennis, squash, business centre, shopping arcade, car rental, and 3 good restaurants (*Lyallpur* Pakistani, *Xuelian* Chinese, *Basant Ct* barbecue). Recommended.

C *Prime*, Allama Iqbal Rd, T600030, F628095. Reasonable rooms, a/c, dish TV, fridge, modern attached bath, phone, good restaurant, even better deal with discounts. **C** *Ray's*, Allama Iqbal Rd, T620062. Carpeted rooms, a/c, dish TV, phone, attached bath, good restaurant. **C** *Sabina*, between Aminpur Bazaar and Kotwali Rd, T628410.

Faisalabad Centre

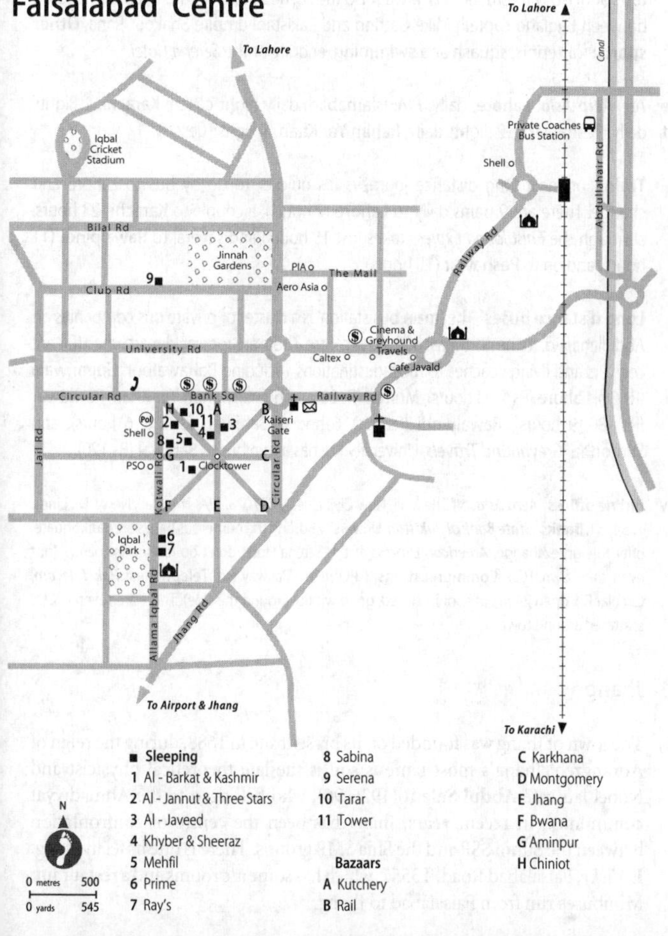

Central a/c, dish TV, clean bedding, attached bath fairly basic, too close to noisy mosque, for half the quoted price it would be a good deal (say, Rs 500).

F ***Al-Barkat***, off Aminpur Bazaar, T634457. Fan, carpet, attached bath, pretty basic and run-down but friendly. **F** ***Al-Jannut***, Chiniot Bazaar, T641335. Reasonable rooms, fan, attached bath, not much English spoken. **F** ***Al-Javeed***, Kutchery Bazaar, T34689. Best of a bad lot in this class, fairly basic. **F** ***Tarar***, Chiniot Bazaar. Filthy rooms, filthy attached and shared bath. **F** ***Three Star***, Chiniot Bazaar, T648667. Friendly, tolerably clean rooms, attached basic bath. **F** ***Tower***, Chiniot Bazaar. Very basic, charpoy beds, basic squat loo and bucket bath, excellent cheap restaurant downstairs.

G ***Kashmir***, Aminpur Bazaar, T642089. Basic and noisy. **G** ***Khyber***, west of Kutchery Bazaar. Very basic. **G** ***Mehfil***, off Chiniot Bazaar, T635303. Basic but reasonably clean, fan, attached basic bath, TV lounge. **G** ***Sheeraz***, west of Kutchery Bazaar. Very basic.

Eating Most hotels have a restaurant. There are plenty of good cheap places around the clock-tower, though for a treat try the *Serena Hotel*.

Punjab

Entertainment **Sports Cricket:** the ***Iqbal Stadium*** is one of Pakistan's finest cricket venues, hosting tests and 1-day internationals. It was also the scene in 1987 of the infamous face-off between England captain Mike Gatting and Pakistani umpire Shakoor Rana. **Other sports:** for **tennis**, **squash** and **swimming**, enquire at the *Serena Hotel*.

Long distance transport **Air** *Aero Asia*: **Lahore**, daily. *PIA*: **Islamabad**, daily night coach; **Karachi**, 2 flights daily; **Peshawar**, 1-2 flights daily; **Rahim Yar Khan**, 1 flight Tuesday.

Train For most long distance journeys it's quicker to go by bus to Lahore and change. There are 9 trains daily to **Lahore** (2 hours), a couple to **Karachi** (23 hours, although the *Faisalabad Express* takes just 15 hours) and several to **Rawalpindi** (11 hours) and on to **Peshawar** (15 hours).

Long distance buses The 'main bus station' is a cluster of private bus companies on Abdullahar Rd, to the northeast of the city centre. There are regular 'depart when full' a/c coasters and flying coaches to most destinations, including **Bahawalpur**, **Gujranwala** (Rs 65), **Lahore** (Rs 50, 3 hours), **Multan** (Rs 200, 10 hours), **Rahim Yar Khan**, **Peshawar** (Rs 180, 9 hours), **Rawalpindi** (Rs 130, 6 hours), **Sahiwal** (Rs 120, 6 hours), and **Sargodha**. ***Greyhound Travels***, University Rd, has a minibus to **Sahiwal** (Rs 120).

Directory **Airline offices** *Aero Asia*, off The Mall, New Civil Lines, T627023. ***PIA***, The Mall, New Civil Lines, T634131. **Banks** ***State Bank of Pakistan***, University Rd, and the numerous banks on 'Bank Square' offer foreign exchange. ***American Express*** at the Serena Hotel don't do foreign exchange (not even their own TCs). **Communications** GPO: is on Railway Rd. **Telephones:** ***Pak Telecom***, Circular Rd, open 24 hrs (if it looks closed, go to window round the side). There are several PCOs scattered around town.

Jhang

Colour map 4, grid B4

The town of Jhang was founded on its present site in 1688, during the reign of Aurangzeb. Jhang's most famous son is the late theoretical physicist and Nobel laureate **Abdul Salam** (1926-96), who belonged to the Ahmadiyyat community. In recent years, Jhang has been the centre of confrontation between the Sunni SSP and the Shia SMP groups. There is one hotel in Jhang, **E** *Vicky*, Faisalabad Road, T3557, which has some a/c rooms and a restaurant. Minibuses run from Faisalabad to Jhang.

Chiniot

Colour map 4, grid B4

Chiniot has ancient origins, with some scholars linking it to a town mentioned in the *Rg Veda*. A town called *Channiwat* is also mentioned in the *Rammayana* and subsequently by Alberuni in his 'Kitab-ul-Hind', and housed one of the three ancient universities of the Punjab (the other two being at Ajodhan and Taxila). Tradition has it that Chandan, a king's daughter who was accustomed to hunting in a man's attire, visited the spot and was so charmed she ordered a town, Chiniot, to be built. A later visitor during the period of British rule was less generous about the town's inhabitants, claiming "the townspeople have an unenviable character for forgery, litigiousness and false evidence, and it is said that any old deed that comes out of Chiniot should be looked upon with the greatest suspicion"!

The town is celebrated for its wood carving and masonry, and craftsmen from Chiniot are known to have worked on such artistically renowned monuments as the Taj Mahal, the Golden Temple at Amritsar and the Wazir Khan mosque in Lahore, as well as the more recent Minar-e-Pakistan. Fine wood carving can still be seen on the doors, windows and balconies of the houses in the central part of the old town. The most prosperous days of Chiniot were during the reign of Shah Jahan, and the elegant Shahi mosque was built during this period. There are no hotels in Chiniot. The town is best reached by minibus from Faisalabad.

Sargodha

Phone code: 0451
Colour map 4, grid B4

Sargodha was established as a colony town in 1903, although its origins are far older. The town's importance today is as a Punjab market town and a Pakistan Air Force base. Legend associates the town with skilled young men in flowing turbans and on white chargers "carrying the day in manly sports like tent-pegging and horse riding". Although comprising mainly low rise buildings, Sargodha sprawls over a considerable area. The road from Chiniot enters through the Sargodha Satellite Town, where the main Flying Coach bus stand is located (on College Rd). Buses, wagons and coasters run when full to **Mianwali, Khushrab, Chiniot, Chakwal, Faisalabad and Lahore.**

Sleeping & eating

D-E ***Sargodha***, College Rd, near Kayyan Cinema, T60722. Some a/c rooms, restaurant.
E ***Malbro***, Court Rd, T66646. Simple rooms, some a/c, attached bath.

Southern Punjab

Lahore to Sukkur

The National Highway (NH), one of Pakistan's main road arteries, heads southwest from Lahore, passing through the heart of the Punjab on its way to Sukkur in Sind state, and eventually on to the sea at Karachi. The road passes through rich agricultural land (though the effects of salinization are becoming increasingly problematic) as well as skirting desert areas. The key attractions en route include the Indus Valley Civilization site at **Harappa**, the great historical city of **Multan**, princely palaces in **Bahawalpur**, desert castle such as **Fort Derawar** in the Cholistan Desert, and spectacular ruined tombs at **Uch Sharif**.

Sahiwal

Phone code: 0441
Colour map 4, grid B4

Some 107 kilometres southwest of Lahore along the NH is the market town of **Sahiwal**. Originally named by way of what is said to be a rather doubtful compliment to Sir Robert Montgomery, Lt-Governor of the Punjab between 1859-65, Sahiwal is at the heart of the Punjab's cotton growing belt. Less than 100 years ago this area was little more than scrub jungle, but the provision of canal irrigation, combined with naturally fertile soils, has made Sahiwal a valuable agricultural region. It is also noted for its own breed of milk producing cows and beef providing bullocks.

The main town lies west of the NH, known locally as GT Road. The main axis is Railway Road, parallel and several kilometres west of GT Road. The GTS bus stand, GPO, PIA office (T2803), Habib Bank (foreign exchange) plus several hotels are here. At the south end of Railway Road is the cricket stadium and a 19th century British-built church. Sahiwal is a good base from which to visit Harappa (see below).

Sleeping & eating

C *Mooren City*, GT Rd, T63403. Plain a/c rooms, modern attached bath, decent restaurant, would be good value with a 50 percent discount. **D** *Sea Rose*, GT Rd, T77377. A/C doubles and cheaper non a/c rooms, restaurant recommended, good value. **E** *Al Habib*, Railway Rd, T778492. Some a/c rooms. **F** *Indus*, Railway Rd, T75476. **F** *Montgomery*, Railway Rd, T2885. **F** *Stadium*, Railway Rd, T74656. Quiet garden, good value. There are cheap restaurants along Railway Road, plus plenty of places around the 'flying coach' stands on the National Highway (GT Road).

Transport

Though the main GTS bus stand is on Railway Road, most of the regular buses and deluxe coaches arrive/depart on GT Road (for **Lahore**, **Multan**, **Bahawalpur**, **Karachi**, plus local buses to **Pakpattan**). To reach **Harappa**, take any south-bound bus passing **Harappa Junction**, and change here to either one of the irregular buses to the site, or a tonga (Rs 40).

Pakpattan

A diversion 47 kilometres southeast of Sahiwal leads to the town of Pakpattan, usually reached by a local bus from the GT Road at Sahiwal. A journey along this road gives a good vignette of typical rural life in Punjab. Small hamlets are scattered amongst the wheat and sugar cane fields, and although most have a small mosque, shopping requires a visit to the road side bazaars. Certain plots of land have been laid waste by salinization. Mid-way between Sahiwal and Pakpattan is the massive Ittefaq sugar mill, owned by the family of the Prime Minister of Pakistan, Nawaz Sharif. The mill is a major local employer.

Colour map 4, grid C5

The prime attraction of the town is the shrine of **Baba Farid-ud-din Ganj Shakkar** (1173-1265), a revered holy man from Afghanistan who came to settle here. Indeed, when Tamerlane marched here with his army in 1398, the town was spared out of respect for Baba Farid. The town is now a major pilgrimage centre, particularly during the saint's Urs (5 Muharram, mid-April 1999, early April 2000). Surprisingly, the oldest looking tomb in the complex, a red brick building with white dome roof, is that of the holy man's grandson, Mooj Dira. Baba Farid's tomb is in the more modern, small marble room. A narrow opening in the wall next to the shrine is known as Heaven's Gate, and any males who pass through here are guarantied entrance into paradise. For further details see Sheikh Parvaiz Amin Naqshbondy's "*Hazrat Baba Farid-ud-Din*" (Umar Publication, available in Lahore bookshops).

Prior to Partition, Pakpattan ('ferry crossing of the pure' – an old crossing on the Sutlej) housed a large Hindu population. On the hill in the centre of town, their tall houses, with carved wooden window frames can still be seen. Most of the Hindu temples on the hill were destroyed following the bulldozing of the Ayodhya mosque in India in December 1992.

Harappa

With Moenjo Daro in Sind (see page 123), Harappa represents the other key city of the Indus Valley Civilization. Excavations are continuing at Harappa under the auspices of the Archaeological Survey of Pakistan. Today the site is rather poorly cared for and has nothing of the grandeur of Moenjo Daro, though the total area of the two cities and key features of their basic layout are similar. The ravaging effects of salinization are blatantly evident all across the site.

Colour map 4, grid C4

Ins and outs

The main junction for visiting the site is **Harappa Road** (sometimes known as **Harappa Station**) on the Lahore-Multan Road. Trains to/from Harappa Station are irregular, so the site is best visited by road. The site is signposted across the rail line and Lower Bari Doab Canal, 7 kilometres away. A tonga costs Rs 40, although there is an irregular bus service. Any buses passing between Lahore and Multan will, **on request**, stop at Harappa Junction. The easiest way to reach Harappa is to take any south-bound bus from Sahiwal passing **Harappa Junction**,

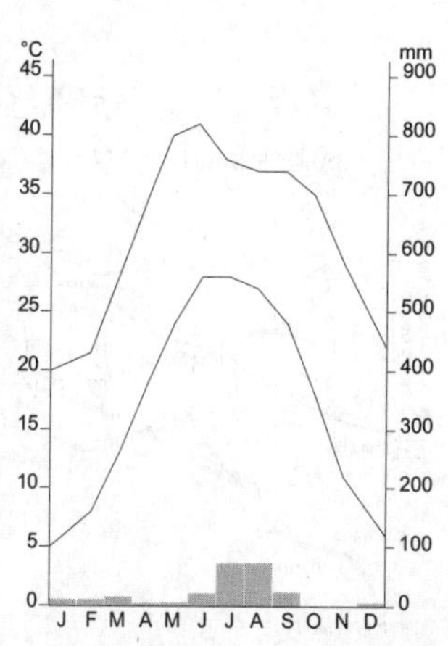

The best time to visit is between November and March

and change there to either one of the irregular buses to the site (7 kilometres), or hire a tonga (Rs 40).

The site is generally open daily from 0830 to sunset, though the museum sometimes closes from 1200-1400. Admission is Rs 10. It is sometimes possible to arrange accommodation at the ***Archaeological Department Resthouse*** here through the Department of Archaeology based at Lahore Fort. Otherwise, the nearest hotels are in Sahiwal (see above).

The site

The discovery of the site The existence of the huge mounds rising nearly 20 metres above the plain, which comprises the Harappan site was reported by Masson in 1826 and visited again by Cunningham in 1853 and 1876. When the railway between **Multan** and **Lahore** was being built in the 1870s the railway engineers found their apparently inexhaustible supply of ready-baked bricks invaluable for

Southern Punjab

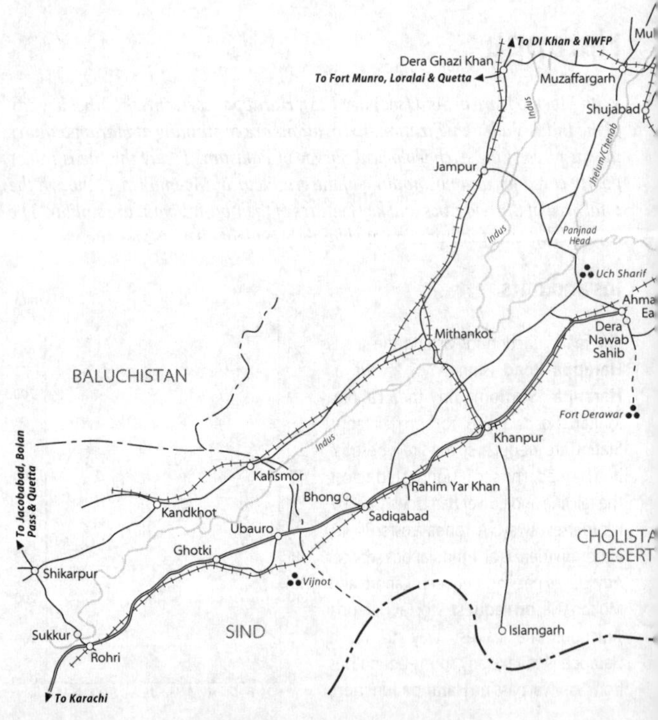

laying the foundations over a distance of more than 150 kilometres.

It was not until the Archaeological Survey started full scale excavations under the Indian Archaeologist **Vats** in 1920, which continued until 1934, that the scale and significance of the buried ruins became clear. Further excavations by **Sir Mortimer Wheeler** in 1946 carried the interpretation of vital features of this Indus Valley City still further.

Tour of the site

The single room **Archaeological Museum** at the site entrance contains some of the most interesting artefacts found at the site. These include terracotta figurines and lingums, copper and bronze objects as well as stone tools including blades and plough shares.

There is also a burial reconstruction showing a female skeleton complete with bangles lying supine in a Deodar wood coffin. Below the coffin pottery vessels are placed in the burial pit, perhaps containing provisions for use in the next life. The museum also contains a male skeleton from Cemetery R-37.

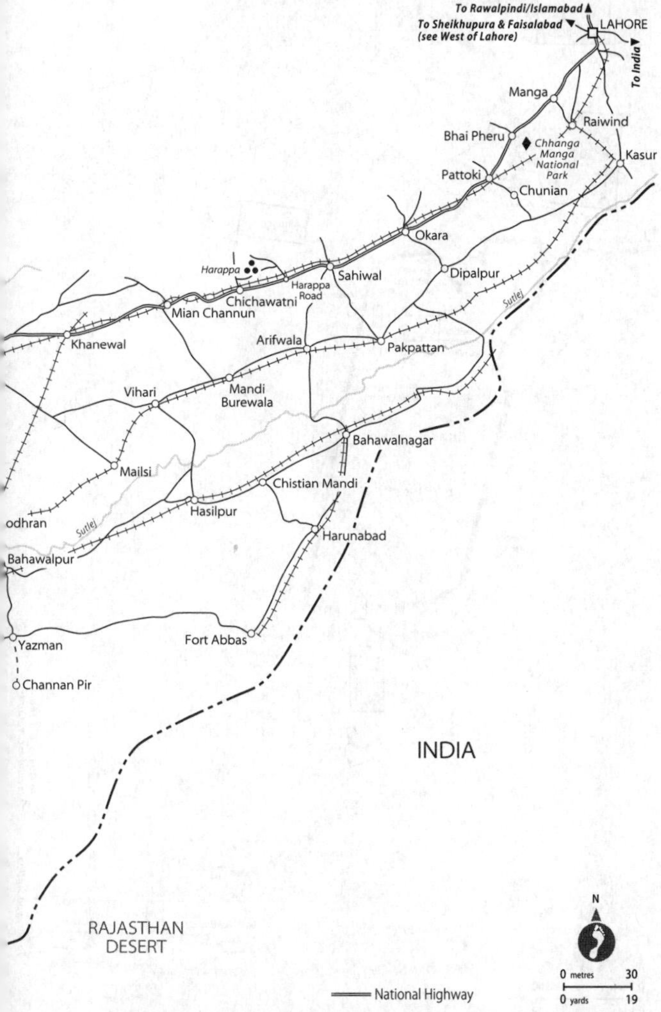

Other notable exhibits include painted burial jars from Cemetery H, a model section of Harappa showing the different levels superimposed upon one another, plus a number of artefacts from Moenjo Daro, Amri, Kot Diji and Rohri.

The path across the site is well laid out and it is possible to walk round the city in about an hour.

Cemetery H The route does not take you past the important sites in chronological order. It starts from the museum at the south edge of the site and passes an area to its left identified as **Cemetery H,** much of which is now grassed over. You get the best view by climbing the path up to the viewing platform and then looking

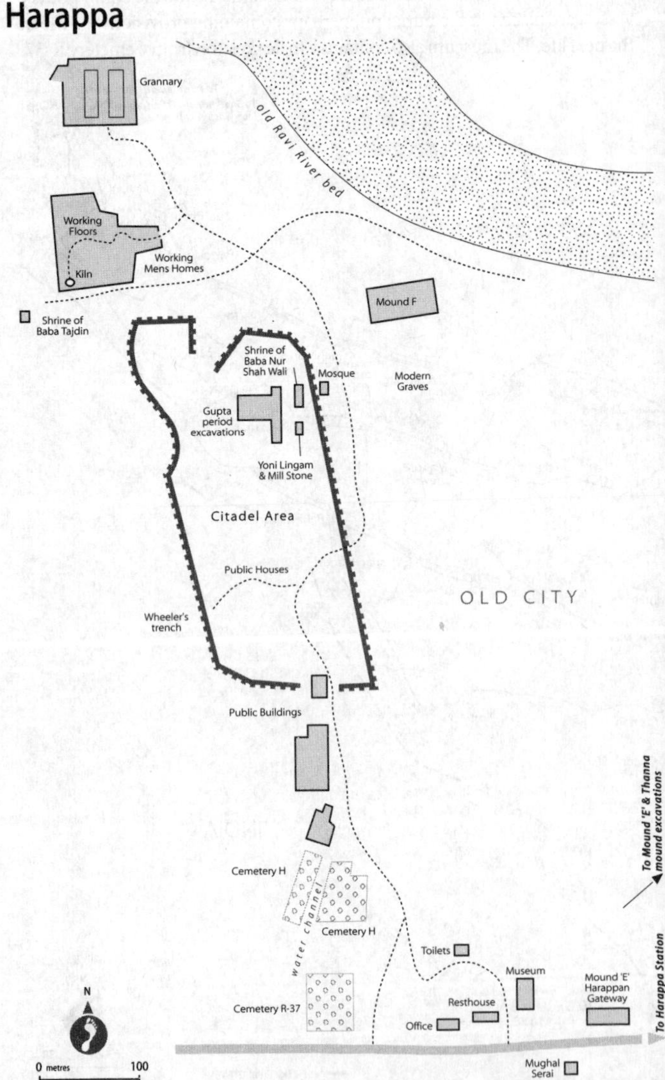

back towards the museum. Cemetery H is a site of vital importance, for as one of the most recent areas of Harappa to be settled it has provided clues to the nature of the last occupants of the town and of the ending of the Indus Valley civilization. Vats found pottery and other grave goods as well as skeletons, and argued that the "**Cemetery H culture**" was the final stage of the Harappan civilization.

The cemetery contained graves dug at two levels. In the lower (and older) of the two, bodies were buried intact and the pottery was similar to that in the main part of the Harappan City. However, in the upper level disarticulated bones were buried in large urns. As Allchin and Allchin point out, "the painted urns from this site tell us all that is so far known about the beliefs of their makers."

Peacocks are a common decorative motif, in some cases showing hollow bodies with small horizontal human forms painted inside. Bulls and cows are another common motif, one of which shows a pipal leaf springing from the hump. All these features have elements in common with the beliefs of the Rg Veda. Vats pointed to further similarities, including, in Allchin and Allchin's words, "two beasts facing each other, held by a man with long wavy hair, while a hound stands menacingly behind one of them; in yet another a little man of similar form stands on the back of a creature which shares the features of a centaur with the Harappan bull-man."

Vats argued that these images bore striking similarities with figures from the Vedas, among them the figure of the hound which he compared with the Vedic God of Death, Yama. Allchin and Allchin suggest that the peacock can be interpreted similarly, "seeing in them the 'One Bird' of the Rg Veda", variously identified with Agni (Fire), Surya (Sunday) and Soma.

All these features suggest that there was a continuity in the use of the site between the Indus Valley settlers and the invading Aryans. The pottery of the upper levels shows strong similarities to pottery found in western Iran at a much later period than that of Harappa itself. Although there are as yet no radiocarbon dates available, the earliest phase of the Cemetery H culture is put by Allchin and Allchin at around 2000 BC, but the distinctive star and bird motifs on the later pottery is contemporaneous with designs from Iran dating from 1550-1400 BC. They supported the earlier conclusion of Vats that "the Cemetery H culture was the final stage of the Harappan, and continuous with it; but that it must indicate the presence of foreign conquerors or immigrants."

Cemetery R-37

To the south of the Cemetery H area, a path leads to another burial site known as **Cemetery R-37**. Discovered in 1937 by Shastri, and further excavated by Wheeler (1946), Mughal (1966) and Dales and Kenoyer (1986-88), 57 graves from the mature Harappan period have been found, with 15-20 pots in each grave in addition to personal toilet instruments. Over time the area became eroded and the graves exposed, and it is suggested that the cemetery became used as a rubbish site. The graves are generally of a poor order, suggesting it was a burial ground of average citizens ranging from 2600-1900 BC. A male skeleton from Cemetery R-37 is in the site museum.

The citadel

From the viewing platform the path climbs north up onto the **citadel**. This has been far less thoroughly excavated than that at Moenjo Daro, and far more of the original brickwork has been removed. However, you can see something of the scale of the central city, the outline of some of its roads, and its drainage system. The path to the left on top of the citadel leads down to the west edge and overlooks the deep trench cut by Sir Mortimer Wheeler into the fortification wall in 1946. It is possible to scramble down to the bottom and get a good view of the impressive scale of this exterior wall.

The citadel had square towers and bastions, and the widest streets within the citadel ran from north to south, as in Moenjo Daro. The path turns right at the top of the citadel mound and descends through the east wall, following this north. It passes the 17th or early 18th century shrine to **Baba Nur Shah Wali**.

Several myths surrounds this site and the stones enclosed behind a fence just to its south. The tomb of the saint is exceptionally long, perhaps nine metres. If you ask the woman attendant you will hear that the tomb is as big as that because the saint was indeed that length. The stones in front were reputed once to have been gold pestle, mortar and ring. When a thief tried to steal them they turned to stone. Only two are visible today.

Old Mosque

Descending from the shrine, the path passes the **Old Mosque**. Originally referred to as the Eidgah, it is thought to date to the Mughal period (1526-1707 AD), and was probably built as a place of worship in honour of a renowned local person (possibly Baba Nur Shah Wali). Measuring 12 metres north-south, it may have been square, but no evidence of a roof has been found. It is built from re-used Harappan bricks, and stands on top of the city walls that date to 2600-1900 BC.

Working floor

Return to the path and continue north. To the right is another mound with a deep excavation made by Sir Mortimer Wheeler, and across in the distance it is just possible to make out the banks of the **Ravi** (flowing from right to left) which once brought boats right up to the north edge of Harappa.

The footpath passes through some low trees, and immediately to its east lies the lower town. Walking across this area you can see the great round brick **working floors**, almost certainly used for grinding grain. Wheat and barley chaff were found in the floors' cracks. Beyond and to the south of the round threshing floors is a group of '**working men's homes**, or single roomed barracks, similar to the small houses in Moenjo Daro.

Granary

The main path continues north to the remains of what Vats termed the **granary**. It comprises the footings of a series of two rows of six granaries, each 16 metres by six metres very close to the old river bank. Allchin and Allchin suggest that the combined floor space was over 800 square metres, similar to that at Moenjo Daro. Although there is no evidence of the superstructure which once covered the brick plinths, their size is still testimony to the sophistication and organization of an urban civilization which both needed and could organize grain storage on such a scale. Evidence of the ever-present problem of increased salinization is particularly prominent here.

Other points of interest

Returning to the site entrance, opposite the museum, across the road, are the remains of a 45 square metres caravanserai that was excavated in 1994, and is thought to either date to the Mughal period (1526-1707) or to the rule of Shah Sher Suri (1540-1545).

Another recent discovery at the Harappa site is the **Mound E** and **Thanna Mound**, located east of the museum. The oldest settlement of the early Harappan period covers eight hectares from the northwest corner of Mound E to the edge of the Thanna Mound, and has been dated at 3300-2600 BC.

The Harappan settlement on Mound E was enclosed by a city wall made of mud-bricks that stood five and a half metres wide and several metres high. It enclosed Mound E on the south side, and turned north along the east ridge of the mound. In 1990 a gateway was discovered in the centre of the south wall, and in 1993 a huge bastion was excavated to the southeast. Excavations are continuing.

Multan

Phone code: 061
Colour map 4, grid C3

The history of Multan is the history of the sub-continent. Every invader from Alexander through the Mauryans, Kushans, Huns, Arabs, Ghaznavids, Mughals, Afghans, Sikhs, right up to the British, have fought for control of the city. The modern city is developing rapidly as an industrial centre, yet has still managed to retain many important historical and cultural attractions.

Seeing the sights of Multan is undoubtedly easier during the cooler months (November-March), though there are some stunning sights that should not be missed even if you can only get to Multan during the height of summer. Most of the sights are located in a compact area around the Fort, of which the Shrine of Shah Rukn-e-Alam is the most beautiful.

Ins and outs

Getting there

Multan is located about 420 kilometres southwest of Lahore (179 kilometres from Harappa) and 945 kilometres northeast of Karachi, and has good transport links. The airport is several kilometres to the west of town (Rs 150 taxi, cheaper by rickshaw), and is connected to all the major cities. Multan is on the main Peshawar-Rawalpindi-Lahore-Multan-Karachi line, and there are special reservation allocations for those joining the train here (Multan Cantt station). Some buses will drop you at the inconveniently located General Bus Stand to the southeast of town (Rs 30 rickshaw), whilst some from the north drop passengers at Officer's Colony Chowk to the northeast (Rs 5 wagon into town). If you are lucky, the bus may drop you at the centrally located Dera Adda Chowk.

From Multan it is possible to continue west into Baluchistan via **Muzzaffargarh**, **Dera Ghazi Khan** and **Fort Munro** (see 'Quetta to Dera Ghazi Khan' section on page 153).

Getting around

The town centre is compact enough for walking, though at certain times of the year the heat, dust and pollution will force you into one of the ubiquitous rickshaws. Bargain hard. Minibuses 1 and 3 make a tortuously slow circuit of the town from Dera Adda Chowk, via Eidgah Mosque, to the General Bus Stand (Rs 5, very crowded).

History

Early history

The first recorded history of Multan is thought to date to the campaign of **Alexander the Great**, who passed through the district in 326-325 BC. Ptolemy describes in great detail the Macedonians' defeat of the Malloi (believed to be the Malavas mentioned in the *Mahabharata*), and how a reckless action by Alexander almost cost him his life. However, it should be noted that the near impossibility of tracing Alexander's exact route means that identification of Multan with this battle is mere conjecture.

The city was then ruled by the **Mauryans** and **Kushans** up to about 470 AD when it was taken by the **Huns**. They remained until the middle of the sixth century.

Arrival of the Arabs

The next source of the early history of Multan can be found in the writings of the early Arab geographers. When the Arabs first penetrated the region, Multan was in the hands of the Brahmin ruler **Chach**. It was during his lifetime that the great Chinese pilgrim **Hiuen Tsang** visited Multan (641 AD). Referring to the city as *Mulosan Pulu*, he described in great detail the magnificent golden statue of Mitra in the city's famed Sun Temple.

Centuries of Muslim rule began when the Arab commander **Mohammad bin Qasim** captured Multan in 712 AD, although it took several centuries for Islam to establish itself as the dominant religion amongst the populace. (It was not until the saint **Makhdum Syed Mohammad Yusuf Shah** settled in Multan in 1088 that significant numbers of the population converted to Islam).

By the end of the ninth century, as the Caliphate weakened, Multan became all but independent of Baghdad. At different points the city came

Multan

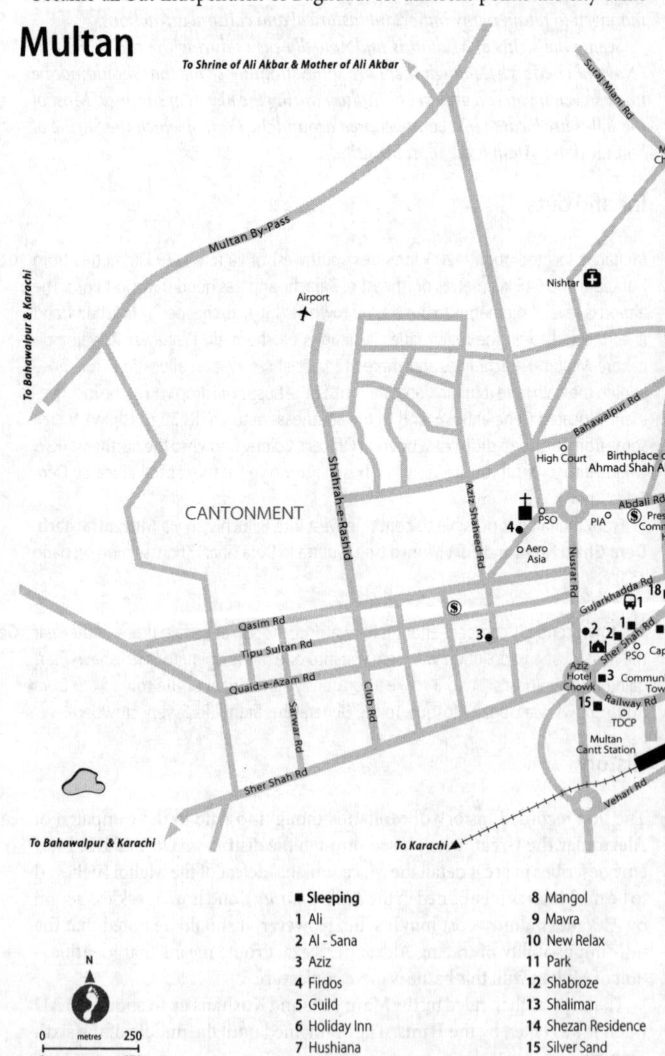

■ **Sleeping**
1 Ali
2 Al - Sana
3 Aziz
4 Firdos
5 Guild
6 Holiday Inn
7 Hushiana
8 Mangol
9 Mavra
10 New Relax
11 Park
12 Shabroze
13 Shalimar
14 Shezan Residence
15 Silver Sand

under the rule of a number of dynasties, including the **Karmatians** (c 915 AD) and the **Ghaznavides** of Afghanistan (c 1004).

The Ghaznavides

Although Multan passed through the hands of a succession of rulers, it was during the reign of the former Turkish slave **Nasir al-Din Qabacha** (c 1206) that Multan developed as a centre of learning and piety. Families such as the Gardezi Syeds and the Qureshis moved to the area, in search of religious education at centres established by the locally born saint **Hazrat Bahauddin Zakaria**. This period also saw the arrival in Multan of other saints such as **Sham-i Tabriz** from Afghanistan, **Kazi Kutb-ud-din** from Kashan, plus **Baba Farid-ud-din Ganj Shakkar** in Pakpattan (see page 291) and **Jalal al-Din Surkh** in Uch (see page 310). Multan continued to be attacked, besieged and conquered by a succession of invaders until coming under the rule of the greater **Mughal** Empire.

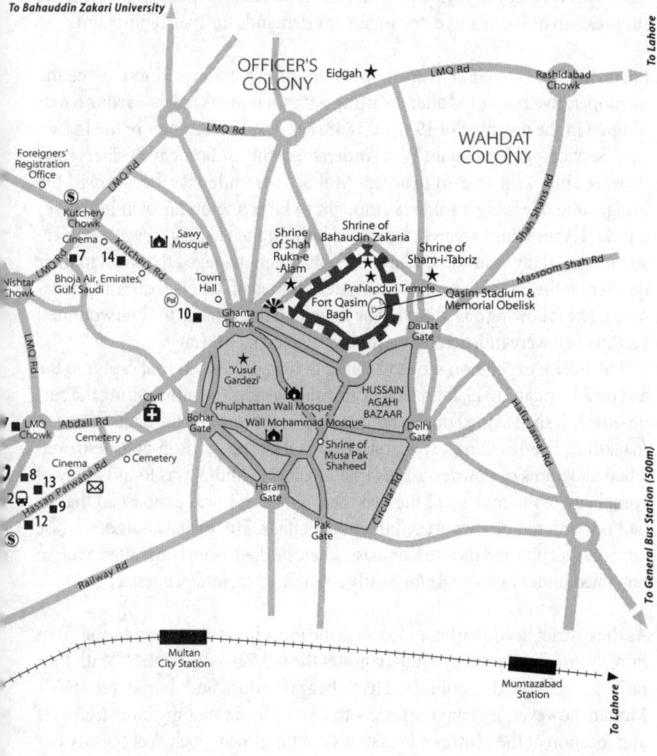

16 Sinbad & Tourist information
17 Taj
18 United

• Eating
1 Multan Chargha Roast
2 New Tabaq
3 Shangrila
4 Xiyuan

Transport
1 Minibuses to Bahawalpur
2 Minibuses to local destinations
3 Minibuses to Sahiwal

Punjab

Mughal period The two centuries of Mughal rule (1528-1752) that Multan enjoyed is regarded as a period of great stability for a city that had experienced so much traumatic upheaval. Coins and documents of the era conferred on Multan the title *Dar-ul-Aman* – 'City of Peace' or 'Seat of Safety'.

Afghans and Sikhs As the Mughal Empire gradually disintegrated, Multan was annexed by the Afghan king, **Ahmad Shah Abdali** (himself born in Multan). Although the Afghans appointed the Governor of Multan, they were only really interested in extracted tribute, so the city was allowed to administer its own internal affairs. This situation continued until 1818 when the Sikh leader, **Maharaja Ranjit Singh**, attacked Multan. During the siege the Sikhs used the famous **Zam zama** cannon that Kipling immortalized (see page 269). The battle for the fort at Multan lasted 84 days during which time thousands were killed on both sides, and most of the buildings within the fort were destroyed. Muslim historians look at the period of Sikh rule as Multan's darkest hour, with the suppression of Islam and extortionate tax demands the main complaint.

The British Following the First Sikh War of 1845, the British attempted to replace the uncooperative ruler of Multan, **Mulraj**, with their own choice, **Sardar Khan Singh**. On the morning of 19 April 1848, Mr. P A Vans Agnew of the Indian Civil Service and Lieutenant W A Anderson of the 1st Bombay Fusiliers rode unarmed into Multan Fort to accept Mulraj's surrender. As they crossed the bridge, one of Mulraj's soldiers (thought to be acting on his own initiative) attacked Agnew and severely wounded him. In the ensuing struggle Anderson was mortally wounded. The two Englishmen managed to return to their quarters at the Eidgah, from where Agnew dashed off letters requesting assistance. The following day, deserted by their Sikh bodyguard, the two wounded Englishmen were murdered by a mob instigated by Mulraj.

The British expedition sent to Multan to bring Mulraj to trial captured the fort on 22 January 1849, following a campaign lasting a month. During the battle, a British shell landed on the Jami Masjid in the fort that the Sikhs used as a magazine. The resulting explosion killed 500 of the garrison and destroyed 2,000 kilograms of powder. At his trial in Lahore, Mulraj was found guilty of complicity in the murder of the two men, although it was established that he had not ordered or encouraged the initial attack. He was taken under house arrest to Calcutta and then to Varanasi, where he died a short time after. Multan remained under British rule for nearly a century until independence.

Modern Multan As the district headquarters, Multan is the most important town in southern Punjab. Any literature on Multan quotes the old Persian couplet, "With four rare things Multan abounds, Heat, beggars, dust and burial grounds". Multan, however, is changing fast, with its rapidly developing industrial base and location at the centre of Pakistan's cotton growing belt. Yet the city has managed to retain its status as ancient cultural capital of the region.

Sights

The Fort area Built on a mound separating it from the city and the dry river bed of the Ravi, the **fort** is a prominent landmark. At its peak the outer walls ran for two kilometres, reinforced by 46 bastions and four gateways each with two towers. Much of the fort was destroyed in the siege of 1848-49, although parts of the outer walls and most of the key shrines survived.

The view from the highest point of the fort, the old gun emplacement just inside the **Bohar Gate**, gives a good idea of Multan's size – something that is hard to appreciate as you make your way through the narrow Hassain Agahi Bazaar. In places the gun emplacement looks ready to collapse, plunging unsuspecting sightseers to the ground below. Binoculars can be hired to admire the sights, although most young men use them to discretley view women! Near to the viewpoint is the **Nigar Khana**, the former armoury that has been turned into a government handicraft shop selling a mixture of beautiful traditional products and pure kitsch.

Within the fort walls are **Qasim Bagh**, a small park offering mini train rides, fairground rides and a children's playground, plus the **Qasim Stadium**, the venue for political rallies and international cricket fixtures. Outside the stadium entrance is a 15 metres high memorial **obelisk** erected to the memory of Agnew and Anderson. The emotional inscription by Sir Herbert Edwardes tells how Agnew and Anderson "being treacherously deserted by the Sikh escort were on the following day, in flagrant breach of national faith and hospitality, barbarously murdered".

When the Chinese traveller **Hiuen Tsang** visited Multan in 641 AD, he described a stunning **Sun Temple** on the fort mound: "There is a temple dedicated to the sun, very magnificent and profusely decorated. The image of the Sun-Deva is cast in yellow gold and ornamented with rare gems. Its divine insight is mysteriously manifested, and its spiritual powers made plain to all". It was thought to have been destroyed in the 11th century, restored and then finally demolished for good by Aurangzeb. The temple was perhaps replaced by the Jami Masjid that the Sikhs used as the ill-fated powder magazine during the 1848 siege. Cunningham identified the site in 1853 as being just to the west of the obelisk. No trace remains today.

At the northern corner of the fort lie the insubstantial remains of the **Prahladpuri Temple**, dedicated to the man-lion form of Vishnu. Although it survived the battle of 1848-49, its fate since then is unclear. However, many recent guides to Multan confuse its remains near to the shrine of Hazrat Bahauddin Zakaria with those of the long since vanished Sun Temple.

Shrine of Hazrat Bahauddin Zakaria

Also known as Bahawal Hakk, **Bahauddin Zakaria** (1182-1266) was born at Kot Aror near Multan and educated in Turan, Iran, Baghdad, Madina and Jerusalem. Having received his doctorate he returned to Multan to preach, in particular spreading the teachings of the **Suhranwardiya Sufi**. The **Khanqah** or University that he founded in Multan became one of the great centres of Islamic learning. He was a great friend of **Farid-ud-din Ganj Shakkar** of Pakpattan.

His shrine stands in the northeast corner of the fort. Built by the saint himself, the only other similar style of architecture is found at Sonepat in India. The base of the tomb is 15 metres square, surmounted by an octagon, and topped by a hemi-spherical white plastered dome. The façade is decorated with blue tiles and superb frescoes. Although substantially damaged in the siege of 1848-49, it was restored by public subscription. The shrine is particularly busy during the saint's Urs (27th Safar, mid-June 1999, early June 2000). Several influential

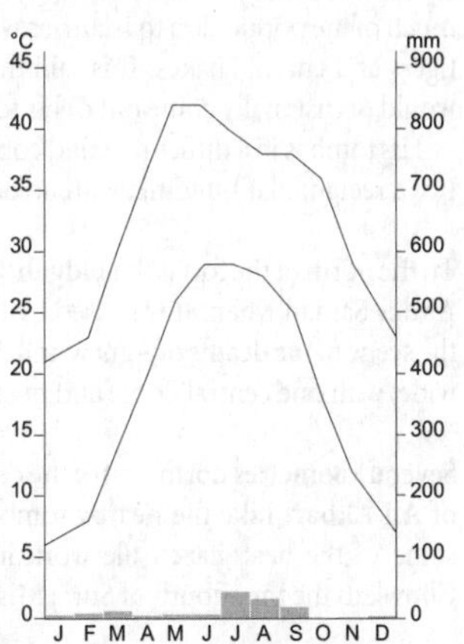

The best time to visit is between November and March

members of the Qureshi family, including Nawab Muzaffar Khan, have their graves nearby.

Shrine of Shah Rukn-e-Alam

On the west side of the fort, dominating both the fort and the city, is the shrine of the saint's grandson, **Shah Rukn-e-Alam** ("pillar of the people"). The tomb was originally intended for the Tughluq family, having been built in 1320 by Emperor Ghiyas ud Din Tughluq, but was given up to the popular Shah Rukn-e-Alam upon his death in 1334.

The shrine is an octagon 15 metres in diameter inside, with perpendicular walls 12 metres high and four metres thick, supported by sloping towers at the corners. This is surmounted by a smaller octagon eight metres high with a small passage around the lower storey from which the Muezzin calls the prayer. The structure is topped by a dome 18 metres in diameter, and said to be one of the largest in Asia. The building stands just over 30 metres high, although the mound upon which it stands raises it to 45 metres, allowing it to dominate the city. At dusk, in the dust laden atmosphere, it seems to rise ethereally above Multan.

The shrine is built of red brick, bounded with beams of sisam wood, with the exterior ornately decorated with calligraphy and blue and white mosaic tile work. It has been brilliantly renovated, winning an Aga Khan Award for architectural restoration. The best time to visit is undoubtedly during the saint's Urs (3rd road Jamaldi ul Awal, mid-August 1999, early August 2000).

Shrine of Sham-i Tabriz

Just northeast of the fort is the tomb of **Sham-i Tabriz**, a Sufi saint born in Afghanistan in 1165. It is said that he raised the dead son of the ruler of Ghazni before coming to Multan in 1202. There are at least three other legends about Sham-i Tabriz (sometimes known as Shams Sabzwari) that associate him with drawing the sun closer to Multan, thus accounting for the city's great heat.

He died in 1276 and the tomb was constructed in 1330, although it was substantially rebuilt in 1780. The main body of the tomb is 10 metres square, eight metres high and surrounded by a richly coloured carved verandah. It is surmounted by an octagon, topped with a green tiled dome, and the whole building stands just under 20 metres high. The interior is rather plain. Try to visit during the saint's Urs (14-16 Rabusani, end of July 1999, mid-July 2000).

Shrine of Makhdum Syed Mohammad Yusuf Gardezi

A direct descendant of the Imam Hassan, this leading member of the influential Gardezi family settled in Multan in 1088. He was influential in converting much of the population to Islam, as well as having the gift of being able to ride tigers and charm snakes. It is said that for 40 years after his death his hand would occasionally come out of his tomb!

His tomb is in a difficult to find compound to the southwest of Bohar Gate. It is a rectangular building, with no dome, but exquisitely tiled.

Eidgah

To the north of the fort is the **Eidgah**, built in 1735 by the Governor of Lahore, Abdus Samad Khan. It was used by the Sikhs for military purposes and was the scene of the deaths of Agnew and Anderson. It is 72 metres long, 16 metres wide, with one central dome and open chambers on either side.

Shrine of Hazrat Ali Akbar Shah

Several kilometres northwest of the centre of Multan is the 16th century tomb of **Ali Akbar**. Like the nearby tomb of his mother, Ali Akbar's shrine has some of the best glazed tile work in Multan. Tongas run from Kutchery Chowk to the the suburb of Suraj Miani where the shrine is located.

Hussain Agahi Bazaar

There are numerous other interesting mosques and shrines scattered throughout the city, many of which you happen to chance upon whilst wandering through the streets. Several are located in **Hussain Agahi Bazaar**, the narrow street market area just to the west and southwest of the Fort. The entrance to the **Shrine of Hazrat Musa Pak Shaheed** is marked by an imposing carved stone gateway that leads into a large courtyard. The shrine is the building to the left, with a green dome and blue tiled façade. Musa Pak Shaheed was born in Uch in 1545, and was killed by bandits just south of Multan in 1600. When his successor brought his body here 16 years later, it is said to have not been decomposed at all, and was indeed brought into Multan seated on a horse. He was a descendant of Abdul Kadir Gilani, and the shrine is popular today with Pathans. The adjacent, low concrete mosque, with three white domes, appears plain from the outside but has a beautifully decorated mihrab inside.

One of the main 'shopping areas' of Hussain Agahi Bazaar is a square variously known as Godri Bazaar, Chopar Bazaar or simply Chowk Bazaar, and it contains a number of attractions. **Wali Mohammad Mosque** was built in 1758 by Ali Mohammad Khakwani. The roof is flat, with no dome, but the frescoes on the exterior walls are exceptional. The three doorways have well executed spandrels.

The Chowk Bazaar is dominated by the minaret of the **Phulhattan Wali Mosque**. This is decorated with blue and pink floral motifs to the cupola at the top. The domed ceiling of the entrance gate is tiled with mirrors. Initially constructed by Emperor Farrukh Siyar, the mosque has been substantially rebuilt. The vivid use of tiles is continued in the interior courtyard, but the mirror work above the prayer chamber entrance is too modern to be appealing.

Opposite the mosque is a small Hindu stupa with Sanskrit engravings. A further 50 metres up the adjacent alley is a stairway leading to the **Girja Ghar Hindu Temple**. The interior is pretty much neglected, but two carvings of Hindu deities can be seen next to the main shrine entrance. The temple is topped by a high stupa. This area of the city has some of the finest examples of the carved wooden balconies and window frames that were a feature of the houses of wealthy Hindus. Prior to Partition, Multan was renowned for its metalwork, particularly jewellery and inlay on gold, silver and copper. Since this trade was primarily done by Hindu craftsmen, it has declined since 1947. Continuing along the Chowk Bazaar will return you to the Hussain Agahi Road below the Fort.

Essentials

Sleeping

■ *on map*
Price codes:
see inside front cover

Multan has a reasonable spread of hotels, though some at the cheaper end are a bit squalid. It may be worth paying extra for a room with an air-cooler (a noisy and primitive version of a/c).

More expensive hotels L *Holiday Inn*, 76 Abdali Rd, T587777, F512511. Best in town, though rooms not as big as others in chain, business centre, health club, pool, *TGI 76* 24 hour coffee shop, *Mehfil* Pak/continental restaurant (buffet/à la carte), *Shang Palace* Chinese, ask about discounts. **A** ***Shezan Residence***, Kutchery Rd, T512235, F512238. Large furnished rooms, carpet, central a/c, dish TV, fridge, attached modern bath, restaurant and bakery, though not as 'luxurious' as the price suggests. **B** ***Sindbad***, Nishtar Chowk, Bahawalpur Rd, T512640, F547144. Large rooms, a/c, fridge, dish TV, attached bath, but no real feel of luxury or quality, restaurant.

Mid-price hotels **C** ***Al-Sana***, Sher Shah Rd, T547501, F512794. Clean rooms, a/c, phone, dish TV, modern attached bath, nice restaurant, good deal if you can get ⅓ off the price. **C** ***Firdos***, Karim Centre, LMQ Rd, T572155, F510070. Furnished a/c rooms, dish TV, modern tiled bath, plus cheaper (hot) non a/c rooms (**D**), above impossibly noisy tape and CD market, staff pushy (tried to solicit a tip just to show the room!), don't bother. **C** ***Hushiana***, Kutchery Chowk, LMQ Rd. Closed. **C** ***New Relax***, Kutchery Rd, T511688. Bed linen clean but rooms rather run-down, a/c, dish TV, attached bath, *Dia Star* restaurant, haggle like mad. **C** ***Silver Sand***, 514 Railway Rd, T42061. All rooms a/c, larger deluxe rooms have sitting area also, but carpets, curtains, furniture and fittings all a but frayed, corridors very run-down, Chinese/Pakistani restaurant, needs a lick of paint to justify price. **D** ***Mangol***, Nawsan Shahr, LMQ Rd, T512865. Some a/c rooms, attached clean bath, though currently looks closed. **D** ***Shalimar***, Hassan Parwana, T583245. Reasonable rooms with fan, small clean attached bath, some a/c rooms (**C**) but a/c "is resting" 0800-1200 and 1700-2100!

Budget hotels **E** ***Mavra***, Hassan Parwana Rd, T511822. Rather smelly rooms, fan, basic attached bath, air-cooled restaurant, poor value. **E** ***Park***, Azmat Wasti Rd, T514407. Good value clean rooms, but foreigners usually told it's 'full'. **E** ***Shabroze***, Hassan Parwana Rd, T544224, F585581. Bed linen not gleaming white but bathrooms reasonably clean, life-saving air-coolers, small restaurant, friendly, best deal at cheaper end. Recommended. **F** ***Aziz***, Aziz Hotel Chowk, Sher Shah Rd. Very basic cell, fan, filthy sheets, dirty attached bath. **F** ***Guild***, Sher Shah Rd. Filthy cell, horrible attached bath, air-cooler. **F** ***Taj***, LMQ Chowk, Abdali Rd, T549319. Basic, attached bath rather grim, huge old-fashioned air-coolers, reasonable restaurant. **F** ***United***, Sher Shah Rd. Very basic, fan, attached bath, pretty grubby, pushy staff. **G** ***Ali***, above snooker hall, Sher Shah Rd. Not interested in foreigners.

Punjab

Eating

• on map

There are numerous **budget** restaurants around Derra Adda Chowk and in Saddar. ***Xiyuan***, Qasim Rd, opposite *Aero Asia* does good **Chinese**, as does ***New Tabaq***, Nusrat Rd, Saddar, although the proximity to the chicken slaughter houses may influence your choice from the menu. ***Shangrila***, Aziz Shaheed Rd, Cantt, also has reasonable Chinese. ***Multan Chargha Roast***, opposite *Sindbad Hotel*, has passable roast chicken. Some of the **hotel restaurants** are good, notably those at the *Holiday Inn* and *Shehzan Residence*.

Entertainment

Sports **Cricket:** *Qasim Stadium* is a low, shade-less concrete bowl inside the Fort area that has previously served as a venue for political rallies and 1-day internationals (though not recently). **Snooker:** *Hot Shot Snooker Club*, LMQ Rd, near Pak Telecom. **Swimming:** try the *Holiday Inn*.

Shopping

Handicrafts The tradition of **silk textiles** existed before the 8th century, when silk from Bokhara was woven into cloth in Multan and then re-exported. Woollen **carpet** weaving is said to have started when families of weavers settled here during the reign of the Ghauris. The carpets are hand-woven on looms and occasionally in addition to pure woollen ones, wool/cotton carpets are also produced.

The town is also famous for **painted and glazed pottery**, particularly *naqqashi* designs in the local *Kangri* style. The old blue and white decorative work is seen in the religious monuments, not only in this town but all across the country. The Mughal emperor Shah Jahan is thought to have ordered these tiles specially when the Mosque in Thatta was built and his son Aurangzeb had done likewise for Abu Waraq's shrine. Today you can buy pottery items for everyday use, crafted with the same skill.

Multan was once also renowned for metal work especially jewellery making and inlay on gold, silver and copper. Since this was done by the Hindu craftsmen, it has

Selected train fares from Multan

	A/c sleeper	*A/c sitter*	*1st class sleeper*	*Economy*
Bahawalpur	*Rs 214*	*Rs 124*	*Rs 61*	*Rs 26*
Hyderabad	*Rs 923*	*Rs 534*	*Rs 347*	*Rs 155*
Larkana	*Rs 726*	*Rs 422*	*Rs 270*	*Rs 120*
Karachi	*Rs 1,086*	*Rs 630*	*Rs 413*	*Rs 195*
Lahore	*Rs 489*	*Rs 287*	*Rs 176*	*Rs 75*
Peshawar	*Rs 962*	*Rs 551*	*Rs 363*	*Rs 165*
Quetta	*Rs 1,001*	*Rs 579*	*Rs 380*	*Rs 175*
Rawalpindi	*Rs 799*	*Rs 467*	*Rs 297*	*Rs 135*
Sukkur/Rohri	*Rs 630*	*Rs 360*	*Rs231*	*Rs 100*

declined since 1947. Multan also produces its particular type of **shoes**, *khussa*, embroidery work on garments, camel skin articles and lacquered wood.

Many of these traditional crafts can be found in the busy bazaars below the fort. Other items can be found in the government handicraft shop inside the fort.

Music There are numerous tape and CD shops, selling everything from bootleg Hindi pop and 'western' hits, through to traditional music, in the Karim Centre, LMQ Rd (below *Firdos Hotel*).

Punjab

Long distance transport

Air *Aero Asia*: **Karachi**, daily; **Lahore**, daily. *Bhoja Air*: **Karachi**, Monday, Wednesday, Thursday, Rs 1,835; **Lahore**, Monday Wednesday, Thursday. *PIA*: **DI Khan**, Monday, Tuesday, Friday, Saturday, Rs 880; **Faisalabad**, Wednesday, Thursday, Friday, Sunday, Rs 1,180; **Islamabad**, 2-3 per day, Rs 2,200; **Karachi**, 1-2 per day, Rs 2,200; **Lahore**, 2-3 per day, Rs 1,480; **Peshawar**, Monday, Tuesday, Friday, Saturday, Rs 2,320; **Rahim Yar Khan**, Wednesday, Saturday, Sunday, Rs 1,240; **Zhob** Monday, Tuesday, Saturday, Rs 880.

Train The main station is Multan Cantt. The Commercial Department (for student and tourist discounts) is just east of the station, towards Multan City station.

Karachi *Shalimar Exp*, 1130, 12 hours; *Tezgam*, 1945, 12 hours. **Lahore** *Tezgam*, 0510, 6 hours; *Khyber Mail*, 1210, 6½ hours. **Rawalpindi** *Quetta Exp*, 0635, 14 hours; *Awam Exp*, 2315, 12 hours. **Peshawar** *Khyber Mail*, 1210, 17 hours; *Awam Exp*, 2315, 16 ½ hours. **Quetta** *Chiltan Exp*, 1905, 19 hours; *Quetta Exp*, 2105, 19 hours. In addition, there are some services to key destinations that originate in Multan (and thus have greater availability of tickets).

Long distance buses The **General Bus Station** is inconveniently located to the southeast of town, on the Multan By-pass (Rs 30 rickshaw ride). Ancient buses run to most destinations. Several private companies, for example ***New Khan Road Runners***, T563055, run more comfortable a/c flying coaches from here: **Bahawalpur** (Rs 35, 5 per day, 2 hours); **Faisalabad** (Rs 100, hourly, 5 hours), **Lahore** (Rs 150, hourly, 7 hours); and **Rawalpindi** (Rs 240, 1 per day, 14 hours). *TDCP*, Railway Road, T580951, run 10 a/c coaches per day to **Lahore** (Rs 150, 7 hours). There are several minibus stands in central Multan, though the former GTS bus stand at Dera Adda Chowk is no longer functioning. On Gujarkhadda Road, just west of Dera Adda Chowk, are minibuses to **Bahawalpur** (Rs 25, 2 hours). Just west of Dera Adda Chowk are minibuses to **Sahiwal**. Just west of the *Shalimar Hotel* on Hassan Parwana Road is a yard running minibuses to local destinations, such as **Alipur**, **Jalapur**, **Kot Mathan**, **Muzaffaragarh**, **Shah Jamal** and **Shujabad**.

Directory

Airline offices *Aero Asia*, 30 Metro Plaza, Qasim Rd, T514135. ***Bhoja Air***, Kutchery Rd, T545581. ***Emirates***, Kutchery Rd, T510747. ***Gulf***, Kutchery Rd, T587617. ***PIA***, 85 Abdali Rd, T570131. ***Saudi***, Kutchery Rd, T580136.

Banks *Emirates Int*, Jalil Centre, Abdali Rd. ***Habib***, Main Cantt. ***National Bank of Pakistan***, Main Branch, Kutchery Chowk. ***UBL***, Main Cantt. All offer foreign exchange.

Communications **GPO:** Hassan Parwana Rd, open Mon-Thur 0900-2000, Friday 0900-1230 1430-1900, Sat 0900-2000, Sun closed. No poste restante. **Telephones:** ***Pak Telecom***, LMQ Rd, open 24 hrs. **Courier:** ***DHL***, T571733. ***TCS***, Bahawalpur Rd, T111123456.

Hospitals & medical services *Civil Hospital*, Abdali Rd, T30539. ***Nishtar Hospital***, off Bahawalpur Rd, T31385.

Places of worship *St Mary's Protestant Church*, Qasim Rd.

Tour companies & travel agents Most are located on Kutchery Rd, though *PTDC* and *TDCP* are a better bet.

Tourist offices *PTDC*, at *Sindbad Hotel*, Nishtar Chowk, Bahawalpur Rd, T512640 (extension PTDC), well meaning but rather disorganized, can arrange city tours, winter tours of Southern Punjab (around Rs 3,000 per person per day all inclusive), very friendly. ***TDCP***, 517-A Railway Rd, next to *Silver Sand Hotel*, T580951. Can arrange city tours, winter tours of Southern Punjab, and offers 10 deluxe a/c coaches per day to Lahore (Rs 150, 7 hrs).

Useful addresses *Foreigners' Registration Office*, Kutchery Chowk, Suraj Miani Rd. ***Police***, Kutchery Rd, T72212/72320.

Bahawalpur

Phone code: 0621
Colour map 3, grid B6

A pleasant town with lots of tree-lined avenues and public parks, Bahawalpur has a relaxed, open feel. Though there are few attractions within the town itself, with the former princely palaces largely out of bounds, Bahawalpur is a good base from which to visit Uch Sharif and the series of forts in the Cholistan Desert.

Ins and outs

Getting there Bahawalpur is some 94 kilometres south of Multan, and about 850 kilometres north-east of Karachi. The airport is 11 kilometres east of town, and incoming PIA flights are met by a bus (otherwise about Rs 100 by taxi). The train station is a couple of kilometres west of the town centre, and is on the main Peshawar-Rawalpindi-Lahore-Multan-Karachi line (though reservations on express trains can be hard to get). The General Bus Station is to the north of town, though a number of destinations to the south are served by 4 small bus yards on Circular Road to the south of town.

Getting around The cycle rickshaws have long since disappeared (apart from the one in the museum), though the centre of the town is compact enough to explore on foot. You will probably need a rickshaw to go to the train station (Rs 20) and General Bus Stand (Rs 15).

History

Formerly the capital of the Princely State of Bahawalpur, the modern town was founded in 1748 by Nawab Bahawal Khan Abbasi I, a direct descendant of the Prophet's uncle Abbas. He raised a wall around the villa of Mohammad Panah Khan Ghumrani and proceeded to build a town that he called

Bahawalpur after his own name. The foundation of the state is attributed to the Abbasis, who ruled for two centuries, although the main seat of the Abbasi family is 55 kilometres southeast at Dera Nawab Sahib.

Entitled to a 17 gun salute, the Nawabs of Bahawalpur were allowed a notional degree of autonomy under the British, until 1903, when the 11th Nawab **Mohammad Bahawal Khan V** took over the full administrative and legislative duties of the state. Many progressive reforms were undertaken during his rule, including the construction of schools and hospitals.

Upon Partition, Bahawalpur immediately acceded to Pakistan and continued as an autonomous province within the federal state until the administrative reforms of 1954 merged the Princely State into the Bahawalpur Division of the Punjab.

It was near Bahawalpur in August 1988 that the plane carrying President **Zia ul-Haq** crashed, killing all on board.

Sights

The Amirs built many fine palaces in Bahawalpur before moving out to Dera Nawab Sahib in the 19th century, but sadly most are now occupied by the army and thus off limits to visitors.

Perhaps the finest is the **Nur Mahal Palace** to the southwest of town. Completed in 1875 in Italianate style, the palace was originally intended as the residence of the 10th Nawab, Sir Sadiq Mohammad Khan IV, although he chose not to stay there due to its proximity to the Maluk Shah graveyard. It is now part of the army's Divisional Battle School, and sightseers are turned away sharply. It is perhaps easier to look at the model of the palace in the museum.

The **Daulat Khana**, completed in 1886, was also built for the 10th Nawab but it is now in a very poor state of repair. Other former residences of the Nawabs, the 1876 **Bahawalgarh Mahal** and the 1902 **Gulzar Mahal**, both to the east of town, are also occupied by the military and impossible to visit. The **Emir of Dubai** also has a palace on the outskirts of town that is used as a base for hunting expeditions into the Cholistan Desert.

In a town of low-rise buildings, the stunning **Jamai Masjid al-Sadiq** stands out magnificently, rising above the bazaar. Built shortly before Partition, the exquisitely carved white stone mosque compares with any mosque built in South Asia this century (Shah Faisal Masjid, Islamabad included). To the southwest of the main bazaar is the **Eidgah**, who's tall yellow minarets and low yellow wall are a distinctive landmark.

The **zoo** on Stadium Road has a representative collection of fauna of the region, plus a successful captive breeding programme that has supplied amongst other things, lions to the other zoos in the country. Opposite is the **Dring Stadium**, one of the country's finest sporting complexes.

The **Museum** (0900-1600, closed Friday) contains galleries dedicated to the Pakistan Movement, Islamic Arts, Archaeology (including exhibits from Cholistan, Gandhara, Moenjo Daro, Harappa, Derawar, Kot Diji, Amri, Soan and Rohri), Ethnography (including cloth, jewellery, pottery from Cholistan, plus Bahawalpur's only cycle rickshaw), and a room of rare manuscripts and calligraphy. Next door to the museum stands the **Sadiq Reading Library**, who's foundation stone was laid in 1924 by the then Viceroy and Governor General of India, Sir Rufus Daniel Isaacs, Earl of Reading.

Short excursion from Bahawalpur

Lal Suhanra National Park

Phone code: 0621

Located 36 kilometres east of Bahawalpur, the Lal Suhanra National Park has been established on either side of the Desert Branch Canal and provides a number of floral and faunal contrasts. Changing from desert to forest, with a large lake and grassland, the park supports a great variety of animal and birdlife. Inside the main gate is a children's playground, and a small zoo housing deer, antelope, Nilgai, and gazelles, plus aviaries containing peacocks, falcons, quails, owls, pheasants and swans, as well as the rare Houbara Bustard. There are also a couple of miserable rhinos from Nepal. Further into the park there are black buck, blue bull antelope and chinkara. In recent years there have been accusations that well connected Pakistani politicians have been using this park as a private hunting reserve.

The TDCP has a **D** *Motel* with six rooms and restaurant, although its not possible to book in advance. Further into the park are two **E** *Resthouses* that

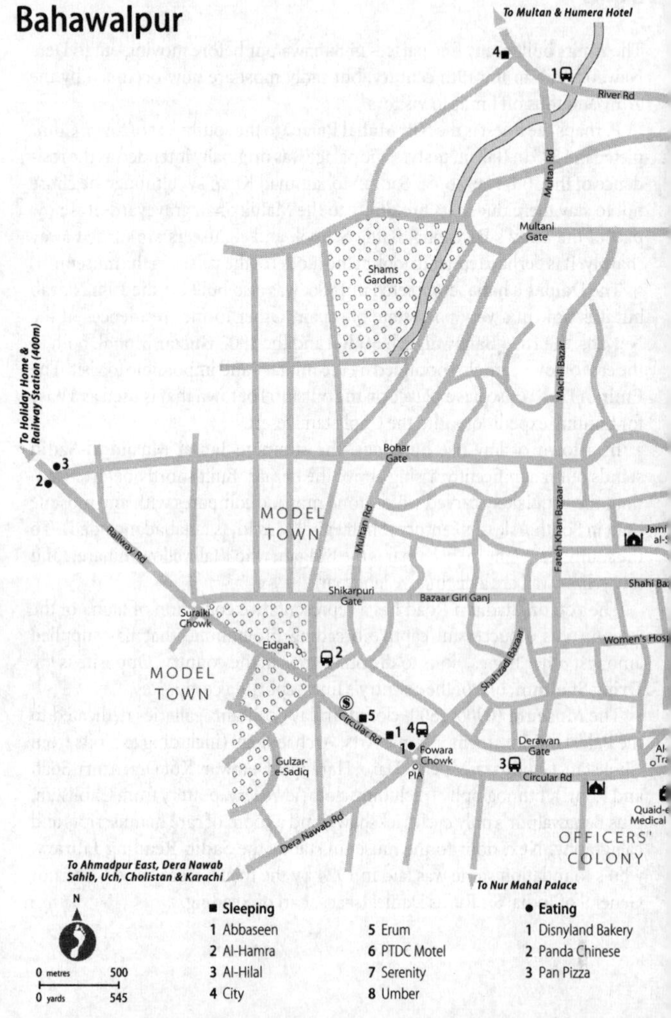

should be booked at the park office at 3a, Trust Colony, Bahawalpur, T80696. The park is quite peaceful, but you will require your own transport to explore it fully. The park can be reached by bus or wagon from Bahawalpur's GTS bus stand (Rs 11, 30 minutes). The bus drops you at Lal Suhanra Chowk, from where it's a three kilometres (Rs 20) tonga ride to the main gate.

Essentials

Sleeping

■ on map
Price codes: see inside front cover

Mid-price hotels C *PTDC Motel*, Club Rd, T84760. Recently opened, "a fantastic hotel ... several little cabins, very clean and modern ... restaurant is excellent", often empty so bargain hard. **C** ***Serenity***, Bobby Plaza, Circular Rd, T876792, F876093. Well furnished rooms with dish TV, modern attached bath, plus some suites (**B**) with a/c, fridge and balconies, restaurant, keen staff. Recommended. **D** ***Holiday Home***, off Railway Rd, Model Town, T874566. Private home-stay. **D** ***Humera***, Multan Rd, near Sutlej Bridge (north of town), T884840. Some a/c rooms, dish TV, restaurant, garden, but remote and looking very forlorn.

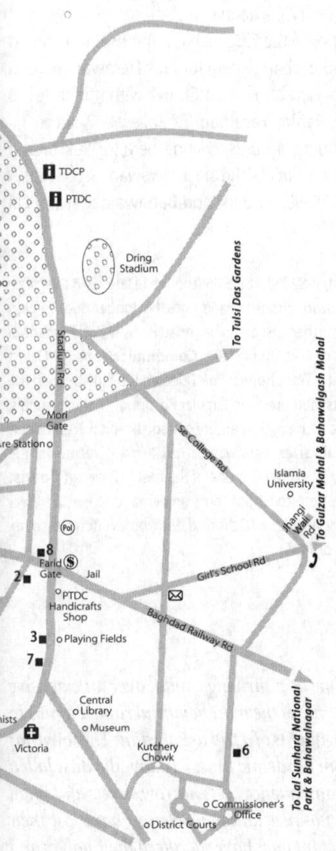

Budget hotels E *Abbaseen*, Circular Rd, T877592. Fairly basic, fan, attached bath, a/c not working, not much English spoken. **E** *Al-Hamra*, no English sign, new location just inside Farid Gate to left. Good clean rooms, attached bath, cheap, "highly recommendable", good choice. **E** *Al-Hilal*, no English sign, Circular Rd, T875942. Fairly basic rooms, attached bath, air-cooler. **E** *City*, Multan Rd, near General Bus Station, T882440. Pretty basic, convenient for bus station, but so noisy! **E** *Erum*, Circular Rd, T7120. Rms not particularly clean but at least they have an air-cooler, some cheaper rooms without, fridge, attached bath. **G** *Umber*, Farid Gate. Very, very basic.

Eating

● on map

Disnyland Bakery (sic), Fowara Chowk, has cakes, sweets, biscuits and bottled mineral water. There's an ice-cream parlour upstairs, and a stall and seats outside. ***Pan Pizza***, Railway Rd, T877140, has been recommended by several readers (Rs 150-200). ***Panda Chinese***, opposite, also comes highly recommended ("Rs 250-300 for 2 sharing, excellent"). There are numerous cheap and basic places just inside Farid Gate and around Fowara Chowk.

Festivals

Channan Mela Each year around the Hindu month of Chaitra (mid-end of March), a huge festival celebrating Cholistani life and culture is held at the small village of **Channan Pir**, located some 40 kilometres south of Bahawalpur.

Punjab

Enquire at the tourist office for further details.

Shopping **Handicrafts** Bahawalpur is the centre for marketing handicrafts produced in the Cholistan Desert region. The ***Punjab Small Industries Corporation*** shop opposite Farid Gate is a good place to start, and gives some idea of what price to pay in the bazaar.

Long distance transport **Air** *PIA*: **Islamabad**, 2 per day, Rs 1,960; **Karachi**, Thursday, Saturday, Rs 2,080; **Lahore**, 2 per day, Rs 1,300; **Sukkur**, Thursday, Rs 1,360.

Train **Karachi** *Shalimar Exp*, 1255, 11 hours; *Tezgam*, 2112, 13 hours. **Multan** 9 trains daily, 1½ hours. **Lahore** *Khyber Mail*, 1014, 8½ hours; *Shalimar Exp*, 1713, 6½ hours. **Rawalpindi** 7 trains daily, 16 hours. Note that there are only limited reserved places available on the express trains.

Long distance buses The chaotic **General Bus Station** is located to the north of town. There are shuddering wrecks to most destinations, though you're better off with the private 'flying coach' companies. There are regular services to **Multan** (Rs 25, 2 hours), with some continuing to **Lahore** (Rs 175, 9 hours).

The small yard just off Circular Rd, opposite the Eidgah, has minibuses that depart when full for **Ahmadpur East** (Rs 15, 1 hour, change here for **Fort Derawar** and **Uch Sharif**). **Shahzadi Bazaar Bus Stand** is a yard off Fowara Chowk with minibuses to **Kanpur**; **Multan** (Rs 25, hourly, 2 hours); **Rahim Yar Khan** (Rs 70, every 2 hours, 3½ hours) and **Sadiqabad** (Rs 80, every 2 hours, 4 hours, change here for Sukkur and places further south). Another bus yard on Circular Rd near Derawan Gate ('Red & White' sign) has coasters to **Sadiqabad** (Rs 80, 4 hours) and **Bahawalnagar** (for **Lal Suhanra**).

Directory **Airline offices** *PIA*, Fowara Chowk, Circular Rd, T882303, F882305 (though in late 1998 this office looked closed). **Banks** ***National Bank of Pakistan***, opposite Farid Gate. No longer does foreign exchange (they send you to their Main Branch further east along Baghdad Railway Rd). ***Prudential Commercial Bank***, next to *Erum Hotel*. Changes cash at terrible rates. **Communications** **GPO:** just off Baghdad Railway Rd, to the east of Farid Gate. **Telephones:** ***Pak Telecom*** is a little beyond the GPO. **Hospitals & medical services** **Chemists:** numerous on Circular Rd, opposite the hospitals. **Hospitals:** ***Victoria Hospital***, Circular Rd. A typical turn of the century cottage hospital. Next door is the huge ***Quaid-e-Azam Medical College***. **Libraries** Bahawalpur has a good record in the provision of education, and the ***Central Library*** (see 'sights') is one of the best in Pakistan. **Tourist offices** *TDCP*, 11-12 Stadium Rd, is frequently deserted. Runs tours on demand to Fort Derawar and Uch Sharif (Rs 600 for guide plus Rs 1,500 for vehicle). ***PTDC*** is next door, but is often closed up. **Useful addresses** ***Edhi ambulance***, T661204 or T115.

Uch Sharif

Colour map 3, grid B5

Although much diminished from its time as a thriving capital over an extensive area, the town of Uch Sharif contains some of the most beautiful ruined tombs in the country and represents one of the highlights of a trip to Pakistan. The town has been described by an eminent Pakistani academic thus: "Today, the dust laden Uchchh Sharif is a small town of little consequence ... Its narrow streets and small houses are mostly unsightly. Even its mosques and mausoleums have lost their splendid colour. In fact, the most important ones have sacrificed their halves and much of their original revetment to the ravages of time and tide. Nonetheless, the city is still revered by the devotees of those who are lying buried there. They flock to their tombs and their Khanqahs ceaselessly to offer fateha and to seek solace from worldly woes. It seems that the practice will continue for ever" (Dr Ahmad Nabi

Khan's attractive book on the history and architecture of Uch is available through the National Institute of Historical and Cultural Research in Islamabad).

The best time to visit Uch is late on a spring afternoon, whilst the air is clear and the temperatures not too hot.

Ins and outs

Most visitors reach Uch from Bahawalpur. A minibus from the wagon yard opposite the Eidgah in Bahawalpur drops passengers in **Ahmadpur East** (Rs 15, 1 hour), a small town 50 kilometres south of Bahawalpur along the National Highway (make sure the driver knows that you are continuing to Uch). From there, a second minibus takes passengers to Uch (Rs 10, 45 minutes). Very occasionally, a minibus will run all the way from Bahawalpur to Uch. From the wagon yard in Uch, walk through the main bazaar, and follow this main street all the way through town and out the other side to the tombs (20 minutes).

History

The etymology of the name is uncertain, but it is thought that the town can trace its origins back to the Buddhist period of rule before Alexander re-named it Askandra (or Alexandria). Following the Arab conquest of Sind and Multan in 711/712 AD, the town came under Muslim influence, but control over Uch was continually contested for the next seven centuries. The Mughal Emperor Akbar eventually annexed Uch to the Delhi Sultanate, and the town developed as an important cultural and literary centre. Indeed, the town reached its peak in the 13th century as a centre of Islamic learning and piety. The town is variously referred to as Uch, Uchchh or Uch Sharif.

Sights

There are two distinct groups of religious buildings in Uch. On the one hand is a group of **square** or **rectangular tombs** with low wood-framed flat roofs and timber columns. The second comprise **domed tombs** built on octagonal plans. Tragically many of the buildings have been seriously damaged or even partially destroyed, mainly by the shifting course of the **Chenab**.

Tomb of Bibi Jalwindi

By far the most striking monument still standing is the **Tomb of Bibi Jalwindi** (see photograph in the colour section at the front of this book). This is one of three such tombs found on the southwest edge of the high mound representing the debris of an ancient fortress. Much of the surface comprises a huge graveyard, the earth over the graves standing up sharply from the surrounding baked mud.

If you approach these tombs from the narrow lanes of the town you get the impression that they are still intact, yet despite their damaged state, they are still among the finest of their kind. The Tomb of Bibi Jalwindi in particular still suggests the magnificence both of form and decoration which was once the hall mark of the completed structures. The structure is essentially brick built, embellished with stunning glazed tile mosaic.

Thought to date to 1494, the mausoleum was erected in three octagonal storeys. The lower storey was supported by rounded and sloping corner turrets, on which a second storey with a narrow gallery for walking round was supported. A hemispherical dome crowned the building. In the west wall is the beautifully carved wooden mihrab. It is one of the finest achievements of

Multani style architecture, for which the Rukn-e-Alam and the Baha al-Din Zakaria, built 150 years earlier, had served as outstanding examples.

The exterior of the tomb is almost totally covered with the glazed tile work which is the hall mark of the style. The spandrel of the arches has a variety of floral patterns, the parapet has a frieze of glazed tiles while the turrets are surmounted with a bunch of broad flowering leaves, unique to this tomb. The first storey rises to a height of nine metres, the second storey surmounting it like a drum. The destruction of nearly half of the tomb allows a clear view of the interior decoration, which is equally remarkable. It is well worth scrambling down the slope to the field below to obtain a more distant view, which in the evening light is particularly rewarding.

Tomb of Baha' al-Din Uchchhi

The mausoleum nearest to the tomb of Bibi Jalwindi is that of **Baha' al-Din Uchchhi**, also known as **Baha al-Halim**, and is thought to be the earliest of the group found here. The architect-mason who constructed it is buried in the third of the domed tombs.

Tomb and Mosque of Jalal al-Din Surkh

Close to the Tomb of Bibi Jalwindi is the tomb and mosque of **Jalal al-Din Surkh** (1177-1272). "It was presumed" writes Dr. Ahmad Nabi Khan "that the devoted visitor coming to the tomb to offer *fateha* and to pay homage to the personage lying buried there, might like to pray in a nearby situated mosque attached to it." The mosque of Jalal al-Din Surkh belongs to the flat roofed class of tombs and mosques in Uch. It too has suffered damage at various times; an inscription in Persian on either side of the Mihrab records that it was repaired by Mulla Ahmad under the orders of Sheikh Hamid in 1617. The key time to visit is during the saint's Urs (19 Jamad Sahri, end of September 1999, mid-September 2000).

Tomb of Jalal al-Din Bukhari

A few minutes walk away stands the tomb of **Jalal al-Din Bukhari** (1303-1383), grandson of Jalal al-Din Surkh. A 14th century saint, he travelled widely to Mecca, Medina, Mesopotamia, Egypt and Persia before settling in Uch, and is credited with popularizing the Sufi Suhrawardiya school in the region. His shrine is a flat-roofed oblong room supported by wooden pillars, with a small room containing a footprint of Imam Ali to the left. It is still visited by pious Muslims today, and is particularly busy during the saint's Urs (10-12th Zilhaj, end of March 1999, mid-March 2000).

Shrine of Sheikh Saifuddin Ghazrooni

Nearby, and a little difficult to find, is the shrine of **Sheikh Saifuddin Ghazrooni**. A Muslim saint who settled in Uch around 980 AD, his shrine is said to be the oldest Muslim tomb in South Asia, although it is now in a poor state of repair.

Fort Derawar and the Cholistan Desert

Colour map 3, grid C5

The **Cholistan Desert** is the largest desert in Pakistan, covering over 25,000 square kilometres. It extends south into the Thar Desert in Sind, and east into India's Rajasthan Desert. Its name is said to derive from the Urdu verb *cholna* – to walk – although its not clear whether this refers to the shifting sand dunes or the semi-nomadic people who roam the desert in search of water and pasture.

The area has experienced a succession of climatic changes over the last 500,000 years, with a deep layer of red soil below the present sand surface suggesting a much moister environment during the Upper and Middle

Palaeolithic periods. The **Hakra River** (known in the Vedas as the **River Sarasvati**, and more recently as the **Ghaggar**) once flowed through the region, supporting a civilization contemporary with Moenjo Daro and Harappa. Over 400 archaeological sites have been uncovered along the dried up bed of the Hakra, in addition to evidence of numerous Stone Age settlements at the lower levels.

A series of desert forts have been built to guard the trade route across Cholistan, the best preserved of which is **Fort Derawar**. PTDC and TDCP in Lahore, Multan and Bahawalpur can sometimes arrange jeep and camel safaris in the Cholistan Desert.

Ins and outs

Getting there

For those not on a tour, Fort Derawar is usually approached from Bahawalpur. A minibus from the wagon yard opposite the Eidgah in Bahawalpur drops passengers at 'Abbasi Chowk' in the small town of **Ahmadpur East**, 50 kilometres south along the National Highway (Rs 15, 1 hour). Make sure that the driver knows you are going to Fort Derawar (*qila*) otherwise he will drop you further away. There is no public transport to the fort but Suzuki mini-vans can be hired easily by asking around 'Abbasi Chowk'. Rates are negotiable, although Rs 500 is the usual day hire fee. The road to the fort has now been sealed so a four-wheel drive vehicle is no longer necessary, although the road does deteriorate as you near the fort. Although less than 50 kilometres away, it takes 1½ hours to reach the fort.

Getting around

The fort remains the property of the Abbasi family and a **permit** is required to go inside. The permit is available from the seat of the Abbasi family – the splendid 19th century **Sadiq Garh Palace** in **Dera Nawab Sahib** (the twin sister of Ahmadpur East, lying 4 kilometres to the east). If travelling as part of a TDCP or PTDC tour, this formality is usually arranged for you. However, the permit is only necessary if you wish to go inside the fort, and since the interior is mostly in ruins, Fort Derawar is still worth a visit even if you do not have the permit.

Snacks and cold drinks are available in the village outside the fort, but it is wise to take water and sun-block. Bottled mineral water can be found in Ahmadpur East but is it rarely refrigerated. PTDC are planning to develop camping facilities at the fort – they have got as far as putting up the sign announcing the project!

Approach

Travelling due south from Dera Nawab Sahib, the road to the fort branches right over the irrigation canal, about 10 kilometres beyond the village of Shahi Wali. Continue to the crossroads and then take the left turn at the 28 kilometres marker stone. Recent provision of irrigation has made the area remarkably green, with wheat and sugar cane being prominent. However, about 24 kilometres from the fort cultivation becomes patchy, with the landscape giving way to dunes and desert scrub.

The deterioration of the sealed road surface coincides with the first view of the fort, some five kilometres away. Many drivers elect to drive on the sand flats on nearing the fort, thus romanticizing the approach to this remarkable structure, as well as providing a smoother ride. Mirages of huge lakes are a common phenomenon. The lost in time feel of the place is enhanced by the flocks of wandering sheep and goats grazing on the scrub around the fort, with shepherds keeping watch from the backs of camels. Two famous Pakistani dramas – *Darya* (River) and *Reigzar* (Desert) – were filmed in the ruins of the village at the base of the fort.

Fort Derawar

The present fort at Derawar was built by the Abbasi family in 1733, although it is believed that there have been fortified settlements on the site for several thousand years. Travelling along the desert road, the fort's massive outer walls loom out of the desert, visible from some distance away. It is an impressive sight.

The outer walls of the fort rise 30 metres out of the desert, and are supported by 40 massive bastions, 10 on each side. The huge defensive tower at the main entrance to the east was added in 1965, during the Indo-Pak war. The fort's defensive walls run for one and a half kilometres, and it is worth walking around the outside of the fort to get a sense of scale.

500 metres to the east of the fort is the royal cemetery of the ruling Nawabs. Many of the tombs are decorated with marble and blue tile mosaic, although the enclosure is closed to visitors. Nearby is the permanent water-hole from which water is drawn up in goatskin bags. Directly outside the fort, to the east, is the attractive **Sadiq Mosque**. Built in 1849 in the same style as the Moti Masjid in Delhi's Red Fort, a marble slab at the entrance covers the carved signature of **Khewja Ghulam Farid**, a revered Sufi saint. In a small enclosure 500 metres northwest of the fort are the graves of four of the Prophet Mohammad's companions.

Most of the interior of the fort is in ruins, although a few of the modern structures remain. The gates to the ladies' section of the Nawab's quarters and the painted pavilion to the northeast are usually locked. There is an extensive network of subterranean passages leading to vaulted chambers, cellars and dungeons beneath the fort, many of which show evidence of being accessible by trolleys. Locals suggest that there is an underground tunnel from the fort through the desert, to Dera Nawab Sahib, some 45 kilometres away. However, the same locals claim that cannonballs fired from the fort's two cannons once landed on Lahore!

Rahim Yar Khan

District headquarters in the Bahawalpur Division, Rahim Yar Khan lies approximately half-way between Karachi and Lahore (and about 114 kilometres southwest of Bahawalpur, on the National Highway via Khanpur). The original site is associated with **Phul Badda**, capital of Phul during the period of Sumra rule over Sind. The present site was laid out in the mid-18th century. It was renamed in 1881 after the eldest son of Nawab Sir Sadiq

Fort Derawar, Cholistan Desert

Mohammad Khan, the Crown Prince Rahim Yar Khan. The modern town is a commercial and industrial centre. The Emir of Abu Dhabi has a palace nearby which is used as a base for hunting expeditions into the Cholistan Desert. He is credited with having financed the construction of Rahim Yar Khan's airport, as well as the huge, modern extension to the district hospital. Rahim Yar Khan can be used as a base from which to visit Bhong Mosque (see below).

Sleeping & eating

D-E *Faran*, Thali Rd, T0731-78426. "A decent, clean, safe hotel with 70s decor". There are a number of budget **F-G** hotels in Railway Chowk, Shahi Rd, around the railway station. The best is probably **F** ***Paras***, T72586, the only one with an English sign.

Transport

Air *PIA*: **Faisalabad**, Tuesday, Rs 1,780; **Islamabad**, Tuesday, Rs 2,860; **Karachi**, daily, Rs 2,200; **Lahore**, daily except Tuesday, Rs 1,900; **Multan**, Monday, Friday, Saturday, Rs 1,000; **Peshawar**, daily except Tuesday.

Train Although on the main Peshawar-Rawalpindi-Lahore-Multan-Karachi line, it is difficult to get a reservation other than 'economy' class in Rahim Yar Khan. For times, look under 'Bahawalpur' and add/subtract approximately 2½ hours.

Bus Wagons leave from Town Hall Chowk for **Sadiqabad** (for **Bhong Mosque**). Coasters to **Bahawalpur** (Rs 80, 4 hours) run from the yard next to Punjab Sweet Mart on Shahi Rd. ***New Khan Road Runners***, T73139, opposite, run deluxe services to **Lahore** (Rs 175, 13 hours) 1845 1945 (via **Faisalabad**) 2115 2215. ***Manthar Travel***, Shahi Rd (next to Galaxy cinema), T76925, run a/c coaches to **Karachi** (Rs 220, 14 hours) 1830 1915.

Directory

Most of the utilities (GPO, Pak Telecom, banks etc) are located east (left) from the station along Shahi Rd (towards Town Hall Chowk). *PIA*, Iqbal Complex, Town Hall Chowk, T75432.

Bhong Mosque

Almost 70 kilometres southwest of Rahim Yar Khan is the extraordinary **Bhong Mosque**. What is remarkable about this complex is that the relatively insignificant town of **Bhong** (*Population*: 5,000) boasts one of Pakistan's most elaborate and ostentatious mosques. What is also remarkable is that some current guidebooks fail to even mention this place!

Ins and outs

To reach Bhong, take a wagon from Town Hall Chowk in Rahim Yar Khan to Sadiqabad (39 kilometres, 1 hour). From there, local buses run the 27 kilometres (1 hour) to Bhong.

Sights

Conceived, designed and financed by a local landlord (Late) **Sardar Rais Ghazi Mohammad Khan**, the complex comprises two mosques, a library, a madrassa and guest quarters. Construction began in 1932 and continued for 50 years. Essentially, the grand mosque reflects the traditional local style integrated with stylistic elements borrowed from regional Islamic architectural forms, notably from Iran, Spain and Syria. Rais Ghazi also chose to include Western colonial influences. The intention was "to represent as many forms of vernacular craft and Islamic religious architectural features as possible using a combination of traditional and modern materials". Does it work? Cynics may argue that the complex has evolved into something of an Islamic architectural theme park, with the designer choosing to include too many competing styles. However, no one can fail to be impressed by the spectacular interior to the grand mosque. Rais Ghazi chose to use only traditional materials and craftsmanship for the mosque interiors, and this is reflected in the superb use of teak, ivory, marble, onyx, coloured glass, glazed tile work, frescoes, mirror work, gilded tracery, ceramics, calligraphy and inlay. The gold leaf on the mihrab is striking.

The building of the Bhong complex has had a major effect upon the local community. During the 50 year construction period, it is estimated that 1,000 workmen and 200 craftsmen have been employed on the project. Although many workers were brought in from outside – master masons and craftsmen from Rajasthan, from Multan for the glazed tile and mosaic work, from Karachi for painting and calligraphy – most of the unskilled labourers came from the local community. Many of the craftsmen trained in the workshop have subsequently been employed by the government on the restoration of national monuments.

The development of the complex has resulted in the growth of local infrastructure, including provision of electricity, running water, irrigation, transport and a market. Further, prior to the development of secular education in the 1960s, the madrassa was the regional centre for education, attracting at its peak students from Turkey, Afghanistan and Iran. In 1986, Bhong Mosque was awarded the Aga Khan Award for Architecture.

Routes The NH goes southwest through **Sadiqabad** (39 kilometres), crosses the Sind border to Ubauro (68 kilometres) and then passes through Ghotki to **Sukkur** (108 kilometres). For details of Sukkur see page 133.

Azad Jammu and Kashmir

Azad Jammu and Kashmir

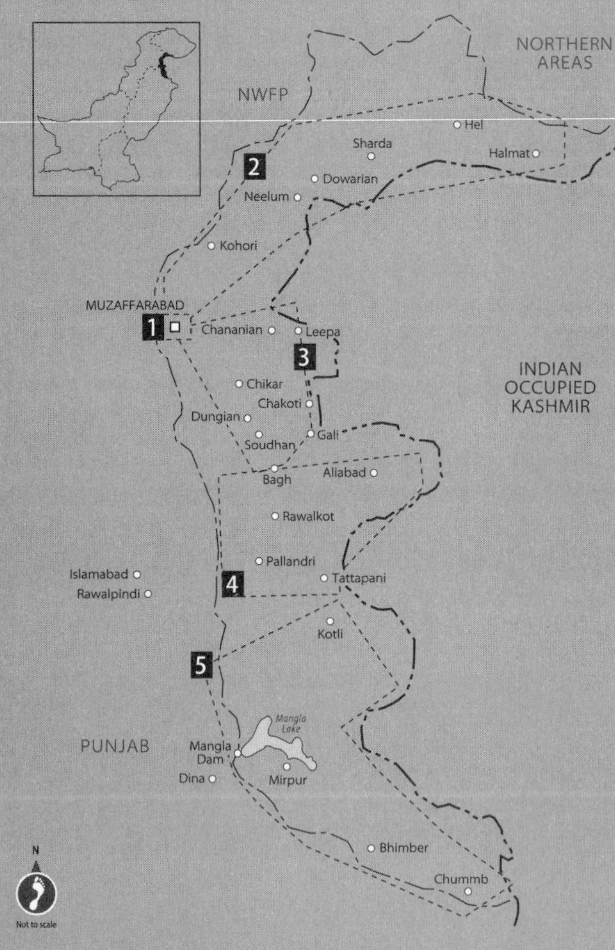

Text Divisions

Azad Jammu and Kashmir's (AJ&K) beautiful valleys, forests, lakes and mountains have been permanently scarred by a 50-year-old political dispute that shows little sign of being resolved. Since Pakistan and India became independent of Britain in 1947, Kashmir has been divided between the two nations in a dispute that totally dominates the bilateral relations of the South Asian neighbours. India currently occupies 63 percent of Kashmir, whilst the rest of Azad ('Free') Kashmir is under Pakistani administration. India and Pakistan have fought a number of wars over the status of Kashmir, and the current de facto border here between the two countries, the 'Line of Control', is in fact a ceasefire line.

For visiting foreign tourists, the sensitivity of this border means that it is currently impossible to visit some of the region's most attractive spots. Information has been included on these areas (compiled with assistance from the AJ&K Tourism Department and local sources), in the hope that a resolution to the dispute will allow access to these beautiful areas. In the near future, however, this seems unlikely. Other parts of Azad Kashmir can be visited quite easily, although a permit must first be obtained (details below).

Best time to visit *The best time to visit the northern parts of Azad Kashmir is from early April until early June, and then from September through to early November, thus avoiding the extremes of winter cold and summer heat, plus the monsoons. The south is oppressively hot in summer, and is best visited between October and March.*

Ins and outs

The travelling text of the 'Azad Jammu and Kashmir' chapter is divided into 5 key sections. It opens with 'Muzaffarabad', detailing the state's capital. The second section describes the beautiful 'Neelum Valley', now largely off-limits to tourists. The third section, 'Jhelum Valley', describes this valley, much of which is accessible to foreigners, as well as the 'Leepa Valley', which isn't. The fourth section describes 'Poonch and Bagh District', whilst the chapter concludes with the southernmost 'Mirpur and Kotli Districts'.

If you intend visiting the northern and central areas, then the best approach is by bus (or plane) from Islamabad/Rawalpindi via Muzaffarabad (it is here that you obtain your NOC, see below). If you are only visiting the southern districts, you can get a direct bus from Rawalpindi to Mirpur, or you can get a bus from Dina (on the GT Road between Rawalpindi and Lahore) to Mirpur. The southern districts are easier to visit if you do not have an NOC.

An understanding of the 'Kashmir question'

Anyone interested in visiting this region should have at least some knowledge of the 'Kashmir question', not just because you will be invited to debate it at every possible opportunity, but to have 'no opinion' on the matter is rather insulting, suggesting that the outside world does not care about, or is ignorant of this situation.

There are two versions of events in Kashmir at Partition; one supported by Pakistan and the other by India. In fact, indigenous accounts of this period of South Asia's history are generally so skewered in their bias that they are rendered unreadable. There is a very fine dividing line between 'law and order' and 'state sponsored terrorism', between 'liberation movement' and 'terrorists'; all terms used regularly by the two sides in the conflict.

Prior to independence, the secular ('Hindu' if you read Pakistani accounts) Congress Party, led by Sheikh Abdullah, had established itself as the leading democratic force in the State of Jammu and Kashmir. As Britain liquidated its empire in the sub-continent, the Muslim League in Kashmir clearly favoured joining Pakistan, whilst the Congress party had a preference for India, or indeed independence. The Hindu Dogra Maharaja **Hari Singh**, ruling a predominantly Muslim state, was still undecided when Pakistan and India became independent in August 1947.

What actually happened immediately after independence is vehemently contested by India and Pakistan to this day. According to Indian historians, Pathan tribesmen from NWFP, supported and encouraged by Pakistan, invaded Jammu and Kashmir, attempting to annex the state for Pakistan. Those writing from a Pakistani viewpoint suggest that there was an insurgency amongst the Maharaja's own people, demanding accession to Muslim Pakistan, and the Kashmiris were joined in their struggle by civilian volunteers from across the border. Either way, with the 'rebels' only a few miles from the capital at Srinagar, on 25 October 1947, Hari Singh signed an instrument of accession to India, and Indian troops were flown into the state. In the meantime, in Gilgit and Baltistan to the far northwest of the State of Jammu and Kashmir, the local people rebelled against the decision, declared their independence from Kashmir, and vowed to join Pakistan.

The war in Kashmir between India and Pakistan was one of the first major crises to be discussed at the **United Nations**, and remains its longest unresolved dispute. India charged that Pakistan had sent "armed raiders" into the

Visiting Azad Jammu and Kashmir

Because of the sensitive nature of the de facto border with India, and the very real danger from firing across the Line of Control, certain areas of Azad Kashmir are off-limits to foreigners. Unfortunately, these areas include the two most attractive valleys in Azad Kashmir – Leepa and Neelum – plus a number of other interesting sites. A permit, or ***No Objection Certificate****, is required to visit any other place in the state, although even equipped with this,* ***you are not permitted to approach within 16 kilometres of the Line of Control****. You will frequently be asked to produce this document, so it is not advised that you attempt to travel around Azad Kashmir without it. In fact, whereas across the rest of Pakistan everybody seems to know one sentence of English – the ubiquitous "what is your country?" – in Azad Kashmir there is an alternative mantra: "prove your identity!" Obviously the result of the tense security situation in the state, this is a phrase that you may well come to loathe. Its usage is not restricted to police officers and members of the security forces that you may meet; school children, bus drivers, hotel managers, the list is endless. Many visitors to Azad Kashmir frequently have their breakfast, lunch, dinner, sleep, and any other activity interrupted by someone demanding that you "prove your identity". The irony is that, invariably, those demanding that you prove your identity are unable to prove their own. Those claiming to be members of the police rarely have the documents to substantiate their claim. As a general rule it is advisable that you only show your No Objection Certificate to those in uniform, or in possession of a police or security services identity card.*

No Objection Certificate: *The No Objection Certificate (NOC) should, in theory, be obtained from the Ministry of Home Affairs within the Ministry for Northern Areas, Frontier Regions and Kashmir Affairs at the Secretariat in Islamabad. However, unless you are a journalist working in Pakistan, it is far more practical to obtain the NOC by going directly to the* ***AJ&K Home Department*** *in the* ***Secretariat*** *at* ***Muzaffarabad*** *(located in the Chattar area, to the south of the town centre, T4157).*

To obtain the NOC you must visit the Home Department (closed Friday afternoon/Saturday afternoon/ Sunday/holidays) and write a short letter explaining the places that you wish to visit, and why. Your letter will then be translated into Urdu, and reproduced into 6 or 7 copies. The various copies will pass through many hands, including those of the police, military intelligence (ISI), Home Secretary and the Tourism Department, and any sensitive areas will be deleted with bold strokes of a red pen. The whole document will then have to be retyped. This process can take upwards of 4 hours, allowing plenty of opportunity for endless cups of tea and discussions on the 'Kashmir situation'. Before being given the NOC, you may well be called for interview by the Home Secretary, ISI or both. Freelance journalists will probably be denied the document. If you have any other problems, it is worth enlisting the help of the friendly AJ&K Tourism Department across the road. There is no guarantee that you will get a NOC.

The NOC, written in Urdu, does not actually list the places to which you can and can't go, although you have to sign a declaration stating that you will not go within 16 kilometres of the Line of Control, nor photograph bridges or military installations. Once you have your NOC, you can book AJ&K Tourism Department Resthouses at places you wish to visit.

It is best to obtain your NOC as soon as practical after arriving in Muzaffarabad. It is quite likely that the police or ISI will hear of your arrival in town remarkably quickly, and you may receive a visit at your hotel.

state, and called upon the UN to demand their withdrawal. Pakistan countered that India had used "fraud and violence" to manoeuvre Hari Singh's accession, and demanded that a plebiscite be held under the supervision of the UN in order to settle the dispute. Hostilities between the two countries continued until 30 December 1948 when a UN sponsored **ceasefire** was agreed upon. The ceasefire line, or **'Line of Control'**, has been the de facto border between the Indian State of Jammu and Kashmir and Pakistani administered Azad Kashmir ever since.

After the war, a **plebiscite** was agreed to by India on condition that the armies of both parties withdraw from all the territories of the former state, and that peace and normalcy be restored first. These conditions, not surprisingly, have never been met and the plebiscite is yet to be held. In 1957 a bill was passed in the Indian parliament integrating the State of Jammu and Kashmir within the Indian Union. In 1965 Pakistan and India began another brief war over the status of Kashmir, although the war rapidly ground to a stalemate.

Following Pakistan's crushing defeat in the 1971 war over Bangladesh, Prime Minister Zulfikar Ali Bhutto was of the opinion that Pakistan could not resolve the issue by military force. In 1972 he signed the **Simla Agreement** with the Indian Prime Minister Mrs Gandhi under which both countries recognized the Line of Control, and agreed that the dispute could only be resolved through bilateral negotiations. Many Pakistanis never forgave Bhutto for 'selling out' on the Kashmir issue.

With no sign of a resolution to the dispute, the **'Kashmir question'** continues to dominate relations between India and Pakistan. In fact, following the uprising, or 'jihad', that began in the Indian occupied part of Kashmir in 1989, there has been a hardening of stances between the two sides. India charges Pakistan with arming, training and funding the 'terrorists', whilst Pakistan insists that it offers just moral support to the 'freedom fighters'. Pakistan further charges India with acts of state terrorism in occupied Kashmir, a charge seemingly substantiated by the reports of independent Human Rights organizations.

In Azad Kashmir the situation remains tense. Much of the state is closed to foreign tourists, with regular reports of firing across the Line of Control. However, as Azad Kashmir becomes more and more integrated within the federal structure of Pakistan, less attention is paid to the voice demanding Kashmiri 'independence'.

Muzaffarabad

Phone code: 0581
Colour map 5, grid B3

Muzaffarabad has retained a strategic importance on the main route between the Punjab and the Vale of Kashmir from at least the Mughal era. However, the town's profile has been raised since the partition of the sub-continent (and the division of Kashmir between Pakistani and Indian control) and Muzaffarabad is now the capital of Azad Kashmir. Ironically, the closing of the trading and communications route along the Jhelum Valley to Srinagar has removed Muzaffarabad's initial raison d'être. Foreigners intending to visit Azad Kashmir are advised to begin their journey in Muzaffarabad because this is the only place at which you can obtain the essential No Objection Certificate.

Ins and outs

Getting there There are direct flights between Islamabad and Muzaffarabad, with less regular flights linking the AJ&K capital to Lahore. The airport is close to the town, with a rickshaw ride costing around Rs 75 (about Rs 150 by taxi). Regular buses run between Muzaffarabad and Rawalpindi (4½ hours) via Murree and Muzaffarabad also acts as the main transport junction for regional bus services to the Neelum, Jhelum and Leepa valleys.

Getting around

The city runs for almost 4 kilometres along the east bank of the Neelum River, from the fort down to the confluence of the Neelum and Jhelum rivers. Below the confluence is the area called Chattar, where the AJ&K Legislative Assembly, Secretariat and Tourist Office are located. Suzuki wagons run between the fort, the main bazaar (Bank Road) and Chattar.

Muzaffarabad

▲ To Neelum Valley

To Garhi Habibullah Khan (for Kaghan Valley), Mansehra & Abbottabad ◄

To Jhelum Valley ▼

To Murree, Islamabad & Rawalpindi ▼

Sleeping
1 Al Habib
2 Gilani
3 Neelum View
4 Palace
5 Sangum
6 Tayyeba
7 Tourist Resthouse

Buses
1 Regional Bus Station
2 'New'Bus Stand
3 Suzuki stand to Chattar

0 metres 250
0 yards 273

Sights

Red Fort

Muzaffarabad's sole tourist attraction is the 16th century **Red Fort** located at the northern limit of the town. Begun in 1549 and completed in 1646 by **Sultan Muzaffar Khan** (who gave his name to the town), the fort was built as a result of border skirmishes between the Mughal Emperor Akbar and the Chak rulers of Kashmir. Once the Mughal rulers claimed the ascendancy, the fort's strategic interest declined, although there was a brief revival under the Afghan Ahmed Shah Durani. The Dogra rulers of Kashmir, **Gulab Singh**, and then **Ranbir Singh**, rebuilt and extended the fort, yet it was abandoned at Partition.

Surrounded on three sides by the Neelum, the impressive red clay outer walls are reasonably well preserved, although the river has caused some damage to the north. The

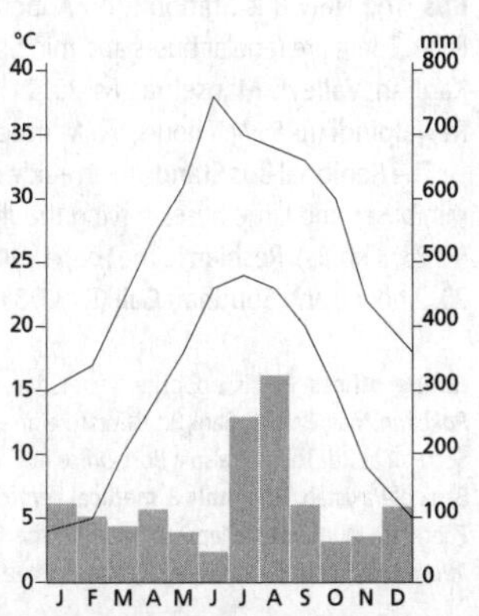
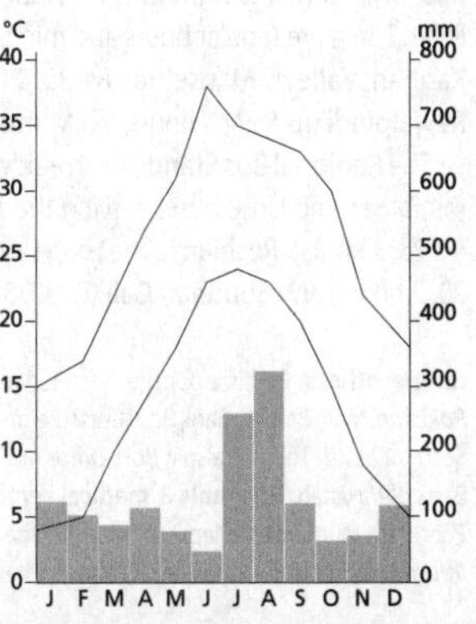

The best time to visit is October to November and March to May

Azad Jammu and Kashmir

entrance to the compact fort is through the adjacent *Resthouse*, and there are some pleasant gardens and lawns once inside. There is also a small museum. The fort is open until quite late, although the museum closes at 1700. The views across the river to the army stables are impressive during the late afternoon.

Essentials

Sleeping
■ *on map*
Price codes: see inside front cover

B ***Sangum***, Secretarial Rd, Domal, T4194, F2587. Best in town, dish TV, fridge, phone, Oriental and Kashmiri restaurant, room service, bakery, car rental, banquet hall. **D** ***Neelum View***, Neelum Rd, opposite Fort, T4733, F5468. A/c, dish TV, phone, room service, laundry, *Lotus* restaurant. **D** ***Tayyaba***, Secretariat Rd, T4800. Reasonable rooms, attached bath, some cheaper **E** rooms also. **E** ***Al Abbas***, Secretariat Rd, T3103. Reasonable doubles with attached bath. **E** ***Capital City***, Secretariat Rd (old PIA building), T4828. **E** ***Tourist Resthouse***, Fort, T3090. Good value government-run resthouse, some a/c rooms, quiet garden, good location, meals available. Bookings through Tourism Department, T4112. There are numerous **F** hotels in Muzaffarabad, generally in and around Bank Rd in the main bazaar, and opposite the New Bus Station on the west bank of the river. The best in Bank Rd are probably ***Palace***, T3189 (no English sign) with cheap rooms, friendly staff, with attached bath and bedbugs, or the ***Gilani***, T3799. The best cheap hotel in town is the friendly **F** ***Al Habib***, Abbottabad Rd, opposite New Bus Station, T3282. With good value rooms and restaurant.

Eating

Not much choice other than the hotel restaurants, although those at the *Sangum* and *Neelum View* are quite good.

Shopping

Handicrafts Although Kashmir is famous for its handicrafts, particularly dyed wools and woodcarvings, they are all distinctly lacking in the main bazaar above Bank Rd. The labyrinth-like properties of the bazaar do make it a fascinating place to wander, however.

Local Transport

Rickshaw There is a rickshaw stand on the slope just above Bank Rd.

Suzuki See the map for the location of the Suzuki stand north to the Fort and south to Chattar (both Rs 3).

Long Distance Transport

Air PIA: **Islamabad**, Monday, Tuesday, Wednesday, Thursday, Saturday, Rs 400; **Lahore**, Monday twice, Tuesday, Wednesday twice, Thursday, Saturday twice.

Bus The **New Bus Station** is on Abbottabad Rd, on the west side of the Neelum River. There are regular buses and minibuses to **Ghori Garhi Habibullah** (change for **Kaghan Valley**), **Mansehra** (Rs 20, 2 hours), **Abbottabad** (Rs 25, 3 hours) and **Rawalpindi** (Rs 55, 4½ hours) via **Murree**.

The **Regional Bus Stand**, down a side road off Bank Rd, next to the *Gilani Hotel*, has minibuses and large buses serving the Jhelum Valley, including all stops to **Chakoti** (Rs 25, 3 hours), **Reshian** in the Leepa Valley, and **Bagh** (Rs 45, 4 hours), via **Chikar** (Rs 20, 2 hours) and **Soudhan Gali** (Rs 32, 3 hours).

Directory

Airline offices *PIA* is opposite Secretariat, Chattar, T3121/4877. **Banks** *National Bank of Pakistan*, Main Branch, Bank Rd. Offers foreign exchange, including TCs. **Communications** **GPO:** Secretariat Rd. There is also a Post Office in Chattar. **Telephones:** Bank Rd, behind the National Bank of Pakistan. **Hospitals & medical services** *Combined Military Hospital*, CMH Rd, T3666. There are numerous chemists opposite the hospital. **Tourist offices** *Azad Kashmir Tourist Information Centre*, opposite Secretariat, Chattar, T4112 (0900-1600, closed Sat/Sun). The helpful office provides essential information to visitors to Azad Kashmir, as well as booking for the various *Tourist Guesthouses, Angler's Huts* and *Tourist Cottages*. However, they will not take any bookings until you have your NOC. **Useful addresses** ***Home Department, AJ&K Secretariat***, Secretariat Rd, Chattar, T4157. The place to obtain your NOC. ***AJ&K PWD Office***, Secretariat Rd (1st courtyard on left up road opposite Kashmir Industrial Emporium), T3247 (0900-1600, closed Sat/Sun) for bookings of *PWD Inspection Bungalows* in Chikar, Neelum and Leepa Valley. Inconveniently, those in Soudhan Gali, Bagh and Pallandri must be booked in Bagh. ***Divisional Forestry Office***, for booking *Forest Resthouses*, is near Jinnah Bridge in Domal, although it may be about to move to a new site. Offices of ***Jammu and Kashmir Liberation Front*** and ***Jammu and Kashmir Peoples' Conference*** are on Neelum Rd, near the Fort.

Neelum Valley

Considered by many to be the most picturesque of all the Kashmir valleys, the 200 kilometre long Neelum Valley runs in a generally northeast direction from Muzaffarabad towards the river's source in the Pir Panjal. The Neelum River, known as Kishanganga prior to Partition and so marked on many maps, runs for much of its journey through Pakistani administered Kashmir broadly parallel to the Kaghan Valley's Kunhar River. The valley is famous for its scenic beauty, with thick fir and deciduous forests cloaking the hills on either side of the river and affording marvellous trekking opportunities.

Colour map 5, grid B/C3

Unfortunately, the bad news is that for almost its entire length, the valley runs parallel and adjacent to the Line of Control with India, and is thus strictly off limits to foreigners (even with a No Objection Certificate). Domestic tourists may still visit the area, but the regular Pakistani press reports of Indian firing across the Line of Control suggest that life is anything but normal in the valley. The following details on the Neelum Valley are for information only, hopefully anticipating a time when the valley can be visited.

Muzaffarabad to Halmat and the border

Colour map 5, grid B4

The road along the Neelum Valley leaves **Muzaffarabad** to the north, past the fort, and is sealed for the first 100 kilometres or so, before becoming a fair-weather road, and finally a jeep track. Public buses run as far as **Khel** (155 kilometres), beyond which jeeps and ponies are the only other transport option.

At **Kohori** (marked on some maps as Ghori), 16 kilometres from Muzaffarabad, a trekking route leads north, passing close to Makra Peak (3,885 metres), and continuing to Shogran in the Kaghan Valley (about two to three days). Another trekking route into the Kaghan Valley begins at **Patikha**, six kilometres further along from Kohori. Beyond Patikha the road comes within 16 kilometres of the Line of Control, and so tourists are currently not permitted to travel beyond this point.

At **Nouseri** (20 kilometres) the Neelum Valley turns sharply to the northeast, the road crossing to the west bank, and continuing up to **Kundal Shahi** (32 kilometres). Here, the Neelum River is joined from the northwest by the Jagran Nala, a tributary well stocked with trout. A jeep track goes up the nala to **Kutton** (eight kilometres) where the AJ&K Tourism Department have several **E** *Angler's Huts*. Another *Angler's Hut* is located at **Salkhata**, three kilometres beyond Kundal Shahi (bookings from the Tourist Office in Muzaffarabad) at a secluded spot close to the trout hatchery.

The road continues northeast to **Athmuqam** (84 kilometres from Muzaffarabad), a larger settlement that serves as the sub-divisional headquarters. Just beyond Athmuqam is the village of **Neelum** (nine kilometres), and there is a riverside AJ&K Tourism Department **E** *Resthouse* at nearby **Keran**.

A further 13 kilometres from Neelum is the village of **Dowarian**, located at 1,615 metres amongst a beautiful conifer forest. There is a **E** *Resthouse*. From Dowarian it is possible to trek northwest across the 4,140 metres Rattigali Pass onto the Kaghan Valley's Lalazar Plateau (2-3 days). There is excellent camping at the Rattigali Sar, a large alpine lake near to the pass.

The road continues on to **Sharda** (30 kilometres), described by the AJ&K Tourism Department as being "a breath-taking green spot at an altitude of 1,981 metres ... a captivating landscape with numerous springs and hillsides covered with trees." The Tourism Department run a **E** *Resthouse* and 22 bed *Youth Hostel*. It is possible to trek north, and then northwest, along the Surgan Nala and across the Nurinar Pass into the Kaghan Valley.

The main road runs as far as **Khel** (155 kilometres from Muzaffarabad), described as being another picturesque village. Even if Khel ever becomes accessible to tourists, it would probably be too risky to attempt the trek north along the Shounter Nala and across the 4,420 metres Shounter Pass to the lawless region around Chilas.

Khel is the point at which to hire a jeep or horses for the 49 kilometres journey on to the border village of **Halmat** (**E** *Resthouse*).

Jhelum Valley

Colour map 5, grid B/C3

The Jhelum Valley runs in a southeasterly direction from Muzaffarabad, and prior to Partition and the subsequent division of Kashmir, provided the main line of communication between Punjab and Srinagar. Today, the Pakistani administered section ends at Chakoti, 60 kilometres from Muzaffarabad. However, because of the proximity to the Line of Control, it is not possible to travel much beyond Dani Baqaian (33 kilometres), the turn off for the chain of hill stations on the road to Bagh District. Thus the beautiful Leepa Valley is off-limits to foreigners, although some information on this valley is included for future reference.

Routes The road along the Jhelum Valley follows the southernmost bank of the river, passing through the small village of Garhi Dopata, before reaching the settlement of **Dani Baqaian**. The main road continues in a southeasterly direction, towards the turning for the **Leepa Valley** and for the Line of Control at **Chakoti**. Another road turns south at Dani Baqaian, giving access to a string of small **hill stations**, before continuing to Bagh, in Poonch & Bagh District.

The Hill Stations

Chikar
Colour map 5, grid B3

The small town of **Chikar** (13 kilometres) is situated on the crest of a ridge, offering fine views of the terraced wheat and maize fields, leading up to the pine topped hills that surround on all sides. These forests offer some cool and relaxing short walks. A very comfortable **D** *PWD Resthouse* is well sited, just above the main bazaar (no sign). It has six large, well furnished rooms, with clean attached bath, shady veranda, and pleasant garden. Meals are by arrangement, although there are several basic restaurants in Chikar's bazaar. Bookings should be made in Muzaffarabad. The **E** *Tourist Resthouse*, belonging to the AJ&K Tourism Department, has recently been refurbished. There are several basic **F** hotels in the bazaar, including *Al Shabaz* and *Shamsa Barri*.

Noonbagla

To the south of Chikar the road forks. Contrary to some maps, and other guidebooks, the four hill stations in this chain are not linked by road on a single north-south axis. The right fork offers a sealed, and then a fair-weather road, to **Noonbagla** (12 kilometres, and sometimes referred to as Loonbagla), a very quiet and relaxing settlement comprising some two dozen or so buildings. There is a very pleasant **E** *Forest Resthouse* just above the bazaar. It offers two clean doubles, with attached bath and terrace views, meals by arrangement. Bookings from Muzaffarabad, but they are not always necessary. There are some excellent walks along the pine clad ridge behind the *Resthouse*.

Noonbagla can be reached by Suzuki from Chikar (Rs 20, 45 minutes), although you should ascertain as to whether you have made a 'booking', or are in a 'service' car.

Routes

The fair-weather road continues beyond Noonbagla to **Dungian** (3 kilometres), another tiny settlement surrounded by pine forests, and on to **Soudhan Gali** (13 kilometres). However, there is no regular transport on this route, and following poor weather, the route is often blocked to vehicles. Having said that, it is a very nice walk.

Soudhan Gali

The main route to **Soudhan Gali** (16 kilometres) is via the left fork beyond Chikar. The road drops down to the river below Chikar, before making a slow, tortuous climb up to Soudhan Gali. Public buses operate on this route from Muzaffarabad (Rs 32, three hours via Chikar Rs 10, one hour), continuing onto Bagh (Rs 12, one hour). The main bazaar is set just below the pass, at the top of the crest.

Soudhan Gali has a good **D** *PWD Resthouse* situated above the bazaar, but the chowkidar will not let you stay without a booking chit. The booking can only be made at the PWD in Bagh, very inconvenient when you'll have almost certainly come from the direction of Muzaffarabad. There is a reasonable private **E** *Resthouse* located near the hairpin bend on the hill (blue and red veranda, no sign), plus some very basic **F** hotels in the bazaar.

Routes

The road from Soudhan Gali gradually descends to the town of **Bagh** (25 kilometres).

Leepa Valley

Colour map 5, grid B3

All of the literature and brochures from the AJ&K Tourism Department go to great length to describe the beauty of the **Leepa Valley**, suggesting that it is the most stunning in Azad Kashmir. Unfortunately, most of it lies within 16 kilometres of the Line of Control, and so is off-limits to foreigners. It is open to domestic tourists, however, from May to November.

Returning to the main route along the Jhelum Valley, beyond Dani Baqaian the road passes through **Naili** (45 kilometres from Muzaffarabad), the turning point for the **Leepa Valley**, before continuing via **Chinari** (6 kilometres) to the border town of **Chakoti** (8 kilometres).

A fair-weather road climbs northeast from Naili up to the 2,750 metres **Reshian Pass**. A path leads west from here to the pleasant meadows at **Danna** (AJ&K Tourism Department **E** *Resthouse*). The main jeep track then drops down into the valley of the Leepa River, a tributary of the Neelum. At the head of the valley the route divides. To the east is **Leepa** (60 kilometres from Naili), a small village at 1,921 metres set amongst the rice paddy fields, and noted for its typical wooden Kashmiri houses. To the west is **Chananian** (58 kilometres from Naili), located at 2,226 metres amongst thick pine forest. There is an AJ&K Tourism Department **E** *Resthouse* here. Public buses from Muzaffarabad run as far as Reshian, beyond which a jeep will be required.

Poonch and Bagh District

Although not as attractive as the Neelum and Leepa Valleys, Poonch and Bagh District does have some attractive hill resorts, most notably Dhirkot, Banjosa and Tararkhel. Poonch District has a long military history, and is noted for its fighting men. Although there are differing interpretations of events, it is through this area that the 'liberation' of Kashmir was launched following the Maharaja of Kashmir's decision to accede to India in 1947. The region had been under Dogra rule since the British handed over the area to Gulab Singh following the signing of the Treaty of Amritsar in 1846. The Maharaja of Kashmir had, however, found it very difficult to establish his rule in Poonch.

Rawalkot
Colour map 5, grid C3

Rawalkot is the district headquarters, and can be reached from Rawalpindi/Islamabad via Kahuta and Azad Pattan, or via Dhalkot, or from Muzaffarabad via Kohala and Dhirkot. The town is also linked to Banjosa. Tararkhel, Pallandri, Tattapani and Bagh. It serves more as a centre to the communications network than as a tourist attraction itself. There is, however, an AJ&K Tourism Department **E** *Resthouse*, plus an office at which to book the other *Resthouses* at Dhirkot and Banjosa. *PWD Resthouses* at Pallandri and Tararkhel should also be booked from Rawalkot.

Ins and outs **PIA** have flights to **Islamabad** Tuesday, Thursday, Saturday 1115 and **Karachi** Tuesday, Thursday, Saturday 1115.

Banjosa Some 20 kilometres southeast of Rawalkot, at Banjosa (1,981 metres), there is a beautifully situated **E** *Resthouse*, in the heart of the pine forest. There are some excellent walks along the ridge, with fine views of the Pir Panjal, plus boating facilities on a small lake.

Tararkhel and Pallandri Another pleasantly located hill station, at a similar altitude, is Tarakhel, to the south. There is a small bazaar and an **E** *PWD Inspection Bungalow*, bookable in Rawalkot. Beyond Tarakhel is Pallandri (64 kilometres from Rawalkot), an attractive small resort surrounded by low hills. There is an **E** *Inspection Bungalow*.

Tattapani Tattapani is situated on the west bank of the Poonch River, a little over halfway between Rawalkot and Kotli, in Kotli District. As well as being an important road junction between the two districts, Tattapani is most famous for its hot sulphurous springs. The AJ&K Tourism Department have built an attractive hotel around the springs. Unfortunately, Tattapani's proximity to the Line of Control means that foreigners are not allowed to visit.

Bagh

Colour map M, grid C3

The sub-district headquarters town of **Bagh** is located on either side of the Mahl and Malwani Rivers, at its confluence with a smaller tributary. Unfortunately, Bagh, like Soudhan Gali, has a plethora of arseholes who will keep demanding that you "prove your identity", and there is not much to see in the town anyway.

Ins and outs On the north side of the river is the main bus yard, with regular buses and minibuses serving Muzaffarabad (Rs 45, 4 hours) and Rawalpindi (Rs 70, 4½ hours). Bagh is connected to Muzaffarabad via the chain of hill stations, and is also connected to Rawalkot to the south.

Sleeping

The **E** ***PWD Resthouse*** is to the west of town, across the main bridge (no sign, but a distinctive red and white surrounding wall). Prior booking at the adjacent PWD office is essential. In the same road is the office of the Forestry Department, where you can book *Forestry Resthouses*. There are several grotty **F** hotels in town, although easily the best bet is the excellent **F** ***Al Noor***, near to the hospital, on a hill above the bus stand. It is friendly, with very cheap, clean, carpeted VIP doubles with attached bath, and a restaurant. Recommended.

Aliabad

Aliabad is located 112 kilometres east of Bagh, set amongst a thick forest of deodar and pine. It is reachable by bus and then jeep from Bagh or Rawalkot. It is currently off-limits to foreigners.

Dhirkot

One of the most attractive resorts in the district that foreigners can visit is Dhirkot, on the road between Kohala and Bagh. At 1,676 metres the climate is a pleasant change from the summer heat of the Punjab plains. The prime attraction is the location of the **E** *PWD Resthouse* and **E** AJ&K Tourism Department *Tourist Huts*, set in the heart of the deodar and pine forest. The accommodation here is very popular, and booking ahead is essential (in Rawalkot or Muzaffarabad). Access is easy from Islamabad (132 kilometres) via Murree and Kohala (24 kilometres).

Mirpur and Kotli Districts

Kotli District

Colour map 5, grid C3

Formerly a sub-district of Mirpur until 1975, Kotli District provides a geographical link between the low hills and plains of Mirpur District to the south, and the more mountainous district of Poonch to the north. There is, however, little of tourist interest in the district.

Kotli town is fairly small, with transport links to Rawalkot, Islamabad (141 kilometres) and Mirpur. It has an **E** *PWD Resthouse* and a number of cheap hotels. About 40 kilometres to the east is the relatively cool hill station of **Nakyal** (1,524 metres), although this is too close to the Line of Control to be open to foreigners. To the west of Kotli, on the Islamabad road, is **Sensa** (53 kilometres), a good base to explore the nearby chir forests around **Bruhian**. There is a *Forest Resthouse* at Sensa.

Mirpur District

Although parts of Mirpur District are hilly, much of the region comprises plains that are geographically and climatically closer to the Punjab than the mountain valleys of the rest of Azad Kashmir. As a result, the district can be incredibly hot in summer.

The district has few tourist attractions (Mangla Dam and Lake are dealt with as an excursion from Dina in Punjab, see page 246), yet has a fascinating background and some remarkable links with the UK. Mirpur district has undergone dramatic transformation since the construction of the massive **Mangla Dam**, including the re-siting of the district headquarters town.

Mirpur

Colour map 5, grid C3

The district headquarters, Mirpur is probably easier to reach from the GT Road at Dina (on the Islamabad/Rawalpindi to Lahore route) than from

'Home from home'

It may seem incredible, but at least three-quarters of all British Pakistanis can trace their origins to an area no greater than 32 kilometres by 48 kilometres, lying mostly in Azad Kashmir. The overwhelming majority stem from Mirpur district, and parts of southern Kotli district. Mirpuris themselves make up well over half of Britain's Pakistani population, and 75 percent of the Pakistani population in the northern English town of Bradford.

Although there was a high level of migration from the area as the Mirpuri peasants saw their land disappear beneath the Mangla Lake in 1968, this was actually the culmination of a process that had begun long before the idea for the Mangla Dam was even conceived.

From the closing decades of the last century, Mirpuri villagers began to take jobs as stokers on British merchant ships operating out of Bombay. Britain was reluctant, except in times of war, to recruit subjects of the Maharaja of Kashmir as soldiers in the Punjab regiments, so the Mirpuris found alternative employment with Britain's merchant fleet. As Britain's coal-powered merchant fleet continued to expand rapidly during the early decades of this century, so the demand for labour steadily increased. As seamen, Mirpuris were in an excellent position to keep a close watch on global job opportunities, and some began to seek work ashore.

When acute industrial labour shortages began to emerge in Britain during the Second World War, Mirpuri ex-seamen were eagerly recruited to fill the gaps. As opportunities began to widen further still in Britain's post-war boom, more Mirpuri seamen began to settle. Having established themselves ashore, they began to call their relatives over, initiating a process of chain migration. Many families who received resettlement grants following the construction of the Mangla Dam chose to join relatives in the UK. In many villages in Mirpur District, well over half the population now lives in Britain.

An excellent book on the subject, "Home From Home: British Pakistanis in Mirpur", with text by Irna Imran and superb photos by Tim Smith, is available from the Bradford Heritage Recording Unit, Administration Section, Bradford Central Library, Prince's Way, Bradford, BD1 1NN (T+44-1274753672), price £7.50.

other parts of Kashmir. Although there is little of tourist interest beside the Mangla Dam, Mirpur must rate as one of the friendliest towns in Pakistan. Because of the links with the UK, do not be surprised if you are hailed in the street by young Pakistani lads with broad Yorkshire accents, halal butchers from Halifax, or if you meet nervous young bridegrooms from Birmingham about to see their future brides for the first time.

Other links manifest themselves in strange forms, such as the ease with which you can direct dial the UK, or the proliferation of new businesses and industries initiated by capital from British Pakistanis.

Sleeping **C** *Jabees*, Allama Iqbal Rd (west end), T3092. A/c, restaurant, some deluxe rooms. **C** ***Kashmir Continental***, Allama Iqbal Rd, T4303. A/c, dish TV, fridge, direct dialling, fax, car rental, coffee shop, restaurant with Chinese, Pakistan and Continental food, corporate and group rates, best in town. **E** ***Roopyal***, Chowk Shaheedian, Allama Iqbal Rd, T3455. Opened in 1992 by Benazir Bhutto, some a/c rooms, good value. Restaurant recommended. **F** ***Nathia Super***, Chowk Shaheedian, Allama Iqbal Rd (east end). Good value doubles with attached bath, run by a Mirpuri from Walthamstow, downstairs is a 3-table snooker hall. Recommended. Number of **F** hotels around bus stand including ***Al-Bilal*** and ***Mir Faisal*** (signs in Urdu only).

Directory **Communications** GPO is north of Chowk Shaheedian roundabout.

North West Frontier Province

North West Frontier Province

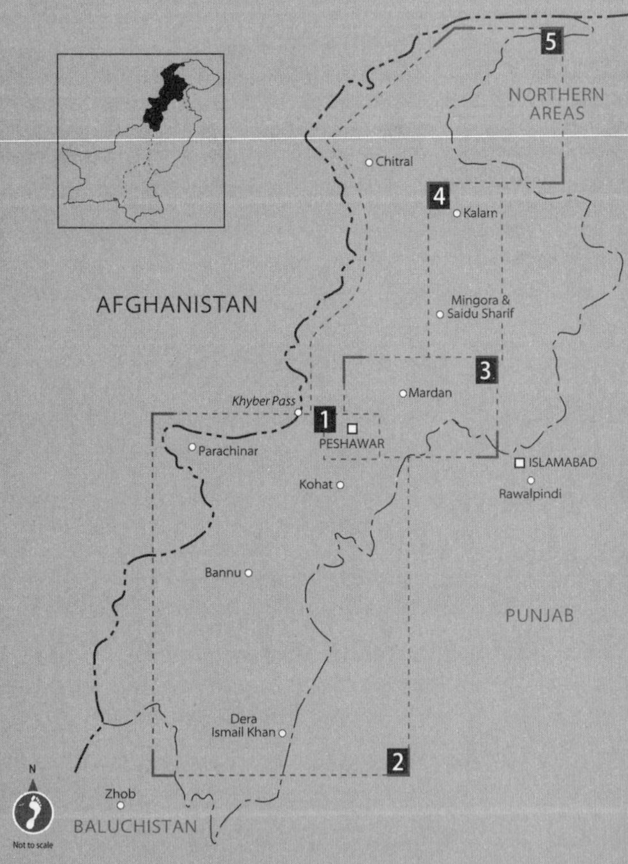

Text Divisions

In many ways, the North West Frontier Province (NWFP) is Pakistan's most diverse province. Covering an area of over 100,000 square kilometres (including the Tribal Areas), NWFP stretches from the Pamir in the extreme north all the way south as far as Dera Ismail Khan on the banks of the Indus, encompassing high mountains, fertile river basins and semi-arid deserts. At the heart of the province is the Peshawar Valley, often referred to as the Vale of Peshawar. Its rich alluvial soils, watered by the Kabul and Swat rivers, make this amongst the most productive agricultural regions in Pakistan. The mountains to the north, particularly the Hindu Kush, are amongst the most spectacular in Pakistan, offering some of the best opportunities for trekking and climbing in the world.

Best time to visit *The northern half of NWFP is best visited from spring through to autumn (April-September), the length of the season broadly speaking decreasing as one moves further north. The southern half of the province is best visited from late autumn through to early spring (November-March), when days are pleasantly cooler. Be prepared, however, for cold nights during this period.*

Ins and outs

Peshawar, the provincial capital and largest city, is for many people the starting point of a visit to NWFP. As well as being a major attraction in its own right, the city provides a convenient base for exploring the surrounding areas (notably the Khyber Pass and Peshawar Valley), and is also the main transport hub. In the mountains to the north of Peshawar there are essentially two options. The green and fertile Swat Valley is easily accessible both by road and air, making it a popular tourist destination amongst Pakistanis, particularly during the summer months when it provides welcome relief from the heat of the plains. Chitral is much more remote, involving a 12 hour journey by road, or a breathtaking, weather-dependent flight in a twin-propeller Fokker F27 plane. Either way, it is a region well-worth visiting, being one of the most fascinating and spectacularly beautiful in Pakistan. The southern half of NWFP is the least visited, its rugged, arid landscape and predominantly tribal society making it a difficult and challenging (though also rewarding) area in which to travel.

NB While the district of Hazara, which includes Abbottabad, the Kaghan Valley and parts of Indus Kohistan, is administratively part of NWFP, these areas are dealt with in the Northern Areas chapter, since in practical terms they form part of the KKH route.

Background to the area

The Pathan tribes that dominate NWFP have for centuries exploited its rugged terrain and thrived on banditry and guerrilla warfare, eluding the attempts of invading powers to control and pacify them. During the Colonial period, this frontier region grew in strategic importance and the British established their 'Forward Policy', struggling to control it as a buffer zone against Russian expansion. Despite the Durand Line of 1893 (which today forms the border with Afghanistan), they never gained full control. Even today, nearly a third of the region is designated 'Tribal Areas', with internal autonomy from Pakistani law.

Throughout history this region has existed as a turbulent zone of contact between the civilizations of Central Asia and the Middle East on one side and South Asia on the other. Yet the province also has a rich cultural history of its own, stretching back to the Indus Valley Civilization. The Peshawar Valley and hills of Swat, along with Taxila to the east, were the focus of the Gandharan civilization which flourished under the Kushans around the second century AD as one of the most important centres of Buddhism on the subcontinent. Today these regions have the highest concentration of archaeological sites in Pakistan, and some, such as the Buddhist monastery remains at Takht-e-Bhai, are beautifully preserved. Gandharan art, with its distinctive fusion of Graeco-Roman and Indian styles, is famous throughout the world. Peshawar, which became the capital of the Kushan kings, reached its zenith under Mughal rule as a wealthy trading town with lavish mosques, palaces and gardens. Tucked away in the remote valleys of Chitral, the unique Kalash tribes have existed for centuries in isolation, their colourful, vibrant culture and way of life still surviving today.

The way of the Pathans

*The **Pukhtunwali** (way of the Pathans) is a strict moral code of behaviour. Hospitality (**Melmastia**) is fundamental to the Pathan code and is extended without question to all strangers and guests. Even the poorest members of Pathan society are expected to adhere to the principle of melmastia, often at great personal sacrifice. Related to this is the concept of **Panah**, by which a Pathan is bound to offer refuge to anyone who asks it. This even extends to protecting a sworn enemy, should they demand it. Once the protected person leaves his host's territory, he once again becomes fair game. Revenge (**Badal**) is the driving force behind the endless cycle of bloody feuding which plagues Pathan society. According to their code, a Pathan must avenge any insult against himself, his family or tribe if he is to keep his honour. Traditionally, badal is taken as a result of quarrels over '**zar, zan, zamin**' (gold, women, land). The obligations of badal are shared by all clan members, and can be passed down from generation to generation until they have been fulfilled. The only escape from this cycle is through **Nanawati** (literally 'giving in'), whereby a tribesman or family can go to the aggrieved party and ask them to drop their vow of revenge. Such a request carries with it a connotation of shame, while the other party is under no obligation to accept. It does however provide a mechanism for forgiveness, albeit a rarely utilized one.*

*Nang, the Pathan code of honour, is shaped by pride (**Ghairet**), bravery (**Tura**), generosity (**Khegara**) and respect (**Wafa**) and determines an individual's or group's standing in society; failure to uphold these virtues brings disgrace (**Tor**) and ridicule (**Paighor**).*

*The **Jirga**, or council of elders, is the institution whereby clan decisions are reached, theoretically on a consensus basis. It acts as an executive, judicial and legislative body, and is also commonly used as an instrument of arbitration and conciliation in the case of long-running disputes. The decisions reached at a jirga are binding and cannot be challenged. The jirga also regulates relations with the outside world. Indeed, the jirgas have proved vital in negotiations between the provincial and federal governments and the Tribal Areas. Where a jirga reaches a decision requiring action on a community level, a **Lashkar** may be assembled; essentially a small army gathered from amongst the clans and tribes, entrusted with the task of carrying out the jirga's decision.*

*The **Hujra** is still very much a feature of Pathan village society. Originally Hujras were established as guest houses by the wealthier members of a village. Later their role broadened to become a focus for the social life of the village; a place where everyone could gather to discuss local matters, exchange views and catch up on news.*

People

Approximately 90 percent of the population of NWFP are **Pathans** (or **Pukhtuns**). Numbering up to 18 million people and inhabiting north Baluchistan, east Afghanistan and NWFP, they are one of the largest tribal societies in the world. Divided into numerous sub-tribes and clans, the Pathans are a fiercely independent people constantly feuding amongst themselves and ever hostile to any threat to their freedom. Mughals, Afghans, Sikhs, British and Russians have tried to control them, and while those tribes that settled on the plains may have paid taxes and token tribute to their temporary rulers, the semi-nomadic tribes of the hills have never been subdued.

Many Pathan tribes claim a common ancestry from a man called **Quais** who was sent by the Prophet to spread Islam in Afghanistan. One of his sons, *Afghana*, had four sons, who left Afghanistan to settle in different parts of the

The "Frontier Gandhi"

Initially at least, the Independence Movement throughout British India was dominated by the exploits of Mahatma Gandhi, a momentous figure who puzzled, confused and worried the British with his non-violent resistance to Imperial rule. However, Gandhi was joined also by another, much more improbable champion of non-violence. In the hills of the Northwest Frontier, another great leader emerged. ***Abdul Gaffar Khan****, the son of the chieftain of a small village, found Gandhi's non-violence to be deeply compatible with his own Islamic faith. Working amongst some of the most violent and lawless Pathan tribes of the Frontier, he inspired such deep respect and obedience that he was able to raise an army of around 100,000 Pathans committed, under oath, to resist the British through entirely non-violent means.*

That the Pathans, whose sacrosanct code of tribal honour requires them to seek revenge, or badal, for any insult, should renounce violence in the face of repeated humiliation, and indeed slaughter, at the hands of the British, was incredible. And yet Abdul Gaffar Khan, or Badshah Khan ('the king of kings'), succeeded in forming such a force, which he named the ***Khudai Khidmatgars****, meaning 'Servants of God'.*

The British suppressed the Independence movement in NWFP particularly ruthlessly. The region was seen as being of crucial strategic significance, guarding the 'Gateway of India' from the aggressive designs of Tsarist Russia. They were deeply suspicious of this army of 'non-violent' Pathans; after decades of guerrilla war they saw it as a contradiction in terms. NWFP was ruled by what amounted to draconian martial law and the full extent of the repression hidden from the public eye. Later, Abdul Gaffer Khan wrote "The British feared a non-violent Pathan more than a violent one ... All the horrors the British perpetrated on the Pathans had only one purpose; to provoke them to violence."

For all the selfless sacrifice and single minded determination of Abdul Ghaffar Khan and his followers, they were in the end ignored and discredited. Like Gandhi, Ghaffar Khan opposed the partition of India as demanded by the Muslim League. Indeed NWFP, choosing the Khudai Khidmatgars over the Muslim League, had originally voted to join India. But at the insistence of the Muslim League and in the end Mountbatten, a second referendum was held, and in his desperation to avoid an explosion of communal violence, Ghaffar Khan instructed the Khudai Khidmatgars to abstain. Thus NWFP became a part of an independent Pakistan, ruled by the former Muslim League. Abdul Ghaffar Khan pledged his support for Pakistan, but lobbied hard for an united Pathan province – 'Pakhtunistan' – within Pakistan. The newly founded state of Pakistan, at war with India over Kashmir, arrested the Khan for "fomenting open sedition" (a charge identical to the one repeatedly levelled at him by the British) and sentenced him to 3 years' rigourous imprisonment.

As Eknath Easwaran comments, "within less than a year of the night that Mountbatten handed over the reigns of power to India and Pakistan, Mahatma Gandhi had been assassinated by a Hindu who feared he was pro-Muslim and Abdul Ghaffar Khan had been jailed by an Islamic government who claimed he was pro-Hindu." (E Easwaran, A Man to Match his Mountains)

province as founding fathers of the various tribes. In contrast the **Wazirs** claim to be one of the lost tribes of Israel which migrated east, converted to Islam and finally settled in Waziristan. However, most experts agree that the Pathans probably originated from an ethnic group in Afghanistan.

The NWFP's non-Pathan populations are found mostly in Chitral and Hazara districts. The **Khowar** language of the **Chitralis**, who call their land

Kho, relates them closely with the nomadic groups of the Wakhan and Pamir regions. Hazara district consists mainly of **Hindko** speaking tribes whose language and culture are closely related to that of the Punjabis to the south. The **Kalash** are a small ethnic group found in Chitral, in the valleys of Rumbur, Bumburet and Birir. Their fair complexions led early visitors to liken them to "handsome Europeans, with brown hair and blue eyes" believed to be descendants of Alexander's armies. More probably, they are related to an ancient Indo-Aryan group from Afghanistan.

Siddharta fasting Buddha, Peshawar Museum

Peshawar

Phone code: 091
Colour map 5, grid C1

The romance of Peshawar has traditionally been linked to its 'frontier' location, close to the historic Khyber Pass. Today it is a large and rapidly growing city, but it has a distinct character all of its own, and much of its unique atmosphere still thrives in the fascinating bazaars of the Old City.

Ins and outs

Getting there

The recent introduction by Emirates airlines of direct international flights between London and Peshawar (via Dubai) has put Peshawar on the map as a highly appealing alternative 'gateway' to Pakistan. PIA and Shaheen Air also operate direct flights between Peshawar and a number of Middle Eastern/Gulf destinations, but otherwise Peshawar's airport only deals with domestic flights. There are regular connections with Islamabad, Lahore, Karachi, Quetta and a number of other smaller towns and cities (the most relevant of these from the tourists' point of view being the daily Fokker 27 flights to and from Chitral). Peshawar is the terminus for Pakistan's main railway artery. There are actually 2 stations; Cantonment and City. The most convenient is Cantonment, both in terms of its location and the fact that the main booking office is situated here. Trains run to Rawalpindi, Lahore and ultimately Karachi, with a branch also to Quetta. If travelling by train, bear in mind the times and distances involved in longer trips (Quetta 39 hours, 1,569 kilometres; Karachi 32½ hours, 1,676 kilometres); unless you have a sleeper, a break of journey is essential. The main bus station and a number of private coach companies, which between them offer services to most destinations north, east and southeast of Peshawar, are all to be found along the GT Road heading east out of town towards Rawalpindi. For southern NWFP (Kohat, Bannu, Dera Ismail Khan) and Quetta, buses and minibuses leave from Kohat road, to the south of the city centre. There are a couple of companies in the Old City operating direct Hiace minibus services to Chitral.

Getting around

Peshawar really consists of 4 distinct areas. In the east, to the south of the GT Road, is the **Old City**, the heart of ancient Peshawar. To the west and southwest of this are the **Cantonment** and **Saddar Bazaar** areas, which between them represent the commercial and administrative centre of modern Peshawar, with most of the hotels, restaurants, shops, banks and government offices etc. To the west of this again, beyond the airport, on the road leading toward the Khyber Pass, is the **University Town**. As well as being the site of Peshawar University, this area has developed as a focus for foreign consulates, NGOs, etc. Even further west is the new residential area of **Hayatabad**. The bus system in Peshawar is almost entirely run by Afghans. Rickety Mercedes and Bedford buses run back and forth between the main bus station on the GT Road and University Town/Hayatabad, passing through the Old City, Saddar and Cantonment en route. Auto-rickshaws are also plentiful in Peshawar, and a convenient way of getting around. Taxis are less prolific than in Islamabad, but in the Saddar and Cantonment areas, or outside the more expensive hotels, you can usually find one without too much problem. Saddar and the Old City are both fairly compact and it is possible to get around them on foot.

History

Peshawar's origins are unclear. The earliest written record, a **Kharoshthi** rock inscription at Ara, near Attock, dated 119 AD, referred to it as *Poshapura* meaning 'City of Flowers'. The Kushan king *Kanishka* is thought to have moved his winter capital from Pushkalavati to Peshawar, at which time the city became a major pilgrimage centre. Various Buddhist sites have been identified with locations in the modern-day city, the most important being Shah-ji-ki-Dheri, site of the Kanishka Vihara, a large monastery and stupa complex. The site was excavated by the archaeologist Spooner in 1907, who discovered the famous bronze reliquary casket of Kanishka, now on display in Peshawar Museum. Nothing remains of the site itself.

After the decline of the Kushans, Peshawar fell to the Sassanians for a period and then reverted to a new dynasty of Kushans, the Kidar (little) Kushans, before being overrun by White Huns in the fifth century AD. They were followed by the Turki and Hindu Shahis in the sixth to seventh centuries AD, although little is known about the fate of the city during this period, except that the Hindu Shahis shifted their capital from Peshawar to Hund on the banks of the Indus. This move appears to have coincided with the spread of Afghan (Pathan) tribes into the Peshawar Valley. Later, at the start of the 11th century, Mahmoud of Ghazni invaded, extending the Ghaznavid Empire to include the city of Peshawar. Following the destruction of the Ghaznavid Empire at the hands of the Ghorids, Peshawar found itself on the margins of both the Central Asian and Indian empires, and all but disappeared from historical records.

The city next acquired importance during the Mughal period, when it flourished as a regional capital. The Mughals planted trees, laid out gardens and built forts and mosques; their monuments are amongst the few to have survived the city's long and turbulent history. The present form of the city's name is attributed to Akbar who changed it from the Persian '*Parshawar*' to Peshawar, meaning 'Frontier Town'. After the decline of the Mughals, the Durranis of Afghanistan gained a firm hold of Peshawar for a time, before being driven out by the Sikh Empire of Ranjit Singh. The city became a major bone of contention between the Durranis and Sikhs, before the British, extending their empire to the north and west, finally brought it under their control.

Sights

Arriving in Peshawar along the GT Road from Rawalpindi, as well as confronting the usual chaos and congestion, you are engulfed by a choking, eye-stinging blue haze of fumes which hangs over the city in a permanent cloud. The congestion and pollution are inescapable aspects of Peshawar, but despite this, most people quickly fall in love with the place. It's not so much that there are any great sights in the traditional sense (though Peshawar Museum is one 'sight' certainly not to be missed). Rather, it's the atmosphere of the

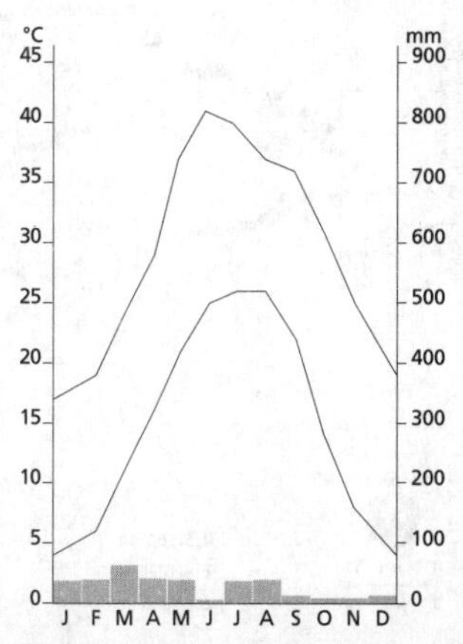

The best time to visit is November to March

place, and in particular the mesmerizing bazaars of the Old City, which buzz with an almost tangible feeling of vibrancy and excitement. This is after all one of the ancient trading centres of Asia, and today, as in the past, people are drawn from far and wide to do business here. You could spend weeks exploring the narrow alleyways and covered markets, hunting out obscure treasures of antique tribal jewellery or bargaining over sumptuous Central Asian carpets, but even an afternoon spent here is enough for something of the romance of this historic frontier city to get under your skin.

The Old City

In traditional Central Asian style, the Old City was formerly completely encircled by a wall and centred on a citadel. Today the wall and its 16 gates survive only in name. The fortified stronghold of **Bala Hisar**, today the most imposing landmark, is almost certainly the site of the ancient citadel. It was the key to control of Peshawar and changed hands many times. When the Mughal emperor Babur arrived in 1509, he occupied and strengthened the existing fort and laid out the **Shalimar Gardens**. After the decline of the Mughals, the Durranis of Afghanistan controlled Peshawar until 1818. The fort at this time was in magnificent condition, as described by Elphinstone when he visited in 1809.

"The throne was covered with a cloth adorned with pearls, on which lay a sword and a small mace set with jewels. The room was open all round. The centre was supported by four high pillars, in the midst of which was a large fountain. The floor was covered with the richest carpets, and round the edges

Peshwar Overview

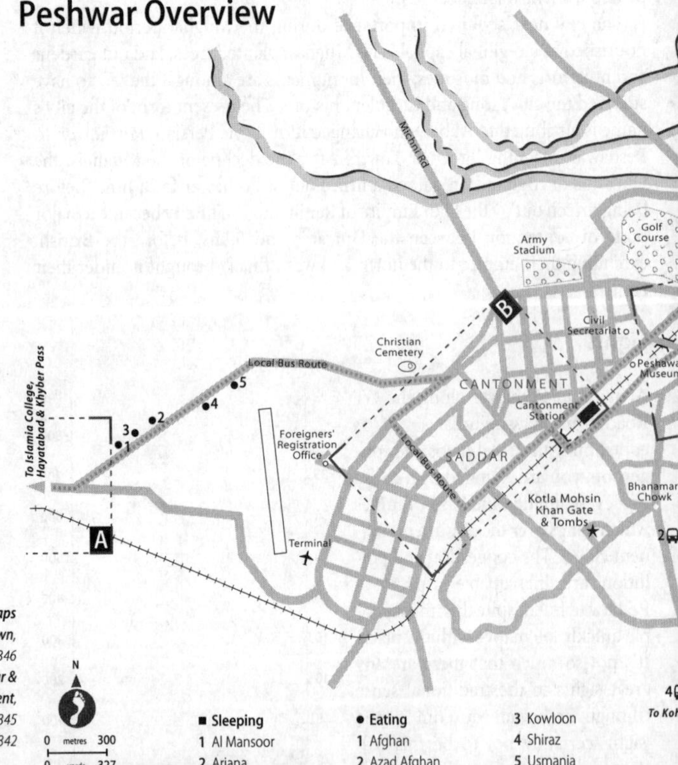

Related maps
A University Town, page 346
B Saddar Bazaar & Cantonment, page 345
C Old City, page 342

were slips of silk embroidered with gold. The view from the hall was beautiful. Immediately below was an extensive garden, full of cypresses and other trees, and beyond was a plain of richest verdure."

The Bala Hisar and the Shalimar Gardens were destroyed by Ranjit Singh who later rebuilt the fort of mud. The present fort was built by the British, who replaced the mud walls with 'pucca' brick. It is currently closed to the public, being occupied by the Frontier Corps, though there are plans to open it for guided tours. Ask at PTDC or Sehrai Travels for more information. **NB** No photography in the vicinity.

The Bazaars

The bazaars of the Old City are a kaleidoscope of colours, sounds and smells. Crowds of people jostle with cars, bicycles, donkey carts and rickshaws and narrow alleys lead off from the main streets, concealing even more colourful and atmospheric bazaars with everything from vegetables to ornate gold and silver jewellery. Trades tend to group together on the whole, though less so than in the past. A brief description of the main bazaars is given below, although there are many more; perhaps the best thing is simply wander at will. For the serious shopper, the Old City is a wonderful hunting ground, although it is not for those in a hurry. Deals are negotiated unhurriedly over cups of green tea (*'khawar'*) and endless small-talk interspersed with bargaining.

The main route into the Old City from Saddar is over Rail Bridge, which brings you to a busy junction known as Shuba Chowk. All around here are numerous carpet shops, and swarthy Pathans walking the streets with carpets on their shoulders in the hope of a quick sale. Going straight on leads to Bajori Road and **Namak Mandi**, where there are several excellent tikka restaurants. Going left into **Khyber Bazaar**, most of the street is lined with shops selling electrical goods ranging from air conditioners to hi-fi systems. Towards the end there are the dentist shops with brightly painted signs showing false teeth. The crossroads at the east end of Khyber bazaar marks the site of the old Kabuli Gate. Turning left here leads up past Lady Reading Hospital and Bala Hisar to the GT Road. Right leads into Cinema Road and back round towards Namak Mandi; as well as its cinemas and feature bill boards, Cinema Road is a treasure trove of lurid Indian and Pakistani film-star postcards. Straight on is **Qissa Khwani Bazaar**, or story-tellers bazaar. Here were the 'Khave Khanas'; tea shops and eating houses where in the past, travellers and traders met to exchange their tales and news of faraway places. Today the tea shops have given way

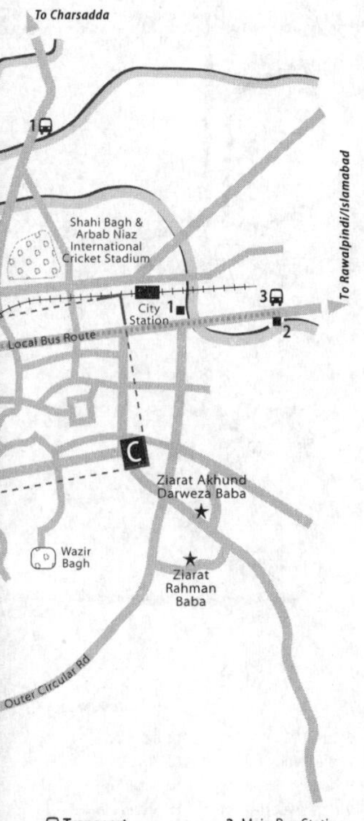

North West Frontier Province

to cold drink stands, as well as bookshops, clothing, luggage and general stores. Turning left at the end, the road runs up past shops selling **brass and copperware**. A fork off to the right takes you into the **Cloth Bazaar** while straight on is a bazaar selling **tea and spices**. The next turning left on either leads up to Chowk Yadgar. To the south of the cloth market is **Pipal Mandi**, the main grain wholesale area where a peepul tree is believed to mark the spot where the Buddha once preached.

Chowk Yadgar lies at the heart of the Old City. Originally a memorial to Col EC Hastings, it was replaced by a plaza and memorial to those who died in the Indo-Pakistani war of 1965. The west side is lined with the shops and stalls of moneychangers with their displays of currencies. An underpass runs under the plaza from east to west.

Sethi Street runs east from Chowk Yadgar. This street was at the heart of the traditional business community and gained its name from the powerful Sethi family which at one time conducted highly profitable trade with Russia, China, India and Central Asia. A few of the old houses remain, some in precarious states of structural repair, with richly carved wooden doorways and ornate balconies. Inside are large airy reception rooms and deep cellars which provided relief from the summer heat. Following Sethi Street east from Chowk Yadgar, the first narrow alley on the left is the **Chappal market**, selling sandals, followed immediately by the vegetable market (**Sabzi Mandi**),

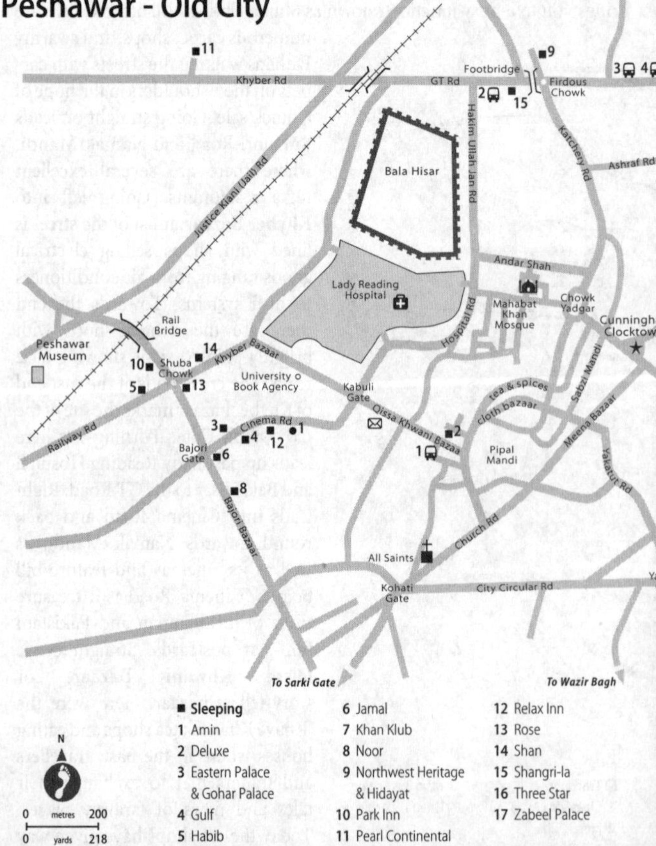

■ **Sleeping**
1 Amin
2 Deluxe
3 Eastern Palace & Gohar Palace
4 Gulf
5 Habib
6 Jamal
7 Khan Klub
8 Noor
9 Northwest Heritage & Hidayat
10 Park Inn
11 Pearl Continental
12 Relax Inn
13 Rose
14 Shan
15 Shangri-la
16 Three Star
17 Zabeel Palace

Related map Peshwar Overview, page 340

covered in summer with matting against the heat. Further along is **Cunningham Clock tower**, built in 1900 by Balmukund to celebrate Queen Victoria's Diamond Jubilee, and in honour of Sir George Cunningham who became Governor of NWFP. Around it tanners practice their trade, joined occasionally by fishmongers. **Karim Pura**, the narrow street which forks off left from Sethi Street at the Cunningham Clock tower, is also lined with ancient houses with intricately carved woodwork, which are in some ways more impressive, or at least more numerous, than those of Sethi Street. The bazaar along here is varied; everything from household goods to meat and spices. Shortly after the clock tower on the right is **Meena Bazaar** (women's bazaar), where *Burqas* and veils for women are sold along with items of embroidery. Towards the end of the street, on the left, is the restored **Sethi House**, which is included in guided tours of Peshawar; if you don't want to join a tour, the beautifully restored *Khan Klub* hotel, near Rampura Gate is if anything more impressive, and boasts an excellent restaurant as well.

At the east end of Sethi Street is **Gor Khattri**. This large walled compound with its impressive Mughal gateway is today a police headquarters. It is usually possible to wander in and look round, although there is not much left to see. It was originally the site of the *'Tower of the Buddha's Bowl'* where the Buddha's sacred alms bowl was believed to have been housed. Later it became an important place of Hindu pilgrimage, perhaps as a site for funeral sacrifices or for the initiation of *Yogis*. The daughter of the Mughal emperor Shah Jahan converted it into a *caravanserai* (the existing compound) and built an accompanying mosque. During the Sikh period the mosque was destroyed and replaced with a temple of *Gorakhnath* (Siva) and its subsidiary *Nandi* shrine, the remains of which still stand.

Andarshah Bazaar (meaning 'inner city') runs west from Chowk Yadgar towards Bala Hisar. It houses the silver and goldsmiths, selling a wide range of ethnic, antique and modern jewellery. The tiny alleys that lead off to the south from the main street contain many more shops, some with quite rare antique items. About half way along on the north side is an arched gateway into **Mahabat Khan Mosque**. Mahabat Khan was twice governor of Peshawar during the reigns of Shah Jahan and Aurangzeb, and is thought to have built it. Although much smaller, it closely resembles the Badshahi Mosque in Lahore and provides an excellent example of Mughal architecture from Shah Jahan's time. During the Sikh period, the two minarets were frequently used as gallows by the Sikh

Eating
1 Salateen

Transport
1 Chitral Hiaces
2 Firdous Chowk Flying Coaches
3 New Khan Road Runners
4 Pakistan Flying Coach

Governor, Gen Avitabile, a mercenary of Italian origin who joined Ranjit Singh's court following the Napoleonic wars. The Prayer Hall is decorated with intricate paint work, aging but still precise and distinct. The fire which swept through Andarshah in 1898 nearly destroyed the mosque but fortunately many of its decorative features were restored.

Other sights around the Old City

All Saints Church Built in 1883 and originally situated in the grounds of the nearby Edwardes High School, this church has a beautiful stained glass chancel window and carved wooden arches. It is open on Sundays from 1000-1300, when masses are held. At other times there is a chowkidar in the house opposite who holds the keys.

Ziarat Rahman Baba Situated to the southeast of the Old City and Ganj Gate, between Outer Circular Road and Hazar Khwani Road, is the shrine of the famous Pashto poet Rahman Baba. There is a new complex here consisting of a library, mosque and shrine, the latter with an imposing white marble dome decorated with blue tiles on the outside and an intricate mirror mosaic on the inside. The much older shrine outside has more character and is a popular meeting place in the evenings. Just before the turning right off Hazar Khwani Road to the shrine, there is a small shrine to **Akhund Darweza Baba**, a famous Sufi saint from the Mughal period.

Kotla Mohsin Khan Gate and Tombs Situated southwest of Bhanamari Chowk, just off Badshahi Road, this crumbling but impressive gate once formed the entrance to a fortified residence or *Kotla*. The identity of Mohsin Khan is uncertain. Nearby there are two large domed tombs; again it is uncertain as to who these were for. Today they are home to large numbers of bats!

Cantonment and Saddar Bazaar

British troops first set up camp in what was to become the cantonment in 1848-49. A barbed wire enclosure with 10 gates was followed by permanent buildings. Following the classical colonial style, ubiquitous throughout British India, a wholly independent town was built with long wide tree-lined boulevards designed for horse drawn traffic and spacious bungalows set back from the road, along with all the social infrastructure of Government buildings, schools, churches, clubs etc. The railway line and station which divides the cantonment from the Old City followed. Today there are still many examples of the distinctive Mughal/Gothic architecture of the British period amongst the more modern buildings, giving glimpses of a bygone age. The oldest markets of Saddar Bazaar are to be found in the grid of narrow alleys centred on Fowara Chowk; in places these are every bit as atmospheric as those of the Old City.

Peshawar Museum

This classic piece of architecture was built in 1905 as the Victoria Memorial Hall. Many of the best artefacts from the various stages of Gandharan civilization are housed here. This is a collection not to be missed, and the presentation is excellent. Upstairs there is an ethnographic section including wooden carvings from the Kalash valleys.

■*0900-1300, 1430-1700, closed Wednesday and public holidays. Free. Buses heading northeast along Sunehri Masjid Road pass the museum en route to the GT Road. An auto-rickshaw from Saddar shouldn't cost more than Rs 15.*

University Town

Situated seven kilometres west of Peshawar on Khyber Road. The impressive **Islamia College** and Collegiate School (1913) was built on a 'parched, barren and uneven tract interspersed by ancient mounds' in Mughal/Gothic style and was followed by the University which was founded in 1930. Today a sprawling residential area of red brick buildings and well kept lawns surrounds the University, and various Medical, Engineering, Forestry, Science and Industrial Institutes and Research Councils line the main road.

Further west is the new development of **Hayatabad**, and beyond this, **Smugglers' Bazaar**, selling luxury western goods. At the end of the bazaar is a check post which marks the start of **Khyber Agency**. Foreigners are not allowed beyond this point without a permit.

Peshawar - Saddar Bazaar & Cantonment

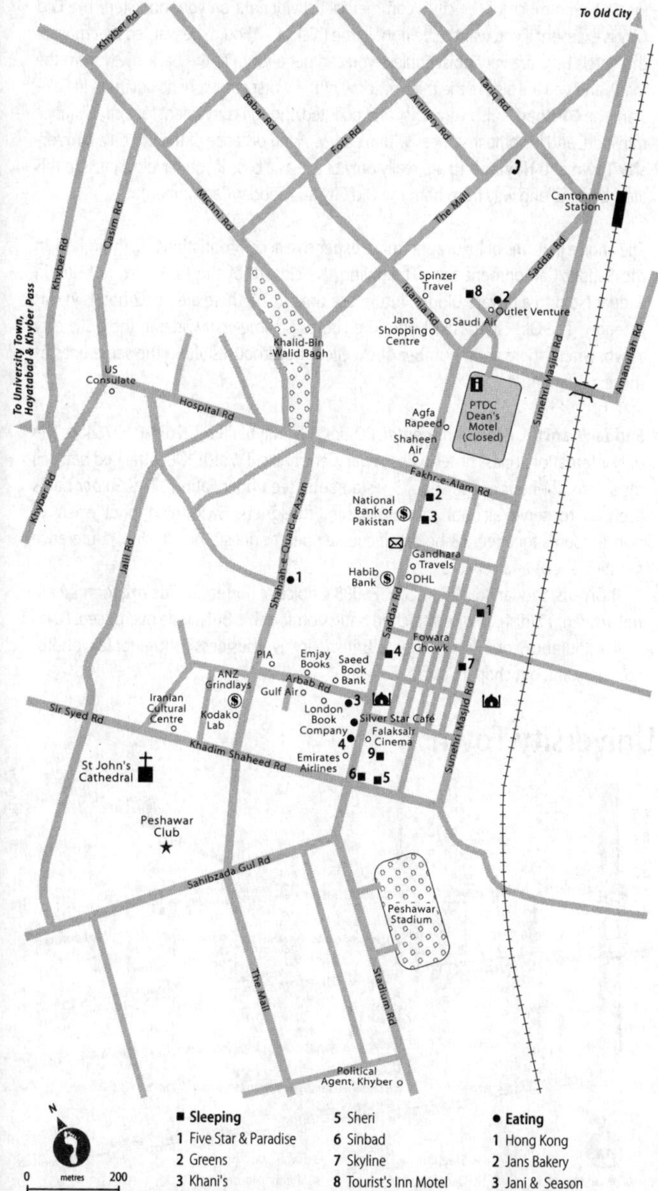

Related map *Peshwar Overview,* *page 340*

Essentials

Sleeping

■ on maps
Price codes: see inside front cover

Each of Peshawar's districts has its own advantages and disadvantages. The **Saddar/Cantonment** area is in many ways the most practical; here you are centrally located, with much of the city's commercial activity right on your doorstep. The **Old City** is excellent if you want to be right in the thick of it, though be warned that most of the hotels here are very noisy (unless you can get a room at the back, away from the road), and you are also in the thick of some of the worst atmospheric pollution in Pakistan. The **GT Road** is also very noisy and polluted, though convenient for long-distance transport, and in some instances within easy walking distance of the Old City. **University Town** and **Hayatabad** are really only of use as a base if you have business in this area, being a long way from both the Old City and Saddar/Cantonment.

More expensive hotels

The choice in terms of luxury and more expensive accommodation is fairly limited. In the Saddar/Cantonment areas, following the closure of the *PTDC Dean's* hotel in Saddar (sold to a private bidder; future use unknown), there are just 2 hotels in this category. The Old City has just one. The choice is somewhat wider in the University Town, where there are a number of excellent guesthouses along the same lines as those in Islamabad.

Saddar/Cantt **L** *Pearl Continental*, PO Box 197, Khyber Rd, T276361, F276456. The only international class hotel in Peshawar. Central a/c, TV/dish, IDD, attached bath, all mod cons. 24-hour coffee shop, 3 restaurants (see under Eating). The *Gulbar* bar is licensed to serve alcohol to non-Muslim foreigners. Swimming pool open to non-residents for a fee. 18-hole golf course open to guests, health club, conference facilities, shops and services.

B *Greens*, Saddar Rd, T276035, F276088. Choice of normal and deluxe rooms, central a/c, fan, TV/dish, phone, attached bath. Comfortable but a little overpriced. *Lala's Grill* restaurant, *Sehrai* Travel Agents, British Airways, business centre (for fax, photocopy etc) and gift shop in lobby.

University Town

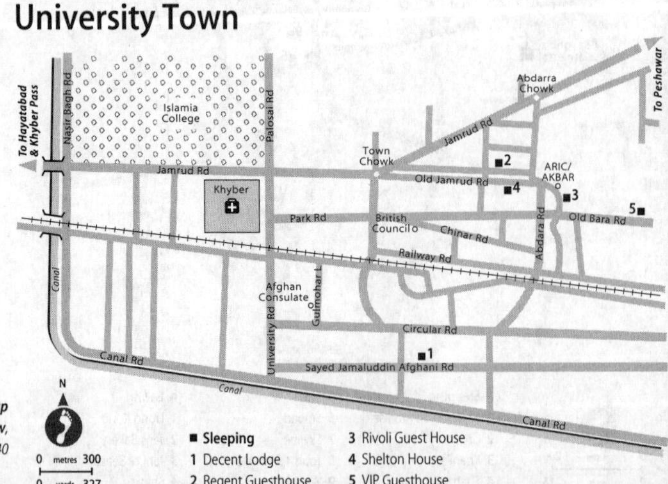

Related map Peshwar Overview, page 340

North West Frontier Province

Old City **A** *Khan Klub*, PO Box 468, New Rampura Gate (Navey Drawaza), T2567156, F2561156, E khan@khanklub.psh.brain.net.pk. This unique hotel is housed in a beautifully restored 200-year-old former Sikh *Haveli* (merchant's house), and is quite unlike anything else you will find in Pakistan. There are just 8 rooms, varying in price from Rs 2,000-4,000. All have a/c, IDD and attached bath, but there the similarities end, each of them being individually decorated and furnished using beautiful locally produced materials. A different semi-precious stone forms the central theme for each room (the Lapis suite, Garnet room etc), complemented by carefully chosen embroidered silks, carved wooden furniture, hand-knotted carpets etc. Downstairs there is an excellent traditional style Pathan restaurant (see under Eating). Highly recommended. Advance booking advisable.

University Town **B** *Decent Lodge*, 62 D/A Syed Jamaluddin Afghani Rd, T840221, F840229. A/c, fan, TV/dish, attached bath. Comfortable and nicely furnished. **B** *Regent Guesthouse*, 44 D-A, Old Jamrud Rd, University Town, T840670, F840082. A/c, fan, TV/dish, phone, attached bath. Comfortable, though perhaps slightly below the standard of the other guesthouses. **B** *Rivoli Guesthouse*, Rehman Baba Rd, University Town, T841483, F844369. A/c, fan, TV/dish, phone, attached bath. Comfortable and nicely furnished, though the most expensive of the guesthouses. **B** *Shelton House*, 15-B, Old Jamrud Rd, University Town, T842087, F828965. A/c, fan, TV/dish, phone, attached bath. Comfortable, nicely furnished and well run. **B** *VIP Guesthouse*, Old Bara Rd, University Town, T/F843392. A/c, fan, TV/dish, attached bath. Comfortable, nicely furnished and well run.

Mid-price hotels

The selection of mid-price hotels is very limited, with just 1 in Saddar, 2 in the Old City and 3 along the GT Road.

Saddar **D** *Khani's*, Saddar Rd, T277512. Rooms with a/c, fan, TV/dish, attached bath. Also some cheaper rooms with fan only (Rs 400), and a couple of basic rooms on the roof (Rs 100; these heat up like ovens in summer). Clean, well run and friendly.

Old City **C** *Park Inn* (formerly *Galaxie*), Shuba Chowk, Khyber Bazaar, T2560048, F2560049. Rooms with a/c, fan, TV, phone and attached bath. Also cheaper rooms with fan, phone and attached bath (Rs 447). Breakfast included. Under new management but still a bit run-down and overpriced. **C** *Rose*, Shuba Chowk, Khyber Bazaar, T250755. Rooms with a/c, fan, TV, phone and attached bath. Also cheaper rooms with fan, TV, phone and attached bath (Rs 350), or just fan and attached bath (Rs 250). Rooms arranged around central courtyard. Recently refurbished, clean and very good value (though noisy). Recommended.

North West Frontier Province

GT Road **C** ***Amin***, GT Rd, T218215, F214772. Rooms with a/c, TV, phone, attached bath. Also cheaper rooms with fan and attached bath (Rs 180). Right on GT Road, so very noisy. Cheaper rooms good value, more expensive ones overpriced. **C** ***North West Heritage***, Firdous Chowk (just off GT Rd), T215881. Near to ticket office for Flying Coach services to Rawalpindi and Lahore. Rooms with a/c, fan, TV, phone and attached bath. Also cheaper rooms without a/c (Rs 600). Recently opened, clean rooms, pleasant airy hotel, friendly staff, surprisingly quiet. Recommended. **C** ***Shangri-la***, GT Rd (opposite Firdous cinema), T210960. Right next door to Flying Coach services to Rawalpindi and Lahore. Clean comfortable (though noisy) rooms with a/c, TV/dish and attached bath. **D** ***Al-Mansoor***, GT Rd, T213106, F217608. Reasonable rooms arranged around central courtyard with a/c, TV, phone and attached bath. **D** ***Hidayat***, Firdous Chowk (just off GT Rd), T2565635. Near to ticket office for Flying Coach services to Rawalpindi and Lahore. Rooms with a/c, TV, attached bath. Also cheaper rooms with fan, phone and attached bath (Rs 250). Rooms arranged around concrete courtyard. Surprisingly quiet. Cheaper rooms good value, more expensive ones overpriced. **D** ***Zabeel Palace***, GT Rd, T218236. Reasonably clean rooms with a/c, TV, phone and attached bath. Also cheaper rooms with fan, phone and attached bath (Rs 230).

Budget hotels

There are numerous budget hotels to be found in Saddar, the Old City and along the GT Road. The cheapest of these are often extremely basic and far from clean. Women travelling alone should exercise caution; in this respect the *Tourist Inn Motel* is fine, as is the *Youth Hostel*. Bear in mind that many of the mid-price hotels listed above also have very good value 'simple' rooms which fall into the budget category.

Saddar **F** ***Five Star***, Suneri Masjid Rd, T276950. Noisy, grotty rooms with fan and attached bath. Best avoided. **F** ***Paradise***, Suneri Masjid Rd, T279027. Noisy, grotty rooms with fan and attached bath. Best avoided. **F** ***Shahzad***, Saddar Rd, T275741. Basic but reasonably clean rooms with fan and attached bath. No natural light, but pleasantly cool in summer. **F** ***Sheri***, Stadium Chowk, T278449. Basic but reasonably clean rooms with fan and attached bath. No natural light, but still hot in summer. **F** ***Sinbad***, Saddar Rd, T275020. Basic but reasonably clean rooms with fan and attached bath. Some rooms are windowless boxes. **F** ***Skyline***, Sunheri Masjid Rd, T270507. Noisy and basic rooms with fan and attached bath. Best avoided. **F** ***Wahid***, Saddar Rd, no phone. Basic rooms with fan and attached bath. Set back from road, so a little quieter. **F-G** ***Tourists' Inn Motel***, 3 Saddar Rd, T279156. 3 double rooms (Rs 200 each), and 3 large dorm rooms jam-packed full of rope-beds (Rs 75 per bed). Share toilet and (hot) shower facilities. Also self-catering kitchen, large fridge and TV in common area. Off-road parking. Popular with backpackers, friendly atmosphere, a good place to meet other travellers and team up in groups for visits to the Khyber Pass. Considerable effort has gone into improving the communal facilities, but the sardine tin approach to the dorms makes staying here somewhat claustrophobic when it is busy.

Old City **F** ***Deluxe***, Qissa Khwani, T216907. Basic rooms with fan and attached bath. Friendly management. **F** ***Eastern Palace***, Cinema Rd, T210260. Fairly clean but very small rooms with fan and attached bath. Relatively quiet. **F** ***Gohar Palace***, Cinema Rd, T218631. Basic but reasonably clean rooms with fan and attached bath. Relatively quiet. **F** ***Gulf***, Cinema Rd, T210103. Reasonably clean rooms with fan and attached bath. Those at front with balconies nicest. *New Lahori* and *Charga House* restaurants downstairs. **F** ***Habib***, 2 Shoba Bazaar, Railway Rd, T216219. Simple rooms with fan and attached bath. Also some a/c rooms (Rs 500). Small courtyard, parking. **F** ***Jamal***, Bajori Gate, T213665. Fairly basic rooms with fan and attached bath. **F** ***Noor***, Bajori Rd, T210916. Cleanish rooms with fan and attached bath, but very little natural light. **F** ***Relax Inn***, Cinema Rd, T215623. Fan and attached bath. Rather basic. Upstairs rooms

OK, downstairs rooms are windowless boxes. **F *Shan***, Khyber Bazaar, T210668. Fairly basic but cleanish rooms with fan and attached bath. No natural light.

GT Road F *Ariana*, GT Rd (opposite main bus station), T252585. Basic but reasonably clean rooms with fan and attached bath. Noisy. **F *Three Star***, GT Rd, T218160. Simple but reasonably clean rooms with fan and attached bath. Courtyard with shops on ground floor.

Hayatabad G *Youth Hostel*, Block B1, Plot 37, Phase 5, Hayatabad (heading west past Islamia College, after crossing the Kabul River Canal, take second turning left off the GT Rd into Hayatabad, then first right; situated near water tower and National Bank of Pakistan building), T813581. Several large dorm rooms and some 3-4 bed rooms, kitchen, common room, basic but clean and good value. A long way from Saddar and the Old City (though walking distance from GT Rd and public transport), no shops nearby as yet. Small garden, parking. Camping also allowed.

Eating

● *on maps*

Peshawar is a great place to sample a Pathan favourite, the *chapli kebab*. This consists of a large, round, flat burger made with mince, chopped onions, eggs and tomato and served with naan. It certainly puts all Western burgers to shame. Other meat dishes include *tikka*, *karahi* and 'roast' (usually lamb). Vegetarian food is limited to the usual *daal* and simple vegetable curries. Afghani pilau rice is a good variation, but take care as a 'veg pilau' often also contains meat. The Chinese restaurants listed below have a reasonable selection of vegetarian dishes.

Pakistani

Saddar/Cantt: at the top of the range, the *Pearl Continental* hotel's ***Marco Polo*** restaurant serves both Pakistani and continental cuisine in elegant surroundings for around Rs 1,000 per head. There is also an outdoor ***Terrace BBQ*** during summer. The fixed price evening buffets are very good value: check with the hotel as to which nights these are offered. More moderate is the *Greens hotel's* ***Lala's Grill***, where you can eat well for around Rs 200-300 per head. The ***Shiraz***, on Saddar Rd, serves good food in clean surroundings. Eat well for Rs 100-200. There are lots of good cheap Pakistani-style restaurants and food stalls in the old bazaars around Fowara Chowk.

In the **Old City**, the ***Khan Klub*** hotel boasts a beautiful restaurant, traditionally furnished with low tables and cushions strewn on the floor. Serving Afghani and Pakistani cuisine, it has been listed as being amongst the top 10 restaurants in Pakistan by *The News*. There are live music performances (*Rabbab* and *Tabla*) at lunch and dinner. Meals cost in the region of Rs 300-350 per head. Advance booking is essential. ***Salateen***, on Cinema Rd, T210279. Has rightly gained a reputation for excellent Peshawari food. A good meal here will cost in the region of Rs 150-200 per head. Namak Mandi (Bajori Rd) has lots of excellent tikka stalls and restaurants. There are also lots of cheap places along GT Rd.

Along Jamrud Rd, heading towards **University Town**, there is the ***Usmania***, T43135. A comfortable a/c restaurant serving good Pakistani and continental cuisine for around Rs 100-200 per head. The ***Shiraz***, a little further along Jamrud Rd on the same side, T842029, is very similar, though slightly more expensive. Cheaper places include the ***Azad Afghan***, further along on the opposite side, T44152, and the ***Afghan***, T42136, both serving kebabs, pilau etc.

Chinese

At the top of the range, the *Pearl Continental's* ***Taipan*** restaurant is probably the best, though also very expensive. The ***Hong Kong***, 24-D The Mall, T274504, is more reasonable, costing Rs 100-200 per head, though the food here is not particularly memorable. Approaching University Town along Jamrud Rd, the ***Kowloon***, offers a fairly similar deal.

Fast food Despite the quality of Peshawar's home grown 'fast food' offerings such as *chapli kebabs*, there still seems to be plenty of demand for Western-style fast food. On Arbab Rd in Saddar are ***Seasons*** and ***Jani***, both serving the usual fare of burgers, chips, milkshakes etc. The ***Silver Star***, on Saddar Rd, offers something of a fusion between Western and Pakistani fast food, serving roasted chickens, chicken spring rolls and various deep fried 'patties' of lentils, cheese etc.

Bakeries On Saddar Rd, ***Jan's Bakery*** is a firm favourite with backpackers staying at the *Tourist Inn Motel* immediately behind. The ***Honey Bakery***, next door to ANZ Grindlays bank on The Mall is also good. There are several others along the central part of Saddar Rd.

Entertainment

If you are after a drink, the only above-board place where you can get one is at the *Pearl Continental's* ***Gulbar***, which is open to non-Muslim foreigners from 1000-2400. You have to fill out and sign a form giving your details and declaring that you are indeed a non-Muslim. The bar is usually empty and always totally lacking in atmosphere. A bottle of Murree beer here will set you back Rs 180. The music put on each day in the *Khan Klub's* restaurant is of a very high standard. If you fancy sampling an authentic Pakistani cinematic experience, the various cinemas in the Old City's Cinema Rd all have the usual selection of lurid films on offer. Otherwise, there is not a huge amount going on in Peshawar in terms of entertainment; it is however worth asking at PTDC for information on any special cultural events which may be taking place.

Sports ***Arbab Niaz Stadium***, near Shahi Gardens is Peshawar's international cricket venue. There is also a polo ground here. Guests at the *Pearl Continental* hotel can make use of the ***Peshawar Golf Course***, off Shami Rd. Non-guests are allowed to use the *Pearl Continental's* **swimming** pool for a daily fee. The oldest and best swimming pool is in the *Peshawar Club*, although it is unfortunately not open to the general public. ***Wazir Bagh***, south of the Old City is a good place to watch (and join in) informal cricket, basketball, badminton, football, *kabadi* etc on Friday and Saturday evenings.

Shopping

The bazaars of the Old City are the most fascinating place to hunt for everything from carpets to spices (see page 341). Note that they more or less completely close down on Fridays, particularly in the afternoon. Saddar Bazaar has many tourist shops selling a wide range of antiques, jewellery, carpets, furniture, embroidery etc. Prices tend to be higher than in the Old City, although there is plenty of room for bargaining. One or two are fixed-price. The ***Outlet Venture***, sponsored by the Ockenden Trust, sells high quality carpets, rugs, embroidery, jewellery etc, all made by Afghan refugees. They have a shop in Saddar Rd, next door to Jan's Bakery, upstairs. Prices are fixed, and a little on the high side, but you can browse without having to worry about any hard sell.

Bookshops There are several bookshops on Arbab Rd, in Saddar. Both the ***London Book Co*** and ***Saeed Book Bank*** have a good selection of books in English, as well as international magazines and newspapers on sale. On Khyber Bazaar in the Old City, the ***University Book Agency*** is the best of several bookshops here, with a wide range of books on Pakistan's history and politics.

Local transport

To and from the airport The easiest way to get to and from the airport is by taxi or

Selected domestic fares and flying times from Peshawar

To	*Fare (Rs)*	*Flying time (approximately)*
Islamabad	*700*	*45 minutes*
Lahore	*1,840*	*1 hour*
Karachi	*3,400**	*1 hour 55 minutes*
Quetta	*1,960/2,620***	*1 hour 25 minutes*
Chitral	*630/2,500****	

** Cheaper 'Night Coach' fares are available to Karachi for around Rs 2,600.*
*** The cheaper fare is by Fokker F27, stopping in Dera Ismail Khan and Zhob, while the more expensive one is a direct Airbus 300 flight.*
**** Flights to Chitral are subsidized for Pakistanis. Foreigners pay the higher rate.*
***NB** The daily Fokker F27 flights to Chitral are weather dependent. If your flight is cancelled due to bad weather, you must go back to the PIA office and reconfirm your ticket if you wish to try again the next day. PTDC have a quota of two seats specifically for tourists on each flight; if there is a long waiting list, it is worth trying for these. Flights to Quetta are almost always oversubscribed and should be booked well in advance.*

auto-rickshaw. From Saddar you should not pay more than Rs 30 for an auto-rickshaw, or Rs 50 for a taxi.

Bus The main artery of public transport is between Hayatabad/University Town and the main bus station on the GT Rd. See the Peshawar Overview map, page 340, for the route. Note that heading from Saddar towards the GT Rd, buses go straight along Sunheri Masjid Rd, past the Cantonment railway station and Peshawar Museum, before turning directly into GT Rd near the Bala Hisar fort; coming from the main bus station on the GT Rd, they turn left just before the Bala Hisar fort, passing right through the heart of the Old City via Khyber Bazaar and Shuba Chowk, and then continue along the south side of the railway line before crossing it by the bridge to the south-west of the railway station and turning left into Sunheri Masjid Rd.

Auto-rickshaws are the most ubiquitous form of local transport after the buses. The fare from the centre of Saddar to Khyber bazaar in the Old City is around Rs 25-30.

Taxis can be found at the airport, outside major hotels, and around Saddar; there is a taxi rank on Fakhr-e-Alam Rd, between Sunheri Masjid and Saddar roads.

Car hire (with driver) is available from the major hotels, or can be arranged through PTDC.

Long-distance transport

Air

Peshawar Airport, T273081. **Domestic:** PIA operates regular domestic services to **Islamabad** 2-4 daily; **Lahore** 2 daily; **Karachi** up to 3 daily; **Quetta** 1 daily except Tuesday and Saturday; **Zhob** 1 daily except Friday; **Bannu** Monday, Wednesday, Friday; **DI Khan** 1-2 daily; **Multan** Monday, Tuesday, Friday, Saturday; **Parachinar** Monday, Wednesday, Friday; **Saidu Sharif** 1 daily except Saturday; and **Chitral** 2 daily (weather permitting). **Shaheen Air** has flights to **Lahore** on Monday, Tuesday, Thursday, Friday. **Aero Asia** has 2 flights daily to **Karachi**. **International**: PIA operates direct flights from Peshawar to Abu Dhabi, Doha, Dubai, Jeddah, Kuwait and Riyadh. There is also a weekly flight (Friday) via Islamabad to Almaty. **Shaheen Air** has flights to Dubai and Abu Dhabi. **Emirates** now have direct flights to London via Dubai. At the time of

Selected rail fares from Peshawar (in Rupees)

	A/c Sleeper	*A/c Sitter*	*1st Sleeper*	*Economy*
Rawalpindi	-	*175*	-	*40*
Lahore	*642*	*366*	*237*	*100*
Quetta	*1,755*	*1,013*	*704*	*330*
Karachi	*1,840*	*1,064*	*732*	*350*

writing, **Qatar** were also due to start direct international flights to and from Peshawar, and were opening an office in *Greens* hotel.

Train Cantonment Railway Station, T274437, or T117. Note that Sleepers and a/c must be booked well in advance; they often sell out as soon as they go on sale (15 days before the departure date). **Rawalpindi:** all the services listed below to Quetta and Karachi (with the exception of the *Khushal Khan Khattak Exp)* stop in Rawalpindi. They take between 3½ and 4 hours. There is also the much slower *212 Passenger*, 1515, 6 hours, which stops at all stations en route, including **Taxila**. Note that trains are liable to lengthy searches when crossing into Punjab. **Lahore:** all the services listed below to Quetta and Karachi (with the exception of the *Chenab Exp* and *Khushal Khan Khattak Exp*) stop in Lahore. They take between 9½ and 10¾ hours. The *212 Passenger* takes 18 hours. **Karachi:** *Awam Exp* (via 'Pindi and Lahore), 0815, 32¼ hours; *Khyber Mail* (via 'Pindi and Lahore), 2230, 32½ hours; *Zulfiqar Exp* (via 'Pindi and Lahore), 1000, 33½ hours; *Chenab Exp* (via 'Pindi, Sarghoda, Faisalabad and Multan), 2015, 39 hours; *Khushal Khan Khattak Exp* (via Attock, Kundian, DG Khan, Jacobabad and Larkana), 1845, 38 hours. **Quetta:** *Abaseen Exp* (via Lahore), 1800, 39 hours.

Bus **Main Bus Station** This chaotic bus station spreads for over half a kilometre along the north side of the GT Road, 3 kilometres to the east of the Bala Hisar fort. There is an assortment of old buses and Hiace minibuses from here to all points along the GT Road as far as Rawalpindi, and north towards Charsadda, Mardan, Takht-e-Bhai, Mingora/Saidu Sharif, Timargarha and Dir. They operate on a 'depart when full' basis.

Firdous Chowk Flying Coaches Just to the east of the Bala Hisar Fort on the south side of the GT Road (beside the *Shangri La* hotel), there are about half a dozen 'Flying Coach' companies offering a/c coach and Coaster services to **Rawalpindi** (Rs 50, 3 hours) and **Lahore** (Rs 125-150, approximately 8 hours). **NB** Some services call first in 'Pindi, while others go directly onto the Lahore motorway. Most of them have at least 1 departure every hour, so you rarely have to wait long, but if you want a good seat it is worth booking in advance.

New Khan Road Runners T219155. Situated on the north side of the GT Road, around 500 metres to the east of Firdous Chowk. Selection of a/c coaches and Coasters to **Abbottabad** (Rs 62), **Mansehra** (Rs 72), **Lahore** (Rs 230), **Faisalabad** (Rs 152) and **Karachi** (Rs 550).

Pakistan Flying Coach T213505. Situated on the north side of the GT Rd, around 600 metres to the east of Firdous Chowk. Selection of a/c coaches and Coasters to **Dera Ismail Khan** (Rs 100), **Multan** (Rs 140), **Sialkot** (Rs 80), **Faisalabad** (Rs 150) and **Karachi** (Rs 550).

Charsadda Adha Situated on the Charsadda road to the north of Shahi Bagh. Local buses operate from here to **Charsadda**, sometimes continuing on to **Mardan**, though for the latter, it is much quicker to get a Hiace minibus from the main bus station.

Chitral Hiaces In Qissa Khwani Bazaar (Old City), there are 2 companies inside the covered arcade opposite the *Deluxe* hotel (inside the same arcade are the entrances to the *Yassar* and *Jamshed* hotels, both very basic); ***New Abasin Flying Coach***, T2567691 and ***Sarhad***, T217968. Both have 1 departure daily, during the evening (usually between 1900-2100, but check). The fare is Rs 250, and the average journey time around 12 hours. If the prospect of this gruelling (and hair-raising) overnight trip does not appeal, a much better option is take a Hiace from the Main Bus Station as far as Dir (it may be necessary to change in Timargarha), spend the night there, then continue on the next day.

Kohat Adha Located on Kohat Rd, to the south of Bhanamari Chowk (see Peshawar overview map). An auto-rickshaw out to here from Saddar will cost around Rs 25, or you can catch bus number 3 from Sunheri Masjid Rd (catch it heading northeast, before it crosses the bridge to the southwest of the Cantonment railway station). Hiace minibuses operate from here to **Kohat** (Rs 20, 1½ hours). **NB** You are allowed to travel direct to Kohat, even if Darra is closed to foreigners, providing you do not get off at Darra). There are also various old buses and Hiace minibuses going as far as **Darra** only, and on to **Hangu** and **Thal** (west of Kohat), and **Bannu** (southwest of Kohat).

Quetta Coaches Everyone has a different name for this bus stand, situated further south along the Kohat Rd, beyond the Outer Circular Rd (the last stop on the bus number 3 route, see above). The PTDC map of Peshawar labels it Sada-Bahar Bus Station, while most locals seem to refer to it as 'Ghaas Phul' or 'Wahokh Phul' (literally 'Grass Bridge' in Urdu and Pashto respectively). A/c coaches operate from here to **Quetta**; they go first to Dera Ismail Khan, then follow the east bank of the Indus, before crossing again at Sukkur to go through Jacobabad and Sibi. Minimum journey time is in the region of 30 hours.

Directory

Airline offices **Domestic:** ***PIA Booking Office***, 33 The Mall, Cantt (entrance in Arbab Rd), T273081 (ext 230 for Chitral flights). Open 0800-2000 7 days (desk for flights to Chitral, open 0900-1700 daily). ***Shaheen Air International***, 16 Fakhr-e-Alam Rd, Cantt, T278409, F278427. **International:** ***Air France***, GSA Capitol Travels, Pearl Continental Hotel, T273386. ***British***, GSA Aviona, Greens Hotel, Saddar Rd, T273252. ***Emirates***, 95-B Saddar Rd, T275912, F276374. ***Gulf***, GSA King Associates, Arbab Rd (opposite PIA building), T275049, F275965. ***Qatar***, Greens Hotel, Saddar Rd, office about to open at time of writing. ***Saudi***, GSA Southern Travels, 6 Islamia Rd (opposite Jan's Shopping Arcade), Cantt, T285071, F285072.

Banks *ANZ Grindlays*, The Mall (opposite junction with Arbab Rd). Fixed fee of Rs 500 to exchange TCs. No charge for cash. Able to give cash advances against Visa cards. ***Habib Bank***, Saddar Rd. Provides a fairly efficient foreign exchange service for both cash and TCs. There are numerous money changers to be found around ***Chowk Yadgar*** in the Old City. They are authorized by the State Bank to deal in foreign currency, both cash and TC, and at the time of writing were offering dramatically better rates than the banks. You are also likely to be approached by unofficial money changers around Saddar; generally they will also try to sell you anything from carpets to hashish, and are best avoided.

Communications **Post:** *GPO*, Saddar Rd, Saddar. Open 0900-1900, Fri 0900-1200, closed Sun. *Poste Restante* service available. **Courier:** *DHL*, 1080 Saddar Rd, T277418, F277417. **Telephone:** (Pak Telecom), 2 The Mall. Open 24 hrs 7 days. Local/international phone, fax, telegram, cable. Note that faxes can only be sent between 0900-2400, when the man responsible for the fax machine is present (Pakistani bureaucracy at its best!). **Internet:** The *British Council* (see below) has its own ***Cyber Station*** where you can hook up to the internet for Rs 70 per hour. Another place is ***Cyberlinks***, Gulhaji Plaza, Jamrud Rd, University Town (opposite *Shiraz* restaurant). The business centre at the *Pearl Continental* hotel also has an internet facility, but it is very expensive.

Cultural centres *Alliance Francaise*, 1 Park Rd, University Town, T843928. ***British Council***, 17-C Chinar Rd, University Town, T841921, F842633. The library (open 1200-1800, closed Sat and Sun) is geared up mainly towards providing information on study in the UK, but has a good selection of British newspapers and international magazines. Internet access also available. ***Peshawar Club***, Sir Sayid Rd, near The Mall, T279048. Established in 1863 for the armed forces. For members and guests only, but you can look around the library and buildings. Facilities include tennis, squash, billiard, gym and swimming pool. Foreigners living in Peshawar can apply for temporary membership.

Embassies & consulates *American Consulate*, 11 Hospital Rd, Cantt, T279801. Open 0800-1630, closed Sat and Sun. ***Afghan Consulate***, 17-C Gulmohar Lane, University Town, T285962. ***Iranian Consulate***, 18 Park Avenue, University Town, T41114. It may be possible to obtain transit visas here, but at the time of writing the best place to do so was in Quetta. However, it is worth checking for yourself before heading off into Baluchistan as the situation can easily change without warning.

Hospitals & medical services Hospitals: The ***Sherpao*** (also known as *Hayat Shaheed*), University Town, T841701 and ***Lady Reading***, Hospital Rd, Old City, T9211430, are the 2 largest. ***Mission***, Dubgari Gate, Old City, T212371, is the least crowded of the main hospitals. The ***Hayatabad Medical Complex***, Hayatabad, T818040, has a good reputation, though it is a long way from the centre of town. The ***Cantonment General***, Sunheri Masjid Rd, Saddar, T272139 is OK for minor problems. The ***Khyber Medical Centre***, Dubgari Gate, T211241, is a good private hospital. There are several private practitioners around Dubgari Gate, and also in Doctor Plaza, Saddar Rd, opposite *Greens* Hotel. Opposite the *Sherpao* there is a free but crowded *Dental Hospital*, or there are private dentists in Saddar Rd. **Chemists:** all the hospitals listed above have their own dispensaries, and there are numerous chemists dotted around Saddar and the Old City.

Libraries As well as the libraries in the various cultural centres (see above), there is the ***Department of Archives and Public Libraries***, next door to Peshawar Museum, T278944, which has an extensive collection of archival materials (of interest mostly to researchers and those with a specific area of interest). ***ARIC*** (Afghan Resource and Information Centre, see under Useful addresses below) has an excellent library/resource centre focusing on Afghan issues.

Tour companies & travel agencies *Gandhara Travels*, Saddar Rd, T273832, F273124. Domestic and international flights, hotel reservations. ***Sehrai Travels and Tours***, Greens Hotel, Saddar Rd, T272085, F276088, E sehrai@psh.brain.net.pk. Efficient and helpful, specializing in large group tours, but also offering tailor-made packages for individuals/small groups. Responsible for organizing the 'Khyber Steam Safari' (see under Around Peshawar, below). Also offer standard trips up to the Khyber Pass, and walking tours of the Old City. Full ticketing service for international and domestic flights. ***Spinzer Travels***, 2 Islamia Rd, T278835. Domestic and international flights etc.

Tourist offices PTDC Tourist Information Centre, Deans Hotel, 3 Islamia Rd, Saddar, T286829. Open 0900-1300, 1400-1630, Fri 0900-1200, closed Sun. Helpful staff, well informed. Ask here for reliable information on the current situation in Khyber Agency and Darra. PTDC have 2 seats per flight to Chitral reserved for foreign tourists; they will issue you with a letter to present to PIA. Also able to arrange tours of Peshawar Old City, the Khyber Pass and major sites in the Peshawar Valley (Charsadda, Takht-e-Bhai, Shabaz Ghari etc). In 1998 they were charging Rs 1,500 for trips by jeep to the Khyber Pass (5 people, all-inclusive). To hire a Land cruiser with driver for longer excursions costs Rs 2,500 per 24 hrs, all-inclusive. ***Sarhad Tourism Corporation (STC)***, Block 13-A Old Courts Building, Khyber Rd, Cantonment (near *Pearl Continental*), T9211091, F921087. NWFPs provincial tourism corporation; there is no public counter here, but you can phone up for information on the dates of the Shandur Polo Festival.

Useful addresses **Police:** T212222 (Emergency T15). **Fire:** T279074. **Foreigners' Registration Office:** Special Branch, near Shaheen Camp, T9210508. Open 0800-1300, closed Sun. **ACBAR (Agency Coordinating Body on Afghan Refugees):** PO Box 1084, 2 Rehman Baba Rd, University Town, T44392, F840471. Also the location of **ARIC (Afghan Resource and Information Centre)**. **Political Agent, Khyber** (Permits for Khyber Pass), Stadium Rd, T278542.

Around Peshawar

Khyber Pass

The Khyber Pass has achieved something of a legendary status and remains one of the great attractions for visitors to Peshawar. Visually it's not particularly impressive, but somehow the journey up through the barren landscape of the lawless Tribal Areas is one which captures most people's imagination. Its historical significance has also been vastly overstated. Billed as the main invasion route from the west since Aryan times, the first recorded conqueror to pass through it was in fact Babur in the 16th century. For many conquerors before, it was the passes to the north and south that provided routes into the subcontinent. To the British, however, it represented the 'Gateway of India', an all important break in the mountainous barrier of their northwest frontier.

Ins and outs

Foreigners are required to obtain a **permit** to visit the Khyber Pass. They must travel by private vehicle and take an armed escort. If you wish to organize it yourself, both the permit (Rs 120 per person, bring photocopies of the relevant pages of your passport) and armed escort can be obtained from the Political Agent, Khyber in Peshawar (see under Useful Addresses). The easiest way to organize a visit, however (and the cheapest if you can get a group of 5 together), is through PTDC or a reputable travel agent such as *Sehrai Travels*. PTDC charges Rs 1,500 for a half-day visit by jeep (maximum 5 people), including permits and escort. *Sehrai Travels* charges Rs 585 per person (minimum 2 people). The *Tourist Inn Motel* offers a similar deal to PTDC. There are also plenty of taxi drivers and freelance 'guides' hanging around Saddar Bazaar who may offer to take you for less. They are less reliable and if you opt for one of these, PTDC strongly advises you to call at their office and inform them before setting off. A recently revived alternative to going by road is to travel on the famous Khyber railway (see below). Note that at the time of writing, the Khyber Pass was open to foreigners, but whenever there is any unrest amongst the Afridi tribes controlling the area, the authorities are liable to close it. There is a ***PTDC Motel*** at Torkham, though at the time of writing, foreigners were not allowed to stay overnight here.

The pass

The pass stretches from Jamrud Fort to Torkham. Heading west out of Peshawar along the Jamrud Rd, you pass University Town, Hayatabad and Smugglers' Bazaar, before entering Khyber Agency. **Jamrud Fort** (18 kilometres) was built by the Sikh General Hari Singh in 1836, provoking an attack by the Afghans which cost him his life. It is of rough stonework faced with mud plaster, and in three tiers; lower and upper forts and a keep. There is also a stone arched gate on the road, the **Bab-e-Khyber**, built in 1964. From the fort, the road zigzags up past viewpoints and watchtowers with good views back onto the Peshawar plain. Next is the 1920s British-built **Shagai Fort** (30 kilometres). It is now manned by the Frontier Force and closed to the public. In the middle of the pass is Ali Masjid (mosque) and high above it the **Ali Masjid Fort** which defends the narrowest point of the gorge, less than 14 metres wide.

From here the pass opens out into a wide valley dotted with fortified Pathan settlements. Just before Landi Kotal, 15 kilometres from Shagai Fort, there is the **Sphola Stupa**, to the right of the road on a hillock above Zarai. It dates from the second to fifth centuries AD and is the last remains (somewhat dilapidated) of an extensive Buddhist monastery. **Landi Kotal** itself is a bustling colourful market town with everything from smuggled electrical goods to drugs. Eight kilometres further on is the border town of **Torkham**, though foreigners are only allowed as far as **Michni check post**, a little beyond Landi Kotal.

The Khyber Railway Built by the British in the 1920s, the Khyber Railway is a remarkable feat of engineering, with 34 tunnels and 92 bridges and culverts. At one point it climbs 130 metres in just over one kilometre, passing through a series of switchbacks with reversing stations and requiring an additional steam engine at the back to help push the train up the steep gradient. Regular passenger services were discontinued some years ago due to insufficient usage (in practical terms it is very slow, prompting most locals to travel by bus). Recently however, *Sehrai Travels* have managed to reinstate a 'Khyber Steam Safari' for the benefit of tourists. The train currently operates monthly, but if there is sufficient demand, more departures may be scheduled. This is a full-day outing costing US$85 per person (including return trip by rail, refreshments en route, picnic lunch at Landi Kotal and guided sightseeing). For more details contact *Sehrai Travels and Tours* (see under Peshawar Tour operators and travel agents).

Peshawar Valley The Peshawar Valley is rich in historical sites from the Gandharan period; perhaps the most impressive visually is the Buddhist monastery of Takht-e-Bhai. This and many others can be visited as long day-trips from Peshawar. See the Peshawar Valley section, page 365.

Darra Adam Khel

Colour map 5, grid C1

Darra is the biggest centre of indigenous arms manufacture in NWFP (and Pakistan for that matter). Home to the Adam Afridi tribe or *khel*, the town consists almost entirely of gun shops where working replicas of anything from pen-guns to Kalashnikovs are meticulously fashioned with only the most primitive of machine tools. These gun-making skills are thought to have arrived here in the 1890s with a Punjabi gunsmith who was wanted for murder and settled in the town, beyond the reach of the authorities.

Ins and outs Darra is situated 42 kilometres south of Peshawar on the Kohat road. At the time of writing, it was closed to foreigners, and had been for the last couple of years. However, nothing is cast in stone in Pakistan, and it may well be opened up to tourists again at some point. Enquire at PTDC in Peshawar as to the current situation. In the past, foreigners were required to obtain a permit from the Civil Secretariat of the Home Department in Peshawar in order to visit. They were then allowed to travel there on public transport without an escort, though once there they would be shown around by a local official who would also keep a close eye on them. Note that the town all but closes down on Fridays. There are regular buses and Hiace minibuses to Darra which depart from the bus stand known as Kohat Adha, to the south of the Old City on Kohat Rd (see under Peshawar Long-distance transport). The journey takes around 45 minutes. On the return journey, any north-bound bus passing through the town will get you to Peshawar.

Southern NWFP

The southern half of NWFP has poorly developed infrastructure and is little visited by tourists. In summer it can get unbearably hot and dusty during the day. The prevailing image – in places an accurate one – is of a region beset by tribal feuding and lawlessness. Nevertheless, it does have a certain wild charm of its own, and for the more determined traveller, this is a fascinating and rewarding, if at times demanding, region in which to travel.

Ins and outs

The main route south from Peshawar passes through the districts of Kohat, Bannu and Dera Ismail Khan (DI Khan), crossing barren semi-arid countryside with hills and mountains averaging around 1,500 metres and occasional fertile oases. To the west, following the border with Afghanistan are the Federally Administered Tribal Areas (FATAs) of Kurram and North and South Waziristan. The Tribal Areas, or Agencies, are off-limits to foreigners unless they have a permit and escort. The main highway is open to foreigners without a permit as far south as DI Khan, although it passes through several pockets of Tribal Areas and you are only allowed to stop in the main towns of Kohat, Bannu and DI Khan. Provided you travel sensibly and take heed of local advice (ask also at PTDC in Peshawar for up-to-date information on travelling in the area), these routes are perfectly safe. Venturing into the Tribal Areas without a permit is however dangerous; this is not an area where the official line on travel restrictions can be ignored. Women travellers are likely to find southern NWFP hard work; travelling alone is inadvisable unless you have some experience of the area.

Peshawar to Kohat

Heading south out of Peshawar on the Kohat road, you pass first through the arms manufacturing town of **Darra Adam Khel** (42 kilometres). See above for details. The road then climbs up to the Kohat Pass, from where there are good views north back towards the arid plains around Darra, and south down onto the wide and fertile Kohat Basin. The town of Kohat, 93 kilometres from Peshawar, lies at the centre of this basin.

Kohat

Phone code: 0991
Colour map 5, grid C1

Although in a 'settled' area, Kohat remains a focus for the surrounding Tribal Areas and still has something of a 'Wild West' feel about it. For the British it was a vitally important military outpost and today the town's military importance continues, with the large Fort and extensive Cantonment area occupied by the Pakistan army. The Old City meanwhile has changed little, retaining many remnants from British and Mughal times. It is still surrounded by walls and marked by four gates. Inside, the bazaars are packed into narrow, bustling streets. The town had a large Hindu population prior to Partition, and a number of Hindu families still live in Tirah Bazaar, near the *Nadria* hotel.

Ins and outs

Coming from Peshawar, soon after reaching the bottom of the Kohat Pass, you arrive at a crossroads and sign reading "Welcome to Kohat". There is usually a Suzuki waiting here to take passengers into the centre of Kohat (straight ahead), but buses and minibuses turn right, bypassing the centre of town and depositing passengers at Peshawar Chowk, to the west of the centre, on the Hangu road. An auto-rickshaw into the centre of town from here will cost around Rs 15, or there are Suzukis which do the trip for a few rupees. To pick up transport heading southwest to Bannu or south to DI Khan, you must get out to the main bus station, which is around 5 kilometres to the south of the centre, just off the Bannu road. Buses run to here from the local bus station in the centre of town, or you can get a Suzuki from near Faisal Gate, or take an auto-rickshaw for around Rs 30-50. Kohat is also connected by narrow-gauge railway with Rawalpindi. The station is a few kilometres south of the city, just off the Bannu road.

History Kohat developed primarily as a garrison town during the British era, and flourished also as a trading post at the intersection of the east-west route between Afghanistan and the Punjab and north-south along the Indus. Its origins however are much older. Local tradition asserts that the town was founded in the 14th century by the Bangash Pathans, who migrated from the Kurram Valley to the east, displacing the indigenous Orakzai. The Khattaks, who are the other main tribal group found here, migrated into the area from the Suleiman mountains to the south in the 15th century. In 1505 the Mughal emperor Babur plundered the town during a raid on the district, but was able to maintain only nominal control. Indeed, throughout its history, Kohat remained for all practical purposes independent, the tribal groups of the area fiercely resisting the control of the Durranis, Dost Mohammad and the Sikhs, until the British firmly established themselves there, though not before undertaking a large-scale campaign against the nearby Mirzanai tribes in 1855. For the British, it formed a vital part of the network of outposts defending the northwest border of their empire, and they lost no time in building roads linking it with Peshawar to the north and Bannu to the southwest.

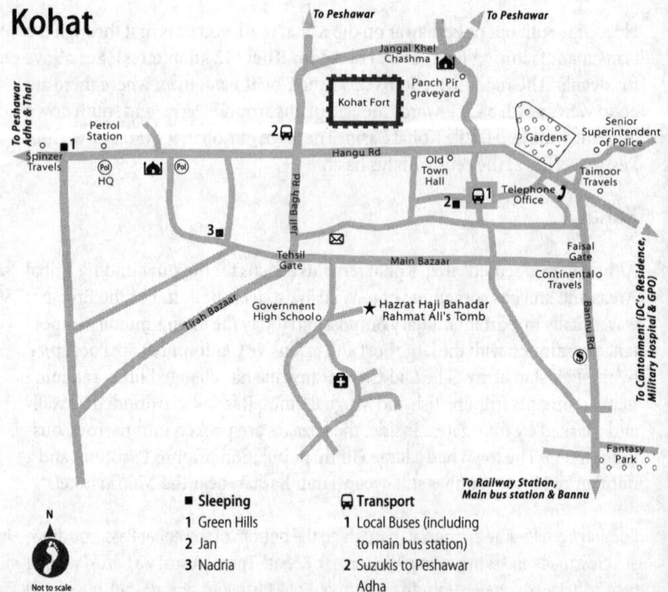

Sights

Kohat Fort, built by the British, is a large imposing structure overlooking the town, although it is now occupied by the military and closed to the public. The **Deputy Commissioner's residence**, formerly the home of Louis Cavagnari, who served as the British Resident in Kabul, is a beautiful white-washed colonial-style building with round-topped French windows, set in immaculate gardens. Still in use by the DC, getting permission to look around the grounds is difficult, although it is worth trying, if only to see the colourful assortment of tribal chiefs usually gathered here in anticipation of an audience. At **Jangal Khel**, near the fort, there is a large spring-fed water tank next to a mosque, where men and boys come to bathe and wash. Next to it is an old graveyard known as **Panch Pir** or 'five saints', with gravestones dating back to the Mughal period (perhaps casualties of Babur's expedition), as well as some British graves and a number of huge shady Banyan trees. In the Old City, the **Tomb of Hazrat Haji Bahadar Rahmat Ali** (also known as Syed Abdullah Shah), a Sufi saint from the time of Aurangzeb, has a beautifully decorated dome. Nearby is the Government High School for Girls, formerly a Hindu pilgrims' resthouse or *Dharamsala*. The **bazaars** of the Old City are colourful and lively, and well worth a visit.

Sleeping & eating

There is only basic accommodation available. **G** ***Green Hill***, Hangu Rd, near Police Line, T512228. Reasonably clean rooms with fan and attached bath, restaurant. **G** *Nadria*, outside Tehsil Gates, T513162. Reasonable rooms with fan and attached bath, also some with a/c. There are a few very basic hotels around the local bus station, but these are very noisy and unappealing.

The restaurant at the *Green Hill* hotel serves reasonable food. More interesting however are the various food stalls to be found in the bazaars of the Old City. Try the street running parallel to the north of the Main Bazaar. Look for yourself to find the most appealing freshly cooked snacks; *chapli kebabs* are widely available, as is *kaleji*, and sometimes deep-fried fish.

Transport

Train A single track narrow-gauge railway runs west from Kohat to **Rawalpindi**. There is 1 service daily, the *187 Passenger*, departing at 1815 and taking 5½ hours.

Bus The regular Hiace minibus services which operate to **Peshawar** (Rs 20, 1½ hours) are best caught from Peshawar Adha (see Ins and outs, above). Services to **Bannu** (Rs 40, 2 hours) and **Dera Ismail Khan** (Rs 80, 5 hours) must be caught from the main bus station, just off the Bannu road. Note that when the new section of the Indus Highway bypassing Bannu is open, services to DI Khan will be much faster. There are also bus and Hiace minibus services from the main bus station to **Kalabagh**, on the Indus River, and to **Thal** and **Parachinar** in the Kurram Valley.

Directory

Communications Post and Telephone: there is a GPO in the Cantonment area; it's a lengthy walk from the centre of town, so it makes sense to take an auto-rickshaw. You can also make international calls from here. More conveniently, there is a Pak Telecom office nearer the centre of town, open 0800-1900, closed Sun. There are also a number of PCOs in the Main Bazaar, and a small post office in the street running parallel. **Useful phone numbers Commissioner:** T510775. **Deputy Commissioner:** T3527. **Senior Superintendent of Police:** T4160.

Routes

From Kohat a good but narrow metalled road leads east towards **Islamabad** (175 kilometres). At **Khashalgarh** (50 kilometres from Kohat), the road crosses the Indus on a rail/road bridge into Punjab Province. From Khashalgarh it is 77 kilometres on to **Fatehjang** and a further 47 kilometres into Islamabad, a journey of about 3-5 hours.

Another road leads west towards **Thal** and **Parachinar**, the latter being the last town in the Kurram Valley and headquarters of the Kurram Agency, a Tribal Area for which permits are required. The valley is a very beautiful one, but it is also very sensitive and has for a long time been closed to foreigners. Permits are issued through the Home Department of the Secretariat in Peshawar, but unless you have connections, or a good reason for going there, you are unlikely to get one.

Southwest to Bannu and DI Khan

At the time of writing, a new section of the Indus Highway was nearing completion. This branches off the old Kohat-Bannu road a little to the southwest of Lachi, bypassing Bannu and rejoining the old Bannu-DI Khan road at Serai Gambila. Near where the Indus Highway branches off the Kohat-Bannu road, there is also a turning which leads southeast to Shakadara and then on to Kalabagh (see page 242).

The old Bannu road crosses the Salt Range passing close to the salt mine at **Jatta**. After about 100 kilometres the road winds down from the Kohat and Wazir hills into the Bannu Basin, an almost circular alluvial plain shut in on all sides by mountains and drained by two rivers, the **Kurram** and the **Tochi** (or Gambila). Between them lies a tract of richly irrigated country, densely populated, wooded and crossed by many water courses. This oasis is the setting for Bannu (125 kilometres), refreshingly green and surrounded by palms and shady mango trees.

Bannu

Phone code: 0928
Colour map 4, grid A2

The old town of Bannu, which has some of its original gates still standing, is as crowded, dusty, noisy and chaotic as the Cantonment area is spacious, clean, peaceful and ordered; the latter even boasts a small golf course. For those interested in the town's colonial legacy, in the Cantonment there is the **Pennell Missionary Hospital** and school, founded at the turn of the century by a British missionary. Otherwise, the main reason for stopping here is to break the journey between Peshawar and DI Khan, although once the new section of the Indus Highway bypassing the town is open, even its usefulness in this respect will diminish.

History Bannu (then called Pona), is first mentioned by the Chinese pilgrim Fa-Hien in 404 AD, who describes a Buddhist monastery with 3,000 monks. The town grew as a result of its position on the original trading route between Kabul and the Indus, later replaced by the Kurram/Miranzai Valley route through Hangu and Kohat.

During the 18th century the Durranis exercised a precarious hold over the area, followed by Ranjit Singh, who built the fort here in 1844. From 1846 the British extended their control over the area through Lieutenant Edwardes, who in turn administered through the Sikhs. He named the town Dulipshehr after the young Maharaja. In1899 it was renamed Edwardesabad and in 1903 Bannu. Edwardes gained the respect of the local tribes and exerted considerable influence, even getting many of the surrounding villagers to pull down their fortifications and accept British protection.

Sleeping & eating **D** ***Bag-e-Sakhoun***, Kohat Rd, T3868. A little out of town (past bus station on road to Kohat). Clean and comfortable rooms with fan and attached bath. Restaurant, nice garden. Recommended. **F** ***Inam Palace***, New Lari Adda, near bus station, T3241. Clean rooms, some with a/c (**D** category), courtyard. Restaurant. Friendly, good value. **F** ***KD's***, Jaman Rd, T4089. Basic rooms with fan and attached bath. **F** ***New Jan's***, Lakki Gate, T2345. Basic rooms with fan and attached bath. Restaurant. **G** ***Sajjad***, Chai Bazaar, T2583. Basic rooms with fan and attached bath. As well as the hotel restaurants, there are lots of good Pakistani-style eating places in the old town.

Women are not allowed

According to a local story, the town of Wana gained its name from a dispute between the British and the local population. Having established their outpost there, the British officers posted to the town began to bring their wives and families to live with them. It was not long before the 'Memsahibs' could be seen wandering around the bazaar, doing their shopping. This raised an outcry amongst the conservative tribal elders, who promptly assembled a jirga in which they voted to ban these immodest white ladies from their town. The British, anxious not to spark a violent confrontation, reluctantly agreed to comply. Subsequently, the town became known by the acronym of Women Are Not Allowed!

Transport

Air Airport T3573. PIA operates Fokker F27 flights to Peshawar on Monday, Wednesday and Friday.

Train The narrow gauge railway connecting Bannu with Kalabagh via Lakki no longer operates passenger services.

Bus Regular bus and Hiace minibus services operate in all directions, leaving when full. **Kohat** Rs 40, 2 hours. **DI Khan** Rs 40, 3 hours.

Directory

Useful phone numbers Commissioner: T2299. Deputy Commissioner: T2502.

Routes

From Bannu one road leads west into the Tribal Agencies of **North and South Waziristan.** These tribal areas can be very dangerous and should not be visited without a permit and escort. Without special connections or a specific reason for visiting, these are not usually granted. The road passes **Razmak** (126 kilometres) with its Army Cadet College, **Wana** the administrative capital of south Waziristan and **Tanai Scout Post** (206 kilometres) with its fort, before crossing into Baluchistan and continuing on to **Zhob** (333 kilometres). At Taudachina (just beyond Ramzak) and at Tanai there are turnings heading east which converge at Jandola before going on past **Khirgi Post** with its impressive fort, **Dabarra**, centre for the local falcon trade, and arriving at **Tank** (110 kilometres). From Tank, 1 road leads east to join the Bannu-DI Khan road at Pezu, while another leads southeast directly to DI Khan.

South to DI Khan

Taking the main road southeast from Bannu, after around 40 kilometres the new section of the Indus Highway joins from the north. Shortly afterwards there is a turning east to Lakki and Kalabagh (see page 242). At **Pezu** (82 kilometres) there is a turning west to Tank, a large town on the edge of the Tribal Areas (see above).

From Pezu a path leads up to the nearby peak of **Sheikh Budin** (1,377 metres) named after the Sufi saint *Sheikh-Baha-ud-din* whose shrine is at the top. The mountain owes its height to a cap of limestone which has prevented erosion. To the southwest is the Suleiman range, dominated by the 3,355 metres **Takht-e-Suleiman** (*Throne of Solomon*). The main road continues south from Pezu crossing the western extremities of the Marwat Range before descending on to the Derajat Plain and reaching DI Khan. About 22 kilometres before DI Khan is **Rahman Dheri**, an Indus Valley Civilization settlement dating from 3200 BC. The site is about three kilometres west of the main road, its low mound barely visible from the road. Today nothing remains of the excavations, which once revealed the town layout and ancient brick walls of houses. Numerous pottery shards are still in evidence however, scattered around the site.

Dera Ismail Khan

Phone code: 0961
Colour map 4, grid B2

DI Khan is a prosperous town situated on the west bank of the Indus. Despite being close to restricted Tribal Areas, it is a safe place with a relaxed, good natured atmosphere. The only exception to this is during the Shia festival of Muharram, when tensions between the town's minority Shia population and the majority Sunnis sometimes erupt into violence.

Ins and outs

Getting there Long-distance coaches, buses, Coasters and Hiace minibuses connect DI Khan with most towns and cities. DI Khan also has an airport providing regular connections with Islamabad, Karachi (via Multan), Peshawar, Quetta and Zhob.

Getting around The old town is encompassed by Circular Road and crossed by four main bazaar streets. At the centre is the Chowkala Tower, a free-standing modern brick structure straddling the intersection. The spaciously laid out Cantonment area is to the east and south, between the old town and the Indus River. Within the old town, the best way to get around is on foot. Auto-rickshaws are plentiful, and useful for getting around the Cantonment, to and from the Indus River, or back to your hotel when you find yourself at the opposite end of town. Most trips shouldn't cost more than Rs 15-20. The airport is situated around 10 kilometres out of town; PIA operates a shuttle bus between its booking office and the airport.

Sights

DI Khan is famous for its brass inlaid woodwork and the narrow bustling **bazaars** of the old town are a fascinating area in which to explore and shop for these and many other goods. Locally produced traditional leather *chappals* are also a good buy, though they are often much prettier than they are comfortable. Another speciality is the local *halwa*, a delicious sweet meat made from sesame seeds, honey, nuts and saffron. Many of the houses in the bazaars and small alleys running between them have beautifully carved wooden balconies.

DI Khan's other great attraction is its setting on the banks of the **Indus River**. The road running along the river bank forms a pleasant tree-lined promenade, the *Midway* hotel and the *Indus View* restaurant both have outside seating by the river's edge; ideal places to relax and enjoy the broad sweep of the Indus, which at this point varies from 10-20 kilometres in width according to the season. The **SS Jhelum**, a paddle steamer which saw service in southern Iraq during the First World War, is moored by the river bank opposite the *Indus View* restaurant. Unfortunately, years of neglect have taken their toll and today it is a rusting old wreck which looks ready to sink at any moment. Small ferries still ply back and forth across the river from here.

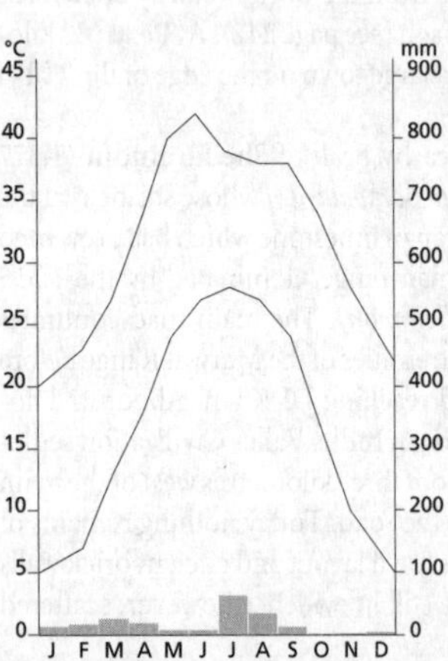

The best time to visit is November to March

Essentials

Sleeping
■ *on map*
Price codes: see inside front cover

D *De Hilton*, East Circular Rd, T711437, F710380. Clean rooms with a/c, TV, phone and attached bath. Rather noisy. Restaurant. **D *Jan's*** (sign in Urdu only), North Circular Rd, T710913. Quiet rooms around central concrete courtyard, a/c, fan, phone and attached bath. Also cheaper non-a/c rooms (double Rs 350). Restaurant. Reasonable hotel, but nothing special. **D *Midway***, Indus River Bank, T812100. Clean and comfortable rooms with a/c, fan, TV, phone and attached bath. Also some slightly larger/nicer 'deluxe' rooms. Waterfront location makes this the most pleasant place to stay. Restaurant. **D *Rose***, East Circular Rd, T711532. Clean and comfortable rooms with a/c, TV, phone and attached bath. Also very good value rooms with fan only (double Rs 230). Restaurant. Friendly staff. Recommended. **E *Nawaz***, North Circular Rd, T713427. Small but clean rooms with fan and attached bath. **F *Al-Habib***, off Topan Wallah Bazaar, T711306. Basic rooms with fan and attached bath. Pleasant courtyard. **G *Gulbar***, East Circular Rd, no phone. Set back slightly from main road. Basic rooms arranged around central courtyard, fan and attached bath. Quiet. **G *Taj Mahal***, East Circular Rd, T710834. Very basic rooms in converted Hindu temple.

Eating
● *on map*

The ***Neelab*** in the *Midway* hotel is the best restaurant. As well as an a/c dining hall, it has its own area of outdoor seating across the road on the banks of the Indus. The ***Indus View*** is pleasantly located overlooking the Indus. The restaurant itself is a/c, though it looks pretty dilapidated inside. The seating area across the road on the banks of the Indus is pleasant enough. The *Rose*, *De Hilton* and *Jan's* hotels also have reasonable restaurants. Cheaper places are in the old town, particularly along Topan Wallah Bazaar.

Dera Ismail Khan

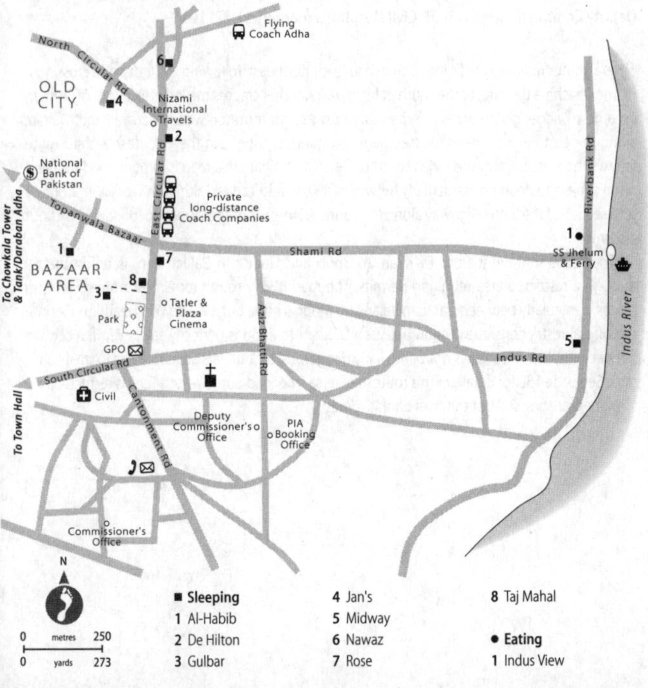

Transport **Air** *PIA Booking Office*, 7-A Aziz Bhatti Rd, Cantonment, opposite DC's office, T710639. Open 7 days, 0900-1700. Airport T740331. *Nizami International Travels*, East Circular Rd, T/F714414, can also book flights. **Peshawar** up to 2 flights daily (with 1 daily onward connection to **Islamabad**). **Quetta (via Zhob)** Wednesday, Thursday, Sunday. **Multan (via Zhob)** Monday, Tuesday, Friday, Saturday.

Bus There are about half a dozen **long-distance a/c coach** companies along East Circular Rd, all on its east side, spread over the first 200 metres to the north of the junction with Shami Rd and Topanwala Bazaar. The 'ticket offices' consist simply of a desk out on the street, most of them in front of sweet sellers' shops. Between them they offer regular services to **Karachi**, Rs 300, approximately 20-24 hours. There is also 1 company offering a daily service to **Quetta** (via DG Khan, Shikarpur, Jacobabad and Sibi) Rs 300, 20 hours.

Flying Coach Adha Situated just off the Bannu Rd at the northern edge of the town. Coasters and Hiace minibuses to **Islamabad/Rawalpindi** Rs 150, 6-7 hours; **Peshawar** Rs 100, 6 hours; **Kohat** Rs 80, 5 hours; **Bannu** Rs 40, 2 hours; **Multan** Rs 70, 8-9 hours (very bad road!); **Sarghoda** Rs 70, 6 hours; **Mianwali** Rs 40, 2 hours.

Tank/Daraban Adha Situated outside the western gate to the old town. Rickety old buses, Datsun pickups and some Coasters operate from here to **Tank** and **Jandola**, and also to **Daraban Kalan** (Rs 15, 1½ hours) and **Zhob** (Rs 80-100, 7-9 hours). See below for more information on the route to Daraban and Zhob.

Directory **Banks** *National Bank of Pakistan*, Topan Wallah Bazaar. Open 0900-1330, Fri and Sat 0900-1230, closed Sun. Changes cash and TCs at the standard bank rate. **Communications Post and Telephone:** the GPO is on the corner of East Circular Rd and South Circular Rd. Open 0900-1500, Fri 0900-1130, closed Sun. The Pak Telecom office is in Cantonment, just off Cantonment Rd. Open 7 days, 0600-2200. There is a small post office next door. **Hospitals & medical services** *Civil Hospital*, South Circular Rd, T811436. There is a dispensary in the hospital, and a number of pharmacies nearby on South Circular Rd. **Useful phone numbers** **Commissioner:** T712413. **Deputy Commissioner:** T713401. **Civil Hospital (emergency):** T711408.

Routes from DI Khan Several routes radiate from DI Khan. One road leads northeast, following the Indus and crossing it on the Chashma Barrage, to the south of Mianwali. Another crosses the Indus just west of DI Khan on a new bridge, giving access to the main north-south route between Mianwali and Multan, along the east bank of the Indus (see page 242 for details of both these routes). A third route follows the west bank of the Indus south to Dera Ghazi Khan; this road is in poor condition and often subject to flooding, particularly between DI Khan and Taunsa, although work is in progress on a section of the Indus Highway along this route. All these routes are open to foreigners without a permit.

The route southwest from DI Khan, to Zhob and Quetta in Baluchistan, is unfortunately through a restricted area requiring permits. The road is very rough (or almost non-existent) in places, particularly between Daraban Kalan and Mughal Khot, but it is also very beautiful. Despite the official restrictions, the section between DI Khan to Zhob is perfectly safe. Even the section between Zhob and Quetta is not particularly dangerous, though it is advisable not to travel after dark. See page 158 for details of this route in reverse. The road northwest to Tank is restricted and foreigners are advised not to travel on this route.

Peshawar Valley

The fertile plains to the north and east of Peshawar form the heartland of the Peshawar Valley and are of enormous agricultural and industrial importance, being the centre of tobacco and sugarcane cultivation and processing. They are also of great historical significance, rich in archaeological remains from the Gandharan Buddhist period, making this a fascinating area to explore. October to April are the ideal months to visit, when the climate is pleasantly cool during the day. Summer temperatures climb well into the forties.

Ins and outs

Mardan is centrally located, and being the main transport hub, is the ideal base from which to visit most of the sites. Unfortunately however, there is only a very limited selection of basic accommodation in the town. Another possibility is to explore the area in short visits from Peshawar, or en route to Swat/Chitral. Alternatively, if you have your own transport, the road via Mardan and Swabi provides a slower but much more interesting and scenic route to Islamabad. In contrast to the busy GT Rd, lined for much of the way with heavy industrial factories, the small tree-lined roads to the north pass through a green, fertile landscape of fields and canals, with isolated hills rising out of the flat plains. The area is ideal for cyclists with the many canals making for excellent traffic-free cycle routes.

Charsadda

The town of Charsadda is situated 28 kilometres northeast of Peshawar. This is the site of the ancient city of **Pushkalavati** (the lotus city), capital of

Phone code: 0921
Colour map 5, grid B1

Peshawar Valley

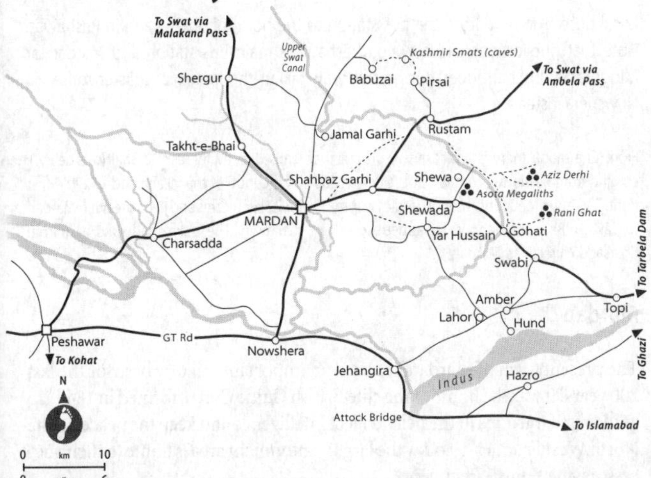

Gandhara from around the sixth century BC to the second century AD. Peshawar later emerged as the regional capital, but Pushkalavati, with its large shrine, remained an important centre of Buddhist pilgrimage. The Hindu epic, the *Ramayana*, describes how it was founded by *Bharata*, Rama's brother, as a twin city of Taxila (both were named after Bharata's sons). Throughout its history, Charsadda has been subject to continually changing river courses, giving rise to the various different sites and finally forcing the move to Peshawar.

Sights Despite its historical importance, there is not much for the visitor to see, with the important sites being marked only by mounds which give little idea of the ancient settlements they conceal. One kilometre west of the modern village of Charsadda, where the road turns sharply right (coming from Peshawar) before crossing a river, a track leads north to the two largest mounds, known as **Bala Hisar**, probably because they were used as a fort in the 18th-19th centuries. The mounds were excavated by Sir John Marshall in 1902 and by Sir Mortimer Wheeler in 1958. All the important finds were removed to Peshawar and Lahore museums, but there are countless pottery shards still scattered all over the site. Across the river to the northeast of Bala Hisar are the mounds of the later city of **Shaikhan Dheri**, excavated by Peshawar University in 1963 and revealing a city founded by the Bactrian Greeks in the second century AD. The contemporary village of **Rajur** (from *'Rajaghar'* or royal palace) is built on some low mounds which almost certainly contain the remains of an extensive city. Little has been excavated, although Indo-Greek, Scythian and Kushana coins have been found. The whole area is surrounded by an ancient graveyard, protecting much of the ground from excavation. Where unprotected, many of the mounds have been dug away by local villagers for use as topsoil and fertilizer. Just north of Rajur are the mounds of **Shah-e-Napursan** (literally 'neglected city') and **Mir Ziarat**, perhaps the site of the legendary stupa built by Asoka and said to contain the remains of the Buddha. **Prang**, to the south of the main crossroads in Charsadda, has more mounds and probably once lay at the confluence of the Kabul and Swat rivers. The name is a corruption of *prayag* or *prayang*, the sacred town at the confluence of the Jumna and Ganges rivers near Allahabad in India, suggesting that Charsadda once held a similar religious significance.

Transport Local buses run here from the bus station to the north of Shahi Bagh in Peshawar. Note that public transport between Peshawar's main bus station and Mardan or Mingora/Saidu Sharif does not go this way, taking the longer but faster route via Nowshera instead.

Routes From Charsadda there is a pleasant short cut that leads directly to Takht-e-Bhai (see below); coming from Peshawar, turn left at the crossroads in the centre of the village and take the first right. This quiet road runs through fertile countryside for 22 kilometres and joins the main Mardan to Takht-e-Bhai road about 1 kilometre south of the town. The main road runs east from Charsadda directly to Mardan.

Mardan

Phone code: 0931
Colour map 5, grid B1

The present town of Mardan has been an important military base for the last 200 years. It was the home of the elite British Guide Corps, formed in 1846 "to guide regular troops in the field, collect intelligence and keep the peace on the North West Frontier". Today the large Cantonment area is home to their successors, the Punjab Regiment.

The Cantonment lies to the south of the main Swabi road and is marked by small bastion gates to the spaciously laid out grounds with their wide boulevards. Inside is the old Catholic church and cemetery, although access is restricted. South of this is the Mall and Saddar area, Bank Road etc. On the east side of the river is the old town of Mardan, known as **Hoti Mardan**, *Hoti* being a prominent family name going back many generations. The remains of an old Hindu temple and a Sikh Gurudwara can be seen here, though both are now private homes.

Standing at a large intersection in the Saddar area is a **Memorial Arch**, built in Gothic-Mughal style. According to the inscription, it is dedicated to the "memory of Sir Louis Cavagnari KCSI, officers and men of the Guides who fell in the defence of the residency at Kabul on 3 September 1879."

Sleeping & eating

Accommodation in Mardan is very limited and basic. **G** *Al-Idrees*, Bank Rd, T63339. Passable rooms with fan and attached bath. Probably the best choice. Restaurant. **G** *Sway Mian Sahib*, Bank Rd, T62211. Really basic rooms with charpoy beds and fan, share toilet. Nice courtyard though, and fairly quiet. Restaurant. **G** *Zaman*. Basic rooms with fan and attached bath. Restaurant. There are also several noisy hotels around the bus station, though none deserve a mention. All the above serve reasonable food, or there are lots of basic restaurants around the bus station. There is a more upmarket a/c restaurant on the Mall, the ***Al Hussain***, T62163, serving Pakistani dishes.

Shopping

Oriental Art Gallery & Old Coin Shop, College Chowk, T62102. Owned by Fazli Mabook Zahid, this shop has an unique collection of antique artefacts and coins from Afghanistan and Pakistan, some of which would be more appropriately housed in a museum.

Transport

Local transport around the town is still mostly by horse-drawn tonga, making the centre slightly less frenetic than comparably sized places. Auto-rickshaws are however becoming more common. The **general bus stand** and **Flying Coach stand** are more or less next door to each other on Charsadda Rd, to the west of Saddar. Rickety old buses run from the general bus stand to local destinations in the Peshawar Valley

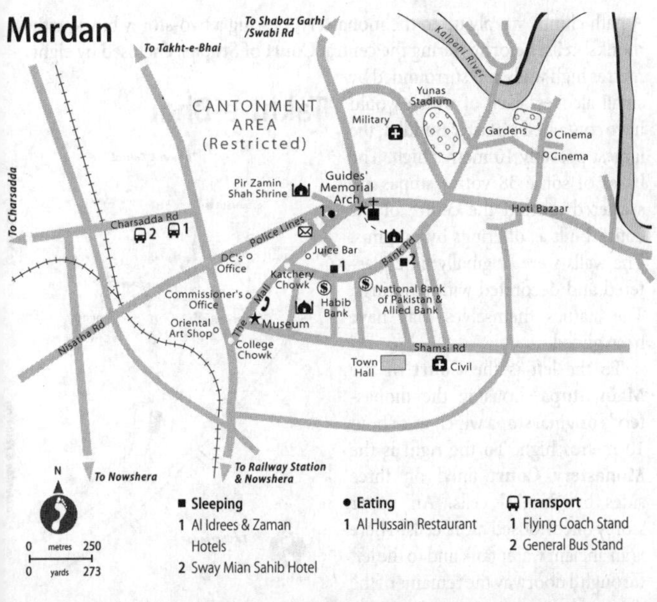

(**Charsadda**, **Takht-e-Bhai**, **Shahbaz Ghari**, **Nowshera**, etc), and also further afield. Faster Hiace minibuses run from the Flying Coach stand to **Peshawar**, **Islamabad**, **Pir Baba**, **Mingora/Saidu Sharif** and **director**

Routes A fast dual carriageway leads south from Mardan to Nowshera (22 kilometres) on the GT Road (see Islamabad to Peshawar, page 225). A main road runs east towards Swabi and Tarbela. Another leads northwest to Takht-e-Bhai and onto the Malakand Pass and Swat Valley.

Takht-e-Bhai

Colour map 5, grid B1

The small town of Takht-e-Bhai is famous for its nearby Gandharan Buddhist monastery. The monastery is perched strikingly on the side of a bare ridge of rock rising abruptly up from the surrounding plains, and is certainly the best preserved and most impressive piece of Gandharan architecture in Pakistan. The sophistication and quality of the building work is clear from the beautifully fashioned walls and well preserved brickwork.

Ins and outs Takht-e-Bhai is 14 kilometres northwest of Mardan on the road to Swat. There is also a direct road from Charsadda (see above). The monastery is 3 kilometres to the east of the main bazaar; the turning is in the centre of town and is well signposted. Tongas are readily available for hire. During summer, an early start is recommended as there is little in the way of shade against the sun. Unfortunately there is no accommodation in the town, short of a charpoy at one of the restaurants, although some travellers report that the caretaker at the monastery is happy to let people camp out there.

North West Frontier Province

History Takht-e-Bhai (literally 'spring on a flat terrace') was probably the largest of more than 1,400 monasteries which thrived in lower Swat and the plains of Peshawar during the Gandharan Buddhist period. The earliest settlement was founded around 40 AD, the main peak of activity was during the Kushana period of the first to fourth centuries AD, and the last stage dates from the fifth and sixth centuries.

Sights A path climbs steeply up to the monastery, passing a two-storey block with monks' cells, before entering the central **Court of Stupas**, enclosed by eight metres high walls and surrounded by small alcoves, each of which would have contained a plaster Buddha, the largest possibly 10 metres high. The bases of some 38 votive stupas are scattered around the centre of the court, built as offerings by pilgrims. The walls were originally lime plastered and decorated with paintings. The statues themselves may have been gilded.

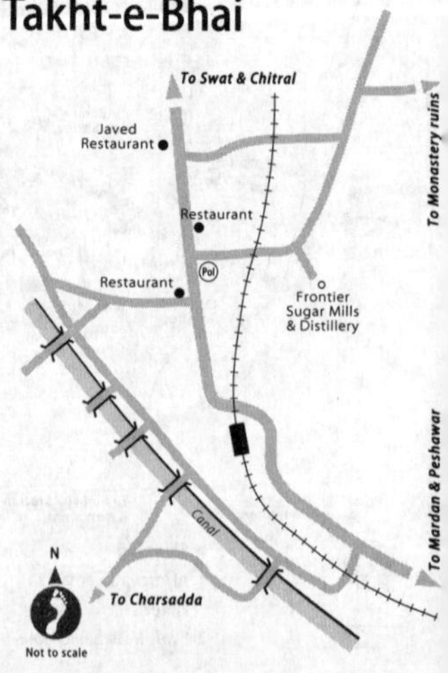

To the left is the **Court of the Main Stupa**, housing the monastery's original stupa which was about 10 metres high. To the right is the **Monastery Court** lined on three sides by monks' cells. An upper storey once housed more cells. There is an ancient water tank and to the left through a doorway the remains of the kitchen and refectory area. Straight ahead is the **Open Court**, beneath which are 10 vaulted chambers probably used either for meditation or as granaries. To the right of the open court, enclosed by high walls, is the **Assembly Court** where the monks would meet. The water tanks here were built during excavation work this century. To the left is a covered area with a sign saying 'museum', enclosing the remains of two small intricately worked stupas and displaying pieces of sculptures and fragments from the site.

On the way up to the monastery, a new path leads off to the left and climbs to some more buildings, less intact but with an excellent view over to the main monastery. The early morning light is perfect for photography from here. The remains of other buildings are scattered across the hillside.

Jamal Garhi

The ruins of another Buddhist monastery near the village of Jamal Garhi are less complete than those at Takht-e-Bhai but still impressive and well worth a visit. The views from the hilltop over the surrounding plains, including across to Takht-e-Bhai, are particularly stunning at dawn when the air is clear, and in the evening light. The site can be easily visited as a day trip from Mardan.

Ins and outs

The turning north to Jamal Garhi is 1 kilometre east of Mardan, across the river on the road to Shahbaz Garhi and Swabi. After 14 kilometres there is a right turn signposted "Jamal Garhi archaeological remains" leading to the village of Jamal Garhi, from where you can climb up to the ruins. Buses from Mardan run fairly frequently on the route past Jamal Garhi up towards Katlang and Babuzai. It is 3 kilometres from the turning to the village (tongas run a shuttle service for a few rupees) and then a gentle half-hour walk in a long zig-zag on a good path up to the monastery.

The site

The path leads in past a long wall, striking for its near perfect brickwork, and into the monastery. On the highest point is a well preserved circular courtyard surrounding the base of a large stupa. You can look down from here onto the main buildings and courtyards filled with stupa bases. Outside the main complex are some small monks' cells built into the side of the hill, some of which are still intact. Illegal digging in various parts of the site is spurred by local legends of gold buried in the ruins.

Routes

The road leading west from the staggered junction on the main road at Jamal Garhi comes out at Shergur, on the Mardan-Malakand road. The road leading north takes you past the village of Katlang, followed by a turning east to Shamozai and later another to Babuzai, before reaching Mian Khan, at the foot of the hills separating Mardan from Buner. From Babuzai there is a pilgrim path that climbs a narrow valley to **Kashmir Smats**, the site of a ruined monastery (of which little remains) and complex of caves still considered holy by Hindus and Buddhists. This is a long day's outing and a guide is advisable as the route is not always clear.

The main road leading east from Mardan passes through Shahbaz Garhi, Swabi and Topi before eventually crossing over the Tarbela Dam and entering Punjab. En route there are a number of interesting sites. Some are close to the road and can be reached by public transport, while others involve a short diversion off it, for which you really need your own transport.

Shahbaz Garhi

The small village of Shahbaz Garhi, 13 kilometres east of Mardan, is surrounded by three important sites and is thought to be the location of the ancient city of **Varusha**. The city lay at the intersection of two major trade routes, from China by way of the Indus and Swat valleys, and from Afghanistan by way of Bajaur and Swat, crossing the Indus at Hund.

Just south of the village, on the edge of a hill visible from the road, are **Asoka's Rock Edicts**, two large boulders inscribed with 14 edicts in the *Kharoshthi* script of Gandhara. There are steps leading up to the rocks and a shelter over them. Having inherited a full-blown empire, Asoka extended it further by conquering Kalinga (modern day Orissa in India), before repenting at the destruction and suffering caused by his military campaigns and preaching the virtues of Buddhist pacifism. He left a series of inscriptions on pillars and rocks across the subcontinent (there are more in Pakistan at Mansehra, see page 434) in which he urged people to follow the code of *Dharma*, encouraging a social order based on tolerance, non-violence and respect for authority.

On a hill to the north of the village, reached from the road leading up to Rustam and the Ambela Pass, are the ruins of **Mekha Sanda** stupa and monastery. Local legend tells how Prince Visvantura, an incarnation of the Buddha, inherited a holy white elephant which brought rains whenever needed. The prince, in a demonstration of generosity designed to inspire his subjects, gave it to a neighbouring kingdom which was hostile but suffering from a drought. His people, however, disowned him and he was banished to Mekha Sanda with his wife and children. He was only accepted back years later after giving away his children to be sold in the market; the ultimate act of self denial. The two rocks on the hill supposedly resemble a pair of water buffalo, giving the site its name. Nearby are the caves where Prince Visvantura and his family took refuge.

A little further along the road to Rustam, down a track leading off to the left, is the site of **Chanaka Dehri** stupa and monastery commemorating the legendary white elephant. There is little to see there today. Back on the main road to Swabi, past the rock edicts, is the site of **But Sahri** convent and stupa, dedicated to the gift of the two children. The mound is covered by later Muslim graves and is unexcavated.

Asota megaliths

At Shewada (literally 'Shewa junction'), 40 kilometres east of Mardan, there is a crossroads. The turning north leads to the village of Shewa. To the right of the road, before the village, there is a small circle of stone megaliths. The standing stones are thought to have once formed a circle with 30 gates, perhaps representing days of the month. Their origins are far from clear. A local legend relates how a party of women on their way to attend a wedding were waylaid by robbers. One of the women prayed out loud, begging that they be saved from being raped by the robbers. According to the legend, her prayers were answered, after a fashion, when the women were all turned to stone. One theory suggests that the site is perhaps a Zoroastrian temple dating from the sixth century BC.

Aziz Derhi

Excavations in 1993-4 of a low mound near the village of **Gangu Dher** revealed extensive remains of a Buddhist Monastery. The site covers four periods; Scytho-Parthian, Kushan, Sassanian and Hindu Shahi. Some distinctive sculptures (not yet displayed) recovered from the site will be useful in determining its exact chronology. The carved stairs and elaborate reliefs found here are comparable only to those found at the Saidu Stupa in Swat. The low mound overlooks a flat expanse of fertile land ringed to the north by mountains.

The site can be reached either from the village of Gohati on the Mardan-Swabi road, or via Asota to the west. From Gohati, follow the east bank of the Upper Swat Canal north (the turning is signposted to Aziz Derhi) for 14 kilometres and then turn right (also signposted). Bear right at a fork and the mound is signposted to the left after two to three kilometres. Coming from Asota you can continue north, bearing right at a fork and crossing a bridge before passing through the village of Shewa. Further on, after crossing a canal, turn right to follow it south until you reach the turning to Aziz Dehri.

Rani Ghat

After one kilometre on the track north from Gohati to Aziz Derhi, there is a turning east which after around seven kilometres arrives at the village of Nogram. Excavations nearby have revealed the archaeological site of Rani Ghat (literally 'queen's rock'), a monastery dating from the Kushan period, complete with stupas and a beautiful gate built of stone blocks.

Routes

The main road continues east from the junction at Gohati to the town of **Swabi**. From here, one road goes to **Topi** and then crosses the base of **Tarbela Dam** (see page 224). Local buses from Mardan generally go as far as Topi, from where there are buses to Tarbela, on the other side of the dam. From Tarbela there are buses to Haripur via Lawrencepur and Hasan Abdal, and direct to Islamabad.

The other road from Swabi heads south to the village of **Amber**. Arriving in the village, you come to a T-junction. Turning left, you rejoin the Tarbela road just before Topi. The turning right heads southwest towards Jehangira on the GT Rd. Just southwest of the T-junction is a turning to the village of Hund on the banks of the Indus.

Hund

Although today only a small village reached by a dirt track, Hund was once an important crossing point on the Indus. Its Sanskrit name was *Wada Bahanda Pura* meaning 'city of the water pots', in reference to the large up-turned ceramic pots that were used to cross the river. It was also known as *Vada Bahind Pur* meaning 'city by the river', and as *Wahind*; 'the way to India'. It became the winter capital of the Hindu Shahi rulers of Gandhara after they defeated the Turki Shahis in Kabul in the ninth century AD. Alexander the Great, the Scythians and Kushans, various Chinese pilgrims, Mahmud of Ghazni, Timurlane, Babur and many others crossed the Indus here on their journeys. The walls, bastions and gates of the 16th century **Akbar's Fort** still survive, surrounding the village. There are also traces of the cobbled road leading down to the river, marking the crossing point. The traces of diaper masonry in the cliff by the river's edge are probably the remains of the earlier Hindu Shahi fort.

The Muslim traveller *Muqaddasi* described the city in the 10th century AD as "a capital city of great glory. Situated on a square open plain, it has many gardens, clean and attractive. The fruits of both summer and winter seasons are plentifully available. Around the city are gardens full of walnuts, almonds, banana and date. Prices are low; three mounds of honey can be bought for one dirham, bread and milk are very cheap. The houses are built of timber covered with dry grass ... it could match with the best cities of Iran."

The road to Swat via the Ambela Pass

An alternative to the main road to Swat over the Malakand Pass is the road via the Ambela and Buner passes. Passing through Buner District, this route then crosses the Karakar Pass to rejoin the main Swat Valley road at Barikot. There is also the option of a detour to the popular shrine of Pir Baba.

From Shahbaz Garhi a quiet, tree-lined road leads northeast through green, fertile countryside to the village of Rustam where there are basic restaurants and tea stalls. Arriving in the village, you come to what is in effect a T-junction. Turning left leads to Pirsai, from where there is a steep pilgrim track up to Kashmir Smats, while turning right takes you up to the Ambela Pass. There are excellent views down onto the plains of Peshawar on the climb up to the pass.

Ambela Pass This pass was the scene of the famous Ambela Campaign in 1863 in which the British set out to punish a tribe of 'Hindustani fanatics' from the village of Malka in the hills east of Buner who had been carrying out raids into British controlled territory. They attempted to march across the Ambela Pass without permission of the Pathan tribes of Buner. This provoked a *jihad* against the British which rapidly gained momentum, leading to a confrontation on the pass. The campaign grew into a major military operation involving around 10,000 men on either side and lasting for two months. Eventually the British won a partial victory and were allowed to carry out token retribution on the people of Malka in return for a truce with the Pathan tribes which guaranteed them their independence.

On top of the pass, the road passes through a landscape of boulder-strewn hills scattered with low scrub and patches of cultivation, before descending into a small, well wooded basin. The main road takes a left fork to skirt round the village of Amber, then climbs to the much lower Buner Pass, before descending into a larger basin. After crossing a river, the road passes through the village of Chinar. Soon after is the larger town of Swari. Turn left at the T-junction in the town and follow the road to Daggar. Shortly after the village, by a small hillock with an old colonial building and a newer fort nearby, there is a fork. The left fork is the direct route to Barikot, passing through the town of Jowar before crossing the Karakar Pass. The right fork leads eventually to Pir Baba, passing first through the small village of Pacha.

Pir Baba (Syed Ali)

Situated in beautiful countryside with Mount Ilam (2,811 metres) to the east dominating the surrounding mountains, the shrine of Pir Baba is very popular, attracting huge numbers of pilgrims, particularly during the *Urs* which is held each year at the beginning of September. Pir Baba, whose real name was Syed Ali Shah (*Pir Baba* is a title of veneration, literally meaning 'great holy man') was reputedly the grandson of the Mughal Emperor Babur, though other sources suggest that his father came from Afghanistan in the service of Babur.

Ins and outs There are several very basic hotels in the village with little to choose between them. Most of them have equally simple restaurants attached. Buses and Hiace minibuses run from here back to Mardan, or on to Barikot and Mingora, departing when full.

To reach the shrine, cross the river in the village and walk up to the large mosque. A path lined with beggars and stalls selling jewellery and perfumes leads directly up to the shrine from inside the mosque. From Pir Baba it is a half hour walk to **Chilla**, the cave on a hillside above the village of Narbatwal where Pir Baba lived his life of meditation. The cave is attended by chowkidars who will show you around inside. They will expect a small offering of money.

Routes The drive to Barikot from Pir Baba is very scenic. Turn right just south of Pacha and follow the road to Jowar, a small town with a bazaar and restaurants etc. Turn right at the T-junction in the town and follow the road up to the Karakar Pass. The road climbs up through well wooded hills, with views of Mount Ilam to the right, and then descends to Barikot, on the main road up the Swat Valley.

Swat Valley

The Swat Valley is one of the most fertile and easily accessible mountainous areas in northern Pakistan. The main attraction is its scenic beauty – lush green valleys with thick pine forests, surrounded by snowy peaks – and pleasant climate in summer. In addition, the area is rich in historical sites dating back to the Gandharan Buddhist period and earlier. Swat is one of the most popular hill destinations for Pakistani tourists, after Murree and the Galis. The down-side of this is that some of the hill resorts have been heavily developed, with new hotels springing up rapidly in a haphazard fashion. The main resorts can also get extremely crowded during the peak summer season. However, there are still plenty of beautiful spots, quiet and unspoilt, just that little bit away from the main tourist centres.

Ins and outs

The Swat Valley is easily reached by road from both Peshawar and Islamabad. In either case, it is necessary to pass first through the Peshawar Valley (see above). From Peshawar, one can either travel east on the GT Rd as far as Nowshera, then head north through Mardan and Takht-e-Bhai and across the Malakand Pass to Swat, or else head northeast through Charsadda and join the road north at Mardan or Takht-e-Bhai. From Islamabad, one can follow the GT Rd west to Nowshera and then head north, or else branch off north at a number of points earlier to join the road running west through Tarbela and Swabi to Mardan. An alternative route into Swat from Mardan is across the Ambela, Buner and Karakar passes. There are also direct flights from Peshawar and Islamabad to the twin towns of Mingora/Saidu Sharif.

Geography

Rising in the **Shandur Range**, the three principle sources of the Swat River – the Gabral, Bahandra and Ushu – unite at Kalam (2,013 metres) into a single hill torrent which then drops 18 metres per kilometre in a narrow gorge for 39 kilometres before reaching **Madyan** (1,312 metres). Here the river broadens out, liberally fed by both monsoon seasonal rainfall and summer snowmelt. Below Mingora the river becomes a huge braided stream up to five kilometres wide and rich in silt deposits. The broad riverine flats are the richest and most populous areas in Swat. The river is controlled by a complex system of canals and river cuttings, combined with terracing. Known throughout the NWFP as the 'Maize Granary', Swat also grows rice, wheat and barley as well as fruits. More recently honey collecting has become popular. Local industries include woollen Swati caps and shawls, blankets, silverware and tribal jewellery. Forestry is also an important source of income with timber being floated down the river to the railhead at Dargai.

However, forest reserves are dwindling rapidly. As well as the activities of logging contractors, there is added pressure from nomadic groups and from a population which has shot up from about 93,000 in 1884 to well over two million in 1998. The joint Pak-Swiss Kalam Integrated Development Project (KIDP) enjoys a high profile and has been remarkably successful in involving local communities in initiatives aimed at ensuring a sustainable pattern of development in the valley.

People

The people of Swat Valley are mostly **Yusufzai Pathans**, displaced from the Peshawar Valley by the related *Mandnar Yusufzais* late in the 16th century. The Yusufzais in turn forced the Dardic speaking *Dilazaks* further up the Swat Valley into the remoter parts of Kohistan and North Hazara. Today, Upper Swat, or Swat Kohistan, is inhabited by two language groups, the *Torwal* and *Gawri*, both Dardic, the former found between Madyan and Kalam, the latter above Kalam up to the Shandur range. In addition there are two nomadic groups, the *Gujars* who mainly herd cattle and the *Ajars* who rear sheep and goats. The Ajars practise extreme forms of *trans humance*, involving annual movements of whole village communities from 600 metres up to 4,500

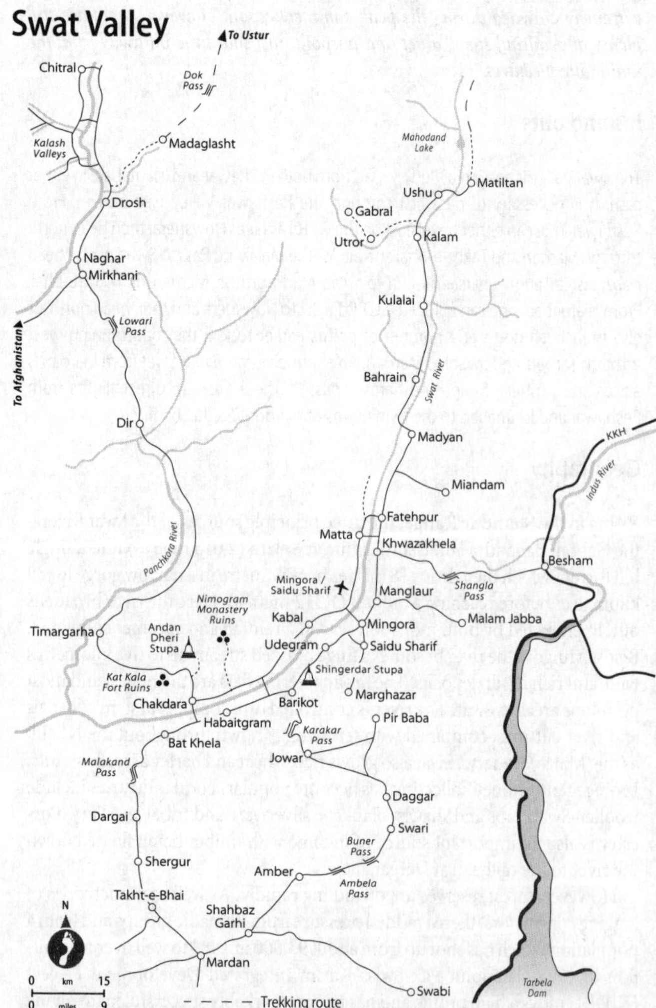

North West Frontier Province

metres, accomplished in four to five moves between appropriate seasonal altitude belts.

Despite its popularity as a tourist destination, the people of Swat Valley are markedly tribal and distinctly conservative in their outlook. Tourism is tolerated in the valley, and for many is the main source of income, but it sits slightly uneasily alongside the traditional Islamic tribal structure of the society. Away from the larger towns, women may feel slightly uneasy if travelling unaccompanied; they should avoid walking alone in the hills altogether.

History

The Swat Valley's favourable environment for settlement has been compared with that of the **Zagros Mountains** in present-day Iran, the traditional '*Cradle of Civilisation*'. The earliest evidence of settlement goes back at least 10,000 years to the early '*Grave Cultures*', so called because the primary evidence of settlement comes from graves. The first written reference to the valley comes from the Vedic literature of the Aryans who called it '*Suvastu*'.

Later, in 327 BC Alexander the Great passed through the valley when he came through Afghanistan, by way of Bajour and Dir. He captured the ancient fort of **Bazira** in present-day **Barikot**, and **Ora (Udegram)** before he went on to the plain of Peshawar.

At the height of the Buddhist Gandharan civilization in the first century AD there were at least 1,400 monasteries in Lower Swat alone. The *Tantric* and the *Mahayana* schools of Buddhism were developed here, spreading throughout the subcontinent. The valley is still rich in Buddhist monastery ruins, stupas, sculptures and rock carvings.

From about the seventh century AD the Swat Valley became the refuge for a much reduced Buddhist culture. Hinduism grew and the *Hindu Shahi* rulers extended their control into the valley during the eighth and ninth centuries AD until they were supplanted by the Muslim, *Mahmud of Ghazni*. Later, under the Mughals, both *Babur* and *Akbar* fought to control the Yusufzai Pathans of Swat, the former marrying into the tribe in 1519.

During the British period, Swat was the scene for the famous Malakand Campaign of 1897 against the *Sayyid Hajji Shoaib Baba* who preached *jihad* against the British and was dubbed the '*Mad Mullah*', *an event covered by the young Winston Churchill for the Daily Telegraph.*

Swat Valley was consolidated into an independent state in 1926 by the **Wali** or ruler, *Miangal Gulshehzada Abdul Wadood,* the grandson of the *Akhund* of Swat, a famous Sufi ascetic and religious leader (Akhund meaning teacher). His son *Miangal Jahanzib* took over in 1940 until 1969 when Swat was integrated into NWFP. They were competent leaders who achieved internal political integration and promoted the building of roads, hospitals and a free school system.

Best time to visit

The peak tourist season is generally from mid-June to mid-August, when the climate higher up the valley is at its best, although lower down it remains very hot. This is also when the valley receives most of its rainfall. If you want to avoid the crowds, spring (April/May) and early autumn (September) are the best times to visit, although you should be prepared for chilly nights higher up. The road above Bahrain is sometimes still blocked in May.

Routes

Heading north from Mardan, through Takht-e-Bhai, the road into Swat passes through fertile countryside. Factories for processing tobacco, one of the major cash crops in the region, line the route. Soon after the small town of **Shergur** there is a check post marking the border between

Mardan and Malakand Districts. **Dargai**, the next major town, is the railhead for the narrow-gauge line from Nowshera. The railway opened up the area for logging, which is still a major industry.

From here the road climbs steadily up to the **Malakand Pass**. On the way up there are good views south onto the Peshawar Valley. The Upper Swat Canal, which carries water from the Swat River on the other side of the pass by way of a tunnel, can be seen snaking its way down towards the plains in a series of rapids. The pass itself is topped by a fort, built by the British following the Malakand Campaign in 1897. A small village has grown up around it, and there are simple restaurants serving tea, cold drinks and food.

The road descends gently from the pass, arriving at the town of **Bat Khela**, which is spread out over a large area. There is a bus stand here and a few very basic hotels. The ruins of a Hindu Shahi fort are visible up on a ridge to the east. The countryside around is green and fertile, and the road lined with trees. Further on there is a bridge across the Swat River to **Chakdara**, marking the border with Dir District, and the start of the route to Dir and Chitral (see page 394). Thana, the next village, with its small bazaar, also spreads up the hillside overlooking the road. Further on is **Habaitgram**, with the ruins of a huge and impressive Hindu Shahi fort above. Below the ruins is the well preserved Buddhist **Top Dara Stupa** and nearby, the ruins of a monastery. The road climbs over a shoulder of the hills and passes **Landakai check post** which marks the start of Swat proper.

Nimogram

Seven kilometres beyond Landakai, a turning left leads across the river, giving access to **Nimogram Monastery and Stupas** (pronounced 'Neemogram'). Cross to the north side of the river and turn left at the T-junction. At the village of **Dedawar** (two kilometres), there are the remains of a stupa above the road. After seven kilometres the road fords the wide stream of the Nimogram Valley, and immediately after is the turning north to Nimogram, in the village of **Zarakhela Shamozai**. The first four kilometres are metalled, then the road turns to a dirt track and follows the stream bed (for short periods after heavy rains this route becomes impassable). Do not cross over to the right bank. The village of Nimogram is eight kilometres up the valley. It is a short steep climb up to the ruins, which are amongst the best preserved in Swat. There are commanding views back down the valley.

Ins and outs Although it is not easily accessible, Nimogram is well worth a visit; if you do not have your own transport, the most practical way of getting there is as an excursion from Mingora, where a car can easily be hired. Alternatively, the valley can be reached from Chakdara, to the west. Public transport up the valley is minimal and erratic. Allow a half-day for the round trip from Mingora/Saidu Sharif.

Lower Swat Valley

From the bridge turning to Nimogram, the main road continues past **Birkot Hill**. Ongoing excavations by an Italian archaeological team have uncovered part of what is thought to be the ancient town of **Bazira**, conquered by Alexander the Great in 327 BC. The excavations have revealed evidence of continuous occupation for 1,000 years between the 5th century BC and 5th century AD.

The small town of **Barikot** is 1 kilometre past the excavations. A road leads southeast from here, across the Karakar, Buner and Ambela passes, and back down onto the plains of Mardan (see page 366).

3 kilometres further along the main road, the ruins of the huge **Shingerdar Stupa** are clearly visible to the right. Local legend attributes the building of this stupa to a king named Uttarasena, who is said to have housed relics of the Buddha inside.

Footprint Handbooks

Travel guides for free spirits

Affix
Stamp
Here

Footprint Handbooks
6 Riverside Court
Lower Bristol Road
Bath
BA2 3DZ
England

BCS99

At **Ghalagai**, 2 kilometres further on, there is a large Buddha carved into the cliff-face beside the road; once in perfect condition, the head has now been completely defaced. Next to it, a set of concrete steps lead to a small cave with more Buddhist carvings, now hardly discernible.

After 7 kilometres, just before the village of Udegram, there is a large rock face known as **Gogdara Rock**, to the right of the road, covered in ancient petroglyphs dating back 3,000 years, depicting stick men riding in chariots and numerous animals. There are also Buddhist carvings dating from around the sixth century AD. More recently, locals have added their names to the rock. (Is it art or is it graffiti?)

Udegram

Colour map 5, grid B2

Udegram is a site of major historical importance. There is a signposted turning right in the village leading to excavations, which have been identified as the bazaar area of the ancient city of **Ora**, site of one of Alexander the Great's battles as he passed through the valley in 327 BC. Nothing is labelled however and the excavations themselves are not particularly impressive. A path to the right leads up through a large graveyard to the shrine of **Pir Khushab**, one of Mahmoud of Ghazni's generals who died in the siege of **Raja Gira's Fortress** on the hilltop above. The climb up to the fortress is worthwhile. Half way up are the well preserved remains of a mosque. Higher up, a flight of steps lead up to the main citadel of the fortress. The huge crumbling walls stretch out along the ridge, enclosing numerous ruined buildings. Most of the visible remains date from the Hindu Shahi period, although the site was first occupied as early as 1000 BC. There are excellent views from here in all directions.

According to a local legend, Mahmoud of Ghazni managed to capture the fort by depriving some of his horses of water for several days. When they were released, they quickly found the source of the fortress's water supply, where Mahmoud then concentrated his attack, eventually cutting off the supply to the fortress.

Mingora/Saidu Sharif

Phone code: 0936
Colour map 5, grid B2

The twin-towns of Mingora/Saidu Sharif have now all but merged into each other. Mingora is the old bazaar town, with most of the cheaper hotels, and all the main markets, while Saidu Sharif, to the south across the river, is the administrative centre. Together they form the largest urban centre in Swat, and Mingora in particular has become heavily congested.

Ins and outs

Getting there

Mingora/Saidu Sharif represents the major transport hub of the Swat Valley. There are regular bus and minibus connections with most towns and cities in the region. Swat's only airport is also situated nearby, providing connections with Peshawar and Islamabad.

Getting around

Suzukis and auto-rickshaws are the primary means of getting between Mingora and Saidu Sharif. Frequent Datsun pickups run to and from Marghazar (see below). Taxis are also readily available.

Sights

Swat Museum Refurbished in 1994 with the help of a 'cultural grant' from Japan, this museum is excellently laid out and well worth a visit. The impressive collection of Gandharan Buddhist statues, freizes, etc demonstrate clearly the remarkable range of styles, from Oriental through to Graeco-Roman, which evolved during this period. There are also various terracotta and stucco pieces, knives, arrowheads, pieces of grave pottery, etc dating back as far as the fourth century BC. The ethnographic section has some particularly fine examples of traditional silver jewellery and embroidery work. ■ *Open seven days, summer 0830-1230, 1430-1730, winter 0900-1300, 1400-1600. Rs 4.*

Shrine of the Akhund of Swat The small colourful shrine to the Akhund of Swat (also known as Saidu Baba) is housed in the marble courtyard of a mosque in Saidu Sharif. It is tucked away amongst the narrow alleys between Marghazar Road and Aqba Road.

Saidu Stupa and Monastery This site consists of a lower terrace with the remains of the main stupa, and a higher terrace with the monastery remains. Excavations were carried out between 1963 and 1972 by an Italian archaeological team. This site is the most easily accessible of the various Gandharan Buddhist remains to be found here, being within walking distance of the main road through Saidu Sharif.

Butkara 1 Identified as the monastery of T'a-lo, mentioned by the Chinese pilgrim Sung Yun in 520 AD, this site (also known as Gulkada, or simply Butkara) is the most important of those around Saidu Sharif, and has yielded a vast array of artefacts. The Italian archaeologist G Tucci identifies the site as part of the ancient city of Uddiyana. The main stupa, thought to have been started by Asoka in the third century BC (at the same time as Dharmarajika in Taxila), perhaps to house some of the ashes of the Buddha, was over the next 12 centuries completely encased by a new, larger stupa no less than five times. Surrounding it are the remains of numerous smaller stupa bases, viharas and columns, as well as various stone sculptures, including a pair of distinctive lion statues. During its long period of occupation, the site was subject to repeated flooding and earthquakes, and the different building techniques and styles of each era are clearly identifiable. The successive building phases are reflected also in the haphazard, cluttered layout of the structures surrounding the main stupa. The turning east off Saidu Sharif Road leading to the site is signposted "Butkara Remains". The site itself is to the north of this road,

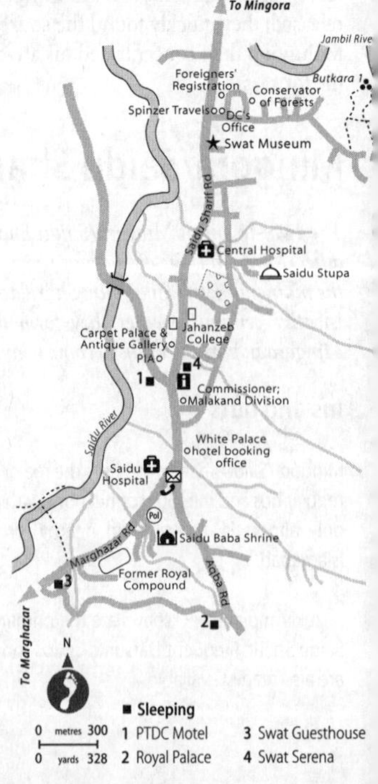

North West Frontier Province

reached by a narrow, easily missed path leading off to the left, just past the turning right up to He'ra School.

Butkara 3

In some ways this site is the most atmospheric, being tucked away in a small, wooded ravine. There is an open stupa court surrounded by small chambers housing stupas, a couple of which are still fully intact. Excavations were carried out between 1982 and 1985 by Dr Abdur Rahman of Peshawar University. The site is thought to have been occupied from second century BC to seventh century AD. To reach the site, continue along the road for about 500 metres past the path leading to Butkara 1. At a culvert, follow the path leading off to the right, up the left side of the stream, crossing to the centre where it divides and passing a small mosque on the right, then bear right across a small patch of flat land. The remains are hidden in a cleft below.

Panr

The ruins at Panr (pronounced 'pahn'), situated on the north side of the Jambil River, consist of a stupa court and monastery. The site is thought to date from the first to seventh centuries AD. This is perhaps the least impressive of the sites, and more difficult to reach than the others. There is a crossing point to the north side of the Jambil River about one kilometre beyond the turning for Butkara 3, or else follow Hajji Baba Road southeast from Mingora. A path leads off to the left from this road, by a small quarry. Follow the path along the course of a small stream for about 500 metres, bearing right where it forks, and soon afterwards climb up the left bank on a small path to the site.

Jambil Valley

The Jambil Valley, running southeast from Mingora, is rich in archaeological remains. As well as the sites of Butkara 1, Butkara 3 and Panr, mentioned above, there are excavated sites at **Butkara 2**, **Leobanr** and **Matelai**, further up the valley.

Marghazar and Mount Ilam

At the head of the Saidu Valley, 14 kilometres from Saidu Sharif, is Marghazar, the former summer palace of the Wali of Swat. The palace has now been converted into a luxury hotel, the *White Palace* (see under Sleeping, below). It is a pleasant 30 minute drive up through terraced fields and small villages, the acacia-lined road running alongside Saidu stream. There is a picnic area under a large shady tree below the hotel, and in summer several handicraft shops by the entrance. From Marghazar there is a trail up to the summit of Mount Ilam, considered sacred by Muslims, Hindus and Buddhists alike, and until recently attracting considerable numbers of Hindu pilgrims each year. It is a rewarding full-day walk to the top and back. PTDC recommend taking a guide. The *White Palace* hotel has English-speaking guides available.

Essentials

Sleeping

■ *on maps*
Price codes: see inside front cover

Most of the luxury and more expensive hotels are located in Saidu Sharif. Mingora is the main focus for budget and mid-range hotels. There are large numbers of budget hotels along GT Rd and New Rd in particular, of which only a small selection are listed. There are several luxury resort-type hotels to the north of Mingora, along the road leading up the Swat Valley, including the *Rock City* hotel, and a newly opened branch of the *Shangri La* chain. **NB** Hotel categories are for the high season; when it is quiet it is often possible to negotiate very large discounts, particularly in the more expensive and mid-range hotels.

Marghazar B *White Palace*, Marghazar (14 kilometres from Saidu Sharif), T812008, F712320 (or book in Saidu Sharif, T710848). Formerly the summer palace of the Wali of Swat, the main attraction of this hotel is its beautiful, peaceful location and cooler climate in summer. Comfortable rooms with TV, phone and attached bath on 3 levels up the hillside, overlooking pleasant gardens with ponds and running water. Restaurant serving Pakistani, Chinese and Continental food. Recommended if you want to get away from it all, and ideal as a base for visits to Mount Ilam.

Saidu Sharif A *Swat Serena*, T711640, F710402. This was a former residence of the Wali of Swat (later it was given to his brother-in-law, while the main block was added in honour of Queen Elizabeth's visit in 1960). Set in quiet, well maintained gardens, its

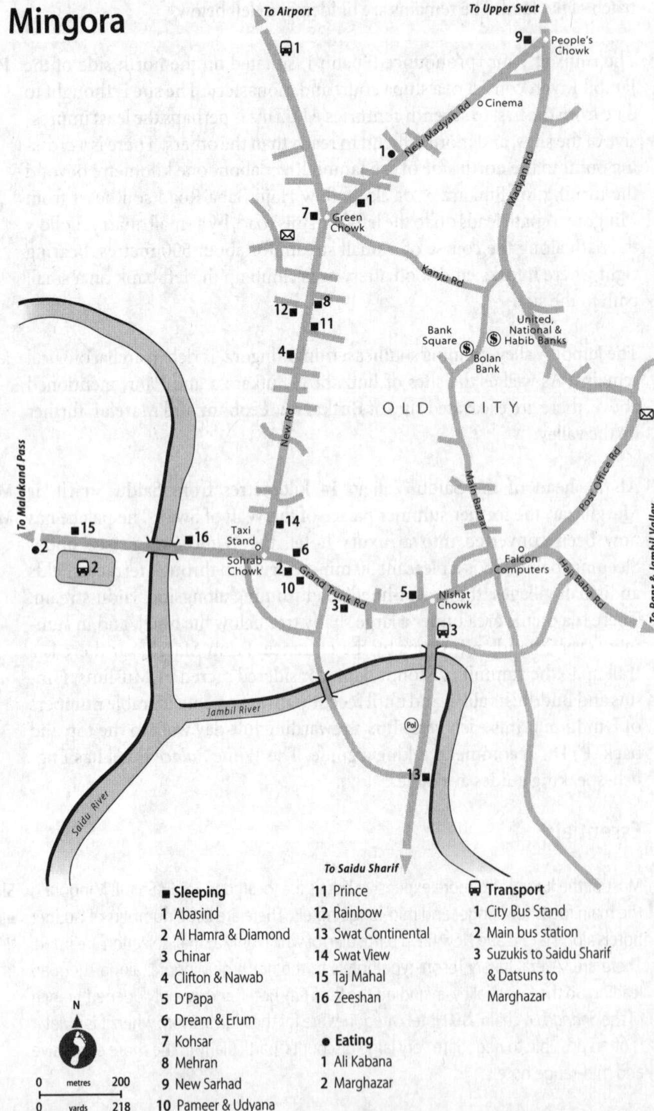

solid, Colonial-style architecture is both impressive and practical, being cool and airy in summer. Rooms are attractively furnished to a very high standard with traditional Swati carved wooden furniture and embroidered fabrics, as well as the usual facilities (a/c, TV/dish, phone, attached bath). *Suvastu* restaurant. Badminton, golf (at Kabbal), children's play area, handicraft shops, car hire, foreign exchange, airport courtesy car. There are often heavily discounted summer deals for couples and families. Well run. Highly recommended.

B *PTDC Motel*, T713774, F713776. Recently opened modern hotel. Rooms with a/c, TV/dish, phone, attached bath. Clean, pleasantly furnished and well run. Tourist information located here. **B *Swat Continental***, T711399, F711199. Rooms with a/c, fan, TV/dish, phone, attached bath. Restaurant. Car hire, foreign exchange, airport courtesy car. Pleasant, well run hotel, comfortable rooms, but unfortunately those at the rear overlook Saidu's open sewer of a river.

C *Royal Palace*, T720239. Another former residence of the Wali. Situated up on a hillside overlooking Saidu Sharif, it makes for a good value and restful retreat, and is noticeably cooler in summer than hotels down in the town. Rooms with a/c, TV/dish and attached bath. Also cheaper non a/c rooms (Rs 600), garden, restaurant. **NB** At the time of going to press, the hotel was due to close for refurbishment: when it re-opens it may well have moved up into the **B** category bracket. **C *Swat Guesthouse***, T720050. A/c and cheaper non a/c rooms, TV/dish, attached bath. Restaurant. Pleasant courtyard and garden, though overall a bit run-down. Closes down out of season.

Mingora **B *Pameer***, GT Rd, T720201, F720206. Rather overly plush rooms with a/c, TV/dish, phone and attached bath. Restaurant. **B *Swat View***, New Rd, T720889. Overpriced rooms with a/c, TV/dish, phone and attached bath. Also cheaper non a/c rooms (double Rs 650). Restaurant. Shopping arcade below.

C *Al-Hamra*, GT Rd, T710966. Rooms with a/c, TV/dish, phone and attached bath. Also cheaper non a/c rooms (double Rs 500). Overpriced but very willing to drop prices.

D *D'Papa*, GT Rd, T/F711618. Reasonable rooms with a/c, TV/dish, phone and attached bath. Best rooms at rear. Also cheaper non a/c rooms (double Rs 350). Restaurant. **D *Zeeshan***, GT Rd, T720325. Rooms with a/c, TV/dish, phone and attached bath. Also cheaper non a/c rooms (double Rs 400/200). Restaurant.

E *Chinar*, GT Rd, T4456. Clean rooms with fan and attached bath. Restaurant. Snooker hall (2 reasonable tables). **E *Diamond***, GT Rd, T710321. Mediocre rooms with fan and attached bath. **E *Dream***, GT Rd, T712250. Reasonable rooms with fan and attached bath. Restaurant. **E *Erum***, GT Rd, T6419. Mediocre rooms with fan and attached bath. Restaurant. **E *Taj Mahal***, GT Rd (opposite bus station), T713521. Clean rooms around central courtyard (set back from the road, so relatively quiet), with fan and attached bath. Also a/c rooms (double Rs 600). **E *Udyana***, GT Rd, T5076. Reasonable rooms with fan and attached bath. Restaurant. **E/F *Abasind***, New Madyan Rd, T710961. Choice of simple or 'deluxe' rooms with fan and attached bath. A/c available for extra Rs 200 per day. Pleasant courtyard. Restaurant. **E/F *Nawab***, New Rd, T720575. Reasonable rooms with fan and attached bath. Also 'deluxe' rooms with carpet and TV/dish. Restaurant.

F *Mehran*, New Rd, T710882. Simple rooms with fan and attached bath. Friendly staff. Restaurant. **F *New Sarhad***, New Madyan Rd, T813347. Simple rooms with fan and attached bath. Restaurant. **F *Prince***, New Rd, T4887. Simple rooms with fan and attached bath. **F *Rainbow***, New Rd, T720573. Fairly clean rooms arranged around central courtyard (set back from road, so reasonably quiet), with fan and attached bath. Restaurant. Friendly. Recommended.

G *Clifton*, New Rd, T720968. Basic rooms with fan and attached bath. Restaurant. **G *Kohsar***, New Rd, T720519. Basic rooms with fan and attached bath.

Eating
● *on maps*

Almost all of the hotels have restaurants. At the top of the range, the *Serena's* ***Suvastu*** is highly recommended. It offers good value buffet lunches and dinners (Rs 250/270 per head respectively, as well as a once weekly outdoor barbecue for Rs 300 per head (provided there are enough guests). The restaurant in the *Swat View* hotel is also good. The cheaper and simpler ***Ali Kabana*** restaurant, on New Madyan Rd, serves good kebabs, *karahi* and *tikka*, and has a pleasant roof-top terrace. Recommended. Mingora is an excellent place to sample grilled kebabs, *tikkas*, *karahi*, and braised liver or *kalaji*, all of which are available from numerous local-style restaurants or road-side stalls, particularly along New Madyan Rd, and also New Rd and GT Rd. There is a lively fruit market around Green Chowk.

Entertainment

Sports The *Serena* hotel has badminton courts, and there is a golf course nearby at Kabbal. PTDC can also arrange pony trekking. Swat has some excellent trout fishing, although the best is higher up the valley.

Shopping

The best buys are the beautiful local hand-embroidered shawls, waistcoats, front pieces etc. There are numerous handicraft shops in Mingora along New Rd and GT Rd selling these goods, as well as intricately carved wooden furniture, traditional silver jewellery and precious/semi-precious stones. The maze of tiny alleys between Main Bazaar and New Rd are worth exploring for handicrafts and jewellery.

Local transport

Car hire (with driver) can be arranged through PTDC. A number of the more expensive hotels also offer car hire. Alternatively you can negotiate your own from the **taxi** stand at Sohrab Chowk. Just to the south of Nishat Chowk there is a stand for **Suzukis** and **Datsun pickups**. Suzukis ply back and forth between here and the southern end of Saidu Sharif (near junction of Marghazar and Aqba roads), while Datsun pickups ply back and forth between here and Marghazar. **Auto-rickshaws** are widely available; away from the main Suzuki and Datsun routes, they represent the most practical means of getting around.

Long-distance transport

Air PIA Booking Office, Saidu Sharif, T711092. Open 7 days, 0830-1300, 1400-1700. Airport T812053. The airport is about 6 kilometres from Mingora, on the opposite bank of the Swat River. A taxi should not cost more than Rs 50-75. Allow around 30 minutes. There are daily flights (except Saturday) to **Islamabad** (at 1545) and **Peshawar** (at 1100) (foreigners pay Rs 1,900 one way for each).

Bus The **main bus station** is on the GT Rd, to the west of Sohrab Chowk. A combination of rickety old buses, Coasters, Bedford vans and Hiace minibuses operate from here to most destinations. Services are more frequent during the summer season; off-season you may have to change to reach more out-of-the-way places. If you are heading north up the Swat Valley to **Madyan** (Rs 13), avoid the Bedford vans as they are hopelessly slow (up to 3 hours); the Hiace minibuses are much quicker (around 1¼ hours). If you cannot find a direct minibus to **Bahrain** (Rs 16, 1½ hours) or **Kalam** (Rs 30, 2½ hours), change in Madyan. Likewise for **Miandam** (Rs 13, 1¼ hours). Direct minibuses to **Besham** (on the KKH, Rs 40, 3 hours) are frequent all-year round, or you can change at **Khwazakhela**. If you are heading to **Chitral**, you are most likely to find a minibus going as far as **Timargarha** only (Rs 22, 1½ hours); change there for Dir, and change again in Dir for Chitral. There are regular Coasters and Hiace minibuses to **Mardan** (Rs 35, 2½ hours) and **Peshawar** (Rs 50, 3½ hours).

During the summer season (June-September), **PTDC** operate daily a/c Coasters from the *PTDC Motel* in Saidu Sharif to Rawalpindi (*Flashman's* hotel), departing at 1600 (Rs 175, 5 hours).

The **city bus station**, to the northwest of Green Chowk, has rickety old buses and Datsun pickups running primarily to local destinations on the west bank of the Swat River (Kabbal, Matta etc).

Directory

Banks *Bolan Bank*, *United Bank Ltd* and *Habib Bank*, all in Bank Square on Main Bazaar (Mingora), are able to change cash and TCs at the official rate. There are also several money changers round here who will change cash for the better 'kerbside' rate, as will most of the tourist shops around Mingora and Saidu Sharif. The *Serena* and *Pameer* hotels do foreign exchange at the official rate, or a little less.

Communications **Post:** there are 2 post offices in Mingora; the main one is hidden away in a small alley off New Rd, while the other is on Post Office Rd. The GPO in Saidu Sharif is on Marghazar Rd, near the junction with Aqba Rd. **Telephone:** The Pak Telecom office is next to the Saidu Sharif GPO, open 0800-2200, Sun 0800-1000, 1500-1700. **Internet:** ***Falcon Computers***, Old Sabzi Mandi, Haji Baba Chowk, Mingora (on GT Rd, to east of junction with Main Bazaar), T713334. Situated on the first floor (look out for *Falcon Computers* sign). Internet access Rs 135 per hour (after 2100). Emails Rs 12 each.

Hospitals & medical services There are 2 hospitals in Saidu Sharif, the ***Central*** and ***Saidu Sharif***. There are chemists in the vicinity of both hospitals and many more in Mingora.

Tour companies and travel agents *Spinzer Travels*, Saidu Sharif, T/F710651. There are also numerous travel agents in Mingora, concentrated around New Rd and GT Rd, most of which are able to make bookings with PIA.

Tourist offices The *PTDC Tourist Information Centre* is in the *PTDC Motel* in Saidu Sharif, T711205. They are helpful and well-informed. They can organize car hire (with driver) and offer a good value guided tour of the main Buddhist sites in lower Swat (half day, Rs 500). PTDC Motels in Malam Jabba, Miandam and Kalam can be booked here. A daily coach service to Rawalpindi departs from here during the summer (see under Transport).

Useful addresses **Police:** the main police station in Saidu Sharif is on Marghazar Rd, south of the junction with Aqba Rd, T711784, or T15. **Senior Superintendent of Police (SSP):** (for Foreigners' Registration) is in Saidu Sharif, in the compound off Jambil Rd, T711965. **Commissioner (Swat) Office:** in same compound as SSP, T710333. **Deputy Commissioner (Swat) Office:** in same compound as SSP, T711864. **Conservator of Forests Office:** in same compound as SSP, T711528.

North from Mingora/Saidu Sharif

Heading north from Mingora, the main road follows the east bank of the Swat River, which flows past rapidly in a wide, shallow, braided course. At **Manglaur** the road crosses a bridge and there is a signposted turning right, up to Malam Jabba, 33 kilometres away at the head of a picturesque side valley. Three kilometres up the valley, on the opposite bank of the river, is the well preserved seventh century **Jahanabad Buddha**, carved on the face of a huge boulder. The carving, directly opposite the village of Malakpur, is visible from the road, although you really need to climb up to it to get a good view and a sense of its scale (it is four metres tall). A small footbridge crosses the river below the village, or there is a larger bridge, suitable for cars, a little further on at the village of Jahanabad. The road continues up the valley, climbing steeply through small villages with places to stop along the way for cold drinks or tea. Higher up, the hillsides become more densely wooded with tall pines.

Malam Jabba

Colour map 5, grid B2

At an altitude of over 3,000 metres, Malam Jabba has snow until May. It was identified as the ideal location in which to develop a ski resort. With Austrian funding a chair lift was built, along with a large luxury hotel. However, due to disputes between the federal and provincial governments over ownership, the resort remained closed for more than 10 years. In autumn 1998 the hotel was finally opened under the management of PTDC as an interim measure, although it was not clear whether the ski-lift would be operational for the winter skiing season. Check with PTDC in Saidu Sharif for more information.

There are excellent views down into the main Swat Valley and some pleasant walks in the area. The resort is a popular picnic venue in the summer. Hidden in a depression to the left as you face up the chair lift, there are the ruins of a **Buddhist Stupa** and other buildings, although little now remains to be seen.

Ins and outs During summer, there is 1 bus daily from Mingora, leaving around 1000 and returning around 1600. It is very slow, taking around 3 hours, stopping frequently and struggling along in first gear for most of the climb from Manglaur. Datsun pick-ups run more frequently, though irregularly, and are quicker. Both leave from a bus stand north of People's Chowk, on Madyan Rd. With the opening of the hotel at Malam Jabba, it is likely that minibus services will also start operating from the main bus station. It is possible to catch public transport bound for Malam Jabba from the junction at Manglaur, although vehicles are often packed full, with people hanging from the roof and sides.

Routes Continuing north from Manglaur, the main road passes through rich, fertile countryside. At the small town of **Khwazakhela**, a signposted road forks right, leading over the **Shangla Pass** (2,134 metres) to Besham (see page 450). This route is very scenic, climbing through fertile terraced fields and rich forests. On top of the pass there is the ***Shangla Top Rest House***, bookable through the Conservator of Forests in Saidu Sharif. There are also Forestry Dept resthouses at ***Yakhtangi*** and ***Alpurai***, on the way down from the pass. There is a bridge across to the west bank of the Swat River at Khwazakhela and a couple of simple hotels in the town, the best being the **F *Awami***, with basic but clean rooms and a restaurant. The main road continues north up the valley, passing through the village of **Fatehpur**, where another bridge crosses to the west bank of the Swat River. Shortly after the town there is a signposted turning east to Miandam. There are several small tea shops by the junction.

North West Frontier Province

Miandam

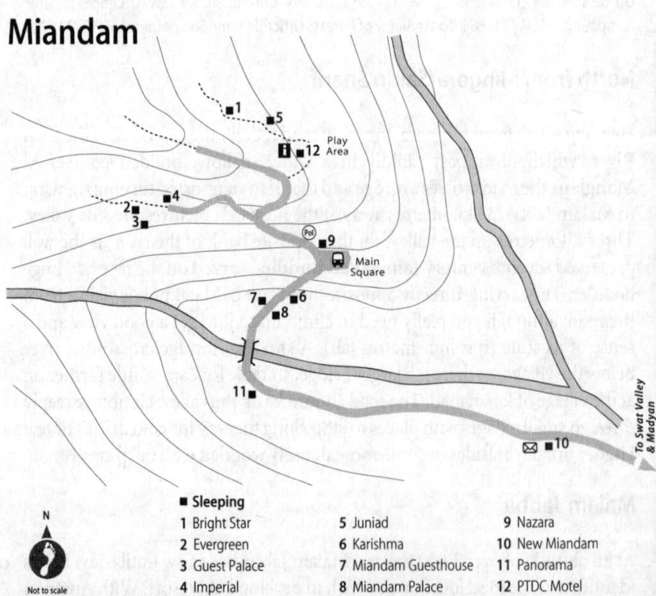

Miandam

Miandam, nine kilometres from the junction on the main road, is a popular resort and can get very busy. The best time to visit is just before or after the peak season (which is during July and August), when it is quieter. Situated at an altitude of 1,820 metres it is pleasantly cooler in summer. There are nice walks in the surrounding valley.

Phone code: 0936
Colour map 5, grid B2

Sleeping

■ *on map*
Price codes:
see inside front cover

Price categories are for the peak season, when it may be necessary to book in advance. Prices are very negotiable off-season. Note that some hotels close during the winter (September to March). The standard of accommodation is generally good in terms of cleanliness. **NB** Miandam has a central telephone exchange (T840309). The phone numbers given below are extensions.

B ***PTDC Motel***, T10. Expensive, but still the most pleasant for its mature shady gardens. Clean rooms with fan, TV/dish, phone and attached bath. As well as the main complex, there are twin room 'cottages' available. Camping is allowed in the grounds. Restaurant. Tourist information. Well run. Open all year round.

C ***Imperial***, T1 (or T780600). Modern 3-storey building with a mirror extravaganza of a lobby. VIP, deluxe and normal rooms, TV/dish, phone, attached bath. Restaurant. **C** ***Juniad***, T17. Situated behind the *PTDC Motel* with nice views down into the next valley. Large rooms, some wood panelled, TV/dish, phone, attached bath. Small garden. Restaurant. A bit run-down.

D ***Bright Star*** is next door to the *Juniad*. Rooms with attached bath. Good views. Restaurant. **D** ***Evergreen***, T34. Pleasant rooms with fan, TV and attached bath. Also simpler rooms without TV (Rs 250). Restaurant. **D** ***Guest Palace***, T35. Clean, pleasant rooms with fan and attached bath. Nice roof terrace. Friendly. **D** ***Miandam Guesthouse***. Rooms with attached bath. Expensive for what you get. Restaurant with TV/dish. **D** ***Panorama***, T31. Situated across bridge from centre of village. Clean, pleasant rooms with fan and attached bath. Restaurant. Good views.

E ***Miandam Palace***, T21. Reasonable rooms with attached bath. Good views. Restaurant. **E** ***New Miandam***, T11. Situated on road leading up to village. Clean rooms with fan and attached bath. Pleasant garden/terrace area with good views.

F ***Karishma***, T4. Reasonably clean rooms with attached bath. Good views. **F** ***Nazara*** T5. Overlooking main square/bus stand. Reasonable rooms with attached bath.

Madyan

Continuing north along the main road up the Swat Valley from the turning for Miandam, you pass various newly-built hotels lining the road before arriving in the centre of Madyan, 56 kilometres from Mingora. The valley begins to narrow here, and one gets a sense of being amongst the mountains.

Phone code: 0936
Colour map 5, grid B2

Madyan (1,320 metres) is a small, lively town with a bustling bazaar, situated on the banks of the Swat River where a side valley drains in from the east. The town has plenty of hotels, although it does not get as busy as Miandam or Kalam, and retains something of its traditional character. It is popular amongst backpackers, having developed a reputation as something of a hippie haven during the 1960s (largely thanks to the venerable Muambar Khan, see under House Rentals, below), and continues to offer a quieter alternative to the busier resorts.

Sights The ancient wooden mosque in the old village, to the north of the main bazaar towards the river, has some beautifully carved wooden timbers. It was being restored at the time of writing, though the carved timbers were being preserved. Nearby, in the same street as the main entrance to the mosque, there is a big old carved wooden doorway to a private family house. Otherwise, Madyan's main attraction is its setting. There are plenty of beautiful walks in the surrounding hills, notably up the 'Chail Road', which leads up the Madyan Valley, past the *Trout Park* trout farm and hotel, to Shanku (where the road ends), and on to the village of Bishigram. Other villages around Madyan are very conservative in their outlook and you are probably better off going with a local guide (this applies particularly to women).

Sleeping

■ *on map*
Price codes: see inside front cover

D *Madyan*, T780031, F780035, away from centre, across bridge and above road to Bahrain. Comfortable rooms around pleasant courtyard/gardens with fan and attached bath. Also 'deluxe' rooms (double Rs 1,200) with river view, TV, phone and sitting room. Restaurant. Recommended. **D** *Swat Holiday*, T780165. Modern, newly opened hotel. Clean, pleasant rooms with fan, phone and attached bath. Shared balconies overlooking river. **D** *Trout Park*, T780029. Situated around 1 kilometre up the 'Chail Road', by the Madyan River. This pleasant hotel forms part of the trout farm located here. Clean rooms with fan, TV/dish and attached bath. Best rooms upstairs. Lovely garden. Restaurant. Friendly and well run. Recommended.

E *Zarin Palace*, T780321. Large (54 room) modern hotel, clean rooms with fan, phone and attached bath, some with TV/dish. Upstairs balcony area, function room. Restaurant. Handicraft shops below.

F *Al Madina*, T780596. Simple but clean rooms with fan and attached bath. **F** *River Palace*, T780242. 3 storeys overlooking river. Reasonable rooms with fan and attached bath. Restaurant. **F** *Hunza Guesthouse*, on riverside near bridge, 6 simple but clean rooms sharing 2 bathrooms. Pleasant balcony. Self-catering facilities. **F** *Imran*, T780263, near bus stand. Simple but clean rooms with attached bath. Nice balconies. Restaurant.

House rentals The tradition started by Muambar Khan in the 1960s of providing overland travellers with local-style accommodation in the old village above the main road still continues, and has been taken up by others nearby. **F/G** *Caravans Guesthouse*. Run by Fida and a Danish Muslim, Michael, this traditional house consists of a downstairs and upstairs wing, each with 2 large double rooms and a 3-4 bed dorm (Rs 60 per bed). Downstairs these open onto a covered verandah, while upstairs there is a balcony and terrace area, as well as a self-catering kitchen. There are 2 shared

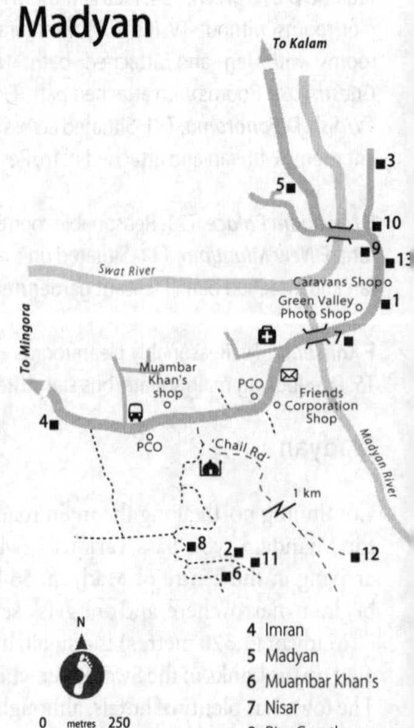

North West Frontier Province

toilets/showers (1 on each floor), with hot water. Booking and information from the *Caravans* handicraft shop in the main bazaar, by the *Zarin Palace* hotel. **F/G *Muambar Khan***. The original house rental, simple rooms with shared facilities. This is the most basic, but also perhaps the most authentic. Certainly, Muambar is quite a character. Watch out for that water pipe of his ... see what it's done to him! During the day you can usually find Muambar at his shop near the bus stand in the main bazaar. **F-G *Riaz Guesthouse***. Run by one of Muambar's sons, Riaz Ahmad, this is the most recent addition to the community of guesthouses here, and the most comfortable. It's a modern concrete building, but well-built and tastefully done. Upstairs there are 4 double rooms, each with its own attached bath (complete with hot water), a 4-bed dorm (Rs 60 per bed), a large common room and a terrace/covered area. Downstairs Riaz is planning a restaurant, self-catering kitchen and a more basic dorm. **F-G *Tourist Inn***. Not yet running at the time of writing, Noor ul-Amin (Muambar's younger brother) is planning to establish his own guesthouse just nearby, along the same lines as the others. Between them, Michael and Muambar Khan's family offer very pleasant alternative budget accommodation with a friendly, relaxing atmosphere.

Eating

Many of the hotels in Madyan have their own restaurants. If you are staying at one of the house rentals in the old village, these serve good value meals (order in advance), and also have self-catering facilities. There are several of the usual basic Pakistani-style eating places in the main bazaar, including some excellent *chapli kebab* joints. The ***Trout Park*** (see Sleeping, above) has its own restaurant serving excellent fresh trout (Rs 250 per kilo) from its trout farm, or you can buy it to take-away.

Shopping

Madyan is a good place to buy traditional Swati embroidered woollen shawls, carved wooden furniture, carpets, rugs, antique jewellery, coins, semi-precious stones etc. There is considerably less of the hard-sell to be found than the more popular resorts, and prices and quality compare favourably. There are plenty of shops to choose from in the main bazaar: ***Caravans***, by the *Zarin Palace* hotel, and ***Friends Corporation***, to the east of the Chail Rd turning, both have a good selection. The latter also have a shop about 2 kilometres north of Madyan on the road to Bahrain, with one of the largest collections of antique carved wooden furniture in Swat.

Transport

Madyan's bus stand is in the main bazaar in the centre of town. Hiace minibuses (and the much slower Bedford vans and big buses) run regularly from here; north to Bahrain and Kalam, and south to Mingora/Saidu Sharif, departing when full. During summer there are regular services direct to Miandam, or else take any south-bound bus as far as the turning for Miandam (ask for 'Fatehpur Tehsil') and then wait for a local Bedford pickup or take a taxi.

Directory

Communications Post: Madyan's post office is a small, easily missed affair on the right as you walk down from the main bazaar towards the bridge over the Madyan River. **Telephone:** there are a couple of PCOs in the main bazaar from where you can make international calls.

Bahrain

Phone code: 0936
Colour map 5, grid B2

Heading north out of Madyan, the main road crosses to the west bank of the Swat River and continues north to Bahrain. The valley meanwhile steadily closes in and begins to climb more steeply. At Bahrain the river is a muddy, fast-flowing torrent, dotted with rapids.

Bahrain is busy with hotels, although most Pakistani tourists seem to stop only to shop at the equally numerous antique and handicraft shops. The town is spread out along the road, on either side of the roaring Darel Khwar as it flows into the Swat River from the west. Away from the road, along the banks of the Darel, there are some interesting old houses with intricately carved woodwork.

Sleeping Price categories are for the high season; when it is quiet practically every hotel will offer you a room for Rs 200 or less.

B *Grace*, T780030. Very lavish and grandiose affair (or aspires to be at least). Rooms with fan, TV/dish, phone and attached bath. Restaurant. **B** *KB5*, T780078. Somewhat cavernous, but OK. Rooms with fan, phone and attached bath. Restaurant. **C** *Marina*, T780168. Overlooking river. Choice of deluxe (TV/dish), moderate and economy (roadside) rooms, all with attached bath. Restaurant. **C** *Deluxe*, T780115. Nice location overlooking river. Clean rooms with attached bath and balconies. Restaurant. **D** *Lachine*, T780300. Reasonable rooms with attached bath. Restaurant. **D** *Swat Valley*, T780152. Reasonable rooms with attached bath overlooking Swat River. Restaurant. **E** *Abshar*, T780122. Overlooking the Daral Khwar. Rooms with attached bath. Food on order. **E** *Bahrain*, T780533, above Muslim Commercial Bank. Mediocre rooms with attached bath. Restaurant. **E** *Dimsun*, T780047. Overlooking Swat River. Reasonable rooms with attached bath. Restaurant. **E** *Jabees*, T780023. Overlooking Daral Khwar. Overpriced rooms with attached bath. Restaurant. **E** *Tower Hill*, T780069. Rooms with fan and attached bath. **G** *Khanzaza*, down by river and reached through the bus depot (on right before bridge, coming from Madyan). Nice, simple place with great riverside location and very friendly owner. Double room Rs 50.

North to Kalam

It is a further 30 kilometres to Kalam from Bahrain. There are several hotels along the way, beautifully situated beside the river, far from all the commotion of the main resorts and ideal if you have your own transport. Opposite the village of **Kulalai**, about half way between Bahrain and Kalam, the **Mankial Valley** drains in from the east. A footpath leads up the valley and over into Kandia Valley, which drains into the Indus north of Dasu on the KKH; this route crosses into the wild and lawless territory of Indus Kohistan and is not safe without a reliable local guide. Around 10 kilometres up the Mankial Valley, PTDC are building the *Mankial Jabba PTDC Motel*, described as being "60 percent complete" in 1998. There is a *Forestry Rest House* in Kulalai, bookable through the Conservator of Forests in Saidu Sharif. The peak of Mankial mountain (5,726 metres) can be seen at various points from the road. Beyond Kulalai, the road deteriorates to a rough track in places; during winter it is often impassable around here. At the village of **Pishmal** there is a traditional Swati mosque by the roadside, with its beautiful and distinctive octagonal wooden minaret still intact.

Kalam

Phone code: 0936
Colour map 5, grid B2

This popular Pakistani holiday resort has seen phenomenal growth over the last decade or so. The new town consists practically exclusively of hotels, and the boom in hotel construction shows no signs of slowing down. Indeed, at the time of researching, Kalam looked more like a building site than a resort. Along the main road into town it's like a competition in extravagance. However, shoddy construction and severe winters combine to ensure that each season's latest fabulously lavish 'palace' is a tatty run-down affair with damp and peeling walls a few years later.

Ins and outs

Kalam basically consists of one main street running north-south, with the Swat River to the east and an area of high ground rising up to the west. The original old bazaar is towards the north end, on both sides of the river, joined here by an old wooden suspension bridge. About 500 metres to the south of this, a surfaced road leads west up onto the hillside. Turning left shortly afterwards at a T-junction takes you towards Jalban village and the *Walnut Heights* hotel. Turning right leads north, parallel to the main road, past the *PTDC Motel*, and then the Fisheries Department and police station opposite each other (turn left here for the *Sangam* hotel), before eventually rejoining the main road to the north of the main bazaar. The bus stand is in the main bazaar, just to the north of the wooden suspension bridge, by the *Khalid* hotel.

Sights

The new town may be something of an eyesore, but Kalam does have its plus points too. Its great attraction to Pakistanis is its higher altitude and therefore cooler climate during the summer months, as well as the beauty of the surrounding valleys and mountains. Across the wooden suspension bridge is the old village of Kalam. The old **mosque**, with its massive carved wooden pillars and scrolls and intricately worked doors, is worth a visit. During summer a favourite is to sit on charpoys placed in the shallow edges of the river with the cool mountain water flowing underneath, sipping cold drinks or tea and chatting. Nearby is a mini fairground. To the north of Kalam there are several very beautiful valleys, accessible by jeep, which offer endless opportunities for day-trips as well as trekking (see below). The rivers north of Kalam offer excellent trout fishing. Permits can be obtained from the Fisheries Department.

Sleeping

There is a complete overload of hotels of all shapes, sizes and prices lining the main road into town; with a few exceptions, these are best avoided. Many of the better hotels are to be found up on the hillside to the east. Only a small selection is listed here. 'Load shedding' is something of a nonsense in Kalam as there is rarely electricity and at night the resort reverberates to the sound of generators. Price categories are for the high season; out of season prices are extremely negotiable.

B *PTDC Motel*, T830014. Located up on hillside overlooking town. Choice of rooms in main block or separate 'huts', comfortable but a bit run-down/overpriced. Restaurant. Great views. Extensive though slightly tacky garden. Foreigners may be allowed to camp for a couple of nights at a time. Tourist information located here. **B *Sangam***, T830015, F830017. Pleasantly situated in quiet spot up on hillside. Comfortable, well-run hotel, good value. Recommended, *Shahzad* restaurant. **B *Walnut Heights***, T830222. Situated 2 kilometres above Kalam, past the village of Jalban. This luxury hotel with its excellent views, large, comfortable and tastefully furnished rooms and homely atmosphere is Kalam's best kept secret and far and away the best value and nicest luxury hotel here. Restaurant. Highly recommended. **D *Seaside***. In main bazaar by footbridge, overlooking river. Reasonable rooms with attached bath. Restaurant. **E *Hill Top***. Up on hillside. Reasonable rooms with attached bath. Restaurant. Good value. **F *Delux Inn***. Located in main bazaar, near bus stand. Basic rooms with attached bath. Restaurant. **F *Khalid***, T830006. Located in main bazaar, near bus stand. One of Kalam's first hotels. Basic but reasonably clean rooms with attached bath. Friendly staff.

Eating

Most of the hotels have restaurants, and there are also a number of tourist-oriented restaurants such as the ***Café Pizzaria*** on the main road (directly opposite the turning west up the hill). In the main bazaar, and in the old part of town across the river, there are various simple Pakistani-style restaurants. Delicious locally caught fresh trout is served in many of the restaurants.

Transport **Jeep hire** For trips up into the valleys to the north of Kalam you really need a four-wheel drive. These can be hired through PTDC, through either of the tour companies (see below), or directly in the main bazaar. Most of the hotels will also arrange jeep hire, but they generally charge more. Prices tend to fluctuate according to demand, escalating when it gets busy. In autumn 1998 it cost around Rs 1,100 for a full-day excursion to Mahodand or Gabral.

Buses and Hiace **minibuses** (much quicker) run frequently from the bus stand in the bazaar to Bahrain, Madyan and Mingora, leaving when full.

Directory **Banks** There are no banks offering foreign exchange in Kalam, but most of the more expensive hotels will change Sterling and US$ cash without any problem. **Communications** There is a post box (but no post office) on the east bank of the river, across the wooden suspension bridge, near the old mosque. International calls can be made from the more expensive hotels, but check their rates first as some are extortionate. **Tour companies & travel agents** *Dardistan Trekking Co*. Located in the main bazaar, near the *Khalid* hotel, this small outfit is run by Aslam Khan, a reliable and knowledgeable local guide, who can organize treks from Kalam to Dir, across the Kachikani Pass to Sor Laspur, and across the Dadaril Pass to Phandur lake. He can also arrange jeep hire etc. *Tourist Information Centre* (a private company). Located on the main road, south of the main bazaar. Run by Shah-e-Room, another reliable and knowledgeable local guide, this outfit offers the same services as above. **Tourist offices** The *PTDC Motel* has a small Tourist Information Centre. They are mainly useful for arranging jeep hire, and for booking other PTDC motels in Swat. **Useful addresses** Police: the police station is up on the hill to the west of the main road. T830008.

Around Kalam

The mountains and valleys around Kalam are extremely beautiful, many of them still thickly wooded, with fast-flowing trout-filled streams, waterfalls and glaciers cascading down from the mountains and numerous lakes and meadows. Locals fondly refer to this region as the "Switzerland of Pakistan".

Socially though this is no Switzerland. Swat *Kohistan*, 'land of mountains', is almost by definition lawless and tribal, or rather governed only by tribal law. The recently removed signs saying "Do not go beyond this point as the area is dangerous and the woods are dense" have been replaced by an uneasy truce between a tribal society which is also very conservative and traditional, and the middle class Punjabis fuelling the tourist mini-boom here. Whether you are going for a day-trip to one of the valleys around Kalam or intend to undertake a longer trek into Chitral or the Ghizar Valley to the north, it is essential that you take a reliable local guide. Permits are required for fishing in any of the rivers around Kalam.

Ushu Valley and Mahodand A bridge crosses to the east bank of the Swat River at the north end of Kalam. Shortly afterwards the road forks; left to Utror and Gabral; right to the Ushu Valley and Mahodand. Following the right fork, the road passes through thick pine forest and climbs up the Ushu Valley to Ushu village. Beyond the village, immediately after a bridge, is the pleasant **D** *Ushu Hotel*, beautifully situated right down by the fast-flowing river, with a small trout farm adjacent. There is also a *PTDC Motel* under construction here. The road then passes through Matiltan village with it sold wooden mosque. There is a *Forestry Rest House* here, bookable through the Conservator of Forests in Saidu Sharif. Beyond the village, the road, previously metalled, becomes a rough jeep track. It climbs through terraced fields of potatoes, corn and maize, and then crosses the snouts of various small seasonal glaciers before reaching Mahodand, 35 kilometres northeast of Kalam. The glaciers have generally retreated sufficiently by late May or early June to be passable. On the way up there are excellent views of Mount Falaksir (6,259 metres) to the east.

Mahodand, meaning 'Lake of Fishes' in Pashto, is in fact a stretch of the Ushu River where it runs across level terrain, allowing it to widen out and giving the appearance of a lake. The 'lake' is surrounded by pine trees and beautiful open grassy meadows; its calmer waters make for excellent trout fishing. Mahodand is a very popular picnic spot in summer, and can get quite busy. A trail continues north from here, and a choice of three trekking routes lead into the Ghizar Valley. (See Dadarili Pass hike on page 499.)

Utror and Gabral

Taking the left fork after crossing the river to the north of Kalam, the road follows the Utror River for 16 kilometres to Utror village. The road is metalled for about the first nine kilometres before becoming a rough track. From Utror, it is a further eight kilometres on to Gabral village. There is a *Forestry Rest House* in both villages, bookable through the Conservator of Forests in Saidu Sharif. There are numerous picnic spots amongst the pine trees by the river, and endless opportunities for walking, although you should take a guide with you, even for short walks. The walk up to Kundalu Lake, two hours to the north of the jeep track between Utror and Gabral, is supposed to be particularly beautiful. The trout fishing in the area is excellent. From Utror, a trekking route leads west towards Dir.

Desan Valley

The Desan Valley, which climbs up from behind the *Walnut Heights Hotel* above Kalam, through pastures and woods, is also very beautiful. There is no jeep track here, although the hotel can organize ponies for an outing or longer trek up the valley.

Other possibilities

There are more than half a dozen lakes in the valleys around Kalam; if you have the time, it is well worth exploring the area with a knowledgeable local guide to find the nicest and most secluded spots.

Chitral Valley

Chitral is an area of outstanding natural beauty, boasting spectacular mountains which offer endless opportunities for trekking and climbing. It is also home to a fascinating variety of peoples, including the non-Muslim Kalash and the semi-nomadic Wakhi. As in Hunza, the people of upper Chitral are Ismaili Muslims and much more open in their outlook. Compared with the Northern Areas, Chitral receives very few tourists, though it has as much, if not more, to offer the visitor.

Ins and outs

Culturally and physically Chitral is the most isolated region of NWFP. Only 2 roads connect it with the rest of Pakistan. The main land route from Peshawar, through Dir and over the **Lowari Pass** (3,118 metres), takes around 12 hours and is closed by snow from late November until May. The lengthy route from Gilgit on a rough jeep track over the **Shandur Pass** (3,734 metres) takes at least 2 days. It generally closes earlier and for longer. In winter, the Fokker F27 flights between Peshawar and Chitral are the region's main link with the outside world. They are subject to frequent cancellation due to bad weather, even in summer. The only land route into Chitral passable in winter is the route detouring around the Lowari Pass and into Afghanistan, which is unfortunately closed to foreigners.

Geography

The rugged and heavily glaciated **Hindu Kush** range (literally 'Hindu Killer') raise a formidable barrier along the western and northern border with Afghanistan. Averaging over 4,500 metres and dominated by Tirich Mir (7,787 metres) and Istora Nal (7,327 metres), these mountains mark the watershed between the valleys draining the Oxus and the Indus basins. To the south and east, the **Shandur** mountains (also known as the Hindu Raj or Mashabar) separate Chitral from Gilgit, Swat and Dir.

The **Chitral River**, known by four different names at various stages along its course, rises in the area of the **Chiantar glacier**, a 40 kilometres sheet of ice which is also the source of the Oxus and Gilgit rivers. Here, as the **Yarkand**, it flows down from an altitude of over 5,000 metres to be joined by the **Laspur River** which drains most of the northern slopes of the Shandur range. It is then known as the **Mastuj** until joined by the Lutkoh branch, draining the Tirich Mir region, where it becomes the Chitral River for much of its course until, close to Afghanistan, it becomes the **Kunar**. In total the river valley runs to over 300 kilometres. Close to Chitral town the river plain widens to over four kilometres in width and runs in a broken pattern of cultivated alluvial fans right down to **Naghar**, 10 kilometres south of Drosh.

Historically the Chitral Valley was one of the main arteries of the Silk Road, across the **Boroghil Pass** to Yarkand and Kashgar, but was later replaced by the more southern routes along the Indus and through Kashmir and Ladakh due to persistent banditry and feuding in the region.

History

Chitral is known to have existed as an unified independent kingdom from at least the 14th century, when **Shah Nadir Rais** established himself as overall ruler. According to some sources Shah Nadir Rais was descended from the Trakhan rulers of Gilgit, while others suggest that he came from Badakhshan.

Following the death of **Sangin Ali**, a powerful adviser to the Rais rulers, in 1570, two of his four sons managed to oust the Rais dynasty, establishing what became known as the **Kator Dynasty**, which ruled right up until the 1960s. The **Adamzada** clan, which form most of the upper class in Chitral, are descended from Sangin Ali's grandsons. The **Khuswaqt** family, who later emerged as rulers of Mastuj, Yarkhun and the Gilgit Valley, are similarly descended from this family. The history of the region from this time is an intricate web of intrigue and conspiracy amongst the various families of the ruling classes, further complicated by almost continual warring with neighbouring kingdoms.

In 1857, **Aman ul-Mulk** emerged as Mehtar (ruler) of Chitral, and by 1880 had extended his rule to include the semi-independent kingdom of Mastuj. The British, fearful of the possibility of the Russians gaining a foothold here, had already sent a mission to Chitral under **Lockhart** in 1855-6. In 1889 they provided Aman ul-Mulk with a subsidy of Rs 6,000 per annum, which they doubled in 1891 on the condition that he accepted British advice on all matters connected with foreign policy and the defence of the frontier. By 1889 the **Trans-Caspian Railway** linking the European provinces of Tsarist Russia with Tashkent had been completed. Russian exploration parties visited Hunza in 1889 and Chitral in 1891, and British speculation at the threat of Russian expansion into South Asia began to appear well founded.

The sudden death of Aman ul-Mulk of a heart attack in 1892, leaving no less than 16 sons to dispute the succession amongst themselves, unleashed a particularly bloody chapter in Chitral's history. Eventually, **Nizam ul-Mulk**, the eldest son, secured the Mehtarship. The British meanwhile lost no time in establishing a Political Agency in Chitral, so as to be better placed to influence events there.

In January 1895 Nizam ul-Mulk was murdered by one of his half-brothers, **Amir ul-Mulk**, triggering another round of bloody in-fighting. This time the British, in whose eyes Chitral had assumed enormous strategic significance, intervened more directly, sending a force from Gilgit under **Major George Robertson**. On his arrival, he forcibly occupied Chitral Fort, a classic piece of British heavy-handedness which only served to turn all the warring parties against him. Robertson soon found himself under siege from the reunited factions of the Chitrali royal family.

The **Siege of Chitral**, as it became known in British accounts, lasted for over a month. Major Robertson managed to hold out until at last a detachment of reinforcements sent from Gilgit under the leadership of **Colonel James Kelly** prompted the Chitrali forces to retreat. Kelly's march across the snow-bound Shandur Pass in early April, complete with two cannons, was recognized as a major achievement, and certainly took the Chitralis by surprise. Soon after, a much larger relief force arrived by way of Malakand and Dir. The British placed **Shuja ul-Mulk** (Amir ul-Mulk's brother), a boy of 14, on the throne and thereafter kept a close eye on the kingdom, supplementing the Political Agent there with a large back-up force in Drosh. Major Robertson, arguably responsible for triggering the fiasco through his indiscretion, was knighted for his "gallant bravery".

The Imperial Gazetteer records how: "Since then [the Siege of Chitral] Chitral has enjoyed an unwonted peace ... Hospitals have been opened ... Cultivation has been extended and the Methar's revenue continues to increase, while at the same time his mental horizon has been much enlarged by his visits to Calcutta, Delhi and Peshawar." In fact the British did very little; not withstanding its strategic significance, they showed minimal interest in the province and made no real effort to develop it.

At Independence, the Mehtar of Chitral acceded to Pakistan, but remained in charge of all internal affairs of the former Princely State. The Pakistani government was represented by a Political Agent, an arrangement that almost exactly mirrored the system under British rule. However, in 1954 there was an internal revolt against the Mehtar, and the Political Agent took over direct control until 1969, when the state was formally merged into Pakistan, becoming a district of the newly formed Malakand Division of NWFP.

People

The Chitrali people, who call their land *Kho*, are not Pathan, though today there are many Pathans to be found in Chitral. Although the Chitrali language, *Khowar*, belongs to the Dardic group, it has strong connections with the languages of the Pamir and Wakhan regions to the north, and with Iran. In addition there are two minorities; the **Kalash**, who number about 3,000 and inhabit the valleys of Birir, Bumburet and Rumbur, just south of Chitral, and the **Wakhi**, a nomadic group occupying the Pamir (literally 'upland grazing zone') and the neighbouring Wakhan Corridor, a thin wedge of Afghan territory separating the former Soviet Union and Pakistan.

The Road to Chitral

The route to Chitral is the same as for Swat as far as Chakdara. Here a road crosses the Swat River and passes through **Dir District**. Like Chitral to the north, Dir existed as an independent kingdom for many centuries, before being incorporated into Pakistan following independence. The people of Dir are predominantly Yusufzai Pathans and away from the main road the region is today still subject only to tribal law. Dir town is the last urban centre before the road climbs over the Lowari Pass into Chitral. There is reasonable accommodation here, making it a convenient place to break the long journey. Much more attractive, though a very long day's drive from Peshawar is the beautiful *Old Fort* at Naghar, on the other side of the Lowari Pass.

Chakdara

Colour map 5, grid B1

The bridge across the Swat River at Chakdara marks the start of Dir district. After the bridge, to the right of the road is **Chakdara Fort**, built by the British in 1896, on the site of an earlier Mughal fort, built in 1586 following Akbar's campaigns in the area. It is now occupied by the Dir Scouts and closed to the public. To the left of the road is **Damkot Hill**, site of **Churchill's Picket** and **Shishi (mirror) Guard**. The main bazaar at Chakdara is two kilometres further on, across a second bridge. Chakdara is a small village, and the only place of interest is the small museum, by the junction with the road which runs along the west bank of the Swat River. One kilometre beyond the main bazaar on the road to Dir there is the **F** *Jamal*, T761063. Clean rooms with fan and attached bath. Also some more expensive a/c rooms with TV/dish and fridge. Restaurant. Small garden.

History

Excavations on and around Damkot Hill have revealed evidence of settlement as early as the second millennium BC when **Aryans** occupied the site, leaving behind distinctive black and grey pottery, wood, stone and iron utensils and copper and gold jewellery. An Aryan graveyard was also discovered at the foot of the hill, on the north side. The site then appears to have been abandoned until around the first century AD. With the flowering of **Gandharan** culture in the region, the site became an important **Buddhist** centre, and a monastery and stupa were built on the hill. This was destroyed by **White Huns** in 528 AD, and in the eighth century AD the **Hindu Shahis** built an extensive fort on the ruins. This fort appears to have housed a fully-fledged town, with houses, shops, stables and blacksmiths' forges. Hindu Shahi rule lasted for over 250 years until the fort was destroyed by **Mahmoud of Ghazni**, who invaded Swat in 1001. Damkot Hill itself then appears to have remained unoccupied until the arrival of the **British**, although Chakdara came under the loose control of the **Mughals** who, not withstanding their initial conquering of the area, gave the recently arrived **Yusufzai Pathan** tribes virtual autonomy. The hill is now occupied by the military and closed to the public.

Chakdara Museum

This small museum has some beautiful pieces and deserves the same treatment as at Saidu Sharif. The central hall contains many small statues and small and medium-sized freizes, some very beautifully carved and well preserved. There are also some stucco pieces and one terracotta figure very similar to those found at Mehrghar in Baluchistan. However, there is no attempt to date or locate any of the pieces. The hall to the left contains impressive traditional embroidered costumes, antique guns and swords, tribal jewellery of silverwork and semi-precious stones and a display of funeral burial items, all gathered from sites around lower Swat.

■ *Officially 0830-1230, 1430-1730 in summer and 0900-1300, 1400-1600 in winter; in practice you may have to track down the chowkidar. Free.*

Transport

There is no bus stand in Chakdara. If you stand out on the main road you can catch local public transport bound for Mingora or Timargarha (both major transport hubs). If you are heading for Mardan or Peshawar, you may be able to find space in a Hiace minibus coming from Chitral or Timargarha, but it may be better to cross the bridge and pick up the more frequent transport coming from Mingora.

Chakdara to Timargarha

Around eight kilometres beyond Chakdara there is a turning right which leads to the ruins of **Andan Dehri Stupa**, less than one kilometre from the main road. Only the base remains, but it is believed to have been 24 metres tall and one of the most important in Swat. This side road continues on to the village of **Shewa**, beyond which, on the range of hills marking the northern border of Dir, are the ruins of the Hindu Shahi fort of **Kamal Khan China**.

The main road bears west soon after the turning for Andan Dehri, entering the Talash Valley. To the south of the road, on the low pass separating the two river valleys, there are the ruins of the Hindu Shahi fort of **Kat Kala**, identified by Sir Olaf Caroe as the site of the ancient city of **Massaga**, captured by Alexander the Great in 327 BC. The road then bears north again, joining the Panjkora River. Across the river are the Tribal Areas of Bajour Agency. The Bajouris, along with other tribal groups from surrounding areas, particularly the Mohmands, Malazai and Kohistani Pathans, were infamous to the British for their lawlessness. The present road was built by the British close to the ridge to avoid sniping gunfire from across the river. As recently as 1977 the

Pakistan Air Force was firing on 'Pathan irregulars' in a dispute over timber rights, and even today the hills of Dir and Bajour are considered a hideout for bandits.

Timargarha

Phone code: 0934
Colour map 5, grid B1

Situated 48 kilometres from Chakdara, Timargarha is the headquarters of Dir District. Across the river at **Balambat** there is an archaeological site which has revealed evidence of continuous occupation since 1500 BC by Aryans, Buddhists, Hindus and Muslims. Fire altars were also discovered, on which juniper would have been burned. Despite its administrative importance (there is also a district hospital here), the town is small and unassuming, and apart from the excavations at Balambat, there is little to stop for here. It is however a major transport hub.

Sleeping

F *Al-Imran*, T821343. Located at the south end of town, near the bus stand (hotel sign in Urdu only). Clean rooms with fan and attached bath. Restaurant. Friendly, well run hotel. Next door is the more basic **G** *New Khyber*, also with restaurant.

Transport

The large bus station at Timargarha has regular Hiace minibuses to Mingora, Mardan, Peshawar (it is sometimes necessary to change at Mardan for Peshawar) and Dir, as well as buses and coaches. There are pick-ups available north of the bus stand in the main bazaar, past the turning across the river. Suzukis operate locally through the town and across the river to Balambat.

Timargarha to Dir

The main road continues north following the river and passing through various small bazaars, including **Khal** (18 kilometres), where a new bridge crosses the river, **Wara** (32 kilometres), **Sahi Baha** (41 kilometre), with its large new mosque and bridge across the river, **Darora** (48 kilometres), **Bibaware** (56 kilometres) and **Chutiatan** (72 kilometres), before arriving at Dir (78 kilometres), by which time the valley has become narrow and thickly wooded. The journey from Timargarha to Dir takes approximately two hours. Near Chutiatan, a jeep track leads east as far as the village of **Thal**, from where it is possible to trek over into the Swat Valley. This trek passes through fairly wild tribal territory; a guide, and permission from the Deputy Commissioner in Dir, is essential.

Dir Town

Phone code: 0934
Colour map 5, grid B1

Although not the district headquarters, Dir seems to have more political significance than Timargarha. This was the seat of power of the Nawab of Dir, whose palace stands on the hillside above the town, still occupied by his descendants during the summer. Below it, the royal guesthouse is now the *Dir Hotel*. It is a small, lively town, and an obvious place to break the journey between Peshawar and Chitral. Dir is famous for its home grown knife industry, producing distinctive small pen-knives as well as larger knives and daggers. There is the potential for some pleasant walks around Dir, although a reliable local guide is essential as the area is tribal.

Sleeping & eating

C-D *PTDC Motel*, T880900. Situated several kilometres north of Dir at Panakot. Comfortable rooms with fan, phone and attached bath. Restaurant. 20 percent discount on room rates from mid-September to end March. **E** *Al Manzar*. Reasonable rooms

■ on map
Price codes:
see inside front cover

upstairs with fan and attached bath. Restaurant. Able to change US$ cash. **E** ***Dir***, T880048. Former royal guesthouse. Cool and airy though slightly dilapidated rooms with fan and attached bath. Pleasant garden. **E** ***Yassar Palace***. Central but very noisy (rear of hotel overlooks main bus stand). Reasonable rooms with fan and attached bath. **F** ***Abshar***, T880735. Situated across the bridge to north of main bazaar, overlooking the river. Clean rooms with fan, attached bath and balconies. Restaurant. Probably the best budget choice.

As well as the hotel restaurants, there are lots of local-style restaurants in the main bazaar serving the usual *karahi*, *chapli kebab*, *daal* etc.

Transport

The main bus station is in a large yard in the centre of town. Regular Datsun pick-ups and Hiace minibuses run from here north across the Lowari Pass to **Drosh** (Rs 140, 3½-4 hours) and **Chitral** (Rs 150, approximately 5 hours). Hiace minibuses for **Timargarha** (Rs 20, 2 hours, change here for **Mingora/Saidu Sharif**), **Mardan** (Rs 55, 5 hours) and **Peshawar** (Rs 65, 6 hours) operate from the small yard by the *Dir Hotel*.

Directory

Communications Post: the post office is on the main road, south of the *Al Manzer* hotel, identifiable only by the post box outside. **Telephone:** there is a small Pak Telecom office opposite the *Yassar Palace Hotel*. More expensive, but more convenient, is the nearby ***International Choice PCO***, T880377. With IDD.

Across the Lowari Pass

The main road crosses the river at Dir and continues north. After about 10 kilometres the road becomes a rough track and begins its long climb up to the Lowari Pass, passing first through the village of Qalandar. At 3,118 metres, the **Lowari Pass** is generally only open from late May/early June through to October, becoming blocked by snow during winter. A tunnel, visible from the road near the foot of the pass, marks the start of an unfinished project which originally aimed to make the route a year-round one; questions about the technical feasibility of the tunnel, and its cost, have put the project on hold. The rough track climbs up to the pass in a long series of switch-backs. Near the summit on the Dir side there are a few tea stalls which also serve simple food.

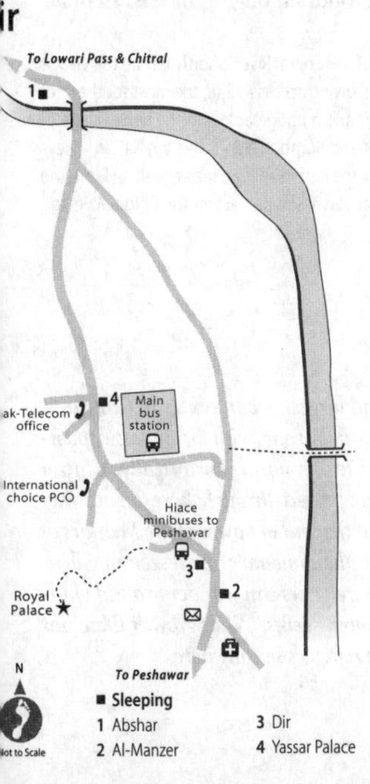

The descent down the Chitral side is even more tortuous. Near the foot of the pass there is a check post at **Ziarat** where foreigners must register. The road continues past another check post at the small village of Ashriat, before arriving at **Mirkhani**, with its fort occupied by the Chitral Scouts. Here a road forks off to the left, following the Kunar River to the Afghan border at Arandu. During winter, under a special arrangement, Pakistanis are able to travel by this route in order to bypass the Lowari, passing through the Afghan province of Nuristan before re-entering

North West Frontier Province

Pakistan via the Nawa Pass and rejoining the Chitral road just south of Dir, at Chutiatan. Foreigners are officially not allowed to travel by this route. It is possible, however, to cross the pass by foot when it is still closed to vehicles. It is a long hike and you should check first with locals as to the depth and condition of the snow.

Naghar A short distance after Mirkhani there is a bridge across to the fort at Naghar. The fort was built in 1919 by Shuja ul-Mulk, the then Methar of Chitral, for one of his sons, Jhazi ul-Mulk. Today it is still occupied by the descendants of the royal family, who have opened a small hotel, the **C** *Old Fort Tourist Resort*, T05333-450 (or book through *Hindu Kush Trails* in Islamabad, T277067, F275031). There are currently six rooms, with more planned. Camping is also allowed, and there is a restaurant. The fort is an almost magically idyllic place to stop for a night and it is even worth contriving to do so just to spend an evening enjoying the setting and the hospitality. Most travellers enthusiastically write of Naghar as a 'paradise' in the visitors' book. The hotel has a small, delightful garden and the rooms overlook the wide swirling waters of the Chitral River, which sweep round the outcrop of Naghar in a huge U-bend. Behind the fort there are large, well maintained gardens and orchards of peaches, apples, plums, pears, apricots and cherries.

Drosh 10 kilometres north of Naghar is the town of Drosh, with its large fort, which is today the headquarters of the Chitral Scouts. The fort is closed to the public and there is little else of interest in the town. Passable accommodation is available in the **F** *Javed Palace*. There are a few other more basic hotels in the bazaar.

Shishi Valley Just beyond Drosh is the Shishi Valley which climbs up to the northeast. This steep, thickly wooded valley is jeepable as far as the village of **Madaglasht**, and there are opportunities for trekking beyond, although a guide is essential.

Routes The main road continues north along the east bank of the Chitral River. Shortly before the village of **Gahiret**, an old steel girder bridge crosses the river, giving access to Birir, the most southerly of the 3 Kalash valleys. Further on there is a turning left and a bridge across to the large village of Ayun, the gateway to the Kalash valleys of Bumburet and Rumbur. **NB** To visit the Kalash valleys you must first have registered in Chitral. (For details of the Kalash Valleys, see page 404.) From the turning to Ayun, it is a further 18 kilometres to Chitral Town, situated across the Chitral River, on the west bank.

Chitral Town

Phone code: 0933
Colour map 5, grid A1

Chitral town is the district headquarters and largest urban centre in Chitral. It boasts a lively, colourful and atmospheric main bazaar, with the majestic splendour of Tirich Mir dominating the skyline to the north. Historically, Chitral gained its importance from the trade that passed through here on its way between Afghanistan and China. It was also the seat of power of the Mehtars of Chitral. Chitral has experienced little of the phenomenal growth seen in Gilgit, and remains a small, friendly place where foreigners can wander around without being pounced on, or even noticed, it often seems. What growth there has been has come mainly as a result of Afghan refugees settling here.

Ins and outs

Getting there

The airport is situated around 3 kilometres to the north of town, on the west bank of the river. There is always at least 1 minibus waiting there to meet people off the plane and shuttle them into town (Rs 10), and more often than not representatives from various hotels offering a free jeep ride, provided you stay at their hotel. There is a new bus station a few kilometres to the north of town, on the east bank of the river, but no one seems to use it, with minibuses and jeeps all operating from various points along the main bazaar.

Getting around

The town is small enough to wander around comfortably on foot. **NB** Foreign tourists arriving in Chitral are required to register with the Superintendent of Police (see below under Useful addresses). It's a straightforward process taking no more than 30 minutes. Registration in Chitral should not be confused with Foreigners' Registration (see page 31); it is a separate formality required of all foreigners, irrespective of whether they have registered elsewhere.

Sights

Chitral Fort

The **Chitral Fort**, situated by the bank of the river was the site of the 1895 Siege of Chitral, and focus for the bloody intrigues which characterized Chitrali politics; whoever held the Fort in effect held power in the kingdom. Today much of the fort is a crumbling ruin, although parts of it have been restored and are still occupied by the descendants of the royal family. Officially it is closed to the public, though if you ask you may be allowed to look round the abandoned parts. Inside, there are five cannons, two dating from the First World War. The best views of the fort are on the way into town from the north, or from across the river. Next to it is the recently restored **Shahi Masjid**, a striking onion-domed mosque dating from the time of Shuja ul-Mulk. To the south of the main bazaar is the **polo ground**, one of the largest in Pakistan. Games are played here on a regular basis between March and October; check with PTDC for dates, or just listen out for the drumming which heralds the start of a match.

Essentials

Sleeping

■ *on map*

Price codes: see inside front cover

A ***Hindu Kush Heights***, Gankorini, T413151, F413153 (or book in Islamabad, T275485, F275475), E hotels@hindukush.sdnpk.undp.org. Perched high up on the mountain-side to the north of Chitral town, this hotel is in a class of its own. Built and managed by Siraj ul-Mulk, a member of the former ruling family, the loving care and attention which has gone into this place is evident the moment you walk in the door. All the rooms are tastefully furnished with traditional Chitrali rugs and hangings, marble floors, wood panelled ceilings and with balconies offering spectacular views out over the Chitral Valley. The restaurant here is excellent as well (see under Eating). **A-B** ***Pamir Riverside Inn***, Noghor Gardens, T412525, F413365. Beautiful and peaceful riverside location with lovely gardens. Choice of rooms from Rs 1,000-2,000, comfortable but overpriced. Restaurant.

B ***Mountain Inn***, T412800, F412668, E mountain@inn.sdnpk.undp.org. Established in 1968, this is the oldest hotel in Chitral town. Comfortable, nicely furnished rooms set around a courtyard of beautiful, mature gardens with bright flowers and large shady trees. Restaurant. Run by the helpful and knowledgeable Haidar Ali Shah. A wonderful oasis of a place with plenty of long-standing afficianos. **B** ***PTDC Chitral Motel***, New Bazaar, T412683, F412722. Comfortable rooms with TV/dish, phone and attached bath. 20 percent discount 16 September-31 March. Restaurant. Tourist information centre.

D/E *Dreamland*, New Bazaar, T412608, F412770. Clean, comfortable rooms with fan and attached bath. More expensive ones with TV/dish and phone (double Rs 550). Restaurant. Pleasant, homely, well run place. Helpful staff.

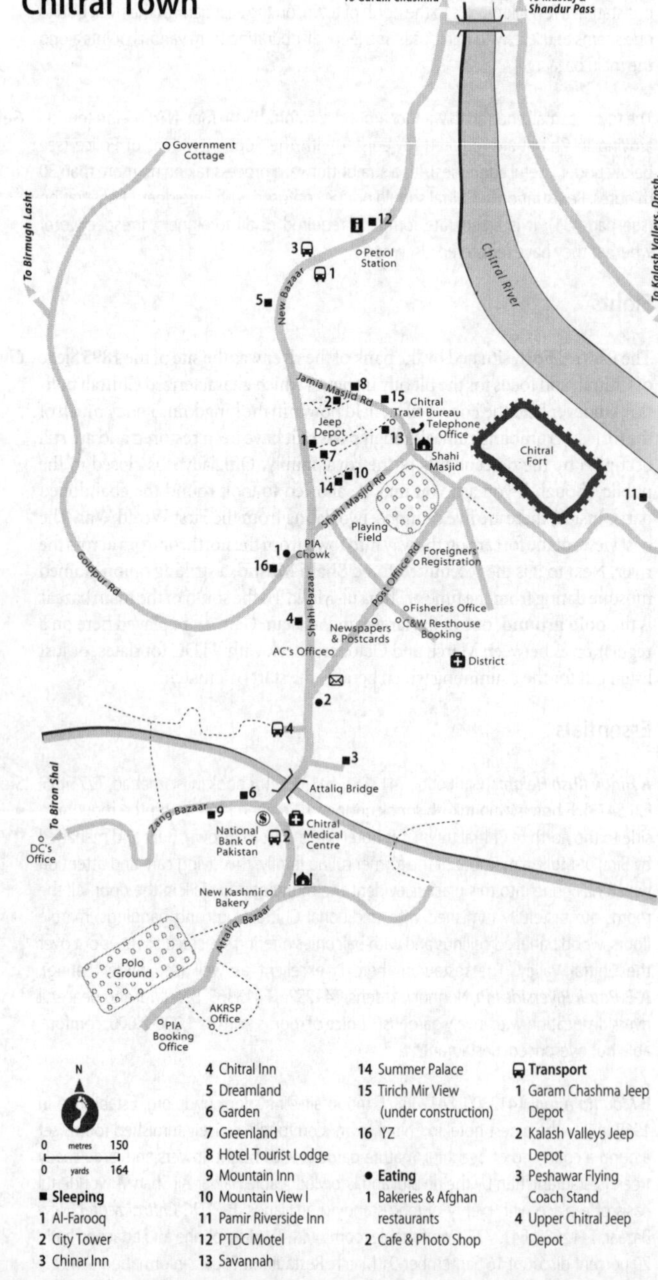

E ***Chinar Inn***, off Shahi Bazaar, near Attaliq bridge, T412582. Clean, pleasant rooms with fan and attached bath, arranged around small, quiet garden. Also very basic rooms in old block (double Rs 50). Set back from the road. Restaurant. Very good value. Recommended. **E** ***Tourist Lodge***, Jamia Masjid Rd, T412452. Basic, not overly attractive rooms with fan and attached bath.

F ***Al-Farooq***, New Bazaar, T412726. Clean rooms with fan and attached bath. Some rooms with balconies. Friendly place, centrally located but noisy. Popular with Punjabis. Restaurant. **F** ***Chitral Inn***, Shahi Bazaar, T412025. Centrally located, but rather unattractive, small-windowed, box-like rooms with fan and attached bath. **F** ***Mountain View***, New Bazaar, T412559. Simple but clean rooms with fan and attached bath. Rather ugly concrete building. Restaurant. **F** ***Savannah***, off Jamia Masjid Rd, T412294. Reasonable rooms with fan and attached bath around concrete courtyard. Bit dank, no views. **F-G** ***Summer Palace***, off Shahi Bazaar, no phone. Simple but clean rooms with fan and attached bath in big concrete building. Also rooftop dorm under awning (Rs 20 per bed). **F-G** *YZ*, Goldpur Rd, no phone. Basic rooms with fan and attached bath, set around pleasant garden/courtyard. Friendly.

G ***Garden***, opposite *Mountain Inn* hotel, no phone. Very basic, charpoy beds, outside toilet, wash in stream, but pleasant, shady garden and friendly staff. **G** ***Greenland***, off Shahi Bazaar, T412084. Basic rooms with fan and attached bath in big concrete building.

Eating

● *on map*

If you fancy something really special, the restaurant at the ***Hindu Kush Heights*** hotel, T413151, serves excellent food, cooked by a truly inspired Bangladeshi resident chef. Treat yourself for under Rs 500 per head. If you are not staying there you will need to book in advance and organize your own transport out there and back, but it's worth it, as much for a chance to see the hotel as to sample their excellent food. Most of the hotels in Chitral itself have their own restaurants. When it is quiet it is better to let them know in advance if you want to eat there that evening. There are dozens of simple Afghan-run eating places and *chai* shops in the main bazaars; particularly around PIA Chowk and along the first stretch of Goldpur Rd (where there are also a couple of bakeries); towards the north end of New Bazaar around the bus stand and jeep depot; and around Attaliq Bridge and along Attaliq Bazaar. On offer is a fairly mundane and limited repartee of meat and vegetable dishes, but it's cheap and filling.

Entertainment

Sports Polo: is played regularly at the polo ground in Chitral, see above. There is excellent **fishing** in many of Chitral's rivers. For permits and more information, contact the Fisheries Office, off Post Office Rd.

Shopping

There are several shops piled high with a wonderful array of Afghan and Chitrali rugs and carpets, as well as all manner of antique tribal jewellery, semi-precious stones (particularly Lapis Lazuli and Turquoise from Afghanistan), embroidery work, carved wooden items etc. The local Chitrali speciality is *Shu*, or *Patti* cloth, a soft handwoven woollen material which is made into intricately embroidered long gowns *(chunghas)*, rugs, bags, Chitrali hats etc. Most of the shops are located in Shahi Bazaar and New Bazaar, and along the first stretch of Goldpur Rd, before you reach the *YZ* hotel.

There is a limited amount of trekking equipment on sale in Shahi Bazaar and New Bazaar; much of it, notably sleeping bags etc, is army surplus stuff (serviceable but heavy). You can often find good second-hand boots, and occasionally bits of equipment left over from mountaineering expeditions. Alternatively, the tour operators have trekking equipment available for hire. For provisions, the shop next door to the *Chitral Travel Bureau* on Shahi Masjid road has a good selection of lightweight, high energy trekking goodies. The various bakeries are also good for biscuits, jam, cakes etc; the ***New Kashmir Bakery*** in Attaliq Bazaar has a good selection.

For postcards, there is a shop on Post Office Rd with a reasonable selection (it also sells local newspapers), or if you are staying at the *Mountain Inn*, see if Haidar Ali Shah still has any of the postcards featuring excellent photos of the Kalash by Hervé Nègre.

Transport **Air PIA Booking Office**, Attaliq Bazaar (by Polo Ground), T412963. Open 7 days 0900-1700. Airport, T412547. Weather permitting, there are 2 Fokker F27 flights daily to Peshawar at 0725 and 1000. If your flight is cancelled due to bad weather and you want to try again for the next day, be sure to reconfirm your seat.

Road Private Jeep Hire: jeeps can be hired privately from any of the jeep depots listed below. Also worth trying is the depot off New Bazaar (behind the *Al Farooq* hotel), where ***Chitral Tourist Travel*** and ***Tirich Mir Travel*** have jeeps for hire. Jeep hire can also be arranged through the *PTDC Motel* and *Mountain Inn*, or through any of the tour operators listed below. Prices vary greatly according to demand; as a rough guide, the following prices were being charged in 1998: Shandur Pass (one way) Rs 3,500; Gilgit (one way) Rs 8,000; Kalash valleys (full day return trip) Rs 800-1,000; Garam Chashma (full day return trip) Rs 800-1.000. Note however that 1998 was a pretty abysmal year for tourism in Chitral and most jeep owners were desperate for business.

Peshawar Flying Coach Stand Ticket office situated towards the north end of New Bazaar, between the *Dreamland* hotel and *PTDC Motel*. Hiace minibuses run from here approximately every hour from 0600-1500. **Peshawar** approximately 12 hours, Rs 250. **Dir** approximately 5 hours, Rs 150. **Timargarha** approximately 7 hours, Rs 200 (change here for **Mingora/Saidu Sharif**).

Garam Chashma Jeep Depot Situated just off New Bazaar, opposite the Peshawar Flying Coach Stand. Passenger jeeps (and occasionally minibuses) operate regularly from here to **Garam Chashma** (2 hours, Rs 20-30), departing when full.

Upper Chitral Jeep Depot Situated just off Shahi Bazaar, a little to the north of Attaliq Bridge. Passenger and cargo jeeps operate from here to Upper Chitral. Most go as far as **Mastuj** (approximately 4 hours, Rs 100). As far as **Buni** takes around 2 hours and costs around Rs 35-50. Some also go to **Sor Laspur** (approximately 5 hours, Rs 100-120). Services are irregular, depending on demand; enquire at least a day before and be prepared to hang around on the day. **Shandur Pass/Gilgit** In the run-up to the annual polo tournament on Shandur Pass, there are regular passenger jeeps departing from here for the pass. At this time there is also plenty of onward transport from Shandur to Gilgit. At other times, it is still worth asking around at the Upper Chitral Jeep Depot in case there are any jeeps returning to Gilgit. If not, your best bet is to get a jeep as far as Sor Laspur, walk or hitch over the Shandur Pass, and then pick up onward transport on the other side. See above for approximate costs of a privately hired jeep.

Kalash Valleys Jeep Depot Situated in Attaliq Bazaar, just south of Attaliq Bridge. Regular passenger jeeps and minibuses leave from here to **Ayun** (45 minutes, Rs 10). Depending on demand, there are usually also several direct jeeps daily to **Bumburet Valley** (generally as far as Anish or Brun, 2 hours, Rs 25) and at least 1 direct jeep daily to **Rumbur Valley** (Balanguru, 2 hours, Rs 25). If not, go to Ayun and catch onward transport from there. Jeeps and minibuses also run to **Drosh** (1 hour, Rs 15) from here.

Directory **Banks** The ***National Bank of Pakistan***, at the junction on the south side of Attaliq bridge, is the only bank licensed to deal in foreign exchange (cash and TCs). Open 0900-1300, Fri and Sat 0900-1200, closed Sun. There are several money changers in Shahi Bazaar and New Bazaar; they give the going 'kerbside' rate, but will only deal with cash (US$ and £ Sterling). They also have large wads of Afghan Rials for sale if you're interested!

Communications **Post:** the GPO is on Post Office Rd, near the junction with Shahi Bazaar. It has a poste restante section at the rear, and you can also send faxes from here. Open 0900-1400, Fri 0900-1200, closed Sun. **Telephone:** the telephone office, for national and international calls, is in a small office off Shahi :Masjid Rd, open 7 days, 0800-1600 (and sometimes as late as 2000), Sun 0800-1200. **Internet:** Haidar Ali Shah at the *Mountain Inn* hotel and Sirajul-Mulk at the *Hindu Kush Heights* hotel both have internet access and are usually happy to let people send Emails and check their messages.

Hospitals & medical services The ***District Headquarters Hospital*** is off Post Office Rd. There are several chemist shops nearby, on Post Office Rd itself. On the south side of Attaliq Bridge is the ***Chitral Medical Centre***, T412768, with its own dispensary which is open 7 days, 0800-1800. There is also a well-equipped DAACAR clinic near the airport.

Tour companies & travel agents ***Chitral Travel Services***, Shahi Masjid Rd, T412461, F412516. Able to organize jeeps and treks (including porters and guides). They also have some equipment (tents, sleeping bags etc) available for hire. ***Chitral Tourist Information***, Dreamland hotel, T412806, F412770. Can also organize jeeps and treks and have some equipment for hire. ***Hindu Kush Trails***, the main tour company in Chitral (run by members of the former royal family), has a liaison office at the *Mountain Inn*. Their head office is in Islamabad; House 37, Street 28, F-6/1, T277067, F275031. They are a good, reliable company, with extensive experience of organizing trekking expeditions and jeep safaris in Chitral and beyond.

Tourist offices There is a helpful ***PTDC Tourist Information Centre*** in the *PTDC Motel*, T412683, F412722. Haidar Ali Shah of the *Mountain Inn*, or either of the other tour companies listed above, are also useful sources of local information.

Useful addresses **Superintendent of Police:** (for registering in Chitral, see under Ins and outs, above), Post Office Rd, T412077. Open 0800-1500, Fri 0800-1200, closed Sun. **Police:** Post Office Rd, T412959. **C&W Sub Divisional Officer:** off Post Office Rd, T412103. Apply here for C & W Rest House bookings. **District Forestry Officer:** off Post Office Rd, T412101. Enquire here about visits to Chitral Gol National Park. **Deputy Commissioner:** on road west of *Mountain Inn*, T412055. If you are planning to stay for more than a week in the Kalash valleys, you must obtain a permit from the DC. **Assistant Commissioner:** Post Office Rd, T412066.

Around Chitral Town

Birmugh Lasht

The Methar of Chitral had his summer palace at Birmugh Lasht, situated high above the town on a small plain. The building is semi-derelict and occupied only by the chowkidar's family. The plain used to be thickly wooded with walnut trees (Birmugh Lasht translates as 'place of walnuts'), but today only a few isolated trees remain. Higher up, on top of the mountain, there is a *Wildlife Department Rest House*, bookable through the District Forestry Officer in Chitral. There are excellent views in all directions, and some trees offering shade, making this an ideal picnic spot.

Ins and outs

A steep, rough jeep track zigzags its way up to the top. Head east out of town along the road past the *YZ* hotel. After the first hairpin bend the jeep track forks off to the left (there is a well-hidden signpost). It is a strenuous 3 hour walk with no shade on the way up. A privately hired jeep will cost around Rs 800 for the return trip.

Chitral Gol National Park

The small side valley (Chitral Gol) that climbs steeply up from Chitral town has been designated a National Park, covering 7,745 hectares. Rich forests of Deodar (Indian Cedar), Blue Pine, Chiligoza Pine and Silver Fir still remain here, as well as stands of willow and birch, and some juniper scrub. Snow Leopards, Black Bears, Markhor and Urial are reportedly still found in the upper reaches of the valley. In theory these are protected under the legislation governing national parks, though in practice hunting still continues, threatening the survival of many species. Encouragingly however, there have been recent sightings of a pair of Snow Leopards. The valley also attracts many migratory birds en route between Central Asia and India, including the Black Throated Thrush, Golden Oriole, Grey Heron, Mallard and Oriental Turtle Dove, as well as being home to an impressive array of indigenous species.

Ins and outs There are several beautiful treks through the park, and some *Forestry Resthouses* offering simple accommodation (you need your own sleeping bag, cooking equipment and provisions). To trek here you need a permit (from the District Forestry Officer) and a guide. See under Tourist offices and Tour operators & travel agents in the Chitral Directory for leads on getting more information and organizing a visit to the park.

Garam Chashma

Situated 45 kilometres northwest of Chitral, Garam Chashma is famous for its hot sulphur springs (hence the name). Regular jeeps and minibuses run between Chitral and Garam Chashma, a two hour drive along the narrow Lutkho River Valley. Approaching Garam Chashma, you pass an old fort still occupied by descendants of the Chitrali royal family, the civil hospital, a police post (where foreigners must register) and the fisheries department office, before arriving in the main village. There is one proper hotel here, the **D** *Injigaan*. It offers comfortable double rooms or dorm beds for Rs 150, and meals to order. The hotel's main attraction however (and the main reason for coming to Garam Chashma), is its own private, **spring-fed hot water pool**, a blissful way to soothe aching limbs after trekking. There are also a couple of very basic Afghan-run hotels in the bazaar. There is excellent trout fishing in the area; permits can be obtained from the fisheries office on the road before the village.

Kalash Valleys

The Kalash, numbering approximately 3,000, are the smallest group amongst the religious minorities of Pakistan. Unlike the other minorities, they live exclusively in a particular geographical area; the three valleys of **Birir**, **Bumburet** and **Rumbur** situated in the Hindu Kush between the Afghan border and the Chitral Valley. Muslims label the Kalash 'Kafirs' ('non believers') and their area Kafirstan. Until 1896 Kafirstan also included present-day Nuristan in Afghanistan, inhabited by the 'Red Kafirs', whereas the Kalash were called the 'Black Kafirs'.

Ins and outs

Getting there and around The Kalash valleys are easily accessible from Chitral. **Bumburet** and **Rumbur** valleys are both reached via the village of **Ayun**, situated on a large alluvial fan on the west bank of the Kunar River. Around 12 kilometres to the south of Chitral on the main road down towards the Lowari Pass, a turning leads down to a bridge across the river and then to Ayun, around 3 kilometres further on. The main square/jeep stop is across another small bridge over the river draining the Kalash valleys. Regular passenger jeeps run from the jeep depot in Attaliq Bazaar (see under Chitral Transport). Most passenger jeeps run as far as Ayun, though many also continue on to Bumburet, the most popular valley. Services to Rumbur are less frequent. If there is nothing going to Rumbur, take a Bumburet jeep as far as the check post and then walk (2-3 hours to Brum/Balanguru).

There are no regular passenger jeep services to **Birir** Valley, to the south of Rumbur and Bumburet, although occasional jeeps do go from Ayun, following a jeep track along the west bank of the Kunar River. The main route is via the bridge at Gahiret, 7 kilometres south of the bridge turning for Ayun. All of the jeep tracks up the valleys are subject to frequent blockages due to floods, landslides and earthquakes. In such cases the track to Bumburet is usually repaired within a few days, but for Rumbur and Birir valleys repairs often seem to take much longer. The track to Rumbur was blocked for almost 3 years following heavy flooding in 1991.

Permits

Visitors to the Kalash valleys must pay a toll (Rs 50, or Rs 10 for Pakistanis, valid for all 3 valleys) at the check post at the junction of Bumburet and Rumbur valleys. The proceeds from this toll are in theory channelled back into the valleys. **NB** You must first

Kalash Valleys

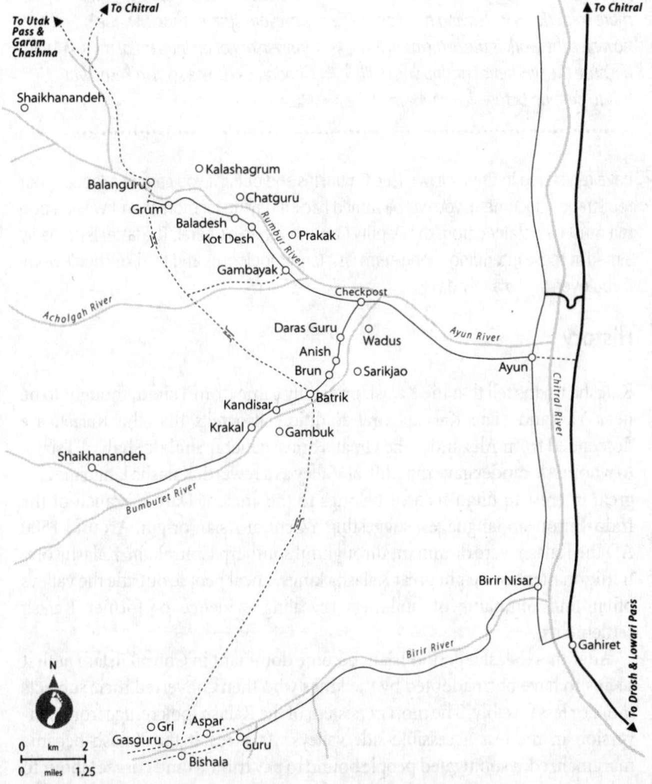

Dress

Kalash women are strikingly colourful in their unique costumes. Their hair is plaited, both at front and back. On their heads they wear the shu'shut, a small head-dress like a ring around the head with a long piece hanging down the back. On top of that the big head-dress or ku'pas is worn for protection against the sun and for ceremonial occasions. Both head-dresses are heavily decorated with cowries, buttons, beads and brass. The decorations reflect the valley of origin and the status of the woman, but nowadays, on the shu'shut in particular, local new fashions gain the greatest influence. When a person dies the close female relatives wear the ku'pas alone for the period of mourning.

The black baggy dress is tied with a broad scarf, or patti. Both used to be woven from home-spun wool. With the cash economy, cloth, borders and yarn from the shops have gained great popularity, allowing the women to be more colourful. For weaving a red patti however, the work is the same as before, because the synthetic knitting yarn still has to be spun before being woven. Huge numbers of glass bead necklaces cover the neck and breast of the woman. They are only taken off altogether by a widow during periods of mourning.

Nowadays the men wear the practical shalwar kameez suit, as well as the Chitrali cap. During the cold winter, decorated woollen leggings are commonly tied around the shalwar. The traditional woollen pants are still used by some of the elders for ceremonial purposes, and are given to 4-6 year old boys for their initiation ceremony during the winter festival of Chaomos. This is also when the small girls receive their first ku'pas. The men used to wear woollen jackets or skin vests during the winter but now modern coats and jackets as well as Chitrali coats are taking over. The former traditional turban is still used for a dead man and for small boys during their initiation ceremony. The traditional men's dress is also seen on the Gandauws – the graveyard statues raised on the anniversary of an influential man. (Many Gandauws can be seen in Peshawar Museum.)

have registered in Chitral town (see Chitral Ins and outs); if you cannot produce your registration document, you will be turned back. If staying for more than 1 week, a permit must be obtained from the Deputy Commissioner in Chitral. The latter is primarily aimed at those intending a long-term visit (anthropologists and the like); don't worry if you overstay by a few days.

History

Kalasha myths tell that the Kalash originally came from **Tsiam**, thought to be near Yarkand. The Kalasha oral tradition also tells that the Kalash are descended from Alexander the Great's brave general **Shalak Shah** of Tsiam, to whom Alexander gave the Chitral Valley as a reward. Kalasha language is of great interest to linguists as it belongs to the ancient Dardic branch of the Indo-European languages, suggesting a Central Asian origin. Around 1500 AD the Kalash were dominant throughout southern Chitral; the Kalasha oral tradition mentions eight great Kalasha kings. Local people outside the valleys often find remnants of buildings revealing evidence of former Kalash settlements.

After this Kalasha period Islam became dominant in Chitral. Islam at first seems to have been adopted by the kings who then converted their subjects more or less forcibly. The most persistent of the Kalash took refuge from conversion in the less accessible side valleys. As a result the Kalash became marginalized; a subjugated people bound to pay tributes and corvée labour to the Mehtars, economically exploited and subject to frequent raids from their neighbours in what is now Nuristan.

When the British established the Durand Line the Kalasha valleys became part of British India and so part of present-day Pakistan. This protected the Kalash from the forcible conversions to Islam carried out by the Afghan king Abdur Rahman in 1896. Groups of Red Kafirs fled these conversions into Chitral. The refugees were given land in the upper parts of the Kalasha valleys and still have their villages there. Ironically they all later gradually converted to Islam. In 1969 the kingdom of Chitral became part of Pakistan. To the Kalash this meant a lifting of their serfdom and the enshrining of their constitutional right to practice their religion.

Religion

The Muslims label the Kalash 'Kafirs' in the misapprehension that they do not believe in God and worship only idols. In fact the Kalash do believe in God, *Khodai* (the Persian word for Allah) or *Dezao*, who is the creator and can be worshipped everywhere. In case of a natural disaster or serious illness, the Kalash try to reconcile God by prayers and sacrifices.

Male and female *Dewalok* (sacred spirits) are responsible for particular parts of daily life and are addressed when necessary through prayers, offerings or sacrifices. The Kalash may ask the *Dewalok* to give their prayers to *Dezao* (in the same way as the Catholics ask the saints to do so). It is important to know and respect that the places of the *Dewalok* belong to the pure sphere, where only men are allowed to go. Exceptions are the temples representing *Jestak*, who protects the families. During menstruation and childbirth, Kalash women stay in the *Bashali* houses where *Dejalik* is represented by a carved piece of wood.

In the Kalasha perception, Nature belongs to other beings than themselves. Through offerings, sacrifices, purifications and prayers, they have to ask for permission to let the animals graze in the high pastures or cut down trees for example.

The pure-impure dualism is central to the Kalasha religion. *Onjesta* (pure, sacred) and *Pragata* (impure, profane) are frequently mentioned in connection with locations as well as with acts, persons and objects. Basically the Kalasha world is divided into complementary spheres of *Onjesta* and *Pragata*, with the divine, the high pastures, the men and the goats belonging to the *Onjesta* sphere, and the women belonging to the *Pragata* sphere, in particular during menstruation and childbirth. For the women, their confinement to the *Bashali* during menstruation provides a monthly holiday from the daily routine of hard work. Anybody entering, or touching anybody there, must be totally washed before returning to the rest of the world.

Tourists should stay away from the *Bashali*. If a female tourist has her period she should keep quiet about it and not leave any sanitary towels or tampons for people to find, as they are considered a strong pollutant in the religious sense (take them out of the valleys, bury them at the 'shitting ground' or burn them secretly, but not in a family house).

The family houses are divided into zones. The fireplace and the area behind it are *Onjesta*. Therefore a woman is not permitted to step over these places, but only to reach with her arms and the top of her body into the area. Inside the house, women have to pour drinking water (considered *Onjesta*) from the common glass into the mouth through her left hand. The valley also is divided into zones – the higher up, the more *Onjesta*.

As women, and also Muslims, are *Pragata*, they can never go to the altars and other places of the *Dewalok* or to the goats' stables above the villages when the goats are down, as these places are *Onjesta*. Acts such as washing the body and braiding the hair are also considered *Pragata* and have to be done at a certain distance from these places.

Purifications are an essential element in the Kalasha religion. These may be done by circling burning juniper or hollyoak, by rinsing the hands in pure river water, by sprinkling goat's blood or by holding something made of iron. Of particular importance is the purification of boys during their gradual transition from the *Pragata* women's sphere into the *Onjesta* male community. Only after several purifications (after the traditional trousers dressing ceremony) at the age of about seven years, are the boys sufficiently *Onjesta* to go to the altars and to the high pastures. When still virgins they are very *Onjesta* and have special religious tasks.

Festivals

Three big festivals are of particular importance and are the milestones of the year. The spring festival *Joshi* in May honours the fairies and so safeguards the goats and shepherds before they go to the pastures. During *Utjao*, in late August, the harvest of goats' cheese is celebrated. At *Chaomos*, lasting most of December, the divine, the living and dead relatives, the crops and the goats are safeguarded, while the community, the village and the valley are purified prior to the coming year. There are also minor religious functions during the agricultural year, like, for instance, the ploughing offering. In summer, tourists attracted by the vivid sound of drums may have the chance of seeing the nightly dances known as *Ratnat*, performed by the young girls and boys in order to safeguard the maize crop.

To the Kalash these festivals are the culmination of religious life and, like the big funerals, they unite the people. Tourists should behave respectfully if visiting the valleys during one of these big functions. As the entire community gathers for festivals, politicians often take advantage of the opportunity to use the occasion, Joshi in particular, as a forum for political propaganda, confusing the religious dances with an ordinary feast.

Social structure

Family relations are extremely important; people rarely call each other by their name, but rather address each other in terms of their relationship to the eldest child of the family. This means that children are very important and everybody know their names. After receiving the proper dress a child is considered a full member of the community. However, the young are expected to behave respectfully towards their elders, listening and obeying their commands.

Households generally consist of the extended family, encompassing many relations and several generations, and forming an integrated economic unit. People belong to their father's clan (even married women) which is very important in terms of identity, and involves sharing the economic responsibility in case of big expenditures such as funerals and the collection of bride price.

As the women are excluded from the *Onjesta* sphere their living space is smaller than the men's. Women mostly stay below the highest water channels in the field and village areas. In the summer they go to the fields of the lower summer pastures. After their return to the villages in the autumn, these areas are purified and closed to the women. Although women are considered *Pragata*, they are not at all looked down upon; they are considered the common pride of the valley, and for instance have to walk first in the procession when coming to another valley for a funeral. The men talk proudly about 'our women' meaning all women from the valley or clan. They have total self-determination in all personal matters. Thus, within the strict rules governing incest and periods of abstention, a woman is able to decide whom to marry and with whom to make love (if the man agrees of course). Men frequently complain of 'women's choice' saying "What can we do?" If a man dares to pull the plaits of his wife or talk rudely to her, she normally leaves the house. She can then take a lover, and nobody can force her back again. After disputes over fields, women's elopements are the main reasons for community conflicts.

Important to the Kalash are the codes of honour that first of all emphasize generosity, living according to their religion, honesty in work and speech (quality of speech is better than quantity) and diligence. Greed is looked down upon – many myths tell how greed leads to disaster.

The Kalasha society has no formal internal leadership. Disputes are settled and decisions made by the male clan elders in common. There are also strong personalities among the women who give their opinions and are heard. Politically the community is split into factions – traditionally around competing clan elders, but nowadays increasingly around competing politicians from outside running for the minority seat in the National Assembly. The Kalasha elected minority member of District Council in Chitral functions as a representative and mediator with the surrounding world. The Kalash have not yet succeeded in winning the minority seat in the Provincial Assembly.

The Kalash in the 20th century

The Kalasha community is at a stage of transition. The building of roads linking the valleys with the outside world has brought with it development; schools, a health system, money, commercial goods, new ideas, electricity and tourism. In particular the Kalash are a major tourist attraction and so of great economic importance for the tourist industry. Tourism is mainly outside Kalasha ownership and control, which leads to concern and frustration among the Kalash; not unanimously, but dependent on the degree to which individuals feel harassed by or benefit from the tourists.

In general the Kalash welcome visitors, if they behave with respect to the people and the culture. Less welcomed are the foreign groups who come just for a brief visit, taking pictures and behaving as if in a zoo. Least welcomed are the gangs of young men from the lowlands; confusing the women's freedom from Purdah with sexual promiscuity, they frequently harass the girls.

The Kalasha culture has always responded to and evolved along with the surrounding world. Some outside tourist interests want the Kalasha culture to be 'frozen' into a museum of the living past. Consequently they complain about modern innovations like electricity. This reflects different perceptions of what 'Kalasha culture' actually is. When asked to define Kalasha culture, a Kalash may reply "Homa Dastur!" – "our tradition" – in brief mainly words and ways, determined by the Kalasha religion. This is not what matters to most of the tourists. In general they come to *see* the 'culture' and catch it with their camera. Thus tourist interests emphasize the spectacular; the big communal rites and the material culture of dresses, houses and technology, leading to complaints about material changes.

The Kalasha religious rites and traditions are central to the unity of the community. As these rites become redefined as tourist events (in the way that dancing has been taken out of the religious context and is done for money in Bumburet and Birir), the basic functions of the rites are eroded along with the unity of the world they sustain.

So far however, contact with other ways and norms has made the Kalash very aware of their own culture. Indeed, there is a growing cultural pride among the Kalash, partly because the interest shown by tourists has made the Kalash aware of the unique nature of their culture. Also, the religious heads tend to interpret disasters like diseases among the goats as caused by cultural slackness, which encourages the people to keep their traditions alive. An increasing dependence on tourist incomes does influence the material culture, although sometimes in positive ways. Thus the women have learnt that their colourful costumes can earn them money, and as their incomes increase, they are able to use the extra money to further embellish their costumes.

Perhaps the greatest threat to the Kalash is the deforestation going on in the valleys. The Kalash valleys are among the few forested areas in Pakistan. Timber is used in increasing quantities for construction of houses for a fast growing population, while firewood is still the main fuel source for domestic use. Far more damaging, however, is the logging carried out by external contractors. The Kalash are fighting to gain control over logging in the valleys, and for their legal right to royalties from the timber. Ultimately however, the only way to protect the ecology of the valleys would seem to involve a complete stop to commercial logging. Without their forest cover, the steep-sided valleys with their large catchment areas are exposed to heavy erosion and flash floods, both of which are occurring with increasing intensity and frequency. The wholesale destruction of the forests in the Kalash valleys for immediate profit seems likely to trigger an ecological disaster which will ultimately destroy the culture and community, and with it a long-term source of income from tourism for many outside the valleys.

Rumbur Valley

Around 45 minutes to the east of Ayun by jeep, the Rumbur and Bumburet rivers merge to form the Ayun River. Coming from Ayun, the jeep track crosses the Bumburet tributary and then forks; left up the Bumburet Valley, or right up the Rumbur Valley. Just by the fork is the check post where visitors must buy their 'permits'. Following the Rumbur Valley, at the village of Gambayak, the Acholgah Valley branches off to the left, leading up to summer pastures. Further on the track passes through Kot Desh and Baladesh before arriving at Grum, where there are several hotels. Just across the river is Balanguru, a picturesque and typically Kalash village shaded by large walnut and jujube trees, with wooden houses built up the hillside, the roof of one forming the front yard of the next. Beyond Balanguru, there are beautiful walks up the valley, past the hydel plant supplying electricity to the village. Higher up the valley is the Muslim (Nuristani) village of Shaikhanandeh (literally 'village of converters'). It is also possible to trek across to Chitral town or Garam Chashma (see below).

Sleeping There are 4 simple hotels in Grum, all offering basic rooms with shared toilet/washing facilities. Meals are prepared to order. **F*Ex-Lant*** (Excellent!). Pleasant garden area opposite with camping. **F *Green Kalash***. **F *Kalash Garden***. Situated about 500 metres before the main village. **F *Kalash Hilton***. Across the river in Balanguru there is **E *Saifullah Jan's Guesthouse***. 6 rooms, shower/toilet block adjacent. Rs 250 per head including all meals and tea on request. This is the nicest place, consisting of a traditional Kalash house set right in the midst of Balanguru. Saifullah Jan was the first Kalash man to receive an education outside the valleys. He speaks fluent English and acts as a spokesman for the Kalash. He has been instrumental in the struggle to protect the valley's forests from various outside logging interests.

Bumburet Valley

The valley of Bumburet is the most popular in terms of tourism and has most of the hotels. As a result, it is the most easily accessible, with the majority of passenger jeeps coming here. In some ways this valley is also the most picturesque, being the widest of the three, with scattered villages and long, fertile stretches of cultivation strung along most of its length. From the check post at the foot of the valley, the jeep track climbs up through the villages of Wadus, Daras Guru, Gadiandeh, Anish (where the first hotels begin to appear), Brun, Sarikjao, Batrik, Kandisar, Krakal and Gambuk. At the top of the valley there is another Muslim (Nuristani) village known, as in Rumbur, as Shaikhanandeh. The village itself is to the left of the main jeep track, piled steeply up the side of a rocky outcrop. Next to the *C&W Resthouse* at the end of the jeep track, there is a trout hatchery. Permits to fish in the river can be obtained here for Rs 50.

Sleeping

Hotels are listed below in the order they appear along the road. Most are able to prepare food to order, even if they do not have a restaurant. Those owned and run by Kalash people are indicated, although some Muslim-run hotels are owned by Kalash, who lease them out. At the time of writing there were a couple more hotels nearing completion in addition to those listed below.

Anish C ***PTDC Motel***, on main road. Hotel under construction at time of writing. Scheduled to open 1999. **F** ***Jinnah Kalash***, set back from main road, opposite hydel station. Kalash owned, upstairs rooms with attached bath. Pleasant quiet location. Restaurant. Camping. Recommended. **E** ***Benazir***, on main road. 4 rooms in new block with attached bath. Cheaper (**F** category) rooms in old block with shared bath. Restaurant. Large pleasant garden, camping, shop. **F** ***Bumburet Tourist Inn***, on main road. Simple rooms in pleasant traditional building. Large garden.

Brun D/E ***Foreigner's Tourist Inn***, on main road. Good clean rooms. Restaurant, shop. Nice garden. **F** ***Taj Mahal***, on main road. Basic rooms, share toilet. Restaurant. **F** ***Kalash Guesthouse***, situated up in the village on the hillside above the main road (to the right going up the valley). Kalash owned. 1 simple double room in traditional house with toilet/washing facilities. Meals prepared to order. Lovely garden and views. Camping. Friendly. Recommended. **F** ***Kalash View***, situated in same village as *Kalash Guesthouse*. More basic (no toilet/washing facilities in building), but equally good views and just as friendly. Food prepared to order. **F** ***Frontier***, on main road. Clean, pleasant rooms. Shop. Restaurant. **E** ***Ishpatta Inn***, behind *Frontier* hotel. Kalash owned. Designed by a Japanese architect in traditional Kalash style. 3 small double rooms with attached bath. Also good value 8 bed dorm (Rs 50 per bed). Camping. Food prepared to order.

Batrik E ***Peace***, just above main road, to the right. Clean rooms. Restaurant. **F** ***Green***, on main road. Kalash owned. Simple but clean rooms with attached toilet. Share shower. **D** ***Kalash Continental***, on main road. Kalash/Lahori joint venture. Clean, pleasant rooms with attached bath. Large, recently opened place of wooden construction with tin roofs. Restaurant. Garden. **B** ***Galaxy***, on main road. Comfortable carpeted rooms with attached bath (some with TV). Also cheaper, better value rooms without carpet (double Rs 300). A big white monstrosity of a concrete hotel. Peculiar layout with rooms facing each other across a narrow rectangular concrete courtyard. Aimed mainly at Pakistani tourists. Circular 'tower' restaurant. Friendly Afghan/Peshawari staff.

Krakal **E** *Lahore Campsite*, on main road. Closed at time of writing, and unclear whether there were plans to reopen it or not. **F/G** *Jahangir*, on main road, opposite *Lahore Campsite*. 3 basic rooms with attached bath and 2 with shared bath. **F** *Kalash Mountain View*, on main road. Kalash owned. Simple rooms with shared bath. Nice verandah with carved wooden posts. Upper storey under construction at time of writing. Pleasant garden (camping) and views. Food prepared to order. **F** *Alexandra*, on main road. Rooms with attached toilet, hot water in buckets. Pleasant garden (camping) and extra camping area on opposite side of the road. **E** *Kalash*, on main road. Kalash owned. 2 rooms with attached bath and western-style toilets. Main block of 8 cheaper rooms (Rs 150) with shared bath. Big garden (camping). Restaurant. Shop. **F** *Sissojak* (pronounced *'Shishoyak'*, Kalasha for 'beautiful'), on main road. Kalash owned. 5 simple rooms, shared bath, in traditional Kalash building with verandah. Lovely large garden (camping), complete with its own orchard. Food prepared to order. Friendly manager. Recommended.

Shaikhanandeh **D** *C&W Rest House*. Comfortable rooms with attached bath. Pleasant garden. Food prepared to order. Book through C&W Sub Divisional Officer in Chitral.

Birir Valley

Situated to the south of Rumbur and Bumburet, Birir Valley is the least visited of the Kalash valleys. It can be reached either from Ayun, or via a bridge crossing at the village of Gahiret, further south along the road to Drosh and the Lowari Pass. From Ayun, a jeep track branches off to the left just above the main square/jeep stop and follows the west bank of the Kunar River to the foot of the valley. Guru is the main village and the only one with any hotels.

Sleeping The main hotels in Guru are on the south bank of the river. They will prepare food to order. **F** *Paradise*. 8 simple rooms with shared bath. **F** *Mehran*. 10 simple rooms with shared bath. Friendly, better value. There is also a **E** *C&W Rest House*. Reasonable rooms with attached bath. Pleasant garden. Book through C&W Sub Divisional Officer in Chitral town. Across the river on the north bank is the **F** *Kalash Guesthouse*, a simple but friendly place with just 2 rooms.

Treks

Trekking routes connect the 3 Kalash valleys. The trek between the Birir and Bumburet valleys can be done in one (long) day. It is a steep, hot climb over a 3,000 metres ridge with little shade along the way. Carry plenty of water and start early. A guide is recommended as it is easy to get lost (particularly going from Birir to Bumburet). From Birir Valley, the path starts at the village of Gasguru and descends into Bumburet Valley at Batrik.

The trek between Bumburet and Rumbur takes 2 days, crossing a 3,000 metres ridge into the Acholgah Valley, and then a second ridge over into Rumbur. From Bumburet the track also starts from Batrik, ending at Balanguru village in Rumbur. A guide is strongly recommended.

From above Bumburet in the Rumbur Valley, the trek across to Chitral town is a fairly easy 2 day trek, although without a guide it is easy to get lost. The trek across the Utak Pass (4,656 metres) to Garam Chashma is said to be a strenuous one taking at least 3 days and involving a difficult river crossing; a local guide who is familiar with the route is strongly recommended.

Upper Chitral

The mountains to the north and east of Chitral town are amongst the most spectacular in NWFP, easily matching any in the Northern Areas; a visit to Chitral is really not complete without at least a brief foray into this beautiful area. Awesome, rocky mountains twisted and eroded into fantastic shapes rear up on all sides, giving occasional glimpses of majestic snowy peaks beyond. The villages along the way appear as isolated oases of rich green irrigated farmland, contrasting strikingly with the surrounding barren rock. The trekking in this region, much of which has recently been changed from a closed to a restricted zone, is particularly beautiful.

Upper Chitral is where the majority of Chitral's Ismailis live, making the area far more open and welcoming than the valleys to the south, particularly for women. The diet is simple, centred around dairy products and wheat. Chitrali bread, either in the form of *Khasta Shapik* or *Chapouti*, is baked in thick round loaves and makes a pleasant change from chappatis or naan. *Machir* is a thin, watery yoghurt-like drink which can be thickened into *Shetu*, or yoghurt, and is in turn used to make *Shupinak*, a delicious thick, creamy cheese.

The Road to Mastuj

The road to Mastuj is undergoing steady improvement and is now metalled as far as Buni. Beyond Buni it reverts to a jeep track, rough in places but easily passable. The journey to Mastuj village can now be made in around four hours.

From Chitral town, cross to the east bank of the river and turn left to head north, and then northeast along the **Mastuj River**. The first village you pass through is **Koghozi**, which boasts its own post office and a few basic shops.

About one kilometre beyond Koghozi, the **Golen Gol** drains in from the southeast. A jeep track leads up this valley as far as the village of **Ustur** (14 kilometres). From there it is possible to trek northeast and then either bear north across the **Shakuh Pass** to Reshun, or continue in an easterly direction across the **Phargam Pass** to Harchin. Another trek leads south from Ustur, over the **Dok Pass**, and then southwest to Madaglasht at the head of the Shishi Valley.

The main road continues along the Mastuj River, passing through the villages of **Maroi, Barenis, Grim Lasht** and soon after **Reshun**. The latter has a small *C&W Rest House* (book through the C&W Sub Divisional Officer in Chitral). Between Grim Lasht and Reshun, the **Barum Gol** drains in from the NW. There is a bridge across to the opposite bank and the village of **Parpesh**. The Barum Gol is jeepable as far as the village of Barum, or sometimes as far as Muzhen. This is the starting point of the trek across the **Owir Pass** and down to the Lutkho Valley.

The Owir Pass Trek

Restricted zone. Maximum elevation 4,338 metres. August to mid-September. Maps: the U502 series sheet covering this trek is restricted; Mountaineering Maps of the World, P 268 Tirich Mir and Buni Zom is reasonable.

Above Barum village there is a track which is in theory jeepable as far as Muzhen (pronounced 'Mujen'), although the bridges along the way are often broken. Alternatively it is a 7 kilometre walk, steep at first but gentle after the village of Shungosh, just over half way. Beside the path above Muzhen there is good camping by the stream, with trees for shade. Above Muzhen the route climbs through open pastures up towards Owir Pass (4,338 metres). There are plenty of potential camping spots on the way up. Be prepared for bitterly cold nights and high winds. The best views of Tirich Mir and Buni Zom are from a small hillock to the north of the pass itself. On the far side the descent is steep, crossing loose slate, before arriving at pastures with good camping. Further down the path passes through small settlements before arriving at Sussoom, the most important village in the Karimabad (previously Ozher) valley, and the head of the jeep track up from Shogore, in the Lutkho valley between Chitral and Garam Chashma. The valley below Sussoom is very narrow with sheer slate cliffs on the south side.

Routes Back on the main road, shortly after Reshun the **Turikho Valley** can be seen draining into the Mastuj River, the two valleys running almost parallel at this point. Almost opposite the junction of the two rivers is the village of **Kuragh**. There is a small hotel here, the **G** *Kohistan*, basic, food available, garden (camping). Just beyond the next village, **Charun**, the road crosses to the north bank of the river on a bridge. The old jeep track into the Turikho Valley branches left just after the

Upper Chitral

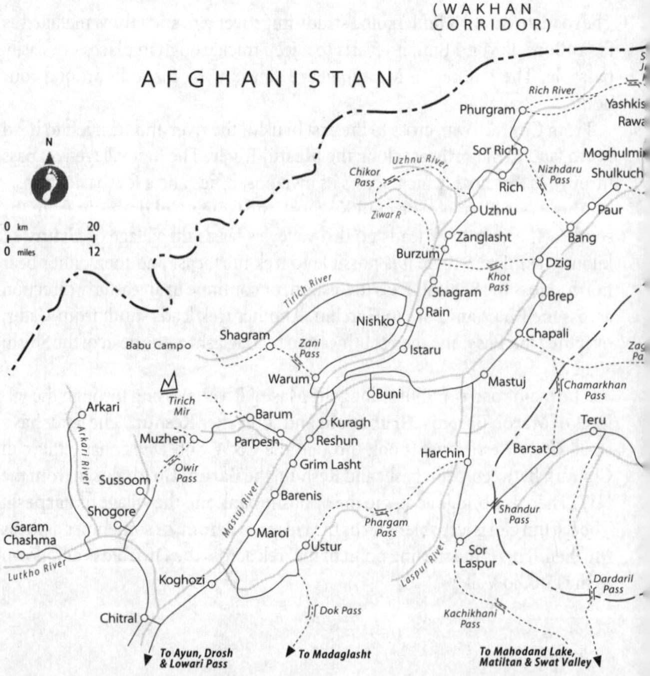

Related map* Gilgit to Chitral (KKH Chapter), *page 489

bridge; these days it is often blocked by landslides. The main road heads east and passes through the village of **Khandan** with its petrol pump, and a turning left which is the start of the new jeep track up the Turikho Valley (see page 418).

Further on there is a bridge across to the village of **Buni**, a large, fertile settlement (the largest in upper Chitral) spread out over a wide alluvial fan. There is a good *C&W Rest House* here. The main jeep track continues straight on, passing through the village of **Parwak** before crossing once again to the south bank of the river. Soon after is the junction of the **Laspur River** with the Mastuj, the former draining in from the south. The jeep track crosses to the east bank of the Laspur River and then forks; left leads into Mastuj village, three kilometres away, while the right fork is the route to the Shandur Pass.

Mastuj Village

Colour map 5, grid A2

Mastuj was once the seat of power of the independent Kushwaqt principality, which in its heyday reached across into the Gilgit River Valley. **Mastuj Fort**, similar in style to the one in Chitral town, is still occupied by Colonel Khushwaqt ul-Mulk, the son of Shuja ul-Mulk, who was made Mehtar of Chitral by the British in 1895, following the siege of Chitral fort. The setting is particularly beautiful, with the village spread out across a large alluvial fan. Bubbling streams and irrigation channels run through golden fields of wheat and barley lined with towering poplar trees, shimmering in the sun and wind, while in the village apricot and *jujube* trees are scattered all around. There is a small bazaar, fairly well stocked with basic supplies (trekkers can stock up on flour, rice, lentils, tea, sugar etc here), a telephone exchange and a post office. The latter was established by the British and was considered to be the most far-flung post office in the Empire.

Sleeping & eating

In 1998 there was a large (40 room) *PTDC Motel* nearing completion in Mastuj which looked set to be ready for the 1999 season. The nicest place to stay however is the **E** ***Mastuj Fort***, situated north of the main village, between the jeep track and the river. There are 2 double rooms or camping in the grounds (Rs 150 per tent, including use of toilet/shower block). In the village itself, there is the friendly **F-G** ***Foreign Tourist Paradise***, with 2 basic but comfortable rooms furnished local-style. Small pleasant garden (camping). Food prepared to order. Next door is the **F-G** ***Tirich Mir View***, offering a similar deal. There is also a ***C&W Rest House***, though getting permission to stay there is difficult. Try in Chitral or Buni.

Shandur Pass

From Mastuj village, the jeep track to the Shandur Pass heads south along the east bank of the Laspur River, passing through the village of **Harchin**. Further on, at **Sor Laspur**, the jeep track bears east and begins the climb up to Shandur Pass, the highest polo ground in the world at 3,734 metres and the site of the annual polo match between Chitral and Gilgit. For details of this section of the route, and the Gilgit River Valley to Gilgit, see page 487.

North of Mastuj: Yarkhun Valley

North of Mastuj village, the Mastuj River becomes known as the Yarkhun. A rough jeep track follows the east bank of the river as it climbs northeast towards the Wakhan Corridor. The jeep track passes first through the village of **Chuinj**, where there is a small basic hotel, the **G** *Khyber*. A little further on is **Chapali**, where a small side valley climbs up to the east, the start of the trek across the **Chamarkhan Pass** to Barsat, just east of the Shandur Pass (see below).

The jeep track continues northeast from Chapali, passing through the village of **Brep**, before crossing to the west bank of the river. Shortly after is the small village of **Dzig**, the start of the trek over the **Khot Pass** and into the Turikho Valley. Further on is **Bang**, consisting of a number of small villages spread out over several kilometres. Here, the **Bang Gol** drains in from the northwest, marking the start of the trek over the **Nizhdaru Pass** to Sor Rich in the Turikho Valley.

Beyond Bang, the jeep track passes through the village of **Pitrangaz**, followed closely by **Paur**, before arriving at **Shulkuch**. A few kilometres beyond Shulkuch the jeep track peters out altogether.

The Yarkhun Valley continues northeast, before eventually swinging round to the east to run parallel with Afghanistan's Wakhan Corridor. A long, strenuous but spectacular trek (around three weeks) follows the Yarkhun Valley, passing the route north over the Boroghil Pass into Afghanistan, then crosses the **Karumbar Pass** (4,300 metres), crowned by a string of lakes, into the Karumbar Valley. After crossing the snout of the Chatteboi glacier, it then climbs up over the glaciated **Chillinji Pass** (5,290 metres) and crosses into the Chapursan Valley to eventually emerge on the KKH to the north of Sust. This trek requires experienced guides and a properly organized and equipped expedition.

An alternative and more manageable trek branches northeast off the Yarkhun Valley, across **Shah Jinali Pass** and down into the Turikho Valley (see below).

Chamarkhan Pass Trek

Open zone. Maximum elevation 4,344 metres. June to October. Maps: U502 series, NJ 43-13 Mastuj is good; Mountaineering Maps of the World, P 212 Central Hindu Raj is better. See trekking notes, page 67.

This is a relatively easy trek taking 2 days (3 going slowly) and offering an alternative route from Chitral into the Gilgit valley, by passing the Shandur Pass. A guide is not necessary, although you need to be fully acclimatized if coming from the Chitral side as there is a height gain of over 1,500 metres on the trek.

From the village of **Chapali**, the path climbs east up the south bank of the small side valley before crossing to the north bank and arriving at a stone shelter at **Malo**. Here the valley forks. The path crosses the stream flowing down from the northeast and follows the right-hand branch southeast, climbing through woods of birch and willow and traversing a scree slope. Higher up the valley forks again.

The valley draining in from the east is the Zagaro, which leads up to the **Zagar Pass** (c5,000 metres). It is possible to continue east across this pass and then across the **Nazbar Pass** (4,977 metres) to arrive at Yasin. Between the 2 passes it is also possible to descend the Bahushtaro Gol to the Ghizar (Gilgit) river at Shamran.

The main track crosses the Zagaro river and heads south up the Chamarkhan Gol. There is good camping and beautiful views at the small shepherds' hut at **Shal**. From here it is a long steady climb up to the Chamarkhan Pass through beautiful pastures carpeted with flowers in summer. The pass itself is wide and flat-topped, and also covered in pasture. Stone cairns mark the route. On the other side, the path descends along the east bank of the river, with plenty of good camping spots along the way, to the junction with the Ghizar (Gilgit) river. There is a police post consisting of a couple of tents by the main Chitral-Gilgit jeep track. **NB** Public transport is infrequent in either direction from here, so be prepared to wait around for a day or two, or walk.

Shah Jinali Pass Trek

Restricted zone. Maximum elevation 4,259 metres. July to September. Maps: U502 series NJ 43-13 Mastuj is good, though some place names are misleading; Mountaineering maps of the World, P 236 Eastern Hindu Kush is good. Trek researched first hand. See trekking notes, page 67

This is a particularly beautiful (though fairly strenuous) trek and well worth the expense associated with trekking in restricted areas. Most people recommend doing it from the Turikho (Rich) to Yarkhun valley due to the steep climb towards the pass coming from the other direction. This depends though on whether you prefer your ascents to be short and sharp, or longer and gentler. The trek is described here going from the Yarkhun to Turikho valley. Allow 4-5 days (not including rest days). Porters charge for at least 6 stages.

The first section from **Shalkuch** is an easy walk climbing gently along the east bank of the Yarkhun River, crossing the Gazin Gol flowing in from the east (the route up to the Thui Pass across to Yasin), and passing through settlements and green, lightly wooded terrain to **Moghulmirir**, where there is good camping.

Above Moghulmirir the main path zigzags steeply up a shoulder of mountain to the village and fields of **Rewak**, situated on a beautiful small plateau with excellent views. On the other side it descends steeply through deep meadows of flowers and wild rose. An alternative route follows the river around the shoulder, but involves crossing to a shingle bank and back, and is not always passable. Further on a bridge leads across the Yarkhun River and the path doubles back before climbing up to the village of **Yashkist**. It is possible to camp in the village, although flat ground is very limited.

Above the village the path enters the Seru Gol, crosses to the south bank of the river, recrosses further up and doubles back to enter the narrow gorge of Isperu Dok Gol. The climb up the gorge is very steep, gaining more than 800 metres before arriving eventually at the summer settlement and pastures of **Isperu Dok**. There is excellent camping on a small grassy patch by the river below the main cluster of stone huts. The setting is a spectacular one and it is well worth spending a day here to explore. It is possible to cover the section from Moghulmirir to Isperu Dok in 1 long day if you are fit.

Above Isperu Dok the valley divides, the left fork being the route to Shah Jinali. Cross to the opposite bank of the river and climb over a shoulder, ascending steadily to the top of the pass. The **Shah Jinali (King's Polo Ground) Pass** is a beautiful area of rolling pasture, covered in flowers in early

July. The greenery is broken in places by snowdrifts, small ponds and crystal clear streams. All around is an amphitheatre of icy peaks. It is a steady descent to **Shah Ghari**, another beautiful spot deep with wild geraniums, onion, hemlock and buttercups.

The next section, down to the village of **Darshal** is subject to frequent change and can follow either bank of the river. Further on, following the right bank after Darshal, there is a precariously perched tiny camp with a rock shelter. A gulley fed by a waterfall runs down from the north. The path then descends steadily, crossing to the left bank and rounding a gradual bend. On the opposite bank, where the Rahozon Gol drains in from the north, there is an area of level ground and trees known as **Moghlong**. Further round the bend, across a side-stream, there is a possible campsite. The valley steadily opens out from its narrow gorge to a wide plain. Further on the path crosses to the right bank of the river on a good bridge and eventually joins the head of the jeep track shortly before Phurgram village.

Turikho Valley

The Turikho Valley is particularly green and fertile, the irrigated patches of settlement blending into each other for most of its length. The lower section of the valley is known as the **Mulkho**, the middle section as the **Turikho** and the upper section as the **Rich** Valley.

From the turning just east of Khandan, the jeep track climbs steeply up to a shoulder of mountain separating the Turikho and Mastuj rivers. On top is a small plateau with pasture known as **Kagh Lasht**, scarred by several jeep tracks which have cut through the ground cover and exposed the sandy soil underneath to erosion. The track descends to the village of **Istaru**, followed soon after by **Warkup**. Further on there is a bridge across to the village of **Nishko** on the west bank.

This bridge gives access to the **Tirich Gol** which drains in from the west, joining the Turikho River higher up, above the village of Rain. The Tirich Gol is jeepable as far as the village of **Shagram** (there are two Shagrams, the second is higher up the Turikho Valley). From Shagram a trek leads southeast over the **Zani Pass** and back into the Mulkho (Turikho) Valley near **Warum**, to join the old jeep track along the north bank of the river. Another trek leads west towards **Tirich Mir Base Camp**.

The main jeep track up the Turikho Valley continues northeast through **Rain** (pronounced 'ra-een'), **Shagram** and across a small side valley draining in from the east (the start of the trek over the Khot Pass to Dzig in the Yarkhun Valley), to **Burzum**. There is a footbridge across to the west bank of the Turikho River here, giving access to the **Ziwar Gol**, which drains in from the northwest. Further along, at **Zanglasht**, another footbridge gives more direct access. A trek follows the Ziwar Gol, branching northwest over the **Chikor Pass** and down the **Uzhnu Gol** to rejoin the Rich (Turikho) Valley at Uzhnu.

The main jeep track crosses to the west bank of the river at **Uzhnu** for a short stretch, then recrosses to the east bank to arrive at **Rich**, a scattered settlement of several villages with a shop selling basic supplies. Further up, beyond **Sor Rich**, the jeep track crosses once again to the east bank to arrive at **Phurgram**. This last stretch of the track, crossing and recrossing the river, is frequently blocked as the bridges here are particularly rickety and easily broken during rains or floods. Further on is the start of the trek over the Shah Jinali Pass and down into the Yarkhun Valley.

Karakoram Highway and the Northern Areas

Karakoram Highway and the Northern Areas

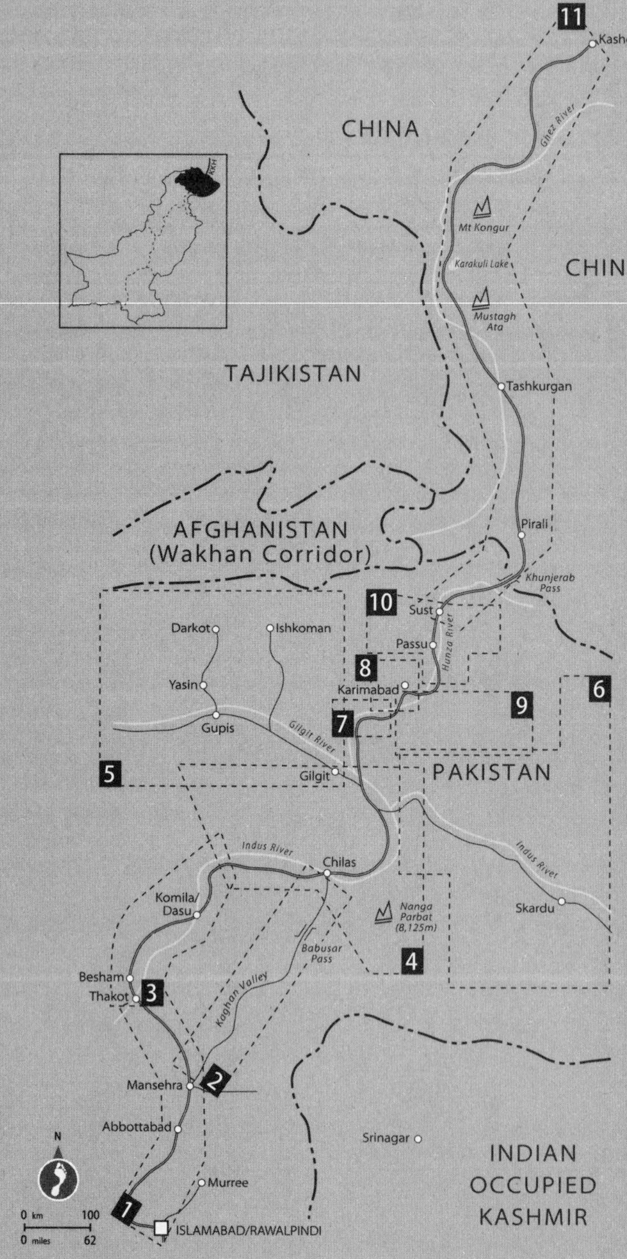

Text Divisions

In the north of Pakistan lie the Northern Areas, a mountainous region containing some of the world's most incredible scenery, a fascinating mixture of different ethnic populations, and some superb trekking and walking routes. The building of a road through the region – the Karakoram Highway – linking Pakistan to China has opened up a spectacular overland route between the two countries, passing through some of Pakistan's most beautiful mountain areas, and providing onward access to Central Asia's historic cities. The opening of this route to foreigners in 1986 has provided adventurous travellers with the opportunity of a unique and exhilarating travel experience. This is the region of Pakistan that is most popular with visitors, and few are disappointed.

Best time to visit *The exact opening and closing times of the Khunjerab Pass between Pakistan and China are weather dependent, though it is officially open from 1 May-30 November. Areas such as Hunza/Nagar are at their best in spring (April) and autumn (October), when the trees are at their most colourful. The main tourist season is June, July, August, September, although July can get very hot in Gilgit and the Indus canyon, and rainy Septembers can lead to landslides and blockages on the KKH. July to September is the main trekking/climbing season.*

Background

On its 1,300 kilometres journey from Islamabad, Pakistan's modern capital on the plains of the Punjab, to Kashgar, the Central Asian market town in China's most westerly province, the **Karakoram Highway** (KKH) threads its way through some of the most dramatic mountain scenery in the world.

As the KKH weaves its way between the peaks, the modern traveller comes across villages and communities that less than a hundred years ago were independent principalities, where the main source of income was relieving passing travellers of their possessions. Nowadays tourism is replacing looting as a key sector of the economy.

Yet the modern day tourist is just the latest in a long line of visitors passing this way. The armies of Alexander the Great, early pilgrims taking Buddhism to China, caravans on a strand of the famous Silk Road, and mysterious explorer-cum-spies playing out the 'Great Game' of imperial rivalry between the Russian and British Empires have all trod this path.

History of the Karakoram Highway

In 1959 work on the Indus Valley Road began. This was to be a 840 kilometres all weather road to link Gilgit to the rest of Pakistan. At Gilgit, the road would join with the old Hunza track making feasible access across the Karakorams to Kashgar. The terrain was so difficult that by 1965 only a natural surface road had been completed.

In 1967, China and Pakistan announced an agreement to build a highway linking Gilgit to Kashgar. Seven battalions of Army Engineers from the Pakistan Army and 10,000 men from the Frontier Works Organisation worked on the road, with heavy machinery having to be airlifted in after construction of improvised airstrips. The road was formally inaugurated on 16 February 1971.

The decision to convert the existing routes into an international highway was taken in 1973. At the peak of construction 25,000 people were at work on the highway, with over 9,000 Chinese employed between Thakot and Hunza alone. The road was fully completed in 1978 and opened to third-country travellers in May 1986. The chief Chinese engineer on the KKH project, stated that "no road any where has been more difficult to build than the Karakoram Highway", and the construction details are impressive: 24 major bridges, 70 smaller ones; 1,708 high class culverts; eight million kilos of dynamite to move 30 million cubic metres of earth and rock; 80 million kilos of cement used; 1,000 trucks consumed in the endeavour; and 400 dead and 314 seriously injured amongst the workforce, although some sources claim that the true figure is significantly higher.

Road Profile: Rawalpindi to Kashgar

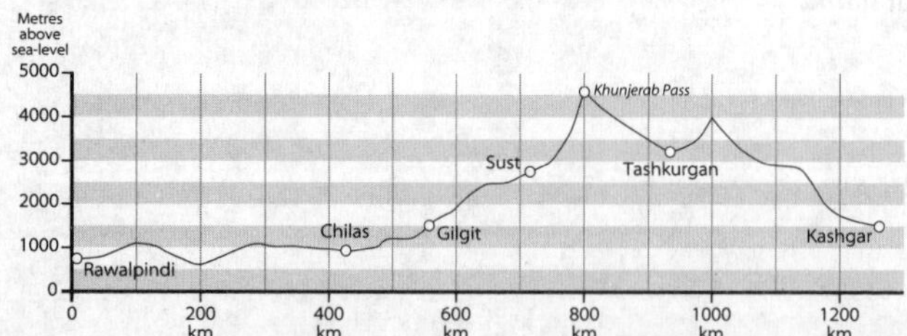

Editorial note

The "KKH and Northern Areas" chapter of the Pakistan Handbook describes a south to north journey along the KKH from Islamabad/Rawalpindi to Kashgar for the simple reason that this is the direction in which most visitors travel (with apologies to those travelling in the opposite direction). Statistics from the Pakistani check post on the border with China suggest that the numbers of foreigners travelling in either direction are roughly the same. However, these figures obviously do not include the large number of visitors who travel along the KKH without continuing their journey into China. Likewise, many visitors arriving from China are in fact 'returnees' who have already travelled through Pakistan, and have just popped up to the Chinese city of Kashgar for a brief visit before returning to Pakistan.

This chapter contains detailed information about all places along the KKH (major and minor), as well as covering the popular excursions off the highway (whether one-day trips or three week treks). Note that in its early stages through Hazara (plus Kaghan Valley excursion) and Kohistan, the KKH is actually passing through North West Frontier Province. Since these regions fall naturally into a journey along the KKH, they are included within this "KKH and Northern Areas" chapter.

So why was the KKH built?

At the time of construction, Pakistani leaders claimed that the KKH would be a "tool in the economic development of the Northern Areas". True, the road has had a major economic and social impact upon the region. Areas that were previously self-sufficient in food are now dependent upon food imports, and the old egalitarian system of land distribution has been disrupted now that land has become a marketable commodity. New technology has come to the area in a variety of forms, and the general opening of the area has encouraged inhabitants to enter the service industries, for example tourism, or to migrate to Pakistani cities in search of employment opportunities. Exposure to new customs and practices has occurred, as contact with foreign tourists and down-country Pakistanis has become more regular, and thus traditional cultures have become more vulnerable to the intrusions of modernity. Further, mountain land use has become a function of access to nearby roads, and thus the settlement pattern of dense nucleated villages has changed to the *strassendorf* model with new structures strung out along the road.

However, border trade with China remains negligible (partly due to the fact that centres of production in both countries are so far away), and despite the 'multiplier effect' that the road has had on these mountain communities, the enormous costs of the road, both in terms of original investment and yearly maintenance costs, could never be rationalized as mere economic development projects. In a similar manner to the period when these northern regions of Pakistan represented the frontiers of British India to be guarded, economic or political development was not the major concern. In fact the economies and societies of areas such as Hunza remained unaffected until the last quarter of this century, and thus when changes did come, they were the result of military and political goals. Therefore, the motivation behind building the Karakoram Highway must be assumed to be political.

The KKH is one of several transmontaine roads built since the 1960s in South Asia that are "manifestations of geopolitical alliances on the mountain landscape" (Allan N.J.R. 1989). China's strongest ties in South Asia are with Pakistan, the KKH being the key piece of Chinese development aid to the

Travel tips

Foreign exchange rates become less favourable the further north along the KKH you travel, so it may be an idea to exchange a reasonable amount into rupees before leaving Islamabad/Rawalpindi.

If you intend travelling as far as Kashgar in China, and then returning to Pakistan, it is advisable to arrange a double-entry Pakistani visa in advance. This is best done when obtaining your initial Pakistani visa, although a single-entry visa can be changed to a double entry visa in Islamabad (see 'Islamabad- useful addresses' for details).

Allow a few 'spare' days for your trip when travelling along the KKH, especially if you have flight connections to make. Although the road crews perform an excellent job, landslides and rock falls can sometimes block the KKH for days (or weeks!). This is particularly likely to happen after rain.

region (the building of the KKH is a relatively inexpensive way for China to deliver economic and military aid to Pakistan). With closening economic and political ties emerging between India and the Soviet Union in the 1960s, as well as American support for India during the Sino-Indian War of 1962, Pakistan increased its efforts to close links with China. The border agreement of 1963 marked improving economic and political relations between Pakistan and China, and the joint collaboration on projects such as the Indus River Road, later the Karakoram Highway, greatly enhanced Pakistan's internal communications. In the same way that China developed transport networks within Xinjiang and Tibet to bring them under central control, Pakistan attempted to integrate the Northern Areas into the fabric of the country.

The government's main programme for the Northern Areas was to establish a network of routes. The constraints of the physical environment meant that for centuries access to peripheral areas of the borderlands was greatly restricted. However, with the perceived proximate danger from India in Kashmir, and the Soviet Union just a short distance away, the construction of routes in the area not only extended central control and lessened the physical distance to the rest of Pakistan, it also contrived, in the form of the Karakoram Highway, to lessen the physical distance to Pakistan's regional ally in China.

In an area that has managed to retain its autonomy for centuries, where inhabitants do not recognize arbitrary borders that intersect their territory, and where 'nation-state' and 'sovereignty' are meaningless concepts, Pakistan desperately needed to integrate the Northern Areas into modern Pakistan. The development of communications infrastructure was the logical way of achieving this.

In terms of practicality the Karakoram Highway is greatly flawed. The nature of the terrain makes it vulnerable to air attack, and should this be successful, as a military supply route there are no terrestrial alternatives (even during peace-time the route is regularly blocked by rock falls and landslides). Being so vulnerable to attack it is not suited to the movement of supplies and troops during a period of war. However, despite this, the perceived potential of the highway in militaristic terms far outweighs its physical ability to deliver, and thus the Karakoram Highway has had a profound effect upon the political manoeuvering in the region.

The changing Northern Areas

The landscape here is dominated by high peaks, rivers, glaciers, plateaux and narrow valleys linked by a network of passes. Historically the political system of the region was one of small kingdoms, with shifting political alliances and boundaries, and dominated by internecinal disputes. The ethnic mix of people in the Northern Areas is reflected in the number and variety of languages and dialects spoken. Indeed, some linguists suggest that the region shows the most intricate pattern of languages in the whole of Pakistan, and in many ways the various groups found in the Northern Areas are largely grouped according to the language that they speak. The key ethnic groups, and the languages and dialects that they speak, are covered in the travelling text as the KKH passes through each individual region.

Despite their perceived isolation (much of which exists only in the minds of tourist brochure writers), the people of the region have always had cultural and commercial links with their neighbours, perhaps best exemplified by the strand of the old Silk Road that passed through the region. In recent years, improved access has brought about a dramatic transformation in the socio-economic structures in place, bringing 'development' but also exposing the vulnerability of traditional systems to the intrusions of modernity.

The most significant recent development in the history of the Northern Areas has probably been the construction of the Karakoram Highway (see above). However, although this has speeded internal communication and helped integrate further the region within the modern state of Pakistan, it is just one of a number of factors that have brought change. It cannot alone account for the socio-economic development, the changing patterns of land use, agricultural practice and settlement patterns that have occurred in recent years. Rapid population growth, increased opportunities in education and government service, labour migration (including both work in the Gulf and down country Pakistan), evolving class structures, are all amongst the dynamic processes that are changing the face of the Northern Areas.

the changing northern areas

Various cultural and social habits which were dictated by environmental constraints have also been eroded. For example, the people of Hunza and Baltistan have abandoned their seasonal raw fruit diet and no longer refrain from cooking during the summer to preserve scarce wood-fuel resources, leading to acute shortages of firewood. However, standards of living have undoubtedly improved, with the spread of schools and hospitals into the remotest areas. Local populations often demand new roads and the benefits they bring, while foreign tourists decry the spoiling of a "paradise", which they often seem to regard as theirs to enjoy.

Development programmes in the region are relatively enlightened, particularly those under the aegis of the Aga Khan Foundation (AKF), such as the Aga Khan Rural Support Programme (AKRSP). Many of their projects encourage local populations to set up village organizations and identify small income generating projects. In return they receive financial and technical assistance from AKRSP. Schemes include land reclamation, irrigation, roads and bridges and training selected village representatives to upgrade their skills in various fields. The programme, involving about 800,000 people, has been particularly successful in involving women. According to a 1986 World Bank report it has "produced outstanding results". The AKF is also highly active with its health (AKHS) and education (AKES) programmes. For further details on the work of the AKF, contact their headquarters at Avenue de la Paix, PO Box 2369, 1211 Geneva 2, Switzerland. For details of the AKRSP locally, see under 'Gilgit'.

The opening of the entire length of the KKH to foreigners has led to a steady flow of tourists along this route. In addition to specialized mountaineering groups, increasing numbers of trekkers, backpackers, and more recently, tour groups are using this route. The government of Pakistan estimate that around 30,000 foreign tourists visit the Northern Areas each year. More and more local people are taking advantage of the income generating opportunities within this sector of the service industry, and it is hoped that a greater percentage of the money spent by tourists on their trip will remain within the Northern Areas (rather than 'leaking out' to tour companies based down country and overseas). There are, however, some concerns about the impact on traditional society of exposure to outside influences (see under 'Central Hunza-Karimabad' for a discussion on varying perceptions of tourism).

Hazara

On the first stage of its journey north from Islamabad/Rawalpindi, the Karakoram Highway (KKH) passes through the district of **Hazara**. This is in fact administratively part of the North West Frontier Province (as is the entire stretch of the KKH up until Shatial, on page 455), though it is dealt with in this 'Karakoram Highway and the Northern Areas' chapter since in practical terms it forms part of the KKH route.

Most visitors only see Hazara through the window of a speeding bus as they head north towards more interesting sections of the KKH (see 'Rawalpindi – Long Distance Buses' for details of bus services from 'Pindi along the KKH). However, those who want to break their journey into more digestible parts may care to stop off in Abbottabad or Mansehra, the latter being the jumping off point for the Kaghan Valley (see following section on page 438).

Land and environment

The leading physical features of Hazara are the mountain ranges that define the boundaries on each side. To the east the main chain is a long ridge of outlying Himalayan spurs that flank the Jhelum and Kunhar rivers, terminating in the hills around Murree. To the northeast, in the Kaghan Valley, another small range marks the boundary between Hazara and Kashmir, and includes the 5,291 metres Malika Parbat. To the west, Hazara is separated from the Swat Valley by the Black Mountains. Between these ranges, the region comprises a series of level tracts of varying size and character. The **geology** of Hazara reflects its position within the area of Himalayan disturbance.

The **climate** of Hazara also shows varied characteristics, with a marked north-south divide in levels of rainfall. Thus, the environment shows marked alterations between the hills and plains, dry soils and moist, and areas of vegetation and barrenness. In the south, the **flora** shows marked similarity to the Punjab, although there is evidence that suggests that prior to environmental change, the region was covered by *chir* forests. The forest tracts of the region are rich in *deodar* and *biar* (blue pine).

History

The ancient name of the region was 'Urasha'; perhaps the 'Uraya' of the *Mahabharata*. The first written account of the district is **Ptolemy**'s description, written at the time of **Alexander's** invasion. The region came under Buddhist rule in the third century BC, and some interesting archaeological sites date from this period, including **Asoka's** Rock Edicts at Mansehra (see below). The region is also mentioned by the seventh century Chinese traveller **Hiuen Tsang**, who referred to the district as the kingdom of *Wu-la-shi*.

The name 'Hazara' is thought to date to the 15th century, following the invasion by the Turkic speaking forces of **Timur** (Tamerlane). The word 'hazara' (thousand) is a translation of the Turkic word *ming*, meaning a regiment of a thousand men. Hazara then came under the control of the **Mughals**, to whom it formed part of the strategic route to Kashmir, but during the decline of their empire it was repeatedly invaded by Pathans from Swat (**Swathis**). In 1752, Hazara eventually came under the control of the Afghan emperor, **Ahmad Shah Durani**.

The **Sikhs** extended their influence into the region at the beginning of the 19th century, and following the conclusion of the First Sikh War in 1846, much to the resentment of the local population the area was ceded to **Gulab Singh** (the Maharaja of Kashmir). In 1847, however, Hazara was transferred to the Lahore Darbar; effectively British rule, and **James Abbott** was appointed as administrator. During the Second Sikh War, the local ruler **Sardar Chattar Singh** was eventually defeated by a predominantly local army headed by Abbott, who was then made Deputy Commissioner of the district. Hazara remained in British hands until independence.

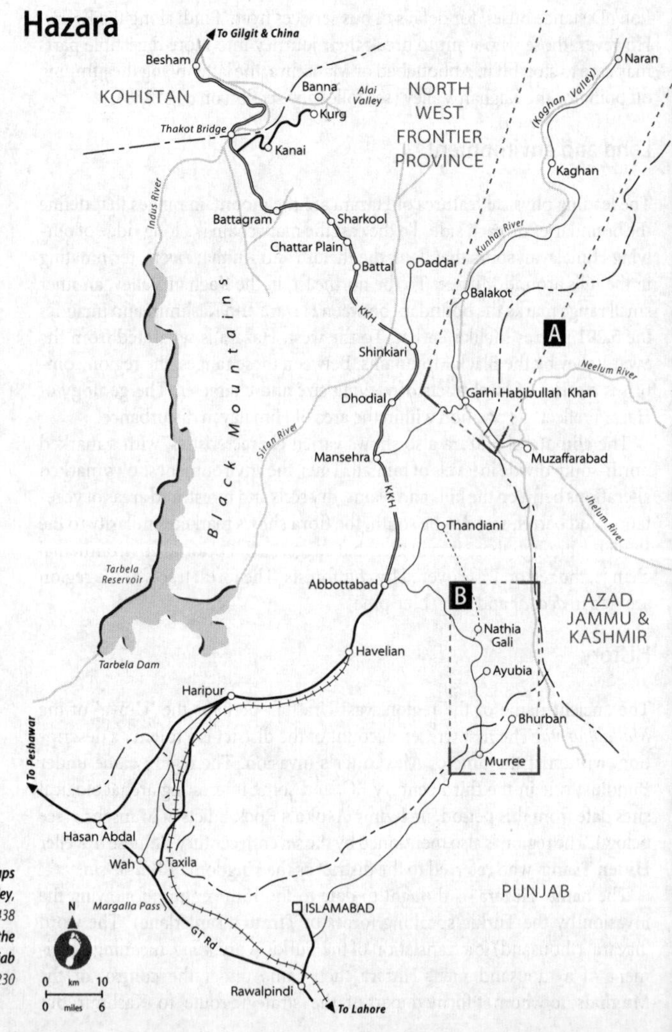

Related maps
A Kaghan Valley, *page 438*
B Murree and the Galis (see Punjab chapter), *page 230*

Culture

There are a number of different tribal groups in the Hazara district, many of whom arrived from the neighbouring valleys within the last 300 years. Most numerous are probably the **Jaduns**, descendants of the Yusufzai Pathans of Swat who migrated to Hazara in the early 17th century. The **Swathis** also share a common background. Other important groups include the **Gakhars**, found predominantly in the south. These traditionally warlike people came to the region with **Mahmud of Ghazni** around 1000 AD, and subsequently fought repeated battles with the Mughals. Another interesting group are the **Mishwanis**, who formed the backbone of Abbott's army in the Second Sikh War. The north of the Kaghan Valley is populated mainly by **Sayyids**, also descendants of the Swathis – the main ethnic group in the lower Kaghan Valley. The oldest inhabitants are probably the **Gujars**, a semi-nomadic group of pasturalists who generally farm lands in the south of the district, and migrate with their flocks in the summer to the northern pastures of the Kaghan Valley, into Swat, and even as far as the Darel and Tangir Valleys near to Chilas.

The main language of Hazara is **Hindko**, a branch of Punjabi, although Pashtu is spoken in the main Pathan areas, and the Gujars have their own language, Gojri.

The start of the Karakoram Highway

Routes

To reach the beginning of the KKH, one must travel west from Islamabad/Rawalpindi on the Peshawar bound GT Road. Having passed through the Margalla Pass, it is possible to turn north either at **Taxila** (31 kilometres), or to continue through **Wah** and turn north at **Hasan Abdal** (16 kilometres). The latter route is quicker, but the former is marginally quieter. Both routes lead to **Haripur** (34 kilometres).

Haripur
Colour map 4, grid A4

Situated in the lush green Dor Valley, **Haripur** (64 kilometres, one hour from Ism) was founded in 1822 by Sardar Hari Singh, one of Ranjit Singh's ablest generals. Just to the east of the town lie the remains of the Harkishangarh Fort, a formidable stronghold built by Hari Singh. Following the building of Abbottabad, Haripur declined in strategic significance, and nowadays is just a small, bustling market town. Haripur is the starting point for visits to the Tarbela Dam (see page 224).

Routes

A further 20 kilometres on is **Havelian**, the terminus for the narrow gauge railway from Taxila, and the official starting point of the Karakoram Highway. Beyond the town the road crosses the Dor River, and then rapidly climbs through denuded hills, before dropping down into **Abbottabad**.

Road Profile: Rawalpindi to Chilas

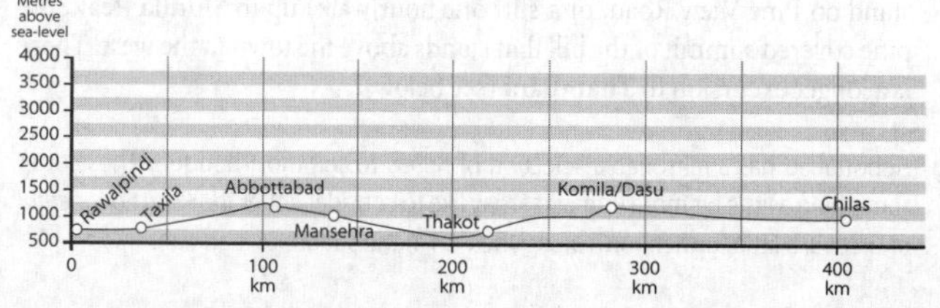

James Abbott

Born in England in 1807, and a schoolfellow of Disraeli, James Abbott received a commission in the Bengal Artillery in 1823 and travelled to India. He later saw action in Afghanistan before being deputed to the 1839 British mission to Khiva. The object of this mission was to effect the release of Russian prisoners and slaves that were being detained by the Khan of Khiva, and despite some resistance (including an incident in which a sabre blow severed 1½ fingers from Abbott's right hand) he was largely successful in negotiating the release of the Russians. He later wrote a lively 2 volume narrative of his adventures.

Upon his return to India, he worked on the survey and demarcation of the boundary between Punjab and Kashmir, and in 1847 became an administrator in Hazara District. When the Second Sikh War broke out the following year, Abbott found allies amongst the Mishwani Pathans of Hazara, and with Colonel John Nicholson, helped defeat the local Sikh ruler Chattar Singh. In 1849 he was appointed the first Deputy Commissioner of Hazara.

Described as "sanguine, chivalrous, warm-hearted and generous", and reputed to be known as Kaka (Uncle) Abbott by local children because of his habit of distributing sweets, Abbott proved to be a good and popular administrator. The local population revered him as their liberator from Sikh and Dogra rule, and it is said that when he left the post in 1853, he was followed to Hasan Abdal by "a weeping and lamenting crowd". It was his successor, Herbert Edwardes, who established the town of Abbottabad.

Abbott retired to the Isle of Wight, and died in 1896.

Abbottabad

Phone code: 0992 (though there is talk of changing it to 05921)
Colour map 5, grid B2

Established in 1853 as a new cantonment town, **Abbottabad** was named after the British soldier turned administrator **James Abbott**. In addition to its role as District Headquarters, Abbottabad has maintained its military tradition, and is today the base of the élite Frontier Force (The 'Piffers'), Baluch Regiment, Army Medical Corps and the Army School of Music. It is also home of some of Pakistan's most prestigious public schools.

Ins and outs

Getting there Abbottabad has several bus stations, plus a number of private coach companies running to a single destination (see 'Transport' below).

Getting around The town is compact enough to walk around, though there are suzuki services to all the outlying spots and short excursion destinations.

Sights

Being less than 150 years old, there is little of historic interest in Abbottabad, although the town does have a relaxed, easy going feel to it. The cantonment area has tree-lined avenues, parks, large bungalows with lush gardens, some old churches, and a morbid Christian cemetery. The bazaar area is crowded, lively and very colourful.

A popular excursion from Abbottabad is to take a minivan (Rs 5 from the stand on Pine View Road, or a stiff one hour walk) up to **Shimla Peak**, the pine covered summit of the hill that stands above the town to the west. There is a longer excursion to **Thandiani** (see below).

Sleeping

Abbottabad has a reasonable selection of hotels to suit most budgets. Those after something a little bit more upmarket may like to consider either the *Pearl Continental* or *Green's*, a little further north along the KKH in the suburb of Mandian.

Abbottabad

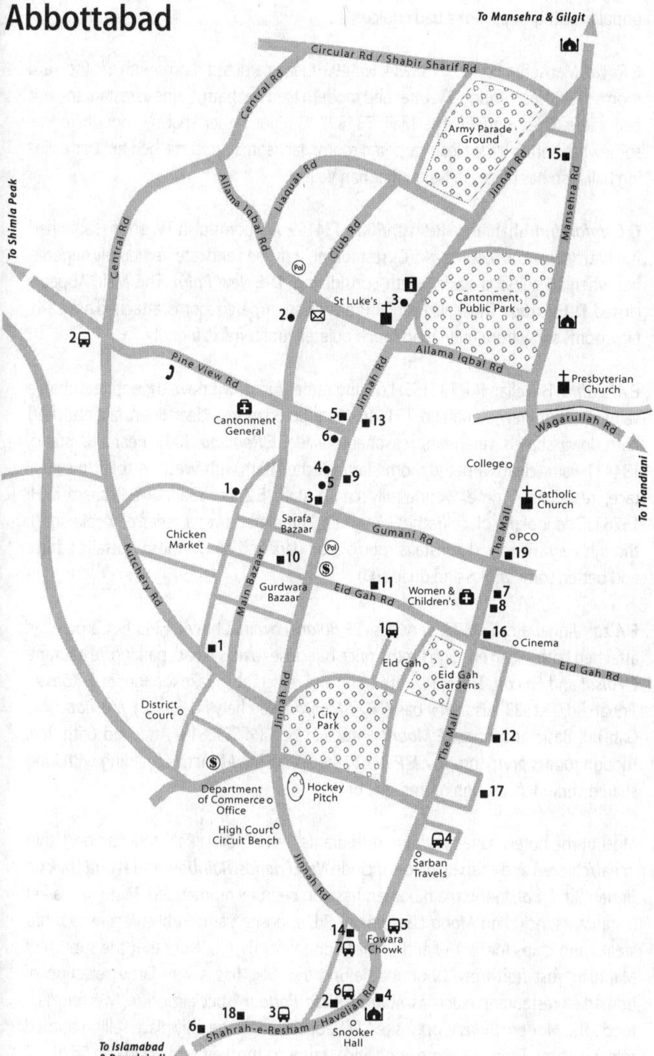

To Mansehra & Gilgit
Circular Rd / Shabir Sharif Rd
Central Rd
Army Parade Ground
Liaquat Rd
Allama Iqbal Rd
Jinnah Rd
Mansehra Rd
15
To Shimla Peak
Club Rd
Central Rd
Cantonment Public Park
St Luke's
3
2
2
Allama Iqbal Rd
Pine View Rd
Presbyterian Church
Cantonment General
Wagarullah Rd
5
13
6
To Thandiani
College
4
9
5
1
3
Catholic Church
Sarafa Bazaar
Gumani Rd
Chicken Market
PCO
The Mall
19
10
Kutchery Rd
Main Bazaar
Gurdwara Bazaar
11
Eid Gah Rd
Women & Children's
7
8
1
16
Cinema
1
Eid Gah
Eid Gah Gardens
Eid Gah Rd
Jinnah Rd
District Court
City Park
12
The Mall
Hockey Pitch
Department of Commerce Office
17
High Court Circuit Bench
4
Sarban Travels
Jinnah Rd
14
5
7
Fowara Chowk
6
2
4
18
3
6
Shahrah-e-Resham / Havelian Rd
Snooker Hall
To Islamabad & Rawalpindi

Sleeping
1 Al Mehran
2 Al-Zahra
3 Alzar
4 Bolan
5 Cantonment View
6 Comfort Inn
7 Faisal
8 Falcon
9 Kohsar
10 Marhaba
11 Mount View
12 New Palm
13 Pines View
14 Ramlina
15 Royal
16 Sarban
17 Springfield
18 Zain
19 Zarbat

Eating
1 Iqbal
2 Modern Bakery
3 Mona Lisa
4 New Friends
5 Rainbow
6 Wood Lock

Buses
1 Main Suzuki Yard
2 Wagons to Shimla Peak
3 General Bus Stand
4 Minibuses to Mansehra
5 Coasters to Lahore
6 Minibuses to Mardan
7 Flying Coaches to Lahore

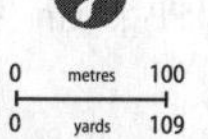

■ on map
Price codes:
see inside front cover

B ***Sarban***, The Mall, T30167, F34436. 3 categories of rooms, 'economy' rooms have fan, phone, attached modern tiled hot bath (**C**), 'deluxe' ground floor rooms slightly larger and with TV, plus a number of rooms with a/c (Rs 300 extra), good restaurant, popular with groups, not a bad choice.

C ***Royal***, Mansehra Rd/KKH, T33234, F34492. Clean carpeted rooms with a/c (non a/c rooms Rs 200 less), fridge, TV, attached modern tiled hot bath, Chinese restaurant, not bad value. **C** ***Springfield***, The Mall, T34397. Exterior rather shabby though rooms somewhat better, large clean carpeted rooms, fan (some a/c), attached hot bath, dining hall, also has places in Naran (Kaghan Valley).

D ***Comfort Inn***, Shahrah-e-Resham/KKH, T34159. All rooms dish TV, phone, attached hot bath (some tubs), some a/c (**C**), restaurant, staff keen and rates extremely negotiable when business is slack, worth considering. **D-E** ***New Palm***, The Mall. Appears closed. **D-E** ***Zarbat***, The Mall, T30608. Pretty clean carpeted rooms, attached hot bath, fan, rooms away from main road much quieter, roof terrace, friendly.

E ***Al-Zahra***, Havelian Rd, T30155. Looking rather run down now, though reasonable value; **E** ***Cantt View***, Jinnah Rd, T31346. 12 carpeted rooms, clean linen, fan, attached bath, long shared verandah, reasonable value. **E** ***Ramlina***, KKH, near bus stand, T34431. Fairly clean carpeted rooms, fan, attached bath with 'western' toilet, nice terrace, restaurant, some wonderfully camp staff. **E** ***Zain***, Shahrah-e-Resham/KKH, T5763. Odd looking place (rather jerry-built, completed over a series of weekends?), though very friendly, downstairs rooms a bit dark and dingy, those upstairs lighter and better, some triples and quads (**D**).

F ***Alzar***, Jinnah Rd, T31672. Very basic. **F** ***Bolan***, Fowara Chowk, T34395. Carpet, fan, attached bath, clean enough for the price but close to noisy road, parking, restaurant. **F** ***Faisal*** and ***Falcon***, The Mall. Both basic and reluctant to take foreigners. **F** ***Kohsar***, Jinnah Rd, T31583. Also fairly basic. **F** ***Al-Mehran***, Kutchery Rd. Basic. **F** ***Marhaba***, Eid Gah Rd. Basic and noisy. **F** ***Mount View***, Eid Gah Rd, T30818. Attached bath, fan, though rooms pretty grubby. **F** ***Pines View***, Jinnah Rd. Attractive building with long shared verandah, though rooms very basic.

Eating
● on map

Most of the hotels have their own restaurants, serving basic Pakistani cuisine. Other 'meat/chicken and chapati' places include ***New Friends***, ***Rainbow*** and ***Wood Lock*** on Jinnah Rd. ***Iqbal***, in the main bazaar, has also been recommended. More upmarket restaurants including ***Mona Lisa***, Jinnah Rd, opposite Cantt Public Park, which has steaks and chips for Rs 150 and Chinese dishes for Rs 100. Note that the suburb of Mandian, just north of Abbottabad along the KKH, has a very large selection of upmarket restaurants such as ***Milano Pizza Parlour***, specializing in 'western/fast food'. The ***Modern Bakery***, opposite GPO, appears to be the only place selling bottled mineral water. There are some good juice stands on the west end of Eid Gah Rd (Rs 12 for 0.5 litre, specify if you don't want ice).

Local transport

Local buses Local transport is provided mainly by suzuki wagons. The main suzuki yard is on Eid Gah Rd, providing services to local villages and up and down The Mall. There are also wagons from here to **Thandiani** (Rs 15, 1 hour). Wagons up to **Shimla Peak** run from the stand at the junction of Pine View Rd/Central Rd.

Long distance transport

Air At the time of going to press, the much heralded (but effectively inconsequential) daily helicopter service to/from **Islamabad** set up by the previous PPP government was not flying. Check with PIA (fare around Rs 1,200 one way).

Long distance buses The completely chaotic **General Bus Stand** on the KKH to the south of town has services to **Rawalpindi** (and beyond, including **Lahore**), **Peshawar, Mansehra** (2 hours), **Murree** (5-6 hours) and **Muzaffarabad** (4 hours) on a 'depart when full' basis, though you're better off using the private services. From the square in front of *Sarban Travels* (Iqbal Shopping Complex), minibuses depart when full to **Mansehra** (Rs 15, 1 hour). A small yard opposite Fowara Chowk has coasters running to **Lahore** (Rs 190, 8-9 hours), T6313398. The small yard in front of the *Hotel Al-Zahra* has minibuses to **Mardan**. Just next to the *Ramlina Hotel* is the office of a company offering 'flying coaches' to **Lahore** (T5238/34431, 0800 0900 1000 1300 2100 2200, Rs 140, 8-9 hours).

For destinations in the **Kaghan Valley** go to Mansehra and change. Both government and private services from Rawalpindi to **Gilgit** pass through Abbottabad, though they are difficult to flag down and are usually full. To get to Gilgit you usually need to change at Mansehra and then at Besham.

Directory

Banks There are several banks in Abbottabad, but changing money can be problematic. ***Muslim Commercial Bank*** on Eid Gah Rd, deals only in US dollars (cash and TCs, not good rates), whilst the ***National Bank of Pakistan*** next door offers no foreign exchange. The *main* ***National Bank of Pakistan*** near to the courts claims to offer foreign exchange, though this isn't guaranteed. **Communications** GPO: is at the junction of Club Rd and Allama Iqbal Rd. **Telephones:** the main telephone office (for international and local calls) is on Pine View Rd. There are PCOs on The Mall and in the Main Bazaar. **Hospitals & medical services** **Chemists:** most of the chemists are located opposite the various hospitals. **Hospitals:** ***Cantt General***, Pines View Rd. ***Women and Children's Hospital***, The Mall (according to a recent newspaper report, this hospital has one of the worst maternal mortality rates in the country). Your best bet is the huge, modern ***Ayub Hospital and Medical Complex*** in Mandian, several kilometres north of Abbottabad along the KKH. **Places of worship** *Catholic* and *Presbyterian* churches are on The Mall, St Luke's *Protestant* church is at Jinnah Rd/Allama Iqbal Rd. **Tour companies & travel agents** ***Sarban Travels***, Iqbal Shopping Complex, The Mall, T5011. Handles tickets for ***PIA***, ***Aero Asia*** and ***Shaheen***. **Tourist offices** ***PTDC***, Jinnah Rd, opposite Cantonment Public Park, T34399. Has a few general brochures on Pakistan, but not much else (Mon-Thur and Sat 0900-1500, Fri 0900-1300, Sun closed). **Useful addresses and phone numbers** **Police:** T15 or T4165. **Fire:** T6289. ***Conservator of Forests***, Jail Rd, T30728/30893. May assist in booking the *Resthouses* at Thandiani and in the Kaghan Valley.

Excursion from Abbottabad

Thandiani

The most northerly of the Galis chain of hill-stations, **Thandiani** is currently reachable by sealed road only from Abbottabad. The winding road climbs the 26 kilometres (one hour) from Abbottabad through fragrant pine forests (take a suzuki from the stand on Eid Gah Road, though ascertain whether it is a regular 'service' or a 'special'). At the summit, a group of shacks serve as restaurants/hotels, including **E** *Green Hills* and **E** *Shalimar*. Some have small one or two bedroom sheds attached, but unless you bargain very hard, they are vastly over priced. The *Shalimar* is clean, with an attached toilet (hole in floor), but ludicrously priced at Rs 300.

The road at the summit forks left, past St Saviour's Church to **D-E** *Far Pavillions* (500 metres downhill). There are two pleasant cottages, a restaurant, plus plenty of camping space on the attractive lawns.

Further along the ridge from the *Shalimar* is the *C&W Inspection Bungalow*, and some fine walks through shady pine forest. A shingle (jeepable) road is being built to **Nathia Gali**, although at present the journey can only be done as a two day hike. There are *Resthouses* enroute at Biran Gali (1,920 metres) and Palakot (2,720 metres). The Asian Study Group (see under 'Islamabad') have produced a route map of the walk.

Routes The KKH continues north from Abbottabad, through the satellite settlement of Sikanderabad, and passing the impressive new Ayub Hospital and Medical Complex in Mandian. There are several hotels on the KKH here, including the **A-B** *Pearl Continental*, **B** *Green's* and **C** *Paradise*.

The KKH itself actually by-passes **Mansehra** (26 kilometres), although two link roads run up into the town. The southern road turns off next to the large **D** *Karakuram Hotel*, and the second road turns off next to **Asoka's Sacred Rocks**. The main bus terminus is 2 kilometres north of Mansehra, on the KKH itself.

Mansehra

Phone code: 0987
Colour map 5, grid B2

Prior to Partition and the unnatural division of Kashmir, **Mansehra** developed as a trading centre on the route to Srinagar, and as a Sikh garrison town. Despite being by-passed by the KKH, the town remains an important transport junction between Muzaffarabad in Azad Kashmir, the Kaghan Valley and points north along the KKH.

Mansehra's main attraction are **Asoka's Rock Edicts**, which date from the third century AD. Inscribed on three large boulders adjacent to the KKH (and now protected by modern roof structures), the edicts give King Priyadarsin's (Asoka) opinions on 'merits of piety', 'prompt dispatch of business', 'true glory', and vegetarianism, amongst other things. However, the *Kharaoshthi* script is so weather-beaten as to be all but invisible.

There are still remains of the Sikh occupation of the town, including a relatively recent Gurdwara (temple) that now serves as the police station, but the old fort has virtually disappeared under the new prison.

Mansehra has a large Afghan refugee population, many of whom speak good English and are keen to engage you in conversation.

Ins and outs Though there is a small bus stand in the town itself, most visitors will either be dropped off down on the KKH just below Mansehra, or at the main bus stand 2 kilometres further along the KKH from the town. Wagons run from the bus station up to Mansehra, though the town is compact enough to explore on foot.

Diversion From Mansehra it is possible to make a diversion to the beautiful **Kaghan Valley** (see page 438). Not only does this trip offer some of Pakistan's most attractive alpine scenery, it also offers a challenging alternative route north, across the **Babusar Pass**, rejoining the KKH at Chilas (see page 457).

Sleeping
■ *on map*
Price codes: see inside front cover

C-D *Karakuram*, KKH just south of Mansehra, T38276. Fairly modern rooms, reasonable value if you possess good negotiating skills, though some distance from town centre and bus stand.

E *Errum*, Shinkiari Rd, T36245. Good value clean carpeted rooms, attached hot bath, good restaurant, friendly, best deal in town. Recommended. **E** *Parbat*, Kashmir Rd, T36979. Simple rooms, fan, attached bath, clean enough, restaurant, this used to be a really good place but has gone downhill somewhat.

F *Al-Junaid*, Kashmir Rd. Basic. **F** *Al-Naz*, Abbottabad Rd. Very basic, reluctant to take foreigners. **F** *Batgram*, Kashmir Bazaar. Extremely basic. **F** *Taj Mahal*, Abbottabad Rd, T2096. Very basic, not really geared up for foreigners. **F** *Zamzam*, Shinkiari Rd, T2127. Small rooms but clean enough, basic but clean attached bath, some cheaper rooms with shared bath, breezy verandah, popular restaurant, good value. Recommended.

Eating
● *on map*

Most of the hotels have their own restaurants. Other basic 'meat and chapati' places include ***Ayaz*** on Shinkiari Rd, and a number of Afghan-run places on Abbottabad Rd. The ***Faqir Bakery*** on Shinkiari Rd appears to be the only place in town that sells bottled mineral water.

Local transport

Local buses Suzukis and pick-ups run from the stand next to the Caltex service station on Shinkiari Rd to the Main Bus Stand down on the KKH (Rs 4). There is also a small minibus yard on Abbottabad Rd which has services to **Abbottabad**, **Haripur** and occasionally **Rawalpindi**, though your best bet is to go to the Main Bus Stand down on the KKH.

Mansehra

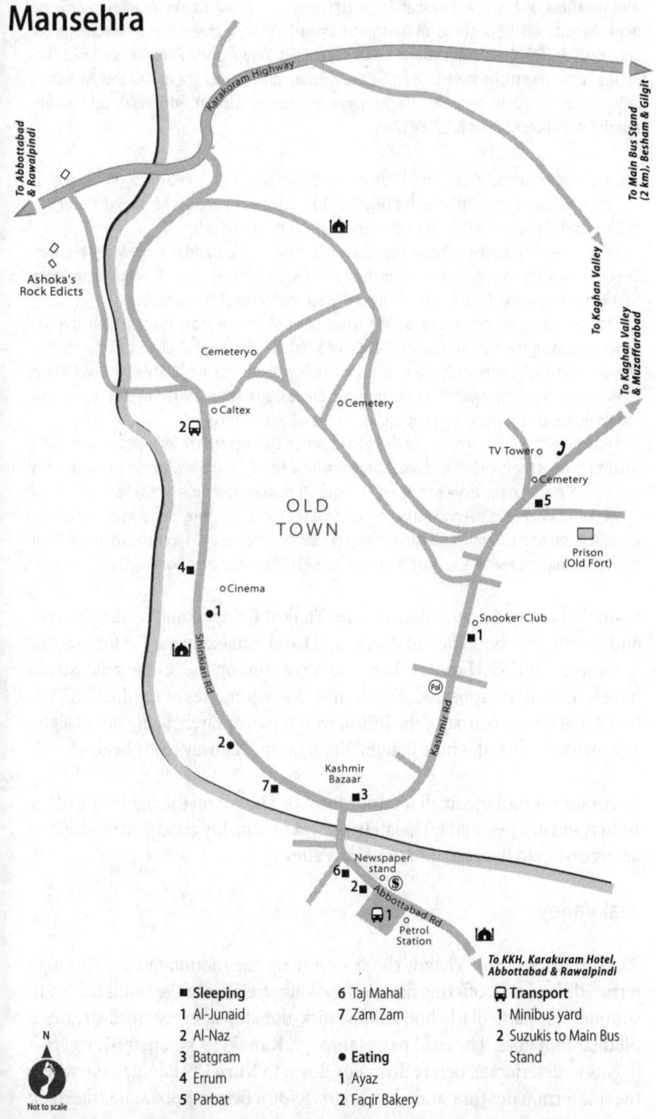

■ **Sleeping**
1 Al-Junaid
2 Al-Naz
3 Batgram
4 Errum
5 Parbat
6 Taj Mahal
7 Zam Zam

● **Eating**
1 Ayaz
2 Faqir Bakery

Transport
1 Minibus yard
2 Suzukis to Main Bus Stand

Long distance transport

Long distance buses The chaotic Main Bus Stand is down on the KKH, about 2 kilometres from Mansehra itself. Almost all the services operate on a 'depart when full' basis. Your best bet is to shout out your destination, then allow yourself to be guided to the relevant stand. There are services to **Abbottabad** (Rs 15, 1 hour), **Besham** (Rs 45, 3-4 hours), **Islamabad/Rawalpindi** (Rs 45, 3-4 hours), **Muzaffarabad** (Rs 30, 2 hours). There are no direct services to **Gilgit**, and the buses coming through from Rawalpindi tend to be full. Your best bet is to go to Besham and change. This is also a major transit point for the **Kaghan Valley**, with minibuses to **Balakot** (Rs 20, 1½ hours), though most go all the way through to **Naran** (Rs 85, 6 hours). Around (and opposite) the Main Bus Stand are various private 'Flying Coach' companies, offering buses to **Lahore** (Rs 170, 9-10 hours) and even **Karachi** (Rs 375, 30 hours+).

Directory

Airline offices *PIA*, is on Abbottabad Rd (just off the map), T36747. **Banks** *Muslim Commercial Bank*, Abbottabad Rd, opposite minibus stand. Open 0900-1230, closed Sun, will exchange US$ only (cash or TCs). **Communications** GPO: Kashmir Rd. **Telephones:** *Paktel*, Kashmir Rd (look for the communications tower). Open 0800-2000, has efficient and cheap IDD and fax (phone charge plus Rs 10 to send, Rs 10 per page to receive). **Useful addresses and phone numbers** Police: Kashmir Rd, T36812.

Routes

Beyond Mansehra the Karakoram Highway gradually begins to climb through a series of switchbacks, passing the settlement of **Dhodial** (10 kilometres), and crossing the Siran River near to **Shinkiari** (16 kilometres). There is the very basic **F** *Dubai Hotel* here.

From here it is possible to follow the course of the river up to **Daddar**, from where there are fine views of Bhogarmang Peak (4,945 metres) in the Kaghan Valley. The KKH winds up to **Battal** (20 kilometres), beyond which is the modest **E** *Green Valley Hotel* (5 kilometres).

The KKH proceeds north through the fertile bowl of Chattar Plain (named after the Sikh general), passing the accommodating **C-D** *Green's Hotel* at **Sharkool** (7 kilometres from Battal). There is also the former *PTDC Motel* here, now privately run as the **C-D** *Affaq Hotel Motel*, T0987-36314 (ext 106), which is a little run down but reasonable value ("rooms close to the road should be avoided as trucks grind up and down the hill in bottom gear").

From here, the KKH continues to the small town of **Battagram** (14 kilometres). Just to the south of town is the impressive new **C** *Battagram View Hotel*, T310194, with some more modest and basic **F** places in the main bazaar, eg *Al-Faqur*, *Al-Kaman*, *Jeddah*, and *Khyber*.

About 12 kilometres beyond Battagram is a small police post, where transport heading north at night is sometimes formed up into convoys (for safety). The next 10 kilometres of the KKH run through a notorious 'slide area' that frequently causes delays after even light rain.

Thakot Bridge

Colour map 5, grid B2

Some 21 kilometres from Battagram is **Thakot Bridge**, built by the Chinese, and marking the boundary of Hazara and **Kohistan** (see page 448 for the continuation of the KKH route). The decorative lions on the bridge's balustrade have long since disappeared. For the next 350 kilometres or so, the KKH virtually follows the course of the Indus, with the river rarely being out of sight. For many visitors, it is here that the Karakoram Highway really begins.

Excursion From the small roadside town of **Thakot** on the right bank of the Indus (and just before the Thakot Bridge), a reasonably good jeep road allows an excursion to the east, into the **Alai Valley**.

Alai Valley

Pick-up trucks from Thakot climb steeply up the mountain road, through terraced rice fields, offering fine views of long stretches of the Indus below. In summer it is particularly hot, and the pick-ups stop at every small stream to fill their radiators. The road passes through **Kanai** (19 kilometres), where it begins to deteriorate, before dropping down to **Kurg** (29 kilometres), where the ride terminates (one and a half hours, Rs 30). Below the bazaar is the main

Anyone for tea?

Despite previous attempts, Pakistan does not produce a single gram of black tea, resulting in foreign exchange expenditure on tea imports exceeding $200 million per year. Thus, Lever Brothers Pakistan Ltd have recently initiated a project in Shinkiari to establish the commercial feasibility of growing tea in Pakistan. The National Tea Research Institute is on the KKH just to the south of the town.

village, a cluster of square, flat-roofed houses near to the Alai River. A partially damaged bridge crosses the river to **Banna**, a newer settlement of mainly breeze-block and tin roof buildings.

Although this is one of the few valleys off the KKH that it is possible to visit, you should ask yourself if it is really necessary to come here. If you are conservatively dressed, you will probably be cordially greeted, but you should bear in mind that the valley's traditional Pathan residents certainly don't invite outsiders into their community. You should not proceed beyond Banna without the support of the former Nawab, and now MNA, Ayub Khan. Nevertheless, the Alai Valley can certainly boast some of the finest henna beards in the whole of Pakistan.

NB To continue the KKH route, turn to page 448.

Kaghan Valley

In a country of outstanding natural beauty, the Kaghan Valley must rank as one of Pakistan's most scenic areas. The 161 kilometres long valley offers fresh alpine forests, deep blue high altitude lakes, lush green meadows, and distant snowy peaks. The Kunhar River that flows through the valley, meanwhile, provides some of the best trout fishing in Pakistan.

Though administratively part of North West Frontier Province, the Kaghan Valley is best visited as an excursion off the KKH and is thus included within the 'Karakoram Highway and Northern Areas' chapter.

Best time to visit During the winter months (November-March), heavy snowfall means that it is generally impossible to go any further north than Kaghan village. The Babusar Pass is usually only open to jeeps from July until early September, although it is possible to cross on foot a little before and after these dates. The

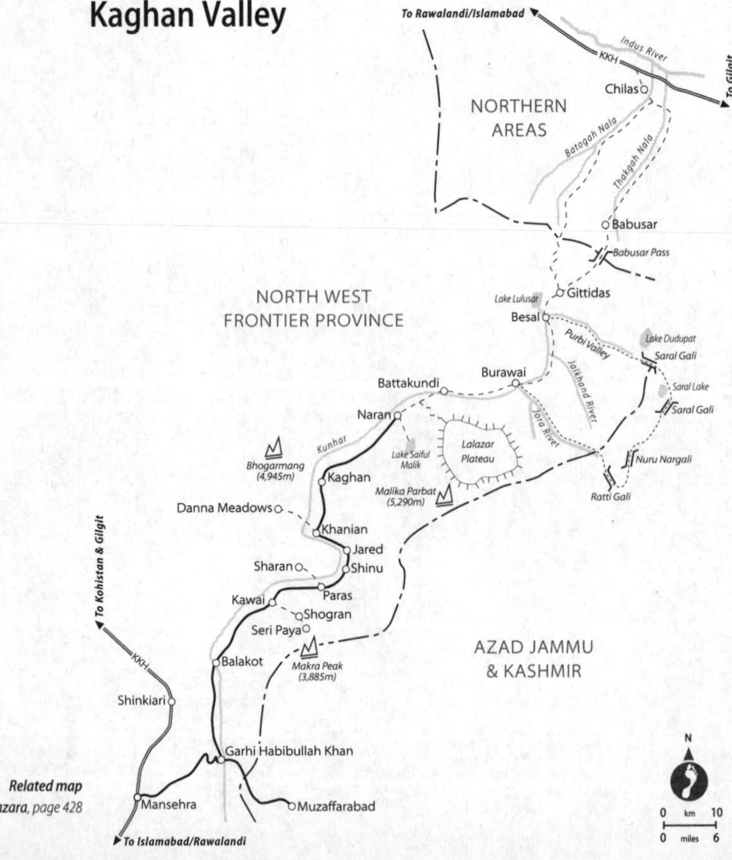

Related map
Hazara, page 428

summer months, May, June and July, show the Kaghan Valley at its best, allowing an escape from the heat of the Punjab plains, although the valley is more crowded with visitors. Late July sees the onset of the monsoon. Autumn can be pleasant, though cold at night.

Ins and outs

There are 2 entrances/exits to the Kaghan Valley. The easiest (and most popular) entry/exit is through Garhi Habibullah Khan at the south end of the valley (usually reached via Mansehra and the KKH). The more adventurous entry/exit to the valley is via the Babusar Pass to the north. This route is weather dependent (see 'best time to visit' above), as well as being extremely challenging. The stretch between Babusar Pass and Chilas (in the Northern Areas) is poorly served by public transport, as well as passing through a potentially dangerous area. For those planning a trip between Islamabad/Rawalpindi and Gilgit (whether travelling north-south or south-north), travelling via the Kaghan Valley provides a more interesting (though more difficult) route than the section of the KKH between Mansehra and Chilas.

Sleeping As with other regions that are popular with Pakistani tourists (eg Murree and Swat), hotel prices in the Kaghan Valley tend to inflate in the high season, at weekends, and when the manager feels like it. It is worth bargaining at any time, though particularly out of season. If you wish to stay in the better hotels at peak times, advance booking is recommended.

Routes

The gateway to the south end of the Kaghan Valley is **Balakot**, which can be reached in 2½ hours from Abbottabad on a good quality winding road. The road passes the bridge at **Garhi Habibullah Khan**, the junction for Muzaffarabad in Azad Kashmir.

Balakot

Phone codes: 0985/0982
Colour map 5, grid B3

There is little of interest in Balakot itself, although the town was the scene of an important battle between the Sikhs and Muslims in 1831. Ahmed Shah Bereli, leader of the Muslim forces, is buried in the small green-tiled tomb down by the river. Those pushed for time may care to stop at more interesting and attractive places in the Kaghan Valley.

Sleeping & eating

■ *on map*
Price codes: see inside front cover

B *(New) Pine Park*. Under construction in 1998, looks very grand, impressive views of unattractive Balakot below.

C *Gateway*, T210591, F210593. Large, clean carpeted rooms, fan, TV, attached tiled bath, breezy garden, restaurant, rather dozy staff, overpriced. **C *PTDC Motel***, T210208. Spacious rooms with shared terrace, set in nice garden, restaurant, reasonable value, tourist info is based here along with a jeep hire service (see below), will also make bookings for *PTDC Motel* in Naran and *Pine Park Hotel* in Shogram.

D *(Old) Pine Park*, T210544. Good views, rooms rather smelly, attached tiled hot bath, public spaces very run down (balconies to the point of being dangerous), this building will almost certainly be abandoned when the 'new' *Pine Park Hotel* is finished. **D *Taj Mahal***, T210321. Carpet, fan, attached bath, rooms are cleaner than the rest of the building, restaurant, overpriced.

E *Balakot*, T210482. Clean carpeted rooms, attached bath, rooms a little dark and hot, uninspiring restaurant. **E *Koh-i-Toor***, T210263. Carpeted rooms, attached bath, those upstairs are better. **E *Kunhar View***, T210229. Small, dark overpriced rooms. **E *Lahore***,

T210031. Simple rooms, clean sheets, basic attached bath, rooms not very private, restaurant. **E** *Paradise*, T210391. Large, fairly clean rooms, fan, carpet, attached bath (some with hot water), upstairs rooms lighter and airier, restaurant, not a bad deal. **F** *Valley View*, T210505. Prices according to floor, but all rather noisy, building run-down.

F *Lalazar* and *Nazir* are both very basic, and reluctant to take foreigners (no English signs). **F** *Mashriq*. Sleazy, noisy, overpriced rooms with shared bath.

Local transport

Car/jeep hire Almost all the hotels offer jeep hire, or you can negotiate your own deal at the jeep yard at the north end of the main road. The official PTDC rates are as follows: Balakot to Naran Rs 1,000 one-way; Balakot to Shogran Rs 700 return; Naran to Lake Saiful Malik Rs 600 return; Naran to Lalazar Plateau Rs 700 return; Balakot to Chilas Rs 6,000 one-way. Similar trips booked through a hotel manager may be marginally cheaper.

Long distance transport

Long distance buses The jeep and minibus yard is at the north end of town (see above for jeep hire deals). The 2 key services are minibuses north to **Naran** (Rs 65, 4-5 hours) and south to **Mansehra** (Rs 20, 1½ hours), both of which 'depart when full'. Occasionally a minibus will head south as far as Abbottabad or even Rawalpindi, though usually you must change at Mansehra.

Directory

Communications Old 3 digit telephone numbers are now pre-fixed by 210. **GPO:** south of the *PTDC Motel*. **Telephones:** *Pak Telecom* is located next to the *Lalazar Hotel*. There is also a PCO just to the north. **Tourist offices** *PTDC* have an office at the *PTDC Motel*, and can arrange jeep hire throughout the Kaghan Valley (and beyond). For rates see 'Transport' above. Short trips are also

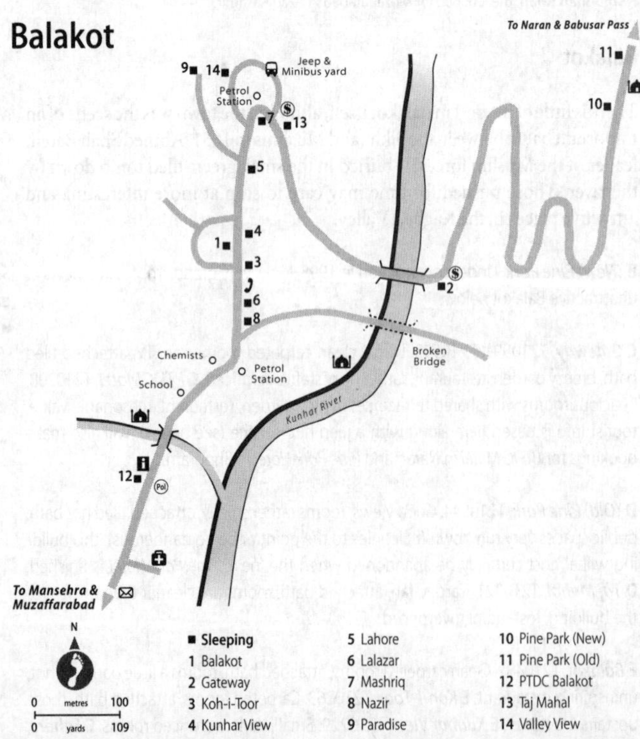

organized: 2 day-1 night tour from Balakot to Naran, Shogran, Seri Paya, and return to Balakot is Rs 3,400; 3 day-2 night trip from Balakot to Shogran, Seri Paya, Lake Saiful Malik, Lalazar Plateau, return to Balakot is Rs 4,300; same trip but 4 days-3 nights is Rs 4,500; Naran to Babusar Top, return to Naran is Rs 2,500. **Useful addresses** **Police:** opposite *PTDC Motel*.

Routes

The road north is currently in a fairly poor state of repair, though it is undergoing upgrading work. From Balakot, the road up the Kaghan Valley climbs quite rapidly, high above the Kunhar River. This very scenic route winds its way to **Kawai** (24 kilometres, 1 hour), a small, beautifully located settlement (though some of the tranquillity has been lost with the basing here of a large FWD road repair camp). Kawai (1,463 metres) is the junction for the jeep track up to the resort of **Shogran**. The recently built **E** *Faisal Hotel* is rather nice, and the **F** *Tourist Hotel* is very good value. Jeeps run the 10 kilometres up the old logging track to Shogran (Rs 200 hire, negotiable), although for those who want to walk, there is a shorter, but very steep, footpath (the manager at the hotel can point you in the right direction).

Shogran

Shogran (2,362 metres) is one of the loveliest locations in the Kaghan Valley, and despite recent hotel construction, remains remarkably unspoilt. Indeed, for many visiting Pakistanis it is the *Pine Park Resort* itself that offers the greatest attraction! The views from Shogran, however, are unsurpassed, especially if you walk up for two hours through the forest to the high summer pastures at **Seri Paya**. The camping here is superb. To the south are views of Makra Peak (3,885 metres), whilst to the north is **Malika Parbat** (5,291 metres), the highest mountain in the Kaghan Valley. The peak was first climbed in 1890 by CG Bruce, and then by the north face by Capt BW Battye in 1920. More sedate visitors prefer to wander through the fragrant pine forest or stroll through the flowers in the lush green meadow.

Sleeping & eating

L-A-B-C *Pine Park Resort*. Open April-December. Main block (double rooms), **B.** Swiss Cottages (1 double room), **A**; Pine Villas (2 double rooms), **L.** Double VIP Suite (2 double rooms and sitting room), **L.** Sin VIP Suite (1 double room and sitting room), **A**. Tourist block (double rooms), **C**. Pakistan and Chinese restaurant, souvenir shop, car rental, excursions arranged, large garden. **C** *Lalazar*. A large cottage, with 4 rooms opening onto a communal lounge, kitchen, fine views. **D** *Faisal*. Rather expensive,restaurant. **E** *Punjab Hazara*. Basic and grossly overpriced.

Routes

The road from Kawai continues high above the east bank of the Kunhar River, before passing through **Paras** (1½ hours from Balakot). On public transport this is generally a chai-stop, although it may be possible to stay overnight on a charpoy at the **F** *Bismillah Hotel* if desperate. A slightly better bet is the reasonable, new **E** *Green Park Hotel*.

Beyond Paras the road drops down to the valley bottom, adjacent to the river. Jeep tracks turns off right for Malakandi and Shogram, and left for **Sharan** (16 kilometres), set in deep forest. A *Youth Hostel* here is currently being renovated.

The next small settlement is Fareedabad, and then **Shinu**, with its trout hatchery, before the road again climbs above the valley floor. A narrow bridge crosses a tributary of the Kunhar River at the miserable little settlement of **Mahandri** (46 kilometres from Balakot), and the road then continues to **Khanian**. *Pine Parks* have a **B** category hotel here that is used to serve as a transit stop on the way to **Danna Meadows**. You can't miss its unattractive red pagoda-style roof. Approachable by a jeep road one hour west of Khanian, Danna is situated in a remote side valley, surrounded by virgin forest, and set in the shadow of Bhogarmang Peak (4,945 metres). It is well worth the effort of getting here.

A further 5 kilometres beyond Khanian is the settlement of **Kaghan**.

Kaghan

This settlement (2,038 metres) gives its name to the whole valley, and is the most northerly point that you can generally reach in winter. During the rest of the year, most visitors continue on to **Naran** (24 kilometres). The valley's main civil hospital is located here. Accommodation is available in Kaghan at the **D** *Lalazar Hotel*, which also has a Chinese restaurant offering 'seafood'! Cheaper options include the **E** *Vershigroom Hotel*, plus some very basic **F** places. On the road leading out of Kaghan is a stand selling 'pure honey'.

Naran

Phone code: 0985 (though some sources give it as 05981)
Colour map 5, grid B3

The centre-piece of the tourism industry in Kaghan Valley, Naran is a combination of stunning scenery and haphazard, unplanned development. The location is beautiful, but the main bazaar is a jumble of unattractive hotels, restaurants and numerous 'handicraft' shops. However, the views are excellent, and a 10 minute walk in any direction from the town centre will lead you to peace and tranquillity. NB The majority of tourists here are groups of young Punjabi men, and visiting foreign women often have to put up with persistent verbal harassment and childish jibes.

Sights

Lake Saiful Malik

Naran's prime attraction is **Saiful Malik Lake**, 10 kilometres to the east. Located at an altitude of 3,215 metres and ringed by an amphitheatre of snow-capped mountains, large blocks of ice can often be seen floating on the sapphire waters. The lake is delightful in summer, when the meadows of alpine flowers are in bloom and the water is reflecting the peak of **Malika Parbat**. It is absolutely de rigeur for visiting Punjabis to be photographed here, preferably with a Westerner also in the shot. Sadly, it also seems de rigeur to scatter as many empty biscuit packets, drink cartons and general litter over as wide a space around the lake as possible. All foreign tourists seem to comment on the nonchalance with which visiting Pakistani's litter this spot (Dave Winter has even overheard Pakistanis saying that the littering is "the government's fault"!). Local legends speak of princes, fairies and jealous demons who visit the lake at night to dance and bathe. Woe betide any mortal who encounters them.

The lake can be reached in a stiff three hour climb from Naran, or by hired jeep (generally Rs 600 return, though this price has been the same for the past three years, and thus must surely increase soon), although the drive across the glacier is exhilarating/petrifying. The lake is impossibly crowded on Friday, Saturday and holidays. There are a number of small snack and cold drinks stalls at the lake, and horses and ponies can be hired. **NB** If you only plan a 20 minute or so stay at the lake, it is possible to hire a jeep late in the afternoon for just Rs 400 (though rushing like this rather defeats the object of visiting such an attractive spot).

Lalazar Plateau

Another pleasant half-day jeep excursion from Naran is up to the **Lalazar Plateau**. A jeep track climbs up to the plateau from Battakundi, some 16 kilometres north of Naran. Located at 3,200 metres, this beautiful meadow is awash with colourful alpine flowers in spring and summer, and set amongst the cool pine forests. A footpath leads from Lalazar Plateau down to Lake Saiful Malik, taking five to six hours. The return jeep trip from Naran costs Rs 700 per vehicle, though this price has been static for at least the last three years and thus must surely increase soon.

Fishing

Kaghan Valley has some of Pakistan's best trout fishing, and there are six authorised reaches in the Naran locality. Permits are available from the NWFP Fisheries Dept Fisheries Office and Trout Hatchery in Naran (Rs 100), just to the right of the path up to Saiful Malik. Several of the shops offer rod hire (Rs 100 per day), as well as offering 'fishing guide' services (Rs 400) and lessons (Rs 100).

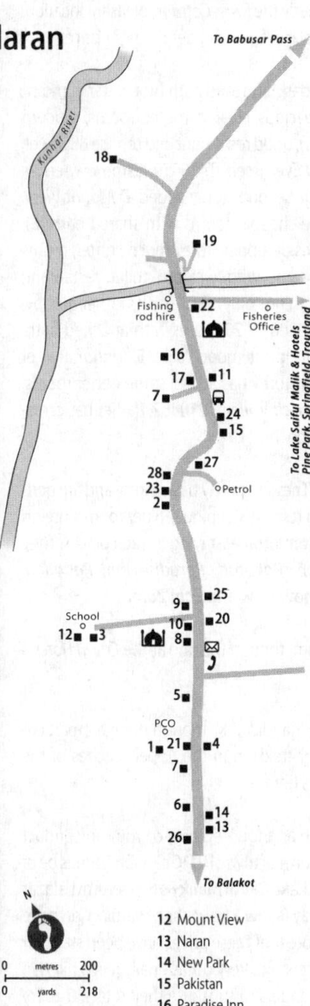

Essentials

Sleeping

■ *on map*
Price codes: *see inside front cover*

Prices in Naran are extremely flexible, and it is worth bargaining hard (or offering to take your business elsewhere if you can't get a good deal). Most of the young Punjabi students sleep 5 or 6 to a room, paying no more than Rs 20 each. Most hotels are vastly overpriced, though during peak periods it is wise to book accommodation at the upper end of the price scale in advance. Most of the hotel bathrooms offer hot water, though for those without their own generator this may only be for a certain period during the day (since there is frequently no electricity during the day).

A-B *PTDC*. Large grounds contain Standard rooms (**B-C**), Surti Cottage (**B**) and some excellent value Economy rooms (**D**). There are also some separate, self-contained cottages; Hill Top Cott (**A-B**), View Cott (**A-B**) and Kunhar Cott (**A**). Book in advance in Islamabad T819384.

B ***Pine Park***, 1.2 kilometres up road to lake, T430045. Red pagoda-style roof is rather lacking in taste and hardly fits in with the environment, rooms are nice though, very modern, pleasant shared balconies, own generator, very popular so bookings essential, good location. **B** ***Springfield Bungalow***, 1.5 kilometres up road to lake, T430055. Very attractive alternative, particularly for families, 1 self-contained cottage with 4 rooms, kitchen, pleasant sitting room, or stay in the 4 room main block with its very cosy verandah, clean bathrooms, resident cook, room service, friendly, book in advance. Recommended. **B** ***Troutland***, 1 kilometre up road to lake, T430088. Quite large carpeted rooms, well furnished, hot water in mornings and evenings only, unless on the top floor rooms can be rather dark, nice location though rooms not much better than competitors in **D** category.

C ***Lalazar***, T430001. Easy winner of 'Naran's ugliest building award', huge, noisy and unsightly, carpeted rooms, attached hot bath, some VIP rooms, also operates the 2 *Lalazar Huts* (2 basic 'huts' at Lake Saiful Malik, each sleeping 2 people, no electricity). **C-D** ***Dreamland Guest House***, T430029. Formerly the *Swiss Cottage*, pleasant location, upstairs rooms particularly appealing, good place if you can get the right price.

D ***Balakot***, T430029. Large rooms but rather dark, attached bath (hot water in mornings only), overpriced; **D** ***Errum***, T430028. Spacious, clean carpeted rooms, modern attached hot bath, some VIP rooms upstairs (**C**), good restaurant and terrace BBQ, well run, probably the best value in this class; **D** ***Evergreen***, T430019. Same owners as *Balakot* and *Dreamland*, currently having huge second storey added. **D** ***Mount View***, T430030. Quieter location than others, some cheaper rooms with shared bath (**E**), camping in garden; **D** ***Naran***, T430008. Rooms on upper storey much lighter, rooms clean, attached bath a little old-fashioned, some with 'western' toilet, restaurant; **D** ***New Park***, T430023. Attached bath (hot mornings only), bed-sheets rather grubby, restaurant, office of *Zeb Travels*. **E** ***Frontier***, T430015. 20 rooms with attached bath, clean enough for the price, restaurant, friendly, pretty good value. **E** ***Kunhar***. Run of the mill. **E** ***Sarhad***. Recent addition of second storey has added some better rooms, though price has increased accordingly. **E** ***Sohrab Valley***, T210482. Rather basic, restaurant. **E** ***Zero Point***. Standard, basic **E** category hotel.

All of the **E-F** category hotels are very similar. They are pretty basic, noisy and are generally aimed at large groups of (male) Punjabi tourists sleeping 4-6 per room. Foreign tourists (and definitely women) may feel uncomfortable staying in such places. They include: ***Bilal***, ***Koh-i-Toor***, ***Madina***, ***Mehran***, ***Pakistan***, ***Paradise Inn***, ***Parwana***, ***Punjab***, ***Qareecha***, ***Saiful Malik***, ***Shalimar***, ***Snow View*** and ***Zam Zam***.

Eating Almost all the hotels have their own restaurant, though the one at the *Errum Hotel* is particularly good.

Shopping There are numerous shops in Naran offering 'handicrafts', though none are particularly recommended. Those heading north, or trekking in the upper reaches of the Kaghan Valley, should stock up on food-stuffs here.

Local transport **Jeep hire** Almost all the hotel managers can arrange jeep hire, or you can conduct negotiations yourself at the jeep yard to the north of town. **PTDC** can sometimes be of assistance here. Standard fares are as follows: **Lake Saiful Malik** Rs 600 return; **Lalazar Plateau** Rs 700 return; **Chilas** Rs 3,500 one-way (allow 9 hours, see 'warning' on page 447); **Naran-Babusar Top-Naran** Rs 2,500. Note that these prices have been static for the past 3 years and thus must surely increase soon. Very occasionally jeeps hired in Chilas tour the cheap hotels looking for passengers to subsidise their return trip. Try the manager at the *Balakot Hotel*.

Long distance transport **Long distance buses** Arriving from the south, minibuses will drop you outside the hotel of your choice. For return trips, head for the transport yard at the north end of town. There is plenty of transport for **Balakot** (Rs 65, 4-5 hours), though if you wish to go all the way to **Mansehra** (Rs 85, 5-6 hours) a morning departure is more likely. Very occasionally there are early morning services all the way to **Rawalpindi**, though such services are demand driven. For transport north see under 'jeep hire' above.

Directory

Communications GPO: towards the south of town, opposite *Kunhar Hotel*. **Hospitals & medical services** The nearest hospital is the *Civil Hospital* in Kaghan village. **Tourist offices** *PTDC* is probably the best place to enquire about hiring a guide for treks and hikes in the northern part of the valley, and all negotiations should really be undertaken in the presence of a PTDC staff member. This is particularly important if trekking north of Besal (eg over the Babusar Pass).

From Naran to Babusar Pass and Chilas

Colour map 5, grid B3

Naran to Battakundi

Beyond Naran, the road becomes a jeep track, passing through some sublime scenery as it traces the course of the Kunhar River. There are some excellent trout fishing reaches here.

The track begins to climb high above the river, through isolated summer settlements that are located amongst fields of peas and potatoes. Gujar shepherds can be seen leading their flocks west, across high passes to pastures in Swat Kohistan. Shortly before Battakundi a jeep track leads five kilometres east, up to the **Lalazar Plateau** (3,200 metres) (see above for details). After 16 kilometres the main road from Naran drops down to **Battakundi** (2,713 metres). There are four or five small, basic **F** hotels – usually a charpoy in a communal kitchen/sleeping area. The **F** *Garaib Nawaz Hotel* (no English sign) at the north end of the village has separate bedrooms. The *Youth Hostel* here is supposedly being refurbished.

Battakundi to Burawai

Leaving Battakundi, the jeep road crosses the river and begins to climb. At **Burawai** (13 kilometres north of Battakundi), the Jora River joins the Kunhar from the southeast, from its source in Azad Jammu and Kashmir. It is possible to hike up this valley in a five day trip which provides a more scenic route to Besal than the jeep road (see 'Burawai to Besal: trekking route' below).

Burawai village is little more than a collection of low shacks, though it is possible to stay on a charpoy at one of the chai-shops overnight if you so wish. A small lodge appears to be under construction on the Battakundi side of the village. It is sometimes possible to get a public jeep between Naran and Burawai (Rs 50).

Burawai to Besal: jeep route

There is a marked change in scenery beyond Burawai, with the silver fir and blue pine trees becoming scantier and the hills barer. There are fine views of the snow-capped **Dabuka** ridge however (4,859 metres). The jeep road also deteriorates considerably beyond Burawai, sometimes being little more than a narrow track high above the river below. This road is very rough. There are, however, some isolated chai stops along this stretch of road, though one wonders how much business they do.

Some 12 kilometres or so beyond Burawai, the Kunhar River is joined from the east by the Jalkhand. A new road to Azad Kashmir is being constructed through this valley, and eventually the whole road through the Kaghan Valley will be vastly upgraded.

The valley begins to open out at **Besal** (18 kilometres from Burawai), with the landscape having been likened to a "bleak Scotch moor". The jeep road drops down to the valley floor, passing the tented settlements of Afghan refugees. Some 20 years ago there were at least 10 shops in Besal, though now only one shop-cum-restaurant has survived. It's possible to sleep on a charpoy here, or bivvy down in the ruins of one of the former shops, though a better bet is to push on to Lulusar Lake (see below). From Besal it is possible to make a short hiking diversion up to Lake Dudupat (see below).

Short hiking diversion

An attractive lake, **Lake Dudupat** (sometimes written 'Dudibach'), lies some 18 kilometres to the east of Besal. For those attempting this excursion, hiring a guide in Besal should be considered essential (around Rs 500 per day). There are no readily identifiable permanent tracks from Besal up to Lake Dudupat: instead you will be following the temporary tracks made during the summer months by villagers bringing their flocks to graze in the Kaghan Valley. In the first six kilometres (two hours) from Besal you may cross as many as five small glaciers (this is where your guide will be invaluable), before entering a 12 kilometres long valley. It takes four to five hours walking through the lush green grass to reach the beautiful circular lake.

Burawai to Besal: trekking route

A very attractive alternative to the jeep road between Burawai and Besal involves a four or five day trekking loop that takes in a couple of 4,000-metre passes and two attractive alpine lakes. A trustworthy local guide should be employed. Read trekking notes, page 67.

From Burawai it is a six to eight hour fairly easy walk to the southeast, along the course of the Jora Valley. The meadows provide good camping. The second day involves a walk up to the **Ratti Gali** pass at 4,115 metres – the boundary between NWFP and Azad Jammu and Kashmir. Follow the stream down from the pass, and where it meets another stream continue north along the stream to **Nuri Nar Gali** pass (also 4,115 metres). This second day should take around five to six hours, and again there is good camping in the meadows (just below the pass). As you follow the stream down on the third day, ignore the Jalkhand River valley (that leads back down to the Kunhar River), and instead take the trail to the northeast over the **Saral Gali** pass (4,191 metres). After four to five hours you reach **Saral Lake**, another good camping spot. Early on day four, as you follow the stream west, the trail splits. The shortest option is to take the route west across the **Saral-di-Gali** pass (4,488 metres), and then along the Purbi River valley to Besal (three to four hours). Alternatively, take the trail north and camp out for a further night at Lake Dudupat. On the fifth and final day it's a five to six hour walk down the Purbi Valley to Besal.

Besal to Gittidas

Continuing north from Besal, after several kilometres (or a two hours walk) you come to **Lake Lulusar**. Shaped like an irregular crescent, two and a half kilometres long, 250 metres wide and 50 metres deep, Lake Lulusar is the source of the Kunhar River that flows through the Kaghan Valley. The water is deep green in colour, and with the sheer mountains rising directly up from the lakeside, it is certainly more beautiful than Saiful Malik. Remote, and at 3,350 metres, there are far fewer tourists too. A legend relates that a blind daughter of Emperor Akbar bathed in its waters and her sight was restored. There is excellent camping potential here, particularly on the west side (away from the road). For those coming from the north, a privately hired jeep from Babusar village to the lake costs around Rs 750.

From Besal it is 12 kilometres along the jeep road to **Gittidas**, the last village before the pass. The valley broadens out considerably here. This village is a summer settlement occupied by Chilasi people, who come here to graze their livestock. The village has a poor reputation and should not be approached unless you are accompanied by a reputable local guide. Camping near here is inadvisable.

A new jeep road is currently in the process of being blasted out of the rock which will eventually link Gittidas to Chilas, but avoiding the Babusar Pass, It in fact follows the **Batogah Nala** to the west of the Babusar Pass. Cyclists and hikers who are travelling south from Chilas to the Kaghan Valley should make sure that they take the correct route as they leave Chilas. (As you leave Chilas,

Warning on crossing the Babusar Pass

In recent years there have been a number of incidents where walkers and cyclists have been either robbed, or threatened by armed Chilasi men whilst crossing the pass, or travelling between Babusar and Chilas. Other travellers, whilst not having been actually assaulted, speak of having been made to feel very "uncomfortable". Take advice, either in Naran or Chilas, before making the trip, and think very seriously about hiring a local guide. This should ideally be done via the PTDC in Naran, with negotiations conducted in front of witnesses. Cyclists should note that the road is extremely rough, and is only really passable on a lightly loaded mountain bike. Because you will be travelling so slowly, you will be particularly vulnerable to the legendary stone throwing kids of the Chilas region. Read trekking on page 67.

you first cross the Batogah Nala. The trail leading from here is this new jeep road to Gittidas. If you want to go to the Kaghan Valley via the Babusar Pass, keep going until you meet the Thak Gah Nala).

Gittidas to Babusar Pass

From Gittidas it is a steady climb of seven kilometres to the summit of **Babusar Pass** ('Babusar Top') at 4,175 metres (though no two sources seem to agree on this height). The actual pass is shaped like a saddle, and the best views are to be had by climbing either flank of the saddle for a further 200 metres or so. There are now a couple of cold drinks stands at the summit.

Babusar Pass to Chilas

From the top of the pass it is a difficult zig-zagging descent down towards Babusar village, though the jeep track here is somewhat better than it is on the Kaghan Valley side. The first thing that you will notice as you make this descent is that the entire valley has been clear-cut. The forest of tree stumps is a staggering, but depressing sight – nothing has been spared. Apparently, a large number of the valley's trees had been cut before the government pointed out that what the villagers had done was illegal. The villagers suggested that "you might as well let us remove the timber since the trees have already been cut down", and when the government agreed, the villagers cut down and removed the rest of the trees virtually overnight. Government plans to reafforest the valley have been so far resisted by the villagers, who fear that in years to come the government may turn round and say "we planted the trees so the land is ours". What a tragic and unnecessary situation.

The road from the Babusar Pass eventually reaches the Chilasi settlement of **Babusar** (13 kilometres). You will probably be asked to sign the book at the police station here, as well as take photos of all the policemen. There is an **F** *NAPWD Inspection Bungalow* in Babusar (bookable in Gilgit if coming from the north) and some basic charpoy hotels, but if you are coming in a jeep from Naran, most drivers prefer to push on to **Chilas** (see page 457). Irregular public cargo jeeps run in either direction between Babusar and Chilas (Rs 50, though possibly not available on Friday), but it is rare to find cargo jeeps going all the way across the pass. These jeeps are uncomfortably over-crowded. Private jeeps can be hired in Chilas or Naran, although at Rs 3,500 one way, the trip is not cheap. A private jeep from Babusar to Lulusar Lake will cost around Rs 750.

The section of the road between Babusar Top and Chilas is quite rough, and it can take up to three hours to cover the 37 kilometres by jeep. Cyclists mention this same journey taking up to 12 hours. The total journey time between Naran and Chilas in a privately hired jeep (with only brief 'photo-stops') is at least nine hours.

Kohistan

The section of the KKH that passes through **Kohistan** is probably one of the most dramatic, as the road clings to increasingly vertical sides of the narrow Indus gorge. This is also one of the wilder areas of Pakistan, with little government control beyond the main highway. The Kohistani people have a warlike history, and are not known for their hospitality to outsiders. Thus it is **not** recommended that you attempt to visit any of the tempting side valleys off the main route. Cyclists may also care to skip this section of the KKH, or else be prepared for Kohistan's stone-throwing kids (though one cyclist has written to say that the kids don't throw stones any more – they all have slingshots!).

Despite the dramatic scenery, many travellers taking the overnight buses between Islamabad/Rawalpindi and Gilgit will pass through this section in darkness. One option is to take the day bus (though you will always end up missing some part of the journey due to nightfall), or to break the trip with a few overnight stops. The problem with this is that despite the fantastic views, none of the stops en route are particularly appealing. Another alternative to the Kohistan section of the KKH is to travel via the Kaghan Valley between Mansehra and Chilas, though this is a challenging route (see section above).

Like the Hazara section of the KKH, and the Kaghan Valley, Kohistan is administratively part of North West Frontier Province. However, it is dealt with in the 'Karakoram Highway and Northern Areas' chapter since it forms part of the KKH route.

Land and environment

Literally meaning 'Land of Mountains', Kohistan is one of the most geologically fascinating places on earth. As the KKH follows the course of the deep Indus gorge, the rock formations take you on a journey from the centre of the earth to its outer crust. Just to the north of Besham, at **Jijal**, the greenish and dark red rocks along the roadside are the result of materials formed 30 kilometres below the earth's surface, and as the KKH continues to **Chalt**, to the north of Gilgit, all the earth's layers are exposed.

Approximately 140 million years ago, a giant landmass floating on the fluid earth mantle broke away northwards from the Gondwanaland supercontinent that forms the modern day continents of Africa, Australia and Antarctica. About 70 million years later, this '**Indian Plate**' began a slow motion collision with the Laurasian landmass, or '**Asian Plate**', that continues today. At the margins of the collision the Indian Plate is subducting beneath the Asian Plate, with the resulting pressure being responsible for the mountain building process that created the Himalaya and Karakoram ranges. Trapped in the middle of the two plates is the small ocean plate that previously supported the **Sea of Tethys**, a shallow sea that used to lie between the Laurasian and Gondwanaland land masses. In the course of the collision between the plates, a narrow chain of volcanic islands that stood in the Sea of Tethys-the **Kohistan Island Arc** – was compressed and contorted, with the result that the metamorphic rock formed at great depth below the oceanic plate has been pushed to the surface, and revealed around Jijal. The younger sedimentary and volcanic materials can be seen at the northern margins of the Kohistan Island Arc, where it joins the Asian Plate near to Chalt. Between the two, the intermediate rock stratas are revealed at the surface. As several signs along the KKH claim, 'Here Continents Collided'.

History

The history of the region is equally fascinating. Although referred to as Kohistan, the region has also been known as *Yaghistan*, or 'Land of the Ungovernable'. British influence in the region was minimal, and even today, Pakistani control beyond the Karakoram Highway is questionable. It is for this reason that tourists are advised **not** to attempt to visit the numerous side valleys away from the main KKH route.

The pattern of settlement in Kohistan has been the occupation of the numerous small valleys, where glacial streams and rivers are more controllable, as opposed to habitation in the Indus Valley itself. The mountain ranges between these valleys proved a barrier to communication, allowing the evolution of numerous independent kingdoms – effectively mini republics. The system of government was by *jirga*, or tribal assembly, but many

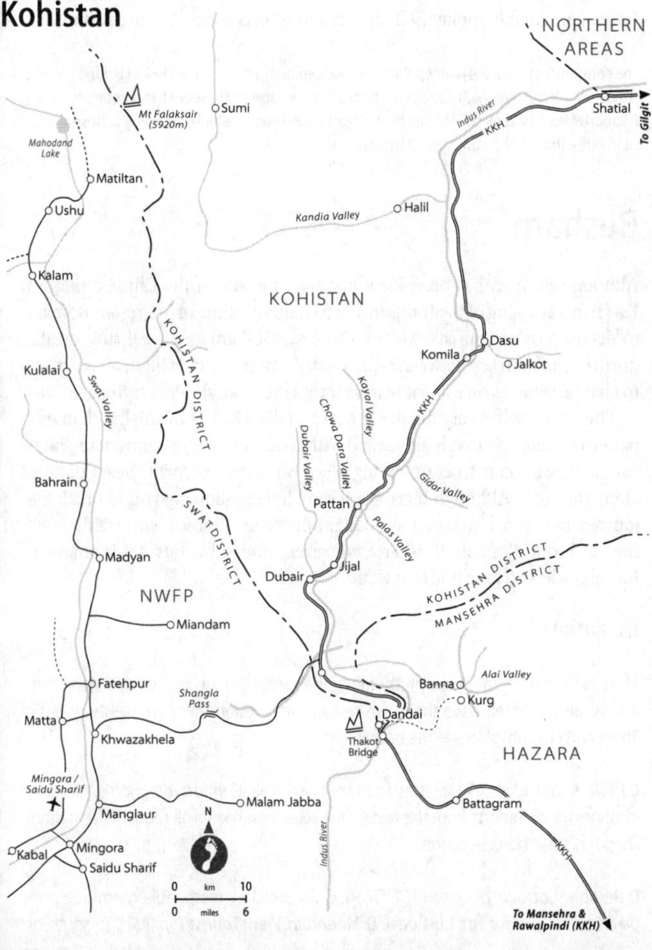

commentators have noted that the independence of thought of the Kohistanis made the area virtually ungovernable. With the exception of Chilas, the British never really established any control over the numerous side valleys.

The situation remains pretty much the same today. Although nominally part of Pakistan, the federal government wields very little influence away from the main road. The societies are very inward looking, fiercely traditional, and reluctant to expose themselves to outside influences. One such example is in the role of women. In some of the valleys female literacy levels are as close to zero as it is possible to get. Following persistant agitation for its introduction, full Shariat (Islamic) law was introduced to Kohistan in early 1999 (taking prescidence over secular civil law).

Culture

Kohistan is an ethnically mixed area, reflecting its history of isolated valleys, with periods of hostile incursions from rival kingdoms. The main ethnic group are descended from the **Shins**, but also linked with **Swathis** and **Yusufzai Pathans** from the Swat Valley. Pushto, Shina, and a language collectively known as 'Kohistani' (various dialects including Maiyum, Chiliss, Gauro) are mainly spoken. The area is almost exclusively Sunni Muslim.

Routes The Kohistan section of the journey along the KKH begins as you cross the **Thakot Bridge**. Having crossed the Indus, the highway passes through the village of **Dandai** (1 kilometre), with the **F** ***Sapari Hotel*** (conveniently located for the nearby gun shops), before continuing to **Besham** (22 kilometres, though the signs says 28 kilometres).

Besham

Phone code: 0941
Colour map 5, grid B2

Although Besham has been identified with the site of the Chinese pilgrim Fa-Hien's crossing of the Indus in 403 AD, there is little of interest in Besham to detain passing tourists. Most visitors see Besham as a meal stop on the north bound journey between Islamabad/Rawalpindi and Gilgit, or as a place to change vehicles on a journey west across the **Shangla Pass** to/from Swat.

The town itself is very much a product of the KKH, showing the changing pattern of land use that is associated with road building in a mountain environment, with construction taking place on a *strassendorf* (linear) pattern along the road. Although there are several hotels, allowing you to break the journey between Islamabad and Gilgit, the town is noisy with traffic at all hours. From Besham it is around seven hours by bus to Islamabad/Rawalpindi, and nine hours to Gilgit.

Essentials

Sleeping & eating
■ on map
Price codes: see inside front cover

Most of Besham's hotels are pretty much the same, though one or two stand out. Almost all the hotels have their own restaurants, though there are plenty of basic 'meat and chapati' places in the bazaar.

C ***PTDC Motel***, KKH, 2 kilometres south of town, T98. Comfortable rooms, pleasing location, mixed reports from the restaurant, reception has some tourist information, shop has small book selection.

D ***Besham Cottage***, close to *PTDC*, T650. Quiet location, reasonable rooms, be prepared to bargain for the best deal. **D** ***Mountain View Tourist Inn***, KKH, to south of police post, T356. Slightly upmarket new hotel, quiet location, picturesque flower garden, clean rooms. **D-E** ***Abu Dhabi Palace***, KKH, T593. Slightly more upmarket than other places in the bazaar, clean rooms, fairly modern attached bath, can be a good deal if you can bargain the price nearer to the **E** price category.

E ***Paris***, KKH, T310. 10 clean, carpeted rooms, becomes good value if you bargain hard. **E-F** ***Abasin***, Mingora Rd, T38. Reasonable value, clean enough, marginally quieter location. **E-F** ***Al-Hayat***, KKH, T366. Another recent, indistinguishable hotel. **E-F** ***Al-Madina***, KKH. Remote, to the south of town, but fairly modern and reasonable value. **E-F** ***Gilgit-Hunza***, KKH. Standard hotel of this price category; **E-F** ***Insaf***, KKH, north of town. New, standard for this category. **E-F** ***International***, KKH, 65. Cheap and good value, friendly staff, restaurant reasonable. **E-F** ***New Hazara***, KKH, T312. Recently completed, not bad rooms, fairly modern attached bath. **E-F** ***North Inn***, KKH, north of town, T679. Another new hotel, fairly standard. **E-F** ***Prince***, KKH, T56. Rooms open onto a fairly noisy courtyard, and none too private, though some cyclists have written to say that the manager is a "real star". **E-F** ***Taj Mahal***, KKH, T82. Fairly basic, restaurant. **F** ***Abshar***, KKH, T614. Fairly new, reasonable. **F** ***Al-Safina***, KKH, T64. Basic and none too friendly. **F** ***Falak Ser***, KKH, T530. Ditto. **F** ***Karachi***, KKH. Very basic charpoy place. **F** ***Rahim***, Mingora Rd. Basic. **F** ***Swat***, KKH, T67. Very basic.

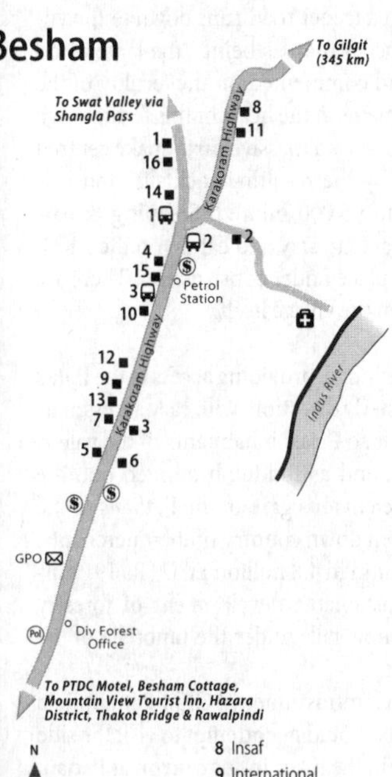

Local transport

Local buses Suzukis run up and down the KKH, linking the main bazaar with the *PTDC Motel* (Rs 3).

Long distance transport

Long distance buses The *NATCO* office is next to the *Swat Hotel*, and though you can buy tickets here, there is no guarantee that the *NATCO* buses passing through will have spare seats. Buses to **Rawalpindi** (Rs 190, 7-9 hours) pass through at around 0200 0400 0600 1800 2300 2400 (though these times are extremely approximate). Buses to **Gilgit** (Rs 200, 9-11 hours) pass at around 0600 1100 1600 1800 2000 2200 2400. The journey times and fares depend upon which sort of bus/minibus/coaster it is. In addition, there are sometimes *NATCO* buses originating in Besham for Gilgit (1100) and Rawalpindi (0500). Likewise, ***Masherbrum Tours***, ***Sargin*** and ***Hameed*** have buses/coasters passing through, though these are generally full.

Minibuses running as far south as **Mansehra** depart when full from outside the fly-blown *Karachi Hotel*. Minibuses running north along the KKH depart from the north end of the bazaar, though many only run as far as **Komila/Dasu** (Rs 40, 2 hours) via **Pattan** (Rs 20, 30 minutes). Minibuses depart when full across the Shangla Pass to **Khwazakhela** and **Mingora** in the Swat Valley (Rs 50, 4 hours).

Directory **Banks** There are a couple of banks in town, though you will need cash US$s (or $ TCs if you're very lucky). **Communications** GPO: south of the main bazaar. **Telephones:** next to the post office. **Hospitals & medical services** Hospitals: *District Hospital* is off the KKH, towards the Indus. **Tourist offices** *PTDC* reception counter can offer some information.

Routes Almost 15 kilometres north of Besham, the Dubair River joins the Indus. The KKH crosses this tributary at **Dubair**, a busy cluster of small wooden shops and houses lining the road and sandwiched on terraces between the river and the highway. The well appointed **F** ***Rest Point Hotel***, T6, is just below the bridge. The restaurant here is very popular.

A trip up the **Dubair Valley** to the original settlement of Dubair (15 kilometres) looks very enticing, but this is one of those Kohistani valleys that is definitely off-limits to tourists. The Dubair Valley continues due north for some 64 kilometres or so, with tracks leading off from the head of the valley into both Swat and Kandia Valley.

Travelling north of Dubair, the KKH continues through **Jijal** (3 kilometres), before the valley opens out into a wide fertile bowl as the Chowa Dara River joins the Indus shortly before **Pattan** (14 kilometres). This stretch of the highway is geologically fascinating; the contact point between the Indian and Eurasian tectonic plates, the latter here exposing layers usually buried 30 metres below the earth's surface.

Pattan

The KKH passes above Pattan, although a feeder road runs down to the village at the north end. Biddulph described Pattan as being "the largest and most flourishing place in Kohistan", and commented on the fertility of the soil and richness of the crops. Pattan remains at the heart of this fertile bowl, although the region was devastated in 1974 by a massive earthquake centred on Pattan. Entire villages were buried by the resulting rockfalls, and it is thought that over 5,000 were killed and 15,000 injured. **Sleeping & eating** Pattan has a couple of miserable places to stay and eat up on the KKH, including the **F** *Kohistan Inn* and a new place under construction. There are also a couple of basic restaurants down in the village itself.

Excursion off the KKH A suspension bridge at Pattan crosses the Indus, providing access to the **Palas Valley**. The valley stretches in a southeasterly direction, with easy access at its head to the Alai Valley. For the 40,000 or so Palasi inhabitants of the valley, the forests represent the only resource, and as Biddulph pointed out, the abundance of this resource attracted the envious gaze of the Pathans of the Alai Valley. Today, this threat comes from down country timber merchants. In 1995, the European Community committed 4.8 million ECU (Rs 191 million) towards the conservation and sustainable development of forestry resources in the Palas Valley. The area now falls under the umbrella of the WWF-backed Himalayan Jungle Project.

Warning The office of the Assistant Commissioner (AC) in Pattan, Raja Gastasab Khan, was insistent that tourists should not attempt to visit the side valleys of **Chowa Dara** and **Palas** that join the main Indus canyon at Pattan, nor the **Kayal** and **Gidar Valleys** slightly further north along the KKH.

Routes Beyond the Pattan bowl, the canyon narrows once more, forcing the KKH high on the valley side. Travelling north, the Indus canyon closes in somewhat, with the KKH perched on a narrow ledge some 300 metres above the river. This section of the Indus gorge is described in graphic detail by the Chinese traveller Fa-Hien, travelling in the early fifth century: "The road was difficult and broken with steep crags and precipices in the way. The mountain-side is simply a stone wall standing up 10,000 feet. Looking down, the sight is confused, and on going forward there is no sure foothold. Below is a river called Sint u-ho (Indus). In old days men bored through the rocks to make a way, and spread out side-ladders, of which there are 700 (steps) in all to pass. Having passed the ladders, we proceed by a hanging rope bridge and cross the river".

Fa-Hien is in effect describing the forerunner of the Karakoram Highway, where men had to be lowered down from above by rope, in order to place explosive charges that would blast a path out of the mountainside. This section of the KKH is said to have been the most difficult to construct, costing more lives per kilometre of road built than any other, and where daily progress was measured in metres rather than kilometres.

A further 8 kilometres north of Pattan, the Kayal River joins the Indus, and the KKH temporarily detours several kilometres up the **Kayal Valley** until a bridging point on the river is reached. There is a small chai shop here. 9 kilometres north of the mouth of the Kayal Valley the KKH crosses the narrow, creaking Keru Bridge; a temporary girder structure that appears to have become permanent.

The highway then drops down nearer to the Indus, although there are still some impressive rock overhangs on the near side. On the east side of the KKH, the deep blue Jalkot Nala joind the Indus. The KKH then runs into **Komila** (63 kilometres from Besham, 30 kilometres from Pattan).

Komila/Dasu

Phone code: 0942
Colour map 5, grid B2/3

The twin settlements of Komila and Dasu sprawl along either bank of the Indus, connected in the middle by the bridge over the river. Komila, on the west bank, is little more than a small bazaar, with a number of hotels, restaurants and transport connections north and south. Dasu, on the east bank, is the administrative centre, with a police station, Deputy Commissioner of Kohistan's offices, Assistant Commissioner of Dasu's offices, and NWFP C&W Ex Engineer's office. A jeep road from Dasu leads east to Jalkot, and eventually to the Babusar Pass and Kaghan Valley, although you should not attempt to follow this ancient communications route.

By bus, Komila/Dasu is more or less the half-way point between Islamabad/Rawalpindi and Gilgit.

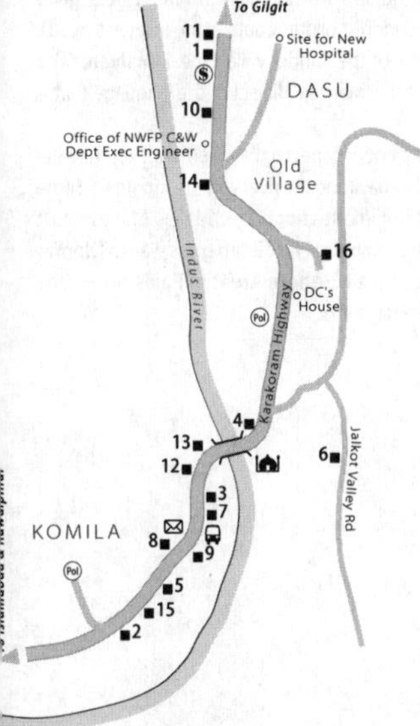

Essentials

Sleeping & eating

■ *on map*
Price codes: see inside front cover

D *Khyber Lodge*, KKH, Dasu, T0942-804. Recently built hotel, 20 clean furnished rooms with fan, attached hot bath (own generator), TV to come, breezy river views from roof terrace, Pak, Chinese and continental food (good place for lunch even if you don't stay here), IDD phone to come, friendly manager, good place, especially if you can bring the price down a bit. **D** *Trungfa Lodge*, just above KKH, Dasu. Recently opened 15 rooms hotel, clean rooms, quite well run, bargain for the best price.

E *C&W Resthouse*, Jalkot Valley Rd. Book with the Executive Engineer in Dasu, reasonable rooms, some a/c (though you'll pay more for this).

KKH and the Northern Areas

F *Afghan Afridi*, KKH, Dasu, T803. 15 basic rooms (doubles and triples), with attached basic bathrooms, all a little pungent, cheap, atmospheric traditional style Afghan restaurant upstairs. **F** *Green Hills*, KKH, Komila, T632. Probably the best of the bunch at this lower end, though it can get noisy since it is used as a meal stop on the Gilgit-Rawalpindi bus route, reasonable cheap restaurant. **F** *Indus Waves*, KKH, Dasu, T968. A little run down, doubles and triple with attached bath, restaurant, basic but friendly and cheap.

There are numerous basic **F-G** places in Komila/Dasu, often with little to distinguish between them. Most have their own restaurants. They include: ***Al-Mashriq, Ameen, Arafat, Azeem, Falcksi, Indus Kohistan Haz, Komila, Lalzar, Moor*** and ***New Abasind***.

Transport Minibuses run from a yard next to the *Indus Kohistan Haz Hotel*, although north bound few go beyond **Shatial** (Rs 35, 1½ hours), or **Besham** south bound (Rs 42, 2 hours).

Routes Just 1 kilometre to the north of Dasu the KKH passes over a temporary girder bridge that seems to have become permanent. It certainly creaks as vehicles cross it. A little further on is a chai shop, very much in the middle of nowhere. Ascending steadily you pass the **D** *PTDC Motel* at **Barseen,** which has reasonable rooms (though you should be able to negotiate a generous discount since few people seem to stay here). 11 kilometres north of Dasu the KKH crosses the iron girder **Barseen Bridge**.

After a further 8 kilometres, the Indus is joined from the west by the Kandia River. A recently completed joint Pak-Japanese suspension bridge over the Indus provides access to the extensive **Kandia Valley**, which runs due west before sharply bending to the north. A jeep track runs tantalizingly along the left bank, to Sumi at the head of the valley, from where a track then leads north around Mount Falaksair (5,920 metres) into the upper Swat Valley. A further track gives access to the valley of Tangir. This was a well worn Buddhist pilgrim route in the first century AD, but is strictly off-limits to visitors today. The people of the Kandia Valley speak **Maiyan**, (also known as Kohistani), although little is known about the 'Manzari' dialect of the language that is used here.

The Indus Valley turns sharply to the east, with plenty of spectacular overhangs on the near side of the KKH, before the canyon walls gradually step back and the river widens and slows. Some 29 kilometres from the Kandia Valley Bridge (and 47 kilometres from Dasu), a new Chinese-built bridge provides access to the Tangir Valley. It is at this point that **Kohistan** gives way to **Diamar District**, as the **North West Frontier Province** meets the **Northern Areas of Pakistan**. For the continuation of the travelling text along the KKH see page 455.

Diamar District and Gilgit District

Anyone taking the late afternoon overnight bus from Rawalpindi to Gilgit will find that, delays permitting, you should be leaving NWFP and entering the Northern Areas at around day break. This is somehow appropriate. Although the scenery along the Indus canyon in Kohistan is breathtaking, in many respects it is here, in the Northern Areas, that the fun really starts.

Diamar District

Diamar District (Dyamar) is one of the administrative regions into which the Northern Areas is divided, covering a vast area of sparsely populated mountainous land on either side of the Indus River. All of the side valleys off this stretch of the KKH have their own histories, though in the context of this administrative division, the history of the regional capital at Chilas is particularly important (see below). Of course the main highlight of Diamar District is the mighty peak of **Nanga Parbat**, with its unlimited trekking and hiking potential on all sides.

Routes

The first settlement of the Northern Areas on the main KKH is **Shatial**, although don't let this miserable collection of shacks put you off the delights to come. There are 2 very basic **G** 'hotels' in Shatial, ***Ittefaq*** and ***Swat***. If your public transport terminates in Shatial, there is usually transport available north to Chilas (Rs 60, 60 kilometres) and south to Dasu/Komila (Rs 35, 1½ hours).

A sign just beyond Shatial reminds you that there are "Petroglyphs for the next 70 kilometres". These rock carvings are part of a chain of inscriptions that reflect historic and prehistoric lines of communications. Concentrations of this rock art are found along the KKH from Shatial to Chilas, along the old Buddhist pilgrim routes through Tangir and Darel to Yasin and Ghizr, at the confluence of the Gilgit and Hunza rivers, on the Sacred Rocks of Hunza near Karimabad, at Passu and Sust in Upper Hunza, along the Gilgit to Chitral route, and also throughout Baltistan.

Excursion off the KKH

A new Chinese bridge to the left of the KKH crosses the Indus, providing access to the infamous **Tangir Valley** (left) and **Darel Valley** (right). Do not be seduced by the azure blue of the Darel River – these two valleys are definitely out of bounds to the casual tourist. This is a great pity since both valleys are rich in archaeological remains, dating particularly from the early centuries AD when Buddhist pilgrims such as Fa-Hien used these routes to travel between China and the great Buddhist sites of south Asia. Gumari in particular is said to have a very nice *NAPWD Resthouse*.

Tangir and Darel Valleys

In describing the people of the Tangir and Darel Valleys, Schomberg suggests that they "know nothing of law and order; the one interest of their lives, their one obsession, is murder." Both valleys were left alone by the British when this area was known as **Yagistan**, 'Land of the Ungovernable', and even today, Pakistani central government control is negligible. However, with both valleys being extremely fertile, the heads of the valleys in particular being thickly forested, it would seem logical for the valley inhabitants to fiercely protect their resources from predatory neighbours. Schomberg's analysis in the 1930s that the people "want to be taken over (by the British administration) and they hope to force the Government to do so by making themselves troublesome" hardly seems credible. Today, the forest tracts are under threat of over-logging, the evidence of which can be seen in the huge timber dumps along the KKH at the entrance to the valleys.

Tangir has many links with Yasin, a function of the ease of communication between the two valleys. Indeed, Yasini rulers used to claim a nominal allegiance and a small tribute from Tangir, although any attempts by Yasin to exercise authority here were fiercely resisted. However, the valley did gain something of a reputation as a place of refuge for princes from Yasin who were seeking asylum.

Similarly, Darel paid a nominal tribute to Kashmir following the invasion of Dogra troops in 1866, although the soldiers did not remain long enough to attempt to impose any rule of law in the valley. In fact, Schomberg claims that only one man, Pakhtun Wali (son of Mir Wali), ever managed to dominate this region, and that was only because he was well qualified as "a blackguard, a treacherous, lawless tyrant, and an accomplished and unflagging intriguer."

Both states remained independent until being incorporated into Pakistan in 1956.

Related maps
A Danyore, Bagrot and Haramosh Valleys, page 484
B Fairy Meadows, Namga Parbat and the Astor Valley, page 461

Routes

The KKH follows the course of the Indus, having made a huge easterly bend at Shatial. In contrast to its passage through the lower reaches of Indus Kohistan, the river here is wide and gentle, frequently flanked by enticing sandy beaches. These beaches will appear particularly seductive if you are crammed into a local bus, because this whole stretch of the journey is particularly hot in summer. Sand dunes border the KKH in what is effectively a high altitude desert.

The road crosses the **Harban Nala** and passes the Harban Dass police post (7 kilometres from Shatial), and then crosses the **Basha Nala** (7 kilometres). The settlement on the opposite side of the valley is Doodishal. A further 6 kilometres along the KKH, the Indus is joined from the north by the **Khanbari Valley**, through which flows a river renowned for its trout. The KKH begins to climb steadily through some very barren landscapes, and as you drive into **Thore** (34 kilometres from Shatial), with its petrol station and abandoned looking settlements, the impression is of arriving in a Mexican desert town (one expects tumble-weed to be blowing down the middle of the street). The only splash of colour is provided by the vivid green cultivation around Hudor, some 10 kilometres further along the KKH, across the Indus via a 650 metres rope suspension bridge. 12 kilometres beyond the bridge turn off is a police check-post (foreigners must enter passport details) at **Chilas**.

Chilas

Colour map5, grid B3

Few tourists stop for long in Chilas; those who do are generally making the trip across the Babusar Pass to/from Kaghan Valley. The incredible collection of rock art in the local vicinity is the main attraction of Chilas. The actual town is some three kilometres above the KKH, and retains something of a reputation for not welcoming outsiders. Yet despite this fearsome reputation, it's not unusual to see groups of Chilasi men sitting around playing Ludo!

The Town

District headquarters of Diamar, (which includes the tehsils of Tangir, Darel and Astor), Chilas is referred to as Silavata (a sort of Sanskrit cum Shina word meaning 'rock or hill of stones') on a nearby sixth century AD rock inscription. Other local inscriptions refer to Chilas as Somanagara, or 'Heroic City of the Moon'.

It was the extraordinary character **Dr GW Leitner** who first brought Chilas to the attention of Europeans. Having visited Chilas in 1866, ostensibly to study the language and customs of the Chilasi people, Leitner later published in 1877 "The Languages and Races of Dardistan"; a monumental volume that included such gems as vernacular greetings in prominent use by the Chilasis. These include "we kill all infidels" and "beat him now, kill him afterwards"!

The Chilasis gained a reputation as fanatical Sunni Muslims, also making frequent raids into the adjacent Kashmir, Neelum, Astor and Gilgit valleys. Following the Sikh occupation of Kashmir, a punitive expedition was sent against Chilas, only to sustain a disastrous defeat. In 1851 the Sikhs returned and captured the fort at Chilas.

Chilas drew the attention of the British during the era of the 'Great Game', when the British were attempting to consolidate their position on the north-west frontier of the British Empire. Colonel Algernon Durand, the British Agent at Gilgit, saw the unpredictable Chilasis as a threat to the recently opened British supply line across the Babusar Pass to the Punjab. In 1892 a situation was engineered that allowed the British to march on Thalpan, opposite Chilas, and after naturally rising to the provocation, the Chilasis were subsequently defeated in battle and their town occupied. Indeed, John Keay notes that during the battle, the Kashmiri troops of the British army "pulled off their trousers the better to give chase."

However, in 1893, in what is referred to as the Indus Valley Rising, the fort at Chilas was attacked, and one third of the garrison was killed or wounded in what was probably the British Army's most disastrous battle fought in Dardistan. For some reason, possibly the lack of food supplies, the Chilasis did not press their advantage and the garrison was relieved. Durand eventually recognized his tactical error in attempting to occupy the Indus Valley death trap; something the Dogra troops of the Maharaja of Kashmir were to experience 54 years later at Partition.

Sights The only real 'sights' in Chilas are the examples of **rock art**, which also form the main sources of information on the early history of the region. Left by pilgrims, missionaries, merchants and conquerors, as well as early inhabitants, they depict various animals, human figures, Buddhist designs etc. The best sites are probably 'Thalpan I' and 'Thalpan V', on the right side of the Indus across the bridge to Thalpan, 'Chilas I' that straddles the KKH next to the Thalpan Bridge, 'Gondophares Rock', the hillock at the mouth of the Batogah Nala, and 'Chilas II to X' to the west of the check post on the KKH. For a full discussion consult Dr AH Dani's *'Chilas: City of Nanga Parbat'* and Karl

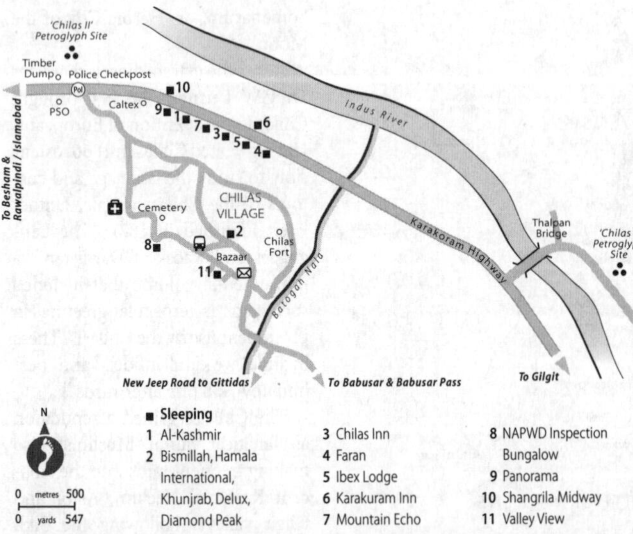

Jettmar's *'Rock Carvings and Inscriptions in the Northern Areas of Pakistan'*, both available in Islamabad bookshops or *GM Beg's Bookshop* in Gilgit.

Essentials

Sleeping & eating

■ on map
Price codes:
see inside front cover

Travelling north, many visitors prefer to press on to Gilgit, whilst those travelling south from Gilgit prefer to put a few more kilometres behind them before stopping for the night. Since Chilas receives so few overnight visitors, the hotels here are desperate for business and hence some excellent discounts are available, particularly at the mid-range places. The good hotels are down on the KKH and the bad ones are up in Chilas village itself (a very steep 3 kilometres climb, especially if carrying luggage). All the hotels have their own restaurants. It may be possible to book the *NAPWD Inspection Bungalow* in Babusar village from here.

B ***Shangrila Midway***, KKH, T235 or Islamabad 813644. 44 rooms with air-coolers, large furnished rooms with clean modern hot bath, a/c restaurant, pleasant long shared verandah, but yet to meet anyone with a good word to say about this place or explain why it's 3 times the price of the *Panorama*, service poor, not good value.

C-D ***Panorama***, KKH, T340. Popular with groups (especially for lunch stops), though excellent discounts available for independent budget travellers, large, clean, carpeted, furnished rooms with modern attached hot bath, towels and soap provided, the air-coolers are real life-savers, some 'deluxe' rooms, nice restaurant is fairly expensive (dhal Rs 50, meat Rs 80) though portions are large. Recommended.

D ***Chilas Inn***, KKH, T211. Because of the heat generated in Chilas, don't take an upstairs room (you'll swelter), large rooms with a/c or air-coolers (but no generator), dining hall, lounge, friendly management, discount for groups. **D-E** ***Karakuram Inn***, KKH, T212. Formerly the *New Shimla*, 4 standard rooms (**E**) are basic but clean, light and airy, modern attached hot bath, fan (though plans for all rooms to have air-coolers in the near future), 10 rooms have air-coolers (**D**), also a 12 person dorm (**G**), good restaurant (Chinese Rs 75 per dish), keen and friendly manager, deserves to do well.

E ***Mountain Echo***, KKH, T315. Simple but smart carpeted rooms, clean linen, fan, attached bath, restaurant, not bad value though the *Panorama* is worth the extra Rs 50. **E** ***NAPWD Inspection Bungalow***, Ranoi Rd, Chilas village. Quite plush though usually full, try booking in Gilgit. **E** ***Valley View***, Chilas village. Basic rooms with basic attached bath, though some have air-coolers.

F ***Al-Kashmir***, KKH. New, simple accommodation block opened, cheap, far cleaner than those up in the village. **F** ***Faran***, KKH. Essentially a restaurant with a few basic rooms round the back. **F** ***Ibex Lodge***, KKH, T247. Used to have good value rooms but the place is now very run down. There are several grotty **F-G** places in the main bazaar (some of which don't have English signs), including: ***Bismillah***, ***Hamala International***, ***Khunjrab***. The best (or least bad) of a bad lot is either ***Delux*** or ***Diamond Peak***.

Transport

Minibuses south to **Komila** (3½ hours) and **Besham** (5 hours) run when full from the main bus yard up in Chilas village, as do buses north to **Gilgit** (3½ hours). *NATCO* buses running between Rawalpindi and Gilgit (in both directions) will pick up passengers down on the KKH, though north bound services seem to have more seats available. Gilgit is Rs 65, Rawalpindi around Rs 230 (depending upon the type of bus).

Chilas to the Babusar Pass and Kaghan Valley

A new jeep road is currently in the process of being blasted out of the rock which will eventually link Chilas to Gittidas (in the Kaghan Valley), but avoiding the Babusar Pass (see page 447). It in fact follows the ***Batogah Nala*** *to the west of the Babusar Pass. Cyclists and hikers who are travelling south from Chilas to the Kaghan Valley should make sure that they take the correct route as they leave Chilas. As you leave Chilas, you first cross the Batogah Nala. The trail leading from here is this new jeep road to Gittidas. If you want to go to the Kaghan Valley via the Babusar Pass, keep going until you meet the Thak Gah Nala. Those contemplating this trip should read the 'warning' on page 448.*

Transport to **Babusar**, and across the Babusar Pass to the **Kaghan Valley** is unreliable. There is usually at least 1 early morning cargo jeep from Chilas bazaar to Babusar (except Friday), though it is very crowded (Rs 50, at least 4 hours). Once you get to Babusar village there is rarely any public transport across the pass (a private hire jeep as far as Lake Lulusar will cost at least Rs 750). A private hire jeep from Chilas to **Naran** in the Kaghan Valley will cost at least Rs 3,500 (9 hours+). See 'box' and 'warning' on page 447.

Routes The KKH continues east from Chilas, crossing the **Batogah Nala** after 1 kilometre and the **Thak Gah Nala** after 4 kilometres. After a further 5 kilometres there is a popular chai stop at **Gini**, at a point where a cool sweet water spring runs down to the KKH (though the water is not suitable for delicate 'western' stomachs). A jeep road runs up to the large village of Upper Gini (population 700, 1½ hours by vehicle), which is situated close to a large lake. The KKH then crosses the Bunar Nala, before arriving at the small settlement of **Bunar Das**.

Bunar The main settlement of **Bunar** is actually on a ridge to the south of the KKH, and often forms the finishing point of the 'Nanga Parbat circuit via Mazeno La' trek (see below). Those wishing to undertake this trek may like to consult Bunar's village lumdadar, Ahmed Mir, or his son Abdul Wakeel, who is a registered mountain guide with *Travel Walji's* (Gilgit T2665, Islamabad T820908). Ahmed Mir may also be able to arrange accommodation for those who get stuck in Bunar (his house is reached on the road signposted 'hydel station' behind the PSO).

Routes On continuing east from Bunar Das, look out for the clumps of vegetation next to the road on the right (south) side; they conceal a hot spring. 2 kilometres from Bunar Das is **Gunar Farm**, with its police fort, petrol station and ***NAPWD Inspection Bungalow***. There are also a couple of very basic charpoy places here which are used to accommodating cyclists. A further 8 kilometres is the tiny settlement of **Jalipur**, which was used earlier this century as a British staging post. It has a *NAPWD Inspection Bungalow*.

Some 6 kilometres further along the KKH is a troublesome area around **Tatta Pani** that is plagued by landslides that often block the road. 5 kilometres beyond here the KKH crosses to the west bank of the Indus over the **Raikot Bridge**. There is a police check-post and the **B *Shangrila Motel*** (this hotel does not appear to be currently operating, though one reader described it as "dirty, with uninviting guest rooms ... uneven service"). A better local accommodation option is at Thalichi (see below).

A jeep track runs up to **Fairy Meadows** (15 kilometres), and a new jeep road to Astor is under construction behind the motel. Distances from Raikot Bridge: Gilgit 78 kilometres north, Dasu 179 kilometres south, Pattan 215 kilometres south, Rawalpindi 520 kilometres south. From Raikot Bridge the KKH swings north.

Fairy Meadows and Nanga Parbat

Colour map 5, grid B4

Situated at the base of Nanga Parbat, **Fairy Meadows** (approximately 3,200 metres) truly is a place of outstanding beauty. The meadows are flower-strewn high altitude alpine pastures situated amongst pine forest, with an imposing backdrop of the massive north or ng' on page 447.Raikot face of the world's ninth highest mountain. It is a wonderful place to camp, has endless possibilities for short walks and longer hikes, and is incredibly photogenic.

Ins and outs

Most visitors to Fairy Meadows actually arrive from Gilgit (including those travelling south-north along the KKH since Gilgit is the nearest place to stock up on supplies, and is a good place to hire guides or meet up with like-minded trekkers). The cheapest option is to take the *NATCO* bus from Gilgit to Raikot Bridge, and then walk up to Fairy Meadows. The problem with this is that even if you take an early bus from Gilgit, it will be getting quite warm by the time you get to Raikot Bridge, and the walk up to Tato is very hot, very dry and particularly miserable. This walk takes at least 4 hours, with a further 2-3 hours to Fairy Meadows. Even those who decide to walk may be trailed for several gruelling kilometres by jeep drivers trying to tempt them into their vehicles! A far better bet is to hire a jeep at Raikot Bridge to take you up to Tato (though the track is gradually being expanded as far as Fairy Meadows). This ride takes about 1½ hours and the Rs 800 charge is not negotiable. Those hiring a jeep all the way from Gilgit to Tato will have a Rs 500 surcharge added to the price, supposedly as a 'tax' collected by the local people who maintain the road. *Travel Walji's* currently charge Rs 2,300 from Gilgit to Tato.

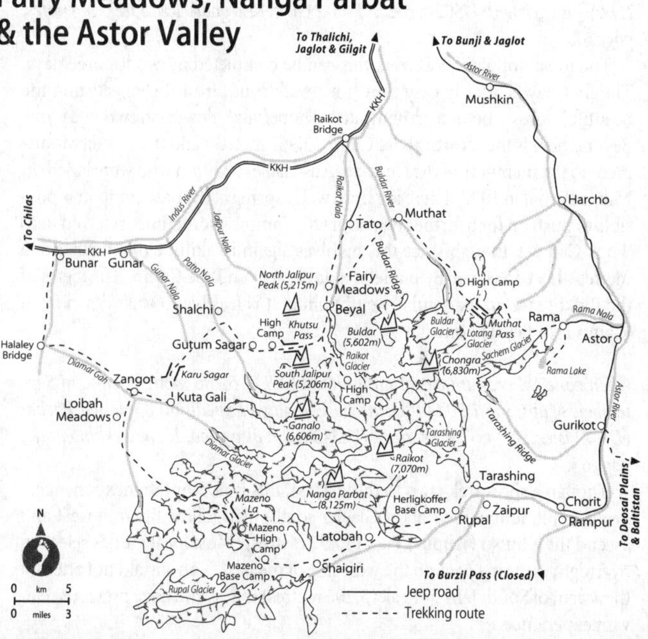

Essentials

Sleeping & eating For many years there was talk that the *Shangrila* chain were going to build a luxury hotel at Fairy Meadows, presumably complete with a tacky and entirely inappropriate red pagoda-style roof. In fact, the local people sold the land to the chain and a large area of forest was clear-cut for the project. Now, thanks to local conservationists, the local people have had a change of heart. At the time of going to press it is believed that the local people were attempting to return the money that they had been paid for the land. It is unclear whether the hotel chain will accept the proposal, though local people that the editors spoke to swore blind that they would not allow the hotel to be built.

Raikot Serai at Fairy Meadows (book at House 1, Street 15, Khayaban-e-Iqbal, F7/2, Islamabad, T276113/8). 1 2-bedded hut (**D**) plus 30 2-person tents (**E**) (mats provided but bring your own sleeping bag), or pitch own tent (**G**), kitchen tent, latrine, some trekking equipment for hire. Very well run. Recommended. A similar camp site has been set up at **Beyal**, an easy 1½ hour stroll beyond Fairy Meadows. It's less well established, though usually quieter, than Fairy Meadows.

Guides and porters Those just wandering around Fairy Meadows and Beyal will not require guides and porters, though for longer trips they are worth considering. Note that Raikot Bridge to Tato is considered 1 full stage, even if your porters travel by jeep! The manager at the *Raikot Serai* can often help arrange guides and porters, though many trekkers employ a guide in Gilgit (Nasir Ahmad, usually found at the *Madina Hotel*, has been consistently recommended).

Treks from Fairy Meadows and Beyal

Beyal to Nanga Parbat (North) Base Camp and 'Camp 1' *Open zone. Maximum elevation optional (3,967-4,467 metres). June to September. Maps; the 1:50,000 Deutsche Himalaya Expedition of Nanga Parbat (DAV) is excellent; U502 series, NI 43-2 Gilgit also good. Read trekking notes, page 67.*

The most popular short trek, this can be completed in two to three days. The first day is a fairly easy four hour walk south from Beyal, skirting the beautiful forest, before arriving at a (hopefully) flower-strewn meadow. Beyond here is the (North) Base Camp (3,967 metres) and the Drexel Monument to the members of the German-Austrian expedition who were killed on Nanga Parbat in 1937. There is a fresh water spring at the base camp. It is possible to push on for a further two hours to 'Camp 1' (sometimes referred to as 'High Camp'), though since this involves a gain in altitude of a further 500 metres, this trip is usually made as a day trip from Base Camp. The views of the Raikot face are particularly enthralling. It is feasible to walk down from 'Camp 1' to Beyal in one day.

Beyal to South Jalipur Peak *Open zone. Maximum elevation optional (4,837-5,206 metres). June to September. Maps; the 1:50,000 Deutsche Himalaya Expedition of Nanga Parbat (DAV) is excellent; U502 series, NI 43-2 Gilgit also good. Read trekking notes, page 67.*

Though a short trek (two to three days), this is not for the inexperienced. From Beyal, follow the Raikot Glacier south, then follow the trail west and ascend the Khutsu (Jalipur) Pass (4,837 metres). Most local guides select an overnight camping spot on the west side of the pass. You should not attempt the ascent of South Jalipur Peak (5,206 metres) unless you have previous relevant experience.

Nanga Parbat

The local name for this 8,125 metres giant is Diamar (correctly Diva-Meru), meaning 'Heavenly Mount', although the mountain is almost exclusively referred to as Nanga Parbat. Kashmiri for 'Naked Mountain', this name is a reference to the massive 4,500 metres wall of the southeast face that is too sheer for snow to stick. However, such is the awesome reputation of the peak that it has been nick-named 'Killer Mountain'.

The mountaineering history of Nanga Parbat begins in 1895 when a British expedition attempted the peak. The leader of the expedition, the famed climber Mummery, along with two Gurkha porters, reached almost 7,000 metres before disappearing without trace. Locals blamed the fairies, spirits, and giant snow snakes that are said to inhabit the mountain, although another explanation may be one of Nanga Parbat's unpredictable avalanches.

In the 1930s no fewer than five separate expeditions attempted the peak. The 1934 Austro-German expedition is believed to have got within several hundred metres of the summit before bad weather forced them back. Four Germans and six Sherpas died in the descent. Just three years later another German party was within striking range of the summit before being wiped out by an avalanche. A later expedition found most of the men lying dead in their tents, as if asleep, their watches all stopped at 1220.

In 1950, a small British expedition attempted the mountain. A member of the party was Tenzing Norgay, later to find fame with Sir Edmund Hillary on the first successful ascent of Everest. However, the expedition were poorly prepared, and Tenzing was later to describe the decision of the British officers to attempt a full ascent as "craziness". Despite a rescue attempt by Tenzing and one of the British officers, the other two members of the expedition died high up on the mountain.

It was not until 1953, less than five weeks after Tenzing and Hillary had 'conquered' Everest, that Nanga Parbat was finally defeated. Hermann Buhl, a noted Austrian climber, eventually stood where no other person had ever been.

The current death toll on Nanga Parbat is thought to be 50. Not only is the mountain's sheer size a huge challenge-its north face slopes down an incredible 7,000 metres down to the Indus – its position as an exposed sentinel at the western end of the Himalayas has led to the formation of its own highly unpredictable micro-climate. Weather conditions change rapidly, and avalanches are common and violent. Yet from the KKH, particularly at sunset, the ethereal beauty of the mountain is sublime.

Beyal to Buldar Peak

Open zone. Maximum elevation (5,602 metres). June to September. Maps; the 1:50,000 Deutsche Himalaya Expedition of Nanga Parbat (DAV) is excellent; U502 series, NI 43-2 Gilgit also good. Read trekking notes, page 67.

Another trek that requires a technical ascent if you wish to make it safely to the top of Buldar Peak (5,602 metres). This trek also requires a crossing of the Raikot Glacier.

Beyal to KKH at Gunar Farm

Open zone. Maximum elevation optional (4,062 metres). June to September. Maps; U502 series, NI 43-2 Gilgit is reasonable. Read trekking notes, page 67.

This trek provides an alternative route back to the KKH from Fairy Meadows/Beyal. There are several options for completing this trek – the route you take will depend largely upon your guide. Note that there is no regular public transport available for you at Gunar Farm.

NB For details of the **Rupal Valley** trek and the **Nanga Parbat Circuit via Mazeno La** trek, both of which are on the south side of Nanga Parbat, see below under the **Astor Valley** section (page 464).

Routes Back on the KKH, just to the north of Raikot Bridge, the Indus is joined by a minor tributary from the east, the **Liachar Nala**. In 1841, a massive landslip, probably triggered by an earthquake, completely dammed the river, creating a giant lake that stretched almost 50 kilometres back to Gilgit. The dam, several hundred metres thick, is said to have raised the water up to 300 metres above its normal level. When breached in early June 1841, having held for several months, the resulting flood is said to have washed away an entire Sikh regiment camped downstream at Chach (although the image of a massive wall of water rushing down is said to be something of an exaggeration). Durand claims that the pile of driftwood left by the flood provided a source of firewood for the local people for almost 50 years.

If the weather is clear, this stretch of road has some of the best views on the entire length of the Karakoram Highway. Directly to the north is the magnificent **Rakaposhi** massif (7,788 metres), flanked by **Dobani** (6,134 metres), with the serrated ridges of **Haramosh** (7,409 metres) to the northeast. Directly behind you, to the south, is the massive north (Raikot) face of **Nanga Parbat** (8,125 metres). A small sign at the settlement of **Thalichi** (10 kilometres from Raikot Bridge) reminds you to look! There is a very pleasant **F** *NAPWD Resthouse* here, popular with cyclists, beautifully furnished (though you may have to be in your room by 2100). Food can be arranged, though it's best to bring your own supplies. Bookings should ideally be made through the Executive Engineer in Chilas or the Chief Engineer's Office in Gilgit.

Across the Indus from Thalichi is the entrance to the **Astor Valley**, gateway to a trekking route round to the naked southeast (Rupal) face of Nanga Parbat. **Thalichi** is in fact the boundary between Diamar District and **Gilgit District**, though the Astor Valley (described below) is part of Diamar. For details of the journey north towards Gilgit turn to page 467.

Just before **Jaglot** (87 kilometres from Chilas, 50 kilometres from Gilgit), a suspension bridge crosses the Indus (look for the sign marked 'NLI Centre'), and a jeep track runs back south through **Bunji** to the **Astor Valley**. A public jeep from Jaglot to Astor is Rs 140 (at least 2-3 per day, 4-5 hours for 50 kilometres).

Astor Valley

Colour map 5, grid B4

Although the route between Gilgit and Srinagar is now firmly closed, the Astor Valley provides a starting point for trips across the Deosai Plains to Baltistan, and for a number of excellent treks around the eastern and southern sides of Nanga Parbat. Refer to the 'Fairy Meadows, Nanga Parbat and Astor Valley' map on page 461.

Routes The Astor Valley is reached from the KKH by the bridge at **Jaglot**. The first settlement along the jeep road is **Bunji**. From here it is a further 4-5 hours or so to the village of **Astor**, via **Mushkin** and **Harcho** (which has the basic **F** *Saiful Malik Inn*). Note that this jeep road is really rough, described by one reader as "dramatic", though it is certainly better once you pass Harcho.

Bunji Strategically placed at a crossing point of the Indus, and guarding the entrance to the Astor Valley, the small, nondescript settlement of Bunji has played a remarkably significant role in the recent history of the Northern Areas. The furthest outpost of the Kashmir state beyond which lay 'Yaghistan', this is the point at which Leitner crossed the Indus in 1866 on his celebrated visit to Dardistan (see John Keay's *The Gilgit Game* for an excellent account).

The British built a fort at Bunji in order to protect the route across the Burzil Pass into Kashmir – the main supply line between British India and the outpost of the Empire at Gilgit. During the Gilgit uprising at Partition, when the people of the Northern Areas fought to throw off the Dogra rule of the Maharaja of Kashmir, Bunji's strategic importance at the head of the the pass into Kashmir was re-emphasized. In fact, Colonel Hasan Khan, one of the key players in the military action, suggests that the capture of Bunji was "the deciding factor in the whole game of Gilgit's freedom struggle" (Dani, 1991).

Such was the terror that the advancing Chilas Scouts struck into the hearts of the Dogra and Sikh garrison at Bunji, that the Maharaja's troops fled during the night, allowing the fort and a huge supply of arms and ammunition to be captured without a shot being fired.

Though the route across the Burzil Pass into Indian occupied Kashmir is closed, Bunji still maintains its strategic significance controlling a vital supply line to Pakistani troops stationed on the Siachen Glacier. It is also the headquarters of the Northern Light Infantry; the successors to the Gilgit Scouts.

Astor

The village (2,345 metres) is about four to five hours from the KKH on a hot, dry and rough jeep road. It is perched high above the river on the shoulder of a mountain, its small and crowded main bazaar consisting of a series of impossibly steep and narrow streets. The restaurants and snack places are fairly basic, and the range of goods on sale in the shops makes stocking up in Gilgit a good idea for trekkers (and those heading across the Deosai).

Sleeping

The best hotel is the **D** ***Kamran***, T140, situated above the bazaar and offering clean, pleasant rooms with fan, attached bath. Up on another hillside, away from the bazaar, is a 2 room **E** *NAPWD Inspection Bungalow* (that should really be booked in Gilgit, though you can try just turning up). The **F** ***Dreamland Hotel*** is described as "over-priced, but still recommended, quiet, good food reliable manager", offering basic rooms with attached bath, nice garden area and views. The **F** *New Ropal Inn* is very basic, with rather pokey rooms.

Transport

There is public jeep transport between Gilgit and Jaglot on the KKH (Rs 25), and then public jeeps from Jaglot to Astor (Rs 140, minimum 2-3 per day, 6 hours, but they are crowded). A privately hired jeep costs around Rs 1,600 to Rs 2,000 one-way from Gilgit to Astor. A couple of public jeeps run daily from Astor to Tarshing (Rs 75). A privately hired jeep all the way from Gilgit to Tarshing costs around Rs 2,700. Frequent Datsuns and cargo jeeps operate to and from Gilgit and Jaglot, and tickets can be bought in the *New Ropal Inn* restaurant in the bazaar. In Gilgit these vehicles arrive at and depart from the *Diamar Hotel*.

Routes

Continuing south from Astor village, the jeep track descends back down to the river level, passing through the village of **Gurikot** (9 kilometres), where there is the very simple **G** *Lalazar Inn* (comprising a restaurant and a couple of rooms upstairs).

The track then crosses and re-crosses the river, before dividing sharply after the second bridge. The main jeep track bears gradually east, climbing steadily upwards towards the **Deosai Plateau** and crossing eventually into Baltistan. The last village before the Deosai is **Chilam**, a tiny, rather forlorn place, swelled in size only by the military presence here. For full details of this extraordinary trip across the Deosai (described in the opposite direction) see page 513.

The other track from Gurikot turns west to the small village of **Tarshing** (40 kilometres), starting point for the excellent Rupal Valley and Mazeno Base Camp trek around Nanga Parbat (see below). Tarshing has the basic **F** ***Nanga Parbat Tourist Cottage*** and is best reached in a jeep privately hired in Astor (Rs 500-600).

Treks and short hikes from the Astor Valley

Rama Lake

From Astor it is possible to walk up to the beautiful **Rama Lake** (3,482 metres), about four to six hours away through dense pine forest (note the altitude change). The camping here is superb, although it is possible to stay at the **F** *NAPWD Inspection Bungalow* about half-way between Astor and the lake (bookings in Gilgit). There is a big luxury **C** *PTDC Motel* nearing completion in the forest below Rama Lake. It is also possible to hire a jeep from Astor up to Rama Lake for around Rs 600.

Rupal Valley trek

Open zone. Maximum elevation optional (4,000 metres). June to September. Maps; the Deutsche Himalaya Expedition of Nanga Parbat is excellent; U502 series, NI 43-2 Gilgit also good. Read trekking notes, page 67.

This trek is a popular with trekking agencies, as well as with self-organized trekkers. It is fairly easy and perfectly possible without a guide (although Nasir Ahmad, usually found at the *Madina Hotel* in Gilgit, has been consistently recommended). This trek begins at **Tarashing**. There are always plenty of guides and porters available here, as well as horses and donkeys for hire. It takes around four to five days to reach Mazeno Base Camp and return by the same route.

The trail climbs the lateral moraine of **Tarashing Glacier** before crossing the glacier on a good path to reach the settlement of **Rupal**, divided into upper and lower villages. There is good camping beyond the upper village, or further on at **Herligkoffer Base Camp** (3,656 metres), an ideal spot with woods, flowers and clear spring water. The path then crosses the Bazhin Glacier (again, this is an easy glacier crossing; there is also a fairly regular flow of locals going back and forth if you don't feel confident on your own). On the far side, below the lateral moraine, is another good camping place known as **Tupp Meadow**, surrounded by summer settlements where sheep, goats, dzo and horses are brought to graze. An alternative route from Rupal village crosses to the south bank of the river on a good bridge and skirts the snout of the Bazhin Glacier to arrive at Tupp Meadow. From here the trail continues up the Rupal valley, passing several possible campsites, to **Shaigiri** (3,655 metres) which offers the best camping and excellent views of Nanga Parbat's south face. The trail then follows lateral moraine as it climbs up to **Mazeno Base Camp**.

Beyond, the trail bears sharply north and begins its steep ascent to Mazeno Pass (5,377 metres). About a third of the way up is **Mazeno High Camp** (4,700 metres). It is possible, instead of returning to Tarashing, to trek over Mazeno Pass and descend into Daimer Valley, which gives access to the KKH via the Bunar Valley (see 'Nanga Parbat circuit via Mazeno La' trek, below).

Nanga Parbat circuit via Mazeno La

Open zone. Maximum elevation optional (5,399 metres). June to September. Maps; the Deutsche Himalaya Expedition of Nanga Parbat is excellent only as far as Mazeno La; U502 series, NI 43-2 Gilgit also good. Read trekking notes, page 67.

This demanding trek offers numerous possibilities and alternatives, though it should be noted that it doesn't make a complete 'circuit' of Nanga Parbat (despite often being referred to as the 'around Nanga Parbat' trek). The first four to five days follow the Rupal Valley trek as far as **Mazeno Base Camp** (see above). You should be fully acclimatized before attempting the six hour climb up to **Mazeno High Camp** (4,700 metres). The following day is long and difficult, and again you should be fully acclimatized. Ascending along the northeast edge of the Manzeno Glacier, you cross it and then head for **Mazeno La** (Pass) at 5,399 metres. The descent from Mazeno La is particularly difficult, largely because the north side is heavily crevassed. Trekkers should have experience of such conditions, and should always be roped (300 metres of rope is recommended). Just to make this trek more complicated, it is often necessary to change porters here (from Tarashing villagers to Bunar residents), though these rules generally only apply to particularly large trekking parties. Having made the descent, the trail meets the Loibah Glacier, which you then follow to the **Upper Loibah Meadows**. The following day features a more relaxing downhill walk to the Loibah Meadows, from where the trail turns north to **Zangot**.

From Zangot there are two options. You can trek for two days down to the KKH at **Bunar**, camping at **Halaley Bridge** on the way (Abdul Wakeel, son of Bunar's lumbador, who is a registered mountain guide with *Travel Walji's*, is very experienced along this route, Gilgit T2665, Islamabad T820908). The second option is to extend the trek by six days, and continue on to **Fairy Meadows**. This option involves overnight camps at **Kuta Gali** (four hours); **Shaichi** via the **Karu Sagar Pass** (4,800 metres), although large parties may have to change porters at Saichi (Bunar to Gunar); **Gutum Sagar** (3,500 metres), six hours; **Jalipur High Camp** (4,400 metres), six hours; before the long descent down to **Beyal** (with the option of a side trip to **Nanga Parbat Base Camp** and **'Camp 1'**, see above).

Gilgit District

Gilgit District is arguably the most important of the five administrative divisions that comprise the Northern Areas and the seat of the regional capital at Gilgit town. It does in fact stretch all the way up to the international border with China, though for the sake of ease of use, its upper sub-divisions such as Hunza, Nagar and Gojal all have their own sections within the 'Karakoram Highway and Northern Areas' chapter of the *Pakistan Handbook*. For those travelling along the KKH from south to north, you will suddenly find that the side valleys off the KKH are now accessible, whilst the towns and villages on the highway itself are more geared up for tourism than their counterparts further south in Hazara and Kohistan.

Gilgit District began life as the **'Gilgit Agency'**, an administrative division created by the British in 1877 in an attempt to increase their influence in a region seen as being vulnerable to Russian incursions.

Back on the KKH

Routes

Returning to the KKH, several kilometres north of Jaglot is the confluence of the Indus and Gilgit Rivers. Here, 38 kilometres from Gilgit, the KKH leaves the Indus and branches along the west bank of the Gilgit River. The **Skardu** road crosses the Gilgit River here on the Alam Bridge, and follows the course of the Indus Valley east to **Baltistan** (see page 502). A sign marks this place as a 'unique spot', at the confluence of 2 rivers and 3 mountain systems. A further 20 kilometres along the KKH is another 'unique spot', marked by a memorial raised by the NLI in 1997 to indicate the place where in 1852 the 'Dards' ambushed and annihilated the Sikh garrison of Bunji Fort.

The KKH continues through another police check-post, before turning north shortly before the confluence of the Gilgit and Hunza Rivers. The KKH crosses the river on a long suspension bridge, and proceeds north for **Hunza** and **China**, whilst the left fork enters **Gilgit** through its eastern suburb of Jutial.

Gilgit

Phone code: 0572
Colour map 5, grid A3/4

Described by John Keay as "the hub, the crow's-nest, the fulcrum of Asia" (The Gilgit Game, 1979), Gilgit is the key junction in the north for travel to all points of the compass. The town has a long and varied history, but each event reflects Gilgit's strategic location. From the numerous territorial disputes between the rival petty kingdoms in the surrounding valleys, through the imperial rivalry of the era of the 'Great Game', up until the Partition war between Pakistan and India and the continuing antagonism between the two states, Gilgit has held its place at the centre of local history.

Cool Gilgit?

Those wishing to escape the oppressive summer heat of the plains by heading up to Gilgit are in for a disappointment. The albedo of Gilgit's brown, barren hills is high, and the heat from the sun just seems to bounce around the bowl that the town sits in: temperatures in the 40°s are not unknown. Further, at only 1,500 metres above sea-level, there are none of the cooling effects of altitude.

In recent years Gilgit has undergone rapid social and economic change, as the upgrading of an ancient trading route in the form of the Karakoram Highway has brought greater integration between the north and the rest of Pakistan, as well as revolutionizing patterns of trade and employment.

Most tourists visiting the Northern Areas spend some time in Gilgit, whether preparing or recovering from a trek, shopping, or just connecting with onward transportation.

Ins and outs

Getting there Gilgit is the transport hub of the Northern Areas, though whereabouts you arrive in the town largely depends upon where you've come from and which company you have travelled with. For details of all the bus and jeep operators, see under 'Long Distance Transport' below.

Getting around Suzuki minivans run up and down the main road, linking the GPO in the west with Jutial in the east (Rs 6 for full journey), and can be flagged down anywhere along this route. Occasionally, if a lone 'western' woman gets in, all the men get out, and the driver will insist that you hire the whole vehicle ('special'). A 'special' suzuki will cost around Rs 30 for most journeys within Gilgit (eg the airport to your hotel). Suzuki minivans also run from Garhi Bagh, via Babar Rd, across the Jinnah Bridges to Danyore.

History

Ancient and medieval history The record for the early and medieval history of Gilgit is rather incomplete, largely because the oral tradition, as opposed to the written form, has been the primary source of transmitting information on the period. The oral tradition has left us with some amusing titbits, however, such as the story of the last Buddhist ruler of Gilgit, Sri Badad (though some sources claim he was Hindu). It is suggested that such was his taste for the flesh of young children, that he ate nothing else!

The Trakhans were the dominant dynasty during Gilgit's medieval period, ruling for eight distinct phases from some time in the eighth century until 1840. It is from the Trakhan line that the rival ruling families of Hunza and Nagyr have evolved.

Modern history Towards the end of the Trakhan dynasty, both **Sikh** and **British** influence was growing in the region. In 1842 a Sikh army from Kashmir, at the request of the beleaguered ruler of Gilgit, succeeded in driving the murderous **Gohar Aman** back to his stronghold in Yasin. Gohar Aman continued to harass the town and the Sikh garrison, and eventually succeeded in recapturing Gilgit in 1852. He ruled there unopposed until his death in 1860, by which time he is alleged to have sold half of the local population into slavery.

In the meantime, following the decisive victory in the First Anglo-Sikh War of 1846, the British had 'sold' Kashmir to the Dogra Raja of Jammu,

Gulab Singh after he had footed the bill for the Sikh's war reparations. Following Gohar Aman's death, the Dogras returned to Gilgit under the direction of Gulab Singh's successor Ranbir Singh. Thus, for the first time since the rule of Sri Badad some 11 centuries earlier, Gilgit found itself under the yoke of a non-Muslim ruler.

It was around this time that the British were beginning to penetrate the region. Vigne and Moorcroft had reached close to Gilgit in the late 1830s, and in 1866 the amazing Leitner had brought back the first written account of the town, albeit after a stay of less than 24 hours. British concern was growing over the perceived threat of a Russian invasion through the unmapped passes to the north, and the vulnerability of the Kashmir frontier became a major issue.

The British response was to appoint a series of 'Political Agents' to Gilgit, perhaps the most influential of whom was **Colonel Algernon Durand** (see 'box' on the Battle of Nilt, page 537). Although in theory just a representative of the British government on the frontier, Durand was the de facto military commander of the region, and as such was the key policy maker. A system evolved by which the Political Agent was responsible for the area of the Agency, reporting to the British Resident in Kashmir, whilst the Maharaja's representative was only answerable for Kashmir State Territories, which at this stage included the district (Wazarat) of Gilgit.

This system of 'dual control' was soon deemed unworkable, and in 1935 the then Maharaja of Kashmir, **Raja Hari Singh**, was 'encouraged' to sign a document leasing the Gilgit Wazarat to Britain for 60 years. This is how the position of Gilgit stood at the partition of the sub-continent in 1947, and the creation of the state of Pakistan.

Recent events

The key event in the recent history of Gilgit has been the development of transport infrastructure in the region, in particular the construction of the Karakoram Highway. Gilgit is now a major staging post in the border trade with China, and potentially with Central Asia in the future. It is also a key market for goods from both China and down country Pakistan, as well as a local centre for labour.

In recent years, Gilgit has had more than its share of sectarian violence. The population is roughly split between Sunni and Shia Muslims, with a sizeable community of Ismailis. Tensions between the Sunni and Shia communities are at their highest around key religious dates, particularly *Ashoura* and the end of *Ramadan*. In 1988 several hundred were killed in gun battles in the Gilgit area, and again in 1993 greater casualties were only avoided by the imposition of a 24 hour curfew. There have been a number of isolated incidents since, though Gilgit remains tense around the key religious festivals and is thus best avoided at these times.

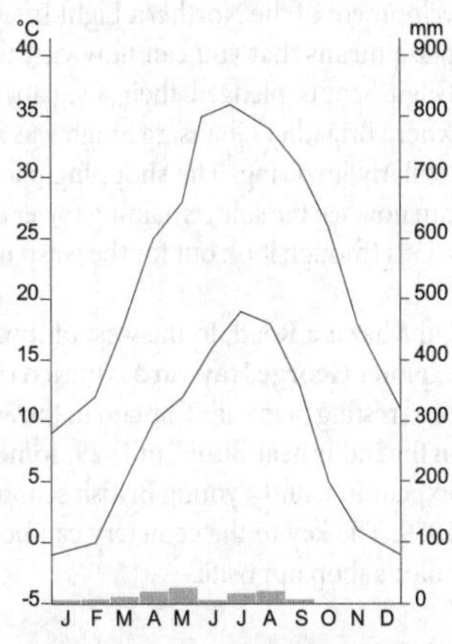

The best time to visit is between March and October

Sights

In terms of tourism, Gilgit's greatest utility is as a base to visit nearby attractions, arrange transport to other places in the Northern Areas,

Partition and the Gilgit uprising

*A radical reinterpretation of the 1935 lease agreement meant that when British paramountcy over India lapsed on 3 June 1947, the whole of the Gilgit Agency was handed over to the Maharaja of Kashmir. His representative, **Brig Ghansara Singh**, took over as governor of the area on 1 August 1947, 2 weeks before the date set for the independence of India and Pakistan. This was despite the fact that all the civil and military officers had expressed a preference to the British to join Pakistan. The local population had not been consulted at all. On the night of 26 October 1947, Maharaja Hari Singh announced his accession to India. How much this decision was influenced by the arrival of Pathan Afridi tribesmen from NWFP on his doorstep proclaiming a jihad, is open to historical debate, but in Gilgit plans for this eventuality had obviously already been made. A small group of army officers serving in the Gilgit Scouts had already secretly pledged their allegiance to Pakistan, and made plans for the liberation of Gilgit. In the early hours of the morning of 1 November 1947, Brigadier Ghansara Singh was arrested at his home, and placed under custody. He was made to sign a surrender document, and the Pakistani flag was raised over Gilgit. Within 4 days the Chilas Scouts had captured the fort at Bunji, thus gaining control of the vital line of communication, and potential counter-attack, with Srinagar.*

Meanwhile, in Gilgit, a Provisional Government had been set up, headed by Shah Rais Khan, a descendant of the former ruling family of Gilgit. Assistance was requested from Pakistan, although this fledgling state's meagre resources meant that the support given was generally moral as opposed to tangible. Major (later Brig) Mohammad Aslam Khan, winner of the Military Cross on the Burma front in 1941 and now proprietor of the Shangrila chain of hotels, was flown in to coordinate the military defence of the country so far acquired, and to 'liberate' as much territory as possible. He formed three forces, nicknamed 'Tiger', 'Ibex' and 'Eskimo', that not only succeeded in holding the territory gained, but also managed to liberate Baltistan and occupy parts of Kashmir. In January 1948 a UN sponsored cease-fire ended the war, leaving the Line of Control as the defacto border between Pakistan and India.

or prepare for a trekking expedition. Although a major tourist centre, there is not really that much to see in Gilgit itself.

There are a number of monuments dedicated to the Gilgit Uprising, including a memorial in **Chinar Bagh**, the municipal gardens down by the river, where the graves of two of the key players are located. The recent redevelopment of the Northern Light Infantry's former barracks into a shopping plaza means that you can now visit the **Oath Hall** where the officers of the Gilgit Scouts pledged their allegiance to Pakistan, and the **Custody Hall** where Brigadier Ghansara Singh was imprisoned. However, neither are particularly inspiring. The shopping plaza redevelopment also means that you can now see the sole remaining tower of the **fort** that Gohar Aman built in the 1850s (though look out for the wasp nests).

European cemetery On Khazana Road, to the west of town, is the cemetery in which the British explorer **George Hayward** is buried (see page 496). The graveyard is also the final resting place of a Captain in the Sikh Pioneers who "accidently drowned in the Indus near Bunji" in 1929, some members of the 1959 Batura Muztagh Expedition, and a young British school teacher who died in a fall near Sust in 1989. The key to the cemetery can be obtained from Mohammad Ali in the tailor's shop opposite.

Polo matches

Gilgit has a number of polo teams (largely drawn from the police and armed forces), with the version played here being far less genteel than the version that Prince Charles enjoys. The 'Old Polo Ground' (see map) is little more than a section of street that is closed off during matches (though some bloody-minded suzuki drivers seem determined to exercise their right of way during the practice matches held here). Important matches are held at the Aga Khan Polo Ground (see map). The army often organizes a tournament at the end of August/beginning of September, and there are generally plenty of practice matches as the area gears up for the Shandur Pass tournament (see 'box' on page 501). The 'Gilgit Uprising' is celebrated with a festival that usually features a series of polo matches (1 November for one week). Enquire about fixtures at the Tourist Office.

Jutial Nala/ Water Channel walk

A popular walk, giving good views of the 'bowl' in which Gilgit sits, involves a stroll along the Jutial Nala above Gilgit to the south. You can extend the walk by continuing along the Jutial water channel, even continuing to the Kargah Buddha (see below). Depending upon which option you follow, this can be a half or a full day's walk. Take plenty of water. **NB** Do not attempt these walks if it has rained recently – there may be the danger of landslides and rockfalls.

Take a suzuki from Saddar Bazaar up to the junction for the *Serena Lodge*, and then walk up the hill past the hotel. About 500 metres past the *Serena Lodge* turn right (west), and follow the irrigation channel (for directions just ask for the 'nala'). For **Jutial Nala**, head for the cleft in the rock near the beginning of the irrigation channel. Follow the goat path into the steep-sided gorge, sticking to the right of the stream. The gorge climbs for some six kilometres up to pine forests and green pastures, with great views back north to Rakaposhi.

Less ambitious walkers can ignore the temptation of climbing up the Jutial Nala, instead continuing west along the **water channel**. There are good views from here down to the Gilgit 'bowl', particularly early on misty mornings. After several kilometres you reach the village of Barmas, a 'suburb' of Gilgit. From here you can drop down into Gilgit (emerging onto Hospital Road, see map), or continue along the channel to the **Kargah Buddha** (see below).

Kargah Buddha

Thought to date to the seventh or eighth century, and showing marked similarities to Tibetan carvings found in Baltistan, this large image of a standing Buddha is found on a cliff face at Kargah, several kilometres west of Gilgit. There is an excellent local legend that provides a far more amusing explanation for the carved figure. The image is actually that of a giant who used to terrorise the local population. A passing saint was enlisted by the terrified villagers to deal with the menace, and he succeeded in pinning the giant to the rock face. The saint explained that the giant would remain pinned there for as long as he was alive, and they would continue to be safe if they buried the saint at the foot of the cliff upon his death. The resourceful villagers killed the saint there and then, and buried him at the foot of the cliff!

Several hundred metres upstream of the Buddha are the remains of a monastery and several stupas, whose excavation revealed a number of Sanskrit Buddhist texts.

■ *Getting there: Kargah is about eight kilometres from Gilgit, and can be reached on foot, or by suzuki. Passenger suzukis heading for Baseen village can be taken from Punial Rd in Gilgit, though they are few and far between. You may be encouraged to hire one (Rs 150 one-way). There are two options for walking there. Either head west along Punial Rd from Gilgit towards Kargah village, before turning left (south) along Kargah Nula, or incorporate the Buddha as part of the Jutial Nala/Water Channel walk (see above).*

Essentials

Sleeping
■ *on maps*
Price codes:
see inside front cover

Gilgit has arguably Pakistan's best range of accommodation options, (minus a truly international standard 5-star hotel), with more and more new hotels springing up each year. At times there are more hotels than tourists. Given that supply now far outstrips demand, some excellent bargains can be negotiated in all price brackets. Backpackers in particular are spoilt for choice.

NB Gilgit is the only place where you can officially make bookings for the ***NAPWD Inspection Bungalows*** in the surrounding area. In some of the more remote areas, particularly to the west between Gilgit and Chitral, this is the only accommodation available. Tourists take the lowest priority behind visiting dignitaries and NAPWD employees, and your booking can be cancelled without notice if someone higher in the pecking order turns up unannounced. If you do not have a booking, (very likely if coming from Chitral side), you will generally be able to use the rest house if it is unoccupied.

Villages that have ***Inspection Bungalows***, but limited alternative accommodation include Chilas, Babusar, Imit, Gahkuch, Gupis, Yasin, Darkot, Phandur, Singal and Gulapur. Those in particularly choice locations, eg Naltar, seem permanently full. Bookings should be made through Administrative Officer (Mr Aktar Hussain), Office of Chief Engineer, NAPWD, Khazana Rd, T3375. Fees are generally Rs 160 for a double room, Rs 200 for a VIP room, and the receipt must be given to the chowkidar at the

Gilgit

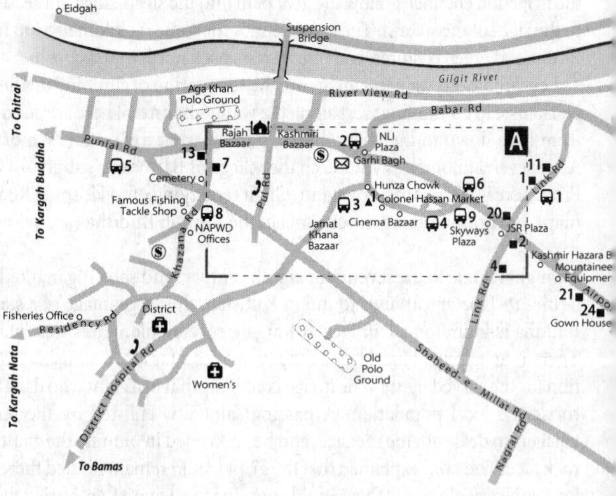

■ **Sleeping**
1 Alflah
2 Al-Imran/Ejaz
3 Chinese Lodge
4 Daimar
5 Dreamland
6 Gilgit Gateway
7 Golden Peak
8 Horizon
9 Hunza Inn
10 Hunza Tourist House
11 Mir's Lodge
12 Mountain Refuge
13 NAPWD Inspection Bungalow
14 North Inn
15 Park
16 PTDC Chinnar Inn
17 Riveria
18 Rupal
19 Shaheen International
20 Tajikistan Inn
21 Top Moon
22 Tourist Cottage
23 Tourist Hamlet
24 Vershigoom

Related map
A Gilgit Centre,
page 474

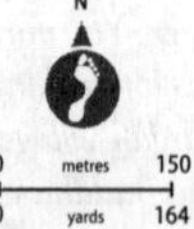

bungalow. Bedding is provided and the chowkidars are usually able to arrange basic meals, although it is certainly worth taking your own supplements.

More expensive hotels A-B *Rupal*, Khomer Chowk, Jutial Rd. Huge, new modern hotel due to open for the 1999 season, reports welcome.

B *Oasis International*, Jutial. Under construction. **B** *Palace*, Cinema Bazzar, T2266. Huge new place, deluxe rooms (**A**) are very big with furnished sitting area, fridge, dish TV, standard rooms are overpriced by comparison, nicely situated *Roof of the World* restaurant. **B** *PTDC Chinnar Inn*, Babar Rd, T2562. Standard and deluxe rooms, all with fan (though they keep reasonably cool even in summer), some a/c rooms planned, pleasant location, good value restaurant, sometimes used by budget tour groups, tourist info and shopping, not a bad deal. **B** *Riveria*, River View Rd, T4184, F3695. Peaceful location near river, high standard, dish TV, phone, hot bath (own generator), large garden used for BBQs (overland companies sometimes camp here), conference facilities, very good restaurant is popular. **B** *Serena Lodge*, Jutial, T55894/9. Luxurious rooms but small and hot in summer, private terrace, heating, dish TV, phone, room service, *Dumani* restaurant is highly recommended for good value buffets, *Jutial* coffee lounge, conference facilities, travel agents, shopping, badminton, tennis, foreign exchange, accepts credit cards. **B** *Shaheen International*, Airport Rd. Huge new place due to open in 1999, noisy location, reports welcome.

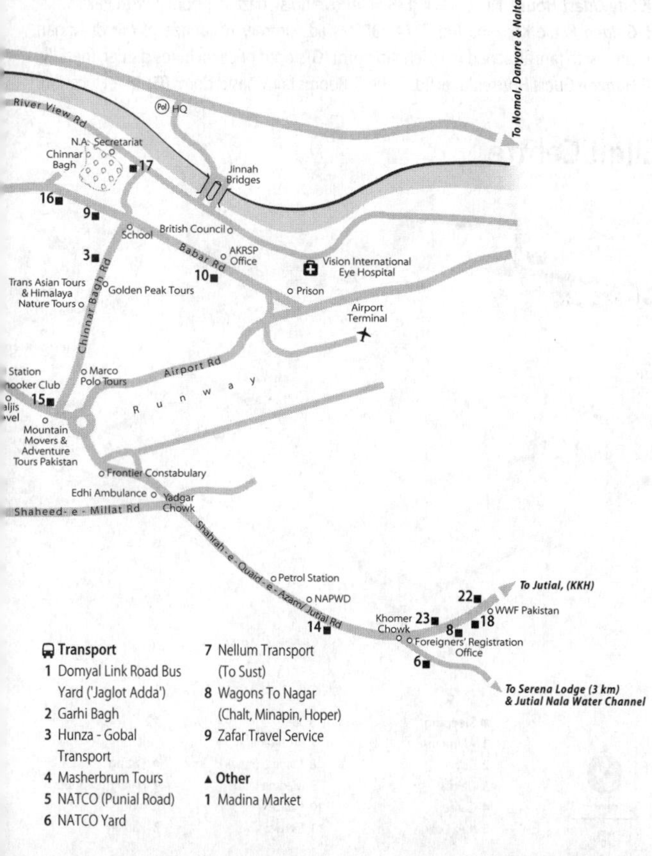

Mid-price hotels C *Hunza Tourist House*, Babar Rd, T2338/3788. Light and airy rooms, pleasant garden, 24 hour hot water, restaurant recommended, popular with NGO staff and tour groups. Recommended. **C** *Mir's Lodge*, Link Rd, T2875. Clean and friendly, nice rooms, some suites with dish TV, excellent restaurant, discounts can make it even better value. **C** *Panorama*, Jutial, T55715. Simple rooms with fan and air-cooler, attached hot bath, a/c restaurant, great (panoramic) views, rooftop BBQ, rather overpriced.

D *Gilgit Gateway*, Khomer Chowk, off Jutial Rd, T55014/55467. Formerly the *Kinbridge*, 'luxury' furnished rooms with dish TV, fan, IDD, carpets a little grubby, modern attached bath, plus overpriced economy rooms, nicely situated *World Roof* restaurant. **D** *Hunza Inn*, Babar Rd, T3814. Nice 'luxury' rooms with attached hot bath, good value simple rooms (attached bath, some hot), quiet location, restaurant, not bad value. **D** *Park*, Airport Rd, T2379, F3796. Service slack and generator noisy, rooms reasonably good value, TV, phone, restaurant gets good reviews. **D** *Tourist Hamlet*, Jutial Rd, T55537/38, F55120. Rooms to suit all pockets, (**B**) luxury suites (dish TV, phone, sitting room and verandah), standard rooms (**D**), dorms and camping (**G**), popular with budget groups, restaurant, Gilgit's only swimming pool, friendly and well run. Recommended. **D** *Yunas*, Shahrah-e-Resham, Cantt, Jutial. 7 kilometres from town centre, quiet, large carpeted rooms, dish TV, restaurant.

Budget hotels E *Chinese Lodge*, Chinnar Bagh Rd, T3950. Clean rooms, fan, attached bath, cheap dorm (**G**), recently refurbished, Chinese food recommended. **E** *City Guest House*, NLI Chowk, T3026. Above noisy bazaar, popular with Pakistanis. **E** *Golden Peak*, Khazana Rd, T2745/3890. Old summer residence of Mir of Nagar, rooms with fan, attached bath, cheap dorm (**G**), room price includes dinner, friendly. **E** *Horizon Guest House*, Jutial Rd, T55465. Rooms fairly basic, dorm (**G**), quiet location,

Gilgit Centre

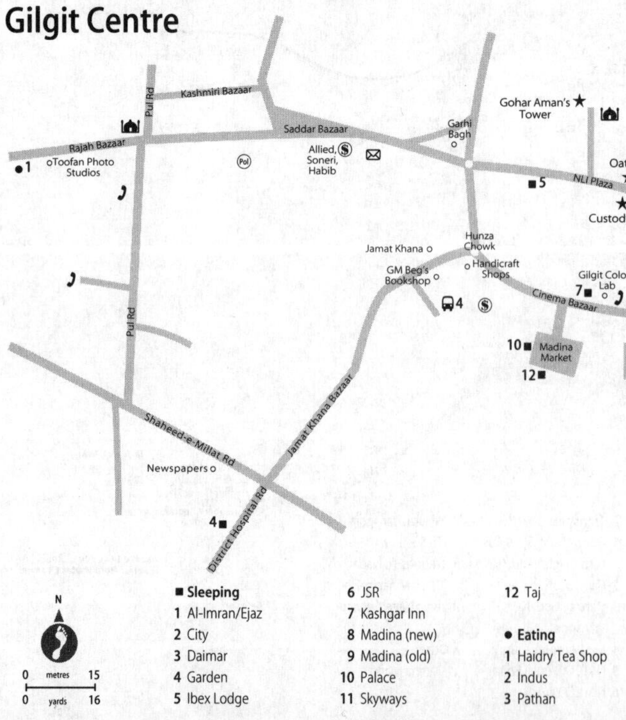

■ **Sleeping**
1 Al-Imran/Ejaz
2 City
3 Daimar
4 Garden
5 Ibex Lodge
6 JSR
7 Kashgar Inn
8 Madina (new)
9 Madina (old)
10 Palace
11 Skyways
12 Taj

● **Eating**
1 Haidry Tea Shop
2 Indus
3 Pathan

well run, has a nice garden and highly recommended food. **E *JSR***, JSR Plaza, Airport Rd, T2308. Much declined, some rooms with attached grubby bath, shared bathrooms very run down. **E *North Inn***, Khomer Chowk, Jutial Rd, T55118/55545. Large carpeted rooms, fan, tiled attached bath, new block under construction, food good. **E *Skyways***, Skyways Plaza, Airport Rd, T3026. Central location, but above noisy music shop. **E *Taj***, Cinema Bazaar, T3716. Rooms nothing special but attached bathrooms are very modern, restaurant. **E** *Top Moon*, Airport Rd, T3828. Indistinguishable from other new hotels built above Gilgit's markets. **E-F *Ibex Lodge***, NLI Plaza, T2334. Some rooms en suite others shared bath, most rooms quite large though either windowless and dark, or too many windows and very public! Restaurant.

F *Alflah*, Link Rd, T3447. Basic place not much used by foreigners. **F *Al-Imran/Ejaz***, Ejaz Plaza, Airport Rd, T3468. Basic, looks structurally unsound (though we said the same thing 3 years ago!). **F *Dreamland***, Airport Rd. Basic place not used by foreigners. **F *Garden***, District Hospital Rd, T2444. Recently renovated after change of ownership, very cheap rooms plus dorm and camping (**G**), quiet garden, restaurant that friendly owner says will specialize in 'McDonalds-style' food! **F *Kashgar Inn***, Cinema Bazaar, T2326. Basic place not used by foreigners. **F *Mountain Refuge***, Babar Rd. Experienced owner, well run, 10 very good value rooms plus some cheap dorms (**G**), number of basic 'huts' planned, rooms available in the family house, excellent communal dinner (Rs 65) served in nicely located restaurant, wonderfully tranquil flower and fruit tree filled garden. Recommended. **F *Tajikistan Inn***, Airport Rd. Basic place not used by foreigners. **F *Vershigoom***, Airport Rd. Basic place not used by foreigners. **F-G *Madina***, NLI Chowk. Gilgit's most popular backpacker hangout for the last 7 years or so, the manager Mohammad Yaqoob and his staff work extremely hard to make your stay a success. Convenient for the bus station, has 'old' and 'new' parts on either side of the road, both with a variety of rooms. Excellent doubles with attached hot bath (**E**), simple doubles with shared bath (**F**), very cheap singles and dorm beds (**G**). Excellent value communal meal served at 1930 (Rs 65), BBC World Service TV, relaxing garden, good place to chat and exchange info. There are a couple of recommended guides who operate out of the hotel. Gets better each year. Highly recommended. **F-G *Tourist Cottage***, Khomer, Jutial Rd, T55516. Backpackers' favourite, run by Japanesse Aisha Keiko, good value rooms (that remain cool in summer and warm in winter), cheap dorms (**G**), shady garden, excellent Japanese set dinner at 1930 (Rs 100, order by 1600 if not resident) plus Japanese lunchtime menu (Rs 30-70). Highly recommended.

G *Tourist Hamlet*, see entry under **D** above.

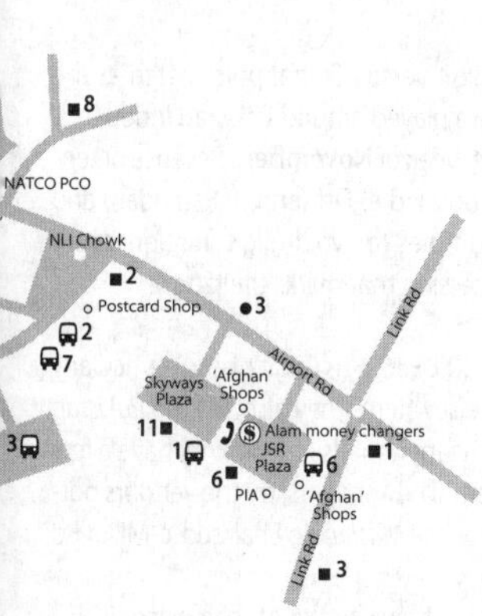

Transport

1 Hameed Travels
2 Masherbrum Tours
3 Masherbrum Yard
4 Minibuses to Karimabad (Hunza-Gojal Transport)
5 NATCO Yard
6 Sargin Travels
7 Zafar Travel Service

Eating

● on maps

Gilgit has a reasonable selection of restaurants, though vegetarians may become bored very quickly. The best *à la carte* menu is offered by the ***Serena Lodge***, and their 'eat-all-you-want' buffet is excellent for a splurge (Rs 250). Other good hotel restaurants where you'll pay up to Rs 200 for a full meal are: ***Hunza Tourist House*** (good breakfasts and 'western' fast foods), ***Gilgit Gateway*** (good Chinese), ***Mir's Lodge***, ***North Inn*** (good Chinese), ***Park Hotel***, ***PTDC Chinnar Inn*** and ***Riveria*** (very good range of Pak, Chinese and continental).

Some of the backpacker places serve tasty communal dinners (usually vegetarian) for as little as Rs 65, though after 3 days they can become a little monotonous. The best ones are at the ***Madina*** and ***Mountain Refuge***. Well worth the trip is the Japanese set menu dinner at the ***Tourist Cottage*** (Rs 100, book by 1600). A final mention must be made of the ***Horizon Guest House***, which delights visitors with milk shakes (Rs 30), pizza (Rs 100), spagetti (Rs 75), mashed potato and beans (Rs 70) and 'pita pockets' (Rs 25).

For local men the main diet comprises meat and chicken, and there's no better sight than the ***Pathan Hotel*** in full flow. Hygiene is a concern in some of Gilgit's restaurants, so make sure what you order is properly cooked and served straight off the hot plate. Spicy chicken karahi is excellent value at Rs 150 (for 2).

Entertainment

Sports **Bicycling:** see under 'tour companies' below. **Badmington:** available at the ***Serena Lodge***, though really for guests only. **Fishing:** licences should be obtained from the ***Fisheries Office***, Napur Rd, T2374 (Rs 100 per day). They have some gear for rent here, or you could try the ***Famous Fishing Tackle Shop*** on Khazana Rd. **Horse riding:** is available at the ***Danyore Horse Club***, Danyore, near Gilgit, T30 (Mr Mir Aman, or through most hotels), including the chance to play polo. Charges: 1 hour, Rs 200; all day Rs 600; polo lessons Rs 350. No insurance provided. **Polo:** see under 'sights' and 'local festivals' above. **Swimming:** Gilgit's only pool is at the ***Tourist Hamlet*** (see 'sleeping'). The water is freezing. Note that women should bathe in full shalwar kameez. **Tennis:** Available at the ***Serena Lodge***, though really for guests only.

Nightlife

Gilgit's nightlife has never been the same since the ***Peephole Club*** closed down and Siobhan moved back to Yorkshire! Some of the hotels have videos, though most of the rental shops just stock 'shoot-em-up' flicks (a notable exception being a place out in Jutial).

Festivals

One of the key 'local' festivals is the annual Gilgit versus Chitral polo match at the Shandur Pass (see page 501). Other matches are played around Pakistan Independence Day (**14 August**) and 'Jashan-e-Gilgit' (first week of **November**). Because of tensions between Gilgit's Sunni and Shia populations, Eid el-Fitr (end of Ramadan) and Ashoura (9th and 10th of Muhurram) are good times to avoid Gilgit (foreigners are usually confined to their hotels during the procession that marks the latter).

Shopping

Bookshops *GM Beg's*, Jamat Khana Bazaar, T2409, F3695, is Gilgit's best, particularly for books on local history that are out of print elsewhere. They also sell the *Pakistan Handbook* and have some maps. Some of the cheaper hotels (eg *Madina*) have a few paperbacks for sale. For English-language Pakistani newspapers, try the vendors outside the 2 banks next to the GPO, or the agent for *The Muslim* on Shaheed-e-Millat Rd near the *Garden Hotel*.

Carpets Try the handicraft stores around Hunza Chowk, or the Afghan places in JSR Plaza.

Clothing For those coming from China, Gilgit is usually the first place that you can buy a shalwar kameez (made-to-measure or ready-wear from numerous places in Saddar and Raja Bazaar). For Chitrali hats, waistcoats, choghas etc, look around Hunza Chowk and Madina Market.

Gemstones and jewellery See under 'handicrafts'.

Handicrafts The main handicraft centres are congregated around Hunza Chowk, Madina Market, JSR Plaza, plus the ***Hunza Handicrafts*** shop at the *Park Hotel*. They sell

Flying between Gilgit and Islamabad

The flight between Gilgit and Islamabad must be one of the most spectacular commercial flights anywhere in the world: the little Fokker F-27 planes have to fly **round** *the mountains because they can't fly* **over** *them! You will often find a number of empty seats on board (even though the flight is always over-subscribed). This enables the plane to get more lift, (with the number of empty seats being at the discretion of the pilot). Being so weather-dependent it is never guaranteed that the flights will actually go, so allow spare time to take the bus instead. Even getting on the plane is no guarantee that the flight will depart, and planes have been known to turn round mid-flight (an Urdu-speaking friend enjoying the flight from the cockpit once witnessed a heated argument between pilot and co-pilot as to whether the plane should proceed or turn round!).*

The cost of the flight used to be heavily subsidized (with foreign tourists enjoying a degree of subsidy). This is no longer the case, though at Rs 2,440 one-way it is still remarkably good value. Two seats per flight used to be reserved for tourists (booked through the PTDC), though officially this is no longer the case. If, however, you can manage to make yourself look pathetic enough in the scrum at the PIA booking office, the airline staff may take pity on you. Note that it is not difficult to buy a ticket for the flight: it's just very difficult to actually book a seat on it. Note that if a plane is cancelled due to bad weather (and this bad weather can be anywhere along the route), ticket holders are re-booked onto the following day's flights. At least one-third of all flights are cancelled! If you do get on a flight, sit on the starboard (right) side Ism-Gilgit, and the port (left) side Gilgit-Ism (though there are incredible views on all sides). It is also worth asking the cabin staff for the captain's permission to come up front, and see the view from the driving seat – it's awesome.

just about anything that you could wish for, including a lot of stuff made nowhere near the Northern Areas. Rubbish from China is seen at its best (or worst) in NLI Plaza.

Maps Trekking maps should really be brought from home. ***GM Beg's*** bookshop and the ***Hunza Handicrafts*** have a small selection.

Photography A lot of shops sell colour print film (check to see how it's stored), some black & white, and occasionally slide film. Processing in Gilgit is not particularly reliable (over-used chemicals, poor storage, dust). Judging by the window display, ***Toofan Photo Studios*** in Rajah Bazzar specialise in photographing the region's retards!

Supermarkets Not quite *K-Mart* or *Sainsbury's*, but ***Kashmir Hazara Bakery***, Airport Rd, has the best selection of imported foodstuffs.

Trekking gear ***Gown House***, ***Hunza Handicrafts*** and ***Mountaineering Equipments***, all on Airport Rd, have an eclectic collection of rather worn trekking and climbing gear (including boots, sleeping mats, some sleeping bags, jackets, tents, stoves, some trekking food, though it's unwise to buy second hand ropes). Renting stuff usually works out more costly than buying it, then selling it back to them. Check the gear before you take it away (eg make sure tents have the right poles). ***Adventure Centre Pakistan*** at *GM Beg's Bookshop* rents better quality gear.

Long distance transport

Air Islamabad: Monday, Tuesday, Wednesday, Friday, Saturday 0700, 0745, 1000. Sunday, Thursday 0700, 0745. Tourist fare Rs 2,440 one-way. See 'box' for further information.

Jeep/Car hire There are a number of destinations around Gilgit (usually trekking trailheads) where hiring a jeep is the simplest option for getting there. When the charge is shared between a group it suddenly becomes more reasonable. A privately hired jeep is an extremely pleasant way to travel, offering the flexibility of being able to stop when and where you like. Hire charges for certain routes are more or less fixed, though you may get a slightly cheaper deal by going through a hotel manager at a backpacker hotel. You'll probably get a more reliable vehicle (and steady driver) by going through one of the reputable travel agencies. The prices quoted below are from ***Travel Walji's***, and should represent the maximum you should pay on any route. For destinations not covered below, the usual rate is Rs 12 per kilometre on shingle/dirt roads, Rs 9 per kilometre on metalled roads, plus a Rs 300 overnight charge. **Astor**, Rs 2,000 one-way; **Chirah** (Bagrot Valley), Rs 1,300 one-way; **Chitral**, Rs 8,000 one-way; **Fairy Meadows**, Rs 2,300 one-way, Rs 2,600 same-day return (**Raikot Bridge** Rs 1,200 one-way); **Kargah Buddah**, Rs 400 return; **Karimabad**, Rs 1,500 one-way, Rs 2,100 same-day return; **Khunjerab Pass**, Rs 4,400 one-way, Rs 4,800 2 day return; **Islamabad/Rawalpindi**, Rs 8,000 one-way (this may be a car rather than a jeep); **Mastuj**, Rs 6,900 one-way; **Minapin**, Rs 1,000 one-way; **Naltar (Upper)**, Rs 1,100 one-way, Rs 1,300 same-day return; **Naran** via **Babusar Pass**, Rs 9,200 one-way; **Tarashing**, Rs 2,700 one-way; **Skardu**, Rs 2,600 one-way. *Travel Walji's* are also agents for ***Avis*** car rental. For details of **bicycle hire**, see under 'tour companies' below.

Long distance buses The main ***NATCO*** (Northern Areas Transport Corporation) yard and booking office is at NLI Chowk. Tickets can normally be bought 1 day in advance. Student card holders get a 50 percent discount (except on 'deluxe' services to Rawalpindi). ***NATCO*** buses run south to **Rawalpindi** via **Raikot Bridge**, **Chilas**, **Komila/Dasu**, **Besham** (Rs 165), **Mansehra** and **Abbottabad** at: 0900 ('normal', Rs 257, 18 hours +), 1400 ('deluxe', Rs 300, 16 hours +), 1500 ('deluxe'), 1700 ('deluxe'), 1900 ('deluxe') and 2100 ('coaster', Rs 320, 14 hours +). There is 1 daily ***NATCO*** bus north bound at 0700 to **Sust** (Rs 100, 6 hours) via **Ganesh** (for **Karimabad** , Rs 50, 3 hours), **Gulmit** (Rs 69, 4 hours) and **Passu** (Rs 76, 4½ hours). They also have a daily service at 0600 to **Skardu** (Rs 100, 6½ hours).

NATCO run services west from their yard on Punial Rd to **Yasin** (Rs 76-90, 1 day 'normal' the next day 'deluxe', 7 hours) via **Gahkuch** (Rs 42-57) and **Gupis** (Rs 62-74) at 0800, with extra services as far as Gupis at 1000 and Gahkuch only at 1200. For details of cargo jeeps to **Mastuj** and **Chitral** see the 'Gilgit to Chitral' section below.

Masherbrum Tours, near to *Indus Restaurant*, T3095/2580. Run daily deluxe minibuses to **Rawalpindi** (arriving Pir Wadhi) at 1300, 1600, 1800, Rs 300; and to **Skardu** at 0700 (Rs 80, 'big bus') and 0800 1000 1200 (Rs 100, minibus). ***K2 Travel Service***, NLI Chowk, next to *NATCO*, T2370, run daily minibuses to **Skardu** (Rs 100). ***Zafar Travel Service*** next to *Masherbrum Tours* has a daily minibus to **Besham** (Rs 200) at 1500.

Hameed Travels, Skyways Plaza, Airport Rd, T3181, have daily coasters to **Rawalpindi** (arriving at Mashriq Hotel) at 1500 and 1700 (Rs 330, 14 hours +). ***Sargin Travels***, JSR Plaza, Airport Rd, also run coasters to **Rawalpindi** (arriving at Raja Bazaar) at 1500 and 1700 (Rs 330, 14 hours +).

Minibuses to **Karimabad** run from the office of ***Hunza-Gojal Transport*** in Jamat Khana Bazaar until mid afternoon (Rs 65, 3 hours). ***Nellum Transport*** have morning minbuses to **Sust** (Rs 100, 5-6 hours) from their office on Airport Rd (near the petrol stations).

Travel to destinations in **Nagar**, such as **Chalt** (Rs 30, mornings), **Minapin** (Rs 50, about 1300) and **Hoper** (Rs 90, early morning) is a little more complicated. At least 1 minibus runs to each of these places from close to the National Bank of Pakistan on Khazana Rd, though currently they don't have destination boards in English or a fixed timetable. There are plans to make these services better organised and more accessible, like the Karimabad services.

The bus/jeep yard on Domyal Link Rd (called 'Jaglot adda') has a daily cargo jeep at 1300 to **Lower Naltar** (Rs 50, 4 hours). Minibuses also run from here to **Chilas** (3½ hours) and **Besham** (9 hours) via **Jaglot** and **Raikot Bridge**, although there's no fixed schedules. For cargo jeeps to **Bagrot** and **Haramosh**, ask the shopkeepers near Garhi Bagh (the scruffy gardens just east of the GPO). Cargo jeeps to **Astor** (Rs 95) depart from the *Diamar Hotel* (see map).

Directory

Airline offices *PIA*, JSR Plaza, Airport Rd, T3390. Open daily 0800-1500.

Banks ***National Bank of Pakistan***, Khazana (Bank) Rd, ***Habib Bank*** and ***Soneri Bank*** next to the GPO. All offer foreign exchange (cash and TCs), though it's a slow process and rates are inferior to those available down country. ***Alam Money Changer***, JSR Plaza, T4148 (open daily 0830-1900) offers better rates on cash and TCs and is far more efficient. Most hotel managers will also change cash US$s.

Communications Most of the phone numbers in Gilgit are 4 digit, although Jutial now has a digital exchange and numbers there are 5 digit with a 55 prefix. Gilgit may soon have a digital exchange too. **GPO:** Saddar Bazaar (open Mon-Thur and Sat 0800-1500, Fri 0800-1200, closed Sun). Go to the 'poste restante' office round the back to get all stamps franked. Gilgit to London takes 7-10 days, slightly quicker in the opposite direction. **Poste Restante:** take the little alley up the side of the GPO building, and enter through the last door round the corner on the left. Mail is kept in a small basket and you are free to browse. Notes adressed to 'Poste Restante-Gilgit' saying "please forward all my mail to ..." end up filed in the basket with all your mail! **Internet:** not yet, although *Adventure Centre Pakistan* have an email address (ikram@acp-glt.sdnpk.undp.org) and this guy will probably be the first to see the potential of email. **Telephones:** the government-run PCO is on Pul Rd, behind Rajah Bazaar, or go to the main Telegraph Office on District Hospital Rd (open 24 hrs). Calls are cheapest from here, but queues are longer. Connection times seem much quicker than they used to be. There are a host of private PCOs in Gilgit, though the most convenient is: ***NATCO PCO FAX***, T0092-5723739/2974, outside the *NATCO* bus yard. The proprietor keeps one line free for foreigners to receive calls (no time limit, though you have to pay for a minimum 3 mins out-going call). Charges (per 3 mins, then per additional min): Austria Rs 350, Rs 116; Canada Rs 410, Rs 135; France Rs 380, Rs 125; Ireland Rs 270, Rs 96; Holland Rs 300, Rs 100; UK Rs 305, Rs 101; USA Rs 320, Rs 106.

Cultural centres *British Council*, English Resource Centre, at AKRSP, Babar Rd, PO Box 506, T2480/2910, F2779 (open Mon-Thur 1300-1700, Fri 1400-1700 females only, Sat closed, Sun 0900-1500), has a small library, copies of the *Guardian Weekly*, Pakistani newspapers. The 'Guest Speaker' evenings have become a significant part of the expat social scene in Gilgit, though it's perhaps a measure of how little there is to do in the evening in this town that crowds are prepared to turn out for talks on "The Problem of Solid Waste in Gilgit"!

Hospitals & medical services **Chemists:** opposite the hospitals and at various places in Cinema Bazaar. **Hospitals:** *District Hospital*, District Hospital Rd, has a reasonable level of competence, though extreme cases are often flown out to Islamabad (weather permitting!). Women should go to the ***Women's Hospital*** opposite, where they should ask to see a female doctor. Certain cases will, however, be referred to a (male) specialist at the District Hospital. The resources at the foreign charity-run ***Vision International Eye Hospital*** on River View Rd (T2878) are too stretched to deal with tourist's general complaints. ***Edhi Ambulance***, Yadgar Chowk, T55156. **Useful addresses** **International agencies:** ***Aga Khan Rural Support Programme (AKRSP)***, PO Box 506, Babar Rd, T2480, F2779. Has an excellent 'development' library, and you may find someone who will explain the organization's role in the Northern Areas. ***International Union for the Conservation of Nature – Pakistan (IUCN)***, is housed in the former *Alpine Hotel* out in Jutial. ***Kashgar Prefecture of the People's Republic of China***, Jutial, T55041, though they don't issue visas. ***United Nations Military Observer Group in India and Pakistan***, Field Station, Jutial. ***WWF-Pakistan*** have an office at Khomer, on the Jutial Rd (near *Tourist Cottages*), T55658. Can offer some information on the region.

Libraries *British Council*, see 'cultural centres' above. ***Gilgit Municipal Library***, Upper Khazana (Bank) Rd (open Mon-Thur and Sun 0900-1500, Fri 0800-1200, Sat closed). Has an excellent range (borrowers welcome for a small deposit), particularly strong on local history, Sherbaz Ali Khan who runs the library is extremely helpful.

Tour companies & travel agents Tour and trekking agencies have proliferated in recent years, although it is difficult to recommend individual guides and agencies unless we have used them personally. Those listed below are the most reputable and longest established, and are ones that the 2 editors (or readers of the *Pakistan Handbook*) have direct experience of. ***Adventure Center** Pakistan*, 468 Sir Aga Khan Rd (at *GM Beg's Bookshop*), T2409, F3698, E ikram@acp-glt.sdnpk.undp.org. Run by the experienced and efficient Ikram M Beg. Recommended. ***Golden Peak Tours***, Chinnar Bagh Link Rd, T4159, F55900. Treks, tours, transport hire. ***Himalayan Nature Tours***, Chinnar Bagh Link Rd, T2946/55359, F55900. Treks, tours, guided expeditions, also rents out Italian-made 21-speed mountain bikes for Rs 400 per day (deposit required). ***Madina Guides***, c/o *Madina Hotel*, NLI Chowk. Recently set up by 2 guides who work out of (but are not attached to) the *Madina Hotel*, this is a good option for backpackers. One of the editors has personally travelled with Nasir Ahmad, and he has also been recommended by several readers. ***Mountain Movers***, Airport Rd, T2967. Long-time established, can also arrange white-water rafting. ***Travel Walji's***, Airport Rd, T2665, F4129. Pakistan's longest established travel agents, a little pricier than others, but reliable and very well run, can also arrange white-water rafting.

Tourist offices *PTDC*, *PTDC Chinnar Inn*, Babar Rd, T2562. New incumbent is far more amenable than predecessor. There is also a small office in JSR Plaza, Airport Rd. Budget hotel managers (eg Yaqoob at the *Madina Hotel*) are also good sources of info.

Useful addresses **Foreigners' Registration Office**, Khomer Chowk, Jutial Rd (open Mon-Thur and Sat 0800-1500, Fri 0800-1200, closed Sun). This is a new location. **NAPWD**, Administrative Officer (Mr Aktar Hussain), Office of Chief Engineer, NAPWD, Khazana Rd, T3375, for booking *NAPWD Resthouses*, see 'sleeping' above. **Police**, T4007/3266, the headquarters are on the other side of the Gilgit River, across Jinnah Bridges.

Excursions from Gilgit

Naltar Valley

Colour map 5, grid A3

Lying to the north and northwest of Gilgit is the beautiful Naltar Valley. An area of glacial lakes, pine forests and alpine meadows penned in by snow covered peaks (with seasonal skiing), this is ideal camping country (though some accommodation is available). There are a number of short hikes that can be made from here, in addition to two short treks.

Ins and outs The road to **Naltar Valley** leaves Gilgit by the Jinnah Bridge, but turns north (left) at the Frontier Constabulary post, rather than crossing the suspension bridge to Danyore and the KKH. This route used to form part of the Old Hunza Road prior to the construction of the KKH. The route is dry and dusty until you reach the extensive cultivated area of **Nomal**. There is a ***NAPWD Inspection Bungalow*** here, as well as a dubious looking footbridge across the Hunza River to the KKH.

At Nomal a rough jeep track turns west, up the Naltar Valley. As Schomberg (1933) points out, this entrance to the Naltar Valley is an "unprepossessing means of access to the lovely valley behind". After 10 kilometres you reach **'Lower' Naltar**, or Naltar Paen. **'Upper' Naltar** is a further 10 kilometres up the valley. The main settlement at 'Upper' Naltar is often referred to as **Dumian** (2,820 metres).

Naltar The lower reaches of the Naltar Valley are confined within a hot, rocky, narrow canyon, but at 'Upper' Naltar the valley opens out to reveal lush green alpine pastures and pine forests surrounded by spectacular snowy peaks. In winter, the scene is entirely different, and it is here that the Pakistan Air Force maintains a winter survival school. Note that Lower Naltar is Shia, whilst Upper Naltar is Sunni.

Sleeping & eating

E *Pasban Inn* has large rooms with attached bath, restaurant with a good menu and dish TV. **F** *Hilltop* has a 4 bed dorm and a 3 bed dorm, both with attached bath, restaurant, karaoke machine and walnut garden with flashing lights. **F** *Prince* has a couple of triples, with separate open air toilet, restaurant, and garden without flashing lights.

Transport

Naltar's cargo jeep drivers have a well deserved poor reputation, and are keen to fleece visiting tourists. You may be asked to pay for a "special booking" only to find another 16 passengers sharing your jeep. If travelling from Gilgit, it is essential to establish whether the fare is to 'Lower' or 'Upper' Naltar. The fare from Gilgit to 'Lower' Naltar is Rs 50, and you may be asked for the same again to continue to 'Upper' Naltar. Cargo jeeps leave from Gilgit's Rajah Bazaar, and from near the minibus stand on Link Rd. A private jeep from Gilgit to 'Upper' Naltar costs Rs 1,100 one-way, Rs 1,300 same day return. Return jeeps leave 'Upper' Naltar early in the morning.

Naltar Lake

The beautiful Naltar Lake is a gentle 12 kilometres walk beyond 'Upper' Naltar, and can be reached in three and a half to four hours. The path passes through pleasant meadows and scattered pine forests, although there is some scrambling over loose scree and boulders at the start of the trek. The gradient is quite modest though. It is worth noting if you are returning the same day, however, that the numerous streams that you have to hop across are considerably higher by late afternoon. There are actually several lakes in the upper

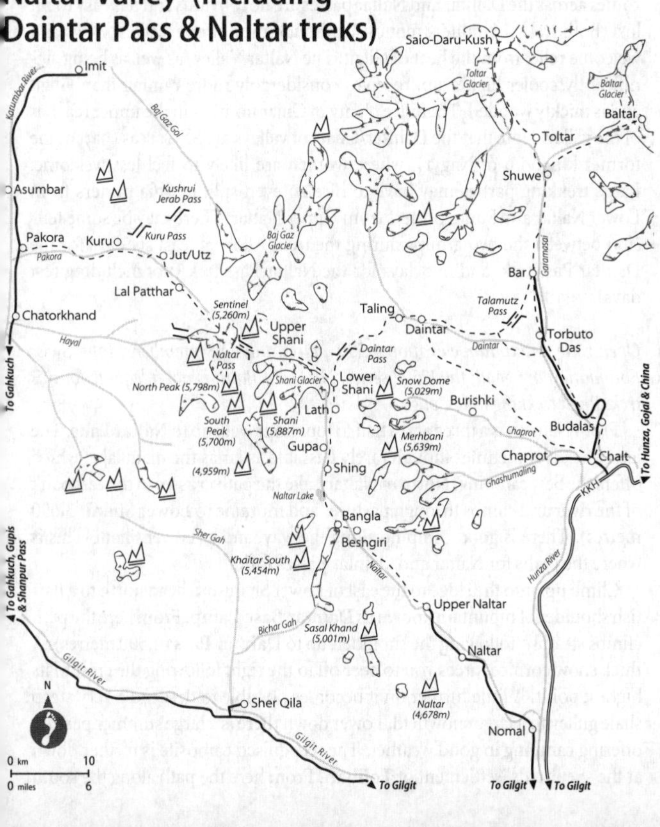

part of the Naltar Valley, although the first one that you come to is probably the most attractive. Set in a hollow of terminal moraine deposited by a long since retreated glacier, Naltar Lake is a stunning vision of colour, with exquisite aquamarines, electric blues and vivid greens. In places it is unbelievably clear. Potential swimmers should note that it is very deep and genital-shrivellingly cold. Diving in may cause unhealthy rapid changes in body temperature. It can also take longer to climb out than you think, so don't leave it until you are turning blue before attempting to scramble out. Upon closer investigation, male swimmers may have the impression of having undergone a sex change.

It is quite possible to camp at this idyllic spot, or to use the tents provided by the **F** *Lake View Hotel*, or *Red Stone Huts*. Both also serve food. The two other lakes beyond Naltar Lake are said to offer the best fishing.

Beyond the series of lakes, there are two more strenuous trekking opportunities. One route travels over the 4,710 metres Naltar (or Pakor) Pass into the Ishkoman Valley, and the other crosses the Daintar Pass (4,500 metres) to Chalt.

Treks from the Naltar Valley

The Naltar valley gives access to two possible treks, one leading over the **Daintar Pass** and via the Daintar Valley to Chalt in the Chaprot Valley, the second leading over the **Naltar (Pakor) Pass** into the Ishkoman Valley. Although in an open zone, a guide is recommended for both treks since the routes across the Daintar and Naltar passes are not obvious and it is easy to get lost. Both treks are quite strenuous, although they offer excellent views and welcome relief from the heat of Gilgit. The Naltar Valley, as well as being significantly cooler higher up, receives considerably more rainfall than Gilgit and is thickly wooded. There are plenty of Gujar nomads in the upper reaches of the valley. Note that the Daintar/Chaprot valleys are Shia areas (part of the former kingdom of Nagyr), where women are likely to feel less welcome. Large trekking parties may have to hire an even split of Shia porters from Lower Naltar and Sunni porters from Upper Naltar. There may be some tension between the two groups during the trek! Allow at least six days for the Daintar Pass trek, and five days for the Naltar Pass trek (not including rest days).

Daintar Pass trek

Open zone. Maximum elevation 4,500 metres. July to September. Maps; Swiss Foundation are good; the U502 series, NJ 43-14 Baltit is not adequate for this trek. Read trekking notes, page 67.

From Naltar it is a three and a half to four hour walk up to **Naltar Lake**. The jeep track is sometimes though rarely passable as far as the main lake, which offers the best camping. North of Naltar Lake the path crosses to the east bank of the river and climbs through pastures and moraine to **Lower Shani** (3,690 metres). There is good camping along the way, and at Lower Shani. This is where the paths for Naltar and Daintar passes fork.

Climb up onto the ridge to the east of Lower Shani and head north to a flattish shoulder of mountain known as **Daintar Base Camp**. From here the path climbs steadily, following the shoulder, up to **Daintar Pass** (4,500 metres). A thick snow cornice forces you to bear off to the right following the crest to its highest point. A little further on it becomes possible to descend a very steep shale gulley to a large snowfield. Lower down there is a large summer pasture offering camping in good weather. The recognised campsite is further down at the shepherds' settlement of **Tolibari**. From here the path along the south bank of the river runs through woods and pastures, fording two side streams and then enters a narrow gorge before arriving at the village of **Taling**, where the Daintar River flows down from the north. There is a polo ground above the village. Taling is at the head of the jeep track, although it is often blocked lower down and jeeps rarely come up this far (if you are planning to arrange for a jeep to pick you up from here, check first as to the condition of the track). It takes around three hours to walk down to Torbuto Das, from where there are fairly regular passenger jeeps. At Daintar just past Taling, a path on the opposite (south) bank of the river climbs up to the ridge behind and leads down to Chaprot village, three kilometres above Chalt (see page 499).

Naltar (Pakor) Pass

Open zone. Maximum elevation 4,710 metres. July to September. Maps: as for Daintar Pass. Read trekking notes, page 67.

From Lower Shani (3,690 metres, see above) the path heads west on a good path alongside the Shani Glacier to **Upper Shani** (4,230 metres), a large area of summer pasture at the foot of the pass. Higher up there is another area of summer pasture on a plateau, also good for camping. **Naltar (or Pakor)** Pass (4,710 metres) is wide and flat topped, with no definite path across it. Shortly after the summit the route bears off to the right (north) across crevassed snowfields, crosses a small side glacier and then follows the crest of lateral moraine before arriving at a meadow surrounded by trees, plus large red boulders known as **Krui Bokht** (in Khowar language, or **Lal Patthar** in Urdu). From here the path follows the Pakora River, passing through pastures, woods and summer settlements, crossing the river three times. The lower section of the valley enters a narrow gorge, with the trail gently climbing up to the Gujar huts at **Jut/Utz** (3,390 metres). The descent towards Pakora is fairly steep, and also hot and dry, before the valley opens out as it approaches Pakora village, at the junction with the Ishkoman Valley (see page 492).

Danyore Valley

Most visitors only see **Danyore** (Dainyor) as a small roadside village on the KKH just north of Gilgit (see page 532). However, this small village actually stands at the head of a little-explored valley – **Danyore Valley** – that provides one of the best views of the South Face of **Rakaposhi**. What is more, there is a relatively easy trek in the Danyore Valley that provides a close up view of the Rakaposhi South Face. Suzuki minivans run via the Jinnah Bridges and another dramatic suspension bridge to Danyore from Gilgit's Garhi Bagh (near Saddar Bazaar). For orientation see the 'Danyore, Bagrot and Haramosh Valleys' map on page 484).

Danyore Valley Trek (Rakaposhi South Face)

Open zone. Maximum elevation circa 4,000 metres. July to September. Maps: Swiss Foundation good; U502 series, NI 43-2 Gilgit and NJ 43-14 Baltit are adequate. Read trekking notes, page 67.

This trek is an excellent way of getting in shape for more strenuous treks; it does not involve crossing any passes, and although the lower sections of the valley are hot and dry, higher up there are beautiful alpine woods and pastures in the ablation valley alongside the glacier flowing down from Rakaposhi. Allow two days (three going slowly) to reach the head of the valley, and two (or one very long day) to return.

The path into the valley climbs up through **Danyore village**, heading towards the "Danyore Hydel Project" on the right bank of the river. It takes four to five hours in a baking hot, bare rock canyon to reach the first spring water. The path then crosses the river three times before climbing steeply over a shoulder and descending once again to the river. Further on, across a wide stony plain, a rock cairn marks the point where a small spring emerges at the base of the low cliffs by the river. The path then climbs steeply up to **Barit village**, situated on a small plateau. Rich green terraced fields extend up the side valley flowing in from the west. The path crosses the side valley on a wooden bridge and then climbs steeply to rejoin the main valley, running along an irrigation channel. It then continues past three bridges giving access to cultivated summer settlements on the east bank before climbing up through pine forests to a small summer settlement high above the river. There is spring water available here. After descending back to the river level, cross to the east bank of the river. The path, marked by stone cairns, runs through lightly wooded, rocky terrain. It crosses a small side stream and then climbs onto the ridge of the glacier's lateral moraine. Follow the ridge until the ablation valley to the right widens out into a large area of alpine pastures, woods and streams, offering numerous idyllic camping spots. It is well worth spending a day or two here to explore and take in the awesome scenery.

Bagrot and Haramosh Valleys

Located to the east of Gilgit, the Bagrot Valley runs roughly southwest-northeast for 20 kilometres or so, before turning east and providing a route into the Haramosh Valley. In addition to offering fine views of the south

Danyore, Bagrot & Haramosh Valleys

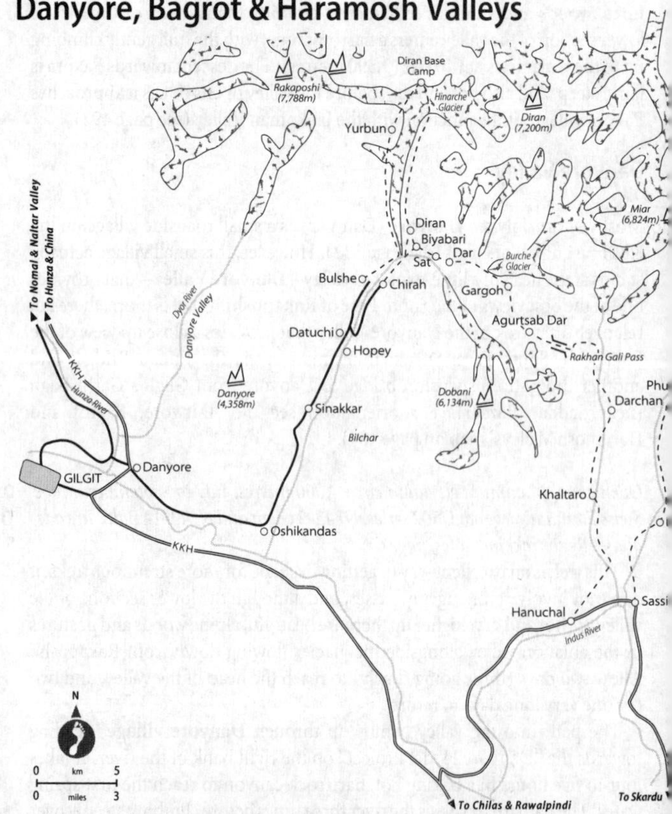

face of the Rakaposhi Massif, this little visited valley offers some excellent walking and trekking.

The highly cultivated entrance to the valley is usually reached from Danyore, on the KKH, although public cargo jeeps are irregular. It may be possible to take a very crowded cargo jeep (Rs 30) from Garhi Bazaar in Gilgit – otherwise you will have to hire a vehicle (Rs 1,300 one-way, two hours). *Bagrote Serai* have a jeep that transfers tourists from Gilgit (T Oshikandas 37). All food supplies should be purchased in Gilgit before setting out for the valley.

The first few kilometres of the valley are rocky and barren, as the jeep track winds its way through the lateral moraine, but after **Sinakkar** this soon gives way to intensively cultivated agricultural land. The jeep track runs as far as **Chirah**, where the run-down **E** *NAPWD Inspection Bungalow* and the basic but friendly **F** *Bagrote Sarai* provide the valley's only accommodation. Beyond Chirah there are walks up to the summer pastures, and a demanding trek across the Burche Glacier into the Haramosh Valley (see below).

The 6,134 metres Dobani (Bilchar) Peak at the centre of the valley is said to be inhabited by fairies, and the belief here in the power of shamans is strong. The population of the valley are Shia Muslims, and traditionally provided the backbone of the army raised in times of war by the rulers of Gilgit. When Durand visited the valley in 1889, he found evidence of an earlier raid by Gohar Aman, a prince of Yasin, in which it is estimated that two thirds of the population had been killed or carried off into slavery. Schomberg, naturally, has his usual quota of negative opinions about the people of this valley, claiming that Bagrotis are "famous for their stupidity". It would be interesting to find out what they thought of him.

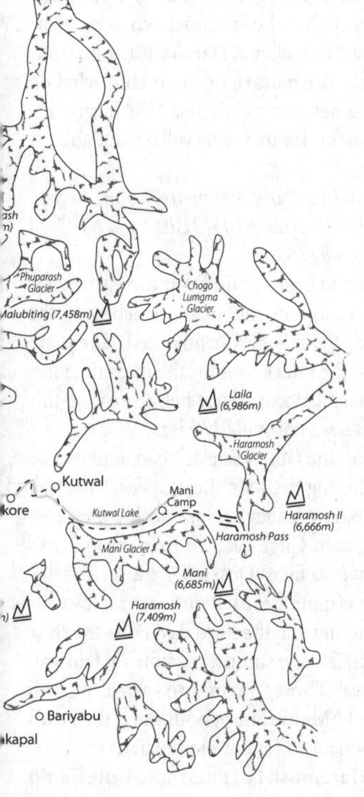

Few people visit this valley, although in recent years a large number of anthropologists (many attached to the joint German-Pak 'Culture Area Karakoram' project) have been studying the rapidly changing social structures within the valley.

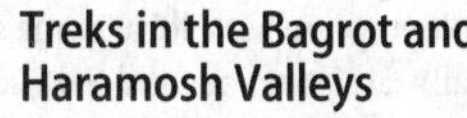

Treks in the Bagrot and Haramosh Valleys

Diran Base Camp

Open zone. Maximum elevation circa 4,000 metres. June to September. Maps: Swiss Foundation good; U502 series, NI 43-2 Gilgit and NJ 43-14 Baltit are adequate. Read trekking notes, page 67.

This is a fairly straightforward short trek, although a local guide should be employed to take you across the Bagrot Glacier. It provides some wonderful views of the less commonly seen faces of Rakaposhi and Diran. Note that Diran Base Camp is referred to locally as **Hinarche Harai**. Perhaps the only drawback to this trek is that the best campsite (**Biyabari**, just below Diran village) after leaving the trailhead at **Chirah** is only a two to three hour walk, making the first day very short and the second very long. The second day involves an unrewarding (seven to eight hours) walk along the east side of the Hinarche Glacier. Once across the glacier it is a further one and a half hours to **Diran Base Camp** (Hinarche Harai). Return by the same route. **NB** The route via the west side of the Hinarche Glacier (via Yurban) is heavily crevassed at the north end.

Bagrot Valley to Haramosh Valley

Open zone. Maximum elevation 4,548 metres. June to September. Maps: Swiss Foundation good; U502 series, NI 43-2 Gilgit and NJ 43-14 Baltit are adequate. Read trekking notes, page 67.

This little attempted trek provides a route from the Bagrot Valley to the Haramosh Valley via the **Rakhan Gali (Pass)**, and is usually attempted from west-east. A guide is essential. Note that upon crossing the pass, large parties will have to change porters.

The first day involves climbing gradually along the lower east side of the Hinarche Glacier from **Chirah**, before bearing east along the north side of the Burche Valley. Beyond **Dar** (three hours) the trail continues along the **Burche Glacier**. After two kilometres the trail divides. Following the branch to the right (heading southeast), it takes two tricky hours to reach the shepherd's hut at **Gargoh**. There is good camping here. The second day involves a short but steep climb up to the camp site at **Agurtsab Dar**. The third day is the most arduous of the trek. It's a three hour slog over the scree up to the **Rakhan Gali** (4,548 metres), and then a very steep three hour drop down to **Ber**. The best camping is a further hour or so down the valley at **Darchan**. The final day is a fairly unrewarding seven hour hike via **Khaltaro** down to **Hunuchal** on the Gilgit-Skardu road. Buses running between Gilgit and Skardu provide onward transport, though there's no guarantee that seats will be available.

Kutwal Lake and Mani Camp

Open zone. Maximum elevation optional (3,260-4,800 metres). June to September. Maps: Swiss Foundation good; U502 series, NI 43-2 Gilgit and NJ 43-14 Baltit are adequate. Read trekking notes, page 67.

Before considering this trek, you should bear in mind that two Americans were shot whilst camping at Mani Camp in the upper reaches of the Haramosh Valley in mid 1998; one of them subsequently died. There are numerous theories as to the reason for the attack, but for the meantime it is essential that potential visitors seek reliable local advice before visiting this area. Employing a reliable local guide seems particularly wise.

The trailhead is just beyond **Sassi** on the Gilgit-Skardu road, and can be reached by taking one of the buses running between these towns. This trek can also be tagged on to the end of the 'Bagrot Valley to Haramosh Valley' trek (see above). From the bridge on the main Gilgit-Skardu road, head north along the east side of the Phuparash River as far as **Dassu**. On the second day continue north from Dassu (the climb is quite steep), then bear east towards **Isekere**, where there is some good camping. On the third day, cross the river above Isekere and follow the winding trail to the summer pastures at **Kutwal**. There are several options beyond Kutwal. Those with time to spare can camp at both **Kutwal Lake** (3,260 metres) and **Mani Camp**, both along the north side of the Mani Glacier. The very experienced (and well prepared) can continue across the difficult 4,800 metres **Haramosh La (Pass)** onto **Laila Camp** and the **Chogo Lungma Glacier** (though this route is usually attempted from Baltistan). Otherwise, follow the same route back to the trailhead at Sassi.

Gilgit to Chitral

The journey west from Gilgit towards Chitral is one of the most beautiful and challenging trips in Pakistan. The route follows the Gilgit River upstream, providing access to the fascinating side valleys of Ishkoman and Yasin, both of which have almost inexhaustible trekking potential. The scenery at Phandur is sublime, before the road crosses the famous Shandur Pass, scene of the most spectacular polo event in the world. The road can be rough, and in places dangerous, but this is a journey you will remember for a long time. Foreigners making this trip will require strong arms; you'll be expected to wave to all the children that you drive past!

Planning this trip

Ins and outs

Your enjoyment of this journey will be directly affected by the mode and style of transport that you select. If you are travelling on a tight budget, then this is the one trip in Pakistan where it is worth splashing out on a private hire jeep. Although the journey is perfectly feasible in a cargo jeep, the public vehicles on this route are very heavily loaded, and it is not unusual to find 20 other passengers also clinging to the back of the jeep. The road can be quite rough in places, and Pakistani cargo jeeps seem to have a disproportionate number of strategically placed sharp metal objects which your swaying body will regularly find. It is difficult to enjoy the scenery under these circumstances. Further, this route offers some sublime camping spots, whereas cargo jeeps tend to stop for the night in relatively uninteresting villages. If you are travelling by cargo jeep, it is recommended that you take your time over the trip, travelling in short bursts, and alighting at points that take your fancy.

Jeeps can be privately hired in Gilgit through most hotels, although the reputable travel agents such as ***Waljis*** are not much more expensive and far more reliable. Expect to pay around Rs 6,900 to Mastuj, Rs 8,000 to Chitral for a 2 to 3 day trip. Jeeps seat 4 comfortably, 5 or 6 at a push, and thus the cost is not excessive when shared.

Cargo jeeps leave from Gilgit's Punial Road, although it's unusual to find a vehicle going the whole way to Chitral. Chitral based jeep drivers, who would otherwise be returning back empty, often tour the cheap hotels such as the *Madina* offering competitive prices for the trip.

A NATCO bus runs daily from the Punial Road NATCO yard in Gilgit to Yasin, via Singal, Gahkuch and Gupis (see 'Gilgit – Long distance buses' above).

For details of transport from Chitral to Gilgit, see the Chitral section.

Sleeping & eating

If you are equipped to camp, this trip offers some great overnight resting places. Particularly recommended are Khalti Lake, the Phandur region, Langar and the Shandur Pass itself. If you require hotel accommodation, then some advanced planning is worthwhile. The **F** category ***NAPWD Inspection Bungalows*** at Gulapur, Singal, Gahkuch, Chatorkhand, Imit, Gupis, Yasin, Phandur and Teru all offer comfortable accommodation, albeit with very basic food. However, they can only be booked in Gilgit (see 'Sleeping', Gilgit) – not much use if you are coming from Chitral. Most will accept casual callers if unoccupied. Singal, Gilmiti, Gahkuch, Gupis, Phandur, Sor Laspur and Mastuj all offer some form of basic **F** accommodation.

Colour map 5, grid A3

Gilgit to Gahkuch

Routes The road to Chitral leaves Gilgit to the west, passing the turn off to the Kargah Buddah. Plans are underway to upgrade the road, initially laying tarmac as far as Gahkuch, and eventually sealing the road all the way along the route to Chitral. If and when this occurs, it is bound to greatly affect the volume and pattern of transport across the Shandur Pass. However, at the moment the road is sealed for just 7 kilometres beyond Gilgit before changing into a fairly good jeep road. It is worth noting that the road deteriorates beyond Gupis.

The jeep road passes along the south side of the Gilgit River. Some 27 kilometres from Gilgit is a rope suspension bridge leading to the village of Bargo on the north side of the river. The jeep road then passes through the small village of **Shenote** (4 kilometres) that marks the boundary between Gilgit and **Punial District**.

The road continues through **Gulapur** (4 kilometres), with its **E** *NAPWD Inspection Bungalow*, and a couple of basic chai shops where you could stay on a charpoy if desperate. The green and fertile village across the river is Rashmal, connected by a new bridge.

Sher Qila Being a relatively fertile and well watered strip of land on either side of the Gilgit River, the former independent kingdom of **Punial** became a bone of contention between the rulers of Yasin and Gilgit. Both states possessed the region in turn, until it was annexed by the Maharaja of Kashmir in 1860. Part of the desire to control Punial was due to the strategic location of the fort at **Sher Qila**.

On the north side of the river, connected to the main road by a suspension bridge, Sher Qila (35 kilometres from Gilgit, one and a half hours by bus) controls the western approach to Gilgit. The word 'Sher' (a Dogra corruption of the Shina word 'Cher') means "an impregnable rock", whilst 'Qila' means "fort". All that remains of the fort today is one 150 year old watch-tower, close

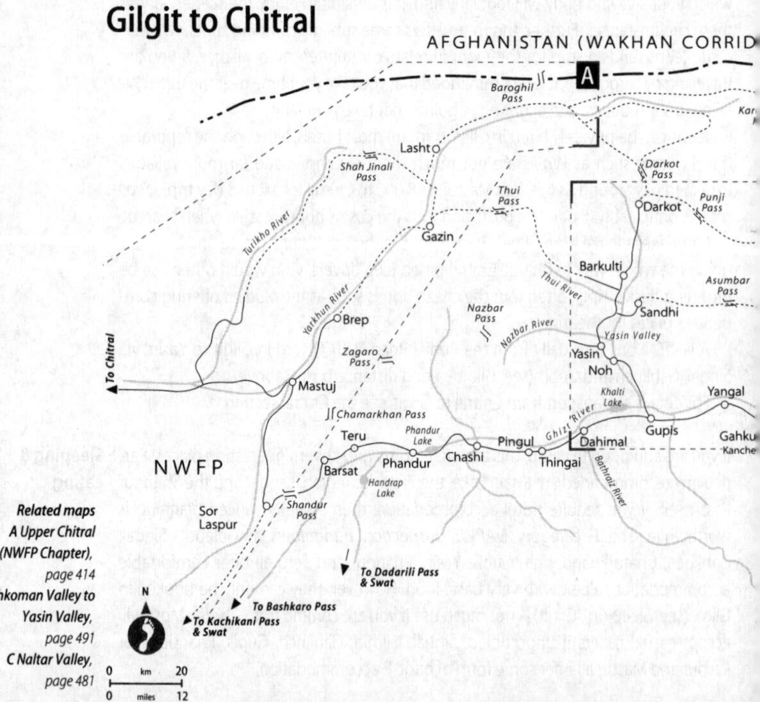

Related maps
A Upper Chitral (NWFP Chapter), page 414
B Ishkoman Valley to Yasin Valley, page 491
C Naltar Valley, page 481

to the river. Sher Qila's most impressive building now is the Aga Khan High School for Girls.

The village is also home of the *Sher Qila Women's Art Group*; a recently established women's cooperative that produces "art that reflects the women's first tentative explorations into self-expression, self-esteem and financial independence". The inexpensive prints are available from the S.W.A.G. studio at the residence of the former Raja of Punial in Sher Qila (visitors welcome), and from a number of handicraft shops in Karimabad. For further information contact Ms Nilusha Bardai, c/o Pilot School Sher Qila, BPO Sher Qila, NA, Pakistan.

Routes

The jeep track continues through the tiny settlement of **Dalnati** (3 kilometres), then through **Goherabad** (4 kilometres), which has a couple of chai and cold drinks stands. 3 kilometres beyond here is a bridge across the river to **Japuky**, which has a basic **F** ***Inspection Bungalow***. At **Gich** (2 kilometres) you may be confronted by graffiti sprayed by the 'Ghizr Student Federation' (GSF) demanding "we want road metalled".

At **Singal** (48 kilometres from Gilgit, 2 hours by bus), you must enter your passport details at the police check-post. Singal is the site of a very plush Aga Khan Medical Centre, a **F** ***NAPWD Inspection Bungalow***, a couple of basic restaurants (***Lucky*** and ***Sungum***) and the basic **F** ***Ghizer Hotel***. Beyond Singal is the tiny 'village' of **Thing Das**.

The road then passes through the small village of **Gilmiti** (16 kilometres), where there is a PSO petrol pump and the basic **F** ***Nadir Hotel***. Kuwait and Bubal, the villages on the opposite side of the river, are famed locally for their wine! Indeed, Schomberg notes how the people of Punial are "inordinately pleasure-seeking", and how "they love the juice of the grape, either as wine or, preferably, in the form of that trebly distilled liquor, potent and unrefined, which would make any Western head ache for weeks." Perhaps Schomberg's judgement was also impaired, for having described the people of Punial as "shrewd and intelligent", in the next breath he is referring to them as "unenterprising and dirty".

Shortly before Gahkuch (having passed through a fairly barren stretch of road) the recently built Chinese **Kanchey Bridge** (65 kilometres from Gilgit) crosses the river, offering one of two alternative routes to the **Ishkoman Valley**. One route passes along the north side of the Gilgit River, through the village of Silpi. The old rope suspension bridge that the Kanchey Bridge replaced was dismantled, and moved up-river to connect Silpi to Gahkuch. The jeep track, shortly to be upgraded, then runs up the east side of the Ishkoman Valley to Chatorkhand. The alternative route is via the bridge just beyond Gahkuch.

Gahkuch

Colour map 5, grid A3

73 kilometres from Gilgit, this is the district headquarters and the most westerly settlement in Punial District. An important fort previously stood at Gahkuch, commanding both the entrance to the Ishkoman Valley and the Gilgit-Chitral road. It was whilst occupying this fort in 1893 that Durand learnt of the Indus Valley Uprising. There is a police check-post here where foreigners must enter their passport details.

"Between the Oxus and the Indus"

A book that may be of interest to travellers undertaking the Gilgit to Chitral journey is "Between The Oxus And The Indus". Amongst all the accounts of travel in the Northern Areas of Pakistan by British military types, that of Colonel R C F Schomberg is one of the most extraordinary. Published in 1933, and received as an authoritative study of the lands and peoples of the region between the two great rivers, "Between the Oxus and the Indus" must be one of the most bigoted pieces of colonial writing ever published. Amongst excellent descriptions of the physical terrain, and the local political scene and social structures, are dotted highly disparaging remarks about the capabilities of the local people. Referring to the people of one particular valley, Schomberg remarks: "It is difficult to describe the luscious beauty of a walk through this countryside when summer is ablaze. The people, stupid, dirty, and but indifferent imitations of monkeys, cannot mar the noble prospect." The only people that Schomberg admired were the Hunzakuts, and only then because they were the best porters, and could tie a load onto a horse.

Although not wishing to give a platform to Schomberg's views, selected quotes have been included in this text in order to give some idea of the British attitudes to the various ethnic groups in the region.

Sleeping & eating The **F** ***NAPWD Inspection Bungalow*** is very luxurious, although you are likely to be turned away if you do not have a booking from Gilgit. **G** ***Snow Drop Inn***, Main Bazaar, T73, is often a meal stop on the Gilgit-Yasin bus trip, has 1 grotty, basic and not very private room, though foreigners are usually referred to the **F** ***Shandur Tourist House*** (right off main bazaar, no English sign), which has reasonable triples with attached bath.

Transport The *NATCO* bus to Gilgit passes through Gahkuch around 0930 and 1200 (having come from Yasin and Gupis).

Routes After Gahkuch is the tiny settlement of **Damas**, and a footbridge across the river to the head of the Ishkoman Valley. A further 10 kilometres beyond Gahkuch, a 100 metres suspension bridge crosses the river to the **Ishkoman Valley**. From this point it is 83 kilometres east to Gilgit, 27 kilometres west to Gupis, and travelling north up the Ishkoman Valley, 20 kilometres to Chatorkhand, 55 kilometres to Imit and 100 kilometres to the Pamir Border with Afghanistan. Currently, there is more traffic to the Ishkoman Valley via this route than the alternative Kanchey Bridge. Cargo jeeps from Gahkuch (Rs 25, 1 hour) are particularly crowded.

For those continuing west, and not making an excursion up the Ishkoman Valley, turn to page 494.

Ishkoman Valley

Although the whole valley is generally referred to as the Ishkoman Valley, the major river that runs through the valley is the **Karumber** (which descends from the Karumber Glacier to the northeast), and some texts refer to the valley as the Karumber Valley. The actual Ishkoman River is a small tributary that joins the Karumber from the northwest, from a valley that is referred to as 'Ishkoman proper'.

The language pattern of the valley reflects the history of migration into the area and conquest by the neighbouring states of Chitral, Yasin and Gilgit, with Shina, Khowar (Chitrali), Burushaski and Wakhi all being spoken.

Our old friend Schomberg visited the area, and as usual, he was not impressed by the people: "The more I saw of the inhabitants of Ishkoman, the more was I struck by their degeneracy; they were poor in physique and lacking in brains." Working himself up into an apoplexy, Schomberg refers to the indigenous population as "absurd pygmies", "no better than cretins", before finally concluding with "I am afraid that the people of Ishkoman represent as low a type of humanity as any in the North-West of India"! Few foreign visitors, bar the odd trekking groups, visit the Ishkoman Valley, which is a great pity because the local people are very friendly and welcoming.

Routes

At the entrance to the Ishkoman Valley is a wide alluvial fan, upon which the green and well cultivated fields of the village of **Hatoon** stand. The jeep road runs along the west side of the valley, before crossing the river on the 75 metres suspension bridge at **Hasis** (8 kilometres). Here, the jeep road joins the alternative route south via Silpi to the Kanchey Bridge. The road north up the valley continues to **Chatorkhand** (12 kilometres).

Chatorkhand

Colour map 5, grid A3

This is the largest settlement in the valley, and was described by Schomberg as being "famous for its pir and its bugs". The Ismaili community venerate their pirs (a hereditary position as a religious leader), and many attain considerable power and social status. The current pir, Syed Karim Ali Shah, is Deputy Chief Executive of the Northern Areas.

Ishkoman Valley to Yasin Valley

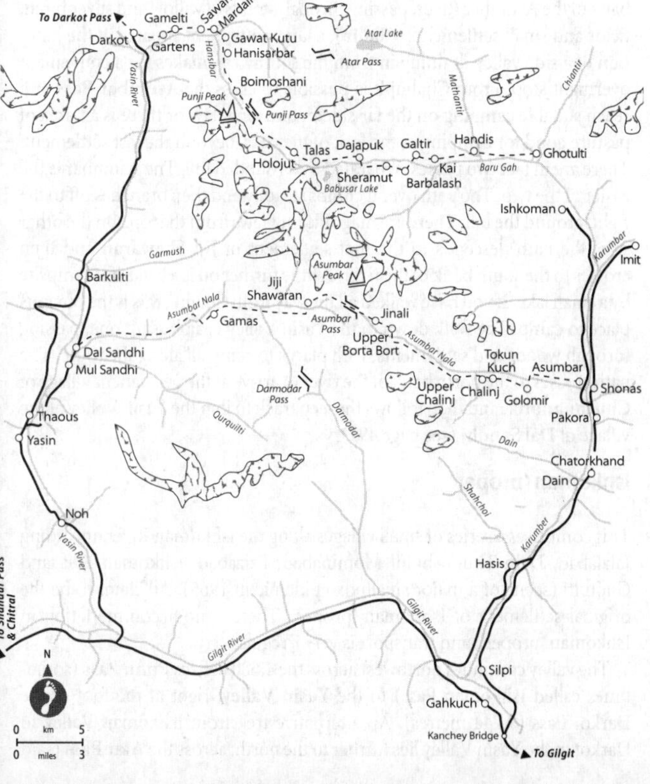

KKH and the Northern Areas

Sleeping & eating The **F** ***NAPWD Inspection Bungalow*** has 3 VIP doubles, with eccentric plumbing, plus 2 standard rms set in a large garden. Basic meals are available through the chowkidar, although you may well want to bring your own supplements. There are several chai shops in the village.

Transport There are extremely crowded cargo jeeps to Chatorkhand from Gahkuch (and usually 1 per day that has come all the way from Gilgit that is even more crowded). The alternative is to get off the Gilgit-Gupis-Yasin bus at the bridge and walk/hitch (20 kilometres).

Routes Several kilometres north of Chatorkhand is the village of **Pakora** (marked on some maps as Phakor or Pakor). A *nala* joins from the east, and it is through the narrow opening to this valley that you can trek east across the **Naltar Pass** (4,710 metres), sometimes marked Pakor Pass, to the **Naltar Valley** (see details of trek, in reverse, on page 483).

Immediately beyond the Jamat Khana in Pakora, the road divides, although both forks re-join several kilometres further north. A steep path several hundred metres along the left fork leads down to a rope suspension bridge across the Karumber River. This route leads along the west side of the valley to **Ishkoman**. It also leads to the valley joining from the west that provides a relatively easy 5 day trek across the **Asumbar Pass** (4,560 metres) to **Yasin Valley**.

Asumbar Pass trek *Open zone. Maximum elevation circa 4,560 metres. July to September. Maps; U502 series, NJ 43-14 Baltit and NJ 43-13 Mastuj are the only ones readily available and are fairly good. Read trekking notes, page 67.*

This is a relatively easy trek passing through villages and summer settlements along the way, and can be done without a guide. From Pakora village, cross to the west side of the valley. A good path heads west along the south bank of the Asumbar River, passing through stands of willow and silver birch, fields and small settlements. **Chalinj**, a large settlement situated at the junction of a side valley draining in from the southwest, makes for a convenient overnight stop. From Chalinj it is possible to cross the **Asumbar Pass** and reach suitable camping on the far side in one long day, or there is an area of pasture good for camping at the foot of the pass, beyond the last settlement. There are in fact two passes, separated by a rounded hill. The Asumbar is the easier of the two. The path over it climbs steadily and then branches off to the right, around the hill. There are magnificent views from the top. On the other side, the path descends to the first settlement of **Jiji Shawaran** and then crosses to the south bank of the river. A little further on is a beautiful campsite by a small lake. If you have walked all the way from Chalinj, this is the obvious place to camp. The walk down to the Yasin Valley is a pleasant one, passing through woods and settlements, with places to camp all along the route. The path crosses to the north bank of the river to arrive at the permanent village of **Chuchuanotik**, and then follows the jeep track to join the Yasin Valley at the village of **Dal Sandhi** (see page 497).

Ishkoman 'proper'

Colour map 5, grid A3

This comprises a series of small villages along the Ishkoman River, including Jalalabad, Dalti Thupushkin, Mominabad, Faizabad, Ishkoman Bala and Ghotulti (scene of a major smallpox epidemic in 1965). All claim to be the original settlement of Ishkoman 'proper'. There is no accommodation in Ishkoman 'proper', and transport is very irregular.

The valley continues northwest across the 4,680 metres **Punji Pass** (sometimes called Ishkoman Pass) to the **Yasin Valley**, right at the foot of the Darkot Pass (4,744 metres). An alternative trek from Ishkoman Valley to Darkot in the Yasin Valley lies further to the north, across the **Atar Pass** (said to be easier, though a guide is essential). The latter is the route that our old friend Schomberg used to reach Darkot from Ishkoman.

Punji Pass trek

Open zone. Maximum elevation 4,680 metres. July to September. Maps: U502 NJ 43-14 Baltit and U502 NJ 43-13 Mastuj can be used, though both have mistakes. Punji Pass is labelled as Ishkuman Aghost (and ignore what is marked as Punji Pass). A guide is essential for this trek since the trail is not always obvious. Read trekking notes, page 67.

The trek really begins at **Ghotulti** village, above Ishkoman 'proper'. Climb steeply for 50 minutes above Ghotulti to the shrine of a local saint (large circle of stones enclosed by a square stone wall). Continue west, high above the Baru Gah River for a further two hours to **Handis** (2,930 metres), and then find a suitable place to camp near to the settlement. (It is from Handis that you can take the alternative northerly route via the Atar Pass to Darkot).

On the second day, head west from Handis high above the Baru Gah River on the north side as far as **Kai** (45 minutes). The trail then continues to **Galtir** (3,280 metres). From here you descend to the river and cross to its south bank, pass through a juniper forest (passing a series of large cairns), then climb gently high above the river (still on its south bank). After two hours or so you reach the small settlement of Babusar, close to a small lake. Just beyond here you cross once more to the north side of the Baru Gah, and head up towards the summer settlement of Talas. Climb steeply up to the superb grassy camp site at **Holojut** (3,870 metres, five to six hours from Handis). There are great views from this spot, as well as good fresh water springs.

The third day can be a long haul, depending upon your level of fitness (five to seven hours). Head broadly northwest along the valley floor towards the small waterfall, then continue across the alluvial plain on the north side of the valley. You may need to cross and recross the stream a number of times, before climbing gently to a flower-strewn meadow. Having crossed the meadow, a series of switchbacks begin to climb to the west. The trail turns sharply east to avoid a deep ravine, before continuing northwest along a rocky ridge. Ascending the shale slope on the south bank of the stream, you climb up to the **Punji Pass** (4,680 metres, marked by two cairns). There are some fine views from the top of the pass. The path from the pass descends in a northwest direction, though you will have to cross a glacier and traipse across the glacial morain. Some trekkers camp close to the cairn here, though you are still fairly high (4,250 metres). A better option is to drop down into the ravine, cross the icy stream, and continue to **Boimoshani** (3,690 metres).

If coming in the opposite direction (ie Darkot to Ishkoman), this following stage should only be attempted over two days, since there is a rapid altitude gain. In the direction described here, however, this final leg can be attempted in one long day (eight to nine hours). From Boimoshani, descend gently along the north side of the river, and proceed north to the settlement of **Hanisarbar**. The route then climbs once more, up to **Gawat Kutu** (3,450 metres). This is an important summer pasture area, and can seem very 'busy' with people in a very pleasing kind of way. Just to the north of here, the river (called here the Hanisar Bar) is joined from the east by another river valley, the Nyu Bar. This latter valley forms part of the alternative Atar Pass route between Ishkoman and Darkot. Having crossed the Nyu Bar, our route turns west, passing through the cultivated fields of **Mardain** village (on the north side of the valley), through **Sawaney** village, across the Alam Bar River that flows in from the north, and then via **Gamelti** (3,139 metres) and **Gartens** (2,880 metres), before the final dry stretch in to **Darkot** (2,760 metres).

Routes Returning to our exploration of the Ishkoman Valley north of Pakora, the jeep track along the east side of the valley hugs the base of the cliffs and continues to **Imit**. During the summer months it is best to cross the river at this point since the high level of the water can make it difficult to cross directly between Ishkoman and Imit further up the valley.

Imit

This is the starting point for another trek across into the Naltar Valley. It is also possible to cross the Karumber Glacier, and then head west across the Chillinji Pass towards Chitral, although this is a difficult trek through a restricted area and a guide is essential. Some basic details of this trek can be found in the 'Upper Chitral' section of the NWFP chapter (see page 416).

There is reputed to be a sulphurous hot spring near to Imit, although local people claim that it has now disappeared. Schomberg's comment on Imit was that it has two claims to distinction, "the flies and dogs."

There is an **E** *NAPWD Inspection Bungalow* at Imit. Public transport to Imit is very limited. Extremely crowded cargo jeeps from Gilgit pass through Chatorkhand between 1500 and 1600 each day, and return from Imit early the next morning.

Gahkuch to Gupis

Colour map 5, grid A3

Returning to the main jeep road between Gilgit and Chitral, the track climbs high above the river for several kilometres, drops down a little, then climbs once more. Just beyond the sign reading 'Gupis 22 kilometres, Yangal six kilometres', the sharp bend in the road is the point at which, in August 1995, a jeep plunged over the side killing the driver and three backpackers. It's a reminder of just how challenging this trip can be.

14 kilometres beyond the Ishkoman Valley bridge are the green cultivated fields belonging to the village of **Yangal**, and beyond here are bridges across the river to the settlements of Sumal (three kilometres) and Moula Abad (two kilometres) respectively. A sizeable river joins the Gilgit River from the south just before the jeep road reaches **Gupis** (37 kilometres west of Gahkuch, two hours by bus). This settlement has a Civil Hospital, Post Office and a newly built fort. Accommodation is available at the **F** *NAPWD Inspection Bungalow* (at the east end of town), and food at the *Snow Leopard Inn*. There are two buses a day from Gilgit to Gupis, and two per day in the opposite direction (at about 0800 and 1000, ask locally).

Routes Several kilometres west of Gupis is the recently Chinese constructed 96 metres **Gupis Bridge**, at the entrance to the **Yasin Valley**. From this point it is 112 kilometres to Gilgit, 42 kilometres to Gahkuch, 54 kilometres to Phandur, 104 kilometres to the Shandur Pass, and 25 kilometres north up the Yasin Valley to 'Central' Yasin.

For those continuing west, and not making an excursion up the Yasin Valley, turn to page 498.

Yasin Valley

Colour map 5, grid A2

The Yasin Valley, and in particular the characters it produced, has played a leading role in the history of the region. Continually fought over by the rulers of both Chitral and Gilgit, the history of the rulers of Yasin reads like a catalogue of patricide, fratricide and avunculicide. Yasin came to the attention of Victorian Britain following the murder of British explorer George Hayward in the upper reaches of the valley.

Biddulph classifies the original inhabitants of the valley as Yeshkuns, although they refer to themselves as Boorushi. The majority of the valley are Ismaili Muslims, speaking Burushaski, although it is a more archaic dialect than the Burushaski spoken in Hunza and Nagar. The ruling class, however, speak Khowar (Chitrali), reflecting their origins in the valley to the west. Today, many residents of Yasin Valley are bilingual. The valley is sometimes referred to as Woorshigum ('Valley of the Boorushi').

The valley is well watered, and in the lower reaches in particular there is extensive cultivatable land. Yasin is probably seen at its best in late August, as the wheat and maize are approaching harvest. Locally, Yasini women have a reputation for great beauty, although it is not uncommon to find that women who originally belonged to the Khushwakht families of Chitral practise purdah.

Routes

The entrance to the Yasin Valley is relatively dry and stony, until you reach the first 'green' settlements at **Damalgan** (6 kilometres) and **Gindaie** (10 kilometres). The road continues through the terminal moraine to the suspension bridge at **Noh**. Previously, *NATCO* bus services terminated here, though the recent construction of a more solid bridge means that the service now continues all the way to 'Central' **Yasin**, or Yasin 'proper' (25 kilometres from Gupis Bridge).

Yasin

'Central' Yasin is a long, sprawling series of settlements collectively known as Yasin. There are still remains of the fort built by **Gohar Aman**, one of the valley's most celebrated rulers. A member of the Khushwakte ruling family, he is remembered as much for his "cruelty of disposition" as his ability as "an able and energetic Soldier" (Biddulph). Naturally, Schomberg is more caustic in his analysis, referring to Gohar Aman as "a mighty murderer and strapping tyrant". Gohar Aman was the father of Mir Wali, the man generally held responsible for the murder of George Hayward.

Antagonistic towards Shias, Gohar Aman made many raids on Gilgit, and later had great success against the Dogra forces. However, following the eventual Dogra victory in 1863, a punitive expedition was sent to Yasin Valley to extract revenge, and it is the details of this massacre at nearby Muduri that Hayward described so graphically in *The Pioneer* newspaper: "They (Dogra troops) threw the little ones in the air and cut them in two as they fell. It is said that the pregnant women, after being killed, were ripped open and their unborn babies hacked to pieces. Some forty women who were not yet dead were dragged to one spot, and were there burnt by the Dogra sepoys. With the exception of a few wounded men and women who ultimately recovered, every man, woman and child within the fort, and, in all, 1,200 to 1,400 of these unhappy villagers, were massacred by the foulest treachery and cruelty" (Keay, 1979 "The Gilgit Game").

Sights

Yasin Fort stands on the west side of the river, although you may have to enlist some local help to find it (it's close to the Tehsil Office). Within the courtyard is a large tree and a new mosque, although the old mosque, complete with carved pillars, remains. There is a school of thought that suggests that the only surviving photo of Hayward, a copy of which hangs with the portraits of other Gold Medal winners at the Royal Geographical Society in London, was actually taken in front of this self same tree.

One tower of the fort still stands, and although the door remains locked, it is possible to scramble inside where part of the wall has fallen away. Down by the river, near to the small plank bridge, is the grave of Gohar Aman. It is a

George Hayward

Of all the players in the 'Great Game', George J Whitaker Hayward must rank as one of the most extraordinary. Little is known about his early life, and even the details of his place of birth are uncertain. To add to the mystery, there only appears to one photograph of the man, currently in the possession of the Royal Geographical Society (RGS) in London. Recent investigations by Charles Timmis suggest that Hayward was born in Headingly, Yorkshire, and not Ireland as initially thought, after which he attended school in Snaresbrook, just east of London.

His movements are uncertain after he resigned his commission in the Cameron Highlanders, yet in 1868 this relatively unknown man was sponsored by the RGS to undertake a journey to the Pamirs, in search of the source of the Oxus. After being pretty much given up for dead, Hayward re-emerged in 1869 to a hero's welcome, following his extensive surveys in the Pamirs and visits to the great Central Asian cities of Yarkand and Kashgar. He was awarded the RGSs coveted Gold Medal.

Within a year, Hayward had returned to this dangerous and unmapped region. As Hopkirk suggests, "to a man like Hayward, the risks merely made it more attractive", and a greater insight into the man is revealed in a line that Hayward wrote to a fellow explorer: "I shall wander about the wilds of Central Asia possessed of an insane desire to try the effects of cold steel across my throat." This line was to prove prophetic. On 18 July 1870, he was murdered at Darkot, in the Yasin Valley.

The reasons for Hayward's murder have never really been established, nor the instigator of the crime identified. One prime suspect is the Maharaja of Kashmir, embarrassed by Hayward's revelations in a newspaper of a massacre committed by his Dogra troops several years earlier in Yasin. Another prime candidate is Mir Wali, the local ruler, with whom Hayward is said to have argued with in public just days before his death. Whatever the facts of the matter, it was Mir Wali who fled from Yasin, himself meeting a grisly end some years later.

Today, Hayward's body lies buried in the graveyard in Gilgit.

simple Muslim shrine, surrounded by a low, jagged tooth wall.

Another place of interest close to Yasin is what is referred to as **Hayward's Rock**. Perhaps sensing that he was in some danger, Hayward carved his initials, "GWH", the figure "20" (the distance in miles to Darkot), and an arrow pointing in the direction he intended to travel. The rock is about one kilometre from Yasin, on the Nazbar Road, and the chowkidar at the *Inspection Bungalow* can show you where it is.

Sleeping & eating Set in a large garden, the well furnished **F** ***NAPWD Inspection Bungalow*** has 1 single and 1 double, both joining a communal dining room, and private bathrooms. There is also a 3 room VIP block. The chowkidar can fix meals but they are very basic. Best to bring your own food.

Transport *NATCO* run a bus from **Gilgit** to Yasin (Rs 76-90 depending upon whether it's 'normal' or 'deluxe', 7-8 hours), each day at 0800 from their yard on Punial Road (not from the main *NATCO* yard). The bus returns to **Gilgit** at 0700. Very crowded cargo jeeps leave early most mornings from Punial Road in Gilgit, and, on the return leg, from near to the *Insp Bungalow* in Yasin. Note that there is very little public transport north to **Darkot**. It is a full day's walk to Darkot. Public transport is very irregular (Gilgit-Darkot Rs 130 in a cargo jeep, leaving from Jamat Khana Bazaar). A private hire cargo jeep Gilgit-Darkot costs around Rs 3,000 (9 hours).

Routes

Travelling north from Yasin, the road crosses the river on a new concrete bridge, and initially proceeds on a very high quality jeep track. The first village north of Yasin is the sprawling settlement of **Thaous** (various spellings), which has recently seen the construction of a new hospital and a number of schools. The valley here is wide, flat and well irrigated, providing extensive wheat and maize cultivation. Beyond Thaous, the terrain becomes barren and stony. The only greenery is provided by the settlement of **Sandhi**, across the river.

The small village of **Muduri**, above Sandhi, has been identified with the site of the Dogra massacres that Hayward wrote about. Visiting the scene 7 years after the massacre, Hayward noted "I have myself counted 147 still entire skulls, nearly all of those women and children. The ground is literally white with bleached human bones and the remains of not less than 400 human beings are now lying on the hill" (Keay 1979). The *nala* above Sandhi runs east across the **Asumbar Pass** (4,560 metres) to the **Ishkoman Valley** (see page 492 for details of this trek, in reverse).

The river bed north of Thaous is wide and stony, with water running through only 1 or 2 main channels. The flow of the river is augmented by that of the Thui River, that joins the main river some 12 kilometres north of Yasin at **Barkulti**. There is a new bridge that crosses the Thui Nala. The **Thui Valley** provides a popular and spectacular trekking route across the **Thui Pass** (4,499 metres) to the Yarkhun Valley in Chitral District. For details of the Thui Pass trek (in reverse) see page 417.

Beyond the large agricultural settlement of Barkulti, the jeep road is enclosed along a narrow lane that threads its way through a series of small settlements. About 15 kilometres beyond Barkulti the jeep track crosses to the east side of the river, continuing along the wide, flat flood plain. After a further 10 kilometres a wide bowl is reached. Directly ahead is the settlement of **Darkot** (about 41 kilometres from Yasin), whilst the valley joining from the east leads over the Punji Pass to the Ishkoman Valley (see page 493).

Darkot

Colour map 5, grid A2

Infamous as the scene of Hayward's murder, the small village of Darkot stands at the head of the narrow gorge that leads to the Darkot Pass. It was this pass that Hayward was about to cross when he was murdered. Ostensibly on his way to the Pamirs and the source of the Oxus, possibly to 'bag' them for the British, it was no coincidence that the information that Hayward would bring back would be vital in assessing the feasibility of a Russian invasion of India through these unmapped passes.

Many accounts have been written of the circumstances of Hayward's death, the most fanciful of which was a cheesy poem by Sir Henry Newbolt that somehow found its way into the official report of the Gilgit Mission of 1885-6, headed by Colonel Lockhart. This tells how, upon his capture and facing certain death, he asked to be allowed to ascend a mound and gaze upon the rising sun one final time. An alleged eye-witness to the murder paints a scene that would appeal to such Victorian romanticism, describing Hayward as he walked up the mound: "as tall against the morning sky, with the rising sun lighting up his fair hair as a glory; he was beautiful to look at." Hayward is then said to have returned, said "I am ready", and was then killed. Subsequent investigations by Drew, who recovered the body and buried it at Gilgit, and later by Schomberg, suggest that Hayward was seized during a meal, and along with his servants, was bound and dragged to the mouth of a small nala where all were killed.

The supposed scene of the murder can still be visited, though it is not possible to determine the exact spot with any certainty. The place is known locally as"farang gee-bar", or the 'place of killing of the foreigner'. Local school teacher Muhammad Murad will show the spot to visitors. To find the site, turn right (east) as you cross the small wooden bridge at the entrance to Darkot, and continue up the slope as if heading for the Punji Pass. You pass a small shop in the middle of nowhere that belongs to a one-armed man (

honest!), beyond which to the right is a natural amphitheatre. Follow the trail beside the nala, and the scene is just around the 'backside'. The large boulder that stood over the site has been washed away. It is interesting to note how concerned local people are about their image to outsiders, some 130 years after the event; you may still be asked "what do people think about this murder in your country?", and villagers are at pains to point out that those involved were not actually from Darkot.

Sleeping There is a basic **E** *Resthouse* in Darkot, although it does not see many visitors.

Routes The approach to the **Darkot Pass** (4,744 metres) from the south side is particularly steep. Having crossed the pass into the Chapsuran Valley, you are now in a restricted area for which a permit is necessary (although there is no check-post).

Gupis to the Shandur Pass

The districts between Gupis and the Shandur Pass are referred to as **Ghizr** (sometimes Ghizer) and **Kuh**. Up until Phandur, the majority of the population of the main valley speak Shina, and beyond Phandur it is Khowar that prevails. Between Gupis and Phandur, there are numerous rock carvings, many on boulders that can be easily viewed from the road. Dani (1991 "History of the Northern Areas") suggests that these art forms illustrate the lives of pastoral nomads who may have moved here in early Christian times, and show great continuity with similar designs found in the Pamir region. Many show mounted horsemen, solar motifs, hunting scenes, and long horned ibexes. **NB** The jeep track west of Gupis deteriorates considerably.

Routes The jeep track heads west from Gupis, passing through the tiny settlements of Hamardas and Jandrote, before arriving at the stunning **Khalti Lake** (10 kilometres).

Khalti Lake Some guidebooks barely mention this place, yet this is not only one of the most scenic spots along the Gilgit-Chitral route, it is also one of the most beautiful places in the whole of Pakistan. Make every effort you can to get here, even if it means taking a bus from Gilgit to Gupis and then walking the final 10 kilometres. At the west end of the lake a bridge crosses to the attractively situated village of Khalti.

This large natural lake was only formed around a decade ago following a major flood. Its deep aquamarine colour is particularly photogenic in bright sunshine, and the lake is a popular spot with trout fishermen. **Sleeping & eating C** *PTDC Motel*, under construction; **E** *Karim Lake View Hotel*, friendly, well run, simple but clean doubles, fresh linen, attached bath, some cheaper doubles with shared baths, restaurant (speciality trout, Rs 20 per fish), terrace is a great spot to enjoy a cold beer (though you'll have to make do with tea). Recommended.

Routes Beyond Gupis, the river is referred to as the **Ghizr River**, and at **Dahimal** (13 kilometres beyond Khalti Lake) it is joined from the south by the emerald green **Bathraiz River** flowing from Swat Kohistan. The Bathraiz Valley leads south towards the Tangir Valley, although you should not attempt to follow this route. This was one route that the early Buddhist pilgrims used on their journeys from China to Gandhara, Swat and other pilgrimage sites in South Asia, as well as the means of access for invading armies from Chitral and the kingdoms to the north.

10 kilometres beyond the bridge over the Barthraiz River, and on both sides of the Ghizr River, is the settlement of **Thingai**. As the jeep track continues west, look out for the numerous petroglyphs on the rocks just past the village of **Pingul** (six kilometres). Sure enough, Schomberg has an anecdote with which to disparage the people of Pingul. Upon asking the villagers why they

live in such run-down houses, bearing in mind that heavy snowfall forces them indoors for long periods of the winter, they are alleged to have replied: "We are too lazy. We like comfort and hate exertion, so are content to live in these houses. They are bad and miserable but we cannot be bothered to build better ones"!

At **Chashi**, the valley widens greatly, and the main river is augmented by tributaries from both the north and south, the latter of which provide access to Tangir and Darel Valleys. When Schomberg saw the small houses at Chashi, with their open skylights in their roof, "the temptation to lob stones into some of them was hard to resist"!

Phandur

Beyond Chashi, a long sprawling village, the road crosses to the north side of the river via a narrow wooden bridge. The trail then begins to climb the hill created by the terminal moraine of a long since receded glacier, passing on the right the attractive **Phandur Lake** (about nine hours by privately hired jeep from Gilgit). The view down to the deep blue lake is magnificent, with the Ghizr River meandering through the green, and highly cultivated flood plain that supports the settlement of **Phandur**. The lake, situated at an altitude of about 2,800 metres, is said to be well stocked with trout. On the crest of the hill (36 kilometres from Dahimal) is the superbly located **F** *NAPWD Inspection Bungalow*, which has a number of rooms (although it is often full, and a booking chit from Gilgit is pretty much essential if you want to stand a chance of being able to stay). The chowkidar may be able to provide basic meals, though it is as well to bring your own. The **F** *Over The Lack Hotel* (sic) has three basic rooms with clean linen, a shared squat toilet (no running water, buckets supplied), occasional electricity, with basic meals available. It appears that the owner of this hotel is the chowkidar of the *Insp. Bungalow*, and thus he prefers visitors to stay in his place (where he makes some money) rather than the government owned place (where he doesn't). Ground has been broken for the construction of a **C** *PTDC Motel*, although the future of this project is uncertain. It is often possible to hire horses in Phandur, offering an almost inexhaustible series of day-trips (and longer excursions).

Routes

A little to the west of Phandur, a side valley leads south to **Handrap Lake**. As well as making a good camp site, this is a good place to get your fishing rod out – trout anyone? The whole area is part of the recently created Shandur-Handrap National Park, though effectively this protected area exists only on paper. It is possible to trek south from here across the **Dadarili Pass** into Swat (though this trek emerges into potentially dangerous areas and an armed escort may be required).

The jeep track continues through **Teru** (22 kilometres) at 3,065 metres (*NAPWD Inspection Bungalow*), and **Barsat** (3,353 metres), the final settlement in the district, before entering a beautiful glen. The camping here at **Langar** is superb, with fresh springs, a trout stocked river, and a lush green meadow set in a natural amphitheatre of snow-capped peaks.

Note that there is very little public transport from Barsat across the Shandur Pass (and privately hired vehicles are very expensive). In fact, for those who are walking the route, it is easier (and arguably more scenic) to trek over the Chamarkhan Pass to Mastuj, rather than via the Shandur Pass.

Chamarkhan Pass trek

Open zone. Maximum elevation 4,328 metres. July to September. U502 NJ 43-13 map is adequate, though a guide is highly recommended. Two days. Read trekking notes, page 67.

From the police check-post at Barsat, head north along the east side of the Chamarkhan River. The trail is rather confusing; when in doubt, stick to the centre of the valley. The upper meadows (after a four to five hour walk) make a good first night camping spot. Having crossed the 4,328 metres

Chamarkhan Pass, it is a steep descent down the east side of the river to the small settlement of **Kulam Shal** (3,429 metres). Just beyond the settlement, the trail is joined from the east by a track towards **Zagaro Pass** (4,920 metres). Ignore this route, and head northwest into the Zagaro River valley, staying on the true right bank of the river. After several hours walking you reach the small village of **Chapali**. From here it is an unrewarding 10 kilometres walk down to **Mastuj** along the jeep road, though you may be able to hitch a ride on a passing jeep or tractor.

Shandur Pass to Chitral

Routes The track then begins to climb up to the **Shandur Pass** (28 kilometres from Teru). The pass is not particularly high at 3,734 metres, and is generally described more as a plateau, with 2 large lakes

Upper Ghizr River Valley (Including Chamarkhan Pass Trek & Dadarili Pass Trek)

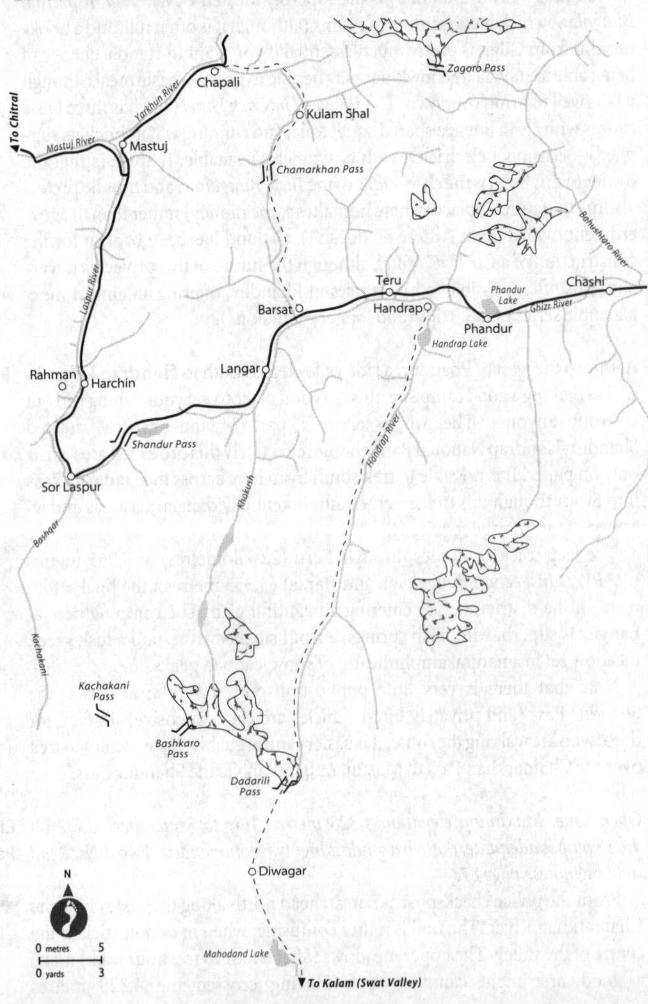

Shandur Pass Polo

In recent years, the 3,735 metres Shandur Pass has become the annual venue for the most spectacular polo event in the world, although the first ever tournament was held here as far back as 1936. Each year, the teams of Gilgit and Chitral compete as the highlight of a three day festival when Shandur Top becomes a huge tent city. In addition to the polo, there are golf and fishing tournaments, cultural shows, as well as the opportunity for the elite of Pakistan to 'be seen'. When it comes to the polo, forget Prince Charles and Windsor Great Park, this is how the game was meant to be played. It's fast, exciting and dangerous.

On the downside, the organisation of the festival is invariably a monumental cock-up. For years the Tourism Department have been trying to fix an annual date for the event, but their attempts are frequently scuppered by the politicians who change the dates at short notice to fit in with their own plans. In 1995 the dates were rearranged with just one month's notice, and the final was played on the first day of the festival because that was the only day that the President of Pakistan could make it. The 500 jeep traffic jam that develops as everyone leaves at the end of the festival isn't much fun either.

Accommodation, food and transport can be arranged in Gilgit just before the festival begins. Shop around for the best deal. Alternatively, bring your own equipment.

lying on it. The polo ground is said to be the highest in the world, and is the venue for the celebrated annual Gilgit vs Chitral match. At the centre of the pass, the Northern Areas give way to the **North West Frontier Province**.

Shandur Pass

The most famous crossing of the pass was perhaps that by Colonel James Kelly in 1895, at the head of an expeditionary force sent to relieve the British forces besieged in the fort at Chitral. Crossing in April, and faced by shoulder deep snow, the decision to bring artillery pieces looked as if it would doom the entire expedition, although they were to prove crucial later as the force battled towards their goal. Inspired by their commander, Lt Cosmo Stewart, the native regiment dismantled the guns and carried them through the snow. As one British officer pointed out: "Nothing can be said too highly in praise of this splendid achievement. Here were some 250 men, Hindus and Mussulmans, who, working shoulder to shoulder, had brought two mountain guns, with their carriages and supplies of ammunition, across some 20 miles of deep soft snow, across a pass 12,300 foot high, at the beginning of April, the worst time of the year."

Routes

The first village in NWFP as you descend from the Shandur Pass is **Sor Laspur**, starting point for a trek across the **Kachikani Pass** (4,766 metres) into Upper Swat. (**NB** This rarely attempted trek is usually attempted from south-north, ie Swat to Sor Laspur. A local guide and armed escort is essential.) There is a basic **F** hotel in Sor Laspur. It is a further 22 kilometres from here to **Mastuj**. For details of the route from Mastuj to **Chitral**, see page 413 in the 'Upper Chitral' section of NWFP chapter.

Baltistan

Baltistan lies right at the heart of the Karakoram mountains, and possesses a landscape that is as spectacular and exhilarating as it is forbidding, inhospitable and isolated. The region's main attractions are the opportunities it offers for climbing and trekking. However, you don't need to be a mountaineer or dedicated walker to appreciate the beauty of these mountains, since many of the most attractive areas are easily accessible by jeep, including Shigar, Khapulu, Hushe and the Deosai plateau. But Baltistan is not just about awesome mountain scenery; it is also home to the Balti people, whose hardy resilience is matched only by their warmth and friendliness. The history and culture of this region, stretching back to Buddhist times and earlier, is also still very much in evidence in the local architecture, language and traditions of its people.

Best time to visit The best time to visit is from mid-May to mid-October. The trekking season lasts from early June to late September. During summer (July/August) it can get quite hot during the day, with temperatures reaching well above 30°C, and even touching 40°C on occasion. Temperatures however drop considerably if there is cloud or rain. Nights are generally pleasantly cool. During winter it is bitterly cold, with temperatures dropping to as low as minus 30°C.

Geography

To the north, the **Karakoram** mountains dominate the region, a huge tangle of rock and ice with 12 of the 30 highest recorded peaks in the world. At its core is the **Baltoro** Glacier, covering some 1,200 square kilometres, and four peaks exceeding 8,000 metres; **K2**, the second highest mountain in the world at 8,611 metres, **Gasherbrum I** (8,068 metres, also known as Hidden Peak), **Broad Peak** (8,060 metres) and **Gasherbrum II** (8,035 metres). There are also dozens of 7,000 metres peaks and literally hundreds of 6,000 metres ones, the majority of them unnamed. To the south is the **Deosai**, an enormous expanse of high plateaux, all above 4,000 metres. Flowing through the middle of Baltistan and dividing these two main features is the **Indus** River. Entering the region from the south across the ceasefire line with India, it then trends northwest, at one point spreading out over a wide glacial plain around Skardu, before raging through a narrow gorge till it loops sharply south to emerge near its confluence with the Gilgit River. Joining it from the east is the **Shyok** River, while near Skardu the **Shigar** River flows in from the north. Although lesser in terms of size, the latter two are of crucial importance in terms of the opportunities for settlement which they afford.

History

Early History Buddhism first emerged in Baltistan during the Kushan period, around the third or fourth century AD. During the fifth or sixth century AD, White Huns are known to have reached into Baltistan. Later, in the eighth century AD, the Tibetans invaded, leaving numerous carvings and establishing Buddhism as the main religion once again. The first references to Baltistan as a distinct region date from around the fifth century when it was known as **Great Bolor** in Arabic literature, or *Po-lu-lo* in Chinese accounts. Internally the region was divided into eight kingdoms, Skardu forming the most important central power, followed by Khapulu, Shigar, and Rondu. Finally there were the lesser kingdoms of Kiris, Parkutta, Tolti and Kharmang, each a "fortress principality" guarding the approaches to Ladakh along the Indus. Astor, along with the sparsely populated Deosai Plateau, was at times loosely connected with Baltistan.

Makpons

It was not until after the decline of Tibetan power around the beginning of the 10th century that the region established some degree of independence. The most important dynasty to emerge in Baltistan was the Makpon dynasty. One legend relates how the dynasty was founded by a man named **Ibrahim Shah** somewhere around the 12-13th century, thought by some to have come from Kashmir, while others hold that he originally came from Egypt. Another tradition identifies the dynasty as having descended from the White Huns. The term 'Makpon' on the other hand translates literally from Tibetan as 'commander of a frontier region' suggesting Tibetan origins.

By the start of the 16th century, Baltistan was united as a kingdom under the ruler **Makpon Bokha**, with Skardu as the capital. He was succeeded by **Sher Shah I** (1515-1540), by which time the dynasty was strong enough to repel the invasion of the Central Asian Mughal **Sultan Abu Said Khan** in 1532. The Makpons continued to extend their rule and by the time of **Ali Sher Khan Anchen** (1595-1633), considered the greatest of the Makpon rulers (the *Anchen* was a title added later, meaning 'great'), they exercised control over all the minor kingdoms of Baltistan. Ali Sher Khan waged war with the Ladakhis, at one point invading their capital. He also attacked Gilgit, Chilas and Astor, and even reached as far as Chitral. However, only the valley of Haramosh was annexed, being integrated into Rondu. He brought back many prisoners from his campaigns, putting them to work on numerous building projects.

Close relations were established between the **Mughals** and the Makpon rulers following Akbar's conquest of Kashmir in 1586. According to local legend, a Mughal princess by the name of **Gul Khatoon** was given in marriage to Ali Sher Khan, although historical sources suggest that he married a Ladakhi princess. Whoever his wife was, she was responsible for building the aqueduct which still survives in Skardu, and for laying out a Mughal-style gardens (no longer remaining) fed by the waters of the aqueduct.

Ali Sher Khan's death was followed by a period of feuding which resulted ultimately in the Mughals establishing suzerainty over Baltistan. However, they hardly interfered in the internal affairs of the region, to the extent that the semi-independent kingdoms were left to fight amongst themselves. This they did with a vengeance, and at one stage the Mughals, fearful of the instability of their northern border, undertook a campaign against Ladakh and Baltistan. Even after this, they appear to have been happy to maintain subsidiary local authority. The rule of **Shah Morad Khan** in Skardu (1660-1680) was considered to be another golden age, equal to that of Ali Sher Khan's; fortresses and palaces were built, craftsmen brought from Kashmir and trade extended as far as Tibet and Kashgar. Campaigns were also undertaken against the other Balti kingdoms, and on two occasions Morad Khan attacked Gilgit.

The 18th century was marked by invasions, internecine wars between the kingdoms, as well as campaigns against Kashmir and Ladakh. Skardu was captured and plundered by the Afghan **Haji Karim Dad Khan** in 1779, and a year later it was absorbed by the powerful ruler of Shigar, **Azam Khan**, who held it for the next five years.

Sikhs and Dogras The Sikhs, who took power in Kashmir in the second half of the 18th century, extended their control also into Ladakh by the start of the 19th century. At this time, **Ahmed Shah** (1800-1840) was the ruler of Skardu. He had already repelled one Sikh attack on Skardu, engaging their troops for long enough to ensure that the majority died in the bitterly cold weather and vicious snow storms during their subsequent retreat across the Deosai. When the British explorer **GT Vigne** visited Skardu in 1835, Ahmed Shah was convinced that his mission was a diplomatic one and that the British would offer him protection against the Sikhs. However, Vigne (officially at least) had no such brief and in 1840 the Raja of Jammu **Gulab Singh**, a Rajput Hindu and member of the Dogra tribe, again attacked, this time taking Skardu and subjugating Baltistan. Gulab Singh forged close links with the British, even siding with them in the Sikh Wars. For his loyalty he was awarded the whole of Kashmir and left to his own devices. Although he taxed Baltistan heavily, the indigenous rulers were allowed to remain in place, watched over only by a *Kardar*, a kind of political agent, and a small force of 100 men.

Independence and Partition At Independence the people of Baltistan followed the lead taken in Gilgit and revolted against their Dogra rulers. While the battle was a swift one in Gilgit, which was able to formally accede to Pakistan in November 1947, in Baltistan the Dogra army resisted until 1948 before being finally driven out. It was not until January 1949 that a cease-fire was declared between India and Pakistan, with the line of control becoming the de facto border between the two countries. The line of control divided a geographically and culturally integrated area and severed an important trade route from Kashmir through Baltistan to the Punjab.

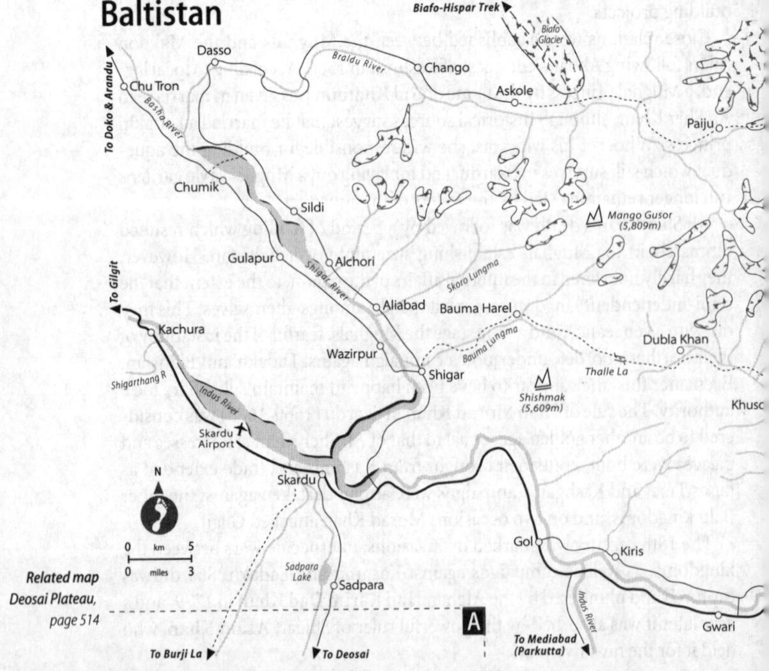

Related map Deosai Plateau, page 514

Religion, culture and society

The majority of people in Baltistan are **Shia** Muslims. According to local legend, the Shia faith was brought to Baltistan by a man named **Amir Kabir Syed Ali Hamadani**, who is said to have arrived in Shigar around 1379 AD. He is thought to have come originally from Iran, by way of Kashmir. Nearly 150 years later a second Muslim missionary, **Mir Shamsuddin Iraqi**, arrived in Baltistan around the time of Makpon Bokha and Buddhism finally died out. The **Nurbakshi** faith of the people of Khapulu and Hushe is traditionally attributed to **Hazrat Syed Mohammad Nur Baksh**, the vice-regent of the son of Amir Kabir, who preached between 1438-1448. It is closely linked to the Shia faith, and according to some sources, Nur Baksh was himself a pious Shia whose teachings were in fact later spread in somewhat adapted form by Mir Shamsuddin Iraqi and subsequent missionaries, thus giving rise to the Nurbakshi sect.

The Shia faith as practiced in Baltistan today is very strict and, apart from in Nurbakshi areas, one is very unlikely to see any women at all. However, this is a relatively recent phenomenon. The spread of Islam, which at the time had a strong Sufi element to it, originally involved a synthesis of the Muslim faith with the cultural heritage of the region. Traces of Sufism can still be seen in the old mosques of Shigar and Khapulu for example, which are known as *Khanqahs* or monasteries, and include special cells for meditation and prayer. Traditions of music, dance and folk literature meanwhile remained very much alive in Baltistan until very recently. Dances depicted different aspects of everyday life and the surrounding environment, songs and music were used to mark religious and social festivals, while epics such as the *Gesar* recounted the Buddhist history of the Baltis. Many observers link the transformation with the revolution in Iran, which coincided with the politicisation of religion and the emergence of more militant sectarian groups in Pakistan as a whole.

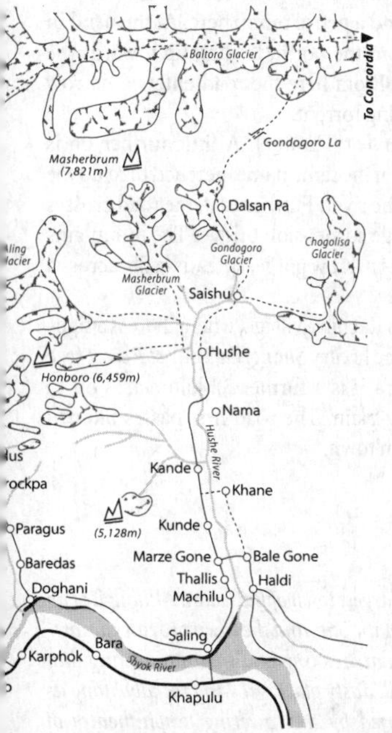

The road to Skardu

This route is a spectacular one following the narrow gorge of the Indus as it cuts its way through sheer rock mountains. In technical terms the road is in many places even more of an engineering triumph than the KKH; certainly, the most difficult sections claimed more lives per kilometre built than any section of the KKH. The right side of the bus gives the best views, but is definitely not for vertigo sufferers!

The Skardu road leaves the KKH 33 kilometres to the south of Gilgit, crossing the Indus River at **Alam Bridge**. There are several rock carvings and inscriptions by the turning. The road first bears northeast, giving excellent views of the Nanga Parbat massif, followed by a glimpse of

An icy romance

The irrigation water which sustains agriculture in Baltistan comes almost entirely from glacier-melt. For the people of Baltistan, glaciers are therefore fundamental to their survival; the body of folklore which has grown up around these life-giving sources of water is fascinating. Glaciers are believed to be either male or female, their gender influencing the fertility of the land they irrigate, as well as the characteristics of the people who cultivate the fields. Thus male glaciers are believed to produce higher yields and a more virile male population, but less attractive women. Female glaciers on the other hand produce lower yields, less 'manly' men, but particularly beautiful women. Not surprisingly, there is little or no consensus between villages as to the gender of the relevant glaciers.

More importantly however, the people of Baltistan believe that they can induce glaciers to 'mate' and produce offspring, thus creating new sources of irrigation water. First a suitable site for the new glacier is selected. Large chunks from two glaciers, one male and one female, are then carried to the spot. According to tradition, the chunks of glacier must be transported in one go, with the bearers observing strict silence along the way. During winter, snow accumulates around the fledgeling glacier, increasing its size. During summer, it must be carefully tended and a canopy of hay is built and kept continually moist to protect it from the melting rays of the sun. Given the right conditions, the new glacier gains a momentum of its own after around seven years, thereafter providing a permanent source of irrigation water.

The practice of breeding glaciers appears to be dying out, with no new ones known to have been created in the last 30 years or so. However, according to village elders, there are dozens such glaciers scattered around Baltistan, a testament to the ingenuity and resourcefulness of the people in the face of their harsh, marginal environment.

Rakaposhi, and then bends sharply southeast at **Sasli** (27 kilometres, also known as Sassi). There are tea shops and a petrol pump here. At the bend in the river, a steep side valley enters from the north, leading up towards the north face Base Camp of **Haramosh**. From here the road enters a narrow gorge and the Indus roars past as a raging torrent.

The gorge begins to widen at **Tuar** (or Thowar). A little further on is **Rondu**, capital of the former kingdom of the same name, perched high up the steep valley side on a flat shelf, across the river. Further east, the road crosses to the south bank of the Indus on a large suspension bridge. The mountains fall back, and the river, released from its narrow gorge, spreads lazily across a wide open plain with rolling sand dunes.

Just east of the bridge the road passes Kachura village, where there is a sign-posted turning to **Kachura Lake** and the luxury *Shangrila Tourist Resort* (see under Around Skardu). From Kachura it is a further 32 kilometres on to Skardu, across the parched and sandy plain. The road first passes **Skardu Airport,** 13 kilometres west of the main town.

Skardu

Phone code: 0575
Colour map 5, grid B5

Skardu is the administrative centre and largest town of Baltistan. Although of no great interest in itself, its setting is a dramatic one, and the town provides a starting point for some of the most spectacular trekking and mountaineering that Pakistan has to offer. The town is a small, dusty place, growing rapidly along its one main street, but still utterly dwarfed by the towering amphitheatre of imposing rock mountains all around, and by the broad sweep of the Indus as it threads its way lazily across an even broader plain. Dominating the town on the north side is the huge rocky outcrop of Karpochu. To the west are rolling sand dunes stretching out into the distance. To the south the wide stony course of the Sadpara Nullah, an irrigated oasis scattered with trees and fields, fans down from Sadpara Lake. Hidden from view by the surrounding mountains is the vast tangle of high Karakoram to the north, and the equally vast high plateaux of the Deosai to the south.

Ins and outs

Getting there

The easiest way to get to Skardu is via the daily weather-dependent flights from Islamabad. The main land route into Baltistan is the road along the Indus River linking Skardu with the KKH. There are regular bus services between Gilgit and Skardu (a 7-hour journey), and less regular services between Islamabad/Rawalpindi and Skardu (a gruelling 22-hour overnight journey).The only other route into Baltistan is by way of a rough jeep track which follows the Astor valley southeast from the KKH at Jaglot and climbs up over the Deosai Plateau before descending eventually to Skardu. This is a demanding two day journey for which you should be properly acclimatized. There is no regular public transport along this route.

Skardu

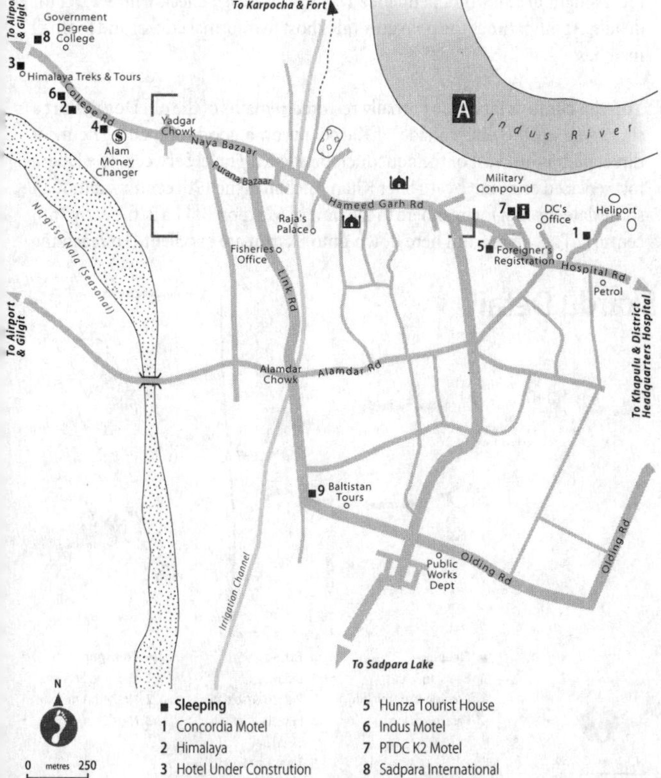

Sleeping
1 Concordia Motel
2 Himalaya
3 Hotel Under Constrution
4 Hunza Inn (5 Brothers)
5 Hunza Tourist House
6 Indus Motel
7 PTDC K2 Motel
8 Sadpara International
9 Yak & Yurt Serai

Related map
A Skardu Detail, page 508

Getting around There are usually Hiace minibuses waiting outside the airport terminal to ferry people into town for Rs 12, and also representatives from the various hotels who will take you for free provided you stay at their hotel. To get from town out to the airport, your best bet is to take a taxi (Rs 75-100 one way). During the day Suzuki minivans ply back and forth along Skardu's main street, running between Yadgar Chowk and the district hospital at the east end of town (Rs 5), or there are plenty of taxis hanging around in Naya Bazaar.

Sights

The modern town of Skardu is seen by most as a place from which to set off from and return to, rather than a destination in itself. It does however have a certain amount of atmosphere and there are parts of it which are worth exploring. There are also several short half or one-day excursions which can be made from here (see under Around Skardu).

Purana Bazaar Running in a short arc to the south of Naya Bazaar, Purana (old) bazaar gives something of the flavour of the town before the arrival of jeeps and concrete, with its wooden houses and shops selling basic supplies, clothes, shoes and household goods.

Polo Ground The large polo ground, just east of the old aqueduct is a lively social focal point during the summer when polo matches are held. There is usually a major tournament around Independence Day (14 August); check with PTDC for details. At other times the polo ground is host to informal cricket and football matches.

Karpochu You can climb as far as the partially restored remains of the old **Dogra Fort** a short way up the eastern side of Karpochu on a good footpath. The most direct path is just east of the aqueduct, beside K2 Travel Services. The Dogra fort replaced one built by Ali Sher Khan Anchan in the 17th century, although some date the first fortress here to the time of Makpon Bokha in the early 16th century. The views from here down onto Skardu are excellent. To reach the

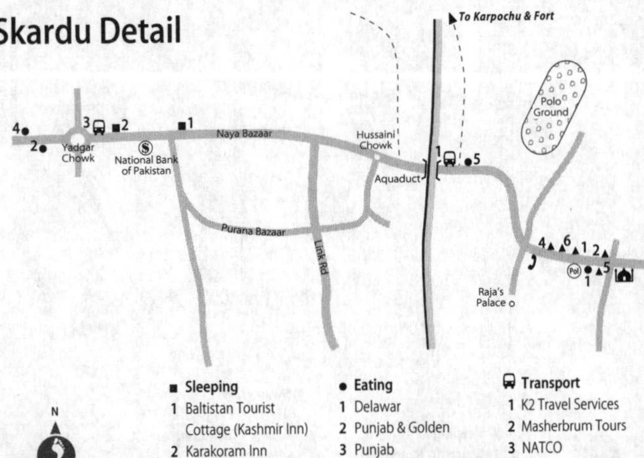

top you need to start from the western end, near the *Sadpara International* hotel. It is a long, dry, exposed climb, and very difficult in places (not recommended unless you have at least a rudimentary knowledge of rock climbing), although the views from the top are spectacular. There are further ruined fortifications here of uncertain origin.

Essentials

Sleeping

■ on maps
Price codes: see inside front cover

B ***PTDC K2 Motel***, off Hameed Garh Rd, T2946, F3322. The traditional focal point for mountaineering and trekking groups, and a good place to get current information or link up with other trekkers/climbers. Comfortable rooms with fan, phone and attached bath (best ones in new block, slightly cheaper in old block). Pleasant garden and excellent views out over Indus. Restaurant. Camping (Rs 100 per tent, including use of toilet/shower facilities). PTDC Tourist Information Centre based here.

C ***Concordia Motel***, off Hospital Rd, near Heliport, T3386, F2547. Pleasant, nicely furnished rooms with fan and attached bath. Peaceful location with excellent views out over Indus. Restaurant. **C** ***Hunza Tourist Lodge***, Hameed Garh Rd, opposite turning for *PTDC K2 Motel*, T2515, F2547. Set back from road, light airy rooms with fan and attached bath. Pleasant garden. Restaurant. Clean and comfortable but a little expensive. **C** ***Yak and Yurt Serai***, Link Rd, T2856. Open April to September only. Rather unusual arrangement of luxury Mongolian-style yurts. Restaurant. A long way from the centre.

D ***Indus Motel***, College Rd, T/F2608. 'Deluxe' rooms at rear with good views south over Sadpara Nullah, comfortably furnished with fan and attached bath. Also simpler rooms at front without the views (double Rs 250-300). Friendly staff. Restaurant.

E ***Himalaya***, College Rd, T2576. Simple but clean rooms with fan and attached bath. Best rooms at rear with balconies and good views south over Sadpara Nullah. Restaurant. **E** ***Karakoram Inn***, Yadgar Chowk, T2449. Mediocre rooms with fan and attached bath. A bit run down, and slightly oppressive interior. Restaurant. **E** ***Sadpara International***, College Rd, T/F2951. Simple but clean rooms with fan and attached bath. Rooms arranged around pleasant (concrete) courtyard. Also some 'deluxe' rooms (Rs 400) and basic rooms (Rs 100). Restaurant. Good value, well-run hotel.

F ***Baltistan Tourist Cottage (Kashmir Inn)***, Yadgar Chowk, T2707. Simple rooms with fan and attached bath. Also basic dorm with shared bath and no fan (Rs 50 per bed). Pleasant restaurant and balcony area upstairs. Helpful manager. **F** ***Hunza Inn (5 Brothers)***, College Rd, T2570. Fairly basic rooms with fan and attached bath. Rooms arranged around pleasant garden/courtyard at rear, some with shared bath only. Restaurant. Nicer than it looks from the outside.

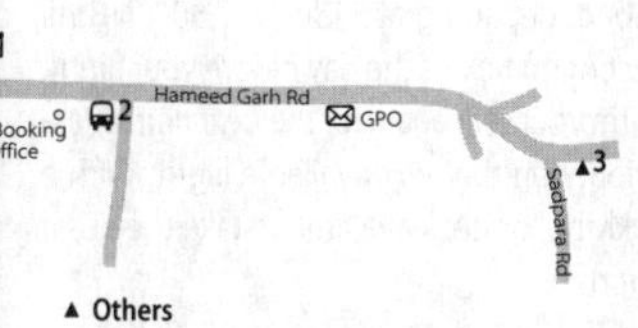

Eating

● on maps

Skardu is not exactly a gourmet's paradise. If you are vegetarian, choice is particularly limited. The restaurant at *K2*

KKH and the Northern Areas

Motel is open to non-guests. When there are 30 or more people staying there is an evening buffet (Rs 225 per head); book in advance if you are not staying. The restaurant at the *Concordia* hotel serves a fixed menu evening meal (Rs 200 per head); again, book in advance if you are not staying. Most of the other hotels have their own restaurants offering reasonable but uninspiring food; the restaurant at the *Indus Motel* is one of the better ones.

There are dozens of cheap local-style restaurants in Naya Bazaar and Hameed Garh Rd. Around Yadgar Chowk there are several places, including amongst others the ***Punjab***, ***Golden*** and ***Qadri Inn***. Just east of the aqueduct, ***Tibet Fast Food*** is good, particularly for soups. Heading east towards the *PTDC K2 Motel* there is the ***Delawar*** and further on another ***Punjab***. All these places are pretty basic, and hygiene standards are often not all they could be.

Entertainment

Sports During the summer there are occasional **polo** matches at the polo ground (see under Sights, above). There is good **trout fishing** on many of the rivers in Baltistan. Permits can be obtained from the Office of the Assistant Inspector of Fisheries on Link Rd. Otherwise you are surrounded by thousands of square kilometres of climbing and trekking territory.

Shopping

There are several tourist-oriented shops along Naya Bazaar selling antiques, souvenirs, jewellery, precious and semi-precious stones etc, most of them concentrated around Yadgar Chowk; for example ***Topaz Gems***, below *Karakoram Inn*, ***Baltistan Gems***, near *Baltistan Tourist Cottage*, or ***Pakiza***, next to National Bank. Another place worth trying is ***Shahbaz Jewellers and Antiques***, on Hameed Garh Rd. Precious and semi-precious stones available include, amongst others, Ruby, Amethyst, Emerald, Topaz, Garnet, Turquoise, Aquamarine (mined locally around Baltistan), Tourmaline and Lapis Lazuli. Some of the antique jewellery and other artefacts are quite striking.

Purana and Naya bazaars are the best place to shop for basic trekking supplies. All staple foods, biscuits etc are readily available, as well as cooking implements (including pressure cookers) and kerosene stoves. High-energy and freeze-dried foods are more difficult to come by, although left-overs from previous expeditions sometimes find their way into stores; College Rd and Naya Bazaar are the best place to look for these. If you are looking for trekking equipment (tents, sleeping bags etc), your best bet is to try renting it from one of the tour operators (see below).

Rockmans, Hameed Garh Rd (next door to *Travel Waljis*), have a good selection of postcards, T-shirts and various handicrafts/souvenirs, as well as a selection of apricot products (dried apricots, apricot candy bars, apricot kernel oil etc).

Further east from *Rockmans* on Hameed Garh Rd, by a crossroads, there are a couple of large metal tanks where kerosene is sold; if there is no one on hand, ask around in the surrounding shops.

Long-distance transport

Air PIA Booking Office, Hameed Garh Rd, T2491. Open 7 days, 0800-1400. Weather permitting, there is 1 flight daily to **Islamabad**, departing at 1130, Rs 2,500. **NB** All flights are effectively on a stand-by basis. Reconfirm tickets the day before your flight. If your flight is cancelled, you need to reconfirm your seat again for the next flight. Passengers from cancelled flights are given priority on the next available flight. With a few days bad weather, a large back-log quickly builds up; leave time to take the bus if you have a tight schedule/onward connections.

Road Private Jeep Hire The tour operators listed below in the Directory, PTDC Tourist Information and most hotels can all arrange private jeep hire. Rates vary greatly depending on demand. The following rates were being charged in 1998, though it should be remembered that this was a disastrous year for tourism in Baltistan, and most jeep owners were desperate for business; Sadpara Lake Rs 400 (half-day excursion); Shigar village Rs 800 (half-day excursion); Kachura Lake Rs 650 (half-day excursion); Deosai plateau Rs 2,500 (full-day excursion); Astor via Deosai Rs 7,000 (2 day trip); Askole Rs 3,000 (one-way drop).

Bus There are three companies operating from Skardu, the government-run Northern Areas Transport Company (NATCO), the private Masherbrum Tours and the private K2 Travel Services.

NATCO Booking office and bus stand situated on Hameed Garh Rd, next to PIA booking office, T3313. **Rawalpindi** 2 buses daily, normal bus 1100, Rs 310, deluxe bus 1500, Rs 360, approximately 22 hours. **Gilgit** 1 bus daily, 0600, Rs 100, 7 hours. **Khapulu** 3 buses daily, 0600, 0800, 1000, Rs 56, 3 hours. **Shigar** 1 bus daily, 1500, Rs 15, 1½ hours. Also various local services from Yadgar Chowk.

Masherbrum Tours Booking office and bus stand by Yadgar Chowk, T2616. **Rawalpindi** 2 buses daily, deluxe bus 1400, Rs 360, a/c Coaster 1430, Rs 450, approximately 22 hours. **Gilgit** 4 buses/minibuses daily, big bus 0600, Rs 80, Hiace 0800, Rs 100, Coaster 1000, Rs 100, Hiace 1300, Rs 100, 6-7 hours. **Khapulu** 1 bus daily, 0700, Rs 56, 3 hours.

K2 Travel Services Booking office and bus stand immediately east of aqueduct, next door to *Tibet Fast Food*. **Rawalpindi** 1 Coaster daily, 1400, Rs 400, approximately 22 hours. **Gilgit** 2 Hiace minibuses daily, 0900, 1300, Rs 100, 6-7 hours. **Khapulu** 1 jeep daily, 0700 or 0800, Rs 60, 3 hours.

Cargo Jeep This is the cheapest way of getting to places not served by public bus. Finding a cargo jeep going to your destination can be difficult, particularly as everyone will try to persuade you to hire a private jeep (a 'special' or 'booking'). They run on an irregular basis up the Shigar valley at least as far as Dassu or Chutron, across the Deosai to Astor and east towards Khapulu and up to Hushe. The most regular services are to Kachura, Shigar village, Doghani (at the foot of the Thalle valley) and Khapulu. They leave from various places along Naya Bazaar, particularly around Hussaini Chowk; ask around.

Directory

Banks *National Bank of Pakistan*, Naya Bazaar, T2958. Will change cash and TCs at the official rate (or often as not the previous day's official rate). Open 0900-1330, Fri and Sat 0900-1230, closed Sun. To the west of Yadgar Chowk, ***Alam Money Changer***, T2120. Will change cash and TCs at slightly below the 'kerbside' rate in Islamabad. Open 0800-1800, Fri 0800-1200, closed Sun. The *PTDC K2 Motel* is able to change US$ cash, or there are plenty of unofficial money changers in Naya Bazaar on the lookout for dollars; try at the PCOs.

Communications **Post:** The GPO is situated on Hameed Garh Rd, east of the PIA and NATCO offices. Open 0800-1600, Fri 0800-1200, closed Sun. **Telephone:** the army-run telegraph office is on Hameed Garh Rd, east of the aqueduct. Open 7 days, 0600-2400. You can make national and international calls from here, though faxes can only be sent within Pakistan. There are a couple of PCOs near Yadgar Chowk, though they charge nearly twice as much as the telegraph office for international calls.

Hospitals & medical services **Hospitals:** The ***District Headquarters Hospital*** is situated east of the main town, beyond the *PTDC K2 Motel*, on Hospital Rd. **Chemists:** there are several chemists opposite the hospital, and some in Naya Bazaar.

Tour companies & travel agents *Adventure Karakoram*, PO Box 636, T55144. Run by Mr Abbas Kazmi, one time manager of the *Baltistan Tourist Cottage*, a local scholar specializing in Baltistan's pre-Islamic history and culture. Offers a wide range of organized/tailor-made treks and jeep safaris. ***Baltistan Tours***, PO Box 604, Link Rd, Satellite Town, T2626, F2108 (Liaison Office; PO Box 1285, House 14, Street 44, F-6/1, Islamabad, T220338, F218620). One of the larger trekking companies, local handlers for ***KE Adventure Travel***, see page 22. Good, reliable service, but a little expensive. ***Himalaya Treks and Tours***, College Rd, T2528 (Liaison Office; 112 Rahim Plaza, Murree Rd, Rawalpindi T/F563014. Mountaineering/trekking expeditions, jeep safaris, equipment hire available for up to 50 people. Good reputation. ***Travel Walji's***, Hameed Garh Rd, T3468 (Head

Office; 10 Khayaban-e-Suhrawardy, PO Box No 1088, Islamabad, T270757-58, F270753). This is Pakistan's largest tour operator. They are not the cheapest, but generally give a good service.

Tourist offices *PTDC Tourist Information Centre, K2 Motel*, T2946, F3322. Helpful staff who will point you in the right direction for organizing treks etc. They have two seats on flights to Islamabad reserved for foreign tourists; they will issue you with a letter to present to PIA. They can also arrange private jeep hire.

Useful addresses **Police:** Hameed Garh Rd, T2444. **Deputy Commissioner:** Hospital Rd, T2955. Contact the DC if you look set to overrun on your visa due to flight cancellations, road blockages, illness etc. He will issue you with a letter of explanation to present to the visa extension office in Islamabad. **Foreigners' registration:** Superintendent of Police, Hospital Rd, T2424. **NAPWD:** Link Rd, T2788 or T2406. (For booking NAPWD Resthouses.)

Around Skardu

Sadpara Lake and Buddha

Situated eight kilometres south of Skardu, Sadpara Lake is a beautiful, tranquil spot and well worth a visit. The lake is fed by the mountain torrent which flows down from the Deosai plateau to the south, and dammed on its northern edge.

It is a three hour walk to the lake, or you can hire a suzuki or jeep, or try hitching. By foot the most scenic option is to follow the aqueduct from the centre of town, joining Link Road by Alamdar Chowk. Continue south along Link Road and then either follow the rough track heading south from the corner where *Yak and Yurt Serai* is situated, or turn east and then south again at the next crossroads. A short detour across Sadpara stream takes you to the **Sadpara Buddha**, a meditating *Maitreya Buddha* surrounded by *Bodhisattvas* carved into a large boulder, thought to date from around 900 AD.

The lake is well stocked with trout. **Fishing** permits can be obtained from the Fisheries Office by the lake or from the office in Skardu (Rs 100 per rod). Note however that fishing is not permitted from November to March, as this is the breeding season. It is a further seven kilometres to the picturesque Sadpara village above the lake. The people of Sadpara are Shina speakers, known in Balti as *Brokpas* (literally 'settlers of high places'). They are descended from the prisoners brought back by Ali Sher Khan Anchan following his campaigns against the people of Chilas, Gilgit and Astor. There is a check post on the road by the turning to the village marking the start of the Deosai National Park (see below).

Sleeping

B *PTDC Sadpara Motel*, situated on an area of high ground on the northwest side of the lake; shortly before arriving at the lake, there is a bridge across the Sadpara Nullah and a track leading up to the hotel. Scheduled to open in 1999 and promising to offer good quality luxury accommodation. Unfortunately, its tin-roofed buildings are something of an eyesore from further up the valley.

D *Sadpara Lake Inn* (**NB** hotel used to rent 2 rooms to PTDC; at time of writing, the sign above the entrance still reads 'PTDC Sadpara Hut'), situated by lake, just off main jeep track. 6 reasonably comfortable rooms with attached bath. Pleasant lakeside garden. Restaurant. Camping allowed. Trekking equipment (including tents) available for up to 25 people. Motorboat, rowing boats and fishing equipment for hire. Friendly manager.

E *Lake View Motel*, situated by lake, on main jeep track. Just 2 simple but clean rooms with attached bath, one with views out over lake. Pleasant garden. Restaurant. Camping allowed. Rowing boats and fishing equipment for hire. Friendly manager.

Eating

Each of the hotel restaurants offer excellent meals of fresh grilled trout served with chips. This will cost around Rs 350-400 for two people (probably slightly more at the *PTDC Sadpara Motel* when it opens).

Kachura Lake

The village of Kachura is situated 32 kilometres west of Skardu, just before the main road to Gilgit crosses to the north side of the Indus River. A turning leads south off the main road up through the village, with its rich fruit orchards, to the luxury **Shangrila resort**, which features its own private lake (see under Sleeping, below).

A much more attractive option is to continue on to the far more beautiful and unspoilt **upper Kachura lake** (known locally as Foroq Lake). Continue past the turnings for the *Shangrila* resort and *Tibet Motel* until you reach the village of Karpia. Bear right in the village to follow a very rough track for around one kilometre, and then take a path off to the left which leads steeply down to the lake (ask directions from the village as the route is not particularly obvious). There are a couple of simple snack places here which open during the summer season only, but otherwise the lake is completely undeveloped.

The **Shigarthang nullah**, which drains into the Indus just to the east of Kachura, is the starting point for treks up onto the Deosai plateau. There are also plenty of beautiful short walks in the area.

Sleeping

L *Shangrila*, T2970, F3369 (or book in Islamabad; House 17 Street 31, F-7/1, T206301, F206304, E resorts@isb.comsats.net.pk). This fancy resort consists of a complex of red Chinese-style pagoda-roofed cottages and carefully manicured gardens arranged around Kachura lake. 'VIP Suite' and 'Swiss Cottage' chalets featuring two double rooms with fan, phone, attached bath and balconies overlooking the lake range from Rs 8,000-11,500, while the presidential suite costs an outrageous Rs 19,000. There are 3 restaurants offering Chinese, Continental and Pakistani cuisine, a café in the fuselage of a crashed DC-3 airplane, conference facilities, shops, boating on the lake and a rather sorry-looking zoo. Overall it's pretty smart, but somehow it doesn't quite live up to its price tag.

B *Tibet Motel*, fronts onto Kachura lake opposite the *Shangrila* resort, T14 (or in Skardu T2518). Just 2 rooms at present, fan and attached bath, OK but nothing special. New 10 room wing under construction at time of writing. Nice lawn on waterfront. Restaurant. Boating. Camping allowed (good value at Rs 100 including use of toilet/shower facilities).

The Deosai Plateau

Covering an area of over 400 square kilometres, all of it above 4,000 metres, the Deosai plateau is an uniquely beautiful region. In China the word translates literally as 'giants abode', and it isn't hard to see how a landscape on such a massive scale could have inspired stories of giants. In Balti, the region is known as *Bhear Sar*, meaning 'place of flowers', an apt description during summer. It contrasts sharply with the ring of jagged rocky mountains that surround it on all sides. Gently rolling hills extend into the distance as far as the eye can see, clothed in a soft cladding of vegetation and carpeted with brightly coloured flowers in summer. The plateau's rivers meanwhile flow past crystal clear and icy cold. You get an unmistakable sense of the elevation here, in the huge expanse of horizon, the wide open space and the clarity of light and colour typical of such high altitudes.

Best time to visit The Deosai is at its best from mid-July to late August. While the weather can be glorious in daytime during this period, temperatures drop dramatically at night, and can also turn nasty very quickly, with intense windstorms often sweeping across the plateau. Note that rivers can be impassable in a vehicle when in spate (usually during June and early July). Take local advice and find out about the current state of the jeep track before setting out. Mosquitoes are a major problem during the early part of the season(June/July) and strong repellent or mosquito nets are essential. On the other hand, this is also when the plateau is in full flower. From November through to May the Deosai is completely snow-bound.

Ins and outs

There is a jeep route across the Deosai which links Skardu with Astor and continues down to the KKH at Jaglot. From Skardu to Astor is 115 kilometres, which is feasible in one very long day, but much more enjoyable if spread over 2 days with an overnight stop on the plateau. There are comfortable hotels at Sadpara and Astor, and during the summer there are several temporary 'hotels' on the plateau offering food and basic accommodation in tents. Even so, you are strongly advised to bring your own supplies. It is essential that you are properly equipped for high altitudes. If you have flown directly up from the plains and are planning a visit to the Deosai, acclimatization is an important consideration.

During the summer, cargo jeeps make the journey from Skardu as far as Chilam or Astor on an irregular basis. Astor is linked by regular public transport with the KKH and Gilgit. Renting a private jeep is fairly expensive (Skardu to Astor was around Rs 7,000 in 1998), but worthwhile, particularly if you can split the cost between several people. Alternatively, the Deosai plateau can be visited as a round-trip excursion from Skardu. This is possible in one long day, but again is better spread over 2 days or more. Part of the Deosai has been designated as a National Park and an attractive option is to arrange a visit through the staff who run it. For details of this, and the jeep route across to Astor, see below.

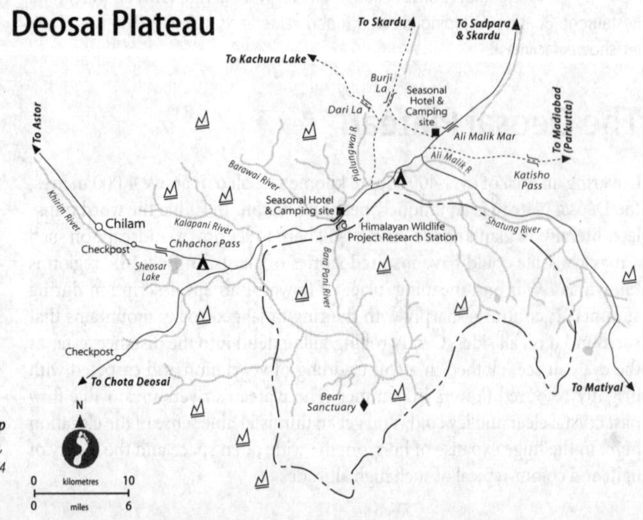

Related map Baltistan, page 504

Geography

The Deosai closely resembles the Tibetan plateau in its topography and environment. It is of enormous significance in hydrological terms, acting as a huge water store. As it gradually melts, the snow that has built up here over the winter accounts for over 5 percent of the total discharge of the Indus. The data from weather stations monitoring snowfall on the Deosai are used to predict the peak flow of the Indus later in the year.

Fauna and Flora

Frozen beneath a deep blanket of snow for much of the year, the Deosai is surprisingly rich in plants and animals, bursting into life during the brief spring and summer months. The plateau is home to the **Himalayan Brown Bear** (*Ursus arctos Isabellinus*), a species of bear unique to this part of the world, and under serious threat due to illegal hunting. Rough estimates place the total number still surviving in Pakistan at around 30-40, with perhaps 25 inhabiting the Deosai. The remainder are found in the Biafo Glacier area and in Khunjerab National Park. Other mammals include the **Golden Marmot** (in large numbers), **Tibetan Wolf**, **Tibetan Red Fox**, **Himalayan Ibex**, **Ladakh Urial** and various small rodents, including voles and shrews.

Reptiles include lizards such as the **Himalayan Agama**, **Ground Skink** and **Glacial Skink**. The unique **Snow Carp** is found in the Deosai's rivers. Below 3,000 metres, in the nullahs leading down off the plateau, the **Himalayan Otter** feeds on the snow carp. This altitude zone and habitat is also home to some **Snow Leopards** and **Musk Deer**, particularly amongst birch and juniper forests. The recently discovered **Alpine Toad** looks set to qualify as a separate species.

The plateau provides spring and summer breeding grounds for many of Pakistan's birds, including the **Himalayan Golden Eagle**, **Lammergier** (bearded vulture), **Northern Hobby** (a falcon), **Kestrel** and **Long-legged Buzzard**, as well as larks, wagtails, warblers and sand plovers. It also lies on the flight path of a number of migratory birds which can be seen from late September to mid-October on their return from Central Asia to the plains of the subcontinent. Species include the **Osprey**, **Damoselle Crane**, **Little Turn**, **Great Black-headed Gull** and ducks such as the common **Teal**, **Pintail**, **Shoveller** and **Marganzer**.

More than 100 species of plants and grasses are found on the Deosai, including colourful flowers such as **Aconitum**, **Rheum**, **Iris**, **Astragalus** and **Spiraea**. There is also a wealth of herbs and medicinal plants, including **Ginger**, **Primula**, **Geranium**, **Mint**, **Artmesia**, **Rubus** and **Barberry**. At lower altitude on the peripheries wild rose is found, as well as trees such as Juniper, Blue Pine, Spruce, Pencil Cedar, White Birch, Himalayan Poplar and Chinese Salix.

Deosai National Park

In an attempt to provide some sanctuary to the remaining Brown Bears, and to monitor them and learn more about their behaviour and habitat, the Deosai National Park was established in 1993 by the **Himalayan Wildlife Project**, in collaboration with the Northern Areas Forestry, Parks and Wildlife Department and local communities. The park has a semi-official status and an important part of the management plan involves gaining official recognition and ensuring proper implementation of recommendations for the protection of the Brown Bear and its habitat. One problem is the inflexible nature of existing regulations for National Parks. The Deosai is vital to the livelihoods of many people, providing important pastures for livestock during the spring and summer. The lesson learnt from similar projects in Pakistan, such as the Khunjerab National Park, is that all-or-nothing measures (eg the complete banning of grazing) are generally unworkable and serve only to alienate local people. The priority for Deosai has been very much to encourage local support and involvement, and to formulate a set of rules that are flexible enough to take account of existing land-use patterns without compromising the integrity of the park area.

Visiting the park There is a check post at Sadpara village, and another one near Sherkuli village, between the Chhachor Pass and Chilam. The hunting of bears or other wildlife and carrying of firearms is forbidden in the park area (line-fishing is allowed). Vehicles are not allowed off the main jeep tracks. People are asked to camp at the recognized campsites, or within 60 metres of the track. Entry into the 'Bear Sanctuary' area (see map) is restricted and permits must be obtained, either from the District Forestry Officer in Skardu, or from the Conservator of Wildlife in Gilgit.

If you want to gain some insight into the wildlife and ecology of the Deosai, or would just like to see a Brown Bear, the staff of the Himalayan Wildlife Project, who are properly trained, familiar with the terrain and experienced in tracking the animals (safely), will take people on tours of the protected area. They have a research station at the Bara Pani bridge crossing, which is manned throughout the season. To organize a visit, contact the *Himalayan Wildlife Project*, Centre One, House 1, Street 15,Khayaban-e-Iqbal, F-7/2, Islamabad, T051-276113, F051-824484. Alternatively, it may be possible to arrange a visit by contacting the staff at the check posts at Sadpara or Sherkuli, depending on who is available at short notice.

The jeep route across Deosai: Skardu to Astor From Skardu the jeep track climbs up past Sadpara Lake (see above; Around Skardu) and, further on, Sadpara village. Above the village, on the jeep track, is **Sadpara check post**, marking the start of the National Park area. As well as the accommodation down by Sadpara Lake, there is a spare tent at the check post which is able to sleep up to four people (bring your own bedding), or you can pitch your own tent. The check post is recommended as an overnight acclimatization stop. Above the check post, where a small nullah joins the main stream, there is an area of cultivated land up on the hillside, strewn with several enormous boulders covered in rock inscriptions from pre-historic, Buddhist and Islamic times.

Beyond the check post the jeep track climbs steeply up the Sadpara Nullah. After the track crosses to the west bank of the stream, the course of the old jeep track which continued along the east bank can still be seen in places. If the new track feels scary, you can comfort yourself with the fact that it is infinitely less hair-raising than the old one. At the top (around two to three hours drive from Skardu) is **Ali Malik Mar** (4,080 metres), the pass marking the start of the Deosai proper. From here, the track descends for a short way to a designated camping site with a seasonal *hotel* consisting of a couple of tents. Tea and basic meals can be obtained here when it is open.

After about 30 minutes, the jeep track forks; the right fork is the main route to Chilam and Astor, while the left fork heads southeast towards Matiyal. The latter route is closed to foreigners. Taking the right fork, further on the track fords the Ali Malik Mar and Shatung streams shortly before they converge. This fording is the most difficult on the route. There is a designated camping site here. The track then continues along the main river to the bridge-crossing at **Bara Pani** (about one hour's drive from Ali Malik Mar). By the bridge there is another designated camping site and a seasonal *hotel* with a couple of tents for sleeping and a kitchen tent serving tea and basic meals. Around 500 metres to the south of the bridge (off to the left as you face the bridge coming from Skardu) is the main summer camp/research station of the Himalayan Wildlife Project.

After crossing the bridge, the track climbs gently but steadily over a watershed and down to the **Kalapani** River. The track crosses the river and then forks further on. The right fork is the Chilam/Astor route, while the left fork leads to the area known as **Chota (small) Deosai**, currently closed to foreigners and guarded by an army check post. Taking the right fork, the main track continues on to the beautiful **Sheosar lake** (around one hour's drive from Bara Pani), where there is good camping. Immediately after is the **Chhachor pass** (4,230 metres), after which the track begins to descend. Around an hour beyond the pass is the **Sherkuli check post**, marking the entrance to the Deosai National Park from the Astor side. Soon after is the small village of **Chilam**, situated near the top of the Das Khirim valley. It takes a further two to three hours to reach the village of Astor. For details of Astor and the Astor valley, see page 465.

Deosai Plateau Treks

Open zone. Maximum elevation optional (4,080-4,820 metres).August. Maps; the U502 series, NI 43-3 Mundik and NI 43-2 Gilgit are not accurate enough to be relied on for treks on Deosai. Partially researched first hand. See trekking notes, page 67. NB Foreigners are not permitted to go south or east of the jeep track between Ali Malik Mar and Chachhor Pass without a permit.

Skardu-Astor The jeep route between Skardu and Astor can also be done as a trek; allow around 5-7 days between Skardu and Chilam. This route has also begun to attract adventurous mountain bikers in search of some thing really challenging.

Burji La The most popular trek is a short loop from Skardu, climbing up past Sadpara Lake, across Ali Malik Mar, then doubling back across Burji La and down to Skardu. This takes around 4 days. It is advisable to do the trek in this direction as the ascent from Skardu to the 4,820 metres Burji La is extremely steep and involves an altitude gain of nearly 2,500 metres in just 2 days. In either direction, it is essential to acclimatize properly first; do not be tempted to do this trek if you have just flown into Skardu. The approach to Burji La from the south does not follow any clear path and the route across the pass itself can be difficult to determine. A guide is strongly recommended (**NB** there is no shortage of people in Skardu claiming to be guides; only go with someone who has references proving they have done the trek).

If walking from Skardu, the best place to camp for the first night is by the check post on the jeep track above Sadpara village. The second day takes you over Ali Malik Mar (4,080 metres) to the camping site and seasonal 'hotel' just beyond the pass. From here follow the jeep track on for a short distance and then branch off sharply to the right to head due north towards Burji La (if you reach the main fork in the jeep track you have gone too far). The approach to the pass leads past 2 small lakes with options for camping wherever there is water. The pass itself gives spectacular views of the Karakoram mountains to the north (including K2 and Masherbrum on a clear day) and south back onto the Deosai. It is feasible to reach Skardu from the top of the pass in 1 long day; an overnight stop half way down is preferable, but make sure you have sufficient water with you as there is none along the way.

Shigarthang Valley From near Kachura Lake trekking routes lead up the Shigarthang valley onto the Deosai. Higher up, the valley divides. The left fork climbs southeast over the **Dari La** and on to the Deosai. From here you can angle sharply northeast over the **Burji La** and drop down towards Skardu, or else join the rough Skardu-Astor jeep track to the south. The right fork continues southwest up the main stream, crosses the **Alam Pir La**, and then follows first the **Bubind** and then the **Das Khirim** valley down towards Astor. An alternative route branches west above the first fork in the valley, across the **Banak La** and descends the **Parishing river** directly to Astor. The editors have not covered these routes, but a survey of the literature reveals some confusion as to names and exact routes; a guide familiar with the area is strongly recommended.

Shigar River Valley

The Shigar River flows into the Indus just north of Skardu. The valley is wide and fertile, carpeted by gently terraced fields of wheat, barley and maize, and rich orchards of apricot, mulberry, peach, plum, apple and pear. Once a powerful independent kingdom, this valley is the gateway to some of the most spectacular treks in northern Pakistan, including the famous Baltoro trek up to Concordia and K2 base camp. The beautiful village of Shigar, near the foot of the valley, is worth a visit in itself and is easily accessible from Skardu.

History Shigar was one of the most powerful semi-independent kingdoms after that of the Makpon rulers of Skardu. A local legend traces the ancestry of the ruling family to a man named **Cha Tham** (or Shah Tham), who was deposed as the ruler of Nagar during the second period of the Trakhan dynasty in Gilgit. He crossed over to Shigar by way of the Hispar and Biafo glaciers and subsequently established the *Amacha* dynasty which continued to rule right up until the Dogra period. It was to Shigar that the Muslim missionaries Amir Kabir Sayed Ali Hamadani and Mir Shamsuddin Iraqi are first said to have come, in the 14th and 16th centuries respectively. Following Sultan Abu Said Khan's invasion of Baltistan in 1532, which brought him by way of the Braldo pass to Shigar, strong links were forged with Yarkand to the north. Later these were replaced by ties with the Mughals of Kashmir. **Imam Quli Khan** (1634-1705) is considered the greatest of Shigar's rulers. He forged close links with the ruler of Skardu, Shah Morad Khan, helping him with his campaigns against Khapulu, Ladakh and Gilgit. It was during the rule of his son **Azam Khan** that Skardu fell under the control of Shigar for a short period.

Skardu to Shigar

The left turn for Shigar is signposted about 10 kilometres east of Skardu on the road to Khapulu. From the turning onwards the road is unmetalled, though in fairly good condition. The old wooden suspension bridge across the Indus has now been supplemented by a much more solid-looking Chinese-built bridge right next to it. After crossing the river, the track runs north across a level plain before climbing over a shoulder of mountain giving excellent views back down onto the Indus and up the Shigar valley. The track then descends to Shigar village, 32 kilometres from Skardu.

Shigar Village

Colour map 5, grid B5

This picturesque village, shady and green, was once the capital of the ancient kingdom of Shigar. Today it retains much of its charm. Many of the houses are still built of wood, with intricately carved doorways and windows.

Ins and outs

Visiting Shigar village as a day-trip from Skardu by public transport is a little tricky, but with a privately hired jeep it is an easy half-day excursion. The bus goes right into the main bazaar. A good place to wait for cargo jeeps is near the polo ground, by the turning leading to the bridge across the Shigar River. It is also worth asking around the restaurants.

Sights

The largely destroyed ruins of the **Raja's Fort** stand on a sharp outcrop of rock overlooking the village. Below it, a short distance up the Bauma stream is the former **Raja's Palace**, in the same style as those at Baltit and Altit in Hunza. It has a beautifully carved entrance doorway and carved wood decoration in the outside wall, but inside it is in a sorry state of dilapidation. Nearby, overlooking the Bauma stream, is a small, beautifully carved wooden **mosque**. By the roadside in the centre of the village there is another wooden **mosque**, where Friday prayers are still held. This is the largest mosque in Shigar, with a three-tiered roof built by Kashmiri craftsmen. Its construction is generally attributed to the Muslim missionary Mir Shamsuddin Iraqi. Unfortunately, entry to either mosque is forbidden to non-Muslims. Scattered around a low ridge to the south of the main village are numerous **rock carvings** depicting ibex, Buddhist stupas and other symbols. The ruins of a **Buddhist monastery** have also recently been excavated in the area.

Sleeping & eating

There is only 1 hotel in Shigar, the **E** ***NAPWD Resthouse***, pleasantly situated by the Bauma stream. 2 rooms, clean and comfortable, good value. Nice garden (**camping** allowed). Food prepared to order. Book through NAPWD in Skardu, or else try just turning up; the chowkidar seems quite happy to let people stay without a booking, provided there is space (which there usually is). There are a few very basic restaurants, including the ***Mohammadi*** and ***K2*** offering simple food, and bedding for the night if you don't mind roughing it on the floor along with whoever else is passing through.

Shigar

To Askole
Chemists
Bauma Stream
Raja's Fort (ruins)
Raja's Palace
To Thalle La Trek
To Bridge across Shigar River
Polo Ground
Rock Carvings
To Skardu

■ **Sleeping**
1 NAPWD Resthouse

● **Eating**
1 K2 Restaurant
2 Mohammadi
3 Restaurant

Not to scale

Transport

There is a daily NATCO bus service from Skardu to Shigar village, departing at 1500. It takes around 1½ hours and costs Rs 15. The bus remains in Shigar overnight and leaves for the return journey to Skardu at around 0630-0700. Cargo jeeps operate fairly regularly on this route (most of these leave Skardu in the late morning or early afternoon; the frequency depends on demand). They cost Rs 30 and complete the journey in around 1 hour. Cargo jeeps also pass through Shigar on an irregular basis (usually in the afternoon) en route to Askole in the Braldu Valley (the start of the Baltoro trek to Concordia and K2), and Chu Tron in the Basha valley. The fare to either destination is around Rs 110-120. Unless you are prepared to risk quite a bit of waiting around, you really need to hire a jeep privately to get to these places.

Excursions from Shigar

Bauma Lungma

The side valley climbing up to the east from Shigar village is known as Bauma Lungma (*lungma* meaning 'stream'). A jeep track leads up as far as the hydro-electric plant at **Chaupi Ol** that provides Shigar with electricity. This is the start (or finish) of the Thalle La trek (see page 522 for a description of the trek going from the Thalle valley to Shigar). If you do not want to undertake the full trek, it makes for a very pleasant walk to follow the valley up as far as feels comfortable and then return to Shigar. From the hydro-electric plant to the picturesque settlement of **Ol** is around two hours away. A little further on there is a bridge across the stream. If you double back along the opposite bank here you can reach the equally picturesque settlement of **Anisgal**. Both settlements offer good camping.

Basha Valley

There is a bridge crossing just to the west of Shigar village and a jeep track leading up the west bank of the river, giving access to the Basha valley which branches off to the northwest. At **Chu Tron**, eight kilometres into the Basha valley, there are hot sulphur springs with separate bathing huts for men and women. There is also a *NAPWD Resthouse* adjacent, bookable in Skardu (also worth trying without a booking). The jeep track continues up the valley as far as the beautiful village of **Doko** (20 kilometres). It is a long day's walk (or two fairly easy days) to **Arondu**, a tiny village at the snout of the awesome 40 kilometres **Chogo Lungma Glacier**. North of the village, the glaciated Kero Lungma valley leads up to the extremely difficult and deeply crevassed Nushik La, and over to the Hispar Glacier. The pass was once used as a route connecting Nagar with Baltistan, but is today considered to be impassable.

The road to Askole

The main route up the Shigar valley continues up the east bank, passing through several green and fertile villages along the way. At the confluence of the Basha and Braldu valleys, a series of bridges provides an alternative point of access to the Basha valley, although after heavy rains the crossing is often impassable. **Dasso**, 11 kilometres into the Braldu valley where the jeep track crosses to the north bank, is the first village. This was originally the starting point for the trek to K2, but the jeep track has now been extended as far as **Askole**. This last section of jeep track is still unstable in places and subject to frequent closures due to landslides. A little way beyond the village of **Chango**, above the jeep track, there are hot sulphur springs suitable for bathing.

Treks in the area

Baltoro Glacier Trek: Concordia and K2

Restricted zone. Maximum elevation optional (5,000 metres plus). June to mid-September. Maps; Swiss Foundation are the best; Leomann's sheets 2 and 3 are also good; U502 series, NI 43-3, Mundik and NI 43-4, Chulung are adequate; the excellent 1977 Japanese-Pakistan K2 1;100,000 map covers the Baltoro glacier only. See trekking notes, page 67.

Since this trek is in a restricted zone and therefore requires a permit and registered guide, no detailed route description is given here. In practice it is only possible to obtain a permit through a recognized trekking agency. This is far and away the most popular trek in Pakistan, attracting large numbers of trekking groups (all the major trekking agencies bring groups here) as well as numerous mountaineering expeditions en route to peaks around Concordia. As a result it can get seriously crowded and some of the main campsites have become heavily polluted.

The trek in along the Braldu and Biaho rivers, and then onto the Baltoro Glacier is a long and extremely demanding one. The reward on the other hand is spectacular, taking you right into the heart of the Karakoram mountains at Concordia, where the Godwin-Austin Glacier descends from K2 to join the Baltoro. Surrounding these huge expanses of ice are some of the highest peaks in the world, with 7 of them (K2, Broad Peak, Gasherbrum IV, Mustagh Tower, Golden Throne, Chogolisa and Masherbrum) clearly visible.

Notwithstanding landslides and blockages, the jeep track now extends as far as Askole. The trek from Askole to Concordia takes around 8 days, not including rest days. Porters on this trek can be difficult, often striking for increased pay, or refusing to go beyond the lower stages of the trek. There are 20 recognized stages between Askole and Concordia. It takes a full day to trek up to the K2 base camp from Concordia. Count 4 to 6 days for the return trip.

Another option which is becoming increasingly popular is to trek out of Concordia into the Hushe valley over the Gondogoro pass. At 5,500 metres the route across this pass is extremely strenuous. An alternative route across the Masherbrum pass is slightly lower (5,364 metres), but extremely difficult, involving technical sections on the descent through an icefall on the far side and requiring ropes, crampons and ice axes.

Biafo-Hispar Trek: Askole to Nagar

Open zone. Maximum elevation 5,150 metres. July to mid-September. Maps; Swiss Foundation are best; U502 series, NI 43-3 Mundik, NJ 43-15 Shimshal, NJ 43-14 Baltit, reliability poor but adequate. Read trekking notes, page 67.

Although this trek is in an open zone, it is extremely strenuous, involving long stretches of glacier walking along this 115-kilometre ice corridor; a guide is essential, as well as crampons and ropes. The trek takes you far from any permanent settlements and is rich in wildlife, including Himalayan Brown Bears. Starting at Askole, the route follows the K2 trek for a short way before branching up the Biafo Glacier. The first part of this trek, up the lower sections of the Biafo Glacier, is particularly difficult. Above the junction of the Sim Gang and Biafo glaciers, off to the north as you approach Hispar Pass, is Snow Lake, a huge expanse of ice covering around 80 square kilometres. Known locally as Lukpe Lawo, it was named Snow Lake in 1892 by the British explorer Martin Conway. The 5,150 metres Hispar Pass provides stunning views in good weather; west down the Hispar Glacier towards Hunza and east back to the peaks surrounding Snow Lake and Sim Gang Glacier. The trek down to Hispar village along the north edge of the Hispar Glacier is difficult in places, crossing four-side glaciers en route. Between these there are several beautiful ablation valleys (small valleys running parallel to the glacier), rich in alpine flora and with plentiful water. Hispar village, the first permanent settlement after leaving Askole, is at the head of the jeep track which runs up past Nagar village from the KKH opposite Karimabad. There is no regular public transport up to Hispar, so unless you have organized a jeep to meet you at Hispar, it is still another two days walk down to Nagar, where you can count on finding public transport. The trek between Askole and Hispar villages takes around 12 days (not including rest days) and involves around 16-18 porter stages (definite porter stages on this route have not been established).

East to Khapulu

The road east from Skardu to Khapulu is now metalled for most of the way. After passing the bridge-turning to Shigar, the road bends southeast across a stony plain to **Gol** (30 kilometres). Just before the village, beside the road, several large boulders bear weather beaten inscriptions in Tibetan and carvings of Buddhist stupas, tridents and other symbols. A bridge at Gol crosses the Indus giving access to a rough jeep track running along the north bank of the Shyok River.

A few kilometres beyond Gol the Shyok River drains into the Indus from the east. A suspension bridge crosses the Indus just south of its confluence with the Shyok. There is a check post at the bridge where foreigners must register their details. The road southeast along the Indus (closed to foreigners) passes through the villages of **Mediabad** (formerly Parkutta), **Totli** and **Kharmang**, once centres of tiny independent kingdoms, and leads towards the Line of Control (effectively the border) with India. The main route east to Khapulu crosses the Indus on the suspension bridge and follows the south bank of the Shyok River. This first stretch of the Shyok was once the home of the tiny kingdom of **Kiris** (the village is on the opposite bank). Beyond was the powerful kingdom of Khapulu, second only to Skardu, guarding the old route to Ladakh.

Just to the east of **Gwari** village, which extends along the road for several kilometres, there is a bridge across to the north bank of the Shyok. Between the villages of **Yugo** and **Karphok** there is a second bridge. Hidden in the mountains above Karphok there is a large lake fed by glacier water. A few kilometres beyond Karphok, there is a third bridge across the Shyok which gives direct access to the village of **Doghani**, at the foot of the Thalle valley. Higher up this valley is the start of the **Thalle La** trek. The main road continues along the south bank of the Shyok, passing through **Bara**, a cluster of villages stretching over several kilometres, before arriving at Khapulu, 103 kilometres from Skardu.

Thalle La Trek

Open Zone. Maximum elevation 4,572 metres. July to September. Maps: Swiss Foundation are the best; U502 series, NI 43-3 Mundik, is reasonably accurate topographically, though place names are mostly redundant. Trek researched first hand. Read trekking notes, page 67.

This trek is easily accessible from Skardu and is ideal if you are looking for something not too demanding, or wish to acclimatize and improve your fitness. It can be done in either direction; the ascent to the pass is gentler from Shigar side, though if you cannot afford to organize jeeps to pick you up at the end of the trek, it is probably best to finish in Shigar, where public transport back to Skardu is readily available (on the Thalle side you are likely to have to walk all the way down to **Doghani** before finding any public transport). The trek is here described from Doghani to Shigar. If you are fit and determined, the trek can be done in three days; four days is more manageable, or five if you wish to go slowly and have time to relax or explore at the end of each day's walking.

From **Doghani**, the jeep track continues up the Thalle valley as far as **Khusomik**, the last permanent village. Up until about 50 years ago, the side valley that drains in from the east at Khusomik was used as a route across to Kande in the Hushe valley. However, glacial advance and deep crevasses have made this route no longer passable.

From Khusomik the trail crosses the side valley on a foot bridge and climbs gently past two small areas of fields and pasture and then crosses to the west bank of the valley. The side valley that leads off to the southwest from here is a trekking route across to Kiris, on the north bank of the Shyok near where it joins the Indus. The trail continues up through beautiful summer pastures with rich green meadows, flowers (July and early August), fields and scattered seasonal settlements of tiny stone houses and animal enclosures. There are numerous places to camp along this stretch. Higher up, near **Metsik Pa**, which consists of two animal enclosures with huts, the valley forks. The left fork is the route up to Thalle La, while the right fork leads up to the much higher and more difficult **Tusserpo La** (5,048 metres) which provides an alternative route over to Shigar. *Metsik Pa* means 'place of fire' in Balti, and according to locals this area was thickly wooded until around a hundred years ago, when a huge fire which raged for more than a month completely destroyed the forests.

The trail continues along the left bank of the stream to **Dumsum** (literally meaning 'junction'), where there are shepherds' huts, before crossing to the right bank. There is one more potential camping place higher up at **La**, again a small seasonal settlement of shepherds' huts, before the final ascent up to **Thalle La** (4,572 metres). From the top of the pass it is a long steady descent along the right bank of the stream. The pastures on either side of the pass abound in Marmots. Lower down, the vegetation gradually gives way to stunted woods of pine, Juniper and wild rose. There are 3 small settlements in close succession, offering good camping places, before reaching **Bauma Harel**, at the junction of the Thalle La and Tusserpo La valleys, again a good camping spot. From Bauma Harel it is a steep descent down the **Bauma Lungma**, which is a narrow, rocky and dry gorge for much of the way. The path follows the right bank, crosses to the left and then back to the right bank. Beyond the second bridge, on the left bank, is the picturesque settlement of **Anisgal**. Further on, the trail passes the similar settlement of **Ol**, before finally reaching the hydro-electric power station at **Chaupi Ol**, from where it is a short walk along a jeep track down to Shigar village.

Khapulu

Colour map 5, grid B5

Khapulu is beautifully situated, spread across a wide alluvial fan which slopes steeply down from an amphitheatre of mountains to the south. It is surprisingly green, with numerous irrigation channels feeding terraced fields and orchards which abound in apricots, apples and even oranges (these are harvested from late August to early September). Situated at an altitude of 2,600 metres, it is also pleasantly cooler than Skardu in summer. There are numerous walks along tree-lined paths and irrigation channels and good fishing in the calmer bits of the Shyok River. Like the village of Shigar, it is a picturesque place where you can experience something of the flavour of traditional Balti culture. The people belong to the **Nurbakshi** sect of Islam, similar to the Ismailis of Hunza and Chitral in their more progressive outlook on life. They are warm and friendly and the women go about their business freely, without observing purdah. As throughout most of Baltistan, however, years of exposure to mountaineering and trekking expeditions have generated a persistent 'one pen' culture amongst the children.

Ins and outs

There are regular bus, Hiace minibus and cargo jeep services between Skardu and Khapulu, which make the journey in 2½ to 3 hours. Unless you are really pushed for time, an overnight stop here is recommended. Arriving from Skardu, you pass first the AC's and DC's houses, a petrol station and the police station (for Foreigners' Registration). A little further on, a rough track leads up from the main road to the main bazaar in the lower part of the village, where the cheaper hotels, bank, post office, PCO and bus station are located.

History Khapulu formed the third major kingdom of Baltistan. It is interesting in that the ruling dynasty, known as the **Yabgu**, are thought to have come from Central Asia, possibly from Yarkand via the Saltoro pass. The term *Yabgu* is certainly of Turkic origin, being a well-known Turkish title. It was during the rule of **Bahram** (1494-1550) that the Muslim missionary Mir Shamsuddin Iraqi is known to have visited Khapulu. According to some sources it is he who was responsible for establishing the Nurbakshi sect (see page 505). Many folk tales talk of the great theological debates which took place at this time. Khapulu was subject to repeated attacks from Skardu, although at a later stage, under the rule of **Hatim Khan** (1650-1715) who was considered the greatest of the Yabgu kings, Khapulu in its turn attacked Skardu. The gates of the Raja's palace in Khapulu are said to have been taken from Skardu at this time. Later, in the early 19th century, Ahmed Shah of Skardu once again attacked Khapulu, installing his own governor, or *Kharpon*. The divisions this caused amongst the people ultimately paved the way for the Dogra invasion of Baltistan.

Sights **Raja Mahal** High up on the alluvial fan overlooking the village (a pleasant 45 minute walk from the main bazaar) is the Raja Mahal, or Raja's Palace. The palace is thought to be around 400 years old, built by Kashmiri craftsmen for the rulers of the Yabgu dynasty. It was occupied until recently by three brothers of the old ruling family. If it is locked, the chowkidar, whose family live in the palace's compound, is usually on hand to open it up. From the outside, the most striking feature of the palace is a four-storey carved wooden balcony. Inside, you can see the beautiful, intricately carved Kashmiri woodwork decorating the doors, windows and some of the ceilings of the various rooms. Overall however the palace is very dilapidated and heading steadily towards dereliction (take great care if you go up onto the roof). It stands out as a fascinating and potentially very attractive monument urgently in need of restoration.

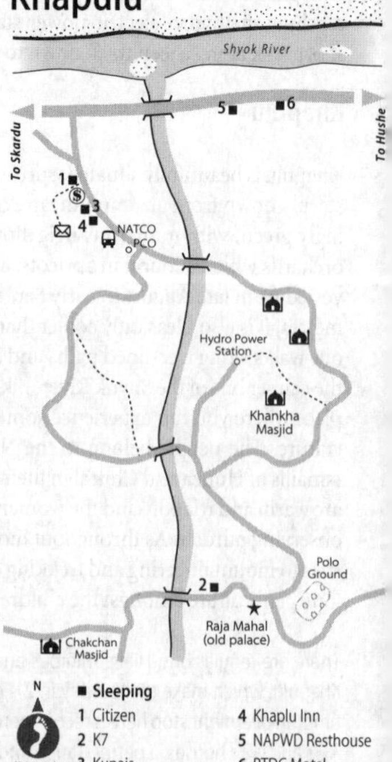

Mosques On the way up through the village en route to the Raja Mahal you pass two old wooden mosques by the track. Further on, below the track, is another large wooden mosque, the **Khankha Masjid**, with some particularly fine carved decoration. Around 15 minutes walk beyond the Raja Mahal, in Chakchan village, the similar **Chakchan Masjid** is also worth a visit. Unfortunately, non-Muslims are not allowed to enter any of these mosques.

Hanjore To the southeast of the main village, up on the shoulder of mountain reaching down to the river, is an area of summer pasture with shepherds' huts, known as Hanjore. From here there are excellent views of Masherbrum (7,821 metres) above the Hushe Valley to the north. Further up, towards the glacier above the pasture, there is a lake. To reach Hanjore, follow the old jeep track which branches off by the polo ground near the Raja Mahal. It is a long and fairly strenuous (but rewarding) climb.

Sleeping

■ *on map*
Price codes:
see inside front cover

B ***PTDC Motel***, situated on main road below village, 10-15 minutes walk past the turning up to the main bazaar, T77090, F77091. Brand new, tastefully built complex. Comfortable chalet-style rooms with fan, attached bath (hot water) and individual balconies. Restaurant.

D ***K7 Motel***, situated above main village, a little past the Raja Mahal. 4 rooms with small sofa-beds, attached bath (hot water) and individual balconies. Excellent views out across the valley. Restaurant. Garden with as yet unused trout tanks (**camping** allowed).

E/F ***Khaplu Inn***, situated in main bazaar. Looks fairly uninviting from the outside, but has some clean, pleasant rooms at the rear with attached bath (hot water). Restaurant. Friendly, helpful manager. Recommended.

G ***Citizen***, situated in main bazaar, entrance on path leading to post office. Basic but relatively clean rooms with shared shower/toilet facilities. Rooms arranged around small, quiet courtyard. The owner has made quite an effort to appeal to backpackers, with welcome signs in English. Restaurant (promising-looking menu, but many of the items listed often unavailable). **G** ***Kunais***, situated in main bazaar. Basic but relatively clean rooms shared shower/toilet facilities. Restaurant.

Eating

The *PTDC Motel's* restaurant is the most comfortable. When there are guests, they serve a fixed evening menu (Rs 225 per head); book in advance if you are not staying here. The restaurant at the *Khaplu Inn* is popular with bus and jeep drivers, and serves the usual meat and rice dishes. Otherwise, there are a couple of places in the main bazaar selling simple snacks (bhajis, samosas etc).There are also a couple of bakeries where you can buy biscuits etc, and shops selling rice, lentils, onions and whatever fruits/vegetables are in season.

Transport

NATCO runs three buses daily to Khapulu from Skardu, Masherbrum Tours one minibus daily, and K2 Travel Services one jeep daily, all leaving in the morning (see under Skardu Transport). There are usually several cargo jeep services departing later in the day. Returning, there is usually a Hiace minibus service to Skardu departing at 0800 each morning, a NATCO bus at 0900, and then at least one Hiace minibus which sets off in the afternoon. The manager of the *Hushe Inn* can book seats in advance. Cargo jeeps to Skardu run largely according to demand.

Hushe Valley

North of Khapulu, the Hushe valley (pronounced 'Hooshay') climbs gently for 30 kilometres up to Hushe village. A rough jeep track, difficult in places, reaches as far as the village, leading past spectacular views of snow-capped peaks on all sides, with Masherbrum to the north dominating. As in Khapulu, the people are predominantly Nurbakshi. Being the only approach route to Masherbrum, as well as numerous other major peaks in the area, the Hushe valley has for a long time attracted mountaineers. With the discovery of the Gondogoro La route across to Concordia and the Baltoro Glacier, the valley has become of major importance, at least in terms of mountain tourism. Trekkers can now make the 10-12 day trek from Askole to Concordia, and then instead of doubling all the way back, climb up over the Gondogoro La (a very strenuous and in places technical 5,500 metres pass) and down into Hushe valley.

Ins and outs Finding public transport heading up the Hushe valley is something of a hit-and-miss affair. Cargo jeeps run on an irregular basis from Skardu or Khapulu to various villages in the valley. Those coming from Skardu are likely to be already full when they pass Khapulu (wait for them on the main road below Khapulu if you want to try). You will probably have better luck asking around in the main bazaar in Khapulu. Fares are open to negotiation; from Khapulu as far as Kande should cost around Rs 100, and as far as Hushe village around Rs 150-200. Jeeps are readily available for private hire in Khapulu's main bazaar; as far as Hushe village will cost at least Rs 1,000, though this depends on your bargaining skills.

The other option is of course to walk. From Khapulu to Hushe is feasible in one very long day if you are fit, but two days is more realistic. There is accommodation at Machilu and Kande, and plenty of opportunities for camping all the way up the valley. The first section between Khapulu and Machilu (around four hours) is the least interesting; if possible, it is worth getting transport for this stretch (or at least across to Saling). From Machilu to Kande is around three to four hours, and from Kande to Hushe the same again.

Khapulu to Hushe Village

Originally locals would cross the Shyok River from Khapulu on rafts known as *dzaks*, made of inflated goatskins, walking several kilometres upstream before paddling their way furiously across the fast-flowing river. Until very recently this was continued, with inner-tubes replacing the goatskins, but the regular fatalities, particularly when the river was swollen, finally convinced the authorities to build a bridge. Completed in1992, this bridge crosses the Shyok four kilometres east of Khapulu, giving direct access to the village of **Saling** on the west bank of the Hushe River.

From Saling, the track climbs up into the valley. At the village of **Machilu** there is a **F** NAPWD Resthouse. Officially this should be booked in Skardu, but in practice you can just turn up and, providing there is room (which there usually is), you will be allowed to stay. Opposite is the village of Haldi, on the banks of the Saltoro River where it drains into the Hushe River from the east. The **Saltoro River Valley** is currently closed to tourists due to the border dispute with India over the Siachen Glacier. The valley is particularly stunning in places with sheer granite pinnacles rising to nearly 1,000 metres above the valley floor. Higher up, the valley divides, the north fork being the **Kondus valley**, while that to the south keeps the name of Saltoro (*giver of life*). Both valleys have the potential for some beautiful trekking and climbing.

The main track up the Hushe valley passes through **Thallis** to **Marze Gone**, where a bridge crosses to the east bank village of **Bale Gone**. From Bale Gone a jeep track leads south back to Haldi. The track north along the east bank is impassable except on foot.

The main track continues north, passing the village of **Khane** on the east bank, reached only by a footbridge, before arriving at **Kande**, a reasonable sized village with a small hotel, the **F-G** *K6 Motel*, with one double room and one 'dorm' room (sleep on the floor). There is a restaurant and small shop opposite. If you are walking up to Hushe, this is a good place to break the journey. Above Kande, the jeep track continues on for a while before crossing to the east bank on a wooden bridge and climbing the final stretch up to Hushe village.

Hushe Village

Colour map 5, grid B5

Hushe Village is beautifully located on a small hillock, surrounded by rocky peaks and pinnacles, with Masherbrum visible from here in all its splendour. This is the starting point for numerous beautiful treks and walks. The village is steadily gearing itself up to the increased flow of trekkers and climbers, with new camping sites and shops opening each year. In 1998, more than a thousand people were estimated to have passed through, going to or coming from Concordia over Gondogoro La.

Sleeping & eating

Hushe's one hotel, the basic **G** ***Masherbrum Inn***, has 3 double rooms with shared toilet facilities. There is a simple kitchen/restaurant, and a store room. The oldest running camping site is the **G** ***Gondogoro***, owned by Ashraf Hussain, consisting of a small walled yard with a simple toilet, kitchen/dining room and a store room. The other camping sites offer similar facilities. They are the **G** ***Gondogoro La***, (Farhat Ali); **G** ***K6-K7*** (Mahmood Hassan); and **G** ***Leyla Peak***, (Hamza Ali). All are able to provide simple meals. Biscuits, snacks etc (often including foreign chocolate and other goodies) can be found in the various small stores in the village. There is also an open campsite (no charge) just beyond the village, down near the spring, but don't expect any privacy or respite from boisterous, inquisitive and demanding children.

Transport

Cargo jeeps run on an irregular basis down to Khapulu, or it is often possible to negotiate something with private jeeps heading back down to Khapulu or Skardu, having dropped their trekking groups at the road head. However, jeep drivers in Hushe tend to charge somewhat inflated prices for private bookings. If you cannot find a cargo jeep or negotiate a reasonable deal on a private booking, it is worth walking down to Kande or further, since cargo jeeps from Khapulu often do not go all the way up to Hushe village.

Treks from Hushe

The village of Hushe marks the start of treks north towards the glaciers of Aling, Masherbrum, Gondogoro and Chogolisa, and numerous peaks in the area. **NB** All these treks, with the exception of the trek to Aling Glacier, have now been officially classified as restricted. However, this is a development which is being strongly contested by the freelance guides in Hushe, who argue that they should be allowed to take trekkers on round-trip treks from Hushe without having to obtain permits. In practice, many trekkers do go up the Gondogoro valley and towards Masherbrum Base Camp without a permit. However, you are advised to obtain a permit if you intend to go to the top of Gondogoro La. On no account should you consider crossing into Concordia without a permit; you are very likely to get caught and are liable to be helicoptered back to Skardu at your own expense.

Guides, Equipment and Supplies Each of the camping sites in Hushe is owned by a government-registered guide, and there are several others from Hushe, including Firma Ali, Mohammad Nazir and Anwar Ali, a free-lancer with plenty of experience and good humour. There is a considerable amount of equipment available for hire, including tents, sleeping bags, crampons, ice axes, ropes etc. Hamza Ali has a good selection of equipment, as does Ashraf Hussain, and the *K2 Shop* claims to have enough to equip a party of 12. The latter, and also a couple of other stores, usually have a reasonable selection of high-energy, freeze-dried and tinned foods leftover from previous expeditions. Unless a large group have hired everyone and everything (fairly unlikely),it is usually possible to simply turn up in Hushe and organize guides, porters, equipment and food.

Gondogoro La

Restricted zone. Maximum elevation 5,500 metres. June to September. Maps: Swiss Foundation are the best; U502 series, NI 43-3 Mundik, is adequate as far as Dalsan Pa. Trek researched first hand. *See trekking notes, page 67.*

This is a very beautiful trek. From the top of Gondogoro La there are excellent close-up views of K2 and a host of other high peaks (provided of course the weather is clear). The panorama is truly breathtaking. It is also an extremely strenuous climb (particularly without the benefit of a couple of weeks walking and acclimatizing that you get if you come from the Baltoro side). The top of the pass is at an altitude of 5,500 metres (another 500 metres and it would qualify as a mountain), and involves a climb along the glacier and a snow traverse. A guide and proper equipment (high-altitude clothing/bedding, crampons, rope) is essential if going this far. The trek to Dalsan Pa (the last stop before heading onto the glacier) is far less demanding but still very beautiful and well worth considering.

From Hushe it is six stages up to Dalsan Pa (three to four days),and a further three stages to the top of the pass (two days). From Hushe the path heads north along the east bank of the river through fields and stands of willow and wild rose. It then bears east along the south bank of the Charaksar River, passing through a summer camp used by shepherds. Just beyond where the Gondogoro River joins from the north, a bridge crosses to the north bank to reach **Saishu**, where there is good camping. A rubbish pit and latrines have been dug here, and in season there are even a couple of simple 'restaurants'. The path then climbs up the east side of Gondogoro River and glacier, following lateral moraine and stretches of ablation valley. There are several possible camping places, the main one being at **Gondogoro summer settlement**. Above here there is a difficult stretch down beside the edge of the glacier before climbing back onto the lateral moraine and then passing through a beautiful meadow area and up to **Dalsan Pa**. Dalsan Pa is particularly beautiful, with two small lakes and a meadow that is carpeted with flowers in spring. The last three stages from Dalsan Pa – onto the glacier, up to **Gondogoro base camp** and then to the top of the pass – is where the going gets really tough. An alternative route crosses the extremely difficult and technical **Masherbrum La.**

Chogolisa and Charaksar Glaciers

From Saishu a route continues east along the north bank of the Charaksar River and then along the north side of the Charaksar Glacier to its junction with the Chogolisa Glacier. The valley is more barren than the Gondogoro or Masherbrum, and the main attractions are the opportunities for climbing **K6** and **K7**.

Masherbrum Base Camp

Restricted zone. Maximum elevation optional (up to 4,200 metres). June to September. Maps: as for Gondogoro La. *See trekking notes, page 67.*

This trek bears off to the northwest above Hushe and follows the left side of the Masherbrum Glacier up to the base camp. Cross the footbridge just north of Hushe village to the west bank of the river. The path crosses the Honboro River, passes through a seasonal settlement and then crosses the Aling River. Higher up is **Dumsung**, and a little further on is **Parbisan**, both good camping spots. As far as Parbisan (one stage) is easy and pleasant, passing through fields and stands of wild rose, willow, juniper and tamarisk. Above Parbisan, there is a difficult section up onto the lateral moraine. Once on top, it is a beautiful walk along the lateral moraine to **Brumbrama**, situated on a wide sandy area between the lateral moraine and the mountains. It is possible to reach this far in one day (two stages). A little higher up is **Chogospang**, with a few stone huts where in summer women tend large flocks of sheep and goats, as well as yaks, cows and *dzo*. Above Chogospang the path follows the lateral moraine before dropping down onto the glacier itself to reach Masherbrum Base Camp (4,200 metres).

Aling Glacier

A trekking route follows the north bank of the Aling River as far as the summer settlement of Ghazala, on the north side of the Aling Glacier. Allow two days to trek as far as here. This is the only trek to the north of Hushe officially classified as being in an open zone.

Lower Hunza and Nagar 2

For the majority of foreign visitors to Pakistan, reaching Hunza is one of their main aims. With a reputation for outstanding natural beauty, welcoming people, endless trekking and hiking potential, and a tourism infrastructure that is sufficiently developed so that you don't have to 'rough it', but not too developed so as to attract hordes of package tourists, Hunza is often considered to be the centre-piece of the North's tourism industry.

True, Hunza is all these things, though the general term 'Hunza' can be a little misleading (see 'box' and 'Lower Hunza and Nagar 2', 'Central Hunza' and 'Nagar 1' maps). The areas that most visitors are interested in are Central Hunza and Gojal (Upper Hunza), though for the more adventurous (and trekkers in particular), there are plenty more delights to seek out.

Brief history of Hunza and Nagar

Both Hunza and Nagar were formerly princely states, each ruled by an unbroken line of *Thums* (kings) for almost 1,000 years. The ruling families occupied their positions sometime during the fourth period of Trakhan rule in Gilgit (1241-1449), and both houses (Ayash in Hunza, Maglot in Nagar) are descended from a pair of brothers. Like many of the other semi independent kingdoms in the Northern Areas, internecine fighting was the usual mechanism of succession. Despite periodic inter-marriages between the two houses, a great rivalry, frequently resulting in open hostility, has continued between the two kingdoms, yet as the British found out when they annexed the region in 1891/92, the two were prepared to unite against a common enemy.

Hunza in particular emerged as a powerful kingdom in the region, establishing relations on equal terms with both China and Kashmir, whilst they, in the words of Durand, "impartially plundered caravans to the north and kidnapped slaves to the south". It was partly this persistent caravan raiding, and

Road Profile: Gilgit to the Khunjerab Pass

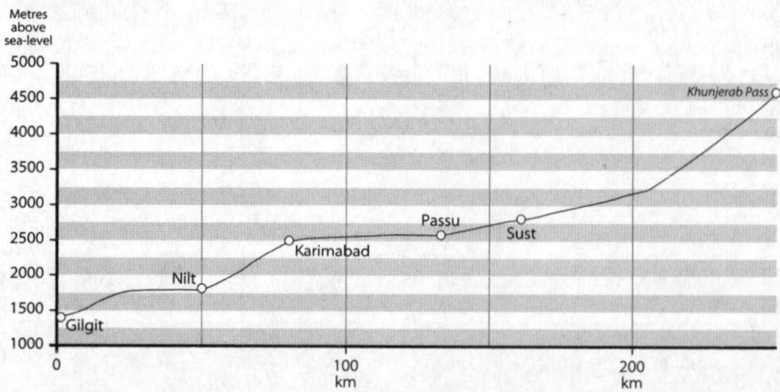

Administrative and geographical divisions of Hunza and Nagar

'Lower Hunza' *This area comprises the villages on the north side of the Hunza River between Khizerabad and Hasanabad. The majority of the villagers here are Shina-speaking (and the area is often referred to locally as Shinaki). Details of this region can be found within the 'Lower Hunza and Nagar 2' section on page 530.*

'Central Hunza' *Sometimes referred to as 'Hunza Proper', this is the area above the Hunza River between Hasanabad and Nasimabad/Shishkut. Its capital was Baltit, which has now been largely integrated within the newer settlement of Karimabad. Most of the inhabitants are Burushashki-speakers. Details of this region can be found within the 'Central Hunza' section on page 540.*

'Gojal' *Also known as 'Upper Hunza', this is the area further north along the Hunza River (and KKH), between Nasimabad/Shishkut and the Khunjerab Pass (into China). Most of the inhabitants are Wakhi-speaking. Details of this region can be found within the 'Gojal (Upper Hunza)' section on page 559.*

'Nagar 2' *This area comprises Chalt and the Chaprot Valley, plus the Bar Valley, as well as the villages along the south side of the Hunza River as far as Minapin. Most of the villages are Shina-speaking. This region is sometimes referred to as 'Lower Nagar'. Details of this region can be found within the 'Lower Hunza and Nagar 2' section on page 530.*

'Nagar 1' *This area comprises the villages on the south side of the Hunza River, from Minapin to the Hispar River. Its capital is the village of Nagar, sometimes referred to as Nagar Proper. The main language spoken in Nagar 1 is Burushashki. Details of this region can be found within both the 'Lower Hunza and Nagar 2' section on page 530 and the 'Nagar 1' section on page 554.*

partly perceived closening links between Hunza and Russia during the era of the 'Great Game' that precipitated the 1891/92 'Hunza Campaign' that resulted in the British annexation of the two states.

Hunza and Nagar both retained a semi-autonomous status in British India until Partition, and then became independent princely states within Pakistan. Prime Minister Zulfiqar Ali Bhutto's reforms of 1973 and 1974 eventually abolished the feudal authority of the Mirs, and incorporated the princely states within the Northern Areas of Pakistan, so ending the 960 year hereditary rule of the two families.

The recent construction of the Karakoram Highway has brought great changes, particularly to Hunza, although the implications of this are discussed elsewhere. In recent years, the various development networks of the Aga Khan Foundation (Aga Khan Rural Support Programme, Education Services, Health Services, Cultural Services) have been highly active in the region, being particularly successful in Hunza.

Gilgit to Lower Hunza and Nagar 2

The majority of visitors to Northern Pakistan usually take a bus or jeep directly between Gilgit and Karimabad (in 'Central Hunza'), though there are a number of attractions in between, all of which can be reached by public transport.

Routes

Travelling north to Hunza there are 2 roads out of Gilgit. Jeeps and Suzukis leave Gilgit by the Jinnah Bridge across the Gilgit River, and then run parallel to the river, before encountering a spectacular suspension bridge across the Hunza River. Vehicles to **Nomal** and **Naltar Valley** continue along the west side of the Hunza River, whilst those travelling to **Hunza** cross a suspension bridge that disappears into a tunnel in the cliff face. The tunnel emerges into the village of **Danyore**.

Larger vehicles (including buses and minibuses) travelling north leave Gilgit via Jutial, on the road leading to the KKH. Several kilometres beyond Jutial, the KKH forks right (south) for Islamabad and left (north) for Hunza/Nagar and China. Travelling north, the KKH crosses the confluence of the Gilgit and Hunza Rivers, and continues along the east bank of the Hunza River. 6 kilometres north of Gilgit is the village of **Danyore**.

Danyore has the **E** *Travel Lodge*, KKH, T399930. Rooms with attached bath, shady garden and quiet location, camping available. This is the HQ of the Danyore Horse Club (see Gilgit sports info). The Danyore Valley also offers some trekking potential (see 'Around Gilgit' on page 483).

Beyond Danyore, the landscape is quite barren on either side of the KKH. Across the river, running like a long scar along the mountainside, you can make out the Old Hunza Road.

The first real splash of green is the village of **Jutal** (15 kilometres), through which the KKH passes. On the opposite side of the river are the sprawling agricultural lands of the village of **Nomal**, gateway to the **Naltar Valley** (see page 480). There is a footbridge across the river several kilometres north of Jutal village, although the footpath down to the bridge from the KKH is very steep (and the bridge itself is in a very poor state of repair). Several kilometres further along the KKH is a memorial to the 103 Corps of Engineers "who preferred to make the Karakorams their permanent abode".

The next village on the KKH is **Rahimabad** (60 kilometres from Aliabad), situated on either side of a small bridge. The **G** *Hassan Shah Hotel* in Upper Rahimabad is often used as a meal stop on north bound buses.

Beyond Rahimabad the canyon wall closes in on the right side, and a 'slide area' begins. At the end of the slide area is a Frontier Constabulary Check post where foreigners may be required to enter their passport details.

At **Jaglot Goor** (5 kilometres) there are a number of chai and cold drink stalls, including the

Lower Hunza, Nagar 2, Central Hunza & Nagar 1

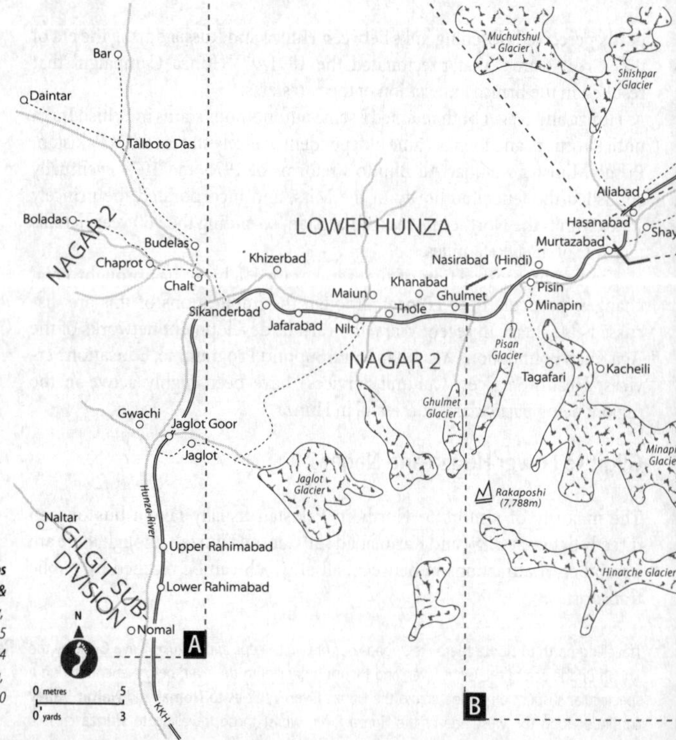

Related maps
A Chalt Region & Chaprot Valley, *page 535*
B Nagar 1, *page 554*
C Central Hunza, *page 540*

New Krakoram Hotel (sic) that serves excellent meat and grisle pies. The **G** *New Hunza Hotel* is basically a restaurant, although it is possible to stay on a charpoy here. Jaglot is also a base for one of the many KKH road maintenance crews.

Kohistan Island Arc

Beyond one of several potential 'slide areas' north of Jaglot Goor, Gilgit District ends and the KKH enters **Hunza and Nagar**. A very small stone high above the KKH to the right bears the inscription "Here continents collided"; a reference to the 'Kohistan Island Arc' geological phenomenon (see page 448). Ironically, a larger, roadside metal sign bearing the same message has been destroyed by landslides triggered by the very action it described. In fact, when Biddulph visited the area in 1876, himself being an experienced Himalayan explorer, he was moved to say: "I suddenly found myself confronted with a more difficult and dangerous piece of ground than I had ever traversed in a tolerably large experience of Himalayan sport. For nearly half a mile it was necessary to scramble over rocky ledges, sometimes letting oneself down nearly to the water's edge, then ascending 300 or 400 feet above the stream, holding on by corners of rock, working along rocky shelves 3 or 4 inches wide, and round projecting knobs and corners where no 4-footed animal less agile than a wild goat could find a path."

Routes

As the KKH leaves Gilgit District and enters **Nagar 2**, the KKH takes a sharp bend to the right, following the course of the Hunza River. To the left, a jeep road drops down to the river and crosses on a new bridge to the village of **Chalt**. This is the gateway to the **Chaprot Valley** and **Bar Valley**. Those continuing along the KKH, turn to page 536.

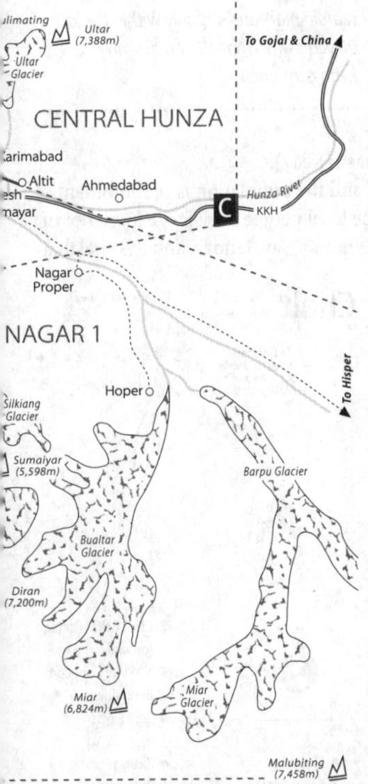

Chaprot Valley and Bar Valley

This whole area has a wonderfully rustic feel to it, reflecting the availability of fertile, well irrigated agricultural land. It is partly for this reason that the Chaprot Valley was a source of contention for so long between the rival kingdoms of Gilgit, Hunza and Nagar. Further, the fort at Chalt used to strategically control the main southern approach to both Hunza and Nagar. As Keay notes: "to both states the control of Chaprot and Chalt represented the difference between being besiegers and besieged" (1979, "The Gilgit Game"). In 1886 the then Mir of Hunza, Ghazan Khan, was so desperate for the restoration of Chaprot to his control that he begged of Colonel Lockhart, "Give me Chaprot and my people shall carry you through the Killik snows as if you were women", adding that the forts at Chalt and Chaprot were "as dear to him as the

Myth-making in Hunza

Many commentators suggest that Hunza has always been the dominant partner in this often bitter rivalry between the two former kingdoms, but this may just be because Hunza has evolved a powerful mythopeiatic force, promulgating many half-truths and legends. Despite a prolonged history of contact with outsiders, the legend of Hunza's perceived isolation remains. It was through the Hunza Valley that Buddhism first reached China, and by 200 AD a branch of the Silk Road connected the region with Central Asia and China. By the time Islam became established here in the 11th century, Turks, Mongols, Persians, Afghans, Taimunis, Dogras and Chinese had all passed through, as soldiers, pilgrims, traders and adventurers. Inscriptions on the Sacred Rocks of Hunza near Karimabad bear testament to 2,000 years of travellers' graffiti. Yet current holiday brochures still advertise the Hunza Valley as being "famed for its isolation". Part of this idealization has been inspired by Hilton's 1933 novel "Lost Horizons", whose 'Shangri-la' is supposedly based on Hunza. Again, some tour companies still advertise Hunza as "a real Shangri-la".

The myth-making process continued into the latter part of this century, with stories of a society free from illness and famed for the longevity of its people. In 1964, Hoffman produced a book titled "Hunza: 15 Secrets of the World's Healthiest and Longest Living People". This romanticisation of Hunza continues in some quarters today, with another current tourist brochure claiming that the Hunzakuts are "a robust people famed for their ageless long life and good looks. Their secret elixir seems to consist of isolation and a spartan diet".

In reality, this idealisation is far from the truth. A WHO report in 1985 estimated that 60 percent of the population of the Northern Areas suffers from iodine deficiency, resulting in cretinism in as much as 7 percent of the population. Although somewhat less in Hunza, infant mortality rates in the Northern Areas remain high, and it is only within the last 20 years or so that TB and dysentry have been contained.

strings which secured his wives' pyjamas" (Keay).

Today, the valley belongs to Nagar, and the population is predominantly Shia. Although remarkably friendly, the local people have less experience of dealing with foreign tourists than the people of , say, Hunza, and it is vital that visitors show a sensitivity to local customs, particularly in terms of modest dress. For orientation, see the 'Naltar Valley (including Daintar Pass and Naltar Pass treks)' map on page 481.

Chalt

Colour map 5, grid A3

Despite being the gateway to the beautiful Chaprot, Ghashumaling and Bar Valleys, Chalt receives remarkably few visitors. In fact, a report by the Aga Khan Rural Support Programme in 1995 found that less than 50 foreign tourists visit Chalt each year. As such, Chalt and the Chaprot Valley can claim to be the Northern Areas best kept secret,

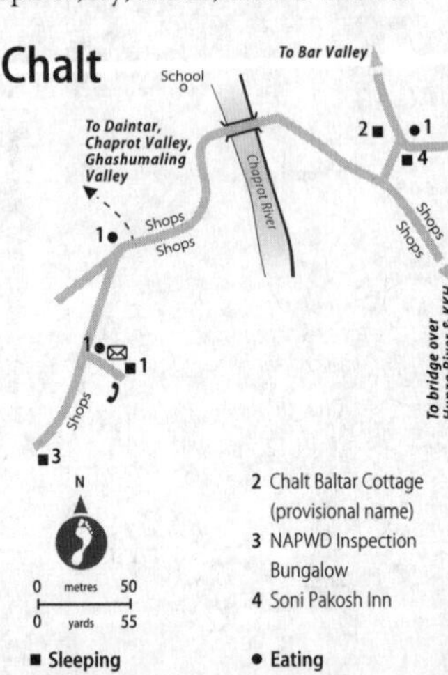

for even Schomberg was moved to say "the Chaprot Valley is lovely, more beautiful than any other in the whole of the Gilgit Agency."

Sleeping & eating

F *NAPWD Inspection Bungalow*, 2 rooms set in its own attractive grounds (book in Gilgit, though casual callers usually admitted). Meals are by arrangement with the chowkidar. **E-F** *Chalt Baltar Cottage*. Former school being converted to 6 rooms guest house, attached bath, large, shady garden (camping permitted), and may offer 'horse safaris'. **G** *Baltar Cottage* has 2 very basic rooms, and the **G** *Soni Pakosh Inn* is more a restaurant than a hotel, though a couple of rooms are under construction round the back.

Transport

At least 1 minibus per day runs from near the National Bank on Khazana Rd in **Gilgit**, though it does not have an English sign-board and there's no fixed departure time: ask around. Minibuses back to **Gilgit** from Chalt run intermittently between 0600-0900 (Rs 30). Alternatively, walk up to the KKH and hitch.

Short walks in the Chaprot Valley

The small village of **Chaprot** in the Chaprot Valley is about an hour's walk beyond Chalt. From Chaprot it is possible to walk southwest along the **Ghashumaling River**, where you will find excellent walks through orchards, pine forest and fields of wild strawberries.

From Chaprot it is also possible to take the path northwest to Daintar, and make the trek over the Daintar Pass to Naltar (see page 482), or to head east (then north) from Daintar to link up with the Bar Valley trek (see below).

Another option is to head up the **Budelas** or **Bar Valley** from Chalt (follow the Bar signpost). Several kilometres beyond Budelas there is a hot, sulphurous spring, said to have healing qualities. At **Talboto Das** the path divides, with the right fork continuing to **Bar** (18 kilometres from Chalt, see 'Bar Valley trek' below), and the left fork leading to Daintar- starting point for the trek across the 4,500-metre Daintar Pass (see page 482).

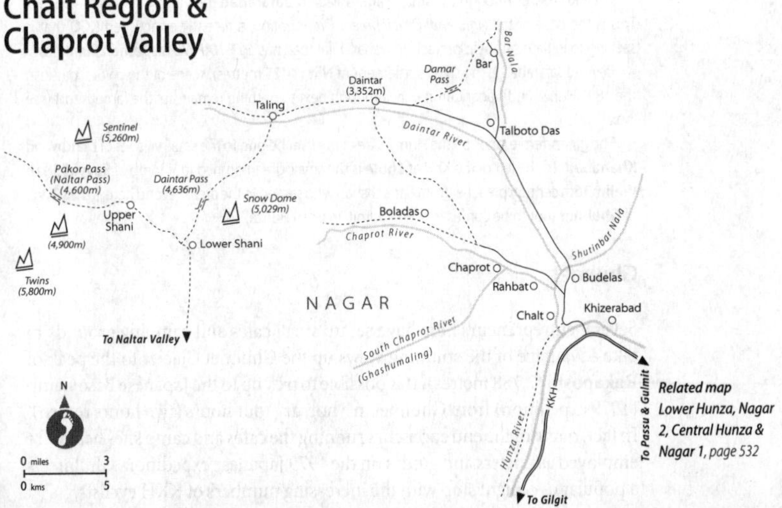

Related map Lower Hunza, Nagar 2, Central Hunza & Nagar 1, page 532

Bar Valley trek *Open zone. Maximum elevation 4,000m. July to September. Maps; Swiss Foundation are good; the U502 series, NJ 43-14 Baltit is just about adequate for this trek. Read trekking notes, page 67.*

The villagers in the Bar Valley, who are keen to promote tourism here, have gone as far as forming the 'Bar Valley Conservation NGO' and producing leaflets extolling the virtues of the valley. They are also encouraging local people to accommodate tourists in their homes, or allowing them to camp on their land (nominal charges). Horse riding can be arranged (Rs 650 per day), as well as cultural events such as polo matches (Rs 11,000), mock marriage ceremonies (Rs 6,000) and dancing (Rs 5,500). They can be contacted in Barkot village (Bar, 2,200 metres), or through the WWF office in Gilgit (see above). The WWF are involved locally in setting up a 'Sustainable Wildlife Project' based on management and utilization of the Siberian ibex (*Capra ibex sibirica*), including trophy hunting (December only, US$3,000 licence fee, 75 percent of which goes to the local people).

There are in fact two options for trekking in the Bar Valley, though day hikers can easily reach Bar in one day. For orientation, see the 'Naltar Valley (incl Daintar Pass and Naltar Pass treks)' map on page 481. The first involves an eight-day return trip from **Torbuto Das**, via **Bar**, heading along the Garamasai River to **Toltar**, before bearing northwest along the Toltar Glacier to **Saio-daru-kush**, from where you retrace your steps. The camping around the **Bar-daru-kush Lake** (3,200 metres) and pastures (beyond Toltar) is sublime. Note, however, that crossing the Toltar Glacier to reach Saio-daru-kush can be treacherous.

The alternative is to head up the Garamasai River from Bar to the summer pastures at **Shuwe**, and then continue northeast to the Baltar Glacier and **Baltar**. This return trip can be completed in three days.

Returning to the KKH

Routes Returning to the route along the KKH, as the Hunza River and the KKH make a 90° bend, there are marvellous views of Rakaposhi straight ahead. Although the KKH continues on the Nagar 2 side of the valley, across the river the first **Hunza** village (Khizerabad) can be seen. Significantly, the rope bridge between **Sikanderabad** on the Nagar side, and **Khizerabad** on the Hunza side, was burnt in mid-1995 during Shia-Ismaili clashes.

The KKH passes through the small Nagar village of **Jafarabad** (previously known as Tondas). This is the base of the *Naunehal Development Organization*, a recently established NGO that is seeking to initiate self-help projects in Nagar. Jafarabad has an **E** ***NAPWD Inspection Bungalow***.

Beyond Jafarabad is the small settlement of **Nilt** (1,425 metres), scene of the pivotal battle in the 1891 Hunza and Nagar Campaign, although next to nothing remains of the famous fort (see 'box').

The green, fertile lands on the Hunza side of the river belong to the small villages of **Maiun** and **Khanabad**. To the left of the KKH at **Thole** is the small, green domed roof tomb of **Sayyid Shah Wali**, a 16th century preacher from Badakhshan who settled in the area. Beyond here is the village of **Ghulmet** (not to be confused with 'Gulmit' in Gojal Hunza).

Ghulmet

Several entrepreneurs here have set up small cafés and camping grounds to take advantage of the stunning views up the Ghulmet Glacier to the peak of **Rakaposhi** (7,788 metres). It is possible to trek up to the Japanese Base Camp (1979 expedition) from Ghulmet in a hot, dry four hours (two hours return). In fact, many of the entrepreneurs running the cafés and camp sites here were employed as porters and guides on the 1979 Japanese expedition. Ghulmet is a popular overnight stop with the increasing numbers of KKH cyclists.

Battle of Nilt, 1891

Although relatively insignificant amongst the many great battles that the British Army fought during their period of conquest of South Asia, the battle for the fort of Nilt on 1st December 1891 is recorded in British military history as an action in which two Victoria Crosses were won. In fact, such was the bravery on display that one local ruler is reported to have commented "This is the fighting of giants, not of men."

Having crossed the Hunza River, the British expeditionary force was stopped in its tracks by the seemingly impregnable stone fortress at Nilt. With the seven pound guns making no impression on the fort walls, the defenders were able to pick off the British troops at will through the narrow peepholes. In fact, the British commander Col Durand, who refused to take cover by crouching behind a rock, received a bullet in a delicate part of his anatomy that meant he had to do quite a lot of crouching in the future!

With casualties mounting, the order was given to blow the main gate. The special Times correspondent E F Knight, who witnessed the battle (and later wrote an excellent, if unintentionally hilarious, account of this period of history in "Where Three Empires Meet"), described what happened next as "one of the most gallant things recorded in Indian warfare." Rushing through a hail of bullets to the gate, Capt Fenton Aylmer, two subalterns and a Pathan orderly laid an explosive charge, lit the fuse and retreated along the wall to await the explosion. Aylmer was hit by a bullet at such short range that the powder charge singed his uniform, and then to make matters worse, the fuse went out. Risking what Knight thought was certain death, the wounded Aylmer returned to the gate, trimmed the fuse and relit it. Whilst doing this, a heavy rock dropped from above by the fort's defenders crushed one of his hands. This time the fuse was good, and with the gates blown, the three British officers and six Gurkhas dashed into the fort. Unfortunately, the rest of the British force did not realize that the walls had been breached, and for many minutes the storming party were isolated. It wasn't until Lt Boisragon, one of the subalterns, dashed back to the breech, thus exposing himself to the fire from both sides, that the British realized their colleagues were inside. Within minutes the reinforcements had stormed the fort and the battle was over. For their gallantry, both Aylmer and Boisragon received the Victoria Cross.

Sleeping & eating

E ***Rakaposhi Paradise*** is the only 'real' hotel, with 4 clean enough doubles with shared bath and toilet. Camping is also available, and there is a small restaurant. ***Rakaposhi Zero Point***, ***Rakaposhi Main Point***, ***Rakaposhi Echo*** and ***Rakaposhi Vieweria*** all allow camping for Rs 25 per person, as well as snacks and meals. The longest established café/camp site is ***Rakaposhi View Point***, which for some inexplicable reason suggests that "sometimes a hot cup of tea is more welcome when it comes with sympathy"!

Routes

At **Pisin**, on the KKH, a jeep track branches right to **Minapin** (4 kilometres). Minapin is the starting point for a magnificent trek to the base camps of **Rakaposhi** and **Diran**.

Minapin

The main reason to visit Minapin is to use it as a base from which to trek to **Rakaposhi base camp**, with the possibility of continuing to **Diran base camp**. This is an ideal introduction to trekking, being relatively easy but still offering superb mountain views of Rakaposhi (7,788 metres) and Diran (7,200 metres). The hotels in Minapin are geared up towards providing guides, cooks, porters and some equipment, though it is as well to stock up with provisions in Gilgit. Minapin, and the accompanying hike up to Rakaposhi base camp, is becoming one of the "must dos" amongst visitors to this part of Pakistan. Even if you don't fancy the trek this is a nice spot to "chill out", or you could make the less demanding walk up to **Shuli** (two hours), which also has excellent Rakaposhi and Diran views.

Sleeping & eating The staff at the hotels here go out of their way to make you feel welcome. In fact, some readers have written to say that they received "more of a Hunza welcome than a Nagar welcome". **D** *Diran Guest House*, excellent facilities, 16 well furnished rooms with views, attached modern hot bath, superb restaurant, bookshop, plans for a pool. The manager, Israr, has decorated the place with pictures of the late Princess of Wales!. **E-G** *Diran Guest House*, run by the same people, excellent value, traditional style house in attractive garden (dorms **G**, 4 cool doubles with attached hot bath **E-F**), camping possible. The friendly staff can also assist with guides, porters and equipment for the Rakaposhi/Diran base camp trek. Recommended. **F** *Alpine Camping*, 2 doubles with attached bath, restaurant and camping facilities, although it's not very private.

Transport There are some wagons to Minapin from **Gilgit** each day (Rs 50, leaving from Khazana Rd, see 'Gilgit' map), though there is no fixed timetable and the destination board is not written in English. An easier option is to take a regular bus or minibus along the KKH, get off at Pisin, and walk the 4 kilometres from there. If you are carrying a lot of equipment for an expedition, you will probably have to hire a jeep all the way from Gilgit (around Rs 1,000). A wagon returns from Minapin to **Gilgit** each morning at 0600 (Rs 50).

Rakaposhi/ Diran base camp trek *Open zone. Maximum elevation optional (2,400-4,400m). April to Oct. Maps: Deutsche Himalaya Expedition map of Minapin is excellent; Swiss Foundation good; U502 series, NJ 43-14 Baltit is reasonable. For orientation, see the 'Nagar 1' map on page 554. There is also a very good sketch map of the route in the visitor's book at the Diran Guest House. Read the trekking notes, page 67.*

Some visitors suggest that the trip to Rakaposhi base camp is less of a trek and more of a hike, and can be attempted as a day trip from Minapin. This is true, though it makes for a very long day with less time available at 'the top' (and you have to be pretty fit). We have received letters from some readers who have reached Tagafari (Rakaposhi base camp) in 4-5 hrs, spent an hour there, then walked back down to Minapin the same day. A far better idea is to take 2 days (or 1 long day) to get there, spend a day there (or add a day by also visiting the Diran base camp), and then take a further (long) day to walk back down to Minapin.

Since the route as far as Tagafari is fairly straightforward, and there are no glacier crossings, it is possible to do this trip without a guide (and without porters if you carry your own gear). For those continuing to Diran base camp near Kacheili, a guide is essential to lead you across the Minapin Glacier. Porters on this route have previously had a reputation for being greedy, attempting to charge for 6 stages from Minapin to Tagafari and back (it's only 4). However, we have not received any complaints recently (and had no problems personally in Aug 1998), so perhaps the situation has improved. If you continue from Tagafari to Diran base camp and back, this is a further 2 stages. Since this is usuually done as a day trip, you can give your porters a day off (ie half-pay), though you will have to pay the guide for the 2 stages.

From **Minapin** village the path follows the irrigation channel and crosses the river on a good bridge. It then follows the right bank of the river before ascending steeply through woods to a summer settlement known as

Bungidas. Higher up is the smaller summer settlement of **Hapakun** with good camping (the overnight stop for those taking 2 days to reach Tagafari). The path continues through woods and pastures, climbing steeply to the crest of lateral moraine which until now has hidden the huge Minapin Glacier to the left. There are spectacular views from here of Diran peak (7,200m). The narrow path then traverses a scree slope which drops away steeply down to the glacier before descending to **Tagafari**, a narrow field between the lateral moraine and Rakaposhi that is generally referred to as **Rakaposhi base camp** (this is officially 2 stages from Minapin). There are a couple of tents at Tagafari where you can stay for around Rs 80 per night (cold drinks and snacks are sometimes available too). If this is as far as you intend to go, it is well worth spending a day or two here exploring the area and taking in the scenery (the possibilities are limitless).

From Tagafari, it is possible to cross the Minapin Glacier to **Kacheili**, a grassy summer pasture with superb views of Rakaposhi that is usually referred to as **Diran base camp** (4-5 hrs). It is perfectly feasible to walk from Tagafari to Kacheili, and back to Tagafari, in 1 day, though a guide is essential to help you negotiate the glacier. It is also quite feasible to walk down from Tagafari to Minapin in 1 long day. There is also the option of continuing from Kacheili up to the beautiful **Kacheili Lake** at around 4,400 m (1 hour). Those who have a guide can make an alternative descent from Kacheili Lake to Minapin, though this can only be attempted at certain times of the year when the streams are lower.

Routes

Returning to the KKH, a little beyond Pisin the road leaves Nagar 2, and crosses the Hunza River by way of a Chinese built bridge onto the **Hunza** side of the river. From here, it is 80 kilometres south to Gilgit, and 21 kilometres north to Aliabad.

The first village in Hunza on the KKH is Hindi, now known as **Nasirabad** (1,500 metres). The *Eden Gardens* cold drinks stand offers great views of Rakaposhi and Diran from its flower-filled garden. Just beyond Hindi is one of the worst 'slide areas' on this section of the KKH.

The KKH passes through **Murtazabad**, with its **F** *Eagle's Nest Hotel* (not to be confused with the hotel of the same name in Duikar). Beyond the village, a jeep road crosses a rope suspension bridge to **Shayar**, on the Nagar side (the bridge is not immediately visible from the KKH). For details of a long, but enjoyable, walk from Shayar on to Askordas and Sumayar, see page 554 in the 'Nagar 1' section.

On the Hunza side of the river, there are magnificent views of the daunting **Ultar Peak** (7,388 metres). As the road enters the mouth of the Hasanabad Valley, you pass from Lower Hunza into **Central Hunza**.

Central Hunza

Central Hunza is the area above the Hunza River between Hasanabad and Nasimabad/Shishkut, and is the region that most visitors think of when they talk of 'Hunza' (it is sometimes referred to as 'Hunza Proper'). The setting is superb: a natural amphitheatre formed by a series of snowy peaks, with seemingly dry and barren canyons opening up to reveal grassy pastures, orchards, and ingeniously terraced fields. The people living here, predominantly Burushashki-speaking followers of the Ismaili sect of Islam, also have a reputation for openness, and visitors are well catered for in the range and choice of hotels and guesthouses. Through the centre of this region, following the course of the Hunza River, snakes the Karakoram Highway, on its journey up to Gojal (Upper Hunza) and on to China.

Routes The KKH swings into the mouth of the Hasanabad Nala, entering the Central Hunza region. The village of **Hasanabad** is located just below the KKH, with the Norwegian Hydel power station here providing a regular supply of electricity to the Karimabad/Central Hunza region. This is one of the most treacherous 'slide areas' on the entire length of the KKH, and consequently a road maintenance depot is permanently located nearby. At the apex of the bend, behind the road maintenance depot, several trails lead north along either side of the Hasanabad Nala; these are the starting points for treks to the **Shishpar Glacier** and the **Muchutshil Glacier**.

Central Hunza (Including Hasanabad Nala & Ultar Nala treks)

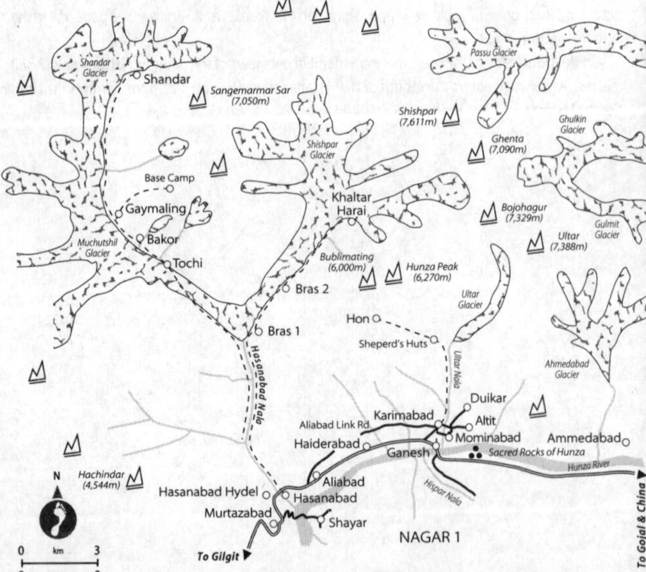

Related map
Lower Hunza, Nagar 2, Central Hunza & Nagar 1, page 532

Treks along the Hasanabad Nala

Shishpar Glacier trek

Open zone. Maximum elevation 3,600 metres. May to October. Maps: Deutsche Himalaya Expedition map of Hunza is good; Swiss Foundation good; U502 series, NJ 43-14 Baltit is unreliable; all the maps have some mistakes, or incorrectly labelled names. For orientation, see the 'Central Hunza (including Hasanabad Nala and Ultar Nala treks)' map below. Read trekking notes on page 67.

This is not a particularly demanding trek (though at some times of the year it is hot and dry), yet it offers alternative views of mountains that become familiar to those staying in Karimabad. Most trekkers complete this trip in four days (two out, two back). From the road maintenance depot on the KKH it is a fairly unrewarding four hours walk along the east side of the Hasanabad Nala to **Bras 1**. The camping site is just above the terminal moraine on the east side of the Shishpar Glacier, although you have to go down to the glacier itself for water. The following day involves a five hour trek along the east side of the glacier moraine to the summer pastures at **Khaltar Harai**, from where there is a view of Ultar Peak that is denied to those who can't get off their backsides in Karimabad. To return, follow the same route.

Muchutshil Glacier trek

Open zone. Maximum elevation 3,600 metres. May to October. Maps: Deutsche Himalaya Expedition map of Hunza is good; Swiss Foundation good; U502 series, NJ 43-14 Baltit is unreliable; all the maps have some mistakes, or incorrectly labelled names. For orientation, see the 'Central Hunza (including Hasanabad Nala and Ultar Nala treks)' map on page 540. Read trekking notes, page 67.

This six day trek also offers rarely seen views of commonly seen peaks, and is again fairly undemanding, though a guide is necessary to cross the glacier. From the road maintenance depot on the KKH, head along the west side of the Hasanabad Nala, camping on the first night below the mouth of the glacier. The second day is fairly long (six to seven hours), beginning with a crossing of the **Muchutshil Glacier** (shown on some maps as the Muchuhar Glacier). The pastures at **Gaymaling** provide the second night's camping. The reward at the end of the third day (six hours) is the camping at **Shandar**, just below **Sangemarmar Sar**; it is worth spending a couple of days here before the three day walk by the same route back down to the KKH.

Routes

As the KKH emerges from the Hasanabad Nala bend, there is a Frontier Constabulary Check post where foreigners sometimes have to enter passport details. Just beyond the check post, a link road to the left runs the 10 kilometres up to **Karimabad** (this is called the 'Aliabad link road', though it is no longer the main route used up to Karimabad).

The main KKH continues through **Aliabad** (incorrectly signposted as being at 2,500 metres). Aliabad is 101 kilometres from Gilgit.

Aliabad

Colour map 4, grid B5

With Karimabad offering better views and a quieter atmosphere, few tourists stop off in what is in effect a typical KKH roadside village (albeit with friendlier people and a nicer atmosphere than those further south in Kohistan). Aliabad does, however, pre-date the building of the KKH, and was the base used by E.O. Lorimer when researching her 1939 book "Language Hunting in the Karakoram". Those intending to trek up the Hasanabad Nala (see above) may care to ask around at the various hotels in Aliabad about hiring **guides** and **porters**.

Sleeping & eating **D** *Aliabad Rakaposhi Inn*, T45096. Large rooms, great views of Rakaposhi. **E** *Village Guest House*, T16. Traditional Hunza style house, sleeps 6, plus 2 doubles. **F** *Dumani*, *Prince/Swat*, *Shishper*, *SR* all pretty basic. All the hotels have some form of restaurant, one of which is used as a meal stop on the daily *NATCO* Sust to Gilgit trip.

Routes Continuing from Aliabad along the KKH, shortly after **Haiderabad** is the **C** *PTDC Motel Hunza*, T69. 29 large carpeted rooms, restaurant, great views, jeep rental and laundry, group/corporate discounts available. Bookings in Islamabad T9203223, F9218233. Pretty good value and well run. Recommended. Opposite is the **D** *Golden Peak View Hotel*, which is popular with Pakistanis, but doesn't have a view of Golden Peak!

Just before Ganesh, a recently constructed jeep track ('New Ganesh Road') runs up to **Karimabad** (2 kilometres). This is the route that most jeeps and minibuses between Gilgit and Karimabad now use. Jeeps waiting at Ganesh to take you up will charge whatever they think they can get away with. On a hot day, it's a steep climb with a back-pack. Half-way up, the right fork leads via the small settlement of Mominabad, across a recently completed bridge, to **Altit** (1½ kilometres). Otherwise, the New Ganesh Road continues up to Karimabad.

The KKH enters a large south bend around the settlement of **Ganesh**, the major Shia village on the Hunza side of the river. North and south bound **NATCO** buses drop and pick up passengers by the KKH memorial, next to the **E** *Karakoram Highway Inn*, T47072. (For bus timings see under Karimabad 'Transport' section). For those continuing north along the KKH to Gojal (Upper) Hunza and onto China, turn to page 559.

Karimabad

Phone code: 0572
Colour map 5, grid A4

The centre-piece of the Northern Areas' tourism industry, Karimabad is a delightful village set in a wonderful location. Panoramic views across the Hunza and Nagar Valleys incorporate three snow-capped peaks over 7,000 metres (Rakaposhi 7,788 metres, Diran 7,200 metres and Ultar 7,388 metres), providing a contrast to the colourful natural environment of Karimabad that includes 30,000 fruit trees, 18,000 poplars and 10,000 other trees. The view of the Hunza Valley from Karimabad in autumn is incredible, though it remains spectacular at any time of the year. Karimabad is the base for a number of short walks and excursions, as well as being a popular place with visitors to relax and unwind.

Ins and outs

Getting there Most visitors arrive by minibus directly from Gilgit (3 hours), and are dropped off in the centre of the village. Those coming from the north (eg Sust, Passu etc) are more likely to be dropped off down on the KKH at Ganesh. Likewise, those coming from Gilgit on the *NATCO* bus will also be dropped off at Ganesh. It's a very steep walk (or an extortionately priced ride) up from Ganesh to Karimabad.

Getting around The number of jeeps roaring in and out of Karimabad can become very unpleasant; there's no excuse not to get around by foot here.

History

The village now known as Karimabad has absorbed the *khun* (cluster of households) around the fort at Baltit, as well as the Khurukushal and Dhirimshal khuns, and has expanded greatly from being just the settlement around the new palace of the *Mir* (King), that was built in 1923.

The state of Hunza was ruled by the same family for 960 years, with their seat of power being the **Baltit Fort**. Famous for their incessant caravan raiding and constant wars against the rival state of Nagar, the modern history of the Hunzakuts of Karimabad begins in 1891/92 when the British occupied the fort at Baltit. Hunza became a princely state within British India, and then retained a similar status within Pakistan following Partition. The administrative reforms of Zulfikar Ali Bhutto's government abolished the feudal authority of the Mir in 1973, and incorporated Hunza within the Northern Areas of Pakistan.

The People

More than 95 percent of the population of Karimabad belong to the Ismaili, with **His Highness Shah Karim al-Husayni Aga Khan IV** as their spiritual head. Traditionally there were only two classes in Hunza: the Mir's family and courtiers, and, the agriculturalists. There is no hereditary occupational class structure (except for the Dom – see Mominabad), with the village hierarchy cutting across a segmentary system of clans of different origin, and no obligation to marry within the clan. Unlike the Nagar subdivision to the south, there is no purdah system in Karimabad, and women work alongside the men in the fields. Some may argue that the women do all the work. Local myths and folklore that pre-date Islam – particularly belief in wizards (*bitten*), fairies (*paris*) and the power of the shaman – are an important cultural aspect of Hunza life.

The population according to the 1981 census was 2,947, although a survey taken in 1990 put the population at 4,596, comprising 616 households at an average size of 7.5 members. A standing joke suggests that the average household composition in Karimabad comprises one grandparent, a husband and wife, four children, a cow, two goats, five chickens and an anthropologist.

The predominant language in Karimabad is Burushashki, although increasing opportunities in education and government service means that Urdu and English are widely spoken. The people of Karimabad are justifiably proud of their achievements in the field of education, and with 95 percent of all children attending school, the implications for future literacy rates are encouraging. The Aga Khan Academy for Girls is the showpiece school.

Foreign tourists find the Hunzakuts of Karimabad amongst the most friendly and welcoming people in Pakistan.

Economy

The nature of the terrain has played a large part in determining the social economy of Karimabad. With annual precipitation below 150 millimetres, rain fed agriculture is not possible, and thus an intricate network of glacier fed irrigation channels serve the limited agricultural land. Previously, a subsistence economy based upon agriculture and pastoral activity, but producing no surplus, evolved. The most pressing social necessity for a household in Karimabad was to be self-sufficient in every way.

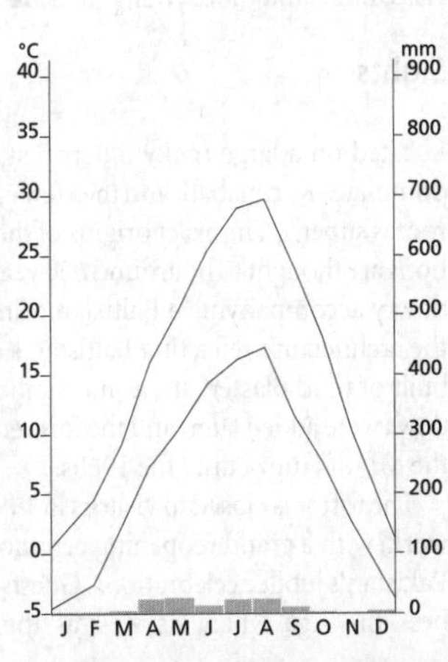

The best time to visit is between June and August

"When in Rome ..."

*Numerous studies have been undertaken into perceptions of tourism amongst the people of Hunza, and Karimabad in particular. A reoccuring theme amongst local people is the **inappropriate dress** that many visitors wear. Tour groups are the worst offenders, although some backpackers who have remained modestly dressed whilst visiting the rest of Pakistan suddenly abandon all sense of modesty here. Unfortunately, most Hunzakuts are too polite to register their complaint, but it must be emphasised that the people **are** offended by shorts, singlets, revealing or tight clothes **on both men and women**.*

Although Hunza women do not observe purdah, this is still a very traditional society. Local women complain about being embarrassed when 'cornered' by (male) tourists wandering around the narrow alleys of the khuns. As with elsewhere in Pakistan, you should ask (and expect a refusal) before photographing women. Children are another matter entirely – bring lots of film!

The improvement of access to the area, in association with other processes of socio-economic change, has had a major impact upon the economy of Karimabad. Previously self-sufficient in food, albeit through a system that entailed frequent winter famines, Karimabad is now dependent upon food imports, particularly cheap subsidised food grains imported from down country. Conversely, new opportunities have been created for exporting crops, particularly fruit, as cash cropping becomes the major system of agriculture. However, attempts to move production to a higher stage to gain value added, eg processing fruit into jam locally, is compounded by problems of transport costs (jars) and power supply.

Recent socio-economic change The influence of improved access to the region, education, introduction of the cash economy, consumerism, land reform and social change has led to the end of the self-sufficiency outlook. A new middle class has emerged, and now about 70 percent of all families have some family member engaged in trade, commerce, tourism related activity, artisanal work, or in government service. Earnings in administrative sectors, service sectors (including tourism) and in trade and commerce are seen as far more lucrative and requiring less physical work than farming, with the result that interest in agriculture has declined. With the population growing so rapidly, and the emergence of an educated class, more and more young men are seeking employment down country.

Sights

Baltit Fort Located on a large rocky outcrop at the base of the Ultar Nala, Baltit Fort dominates Karimabad, and the view of the Hunza and Nagar Valleys from the roof is superb. The exact origins of the fort are unclear, although the foundations are thought to be around 600 years old. It was seemingly built as part of a dowry accompanying a Baltistan princess who came to marry the Mir, with the architecture reflecting Baltistan's ancient links with Tibet. It is primarily built of mud plaster, stone and timber beams. The balconies and bow windows were added later, and the fort remained in use as the official residence of the Mir of Hunza until the 1960s.

The fort was closed to visitors in 1991 in order to complete vital restoration work, with a grand reopening ceremony being held in 1997 to coincide with Pakistan's jubilee celebrations. Guests of honour that day included His Highness the Aga Khan, as well as the President of Pakistan. Prior to the

Tourism in Karimabad

Tourism has become an important, and highly conspicuous sector of Karimabad's economy. In fact, some visitors would argue that it has become too conspicuous. With Karimabad's scenic beauty being the main attraction drawing tourists, there is the danger that the infrastructure that is being built to cater to these tourists is making the village less attractive, with the long term consequence being that tourists will move elsewhere. However, despite the fact that there have been some real monstrosities built lately, much of this view that Karimabad is "too touristy" or "has been spoilt", is down to the snob mentality of backpacker tourism. Many 'travellers' who claim that Karimabad is "too touristy" have decamped to the nearby village of Altit, presumably to repeat the process there. The ultimate irony is to listen to 40 or so 'travellers' at the Kisar Inn in Altit explaining that they are escaping the tourist ghetto of Karimabad, when in fact all the hotels there are empty.

Little attention appears to be paid to the fact that it is local people, albeit a relatively small elite, who are encouraging the development of tourism infrastructure in Karimabad. Larger and more upmarket hotels are being built because the people want to attract higher spending tourists. Likewise, new link roads are being built to serve the needs of the local community and as such, is a form of development encouraged by local people. Yet many tourists see the development of access as "spoiling" the region. Dichotomous views of the environment is a common phenomenon: host communities rarely see themselves or their everyday environment as a 'tourist attraction', whereas for the tourist it is an integral part of the travel experience.

Like many other parts of the world, Hunza children are not adverse to pestering foreigners for "one pen, one rupee" etc.

commencement of the maintenance work, the fort was in grave danger of collapse. The solid rock upon which it stands is subject to the constant attention of the shifting Ultar Glacier, and the subsequent movement had made the fort highly unstable. The entire structure has been completely repinned, in addition to major cosmetic refurbishment.

Formerly in the possession of the Mir, the fort has been donated to the Baltit Heritage Trust – a semi government organization entrusted with the running and maintenance of the building. Local young men now provide an informed guided tour of the fort, as well as some of the surrounding traditional houses. In addition to the fine views, an eclectic slide show is the highlight. ■ *T77110. Open 1 April-31 October 0900-1300 1400-1730. Foreign tourists are charged Rs 200 to enter. Photography is permitted (but no flash).*

Walks around Karimabad

In addition to sitting around admiring the view, you can undertake a number of short walks around Karimabad. More sedate strolls can be taken along the numerous water channels, or down to the neighbouring village of **Altit** (see below). More energetic visitors may wish to visit the summer pastures below the Ultar Glacier (see below).

Ultar Glacier hike/trek

The view from the pastures sited below the imposing Ultar Peak is one of the highlights of a visit to Karimabad. The main **Ultar Peak**, at 7,388 metres (and 73rd highest mountain in the world), is one of the lowest unclimbed peaks. It also has a fearsome reputation and has claimed three Japanese lives in the last few years. **Bubulimating** (also known as Lady's Finger), the 6,000 metres high granite spire to the left, is so sheer that it cannot hold snow. To the right (northeast) of Bubulimating is the 6,270 metres **Hunza Peak**. For those

Karimabad

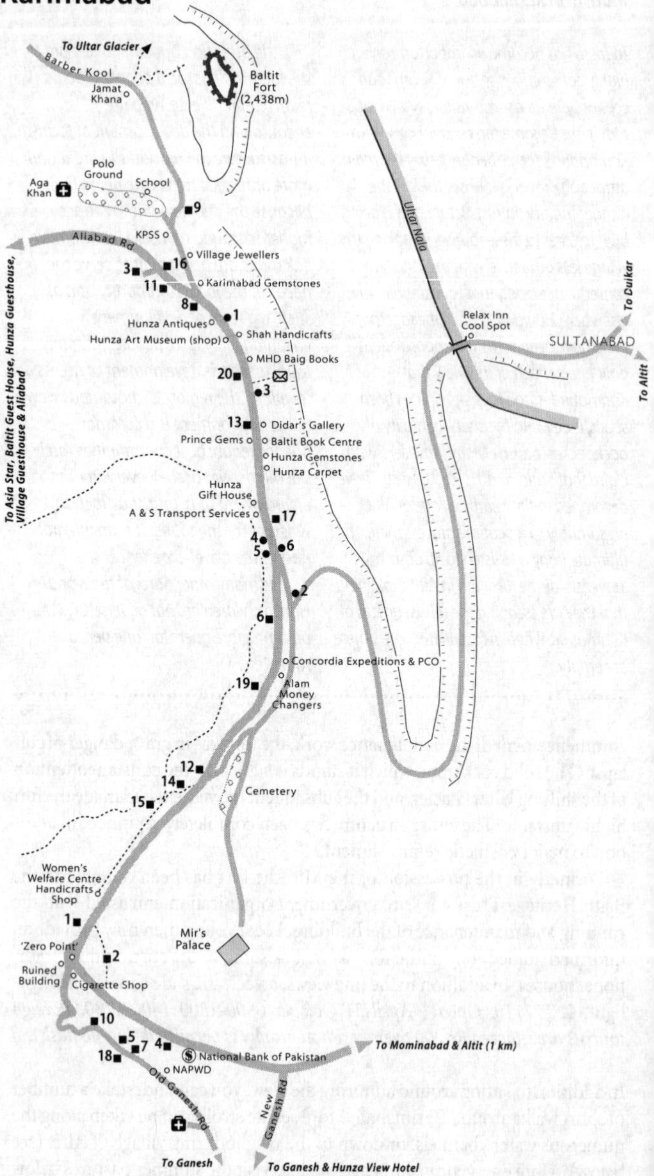

To Ultar Glacier
Barber Kool
Jamat Khana
Baltit Fort (2,438m)
Polo Ground
School
Aga Khan
KPSS
Aliabad Rd
Village Jewellers
Karimabad Gemstones
Hunza Antiques
Shah Handicrafts
Hunza Art Museum (shop)
MHD Baig Books
Ultar Nala
Relax Inn Cool Spot
To Duikar
SULTANABAD
To Altit
To Asia Star, Baltit Guest House, Hunza Guesthouse, Village Guesthouse & Aliabad
Didar's Gallery
Prince Gems
Baltit Book Centre
Hunza Gemstones
Hunza Carpet
Hunza Gift House
A & S Transport Services
Concordia Expeditions & PCO
Alam Money Changers
Cemetery
Women's Welfare Centre Handicrafts Shop
'Zero Point'
Mir's Palace
Ruined Building
Cigarette Shop
National Bank of Pakistan
To Mominabad & Altit (1 km)
NAPWD
Old Ganesh Rd
New Ganesh Rd
To Ganesh
To Ganesh & Hunza View Hotel
N
0 100 metres

Sleeping

1 Baltit Inn
2 Darbar Hunza
3 Garden Lodge
4 Golden Refuge
5 Haider Inn
6 Hill Top
7 Hunza Inn
8 Hunza Lodge & Moon Restaurant
9 Karim
10 Karimabad
11 Mountain Refuge
12 Mulberry
13 New Golden Lodge
14 New Hunza Tourist
15 New Karakoram
16 Rainbow
17 Sunshine
18 Tourist Cottage
19 Tourist Park
20 World Roof

Eating

1 Baltit Bakery & Al Rahim General Store
2 Friends
3 Ghizayyat
4 Hogan
5 Shuq
6 Ultar

camping at the meadow, prepare to have your sleep interupted by the creaking Ultar Glacier, and the sound of distant avalanches.

There is some dispute as to whether the trip up to Ultar Glacier is a 'hike' or a 'trek'. It can be visited as a (long) day trip (ie a 'hike') from Karimabad, though you will almost certainly enjoy the trip more if you camp up at the meadow for at least one night (ie a 'trek'). It is not essential to take a guide up to Ultar, although if you feel more comfortable taking one they are not difficult to find in Karimabad (expect to pay about Rs 300). It should be noted that the number of rockfalls that have occured in recent years means that the route is no longer as clear as it once was. Do not, however, go alone – ask around at the various hotels and see if you can team up with others who are making the trip. An early start is advised, and you should carry plenty of water. Stick to the west (left) side of the stream on the way up – the route is not always obvious. Do not make the trip after heavy rain, or during high winds, since there is a great risk of rockfalls. Whilst up at the meadows, do not attempt to go down onto the glacier.

Although the nala, or canyon, that leads to the Ultar Glacier from just behind Baltit Fort looks quite narrow at the entrance, a strenuous climb of three to four hours along the lateral moraine reveals a wide grassy bowl, surrounded by a spectacular mountain amphitheatre. Shepherds occupy the stone huts during the summer, and are keen to sell chai and fresh dairy products to visitors. It's possible to camp here (at about 3,000 metres), although if you are too close to the huts and the corals holding the 600 or so sheep and goats, you may wake up the next day scratching. You should ask permission from the shepherds before camping near to their huts.

A recent sign of change here has been the opening of a small place amongst shepherds' huts called Lady Finger Restaurant, offering mattresses in a crowded tent for Rs 50 each (blankets provided), lunch for Rs 40, tea for Rs 10, coke for Rs 30 a can, all served on tables and chairs made from the rocks.

A further four hours up to the left of the shepherds' huts brings you to **Hon** (4,600 metres), which offers even better views. There is no water on this route, and it should only really be tackled if you are overnighting at the meadow. There is a rock shelter near the top, plus some obvious camping spots just below. You can walk down from Hon to Karimabad in one long day (six to eight hours). For orientation, see the 'Central Hunza' map.

Essentials

Sleeping
■ *on map*
Price codes: see inside front cover

More expensive hotels **A** *Darbar Hunza*, T Gilgit 4238, T Islamabad 818537, F Islamabad 270608. 40 rooms (including 5 deluxe rooms and 5 suites in the **L** price range), nicely furnished with picture windows, dish TV (though no a/c), bath tubs (bathrooms suprisingly small), public areas very grand, Chinese restaurant (and bar!). Groups get up to 50 percent discount, and individuals may be able to bargain down to the **B** category. **B** *Baltit Inn*, T77012. *Serena*-run, so service excellent and food very good, but rooms are tiny. **B** *Hunza View*, on hill below hospital, T47098, F0572-3695. Rather over-bearing building, described by one reader as "clean, nicely furnished, stunning views, helpful staff, good, above average restaurant".

Mid-price hotels **C** *Hill Top*, T77129/77145. Own generator so hot water guaranteed, rooms facing garden cheaper than those with views, popular with groups, cultural shows sometimes organized, Hunza/Chinese/continental restaurant. **C** *World Roof*, T77153. New, 8 doubles with wonderful views, private balconies, modern clean bathrooms with hot water, 3 singles without views (**E**), prices flexible though usually full in season, restaurant, dish TV lounge planned, rooftop BBQs. **D** *Tourist Park*, T77087. 15 doubles with attached hot bath, restaurant, garden.

 ***Travel tip***

A lot of foreign visitors get ill in Karimabad; could it be the mica-filled water supply that the locals drink with relish, and to which they attribute good health? Bottled water is readily available for those in doubt. Likewise, fresh apricots and mulberries that will be showered upon you are virtually guaranteed to give you diarrhoea.

Budget hotels **E** ***Asia Star***, Aliabad Rd. Formerly *Hillview*, keen manager let down by poorly designed building, excellent Rakaposhi views from restaurant and rooftop terrace, 6 rooms (ones at back cheaper), quiet location. **E** ***Baltit Guest House***, Aliabad Rd, beyond the Aga Khan Academy. An excellent choice for anyone who values peace and quiet, stunning views, 'home-away-from-home' atmosphere, double rooms with attached bath, dorm (**G**) with fine views, though it needs a lick of paint. Recommended. **E** ***Garden Lodge***, Aliabad Rd, T77019. Fairly basic rooms with attached bath, camping in big garden, restaurant. **E** ***Golden Refuge***. 4 carpeted rooms with attached hot bath and fan, dorm (**G**), camping, laundry service. **E** ***Hunza Guest House***, Aliabad Rd, T77164. 1 master room, plus 3 doubles with attached hot bath, 1 traditional style room (sleeping 6, **F**), a little musty and cramped. **E** ***Hunza Inn (Old/New)***, T77186/77086. 5 rooms, 1 with attached hot bath, cheap dorm (**G**), restaurant, supposed villain in the *Haider Inn/Hunza Inn* saga (see below). **E** ***Mountain Refuge***, Aliabad Rd, T77168. Fan, attached hot bath, though rather overpriced, noisy dish TV in restaurant. **E** ***Mulberry***, T77178. Formerly the *Karakoram*, 4 carpeted rooms with shared terrace, attached hot bath, had reports of very good food and friendly service. **E** ***New Golden Lodge***. 5 doubles and 1 triple, most with attached hot bath, views from terrace. **E** ***New Karakoram***, still under construction (since 1995!). **E** ***Sunshine***. Essentially a restaurant that has recently added 2 rooms with attached bath. **E-F** ***Hunza Lodge***. Long time established, older basic rooms with dark cold bath and great terrace views remain good value (**F**), 3 new VIP rooms (**E**) with modern hot bath, small balconies, and unobstructed views are also a very good deal, but often full. Popular *Moon* restaurant upstairs. Recommended. **E-F** ***Karim***, T77091. 3 new doubles with attached cold bath, 2 triples with shared bath, 1 double with shared bath, plus very run down traditional dorm, fine views from the terrace (great spot for lunch or a cold drink). **E-F** ***New Hunza Tourist***. Cheap and basic rooms, plus dorm, brothers who run it are more interested in taking foreigners out on jeep trips (especially if girls are involved). **F** ***Haider Inn***, T77053. Run by the owner of the original *Hunza Inn* (one of Karimabad's first hotels) who didn't register the name and subsequently had it 'stolen' by a competitor (a brother!) who wished to cash in on the reputation. He then changed the name to the *Old Hunza Inn*, but didn't register that either, so subsequently had this name copied by another competitor (another brother!). This is more complicated than Eastenders. Has 5 new rooms with attached hot bath, superb communal evening meals, an entertaining host, and is very popular with the Japanese. **F** ***Rainbow***, Aliabad Rd, T47049. Basic, shared baths, restaurant with noisy dish TV. **G** ***Karimabad***. 3 very basic rooms, rather run down now, possibly about to close. **G** ***Tourist Cottage***. 4 very cheap 4-bed dorms, attached cold bath though hot bucket available, part of the *Haider Inn/Hinza Inn* saga (see above).

Eating
● *on map*

Most visitors eat lunch in one of the small restaurants in the bazaar (see below), and then sit down for a communal meal at their hotel in the evening. Karimabad's grandest (and most unusual) dining experience is at the ***Atiqa Chinese*** in the *Darbar Hunza Hotel*. Managed and staffed by Chinese, the food is excellent (main courses Rs 190, vegetarian Rs 100), but the biggest shocks are seeing a fully stocked bar and mini-skirted waitresses. Whenever these minimally attired girls go shopping in the bazaar, the whole of Karimabad grinds to a halt! ***Ghizayyat*** sells very cheap local food, in a basic setting, though for some reason is very popular with Japanese backpackers. ***Ultar*** and ***Friends*** offer simple, predominantly vegetarian local dishes, and both have pleasant gardens. ***Shuq*** is a popular spot in the mornings when the sun is too hot to sit in the gardens mentioned above. Its dish TV also draws a crowd. Another meeting place for *ZeeTV* fans is ***Hogan***.

Bars & nightclubs

Bars The restaurant at the *Darbar Hunza Hotel* has a bar stocked with alcohol from China (beer and spirits). Officially it's for guests only, though diners are free to order. You may well be offered some 'Hunza Water' (an *arak* derived from fermented mulberries) by your hotel-wallah. It tastes how I've always imagined paint-stripper to taste. A 1½ litre bottle costs about Rs 600 (making paint-stripper a cheaper option).

Festivals

When a large tour group is staying, there is often an evening of music and dancing at the *Hill Top Hotel* (ask at reception). At least once per year there is a grand festival of music and dancing (timings vary), though this is designed with local people in mind; it's held on the old polo ground, to which only villagers are admitted.

Shopping

Bookshops *Baltit Book Centre (BBC)* has books on local subjects plus some maps. ***Mhd Baig Books Stall*** has a selection of 'bestsellers', plus books on local history.

Carpets *Threadnet Hunza Carpet* is part of the Karakoram Handicraft Development Programme (KHDP), and run under the auspices of the AKRSP. It is a community based programme "aimed at reviving the traditional mountain culture and crafts of Hunza". The vegetable dyed carpets, made by local women from Haiderabad, are superb though not cheap (a 3 square metres wool carpet can cost $1,200, or $2,000 for a similar size in silk). Bargaining is expected and credit cards can be used.

Gemstones and jewellery *Prince Gems*, T77115. Has been recommended for gems, semi-precious stones, local handicrafts, credit cards accepted and no commission paid to guides/tour leaders. ***Hunza Gemstones*** has stones and handicrafts, credit cards accepted.

Handicrafts There are so many 'handicraft' shops now established in the main bazaar that it is difficult to recommend any individually; it's just a matter of browsing until you see something that you like, and then negotiating a price that you're prepared to pay. Note that many of the goods on display are not produced locally. (See also entry above.)

Photography Colour print film is readily available (check to see how it's stored), and occasionally slide film (though the freshest stocks are in Rawalpindi).

Supermarkets There are a few 'supermarkets' that should be able to stock you up for a few days of trekking, though the choice is more limited than Gilgit. If you're heading north, this really is the last chance.

Long distance transport

Jeep hire Just about every hotel can organize jeep hire, though one particularly reputable agency is ***A&S Transport Services***, T77084 (they have an office on the main street). They employ reliable drivers and mechanically sound vehicles. A sample of their fares are as follows: Ganesh-Karimabad Rs 120; PTDC (KKH)-Karimabad Rs 120; Karimabad-Altit Rs 400; Karimabad-Hoper Rs 950 (return); Karimabad-Gulmit Rs 800; Karimabad-Duikar Rs 750; Karimabad-Borit Lake Rs 1,000; Karimabad-Sust Rs 1,400; Karimabad-Gilgit Rs 1,400; Karimabad-Passu Rs 1,200; Karimabad-Minapin Rs 900; Karimabad-Khunjerab Pass Rs 2,400. Overnight charge is Rs 300. Other rates on request.

Long distance buses A daily minibus leaves from outside the *Hunza Lodge* at 0500 for **Gilgit** (Rs 60, 3 hours); it doesn't stick around so don't be late. If you only want to go as far as **Pisin** (for **Minapin**) you'll still have to pay the full Gilgit fare. The alternative for south bound travellers is to go down to the KKH at Ganesh. The *NATCO* bus between Sust and Gilgit passes through Ganesh at about 0800 (it usually has seats). If you miss this, there are minibuses running from Sust to Gilgit that pass through about once per hour until mid-afternoon (though they are often full). Travelling north to **Gulmit**, **Passu** and **Sust** is a little more difficult. There are sometimes a couple of minibuses running north from Ganesh at about 0800-0900. The *NATCO* bus from Gilgit to Sust passes through Ganesh at about 1030. If you miss this you'll have to either hire a vehicle, or hitch (though there isn't much traffic). There is no public transport from Karimabad to **Hoper** (see jeep hire above), though there is occasionally a very crowded cargo jeep from Ganesh.

Directory

Banks *Alam Money Changers*, T47109, opposite the *Tourist Park Hotel*. The best place to change cash and TCs, though rates are marginally inferior to those in Gilgit. ***National Bank of Pakistan***, New Ganesh Rd, T47050. Does foreign exchange, though the money changers is quicker. **Communications** **GPO:** the very quaint post office is just above the main road (1-2 days for mail to reach Gilgit, open Mon-Sat 0830-1600, Fri 0830-1200, closed Sun). **Telephones:** nearest international call facility is in Gilgit. **Hospitals & medical services** **Chemists:** on the Aliabad Rd. **Hospitals:** *Civil Hospital*, Old Ganesh Rd, just below the village. But for emergencies go to Gilgit if possible. **Libraries** See under 'Altit' below. **Tour companies & travel agents** *A&S Transport Service*, T77084. Recommended for jeep hire (see under 'Transport' above). *Concordia Expeditions*, opposite *Hill Top Hotel*, T47010. 2 local mountain guides who have been recommended are Rehmat Karim and Arifullah Baig, who can be contacted at the *Karim Hotel*. Another recommended local guide is the English and Japanese speaking Illias Khan, known to local children as 'emushe toro' (don't ask!).

Around Karimabad

Altit

A one and a half kilometres walk to the east of Karimabad (follow the sign) leads you to the charming village of Altit. A sort of scaled down, quieter version of Karimabad, the village is becoming increasingly popular with visitors as a place to spend time relaxing. There are a number of pleasant walks around the neighbourhood, and a fort dramatically positioned on the cliff, 300 metres above the Hunza River. The people of Altit are aware of the impact that tourism appears to be having on neighbouring Karimabad, and though some members of the village are seeking to 'get in on the business', others are concerned that contact with foreigners may adversely affect the traditional way of life. For this reason, there are sometimes signs on display requesting visitors not to wander around the narrow alleys at the heart of the old village. A pleasant way to spend some time is to wander out the other (east) side of Altit, along the quiet track to **Ahmedabad** (about seven kilometres).

Altit Fort is thought to be about a hundred years older than the one at Baltit, and prior to the annexation of Gojal (Upper) Hunza, it marked the northern most extremity of the state. The fort is approached through an apricot orchard, where the chowkidar usually meets you with the key (Rs 25 entrance). The fort is a intricate maze of rooms connected by small doorways, ladders and trapdoors, built on three levels. The dungeon, said to be the scene of one of the many cases of fratricide that litter the history of the ruling families of Hunza and Nagar, has been sealed off. From the balcony of the modern royal apartments there is a tremendous view down to the cluster of houses of old Altit village. Because the densely packed rooftops are regularly used by women for drying fruit and washing, photography of this very appealing scene is forbidden. Pointing your camera in any other direction is permitted (and recommended). The photo on the cover of this book was taken at Altit Fort.

It is no longer possible to climb the 16th century watch-tower (surmounted by a carved wooden goat complete with ibex horns), though you can still appreciate the grand view down the Hunza Valley. A glance down the 300 metres vertical cliff face to the river below is not recommended for sufferers of vertigo.

Hunzuktz Library of International Studies is located at the heart of the village, close to the swimming pool that is so popular in summer with the village children. The rather grand name obscures the fact that the library is little more than a single room, though the staff here are extremely keen to promote the use of English amongst the younger population. There are plenty of books on local history, plus a selection of fiction and 'bestsellers' (tourists can rent books for Rs 5 per day). The library is run entirely through donations, and this is a good place to leave books that you have finished with.

Sleeping & eating

C *White Apricot Lodge*. Large, carpeted rooms with attached hot bath, though this place is generally only open when a group have booked in advance, rather claustrophobic setting with no real views.

D-E *Amir Jan Village Guest House No 1*, T77076. Excellent place, 3 doubles and 1 triple with attached 24 hour hot bath, pleasant dining room (good home cooking), lovely flower-filled garden (visitors can help themselves to fruit from the trees), friendly and smiling owner. Recommended.

F *Kisar Inn*, T77074. One of the most popular backpacker hangouts in Pakistan, very well run, choice of quiet, clean rooms (**F**) with attached bath, cheap dorm (**G**), shady outdoor sitting area, and a sumptuous communal dinner in the evening (Rs 60). Ali Madad also owns the *Eagle's Nest* up at Duikar (see below), and can arrange discounted prices for backpackers/students, as well as organizing jeep trips. Highly

Altit Fort

recommended. **F** ***Village Guest House No 3 (Wilayat Ali)*** and ***Village Guest House No 4 (Ghulam Murtaza)*** do not appear to be currently operating.

G ***Relax Inn***. This is the place next to the bridge, on the road from Karimabad to Altit. It started life as a 'cool spot' selling drinks, though there are now 2 basic rooms with shared bath. Views are nice at sunset (but what a noise from the waterfall), though it's a little remote.

Transport A minibus leaves for **Gilgit** (Rs 60, 3 hours) from outside the *Kisar Inn* at 0500 each morning. Otherwise see under 'Karimabad'. A jeep ride up to **Duikar** costs Rs 700, although you may get it for Rs 300-350 if you're staying at the *Kisar Inn*.

Duikar

Duikar is the latest attraction in the Karimabad area. For some of the finest views in the whole of the Hunza Valley, a climb up to Duikar (pronounced 'Dweekar') is highly recommended; don't miss this place. On a clear day, the scenes at sunrise and sunset are unrivalled, particularly late on a summer's afternoon when the rays of the setting sun illuminate the 7,027 metres Spantik Peak far to the east. It is easy to see why the local people refer to this mountain as Golden Peak. From Duicar, a pathway to the west provides a good two hour walk to **Hosht**, the spectacular ridge high above Baltit Fort. Alternatively, head east to the Hazrat Abbas shrine near **Shabbat** village, from where there are impressive vertical views down to the KKH, as well as across to Golden Peak.

Sleeping & eating **D-E** ***Eagle's Nest***, T77074. Owned by the proprietor of Altit's *Kisar Inn*, and run by his parents, well thought out, 8 clean, large carpeted rooms (blankets provided), with dressing room, attached modern hot bath, shared verandah, and stunning views across to Rakaposhi (you can lie in bed and watch the mountain change colour as the sun comes up!). The rooms are priced in the **D** category, though backpackers from the *Kisar Inn* may be able to negotiate down to the **E** category. There are plans to build a separate block just for backpackers, with **E** price rooms and a **G** priced dorm. It is also possible to take a bed in the tent dorm for Rs 50, or to camp for Rs 40. The restaurant has the choice of à la carte or a communal meal, and is popular with tour groups for lunch. To book, contact the *Kisar Inn* or their office in Karimabad's main bazaar that is shared with *A&S Transport Services*. Highly recommended. **F** ***Edelweiss Lodge***. Located on the road up to Duikar, has 2 rather basic (but very cheap) rooms with attached bath, though you have to walk for 10 minutes for the best views. **G** ***Duikar Tourist Campsite***. Also on the road up to Duikar, Rs 50 for a bed in 1 of the 4 tents. The tents look very basic from the outside, though they are charmingly furnished and decorated inside. Shared bath/toilet, very cheap meals available.

Transport Duikar is reached in a stiff 1½ hour climb above Altit, although it is possible to hire a jeep up the rough track for about Rs 700 (although those staying at the *Kisar Inn* in Altit may be able to negotiate a discount). The road up to Duikar begins at Sultanabad, the small settlement halfway between Altit and Karimabad. The local villagers have requested that the government build a proper link road up to Duikar, so in future it may be possible to make the trip by Suzuki.

Mominabad

Another interesting village between Altit and Karimabad is **Mominabad**, a community of 65 or so houses. The occupants of Mominabad are the Dom, or Berichos, the hereditary lower caste members of the Hunza society who occupy the lower professions, such as those of blacksmiths, cobblers and musicians. They have their own language, Domaki, although the higher cast Burushaski speakers refer to this language in a derogatory way as Beriski.

However, linguists studying Domaki fear that this language may be dead within one generation. The elders of the village believe that they will continue to be discriminated against as lower class citizens if they continue to use their own language, and thus the younger generation is being encouraged to use Burushaski, Urdu and English. Many five and six year olds now have a very narrow Domaki vocabulary. This is an interesting reversal of the normal pattern of a language going out of general usage, where it is the younger generations who make the decision to dispense with the traditional language.

Nagar 1

Sometimes referred to as 'Upper Nagar', the sub-division of **Nagar 1** includes all the land from Minapin to the Hispar River on the south side of the Hunza River, including Nagar Proper, Hoper village and Hispar village. Nagar has a greater land area than Hunza, and since it receives more rainfall (and snow melt), the area of land under cultivation is also greater. The region is famous for its apricots, which are dried and exported to the Punjab in considerable quantity, whilst the streams are supposedly rich in gold!

Nagar's greatest appeal is as the starting/finishing point for a number of highly rewarding treks, though it is certainly worth spending some time exploring villages and hamlets that are barely touched by tourism. For a general history of Nagar, turn to the beginning of the 'Lower Hunza and Nagar 2' section (page 530), where we have committed the cardinal sin of lumping Nagar in with Hunza.

Sumayar, Askordas and Shayar

Looking across the Hunza River from Karimabad towards the Nagar side of the valley, the small village perched on the wide alluvial fan is **Sumayar**. The most interesting way to approach the village is from the west, via Shayar and Askordas. This involves hiking (or hitching) south along the KKH, to the point where the road emerges from the entrance to the Hasanabad Nala (see

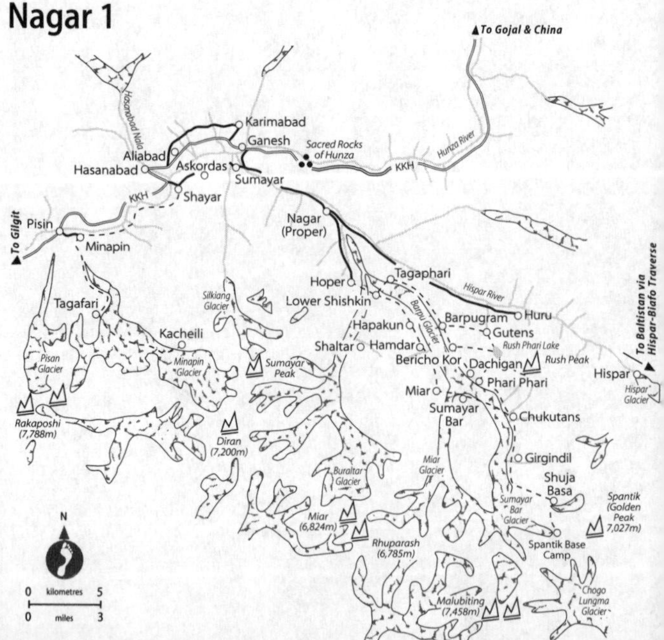

Related map
Lower Hunza, Nagar 2, Central Hunza & Nagar 1, page 532

end of 'Lower Hunza and Nagar 2' section, above). A snaking jeep road drops down to the Hunza River, crosses via a suspension bridge, and then up to the settlement of **Shayar**. From here, it is an enjoyable one and a half hour walk along the track to **Askordas**. This small village is notable for its ostentatious new mosque, built with proceeds from the rich mineral strike above Sumayar. There's a small chai-shop in Askordas. A further one hour brings you to **Sumayar**. The camping site up above the village is now open again, and is a fine place to stop. The more energetic may like to continue up the hillside along the Sumayar Nala to Mamubar, the former hunting grounds of the Mir of Nagar. Some four hours above Sumayar are the summer pastures of Madur Kushi, where it is also possible to camp (though the Mir of Nagar is still entitled to collect rent from campers here). It is high up here, above the Sumayar Nala valley and Silkiang Glacier, that Nagar derives much of its wealth: the aquamarine crystal mines at Chuman Bakhur (a further three hours up the mountain!). In theory, there is a three day trekking route from here to Hoper, although it is rarely used and a guide is essential.

From Sumayar it is a further two hours walk down to Nagar Proper. From here, you can return to the KKH, or head up to Hoper.

Nagar (Proper)

Colour map 5, grid A4

To reach Nagar (Proper), cross the KKH on the bridge just below Ganesh, and then head along the jeep track in a southeasterly direction alongside the Hispar River. The road is sealed as far as the bridge across the river (six kilometres). The road continuing alongside the river from the bridge is the old track to **Huru**. From the bridge it is a short, steep climb up to **Nagar (Proper)**. Note that there is very little public transport on this route. The former capital of the independent state of Nagar, this is still home to the Mir. Few people stop off here, most continuing on to Hoper. Those with a booking from Gilgit can stay in the basic **F** *NAPWD Inspection Bungalow*, or it may be possible to doss down on a charpoy at one of the restaurants, such as the *Distaghil Sar Hotel*. Leaving Nagar towards Hoper, it may be necessary to record your passport details at the police station. Note that the first left turn on leaving Nagar (Proper) is the new road to **Huru** and **Hispar** (20 kilometres).

Hoper

A further 15 kilometres beyond Nagar (Proper), through colourful cultivated fields, the jeep road enters an impressive wide fertile bowl ringed by high peaks. The five small hamlets clustered together here (Shakoshal, Hakalshal, Borushal, Holshal and Ratal) are collectively referred to as **Hoper** (or 'Hopar'). This is the starting/finishing point for a number of impressive treks (see below; for details of the 'Biafo-Hispar Traverse', see page 521 in the 'Baltistan' section). Those with limited time can still admire the dirty **Bualtar Glacier** down below, and the **Barpu Glacier** on the other side. **NB** Do not go down onto the glacier without a reliable guide.

Sleeping & eating

Competition between the two hotel owners in Hoper is so fierce, you may find them literally fighting each other for your custom. They may also tempt you to their place by the offer of three (as opposed to two) eggs in your omlette! Note that when ordering food and drinks, nothing on the menu is priced. This "as you like" system is designed to allow the owners to charge you what they think you will be prepared to pay; fix all prices in advance and double-check your bill. **E** ***Hoper Inn***. 3 double rooms with

Promoting tourism in Nagar

In many regards this is the 'forgotten' part of the Northern Areas. Despite having its own cultural identity (the people are predominantly Shia Muslim, and markedly different to their neighbours and rivals across the Hunza River), Nagar is often mistakenly lumped together with Hunza. It is not unusual, for example, to see Rakaposhi described as being 'in Hunza' (even on government produced PTDC literature), whereas it is indisputedly in Nagar. Through the work of a number of NGOs in the area, particularly the Naunehal Development Organisation based in Jaffarabad, the residents of Nagar are beginning to assert their own cultural identity, largely in an attempt to enjoy some of the tourism-derived income that Hunza seems to generate. Locally produced postcards sporting spectacular views of Rakaposhi, Diran and Golden Peak now proudly, and prominently, bear the word 'Nagar', whilst it is becoming increasingly common to hear Nagaris questioning outsiders as to why they refer to the river running through the centre of the valley as the 'Hunza River'.

Of course these are just cosmetic issues, though they do underline a genuine effort by Nagaris to express a distinct cultural identity. Of course, Nagar has a number of problems, and perceived problems, to overcome if it is to compete with Hunza on an equal footing. In a report prepared by the Naunehal Development Organization, a criticism is made of various guidebooks to the region suggesting that they present a negative image of Nagar. Porters and guides are described as "money-grabbing" and keen to overcharge, whilst children are noted for their "stone-throwing" tendencies. What the report fails to understand is that, in the past at least, these comments were more than justified. For example, the famous Hispar-Biafo Traverse, one of the great Karakoram treks, became the Biafo-Hispar Traverse instead, since trekkers prefered to travel from east-west as Balti porters were more amenable than Nagari ones. There has now been a realization that Nagari porters are on the verge of 'killing the goose that lays the golden egg', and hence great efforts are being made to clean up their act. Likewise, children are being educated in the ways of foreign tourists, and are being actively encouraged not to beg and generally hassle visitors. Of course, respect for alien culture is a two-way business, and visitors to Nagar have a responsibility too. This is a conservative area, and thus visitors must be respectably dressed (no bare flesh, on either sex), not indulge in public displays of affection, and be careful about who and what they photograph (ask permission, particularly when women are around).

Nagar's other great problem is one of access. Although there are public bus services to Nagar Proper and Hoper from Gilgit (near the bank on Khazana Road), services don't run to any fixed schedule, and more importantly, do not have destination boards written in English (compare with, for example, how easy it is to get a minibus to Karimabad). This is a problem that the Nagaris are seeking to resolve.

To see exploitative tourism at its very worst, a visit to Hoper is suggested. Since transport is such a problem, almost all foreign tourists arrive by jeep (and since these are all hired in Karimabad, Nagaris do not derive any income from this). The majority of these day-trippers spend just about long enough to drink a coke, and peer down to the Bualtar Glacier for a couple of photos. Thus, the traders and businessmen in Hoper have little more than 20 minutes to make any money from these visitors. As a result, there is a tendency for the restaurants to grossly over charge, whilst the abiding memory of most visitors is of persistant hustlers trying to flog them 'gemstones' and souvenirs. Until Nagar can attract visitors for longer periods, this sorry situation is set to continue. However, at least there has been a recognition that Nagar has an image problem, and that is the first step towards addressing the issue.

attached bath (possibly hot water), more rooms and new restaurant planned, Rs 30 per bed in 2-person tent. **E *Hoper Hilton*.** 2 triple rooms with 5 more due to be built, clean, carpeted, attached bath (currently cold though plans for hot water), prices negotiable, or take a bed in a tent for Rs 60, restaurant. **F *NAPWD Inspection Bungalow*.** Next to *Hoper Inn*, book in Gilgit.

Transport

A same day return trip by jeep from **Karimabad** costs Rs 950, though you only get about ½ hour here. In theory, a minbus leaves **Gilgit's** Khazana Rd at about 0800 each day (Rs 90, 4 hours), though this is not definite (and there's currently no English destination board). A wagon returns from Hoper to **Gilgit** at 0600. Sometimes there is a cargo jeep from Hoper to **Ganesh** at 0600, returning at 0730.

Treks from Hoper

Barpu Glacier Trek

Open zone. Maximum elevation 4,000 metres. Mid-June to October. Maps: Swiss Foundation reasonable; U502 series, NJ 43-14 Baltit is unreliable. For orientation, see the 'Nagar 1' map on page 554. Read trekking notes, page 67.

This trek is usually undertaken in six days, though it does involve nine stages. The walking is fairly easy, though the fact that there are five glacier crossings makes a guide essential. Leaving Hoper (2,790 metres), you cross the **Bualtar Glacier**. The trail across changes daily, and can take anywhere between 20 minutes and two hours to cross! Make sure that you are carrying water since there is none until the first night's camp. Having crossed the Bualtar Glacier to **Lower Shishkin**, you must then cross the **Barpu Glacier** to **Tagaphari**. Proceed in a southeast direction along the ablation valley via the shepherd's huts at **Barpugram** (45 minutes), and camp the first night at **Bericho Kor** (3,300 metres), a further one hour, and four to five hours from Hoper altogether. From here there is the option of a strenuous two day climb up to Rush Phari (see below).

The second day is a simple, straight-forward two hour hike via **Dachigan** to **Phari Phari** (3,450 metres). The third day is particularly pleasant, passing through the grassy meadows of **Chukutans** to the pastures at **Girgindil** (four hours). From here it is possible to make a two day detour up to **Spantik Base Camp**, known locally as Shuja Basa (a further six stages). To return to Hoper retrace your route back down to Chukutans, then cross the **Sumayar Bar Glacier** to the shepherd's huts at **Sumayar Bar** (five hours). On the fifth day, cross the **Miar Glacier** to **Miar**, then follow the Barpu Glacier via **Hamdar** (two hours) to **Hapakun** (one hour). On the final day, walk down to **Lower Shishkin**, recross the Bualtar Glacier, and return to Hoper (four hours).

Rush Phari Trek

Open zone. Maximum elevation 4,694 metres. Mid-June to October. Maps: Swiss Foundation is usable, though it has some mistakes; U502 series, NJ 43-14 Baltit is unreliable. For orientation, see the 'Nagar 1' map on page 554. Read trekking notes, page 67.

This is a fabulous extension to the Barpu Glacier Trek, though several serious considerations must be borne in mind. Rush Phari, a breathtaking turquoise lake from where a 360° panoramic view takes in all the most spectacular peaks of the region (including K2, Broad Peak and Gasherbrum IV), is located at an altitude of 4,694 metres. Consequently, it is only for trekkers who are already acclimatized. There are also long stretches on this trek where water is not available.

Follow the first day description of the Barpu Glacier Trek from **Hoper** to **Bericho Kor** (3,300 metres). The second day involves an altitude gain of over 1,100 metres, and should only be attempted by those who are fully acclimatized. What's more, this five to six hour climb is very hot, and has no water en route (so you should stock up in Bericho Kor). The first four hours of the climb up from Bericho Kor heads east, up to a 4,020 metres ridge (marked by a cairn). If you experience altitude sickness, you will have to descend since there are no alternative camping options. Having reached the ridge (where a trail joins from Gutens, to the northeast), head southeast along the ridge to the camping spot near shepherd's huts at **Chidin Harai** (two hours, 4,400 metres). There is water here.

The following day it should not take more than two hours to reach **Rush Phari** (4,694 metres), although the trail is not always obvious. It is worth spending some time here, perhaps an extra day, in order to ascend some of the surrounding hilltops (eg Rush Peak) in order to get even better views. Note that it can get very cold and very windy at Rush Phari.

There are two options for the return trip: you can descend the way that you came, or you can make the steep descent down to Phari Phari (three hours). See the 'Barpu Glacier Trek' details above for the return to Hoper.

Gojal (Upper Hunza)

The upper part of Hunza is referred to as **Gojal** (Guhjal), and comprises the area along the upper section of the Hunza River from the village of Shishkut/Nazimabad up to the Khunjerab Pass. It also includes the Shimshal Valley that lies to the east of the KKH, and the Chapsuran Valley that lies to the west of the KKH along the border with China (towards Afghanistan's Wakhan Corridor).

Gojal is populated by Wakhi speaking communities who settled here several generations ago. Originally nomads from the grazing pastures of the Upper Oxus, they are thought to have arrived through the Irshad Pass which connects the Wakhan, Yarkun, Ishkoman and Chapsuran Valleys, and settled down to sedentary agriculture. They were previously ruled by their own Raja, but later came under the suzerainty of the Mir Of Hunza. The people are almost exclusively Ismaili.

For the tourist, Gojal Hunza offers good trekking, and some excellent walks, usually within easy range of the Karakoram Highway.

Routes

Just beyond Ganesh, the KKH crosses onto the south side of the Hunza River, where there is a turning for the jeep track to Nagar (see above). Just after the turning, to the left of the KKH, are the **Sacred Rocks of Hunza**. Beyond this is the Chinese built and run brick factory.

The Sacred Rocks of Hunza

Carved onto a number of boulders at a place known locally as 'Haldikish', or 'Place of Rams', are a series of petroglyphs that date from the first century AD right up until modern times. Generally referred to now as the Sacred Rocks of Hunza, a more detailed explanation of the inscriptions on show can be found in Karl Jettmar's *'Rock Carvings and Inscriptions in the Northern Areas of Pakistan'*, or AH Dani's *'Human Records on the Karakoram Highway'*, both available from Islamabad bookshops. The Sacred Rocks can also be

Related maps
A Walks & Hikes around Passu, page 565
B Shimshal Valley & Shimshal Pamir, page 568
C Sust to Kashgar (Chapursan Valley), page 577

reached by a longish walk from Karimabad (steep uphill climb on the way back).

Routes The KKH passes through the small settlement of **Ayeenabad**, and then continues on to **Nazimabad** (formerly known as Shishkut). This is the boundary of Central and Gojal Hunza. The KKH re-crosses the Hunza River and continues to the police check post 2 kilometres before **Gulmit**. Foreigners sometimes have to record their passport details.

Gulmit

Colour map 5, grid A4

Former summer residence of the Mir of Hunza, Gulmit (2,370 metres) is a sleepy village set amongst productive agricultural land, and offers some easy short walks. The main village is centred around the old polo field several minutes walk above the KKH. As recently as the 1950s the polo ground was a lawn of lush grass hosting regular matches, though the arrival of the internal combustion engine made the keeping of horses an expensive luxury as opposed to an everyday necessity.

There is an excellent, if somewhat eccentric **Cultural Museum** (Rs 20, ask at *Hunza Marco Polo Inn* if it's shut), including the gun that is said to have

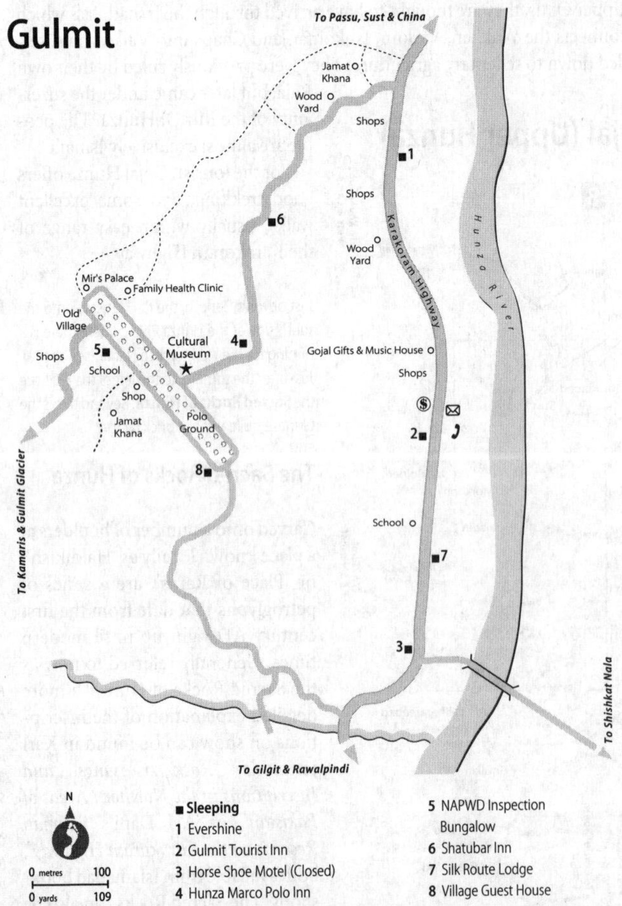

caused Colonel Durand to walk in such a funny way (see Battle of Nilt, page 537). The museum is currently in the process of being restored, with improved labelling and the placing of exhibits into protective showcases.

Next to the Mir's former palace is the original settlement of Gulmit, a labyrinth of alleyways running between the old stone, mud and wooden houses. There is an 'Old House' museum that is sometimes open to visitors (Rs 20), and an even older Shia mosque.

Sleeping & eating

■ *on map*
Price codes: see inside front cover

C *Hunza Marco Polo Inn*, T46107. Very well run, 20 attractive rooms with verandah, attached modern tiled bath with 24 hour hot water. Plus recently constructed VIP guesthouse featuring traditional style Hunza bedroom (sleeps 5), 5 en suite bedrooms, sitting room, dining room, fully equipped kitchen (Rs 2,000 per double). Good restaurant, handicraft shop, all set in flower filled garden, can also arrange guides and transport. Recommended. **C** *Silk Route Lodge*, KKH, T46118. Change of management has improved this place no end, 20 large furnished rooms, very modern attached bath (24 hour hot water), upper floors best with private balconies, light and airy restaurant, pleasant garden, good value. **C-F** *Gulmit Tourist Inn*, KKH, T46119. 2 carpeted, furnished deluxe rooms with attached modern hot bath (though a little overpriced), 13 carpeted doubles, attached modern hot bath, 3 basic doubles with shared cold bath (**F**), 6-bed dorm (**G**) in traditional Hunza room with attached cold bath, or use hot bath in new block, good restaurant, shop, friendly and well run. **C-F** *Village Guest House*, near polo ground, T46112. Set in very pleasant orchard (good camping, **F**), has a variety of rooms at different prices. 1 family room (2 doubles sharing 1 bath, **C**), doubles with rather old fashioned attached hot bath (**D**), some rather overpriced doubles with shared bath (**E**), and a couple of cosy traditional style double rooms with shared bath (**D**). Some readers have written to say "now discovered by tour groups ... prices have gone up ... charges tour group prices ... no longer such good value", though it can be good value if you can negotiate the right price. The proprieter, former 2nd Lt Shah Khan (and commander of 'Eskimo Force', see Gilgit history above), is possibly the most interesting man you'll meet in the Northern Areas!

D *Horse Shoe Motel*, KKH. Closed. **D** *Shatubar Inn*. 11 simple rooms, fairly modern attached hot bath, light and airy restaurant, not bad value (though you should get a discount because it's usually empty).

F *Evershine*, KKH. 2 very run-down and rather dirty doubles with attached hot bath (but cheap), cheap dorm (**G**), good value restaurant (dhal, sabzi and chapatti Rs 60).

Transport

Heading **north**, you have to rely on transport heading from Gilgit to **Sust**. Private minibuses don't really start passing through until 1200, with the *NATCO* bus coming through at 1230-1300. **South** bound you are waiting for transport heading from Sust to **Gilgit**. Minibuses start coming through at 0600, with the *NATCO* bus trundling through at about 0700. Occasionally there is a local minibus from Gulmit to Gilgit at 0600. Sust is 1½ hours, Passu 30 minutes, Ganesh (for Karimabad) 1 hour, Gilgit 4 hours. Alternatively, try hitching, or walk.

Directory

Banks *National Bank of Pakistan*. Open Mon-Sat 0900-1330, deals in US$ only (cash and TCs). **Communications Post Office:** open Mon-Sat 0900-1600, Fri 0900-1200, closed Sun. **Telephone:** the PCO only offers local calls.

Short walks around Gulmit

Warning Glaciers are active and highly unstable, especially in summer. Note that if a foreigner is killed or injured on the glaciers, the local people tend to get the blame from the authorities. It is for this reason that they are so insistent on you taking a guide.

Gulmit Glacier It is possible to walk up to the **Gulmit Glacier** above the village as a long day trip, or as an overnight. The track behind Gulmit climbs steeply to the small village of **Kamaris**, from where a footpath continues for some four hours or so to shepherds' huts on the south side of the Gulmit Glacier. On your return, it is possible to take the path leading down to the east of Kamaris, past the insubstantial remains of the 200 year old **Andare Fort**, and back to Gulmit.

Ghulkin, Ghulkin Glacier and Borit Lake The small village of **Ghulkin** can be reached by either crossing the snout of the Gulmit Glacier, or from a link road off the KKH, 500 metres north of Gulmit. There is an **E** *Village Guest House* at Ghulkin, and the **E** *Al-Rahim Hotel* at the link road turn off on the KKH.

From Ghulkin a footpath crosses the snout of the **Ghulkin Glacier**, before climbing up the lateral moraine. If you are unsure about crossing the glacier, ask for local advice or hire a guide. A further two and a half hours walk brings you to **Borit Lake**, a large brackish glacial lake that attracts a number of migratory birds in February-June and September-November. There is a basic **F** *Borit Lake Hotel* here, or some good camping. From the lake you can either return to Gulmit (four hours), or continue on to Passu (five hours – route described in Passu section). To walk from Gulmit, via Borit Lake, to Passu all in one day is quite a slog.

Routes Returning to the KKH, 1 kilometre north of Gulmit is a jeep road turn off for **Ghulkin**. At the junction is the **E** ***Al-Rahim Hotel***. Several kilometres further on, the KKH passes the small village of **Hussaini**, where you can cross the river on one of two spectacular rope bridges (see Passu section below). Beyond Hussaini, the KKH climbs through a series of bends to the small, but important, village of **Passu**.

Passu

Colour map 5, grid A4

The region around Passu (2,543 metres) offers some of the best walking in the entire Northern Areas, from half and full day trips, to short, multi day walks, right up to long, strenuous treks, and all within easy reach of the KKH.

The actual village of Passu is situated to the east of the KKH, on a wide alluvial fan, with houses scattered among the irrigated fields and orchards. Flooding that follows periodic damming of both the Shimshal and Hunza rivers has done irreparable damage to the agricultural system in Passu, and greatly reduced the amount of land available for cultivation.

To the south of the village, the KKH bridges the stream of the **Passu Glacier**, strikingly white in contrast to the dirty grey morainal glaciers common to this region. On hot days, come and stand here to appreciate the icy drafts off the glacier. To the north of Passu is a wide stony plain, once the site of the Chinese KKH construction headquarters, but now slowly being brought under cultivation with technical assistance from the AKRSP. Also to the north of the village is the immense **Batura Glacier**, stretching some 58 kilometres from the Batura Muztagh group of peaks to the west, right down to (and sometimes through) the KKH. Across the river is a huge and ruggedly beautiful multi-pinnacled ridge of crumbling granite spires, sometimes referred to as The Cathedral but known locally as **Tupopdan**. (See photographs in the colour section at the front of the book.)

Essentials

Sleeping & eating

■ *on map*
Price codes: see inside front cover

Passu has an excellent selection of accommodation to suit all budgets. Most visitors eat at their hotel, though for a treat head out to the *Passu Tourist Lodge*. There is a small shop opposite the *Passu Inn* which should have enough provisions for hiking, though those intending to trek (or go to Shimshal) should stock up in Gilgit.

It has been reported that the people of Passu are not particularly happy about the guesthouses being opened in the heart of the village; local women in particular are nervous about coming across (male) tourists as they go about their daily business. With plenty of space available along the KKH for commercial expansion, do not be surprised if all the village based hotels are shifted out here (a village meeting was due to discuss this issue as we went to press). In the meantime, tourists in the village must be on their best behaviour (and suitably dressed).

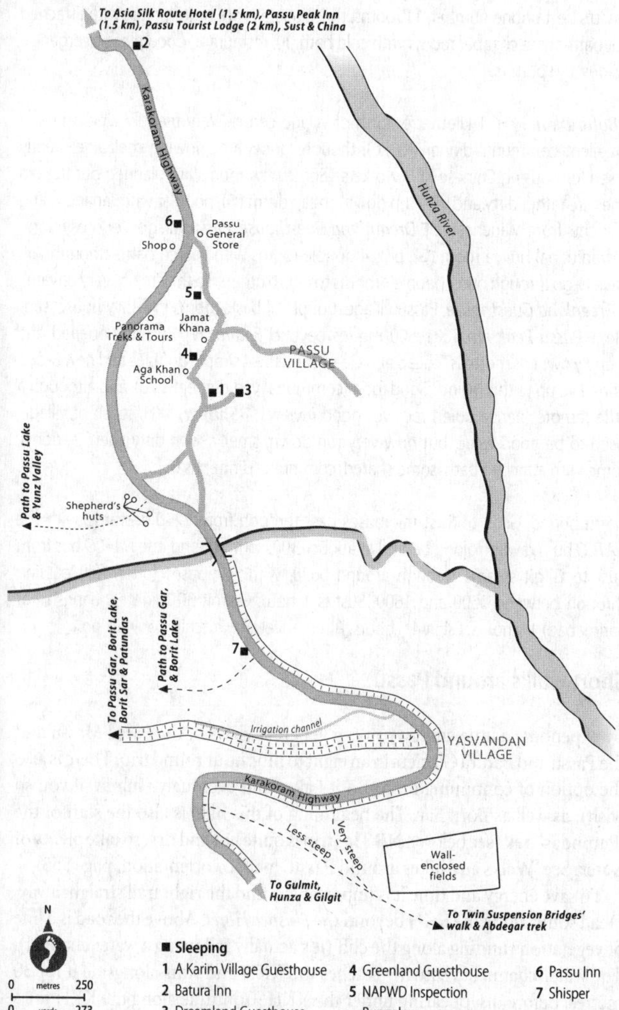

C ***Passu Tourist Lodge***, KKH, 2 kilometres north of village. Although it looks rather like an army barracks, the 20 rooms (in self-contained 4-room blocks) are very nice, with modern tiled bathrooms (24 hour hot water), 15 percent discount for groups (worth asking for anyway). The co-owner formerly worked as a chef at the Gilgit *Serena*, so hence the food is a real treat ("best in the Northern Areas"). Chinese Rs 130, Mexican BBQ chicken Rs 115, spaghetti carbonnera Rs 110 etc. Recommended.

D ***Asia Silk Route*** (provisional name), KKH, just north of *Passu Peak Inn*. Still under construction towards end of 1998, 14 rooms planned.

E ***A. Karim Village Guest House***, Passu village. Beautifully located in heart of village, receives good reviews from visitors, "excellent place ... clean ... food good value", 3 very clean doubles with attached hot bath, 1 triple with shared bath, cosy dorm in traditional Hunza room (**G**), communal dinner (veg Rs 65, meat Rs 75), becoming popular with budget groups, friendly and well run. Recommended. **E** ***Passu Inn***, KKH, T1. Passu's best phone number, 11 rooms, those upstairs are better, most with attached hot bath, some cheaper rooms with cold bath (**F**), restaurant, good place to organize guides and porters.

F ***Batura Inn***, KKH, 1 kilometre north of village centre. Very friendly welcome and excellent communal dinner (Rs 70), though rooms are showing their age greatly (used for housing Chinese KKH workers). Some new rooms are planned but the old ones are rather dirty and very run down, cheap dorm (**G**), popular with Japanese and students from Manchester. **F** ***Dreamland Guesthouse***, Passu village. Very cosy dorm in traditional Hunza room (**G**), plus 4 double rooms with shared baths (though you have to go through other people's rooms to get to others, so they're not very private). **F** ***Greenland Guesthouse***, Passu village. Couple of basic rooms in family house, simple. **F** ***Passu Peak Inn***, KKH, 500 metres beyond *Batura Inn*. Recently opened, the friendly owner's motto is "cheap and clean", and the 4 simple doubles and new 8-bed dorm live up to this billing. Good food (communal veg dinner Rs 70), and although a little remote (hence quiet) receives good reviews. **F** ***Shisper***, KKH, south of village. Used to be good value, but now very run down, smelly, with dirty linen, 7 rooms, some with attached bath, some shared, communal dinner Rs 65.

Transport North bound, Gilgit to **Sust** minibuses pass through from 1230 onwards, with the *NATCO* bus crawling along behind at about 1300. south bound, the *NATCO* bus from Sust to **Gilgit** steams through around 0630, with minibuses (often full) passing through between 0600 and 1600. Sust is 1 hour, Gulmit 30 minutes, Ganesh (for Karimabad) 1½ hours, Gilgit 4½ hours. Alternatively, try hitching or walking.

Short walks around Passu

Passu Gar (and Borit Lake/Borit Sar) By expending a little energy you can get great views of the Passu Massif and the Passu and Batura Glaciers in an eight to nine hour round trip. There is also the option of continuing on to Botit Lake (and eventualy Gulmit, if you so wish), as well as Borit Sar. The beginning of this hike is also the start of the 'Patundas' trek (see below). **NB** This trip is quite hot and dry, so take plenty of water. See 'Walks and hikes around Passu' map for orientation, page 565.

To save energy and time it is important to find the right trail straight away. Head south along the KKH beyond the *Shisper Hotel*. Above the road is a line of vegetation running along the cliff (it's actually following a water channel). The water channel eventually reaches the KKH and runs alongside it for 30 metres, before disappearing under the KKH. Continue along the KKH for a further 30 metres and you'll see a distinct path climbing up the cliff. Follow this in the direction of the electricity pylons until you reach a low saddle. The trail that heads off left (southeast) continues to **Borit Lake** (a further two hours). The trail that ascends straight ahead (west) continues for a further one hour to a large slate platform (2,730 metres), from where there are good views down to Passu Glacier and Passu Lake. There are two options here. A stiff three hours straight up the slate covered mountainside leads you to **Borit Sar**, the viewpoint overlooking Borit Lake and the Passu and Ghulkin Glaciers. Alternatively, head from the slate platform along the old water channel above the Passu Glacier for half an hour, then climb sharply at the end of the ablation valley to a distinct rest point. A second abandoned water channel heads west along the ablation valley, after 40 minutes or so arriving at the shepherd's huts at **Passu Gar** (3,100 metres). You can either camp here, or return to Passu in a further four to five hours. This is the usual first night camp on the 'Patundas' trek (see below).

Twin suspension bridges

Probably the most popular day hike from Passu, this trip crosses and then recrosses the Hunza River on two dramatic suspension bridges, passing through some delightful Upper Hunza villages, and affording fine views of the Passu Glacier. Frequent comparisons are made whilst crossing the river with a certain series of movies starring Harrison Ford. See the colour section at the front of the book for an example. **NB** This trip is quite hot and dry, so take plenty of water. See 'Walks and hikes around Passu' map for orientation, below.

South of the *Shisper View Hotel*, just past the first hairpin out of Passu (and just before the second hairpin), follow the path down from the KKH (it may be marked by some white cairns). Follow the path, and don't be tempted to drop down to the river too early. About 45 minutes downstream, you come to the first bridge. Irregular planks and branches, in places up to metre apart, supply the footholds, whilst two rusty metal cables provide a handrail. The bridge sways as you walk across it , even more so on a windy day or if more

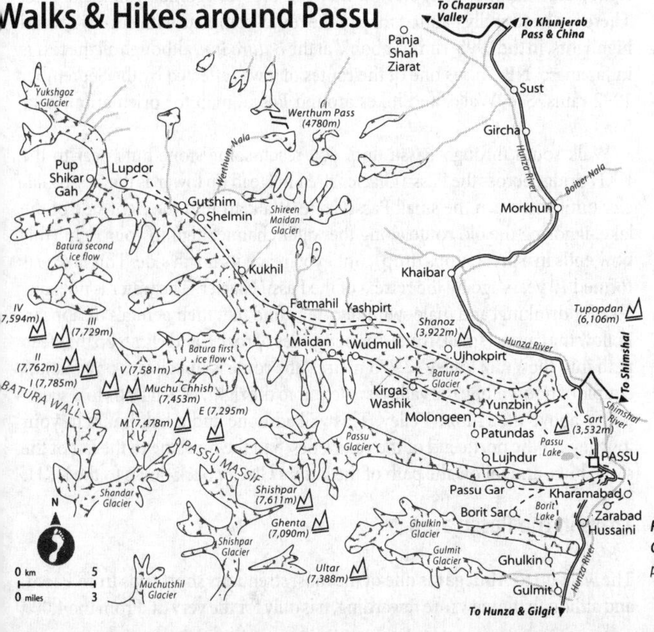

Related map Gojal (Upper Hunza), page 559

Warning

Those planning to hike or trek should note that the trails change somewhat from year to year. In fact, the catastrophic rains of September 1992 changed some routes significantly, and thus you should be sceptical of any route descriptions written before then. Check the latest 'rumour books' in the various hotels (eg Batura Inn). The glaciers here are active and highly unstable, especially in summer. Note that if a foreigner is killed or injured on the glaciers, the local people tend to get the blame from the authorities. It is for this reason that they are so insistent on you taking a guide.

than one person attempts to cross at a time. Having crossed the river, continue straight ahead across the rocky, alluvial fan, and aim to cross the ravine to your right as high as possible. Near the top, to the left, is the route to Abdegar (see below).

The village of **Zarabad** to the right, is well cultivated, and the people are very friendly. It is particularly photogenic in autumn, when the crops are ripening against the distant white background of the Passu Glacier. Follow the path through the village, and then descend by way of the path and steps cut in the cliff-face to the second bridge. There are two bridges here, although the one furthest downstream is too dangerous to use. Across the river is **Hussaini**, another small village situated below the KKH. Near to the bridge are some hot springs with segregated bathing times for men and women. From Hussaini it is about eight kilometres to Passu along the KKH, although you should be able to hitch-hike quite easily.

Yunz Valley The one-day, but hot, dry and strenuous walk through the **Yunz Valley** offers good views of the Passu and Batura glaciers. The route passes behind Skazart, the massive yellow rock that looms over Passu, and takes between six and eight hours depending upon how many of the 'viewpoints' you make it to. There is a beautifully painted map of the route, complete with cut-aways and highlights, in the 1995 'rumour book' at the *Batura Inn*, although all the text is in Japanese. **NB** This is one of the routes that was affected by the September 1992 rains. See 'Walks and hikes around Passu' map for orientation, page 565.

Walk south through Passu until you reach some stone huts near to the KKH bridge across the Passu Glacier stream. Head up towards the Passu Glacier until you reach the small Passu Lake. Walk around the right side of the lake, ignoring the old route along the water channel high to your right (this now ends in a precipitous drop), until you reach its north side. This lake was formed 10 years ago by the retreat of the Passu Glacier. The water is not suitable for drinking, and male swimmers may find that their genitals disappear. Follow the cairns (small, route-marking piles of rock), and climb up the steep path into the Yunz Valley (2,775 metres, the route is not always obvious). A couple of hours along the valley is a detour to the right, which leads to a 'viewpoint' above the Hunza Valley. This will add one and a half hours to your journey. At the north end of the valley, descend the moraine to the left of the stone huts, and follow the path of the Batura Glacier back down to the KKH.

Treks in the Passu area

Abdegar trek The walk up to **Abdegar** is one of the most strenuous short trips from Passu, and although the views are rewarding, it is only for the very fit. From the 4,000 metres ridge across the river from Passu, there are incredible panoramic views back towards the entire Batura Muztagh cluster, including Passu Peak (7,284 metres), Batura Muztagh itself (7,785 metres), numerous other 7,000 and 7,500 metres peaks, plus the Passu and Batura glaciers. For those wanting an idea of the view, there is a panoramic photo of the scene on the reception counter at the *Batura Inn*. It is also worth checking the 'rumour books' here for comments on the best route. See 'Walks and hikes around Passu' map for orientation, page 565.

This is really an overnight trip for which you should be fully prepared. Whatever the day time temperature, it will be freezing cold at night so a good sleeping bag and a tent are essential. You may be able to hire these in the shop near to the *Passu Inn*. It is also worth bearing in mind that you will be sleeping almost 1,500 metres higher than you were in Passu, and the dangers of altitude sickness are very real. There is water at the camp-site, and at the foot of the hill, but none in between. And finally, the route up the scree to the camp-site is not always obvious, and in order to avoid needless, energy-sapping backtracking, it may be wise to hire a local guide. Having said all this, the views on a clear day truly are magnificent.

Having crossed the rope bridge to Zarabad, bear left towards Kharamabad village, and then head up to the bottom of the main hill. There is a freshwater spring emerging out of the cliff next to the waterfall pool. Cross the stream, and the path upwards begins 100 metres downstream of the waterfall. It is a pretty vertical three and a half hours to the camp-site at 3,600 metres (six hours in total from Passu). The following morning you can climb for a further three hours up to the viewpoint (4,000 metres), although if you don't really feel up to it, take some consolation in the fact that the view from the camp-site is 90 percent as good. It takes one and a half hours to descend from the ridge to the camp-site, and then four hours back to Passu.

Patundas trek

Although this trek is fairly short (three days, four stages), it is not for novices. You will need an experienced guide to cross the extremely dangerous Passu Glacier (you will need to be roped, and crampons are recommended), and since there is a rapid altitude gain you will need to be already acclimatized (many people attempt this trek on the back of the Batura Glacier trek, see below). Note that you will have to use Ghulkin guides and porters for this trek. See 'Walks and hikes around Passu' map for orientation, page 565.

For the description of the first day, see under 'Passu Gar' above. The second day begins with the difficult crossing of the dangerous Passu Glacier (a feat that takes anywhere between one and three hours). From here, your guide will lead you the three hours or so via **Lujhdur** (3,400 metres) to the pastures at **Patundas** (4,100 metres). Note that water supplies are problematic along this entire trek. The return to Passu is via the same route, though it can be done in one day.

Batura Glacier trek

Open zone. Maximum elevation optional (up to 4,000 metres). Early June to late September. Maps; the Chinese Institute of Glaciology map of Batura is excellent; Swiss foundation is good; U502 series, NJ 43-14 Baltit is just about adequate. See 'Walks and hikes around Passu' map for orientation, page 565. Read trekking notes, page 67.

The Batura Glacier trek is a popular one and relatively easy, apart from the crossing of the glacier at the beginning of the trek. It can be completed in six to eight days, although you may want longer to explore higher up the glacier.

There are two ways to start the trek, either via the **Yunz** Valley (see under 'Short Walks around Passu'), or by following the south side of the Batura

Glacier from the KKH to the north of Passu. If taking the latter route it is well worth trying to find transport to drop you off by the Batura Glacier itself. Both ways lead to the shepherds' hut at **Yunzbin**, where you can camp. From here the main route crosses to the north side of the Batura Glacier, although it is possible to continue along the south side as far as **Kirgas Washik** and then cross near there. The exact route across the glacier from Yunzbin changes each year and is marked by small stone cairns set up by the locals at the beginning of the season. A guide is recommended for the crossing unless you have experience of glaciers; the most difficult part is getting off the glacier again from its northern edge. Once off the glacier, the path climbs through a series of lightly wooded ablation valleys to **Yashpirt**, the main summer settlement for the people of Passu. There are spectacular views from here of the glacier and surrounding mountains; it is also a beautiful place to spend a day or two exploring. The path continues up through the summer pastures and settlements of **Fatmahil**, **Kukhil** and **Shelmin** to **Gutshim**, the last summer settlement. All of these are good for camping. Higher up at the pasture of **Lupdor**, the ablation valley ends and the only way to continue further is on the glacier. The return journey is back along the same route.

Routes Beyond Passu the KKH crosses the snout of the **Batura Glacier**, an ever present threat to the road. A bridge crosses the Hunza River here, and a new jeep track proceeds a short distance up the difficult gorge of the **Shimshal Valley** (see below). For those continuing along the KKH, turn to page 571.

Shimshal Valley & Shimshal Pamir

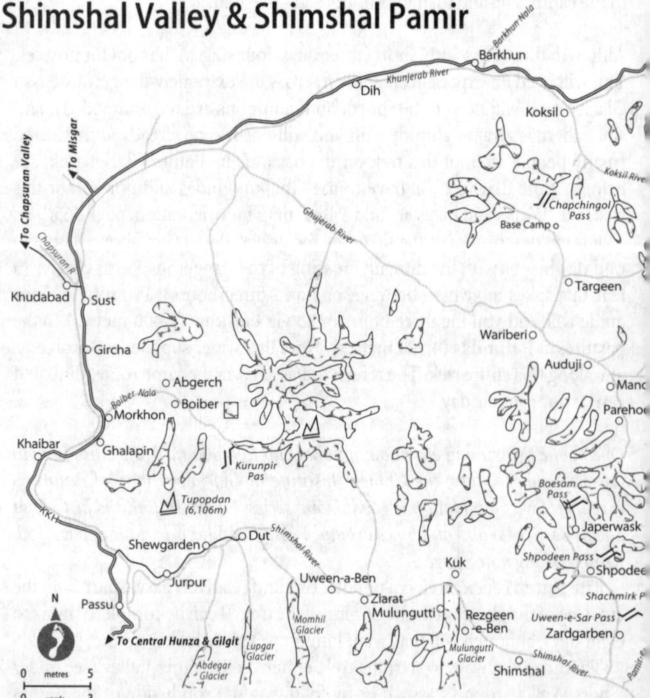

Shimshal Valley

Colour map 5, grid A4

This remote valley was at one time used by the Mirs of Hunza as a penal colony, although its primary usage was as a secret route by which the Hunzakuts could raid the Kashmiri and Ladahki caravans. The area was extensively explored and mapped by the indefatigable Younghusband in 1889. It receives relatively few visitors, which is a shame since the trekking is superb, and the Shimshali guides and porters are amongst the finest specimens of mountain men. Tourism is in its infancy here still, so outsiders should strive hard to leave a good impression.

Passu to the Shimshal Valley

Part of the reason so few outsiders come here is because Shimshal is so difficult to reach. In fact, you have to trek just to get there. For a decade or so the local villages have been constructing a jeep road to link them the 60 kilometres to the KKH, and the outside world. The road is a miracle of engineering, but still only reaches just beyond **Dut** (a distance of some 15 kilometres, or 1¼ hours, from the KKH). Very crowded cargo jeeps run intermittently from Passu to Dut (Rs 7), although if you are carrying all your food and equipment for a trek, you'll probably have to hire a vehicle (Rs 700). If walking, it is two porter stages from Passu to Dut. There are a number of huts at Dut (2,580 metres) where travelling Shimshalis overnight. You can use the communal cooking facilities, though obviously you must clear up after yourself.

Beyond Dut you'll have to walk (three porter stages from Dut to Shimshal). Locals often make it to Shimshal in one long day, though foreigners generally only make it as far as **Ziarat** (2,600 metres) in five to six long hours. A local guide is essential for this trip, not only to assist with the multiple river crossings, but also to alert you to the very real danger of rock-falls. There are some well equipped huts at Ziarat, and it is customary to leave a donation. It's a very long nine hour day from Ziarat to **Shimshal** (2,880 metres), with the route sometimes changing daily. There's at least one tricky glacier crossing, plus several river crossings (if you have porters they may prefer to carry you!).

Sleeping & eating

Your guide generally arranges accommodation (usually with his family), though in 1998 a couple of **F** ***Village Guesthouses*** had opened to compliment the long established **F** ***Disteghil Cottage***. You should really bring all your food supplies with you (preferably from Gilgit). If meals are offered, remember that the high transport costs should be added into the price that you pay.

Treks from Shimshal

Shimshal Pamir trek

'Restricted' zone. Maximum elevation optional (4,420 metres if going all the way to Shewert). July to August. Maps: Swiss Foundation is adequate, though there are several glaring inaccuracies; U502 series, NJ 43-14 Baltit and NJ 43-15 Shimshal likewise. NB Although not officially listed as being in a restricted zone, you are required to take a local guide for all treks from Shimshal village. This was largely the result of a British climber, Peter Thompson, trekking across into China from Shimshal, which led initially to a permanent police post in the village. Shambi Khan, the village headman, subsequently negotiated a deal whereby all foreigners would be accompanied by guides. It may also be neccessary to get a permit from Gilgit; enquire with the DC there. For orientation, see 'Shimshal Valley and Shimshal Pamir' map below. Read trekking notes, page 67.

The trek from Shimshal to Shujerab is a demanding one, crossing three passes, and taking eight days for the return trip. It is also very beautiful. Porters charge for 12 stages for the return trip. The path leads east from the village (entering the Khunjerab National Park) and then crosses to the north bank of the river on a good bridge. Further on it climbs steeply north up the west bank of the **Zardgarbin** Valley before crossing to the east bank and climbing east to an area of pasture with good camping by a large boulder below **Vween-e-Sar Pass** (4,420 metres, also referred to as Zardgarbin Pass or Wyeen Pass). Another route continues up the Zardgarbin River, across the **Boesam Pass** (4,725 metres) and follows the Ghujerab River to rejoin the KKH to the north of Sust (see 'Gujerab Valley trek' below).

The climb over Vween-e-Sar Pass is strenuous and, immediately after the steep and difficult descent from the pass, it climbs once again, zigzagging steeply up the mountainside, to cross the **Shachmirk Pass** (4,160 metres), marked near the summit by a wooden gateway. On the far side there is camping at the foot of the pass at **Targeen** (3,597 metres), near a side river which flows into the Shimshal River from the north. Alternatively, continue for an hour on to **Purien-e-Ben** (3,322 metres). The path then runs along a barren plateau, through an area which was once well wooded, following the Shimshal River to arrive at the shepherds' settlement of **Shujerab** (4,084 metres) with its complex of small stone huts.

From here, the path climbs up to the pastures of **Abdullah Khan Maidan** (4,389 metres). You can now relax and enjoy a wonderfully pleasant stroll through the pastures to the **Shimshal Pass** (4,402 metres), a beautiful open plateau with two lakes. A little further on is the main summer settlement of **Shewert**. Here huge numbers of sheep, goats and yaks are tended by the women of Shimshal, who collect the milk to produce butter and cheese. The spectacle of the animals returning to their night enclosures in the dying light of the sun is a spectacular one. Lovingly referred to by Shimshalis as their "Pamir" (upland grazing area), this area is incredibly beautiful, though extremely harsh as well. The minute the sun drops below the mountains, temperatures fall dramatically. In winter, the yaks are taken to the Shorlik pastures on the Oprang River, while the sheep and goats are brought down to Shimshal.

It is possible to continue southeast from Shewert and then follow the Braldu River south onto the Braldu Glacier and over the Lupke Pass to Snow Lake, joining the Biafo-Hispar Glacier trek. This is an extremely difficult and technical route which should only be attempted by properly equipped, experienced mountaineers and with an experienced guide familiar with the route. The return to Shimshal village is via the same route.

Ghujerab Valley trek

'Restricted' zone. Maximum elevation 4,725 metres. June-September. Maps: Swiss Foundation has many glaring inaccuracies; U502 series, NJ 43-14 Baltit and NJ 43-15 Shimshal likewise. NB Although not officially listed as being in a restricted zone, you are required to take a local guide for all treks from Shimshal village. For orientation, see 'Shimshal Valley and Shimshal Pamir' map on page 568. Read trekking notes, page 67.

This difficult seven day, 12 stage trek should only be attempted by the most experienced and fully equipped trekkers, who are accompanied by a local guide who is well acquainted with the route. There are two high passes to cross, a rushing river to ford, as well as some roped ascents/descents and glacier crossings. That said, it's supposed to be very rewarding! The trek is done from south to north and emerges at Koksil, on the KKH above Sust. You will have to arrange transport in advance to collect you.

Routes

The KKH continues northwards, passing the small settlements of **Khaibar** (Khyber), which offers basic rooms at the **F** ***Khyber Inn***. Beyond this village, the local people are predominantly Wakhi Tajiks, and sometimes refer to this area as 'Upper Gojal'. The next hamlet is **Ghalapin**, before you arrive at **Morkhon** and the adjacent settlement of **Jamalabad** (9 kilometres south of Sust).

Morkhon and the Boiber Valley

The Boiber Valley was probably first settled by Wakhi Tajiks in the 16th century, and was previously the route used by Shimshalis to reach the Hunza River (crossing the 4,873 metres Karun Pir Pass). It is possible to make a longish day hike up the valley to the original settlement of **Abgerch** (3,200 metres, two to three hours) or continue up to **Boiber** (3,505 metres, further one and a half hours). A guide is more or less essential (ask around in Morkhon). For orientation, see 'Shimshal Valley and Shimshal Pamir' map on page 568. It is possible to overnight in Morkhon/Jamalabad at the very basic **F** *Greenlands Hotel.*

Routes

Beyond Morkhon/Jamalabad the KKH continues through the other 'Abgerchi' village of **Gircha** to **Sust**.

Sust

The Pakistani border town of Sust has changed beyond all recognition within the last four to five years. Since the construction of a new Customs and Immigration House two kilometres to the north of the original village, a whole new town has sprung up around it (sometimes referred to as **'Afiyatabad'**). Built entirely to cater for the cross border trade, it is a jumble of hotels, restaurants and shops selling imported/smuggled goods. Most of the services are here (eg booking bus tickets to China, and south towards Gilgit), as well as the more upmarket hotels. Unless you want to pay Rs 50, you'll have to walk between 'Old' and 'New' Sust.

Most visitors spend just one night in Sust, though if you are stuck here longer you could consider walking up to the village of Sust itself (largely hidden from the KKH), or across the river to Khudabad. Alternatively, hire a jeep and take a day trip up the Chapursan Valley to Ziarat (see 'Chapursan Valley trek' below).

Sights

Day trips to the Khunjerab Pass Because transport is so unreliable to/from the pass, and buses passing through are invariably full, this trip is only really feasible if you have your own transport (eg bicycle), or if you hire a vehicle (about Rs 800 for a Suzuki that holds up to eight, Rs 1,000 for a jeep). You have to tell Immigration that you are going, and they generally hold onto your passport until you return. If you are camping the night, bear in mind that it will be very cold, and there is nowhere to get any food. Officially you require a permit, but if you stay away from the Chinese check post on the road, you should be okay. **NB** Do not attempt to by-pass the Chinese check post, or attempt to enter China.

Essentials

Sleeping & eating **'Old' Sust** most of the hotels here have closed down now, although a few are still clinging on. **D** *Khunjerab*, KKH, entrance to Sust, T46213. Reasonable doubles, some with hot water, though rather overpriced. **E** *Hunza Dreamland*, KKH, 2 kilometres south of Sust, T46212. Some reasonable rooms, cheap dorm (**G**), but a little remote.

"Old" Sust & "New" Sust (Afiyatabad)

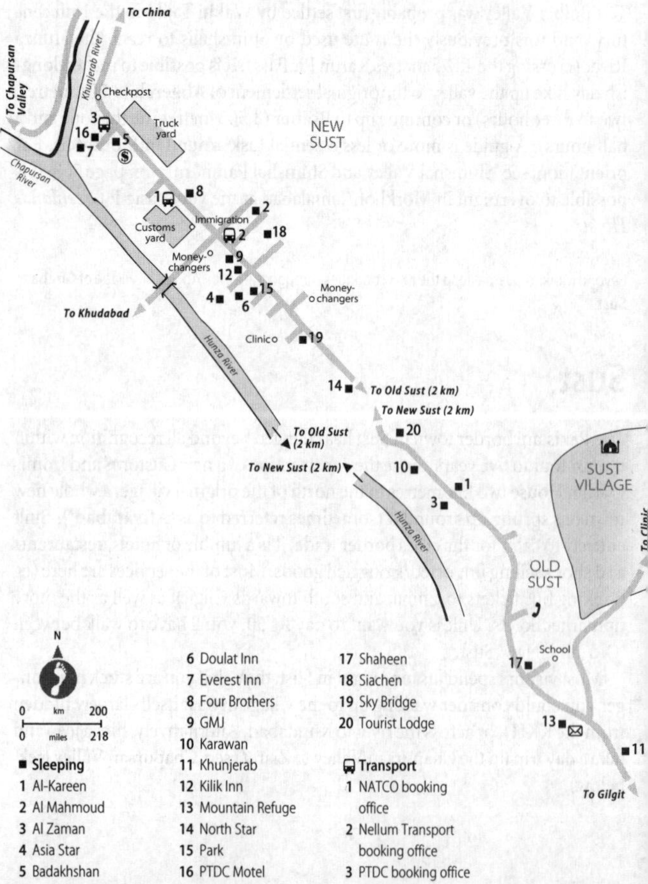

■ *on map*
Price codes:
see inside front cover

E ***Tourist Lodge***. Miserable, overpriced pre-fab tin rooms that are very hot in summer. **E-G** ***Mountain Refuge***, T46219. Long established backpacker favourite, this is probably one of the best deals in town for budget travellers (though the legendary Ibrahim Baig no longer runs it). Some doubles with attached hot bath (**E**), very cheap doubles with attached cold bath (**F**), plus dorm beds (**G**), though you can sometimes pay to have a hot shower. Communal dinner served each night (vegetarian Rs 80, meat Rs 120), the manager can also sell you commission-free tickets to China, and provides free pick-up and drop off at 'New' Sust. Recommended. **F** ***Al Kareem***, ***Al Zaman*** and ***Karawan*** are only worth considering in a real emergency. **F** ***Shaheen*** is very basic, but for some reason a favourite of the Japanese.

'New' Sust (Afiyatabad) Competition, and lack of business, means that many of the prices here have dropped dramatically; just as well since most of these hotels are rather jerry-built (Dave Winter once went from Sust to Kashgar, and by the time he returned 10 days later 2 new hotels had been built!). **B** ***PTDC Motel***, T46240. Best in town, carpeted furnished rooms, modern attached bath (24 hour hot water), although not as luxurious as the price tag suggests, management rather off-hand (more interested in the dish TV), restaurant. **E** ***Al-Mahmoud***. Mainly triples, though rather overpriced, upstairs rooms much airier. **E** ***Asia Star***. Friendly and well run, away from road so marginally quieter, some carpeted furnished rooms with modern attached bath, some cheaper and more basic rooms (still with hot water), cheap 5-bed dorm (**G**), restaurant. Recommended. **E** ***Sky Bridge***, T46225. A very good deal, although cracks in the walls are rather alarming. Large carpeted rooms with modern tiled bath (hot water in mornings), towel and soap provided, balcony views, a 3-bed dorm (**G**), good restaurant, friendly staff. Recommended. **F** ***Badakhshan***. Reasonably clean carpeted rooms, attached bath (some hot), good restaurant (dhal, veg, chappati Rs 60), not bad value. **F** ***Everest Inn***. 10 basic and run down rooms with attached bath, but very cheap, popular with Pakistani traders. **F** ***Four Brothers***. Fairly basic rooms, pay Rs 50 more for carpet and Rs 100 more for hot water, restaurant popular with local men. We can't really recommend the basic **F** ***Doulat Inn***, ***GMJ***, ***Kilik Inn*** , ***Park*** or ***Siachen***. ***North Star*** is still under construction.

Transport

NATCO bus to **Gilgit** (Rs 100, 6½ hours) via **Passu** (Rs 30, 1 hour), **Gulmit** (Rs 36, 1½ hours), **Ganesh** (for **Karimabad**, Rs 50, 2½ hours) and **Pisin** (for **Minapin**) leaves promptly from the *NATCO* office at 0500 Monday-Saturday. ***Nellum Transport***, in a yard next to the *Al-Mahmoud Hotel* in 'New' Sust, have minibuses that 'depart when full' to **Gilgit** (Rs 100, 6 hours) via **Ganesh** (for **Karimabad**, Rs 50) from 0400-1600 daily. Note that if you want to get off at **Passu** or **Gulmit** you'll have to pay the Ganesh fare at least. For details of transport options to China, see 'box'.

Directory

Banks *National Bank of Pakistan* offers poor rates on cash and TCs, and is usually closed when you need to use it (open Mon-Thur 0900-1330 1430-1700, Fri 0900-1300 1500-1700, Sat 0900-1330, Sun closed). There are money changers opposite Immigration office and opposite *Park Hotel* that offer better rates, keep longer hours, and also deal in Chinese currency. **Communications** **Post Office:** is next to the *Mountain Refuge* in 'Old' Sust. The PCO in 'Old' Sust claims to offer international calls, but I've never been successful. **Hospitals & medical services** **Hospitals:** there is a clinic in 'Old' Sust village itself, or try Dr Sher Baz's clinic (0800-0930 1700-1930) near the *Sky Bridge Hotel*.

Crossing the border between Pakistan and China

Leaving Pakistan

It can take several hours for the entire bus to clear Pakistani customs when leaving the country, although Westerners' luggage is rarely checked in any detail. **NB** Do not attempt to smuggle illegal drugs into China – the penalties

Transport options to China

There are several options for travel on to ***Tashkurgan*** *in China, from where you change transport and buy onward tickets to* ***Kashgar****. Whichever option you choose, book as early as possible in order to get a better seat. Note that the devaluation in the price of the Rupee, the change in rules vis-a-vis foreign currency accounts, and the difficulty that Pakistanis now experience in getting Chinese visas, means there are fewer and fewer Pakistani traders heading up to Kashgar. Thus, if you plan to head up to China on one of the days when fewer visitors go (eg Saturday, Sunday, Monday, as opposed to Wednesday, Thursday, Friday when people are aiming to catch the Sunday Market), there may be insufficient people for NATCO to justify sending a vehicle (the minimum is 6).*

The border is officially open from 1st May until mid/late November, although these dates are weather dependent. Chinese and Pakistani traders, as well as the postal service, continue to cross outside these dates, though we've yet to meet any foreign tourists who have been allowed to make the trip.

NATCO *send a combination of coaches, coasters and landcruisers on a daily basis, depending upon demand. All cost the same price, at the time of going to press Rs 1,050 (though bear in mind that this fare tends to go up 15 percent per year). However, before requesting a seat in the land cruiser, note that a vehicle that in the 'West' that would hold 4-5 passengers plus luggage, here holds 10 passengers plus luggage. Avoid at all costs the inwards facing seats in the luggage area, or the 2 middle seats in the second row. Only sit in the front if you know (or want to get to know) the other passenger very well. NATCO vehicles leave at 0830, drive into the Customs and Immigration yard, and then take anything between 15 minutes and 3 hours to complete these formalities. The actual journey time from Sust to Tashkurgan is about 6 hours (if road conditions are OK), though you should note the time zone change (see below).*

PTDC *also run coasters to Tashkurgan from their booking office at the PTDC Motel. The fare is currently Rs 1,050, and though this is the most comfortable way of making the trip, if they have less than 8 passengers you will just be shunted onto a NATCO vehicle. PTDC vehicles leave at 0830, but have to undergo the same Customs and Immigration formalities.*

are severe. Make sure you get an exit stamp from Pakistani Immigration, otherwise you will not be able to enter China (Chinese officials will check for an exit stamp at the various check posts en route to Tashkurgan). **NB It is not possible to get a Chinese visa on the border**. Almost all nationalities need a visa for China. The nearest Chinese embassy is in Islamabad. It is not possible to bring private vehicles into China, unless arranged in advance (and this can take months). The Chinese officials are so used to seeing cyclists pedalling this route, they no longer attempt to force them onto buses. However, please note that on the visa application form at the Chinese embassy in London, for example, it specifically states that it is not permitted to take bicycles into China. Details of Chinese entry/exit formalities at the border post at Tashkurgan are discussed on page 578.

Arriving in Pakistan If you have a visa before arriving at the border post, your crossing will be a much smoother operation. Unfortunately, the immigration post at Sust enjoys a fair deal of autonomy, and rules that apply to visa requirements elsewhere in Pakistan are at the whim of the immigration official on duty here. For example, according to the Pakistan High Commission in London, holders of a British passport do not require a visa for Pakistan if staying for less than 30 days. However, they choose to ignore this rule in Sust, and if you arrive without a visa (whatever your nationality) you will be told that it is a "big problem". You may be asked why you didn't get a visa in advance (try saying that you didn't intend coming, but everybody in Kashgar said how wonderful the Pakistani people are, so you just had to see for yourself!). Persistence pays off, and eventually you will be given a piece of paper authorising you to enter and stay for up to seven days. If you wish to remain longer, you will have to go to Islamabad within the seven day period and extend the visa there (see Islamabad section). Women arriving at the border without a visa seem to have to endure more hassle than men. This is a real pain in the arse when the country is trying to promote tourism (after the nuclear tests in 1998, the government actually temporarily did away with visa requirements for most nationalities in an attempt to attract visitors, yet the immigration staff at Sust denied all knowledge of this directive).

Also, the immigration officers never seem to have, or voluntarily offer, this mysterious Form 'C' that some nationalities used to require. On the positive side, customs checks for arriving foreigners are usually only cursory and very quick.

Therefore, to conclude, it is possible for most nationals of Western countries to get a seven day transit visa on arrival, although it will save hassle if you get a visa beforehand. **NB** Currently, you cannot get a Pakistani visa in Kashgar, and the only Pakistani embassy in China is in Beijing (though they often only issue one month visas).

Treks in the Sust Region

Chapursan Valley trek

Open zone. Maximum elevation optional (up to 5,160 metres). Early June to late September. Maps: Swiss foundation is reasonable, although place names are inaccurate; U502 series, NJ 43-14 Baltit and Leomann Sheet 1 are as good as useless. For orientation see the 'Chapsuran Valley' map on page 577. Read trekking notes, page 67.

This spectacular three week trek is becoming increasingly popular with the large trekking companies, such as *Karakoram Experience* and *Hindu Kush Trails*, largely because it offers so many variations. The Chapursan Valley is effectively a communications route that runs right along the 'top' of Pakistan, parallel to its borders with China and Afghanistan. It is usually combined with the 'Chilinji Pass trek' (see page 416), which links the Chapursan Valley to the Karambar Valley, thus allowing access via the Yarkhun Valley to Mastuj and Chitral, or via the Darkot Pass into Yasin. It can be attempted from east-west (using Chapursan porters) or from west-east (using Chitrali porters). Those travelling east-west from Sust can hire a jeep to take them as far as **Ziarat** (in fact, it is certainly worthwhile for non-trekkers to hire a jeep for this one day excursion).

Sust to Kashgar

The journey from Sust to Kashgar provides some of the most spectacular and varied scenery along the entire Karakoram Highway route, not least of which is the dramatic change in landscape as you cross the Khunjerab Pass that marks the border between Pakistan and China. There is also a marked cultural change too, giving most visitors their first taste of the magic of Central Asia.

By public transport it is usually two days of hard travelling from Sust to Kashgar (breaking the journey and changing buses in Tashkurgan), though you should really make the time to spend some days at Kara Kuli (lake). Cyclists, on the other hand, usually take the best part of a week to complete the trip.

Sust to Tashkurgan

Colour map 5, grid A4

Routes

There is a check post at the north end of Sust where your exit stamp may be checked. Those making a day trip to the Khunjerab Pass may have to register here (some readers have suggested that the guards here may even assist you in hitching a ride).

The KKH to China travels north, entering a narrow canyon about one kilometre above Sust. Here, the Hunza River is joined from the west by the **Chapsuran Valley** (see page 416 for details of trekking here). A further one kilometre north is a petrol station where most vehicles stop to fill up. A little further along the canyon, a jeep road leads off to the west along a side valley for 17 kilometres to **Misgar** (3,708 metres). An ancient strand of the Silk Road trading route used to run north from Misgar, crossing into Chinese territory by way of either the Mintaka Pass (4,709 metres) or the Killik Pass. These two passes were of great strategic concern to the British who feared a Russian invasion of India in the 19th century, particularly when they received a report in 1874 claiming the Killik Pass to be "remarkably easy of access". However, Lockhart's Mission of 1885 found the pass to be a nightmare, losing two porters through exposure, with all the party suffering from snowblindness, and by 1893 the Pamir Boundary Commission had concluded "we have no reason to fear a Russian advance through the passes" (Keay, 1979). When the KKH was being constructed, the route through the Mintaka Pass was considered, but rejected as lying too close to the Afghan and Soviet borders.

Above the junction of the Chapsuran and Killik valleys, the Hunza River is referred to as the Khunjerab River. The KKH follows this narrow gorge in a northeast direction, before turning north at the Khunjerab River's confluence with the Ghujerab River. The bridge here marks the entrance to the Khunjerab National Park, although you are unlikely to see any of the endangered Marco Polo sheep (*Ovis ammon polii*) that the park is designed to protect. The road here is still a very gentle incline.

Sust to Kashgar Road Profile

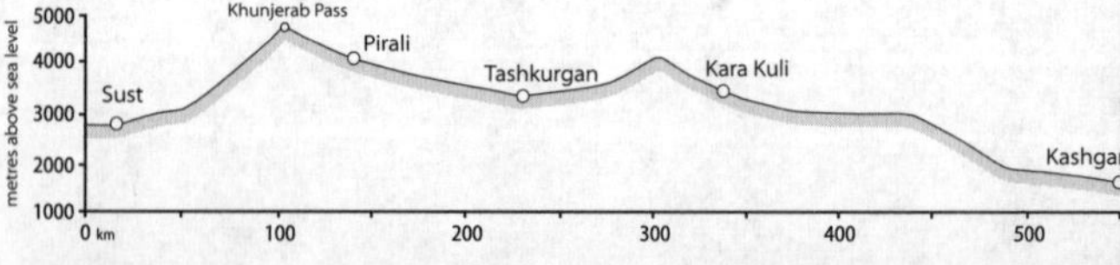

Dih

At the Khunjerab Security Force (KSF) check post of **Dih** (Dhee), 35 kilometres from Sust, Pakistani exit stamps are examined, and foreigners must make an entry of passport details in the book. Those making a day trip to the pass must check-in here too. Cyclists may be permitted to stay at the *Khunjerab Rest House*, or can find plenty of places to bivvy down amongst the road maintenance camps.

Routes

Beyond Dih is a section of road that is particularly susceptible to landslides and flooding. In 1998 a huge landslide dammed the river here, preventing all traffic from passing, and forcing passengers to make a difficult 30 minute detour on foot around the blockage. Local people made a killing, charging $10 a time to carry bags over the difficult terrain. Beyond the slide area the Khunjerab River is joined by the Barkhun Nala at **Barkhun**. There is an 'anti-hunting' check post here, though it is rarely manned. There are some huts here for cyclists to bivvy down in.

The road climbs gently to the check post at **Koksil**, which also has some abandoned work camp buildings. The check post here is rarely manned. The Koksil Valley that heads south here is at the end of the 'Ghujerab Valley trek' from Shimshal (see above). From Koksil to the Khunjerab Pass is 17 kilometres.

After Koksil, the KKH gains altitude rapidly, climbing through a series of 12 tight switchback bends. Some cyclists have pointed out that the descent is harder than the ascent if a head-wind is blowing. Look out for Golden marmots (*Marmota caudata aurea*) along this section of the road. Having climbed significantly, albeit gently, through the series of hairpin bends, the KKH reaches the **Khunjerab Pass** (86 kilometres from Sust). From the Khunjerab Pass to Tashkurgan is a further 125 kilometres.

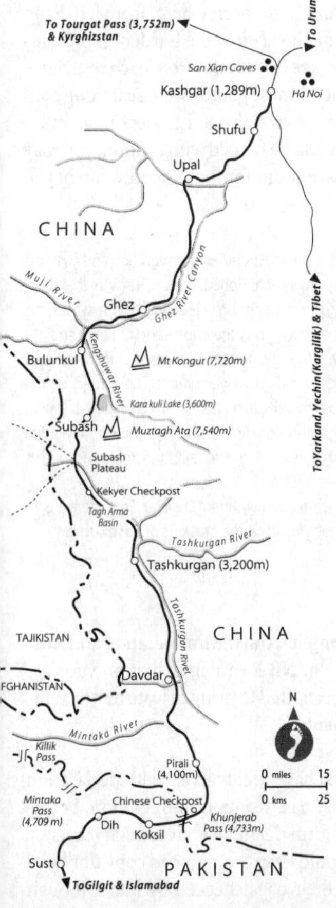

Khunjerab Pass

Although no two sources seem to agree on the exact altitude of the pass (although 4,733 metres is probably the most accurate of a series of estimates that range from 4,602 up to 4,877 metres), it is still thought to represent the highest paved-road international border crossing in the world. Also referred to as Khunjerab Top, the pass is a broad, grassy saddle, flanked on all sides by snowy peaks. How close to the road the snow reaches depends upon the time of year that you cross.

The pass is significant in terms of physical geography in that it marks the continental watershed, (with rivers to the south flowing down towards the Indian Ocean, and rivers to the north flowing into the Tarim basin), as well as a convenient junction between two major mountain chains (the Pamirs and the Karakorams). Further, the physical terrain varies considerably on either side of the pass, with the tight, narrow canyon valleys that have been

Travel tip

*On crossing into China, you move into a different **time-zone**; something that seems to confuse most visitors for the duration of their stay in Xinjiang province. The whole of China runs on Beijing time, which is 3 hours ahead of Pakistan time. However, due to daylight-saving (also known as summer time), from May to September, Beijing time is 4 hours ahead of Pakistan time. The problem is further compounded by the fact that Xinjiang works on an unofficial Xinjiang time, sometimes referred to as 'local time'. In summer this is 2 hours ahead of Pakistan time and 2 hours behind Beijing time (the rest of the year the differences being 1 hour ahead of Pakistan, and 1 hour behind Beijing). Unfortunately, whenever you are quoted departure times for planes, trains and buses in Xinjiang Province, it is never quite specified which time is being used, unless you ask.*

the main feature of the KKH on the last 650 kilometres of its journey through Pakistan, giving way to wide, grassy high altitude plateaux on the Chinese side.

A number of stone markers indicate the international border between the two countries, and it is not unusual for south bound Pakistani traders returning from Kashgar to hop off the bus in order to piss on the Chinese side, before entering Pakistan. Bus drivers make a dramatic swerve here, from left-hand drive Pakistan to right-hand drive China. Just below the border on the Chinese side is a small Chinese check post where exit stamps from each respective country are checked, though in 1998 the Chinese guards were searching bags thoroughly and stealing desirable items from Pakistani traders (cigarettes, tapes etc). Accepting hospitality here should be treated with caution; you may subsequently be charged an outrageous amount for that 'friendly cup of tea' that you have been given.

Routes A further 30 kilometres on is **Pirali** (4,100 metres), the former Chinese immigration and customs post, but now just an 'animal disinfection' post. It is largely abandoned, and cyclists note that there is too much broken glass around to make bivvying down an option. A jeep road to the west leads off to the Killik and Mintaka Passes. Beyond Pirali the KKH gives the impression of being straight and flat, although at speed it is remarkably bumpy. In fact, the deterioration in the state of the road on the Chinese side compared to the Pakistani side is immediately apparent. The scenery on the road is a mixture of green pastureland, being grazed by yaks, dzou (a yak/cow crossbreed), cattle, sheep and goats, followed by long stretches of high altitude sandy desert. Twin-humped Bactrian camels are a common sight, as are the spectacularly dressed nomadic Tajik horsemen. The route is lined by the distant Pamirs.

Several hours beyond Pirali is the relatively large Tajik settlement of **Davdar**. From here it is 77 kilometres to the Chinese Customs and Immigration House on the outskirts of **Tashkurgan**

Chinese entry/exit formalities

Chinese entry and exit formalities are completed at the Immigration and Customs House one kilometre south of town. **NB** Please note that no visas are granted upon arrival, and that it is not permitted to bring private motor vehicles into China without prior arrangement.

Arriving in China For those arriving in China, you will first have to fill out a health declaration form, and then a landing card. You then pass through Immigration, before having to fill out a customs declaration form detailing your foreign currency and expensive consumer items. You should keep the stamped copy until you depart China. Westerners rarely have their bags checked by hand, though their luggage will have to pass through a suspiciously high dosage looking X-ray machine (discreetly put all your film in your pockets). Some readers have written to say that if you're delayed en route from Sust, the immigration post may be shut when you arrive. Your bus (and luggage) plus passports may be impounded until next day. By the time the immigration post opens next day, the Kashgar bus may have gone. You then have the option of staying in Tashkurgan, or hiring a land cruiser to Kashgar (¥1,000).

Beyond Customs and Immigration is a **Bank of China** counter, changing cash and travellers' cheques at the market rate. Outside the Customs House is a Uigyur run bank, though it is not always open. As you leave the Customs House, there is sometimes a (reasonably comfortable) bus waiting for people who want to continue directly on to Kashgar. The fare depends upon the number of passengers wanting to make the trip. The official fare to Kashgar is ¥77, though if there are less than 15 you will be asked for ¥120-130. This fare appears to be negotiable, with the bus company staff presumably pocketing the difference. Don't be afraid to haggle hard. For details of onward transport, see under 'Tashkurgan-Transport' below. The bus waiting outside the Customs House will give you a lift into Tashkurgan, or you can walk the one kilometre.

Leaving China

The exit formalities rather depend upon where you boarded the bus. If you boarded the Pakistan bound bus in Kashgar, and the passenger manifest (list) matches the passports of those on board, you can clear Customs and Immigration fairly quickly. If, however, any passengers have been picked up en route, or at Tashkurgan, the process of putting them on the passenger manifest can delay your departure for hours. You may still have to take all your luggage off the roof and put it through the X-ray machine, even though it should have been 'cleared' at customs in Kashgar.

If you are unable to get a place on a Pakistan bound bus in Tashkurgan, it may be worth walking out to the Customs Hall and trying to arrange transport from there. The *NATCO* landcruisers and buses generally return to Pakistan empty, although they are not allowed to take passengers unless the uncooperative Chinese Immigration officials give their permission. You are not generally allowed through Immigration unless you have south bound transport arranged.

Exchange rates

The Chinese unit of currency is the Yuan (¥), sometimes referred to in the slang term as Kwai (like the English 'quid' or American 'buck'), though officially titled *renminbi* (RMB, or 'people's money'). The two currency system, with RMB for locals and FEC for foreigners, has now been abandoned, although the policy of charging foreigners double, treble, quadruple and beyond for goods and services has been retained (in Xinjiang at least). Banks in the major cities (including Kashgar) change travellers' cheques, generally with small commission charges. In late 1998, the approximate exchange rates for cash were as follows: £1 = ¥13.07; $1 = ¥8.07. Note that you get slightly better rates for travellers' cheques.

Tashkurgan

For a town that everyone has to stop in, Tashkurgan (around 3,200 metres) has remarkably little to offer besides some over-priced hotels and rip-off restaurants. Capital of the Tajik Autonomous County, within the Xinjiang Uiygur Autonomous Region of the People's Republic of China, Tashkurgan is a town of around 6,000 predominantly Tajik people, although there are representations of other minorities such as Uiygurs, Kyrghiz, Uzbeks and of course, Han Chinese.The town has a long history and is said to have been mentioned in the second century AD by Ptolemy. The word Tashkurgan means 'Stone Tower' or 'Stone City', although the town, little more than one main street, hardly lives up to the billing given to it under this title by the Chinese tourism department. Its one attraction is the ancient crumbling **fortress**, mentioned by the Chinese traveller Hieun Tsang when he passed through 13 centuries ago. Much of the outer walls and battlements are intact, and the views of the surrounding plains are good, but it is hardly worth paying the ¥5 to go inside and look at a pile of rubble.

Sleeping
■ *on map*
Price codes:
see inside front cover

Travelling between Pakistan and Kashgar you will almost certainly have to spend a night in Tashkurgan. This means experiencing some of the most disgusting hotels in China (and there's quite some competition). ***Traffic Hotel (Jiaotong Binguan)*** is where the bus drops off most passengers. In the 1996 edition I suggested that this was the worst hotel in the world, with indifferent staff (telling you the place was 'full' when you knew they had at least 200 empty beds), no water in the taps and plumbing but plenty on the hall floor, and disgusting shit-filled toilets. We then received a number of letters saying "not bad ... staff friendly and reasonably efficient ... helpful manager ... speaks good English ... nice double on top floor with attached cold bath ... floor girls bring hot water". In 1998 I found the staff friendly but inefficient (more interested in watching TV, and if only 2 people were staying in the entire hotel they would still put them both in the same room), the linen looked clean but the smell suggested it hadn't been changed for a long time, and although the hallway wasn't flooded when I arrived, it was when I left since my toilet decided to leak all night! A 4-bed dorm is ¥15 per bed with a disgusting shared toilet and no showers, or a double room with a dirty attached hot shower and toilet and TV is ¥50 per bed. ***Ice Mountain Hotel*** has doubles for ¥25 per bed, triples for ¥20 per bed, and quads for ¥10 per bed. Although this Pakistani run hotel is very friendly, the shared toilets are a disgrace and there are no showers. It has a good 'rumour' book that may be of use to cyclists. ***Pamir Hotel*** is used

Tashkurgan

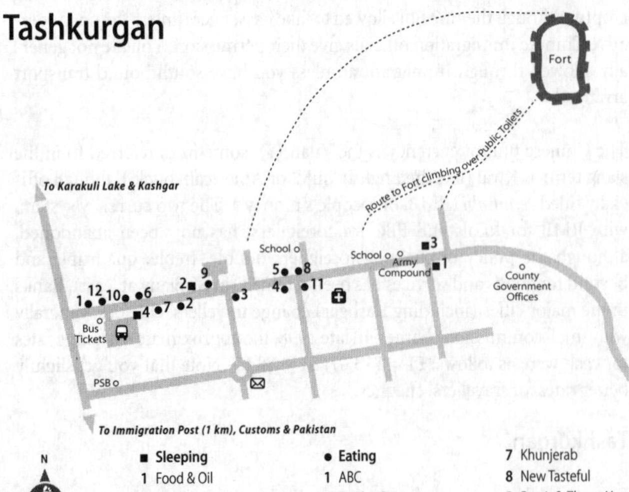

■ **Sleeping**
1 Food & Oil
2 Ice Mountain
3 Pamir
4 Traffic

● **Eating**
1 ABC
2 Border City
3 Flying Dragon
4 Happiness
5 Huanche
6 Huili Comprehensive Shop
7 Khunjerab
8 New Tasteful
9 Pamir & Zhong Yuan & Yiyin
10 'Tajik' Place
11 UBLZC House
12 Un-named places

mainly by tour groups. It has reasonable doubles with attached bath (hot water mornings and evenings) and TV for ¥200, triples with attached cold bath for ¥100, or 4-bed dorms with unappealing shared toilet and no shower facilities for ¥15 per bed. The superbly named ***Hotel of Tashkurgan Food and Oil Trade Corporation*** is not interested in foreigners.

Eating
● *on map*

This is a town where you have to agree the price of everything before you order – you may even find that your second beer costs more than the first. This is not really the place to go out to eat in a big group. We have had letters suggesting that the restaurant opposite the *Traffic Hotel* is not recommended ("bill triple agreed price ... held hostage until bill paid"), and that the ***Flying Dragon*** is a "complete rip-off", although it is difficult to identify individual restaurants since few have English signs. Likewise, some suggest that the ***Huanche*** is a rip-off, whilst others have written to say that it is "good and honest". The Tajik place opposite the *Traffic Hotel* does a good plate of noodles and vegetables for ¥7, and beer for ¥5, whilst the ***Ublzc House*** looks OK. The restaurant at the ***Pamir Hotel*** has plates of fish for ¥20, chicken for ¥20 and vegetables for ¥9.

The best advice is to choose what you want by going into the kitchen, then making very clear what the price is to be. The way the meat is stored (wrapped in a cloth and hung from a tree in the street) may persuade you to become vegetarian whilst in Tashkurgan. Early morning there are stalls outside the *Traffic Hotel* selling overpriced bread, biscuits, sweets and bottled water. Note that food stops en route to Kashgar and Pakistan are extremely limited.

Transport

Those travelling to **Kashgar** may be able to continue straight on from Tashkurgan without over-nighting here (see under 'Entry formalities' above). It is worth asking the bus staff at the Customs Hall if you can buy an onward ticket for the following day straight away. Otherwise, the ticket office (located just inside the entrance gate to the *Traffic Hotel*) opens at 0600 'local time' (0800 Beijing time) and the bus departs at 0700 'local time' (0900 Beijing time). The fare to **Kashgar** for foreigners is ¥77, or ¥40 to **Kara Kuli** (for further details about transport connections to/from Kara Kuli, see page 582). Even though the ticket states that you are allowed one piece of luggage up to 10 kilos, you may be asked an additional ¥5 per piece of roof luggage. Arguing about this can delay the bus departure indefinitely. The journey time to Kashgar is about 7 hours, and the bus is invariably a real bone-shaker. Note that there are no real meal stops on this trip until Upal, just 1 hour short of Kashgar. This route is at its busiest on Thursday, Friday and Saturday.

There are 2 options for heading south to **Sust** in Pakistan. The 'international' through-bus from Kashgar overnights at the *Traffic Hotel*, and leaves for **Sust** at 0800 'local time' (1000 Beijing time) the next morning. Spare seats are sold on a standby basis from the ticket office at the *Traffic Hotel*, though you will have to pay the full ¥220 fare even if you don't get a proper seat. Sometimes, if there is the demand, there is a second bus to **Sust** that originates in Tashkurgan (¥220, 8 hours excluding immigration delays). There are no food stops en route to Pakistan.

Tashkurgan to Kashgar

Improvements on the road north to Kashgar (285 kilometres) mean that the journey generally only takes seven to eight hours, although there is one point in particular where you may be delayed by landslides. The scenery, however, is amongst the most spectacular anywhere in the world.

Routes

Heading north from Tashkurgan, the KKH passes for 20 kilometres through a flat basin before entering a narrow canyon. It emerges on the other side into the marshy pasture of the **Tagh Arma**

Basin. Some 35 kilometres from Tashkurgan is the largish Kyrghiz settlement of **Kekyor**, although the check post here is not usually functioning. The road then climbs in a barely discernible way up to the **Subash Plateau** (although cyclists pedalling into a head-wind may dispute this statement).

Muztagh Ata To the west, tantalisingly close, the Pamirs mark the boundaries with the Wakhan Corridor of Afghanistan, and of Tajikistan. A number of jeep roads lead west towards passes that thread their way through these mountains into the two states, although at the time of writing they are off-limits to tourists. To the east, the spectacular 7,540 metres **Muztagh Ata** (Father of Ice Mountain) comes into view. Possibly the most attractive peak in the entire Pamir range, Muztagh Ata was first mapped in 1886 by the British explorer Ney Elias, although the name he gave it, Mount Dufferin, did not stick. The geological age of the Pamirs (considerably older than its Himalayan and Karakoram neighbours), accounts for the rounding of the peaks, with Muztagh Ata being no exception. The mountain is popular with 'ultimate skiing' enthusiasts, and a great source of revenue for the Chinese government, although this commercial exploitation does not sit well with the local Kyrghiz who revere the holy spirits that are said to live on the summit.

Routes Having reached the top of the plateau (about 1¾ hours from Tashkurgan by bus), the KKH descends steeply through a series of long zig zag bends. Upon reaching the basin floor, you are greeted by the endearing sight of numerous Kyrghiz summer settlements set amongst their grazing herds of yaks. The main settlement here is **Subash**. The KKH continues along a fairly flat road to **Kara Kuli** (about 2 hours from Tashkurgan).

Kara Kuli

Sitting below **Muztagh Ata**, and flanked by 7,720 metres **Mount Kongur** to the northeast, is the beautiful Kara Kuli. Without doubt, this is one of the most stunning places on the entire length of the Karakoram Highway, as the dark, deep waters of the lake reflect the giant peaks that flank two sides. It is a photographer's dream, with the local Kyrghiz population being as photogenic as the remarkable scenery.

It is a good five hour walk around the lake, with the soggy marsh terrain to the southeast of the lake adding time to the journey. Another popular walk is north along the KKH, to two other smaller lakes (Besekh Kul and Shor Kul), and a friendly Kyrghiz village. Donkey, horse and camel rides are also available at the lake. At 3,600 metres, you may well feel the effects of the altitude, particularly if you have come from Kashgar, and it is essential to wear plenty of sunblock. The blistered and weather beaten features of the local children will serve as a painful reminder. The kids here don't beg for pens or money, but moisturiser. The weather is very changeable, and you should prepare for all eventualities if going on a long walk. It gets very cold at night, although the yurts are provided with thick duvets.

An 'Alien Travel Permit' is no longer officially needed for Kara Kuli, although the Public Security Bureau (PSB) in Kashgar or Tashkugan will sell you one if you ask! Treks that lead you any real distance away from the lake, however, are another matter, and enquiries should be made with the PSB in advance.

NB The lake is called a variety of names along the 'Kara Kuli' theme ('Kara Kul' is Uighur for 'black lake', or 'Kalakuli Hu' in Chinese), although we refer to it here as 'Kara Kuli' (or 'little' Karakul Lake) in order to distinguish it from the more famous Kara Kul in Tajikistan.

Sleeping & eating

One of the attractions of Kara Kuli is the opportunity to stay in a traditional Kyrghiz **yurt**, or circular nomad's tent. The Chinese have recognized this desire, and the cost of accommodation has spiralled in recent years. It now costs ¥40-50 per person per night for a place in a yurt, and they are not adverse to trying to crowd everyone into the same tent. Independent travellers may be able to negotiate a better deal – at these prices it is worth trying. An alternative is to walk a couple of hundred metres north of the main settlement, where an enterprising Kyrghiz rents out space in his family yurt for ¥10-15 per person. It can get crowded, along with his wife and kids, although it's great fun. He may be able to offer basic meals. Note that if he gets too popular, he gets hassle from the Chinese running the 'official' site. The only washing facilities at Kara Kuli are in the lake itself, and the public toilets are very unappealing (a new mountain called "Poo Feng", who's approach is said to be "difficult", is beginning to compete in size with Muztagh Ata and Mount Kongur – it's the pile of shit in the men's toilet!).

The restaurant offers reasonable portions of tasty food, and service with a scowl, although the prices are astronomical (¥20-25 for a main dish, ¥5 for rice). If you arrive at Kara Kuli with your own tent, and are self-sufficient in food, you'll have a great time here. Nevertheless, do not let the cost of sleeping and eating put you off coming to this great place.

Transport

Northbound The 0600 'local time' (0800 Beijing time) bus from Tashkurgan to Kashgar will drop passengers off at Kara Kuli (¥40, 2 hours). Continuing north to **Kashgar**, you will have to stand by the road and flag this bus down (presuming it has seats). It passes through at about 0800 'local time' (1000 Beijing time) and the fare is ¥43 (or whatever figure comes into the driver's head). It is 5-6 hours to Kashgar.
Southbound From Kashgar to Tashkurgan, the 'international' through bus to Pakistan leaves Kashgar at around 0930 'local time' (1130 Beijing time), passing through Kara Kuli about 5-6 hours later (fare ¥43). Alternatively, a 'local' bus leaves Kashgar long distance bus station for Tashkurgan at 0700 'local time' (0900 Beijing time), passing through Kara Kuli around 5-6 hours later (fare ¥40). Continuing south to **Tashkurgan** (2 hours, ¥40) you will have to stand by the road and flag down either of these buses. If you are travelling up from Pakistan to Kashgar, and are then returning back to Pakistan, it is best to save your stop-off at Kara Kuli until the return leg since it is easier to flag down buses with spare seats.

Routes

North of Kara Kuli the KKH makes a number of steady climbs and descents, before leaving the pastures of the plateau and descending into the southern reaches of the rocky canyon of the **Ghez River** (sometimes referred to as Tiger's Mouth Gorge). The road here is rough in parts, and subject to rockfalls and landslides. A sign here advertises the *Gonger Ice Peak Hotel* and *Hot Room Sanitorium* but this development is little more than a sign.

Following a long switchback descent, the KKH arrives at the small Kyrghiz settlement of **Bulunkul**, about one hour north of Kara Kuli. Passports are examined at the police check post, whilst photogenic young children sell cold drinks and snacks, including delicious parathas stuffed with spicy fried vegetable (¥2, though this may be too much), although you have to be quick because the bus doesn't stop for long. Pakistani traders claim that the boiled eggs here should be avoided at all costs (as should the toilets!).

The road through the canyon is very rough, although the views are endearing. The enclosing mountains are highly folded, with stratas of multicoloured sandstone providing a dramatic impression. Some of the deep burgundy reds are particularly striking.

After 70 kilometres or so (and 3 hours), the KKH begins to emerge from the north end of the Ghez Canyon. There is a military check post at **Ghez**, at the north end of the canyon, though passports are not checked. The restaurants here do not appear to be open, and the bus does not generally stop anyway.

The KKH finally leaves the canyon and continues for the last 80 kilometres (1½ hours) to Kashgar along a wide, flat plain. Trees line the road that effectively links a chain of smaller oases to the major city of the region. Frustratingly, the bus always seems to stop for a meal break at **Upal**, just 1 hour short of **Kashgar** (even if you're heading south bound).

Kashgar

Phone code: 0998

The oasis city of Kashgar (1,289 metres) has been strategically important for the last 2,000 years. Lying on the ancient trans-Asian trading route, later dubbed the Silk Road, the list of visitors and conquerors is long and varied. Today, the city of Kashgar remains a major Central Asian market town, but has also developed into a thriving tourist attraction. Despite what you may read in other publications, Kashgar is very much on the tourist trail. It has, however, managed to retain some of its original character, and its prime attraction, the weekly Sunday Market, remains a spectacular sight.

Ins and outs

Getting there Kashgar's airport is located about 12 kilometres northeast of the town. Shuttle buses meet incoming flights and take passengers to the CAAC offices in town (¥10). Alternatively, taxis charge about ¥30. Those arriving by bus from Urumqi, Yarkhand, Khotan and Artush are likely to be dropped at the long distance bus station on Tiannan Road. Those arriving from Pakistan, Tashkurgan and Kara Kuli may be dropped in any one of three places. 'International' buses from Tashkurgan currently drop passengers at the *Chini Bagh Hotel*, although a new 'international' bus station is under construction on Jeifang Bei Lu (see map). 'Local' buses from Tashkurgan (via Kara Kuli) usually drop passengers at the long distance bus station, although some terminate in a small yard some 1½ kilometres short of Kashgar (see map).

Getting around The local bus services around town are very crowded and pretty much inpenetrable to short term visitors. The formerly ubiquitous donkey-cart taxis have largely disappeared (much to the disappointment of visiting tourists), as have the motorcycle-sidecar combination taxis (much to the disappointment of visiting *George and Mildred* fans). Fume-belching motor-rickshaws and numerous red taxis (some driven by women) now prowl the streets. Agree the fare in advance (*Seman Hotel* to long distance bus station, ¥10 maximum). A very pleasant way to get around is by bicycle (see 'Local Transport' below), though do not cycle to the Sunday Market (it's too crowded).

History

Early history By the first century AD, the **Han Chinese** had grabbed control of Kashgar, following the extension of the Great Wall westwards, and the construction of a chain of beacons that warned of attack by marauding raiders. However, following the collapse of the Han Dynasty in the third century, Kashgar was sacked by the Huns and a great period of instability ensued. It wasn't until the end of the seventh century that the **Tang Dynasty** reimposed Chinese rule in the region, although they were to be defeated by an alliance of Western Turks and Arabs in 752 AD. The **Arabs** had the upper hand in this one-sided alliance, and subsequently Islam became the dominant religion in the region.

In 1219 the city fell to the great Mongol ruler **Genghis Khan**, as he established an empire that stretched from Asia to eastern Europe. Ironically, the fear generated by the Mongol Horde brought great stability to the whole region, and trade along the Silk Road flourished. In 1265 **Marco Polo** visited Kashgar, and registered his comments on the city.

As the power of the Mongol empire waned towards the end of the 14th century, the city was sacked by **Tamerlane**. However, his death in 1405 marked the beginning of another era of instability that was to last almost 350 years.

Middle history

In the middle of the 18th century, the Manchu Dynasty of the **Ching** returned to the Tarim Basin, ending the isolation from China that was imposed by the insular Ming Dynasty. The Ching rule over the region was tenuous however, and in 1865 the Turkic leader **Yakub Beg** crossed the Pamirs, and having seized control of 'Kashgaria', declared it independent.

In 1868 the first British visitor, a tea planter cum adventurer named Robert Shaw, arrived in Kashgar, followed closely behind by George Hayward (see page 496). Although they were held under virtual house arrest for three months by Yakub Beg, they fared better than the earlier European traveller Adolf Schlaginweit, who in 1857, was tortured and beheaded in the main bazaar.

The Great Game

In the era that followed, Kashgar became the furthest extension of the rival British and Russian empires, acting as a listening post in the great game of imperial rivalry. A British mission headed by Sir Douglas Forsyth, and including John Biddulph, had been received at Kashgar in 1873 by Yakub Beg. However, in 1877 the Ching army put down Yakub Beg's rebellion, and Kashgar was incorporated within the Xinjiang ('New Frontier') Province of China. As a snub to the British for their dealings with Yakub Beg, in 1882 the Chings allowed the Russians to open a Consulate in the city, not sanctioning a British presence there until eight years later.

The first British representative was the 24 year old **George Macartney**, who was to remain in Kashgar for the next 28 years. A shrewd tactician and 'Great Game' player, Macartney is remembered as one of the most extraordinary characters from the latter era of Kashgar's history. In 1898 he returned from brief home leave with a young wife, **Catherine Theodora Borland**, and so began the dramatic transformation of the consulate building, the Chini Bagh (Chinese garden), into a little island of Britain in the heart of Central Asia. Catherine was later to write a book, *An English Lady in Chinese Turkestan*, detailing such exploits as culinary disasters with soggy Christmas puddings.

In 1908 the Chinese finally recognized the British representative in Kashgar as a Consul, although within three years the Manchu government had fallen and China was declared a republic. In the resulting upheaval, the Manchu appointed ruler, the Taotai, was subsequently murdered, and Kashgar threatened to descend into another period of savagery. Order was only restored at the intervention of Russian troops.

As the 1917 Russian Revolution spread slowly eastwards towards Kashgar, the Russian Consulate there remained briefly as a refuge for White Russians. By 1924, however, the Bolsheviks had taken over. Kashgar, in the meantime, continued to be ruled from Urumqi by Governor Yang until his assassination at a banquet in 1928. In the resulting bloody conflict between the Han Chinese and the **Tungans** (Chinese Muslims), Kashgar was briefly captured in 1934 by the Tungans, although they were soon driven out by a local warlord backed by the Soviets.

The warlord, **General Sheng Shih-tsai**, appointed himself as Governor of Xinjiang, and ruled until 1944 when he was pensioned off by the Chinese.

Recent history

Following Indian independence, and the creation of Pakistan, the last British Consul-General, Eric Shipton, left Kashgar. Within a year **Mao Zedong** had declared the foundation of the People's Republic of China and a major modernization of Kashgar began. Much of the old city, including the 500 year old city walls, have been bulldozed to make way for uninspiring concrete blocks, although a few pockets remain. In recent years there have been reports of

Uiygur uprisings in Kashgar, although news of such incidents is suppressed. A building opposite the *Seman Hotel* was supposedly blown up, although it has since been rebuilt, but foreigners who hang around there asking questions and taking photos seem to end up down at the PSB answering questions themselves.

The people Like the rest of Xinjiang Province, Kashgar is predominantly populated by **Uiygurs** (pronounced 'Weegur'), a Turkic Muslim race thought to have arrived in the area around 700 years ago. There are significant numbers of minority groups in Kashgar, including Tajiks, Kyrghiz, Uzbeks, Kazakhs and of course ever expanding numbers of Han Chinese. Although Mandarin Chinese is the official language, Uiygur (written using the Arabic script) is the most widely used in the bazaar. It is not unusual to meet Pakistani traders who are well versed in both languages.

Sights

Sunday Market Without any doubt Kashgar's prime attraction is the weekly Sunday Market, and the city seems to fill with tourists in the days leading up to the event, and empty shortly afterwards. No doubt some will claim that the market is "too touristy", but the sheer scale of it, particularly the livestock market, still seems able to accommodate the number of visitors. **NB** The volume of tourists is considerably lower outside the May-October period when the Khunjerab Pass route to Pakistan is closed.

The main market grounds are within a walled area to the east of the old town, but on a Sunday the entire surrounding area is one enormous donkey-cart and pedestrian traffic jam. Along a side road, just to the west of the main market, is the most fascinating part of the whole spectacle – the livestock enclosure. Throughout the morning, from 0600 onwards, the enclosure gradually fills with sheep, goats, donkeys, horses, bullocks, cows, buyers, sellers, hangers-on, sightseers and tourists (in my four visits I've never seen a camel, though some readers have written in to say that they have), until there's no more open space bar the run where men test-drive the animals. It truly is a photographer's dream, with a sea of fascinating faces, and a superb collection of old bearded men. The livestock deals are so important, and the negotiators so intent upon their bargaining, that they hardly seem to register the presence of several hundred thousand pounds worth of Japanese photographic technology on display.

The main enclosed market grounds contain an astonishing array of goods, from avenues of brightly and elaborately coloured cloth, through fruit and veg, to primitive radio cassette players and electrical goods. There are also traditional Uiygur handicrafts such as elaborately carved knifes and daggers, as well as numerous types of hats. The area behind the main market, outside the walls, is where the poorer dealers trade, some of whose stock merely comprises several odd shoes. It's quite depressing. Equally depressing is the way in which the land around the market has been allowed to be developed, into a modern but largely unused business park (though some carpet showrooms are here).

It's best to arrive at the market as early as possible, (before most of the tour groups), in order to watch it gradually filling up. Shared rickshaw taxis can be hired from outside the main hotels (about ¥5 per person from the *Seman*), and it is not recommended that you take a bicycle. *John's Café* sometimes arrange a free shuttle bus. **NB** Beware of pickpockets. Food served at the Sunday Market always looks a bit dodgy, and there is little on offer for vegetarians.

Old City, bazaars and city walls

With the exception of the livestock market, a mini version of the Sunday Market seems to occur every day within the old city area. To the east of Idkah Square lies the old city, a narrow labyrinth of mud-brick built houses, shops and mosques built on traditional Islamic city design of enclosed courtyards, tight passages and numerous cul-de-sacs. On the edge of this old town lie the bazaars, selling all manner of products, and covering all possible occupations. The hats, knives and handicrafts are probably a better bargain here than at the Sunday Market.

On Seman Road, not far from the *Seman Hotel*, two short stretches of the ancient city walls remain.

Idkah Mosque

When the original **Idkah Mosque** was built in 1442 it was located on the edge of town, but Kashgar's gradual expansion means that the mosque is now pretty much at the centre of town. The mosque currently standing is considerably larger than the original, and has been rebuilt or repaired many times. The main features are the now restored yellow-tiled tower gate, a victim of the excesses of the Cultural Revolution, and the large 16,800 square metres courtyard, said to be capable of holding 20,000 people. Visitors are welcomed if respectfully dressed (arms, legs, and women's heads covered), and the quiet atmosphere in the shady courtyard is certainly worth the ¥3 entrance fee (plus small camera fee).

The main **Idkah Square** outside the mosque, and the surrounding street markets, are enormously interesting (not least the fabulous shots taken by the portrait photographers around the clocktower). Check out the card schools, pigeon swaps, or the old bearded men just hanging about. The barbers' chairs near the mosque always draw photographers.

Abakh Hoja's Tomb

To the east of the town, several kilometres beyond the Sunday Market grounds, is the beautiful **Tomb of Abakh Hoja**. Probably dating to the 18th century, although some sources place it earlier, the mausoleum shows a distinct Persian influence in its use of green and blue tile work on its façade and dome. Although there are some 70 graves in the main domed chamber, the tomb is named after a local Uiygur aristocrat, Abakh Hoja, sometimes referred to as the 'patron saint of Kashgar'.

The tomb is also claimed to be the burial place of Abakh Hoja's grand daughter, popularly known as **Xiangfei**, or Fragrant Consort. Legend suggests that she was the leader of a failed Uiygur uprising in 1759 and was subsequently carried off to the imperial court of the Qing Emperor Qian Long to be a concubine. The Emperor is said to have become so besotted by his new acquisition, that his mother, fearing the growing influence of Xiangfei, ordered her to commit suicide.

The tombs are best reached on a pleasant bicycle journey (45 minutes from the *Seman Hotel*). The large Muslim graveyard located behind the tomb is particularly attractive during the late afternoon, although the main tomb may be closed by then.

Tomb of Yusup Khass Hajib

Built during the Song Dynasty circa 1130, the Tomb of Yusup Khass Hajib was superbly rebuilt and restored in 1993. An 11th century Uiygur poet and philosopher, **Yusup Khass Hajib** was the author of what is considered to be the most important Uiygur text ever produced, '*The Wisdom of Royal Glory*'. He was born near to the Central Asian city of Tokhmahk in 1019, when it was the summer capital of the Karakhanid Dynasty, but later moved to study at the Royal Islamic College in Kashgar.He wrote his 13,290 line "didactic lyric epic" in 18 months between 1069 and 1070, and presented his work to the

Great Khan of the East Karakhanid Dynasty, Talughach Bughra Khan Abdul Ali Hasan bin Sulaiman Arslankhan (!). He was rewarded with the title of 'Khass Hajib', or Privy Chamberlain (King's adviser). Yusup Khass Hajib died in 1085 and was buried in Kashgar, although when the tomb was destroyed by a natural disaster he was reburied at the present site.

A political, economic and cultural history of the Karakhanid Dynasty, the original manuscript of '*The Wisdom of Royal Glory*' has never been found, although three ancient copies survive in Vienna, Cairo and Namangan (in the Fergana Valley).

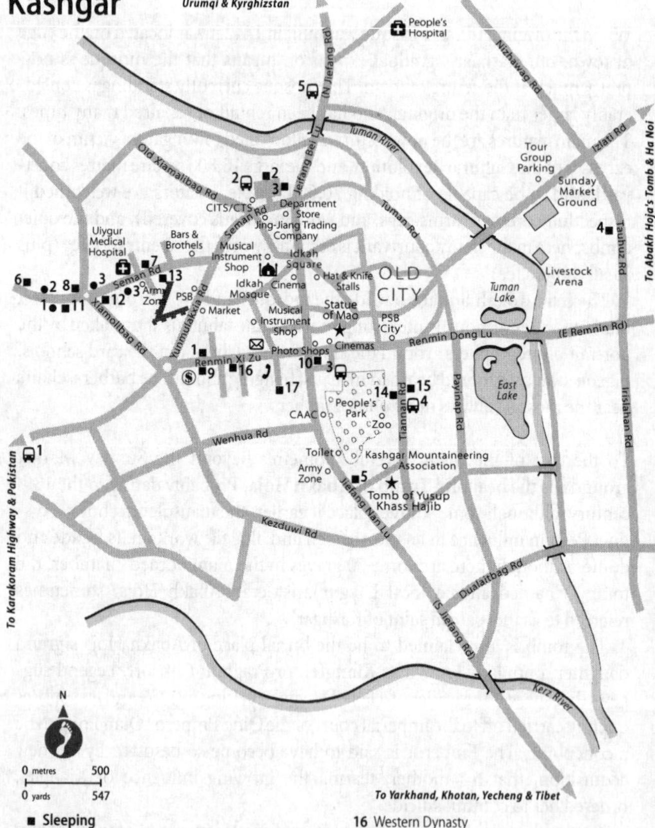

■ Sleeping
1 Cahou
2 Chini Bagh/Qiniwake
3 International
4 Kashgar Guesthouse
5 Labour Union
6 Oasis
7 Old Guesthouse
8 Overseas Chinese & Old City Restaurant
9 Qian Hai
10 Renmin/People's Hotel
11 Seman
12 Seman No 3 & John's Cafe
13 Silk Road Hotel
14 Tian Nan
15 Traffic
16 Western Dynasty
17 Wuzi

● Eating
1 Bar of Wien/Grapevine
2 Oasis Cafe Limin
3 Uiygur Restaurants

Buses
1 Alternative drop off point for local buses from Tashkurgan
2 'International' Bus station & Customs Hall
3 Local Bus stand
4 Long Distance Bus station
5 Proposed site of new 'International' Bus station & Customs Hall

The shrine is entered through the large tiled north gate. The main façade of the tomb features superb blue and white tile work, and is topped by a tall, blue tiled dome. The restoration work really is first rate. Inside the chamber, the sarcophagus stands on a large plinth. The walls are engraved with fine calligraphy, and excerpts from the Qu'ran in Arabic, Chinese and Romaniced Uiygur. In the surrounding cloistered courtyard is a small exhibition detailing the life and work of Yusup Khass Hajib. ■ *Open daily 0930-2000 Beijing time. Admission ¥5, camera fee ¥2.*

Parks

There are a number of pleasant public parks in Kashgar, including one set around the **East Lake** to the east of the city. The central **People's Park**, opposite the incongruous giant **Mao statue**, is a great place to watch the Chinese and Uiygurs at leisure, although the new paved plaza has replaced a large grassy area (¥1 entrance). The **zoo**, however, must rank alongside the cruellest and most depressing in the world (¥1 entrance). To our personal knowledge, the totally insane Himalayan bear has been pacing that same tiny cage since 1990 at least. The monkeys have a rather laissez-faire attitude towards their cages (some prefer to live outside them).

Essentials

Sleeping
■ *on map*
Price codes: see inside front cover

It is difficult to classify Kashgar's hotels by price categories since most offer a range of accommodation to suit all budgets. Those listed below are ranked in order of popularity. The ***Cahou, Labour Union Hotel, Oasis, Old Guesthouse, Renmin/People's, Silk Road, Western Dynasty*** and ***Wuzi*** hotels are either closed, undergoing renovation, or unwilling to accept foreigners. You do not usually get given your own room key – you have to rely on the floor attendant to lock and unlock your room. In theory, this should make your room more secure, but in practice it is not to be trusted: never leave valuables in your room.

Seman Hotel, Seman Rd, T2822147, F2822861. This hotel is divided into a number of different blocks. The 'Main' block is where most visitors to Kashgar stay, though it offers a bewildering choice of rooms. The various dorms (¥15 per bed) have anywhere between 2 and 12 beds, sharing toilets and hot showers on each floor (hot water in morning and evenings, watch valuables carefully when showering). There are also some crumbling 2-bed dorms with attached hot bath in a dilapidated block out the back. Double rooms with TV and attached hot bath in the main block are ¥120, with doubles with shared bath for ¥60 (though how a double with shared bath is different to a 2-bed dorm is not clear). 'Block A' caters mainly to pre-paid tour groups, and offers carpeted doubles with attached bath (¥120-200). 'Block 1' is the best maintained part of the old Russian Consulate, and has luxury suites with antique furniture, TV, phone, fridge and bath tubs for ¥500. The *Peacock Dancing Hall* appears to be currently closed, although the *Seman Kayoke Bar* (karaoke) is up and running (beware of hidden cover charges and overpriced drinks). The uninviting swimming pool is currently empty. The *Seman* has a travel agents and business centre, although all services are overpriced. Unlike in the recent past, the reception staff now greet guests with a smile.

Seman Hotel No3, Seman Rd, above *John's Café*, T2825969. Privately run (not part of *Seman Hotel*), this is the best bet for those after the cheapest double rooms. Comfortable doubles with TV and attached bath (hot water mornings and evenings) are ¥40-60, depending upon the floor.

Chini Bagh/Qiniwake Hotel, Seman Rd, T2822103. On the site of the former British consulate, features comfortable doubles with attached hot bath in the new block

(¥220), similar standard doubles in the old block (¥160), 3-bed dorms with attached hot bath (¥30 per bed) or 4-bed dorms with attached hot bath (¥25 per bed). This place is popular with Pakistani traders, though some women have written with tales of low-levels of harrassment. The compound also features Chinese and Uighur restaurants, a clinic, and currently the customs yard and departure point for the bus to Pakistan.

International Hotel, (formerly the *Kashgar-Gilgit International*), Seman Rd (in the *Chini Bagh Hotel* compound), T2833235. Used to feature friendly Pakistani service, but not anymore. Large, carpeted doubles with attached bath, TV, phone, fridge (¥280), plus some suites (¥600), all with great views over Kashgar, though some guests have complained that the rooms are too tatty for the price. Restaurant, shop, and horrible bar.

Overseas Chinese Hotel, Seman Rd, T2833262. All nationalities welcome, doubles with attached bath ¥120, suites ¥300, or 3-bed dorms for ¥30 per bed. New hotel but facilities not very modern.

Tian Nan Hotel, Tiannan Rd, T2824023. Doubles with attached bath ¥180, 3-bed dorm with attached bath ¥25 per person, cheap 10-bed dorm with shared bath ¥10 per person.

Traffic Hotel, Tiannan Rd, T2825208. Noisy rooms and dorms at the bus station.

Kashgar Guesthouse, Tauhuz Rd, T2822367, F2824679. Convenient for the Sunday Market, though little else, large doubles with attached bath ¥200, cheaper 4-bed dorm with private bath ¥50 per person, restaurants.

Qian Hai Hotel, Renmin Xi Zu, T2822922. Luxury doubles and suites (¥320-800) aimed at the party cadres, friendly but no English spoken.

Eating

● *on map*

Chinese There are any number of upmarket Chinese restaurants along the 'fashionable' Renmin Xi Lu, though most have prices to match their 'trendy' status. Cheaper dining halls can be found at many of the hotels, notably *Tian Nan* and *Chini Bagh*. Little (or no) English is spoken at most of these places, so it is a matter of going into the kitchen and pointing. Make sure that the price is clearly established.

Uiygur All Uiygur dishes are accompanied by *nan*, a thick bread similar to its counterpart served in Pakistan. The other staple is *shashlik*, skewers of barbecued mutton or minced meat served with nan. Hygiene is always a consideration when you order this dish (or anything containing meat). The other Uiygur speciality is *laghman*, the thick noodles that you see being spun out by the food stall holders. They are often served as part of a spicy soup. Other ubiquitous dishes around Kashgar include *chuchureh* (the boiled dumplings with a minced meat filling) and *samsa* (a Central Asian style of samosa). ***Old City***, next to the *Overseas Chinese Hotel*, is a good place to try reasonably priced Uiygur food (¥7-15 per plate), though little English is spoken so you'll have to go into the kitchen and point. Otherwise, the night markets around Idkah Square or along Yunmulakxia Road also serve cheap Uiygur dishes, and are as interesting for their atmosphere as their food. Make sure any dishes that you order are freshly cooked and served hot. The dining halls at the *Seman* and *Chini Bagh* hotels provide a good introduction to Uiygur food. The region is famous for its variety of melons, and fresh slices are extremely cheap. Bear in mind that melons absorb liquid through their skins, and that many stallholders lay their melons in the drainage ditches to keep them cool! Fresh fruit and vegetables are sold each evening at the informal market on Yunmulakxia Road.

'Western' Many visitors do not venture beyond the 2 places close to the *Seman Hotel*. ***Oasis Café Limin*** (formerly *Limin* and *Seman Road* cafés) offers 'sanitized' versions of Chinese dishes (meat ¥15-17, veg plates ¥6-15, fish ¥20, soup ¥5, noodles ¥7, rice ¥2) as well as having a stab at a few typical 'traveller' plates (pancakes ¥4, yogurt with fruit salad ¥4, chips ¥7 etc) that come as a welcome change for those arriving from Pakistan. ***John's Café & Information Service*** has an almost identical menu, though it also offers 'Kashgaria pizza'. Both places are popular as venues for a beer or ten (¥4), and to chat and exchange information (see also 'Tour companies & travel agents' below). It's suprising how often breakfast turns into lunch turns into dinner. Many male travellers also fall in love with the waitresses here! In late 1998 *John's Café* seemed the more popular of the two, though in my humble opinion the food at the *Oasis* is marginally better. However, by only dining at these two places you risk missing out on part of the Kashgar cultural experience. These two places are the best options for **vegetarians**.

Nightclubs

Be wary of the numerous nightclubs/bars along Renmin Xi Lu. They are expensive, generally with a cover charge of ¥40 (including 1 drink), and beer priced at ¥10-15. Many of the places along Seman Road that masquerade as nightclubs/bars are actually brothels.

Entertainment

Café society Kashgar is also a fine place to relax, and many visitors do little more than sit around the ***Oasis Café Limin*** and ***John's Café & Information Service*** outside the *Seman Hotel*, enjoying the food and drink. Recent arrivals from Pakistan revel in the availability of cheap Chinese beer whilst being shocked at the lack of clothes worn by tourists and Chinese women alike. Despite being a predominantly Muslim town, there is little reaction to tourists (including women) wearing shorts – hardly surprising when most young Han Chinese women are wearing shorter and shorter miniskirts. The ***Bar of Wien (GrapeVine)*** café serves drinks and meals in a nice setting in the grounds of the *Seman Hotel*.

Theatres The *Seman Hotel* occasionally puts on Uiygur cultural shows for groups. Enquire at reception.

Sports **Swimming:** the unsavoury looking pool at the *Seman Hotel* (¥10) is currently empty, and looking pretty forlorn.

Shopping

Bookshops ***Xinhua Bookshop*** on Jeifang Bei Lu is the best of a bad lot. ***John's Café*** (see below) has a few books, including usually some guides to China, Tibet and Pakistan, and also has a noticeboard used by travellers wanting to swap books.

Carpets The new 'business park' at the Sunday Market grounds has been largely taken over by carpet traders, and this is the best place to see locally produced (and other) carpets.

Clothing Upwardly mobile young Chinese women shop for latest fashions on the 'trendy' Renmin Xi Lu. Chinese army surplus is available from a store close to the PSB on Yunmulakxia Road. The spectacularly colourful cloth bazaars are located on the arcade running north from Idkah Square, and on the road running north from the post office. Come and see where the Kashgar women buy those spangly dresses.

Handicrafts Hats, knives and brassware are the most popular buys. These and other souvenirs are cheaper in the stalls on either side of Idkah Square than at the Sunday Market, though be prepared for ruthless bargaining. Some very attractive traditional musical instruments (including minature replicas) are available from a number of outlets, including one just north of Idkah Mosque and several on the road running north from the post office.

Photography All the 'department stores' sell a selection of none-too-fresh-looking colour print film. ***Camera and Film*** next to the *Renmin Hotel* has fresher stock plus some Fuji slide film (¥85 for Sensia 100). The photo shop opposite also has slide film. If you can, wait until Rawalpindi. Numerous places on Renmin Dong Lu and Jeifang Bei Lu offer processing, but none look reliable.

Shopping complexes Though it's unlikely that you'll actually find anything worth buying (apart perhaps from a few toileteries), strolling around Kashgar's 'department stores' is a great way to while away the hours. Unattractive products displayed in unappealing ways, sold by poorly motivated sales-staff who prefer to sleep with their heads on the counters. Great stuff.

Local transport

Bicycle: the best bike hire is from *Chini Bagh Hotel* (¥2 per hour, ¥100 deposit, check the condition and lock). A couple of places on Jeifang Bei Lu (north and south of Idkah Square) sell reasonably good quality Chinese made mountain bikes (US$50-120), which could potentially be ridden to Pakistan and sold there.

Long distance transport

Air *Xinjiang Airlines/CAAC* have between 1 and 3 daily flights to **Urunqi**, depending upon demand (usually mornings and evenings). Fare is ¥980 plus ¥50 tax. Book as far in advance as you can.

Train Construction has begun on a line linking Kashgar to the 'outside world', ie Urumqi. It's provisionally due for completion by summer 2000.

Long distance buses The 'international' through-bus to **Paksiatan** (overnighting in Tashkurgan) currently departs from the yard next to the *Chini Bagh Hotel*. Tickets can be bought several days in advance (currently priced at ¥270 to Sust) between 0930-1330 daily (Beijing time). The bus departs (in theory) at 1200 (Beijing time) once customs formalities have been completed and the passenger list typed out (in triplicate). Few 'westerners' have their bags searched, though an additional ¥5 is being stolen from passengers in the form of a 'customs charge'. Note that in theory, you do not have access to your luggage until you arrive in Pakistan, though if the bus is not particularly full the driver may let you retrieve your luggage for the overnight stop in Tashkurgan (don't count on it). In late 1998 further customs checks (including baggage x-rays) were being conducted in Tashkurgan. If demand is slack, it may be possible to buy seats on this bus to **Kara Kuli** (¥43) and **Tashkurgan** (¥63). **NB** In late 1998 a new 'international' bus station and customs yard was under construction on Jeifang Bei Lu (see map).

The **long distance bus station** is on Tiannan Rd, east of People's Park, T2821475/2823796. Tickets can be bought at least 1 day in advance, although if you want to travel on a popular route at a peak time (eg to Urumqi immediately after the Sunday Market), it is best to book early. The system is supposedly now computerized. When buying a ticket, ascertain as to whether the departure time is Beijing or Xinjiang (local) time. Fight for your place in the queue. Information boards are in Chinese and Uighur only. Beware of pickpockets and bag-snatchers.

Urumqi: there are at least 5 different options available on the trip to Urumqi. Most comfortable is the non-stop, 36 hour 'sleeper bus', which has semi-reclining beds as opposed to seats. Upper berths are ¥380, Lower ¥440. Departure times vary, although there's generally an early morning and early evening bus each day. There are several other buses, with varying degrees of comfort/misery, for ¥188, ¥214, ¥253, some of which take 3 days, stopping at revolting hotels for the night where you have no access to your roof luggage. Urumqi tickets from windows 5 and 6. **Tashkurgan**: Daily, 0900 Beijing time, ¥43, 7 hours. This is the bus for **Karakuli Lake** (5 hours), although you generally have to pay the full Tashkurgan fare. Ticket window 7. **Yarkhand (Shache)**

(¥30) and **Yecheng (Kargilik)**: 6 daily buses serve both destinations, every 2 hours from 0900 Beijing time. Ticket windows 1-4. **Khotan (Hotan/Hetian)**: daily, 0830 1900 Beijing time (¥90). Ticket windows 5-8.

The **local bus station** is next to People's Park. Minibuses to **Artush** run from close to the People's Hospital (¥20).

Directory

Airline offices *China Xinjiang Airlines* have a no-English speaking counter just inside the *Renmin Hotel*. *CAAC*, Jiefang Nan Lu, T2822113. Open Mon-Sat 1000-1300 1630-1930, Sun 1100-1300, very inefficient office (try *John's Café*).

Banks *Bank of China*, Renmin Xi Zu. Open Mon-Fri 0930-1330 1600-2000, Sat 1100-1500 Beijing time, offers efficient foreign exchange for cash and TCs, plus Yuan cash advances on Visa/Diners/Amex/Mastercard (1.8% commission). Hotel reception at the *Seman* and *Chini Bagh* change cash and TCs at the set bank rate. Uiygur money changers hassle anyone walking past the *Chini Bagh Hotel*, though you take an unacceptable risk by changing money in this way.

Communications **GPO:** Renmin Xi Lu. Open Mon-Sat 0930-2000, Sun 1000-1930, Beijing time. Upstairs for international mail and poste restante (small fee charged for collecting each item of mail). **Internet:** see under 'Tour companies & travel agents' below. **Telephones:** ***China Telecom***, Renmin Xi Lu. Open Mon-Sat 0930-2000, Sun 1000-1930, Beijing time. Upstairs (to the left) for efficient international calls (UK and Europe ¥21 per minute, Austria ¥19 per minute, USA ¥21 per minute). Also see under 'Tour companies & travel agents' below.

Hospitals & medical services **Hospitals:** ***Renmin Yiyuan/People's Hospital***, T2822337. To the north of Kashgar (see map). The ***Uiygur Medical Hospital*** on Seman Rd is unappealing. There's a clinic at the *Seman Hotel*.

Tour companies & travel agents The government-run ***China International Travel Service (CITS)***, T2825390, F2823087, and ***China Travel Service***, T2832875, F2822552, are both located in the same building within the grounds of the *Chini Bagh Hotel*. They can arrange most things, such as airline tickets, guides, transport, visa extensions and travel permits, but at a price. Local excursions are arranged to **San Xian (Three Immortals) Caves** (¥60 for vehicle to seat 4) and **Ha Noi** (¥100 for 4 passengers). You can do all of the same, but cheaper, through ***John's Café & Information Centre***, Seaman Rd, E john@hotmail.com. (see also 'eating' and 'cafés' above). This is more than just a restaurant and a good place to hang out for a beer and exchange travel information. John Hu can also provide information on travel and activities in the surrounding area (though a classic 'traveller's tale' is that he is a government spy who will grass-up anyone intending to head from Kashgar to Tibet!). He can arrange documentation and transport for those wanting to cross the **Tourgat Pass** into Kyrghizstan (see below), though itineraries and passport information is required up to 2 weeks in advance. ¥100 per person for documentation and ¥1,000 per vehicle seems to be his going rate. He organizes day trips to the **Takla Makan Desert** (¥1,000, maximum 4 persons), or tailor made 2-3 day trips, plus transport and organized trips to **Kara Kuli**. He also sells bus and airline tickets for a negligible mark up. *John's Café* also offers **internet/email** services (¥1 per minute), though some users have suggested that the system is very slow, prone to crashing, you get charged for boot-up time, and the system is shut down between each user. Good international **telephone** connections are available at the government price plus ¥5 per minute, or you can call collect for a ¥5 fee. Another local hustler/fixer in the John Hu mould is 'Elvis', who can usually be found at the *Oasis Café Limin*. ***Kashgar Mountaineering Association***, 8 Tiyu Lu (Sport's Rd), off Jiefang Nan Lu, T2823680, F2822957. The place to ask about trekking and climbing in the Kara Kuli area.

Tourist offices None. See under 'Tour companies & travel agents' above.

Useful addresses *Public Security Bureau ('regional') (PSB)* for **visa extensions** is located on Yunmulakxia Rd (efficient, prices according to nationality). This is where 'Alien Travel Permits' are issued (open Mon-Fri 0930-1330 1600-1930 Beijing time). The ***PSB ('city')***, where you report crimes, lost passports etc, is on Renmin Dong Lu, opposite Tiannan Rd.

Excursions from Kashgar

Ha Noi and Mor Pagoda The insubstantial remains of this Tang dynasty town (seventh-11th century) lie some 35 kilometres northeast of Kashgar, and are usually reached as part of an organized tour (see 'Tour companies & travel agents' above).

San Xian (Three-Immortals) Caves The three caves here, 20 kilometres north of Kashgar, feature the rapidly deteriorating remains of a number of Buddhist frescoes. They are usually reached as part of an organized tour (see 'Tour companies & travel agents' above).

Travelling on from Kashgar

Rest of China In many regards, all roads lead to Urumqi (see 'Transport' above). An alternative to the usual route from Kashgar to Urumqi is to travel via an old branch of the Silk Road that passes along the south side of the Takla Makan Desert. First stop is **Yecheng** (270 kilometres, also jumping off point for Tibet), although it is possible to get a bus from Kashgar all the way to **Khotan** (Hetian, 12 hours). The latter also has an engaging Sunday Market, and is a local centre for the carpet making industry. Both towns have pretty basic hotels and restaurants. From Khotan you can take the bus to Mingfen (Niya), from where a new road runs across the heart of the Takla Makan Desert to Korla. From here you can continue to Urumqi or Turufan (Turpan).

Kyrghizstan The PSB in Kashgar point out that the border crossing across the **Tourgat Pass** (3,752 metres) into Kyrghizstan is a trade route, as opposed to a tourist route, and thus they are reluctant to issue the necessary travel documents. The Chinese side of the border is a restricted military zone, so it would be unwise to attempt this journey without the relevant paperwork. Further, there is no reliable public transport to the border, although a jeep (seats five) can be hired for around ¥1,400. The road to the pass from Kashgar (160 kilometres, six hour) is pretty poor, although it is being improved. Chinese formalities are completed at 'Topa', 60 kilometres south of the pass (and the pass is only open until 1300). You cannot walk across the pass, so if you haven't hired your own transport, you will be quoted outrageous prices for the ride across to the Kyrghiz side (there may be a shuttle bus). From the Kyrghiz side (where extravagant attempts will be made to garner bribes from you by the customs and immigration officials), you can hire a taxi to Naryan for about US$15, and then take a public bus to Bishkek for US$5.

The 'international' bus departure place at the *Chini Bagh Hotel* has an occasional bus to Bishkek (US$50), and a place above the *Wuzi Hotel* (T2826693) also advertises a similar service. Neither seem to run with any regularity.

Several places in Kashgar can arrange the necessary paperwork and transport, although 14 days notice is often required (see Kashgar 'Tour companies and travel agents'). Note that you will require a **visa** whichever direction you are coming from; Chinese visas are definetely **not** issued on the border, although a Kyrghiz one may be if you offer a big enough bribe (but the Chinese may not let you proceed without a Kyrghiz visa, and will not let you back in if the Kyrghiz turn you away). The Chinese will not let you in if you don't have the relevant travel documents to pass through the restricted zone.

Tibet The 'easiest' way to get to Lhasa (Tibet) from Kashgar is the way the Chinese authorities 'approve' of: via Urumqi, Dunhuang and Golmud (a diversion of over 3,500 kilometres!). The route most travellers in Kashgar are interested in is via Mount Kailash in Far-west Tibet. The problem with this route is that it travels via China's 'Western Military Road' across the Aksai Chin, the ownership of which is disputed between China and India. Officially this region is 'closed' to foreigners, which for many 'travellers' is reason enough to attempt it. Gyurme Dorje, writing in Footprint's *Tibet Handbook*, however, perhaps best describes the true appeal of the region: "The traveller who is prepared to undergo the rigours of this journey will come into contact with a way a life that has undergone little change for centuries, and experience the wonder of a unique wilderness and culture largely untouched by the modern world. Therefore, despite all drawbacks and hardships, to participate in a pilgrimage to Mount Kailash or simply to travel in this unique and stunningly beautiful and unpolluted natural environment can be one of life's most rewarding experiences."

In recent years it has become increasingly 'easy' to complete this trip in an east-west direction (ie Lhasa-Mount Kailash-Kashgar). The PSB in Lhasa is prepared to issue the relevant travel documents to groups as long as they book through a travel agency. The normal mode of transport is a truck, taking about one month to complete the journey (including a visit to Mount Kailash), and costing around $1,000 per person.

Attempting the trip in the opposite direction is officially impossible, although those employed in the tourist industry in Far-west Tibet are lobbying hard to have the region 'opened'. In Kashgar the PSB do not seem willing to issue the necessary travel documents. Rather than actually refuse to issue the permit, they claim that the road is 'under-repair', or 'temporarily closed'. Even John Hu, who seems to be able to 'fix' most things in Kashgar, cannot arrange this permit. However, a number of determined individuals do make it, and the information given below is taken from a number of letters about the trip that we have received, as well as Footprint's *Tibet Handbook*. Note that this journey passes through some of the world's most challenging terrain. Passes are high, temperatures are low, and food and shelter unreliable. You will need to be properly equipped otherwise you risk death. It is some 1,671 kilometres from Kashgar to Mount Kailash, and then a further 2,021 kilometres to Lhasa via the 'Northern Plateau' route, or 1,198 via the 'Southern Brahmaputra' route described below. The notes below are how the situation stood in late 1998; the situation in the region could change very quickly.

Routes

The first step is easy: take the bus from Kashgar to **Yecheng** (Kargilik, 270 kilometres), see 'Transport' above. This is in fact where most people get turned back since there is a police check in Yecheng, and then again 15 kilometres beyond it. From here you will have to hitch a ride on a truck. Most are going all the way through to the next major junction, **Ali** (Senge Tsangpo), though you may be forced to take a number of rides via **Mazar** (249 kilometres), **Tserang Daban** (456 kilometres), **Domar** (172 kilometres), **Rutok** (123 kilometres) before the final leg to Ali (117 kilometres).

Accommodation in Ali is available at the ***Ali Hotel***, though you may just as well go for the cheapest bed available (US$10) since water is not generally available in the more expensive en suite rooms (US$30). There is a hotel canteen here and a 'friendship shop' selling food supplies. If you arrive at Ali without the relevant travel permit, the PSB will find you and fine you. Officially this is ¥500, though you can usually bargain it down to ¥350. What happens next is unpredictable. You may be packed off back to Kashgar (at your own expense) or you may even be given assistance by police in finding a ride for your onward journey! The bridge on the exit south of town is the place to hitch a ride via Mount Kailash, although you're better off asking around the truck stops. Note that the road leading east out of Ali takes the alternative 'Northern Plateau' route via Gegye (112 kilometres), Gertse (370 kilometres), Tsochen (260 kilometres), Raga (242), Lhartse (241 kilometres) to Lhasa (351 kilometres).

From Ali the road heads southwest to **Ridong** (30 kilometres), at the confluence of the Indus and Gar Tsangpo. From here the main road to Mount Kailash follows the Gar Tsangpo upstream. It passes through **Lungmar** and then bypasses the site of the former ancient winter capital of Ngari District at **Gar Gunsa** (shown as Gartok on some old maps, and 111 kilometres from Ali). The road continues through **Namru** (23 kilometres), then via **Gar Yersa** (ancient summer capital of Ngari) to **Sogto**. Beyond here the road leaves the Gar Tsangpo, and continues along the southwest side of the Gangtise range into a wide sandy valley which forms part of the upper Sutlej basin. The road here is frequently washed out. Eventually the route reaches the modern coal mining town of **Montser** (237 kilometres from Ali), which has a couple of basic truck stops and a restaurant. Montser can be used as a base from which to visit the pilgrimage site of Tirthapuri (6 kilometres southwest) or the Gurugam Monastery (8 kilometres southeast, then 15 kilometres southwest). The main road continues from Montser to **Darchen** (68 kilometres), the main junction for the circuit of Mount Kailash. The *Darchen Guesthouse* here has dorm beds for ¥25, and food can also be bought. To hitch a ride in a truck all the way from Ali to Darchen will cost between ¥50-70, depending upon your negotiating skills.

The next stage of the journey, largely along the Southern Brahmaputra valley, is some 600 kilometres long as far as **Saga** (you may well get a ride in a truck all the way). There are at least 4 check-posts along this stretch of road. From Darchen to **Barka** is 22 kilometres (the administrative base for the Mount Kailash region), and then 28 kilometres to **Hor**. This is the starting point for the circumambulation of **Lake Manasarovar**. The road continue SSE to **Nyoktse** and then crosses the **Mayum La pass** that marks the frontier between Far-west Tibet and West Tibet. Note that the pass is impassable in wet weather. From here it is 50 kilometres to **Satsam**, and then a further 50 kilometres through the sandy grasslands along the north bank of the Brahmaputra to **Horpa**. The road continues 20 kilometres to **Baryang** and then a further 14 kilometres to the small township of **Gacho**. The road climbs for 36 kilometres up to the **Soge La pass** (4,725 metres) and then follows the Brahmaputra valley to **Drongpa Tradum** (71 kilometres). This was originally founded as a military base, and a main check post for intercepting foreigners travelling without permits. In 1993, however, all the military and administrative functions moved 25 kilometres west, leaving Tibetans to occupy this semi ghost town. Accommodation and food can be hard to come by.

From Drongpa the road continues 145 kilometres southeast via **Lhaktsang**, **Dargyeling** and **Garshok** to **Saga** (*Tibetan:* Kyakyaru). This is a large military town, administering the entire border with Nepal as far west as the Indo-Nepalese border. The truck stop here has a basic 'hotel' and restaurant. From Saga it is often possible to pick up a ride via **Raga** (52 kilometres) all the way to **Chushar Town** (241 kilometres, county capital of modern Lhartse), although there is a check post just before the town. From here it is a further 157 kilometres to **Zhigatse** (Xigaze, Shigatse), a good place to extend visas, and then a further 194 kilometres to **Lhasa** (a bad place to extend visas).

Trekking

Background

Background

History

Pakistan was born out of the partition of the South Asian subcontinent in 1947, when the British transferred power to the newly independent countries of India and Pakistan. Although the modern Islamic Republic of Pakistan is less than half a century old, the land and the people have far more ancient origins. Moreover, the history of Pakistan is far more than just an appendage to the history of India; for long periods Pakistan has been the "arbiter of India's historical destiny". Over the centuries successive groups have arrived from the west, crossing the Indus Plains and moving into present-day India. Sometimes these new arrivals were traders, sometimes conquering armies, whilst others were merely agriculturalists seeking new land to cultivate. All left their mark upon the landscape and culture of South Asia.

There is no one single history of Pakistan. In many cases, the history of Pakistan has been shaped by events beyond its borders, in Central Asia, Persia, Europe and India. Furthermore, numerous dynasties have operated within varying spheres of influences, with contemporary empires frequently being unaware of each other's presence. Thus the following history is just a brief overview of the events that have shaped the modern state of Pakistan.

Settlement and early history

Prehistory

The territory of modern Pakistan has always been a frontier zone between settled agriculture and nomadic pastoralism. At the beginning of the Mesolithic period some 10,000 years ago, settled agriculture was developing in the foothills of Baluchistan. At **Mehrgarh**, where the Indus plains meet the Baluchistan hills, pottery finds have provided evidence of settled agriculture dating back to 8500 BC; the earliest evidence in South Asia. Settled agriculture began to spread east, supported by the Indus, although nomadic tribes continued to occupy the arid western margins of Pakistan, migrating down to the valleys and plains from their summer pastures in the hills as winter arrived. By 6000 BC farming was widespread on the margins of the Indus plains, and within 2,500 years it had spread throughout the region. This development of settled agriculture represents the origins of the Indus Valley Civilization.

Indus Valley Civilization

The discovery of the two major Indus Valley Civilization sites of **Moenjo Daro** and **Harappa**, and their subsequent excavations from the 1920s onwards, have been described as the "most glorious achievement of South Asia's archaeology", fundamentally changing all previous concepts of the origins of South Asian culture. Previously it was believed that the Aryans were the forbears of South Asian culture.

At its height the Indus Valley Civilization covered an area as great as two other empires with which it maintained trading links, Egypt and Mesopotamia, and nearly 300 sites of this culture have been discovered. Perhaps the key feature about the Indus Valley Civilization, however, is the fact that the culture developed was distinctively South Asian. Although commerce played a part, the basis of this civilization was the development of urban centres rooted in the agricultural economy of the Indus basin, where local villagers could take their surplus for sale and exchange; a system continuing in much of rural Pakistan today. The Indus Valley

Civilization is perhaps unique in that it displayed a strict cultural uniformity over its entire area of approximately 1.3 million square kilometres.

Aryan arrival The Indus Valley Civilization reached its peak around 2500 BC with the development of great centres such as Moenjo Daro and Harappa, yet by about 1750 BC Moenjo Daro had been deserted and the entire civilization had disintegrated. Many causes of this decline have been presented: environmental change increasing desertification in an already semi-arid landscape, perhaps as a result of a shift in the course of the Indus; internal political decay accelerating a continuing process of decline; or even the violent arrival of a new wave of immigrants, the Aryans, from the northwest. Whatever the causes, the collapse of this civilization precipitated a major shift in the cultural evolution of the South Asian region.

The origins of the **Aryan** invaders are not precisely known, although it is clear that they do not belong to one single ethnic group. Their arrival, however, did open up a route into the frontier regions of Central Asia and Persia. By 1500 BC the Indo-Aryan language had begun to develop, with the centre of population and culture shifting east from the banks of the Indus to the land between the Ganges and Yamuna. This region became the heart of the Aryan culture, and through the literary traditions of the *Vedas* (such as the *Rig Veda*), laid the foundations of what ultimately became Hinduism.

Ancient Empires In the period that followed the Aryan colonization of large parts of South Asia, a number of empires and dynasties with varying spheres of influence became established in the region of modern Pakistan. The Persian Empire of the **Achaemenians** for example established itself in the Indus basin, with **Taxila** evolving as a great cultural centre.

In 326 BC **Alexander the Great** invaded South Asia, marching his armies from Bactria to the north, through modern-day NWFP and Punjab into Sind, and then leaving to the west, along Baluchistan's Makran coast. There are varying interpretations of the impact of Alexander's brief stay in what is now Pakistan. Although the Hellenistic influence did give rise to a distinctive style of Graeco-Indian art (later termed Gandharan) that persisted until the fifth century AD,

Major Indus Valley Civilization Sites

After Allchin & Allchin

the lands conquered by Alexander and the vassals that he placed on their thrones were swiftly defeated and incorporated into other empires shortly after his departure. Indeed, this Hellenistic influence is often traced to the Bactrian Greeks who arrived over a century later.

Within a year of Alexander's retreat, **Chandragupta Maurya** established the first indigenous empire to control most of the South Asian subcontinent. By the middle of the third century AD the **Mauryan** Empire had reached its zenith under the rule of **Asoka**, one of South Asia's greatest kings. Asoka's empire extended from Afghanistan in the west to Assam in the east, from the Himalayas in the north to Mysore in the south. However, the horrors of the war with the Kalingans left a lasting impression upon Asoka, and though it is not certain as to whether he embraced Buddhism, he certainly embraced many of its pacifist doctrines. He left a series of edicts in the form of inscriptions on rocks and pillars right across the subcontinent (some of which can be seen at Mansehra). Yet within 50 years of Asoka's death in 232 AD, the entire Mauryan Empire had disintegrated.

In the northwest margins of the subcontinent, in the territory of modern Pakistan, a series of invaders from the northwest attempted to exert their hegemony over the region. The **Bactrian Greeks**, **Sakkas**, **Parthians** and ultimately the **Kushans** all established empires of varying size. The Kushans controlled a large empire across much of Central Asia, Afghanistan, and the upper reaches of the Indus and Ganges valleys for almost a century. Under the patronage of the Kushans' great Buddhist ruler **Kanishka** (around 120 AD, although this date is strongly contested), a famous art and cultural school referred to as **Gandharan** flourished in the Vale of Peshawar and the surrounding valleys. It was through these valleys that Buddhism spread into Central Asia and China.

The decline of the Kushan Empire was precipitated by the **Sassanian** invasion and then by the arrival from Central Asia of the **Huns**. Regional kingdoms began to develop as local rulers asserted their influence, and thus the history of the era is highly fragmented.

Spread of Islamic power

Arrival of Islam

South Asia's first contact with Islam came through the Arab traders and sailors using the ancient trade routes through the Persian Gulf into the Indian Ocean during the seventh century AD. However, the mission was commerce and not evangelism, and though some conversions undoubtedly took place, the impact of Islam on the subcontinent at this stage was minimal. Even the Muslim conquest of Persia, including the province of Makran, failed to raise the profile of Islam in South Asia.

Throughout the 6th and 7th centuries, bitter rivalries continued between the Persian, Byzantium and Arab Empires for control of these lucrative maritime trade routes between India and the Mediterranean. As the Arabs gained the ascendency, it became essential for them to control the ports and sea routes along the coast of Sind. Arab dominance in maritime commerce was being challenged by the Hindu merchants of Debal, who, with the tacit support of the Medes of Sind, encouraged pirates to harass the Arab trading ships. Several punitive expeditions were sent by both land and sea to Sind, though they were largely unsuccessful.

In 711 AD, the Governor of Iraq sent the 17 year old Arab governor of Fars to conquer the troublesome region for the Umayyad Dynasty. Accompanied by 6,000 Syrian cavalry and 6,000 armed camel cavalry, this young man, **Mohammad bin Qasim**, marched through the Makran and laid siege to Debal. With the help of six huge catapults, Debal was quickly conquered and most of its population put to the sword or enslaved. The Arab armies then marched north, taking Nerun (Hyderabad), Siwistan (Sehwan), Brahmanabad, al-Rur (Rohri), Askalanda (Uch), before crossing the Chenab and taking Multan, the most important town of the Upper Indus Valley.

Thus Islam gained its first foothold in South Asia.

However, the impact of the Arab conquest of Sind and southern Punjab was more cultural and commercial than religious, and though many learned Islamic scholars arrived to propagate the faith, there was no mass movement towards Islam. In fact, it was almost 300 years before Islam became widely established in South Asia.

Ghaznavid Empire and the Delhi Sultanate

The effective introduction of Islam into South Asia came in the 11th century with the invasion from the northwest of the Turks and the establishment of the Ghaznavid Empire. However, once more the mission was not the propagation of Islam, but plunder. **Mahmud of Ghazni**, successor to the Ghaznavid Sultanate of Afghanistan that was established in the 10th century by a former Turkish slave of the Samanids, raided the Punjab virtually every year between 1000 and 1026, attracted by the agricultural surpluses and the enormous wealth of India's temples. These raids were used to finance his exploits in Central Asia where he maintained an extensive empire. Mahmud of Ghazni is remembered for his patronage of the arts and learning, and during his period of rule many Islamic scholars, particularly those of the *Sufi* order, were active in spreading Islam in the region.

Muslim political power in South Asia was consolidated by the raids of one of Mahmud's successors **Mu'izzu'd Din** (referred to in some texts as Mohammad Ghauri), and the defeat of the Rajput forces at Tarain in 1192. This conquest established a period of Muslim rule in India that was to last 500 years. Mu'izzu'd Din's lieutenant, **Qutb u'd Din Aibak**, made further territorial gains and in 1206 the **Delhi Sultanate** was established. At its peak, under the stewardship of **Iltutmish**,

Delhi Sultanate in 1236

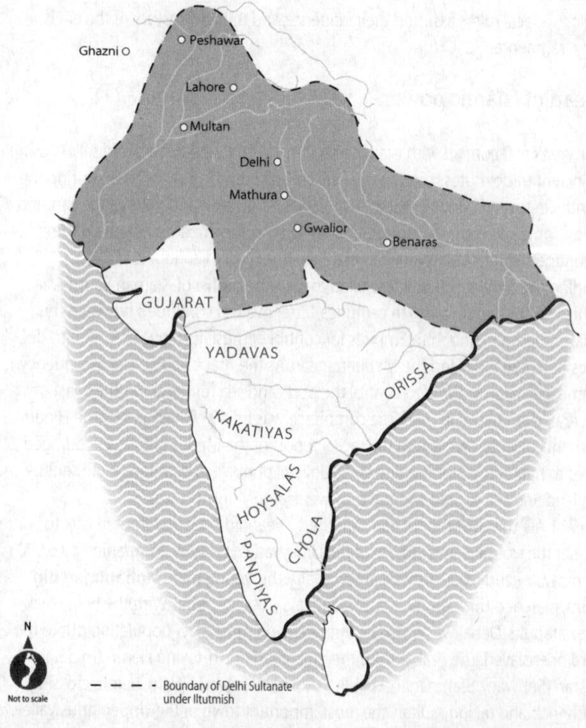

another former Turkish slave, the Delhi Sultanate stretched across a huge swathe of North India, from Afghanistan to Bengal.

These early Muslim rulers looked to the Turkish ruling class and to the Arab caliphs for their Islamic legitimacy, and to the Turkish élite for their cultural authority. However, the plundering raids of Genghis Khan through Central Asia in the 13th century all but cut the Delhi Sultanate off from its cultural, religious and political heritage. As a result, Islam itself underwent major modifications in response to its new social and religious environment, accounting partly for the distinctive form of Islam found in South Asia today.

A succession of dynasties followed, including the **Khaljis** and **Tughluqs** before Delhi was sacked in 1398 by the Mongol warlord **Timur** (Tamerlane). The Delhi Sultanate never really recovered from Timur's murderous attack, although their successors, including the **Lodis**, nominally controlled parts of what is now Pakistani Punjab.

Meanwhile, in Sind, a series of dynasties that included the **Sumas** (1026-1352), **Samnas** (1353-1520), **Arghuns** and **Tarkhans** (1520-1592) ruled over much of the Lower Indus Valley. The 15th century saw the Baluch tribes of Baluchistan united for the first time under a confederacy led by **Mir Chakar Rind**. Although this unity was short-lived, the period is still often referred to as the 'Classical Age' of Baluch history, when many of the great traditions of tribal honour and chivalry were established. It was not until the **Mughals** came to power, however, that one dynasty actually ruled over the majority of the territory that comprises Pakistan.

Mughal Empire

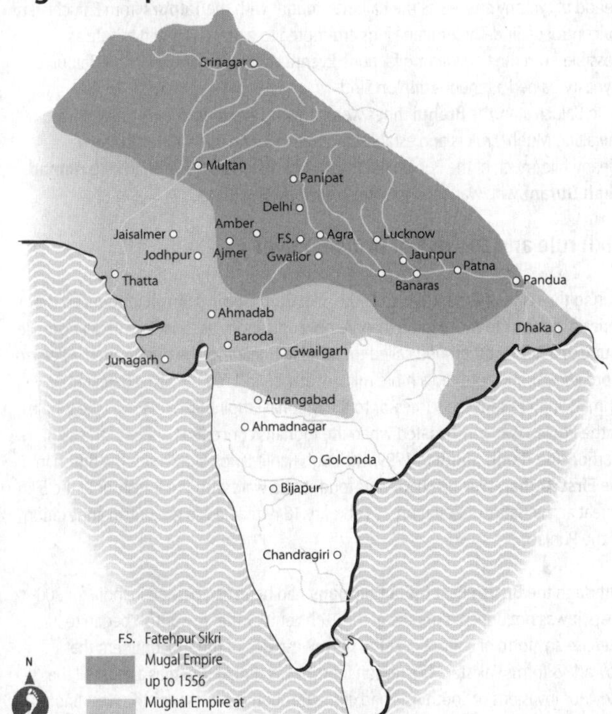

The Mughals The founder of the Mughal Dynasty, **Babur** (The Tiger), defeated the armies of the last ruler of the Delhi Sultanate at Panipat near Delhi in 1526. Although the Mughal Empire stretched across much of what is now Pakistani Punjab and NWFP, within 15 years the attentions of the Afghan **Sher Shah Suri** had forced Babur's successor **Humayun** into exile. These northern and central parts of Pakistan returned to Mughal rule following Humayun's return from exile in 1555.

However, it was not until 1592 that the majority of the Lower Indus Valley joined the Upper Indus Valley as part of the Mughal Empire. **Akbar** took the throne in 1556, and by the mid 1580s had retaken Kabul and established a presence in Kashmir and Baluchistan, whilst establishing his capital at Lahore. Following the defeat of the last Tarkhan ruler of Sind in 1592, the Mughals ruled the greater part of what is now modern Pakistan. Akbar and his successors, **Jahangir**, **Shah Jahan** and **Aurangzeb**, left a lasting impression upon Pakistan, not least in the form of some magnificent Mughal monuments. Following the death of Aurangzeb in 1707, the Mughal Empire declined rapidly, although nine further emperors did succeed Aurangzeb and continued to rule from Delhi until 1858.

Across the territory of Pakistan a number of rulers began to assert their independence. The Mughals ruled Lower Sind until 1737, when the last Mughal Governor of Thatta handed over power to **Mir Nur Mohammad Kalhora**. The Kalhora's had already assumed control of much of Upper Sind by the early 1700s, and upon acquiring Thatta from the Mughals, Nur Mohammad Kalhora became regarded as the ruler who made Sind one province. The Kalhora capital was initially established at Khudabad, although this was removed to the new city of Hyderabad in 1768 by **Ghulam Shah Kalhora**. His period of rule is remembered as a time of great stability, with progress in agriculture and the flowering of Sindhi literature in the works of **Shah Abdul Latif** (see page 116). However, upon his death in 1772, a period of tyranny ensued as the Kalhora's fought with the **Talpurs** from Baluchistan for control of Sind. The Afghan kings attempted to extract as much tribute as possible from the two warring factions. Eventually, three branches of the Talpur Dynasty gained a tenuous grip on Sind.

In Baluchistan, the **Brahui** tribes were growing in strength, eventually driving out the ailing Mughal rulers and establishing their own Khanate: **Kalat State**. Meanwhile, much of the Punjab had been subjugated by the Afghan king **Ahmad Shah Durani**, who was soon to be displaced by **The Sikhs**.

Sikh rule and the rise of British power

The Sikhs During the reign of Aurangzeb, the 10th Sikh Guru **Gobind Singh** introduced the series of reforms to the religion that are now universally associated with Sikhism. He founded a new brotherhood called the **Khalsa** (meaning 'the pure' from the Persian word *khales*), and adopted a more militant stance. In 1764 the Sikhs defeated Ahmad Shah Durani, the successor to the Mughal Empire. Sikh rule over the whole of the Punjab was consolidated when the Afghans conceded Lahore to the Sikh warrior king **Ranjit Singh** in 1799. Although Ranjit Singh sided with the British in the **First Afghan War**, his successors fought two wars with the British, until the Sikh defeat at the Battle of Gujrat on 21 February 1849 that led to the British annexation of the Punjab.

The British Although the **British East India Company** had been established in India for 200 years, it was not until the middle of the 19th century that the British began to exercise any form of control over the northwest area of the subcontinent that nowadays forms Pakistan. The reason for this was simple: whereas almost all the previous invasions of South Asia had come through the passes to the west and northwest, the British had come by sea, and most of these ports were some considerable distance from this northwest frontier region.

Although there is a separate history of the British in all the different regions that now comprise Pakistan, all these histories follow a roughly similar pattern.

Sind Having become the dominant power in India, two factors attracted the British to Sind. Firstly, the British were keen to survey the Indus in order to assess its potential as a trade route. Indeed, when the British completed this survey in 1831, a Sindhi Sayyid, recognizing the implications, remarked "Alas, Sindh has now gone since the English have seen the river". Secondly, Sind became part of the British forward-bloc 'frontier strategy', to counter the perceived threat of Russian expansion through Afghanistan.

In 1842, **Sir Charles Napier** was appointed British Resident in Sind. A treaty was offered to the Talpurs requiring that: one side of the coin of Sind should bear the name of the King of England; the Talpurs should surrender Karachi, Shikarpur, Sabzalkot and Umarkot to the British; and a strip of land 30 metres wide on either side of the Indus be given to the British. Historians agree that the British knew these terms would be unacceptable, and in the inevitable resulting war, Napier's forces rapidly defeated the Talpurs.

Napier's actions were strictly against instructions from London not to interfere in Sind, and having accepted the Talpur surrender in February 1843, he telegraphed his news of the capture with the Latin word *Peccavi* ('I have sinned'). The annexation came within the background of a disastrous campaign in Afghanistan, and many feel that Napier was looking to restore some military pride to the British army. The great Indian adventurer Mountstuart Elphinstone suggested that the British action was "done in the spirit of a bully who has been kicked in the streets and goes home to beat his wife in revenge".

Baluchistan Meanwhile, the British were also becoming embroiled in the internal political machinations of the Kalat state in Baluchistan. One of the ministers in the Kalat state, Mulla Mohammad Hasan, bore a grudge against the then Khan, Mir Mehrab Khan, and managed to engineer a situation in which the British were led to believe that the Khan was working against their interests in Afghanistan. The result was decades of repeated clashes between the British and the various Baluch and Brahui tribes before the British were able to impose a settlement to their liking. In 1877 the British occupied Quetta permanently, and in 1879 signed the **Treaty of Gandamak** in which they gained formal control over much of north and eastern Baluchistan. By 1887 they had gained effective control over most of Baluchistan, though as in NWFP their control remained indirect, relying on the tribal chiefs to administer the region at the local level.

North West Frontier Province (NWFP) British policy in what was to become NWFP was largely a result of their actions in Afghanistan, and their relations with the Sikhs. Afghan pride had been seriously wounded over the loss of Peshawar to the Sikhs, and **Dost Mohammad**, who was on the throne in Kabul, was keen to regain the city. In 1836 **Alexander Burnes** led a mission to Kabul, hoping to gain the allegiance of Dost Mohammad. His task was however complicated by the fact that the British were undecided on the question of Peshawar; on the one hand they could hardly afford to antagonize the Sikhs by handing Peshawar back to him, but on the other hand, nothing less would satisfy Dost Mohammad. Sir Olaf Caroe comments that "It has never been sufficiently stressed that the desire to posses Peshawar ... was the real cause of the First Afghan War."

In the event, Burnes was outmanoeuvred by the Russians, who offered to support Dost if he were to attack the Sikhs. At the same time, Herat to the west (at that time an independent kingdom opposed to Kabul) came under siege from a Persian force supported by the Russians. Burnes's mission had failed and he was forced to return to India. The British opted to install a sympathetic ruler, acceptable to the Sikhs, on the throne of Kabul. In 1838 the **Tripartite Treaty** was signed between the British,

Ranjit Singh and **Shah Shuja**, a Durrani and former ruler of Kabul. The British despatched their **Army of the Indus**, invading Afghanistan and installing Shah Shuja on the throne. In 1841 the Afghans got their revenge, killing Shah Shuja and the two British envoys, Burnes and Macnaghten, and triggering a general uprising. The Army of the Indus, still in occupation of Kabul, started its retreat. They were shown no mercy by the Afghans. In what was later described as the worst ever defeat of the British army in Asia, just one man, Dr William Brydon, reached Jalalabad alive. "Thus is verified" wrote a civilian captive who was later rescued, "what we were told before leaving Kabul; that Mohammad Akbar would annihilate the whole army except one man, who should reach Jalalabad to tell the tale". A year later the British returned with a second army to seek revenge in Kabul, before marching "as swiftly as terrain and dignity permitted" back to British India.

Meanwhile, the death of Ranjit Singh in 1839 signalled the beginning of the end for Sikh power in the region. Two major wars with the Sikhs, in 1845 and 1848, followed before the British formally annexed the Punjab and NWFP. Initially the whole region was controlled from Lahore, by occupying frontier forts and maintaining military roads between them. Outside the settled areas, agreements were made with the tribes, in an attempt to maintain peaceful relations in return for subsidies and allowances.

In 1893 the **Durand line** was drawn up, dividing British India from Afghanistan. The border cut through the tribal areas of the Pathans. This fact, together with the fear that Britain's *Forward Policy* advocating more direct control of the region would compromise their freedom and independence, prompted them to rise up in a series of revolts in 1897. 70,000 troops were mobilized in seven military operations to put down the rebellion, and eventually, in 1901, **Lord Curzon** established the North West Frontier as a separate province administered from Peshawar. The British never really attempted to rule the province directly. Instead they allowed the small chiefs of the tribal areas to govern themselves under the watchful eye of a Political Agent. Force was continually necessary to maintain the status quo. As late as 1937, 40,000 British troops took part in a series of campaigns which ultimately left the tribes of Waziristan "masters of their own house".

Azad Jammu & Kashmir In 1819, after a series of campaigns, the Sikh ruler **Ranjit Singh** eventually succeeded in annexing Kashmir. For the next 25 years or so Kashmir was ruled "quietly, if oppressively" by a Sikh Governor appointed by the court at Lahore. This situation continued until the outbreak of the First Sikh War between the British and the Sikhs in 1845-46. The Dogra Maharaja of the mainly Hindu state of Jammu, **Gulab Singh**, was a very shrewd ruler, and managed to avoid getting embroiled in the war. Had his great ally Ranjit Singh been the man fighting the British there is little doubt that Gulab Singh would have entered the war on the Sikh side. Having less respect for Ranjit Singh's successors, however, and having consolidated his own power-base in Jammu, Gulab Singh remained aloof from the conflict. He was a great opportunist though, and at the conclusion of the war, he acted as a mediator between the British and the defeated Sikhs.

On 9 March 1846, a treaty was signed in Lahore that handed over all Sikh territory, including Kashmir, to the British. When Gulab Singh offered to pay the Sikh war reparations (a sum in the region of Rs 750,000), a second treaty was signed at Amritsar one week later. The **Treaty of Amritsar** stated that "The British Government transfers and makes over for ever, in independent possession, to Maharaja Gulab Singh and the heirs male of his body, all the hilly or mountainous country, situated to the eastward of the River Indus and westward of the River Ravi." Thus Jammu and Kashmir came under Hindu Dogra rule. The name 'Jammu and Kashmir' refers to this administrative district assembled by the British that included not only the Muslim dominated Vale of Kashmir, but the largely Hindu region of Jammu to the south, and Ladakh, the predominantly Buddhist eastern highlands of the great Himalayan axis. It is interesting to note that in hindsight, the British believed that they made a gross error in separating Kashmir from the Punjab, for had it remained part of the Sikh Empire, it would have fallen into British hands following victory in the Second Sikh War in 1849.

Northern Areas The various small kingdoms in what is now the 'Northern Areas' feuded repeatedly among themselves, but periodically succeeded in repelling the Dogras and the Sikhs. Under the terms of the 1846 Treaty of Amritsar, it was understood that Gilgit and Baltistan were to come under the suzerainty of Gulab Singh. In practice, however, his control over the Northern Areas remained entirely nominal.

Towards the end of the 19th century, British interest was heightened by Russian expansion into Central Asia. The 'Great Game' between the two regional powers followed. In 1877 the first **British Agency** was established in Gilgit, only to be abandoned in 1881 after a major revolt of Kohistani tribes. In 1889 a second British Agency was established, this time with improved road and telegraph links as well as a permanent British military presence. Throughout the 1890s, a tenuous control was maintained. Later the **Gilgit Scouts** were established as a well trained force which could keep internal order and respond to any external aggression.

Impact of British colonial rule

When studying the history of the British in India, it has to be said that the turning point was the **Mutiny** in 1857 (or 'War of Independence' depending upon your viewpoint). The Mutiny effected the end of Company rule in India, and in 1858 the Government of India Act transferred the empire of the Company to the British Crown. Having now acquired this resource-rich new colony, the British were keen to hang on to it, and the most pressing concern was to secure the vulnerable and ill-defined northwest frontier. Although Sind and Punjab had already been annexed, the unpredictable frontier tribes of modern NWFP and the Northern Areas proved to be a major source of anxiety to the British administration. When they weren't raiding into British territory, they were flirting with Britain's imperial rivals across the frontier. This era of the 'Great Game' led to the British annexation of territories such as Hunza and Nagar and the establishment of the Durand Line that remains today as the international border between Pakistan and Afghanistan.

The impact of British colonial rule in the territory of Pakistan is complex. The extension of the railway network into this northwest frontier of British India changed patterns of trade and communications, although the tracks were laid primarily to allow the rapid transportation of troops to potential trouble spots. The key feature of the period of British rule in the Punjab and Sind was the development of agriculture. The digging of canals and the construction of barrages across the rivers transformed much of what was previously uncultivatable scrub jungle into prime agricultural land. These irrigation projects, along with the establishment of canal colonies, continued from the 1850s right up until independence in 1947. However, the use of unlined canals and a degree of poor planning has left a legacy of waterlogging and salinization. Even the administrative divisions imposed by the British, including the Durand Line, have created problems for the modern state of Pakistan. The unnatural division of contiguous Pathan, or Pushto-speaking communities by an arbitrary line on a map have precipitated calls for an independent, unified Pathan state that the Pakistani government is desperate to resist.

Independence and partition

Birth of the Independence movement

Within 30 years of the Mutiny, the new western educated élite of Indian society were again articulating a demand for greater political rights, and ultimately self-government. The main vehicle for these demands was the **Indian National**

Congress, formed in 1885. Although founded as a secular organization, the Congress was viewed with suspicion by the educated Muslim élite of north India, who saw it as a tool of Hindu nationalism. The Muslims sensed a threat to their political rights, even their own identity, with the emergence of a democratic system that would give the Hindus of India, with their greater population and built-in natural majority, significant advantages. Many leading figures within the Muslim community, including Sir Sayyid Ahmad Khan, founding father of the Muslim University at Aligarh, advised Muslims against joining the Congress, and come the turn of the century Muslims made up less than eight percent of those attending the party's conferences.

In 1906, with the British Viceroy of India, Lord Minto, announcing planned constitutional changes in India, a delegation of Muslims led by the Aga Khan presented their demands to him for a separate electorate to safeguard their rights and interests. The Viceroy accepted the demands, and following this limited success, the Muslim élite thought it expedient to form an organization that could act as a platform for their views and aspirations. In December 1906 the **All-India Muslim League** was founded, and seven years later it defined its goal for the first time as self-government for the subcontinent.

The demands of the Muslim League were not always opposed to those of the Congress, although great stress was laid upon safeguarding the rights of Muslims in South Asia. In 1916, the League and Congress concluded the **Lucknow Pact** in which the Congress won League support for self-government whilst conceding the principle of separate electorates for Muslims. The League's demands were presented by its newly elected President, **Mohammad Ali Jinnah**. Although the Secretary of State for India announced in Parliament in 1917 that the British goal in India was the gradual development of self-government institutions within the British Empire, this fell far short of Congress and League expectations.

Independence movement gathers pace

In 1927 the British appointed a Commission to make recommendations for a new constitution for India. The **Simon Commission** was rejected by both the Congress and the Muslim League because it contained no Indian members. Congress founded their own commission and prepared its own document, referred to as the **Nehru Report**. The report demanded 'Dominion Status' for India, but rejected the Muslim League's demands for separate electorates and reserved seats for Muslims in Punjab and Bengal. The Muslim League countered with their own report, **'Jinnah's 14 Points'**, setting out the demands of the Muslims, and at the League's annual conference in 1929, a resolution was adopted calling for a federal rather than a unitary structure of government.

The following year, at their annual conference, the Muslim League's President, **Dr ('Allama') Mohammad Iqbal**, articulated the demand for a separate state for South Asia's Muslims. This became known as the **'two-nation theory'**.

Attempts to break the deadlock between the British, Congress and the Muslim League resulted in a series of 'Round Table Conferences' held in London. The deliberations of the conferences led to the ratification of the **Government of India Act of 1935**, a document that envisaged self-government for the people of South Asia. Although both Congress and the Muslim League found fault with the act, it did concede to many of the Muslim demands, including separate electorates, weightage, and a one-third Muslim representation at the centre. The act envisaged a federal structure at the centre, with autonomous governments responsible to the legislature at provincial level.

Both Congress and the All-India Muslim League contested the provincial elections of 1937, but the League performed very poorly, gaining just four of the 11 provinces. A massive reorganization of the structure of the Muslim League took place under the stewardship of its returning President, Mohammad Ali Jinnah, and

Mohammad Ali Jinnah

The death of Mohammad Ali Jinnah little more than a year after Pakistan gained independence left a vacuum that has never been filled. At the time of his death he held 3 key political posts (Governor General of Pakistan, President of the Muslim League and President of the Constituent Assembly),and had become universally known throughout Pakistan as Quaid-i-Azam, or 'Great Leader'.

Much has been written about the personalities involved in the independence movement of the subcontinent, yet almost without fail the part played by Gandhi is vastly overstated, whilst Jinnah's role is diminished. However, in his single-minded drive for Pakistan, Jinnah probably had more impact in the shaping of South Asia's future than any other personality. As Wolpert, Jinnah's principal biographer, points out: "Few individuals significantly alter the course of history. Fewer still modify the map of the world. Hardly anyone can be credited with creating a nation-state. Mohammad Ali Jinnah did all 3."

Part of the fascination with Jinnah is the dichotomy between his personal and public persona. Here was a man who called for the establishment of a separate homeland for the Muslims of South Asia, yet had a penchant for fine whisky and pork sausages. He married a Parsi girl over half his age (despite the girl's father attempting to get a court injunction to stop the marriage), but disowned his own daughter when she married a Parsi-born Christian. Yet there can be little doubt that without Jinnah's indomitable will, it is unlikely that Pakistan would have come into being.

The "apparent paradox of Jinnah's strange story", with the "fascinating complexity of its brilliant light and tragic darkness" can be found in Stanley Wolpert's excellent "Jinnah of Pakistan", 1984, Oxford University Press. Another very accessible means of getting some sort of handle on his life is through the recently released film, "Jinnah".

Mausoleum of Mohammad Ali Jinah, Karachi

the party was revitalized. It was in the light of this rejuvenation that Jinnah presented the Lahore Resolution.

Lahore Resolution of 1940

On 23 March 1940, Jinnah presided over the annual session of the Muslim League in Lahore. A resolution was passed that called for the partition of India. Jinnah suggested that "geographically contiguous units are demarcated into regions which should be so constituted, with such territorial readjustments as may be necessary, that the areas in which the Muslims are numerically in the majority as in the Northwestern and Eastern zones of India, should be grouped to constitute 'Independent States' in which the constituent units should be autonomous and sovereign." Although Jinnah did not specifically use the word 'Pakistan', this **Lahore Resolution** also became known as the 'Pakistan Resolution'. The 23rd of March is celebrated as 'Pakistan Day.'

Some seven years earlier, a Punjabi 'student' at Cambridge, **Chaudhuri Rahmat Ali**, had coined a name for a new Muslim state in South Asia – PAKISTAN. This acronym referred to **P**unjab, **A**fghania, **K**ashmir, **S**ind with the suffix *stan*, Persian for country (although the 'stan' is said by some to stand for Baluchistan). By coincidence, 'Pakistan' also means "land of the pure".

Independence and partition Following the Allies' victory in Europe and the conclusion of the Second World War, the then Viceroy of India, Lord Wavell, convened a meeting in Simla to discuss the future of India. The divide between the viewpoints of the Congress and the Muslim League could not be bridged and the conference ended in failure. In Britain, meanwhile, the Labour election landslide had brought Attlee to power with a resounding majority in the House of Commons. With Britain virtually bankrupt following the war, and a new socialist government in power in London, the writing was on the wall for the British colonial empire in India.

A Cabinet Mission arrived from Britain to discuss the future of India, but failed to secure an agreement between the main political parties, and so proposed their own plan. It was accepted by Congress and by the Muslim League, and although there were certain reservations, an interim government was formed.

In 1947, with the gulf between the Hindu and Muslim communities as wide as ever, Attlee, the British Prime Minister, declared that power would be transferred to responsible Indians by June 1948 at the latest. In March of that year, **Lord Mountbatten** was appointed as Viceroy, to oversee the transfer of power. Mountbatten's plan for the transfer of power envisaged a vote in both the Bengal and Punjab legislative assemblies on the partition of their provinces. On 3 June 1947, the Congress leader Nehru, and Jinnah on behalf of the Muslim League, broadcast their acceptance of the plan. Three weeks later both provinces voted a resounding "yes" to partition.

The Indian Independence Bill was passed in July 1947, and the date of the transfer of power was brought forward to 14/15th August (the 15th was deemed by Indian astrologers to be more auspicious!). Mohammad Ali Jinnah was appointed Governor General of Pakistan, and on **14 August 1947**, Pakistan became an independent nation consisting of two wings, East and West, separated by 1,600 kilometres of potentially antagonistic Indian territory between.

Radcliffe Boundary Commission When Independence arrived, many questions remained unanswered. Several key Princely States had still not decided firmly to which country they would accede; the most notable being Kashmir, a situation still unresolved today.

The question of the borders, most notably in Punjab and Bengal, was to be resolved by a Boundary Commission headed by the distinguished British barrister, **Sir Cyril Radcliffe**. Radcliffe's main qualification for the job, according to Wolpert, was that he "had never even visited India and expressed no known opinions on its problems." To further complicate a task that was to decide the destiny of millions of Muslims, Hindus and Sikhs, he was given just five weeks to complete the task. Many Pakistani historians accuse Radcliffe of bias in his 'awards', particularly of granting two predominantly Muslim tehsils that were adjacent to Kashmir to India. However, it should be noted that it was Jinnah who suggested that Radcliffe head the commission, to the consternation of Nehru.

When the boundary 'awards' were announced on 17 August 1947, the Punjab and Bengal descended into chaos as millions of Muslims, Hindus and Sikhs fled across the respective borders. According to Wolpert: "In and around Amritsar bands of armed Sikhs killed every Muslim they could find, while in and around Lahore, Muslim gangs – many of them 'police' – sharpened their knives and emptied their guns at Hindus and Sikhs. Entire train-loads of refugees were gutted and turned into rolling coffins, funeral pyres on wheels, food for bloated vultures who darkened the skies over the Punjab and were sated with more flesh and blood in those final weeks of August than their ancestors had enjoyed in a century." It is estimated that between a quarter and one million people died in the massacres that accompanied Partition.

Problems of massive population migration

The result of the movement of eight million immigrants into Pakistan's towns and cities was a sharp conflict of interests that has remained a fundamental problem for independent Pakistan. In Javed Burki's words, "it was a trauma because it resulted in a clash between two systems based on totally different traditions, beliefs and values. The much older indigenous system was rigidly hierarchical, that imported by the migrants broadly participatory. The first was a tightly organized and stable system with vertical links between different participants; the second was a loosely clustered system of horizontal linkages between members of different social groups who did not owe allegiance to any particular individual."

These conflicts of style and interest have dogged Independent Pakistan's political history to the present day, nowhere more so than in Sind. Prior to Partition, most positions in business, education, bureaucracy and trade had been filled by Hindus. At independence, the mass exodus of Hindus was matched by an equally large influx of Muslim settlers from India. Taking advantage of these new opportunities, the immigrants filled the vacuum created by the Hindus, settling mainly in the urban areas of Karachi, Hyderabad and to a lesser extent, Sukkur. Known as **mohajirs**, these recent arrivals brought a whole new culture to Sind, with very different aspirations to the predominantly rural ethnic Sindhis.

The massive influx of mohajirs to the urban areas led to the dramatic growth of cities such as Karachi and Hyderabad, and began to alarm the ethnic Sindhis who now only constituted 48 percent of the state's population. Because of their traditionally low levels of education and the lack of a middle-class, the Sindhis were unable to take advantage of new opportunities created at Partition, particularly in government positions, and felt resentful that these opportunities were being taken by Punjabis and mohajirs. Grievances between ethnic Sindhis and mohajirs continue to manifest themselves today in an extremely violent form on the streets of Karachi.

The Kashmir dispute

This state was given concrete form by the Radcliffe Commission, which drew the boundary between India and Pakistan according to the distribution of the Muslim and non-Muslim populations. The main variation from that principle was made in the case of Princely States, where as a result of pressure from Jinnah and the Muslim League, the Princes themselves were allowed to choose which country they would accede to. This caused a number of problems, the most difficult being that of Kashmir. On 14 August 1947 the Dogra **Maharaja of Kashmir** had not decided whether to accede to India or Pakistan, and still cherished the hope that Kashmir could remain fully independent. Within weeks, however, an uprising of Muslim tribes in the northwest threatened to move down into the Vale of Kashmir and to capture Srinagar with Pakistan army support.

Under this pressure the Maharaja asked for Indian help, which Lord Mountbatten insisted should only be given if Kashmir first acceded to the Indian Union. This was done, and the Indian army moved rapidly north to confront the Pakistan army in a war which dragged on until the ceasefire of January 1949. From then on the *de facto* border between India and Pakistan has divided Kashmir in two, though 'legally' the whole of the former Princely State is Indian territory.

Post independence

Early years of independence

On 11 September 1948, little more than a year after Pakistan became independent, Mohammad Ali Jinnah, the father of the nation, died. In Pakistan today there still remains the feeling that the nation was 'orphaned at birth'. Indeed, Pakistan's lack of political direction and instability is often blamed on Jinnah's early demise. Jinnah left no clear view of his vision of Pakistan; was it to be an Islamic state or a secular one, a theocracy or a democracy? There are numerous reinterpretations of speeches Jinnah gave prior to and post independence, but they are often ambiguous. Jinnah's

Troubled history in the making: Jinnah, the movie

There are few people interested in South Asian affairs who have not seen Richard Attenborough's 1982 multi Oscar-winning epic Gandhi, *yet the film remains banned in Pakistan. This is not just because it presented a highly distorted view of Gandhi and his role in Partition (read* The Myth of the Mahatma *by Michael Edwardes for an enlightening read that does not follow the usual fawning approach), but because of the highly unfavourable light in which it presented Jinnah, as "a cadaverous cynic who divided British India to sate his ambition". As the Cambridge academic Professor Akbar Ahmed observes, "It was a great film, but Jinnah's role was a travesty, a distortion of history".*

Thus, Ahmed set about bringing to the screen a film of Jinnah's life that would lay to rest the ghost of Attenborough's Gandhi. *Yet from the very beginning of the project, Ahmed has had to surmount a series of obstacles set in his path. The first controversy over the film concerned the choice of actor chosen to portray Jinnah.*

Mohammad Ali Jinnah

Seeing the renowned British actor Christopher Lee in the role of Jinnah, one is immediately struck by the physical likeness between the two men (and most who have seen the film agree that it is a remarkable portrayal, and a fitting swan-song to Lee's lengthy career). Yet the 75-year-old Lee is best known for his horror film roles as a blood-sucking vampire, and many saw him as unfit for the job of playing such a revered person as Jinnah. One commentator even noted that "Perhaps only Madonna, attacked by some Argentinians as unworthy of Eva Peron, might understand what he was going through" (Alex Spillus, The Independent, 28/6/97). Lee was later to admit that this was the most demanding film he had ever been involved with.

No sooner had the controversy over the choice of leading man died down, when a new rumour began to do the rounds in Pakistan. Supposedly started by a disgruntled journalist who was rejected as a script-writer on the project, the rumour was that none other than Salman Rushdie was writing the screenplay. This was followed by attempts to whip up a storm of frenzy over the casting of a Hindu Indian actor in the role of the Archangel Gabriel (though as Alex Spillus observed, "some in the film world asked – not unreasonably – what an archangel was doing in the story anyway").

Despite these obstacles, including withdrawal of funding from principal partners, the film is scheduled for release as this Handbook goes to press. Whether it will have the same global impact as Attenborough's "Gandhi" remains unlikely, though this is a film that deserves to be seen, and should be considered a "must see" by anyone seeking a greater understanding of Pakistan.

untimely death was most unfortunate for a nation that needed a strong, honest and well respected hand to guide it through those early, vulnerable days and to lay a solid foundation for the future.

Following Jinnah's death, **Khawaja Nazim-ud-Din**, Chief Minister of East Pakistan, was appointed as the Governor General of Pakistan, although he acted merely as a constitutional head of state. The real power lay in the hands of Jinnah's long time associate, the new Prime Minister, **Liaqat Ali Khan**. However, Pakistan was yet to frame a new constitution when Liaqat Ali Khan was assassinated in 1951. India had framed its new constitution by the end of 1949 and held its first general elections in 1951, whilst Pakistan was still effectively being governed by the 1935 Government of India Act.

One of the key issues to dominate the political scene in Pakistan during this period was the state of relations between East and West Pakistan. Since independence, the East wing felt it had been getting a raw deal, being treated as a colony of the West. One of the greatest causes of mistrust between the East and West was the language issue. Attempts by the central government to make Urdu the national language of both wings had been fiercely opposed in 1948 by the Bengali speaking East, so attempts to impose the Arabic script for the Bengali language in 1952 were particularly insensitive. The Muslim League were routed in the Provincial Assembly elections held in the East in 1954, but the Ministry was dissolved and placed under Governor's rule.

From 1953 the bureaucracy played an increasingly important role in economic and social policy. In Javed Burki's words "in the 1953-62 period, Pakistan moved from a Parliamentary to a bureaucratic form of government and from an economy dominated by the private sector to an economy guided by the civil service."

The change was partly a result of the **economic crisis** brought on by the end of the Korean War boom. The War had caused a tremendous increase in prices of cotton and jute. The slump produced a major economic crisis, and encouraged the government to take an active hand in industrial policy and management. The Pakistan Industrial Development Corporation, which had been set up in 1950, embarked on a number of projects after 1953. It became strongly allied to the landed families of the Indus plains, for while the wealthy refugee families had liquid capital to invest in industry, the landlords of the Punjab and Sind had most of their capital tied up in the land. If they were to share in industrial expansion they therefore needed support from the government to enable them to become industrial entrepreneurs. They played a prominent role in the PIDC, which by 1959 accounted for 16 percent of Pakistan's industrial wealth.

The enormous public sector push was highly successful in bringing in new industrial entrepreneurs from the landed class. This group continued to enjoy control of the major share of agricultural land and, most importantly, control of Pakistan's vital irrigation network. Their developing economic power was matched by a transformation of their political significance. The Muslim League, which had been the vehicle for Pakistan's independence, was converted during the 1950s from a party of the Indian refugees into a party re-organized to take account of the interests of West Pakistan's landlords. Party democracy was replaced by a highly centralized party system.

In 1954, despite the objections of the regional assemblies, most notably Sind, the four provinces of West Pakistan were merged into "One-Unit". This move undoubtedly helped frame a new constitution, but was probably an attempt to break the dominance in the National Assembly of East Pakistan. On 23 March 1956, the new constitution was drafted and passed (a day celebrated as 'Pakistan Day').

First Martial Law Government

Despite passing a new constitution, a series of weak governments had brought Pakistan to a point of economic and social collapse, with regionalism running rife. On 7 October 1958, the Commander-in-Chief of the Pakistan Army, **General Ayub Khan**, seized power in a bloodless coup and declared martial law stating "there is no alternative except the disintegration and complete ruination of the country". A purge of corrupt politicians and officials was announced, and some 6,000 people were charged.

One of the first acts of the martial law administration was to shift the capital from Karachi to a new site, Islamabad. A decision resented by most Karachites, for many this brand new federal capital was suspiciously close to the army GHQ at Rawalpindi. The second major programme of the Ayub Khan administration was an attempt to introduce a new system of government – **Basic Democracy System** – that was more geared towards Pakistani society. Ayub Khan's object was to give Pakistan the stable government it had so evidently lacked. He decided to create what he termed basic democracies. Every village or town area had up to 400 electors, selected according to criteria such as land ownership or literacy, whose responsibility was to elect a town or village council. These councillors in turn elected councils at a higher level such as the district. They in turn then elected representatives to Provincial councils. Ayub Khan hoped to ensure both limited political answerability down to the village level and political stability.

The 1960s witnessed unprecedented economic growth and a major change in Pakistan's political structure. **Land Reforms** passed in 1959 began to limit the power of the landlords, particularly increasing the power of the middle rank land owners. Ayub Khan also began to curb the bureaucracy, liberalizing the economy and dismantling the economic controls that had been imposed through the 1950s. But the rapid economic growth was not without costs. Liberalizing the imports of agricultural machinery, for example, has been estimated to have cost 12 jobs for every tractor imported. The cost of 80,000 tractors was thus one million rural jobs lost in the course of a decade during which Pakistan's rural population grew by over 10 million.

Ayub Khan also allowed himself to be 'elected' as President of Pakistan, and succeeded in reframing the constitution. In the 1965 Presidential Elections Ayub Khan narrowly defeated Jinnah's sister Fatima, although there were widespread allegations of cheating.

Indo-Pak War of 1965

Some commentators suggest that the Indians interpreted the alleged rigging of the Presidential elections as a sign of weakness on the part of Ayub Khan, and took full advantage by passing a bill that integrated the disputed state of Kashmir into the Indian Union. The result was a full scale war along the Indo-Pak border that was to last for 17 days until a ceasefire was agreed on 23 September 1965. Reading Pakistani newspaper analysis of the war that appears each year on 'Defence of Pakistan Day' (6 September), you would get the impression that the war was a great military victory. Impartial observers would suggest that a stalemate is the most generous interpretation of the 1965 war. In 1966, with a degree of Soviet encouragement/pressure, the two side signed a declaration in Tashkent agreeing to settle the dispute through "peaceful means".

In 1967, in an action that would have great significance for the future of Pakistani politics, Ayub Khan's Foreign Minister, **Zulfikar Ali Bhutto**, resigned his post and founded the **Pakistan People's Party** (PPP). Two years later, in 1969, amidst growing unrest in East Pakistan, Ayub Khan stepped down and handed over power to the Commander-in-Chief of the army, **General Yahya Khan**.

Second Martial Law Government

Upon becoming the Chief Martial Law Administrator and President of Pakistan, Yahya Khan swiftly abrogated the constitution of 1962, banned all political activity, and dismissed the central and provincial assemblies. In a popular move he then dissolved the 'One-Unit' of West Pakistan, and scheduled elections for 1970.

General Election of 1970 and the War of 1971

The elections were originally due to be held in October 1970 but a devastating cyclone in the East put back the date by two months. Whilst the main focus of the PPP's campaign in the West was one of economic reform and Islamic socialism, in the East the main issue was regional autonomy. In the West, the PPP won 82 of the

138 seats, but in the East the **Awami League** won a comprehensive 160 out of 162 seats. The first session of the new assembly, scheduled to be held in Dhaka, was postponed at short notice, and it soon became obvious that West Pakistan was reluctant to share power with the East, least of all be ruled by a government from there. Agitations in the East were ruthlessly suppressed by the army, and the country soon dissolved into civil war.

The civil war, and the secession of East Pakistan, is often marked as the most inglorious moment in Pakistan's history. With the Awami League calling for all out secession from Pakistan (the Bangla Desh movement), the Punjabi-dominated army was ruthless in its suppression of the insurgency. In fact, most Pakistani historians prefer to gloss over the atrocities committed on civilians by the Pakistan army, or merely suggest "we do not need to go into the details of the army's actions in East Pakistan". Amidst growing atrocities by the Pakistan army in East Pakistan, India lent her mighty force to the Bangla Desh movement, and with such a long supply line to maintain, it is little wonder that the Pakistanis were swiftly defeated. By December 1971 Pakistan had been dismembered, and a new nation, **Bangladesh**, was born.

Return to civilian rule

On 20 December 1971, General Yahya Khan handed over control to Zulfikar Ali Bhutto. Bhutto had come into government under the slogan of *roti* (bread), *kapre* (clothes), *makan* (houses/homes), and not surprisingly soon embarked upon a programme of revolutionary land reform. Like many land reform programmes it failed miserably, not least because many of the PPP leaders and politicians were (and still are) major landowners, and thus this policy was against their vested interests. Further, with no proper land registry, plots above the threshold size were simply divided between family members and re-registered. Bhutto also launched a programme of nationalization that now, 30 years later, is considered by many economists as being the key economic decision that prevented Pakistan from developing as one of the so-called 'Asian economic tigers'.

Martial law was lifted on 20 April 1972, and an interim constitution enforced. By this stage Pakistan had lived under 16 years of martial law and five constitutions. Bhutto also sought to normalize relations with India, and in 1972 signed the 'Simla Agreement' with Indira Gandhi, the Indian Prime Minister. The agreement effected troop withdrawals following the 1971 war, and facilitated the exchange of prisoners. In 1974, Lahore was the venue for the Second Islamic Summit Conference that was attended by most of the heads of state from the Muslim world. Although the summit achieved little, the conspiracy theorists in Pakistan would have you believe that Bhutto's efforts to bring the Islamic world closer together is the reason the 'Americans had him hanged'!

Bhutto's main opponents in the 1977 General Elections were the **Pakistan National Alliance** (PNA), an alliance of mainly religious parties, plus the Pakistan Muslim League (PML). In the event, Bhutto's PPP won 155 of the 200 seats in the National Assembly, amidst charges of massive poll rigging. In a deteriorating law and order situation, the PNA contested the result, and on 5 July 1977 the army stepped in once more.

Third Martial Law Government

The army's Chief of Staff, **General Zia ul-Haq**, declared that he had taken over "to enforce Islam in the country". Zia claimed that he had no political ambitions and would return the country to democratic rule through elections within 90 days. His administration was to last 11 years. The 1973 Constitution of Pakistan was suspended, the national and provincial assemblies dissolved, the Prime Minister, cabinet members and leaders of the main political parties arrested and placed under protective custody. Not surprisingly the elections were suspended. Elections were rescheduled for November 1979, but in the meantime Zia had started a process of accountability directed primarily against the PPP, whilst the PNA joined the martial law administration.

Bhutto's trial and execution

Under Zia, a case against Bhutto dating back to November 1974 was reopened. It was claimed that the Federal Security Force (FSF), acting under Bhutto's orders, had opened fire on a car carrying Ahmad Razi Qasuri, a dissident PPP MNA, killing his father. Commenting later on the court proceedings that he had witnessed, Ramsey Clark, former Attorney General of the US noted: "The prosecution case was based entirely on several witnesses who were detained until they confessed, who changed and expanded their confessions and testimony with each reiteration, who contradicted themselves and each other, who, except for Masood Mahmood (Director General of the FSF) were relating what others said, whose testimony led to four different theories of what happened, who were absolutely uncorroborated by an eyewitness, direct evidence, or physical evidence." Bhutto was found guilty, and on 4 April 1979 was hanged.

Zia's Islamization programme

By the end of 1978 Zia had made himself President of Pakistan, but the elections scheduled for 1979 were cancelled. A process of Islamization began with the enforcement of Islamic laws against drinking alcohol, theft, adultery and Qazf. Severe punishments were introduced for those found guilty: for drinking, 80 stripes of the whip; for a first offence of theft (if the goods stolen were valued more than 4.457 grams of gold), amputation of right hand, for a second offence amputation of left foot, for a third offence, life imprisonment; for adultery, stoning to death, for unmarried sex, 100 stripes; for Qazf (false allegation of adultery) 80 stripes. However, despite the uproar in the West over these 'inhumane' punishments, a review of the period suggests that far fewer punishments were actually carried out than first suggested.

The economic system of Pakistan was further Islamicized, with greater emphasis placed on the payment of *Zakat* (tax). The military further took over the judiciary, and in 1981 the High Courts were stripped of their powers of judicial review and writ jurisdiction. The same year saw the formation of the **Movement for Restoration of Democracy** (MRD), involving major parties including the PPP.

In 1984 Zia engineered a referendum that was taken by him as a mandate to remain as President for the next five years at least. One of the key reasons for the security of Zia's position was the huge Soviet presence in Afghanistan. Indeed the Soviet invasion of Afghanistan in December 1979 is often referred to as "Brezhnev's Christmas present to Zia". With both Afghan refugees and Soviet troops on the doorstep, Pakistan received massive quantities of foreign aid, becoming the third largest recipient of US aid after Israel and Egypt. Such was the strength of Zia's position, with the American's fearing the spread of communism, that Zia was able to dismiss a $400 million aid package from the American President Jimmy Carter as "peanuts".

'End' of Martial Law

In 1985 Zia allowed elections to be held, but they had to be contested on a non-party basis. The MRD boycotted the event. Zia was 'elected' President for a further five years and **Mohammad Khan Junejo** was appointed as Prime Minister. Amendments were made to the constitution, effectively protecting and justifying all martial law promulgations and laws. On 30 December 1985, Martial Law was lifted, but in name only.

In May 1988 Junejo was dismissed by Zia, who claimed that he had not enforced the Islamic system in the country. In July that year Zia promulgated the Shariah ordinance, bringing stricter interpretations of Islamic law. Elections were scheduled for November 1988, but on 17 August 1988, Zia ul-Haq was killed in a mysterious aircrash at Bahawalpur. The chairman of the Senate, **Ghulam Ishaque Khan**, took over the temporary reigns as President.

Pakistan's 'experiments' with democracy: 1988 to present day

Pakistan's 'experiments' with democracy from 1988 until the present day do not make encouraging reading. At the time of going to press, none of the democratically elected governments have served their full term in office. Yet in a country with such a record of military intervention in the functioning of government, none of these failed governments have had their period of governance terminated by an army inspired coup d'état; they have in fact all been driven out of office through their own incompetence and corruption.

National elections of 1988

There was a real feeling of hope throughout Pakistan (and across the rest of the world for that matter), when **Benazir Bhutto**, daughter of Zulfikar Ali Bhutto, was sworn in as Prime Minister in December 1988. Yet Bhutto's PPP government was dismissed by the President just 22 months later, with "corruption, mismanagement and violation of the Constitution" cited as the reasons. Looking back at this period now, there is a real feeling that Pakistan missed its big chance. In the words of Christina Lamb, "on few occasions in history has a ruler squandered so much goodwill so quickly" (*Waiting for Allah*, 1991, an excellent analysis of Bhutto's first government). Many historians feel that those in power were simply seeking to make as much money for themselves as quickly as possible, fearing that the military were poised to resume control of the country at any time. In fact, graffiti appeared on walls all across Pakistan explaining: "We apologize for this temporary democratic interruption. Normal martial rule will be resumed shortly". Bhutto's excuse, "if there was corruption why did no one bring me the facts?" (C. Lamb, *ibid*) seems exceptionally weak, especially when the entire country was referring to her husband **Asif Zardari** as "Mr 10 percent"!

National elections of 1990

The 1990 elections were won by the IJI alliance, with the Pakistan Muslim League's (PML) **Mian Mohammad Nawaz Sharif** installed as Prime Minister. Former Chief Minister of Punjab and a Zia protégé, Nawaz Sharif embarked upon an economic policy of increased privatization, de-nationalization and de-regulation. In many regards, Nawaz Sharif's term as Prime Minister was merely a re-run of Benazir's previous government. An anti-corruption drive launched by the government was seen as a process of victimization by the opposition; a return to that Machiavelli an axiom that "the first rule of politics is to stay in power", mainly through discrediting the opposition. Nawaz Sharif was virtually saying 'you did it to me and now I'm doing it to you'.

Relations between the Prime Minister and President deteriorated rapidly, partly over the performance of the government, and significantly over Nawaz Sharif's attempts to scrap the Eighth Amendment. Ironically, this is the amendment to the Constitution introduced by Zia which allows the President to dismiss the government (one that Benazir had already fallen victim to). In April 1993 the President dismissed the government, and though Nawaz Sharif took the matter to the Supreme Court, the perceived threat of army intervention led to both Prime Minister and President tendering their resignations.

National elections of 1993

A caretaker government run by the noted Pakistani economist **Moeen Qureshi** took over the day to day administration of Pakistan in the intervening period, publishing an extensive and damning list of government loan defaulters who were barred from contesting the forthcoming election. Benazir Bhutto's PPP were narrowly returned to power in the national elections of 1993, although the remarkably poor turn-out (just 40 percent) seems to illustrate succinctly the people's disenchantment with their politicians. A PPP nomination, **Sardar Farooq Ahmad Khan Leghari**, was elected President.

However, 'normal service' was swiftly resumed, with charge and counter-charge of corruption being tossed between government and opposition, and the 'man on the Karachi omnibus' getting screwed by both. By now Bhutto's husband was being referred to as "Mr 50 percent"! By November 1996 the President had dismissed the government through his powers under the Eighth Amendment, once more citing rampant corruption as the reason. Another list of loan defaulters was drawn up, barring them from contesting the forthcoming election, though this time the colossal sums involved took the breath away: over 140 billion rupees had been borrowed from nationalized commercial banks and development finance institutions by about 13,000 individuals, businesses and government departments. This is a staggering amount of money in a country where the average man earns just 65 rupees a day.

National elections of 1997

Although there was a record low turn-out for the February 1997 elections (36 percent), Nawaz Sharif was swept back into power with a resounding victory (some two-thirds of the vote). Bhutto's PPP could only claim a handful of seats in the 217-seat National Assembly, effectively being reduced to a regional party in her native Sind province. She accused the opposition of rigging the election, although she was quoted by journalists of clearing Nawaz Sharif of any complicity since "he has no idea. I've told you before, he doesn't have a brain"! Some commentators claim that Benazir is finished as a major political force, and her call for a government of national unity "minus Nawaz Sharif and myself" (*Newsline*, September 1998) does sound like a desperate measure, but don't write her political obituary just yet.

Imran Khan's anti-corruption party, **Tekreek-e-Insaaf**, also faired poorly and failed to gain a single seat (allowing joyful British newspapers to write that Imran was "clean bowled for nought"). Imran allowed a BBC TV crew to film him on the 1997 campaign trail (*"Imran's Final Test"*), and there is one particularly light-hearted moment when Imran is on the phone to his wife Jemima as the results come in. "It's a landslide" he says, and as Jemima begins to congratulate him, he cuts in to say "no, the other way"!

Recent events

Nawaz Sharif's first act in power was to consolidate his authority. Within weeks of coming to power, the 13th Amendment was unanimously passed (fully supported by his biggest political foe, Benazir Bhutto), and thus Zia's Eighth Amendment (allowing the President to dismiss the government) was cancelled. Almost immediately a 14th Amendment was passed, ruling out 'lotaism' (effectively floor-crossing by elected members of the assembly). According to the Pakistani political commentator Zaffar Abbas, "the idea was to replace governance through presidential decrees with legislation passed by the elected forum", although critics suggested that "the government was using its brute majority to make parliament into a rubber-stamp for its whims" (*Herald*, March 1998).

But Nawaz Sharif's biggest political battle, and victory, was to come later in the year. An apparent disagreement with the Supreme Court Chief Justice (largely over the Eighth Amendment) developed into a full-scale power struggle that eventually led to President Leghari's resignation (to be replaced by **Rafiq Tarar**, Nawaz Sharif's "hand-picked choice") and the dismissal of the Chief Justice. Assessing Nawaz Sharif's first year back in power, Zaffar Abbas suggests that "at the end of the day, the people who voted him into power expect a qualitative change in their lives. No amount of constitutional or economic reforms will compensate for real benefits on the ground."

Yellow taxi scheme

Nawaz Sharif sought to solve Pakistan's chronic urban transport problem and to reduce massive unemployment in one fell swoop. Enter the 'Prime Minister's Public Transport Scheme', also known as the 'Yellow Taxi Fiasco'. The scheme involved the import of thousands of yellow taxis (and also minibuses) primarily from South Korea. Customs duties were waived, and the vehicles were offered to unemployed men at competitive rates. Only a 10 percent deposit was required, with the balance paid to the banks by instalment. In addition to virtually draining Pakistan's foreign exchange reserves, the scheme almost bankrupted a number of banks. Few of the taxi-owners ever repaid their loans. Further, it was later found that many of the vehicles imported duty-free ended up in the possession of influential persons who used them for their own personal use. Perhaps the only positive aspect of this affair is the fact that it is now very easy to get a modern taxi in any city in Pakistan.

His second year in power has been equally dramatic. When India reasserted itself as a nuclear power on 11 May 1998, Pakistan was left with a difficult choice between following suit or stepping back. Despite the threat of US inspired sanctions, and possible withdrawal of international financial assistance at a time when the economy was teetering on the edge, there are few political analysts who would deny that Pakistan had little option than to follow suit. Thus, on 28 May 1998, following a series of underground tests at Chagai in the Baluchistan desert, Pakistan declared itself a **'nuclear state'**. But now that the euphoria is beginning to die down (and there was a very real sense of jubilation in Pakistan at the time of the tests), people are beginning to question not just the seriousness of this escalation in the arms race, but also the economic cost of diverting resources away from health, education and public services.

Whilst Pakistan stared the threat of economic meltdown in the face during late 1998, and as widespread political discontent became more vocal, Nawaz Sharif played what many described as the 'religious card'. He told the National Assembly, "The nuclear tests changed the colour of the Chagai mountains and the Shariat bill will change the colour of society" as he announced plans to move a **15th Amendment** that would replace the existing British-style legal system with Islamic courts and make the "Qur'an and Sunnah the supreme law of the land". Nawaz Sharif's 'playing of the religious card' largely united the nation – against him! Whilst opposition leaders accused him of trying to turn Pakistan into a Taliban-style state, human rights groups called it "the last pill for the demise of this state", minority group leaders decried it, and even the religious parties rejected the bill as having "nothing to do with Islamic Shariat".

What concerned most commentators was not so much the prospect of Pakistan's drift towards becoming a theocracy (after all, the present Constitution already states that "there will be no law contrary to the Qur'an and Sunnah", and Pakistan already has a Federal Shariat Court), but more the concentration of absolute powers into one person's hands. As *Newsline* pointed out, "Under the new amendment, the ruling party (actually the Prime Minister, since dissent is curtailed under the 14th Amendment) could, with a simple majority, pass a law suspending all fundamental freedoms as being contrary to Islam" (September 1998). Eventually a watered-down version of the amendment was passed in the National Assembly, though it didn't really say anything about the supremacy of Shariat not already in the Constitution. At the time of going to press, however, the amendment was being held up in the Senate.

Perhaps inevitably, that old bug-bear of corruption in high places is beginning to dominate press headlines in Pakistan again – the usual signal for a change of government. Whilst Benazir and her immediate family answer charges from Swiss prosecutors about millions of dollars found in accounts there, Nawaz Sharif is being closely questioned about his own source of wealth. Journalists are questioning how the declared wealth of the Sharif family allegedly" increased by nearly 800 percent between 1990-93 during Nawaz Sharif's first tenure as Prime Minister, and by an astronomical 3,600 percent during the last 10 years" (*Newsline*, July 1998). And as Nawaz Sharif launches a drive to bring loan defaulters to book, commentators are asking when his extended family (at least 87 members who are involved in the erstwhile Ittefaq Empire) are going to start to repay their debts (at least 1,149 billion rupees was identified by the Election Tribunal in January 1997, though the figure was estimated by *The Herald* in August 1998 to stand at 5,679 billion rupees).

For visitors to Pakistan, the Machiavellian workings of the political system are morbidly fascinating, but to those living there and directly affected by them, they must be spirit crushing.

Land and environment

Geography

The landscape of Pakistan is one of extraordinary contrasts. To the north lies a mountainous region that features the greatest concentration of high peaks in the world, and the longest glaciers outside the polar regions, while to the south is a vast river plain, with a catchment area of over 450,000 square kilometres. Yet were it not for the complex irrigation schemes that allow cultivation of large tracts in the east and south, 90 percent of Pakistan would be desert.

The physical geography of Pakistan falls into two major regions, each formed by distinct geomorphic processes: 1) The extensive flat plains of the Indus and its tributaries resulting from the deposition of sediments washed down from the Himalaya; 2) The mountains to the north and west produced by the action of the Indian plate that carries the ancient rocks of the subcontinent, subducting beneath the Eurasian landmass.

Rivers

Indus Plains

The Indus Plains include most of the provinces of Punjab and Sind. They have been formed by the alluvium laid down by the **Indus** and its major tributaries. The Indus

Regional Setting

The Indus Waters Treaty

Following Partition, the new international border between Pakistan and India cut indiscriminately across the natural drainage system of the Indus. As a downstream neighbour, Pakistan was at the mercy of upstream usage of its key river and major tributaries, and became particularly alarmed by India's plan to stop the flow of the Ravi and Beas into Pakistan by diverting them into the Sutlej. Further plans were also made to divert part of the Chenab, thus depriving Pakistan of water used to irrigate 3.2 million hectares of agricultural land.

*As a solution to this potentially explosive situation, the World Bank proposed a legal division of the Indus River system between the 2 countries. The plan, accepted by both sides in 1960 as the **Indus Waters Treaty**, allocated the 3 western rivers (**Indus, Jhelum, Chenab**) to Pakistan, and the 3 eastern rivers (**Ravi, Sutlej, Beas**) to India. Technical and financial assistance was provided by the World Bank and donor countries for construction of dams, link canals, barrages, drainage canals, ancillary works, bridges, roads and railways as part of an integrated development plan.*

*However, of the 5 water storage dams that the plan envisaged being constructed in Pakistan by 1995, only 2, **Mangla** and **Tarbela**, have been built. Estimates suggest that if a 3rd dam is not built by the year 2000, Pakistan will be forced to import 4 million tons of wheat, 2 million tons of rice and 3 million tons of edible oils to meet the production shortfall. The proposed construction of the 3rd dam at **Kalabagh** in Punjab, however, has become a major political issue.*

is one of the world's great rivers, stretching 2,880 kilometres from its source at 5,180 metres in Manasarovar Lake in Tibet, to its mouth in the Arabian Sea. From its source, the river runs east-west, cutting a deep gorge through the Himalaya and Karakoram ranges, before turning sharply south at Sazli. It then makes a tortuous journey through the dramatic gorges of Kohistan before emerging onto the Punjab plains at Attock, still 1,600 kilometres from the sea.

Mountains

Large areas of Pakistan comprise of mountain systems and plateaux, and though there are great variations in height and extent, the origins of the building process are common to all. The dramatic slowmotion collision between the Indian plate and the Eurasian landmass, a process which continues today, resulted in uplift that formed the major mountain chains of South Asia. The process of mountain building has been a relatively recent phenomenon on the geological timescale. Although the Karakoram range may have begun to form 100 million years ago, the core of the Himalayas date to about 35 million years ago, with two further major movements between five and 25 million years ago. Sub-Himalayan ranges such as the Siwaliks are even more recent. The rocks at the core of the Himalayas were formed under the intense pressure and heat of the mountain building process.

The mountain and plateaux regions of Pakistan can be divided into five main divisions: Mountainous North; Safed Koh and Waziristan Hills; Suleiman and Kirthar Mountains; Baluchistan Plateau; Potwar Plateau and the Salt Range.

Mountainous North This extends across the whole of the Northern Areas, much of NWFP, and into parts of Punjab. The geological region extends across the international borders into Afghanistan, Tajikistan, China (including Tibet), India and Nepal, and includes most of the world's great mountain ranges. The western most extension of the **Greater Himalayas** is marked by the massive Nanga Parbat (8,126 metres), in the Northern

Areas. The chain is dominated by high peaks, many over 4,500 metres. To the south are the **Lesser Himalayas**, a highly folded and faulted chain that includes Murree and the Galis, the **Pir Panjal** range in Kashmir, and much of Hazara District. Heights vary from 1,800 metres to over 4,500 metres. Finally, the southernmost ranges of the Himalayas are the **Siwaliks**, or **Sub-Himalayas**. Rising to only 1,200 metres, they are deeply folded and faulted.

The dominant chain in the Mountainous North is the **Karakoram**, an awesome blend of high peaks, glaciers, plateaus, lakes and river valleys. The Karakoram range, and the various sub-ranges that bifurcate from the main chain, rise to an average height of 6,100 metres, and include some of the world's highest peaks. The Northern Areas are home to 12 of the world's top 30 peaks, with five over 8,000 metres, 25 over 7,500 metres and almost 100 over 7,000 metres. In **K2** (8,611 metres), Pakistan can boast a mountain second only to Everest in height, whilst **Nanga Parbat** (8,126 metres), graveyard to 47 climbers, can surely be acknowledged as the largest solid lump of rock anywhere on earth. The Karakoram chain contains some of the longest glaciers outside of the polar regions, including **Siachen** (72 kilometres), **Biafo** (62 kilometres), **Hispar** (61 kilometres), **Batura** (58 kilometres), **Baltoro** (58 kilometres), **Gasherbrum** and **Chogo Lungma** (both 38 kilometres). Ice cover in the Karakoram is estimated at 23-25 percent as opposed to eight to 10 percent in the Himalaya and 2.2 percent in the Alps. The region's glaciers provide both a creative and destructive force, being responsible for loss of agricultural land and damage to road networks through encroachment, but also providing the source for irrigation in a region where rain-fed agriculture is not possible.

To the west of the Karakorams are the rugged and heavily glaciated **Hindu Kush** range (literally 'Hindu killer'), which raise a formidable barrier along the western and northern border with Afghanistan. Averaging over 6,000 metres, the highest mountain **Tirich Mir** reaches 7,708 metres. Further north the **Pamir** mountains with their high plateaux reach over into the Wakhan Corridor and the Central Asian states of the former Soviet Union. The lower **Shandur** range (referred to during colonial times as the Hindu Raj) separates the Gilgit River basin to the north from the hills and mountains of Dir, Swat and Indus Kohistan.

Safed Koh Ranges and Waziristan Hills

In the south of NWFP, the **Safed Koh** mountains, averaging 3,600 metres (the highest peak **Sikeram** reaches 4,760 metres), run east-west from around the Khyber Pass and, along with the **Waziristan Hills** to the south, also form a boundary with Afghanistan. These were formed by the same processes as the Mountainous North, but have been subject to later igneous activity. These ranges have played a significant role in the settlement pattern of South Asia. Although now forming a boundary between Pakistan and Afghanistan, the ease of access through the passes of the chain, such as the Khyber, has provided a natural route into South Asia for invading armies, traders, new religions and cultures. Further, some of the valleys created by rivers draining off these ranges, for example the Vale of Peshawar, have

Himalayan Profile

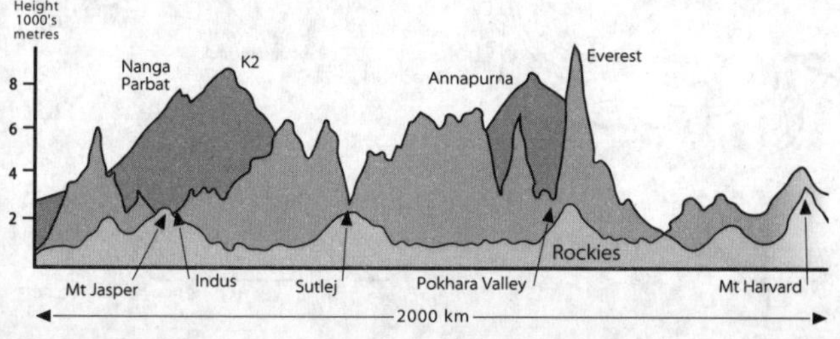

become the centres of major cultures.

Suleiman-Kirthar Mountains Also formed by the Himalayan mountain building process, the **Suleiman-Kirthar Mountains** define the administrative border between Sind and Baluchistan. They run 240 kilometres north to south in a gently curving easterly arc and are topped by Spitangi limestone, between 25 and 50 million years old. The highest point in the Suleiman range is Takht-e-Suleiman (3,375 metres) in the north, while the highest point in the Kirthar range is Kutte-ji Qabar, or Dog's Grave (2,060 metres) in the southern part of the system known as Sindh Kohistan.

Baluchistan Plateau To the west of the Suleiman-Kirthar Mountains lies the **Baluchistan Plateau**, an extensive area crossed by a number of low ranges (Makran Coast Range, Central Makran Range, Siahan, Ras Koh, Chagai, Toba Kakar), with a number of important basins lying between the upland areas (Zhob Valley, Quetta Valley, Baji Valley, Mastung Valley, Kech Valley). The east of Baluchistan is occupied by the Lasbela Plains, with a narrow coastal plain referred to as the **Makran Coast** to the south.

Potwar Plateau and the Salt Range These are two other important areas, located in north Punjab. Running northeast-southwest from Mandra to Kalabagh is the **Salt Range**, two lines of low rugged hills whose seasonal rivers have carved out deep, colourful gorges interspersed with vibrant, fertile oasis. The range is rich in ancient Palaeolithic sites, and rock salt has been mined here for over 2,000 years. The mine at Khewra is the world's most extensive salt mine, and the second largest in terms of production.

In the north of the state is the **Potwar Plateau**, an extraordinary landscape covering almost 13,000 square kilometres. The result of recent uplift, the plateau has deep canyons and gorges carved into the soft rock by ancient rivers such as the **Soan**, and covered by varying depths of loess (wind blown silt). The Potwar is the earliest proven oil producing region in Pakistan, with the country's oldest refinery at Rawalpindi. Despite modest rainfall making it a hard land to cultivate, the Potwar Plateau is rich in ancient sites of some of South Asia's earliest settlements.

Tectonic Map

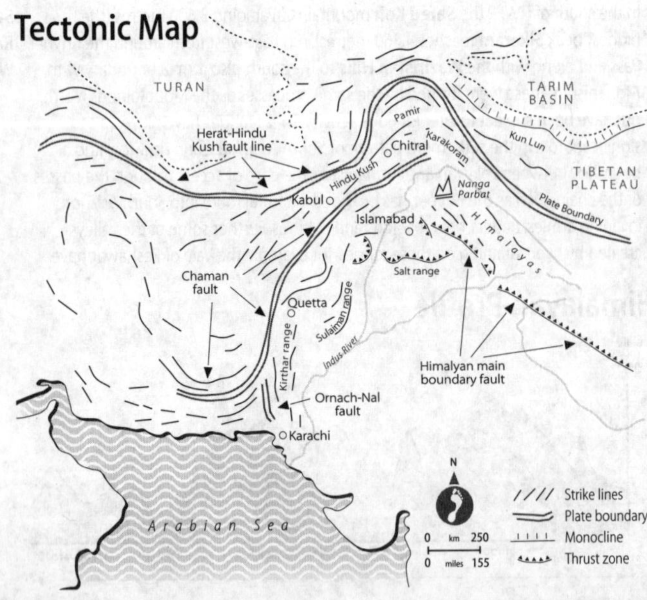

Deserts

The east and northeast margins of Sind are defined by desert. The **Thar Desert** straddles the international border with India, where it extends into the Rajasthan Desert. The northern reaches of the Thar are known locally as the *Pat*. The surface configuration of parts of both deserts has been transformed by irrigated agriculture. To the northeast, the Thar extends into the **Cholistan Desert** in Punjab. Covering over 25,000 square kilometres, the Cholistan is the largest desert in Pakistan. Much of Punjab's other great desert, the **Thal**, lying between the Indus and the Jhelum, is undergoing rapid transformation through irrigation. Much of the mountainous north of Pakistan may effectively be described as 'high-altitude desert'.

Climate

There are three main climatic regimes in Pakistan, although each is modified by factors such as latitude and altitude. The climate over most of the country is predominantly dry, with less than 10 percent of the land area receiving more than 500 millimetres of rainfall a year. A narrow east-west belt of land from Lahore to Peshawar experiences a humid subtropical climate, where rainfall totals exceed 800 millimetres. To the north, the moderating effect of altitude produces a Highland climate, with little rainfall, and arctic temperatures at great heights. **NB** For further details on the best time to visit, see 'Planning your trip' in the 'Essentials' section, plus the regional chapter introductions.

Rainfall

Much of the southern region of Pakistan, including Sind, Baluchistan and south Punjab receives less than 250 millimetres per year, with many large areas receiving less than 125 millimetres. Parts of the central Northern Areas, in the rain shadow of the high mountain chains, also receive less than 125 millimetres annually, mostly in the form of snow at the higher altitudes.

The two main sources of rainfall in Pakistan are the **monsoon**, and the **winter depressions**. Pakistan is at the northwest limits of the monsoon, with over half the rainfall on the Indus Plains arriving in the three monsoon months of July to September. However, much of the rainfall has already been deposited over India, and the secondary monsoon winds that enter south Punjab and Sind have generally lost most of their moisture. The winter depressions, travelling east from the Mediterranean across Iran and Afghanistan, bring some rainfall to the humid subtropical belt, hilly areas of NWFP and parts of north Baluchistan. The timings of these depressions, generally between December-March, are highly unpredictable.

A further source of rainfall is thunderstorms that often cause catastrophic flooding throughout the entire Indus Basin. These usually occur when the summer high pressure cell, stretching from the Sahara and across Arabia to Pakistan, is replaced by great moist monsoon air masses sweeping across the Arabian Sea.

Temperatures

Pakistan experiences great extremes of temperature, with figures varying sharply with latitude and altitude. The desert areas of Sind and Baluchistan experience some of the hottest temperatures on earth (as much as 52.8°C has been recorded). By contrast, temperatures of 30°C are not uncommon at altitude in the mountainous north. There can also be great diurnal (day/night) temperature ranges in many areas of the country.

Fazle Karim Khan (1991) identifies four main temperature regions in Pakistan (see map). 1) Hot summer and mild winter: temperature of the hottest month 32°C+, winter temps 10-21°C. 2) Warm summer and mild winter: summer temps 21-32°C, winter temps 10-21°C. 3) Warm summer and cool winter: summer temps 21-32°C, coolest month 0-10°C. 4) Mild summer and cool/cold winter: summer temps 10-21°C and coolest month well below 0°C in some areas, 0-10°C in others.

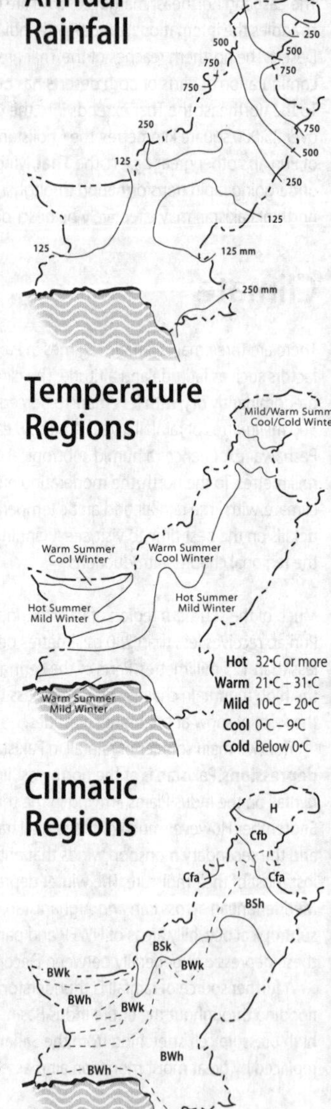

Flora and fauna

Vegetation

There are around 5,700 different plant species in Pakistan, with 500 of them being listed as endangered. Many are of great value in medicinal terms. However, since the greater part of the country experiences a dry climate, vegetation cover is for the most part scarce. There are also three large desert areas in Pakistan (Thar-Cholistan, Thal, Kharan), in addition to vast regions of the mountainous north that are under snow and ice, or above the tree-line (approximately 3,800 metres).

Although parts of Azad Kashmir, Kohistan, Swat Valley, Murree and the Galis, Chitral, Kaghan Valley and Hazara are heavily forested, less than four percent of the land area of Pakistan is under forest. (**NB** This figure excludes the Northern Areas). As in many other parts of the world, figures on forest cover, afforestation and regeneration are highly sensitive and subject to manipulation. Current figures suggest that forest cover in Pakistan has actually doubled since Partition, despite the fact that deforestation is seen as a major threat in many areas. In 1995 the Federal Government unveiled an ambitious new campaign to double forest cover within the next generation.

There are seven forest types recognizable in Pakistan. **Alpine Forests** occur above the tree-line in parts of NWFP and the Northern Areas, although the severity of the environment means that they are not extensive. **Coniferous Forests** extend across parts of Baluchistan and NWFP, including Swat, Dir, Malakand, Kohistan and Hazara, plus Rawalpindi District of Punjab, and parts of the Northern Areas. They occur between 1,000 and 4,000 metres and are dominated by fir (*Abies spp*), spruce

(*Piceamorinda*), deodar (*Cedrus deodara*), kail (*Pinus excelsa*) and chir (*Pinusroxburghii*). Coniferous forests are often mixed with **deciduous** trees, including oaks (*Quercus*), maple (*Acer*), birch (*Betula*), poplar (*Populas*), walnut (*Juglans*) and juniper (*Juniperus*). Such forests are generally key sources of timber.

Sub-tropical Dry Forests occur in many of the foothill regions of Punjab and NWFP up to 1,000 metres, and provide mainly a supply of firewood. The key trees are phula (*Acacia modesta*), kao (*Olea cuspidata*) and the main deciduous trees mentioned above. In areas of Punjab and Sind, xerophytic scrubs such as *Acacia spp* are found as part of patchy **Tropical Thorn Forests**, whilst along the banks of the key rivers such as the Indus, there are narrow belts of **Riverain Forests**. The key species here are babul (*Acacia arabica*) and shisham (*Dalbergia sissoo*).

On the coasts, particularly at the Hub and Indus deltas, there are the ecologically important **Mangrove Forests**. These forests act as an interface between the land and the sea, moderating sea water incursions and controlling the over-quick export of waste into the sea. These forests are ecologically very sensitive, and are greatly under threat due to the over-usage of the main species *Rhizophoras* in the charcoal industry.

Finally, there are a number of man-made **Irrigated Forests** in Pakistan, including South Asia's oldest at Chhanga Manga, 68 kilometres southwest of Lahore (see Longer Excursions from Lahore). Many of these forests form part of national parks, although most are still farmed as sustainable sources of timber and firewood.

In addition to forest areas, there are a number of important **Wetlands** around Pakistan. Amongst the world's most productive environments, wetlands regulate flood levels, purify water, in addition to providing a habitat to many migratory birds. Haleji Lake, near to Thatta in Sind, has recorded as many as 222 different species of birds in the immediate environs.

Soils

The soils of Pakistan are derived primarily from alluvium (river-bourne silt) and weathering action on underlying rocks. The scarce vegetation cover results in soils which are generally rich in basic materials, but poor in organic matter. The topography of the country also has a great role to play, with the nature of the terrain in the mountainous north making it vulnerable to erosion.

Soil erosion is a major problem in Pakistan and is increasingly common in regions subject to deforestation and overgrazing. A further threat to agricultural productivity comes from the twin concerns of **waterlogging** and **salinization**. These problems are particularly acute in large areas of Sind and Punjab that are irrigated by canals. Many of the canal irrigation schemes begun by the British in the 19th century, and continued ever since, were poorly planned, cutting across natural lines of drainage. As much as a third of irrigation water may be lost through seepage, particularly in schemes where canals are unlined. A further third may be lost through evaporation. Excess water percolating downwards can lead to a rise in the water table, causing waterlogging. With high temperatures and low humidity causing extremely high rates of evaporation, the static water rapidly dries out leaving a layer of minerals and salts on the surface. The problem is so great in Pakistan that it is estimated that by the middle of the 1970s, over one-third of the irrigated land in Sind and Punjab was moderately to severely affected by waterlogging and salinization.

Major programmes have been implemented by the Government of Pakistan in order to combat this problem, including the **Salinity Control and Reclamation Projects (SCARPS)**, but the problem is compounded by the fact that large areas of Sind are underlain by severely saline ground water. The only solution is to drain away the water, at great cost to the programme.

Wildlife

Despite its often harsh environment, Pakistan is home to a surprisingly rich diversity of wildlife. Over 1,000 different species, comprising of 666 bird species, 178 mammal species, 176 reptile species and 16 amphibian species, are found in the country. Five out of six of the **Markhor** species (a type of goat) found in the world occur in Pakistan (the Chiltan, Kabul, Suleiman, Astor and Pir Panjal Markhor). **Wild sheep** species include the Afghan, Punjab and Ladakh Urial, as well as the famous Marco Polo (Great Pamir) Sheep and Blue Sheep (or Bharal). **Himalayan Ibex** and **Sind Ibex** (more correctly the Persian Wild Goat) are also found. Mammals such as the **Indus River Dolphin**, **Chiltan Markhor** and **Suleiman Markhor**, are unique to Pakistan. However, many animals and birds found in Pakistan, including the **Baluch** and **Himalayan Brown Bears**, **Snow Leopard**, and seven different species of **pheasant**, are either rare, seriously endangered or on the point of extinction. Others, such as the **One Horned Rhino** and **Black Buck**, have been completely eliminated from the country, although there are efforts to reintroduce them.

Many migratory birds pass through Pakistan, flying along what is known as the **Indus Flyway** as they migrate from Central Asia to South Asia and East Africa. One of the most important of these is the **Houbara Bustard**, which breeds in Central Asia, mainly in the Kizil Kum Desert region southeast of the Aral Sea, before migrating to Pakistan, Afghanistan, Iran and India for the winter. In Pakistan its main habitats are in Baluchistan, Punjab and Sind. Due to excessive hunting, the Houbara Bustard is under serious threat in Pakistan . Ironically Sakar Falcons, captured in Chitral (and themselves a threatened species) are used by visitors from the oil-rich Gulf States to hunt the bird. Many endangered duck species, including the **Marble Teal** and **White Headed Duck** also pass through. In Chitral migrating ducks have been hunted for centuries with local people going to great lengths to build artificial ponds alongside rivers in order to encourage the birds to land there.

Conservation

Pakistan is a signatory to the Convention on Trade in Endangered Species (CITES), the Convention on Wetlands of International Importance (Ramsar) and the Convention on the Conservation of Migratory Species of Wild Animals (Bonn). It is also a member of the World Conservation Union (IUCN), World Wide Fund for Nature (WWF), and International Waterfowl and Wetland Research Bureau (WRB), all of which are active in Pakistan. There are a total of 11 National Parks; Kirthar in Sind; Darun Hingol and Hazerganji Chiltan in Baluchistan; Lal Suhandra, Chinji and Margalla in Punjab; Chitral Gol and Ayubia in NWFP; Khunjerab and Deosai in Northern Areas; and Matcharia in Azad Jammu and Kashmir. In addition there are more than 100 wildlife sanctuaries, wilderness parks and game reserves.

However, the establishment of National Parks and other protected areas often leads to a conflict of interests with local populations. The Khunjerab National Park in particular was the focus of bitter disputes between park authorities and local people, who resented the outright ban placed on their traditional grazing and hunting rights in the area. Initially the park was a failure, with people continuing to graze their livestock and hunt in the area. Indeed the population of Marco Polo Sheep fell from over 1,000 when the park was established in 1975 to less than 50 by the early 1990s. The experience demonstrated the importance of first gaining the active support and participation of local people. Central to this is the need to raise public awareness and to demonstrate tangible benefits of conservation strategies. The Western concept of protecting wildlife and its environments for largely aesthetic reasons has little relevance in a country where many people, particularly those most affected, are living close to subsistence level.

Arts and architecture

Architecture

The major styles of monumental architecture found in Pakistan clearly trace the history of the region and its major civilizations, as well as illustrating the many external influences. The great **Indus Valley Civilization** cities of Moenjo Daro and Harappa provide the earliest examples, with their carefully organized layout and clearly defined functional zones around the main citadels.

The excavated remains of the **Gandharan** civilization at Taxila and elsewhere show the succession of Persian, Greek, Central Asian and Indian influences that came with the Greeks (Hellenistic and Bactrian), Mauryans, Scythians, Parthians and Kushans. The architecture here also demonstrates the fundamental importance of religion, in this case Buddhist, in shaping its forms; remains of the distinctive Stupas of the Buddhists can still be found spread across the Peshawar and lower Swat valleys.

Evidence of the period of Hindu rule in the region can still be seen in the forts and temple remains of the **Hindu Shahis** to be found in the Salt Range, the hills around Dera Ismail Khan and in the lower Swat valley. The styles demonstrate a strong Kashmiri influence as well as replicating the mediaeval architecture of northwest India. However, many of the Hindu temples (most of them derelict) date from the 19th century.

The early Arab invaders left their mark on Sind and southern Punjab, and represent the first evidence of the enormous **Islamic** influence on the architecture of Pakistan. They were followed by the Ghaznavids, who arrived from the northwest. The magnificent tombs at Multan and Uch Sharif, dating from the period of the Delhi Sultanate which followed, bear witness to the growth of Muslim political power in the region, while the numerous Sufi shrines of Sind and southern Punjab demonstrate the diversity of Islamic influences on the region. The striking Chaukundi Tombs and the massive necropolis of Makli Hill, both in lower Sind, display a remarkable independence from contemporary styles in the region, borrowing more from Rajput and Gujerati traditions than from Persian forms, particularly in the stone structures of the Chaukundi Tombs.

However, the most prominent flowering of Islamic architecture in Pakistan dates from the **Mughal** period. It was during this period that the great monuments of Lahore such as Akbar's

Makli Hill, near Thatta, Sind

Background

Fort, the Badshahi Mosque, Jehangir's Tomb and Shalimar Gardens, as well as those of Peshawar such as the Mahabat Khan Mosque, were built and subsequently embellished. Other impressive examples of Mughal architecture include the massive Rohtas Fort near Jhelum and Attock Fort between Islamabad and Peshawar. **Sikh** architecture meanwhile was based almost entirely on that of the Mughals, although they greatly embellished and adapted the original styles to produce their own distinctive forms. The best known examples are the *samadhs* (funerary memorials) of Guru Arjun Dev and Maharaja Ranjit Singh in Lahore. In some cases, such as the Gurdwara Damdama in Gujranwala, the characteristic Islamic dome is replaced by a tall *sikhara* tower, reflecting the Hindu influence in Sikhism.

The **British** also left a lasting and prominent influence, particularly in the cantonments which they built alongside so many of Pakistan's cities. These existed as entirely separate and self contained areas with wide, spacious boulevards and buildings which generally blended Gothic and Mughal styles to produce some striking pieces of architecture, most noticeably in Lahore and Peshawar.

Modern architecture in Pakistan has tended to rely heavily on foreign architects and be driven by a desire to impress, often seemingly by resorting to designs to a huge scale. It encompasses the extremely ugly, the self-consciously bold, the blatantly inappropriate and the inspired. The most prominent examples of modern architecture can be found in the planned capital Islamabad, which in parts succeeds very well in achieving a combination of modern and Islamic styles.

The vernacular traditions represent another important aspect of architecture in Pakistan. These display a diversity as great as the cultural diversity of the country and in terms of design and the building materials used, strongly reflect the social and physical environments in which they have developed. Rural architecture is determined primarily by the availability of building materials; throughout the Indus plains the alluvial soils and clays are used to make sun-dried bricks, often plastered over with mud to give villages and houses a characteristic moulded earth style.

The fortified stone and mud-built compounds of the Pathans found in the tribal areas around Peshawar evolved in response to the need for defence, the requirements of privacy within family and clan units, and the scarcity of timber for building. Those of northern and central Baluchistan show a similar pattern, though with greater emphasis on mud and straw construction and local stylistic differences.

Further south, and in much of Sind, the scrub vegetation is utilized in wicker fencing and thatching. Many of the houses have distinctive wind catchers built into the roofs to funnel cooling breezes inside. In the valleys north of Peshawar and Islamabad there are rich pine forests, and timber forms a major component of buildings. The Swat valley has developed the richest timber building traditions, with intricately carved decorations to both houses and mosques. Throughout the mountainous north, houses are built around the central fireplace to maximize warmth during the winter.

Art

Early painting in Pakistan was patronized almost exclusively by the Mughals, with their famous miniatures depicting scenes of court life, romance and legends. The best sculpture of the region, meanwhile, emerged during the Gandharan period, displaying an unique fusion of Graeco-Roman and Indian styles. However, in modern Pakistan, painting in particular has emerged as an important art form with many excellent artists developing their own unique 'Pakistani' forms and styles. Each of the provincial capitals have a number of art galleries where contemporary works can be seen; regional newspapers give details of the exhibitions and shows.

Literature

There is evidence of a type of pictographic writing from the Indus Valley Civilization, although it has never been deciphered. The Aryan invaders who followed developed a collection of hymns to direct priests in the worship and sacrifices central to their religion. These developed into the **Rig Veda**, the most famous of the Sanskrit Vedas and the forerunner of the great Hindu epics such as the Mahabharata and Ramayana. Like the Vedas, the early literature of Pakistan was essentially sacred in nature. And like the Vedas, it was initially memorized and passed down from generation to generation orally, only being committed to writing later, in some cases not until the 18th and 19th centuries.

The majority of Pakistan's surviving early literature dates from after the arrival of Islam. The Sufis were particularly fond of music and poetry as a medium for their message. The Sufi poet **Kabir** is well known for his treatise attempting to reconcile Hinduism and Islam. Later Sufi poets worked in the regional languages; just a few examples of those whose works still survive today include the Pashto poet **Khushal Khattak Khan** in NWFP, **Abdul Latif Shah** in Sind, **Ghulam Farid** in Punjab and **Mast Tawakali** in Baluchistan. Under the Delhi Sultans, Islamic literature of Persian and Central Asian origin began to be patronized and found new expression within the region. As well as purely sacred literature, the Muslims developed a new emphasis on scholarly literature, particularly in the fields of maths, science, medicine, astronomy and history. Each of the provinces developed their own unique literary traditions, expressed in the various regional languages and often centred around ballads and poems recounting the deeds of specific tribes and their genealogies. Many of these have subsequently proved vital in the reconstruction of history at a local level. However, religion and philosophy always remained amongst the most important themes, as did the influence of Sufism. The 17th century saw the birth of Sikh holy literature in the **Adi Granth** of Sikhism's founder Guru Nanak. The most respected poet nationally is undoubtedly **Mohammad Iqbal**; his poetry is considered by many to be amongst the finest examples of Urdu literature, while his political works – most notably his espousal of the 'two-nation theory' – formed an integral part of the move toward a separate Islamic state.

Literature continues to be of major importance in modern day Pakistan. There is a wealth of novels, short stories and poetry in Urdu and Punjabi in particular, many of which have been translated into English, and which provide an excellent insight into the psyche of the country. Pakistan has a prolific publishing industry, and in addition to fictional works, there is a bewildering array of books on all subjects. Many are admittedly of variable quality, and those on history are often hopelessly subjective, but there are also some excellent works to be found, and at far lower prices than in the West.

Music, songs and dance

The origins of music in South Asia are often traced to the hymns and chanting of the Rig Veda. These were later supplemented by the *Sama Veda*, or Veda of melodies, and there followed a

Mohammad Iqbal

process of embellishment and refinement; originally it is thought that all the melodies created in the Sama Veda consisted of just three notes, sung in strictly descending order. The religious music of the temples was restricted to the high caste Brahmins and therefore excluded the vast majority of people, with the result that parallel folk traditions of music developed amongst the common people.

Around the 13th century, the Muslim influence began to make itself felt in the sphere of music. This influence is generally attributed to **Amir Khusrau** who brought with him from Persia what is known as the **Persian Muqaam System**. The 'Hindustani' style of music subsequently developed in north India, influenced strongly by the Sufis, who blended the distinctive folk melodies of the region and their own Persian and Arabic traditions. It was during the Mughal period, under the reign of Akbar, that the classical (Hindustani) music of north India reached its peak, and it is those traditions which form the basis of Pakistan's classical music. Many of the instruments used in Pakistan are identical, or closely related, to those found in India; the *tabla* (small drums, believed to have been introduced by Amir Khasrau),the long-necked *sitar* and related *sarod*, the *sarangi* (a type of violin), the *shenai* (similar to a flute or oboe) and the *tambura* (a harmonium which was introduced later from the West and is now used extensively throughout the subcontinent). Likewise the structure of melodies is based on the *raga*, a framework within which musicians elaborate through improvisation.

Musical ragas provide the basis of both devotional and folk songs. The distinction between song and poetry is anyway a somewhat arbitrary one; in Pakistan it is all the more so given that most poetry is freely expressed both to music and in spoken form. Thus the *Ghazal* is basically Urdu poetry sung to music. It first developed in the Mughal courts as a form of light entertainment, although it was subsequently refined into a high art form. During the 1930s and 40s, it was used extensively in films. Within Pakistan it is perhaps the most popular form of traditional singing. Some of the best known exponents of the art include Mehdi Hasan, Iqbal Bano, Ghulam Ali, Farida Khanum and Abida Parveen. *Tappa*, meaning literally 'stage' or 'halting place' developed amongst the camel traders and the songs are generally divided into four stages, usually recounting a popular love story. It is performed all over Punjab, and in part of NWFP, being sung in Punjabi, Seraiki and Hindko. There are numerous other regional traditions in folk music, and as many famous exponents of the various traditions.

Of the devotional forms of singing, perhaps the best known is the *Qawwali*, generally attributed to the great Sufi poet **Abdul Latif Shah**, who used the form to express his *surs* (religious truths in musical form). Qawwali is usually sung by a group of up to 12 people with one lead singer. It begins in a slow and measured style, gradually building up to a climax. There are many well known performers of Qawwali, perhaps the most prominent of them being **Nusrat Ali Fateh Khan**, who toured extensively in the West before his untimely death. There are various other branches of Sufi devotional singing. *Vayee* is very close in form to the Qawwali. *Kafi* is generally classified as either 'folk' or 'classical', the former being simpler and in some opinions purer while the latter is far more complex. One of the best known exponents of Kafi was the late Ustad Manzoor Ali Khan. Today his one time students Mohammad Yousif and Abida Parveen keep the form alive. In *Sadarangi* the verses of Sufi poets are sung as ballads, the words of the 'story' conforming to a strict rhythm.

Culture

People and language

From the earliest beginnings of history, this part of the subcontinent has been a zone of contact. As such, it is not surprising that today there is an enormous diversity of peoples, the result of centuries of new settlement that came with the repeated waves of migrations and invasions, and the intermingling of these new arrivals with indigenous populations. Most of the ethnic groups found in Pakistan are descendants of the Aryans, who spread into the region from the northwest. This is reflected also in the languages spoken in the country, the majority of which belong to the Aryan branch Indo-European group. These are divided into three further groupings under the Aryan branch; Iranian (Baluchi, Pashto), Dardic (Khowar, Shina, Kohistani, Kashmiri) and Indo-Aryan (Punjabi, Seraiki, Sindhi, Urdu).

Urdu, the official language of Pakistan, was not widely spoken (except amongst the urban Muslim élites) anywhere in the country at Independence. Indeed, it was adopted primarily because of its neutral status in a country where each region had its own dominant languages. Urdu first developed as the common language of the Mughal courts, blending the Persian of the rulers with the local languages of north India. In its spoken form it closely resembles Hindi, the national language of India, though with a greater emphasis on words with Persian and Arabic, as opposed to Sanskrit, roots. The Urdu script in contrast is a distinctive modification of the Arabic script and wholly different from the Sanskrit-based Devanagari of Hindi. Originally, the two languages were identical (referred to as Hindustani by the British), and it was only in the 19th century that they began to diverge along religious lines. Today, Urdu is most widely spoken as a first language in Sind, amongst the **Mohajirs** (migrants) who came from India at Partition. Nationally, it is only spoken in around eight percent of households, although it is also widely spoken as a second language throughout Pakistan.

The **Punjabis**, a blend of Aryan and Indian stock, are by far the largest single group, accounting for over half of Pakistan's total population. They dominate public life at a national level, with a disproportionate representation in government, the civil service and army, even given their majority status. They also consider themselves to be the 'cultural heart' of Pakistan; as well as possessing most of the great monuments of the Mughal era, the provincial capital Lahore is one of the main intellectual centres of the country. Not surprisingly, their dominant position is often a source of resentment amongst other groups. Their language, **Punjabi**, is also numerically the most important in Pakistan, being spoken in around 48 percent of households. There are a variety of dialects and, as one would expect, it is spoken mainly in Punjab province, where it represents the first language of around 80 percent of households. There are also significant minorities of Punjabi speakers in Sind, and smaller ones in NWFP and Baluchistan.

The **Seraikis** are an important minority in Punjab, and are also found in adjoining parts of Sind, Baluchistan and NWFP. Their language, **Seraiki**, is spoken by around 15 percent of households according to the 1981 census, although the true number is disputed. Punjabis generally tend to emphasize the close links with Punjabi, although it also has considerable affinity with the Sindhi language. Seraiki speakers themselves emphasize the uniqueness of both their language and culture. They have campaigned hard for their own province, arguing that they are discriminated against by the majority Punjabis, and in the other provinces where they live. Speakers of **Hindko** are found primarily in the Mansehra and Abbottabad districts of NWFP. They are closely related to Punjabis both culturally and linguistically, with speakers of the two languages being able to understand each other easily.

The next largest group are the **Pathans**, who represent the majority in NWFP and roughly half the population of Baluchistan, where they are concentrated in the north of the province. Fiercely independent and more obviously Aryan in descent with their often fair complexions and green or blue eyes, the Pathans are a formidable people whose social structure is deeply tribal in nature. As an ethnic group, they extend beyond the political boundaries of Pakistan, accounting for around half of the population of Afghanistan (the present border between the two countries was a highly artificial one created by the British and based on strategic rather than cultural considerations). Their language, **Pashto**, represents the first language of around 13 percent of households nationally. It has numerous dialects, reflecting the fragmented nature of their tribal society.

The **Sindhis** represent a similar percentage of the population to the Pathans. Their language, **Sindhi**, is spoken by around 12 percent of households nationally and by over half in Sind province. There are many different dialects, including *Vicholi*, the most important; *Lar*, spoken in lower Sind; *Lassi*, spoken mostly in Lasbela district of Baluchistan; and *Thari*, spoken in the Thar desert regions of eastern Sind. The exact origins of the Sindhis are uncertain, although it is clear that as an ethnic group they are the result of centuries of diverse influences, a fact borne out by the diverse roots of their language and indeed the history of the region.

The **Baluch** are another of Pakistan's great tribal societies and, like the Pathans, as an ethnic group they extend far beyond the boundaries of Pakistan, in this case encompassing Iran as well as Afghanistan. Their language, **Baluchi**, is the second main language of Baluchistan (after Pashto), being spoken by around 36 percent of households, the majority being in the southern half of the province, where the Baluch tribes dominate. There are also significant minorities of Baluchi speakers in Sind. Nationally it is the first language of only three percent of households, a reflection mostly of the very low population densities found in this vast province. The Iranian (Persian) influence on Baluchi language is strong, and increases in the dialects spoken to the west. This is often cited as evidence of the Persian origins of the Baluch, although according to their own legends, they are descended from tribes which migrated from present-day Syria. Their nomadic origins are certain; the word 'Baluch' translates literally as 'wanderer'.

The **Brahui** are the third main group found in Baluchistan. Their origins are unclear and the subject of much debate. Their language, **Brahui**, is spoken by just over 20 percent of households in Baluchistan. It is amongst the very few languages of Pakistan not apparently belonging to the Indo-European group, being generally identified instead with the Dravidian languages of south India. It has however absorbed much of the vocabulary of the Iranian and Indo-Aryan language groups surrounding it. The apparent Dravidian roots of the Brahui language seems to suggest that they represent a remnant of the indigenous Dravidian population which once occupied most of South Asia before being pushed south by successive waves of Ayrans arriving from the northwest. This is however disputed by some scholars (particularly Baluch and Brahui), who argue that they are in fact one of the Baluch tribes which migrated from Syria.

The mountainous north of Pakistan displays an enormous diversity of peoples and languages, reflecting the influence of centuries of migration and trade along the Silk Routes. Many of the languages of the region are generally identified as belonging to the Dardic group (see above), a blend of indigenous languages with those of the Aryans. **Wakhi**, spoken in upper Hunza, is generally classified as being of the Iranian branch. **Burushaski** however, spoken in central Hunza, defies any such classification and its roots have not been identified. **Balti** meanwhile, spoken in Baltistan, is closely linked with Tibetan.

Religion

The land which now constitutes Pakistan has a rich history of religions. It gave birth to Brahmanism, which later developed into Hinduism. It saw the flourishing of Buddhism in Gandhara and the establishment of the *Mahayana* school. Prior to the arrival of the British, the Sikhs established their powerful empire which centred on the Punjab.

Today, Pakistan is an Islamic state and 97 percent of the population are Muslim. Despite its monotheism, Islam displays a remarkable diversity within Pakistan, as well as having its own 'Asian' feel to it, distinctive in many ways from Islam in other parts of the world. This is a reflection of its diverse origins in the region, as well as the many different influences which acted on it.

The Sufis, responsible for spreading the faith in much of the country, have left their unique mark, particularly in Sind and southern Punjab. While the Arabs brought the first Islamic contact, it was the Ghaznavids who were responsible for establishing Islamic political power in the region. They came from the northwest and were Turks of slave extraction. From the middle of the 13th century, when the Mongols crushed the Arab Caliphate, the Delhi Sultans were left on their own to exercise Islamic authority in the subcontinent, and the main influence came from Persia. Meanwhile, there was a constant process of assimilation and accommodation between the Muslim rulers and local peoples. While the Islamic élites who arrived from Iran or Turkey maintained 'pure' forms of Islam, isolated and less literate communities developed devotional and pietistic forms, incorporating many of their pre-Islamic beliefs, customs and practices. The caste system for example, completely at variance with Muslim injunctions regarding discrimination, remain a fact of life even today in much of the country.

A number of other religions are also represented in Pakistan, albeit as small minorities; Christian, Hindu, Sikh and Parsee (Zoroastrian) communities are all to be found in different parts of the country.

Islam

Mohammad, the founder of the Islamic faith, was born around 570 AD in the city of **Mecca** in present day Saudi Arabia. His family were of noble descent, members of the house of **Hashim**, belonging to the **Abd Manaf** clan and part of the **Quraish** tribal confederacy of Mecca. The Abd Manaf clan had a semi-priestly status, being responsible for certain functions during the annual pilgrimage to the *Ka'ba* in Mecca (the Ka'ba, the cube shaped building to which Muslims face when praying, predates Islam; Muslims believe that it was established by Adam and revere it as a sanctuary where closeness to God can be achieved).

At the age of 40 Mohammad received his first revelations of the Qur'an and began preaching his message. He encountered stiff opposition from the powerful Quaish leaders, the temple guardians and the rich traders, and was eventually forced to flee to **Medina**, known then as Yathrib (the famous *Hijra* which marks the beginning of the Islamic calendar). There he established himself and achieved a position of power, fighting three major battles with the Meccans before finally returning to Mecca in triumph two years before his death in 632 AD.

In his lifetime he had become recognized as a prophet and founded the Islamic faith. Part of his success was in incorporating many aspects of the ancient Arabian religions, such as the pilgrimage to Ka'ba, as well as aspects of Judaism and Christianity. But his success was not purely in religious terms. He was also an accomplished statesman who laid the foundations for what would later become a great Islamic Empire.

Islamic Sects In the century following Mohammad's death, Islam divided into two major sects. Mohammad left no sons and therefore no obvious heir, and gave no instructions as to who should succeed him. There were two main contenders; **Abu Bakr**, the father of Mohammad's wife, and **Ali**, the husband of Mohammad's daughter Fatimah and his cousin. In the event Abu Bakr assumed the title of *Caliph* (vice-regent). He died two years later in 634 AD and was succeeded by **Omar** who was killed in 644. **Uthman**, a member of the powerful **Umayyad** family, was chosen to succeed him, but proved to be a weak leader and was murdered in 656.

At this point the aggrieved Ali managed to assume the title of Caliph, thus ousting the Umayyads. However **Muawiya**, the governor of Syria and a member of the Umayyad family, soon rose up in revolt. He managed to gain the upper hand; in 661 Ali was murdered (by one of his own supporters) and Muawiya proclaimed himself Caliph. Ali's eldest son **Hassan** set up a rival Caliph in Iraq, but was soon persuaded to abdicate. However, the seeds of the schism in Islam had already been sown; between the Sunnis (those who accepted the legitimacy of the first three Caliphs) and the Shias (those who recognized only Ali as the first legitimate Caliph). Later, when Muawiya died in 680, Ali's second son **Hussain** attempted to revolt against the Umayyads, but was defeated and killed in 681 at Karbala, providing the Shias with their greatest martyr.

Followers of the **Sunni** sect, generally termed 'Orthodox', account for around 80 percent of Muslims in Pakistan (globally they represent a similar majority). They base their *Sunna* (path, or practice) on the 'Six Books' of traditions. They are organized into four orthodox schools or rites named after their founders, each having equal standing. The *Hanafi* is the most common in Pakistan, and the most moderate. The others are the *Shafii*, *Maliki* and *Hanbali*, the latter being the strictest. Many Muslims today prefer to avoid identification with a particular school, preferring to call themselves simply Sunni.

Followers of the **Shia** sect account for most of the remainder of Muslims in Pakistan. Those that can trace their descent from Hassan bear the title *Sharif*, and those that trace their descent from Hussain, the title *Sayyid*. However there are also many Sharif and Sayyid families in Pakistan who are Sunni. Both lineages hold a position of religious aristocracy in Islam. Aside from the dispute over the succession of Mohammad, Sunnis and Shias do not generally differ on fundamental issues since they draw from the same ultimate sources. However, there are important differences of interpretation which partly derive from the practice of *ijtihad* ('the exercise of independent judgement') amongst Shias, as oppose to *taqlid* (the following of ancient models) as adhered to by Sunnis. Thus Shias divest far more power in their *Imams*, accepting their role as an intermediary between God and man and basing their law and practice on the teachings of the Imams. (**NB** the term Imam is also used more generally by both Shias and Sunnis to refer to the prayer leader of a mosque.)

Badshahi Mosque, Lahore

The majority of Shias are known as *Ithna asharis* or 'Twelvers', since they recognize a succession of 12 Imams. They believe that the last Imam, who disappeared in 878 AD, is still alive and will reappear soon before the Day of Judgement as the *Mahdi* (One who is rightly guided) who will rule by divine right.

An offshoot of the Shias, and an important minority in Pakistan, are the **Ismailis**. The Ismailis reject the seventh Imam acknowledged by the Twelvers, recognizing instead Ismail, the elder son of the sixth Imam. They are also sometimes referred to as *Sab iya* or 'Seveners'. There was however much dispute amongst themselves as to who was in fact the seventh Imam. The Fatamid Ismailis of Egypt recognized a grandson of the sixth Imam and in turn gave rise to several schismatic offshoots, including the Nizari Ismailis found in Pakistan. The latter recognize the **Aga Khan** as their spiritual head and trace his descent directly to the Prophet Mohammad through his daughter Fatimah. The philosophy of the Ismailis is a largely esoteric one; their theology is based on a cyclical theory of history centred around the number seven, which is considered to be of enormous significance. They are less restrictive in their customs and practice, allowing much greater freedom to women. Likewise, prayers are not linked to a specific formula. The mosque is replaced by a *jamat khana* which also serves as a community centre. Within Pakistan they are found mostly in the Northern Areas and Chitral region, where the Aga Khan is very active in development work.

Various other Muslim minorities are found in Pakistan. Notable amongst these are the **Ahmadis**, another offshoot of the Shias founded by **Mirza Ghulam Ahmad** in 1889. Ghulam Ahmad made a number of claims, including being a recipient of revelations, the Promised Messiah, the *Mahdi* and an *avatar* (incarnation) of Krishna. The Ahmadis believe that Jesus escaped from death on the cross and went to Srinagar where he died and was buried. They split into two main groups, the **Qadiyanis** who hold that Ghulam Ahmad was a Prophet, and the **Lahories** who believe that he was merely a *Mujaddid* or 'Renewer'. The headquarters of the Ahmadis is at Rabwah in Pakistan. The official periodical of the Ahmadis, the Al-Fazl, is the oldest surviving periodial in Pakistan. The Ahmadis were declared non-Muslims in Pakistan by General Zia in 1984, making them liable to prosecution (potentially under the blasphemy law which carries a mandatory death sentence) if they adopt any of the religious forms or observances of Islam. Thus they are forbidden to call their place of worship a 'masjid', to recite the formal call to prayers, or display the *Kalim-e-Tayyaba* (the formal declaration of the oneness of God). They have been increasingly persecuted in Pakistan in recent years and in 1994 Zia's ordinance against them was again upheld. There were even demands that a law be passed obliging them to alter the architecture of their places of worship so that they did not resemble mosques.

Another group, the **Zikris**, are found mainly in the Makran region of Baluchistan. Like the Ahmadis, they have suffered persecution for their unorthodox beliefs. Attempts to have them declared non-Muslims have so far been resisted. Their annual pilgrimage to the Koh-e-Murad near Turbat (which replaces the orthodox pilgrimage to Mecca) is the focus for frequent violent attacks and there have been repeated calls to have their Zikri *Baitullah* (house of God) situated there destroyed.

The **Nurbakshi** are a small minority found only in parts of Baltistan. They are closely linked with the Shias Sufis. The Sufis do not represent a separate sect of Islam; rather they aspire to transcend secand suffer none of the persecution to which the Ahmadis and Zikris are subjected.

Sufism is the mystical aspect of Islam, often described as the "science of the heart". The word *Sufi* is most probably derived from the Arabic word *suf* meaning 'wool', a reference to the woollen garments worn by the early t, emphasizing the importance of personal spiritual development, to be found only through the Qur'an. The Sufis were instrumental in spreading the Islamic faith in Pakistan, and numerous shrines dedicated to Sufi saints are to be found scattered throughout the country. These shrines still draw large numbers of pilgrims during the annual Urs, or death

The Five Pillars of Islam

There are 5 practices or Akran, known as the Five Pillars of Islam, which are generally accepted as being obligatory to Muslims:

Shahada *The profession of faith ("There is no god but Allah..."), which also forms the basis of the call to prayer made by the muezzin of the mosque.*

Salat *The ritual of prayers, carried out 5 times a day at prescribed times; in the early morning before the sun has risen above the horizon, in the early afternoon when the sun has passed its zenith, later when the sun is halfway towards setting, immediately after sunset and in the evening before retiring to bed. Prayers can be carried out anywhere, whether it be in a mosque or by the roadside, and involves facing towards the Ka'ba in Mecca and prostrating before God while reciting verses of the Qur'an.*

Zakat *The compulsory payment of alms. In early times this was collected by officials of the Islamic state, and was devoted to the relief of the poor, debtors, aid to travellers and other charitable purposes. In many Muslim communities, the fulfilment of this religious obligation is nowadays left to the conscience of the individual. In Pakistan it was enshrined in law by Zia ul-Haq and is still levied today.*

Sawm *The 30 days of fasting during the month of Ramadan, the 9th month of the Muslim lunar calendar. It is observed as a fast from sunrise to sunset each day by all Muslims, although there are provisions for special circumstances.*

Hajj *The pilgrimage to Mecca. Every Muslim, circumstances permitting, is obliged to perform this pilgrimage at least once in his lifetime and having accomplished it, may assume the title of Hajji. The pilgrimage to Mecca involves a massive logistical exercise in Pakistan, where around 90,000 people undertake it each year.*

anniversary of the saint, a testimony to their popularity amongst the people.

Islamic beliefs and practices

The word Islam translates roughly as 'submission to God'. The two central tenets of Islam are embodied in the creed "There is no god but Allah and Mohammad is his Prophet" ("*Lah Illaha illa 'llah Mohammad Rasulu 'llah*") which affirms the belief in the oneness of God and recognizes Mohammad as the divinely appointed messenger of God.

The *Qur'an* (generally referred to as the Koran in English) is Islam's holiest book. The word translates literally as 'recitation' and unlike the Bible, is considered to be the *uncreated* (that is direct) word of God, as revealed to Mohammad through *Jibril* (the angel Gabriel). The text consists of 114 chapters, each known as a *sura*. Each sura is classified as Meccan or Medinan, according to whether it was revealed to Mohammad in Mecca or Medina. Most of the text is written in a kind of rhymed prose known as *saj*, and is considered by Muslims to be inimitable. Each chapter of the Qur'an begins with the words "*Bismillah al-Rahman al-Rahim*" ("In the name of Allah, the Merciful, the Compassionate"), an invocation which can also be heard being uttered by Muslims in numerous everyday situations; when boarding a bus or before eating food for example.

In addition to the Qur'an, there is the *Hadith* body of literature, a record of the sayings and doings of Mohammad and his followers, which forms the basis of Islamic laws (*Shariat*), and precepts. Unlike the Qur'an, the Hadiths are recognized to have been written by men, and are therefore potentially flawed and open to interpretation. Thus they are commonly classified into four major categories according to their trustworthiness; *Sahih* (sound, true, authentic), *Hasan* (fair, good), *Da'if* (weak) and *Saqim* (infirm). The two most revered compilations of Hadiths are those of *al-Bukhari* and *Muslim*. It is in the interpretation of the Hadiths that most of the controversy surrounding certain Islamic laws and their application originates.

Jihad: the sixth pillar?

Jihad, literally 'holy war' is considered by some Muslims to constitute the 6th pillar of Islam, although it has never been officially elevated to this status. The concept of jihad was the basis for the early expansion of Islam and was carried out very much in the literal sense of the word. A similar concept underpinned the Crusades of Europe's Christians. There are many contemporary examples of jihad. The Afghan guerrillas fighting against Soviet occupation called themselves Mujahideen, that is those who wage jihad against the enemies of Islam. Other examples are more controversial. The current situation in Indian-held Kashmir is often characterized as a jihad against Hindu domination, while Saddam Hussein has repeatedly tried to cast his plight as a jihad against the evil designs of American infidels.

Many of the attitudes surrounding western perceptions of Islam are based on fears as to the wider implications of the concept. On the other hand, the word actually derives from an Arabic root meaning basically 'to strive', and many Muslims emphasise a less literal interpretation in terms of a personal spiritual striving against sin to attain greater closeness to God.

While Mohammad is recognized as the founder of the Islamic faith and the principle messenger of God, Muslims also regard him as having been the last in a long line of Prophets, starting with Adam and including both Moses and Jesus. They do not accept Jesus as the son of God, but simply another of God's Prophets. Both Jews and Christians are considered *Ahl-e-Kitab* ('People of the Book'), the Torah and the Gospels being completed in Islamic belief by the Qur'an.

Nearly all Muslims accept six basic articles of the Islamic faith; belief in one God; in his angels; in his revealed books; in his Apostles; in the Resurrection and Day of Judgement; and in his predestination of good and evil. Heaven is portrayed in Muslim belief as a Paradise filled with sensuous delights and pleasures. The idea of heaven as paradise predates Islam. Alexander the Great is believed to have brought the word into Greek from Persia, where he used it to describe the walled Persian gardens that were found even before the birth of Christ. Hell on the other hand is portrayed as a place of eternal terror and torture, which is the certain fate of all who deny the unity of God.

Islam has no ordained priesthood or clergy. The authority of religious scholars, learned men, Imams, judges et cetera (referred to collectively as the *Ulema* and individually as *Mullahs* in Pakistan), derives from their authority to interpret the scriptures, rather than from any defined status within the Islamic community. Many Muslims in Pakistan complain that the growing influence of Mullahs interferes with the direct, personal relationship between man and God which Mohammad originally espoused (and was indeed one of the reasons he was driven from Mecca, as it threatened the privileged position of the temple priests).

NB For full details of the Islamic calendar and the significance behind Islamic festivals, see 'Holidays and festivals' on page 53.

Non-Muslim minorities

The **Christian** community in Pakistan represents the largest non-Muslim minority, accounting for around one and a half percent of the population and numbering nearly two million. They are divided roughly 50-50 between the Church of Pakistan, which represents an amalgamation of the various Protestant groups, and Catholics, for whom Pakistan represents an arch diocese. **Hindus** are the next largest minority, numbering around one million, concentrated mainly in Karachi, where there are a number of prominent Hindu temples, and other urban centres.

Both Christians and Hindus suffer considerable discrimination, in the latter case aggravated by incidents such as at Ayodhya in India, and the growing atmosphere of animosity between Hindus and Muslims over Kashmir. Human rights groups reported numerous cases of girls, particularly Hindus, being kidnapped, forced to 'convert' to Islam and then married off to Muslims. There is also increasing evidence that Hindus have begun to sell off their properties in Pakistan and migrate to India.

Tiny communities of **Parsees**, descendants of the **Zoroastrians**, are found in Lahore and Karachi where, as in India, they have established themselves very successfully in the business community.

Modern Pakistan

The challenges facing Pakistan at its inception were enormous. Quite apart from the massive upheaval and human trauma that came with partition, the newly created country inherited very little of the administrative infrastructure left behind by the British, and so had to build a new system practically from scratch. Although it inherited much of the canal-irrigated agricultural land in Punjab, and all in Sind, it was nowhere near self-sufficient in food grains. It had a minimum of modern factory or heavy industry, while its mineral wealth and power potential were for the most part unexploited. Looking at the problems and shortcomings of the country today, it is easy to forget its achievements as well.

Government, politics and institutions

Parliament consists of an upper and lower house, the Senate and National Assembly respectively, with the former occupying a largely advisory role (rather like the House of Lords in the UK) while the latter is primarily responsible for the day-to-day business of government. Its ability to formulate policy is however severely restricted. The 1973 constitution is still nominally in force, although it was substantially amended, first by Zulfikar Bhutto, and then by Zia, who in 1985 gave the President (himself at the time) amongst other things the power to dissolve the National Assembly without the prime minister's consent. This clause allowed the dismissal of Benazir Bhutto's two governments, and the first of Nawaz Sharif, although the latter did away with this 'Eighth Amendment' in 1998 (see 'History' above).

The constitution provides for a federal democratic structure, with four Provincial governments of Sind, Baluchistan, Punjab and NWFP. In addition there is the Federally Administered Tribal Areas (FATA), a semi-autonomous region governed directly by the Federal government largely according to the model left behind by the British, and the Capital Territory Area (Islamabad). Both Azad Kashmir and the Northern Areas, due to their disputed status, are also administered directly by the Federal government and not strictly speaking constitutionally part of Pakistan. However in the 1980s an elected Northern Areas Council was established, while a package of administrative reforms in 1994 have given the region the basic administrative features of a Provincial government. Azad Jammu and Kashmir meanwhile exists as a 'state' with its own president, prime minister and Legislative Assembly.

As noted earlier, one of the most prominent features of Pakistan's fragile democracy is the deep cynicism and disenchantment with which it is viewed. It is not at all uncommon to hear people referring nostalgically to the days of Zia's Martial Law régime; Pakistan's army, if not perhaps one of the most successful militarily, at least has a reputation for efficiency. Democratic government on the other hand has been characterized by inertia, corruption and patronage. Many people argue that real power remains in the hands of the traditional landlord class, religious leaders (*ulema*), the civil service and the army.

Legal system and judiciary

The legal system illustrates many of the problems inherent in reconciling Islamic and secular ideals. Under Zia, a Council of Islamic Ideology was created to bring existing laws into conformity with Islamic injunctions and advise on new legislative

A religious or secular state?

Pakistan is officially an Islamic Republic, and was created in order to provide the Muslims of India with their own homeland. Yet the 1973 constitution, in theory at least, is a secular one, while the legal system was formulated almost entirely on that of the British. This paradox (if indeed it is a paradox) is the source of heated debate in Pakistan. Part of the problem is in defining an Islamic state and many have characterized Pakistan as a country in search of an Islamic ideology with which to underpin its existence. Jinnah, in a much quoted speech to Pakistan's constituent assembly on 1 August 1947, made the following statement:

"You are free; you are free to go to your temples, you are free to go to your mosques or to any other places of worship in this State of Pakistan... You may belong to any religion, caste or creed – that has nothing to do with the business of the State. We are starting with this fundamental principle that we are all citizens and equal citizens of one State ... You will find that in the course of time Hindus would cease to be Hindus and Muslims would cease to be Muslims, not in the religious sense, because that is the personal faith of each individual, but in the political sense as citizens of the State."

Equality and freedom of worship were clearly central to his vision, but then most Muslims would argue that these are central features of Islam anyway. Likewise, the socialism which Zulfikar Bhutto initially promoted so forcefully has many parallels in Islam. Some would argue that the existing democratic system is a purely western model, for which an Islamic parallel exists. But then the country appears to be set against a theocracy on the model of post-revolution Iran; free elections in Pakistan have always resulted in the electorate voting overwhelmingly in favour of secular parties with secular programmes.

proposals. In addition to the provincial High Courts and the Supreme Court, a Shariat (Islamic) Court was established with the power to overrule any law considered 'repugnant' to Islam. Various of the Islamic laws passed during Zia's time, particularly the *Hadood* ordinance, raised great controversy and strong protest from minority rights and women's groups both within Pakistan and abroad. Some, such as the law on the payment of *zakat* (a tax collected for distribution to the poor), highlighted the differing interpretations of Islam; Shia Muslims do not recognize the tax as part of Islamic law. Others, such as those proposing to abolish interest on the grounds that it is un-Islamic, have proved largely unworkable and their implementation remains unresolved.

In 1995 the so called 'blasphemy law' (an amendment to the Penal Code which made the death sentence mandatory for blasphemy) was brought under the public spotlight following a much publicized case in which two Christians were sentenced to death after being charged with writing blasphemous graffiti on the walls of a mosque. A third Christian, also involved in the case, had already been shot dead while returning from one of the court hearings. In a subsequent appeal to the High Court, the judgement was overturned, the judge noting amongst other things that the accused were illiterate. The case served to illustrate the potential for misuse of such laws by extremists and was a source of acute shame for most Muslims. **NB** For details of the '15th Amendment' to the Constitution, and the efforts to replace the British-style legal systems with a Shariat court, see 'Recent events' at the end of the 'History' section.

Many argue that disillusionment with the legal system and judiciary is due to its inefficiency and corruption. Even relatively simple cases can drag on for months or years, at prohibitive cost to all but the most wealthy, and with no guarantee of a fair judgement at the end of it. Even more serious at a national and provincial level is the issue of the independence of the judiciary. Effectively, appointments to the judiciary are controlled by the executive (that is the government) and so obviously open to political manipulation and abuse. This was a set-up initially inherited from the British, but subsequently reinforced by both Zulfikar Bhutto and Zia ul-Haq. There have been growing calls and various attempts to separate the two. To demonstrate the power of the executive over the judiciary, following a highly publicized run-in with the Prime Minister in 1997, the Supreme Court Chief Justice was forced to step down; in the words of one Pakistani journal, "he [Prime Minister] had managed to neutralize the otherwise hostile judiciary ... [and create] divisions within the most hallowed judicial institutions of the country" (*Herald*, March 1998).

In 1998, under the banner of 'speeding up justice' and making 'justice available to all', Nawaz Sharif introduced a 'military court' system whereby cases were to be heard and dealt with within a short period of time (one month was mentioned), with the trial taking place before three senior military 'judges'. Once the verdict was given, one appeal to a higher military court was permitted, but cases could not subsequently be appealed to a civil court. While recognizing the need to speed up the process of justice in Pakistan, most human rights organizations (in Pakistan and abroad) condemned such trials as potentially unsafe. In late 1998, a man convicted of rape by a military court was the first to be executed under this new system.

International Relations

India Pakistan's international relations are dominated by relations with India, with the **Kashmir Dispute** being the greatest bone of contention. The two countries have gone to war no less than three times over the issue, with both maintaining massive deployments of troops along the Line of Control and regularly shelling each other across it. The current deployment of an estimated 300,000 Indian soldiers within Indian-held Kashmir in an attempt to control the insurgency against direct Indian rule there has served to further inflame what has always been a deeply emotive issue to Pakistanis. The Indian army and government has been widely accused of human rights abuses, while Pakistan has been blamed by the Indians for fomenting the current unrest. Officially Pakistan denies any direct involvement, although unofficially it openly admits to supporting the Kashmiri 'Mujahideen' and there are regular calls in the press for the people of Pakistan to rise up in a 'jihad' to aid their brethren in Indian Kashmir. For Pakistani politicians Kashmir is a gift, allowing them to rally populist support and divert attention away from problems at home. The question as to what the people of Kashmir actually want themselves – to remain part of India, join Pakistan or have independence – tends to be ignored. While India blames Pakistan for its problems in Kashmir, Pakistan generally places much of the blame for the problems in Karachi on India. Another less well known and little publicized territorial dispute is over **Junagadh** and **Manavadar** in India's Rann of Kachchh.

The abysmally poor relations between Pakistan and India have their roots in the history of British colonial rule, the Independence movement and Partition. Today those relations continue to have a devastating social, economic and military impact on what would otherwise be a geographically and culturally integrated region. The recent nuclear escalation has dramatically raised the stakes between the two countries, and potentially threatens the stability of the region as a whole. Interpretations and perceptions on both sides remain highly charged and highly subjective, but nobody can deny that there are only losers in the conflict.

Afghanistan Pakistan's involvement in the Mujahideen struggle against the Soviet occupation of Afghanistan was on a massive scale. Mohammad Yousaf, the head of the Afghan Bureau of the Inter Services Intelligence (ISI, akin to the US's CIA) from 1983-87, wrote in his book *The Bear Trap*; "During my four years some 80,000 Mujahideen were trained; hundreds of thousands of tonnes of arms and ammunition were distributed, several billion dollars were spent on this immense logistic exercise and ISI teams regularly entered Afghanistan alongside the Mujahideen." Since the Soviet withdrawal from Afghanistan, Pakistan has constantly maintained that its position is a neutral one, reiterating its respect for the sovereignty of other nations and the principles of non interference. But Pakistan undoubtedly remains inextricably involved in Afghanistan. The **Taliban** movement, which now controls most of the country, originated from religious schools (*madrassas*) along the Pakistani border, and is widely believed to have been funded, equipped and trained by Pakistan. Many believe that Pakistan's ultimate objective is to see the country united under a pro-Pakistani Taliban government. The instability of Afghanistan has serious implications for Pakistan's own security, as well as for its ambitions to form close economic links with the Central Asian States. Yet the Taliban's extremist Islamic position is a source of growing concern within Pakistan. Even more worrying perhaps is the prospect of the Pathan-dominated Taliban agitating for an independent 'Pakhtunistan' which included Pathan majority areas inside Pakistan.

Iran and the Middle East Locked in a seemingly intractable dispute with India to the east, Pakistan has traditionally tried hard to forge close links instead with its Islamic neighbours to the west. Iran, however, is a predominantly Shia country, while Pakistan has a Sunni majority. In the past, the two countries have succeeded in maintaining cordial relations, but conflicting interests in Afghanistan have seriously strained those relations. While Pakistan has backed the Sunni Muslim Taliban movement, Iran has sought to protect its own interests there (in the form of the country's Shia population) by supporting the opposition forces of the so-called Northern Alliance. When in August 1998 the Taliban finally captured the northern town of Mazar-i-Sharif, they are alleged to have massacred thousands of civilians, mostly from the minority Shia Hazara community, as well as executing a number of Iranian 'diplomats' that they found there. Tension between Iran and the Taliban escalated rapidly, with Iran amassing thousands of troops along the Afghan border. With the Taliban and Pakistan so inextricably linked, the stand-off between Iran and the Taliban has had a fundamental impact on Pakistani-Iranian relations.

On a regional level, Pakistan is an active member of the Organization of Islamic Countries (OIC) and a regular participant in regional Islamic Summits. In economic terms, the oil producing countries of the Middle East have been a major source of employment and foreign exchange remittances for Pakistan.

Central Asia The break up of the Soviet Union and the formation of a host of independent states in Central Asia with Muslim majorities was a welcome development for Pakistan. Historical and cultural links with the region are strongly emphasized; more importantly, Pakistan is keen to promote close economic ties. The great prize in this respect is the prospect of providing an outlet for the substantial oil and gas reserves of these land-locked countries. However, Pakistan's ambitions of opening up a land route (and constructing oil and gas pipelines) connecting them, via Afghanistan, with the sea port of Karachi remains for the moment more of a fantasy than a realistic prospect.

China The old maxim that "my enemy's enemy is my friend" was perhaps initially the main driving force behind the close relations which Pakistan established with China. While India's border disputes with the latter are still unresolved, having led to war at one stage, Pakistan was only too pleased to agree her international border with China. The building of the KKH meanwhile is the most tangible manifestation of the two countries' close economic links.

USA Relations with the USA are perhaps the most fraught with hypocrisy and contradictions. America is held up as the devil incarnate in Pakistan; the embodiment of Western decadence and immorality, an enemy of Islam and worse still, a Zionist stooge. The US air-strikes against Afghanistan in August 1998 only served to unleash new waves of popular anti-American sentiment. Yet Pakistan enjoyed unprecedented levels of US economic and military aid during the Afghanistan war. The economic crisis which followed Pakistan's nuclear tests and the subsequent sanctions against it have highlighted the country's dependence on the West for aid. Having lost the status of a 'front-line state' in the fight against communism, it seems unlikely however that Pakistan will be able to regain its close relations with the US; indeed, the latter has done much to build closer links with India instead.

Economy

Until recently, Pakistan's economy has shown remarkable growth, averaging over six percent since the 1970s. However, this has to be weighed against the country's equally high rate of population growth, which negates most of the benefits of economic growth. More importantly, there are many structural weaknesses. In terms of exports there is still a heavy reliance on a few products, with seven major items (raw cotton, rice, cotton cloth, cotton yarn, garments, leather and carpets) accounting for over 60 percent of the total. As well as the fact that most of these have a low value-added component, such a concentration makes Pakistan's economy highly vulnerable to changing demand and price fluctuations on the world market. Government spending is extremely high, with little of it going to the most needy. The military continues to be a massive burden, with around a quarter of each year's domestic budget being allocated to defence. Debt servicing meanwhile accounts for an even larger proportion. Set against this are consistently low levels of tax collection. Wealth continues to be concentrated in the hands of a tiny minority, while inefficiency, corruption and patronage remain major problems.

On the other hand, there have been concerted efforts over the years to encourage the growth of the private sector, ease import restrictions, relax bureaucratic controls on investment, stimulate investment in manufacturing and promote exports. In addition, the privatization of many public sector industries and services was initiated in the early 1990s, while vigorous efforts to encourage foreign investment produced considerable results. Whatever progress was being made suffered a dramatic setback in 1998, which proved to be a disastrous year for the Pakistani economy.

In response to Pakistan's nuclear tests in May 1998, the international community imposed economic sanctions which had an immediate and devastating impact. Within the space of a month, the Pakistani Rupee had depreciated in value by nearly 30 percent against the US dollar. Foreign investment in the country, which had previously reached a peak of US$1.86 billion, rapidly plummeted to US$500 million. Partly as a result of the sanctions, the government's foreign exchange reserves fell to an all-time low of just US$1.2 billion. In response, on 28 May 1998 the government froze all foreign exchange ('forex') accounts held in Pakistani banks and forcibly converted the US dollars held in them into Rupees in order to bolster its own reserves. This completely destroyed foreign investors' confidence in the country and, according to some, left Pakistan with "the worst credit rating in the world." Prior to this, in April 1998, the government reneged on international agreements with private foreign power-generation companies investing in power projects in Pakistan (known as IPPs, or Independent Power Projects). According to these agreements, foreign investors were allowed to repatriate part of their profits, a provision which the government cancelled, dealing an equally devastating blow to investor confidence.

With an external debt of US$31 billion, the government faced a situation where its total debt servicing amounted to US$2.8 billion for 1998-99, almost equal to its gross inflows of around US$3 billion. At the end of July 1998 the government responded by ceasing all repayments on its commercial and institutional debts, effectively precipitating (in technical terms at least) the first ever default in the country's history. Fearing the possibility of a total economic melt-down, the IMF began negotiations for a bail-out package. Pakistan found itself under heavy pressure to sign up to a Comprehensive Test Ban Treaty (CTBT) with regards to its nuclear programme, and also to undertake a range of economic reforms, including an increase in utility prices, revenue expansion through new taxes (including a tax on agricultural income), drastic cuts in expenditure and a further reduction in import bills. Negotiations dragged on, but finally, on 15 January 1999 it was announced that a US$5 billion loan package had been agreed with the IMF. The exact details of the 'conditionalities' attached to the package were not clear at the time of going to press, but they are certain to have serious social consequences, and to further damage the government's political standing.

Agriculture Agriculture (including forestry and fishing) still dominates the economy, employing 47 percent of the labour force and accounting for 25 percent of GDP. This represents a relative decline in economic importance over the years (during the early 1960s it accounted for around 50 percent of GDP), though largely due to the growth of industry. Indeed, growth in agricultural output has kept up with population growth in recent years, to the extent that Pakistan is not only self sufficient in food grains, but like India is also a net exporter of food. The importance of agriculture is demonstrated by the fact that over a quarter of Pakistan's total land area is cultivated. Irrigation meanwhile is crucial to that agriculture, with more than three-quarters of cultivated land being irrigated. The extension of irrigation systems, along with mechanization, improved seed varieties, fertilizers and insecticides, are together responsible for increased output and higher yields.

Wheat is the most important food grain crop, vital to a diet based around *chapattis* and *nan*, and production has grown steadily over the years. **Rice** has become increasingly important, with production concentrating on high quality *basmati* for export to the Middle East, although other varieties are also grown for home consumption. Other major food grains, which are grown on the unirrigated *barani* lands, include local varieties of winter wheat and other hardy crops such as barley, maize, and pulses. Potatoes, onions, oil seeds, sugar beet, and fruits are the other main crops. The millets *bajra* and *jowar* are primarily grown as animal fodder. By far the most important cash crop and largest agricultural export is **cotton**, of which Pakistan is one of the largest producers in the world. **Sugarcane** is also increasingly important, along with **tobacco**, which is grown mainly in the Peshawar valley.

In a society where meat is central to the diet, the rearing of **livestock** is of considerable significance, particularly in marginal areas. As well as being increasingly important as a source of leather, animals are still vital to agriculture for ploughing and as beasts of burden. **Forestry** is of minimal economic importance at the national level, a reflection mostly of the scarcity of forest cover. However, afforestation schemes focusing on fast-growing species and irrigated tree plantations in the Indus basin could provide a sustainable source of timber and fuel wood, both of which are desperately needed. **Fishing** is an important industry along the coast and a cheap source of protein for many local communities. Shellfish such as shrimps, prawns and lobster are of great commercial value and account for around 2.6 percent of export earnings. Many of the rivers in the mountains of northern Pakistan were stocked with trout by the British and trout farming is important locally.

Despite the great progress in agriculture since Independence, it still remains highly vulnerable to the vagaries of Pakistan's climate, with heavy flooding and droughts regularly devastating harvests. Crop infestations, particularly of cotton, are also a major problem. This vulnerability periodically causes major setbacks to the overall economy. The twin problems of waterlogging and salinity leading to the loss of fertile land are also causing increasing concern.

A major constraint on agriculture is the feudal patterns of land ownership which have persisted since Independence, despite attempts (some would say half-hearted) by both Ayub Khan and Zulfikar Bhutto to introduce land reforms. Up-to-date figures are hard to come by, but it was estimated in 1959 that amongst the more powerful *zamindars* (landowners), a mere 6,000 people (0.1 percent of landowners) held 15 percent of all cultivated land in holdings of over 208 hectares, while in contrast 3.3 million people (65 percent of landowners) held an equal percentage of all cultivated land in holdings of less than two hectares. Most observers agree that such figures remain little changed today.

Industry

Manufacturing now accounts for 17.3 percent of GDP and employs 12.4 percent of the labour force, a major achievement given its negligible importance at Independence. Growth in manufacturing was greatest in the 1950s and '60s, when it averaged nine percent per year. Manufactured goods now account for over 60 percent of all exports, the bulk of these being processed foods, cotton textiles and garments. The fashion industry goes from strength to strength, with leather garments becoming increasingly important. Many of the designer labels found in western shops are in fact both designed and manufactured in Pakistan. Sports goods are another area of Pakistani expertise; the footballs used in the world cup come from Pakistan, while cricket bats, squash rackets and hockey sticks (all sports in which Pakistan excels) are considered to be of the highest quality.

Heavy industry and large scale manufacturing have grown more slowly, and one of the main criticisms generally made of Pakistan's economy is that it lacks any real 'depth', relying heavily on imports. Nowhere is this more apparent than in the transport sector; the overwhelming majority of vehicles on the roads are Japanese, and although many are now assembled in Pakistan, the country has no indigenous vehicle industry. Pakistan's first integrated iron and steel mill at Pipri, 40 kilometres east of Karachi, was built with Soviet assistance and is now finally fully operational. However, it has yet to achieve sustained profitability and iron and steel remain major imports. With a huge amount of Pakistan's industry concentrated around Karachi and Hyderabad, the ongoing violence there is having a significant impact on the overall economy.

Tourism

Tourism in Pakistan remains at a modest level, with the country acting as a classic example of what a fickle friend tourism can be. A huge leap in tourist arrivals in the late 1980s (largely as a result of the opening of the KKH to foreigners) had Pakistani financial planners (as well as those involved in the tourism industry) licking their lips in anticipation of the revenues to be accrued from this sector of the economy. However, a series of events, many beyond Pakistan's control, have meant that the anticipated number of visitors never actually arrived. The 1991 Gulf War, sectarian violence in Gilgit during the mid 1990s, the continued violence in Karachi, the nuclear tests in May 1998, and the US cruise missile attack on Afghanistan in mid 1998 have all deterred tourists from visiting. Tourism receipts for 1996 were down to US$145.9 million (down seven percent on the previous year, when the National Tourism Policy had predicted $573 million), with the 1997 receipts expected to be even more disappointing. Although this may sound like a significant amount, the tourism receipts of India, The Maldives and Mauritius for the same period were US$3 billion, US$2 billion and US$1.5 billion respectively.

Although there is no legislating for events such as the Gulf War, Pakistan has not helped itself in the way in which tourism policy is organized. For example, even prior to the May 1998 nuclear tests (which led to many tourist cancellations), the cabinet had taken the decision to abolish the pre-visa system for tourists. Yet none of the Pakistani embassies abroad, nor the immigration officials at the point of entry, attempted to implement this new directive (most denied all knowledge of it). Likewise, PIA offices around the world refused to sell tickets for flights to Pakistan unless potential buyers already had visas. And perhaps most disappointing of all has been the Ministry of Tourism's much-hyped attempt to have the World Tourism Organization (WTO) declare 1999 'Visit Pakistan Year'. All they actually got round to doing was design a logo, and the project has now fizzled out (though there are attempts to have the year 2000 so designated).

Resources and power By far the most important single resource is **natural gas** which, as well as supplying growing energy needs, provides a raw material for the fertilizer industry. There are 25 fields in operation, concentrated around the Indus plains with the largest, at Sui in Baluchistan, accounting for almost half of all production. Gas is piped from here to both Karachi and Lahore. **Oil** production, although limited, has expanded considerably with a vigorous exploration policy being rewarded by a number of finds. Imports from the Middle East (Kuwait in particular), are however still the major source of supply. The discovery in May 1992 of a huge **coal** field in Sind's Thar desert boosted known reserves significantly, although most reserves are of a low quality and production remains limited. Non-fuel minerals found in Pakistan include uranium, rock phosphate, gypsum, iron ore, copper, gold, silver, magnesium, chromite, antimony, barite, rock salt, sulphur, porcelain, china clays and gemstones. **Hydro-electricity** has been developed as a major power source, with the two largest projects, the Tarbela and Mangla dams, being complemented by numerous smaller schemes. The potential generating capacity from this source has been estimated at 10,000 MW; over a third of this has now been achieved and nearly half of Pakistan's electricity is hydro-electric. Despite rapid expansion of overall electricity capacity, demand still far outstrips supply, making power shortages a major constraint on industrial growth.

Population and settlement

After a series of postponements, a nationwide census was eventually held in March 1998 (see 'box' and table). Pakistan's population is now estimated at 130.580 million, making it the ninth most populous country in the world. If the figures for the average annual growth rate are correct (2.61 percent per annum), Pakistan is now much closer to the South Asian average of 2.4 percent. There are those who doubt these figures, maintaining that the annual growth rate is more like 2.9-3.1 percent (which would make it one of the highest in the world).

Even if the 2.61 percent figure is correct, this is still a rapid rate of growth. This reflects a rapidly declining infant mortality rate alongside a much slower decline in the birth rate. The total fertility rate (the average number of children a woman will have in her lifetime) was estimated at 5.4 in 1992 (1998 figures not available yet) and although this is extremely high (the rate in the UK is 1.9), it is an improvement on the 1981 level of 6.4. Interestingly, Pakistan was one of the first countries in Asia to implement family planning schemes, although today only 12 percent of married women are estimated to use contraception, and while three quarters of women are aware of a modern contraceptive method, less than half have access to these. Education is seen as a key factor in successful family planning, with women who have had at least some secondary education having significantly fewer children than those with no formal education. The most significant contribution to falling fertility rates is generally attributed to an increase in the average age of marriage and in the interval between pregnancies, both of which are linked to education and increased prosperity.

The settlement pattern of Pakistan is highly uneven. The largest province, Baluchistan, which accounts for almost half of the total land area, has a population that is about the size of Pakistan's largest city, Karachi. The population density of the various regions reflects the nature of the physical terrain, and the climatic conditions. The predominantly mountainous Northern Areas has a population density of just eight persons per square kilometre. Punjab, however, with a quarter of the land surface, has almost 60 percent of the population (at a density of 353 people per square kilometre), reflecting the easier nature of the terrain and its agricultural potential. Although less than 25 percent of Pakistan's population is urban, in Sind the urban population stands at around 50 percent, due almost entirely to the urban primacy of Karachi.

Education

Education remains one of the most neglected sectors in Pakistan, attracting spending of just 2.2 percent of GNP (the recommended UNESCO level is four percent). Teachers' salaries are abysmal and the profession has low public esteem. Education has also become highly politicized in recent years, with huge variations in statistics, depending on the source. Thus, according to the government's 1994-5 Economic Survey the literacy rate was 37 percent, a five percent improvement on the previous year and a 'valuable achievement', while UNESCO estimates put the figure at around 18 percent. Part of the discrepancy relates to the government's definition of literacy as merely the ability to read and write one's name.

Whichever sources and definitions are used, the absolute figures also conceal massive variations between men and women and between urban and rural areas. The literacy rate is more than twice as high for men (48.9 percent) as for women (23.5 percent), and likewise between urban and rural areas (57 percent as against 27.5 percent). Literacy rates amongst rural women is often as low as five percent. Progress in literacy has also been extremely slow as compared with other South Asian countries; Nepal, which had a literacy rate of just two percent at Independence as compared to Pakistan's 15, now has 48 percent literacy.

Although universal and free primary education is enshrined as a constitutional right in Pakistan, it is not compulsory and actual provision of primary school places nowhere near matches the demand. Facilities are generally very basic, particularly in rural areas, and teachers often poorly qualified. There is also widespread evidence of corruption and embezzlement in the system, with many schools existing only on paper in order to draw the relevant government funding.

Less than one-third of children who complete primary education go on to middle and secondary schools; for girls the proportion is one-fifth. Competition for places at secondary level is intense and the private sector now provides a significant proportion of facilities, although these are fee-paying and therefore only accessible to middle and upper class families.

Facilities in higher education are also under extreme pressure. Less than 10 percent of young people go on to higher secondary (intermediate) level, and as few as 1.6 percent into technical and vocational education. Only about three percent go from intermediate level into degree courses. There are 21 government-established universities and 774 affiliated colleges, with proposals to establish 20 new universities in the next 10 years. There are however serious administrative and financial problems in all the existing universities. On average teaching staff represent just one-fifth of the administrative and support staff. An investigative committee recently found that the prestigious Peshawar University kept no accounts, had no auditor and considered itself answerable to no-one.

 ***Provisional results from the 1998 population census***

Administrative Unit	***1981***	***1998***
	Population (000s)	
Pakistan	*84,254*	*130,580*
Baluchistan	*4,332*	*65,11*
FATA	*2,199*	*3,138*
Islamabad	*340*	*799*
NWFP	*11,061*	*17,555*
Punjab	*47,292*	*72,585*
Sind	*19,029*	*29,991*
	Annual Growth Rate (percent)	
Pakistan	*3.06*	*2.61*
Baluchistan	*7.09*	*2.42*
FATA	*-1.47*	*2.11*
Islamabad	*4.34*	*5.15*
NWFP	*3.32*	*2.75*
Punjab	*2.74*	*2.55*
Sind	*3.56*	*2.71*
	Population Density (per square kilometre)	
Pakistan	*105.8*	*164.0*
Baluchistan	*12.5*	*18.8*
FATA	*80.8*	*115.3*
Islamabad	*375.6*	*882.0*
NWFP	*148.4*	*235.6*
Punjab	*230.3*	*353.5*
Sind	*135.0*	*212.8*

Despite the serious physical constraints on education, the poor quality of services, widespread corruption and the economic pressures on children and young people to earn a living, one of the most striking things in Pakistan is the obvious thirst for knowledge and determination with which people pursue their schooling. Education is widely perceived as the single most important factor in opening up new opportunities and achieving a better standard of living.

Health Government spending on health is even lower than on education, amounting to just 0.8 percent of GNP. On average there was estimated to be one doctor for every 2,037 people, one nurse per 5,969 people and one dentist per 50,329 people. However, the majority of facilities are concentrated in urban areas, which account for less than one-third of the population. Basic Health Units and Rural Health Centres form the basis of health care provision in rural areas, although facilities are often woefully inadequate; more than half have no piped water or sewerage, while staff are often poorly trained. One survey suggested that 70 percent offered no contraceptive services. Wastage and corruption are major problems throughout the health sector.

However, there has been considerable improvement in facilities over the years, as well as a number of relatively successful immunization programmes, which have contributed to a 60 percent drop in infant mortality rates since the 1960s. Nevertheless, the rate is still extremely high; nearly one in 10 children die before their first birthday and a third of these deaths occur within one week of birth. A

Making sense of the census

For almost the past 20 years it has not been possible to say with any degree of certainty what the actual population of Pakistan is. Until the 5th Population and Housing Census was undertaken in March 1998, no census had been held in Pakistan since 1981 (and recent investigations suggest that even this census may be deeply flawed). Censuses are important because they allow governments to plan for the future, so why has Pakistan allowed 17 years to pass between counts?

The census is doubly important in Pakistan because it determines not only the regional representation in the National Assembly, but also the allocation of national resources and federal job quotas to the provinces. Article 51 of the Constitution states: "The National Assembly seats shall be allocated to each province, the Federally Administered Areas and the Federal Capital on the basis of the population in accordance with the last preceding census officially published". The classic example of attempts to manipulate the census is the aborted 1991 census (held in 1995). Early reports showed some remarkable abnormalities, such as the suggestion that Sind's population had grown from 19 million to 46 million in the period 1981-95. The census commissioner smelt a rat and the President cancelled the census. It seems that the data on Sind had been deliberately manipulated to show an increase in the population in order to influence the allocation of seats in the National Assembly, jobs in the federal service, and the distribution of federal resources. There had been further manipulation to influence these allocations between urban and rural Sind. If the results of the 1991 census had been accepted, Sind would have gained 26 seats in the National Assembly, whilst Punjab would have lost 22 and NWFP 3, in addition to affecting their allocation of resource and job quotas. If this had happened in 1991, did it also occur in 1981? And if it happened in Sind, surely it happened elsewhere?

It is feared, though, that however transparent the census procedure is, when the full results of the 1998 census are presented, it will be impossible to satisfy everyone. Undoubtedly the demographics of the country have changed dramatically since 1981, with a marked shift of population from rural to urban areas, thus reducing the power of the feudal leaders of the rural areas. Also present is the fear that the census may reveal the extent of internal divisions within Pakistan. An accurate census may reveal a situation in Sind where the indigenous Sindhi speakers are now outnumbered by an Urdu speaking majority; Punjab's homogeneity may be challenged by the revelation of the true numbers of the Seraiki community; in NWFP, what will be the impact of Afghan refugees who have managed to obtain Pakistani identity cards? And even before the provisional results of the 1998 census had been released, it was generally expected that they would be manipulated in favour of the Punjab. In fact, Prime Minister Nawaz Sharif(a Punjabi) had already announced prior to the census count taking place, that the results would not affect the allocation of National Assembly seats as well as the distribution of federal funds to the provinces: one of the primary purposes of the census in Pakistan in the first place.

As the census was taking place in March 1998, The Herald magazine interviewed representatives of almost every political party and pressure group in the country (including: MQM, PML, Chief of the Pashtun Ulsi Jirga, Sindh Democratic Party, Supreme Court Bar Association, PPP, Pakistan Seraiki Party, Tehrik-e-Insaaf, Baluchistan National Party and Jamaat-e-Islami). Whilst all recognized the need for a census enumeration, everyone interviewed expressed reservations about the outcome. And when the provisional results were announced in late 1998, they were rejected by all but the Punjab.

great many deaths amongst infants are as a result of easily treated problems such as diarrhoea and pneumonia. Under-nourishment and malnutrition are also widespread. Most women receive no ante-natal care and 85 percent of births take place at home, often without any trained assistance. Pakistan is estimated to have one of the highest rates of maternal mortality, although this is in part attributable to high birth and fertility rates.

10

Footnotes

Footnotes

Urdu words and phrases

Pronounce **ā** as in ah **i** as in bee
ō as in oh **u** as oo in book
nasalized vowels are shown as **aṉ uṉ** etc
Note These marks to help with pronunciation do not appear in the main text.

Useful words and phrases

Hello, good morning	*alsalām aleikum*
Goodbye	*hudā hāfiz*
Thank you/ no thank you	*shukriyā / nahīṉ shukriyā*
Excuse me, sorry	*mihrbānī*
Yes/ no	*jī hāṉ / jī nahīṉ*
never mind/ that's all right	*koi bāt nahīṉ*
Very well/ I see/ OK	*āccha*
What is your name?	*āpkā nām kyā hai?*
My name is	*merā nām .... hai*
Do you speak English?	*āp kō angrezī āti hai?*
a little	*thorī -sī*
How are you?/ are you well	*kyā āp kaise hain?*
I am well, thanks, and you?	*main thīk huṉ, aur āp?*
I am not well	*main thīk nahīṉ huṉ*
Where is the ....?	*......... kahāṉ hai?*
Who is ....?	*......... kaun hai?*
What is this?	*yeh kyā hai?*
I like/ I don't like	*mujhe pasand hai / mujhe pasand nahī*
What time is it?	*Yeh kitnī baaje hai?*
Please sit down	*tashreef rakhiye*
Please come	*tashreef lāiye*
Please tell me	*farmāiye*
God willing	*inshallah*
As quickly as possible	*jitni jaldi ho sake*

Shopping

How much is this?	*kitnā / iskā kitnā paisa hai?*
That is very expensive!	*yeh bahut mahangā hai!*
Make it a bit cheaper!	*thorā kam kījiye!*

The hotel

What is the room charge?	*ek din kā kirāyā kitnā hai?/ ek kamrā kitnā paisa hai?*
Please show me the room	*zarā mujhe kamrā dekhāiye*
Is there an air conditioned room?	*kyā a/c kamrā hai?*
Is there hot water?	*kyā kamre meṉ garam pānī hai?*

... a bathroom/ fan/mosquito net	*....ghusal khana/ pankhā/ machhar a*
Is there a large room?	*barā kamrā hai?*
The room is not clean	*yeh kamrā sāf nahīn̠ hai*
Please clean the room	*yeh kamrā sāf karwā dījiye*
Are there clean sheets/ blanket?	*sāf chādaren̠/kambal hain̠?*
This is OK	*yah thīk hai*
Please give the bill	*mihrbānī, bill dījiye*

Travel

Where's the railway station?	*railway station kahān̠ hai?*
How much is the ticket to Karachi?	*Karachi kā ticket kitnā paisa hai?*
When does the Karachi bus leave?	*Karachi bus keb jāegī?*
How much to go to the (Fort)?	*killa jāne ke liye, kitnā?*
Will you go for 10 rupees?	*das rupiye lenge?*
Is it far?	*kyā yeh dur hai?*
left/right	*bāien̠/dāhinā*
go straight on	*sīdhā chaliye*
nearby	*nazdīk*
Is it near the station?	*station ke nazdīk hai?*
Please come here at 8	*āth bajai yehān̠ ānā*
Quickly	*jaldi*
stop	*rukiye*
train	*rel gari*
north	*shimal*
south	*junub*
east	*mashriq*
west	*mahgreb*

Restaurants

Please show the menu	*menu dekhāiye*
No chillis please	*mirch nahīn̠ dālnā*
....sugar/ milk/ ice	*chīnī/ doodh/ baraf....*
I do not like meat	*mujhe gosht pasand nahīn̠*
I do not want chicken	*mujhe murghi chāhiye nahīn̠*
I don't like the food	*khānā mujhe achhā nahīn̠ lagta*
...do not open it	*......kholnā nahīn̠*
sweet/ savoury	*mīthā/ namkīn*
spoon, fork, knife	*chamach, kān̠tā, chhurī*

Time and days

right now	*abhī*	eg ¼ past 7	*sava sāth baaje*
morning/ early morning	*suba/ suba saveray*	eg ½ past 7	*sarhe sāth baaje*
Midday	*dopahar*	eg ¼ to 8	*paune āth baaje*
afternoon/ evening	*shām*	nb half past 1	*desh baaje*
night	*rāt*	nb half past 2	*dhaj baaje*
today	*āj*	Sunday	*itvār*
tomorrow/ yesterday	*kal/ kal*	Monday	*pir*
day	*din*	Tuesday	*mangal*
week	*haftā*	Wednesday	*budh*
month	*mahīnā*	Thursday	*jum'erāt*
year	*sāl*	Friday	*jum'ā*
quarter to	*paune*	Saturday	*haftā*
half past	*sarhe*		
quarter past	*sava*		

Ordinals

first	*pahla*	sixth	*chhata*
second	*dussa*	seventh	*sātvan*
third	*tissa*	eight	*āthvan*
fourth	*chaudtha*	ninth	*nauvan*
fifth	*pānchvan*	tenth	*dasvan*

Numbers

1	*ek*	23	*teīs*
1 ½	*derh*	24	*chaubīs*
2	*dō*	25	*paccīs*
2 ½	*dhāī*	26	*chabbīs*
3	*tīn*	27	*sataīs*
3 ½	*sārhe tīn (etc)*	28	*athaīs*
4	*chār*	29	*untīs*
5	*pānch*	30	*tīs*
6	*chhai*	35	*paintīs*
7	*sāt*	40	*chalīs*
8	*āth*	45	*paintālīs*
9	*nau*	50	*pachās*
10	*das*	55	*pachpān*
11	*gyāra*	60	*sāth*
12	*bārāh*	65	*painsāth*
13	*terāh*	70	*sattar*
14	*chaudāh*	75	*pachattar*
15	*pandrāh*	80	*assī*
16	*solāh*	85	*pachasī*
17	*satrāh*	90	*navve*
18	*athārāh*	95	*pachanve*
19	*unnīs*	100/200	*sau/do sau*
20	*bīs*	1,000/2,000	*hazār/do hazār*
21	*ikkīs*	100,000	*ek lākh*
22	*baīs*	10,000,000	*ek karor*

Basic vocabulary

airport, bank, bathroom, bus, doctor, embassy, ferry, hotel, hospital, juice, police, restaurant, station, stamp, taxi, ticket, train (these English words are used locally though often pronounced differently eg *daktar, haspatāl*)

and	*aur*	difficult	*mushkil*
after	*ke bād*	dirty	*gandā*
alone	*akela*	English	*angrezi*
bathroom	*ghusl khānā*	excellent	*bahut achhā*
beautiful	*hūbsūrat*	food/ to eat	*khānā*
before	*se pahle*	hot (spicy)	*jhāl*
behind	*ke piche*	hot (temp)	*garam*
big	*barā*	hunger	*bhūk*
brother	*bhai*	luggage	*samān*
chemist	*dawāi kī dukān*	marriage	*shadi*
Christian	*isai*	medicine	*dawāi*
clean	*sāf*	Muslim	*musalman*
cold	*thandā*	name	*nām*
day	*din*	newspaper	*akhbār*
delicious	*lazeez*	of course, sure	*zaroor*

old	*puranā*
pen	*qalam*
post (office)	*dāk khānā*
road/ route	*rāstā*
room	*kamrā*
shop	*dukan*
sick (ill)	*bīmār*
silk	*reshmī/ silk*
sister	*bahīn̲*
small	*chhotā*
sometimes	*khabī khabī*
student	*talib-ilm*
summer	*garmiyān*
tea	*chai*
tea-shop	*chai-khānā*
that	*woh*
thirst	*pyas*
this	*yeh*
tourist	*sayyah*
town/ city	*shahar*
water	*pānī*
what	*kyā*
when	*kab*
where	*kahān̲/ kidhar*
which/who	*kaun*
why	*kiun̲*
wife	*bivi*
winter	*sardiyan*
with	*ke sāthh*

Fruit (phal)

apple	*seb*
banana	*kelā*
coconut	*nāriyal*
green coconut	*dāb*
lemon	*nimbu*
lychee	*lichi*
mango	*āmb*
orange	*santrā*
pineapple	*anānās*

Eating out - food and menus

Pronounce **ā** as in ah **ī** as in bee
ō as in oh **u** as in oo in book
nasalized vowels are shown as **aṉ uṉ** etc

Note These marks to help with pronunciation do not appear in the main text

Basic food and vocabulary (Urdu)

khana food, to eat (verb)
anda egg
chāwal rice
chini sugar
gosht meat, usually mutton (sheep)
macchli fish
murghi chicken
panīr drained curds
phal fruit
roti bread
sabzī vegetables

Vegetables

āloo potato
baiṉgan aubergine
band gōbi cabbage
bhindi okra, ladies' fingers
dāl lentils
matar peas
piāz onion
phool gōbi cauliflower
sāg spinach

Pulses (beans and lentils)

masoor dāl pink, round split lentils
moong dāl most common form
chanā dāl chick peas
rājmā red kidney beans
urhad dāl small black beans

Roti - breads

chapāti thin, plain, wholemeal unleavened bread cooked on a *tawa* (griddle), usually made from *ata* (wheat flour). *Makkai-ki-roti* is with maize flour
nān oven baked (traditionally in a *tandoor*) white flour leavened bread often large and triangular
parāthā fried bread layered with ghī (sometimes cooked with egg or stuffed with vegetables)
poori thin deep-fried, puffed rounds of flour (in Punjabi *bhaturā*)

Rice

chāwal plain boiled rice
biriyani partially cooked rice layered over meat and baked with saffron
pulao/pilau fried (and then boiled) rice cooked with spices and vegetables

Accompaniments

achār pickles (usually spicy and preserved in oil)
chutnī often fruit or tomato, freshly prepared, sweet and mildly spiced
dahī plain yoghurt
mirch chilli
numuk salt
raita yoghurt with shredded cucumber
salat salad, usually onions, tomato or cucumber

Methods of preparation

bhoona in a thick, fairly spicy sauce
chargha similar to tandoori (see below)
chops minced meat, fish or vegetables, covered in mashed potato, crumbed and fried
cutlet minced meat, fish, vegetables formed into flat rounds or ovals, crumbed and fried
jhāl frāzi spicy, hot sauce with tomatoes and chillies
karahi (balti) cooked and served in a metal wok, with onions, tomatoes and spices

Kashmiri cooked with mild spices, ground almonds and yoghurt
kebab skewered (or minced and shaped) meat or fish
kīma minced meat (usually mutton)
kofta minced meat or vegetable balls
korma in fairly mild rich sauce using cream/yoghurt
Mughlai rich north Indian style
Peshwari rich with dried fruit and nuts
tandoori baked in a *tandoor* (special clay oven) or one imitating it
tikka marinated meat pieces, baked quite dry

Some typical dishes
aloo gosht potato and mutton stew
aloo gobi dry potato and cauliflower with cumin
aloo matar potato and peas in a dryish mildly spicy sauce
bhaji, pakora vegetable fritters (onions, potatoes, cauliflower etc) deep-fried in batter
bhindi bhaji okra fried with onions and mild spices
boti kebab marinated pieces of meat, skewered and cooked over a fire
chana choor ('Bombay mix') lentil and flattened rice snacks mixed with nuts and dried fruit
chapli kebab spicy burger made with mince, eggs and tomato and served with na-n
keema matar minced meat with peas
matar panīr curd cheese cubes with peas and spices (and often tomatoes)
rogan josh rich, mutton-beef pieces in creamy, red sauce
sāg aloo potato and spinach
sāg gosht mutton and spinach
samosa cooked vegetable or meat wrapped in pastry circle into 'triangles' and deep-fried

Sweets
barfi fudge-like, rectangles/ diamonds often with nuts
gulāb jāmun dark fried spongy balls, soaked in syrup
halwa dry sweet made with thickened milk, carrots and spice
kulfi cone-shaped Indian ice cream with pistachios/almonds

Drinks
chai tea boiled with milk and sugar
doodh milk
lassi cool drink made withyoghurt and water, salted or sweetened
pāni water

Shorts

Special interest pieces on and about Pakistan

Index

Note: grid references to the colour maps are shown in italics after place names. So 'Abbottabad *M5B2*' can be found on Map 5, square B2.

Maps

Sales & distribution

Footprint Handbooks
6 Riverside Court
Lower Bristol Road
Bath BA2 3DZ
T 01225 469141
F 01225 469461
E Mail handbooks@
footprint.cix.co.uk

Australia
Peribo Pty
58 Beaumont Road
Mt Kuring-Gai
NSW 2080
T (02) 9457 0011
F (02) 9457 0022

Austria
Freytag-Berndt Artaria
Kohlmarkt 9
A-1010 Wien
T 01 533 2094
F 01 533 8685

Belgium
Craenen BVBA
Mechelsesteenweg 633
B-3020 Herent
T 016 23 90 90
F 016 23 97 11

Canada
Ulysses Travel Publications
4176 rue Saint-Denis
Montréal
Québec H2W 2M5
T (514) 843 9882
F (514) 843 9448

Caribbean
Kingston Publishers
10, LOJ Industrial Complex
7 Norman Road
Kingston CSO
Jamaica
T 001876 928 8898
F 001876 928 5719

Europe – Central & Eastern
Michael Timperley
MTM
E Mail 100421.2070@
compuserve.com
T +852 2525 6264
F +852 2918 1034

Europe – Germany, Austria, Scandinavia, Spain, Portugal
Bill Bailey
16 Devon Square
Newton Abbott
Devon TQ12 2HR.UK
T 01626 331079
F 01626 331080

Denmark
Kilroy Travel
Skindergade 28
DK-1159 Copenhagen K
T 33 11 00 44
F 33 32 32 69

Nordisk Korthandel
Studiestraede 26-30 B
DK-1455 Copenhagen K
T 33 13 26 38
F 33 91 26 38

Scanvik Books
Esplanaden 8B
DK-1263 Copenhagen K
T 33 12 77 66
F 33 91 28 82

Finland
Akateeminen Kirjakauppa
Keskuskatu 1
FIN-00100 Helsinki
T 09 12141
F 09 121 4441

Suomalainen
Kirjakauppa
Koivuvaarankuja 2
01640 Vantaa 64
F 08 52 78 88

France
L'Astrolabe
46 rue de Provence
F-75009 Paris 9e
T 1 42 85 42 95
F 1 45 75 92 51

VILO Diffusion
25 rue Ginoux
F-75015 Paris
T 01 45 77 08 05
F 01 45 79 97 15

Germany
GeoCenter ILH
Schockenriedstrasse 44
D-70565 Stuttgart
T 0711 781 94610
F 0711 781 94654

Brettschneider
Fernreisebedarf
Feldkirchnerstrasse 2
D-85551 Heimstetten
T 089 990 20330
F 089 990 20331

Geobuch Gmbh
Rosental 6
D-80331 München
T 089 265030
F 089 263713

Gleumes
Hohenstaufenring 47-51
D-50674 Köln
T 0221 215650

Globetrotter Ausrustungen
Wiesendamm 1
D-22305 Hamburg
F 040 679 66183

Dr Götze
Bleichenbrücke 9
D-2000 Hamburg 1
T 040 3031 1009-0

Hugendubel Buchhandlung
Nymphenburgerstrasse 25
D-80335 München
T 089 238 9412
F 089 550 1853

Kiepert Buchhandlung
Hardenbergstrasse 4-5
D-10623 Berlin 12
T 030 311880

Greece
GC Eleftheroudakis
17 Panepistemiou
Athens 105 64
T 01 322 2255
F 01 323 9821

India
Roli Books
M-75 GK II Market
New Delhi 110048
T (011) 646 0886
F (011) 646 7185

Israel
Geographical Tours
8 Tverya Street
Tel Aviv 63144
T 03 528 4113
F 03 629 9905

Italy
Librimport
Via Biondelli 9
I-20141 Milano
T 02 8950 1422
F 02 8950 2811

Kenya
Novelty Wholesalers
PO Box 47407
Nairobi
T 2 743157 F 2 743157

Netherlands
Nilsson & Lamm bv
Postbus 195
Pampuslaan 212
N-1380 AD Weesp
T 0294 494949
F 0294 494455

Norway
Narvesen Distribusjon
Bertrand Narvesens Vei 2
Postboks 6219 Etterstad
N-0602 Oslo 6
T 22 57 32 00
F 22 68 24 65

Schibsteds Forlag A/S
Akersgata 32 - 5th Floor
Postboks 1178 Sentrum
N-0107 Oslo
T 22 86 30 00
F 22 42 54 92

Tanum
PO Box 1177 Sentrum
N-0107 Oslo 1
T 22 41 11 00
F 22 33 32 75

Pakistan
Pak-American Commercial
Zaib-un Nisa Street
Saddar
PO Box 7359
Karachi
T 21 566 0419
F 21 568 3611

South Africa
Faradawn CC
PO Box 1903
Saxonwold 2132
T 011 885 1787
F 011 885 1829

South America
Humphrys Roberts
Associates
Caixa Postal 801-0
Ag.Jardim da Gloria
06700-970 Cotia SP
Brazil
T 011 492 4496
F 011 492 6896

Southeast Asia
APA Publications
38 Joo Koon Road
Singapore 628990
T 865 1600
F 861 6438

Spain
Altaïr,Balmes 69
08007 Barcelona
T 93 3233062
F 93 4512559

Bookworld España
Pje Las Palmeras 25
29670 San Pedro
Alcántara,Málaga
T 95 278 6366
F 95 278 6452

Sweden
Hedengrens Bokhandel
PO Box 5509
S-11485 Stockholm
T 8 6115132

Kart Centrum
Vasagatan 16
S-11120 Stockholm
T 8 111699

Lantmateriet Kartbutiken
Kungsgatan 74
S-11122 Stockholm

Switzerland
Artou,8 rue de Rive
CH-1204 Geneva
T 022 311 4544
F 022 781 3456

Office du Livre OLF SA
ZI 3,Corminboeuf
CH-1701 Fribourg
T 026 467 5111
F 026 467 5466

Schweizer Buchzentrum
Postfach
CH-4601 Olten
T 062 209 2525
F 062 209 2627

Travel Bookshop
Rindermarkt 20
Postfach 216
CH-8001 Zürich
T 01 252 3883
F 01 252 3832

USA
NTC/ Contemporary
4255 West Touhy Avenue
Lincolnwood
Illinois 60646-1975
T (847) 679 5500
F (847) 679 2494

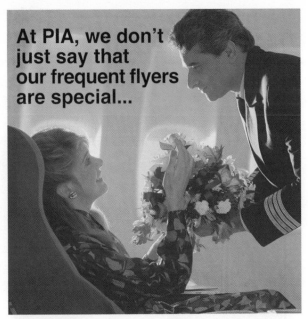

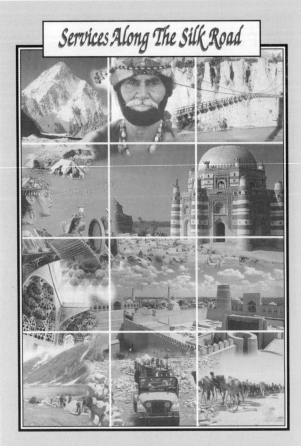

akistan

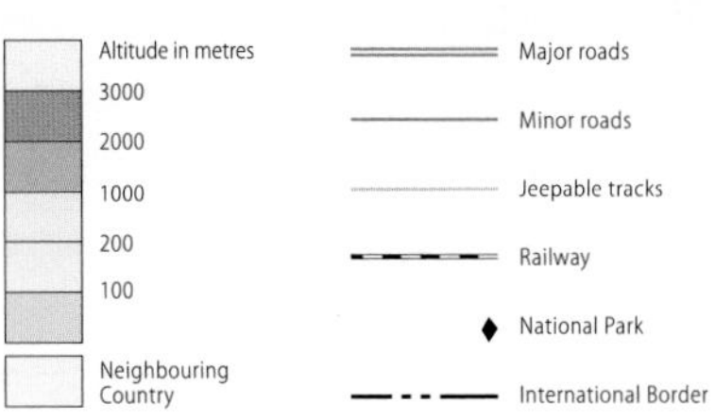

CHINA

5

GILGIT

CHITRAL

SKARDU

MUZAFFARABAD

Line of Control

PESHAWAR

4

ISLAMABAD

RAWALPINDI

The Government of Pakistan states that "the accession of Jammu and Kashmir to Pakistan or India remains to be decided"

AFGHANISTAN

3

LAHORE

QUETTA

AN

INDIA

HYDERABAD

KARACHI

2

Arabian Sea

N

km 100

miles 62

MAP 1
A
B
C
1
2
3
IRAN
Mirjawa
Taftan
To Zahedan
Koh-i-Dalil
Tozghi
Nok Kundi
Yakmach
Kalandi
Gwalishtap
Muksuhte
Rajab
Qila Ladgasht
Washap
Dashtak
Qila Khudabad
Gar
Sari-i-Parom
Zamuran Pass
Nivano
Ispakan
Mand
Tump
Nihing River
Nasirabad
Miri Kalat
Kalatuk
Turbat
Kech River
Sami
Kapput Kum
Piderak
Piri Chat
Makran Coast Range
Ghulaman-e-Bent
Suntsar
Dasht River
Talar
Shadi River
Rumra
Nalent
Kappar
Kandasol
Pishkurgan
Gwadar West Bay
Gwadar Bay
Gunz
Gwadar
Pasni
Jiwani
N
0 km 50
0 miles 31

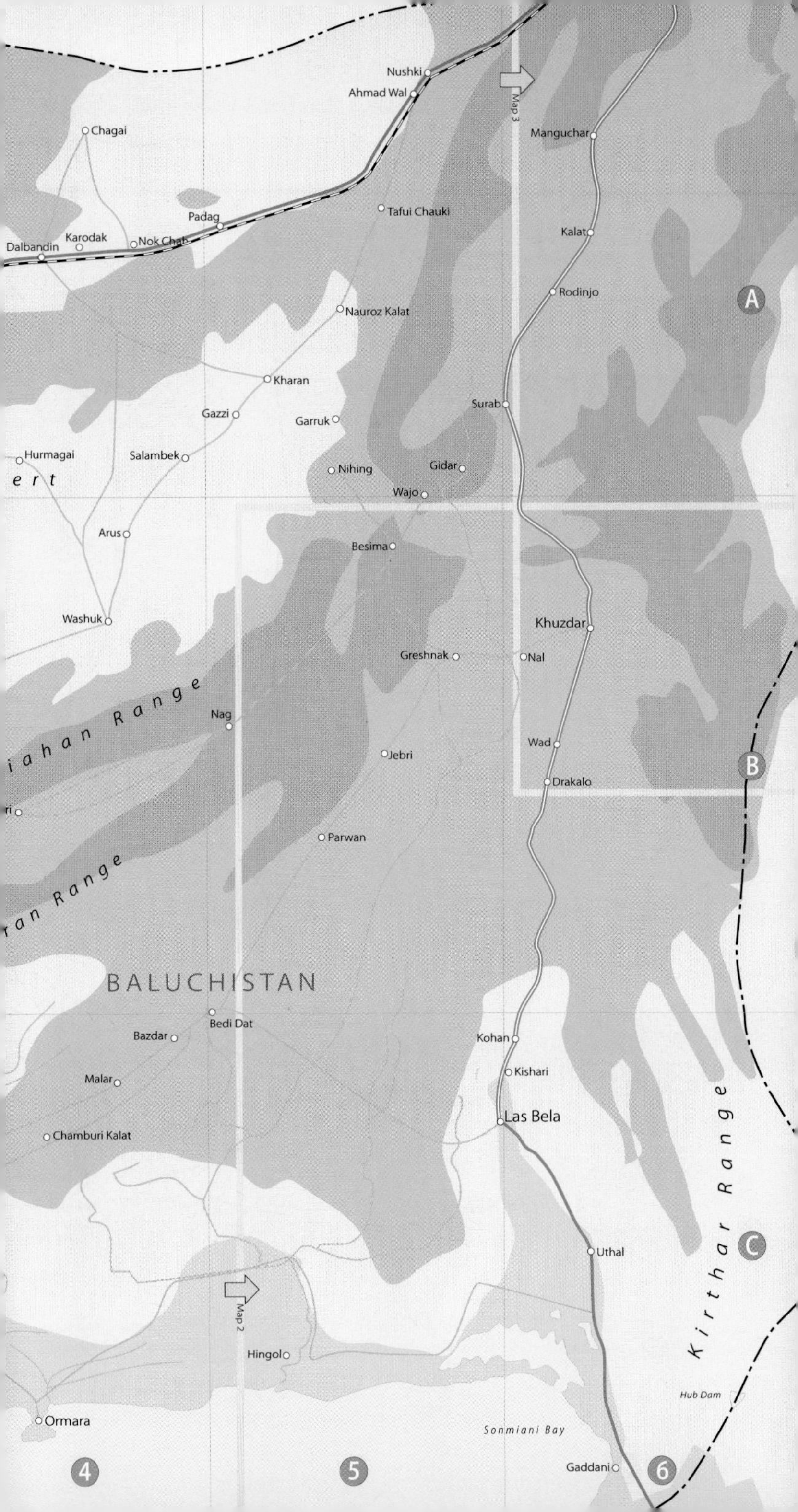

Nushki
Ahmad Wal
Map 3
Chagai
Manguchar
Tafui Chauki
Padag
Karodak
Nok Chah
Dalbandin
Kalat
Rodinjo
A
Nauroz Kalat
Kharan
Surab
Gazzi
Garruk
Hurmagai
Salambek
e r t
Nihing
Gidar
Wajo
Arus
Besima
Washuk
Khuzdar
Greshnak
Nal
iahan Range
Nag
Wad
Jebri
B
Drakalo
Parwan
ran Range
BALUCHISTAN
Bedi Dat
Bazdar
Kohan
Malar
Kishari
Las Bela
Chamburi Kalat
Kirthar Range
Uthal
C
Map 2
Hingol
Hub Dam
Ormara
Sonmiani Bay
Gaddani
4
5
6

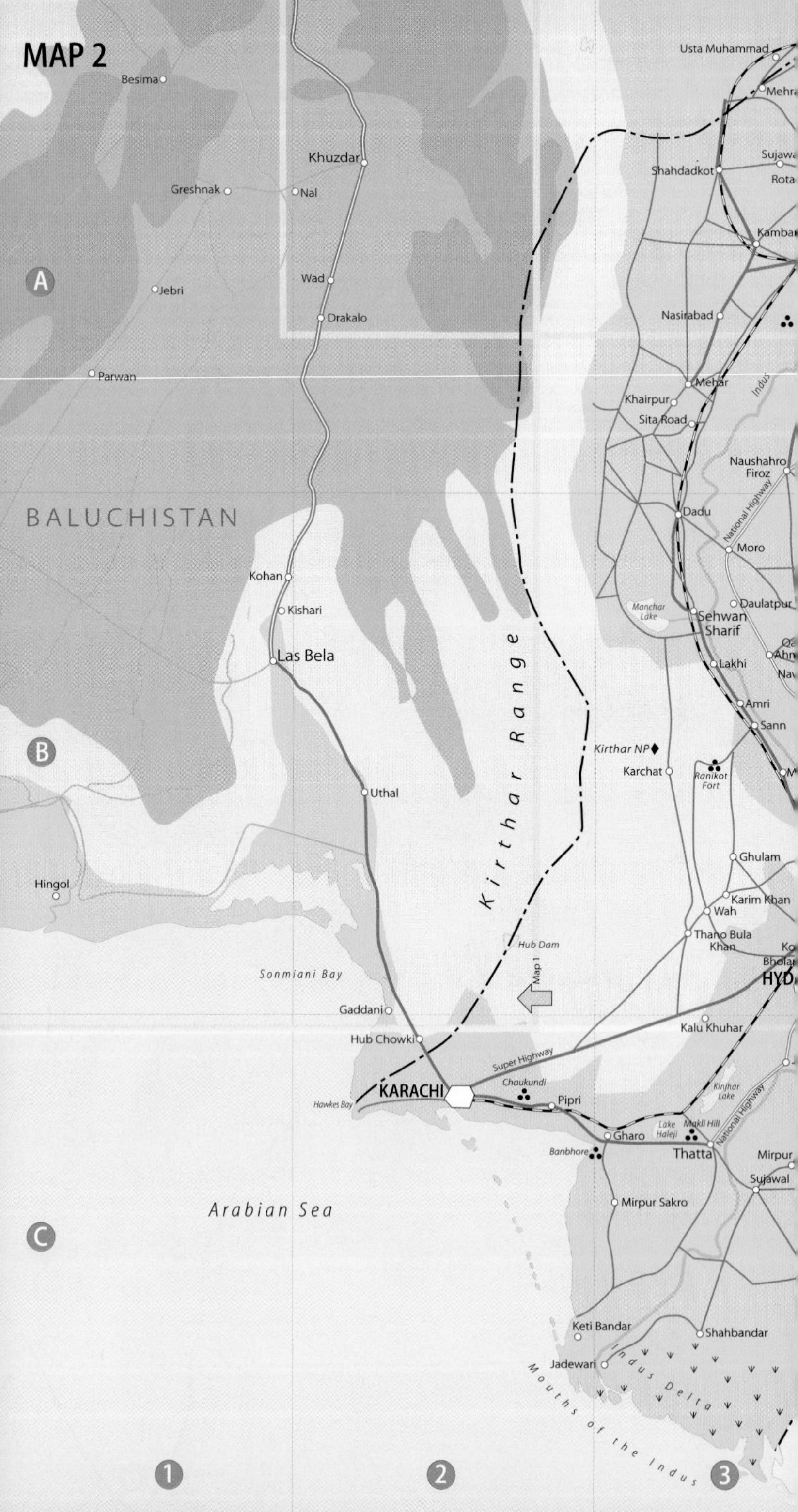

MAP 2
Besima
Khuzdar
Greshnak
Nal
Wad
Jebri
Drakalo
Parwan
BALUCHISTAN
Kohan
Kishari
Las Bela
Uthal
Hingol
Sonmiani Bay
Gaddani
Hub Chowki
KARACHI
Hawkes Bay
Arabian Sea
Kirthar Range
Hub Dam
Map 1
Super Highway
Chaukundi
Pipri
Gharo
Banbhore
Lake Haleji
Makli Hill
Thatta
Kinjhar Lake
National Highway
Mirpur Sakro
Keti Bandar
Jadewari
Shahbandar
Indus Delta
Mouths of the Indus
Usta Muhammad
Shahdadkot
Nasirabad
Mehar
Khairpur
Sita Road
Indus
Naushahro Firoz
National Highway
Dadu
Moro
Manchar Lake
Daulatpur
Sehwan Sharif
Lakhi
Amri
Sann
Kirthar NP
Karchat
Ranikot Fort
Ghulam
Karim Khan
Wah
Thano Bula Khan
Kalu Khuhar
Mirpur
Sujawal
A
B
C
1
2
3

Thul
Kandkot
Ghauspur
Ubauro
Mirpur Mathelo
Ghotki
Vitnot
Shikarpur
Daharki
Pano Aqil
Sukkur
Rohri
Therhi
Khairpur
Mithram
Cholisthan Desert
RAJASTHAN
A
Kot Diji
Map 3
Tajal
N
0 km
50
0 miles
31
Shapur Chakar
Sanghar
Sinjhoro
INDIA
Mansura
B
Khipro
line closed
Tando Adam
Gadra
Mirpur Khas
Tando Allahyar
Jam
Umarkot
Thar Desert
Jamesabad
Digri
Kunri
Chachro
Matli
Jhudo
Naukot
Satidera
Dharindharo
Talhar
Lunic Sond
Tando Bago
Pangri
Gori
Mithi
Islamakot
Panhario
Badin
Virawah
C
Diplo
Nagar Parkar
GUJARAT
4
5
6

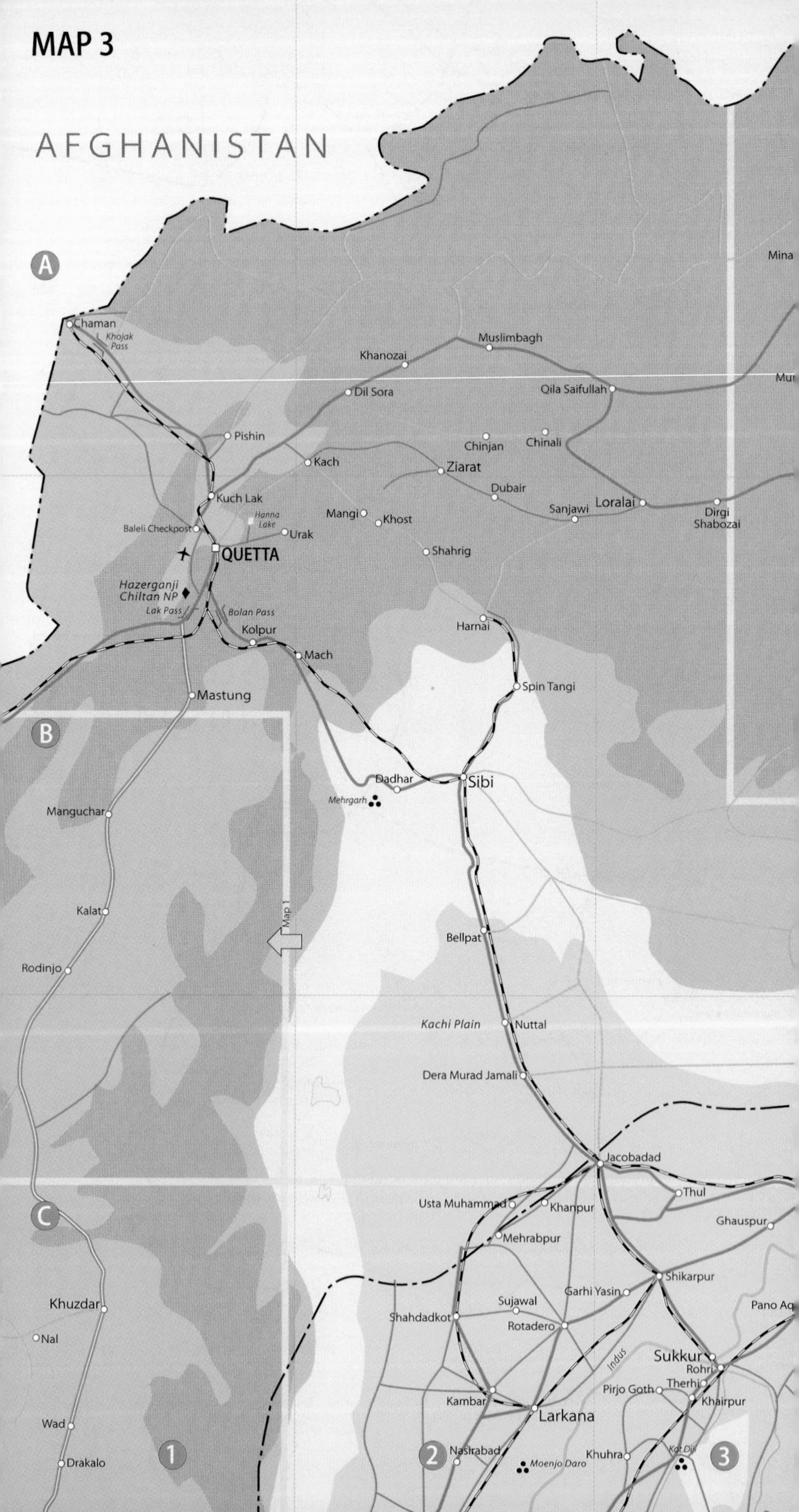
MAP 3
AFGHANISTAN
A
B
C
1
2
3
Chaman
Khojak Pass
Khanozai
Muslimbagh
Dil Sora
Qila Saifullah
Mina
Pishin
Kach
Chinjan
Chinali
Ziarat
Kuch Lak
Dubair
Sanjawi
Loralai
Dirgi Shabozai
Hanna Lake
Mangi
Khost
Baleli Checkpost
Urak
QUETTA
Shahrig
Hazerganji Chiltan NP
Lak Pass
Bolan Pass
Harnai
Kolpur
Mach
Spin Tangi
Mastung
Dadhar
Sibi
Mehrgarh
Manguchar
Kalat
Map 1
Bellpat
Rodinjo
Kachi Plain
Nuttal
Dera Murad Jamali
Jacobadad
Thul
Usta Muhammad
Khanpur
Ghauspur
Mehrabpur
Shikarpur
Khuzdar
Sujawal
Garhi Yasin
Pano Aq
Shahdadkot
Rotadero
Nal
Indus
Sukkur
Rohri
Therhi
Pirjo Goth
Khairpur
Kambar
Larkana
Wad
Nasirabad
Khuhra
Kot Diji
Drakalo
Moenjo Daro

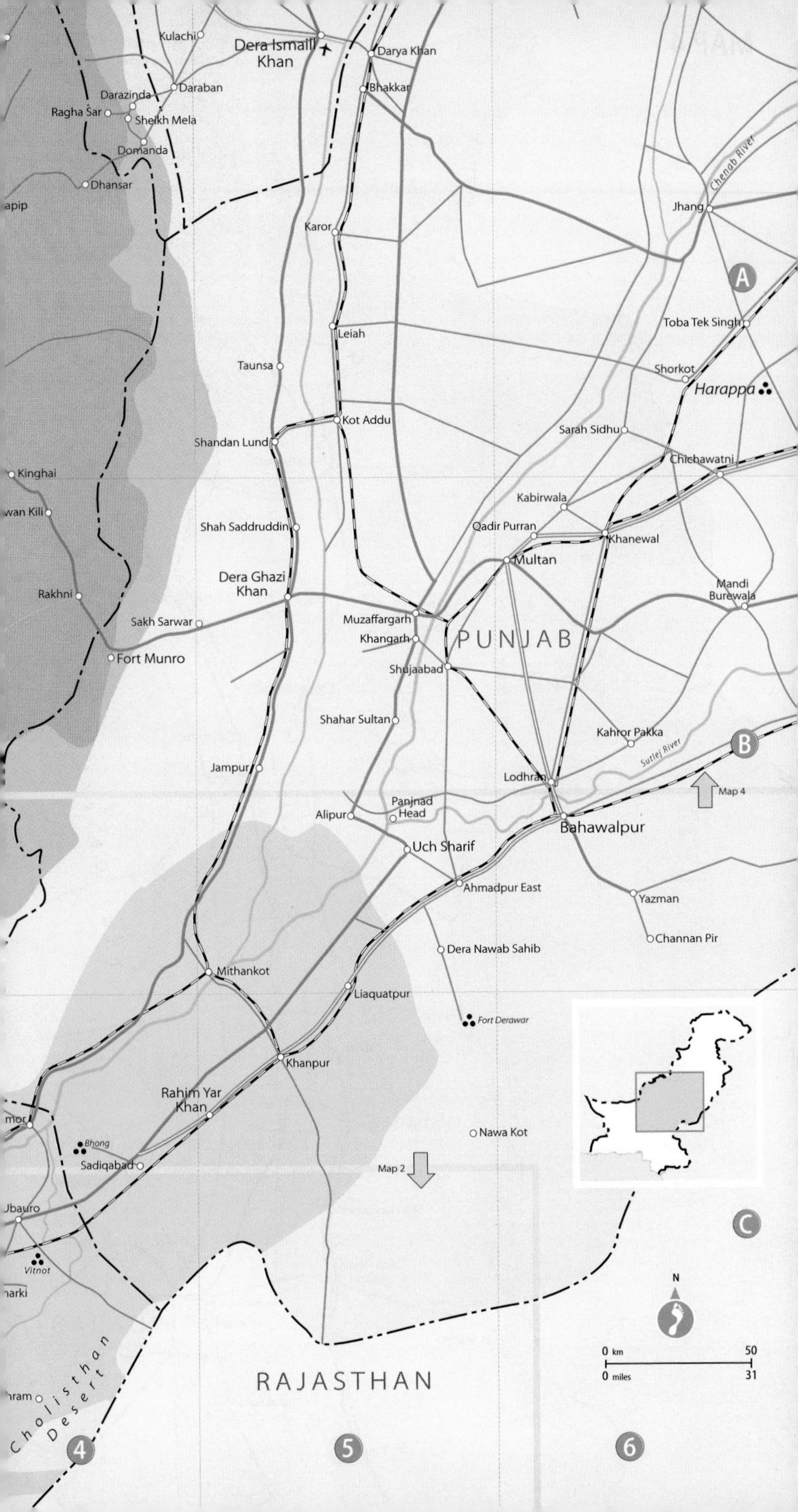

Kulachi
Dera Ismail Khan
Darya Khan
Bhakkar
Darazinda
Daraban
Ragha Sar
Sheikh Mela
Domanda
Dhansar
Chenab River
Jhang
Karor
A
Leiah
Toba Tek Singh
Taunsa
Shorkot
Harappa
Kot Addu
Shandan Lund
Sarah Sidhu
Kinghai
Chichawatni
Kabirwala
Shah Saddruddin
Qadir Purran
Khanewal
Multan
Dera Ghazi Khan
Rakhni
Mandi Burewala
Muzaffargarh
Sakh Sarwar
PUNJAB
Khangarh
Fort Munro
Shujaabad
Shahar Sultan
Kahror Pakka
B
Sutlej River
Jampur
Lodhran
Map 4
Panjnad Head
Alipur
Bahawalpur
Uch Sharif
Ahmadpur East
Yazman
Channan Pir
Dera Nawab Sahib
Mithankot
Liaquatpur
Fort Derawar
Khanpur
Rahim Yar Khan
Nawa Kot
Bhong
Sadiqabad
Map 2
C
Vitnot
N
0 km 50
0 miles 31
Cholisthan Desert
RAJASTHAN
4
5
6

MAP 4
Parachinar
Safed Koh Range
Jamrud Fort
Pabbi
Darra Adam Khel
PESHAWAR
Kohat Pass
Kohat
Samana Ridge
Hangu
Gumbat
Kushalgarh
Thal
Kohat Plains
Indusr
Lachi
A
Salt Range
Miram Shah
Bannu
Kalabagh
Bannu Plains
Daud Khel
Ramzak
Tauda China
Serai Gambila
Isa Khel
Musa Khel
Lakki
Mianwali
Jandola
Wana
Khirgi Post
Pezu
Khudian
Chasma Barrage
Manzai
Tanai Scout Post
Dabarra
Tank
Suleiman Range
Dera Ismaill Khan
Map 3
B
Kulachi
Darya Khan
Darazinda
Daraban
Bhakkar
Ragha Sar
Sheikh Mela
Domanda
Thal Desert
Dhansar
Zhob
Kapip
Badinzai
Mina Bazaar
Karor
Leiah
Taunsa
Kot Addu
Sarah Sidh
Shandan Lund
Kinghai
Mekhtar
Jalwan Kili
Kabirwala
C
Shah Saddruddin
Qadir Purran
Multan
Dera Ghazi Khan
Rakhni
Muzaffargarh
Sakh Sarwar
Khangarh
PUNJAB
Fort Munro
Shujaabad
Shahar Sultan
Kahror Pa
1
Jampur
2
Lodhran
3

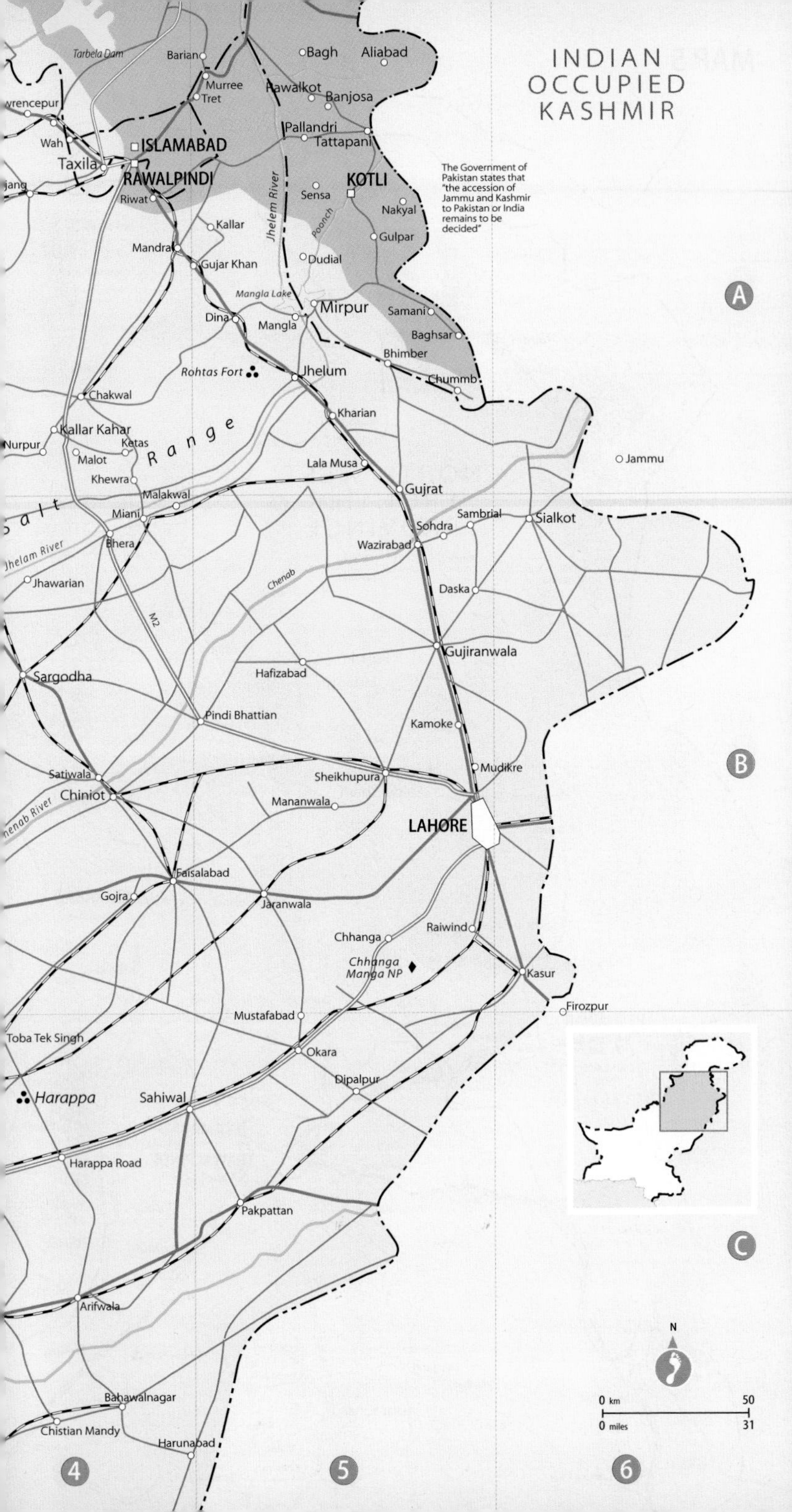

INDIAN OCCUPIED KASHMIR
The Government of Pakistan states that "the accession of Jammu and Kashmir to Pakistan or India remains to be decided"
Tarbela Dam
Barian
Murree
Tret
Bagh
Aliabad
Rawalkot
Banjosa
Pallandri
Tattapani
ISLAMABAD
RAWALPINDI
Taxila
Wah
Riwat
KOTLI
Sensa
Nakyal
Gulpar
Kallar
Mandra
Gujar Khan
Jhelem River
Poonch
Dudial
Mangla Lake
Mirpur
Samani
Dina
Mangla
Baghsar
Bhimber
Chummb
Rohtas Fort
Jhelum
Chakwal
Kharian
Kallar Kahar
Nurpur
Ketas
Malot
Salt Range
Lala Musa
Jammu
Khewra
Gujrat
Malakwal
Miani
Sambrial
Sialkot
Sohdra
Bhera
Wazirabad
Jhelam River
Jhawarian
Chenab
Daska
M2
Gujiranwala
Sargodha
Hafizabad
Pindi Bhattian
Kamoke
Mudikre
Satiwala
Sheikhupura
Chiniot
Mananwala
Chenab River
LAHORE
Faisalabad
Gojra
Jaranwala
Chhanga
Raiwind
Chhanga Manga NP
Kasur
Firozpur
Mustafabad
Toba Tek Singh
Okara
Dipalpur
Harappa
Sahiwal
Harappa Road
Pakpattan
Arifwala
Bahawalnagar
Chistian Mandy
Harunabad
A
B
C
4
5
6
N
0 km
50
0 miles
31

MAP 5

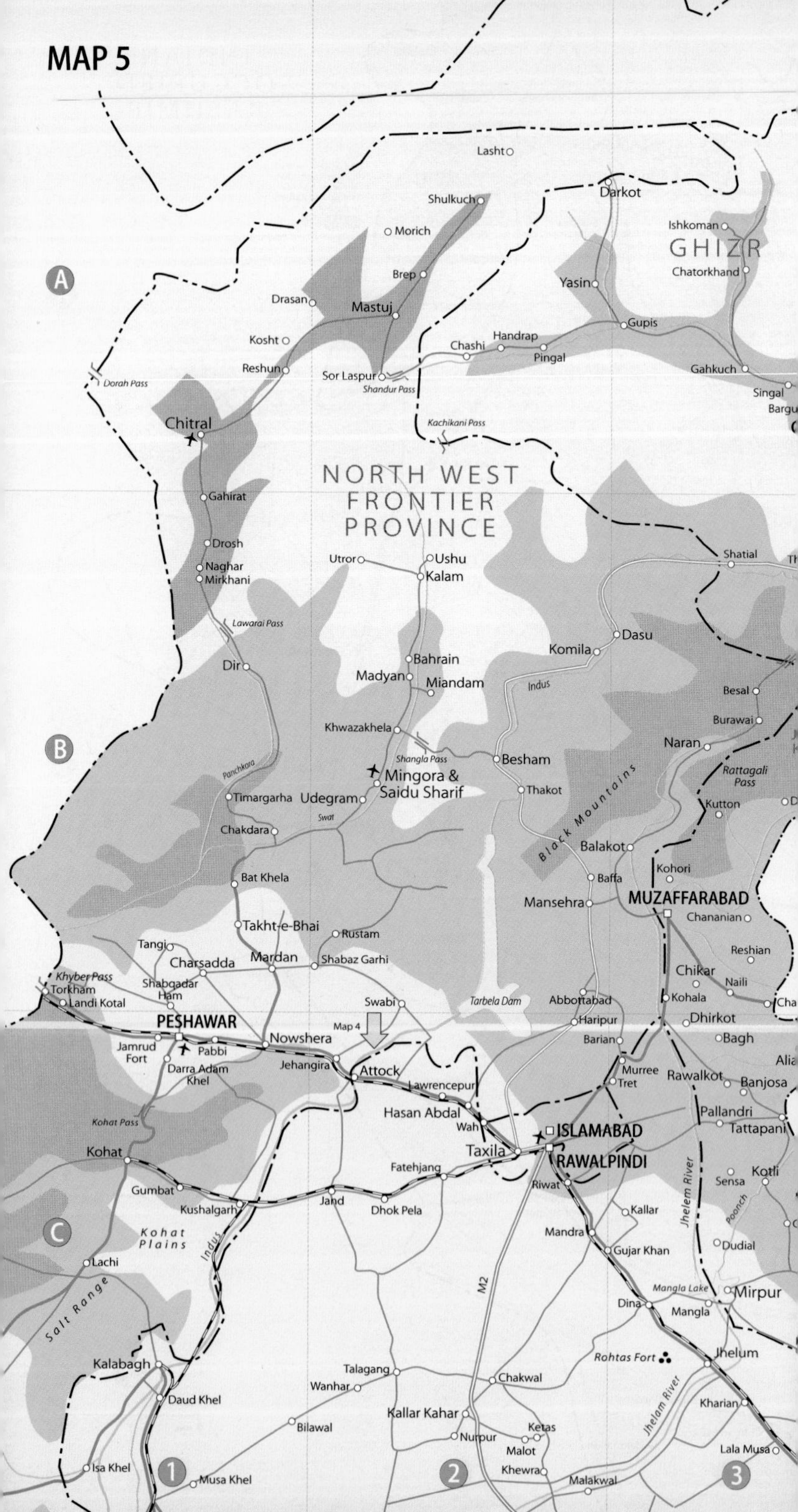

A
B
C
1
2
3
NORTH WEST FRONTIER PROVINCE
GHIZR
Lasht
Darkot
Shulkuch
Morich
Ishkoman
Chatorkhand
Brep
Yasin
Drasan
Mastuj
Gupis
Kosht
Handrap
Chashi
Pingal
Reshun
Sor Laspur
Shandur Pass
Gahkuch
Singal
Dorah Pass
Chitral
Kachikani Pass
Gahirat
Drosh
Naghar
Mirkhani
Utror
Ushu
Kalam
Shatial
Lawarai Pass
Dasu
Komila
Bahrain
Dir
Madyan
Miandam
Indus
Besal
Burawai
Khwazakhela
Naran
Shangla Pass
Besham
Panchkora
Mingora & Saidu Sharif
Rattagali Pass
Thakot
Timargarha
Udegram
Black Mountains
Kutton
Swat
Chakdara
Balakot
Kohori
Bat Khela
Baffa
Mansehra
MUZAFFARABAD
Chananian
Takht-e-Bhai
Rustam
Reshian
Tangi
Charsadda
Mardan
Shabaz Garhi
Chikar
Khyber Pass
Naili
Torkham
Shabqadar Ham
Landi Kotal
Swabi
Tarbela Dam
Abbottabad
Kohala
PESHAWAR
Map 4
Haripur
Dhirkot
Nowshera
Barian
Bagh
Jamrud Fort
Pabbi
Jehangira
Attock
Murree
Tret
Darra Adam Khel
Rawalkot
Banjosa
Lawrencepur
Hasan Abdal
Pallandri
Kohat Pass
Wah
ISLAMABAD
Tattapani
Taxila
RAWALPINDI
Kohat
Fatehjang
Jhelem River
Riwat
Sensa
Kotli
Gumbat
Jand
Kushalgarh
Dhok Pela
Kallar
Poonch
Kohat Plains
Mandra
Indus
Gujar Khan
Dudial
Lachi
M2
Mangla Lake
Mirpur
Salt Range
Dina
Mangla
Rohtas Fort
Kalabagh
Jhelum
Talagang
Chakwal
Wanhar
Jhelam River
Daud Khel
Kharian
Kallar Kahar
Ketas
Bilawal
Nurpur
Malot
Lala Musa
Isa Khel
Khewra
Musa Khel
Malakwal

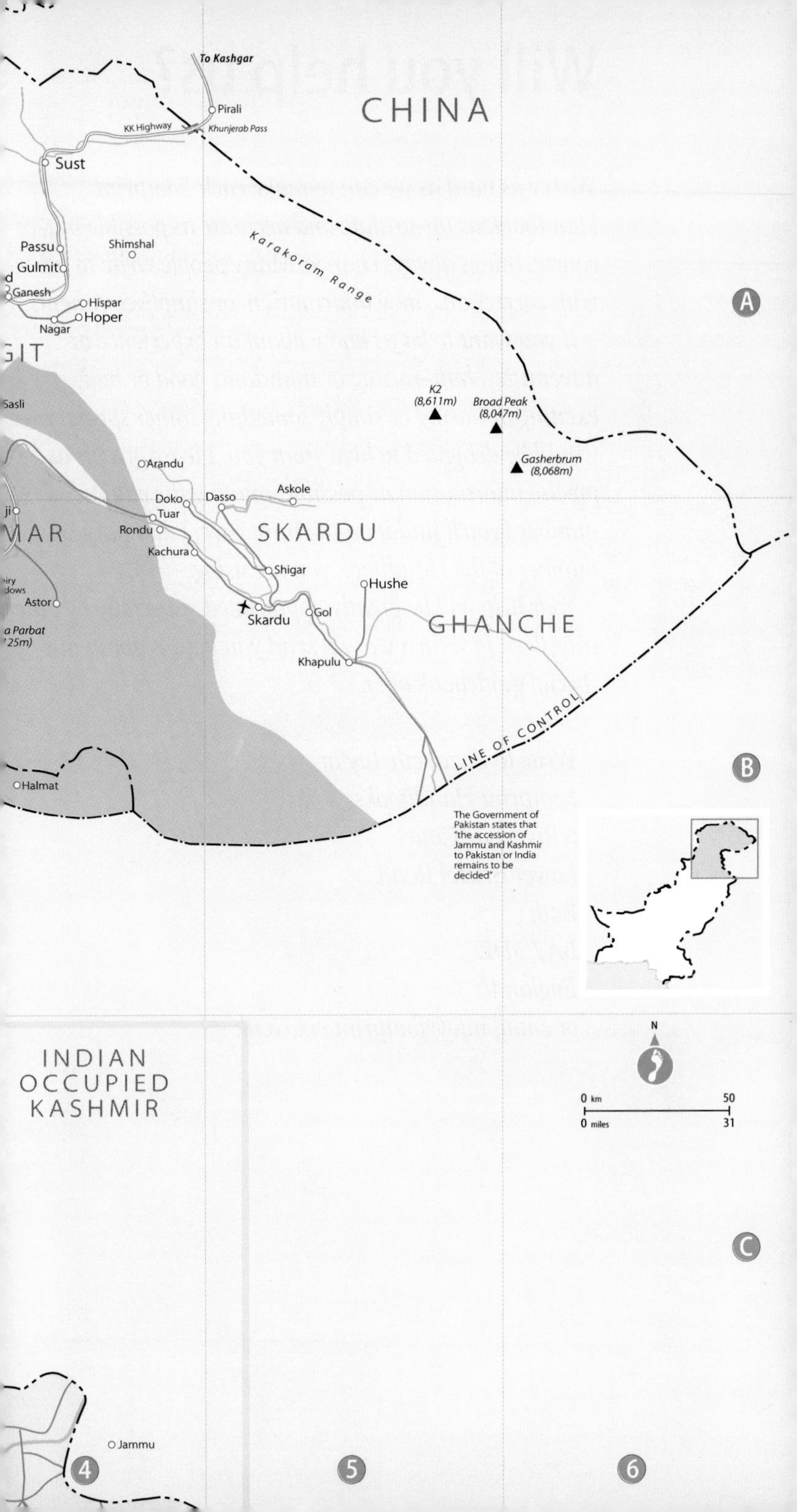

CHINA
To Kashgar
Pirali
KK Highway
Khunjerab Pass
Sust
Passu
Shimshal
Gulmit
Ganesh
Hispar
Hoper
Nagar
Karakoram Range
K2 (8,611m)
Broad Peak (8,047m)
Gasherbrum (8,068m)
Sasli
Arandu
Askole
Doko
Dasso
Tuar
Rondu
SKARDU
Kachura
Shigar
Hushe
Astor
Skardu
Gol
GHANCHE
Khapulu
LINE OF CONTROL
Halmat
The Government of Pakistan states that "the accession of Jammu and Kashmir to Pakistan or India remains to be decided"
N
0 km 50
0 miles 31
INDIAN OCCUPIED KASHMIR
Jammu
A
B
C
4
5
6

Will you help us?

We try as hard as we can to make each Footprint Handbook as up-to-date and accurate as possible but, of course, things always change. Many people write to us - with corrections, new information, or simply comments.

If you want to let us know about an experience or adventure - hair-raising or mundane, good or bad, exciting or boring or simply something rather special - we would be delighted to hear from you. Please give us as precise information as possible, quoting the edition number (you'll find it on the front cover) and page number of the Handbook you are using.

Your help will be greatly appreciated, especially by other travellers. In return we will send you details about our special guidebook offer.

Write to Elizabeth Taylor
Footprint Handbooks
6 Riverside Court
Lower Bristol Road
Bath
BA2 3DZ
England
or email info@footprint.cix.co.uk

Complete listing

Latin America

Argentina Handbook
1 900949 10 5 £11.99

Bolivia Handbook
1 900949 09 1 £11.99

Brazil Handbook
0 900751 84 3 £12.99

Caribbean Islands Handbook 1999
1 900949 23 7 £14.99

Chile Handbook
0 900751 85 1 £10.99

Colombia Handbook
1 900949 11 3 £10.99

Cuba Handbook
1 900949 12 1 £10.99

Ecuador & Galápagos Handbook
1 900949 29 6 £11.99

Mexico & Central America Handbook 1999
1 900949 22 9 £16.99

Peru Handbook
1 900949 31 8 £11.99

South American Handbook 1999
1 900949 21 0 £22.99

Venezuela Handbook
1 900949 13 X £10.99

Africa

East Africa Handbook 1999
1 900949 25 3 £14.99

Morocco Handbook
1 900949 35 0 £11.99

Namibia Handbook
1 900949 30 X £10.99

South Africa Handbook 1999
1 900949 26 1 £14.99

Tunisia Handbook
1 900949 34 2 £10.99

Zimbabwe Handbook
0 900751 93 2 £11.99

Asia

Cambodia Handbook
0 900751 96 7 £9.99

Goa Handbook
1 900949 17 2 £9.99

India Handbook 1999
1 900949 24 5 £16.99

Indonesia Handbook
1 900949 15 6 £14.99

Laos Handbook
0 900751 89 4 £9.99

Malaysia & Singapore Handbook
1 900949 16 4 £12.99

Myanmar (Burma) Handbook
0 900751 87 8 £9.99

Nepal Handbook
1 900949 00 8 £11.99

Pakistan Handbook
1 900949 37 7 £12.99

Singapore Handbook
1 900949 19 9 £9.99

Sri Lanka Handbook
1 900949 18 0 £11.99

Thailand Handbook
1 900949 32 6 £12.99

Tibet Handbook
1 900949 33 4 £12.99

Vietnam Handbook
1 900949 36 9 £10.99

Middle East

Egypt Handbook
1 900949 20 2 £12.99

Israel Handbook
1 900949 01 6 £12.99

Jordan, Syria & Lebanon Handbook
1 900949 14 8 £12.99

Europe

Andalucía Handbook
1 900949 27 X £9.99

Wexas

Traveller's Handbook
0 905802 08 X £14.99

Traveller's Healthbook
0 905802 09 8 £9.99

What the papers say

"I carried the South American Handbook in my bag from Cape Horn to Cartagena and consulted it every night for two and a half months. And I wouldn't do that for anything else except my hip flask."

Michael Palin

"Of all the main guidebook series this is genuinely the only one we have never received a complaint about."

The Bookseller

"All in all, the Footprint Handbook series is the best thing that has happened to travel guidebooks in years. They are different and take you off the beaten track away from all the others clutching the competitors' guidebooks."

The Business Times, Singapore

"Footprint's India Handbook told me everything from the history of the region to where to get the best curry."

Jennie Bond, BBC Correspondent

"Footprint Handbooks, the best of the best!"

Le Monde, Paris

Acknowledgements

Special thanks are due to Birgitte Glavind Sperger, who wrote the excellent piece on the culture of the Kalasha people of Chitral. Thanks also to all at Footprint in Bath for their help and support.

Letters and emails There are a number of people who were of great assistance in the updating and writing of this second edition of the *Pakistan Handbook*. Of all the letters and emails that we received, those from Pierre Willems, Brussels, Belgium, and Graham Williams and Louise Jones, Watford, UK, were particularly helpful. We are also grateful to the following for their emails and letters: Paul Bottell, Surrey, UK. Marco Bronckers, Brussels, Belgium. Dr Alex Duncan, Kent, UK, Gujranwala fan. Agha Sami Durrani, USA. Philippe Fabry, Paris, France. AJB Fryer, Somerset, UK. Kalim Uddin Ghauri, Karachi, Pakistan. Cees de Gruyter and Gerdi ter Heegde, email. Carol Hahn, email. Takeshi Hamada, Kanagawa, Japan. Harold Hochreiter, Salzburg, Austria. David Hodges, Herts, UK. Marie Javins, New York, USA. Kaiser Khan, Rawalpindi, Pakistan. Liz Lambert, Barnsley, UK. John Lane and Eithne Courtney, Co Limerick, Ireland. Giles Lunan, Middlesex, UK. Martin Riexinger, email. Farian Sabahi, London, UK. Charlie Walford, Surrey, UK.

Dave Winter would particularly like to thank the following for their help and friendship: Imran Khan, for writing the foreword. Rizwana Aziz, Assistant Manager Media, Shaukat Khanum Memorial Trust, Lahore. Karim Imamdad of the Embassy of Pakistan, Paris. Gaston de Challus, PR advisor to PIA, and Mrs Sadiqa Ansari, Secretary to the Chairman, PIA (London). Ali Madad and his family of Altit, for his great friendship and help, despite my (accidental) attempt to burn down his hotel! Mohammad Yaqoob of Gilgit, who should be the backpacker hotel manager role-model. Israr Hussein of Minapin,Nagar. Ejaz Ahmed of Gulmit, Gojal, Hunza. Sheraz Akram, Saeed Ahmed and Ashfaq Ahmad Dogar, of TDCP in Lahore. Joe Perkins, Chester City fan and KKH cyclist. Michael Owen of Liverpool and England, for almost making the summer of 1998 bearable. Claire Philips for the use of her kitchen table. Sahra Carter and Gareth (Tash) Courage for their engaging line drawings. Most of all I would like to thank my wife Laurence for all her love and support, and for putting up with long periods of absence from home whilst writing this book.

Ivan Mannheim would like to thank the following people, all of whom have helped in numerous different ways: Sajid and Ibtesam Qaissrani in Islamabad. Liaqat Baig at the British High Commission in Islamabad. Jalal Torr and Mujahid Ahmad at Hagler Bailly in Islamabad. Vaqar Zakaria, co-ordinator of the Himalayan Wildlife Project in Islamabad. Raja Riaz Ahmed Khan at PTDC in Skardu. Mayoun Khan from Altit, Hunza. Rafiq Rajput, Yunus, Haleem and all the other staff at the Himalayan Wildlife Project on Deosai. Abdul Akbar at the British Council in Peshawar. Salahuddin at PTDC in Peshawar. Zahoor Durrani at Sehrai Travels in Peshawar. Qazi M Mohsin, manager of the Swat Serena hotel in Saidu Sharif. Riaz Ahmad, Fida, Noor ul-Amin and Muambar Khan in Madyan, Swat valley. Haidar Ali Shah manager of the Mountain Inn in Chitral. Amir Mohammad Khan at PTDC in Chitral. Saifullah Jan in Rumbur. Salahudin, Haroon Rashid, Shah Jahan and Abdul Wahid from Daraban Kalan. Qamaruddin Mir and Iqbal Qasi at PTDC in Quetta. Yacoob Shah at CTC in Quetta. Sher Bahadur at Geonet in Quetta. Finally, I would especially like to thank Klair Allbuary for her patient support throughout this project, for her help in proof-reading sections of the text, and for plying me with all those delicious organic vegetables which helped to keep me alive (and all those bottles of wine which helped to keep me sane).

HOLYOKE COMMUNITY COLLEGE
LIBRARY
303 Homestead Ave.
Holyoke, MA 01040-1099